Today's Handguns for Sport & Personal Protection

HANDGUNS 2005

17th Edition

Edited by

Ken Ramage

Published by

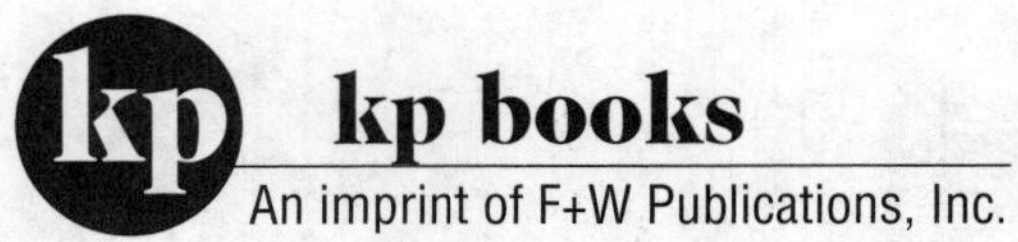

700 East State Street • Iola, WI 54990-0001
715-445-2214 • 888-457-2873

Our toll-free number to place an order or obtain a free catalog is 800-258-0929.

Manuscripts, contributions and inquiries, including first class return postage, should be sent to the HANDGUNS Editorial Offices, Krause Publications, 700 E. State Street, Iola, WI 54990-0001. All materials received will receive reasonable care, but we will not be responsible for their safe return. Material accepted is subject to our requirements for editing and revisions. Author payment covers all rights and title to the accepted material, including photos, drawings and other illustrations. Payment is at our current rates.

CAUTION: Technical data presented here, particularly technical data on the handloading and on firearms adjustment and alteration, inevitably reflects individual experience with particular equipment and components under specific circumstances the reader cannot duplicate exactly. Such data presentations therefore should be used for guidance only and with caution. Krause Publications, Inc., accepts no responsibility for results obtained using this data.

Library of Congress Catalog Number: 2004094033

ISBN: 0-87349-882-8

Designed by Patsy Howell and Tom Nelsen
Edited by Ken Ramage

Printed in the United States of America

— Handguns STAFF —

Ken Ramage, Editor

Firearms & DBI Books

CONTRIBUTING EDITORS

Holt Bodinson — Charles Petty
John Malloy — John Taffin

Editorial Comments and Suggestions

We're always looking for feedback on our books. Please let us know what you like about this edition. If you have suggestions for articles you'd like to see in future editions, please contact.

Ken Ramage/HANDGUNS
700 East State St.
Iola, WI 54990
email: ramagek@krause.com

About Our Covers...

Developed after 4-1/2 years of r&d, the Taurus Model 24/7 semi-automatic service pistol incorporates useful features and safety devices not found on a semi-automatic duty pistol.

The 24/7 has a steel slide and lightened internal metal frame inside an external molded frame and grip of high modulus dense molecular polymer.

Other features include an onboard lock that renders the firearm inoperative with a quarter-turn of the special key provided, a loaded chamber indicator, a striker safety and a brand new trigger bar latch that allows the firearm to discharge only when the trigger is held back. With a Picatinny accessory rail, the Taurus Model 24/7 will carry all accessories designed for this standardized system.

To help manage recoil and improve grip retention, the polymer grip is over-molded with a unique "Ribber" style patented surface. The grip's ergonomic design, textured surface and integral finger grooves comfortably accommodates all size hands while contributing to the secure grasp so necessary during recoil, particularly if the shooter's hand is wet.

The grip/slide relationship is set to the 11-degree angle preferred by professional shooters. The deep-cut beavertail ensures a sure, firm draw and repeatable grasp for all hand sizes.

The slide catch, ambidextrous magazine release, takedown lever and safety are all easily reached and operated. The controls fit flush with the frame and slide to prevent snagging.

The magazine has an integral finger rest for firmer grip and greater firearm control. The magazine well is a new design incorporating an extended back strap that makes it easier to locate the magazine well and insert a fresh magazine under stress, and avoids the extra bulk of a large funnel magazine well opening.

The 9mm and 40-caliber versions are available now and the 45 ACP should be available the last quarter of 2004. The Taurus Model 24/7 is manufactured in both blue and stainless steel.

For more details on features and performance of the Taurus 24/7, see author Dave Workman's article within.

Handguns 2005

Handguns for Sport and Personal Protection

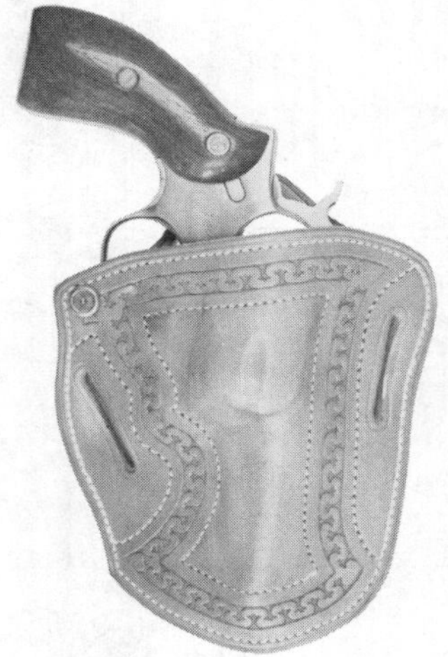

Page 87

Page 92

Page 108

CONTENTS

Handgun News

Gun Tests

CATALOG OF TODAY'S HANDGUNS

Page 140

SEMI-CUSTOM HANDGUNS

Page 170

COMMERCIAL HANDGUNS

CENTERFIRE & RIMFIRE

BLACKPOWDER

Page 183

AIRGUNS

ACCESSORIES

Page 197

REFERENCE

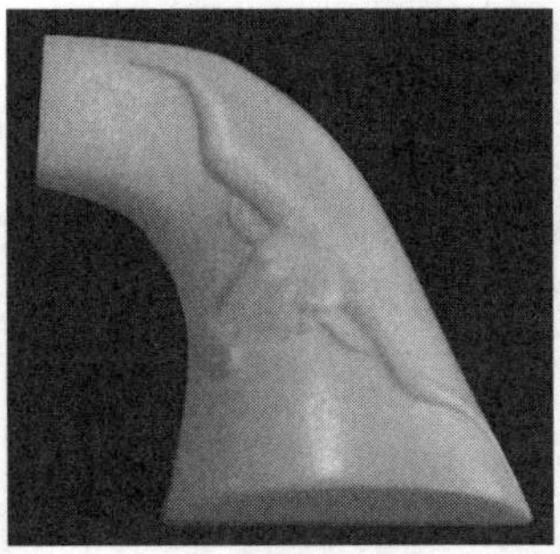

Page 207

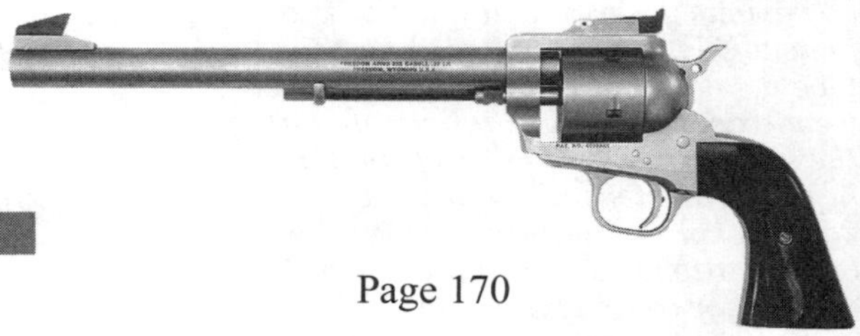

Handgun News:

AUTOLOADERS

by John Malloy

IT IS SOMETIMES difficult to understand some of the factors that influence the world of autoloading handguns.

Certainly, the purchase of sidearms by various governmental bodies is a factor. Companies who make service-type pistols would naturally like to get a contract for a large number of guns of the same type. A number of companies have supplied semiautomatic pistols to various police and military organizations, and then make similar models for commercial sale.

Sometimes, things are not so straightforward. In November 2002, President George Bush approved arming of the pilots of commercial passenger aircraft. The Transportation Security Administration (TSA) apparently opposed the program and set up requirements that tended to discourage participation. A year later, in November 2003, only some 200 pilots had reportedly been armed. Yet, in July 2003, the TSA contracted for up to 9600 40-caliber pistols to arm pilots who completed the program.

The economy appears to be improving, and according to one report, handgun sales are up, and about three-quarters of all new handguns sold now are semiautomatics. Most autoloading handguns can be used for personal protection, and many–perhaps most–are bought with this factor in mind. Personal protection is a valid reason for handgun use, and most states now recognize this fact.

"License to carry" or "carry of concealed weapons" (CCW) legislation continues to grow across the country. Forty-seven states are reported to allow some sort of concealed carry. Only Vermont and Alaska have true "right-to-carry" provisions, under which citizens do not need the government's permission to be armed. (New Hampshire, at the time of this writing, is considering a similar program). In the other states, those with "shall issue," license provisions avoid the bias and favoritism that characterizes states with "may issue" provisions.

How many "shall issue" states are there? Probably about 37 at the time of this writing. Hard to tell at any given moment, though, as anti-gun forces are constantly trying to undermine such laws, and things keep changing.

In Missouri, the legislature passed a CCW law, then the Governor vetoed it, then the legislature overrode the veto, then a judge struck down the law, then the Missouri Supreme Court upheld the law…except in four counties! In addition, the court decided the law imposed an unfounded mandate, and at the time of this writing, no permits have been issued.

In Wisconsin, the legislature passed a CCW law, then the Governor vetoed it, then the state Senate overrode the veto, but then one of the Representatives who had originally cosponsored the legislation changed his mind and the state House failed to override the veto by one vote.

In Ohio, after ten years of effort, a "shall issue" law was passed by the legislature and signed by the Governor, but it contained some ludicrous provisions. Motorists who carry must wear the handgun visible to law enforcement (and everyone else) while in a vehicle, then must immediately put on a concealing outer garment when exiting the vehicle.

Texas has had a "shall issue" law for some time, but anti-gun municipal leaders, with disregard for the law, have held that any public property—including municipal transit and parking areas—is off-limits for concealed carry. Such municipalities have had to be taken to court, one by one, and forced to obey the law. In Houston, the mayor conceded that licensed people could carry concealed on city property, but required that armed citizens wear a special red identification badge.

Georgia also has had CCW for some years, the Metropolitan Atlanta Rapid Transit Authority (MARTA) has required that legally-carried handguns must be separate from their ammunition (illegally-carried handguns are apparently not restricted). I guess, in a way, such a ridiculous provision actually favors autoloading handguns for honest people. In an emergency, it is generally easier to charge a semiauto with a loaded magazine than to draw, open and load a revolver.

In spite of these occasional setbacks and absurdities, we should take heart. Public acceptance of individual carry is growing, as people realize that Wild West shootouts do not occur, and that crime rates go down.

Autoloading handguns are used for many purposes other than for military and police use, or for personal protection. Competitive target shooting of many kinds, small game and/or big game hunting, informal target shooting and plinking, collecting, or just for pride of ownership—all these are reasons for semiautomatic pistols. At times, decorated pistols have been used as a way of raising money for worthy causes.

So, what are the trends in autoloading handguns today?

The Colt/Browning 1911 design seems to be going stronger than ever. Most new pistols introduced are variations on the 1911 theme. However, long-time manufacturers of other types of autoloading pistols now also offer their own 1911 models.

The 22 Long Rifle cartridge remains immensely popular, and new 22 pistols—and conversion kits for centerfire pistols—continue to be introduced.

The stainless-steel Accu-Tek AT380 pistol has a new longer grip frame and a magazine that provides an additional round.

In a sense, cartridge choices remain the same. The 45 Automatic Colt Pistol (45 ACP) cartridge celebrates its 100th birthday in 2005, and still seems to be king of the hill. 9mm and 40 S&W are very popular. Pocket pistols are still mostly 32 and 380.

In another sense, however, cartridge innovation has seldom offered a wider range of calibers than this year's new offerings. New cartridges ranging from 17- to 50-caliber were introduced, with new 25-, 32- and 45-caliber options in between.

The 38 Super cartridge, never a first choice for military or police use, has maintained a certain popularity since its introduction in 1929. It seems to be undergoing a small rejuvenation now, as several companies are bringing out new 38 Super pistols.

The resurrection of good things from the past continues to the guns themselves. Two names too long absent from the pistol scene are now back. Look for them in the report below.

Collectable and commemorative pistols seem to find a following, and a number have appeared this year. An interesting new twist consists of pistols with grips made of the wood of historic trees. Some special pistols offer a way of contributing to worthy causes.

Pistol-carbines are popular. Lacking a better definition, let's include pistols that can be made into carbines, and carbines based on pistols. Not really the proper subjects for this report, perhaps, but related and certainly interesting.

Much is going on. Let's take a look at what the companies are doing:

ADCO is importing the TT 45, a new 45 ACP polymer-frame pistol made in the Czech Republic. This is a peek at one of the first to be displayed.

The new nickel-plated Beretta Cheetah has wood grips and comes in 380 ACP.

ADCO

ADCO, a Massachusetts firm, is now offering a 45-caliber pistol. The new TT 45 is being imported from the Czech Republic. The original CZ firearms factory, established in 1919, began making firearms again after the end of the Soviet Union. That Czech company is now producing the TT 45, and ADCO describes the new pistols as "original CZ."

The mechanism is basically that of the CZ-75, in a polymer-frame package. The design allows carrying the pistol hammer down *(for a double-action first shot)* or cocked-and-locked with the frame-mounted thumb safety. The pistol has a 3.77-inch barrel and measures 7.6 x 5.9 inches. Unloaded weight is about 26 ounces.

The new 45 will probably be followed by other variants in other calibers, and various accessories are available.

Advantage Arms

Advantage Arms has offered, for several years, 22 Long Rifle (22 LR) conversion kits for most models of Glock pistols. Now, the company has introduced a new 22 LR conversion kit for 1911-type pistols. The conversion features Millett adjustable Sights, and has last-round hold-open. Availability was scheduled for summer 2004.

Beretta

Beretta has introduced a number of new models, primarily modifications of the company's basic pistol line.

The Model 92/96 STEEL 1 is designed for the competitive shooter. It has a heavier steel frame, vertex grip, a heavier "Brigadier" slide, and a nickel-alloy finish. With a frame-mounted safety, the STEEL 1 can be carried cocked-and-locked. Recall that Model 92 pistols are 9mm, and Model 96 pistols are 40 Smith & Wesson (40 S&W).

The Model 92 / 96 FS Olive Drab pistols are similar to the United States' M9 military pistol, with an OD finish.

The 92 INOX Lasergrips model is a 9mm in stainless-steel finish with a laser-aiming device contained in the grip panels.

New Cougar INOX pistols are stainless steel with checkered wood grips, a nice-looking combination. The new pistols feature the Cougar's

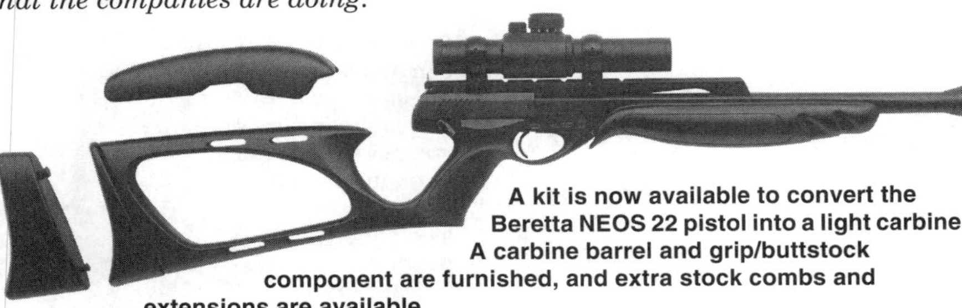

A kit is now available to convert the Beretta NEOS 22 pistol into a light carbine. A carbine barrel and grip/buttstock component are furnished, and extra stock combs and extensions are available.

Ever wonder if Ken Ramage, the editor of this publication, can shoot a handgun well? He proves that he can at a windswept range in Nevada. The pistol is Beretta's new stainless-steel Cougar in 40 S&W.

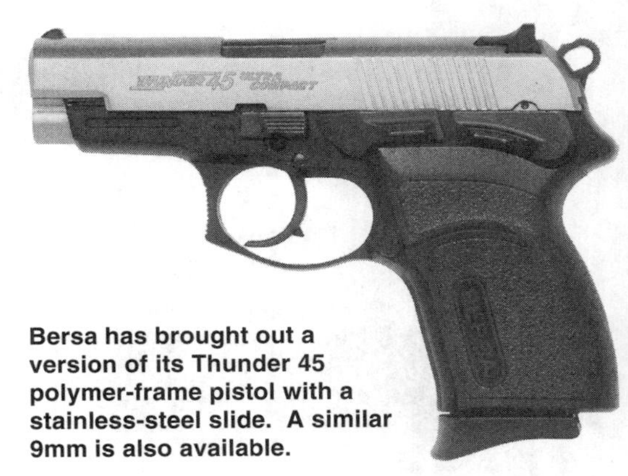

Bersa has brought out a version of its Thunder 45 polymer-frame pistol with a stainless-steel slide. A similar 9mm is also available.

The Browning Hi-Power pistol, gone for a while, is back in the lineup, in 9mm and 40 calibers.

rotating-barrel locking system and are available in 9mm and 40 S&W.

The 84 / 85 FS Cheetah Nickel variant has wood grips and comes in 380 ACP. The Model 84 has a 10-shot magazine. The lighter Model 85 has an 8-shot magazine.

The U22 NEOS carbine kit is now available to convert the NEOS 22-caliber pistol into a light semiautomatic carbine for plinking or small-game hunting. Simply removing the pistol's grip frame and barrel allows installation of the carbine stock and barrel.

Bernardelli

The Bernardelli polymer-frame pistol, based on the CZ-75 mechanism, is now in full production, and a new variant has been introduced. Resurrecting the company's former "Baby" terminology, the new compact version is called the Bernardelli 2000 Baby.

Bersa

New versions of the Thunder 45 and Thunder 9 Ultra Compact pistols are now available with stainless-steel slides. The new Bersa pistols have alloy frames with polymer grips, and are of the tilting-barrel locking system. Barrel length is 3.6 inches, and the pistols measure 4.9 x 6.7 inches. Weight is about 27 ounces. Bersa pistols are made in Argentina and are imported by Eagle Imports.

Browning

The standby Browning Hi-Power pistol was absent for a while, but is now back in the Browning lineup. It is available in 9mm and 40 S&W, in several options.

The PRO-9 and PRO-40 double-action-only (DAO) polymer-frame pistols were introduced last year. The 9mm version, the PRO-9, is now in production. The 40-caliber variant may arrive soon.

At the 2004 SHOT Show, Browning also displayed a "Liberty Tree" Hi-Power pistol. The grips of the pistol are made from the wood of the last surviving Liberty Tree. The Liberty Tree story is an interesting part of American history. In the 1770s, Great Britain sought to prevent rebellion by forbidding private meetings in the colonies. Each colony selected a tree, a "Liberty Tree," as a meeting place, in order to get around the British order. The last tree, a tulip poplar in Maryland, came down during a hurricane in 1999. The wood was harvested and preserved by the American Forests organization, and the wood has been used for the grips. For each of the 228 pistols sold (numbered 1776 to 2004) trees will be planted in environmental restoration projects.

The new polymer-frame Browning PRO 9 pistol, announced last year, is in full production.

Bushmaster

Late in 2003, Bushmaster Firearms, Inc. acquired the Professional Ordnance firm. Professional Ordnance's 223-caliber Carbon 15 pistols (and rifles) now are part of Bushmaster's product line. The former Professional Ordnance facility in Arizona has become Bushmaster's western division. The Carbon 15 arms are made on the AR-15 pattern, but are built from a carbon composition material instead of aluminum. The weight reduction allows pistols that weigh about 46 ounces.

The new Bushmaster Carbon 15 pistols are designated Type 97 (fluted barrel) or Type 21 (unfluted barrel). Two variants of the Type 21, mechanically the same, are offered. The commercial version has a bright stainless-steel barrel and comes with a 10-round magazine. The law-enforcement pistol has a black-coated stainless-steel barrel, and can be had with a 30-round magazine.

Century

New additions to Century's line of Philippine-made 45-caliber 1911-type pistols are twofold. The first type

◀ The Korean Daewoo pistol, absent for some time, is now being imported by Century International Arms. This is the compact DP51C in 9mm. Full-size variants in 9mm and 40 S&W are also available.

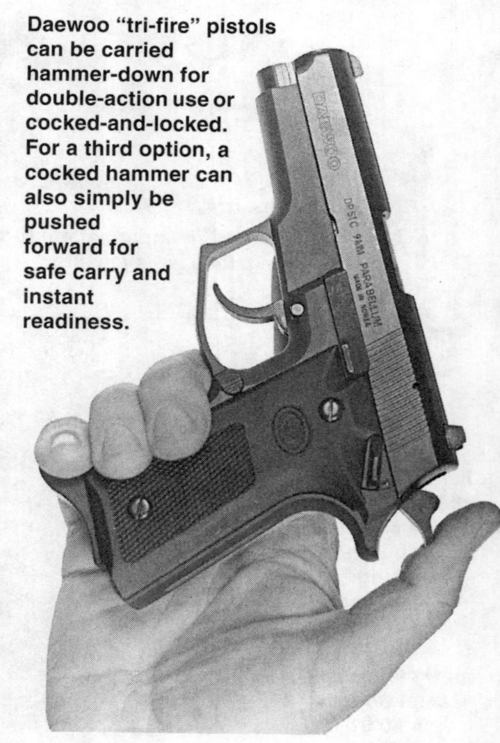

Daewoo "tri-fire" pistols can be carried hammer-down for double-action use or cocked-and-locked. For a third option, a cocked hammer can also simply be pushed forward for safe carry and instant readiness.

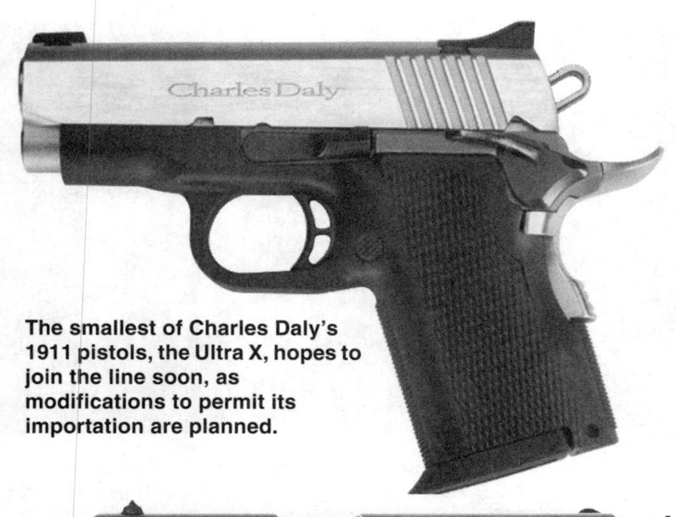

The smallest of Charles Daly's 1911 pistols, the Ultra X, hopes to join the line soon, as modifications to permit its importation are planned.

Colt has brought back the 38 Super, and a blued version with enhancements is standard.

▲A brand-new Colt Model 1911, in the pattern of the WWI pistols, is now a catalog item.

has most of the features modern shooters seem to like—beavertail grip safety, low profile rear sight and round spur hammer. Another variant has these features, but in addition, the top of the slide is flat and the front of the frame is squared. This treatment adds weight, mostly forward, to help control recoil and muzzle rise. The new 45s were scheduled for mid-2004 availability.

Century is importing the Korean Daewoo pistols, which have been absent for a while. Recall that these pistols use the "tri-fire" system that allows the pistol to be carried hammer-down for a double-action (DA) first shot, or cocked-and-locked for a single-action (SA) first shot. In addition, a third method may be used. A cocked hammer can simply be pushed forward for safe carry, after which a light pull on the trigger will cock the hammer again.

Century also offers newly-manufactured Egyptian 9mm Helwan pistols, and also Arcus 9mm pistols in several variations.

Charles Daly

Brand new in the Charles Daly lineup is the ZDA pistol, which bears something of a resemblance to the SIG P 226, both in looks and function. The new ZDA has a 4-inch barrel and will be available in 9mm and 40 S&W.

A new variant added to the HP (Hi-Power) line has a chrome finish and express sights. This pistol will probably be cataloged as an Empire Grade entry.

The M-5 line of 1911-type polymer-frame pistols has a new addition. A 5-inch bull-barrel version is now available, made on the 10-round high-capacity frame. The Ultra X version of the Daly M-5, the little 3-inch barrel variant, was announced last year but will probably not make an appearance until late in 2004. It ran afoul of the BATF's absurd point system and could not be imported. The company hopes that by adding features such as a loaded-chamber indicator, the Ultra X will gain approval.

Colt

The 38 Super is back in the Colt lineup! Introduced in 1929, Colt's 38 Super pistol for a time held the position of being the most powerful handgun made, in terms of energy and penetration. The pistol and cartridge developed a following among lawmen and outdoorsmen. More recently, the 38 Super has become a favorite for action- and practical-style shooting competition.

Colt offers the 38 Super in three different models, all full-size with 5-inch barrels. The blued version has a Commander hammer, aluminum trigger and rubber composite grips. The stainless variant has these same features in a stainless-steel pistol. The top of the line Super is made of stainless steel, polished bright to resemble the early nickel finishes. It features a traditional spur hammer and checkered "big diamond" wood grips.

The World War I-style 1911 pistol, displayed in prototype last year at the 2003 SHOT Show, is now a standard catalog item. A WWI-type screwdriver and copy of an original manual are included with each pistol.

CZ USA

The new CZ Model 2075 "RAMI" is a compact little pistol based on the CZ 75 mechanism. This version is the smallest yet made, with a 3-inch barrel and weight of less than 25 ounces. At 4.7 x 6.5 inches, it falls just between our arbitrary categories of compact (5 x 7) and subcompact (4 x 6). The pistol is offered in 9mm and 40 S&W. The staggered-column magazine gives 10+1 capacity in 9mm and 8+1 in 40.

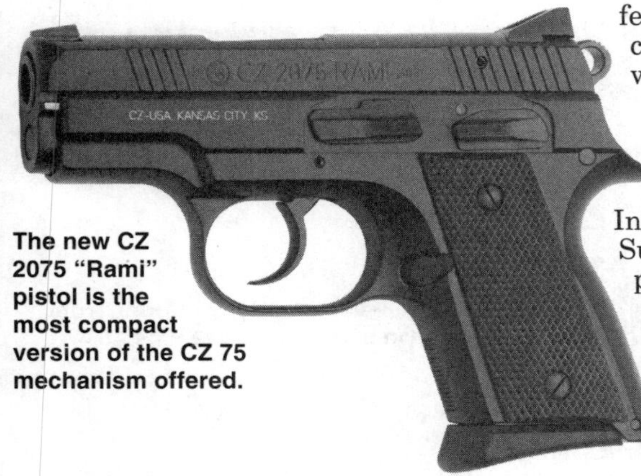

The new CZ 2075 "Rami" pistol is the most compact version of the CZ 75 mechanism offered.

The Detonics pistol is back! Here is a pre-production specimen of the CombatMaster, offered by a new company, Detonics USA.

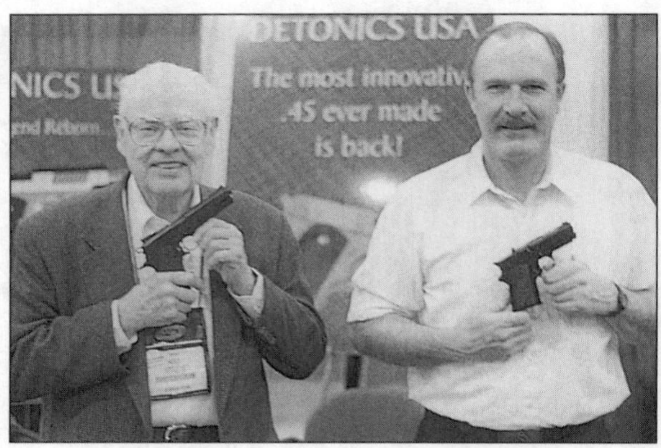

Principals of the original Detonics company are involved with Detonics USA. Sid Woodcock *(left)* the original designer, and Peter Dunn, gunsmith, hold variants that will be offered by the new company.

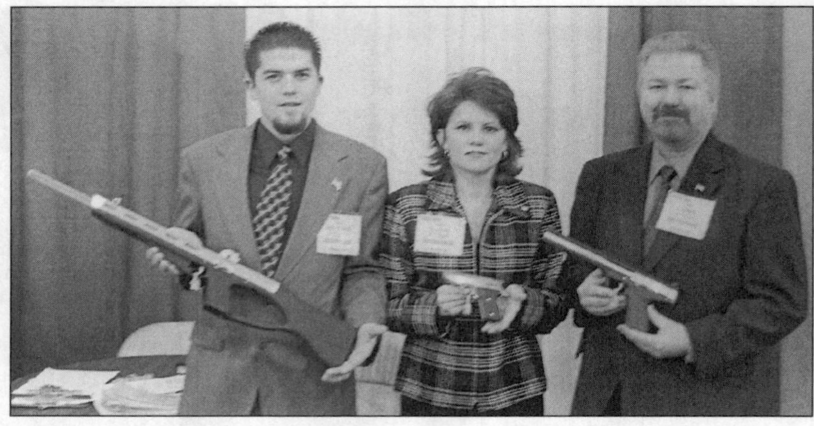

New offerings by Excel Arms: Richard Gilliam holds the 17 HRM carbine, Kathy Gilliam shows the Accu-Tek AT 380 II pistol, and Excel President Larry Gilliam displays the 17 HRM pistol.

▲As companions to their new 17 HRM and 22 WMR pistols, Excel Arms offers carbines in the same calibers.

Detonics

Detonics is back! The original Detonics company was formed in Washington state about 1976 and stayed in business until 1988. It was sold to another group in Phoenix, AZ who did business as New Detonics Manufacturing Co. Within a few years, however, at least by 1992, that company had ceased to do business.

Now a new company, Detonics USA, has been formed in Atlanta, GA by some of the principals of the original firm. Designer Sid Woodcock and gunsmith Peter Dunn are back making Detonics pistols. Author Jerry Ahern, an early proponent of the Detonics design, is also involved with the company.

Woodcock, with his background in explosives, named the first pistol "Detonics," a word related to the science of explosives. That early pistol, the first compact 45-caliber pistol, introduced a number of concepts that are widely used today. The cone-shaped bushingless barrel, captive counter-wound recoil spring and enlarged ejection port were all introduced with the early Detonics pistols. The company was also one of the early users of stainless steel as a suitable material for autoloading pistols.

Detonics USA will offer the small version—the 3 1/2-inch barrel CombatMaster—as its first product, because "that is the Detonics that people remember." The mid-size ServiceMaster and full-size ScoreMaster—also produced by the original company—will be offered later. Initial production was scheduled for October 2004.

EAA

European American Armory (EAA) has added a few new variants to its popular Witness line of Tanfoglio-made pistols.

A Witness P variant with a polymer frame and stainless-steel slide is now available in 10mm chambering with the short 3.6-inch barrel. A Witness PS can be had in 9mm with an accessory rail on the forward part of the frame.

The Witness Limited target pistol, a big single-action pistol in chrome finish and with adjustable Sights, is now available in 38 Super chambering.

Ed Brown

Ed Brown Products of Perry, MO, offers the Executive Elite (5-inch barrel) and Executive Carry (4 1/4-inch barrel) lines. These 1911-type pistols are offered in three finishes—blue, stainless steel, and blue slide on a stainless-steel frame. Front straps and mainspring housings are checkered at 25 lines per inch (lpi), and grips are checkered Cocobolo wood.

The larger Elite pistols have straight mainspring housings. The smaller Carry guns feature the Ed Brown "Bobtail" treatment, in which

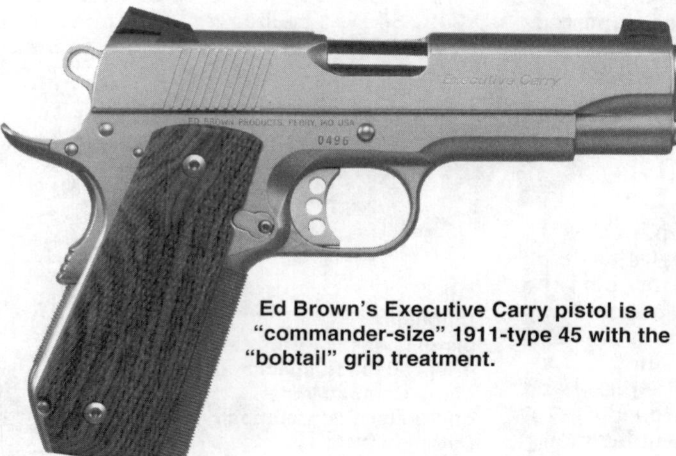

Ed Brown's Executive Carry pistol is a "commander-size" 1911-type 45 with the "bobtail" grip treatment.

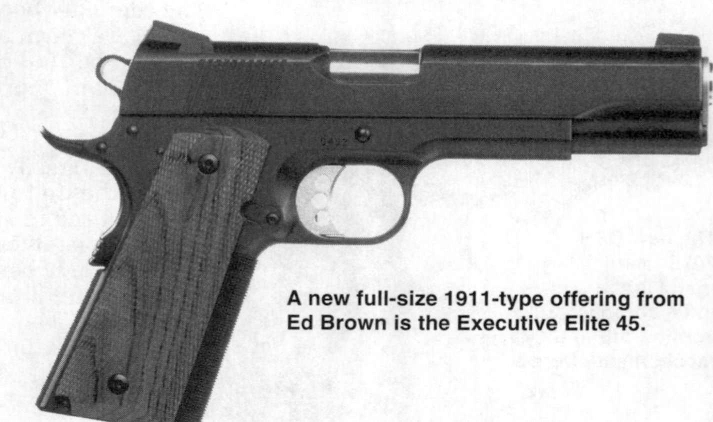

A new full-size 1911-type offering from Ed Brown is the Executive Elite 45.

▶ The Excel Arms MP 17 is a new semiauto pistol for the 17 HRM cartridge. A similar pistol is also made for the 22WMR.

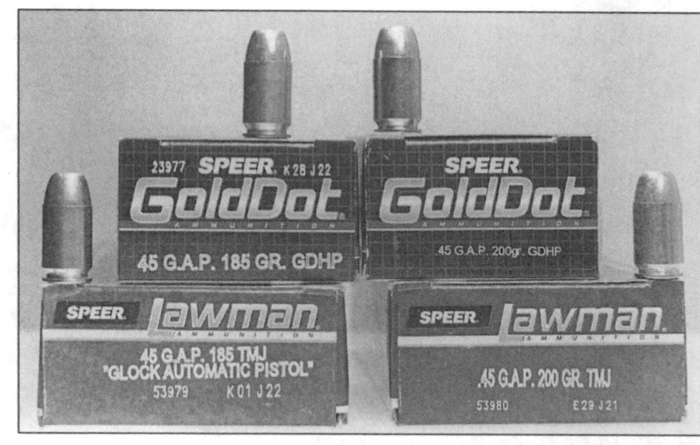

The 45 GAP (45 Glock Automatic Pistol) cartridge, introduced last year, already has a number of different loads offered for it.

the end of the mainspring housing and grip frame angles forward. The Bobtail shape makes concealment easier, and many like the feel of the modified grip.

Excel

Excel Industries makes the Accu-Tek AT-380 pistol, and for 2004, the Accu-Tek was designed with a slightly longer grip and a magazine holding an extra round. Measuring just over 4 x 6 inches, the little stainless-steel 380 is still in the subcompact class, and has 6+1 capacity. Each new AT-380 pistol comes with two 6-round magazines, a hard case and a lock.

A totally new pistol, the Accelerator, is now offered, chambered for either the 17 Hornady Magnum Rimfire (17 HMR) or 22 Winchester Magnum Rimfire (22 WMR). Model numbers are MP-17 and MP-22, respectively. Either pistol has an 8 1/2-inch barrel and weight of about 54 ounces. The big pistols are constructed from stainless steel, with a polymer grip. An aluminum top rib contains fully adjustable sights and allows mounting of optical or other types of Sighting devices. The Excel Accelerator is the second semiautomatic pistol to be offered for the 17 HMR cartridge.

A carbine with a related mechanism is also offered in the same calibers. This will not convert to a pistol, or vice versa, but it uses the same ammunition and same 9-shot magazine, and would make a neat companion piece with the pistol.

Excel also makes a conversion kit that will adapt a 1911 pistol to use either the 17 HMR or the 22 WMR cartridges, in 8-round magazines. This is a serious conversion, with an 8 1/2-inch barrel and fully adjustable Sights.

FNH

FNH USA is the American arm of FN Herstal, offering some firearms similar to those sold under the Browning name.

The 9mm FNP-9 was introduced last year, and it has now been joined by the FNP-40, in 40 S&W caliber. The pistol is a conventional double action with a high-capacity polymer frame and an ambidextrous decocker. With a 4-inch barrel, the FNP-40 is only 7 inches long, and weighs about 25 ounces.

Glock

The Glock Model 37—chambered for the new 45 Glock Automatic Pistol (45 GAP) cartridge—was introduced last year and is now in production. The 45 GAP uses a shorter case (about 0.750") and shorter overall length (about 1.10") than the standard 45 Automatic Colt Pistol (45 ACP) cartridge. Some changes have been made since the introduction of the Model 37, noticeably the use of a heavier slide—a modified Model 21 slide.

However, the Model 37 is still about the same general size as the original Model 17 9mm pistol. The shorter 45 GAP cartridge allows the use of a smaller frame, but limits the loadings to the shorter-length 45-caliber bullets. Chamber pressure of the 45 GAP is somewhat higher than that of the 45 ACP, but several companies have begun to produce it, and at least one other manufacturer plans to offer a 45 GAP chambering in its pistol line.

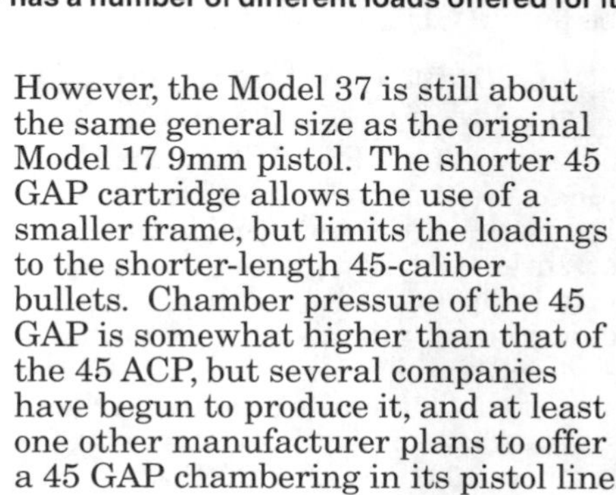

▲ Glock or 1911 pistols can be converted into carbines with Mech-Tech's Carbine Conversion Unit. This is a Glock conversion.

▲ Here is a pre-production version of the Glock Model 37. The production model has a heavier slide, and the cartridge is now called the 45 GAP (45 Glock Automatic Pistol).

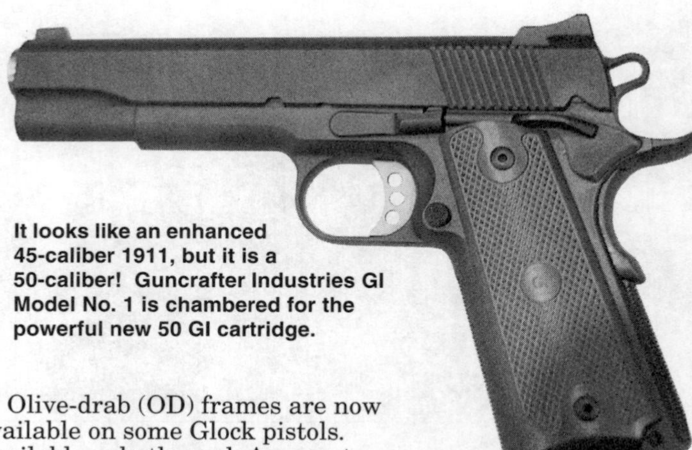

It looks like an enhanced 45-caliber 1911, but it is a 50-caliber! Guncrafter Industries GI Model No. 1 is chambered for the powerful new 50 GI cartridge.

Three different loadings of 50 GI cartridges are offered. The rebated rims are the same diameter as that of the 45 ACP, and the overall length is about the same. A 45 ACP is on the right for comparison.

Olive-drab (OD) frames are now available on some Glock pistols. Available only through Acusport, Models 17, 19, 21, 22, 23 and 27 can be had in OD after June 2004.

Guncrafter Industries

Displayed for the first time at the February 2004 SHOT Show, the GI Model No. 1 from Guncrafter Industries attracted considerable attention. At first glance, the new pistol appears to be another modernized full-size 1911 of normal size and weight. Until one notices the size of the bore. It is a 50-caliber!

The new GI pistol is chambered for the new 50 GI cartridge. The cartridge is a new one, with a case slightly shorter in length than a 45 ACP, and with a rebated rim the same diameter as the 45 ACP. The loaded 50-caliber round is about the same overall length as the 45 ACP. Ammunition, brass, bullets and reloading dies *(dies made by Hornady and Lee Precision)* are available from the company. The 50 GI ammunition, as loaded, features a light load (300-grain bullet at 725 fps) and a heavier load (300-grain bullet at 900 fps). At the introduction, three bullet types—jacketed flat point, soft point and hollow point—were displayed.

Although the pistol is externally the same as a 45-caliber 1911, there are internal dimensional differences. The pistol uses a cone barrel that is fitted directly into the front of the slide. The magazine well in the frame is machined larger to accept the fatter 50-caliber magazine. These changes preclude using those standard 1911 parts, but GI offers a conversion kit of their special parts to convert their Model No. 1 to 45 ACP.

Heckler & Koch

In July 2003, the Transportation Security Administration (TSA) made plans to acquire up to 9600 40-caliber pistols. The pistols were to be used to arm U. S. commercial airline pilots who passed the Federal Flight Deck Officer (FFDO) program administered by the TSA. The contract was awarded to Heckler & Koch (HK) for their USP 40 pistol. In August 2003, HK announced its first U. S. factory, which would be at a site at Columbus, GA. The official groundbreaking for the plant was on October 14, 2003. Reportedly, the contract USP pistols will be made at this location. The USP 40 is a conventional double-action pistol *(although it can be converted to DAO)*, with a 4 1/4-inch barrel. The pistol measures 5.3 x 7.6 inches. The USP is a polymer-frame pistol with a blued slide.

Newly introduced at the February 2004 SHOT Show were two variants of the P 2000 K subcompact pistol, in 9mm and 40 S&W. Smaller and lighter than the USP series, the P 2000 series pistols have different trigger mechanisms. With 3.6-inch barrels, the pistols measure 5 x 7 inches.

High Standard

High Standard and Aguila worked together, and last year introduced the 17 Hi-Standard cartridge, basically a 22 Long Rifle case necked down to 17-caliber, and loaded with a 20-grain bullet. The new round worked perfectly in rebarreled Hi-Standard semiautomatic pistols. However, High Standard has held off marketing the 17-caliber pistols.

The 17-caliber rimfire scene has seen a surprising amount of activity. From left, a 17 Hi-Standard, made by Aguila; a 17 Mach 2, made by CCI and the 17 Mach 2 as made by Eley. The earlier 17 Hornady Magnum Rimfire is at the right for comparison.

The 40 and 45-caliber polymer-frame Hi-Point pistols are in full production. Here, Malloy shoots the new 45.

The new Hi-Point polymer-frame 40 and 45-caliber pistols have undergone some refinements and are now in full production. Adjustable Sights and accessory rails are standard.

In February 2004, a new 17-caliber cartridge based on the 22 LR case was announced. Hornady and CCI worked together to develop a similar—but not quite the same—short 17 round, the 17 Mach 2, with a 17-grain bullet. Eley also plans to make the ammunition. There seems to be a substantial amount of interest in a Long Rifle-length 17, and it will be interesting to see how this situation plays out.

High Standard continues its line of 22 LR target pistols, 45-caliber 1911-type pistols and conversion kits to adapt the 1911 to 22 LR.

Among the new items is the Shea Custom 10X pistol, a 22 target pistol to be hand-built in small quantities by High Standard gunsmith Bob Shea. Shea worked for High Standard from 1943 to 1984, then as an independent gunsmith specializing in Hi-Standard pistols after that. He apparently knows what he is doing.

Another new item is the Marine Corps Trial Pistol, a 45-caliber 1911-type pistol that has the features of the pistol that High Standard submitted for the United States Marine Corps (USMC) sidearm trials.

Hi-Point

Last year, Hi-Point introduced new polymer-frame 40- and 45-caliber pistols. Some minor refinements have been made, and the pistols are now in full production. These are the least expensive new handguns made in these calibers, but seem to work fine and shoot well. Recall that these are blowback pistols, yet are rated for +P ammunition, and have a lifetime warranty.

New for 2004 is the Hi-Point carbine in 40 S&W. The carbine, of course, belongs in another report, but is mentioned here because the 10-shot magazine is identical to, and interchangeable with, that of the new 40-caliber pistol. In the Old West, it was an advantage to have a carbine and a handgun that used the same ammunition. Hi-Point offers that advantage with the added factor that extra magazines will work in either carbine or pistol.

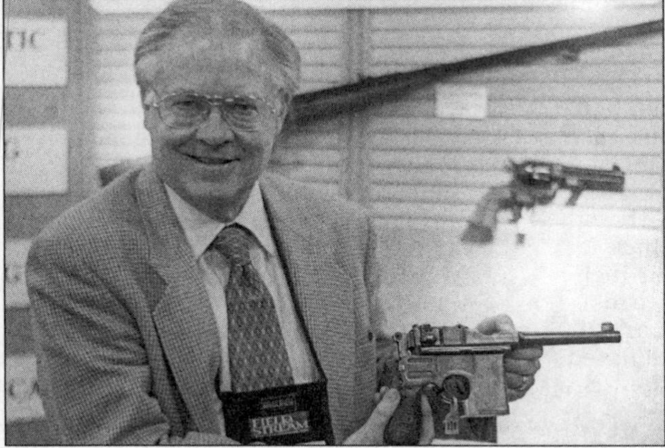

Best-known for replicas of 1800s firearms, IAR also offers a small number of 45 ACP Chinese copies of the Mauser "broomhandle" pistol. IAR president Will Hanson holds a specimen.

IAR

One thinks of the IAR (International Antique Reproductions) firm as a source of shooting replicas of 19th century historical firearms. However, they have a small quantity of the original big 45 ACP Chinese "broomhandle Mauser" copies made in the 20th century. It may be of interest to collectors to know that a small stock of these interesting and historical autoloading pistols still exists.

Kahr

Kahr has introduced a number of new models, all variations of the company's patented DAO mechanism. As the number of models has grown, so have the designations for these models. Here is a breakdown that may help in understanding the Kahr offerings:

"K" alone before a number indicates the original stainless-steel Kahr offering, a mid-size pistol with a 3.5-inch barrel. The numbers 9 or 40 following always indicate the caliber. A "P" prefix indicates a polymer-frame pistol. "M" indicates a Micro Compact, with a 3-inch barrel. "T" represents target or tactical pistols, which have 4-inch barrels.

With this in mind, the new PM 40 pistol is a small 40-caliber, polymer-frame pistol with a 3-inch barrel. The slide is matte stainless steel, and the pistol comes with two magazines—one flush, one elongated for extended grip and an extra round.

The TP 9 is a new 4-inch barrel, polymer-frame 9mm pistol. The polymer frame is black and the slide is matte stainless steel. Either 3-dot sights or tritium night sights are available. Delivery was scheduled for mid-2004.

The T 40 is a 29-ounce 40-caliber stainless-steel frame pistol with a 4-inch barrel. Checkered wood Hogue grips offset the matte-finish stainless steel, and make a sharp-looking pistol. This variant began shipping in February 2004.

Recall that Kahr also offers the Auto-Ordnance line of Thompson 45-caliber pistols. The Custom 1911 pistol, announced last year, is now a catalog item. It is all stainless steel, a full-size pistol with a 5-inch barrel. It features a beavertail grip safety, lightened hammer, adjustable trigger and other niceties. Grips are laminate with big-diamond checkering and have the Thompson bullet logo inlaid.

Kel-Tec

Kel-Tec's little 380 pistol, the P-3AT, which was introduced last year, is now in full production. Like its predecessor, the P-32, it uses a tilting-barrel locked-breech system.

The 380 is very slightly longer than the 32, and weight has gone up a bit over 1/2-ounce to 7.3 ounces. Visually, about all that distinguishes the new 380 are the wider spacing of the grasping grooves and the absence of some lightening cuts on the slide.

Mechanically, the P-3AT does not have the internal slide lock of the P-32. This apparently was omitted to make

Impress your friends by being able to tell the difference between the P-3AT *(above)* and the earlier P-32. The P-32 *(right)* has narrower grasping grooves and a lightening cut at the front of the slide.

space for the larger-diameter 380 cartridge and still keep the width to 3/4-inch. The greater diameter of the cartridge also decreases the magazine to six rounds (6+1 total) capacity. However, a magazine extension is available as an accessory to increase the capacity by an extra round.

Other accessories avail for the P-3AT are a belt clip *(very useful in some carry situations)* and a lanyard kit. The lanyard kit includes an attachment unit for the rear of the pistol, and an elastic lanyard with a latching hook. Handgun guru Jeff Cooper pointed out the benefits of using a lanyard over 40 years ago, and it is interesting that Kel-Tec is offering the option.

Kimber

In 2004, Kimber celebrated its 25th anniversary. To commemorate this special event, the company decided that a number of special 1911 pistols would be made. A total of 1,911 *(a logical number)* 25th Anniversary "Custom" pistols would be made. In addition, 500 25th Anniversary "Gold Match" pistols would be produced. 250 pairs of one each of the Custom and Gold Match pistols, with matching serial numbers, would also be put up in wood presentation cases.

In their regular line, the company offers the Stainless TLE II pistol, a 45 ACP version of the Kimber selected for duty carry by the LAPD's SWAT team. The gun is a full-size 1911-type pistol with a 5-inch barrel. It has tritium night sights.

From the Kimber Custom Shop, the 22 LR pistol introduced last year now is available in a "Rimfire Super" version, with two-tone finish, adjustable Sights, ambidextrous thumb safety, big diamond wood grips and other niceties. Performance has not taken a back seat to looks, though—the 22 pistol has turned in 1 1/2-inch groups at 25 yards.

The 7-ounce Kel-Tec 380-caliber pistol, the Model P3AT, is now in full production.

As of February 2004, Kimber had donated $200,000 to the USA Shooting team. Kimber is thus the largest firearms corporate donor in USA Shooting Team history. The money comes from the sales of special guns, and goes straight to benefit the team. Way to go, Kimber!

Korth

Willi Korth began business by making blank revolvers in 1954, so 2004 became the 50th anniversary of the German Korth company. The firm now has a reputation for making very fine *(and very expensive)* handguns. To commemorate this 50-year milestone, a few specially–embellished Korth pistols and revolvers were scheduled. Five semiautomatic pistols, in 9mm, and five 357 Magnum revolvers will be available, Korth USA reports.

Les Baer

New from Les Baer Custom are two 1911-type 45-caliber pistols in the Thunder Ranch series, which was introduced last year. The Commanche is a serious self-defense pistol with a 4 1/4-inch barrel. It is chrome-plated.

The Home Defense pistol is designed for use in dark environments. It has an M3 tactical illuminator mounted to the front of the "Monolith" frame. The light can be selected to be on for constant or momentary time periods. Night Sights are also provided.

Lone Star

In February 2003, Lone Star Armament introduced a new series of 1911-type pistols. In November 2003, it was announced that Lone Star had been acquired by STI. ***(see STI)***

Mech-Tech

Mech-Tech offers a Carbine Conversion Unit (CCU) that uses the frame of a 1911 or Glock pistol to form a pistol-caliber carbine. Pistol-carbines seem to be of interest now, and this is an interesting device.

Mitchell

The new 1911-type pistols shown in prototype last year are now in production. The first display of production models was at the February 2004 SHOT Show in Las Vegas, NV. The guns are called "Mitchell Gold Series" 1911s, and combine the original 1911 mechanism with 21st century enhancements.

Chamberings have been expanded from the original 45 ACP to also include 40 S&W, 9mm and 38 Super. Standard features include beavertail grip safety, lowered ejection port, skeletonized hammer and trigger, extended thumb safety, walnut big-diamond grips and other niceties.

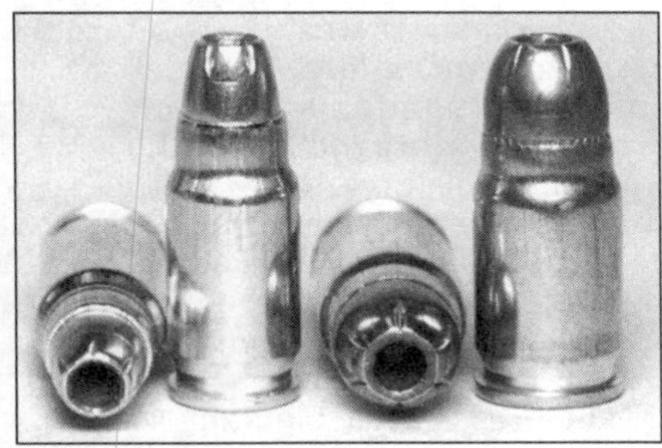

North American Arms has provided two new cartridges for pocket pistols. The 32NAA has been joined this year by the new 25NAA round.

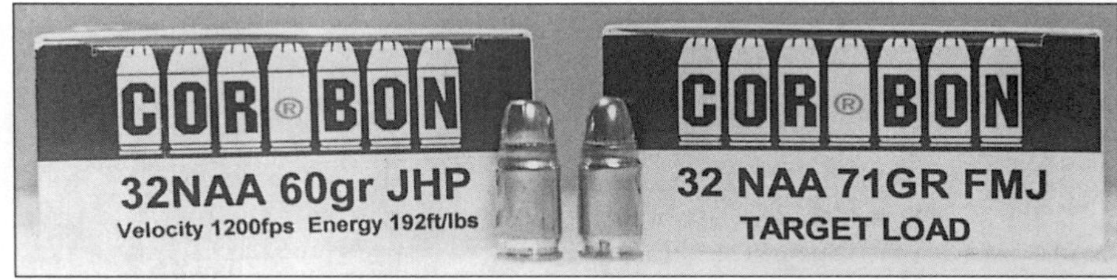

Ammunition for the potent 32NAA is in production. Cor-Bon now produces two loads—a zippy 60-grain jacketed hollow-point, and a 71-grain full-metal-jacket "target load."

North American

North American Arms (NAA) has introduced a new pistol in its Guardian series, chambered for the new 25 NAA cartridge. The pistol is the same size as their 13-ounce 32 ACP Guardian, and has been in development for several years. The first concept was to neck down the semi-rimmed 32 ACP to 25-caliber. That approach was tried, but did not give the 100-percent reliability desired. Working with Cor-Bon, NAA developed a new rimless case with a longer body, and the body diameter of the 32 Harrington & Richardson Magnum (32 H&R Magnum). Although this newer case is longer than that of the 32 ACP, the overall length of the loaded cartridge is about the same.

The performance of the 25 NAA is of some interest. A 35-grain Hornady XTP bullet screams out of its 2.2-inch barrel at about 1200 feet per second (fps). Considering that the case is about three-quarters of an inch long, the bullet only has about 1-1/2 inches to get up to speed. Pretty impressive.

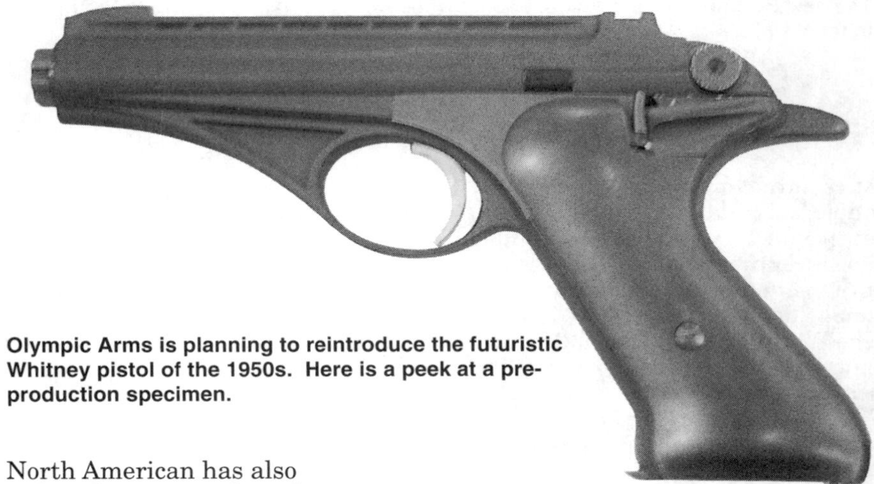

Olympic Arms is planning to reintroduce the futuristic Whitney pistol of the 1950s. Here is a peek at a pre-production specimen.

North American has also introduced an optional 10-shot extended magazine adapter for its 32 ACP and 380 ACP Guardians. Made by Hogue, the adaptor uses the original magazine and floorplate. It increases capacity, while providing additional grip surface.

Olympic Arms

The Whitney is back! At the February 2004 SHOT Show, Olympic Arms announced the return of the Whitney Wolverine. As many old-timers may remember, the original Whitney pistol appeared about 1955 or 1956. Its streamlined, futuristic styling and light aluminum-alloy frame made it stand out from other postwar pistols. The company, however, ran into financial problems, and production stopped after fewer than 14,000 pistols had been produced.

Olympic Arms has improved the Whitney design, and displayed a pre-production specimen at the show. Handguns with aluminum-alloy frames were a novel idea in the 1950s. Now, half a century later, polymer

The 25 NAA cartridge was developed for a small 32-size pistol. From left, a 32 ACP; an experimental 25 formed by necking down the 32 ACP; and the final 25 NAA with a longer rimless case, but of about the same overall length as the 32.

After several years of development, the hot new 25 NAA version of North American Arms' Guardian series has been introduced.

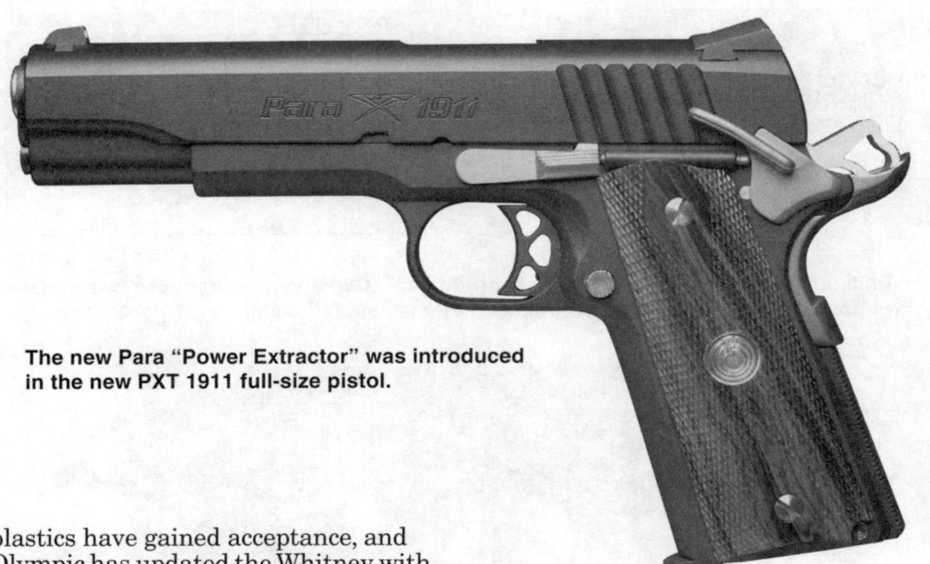

The new Para "Power Extractor" was introduced in the new PXT 1911 full-size pistol.

plastics have gained acceptance, and Olympic has updated the Whitney with a new polymer frame. Other additions will be a ventilated rib, a dovetailed rear Sight, and better distinction of the manual safety positions.

The Whitney name was on the pre-production specimen, and is planned to appear on the final production model.

The original designer, Bob Hillberg, reportedly requested that the name be retained. Production was scheduled to begin in mid-2004.

Many older shooters liked the original Whitney pistol and hoped for its return to production. Olympic's new version should please them, and introduce younger generations to the Whitney.

Pacific Armament

Pacific Armament has introduced a line of Argentine-made FM Hi-Power 9mm pistols. These have the original-style round hammer spurs of the early Belgian-made Hi-Powers, and come with 10-round magazines. The standard "Military" model has a 4.65-inch barrel. A more compact version, the "Detective" model, has a 3.65-inch barrel. Kits to convert existing pistols to Detective configuration are offered. Also, a conversion kit to adapt the Hi-Power pistols to 22 LR is available.

The company also imports a line of Philippine-made 45-caliber 1911-style pistols in full-size (5-inch barrel), mid-size (4-inch barrel) and compact (3 1/2-inch barrel) variants. These pistols are offered in the United States under the Rock Island Armory name.

Para-Ordnance

Para-Ordnance's big news is the introduction of its new "Power Extractor." In the past several years, many makers of 1911-type pistols have begun using coil-spring-loaded external extractors instead of the tempered-steel internal extractor of the original 1911 design.

Para's answer was a new internal extractor, spring-loaded, that reportedly maintains constant pressure against the rim of the cartridge case and has twice the surface area of the original 1911 design. The rear of the Power Extractor is the same size as that of the original, and thus maintains the classic 1911 appearance.

The first two Para pistols with the new extractor are the 5-inch barrel PXT 1911, and the 4 1/4-inch barrel PXT LTC. The Power Extractor will soon become standard on all Para models. Both new PXT pistols also have ramped barrels and supported chambers, features that have been made standard on all Para pistols. As with all Para-Ordnance pistols, they are shipped with two magazines.

The company has a number of new introductions. Of interest to those who favor small, big-bore pistols with as many shots as possible is the new Warthog. It is a 3-inch barrel 10-shot 45 that weighs only 24 ounces. Para is coming up with so many new options that the company plans to publish two catalogs a year to keep shooters current on their offerings.

Para-Ordnance is proud that the Para CCW pistol was chosen as the winner of the *Guns & Ammo* "Gun of the Year" award for 2003. This makes the fourth time one of the company's products has won the award. The Para CCW introduced "Griptor" grasping grooves on the frame front strap and sides of the slide.

World Champion shooter Todd Jarrett has used different Para pistols to win all four United States Practical Shooting Association (USPSA) national championships—Open, Limited, Limited 10 and Production. This seems to speak well for Para's accuracy and functioning.

▲This cutaway slide shows the enlarged gripping surfaces of the new Para Power Extractor.

Para-Ordnance's CCW pistol introduced "Griptor" grooves on the frame front strap and sides of the slide.

A "commander-size" Para pistol, the PXT LTC, comes with the new Power Extractor.

Phoenix

Phoenix Arms, maker of affordable 22- and 25-caliber pistols for personal protection and informal target shooting, is working on a larger-caliber 380 pistol. No prototype was available for observation at the February 2004 SHOT Show. However, a representative said the pistol would probably be similar in design to the present pistols in the Phoenix line. The new 380 was expected to be announced during Summer 2004.

Professional Ordnance

Late in 2003, Professional Ordnance was acquired by Bushmaster Firearms, Inc. Professional Ordnance's Carbon 15 pistols (and rifles) will be manufactured under the Bushmaster name. ***(see Bushmaster)***

Rock River Arms

Rock River has added a new "basic carry" pistol to its offerings of 1911-type pistols. This is a lower-priced model in Parkerized finish, but still includes a beavertail grip safety, and ventilated trigger and hammer.

A 9mm long-slide version with a 6-inch barrel is also new. This configuration is aimed toward PPC shooters, and has a supported chamber.

For those who want to build their own pistols, a frame and slide kit is available. Most of the fitting is done, and a shooter can build a 1911 to his own specifications.

Rohrbaugh

The little DAO Rohrbaugh R9 pistol, introduced as a prototype two years ago, and as a pre-production specimen one year ago, is now in production. Several hundred guns had been made by early 2004.

Recall that the pistol uses standard 9mm ammunition, and has a tilting-barrel locked breech action. It is all metal, with 7075 aluminum frame and 17-4 stainless-steel slide and barrel. With a 2.9-inch barrel, the pistol measures only 3.7 x 5.2 inches, putting it in the smallest part of the subcompact class. Weight is 12.8 ounces, and capacity is 6 +1. The R9 is available with or without Sights.

Ruger

All Ruger adjustable-sight 22-caliber pistols will now be drilled and tapped for a Weaver-type base, and the base itself will be included with each drilled pistol. The base fits in front of the rear sight, and does not interfere with the pistol's metallic sights, but allows easy mounting of optical or electronic sights.

Two special model 22 pistols were scheduled for production during 2004. The first, the William B. Ruger Endowment Special NRA Edition pistol, is a blued Mark II with simulated ivory grips, with red eagle Ruger grip medallions. William B. Ruger's signature is rollmarked on the top of the receiver, along with the Ruger and NRA crests. For every pistol sold, a donation is made to the National Rifle Association's basic marksmanship training program.

The U. S. A. Shooting commemorative is a Mark II with gold plating on the bolt, and black laminate grip panels. For every pistol sold, a donation is made to the United States Shooting Team, which is preparing for the Olympic contests in Athens, Greece. As of February 2004, Ruger had contributed $30,000 to the U.S.A. Shooting Team. Bravo!

SIGARMS

Will the popularity of the 1911 design ever level out? Last year, Smith & Wesson added a 1911 to that company's offerings. In February 2004, SIGARMS unveiled their own 1911.

SIGARMS realized that American practical shooting is dominated by the 1911, and in order to be competitive, the company needed to add a 1911 to their line. The result was the GSR pistol. "GSR" stands for "Granite Series Rail," and denotes the accessory rail on the front portion of the slide. The rail is one thing that makes the SIG 1911 GSR visually distinctive from some other 1911s. Another factor is the shape of the slide's top and side cuts, which make the GSR look a little bit more "SIGgy." The GSR is a high-end pistol, and has an external extractor and many of the enhancements that are now in favor. It

The Ruger NRA pistol has special markings and simulated ivory grips. For each pistol sold, a donation is made to NRA's training programs.

comes as a stainless-steel, or a blued stainless-steel finish.

Other SIGARMS models now have variants that incorporate an accessory rail. Among them are the P 220, P 226 and P 229. The single-action P 210 is now available with a U. S.-style magazine release on the left side of the frame.

An interesting new development is the "K trigger" option for some of the company's pistols. The K trigger is a new DAO with a pull similar to the best double-action revolver triggers. The frame of the pistol has to be changed to accommodate the new trigger mechanism, which involves new parts, spring rates and cam angles.

Smith & Wesson

The SW1911, introduced last year, has been out long enough to warrant a minor recall. Some specimens might need to have the firing pin safety plunger repaired. If you have an SW1911 between the numbers JRD 0000 and JRD 4750, call 1-800-331-0852 for information on the free repair program.

Two variants of the SW1911 are new. The SW1911 adjustable-sight target pistol is a full-size 5-inch model, with ambidextrous manual safety controls. A 1911 Sc, a scandium Commander-size arm, is available as a lighter (28-ounce) variant with a 4 1/4-inch barrel.

The Model 952 is now available in stainless steel. Recall that the 952 is a 9mm target pistol based on the earlier Model 52.

The Model 22A, the full-size 22 LR autoloader, is now available as the 22A Camo. The entire gun is covered with a Mossy Oak camouflage finish.

▲Smith & Wesson's 22A pistol is now available with a camouflage finish.

▼A shorter, lighter "commander-size" version of the SW1911 is available with a scandium frame.

Springfield

It is back to basics for part of Springfield Armory's new 1911A1 offerings. The "GI" series guns are made with low-profile military-type sights and standard hammer, trigger and grip safety. The ejection port is standard, not lowered, and a lanyard loop again appears at the rear of the butt. Slide serrations are the older narrow vertical type. Some concessions have been made to the modern era, as the barrels have ramped barrels with fully supported chambers. Except for the big-diamond walnut grips, the 5-inch Parkerized version is a dead ringer for the World War II 1911A1 configuration. There are also other versions in the GI line—a 5-inch OD green Armory Kote, a 5-inch stainless steel variant, and 3-inch and 4-inch Parkerized variants. It is good to have these basic models available again, so that new shooters do not think that every 1911 has to look like a racegun.

In the XD line of polymer-frame pistols, some variants now will be available in the 45 Glock Auto Pistol (45 GAP) chambering from Springfield's Custom Shop.

A special edition "Sergeant York" 1911 has been prepared by Springfield in connection with Investment Arms.

These special pistols honor Sgt. Alvin C. York, an excellent marksman with both rifle and pistol, who almost single-handedly captured 132 German prisoners during World War I. His actions stopped a German counterattack in France's Argonne Forest. York was awarded the Medal of Honor and the French Croix de Guerre, and became the most decorated soldier of that war. The commemorative pistols are special because the grips are made from the wood of trees that actually grew on York's land. A nonprofit conservation organization, American Forests, kept track of the trees on the York farm and harvested the wood when the trees died. For every pistol sold, new trees will be planted in special Liberty Forests. 132 Peerless Grade pistols, plated and engraved, and with grips made of cherry wood from York's farm will be made. 5000 additional Issue Grade pistols, with grips made from

▲A stainless-steel version of the S&W Model 952 9mm target pistol is now available.

▲A target version of the SW1911 pistol is now offered, with adjustable sights.

▲A 4-inch barrel Parkerized version of Springfield's new "GI" series is available.

▼Springfield's new "GI" series includes a stainless-steel version.

▲A full-size Parkerized 45 with a 5-inch barrel, Springfield's new "GI" pistol resembles previous military pistols.

Springfield has introduced "GI" series pistols. This is a Parkerized version with a 3-inch barrel.

Springfield's two special Sgt. York commemorative pistols, the Peerless Grade and the Issue Grade, rest on a piece of cherry wood from the York farm, from which the grips of the Peerless pistols are made.

the black walnut tree that actually shaded the cabin in which York was born, will also be made.

STI

STI, of Georgetown, TX, in November 2003 acquired Lone Star Armament of Stephenville, TX. The acquisition essentially doubled STI's capacity for producing 1911-type pistols and parts. Beside the increase in pistol production, STI planned to begin providing a full line of parts to other manufacturers.

The Lone Star name has been phased out. Recall, however, that Lone Star offered two basic single-column 1911 pistols—the 5-inch Lawman and the 4-inch Ranger. The Ranger has been dropped, but the full-size pistol continues on as the STI Lawman. The Lawman is suitable for IDPA competition as well as IPSC and USPSA.

Taurus

In mid-2003, Taurus announced its new polymer-frame DAO service pistol, the 24/7. It was introduced in 9mm and 40 S&W, and those options are now available. In the meantime, Taurus developed a larger-bore version, and the 24/7 in 45 ACP was introduced at the February 2004 SHOT Show. The new 45 has a bushingless flared barrel and a

◀ The Taurus 24/7 service pistol, introduced last year in 9mm and 40, is now offered in 45 ACP.

▼ A Taurus pistol in 38 Super, the Model PT38S, is now available.

captive flat-coil recoil spring. An accessory rail is present at the front of the frame. The 45-caliber was scheduled for production in late 2004.

The nice PT 922 22-caliber pistol has undergone some revisions in the past two years, and is now in final form. It has a 6-inch barrel, 10+1 capacity and weighs 29 ounces. The polymer frame has a slanty "Woodsman" look and feel, and the pistol has an adjustable rear sight and fiber-optic front sight.

The 38 Super cartridge came on the scene in 1929, and although it has never been a standard military or police service round, it has remained popular. Taurus has introduced its first 38 Super pistol, the PT 38S. The pistol is conventional double-action, and comes in either blue or stainless steel finishes. With a 4 1/4-inch barrel, it weighs 30 ounces. Availability was scheduled for late 2004.

Uselton

A new line of 1911-style pistols was presented for the first time at the February 2004 SHOT Show, under the name Uselton Arms. Made on Caspian steel frames, the pistols have Uselton stainless-steel slides, barrels and triggers. The Uselton trigger is very distinctive, and has a flat vertical front surface. Other features now in vogue, such as beavertail grip safeties and extended manual safety levers, are also present.

Variants with 5-inch, 4 1/4-inch, 3 1/2-inch and 3-inch barrels are offered. Special features such as titanium frames and Damascus slides are also offered on select models. Calibers are 45 ACP, 40 S&W and 357 SIG. In some versions, interchangeable barrels are provided to make the pistol both a 40 S&W and a 357 SIG, at the choice of the shooter.

Uselton considers their pistols "totally customized" out of the box.

Volquartsen

Known for their Ruger-style 22-caliber pistols, Volquartsen plans to introduce a new lightweight version. The pistol will have a steel receiver and a barrel of 12mm diameter sleeved in titanium. They will offer it in 22 LR, and tentatively plan to offer the 17 Aguila (17 Hi-Standard) when the ammunition becomes available.

Walther

Walther didn't really offer anything new in the autoloading pistol line this year. However, they introduced a 22 LR carbine. It is not really a pistol-carbine, but it is related, so let's give it a quick look. The new G22 carbine is of the bullpup design, so the action is under the stock's cheekpiece. With a 20-inch barrel, the overall length is only 28 inches. The grip of the polymer stock is similar to that of Walther's P22 rimfire pistol, and the carbine can use the same magazines.

Wildey

Wildey is working with the government of Jordan on the Jordanian Armament Weapons Systems (JAWS) pistol project, and the new pistol, introduced last year, is well into development. Recall that the pistol is service-type, with a conventional double-action trigger system. One of its distinctive features is the ability to convert from 9mm to 40 S&W to 45 ACP with the change of a few parts. The replaceable bolt face can be changed by removing the extractor. The rotating barrel and the magazine can both be readily replaced when the pistol is stripped for cleaning. Internal parts can be reached by removing a frame sideplate, which is retained by the slide.

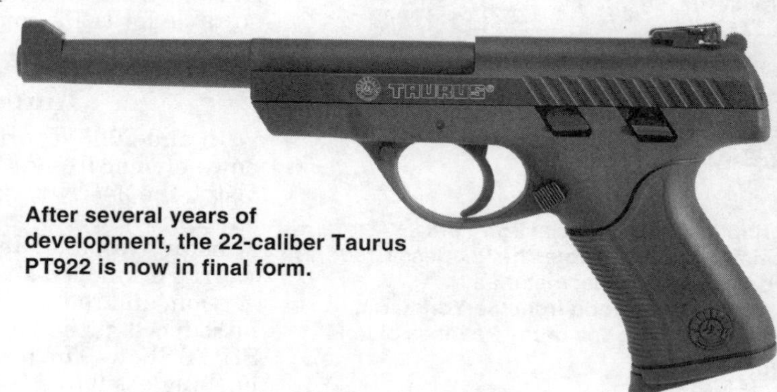

After several years of development, the 22-caliber Taurus PT922 is now in final form.

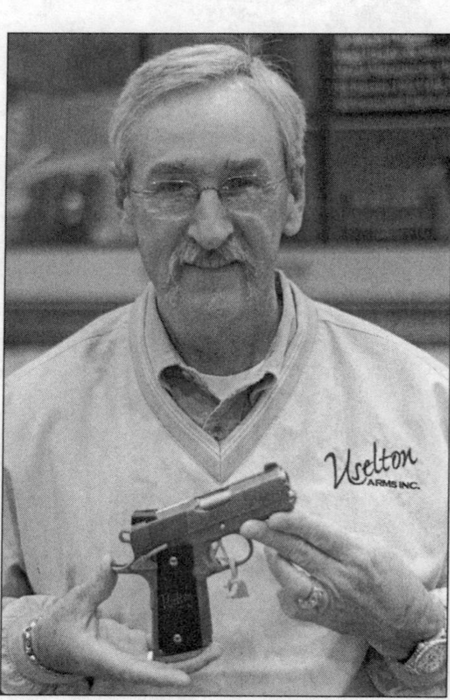

Uselton Arms president Rick Uselton holds one of his company's 1911 variants, built with a titanium frame and a Damascus slide.

▲The Walther 22-caliber G22 carbine has a grip similar to that of the P22 pistol and uses the same magazines.

▶ Optical sights can be added to the Walther G22 carbine.

The pistol has a name now. It will be called the JAWS "Viper." A standard model will have a stainless-steel frame, either natural or blackened, and a lightweight version will have an aluminum-alloy frame and shorter barrel. The design has a true ambidextrous magazine catch, which can be pressed from either side.

Wilson

Wilson Combat has added the Professional Model to its line of 1911-based pistols. It has a full-size frame with a compact slide and matching 4.1-inch barrel. Features such as beavertail grip safety, lightened hammer and extended thumb safety are standard. It is available in all-black, gray-and-black, and green-and-black. Available in 45 ACP, it weighs 35 ounces. The match barrel is hand-fitted, and the accuracy guarantee is an impressive one inch at 25 yards.

POSTSCRIPT

As this is written in 2004, a number of things lie ahead in the remainder of this year and into 2005 that hold great importance for the industry and for the shooters involved with autoloading handguns. Things unknown to me now—such as the fate of the 1994 "Assault Weapon" and magazine ban (due to sunset in September 2004), and the results of the November 2004 elections—may be history when you read this. Regardless of the outcomes, we know we will face continuing battles over license-to-carry legislation and reciprocity, and the enemies of freedom continue to call for greater restrictions on firearms. Please resolve to know where your legislators stand, and to let your legislators know where you stand. ●

The pistol developed by Wildey and the country of Jordan has been given a name, and will appear as the Jaws Viper.

▲The Wilson Combat Professional Model has a full-size frame with a 4.1-inch barrel and shorter slide.

Handgun News:

REVOLVERS, SINGLE-SHOTS & OTHERS

by John Taffin

IT WAS 50 years ago, in 1955, when Smith & Wesson produced the first 44 Magnum. Everyone knew we had reached the top; there was simply no way six-guns could ever be made more powerful. Then, in 1983 Freedom Arms produced their first 454 Casull. John Linebaugh arrived on the scene giving us the 475 and 500 Linebaughs and then stretching both to approximately 1.60 inches for "Maximum" versions of the same two cartridges. Custom revolver-builders offered heavy-duty, five-shot 45 Colt six-guns to allow heavy loading of this grand old cartridge, and Hornady and Ruger collaborated on the 480. Had we reached the end of powerful six-gun cartridge development?

Not quite. The big news last year was the 500 S&W Magnum cartridge and the new Smith & Wesson X-frame revolver. We have now had a year to test this largest of all double-action six-guns, as well as the 500 cartridge. Other manufacturers have joined with Smith & Wesson in supplying 500-chambered revolvers–with Magnum Research offering a single action BFR revolver while Taurus has countered with their Raging Bull version in 500 S&W Magnum. Two custom makers, Gary Reeder Custom Guns and SSK Industries, have offered their 500 Magnums in revolver and single-shot form, respectively. It has been my good (?) fortune to have test-fired the 500 Magnum extensively over the past year, chambered in the original 8 3/8-inch Smith & Wesson Model 500, a 10 1/2-inch BFR, an SSK Custom Encore, and a Gary Reeder single action. The cartridge has proven to be extremely accurate, as well as speaking with authority and finality when used on game.

One might think this would be the end of cartridge development; however, I have been shown three new cartridges that will be arriving on the scene this year. As this is written they must remain as "mystery cartridges", however I can share the fact that two of them will be standard length 50-caliber cartridges for use in single-action revolvers, while the other will be a "Maximum"-length 45-caliber cartridge. We are still looking and hoping for a five-shot Ruger single action in 480 Ruger or 50-caliber, however none of these will be in handguns marked with the Ruger label. Once again it is time for our annual alphabetical trip down the path labeled "Six-guns, Single Shots, and Others."

American Western Arms: AWA has been offering both the Longhorn and Peacekeeper traditionally-styled SAAs for several years. Available in most of the standard frontier calibers, these six-guns were offered in the blue and case-colored finish, as well as in hard chrome. Normally, I would say chrome belongs on the bumpers of a '49 Ford Club Coupe. However, I must admit AWA's hard chrome is very attractive, much like brushed stainless steel. The combination of hard chrome and 45 Colt make an excellent outdoorsman's revolver.

Last year AWA made a major change in their Peacekeeper and Longhorn revolvers. As one takes a close look at the back to the hammer, one notices something quite strange for a traditionally-styled single action. The area of the hammer between the two ears of the back strap is slotted to accept a strut. AWA began fitting their revolvers–on special order–with a coil mainspring system, as well as offering a kit consisting of a new hammer with an attached strut, a coil spring, and a shelf that attaches to the back strap to accept the strut. Changing from a flat mainspring to a coil spring is not quite a drop-in, as the inside of the back of the front strap must be milled out to accept the coil spring. With a coil spring-operated hand and hammer mated up with a Wolff trigger and bolt spring, the action of a single action comes

The Ultimate by AWA features a coil mainspring.

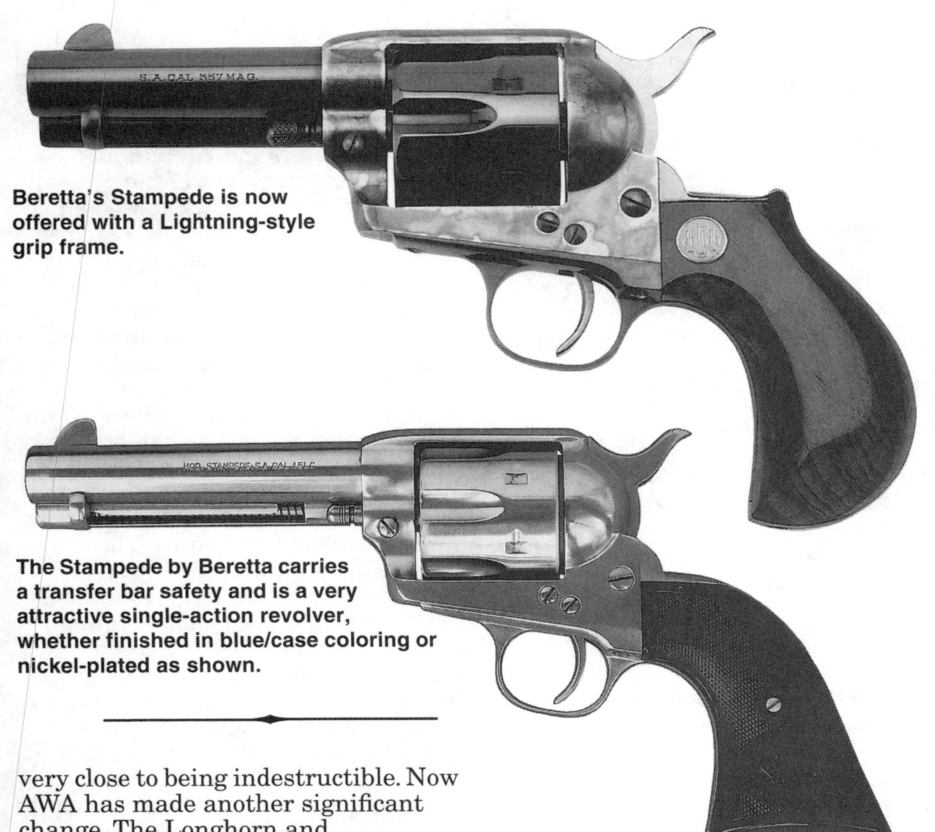

Beretta's Stampede is now offered with a Lightning-style grip frame.

The Stampede by Beretta carries a transfer bar safety and is a very attractive single-action revolver, whether finished in blue/case coloring or nickel-plated as shown.

very close to being indestructible. Now AWA has made another significant change. The Longhorn and Peacekeeper have been dropped and replaced by The Ultimate featuring the new coil mainspring system. These revolvers are made by Matiba and can be specially ordered with one-piece *faux* ivory grips by Tru-Art. Those six-guns I have seen have been very well finished and timed.

Beretta: This is not only the oldest firearms manufacturer in existence, it is the oldest company of any kind–dating back nearly 500 years. In the early 1990s it was my pleasure to be escorted through the Beretta factory, which included a personally conducted tour of their private museum housing several centuries of firearms development. We've all known Beretta as a manufacturer of high quality semi-automatic pistols and shotguns. Then the unexpected happened. Beretta, of semi-automatic fame, purchased Uberti, known for producing replicas of 19th-century firearms. Suddenly, Beretta was in the business of producing single-action six-guns.

In addition to now owning Uberti, Beretta is also offering a revolver under the Beretta name. That single-action six-gun is known as the Stampede. Although traditionally sized and styled, it contains a transfer bar safety, making it safe to carry with six rounds. Available in both the standard grip frame style as well as the Lightning grip frame, the well-built and smoothly operating Stampede has been warmly accepted by single-action shooters. Currently it is available in both 45 Colt and 357 Magnum, in either the standard blue and case-coloring, or nickel finishes.

Bond Arms: Most of us six-gunners will probably admit a fascination with derringers. When I was the kid growing up, one could still find original Remington 41RF derringers at very reasonable prices. They were, of course, chambered for hard-to-get rimfire ammunition. Then Great Western came along and, in addition to bringing out the first true replica single action army, also duplicated the Remington double-barreled derringer in 38 Special. Great Western Arms is long gone now and in the intervening years several companies have offered derringers that run the gamut from excellent quality all the way down to extremely poor. Unfortunately the latter is what too many folks have purchased to use for self-defense.

Bond Arms offers extremely high quality double-barreled derringers in both the spur trigger and trigger guard style. All Bond Arms derringers are made of stainless steel with a spring-loaded extractor, rebounding firing pin, cross-bolt safety, and a nearly endless list of available chamberings. Barrels are interchangeable, allowing the use of 26 different cartridges—all the way from 22 Long Rifle up to the 45 Colt—as well as a special rendition that not only accepts the 45 Colt but .410 shotshells as well. The standard offering, looking much like the traditional Remington Derringer, is known as the Cowboy Defender. Add a trigger guard and it becomes the Texas Defender. For those desirous of the ultimate in snake protection, there is the Century 2000, which handles 3-inch .410 shells. I have been in some places, while hunting, where I would have felt a lot more comfortable packing a Century 2000.

Cimarron Firearms (CFA): Cimarron recently celebrated its 20th year as a leader in supplying authentic replica revolvers, leverguns, and single-shot rifles to cowboy action shooters and those who appreciate the

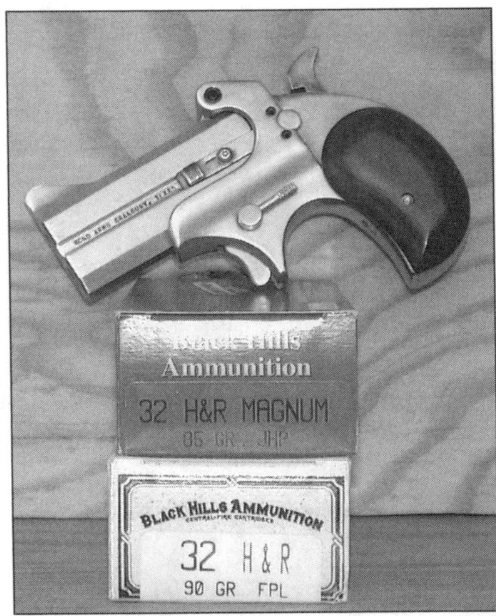

The Bond Arms Cowboy Defender is offered in 26 chamberings, including the easy-handling 32 H&R Magnum.

This Texas rattler met up with a .410-chambered Bond Arms Cowboy Defender.

Cimarron's Model P Jr. is an easy-to-handle, lightweight single action chambered in 38 Special/38LC and 32-20.

firearms of the Old West. Cimarron's Model P, a traditionally styled SAA, is now offered in stainless steel as well as blue/case-coloring and nickel. Barrel lengths are 4 3/4- and 5 1/2- with 7 1/2-inch versions now arriving. Thus far, chamberings offered are 45 Colt and 357 Magnum.

▼Colt's 44 Magnum offering is the stainless steel Anaconda.

▲The Colt Single Action Army is once again offered with a 7 1/2-inch barrel in 45 Colt, 44-40, 38-40, 38 Special, 357 Magnum, and 32-20.

For those desiring a specially tuned and smoothed single action for cowboy action shooting, Cimarron offers the Evil Roy Model P. Evil Roy is one of the top shooters in CAS and has incorporated his ideas of the perfect single action in this latest Model P including easy-to-see square-shaped sights. All of the special guns feature Evil Roy's signature on the barrel. Cimarron says of this revolver: "Featuring internal parts produced exclusively for Cimarron, and springs from U.S. manufacturers. The rear sight notch is large and square while the front sight is wide–with no taper–giving the shooter the finest sight picture.... Grips are hand-checkered or smooth walnut; very slim and trim for fast and safe handling. The actions are set up in the U.S.A. to function safely with lighter hammer action, no creep, and safe but crisp trigger pull. Each revolver is regulated to shoot dead-center left and right windage." Shooters have a choice of the standard finish or a special U.S.A. premium finish with case-coloring by Doug Turnbull.

Normally I am known for shooting the biggest six-guns available; however, I have a kinder, gentler side that has been indulged by shooting Cimarron's Model P Jr. These little six-guns have the standard single-action grip frame of the Model P with a smaller frame and cylinder. Chambered in 38 Special/38 Long Colt, or 32-20, they are not only fun guns for experienced six-gunners, they are also just the ticket for younger shooters—or anyone who cannot handle the recoil of larger six-guns.

There are several classes of shooters under the banner of cowboy action shooting. One group looks to authenticity in their costumes and firearms, especially their six-guns. For these folks, Cimarron offers their Model P with what they call an Original Finish, which is actually no finish at all, or perhaps we should say a specially-induced finish to make a six-gun look like it has been in use since the 1870s—although literally brand-new and in perfect mechanical shape. Original Finish six-guns may be used with either smokeless or

The top and middle 44-40s are original Colt Single Actions; the bottom six-gun is Cimarron's Model P with the antique-looking Original Finish.

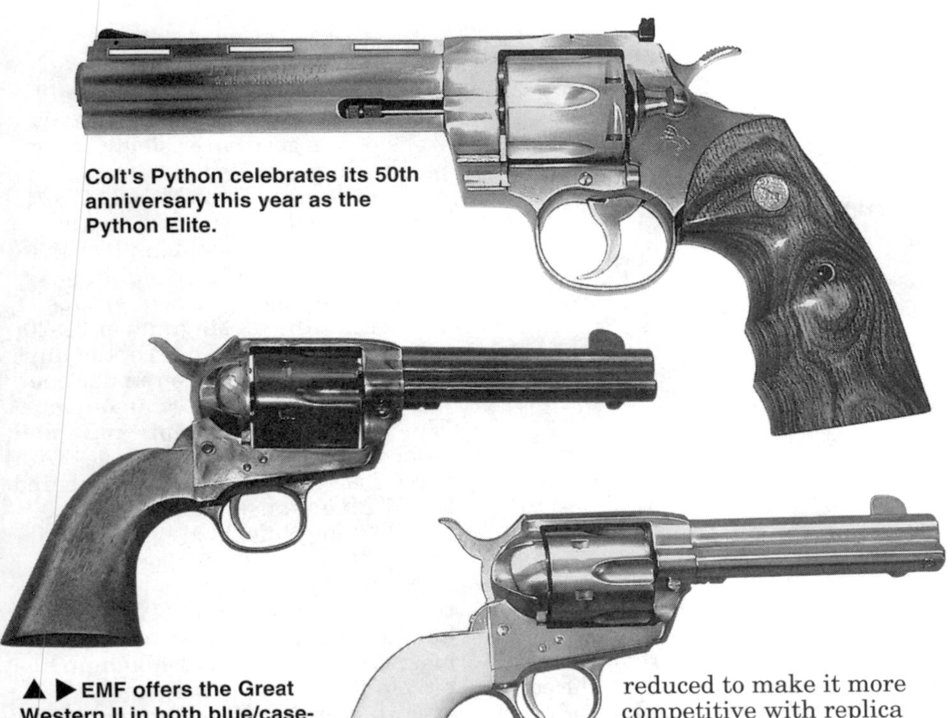

Colt's Python celebrates its 50th anniversary this year as the Python Elite.

▲ ▶ EMF offers the Great Western II in both blue/case-coloring and nickel-plated finishes.

blackpowder loads; however, they are an excellent choice for those who shoot blackpowder as they not only sound like the Old West, they also look like a six-gun with a definite story to tell.

Colt: Colt has made a lot of drastic, and very welcome, changes over the past few years. Three years ago Colt Single Actions were offered only in 45 Colt and 44-40, only in barrel lengths of 4-3/4 and 5-1/2 inches, and with a price tag coming very close to $2000! The last two years the price was reduced to make it more competitive with replica single actions, while still remaining a genuine Colt Single Action. Now, for this year, the Single Action part of the catalog has been greatly expanded as to calibers offered and barrel lengths. Shooters now have a choice of the three standard barrel lengths of 4-3/4, 5-1/2, and 7-1/2 inches, in either the traditional blue/case-colored finish or full nickel finish; chambered for the 45 Colt, 44-40, 38-40, 38 Special, 357 Magnum, and—for the first time in nearly three-quarters of a century—32-20. Just to prove shooters can never be satisfied, I have to ask, "Where is the 44 Special?"

Every day, in nearly every way and every location, single-action shooters argue the merits of replica single actions and the original Colt Single Action Army. When all the arguing and debating is through—there is only one genuine Single Action Army that says COLT on the barrel. No replica, no matter how well it is finished and tuned, can make that statement. While the Colt Single Action Army remains in 36 different versions when one considers calibers, barrel lengths, and finish, the Colt Cowboy is no more.

At one time Colt had a whole stable full of snakes. The Viper, Cobra, King Cobra, and Diamondback are all gone; however, the Anaconda and the Python remain. Although originally offered in both 45 Colt and 44 Magnum, currently the Anaconda is offered only in a stainless steel 44 Magnum with barrel lengths of 4, 6, and 8 inches, complete with fully adjustable sights and finger-groove rubber grips. It has proven to be a sturdy, reliable, accurate hunting handgun. Many shooters would argue that the Python is the finest double-action revolver ever offered at any time. I don't argue; I just enjoy shooting the Python. It continues in the Colt lineup as the Python Elite, in either blue or stainless with a 4- or 6-inch barrel.

Early And Modern Firearms (EMF): Last year EMF introduced the Great Western II. The Great Western originally appeared in 1954 as a totally American-made replica of the Colt Single Action Army. EMF was one of the early distributors of the Great Western, which disappeared in the early 1960s. The Great Western II line has been greatly expanded this year. The Custom Great Western is offered in nickel, satin nickel, blue/case colored, and all-blue finish, in the three standard barrel lengths of

50 years separates these two Great Westerns. The top six-gun is an original Great Western, while the bottom revolver is EMF's Pietta-manufactured Great Western II.

The two greatest 44 Specials of all times? The S&W 1907 Triple-Lock and the Freedom Arms Model 97.

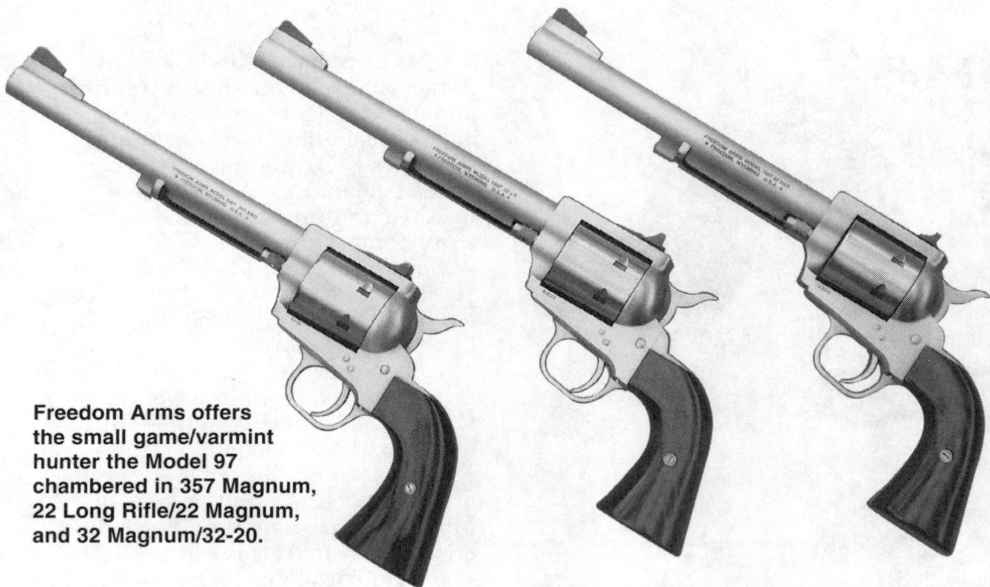

Freedom Arms offers the small game/varmint hunter the Model 97 chambered in 357 Magnum, 22 Long Rifle/22 Magnum, and 32 Magnum/32-20.

4-3/4, 5-1/2, and 7-1/2 inches; in 45 Colt, 44-40, and 357 Magnum with other calibers–as well as engraving–available on special order. All Custom Series Great Westerns are fitted with one-piece ivory-style grips.

In addition to the Great Western, which is made by Pietta, EMF also offers the Hartford Premiere in the three standard barrel lengths and chambered in 45 Colt, 44-40, 44 Special, 38-40, and 32-20. Special versions offered include the Bisley Model in all three barrel lengths, a 3-inch ejectorless Sheriff's Model, the round-butted 4-inch Pinkerton Model, and the 3 1/2-inch Deputy Model—all chambered in 45 Colt. Both the 1875 and 1890 Remingtons are offered and the Remington and the SAA models are also offered with the Antique Finish, making them appear to have experienced more than a century of service. Finally, EMF also offers a Buntline Special version of their 1873 six-guns.

Freedom Arms: Last year Freedom Arms introduced their Model 97 five-shot 44 Special, which I have now had a pleasurable year shooting. In addition, two more six-shot Model 97s have arrived on the scene. One is a 32 Magnum *(with an extra 32-20 cylinder available)*, while the other is chambered in the hot new 17 HMR. Since its inception in 1907, the 44 Special has been chambered in some of the finest revolvers ever produced. From Smith & Wesson we have the Triple-Lock, the Model 1926, the 1950 Target and, in more recent times, the Model 24 and Model 624—as well as a five-shot 296 and 696. Colt waited a while to chamber the 44 Special; however, when they finally moved in that direction they gave us the New Service, the Single Action Army, and the New Frontier. All great six-guns; however, the 44 Special Triple-Lock is most often considered the finest 44 Special—if not the finest revolver-period—ever manufactured. It now has a rival. The 44 Special Model 97 from Freedom Arms is surely the finest single-action 44 Special ever offered, and may just be every bit as good as that first Special 44.

Freedom Arms spent a long time studying barrel twists and different loads in both the 32 Magnum and the 32-20 before deciding to offer this combination in their Model 97. I personally supplied some loads for testing, and spent time with Bob Baker of Freedom Arms shooting the prototype model–both on paper for accuracy and over Oehler's Model 35P chronograph for muzzle velocity. Shooting 32s is always educational and this was no exception as some loads that were expected to do well performed poorly, while others gave surprisingly better results than expected.

The Freedom Arms Model 97 32 is superbly accurate. All testing was done with a 2x Leupold in place to remove as much human sighting error as possible. Five-shot groups, with either the 32 Magnum or 32-20 cylinder in place, were exceptionally small with groups of well under one inch at 25 yards being commonplace. When it comes to varmints and small game one can cover all the bases with three 7 1/2-inch Model 97s chambered in 357 Magnum, 32 Magnum/32-20, and 22 Long Rifle/22 Magnum. While excellent ammunition abounds in both the 357 Magnum and both 22s, the 32 Magnum and 32-20 require handloading for the best results. The most accurate load in 32 Magnum has proven to be Sierra's 90-grain JHC over 10 grains of H110 for five shots in 1/2-inch and a muzzle velocity of 1260 fps, while the 32-20 shoots best *(thus far)* with Speer's 100-grain JHP over 10.0 grains of #2400 for slightly under 1200 fps and five shots in 5/8-inch. This year the Model 97 chambered in 17 HMR has joined the three small game/varmint-gathering Model 97 six-guns.

As expected, this has also proven to be an exceptionally accurate revolver; my 10-inch test gun from Freedom Arms is capable of groups well under 1/2-inch at 25 yards, and probably even better in the hands of the younger, steadier shooter.

Hartford Armory: A new six-gun manufacturer has arrived on the scene. Hartford Armory is now offering the Remington 1890 and 1875 Single Actions. Go back 125 years. Colt, Remington, and Smith & Wesson all made beautiful single-action revolvers. The Colt handled blackpowder extremely well, while the Remington and Smith & Wesson had such tight tolerances they were actually smokeless-powder guns in a blackpowder age. In other words, they were so tightly fitted and closely machined they fouled easily when used with blackpowder. Fast-forward to today and we have the return of the Remington at a time when most shooters use them with smokeless powder. At last we will find out what excellent six-guns the Remingtons actually were. Hartford Armory is building truly authentic versions of the originals that have, at least in my hand, a different feel from the Italian replicas. Both the 1875 and 1890 will

The newest offering from Freedom Arms is the Model 97 chambered in 17 HMR.

The BFR from Magnum Research has proven to be an exceptionally accurate revolver.

be offered in a full blue finish, classified as Hartford Armory Dark Blue, or with a Turnbull case-colored frame; and also in stainless steel. Stocks are two-piece walnut.

Now comes the real surprise: this new version of the old Remington Single Action is chambered in 45 Colt and rated for +P loads; and is also offered in 44 Magnum. Other calibers will be 357 Magnum and 44-40. Although sights are the traditionally fixed single-action style; the front sight, which screws into the barrel, will be offered in different heights for sighting-in heavy-duty hunting loads. I am definitely looking forward to fully testing of this new/old revolver.

Magnum Research: Magnum Research offers the all-stainless steel BFR *(Biggest Finest Revolver)*. The BFR looks much like a Ruger Super Blackhawk; the grip frames will accept the same grips—however, unlike Ruger six-guns, the BFR has a freewheeling cylinder that rotates either clockwise or counter-clockwise when the loading gate is opened. It is offered in two versions: the Short Cylinder chambered in 454 Casull and 480 Ruger/475 Linebaugh, and 22 Hornet; the Long Cylinder is offered in 444 Marlin, 450 Marlin, 45-70, a special 45 Colt that also accepts 3-inch .410 shotgun shells, and–new for this year–500 S&W Magnum.

All BFR revolvers are American-made with cut-rifled, hand-lapped, recessed-muzzle-crowned barrels; tight tolerances; soft brushed stainless steel finish; and are normally equipped with an adjustable rear sight mated with a front sight with interchangeable blades of differing heights. They can be ordered from the factory set up with a scope and an SSK base. The SSK mounting system is the strongest available anywhere for scoping hard-kicking handguns. For the past year I have been extensively testing two BFR six-guns in 480/475 Linebaugh and 500 S&W Magnum. They have proven to be exceptionally accurate and have performed flawlessly.

Navy Arms: When it comes to replica firearms, Val Forgett of Navy Arms started it all. With the passing of Val Forgett this past year, Navy Arms is now headed up by his son, Val Forgett III. The leadership may have changed, but Navy Arms continues to offer some of the finest replicas available. These include The Gunfighter, a specially-tuned single-action army offered in the three standard barrel lengths, chambered in 357 Magnum, 44-40, and 45 Colt. Finish is blue with a case-colored frame and the German silver-plated back strap and trigger guard. Springs are all U.S.-made Wolff springs, and the standard grips are black-checkered gunfighter style.

Navy Arms has also added the stainless steel Gunfighter with the same barrel lengths and chamberings. Stainless steel may not be authentic Old West, however it sure makes a lot of sense for shooting blackpowder loads. Navy Arms also continues to offer the standard 1873 Cavalry six-gun, the 1895 Artillery Model, the Bisley Model, and the two great Smith & Wesson single actions: the 1875 Schofield and the New Model Russian. The latter is offered only in 44 Russian with a 6 1/2-inch barrel, while the Schofield comes in the original 7-inch version, the 5-inch

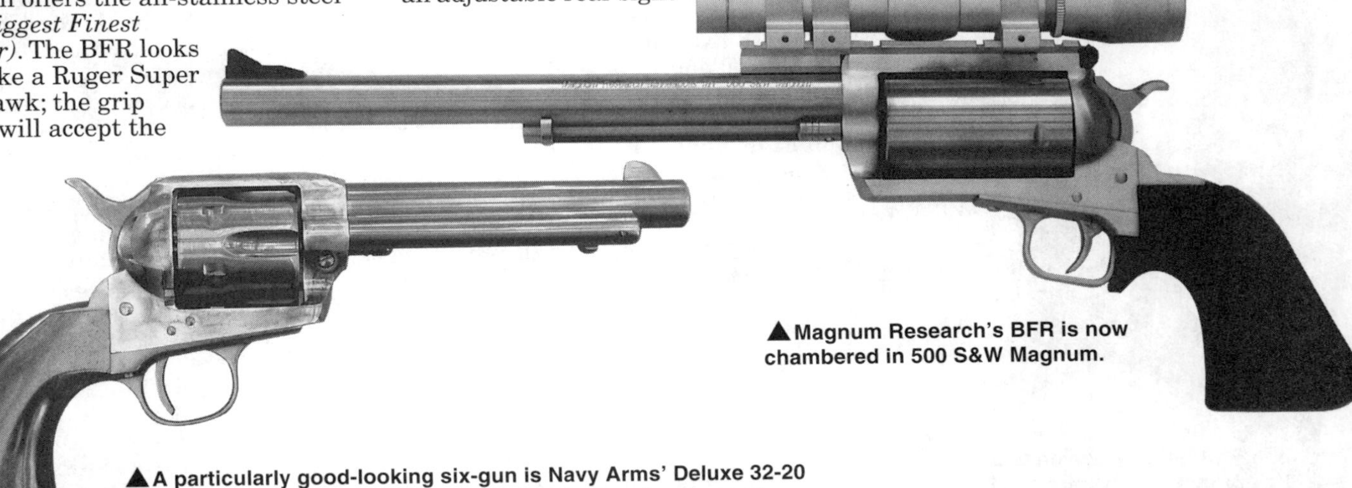

▲Magnum Research's BFR is now chambered in 500 S&W Magnum.

▲A particularly good-looking six-gun is Navy Arms' Deluxe 32-20 with its case-colored and fire-blued finish. It also shoots great.

◀ ▼ Navy Arms Gunfighter features a specially-tuned action, gunfighter grips, blue/case colored finish, and a German silver-plated backstrap and trigger guard.

Ruger's Ken Jorgensen with the new Ruger Hunter Model 22 Long Rifle/22 Magnum version.

▲ ▼ The 1875 Schofield from Navy Arms is offered as the Cavalry, Wells Fargo, and Hideout Models. Custom grips are by Buffalo Brothers and Eagle Grips.

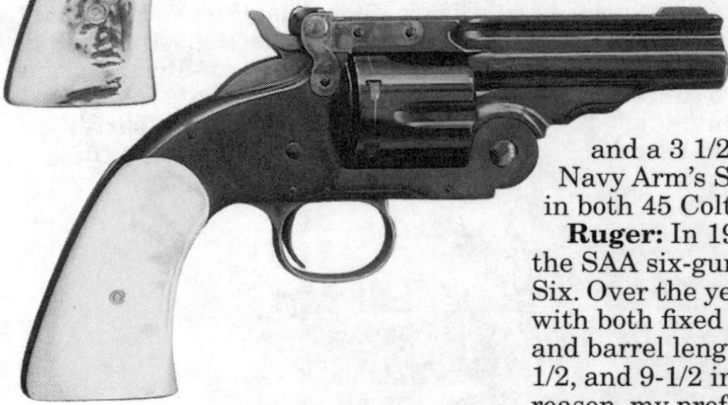

Wells Fargo Model, and a 3 1/2-inch Hideout Model. Navy Arm's Schofields are available in both 45 Colt and 38 Special.

Ruger: In 1953 Ruger resurrected the SAA six-gun with their 22 Single-Six. Over the years it has been offered with both fixed and adjustable sights, and barrel lengths of 4-5/8, 5-1/2, 6-1/2, and 9-1/2 inches. For whatever reason, my preferred barrel length for a hunting handgun — 7-1/2 inches — has never been offered during the first 50 years of the 22 Single-Six.

However, Ruger starts off their second half-century with the most popular 22 single-action revolver ever offered by correcting this mistake.

Ruger single actions have always been favorites of handgun hunters—especially their Hunter Models which continue to be offered in both the Super Blackhawk and Bisley models, in stainless steel, chambered in 44 Magnum, and wearing 7 1/2-inch heavy-ribbed barrels set up to accept Ruger scope rings. These are exceptionally popular hunting handguns and it is proper and fitting that they are now joining by a 22 RF model. The newest Hunter Model is a 7 1/2-inch 22 Long Rifle/22 Magnum version with a heavy-ribbed barrel set up to accept Ruger scope rings.

For those of us who have been shooting the original 22 Single-Six since the 1950s, a longer-barrel scope-sighted version has arrived none too soon. I don't know what goes on in the gun safe but something causes those sights to become a little fuzzier every year. The scope-sighted 22 Hunter Model can take care of this problem. This new Hunter Model is also being offered in 17 HMR. There is still no word from Ruger on a five-shot, large-bore single-action six-gun. *Maybe next year….*

Ruger continues to offer their excellent lineup of six-guns: the Blackhawk, the Bisley Model, the Vaquero, the Bisley Vaquero, the Redhawk, the Super Redhawk, the GP-100, and the Single-Six. This year marks the Golden Anniversary of the immensely popular Ruger 357 Blackhawk. Also new this year from Ruger is the Ruger Studio Of Art and Decoration for providing engraved versions of Ruger firearms. There will be no set patterns; rather, each firearm will be individually embellished to fit the desires of the owner. The work will be performed only on new Ruger firearms. In the past this service has only been available for special presentations or occasions, and for Bill Ruger's personal collection.

◀ Ruger's Single-Six chambered in 17 HMR has proven to be an accurate varmint pistol.

Savage: Savage continues to offer their excellent Striker series of bolt-action pistols. The Sport Striker,

A half-century of Ruger 44 Magnums. *From top right*: original Flattop, Super Blackhawk, Bisley Model, Super Blackhawk Hunter, and the Bisley Hunter.

▶ The Savage Striker is a stainless steel, synthetic-stocked, bolt-action pistol chambered for such cartridges as the 7-08 Remington and 308 Winchester.

designed for small game and varmints is chambered in 17 HMR, 22 LR, and 22 Magnum. The stainless steel Striker comes with a black synthetic stock, muzzle brake, left-hand bolt, and chambered in 223 Remington, 270 WSM, 7-08 Remington, 7mm WSM, 308 Winchester, and 300 WSM

Smith & Wesson: Thousands of the Model 500 X-Frame 500 S&W Magnum were sold in its first year of production and now a new, easier-packing version is offered. The newest Model 500 has a 4-inch barrel–actually 3 inches of barrel, plus a compensator. This could be just the ticket for those who regularly travel areas where four-legged beasts can be mean and nasty. This new version also wears the finger-grooved rubber grips of the original 8 3/8-inch Model 500. As far as grips go, I have found a better way—I should say the better way has been shown to me by Rod Herrett of Herrett's Stocks.

Some shooters experience a phenomenon when shooting the 500 Magnum in that the cylinder unlocks and rotates backwards. One of the reasons for this–and it does not happen with every shooter–is the rubber grips cause the Model 500 to bounce off the web of the hand, resulting in the trigger hitting the trigger finger–which naturally causes the trigger to start backwards and the cylinder to unlock. The solution from Rod Herrett was a pair of smooth-finished walnut Jordan stocks. These grips fill in the backstrap and do not bounce off the hand, as the rubber grips have a tendency to do with some shooters.

Other new offerings from Smith & Wesson this year include the Model 325PD, a lightweight, 21 1/2-ounce scandium and titanium 45 ACP revolver with a 2 1/2-inch barrel and Hi-Viz front sight. Used with full-moon clips, this lightweight but powerful revolver should become very popular for those with concealed weapons permits. When it comes to concealed firearms, one of the most neglected groups has been senior citizens. The AARP, which should be doing everything they can to protect their vulnerable members, instead is rabidly anti-gun. Quite often, senior citizens have a hard time finding a firearm they can easily handle. Smith & Wesson has greatly solved this problem by offering their Air-Lite PD in a seven-shot 22 Magnum version. Bill Jordan often asked for a J-Frame 22 Magnum, and it is now reality.

Smith & Wesson also offers two other special CCW packages with the J-Frame Model 642 hammerless 38

Two of the greatest bargains offered to handgun hunters are Ruger's Hunter Model 44 Magnum in the Bisley and Super Blackhawk versions.

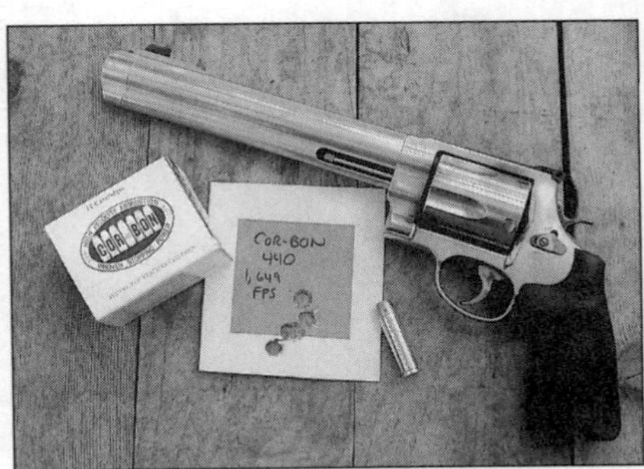

Recoil is heavy with Cor-Bon's 440-grain 500 Magnum load; however accuracy is excellent.

◀ Taffin shooting the 500 Smith & Wesson X-Frame revolver.

Herrett's Jordan stocks improve the handling of Smith & Wesson's Model 500.

◀ Eight shots and a 2-inch barrel—Smith & Wesson's latest 357 Magnum.

▲ Senior citizens rejoice! At last we have a J-framed Smith & Wesson chambered in 22 Magnum.

▲ The Smith & Wesson Mountain Gun is offered this year in 45 Colt.

Smith & Wesson now offers an Airweight 38 Special, paired with a Kydex holster.

Special equipped with Crimson Trace Laser Grips and the Model 637 Airweight 38 Special matched up with a Kydex holster. The Smith & Wesson Performance Center offers several versions every year and this year is no exception. The extremely popular Mountain Gun with its tapered 4-inch barrel is back, this time as a 45 Colt with the Model 25; the Model 686 is offered as a seven-shot 357 Magnum with a 5-inch standard barrel *sans* the heavy underlug; the Model 327 is offered as an eight-shot 357 Magnum with a 2-inch barrel. Hopefully, these special 25 and 686 Models will start a trend back to standard barrels.

Taurus: Taurus, which always has an extensive lineup of new firearms each year, did not disappoint shooters this year. However, they caught everybody off-guard with a totally new offering, a single-action revolver. It wasn't too many years ago that self-styled "experts" told us the single-action revolver was dead. Now in two successive years, two major companies, Beretta and Taurus, have introduced single-action six-guns.

Taurus' version is the Gaucho. Original versions are chambered in 45 Colt with 5-1/2-inch barrels and four finish choices: blue, blue/case color, stainless, and nickel-looking polished "Sundance" stainless. Grips are checkered wood and when I handled the Gaucho I informed the folks at Taurus the grips were 'way too thick. They responded that this problem has already been taken care of. Although the Gaucho has a transfer bar safety it also has a traditional half-cock notch and trigger. The Gaucho is scheduled to be available about the time you read this.

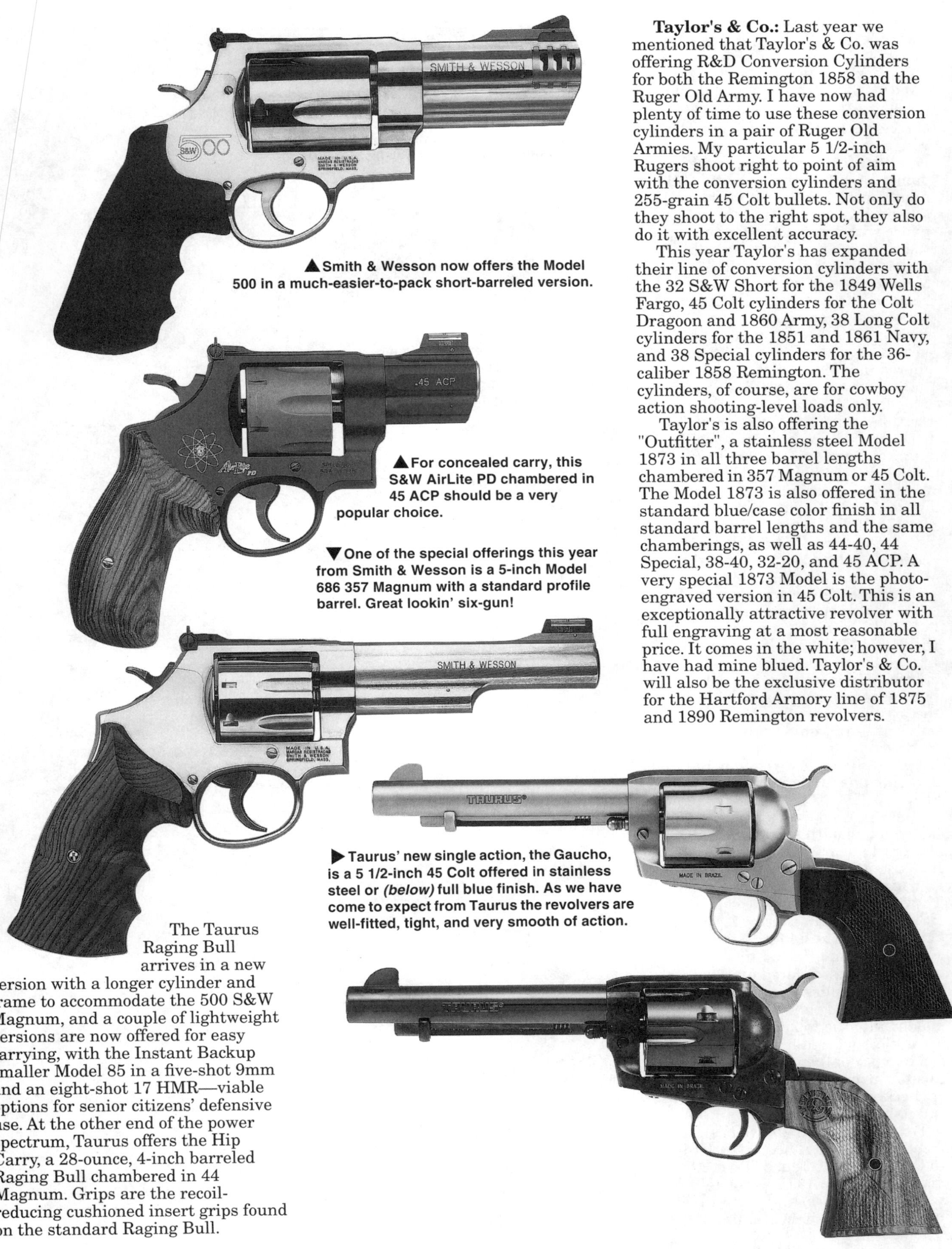

▲Smith & Wesson now offers the Model 500 in a much-easier-to-pack short-barreled version.

▲For concealed carry, this S&W AirLite PD chambered in 45 ACP should be a very popular choice.

▼One of the special offerings this year from Smith & Wesson is a 5-inch Model 686 357 Magnum with a standard profile barrel. Great lookin' six-gun!

▶Taurus' new single action, the Gaucho, is a 5 1/2-inch 45 Colt offered in stainless steel or *(below)* full blue finish. As we have come to expect from Taurus the revolvers are well-fitted, tight, and very smooth of action.

The Taurus Raging Bull arrives in a new version with a longer cylinder and frame to accommodate the 500 S&W Magnum, and a couple of lightweight versions are now offered for easy carrying, with the Instant Backup smaller Model 85 in a five-shot 9mm and an eight-shot 17 HMR—viable options for senior citizens' defensive use. At the other end of the power spectrum, Taurus offers the Hip Carry, a 28-ounce, 4-inch barreled Raging Bull chambered in 44 Magnum. Grips are the recoil-reducing cushioned insert grips found on the standard Raging Bull.

Taylor's & Co.: Last year we mentioned that Taylor's & Co. was offering R&D Conversion Cylinders for both the Remington 1858 and the Ruger Old Army. I have now had plenty of time to use these conversion cylinders in a pair of Ruger Old Armies. My particular 5 1/2-inch Rugers shoot right to point of aim with the conversion cylinders and 255-grain 45 Colt bullets. Not only do they shoot to the right spot, they also do it with excellent accuracy.

This year Taylor's has expanded their line of conversion cylinders with the 32 S&W Short for the 1849 Wells Fargo, 45 Colt cylinders for the Colt Dragoon and 1860 Army, 38 Long Colt cylinders for the 1851 and 1861 Navy, and 38 Special cylinders for the 36-caliber 1858 Remington. The cylinders, of course, are for cowboy action shooting-level loads only.

Taylor's is also offering the "Outfitter", a stainless steel Model 1873 in all three barrel lengths chambered in 357 Magnum or 45 Colt. The Model 1873 is also offered in the standard blue/case color finish in all standard barrel lengths and the same chamberings, as well as 44-40, 44 Special, 38-40, 32-20, and 45 ACP. A very special 1873 Model is the photo-engraved version in 45 Colt. This is an exceptionally attractive revolver with full engraving at a most reasonable price. It comes in the white; however, I have had mine blued. Taylor's & Co. will also be the exclusive distributor for the Hartford Armory line of 1875 and 1890 Remington revolvers.

Thompson/Center: Thompson/Center single-shot pistols have long been favorites both at long-range silhouette matches and in the hunting field. They have been chambered for dozens of factory and wildcat cartridges for those looking for long-range accuracy and adequate power for either target shooting or taking big game. T/C offers two versions of their break-open, single-shot pistols: the standard Contender now in its second phase with the easier-opening G2, and the Encore. The G2 will handle cartridges in the 30-30 and 44 Magnum range, while the larger, heavier Encore feels quite at home with the higher-pressure cartridges such as the 308 and 30-06. Some cartridges, such as the 45-70, are offered in both versions.

Two new cartridges have been added this year, both chambered in the Contender and the Encore. The first cartridge is the new 20-caliber varmint cartridge, the 204 Ruger; while the second is capable of taking any big-game animal found anywhere in the world. The latter cartridge is the 375 JDJ, designed by J.D. Jones of SSK Industries. J.D. is a longtime friend and the absolute authority when it comes to many things concerned with firearms, especially with single-shot pistol cartridges. The 375 JDJ is to single-shot pistols what the 375 H&H is to bolt-action rifles. It may be larger than necessary for some critters and a little light for others, but in capable hands it will always do the job with authority. If I could have only one–and wouldn't that be terrible–single-shot pistol for hunting big game, it would be chambered in 375 JDJ. I have been using my custom SSK 375 JDJ with great satisfaction for nearly two decades now. The introduction of this cartridge in a standard factory handgun should increase its popularity even more.

United States Firearms (USFA): The first thing most notice about the USFA Single Action Army is the absolutely beautiful finish with the main frame and the hammer beautifully case-colored by Doug Turnbull. Standard grips, of checkered hard rubber with a "US" molded into the top part of the grip, are perfectly fitted to the frame and feel exceptionally good to my hand. Custom grips are available in smooth or checkered walnut, as well as ivory and pearl.

For the past year I have been shooting two USFA SAAs, a 4 3/4-inch 45 Colt and a 7 1/2-inch 38-40. All six chambers on the 45 Colt from USFA measure a uniform and perfect 0.452-inch, and the 38-40 is also uniform

▲The 500 S&W Magnum has now found a home in the stainless-steel Raging Bull from Taurus.

▲For those wanting a powerful but lightweight, easy-to-pack big-bore six-gun, Taurus offers the Ultra-Lite in 44 Magnum.

▲A fully engraved single-action six-gun at a very reasonable price is Taylor & Co.'s fully engraved 45 Colt. Custom grips are by BluMagnum.

Thompson/Center's Encore is now offered in 375 JDJ.

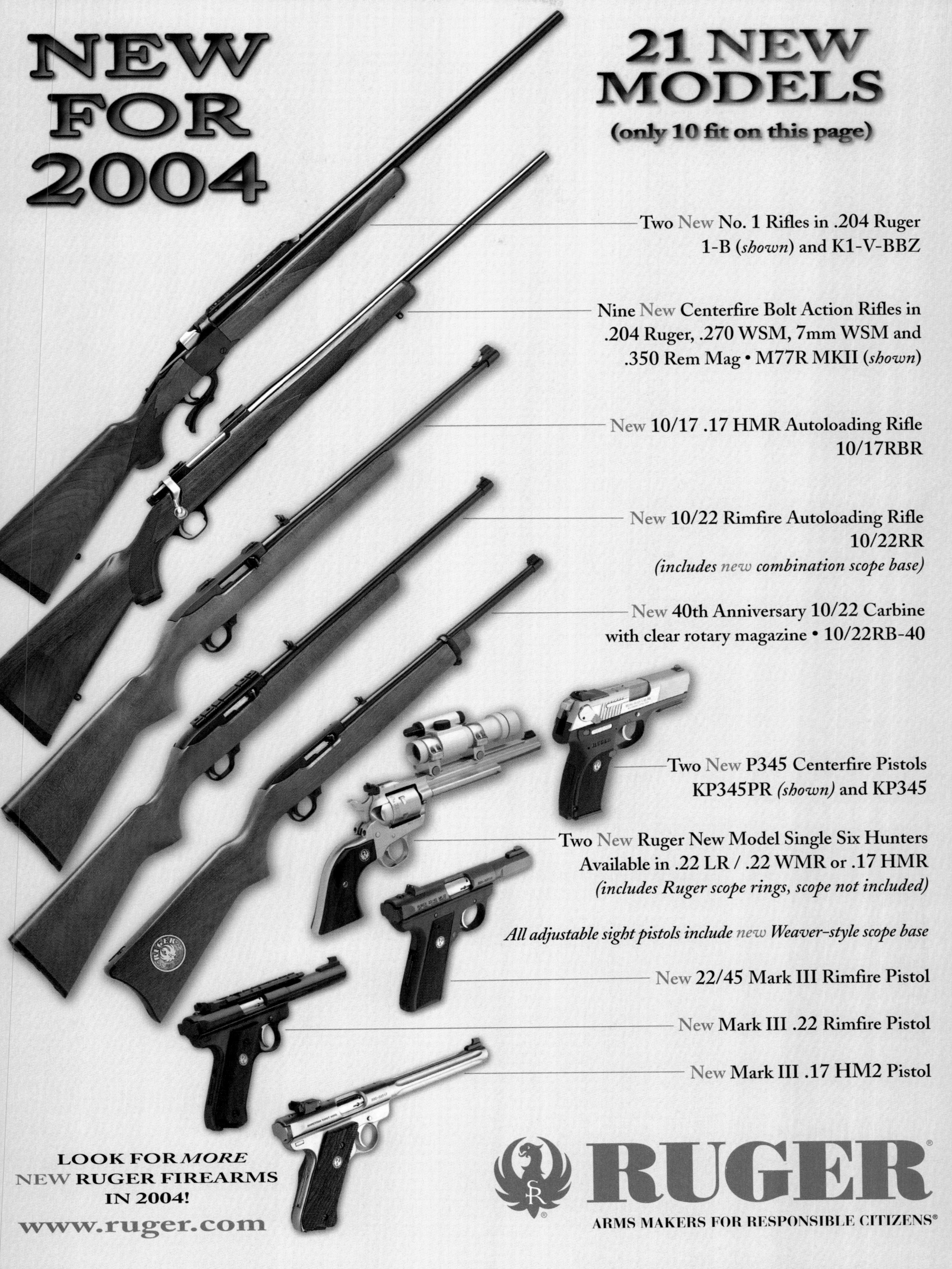
NEW FOR 2004
21 NEW MODELS
(only 10 fit on this page)
Two New No. 1 Rifles in .204 Ruger
1-B (shown) and K1-V-BBZ
Nine New Centerfire Bolt Action Rifles in
.204 Ruger, .270 WSM, 7mm WSM and
.350 Rem Mag • M77R MKII (shown)
New 10/17 .17 HMR Autoloading Rifle
10/17RBR
New 10/22 Rimfire Autoloading Rifle
10/22RR
(includes new combination scope base)
New 40th Anniversary 10/22 Carbine
with clear rotary magazine • 10/22RB-40
Two New P345 Centerfire Pistols
KP345PR (shown) and KP345
Two New Ruger New Model Single Six Hunters
Available in .22 LR / .22 WMR or .17 HMR
(includes Ruger scope rings, scope not included)
All adjustable sight pistols include new Weaver-style scope base
New 22/45 Mark III Rimfire Pistol
New Mark III .22 Rimfire Pistol
New Mark III .17 HM2 Pistol
LOOK FOR MORE
NEW RUGER FIREARMS
IN 2004!
www.ruger.com
RUGER®
ARMS MAKERS FOR RESPONSIBLE CITIZENS®

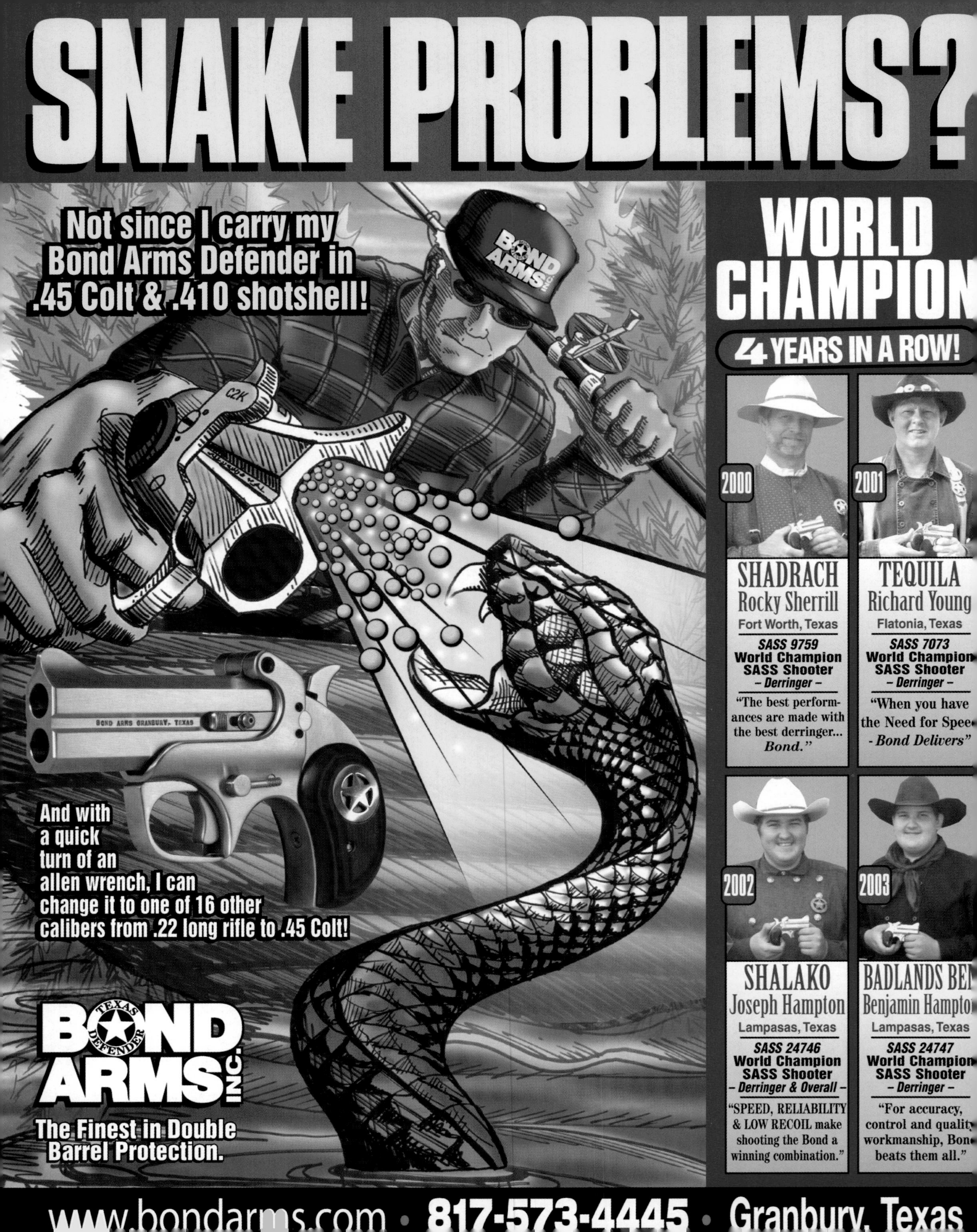

SNAKE PROBLEMS?

Not since I carry my Bond Arms Defender in .45 Colt & .410 shotshell!

And with a quick turn of an allen wrench, I can change it to one of 16 other calibers from .22 long rifle to .45 Colt!

BOND ARMS INC.

The Finest in Double Barrel Protection.

WORLD CHAMPION

4 YEARS IN A ROW!

SHADRACH
Rocky Sherrill
Fort Worth, Texas
SASS 9759
World Champion SASS Shooter
– Derringer –
"The best performances are made with the best derringer... Bond."

TEQUILA
Richard Young
Flatonia, Texas
SASS 7073
World Champion SASS Shooter
– Derringer –
"When you have the Need for Spee
- Bond Delivers"

SHALAKO
Joseph Hampton
Lampasas, Texas
SASS 24746
World Champion SASS Shooter
– Derringer & Overall –
"SPEED, RELIABILITY & LOW RECOIL make shooting the Bond a winning combination."

BADLANDS BE
Benjamin Hampto
Lampasas, Texas
SASS 24747
World Champion SASS Shooter
– Derringer –
"For accuracy, control and qualit workmanship, Bon beats them all."

www.bondarms.com · 817-573-4445 · Granbury, Texas

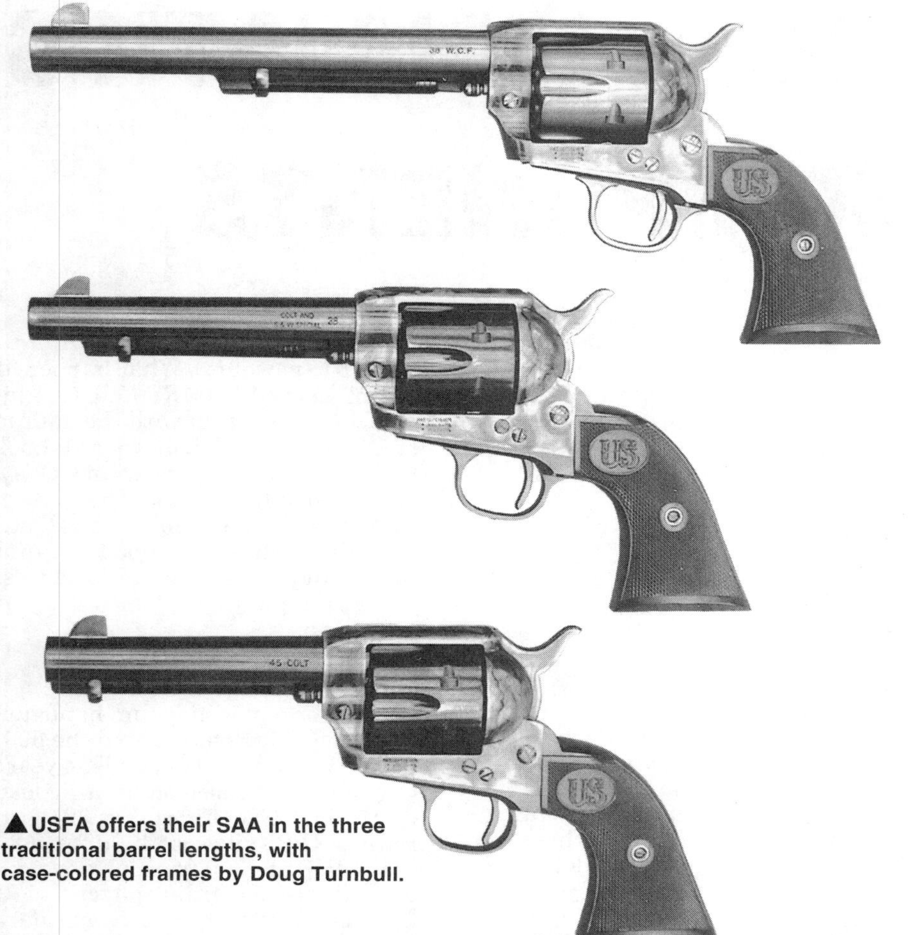

▲USFA offers their SAA in the three traditional barrel lengths, with case-colored frames by Doug Turnbull.

These three "Mystery Cartridges" should be revealed by the time you read this. The first two are 50-caliber for standard-sized single actions, while the Maximum length 45 is for use in stretch-framed, long-cylindered revolvers.

and correct at 0.400-inch. Trigger pulls on both six-guns are set at three pounds. Cylinders lock up tight when the hammer is down on an empty chamber, as well as when the hammer is in the cocked position.

All USFA six-guns are available with a V- or square-notch rear sight and a choice of a cross pin or screw-in blackpowder-style cylinder pin latch. Standard chamberings for USFA single actions are 45 Colt as well as 32-20, 41 Long Colt, 38 Special, 38-40, 44-40, 45 ACP, and 44 Special/44 Russian. The latter can be marked "RUSSIAN AND S&W SPECIAL 44" as early Colt Single Actions were marked. USFA also offers the Rodeo in 45 Colt, 44-40, and 38 Special in 4 3/4-, 5 1/2-, and 7 1/2-inch barrel lengths. This less expensive six-gun is the same basic revolver as the single action army; however, it comes with bead-blasted satin blue finish instead of the beautiful finish of the standard revolver.

Last year, as the switch to all American-made parts was completed, the USFA catalog line was drastically reduced to only traditional single action army six-guns with the three standard barrel lengths. However, this year the Bisley, the Flat-Top Target, and the Omnipotent have all returned with all the parts, finishing, and fitting being totally American.

It has been another most interesting handgun year with many new models and cartridges being offered. It is easy, at least at my age, to wax nostalgic and long for the good old days with hand-fitted double-action revolvers with beautiful bright blue finishes. *(Remember S&W Bright Blue and Colt Royal Blue?)* I still look for such guns at gun shows–especially if offered at bargain prices. We will never see guns like this again. The upside is that with today's machinery and manufacturing processes, guns are better than ever and, relatively speaking, much less expensive. They are stronger, built to tighter tolerances, and in every case in which I have run one of the new production revolvers against one of its counterparts from back in the "good old days", the new gun always wins in the accuracy department. Today's shooters have a wide and varied choice of the best guns ever offered. Yep, it looks like another great six-gunnin' year! •

Gary Germaine of United States Firearms with a pair of USFA's SAAs.

AMMUNITION, BALLISTICS AND COMPONENTS

by Holt Bodinson

HODGDON BUYS THE IMR Powder Company. Imagine what Bruce Hodgdon would have thought. Here was an entrepreneur at the end of WWII, shoveling surplus 4831 out of a boxcar and selling it in paper bags, whose company has gone on to acquire one of Dupont's former crown jewels, IMR. It's a great American business story.

Making a rather dramatic, surprise appearance was the short 45 Glock Automatic Pistol (G.A.P.) cartridge that permits Glock to pack the punch of the 45 ACP into a smaller framed pistol.

In the "Why didn't I think of it" category is Hodgdon's "Xperimental Pack." There may be a trend developing here--small samples of various reloading components that allow handloaders to develop the best load at the least cost for each firearm.

The commercial bullet makers are doing well as more and more Barnes, Hornady, Nosler, and Sierra bullets are integrated into the major ammunition lines.

It's been a busy year in ammunition, ballistics and components.

Aguila

The race is on at Aguila to get their little 17-caliber rimfire, the 17 Aguila, into production and into the marketplace after the surprise introduction by Hornady of its 17-caliber Mach 2 cartridge that is also based on the 22 Long Rifle case. www.aguilaammo.com

Alliant

No new formulations this year in a line that now includes ten shotguns powder, three pistol powders and six rifle powders; however, there is a new, free reloading manual this year chock-full of recipes. www.alliantpowder.com

American Pioneer Powder

Offering a sulfurless, volume-for-volume, replacement for blackpowder that cleans up with water, American Pioneer is supplying its FFG and FFFG formulas as granular powder, as 100- and 150-grain pre-measured loads, and as 45- and 50-caliber compressed stick charges. Ballistics and accuracy data for muzzle-stuffers and cowboy action cartridges look very good. www.americanpioneerpowder.com

Barnes

Over in their XPB pistol bullet line, which is also based on a solid copper HP design, there are two new 500 S&W spitzers in 325- and 375-grain weights. In their more conventional XPB pistol designs, new offerings include a 115-grain 9mm; 155-grain 40 S&W; 185-grain 45 ACP; and 275-grain 500 S&W. Finally, for the big, booming 577 Nitro Express, there is a 750-grain XLC coated X-Bullet. www.barnesbullets.com

Berry's Manufacturing

This is the home of the copper-plated, swaged lead core bullet readily available in all popular handgun and rifle calibers. They're inexpensive, too. New in the handgun line this year is a 350-grain 500 S&W bullet. www.berrysmfg.com

CCI

Combine CCI's mastery in the rimfire world with a Hornady 17-caliber V-Max bullet and what do you get? The Hornady 17 Mach2, that's what. Based on a CCI 22 LR case, this new little varmint cartridge pushes a 17-grain V-Max along at 2100 fps. Accuracy is reported to be exceptional, and the target price for the ammo affordable. Gun makers are lining up to chamber this little mosquito. What happened to last year's 17 HMR? Well, CCI just made it more lethal with the addition of a 17-grain TNT hollowpoint. Look for reloadable brass cases in CCI's inexpensive Blazer line. The throwaway aluminum cases will still be with us while the reloadable brass cases will prove a boon to reloaders. www.cci-ammunition.com

Cor-Bon

When Smith & Wesson went looking for a new magnum handgun cartridge, Cor-Bon designed the 500 S&W Magnum cartridge. This year Cor-Bon has focused on hunting loads for the big 50 that include a 325-grain Barnes XPB spitzer at 1800 fps; a 350-grain JHP at 1600 fps; and a heavy bonded core 385-grain spitzer at 1725 fps, just right for those African safaris. For those of us who like to carry *(and shoot!)* the new titanium lightweights, Cor-Bon has added three new loadings based on their light-kicking 100-grain "Pow'Rball" bullet—a 38 Special+P at 1400 fps; a 9x23 at 1600 fps; and a 357 Mag. at 1600 fps. Teaming up with Barnes, Cor-Bon has created an

Cor-Bon now offers the 325-grain Barnes XPB spitzer in their extensive 500 S&W ammunition line.

Built on the 32 ACP case by Cor-Bon, the 25 NAA propels a 35-grain JHP at 1200 fps from NAA's little Guardian automatic.

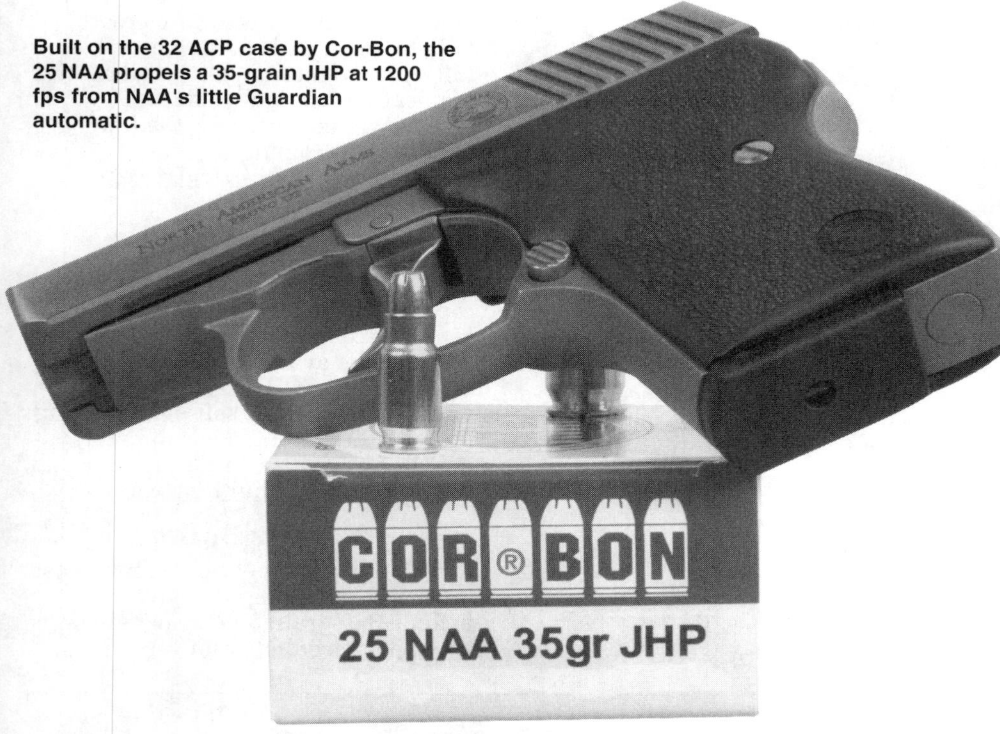

Graf & Sons

For everyone who enjoys shooting the military warhorses, Graf has done an outstanding job of supplying obsolete cases and bullets being produced under contract by Hornady. Brass only is available for the 455 Webley and 9mm Steyr. Buy them while you can. www.grafs.com

Hodgdon Powder

The BIG news this year is Hodgdon's acquisition of the IMR Powder Company. It's too soon to know what the future holds, but it's certainly an exciting development for both companies. In a brilliant marketing move, Hodgdon has developed the "Xperimental Pack." For approximately the price of one pound of powder, the handloader can now buy a pack of four 4-oz. canisters of Hodgdon powders organized by burning rate. The Xperimental Packs enable the handloader to test a variety of powders without having to buy, and possibly never use again, full pounds of powder. Hodgdon's latest and best *Handloading Annual* is packed with 5000+ loads for even the most recent factory cartridges and contains some great, old stories by Elmer Keith and Bill Jordan. www.hodgdon.com

entirely new DPX (Deep Penetrating X) line. The DPX bullets are a proprietary design and are currently available as a 115-grain 9mm+P at 1275 fps, a 140-grain 40 S&W at 1300 fps and a 185-grain 45ACP+P at 1075 fps. It really has happened. Cor-Bon in concert with North American Arms has released the 25NAA—a 25-caliber cartridge based on the 32 ACP case and chambered in NAA's little Guardian automatic. Ballistics of the wee round are pretty hot—a 35-grain JHP at 1200 fps. In the pipeline are a variety of new Cor-Bon recipes for the 45 G.A.P. www.corbon.com

Federal

The 45 Glock Automatic Pistol (G.A.P.) cartridge is a hot new item this year, and Federal is fielding a 150-grain Hydra-Shok JHP and 150-grain FMJ at 1090 fps. In the Premium line, there are two V-Shok loadings for the 17 HMR—a 17-grain Speer TNT and a 17-grain Hornady V-Max bullet. Velocity of both loads is a sizzling 2550 fps. It appears the marriage between Federal and ATK is working very well! www.federalcartridge.com

Fiocchi

There's an interesting 9mm Luger leadless loading featuring a 100-grain, truncated cone, encapsulated base bullet at 1400 fps. Delivering less recoil, the new cartridge is also said to be more accurate than standard 9mm ammunition. www.fiocchiusa.com

Hornady

The creative cartridge designers at Hornady seem to generate a new cartridge each year, and this year is no exception. The 17 Hornady Mach2 rimfire is a petite bottleneck cartridge based on the 22 Long Rifle case. The Mach2 was developed cooperatively with CCI. It zips a 17-grain V-Max bullet downrange at 2100 fps and tests indicate its accuracy exceeds that of its 22 LR parent. Also, Hornady has introduced a new loading for the 500 S&W—a 350-grain XTP Mag. bullet at 1900 fps. www.hornady.com

Cor-Bon has developed an entirely new Deep Penetrating X line of bullets for its high-velocity handgun cartridge line.

The 45 G.A.P. cartridge in the Federal line this year gets a 150-grain Hydra-Shok JHP and a 150-grain FMG at 1090 fps.

Huntington

If you need brass, bullets, or RCBS products, Huntington is the first stop. They are particularly strong in the rare and obsolete caliber department. For example, this year they're adding brass for the 7.62 Nagant Revolver. Huntington offers a unique service for cartridge collectors and handloaders. They will sell you a single case in every conceivable caliber for a very reasonable price. See their extensive catalog at www.huntington.com

Igman

Just beginning to appear on dealers' shelves are sporting rifle and pistol cartridges produced by Igman, a Bosnian company. Igman International USA is the importer.

Phone number (203) 375-8544.

Hodgdon's latest and best "Handloading Annual" is packed with 5000+ loads for even the most recent factory cartridges.

International Cartridge Corp.

International is a 100 percent "green" cartridge maker using copper/tin composites and sintered, powder metal technology to create bullets, slugs and shot. They offer a full range of tactical, duty, and special application handgun, rifle and shotgun ammunition for the law enforcement community.
www.internationalcartridge.com

Magtech

"First Defense" is the label for Magtech's latest line of 100 percent copper hollow-point ammunition for law enforcement and personal defense. It's available in 9mm, 40 S&W and 45 ACP. There's a new 400-grain semi-jacketed soft point loading for the 500 S&W, and a completely new line of rimfire ammunition.
www.magtechammunition.com

Meister Bullets

This well-known brand of hard cast bullets is expanding this year to include 330-grain 500 S&W bullets.
www.meisterbullets.com

Hornady and CCI teamed up to build the Hornady Mach2—an exciting 17-caliber rimfire based on a necked-down 22 LR case.

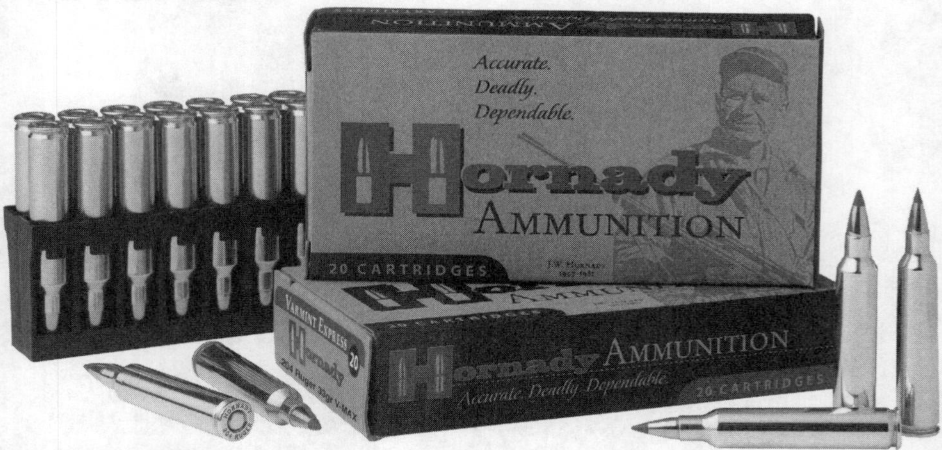

The Ruger 204 loaded by Hornady delivers 4225 fps from a 32-grain V-Max bullet and is the fastest factory cartridge currently offered.

First Defense Box: "First Defense" is Magtech's latest line of 100-percent copper hollowpoint ammunition in 9mm, 40 S&W, and 45 ACP.

Norma

Finally, Norma has produced a complete and thoroughly fascinating reloading manual. The history of the Norma Company and the technical manufacturing and ballistics data contained in the first 150 pages are worth the price of the book alone.

Excellent text and illustrations and very clearly written. Of course, the powders are all Norma, but the bullets span the spectrum of makers including Hornady, Nosler, Sierra, Swift and Woodleigh. Don't miss this new manual. www.norma.cc

Oregon Trail Bullet Co.

Home of those beautiful, accurate "True Shot" silver alloy bullets, Oregon Trail has developed new gas-checked designs of interest to handgunners: 41-caliber 265-grain WNFP; 44-caliber 310-grain WNFP; 45 Long Colt (.452) 360-grain WNFP; 480-caliber 355-grain WNFP; and a 500 S&W 370-grain WNFP. Top quality. Great folks. www.trueshotbullets.com

Oregon Trail has expanded its silver alloy True Shot cast bullet line to include new gas check designs in 308-, 41-, 44-, 45-, 480-, and 500-caliber.

Sellier & Bellot

The 32 S&W Long loaded with a 100-grain bullet at 886 fps has been added to the pistol line, and a 22 WMR with a 45-grain bullet at 1562 fps to the rimfire offerings www.sb-usa.com

Speer

Finally, a carefully crafted cartridge is available for 38-caliber snubbies. Speer is offering a 38 Special +P loading featuring a 135-grain Gold Dot HP bullet at 975 fps. The load is designed to provide optimal ballistics from a 2-inch barrel. New to the Gold Dot Hunting ammunition line is the 41 Mag. loaded with a 210-grain Gold Dot HP at 1280 fps. The 45 Glock Automatic Pistol round gets four new loadings: a 185-grain Gold Dot HP at 1050 fps, a 200-grain GDHP at 950 fps and two similar weight FMJ loadings for training purposes. New component bullets this year in the Gold Dot HP handgun line include 110-, 135- and 145-grain bullets for the 38 Spl., and the 210-grain 41 Mag. www.speer-bullets.com

Starline

At the request of S&W and Cor-Bon, Starline has re-designed the 500 S&W case to accept a large magnum rifle primer to eliminate pierced primer problems that have occurred with the big boomer. The new cases are clearly marked with an "R" after the word "MAG" on the head stamp, so be forewarned. www.starlinebrass.com

Winchester selected the classic 230-grain bullet for their line of 45 G.A.P. cartridges that includes four commercial and two law enforcement loads.

Vihtavuori and Lapua

Vihtavuori and Lapua have created a new website this year. See their products at www.vihtavuori-lapua.com.

Winchester Ammunition

The 45 G.A.P. is getting quite a play this year. In their economically priced "USA" line, Winchester is fielding a 230-grain FMJ round at 850 fps and a 230 JHP loading at an impressive 880 fps. For personal protection purposes, there is a hot 185-grain Silvertip HP loading at 1000 fps on your dealer's shelf. The folks at Winchester Ammunition have been very busy this year! www.winchester.com

Zanders Sporting Goods

Zanders is stocking a new line of Eley Tenex and Eley Match 22 LR loads engineered specifically for semi-auto pistols and rifles. The new Eley ammunition features a special round-nose bullet profile and lubricant that facilitate feeding while reducing fouling build-up to a minimum. www.gzanders.com

Zanders is importing Eley's new semi-auto 22 LR cartridges featuring a special round-nose bullet and lubricant to facilitate feeding and reduce fouling in semi-auto 22s.

CENTERFIRE HANDGUN CARTRIDGES — BALLISTICS & PRICES

Notes: Blanks are available in 32 S&W, 38 S&W and 38 Special. "V" after barrel length indicates test barrel was vented to produce ballistics similar to a revolver with a normal barrel-to-cylinder gap. Ammo prices are per 50 rounds except when marked with an ** which signifies a 20 round box; *** signifies a 25-round box. Not all loads are available from all ammo manufacturers. Listed loads are those made by Remington, Winchester, Federal, and others. DISC. is a discontinued load. Prices are rounded to nearest whole dollar and will vary with brand and retail outlet. † = new bullet weight this year; "c" indicates a change in data.

Cartridge	Bullet Wgt. Grs.	VELOCITY (fps)			ENERGY (ft. lbs.)			Mid-Range Traj. (in.)		Bbl. Lgth. (in).	Est. Price/ box
		Muzzle	50 yds.	100 yds.	Muzzle	50 yds.	100 yds.	50 yds.	100 yds.		
221 Rem. Fireball	50	2650	2380	2130	780	630	505	0.2	0.8	10.5"	$15
25 Automatic	35	900	813	742	63	51	43	NA	NA	2"	$18
25 Automatic	45	815	730	655	65	55	40	1.8	7.7	2"	$21
25 Automatic	50	760	705	660	65	55	50	2.0	8.7	2"	$17
7.5mm Swiss	107	1010	NA	NA	240	NA	NA	NA	NA	NA	NEW
7.62mmTokarev	87	1390	NA	NA	365	NA	NA	0.6	NA	4.5"	NA
7.62 Nagant	97	790	NA	NA	134	NA	NA	NA	NA	NA	NEW
7.63 Mauser	88	1440	NA	NA	405	NA	NA	NA	NA	NA	NEW
30 Luger	93†	1220	1110	1040	305	255	225	0.9	3.5	4.5"	$34
30 Carbine	110	1790	1600	1430	785	625	500	0.4	1.7	10"	$28
30-357 AeT	123	1992	NA	NA	1084	NA	NA	NA	NA	10"	NA
32 S&W	88	680	645	610	90	80	75	2.5	10.5	3"	$17
32 S&W Long	98	705	670	635	115	100	90	2.3	10.5	4"	$17
32 Short Colt	80	745	665	590	100	80	60	2.2	9.9	4"	$19
32 H&R Magnum	85	1100	1020	930	230	195	165	1.0	4.3	4.5"	$21
32 H&R Magnum	95	1030	940	900	225	190	170	1.1	4.7	4.5"	$19
32 Automatic	60	970	895	835	125	105	95	1.3	5.4	4"	$22
32 Automatic	60	1000	917	849	133	112	96			4"	NA
32 Automatic	65	950	890	830	130	115	100	1.3	5.6	NA	NA
32 Automatic	71	905	855	810	130	115	95	1.4	5.8	4"	$19
8mm Lebel Pistol	111	850	NA	NA	180	NA	NA	NA	NA	NA	NEW
8mm Steyr	112	1080	NA	NA	290	NA	NA	NA	NA	NA	NEW
8mm Gasser	126	850	NA	NA	200	NA	NA	NA	NA	NA	NEW
380 Automatic	60	1130	960	NA	170	120	NA	1.0	NA	NA	NA
380 Automatic	85/88	990	920	870	190	165	145	1.2	5.1	4"	$20
380 Automatic	90	1000	890	800	200	160	130	1.2	5.5	3.75"	$10
380 Automatic	95/100	955	865	785	190	160	130	1.4	5.9	4"	$20
38 Super Auto +P	115	1300	1145	1040	430	335	275	0.7	3.3	5"	$26
38 Super Auto +P	125/130	1215	1100	1015	425	350	300	0.8	3.6	5"	$26
38 Super Auto +P	147	1100	1050	1000	395	355	325	0.9	4.0	5"	NA
9x18mm Makarov	95	1000	NA	NA	NA	NA	NA	NA	NA	NA	NEW
9x18mm Ultra	100	1050	NA	NA	240	NA	NA	NA	NA	NA	NEW
9x23mm Largo	124	1190	1055	966	390	306	257	0.7	3.7	4"	NA
9x23mm Win.	125	1450	1249	1103	583	433	338	0.6	2.8	NA	NA
9mm Steyr	115	1180	NA	NA	350	NA	NA	NA	NA	NA	NEW
9mm Luger	88	1500	1190	1010	440	275	200	0.6	3.1	4"	$24
9mm Luger	90	1360	1112	978	370	247	191	NA	NA	4"	$26
9mm Luger	95	1300	1140	1010	350	275	215	0.8	3.4	4"	NA
9mm Luger	100	1180	1080	NA	305	255	NA	0.9	NA	4"	NA
9mm Luger	115	1155	1045	970	340	280	240	0.9	3.9	4"	$21
9mm Luger	123/125	1110	1030	970	340	290	260	1.0	4.0	4"	$23
9mm Luger	140	935	890	850	270	245	225	1.3	5.5	4"	$23
9mm Luger	147	990	940	900	320	290	265	1.1	4.9	4"	$26
9mm Luger +P	90	1475	NA	NA	437	NA	NA	NA	NA	NA	NA
9mm Luger +P	115	1250	1113	1019	399	316	265	0.8	3.5	4"	$27
9mm Federal	115	1280	1130	1040	420	330	280	0.7	3.3	4"V	$24
9mm Luger Vector	115	1155	1047	971	341	280	241	NA	NA	4"	NA
9mm Luger +P	124	1180	1089	1021	384	327	287	0.8	3.8	4"	NA
38 S&W	146	685	650	620	150	135	125	2.4	10.0	4"	$19
38 Short Colt	125	730	685	645	150	130	115	2.2	9.4	6"	$19
39 Special	100	950	900	NA	200	180	NA	1.3	NA	4"V	NA
38 Special	110	945	895	850	220	195	175	1.3	5.4	4"V	$23
38 Special	110	945	895	850	220	195	175	1.3	5.4	4"V	$23
38 Special	130	775	745	710	175	160	120	1.9	7.9	4"V	$22

Notes: Blanks are available in 32 S&W, 38 S&W and 38 Special. "V" after barrel length indicates test barrel was vented to produce ballistics similar to a revolver with a normal barrel-to-cylinder gap. Ammo prices are per 50 rounds except when marked with an ** which signifies a 20 round box; *** signifies a 25-round box. Not all loads are available from all ammo manufacturers. Listed loads are those made by Remington, Winchester, Federal, and others. DISC. is a discontinued load. Prices are rounded to nearest whole dollar and will vary with brand and retail outlet. † = new bullet weight this year; "c" indicates a change in data.

	Cartridge	Bullet Wgt. Grs.	VELOCITY (fps)			ENERGY (ft. lbs.)			Mid-Range Traj. (in.)		Bbl. Lgth. (in).	Est. Price/ box
			Muzzle	50 yds.	100 yds.	Muzzle	50 yds.	100 yds.	50 yds.	100 yds.		
38	38 Special Cowboy	140	800	767	735	199	183	168			7.5" V	NA
	38 (Multi-Ball)	140	830	730	505	215	130	80	2.0	10.6	4"V	$10**
	38 Special	148	710	635	565	165	130	105	2.4	10.6	4"V	$17
	38 Special	158	755	725	690	200	185	170	2.0	8.3	4"V	$18
	38 Special +P	95	1175	1045	960	290	230	195	0.9	3.9	4"V	$23
	38 Special +P	110	995	925	870	240	210	185	1.2	5.1	4"V	$23
	38 Special +P	125	975	929	885	264	238	218	1	5.2	4"	NA
	38 Special +P	125	945	900	860	250	225	205	1.3	5.4	4"V	#23
	38 Special +P	129	945	910	870	255	235	215	1.3	5.3	4"V	$11
	38 Special +P	130	925	887	852	247	227	210	1.3	5.50	4"V	NA
	38 Special +P	147/150(c)	884	NA	NA	264	NA	NA	NA	NA	4"V	$27
	38 Special +P	158	890	855	825	280	255	240	1.4	6.0	4"V	$20
357	357 SIG	115	1520	NA	NA	593	NA	NA	NA	NA	NA	NA
	357 SIG	124	1450	NA	NA	578	NA	NA	NA	NA	NA	NA
	357 SIG	125	1350	1190	1080	510	395	325	0.7	3.1	4"	NA
	357 SIG	150	1130	1030	970	420	355	310	0.9	4.0	NA	NA
	356 TSW	115	1520	NA	NA	593	NA	NA	NA	NA	NA	NA
	356 TSW	124	1450	NA	NA	578	NA	NA	NA	NA	NA	NA
	356 TSW	135	1280	1120	1010	490	375	310	0.8	3.50	NA	NA
	356 TSW	147	1220	1120	1040	485	410	355	0.8	3.5	5"	NA
	357 Mag., Super Clean	105	1650									NA
	357 Magnum	110	1295	1095	975	410	290	230	0.8	3.5	4"V	$25
	357 (Med.Vel.)	125	1220	1075	985	415	315	270	0.8	3.7	4"V	$25
	357 Magnum	125	1450	1240	1090	585	425	330	0.6	2.8	4"V	$25
	357 (Multi-Ball)	140	1155	830	665	420	215	135	1.2	6.4	4"V	$11**
	357 Magnum	140	1360	1195	1075	575	445	360	0.7	3.0	4"V	$25
	357 Magnum	145	1290	1155	1060	535	430	360	0.8	3.5	4"V	$26
	357 Magnum	150/158	1235	1105	1015	535	430	360	0.8	3.5	4"V	$25
	357 Mag. Cowboy	158	800	761	725	225	203	185				NA
	357 Magnum	165	1290	1189	1108	610	518	450	0.7	3.1	8-3/8"	NA
	357 Magnum	180	1145	1055	985	525	445	390	0.9	3.9	4"V	$25
	357 Magnum	180	1180	1088	1020	557	473	416	0.8	3.6	8"V	NA
	357 Mag. CorBon F.A.	180	1650	1512	1386	1088	913	767	1.66	0.0		NA
	357 Mag. CorBon	200	1200	1123	1061	640	560	500	3.19	0.0		NA
	357 Rem. Maximum	158	1825	1590	1380	1170	885	670	0.4	1.7	10.5"	$14**
40, 10mm	40 S&W	135	1140	1070	NA	390	345	NA	0.9	NA	4"	NA
	40 S&W	155	1140	1026	958	447	362	309	0.9	4.1	4"	$14***
	40 S&W	165	1150	NA	NA	485	NA	NA	NA	NA	4"	$18***
	40 S&W	180	985	936	893	388	350	319	1.4	5.0	4"	$14***
	40 S&W	180	1015	960	914	412	368	334	1.3	4.5	4"	NA
	400 Cor-Bon	135	1450	NA	NA	630	NA	NA	NA	NA	5"	NA
	10mm Automatic	155	1125	1046	986	436	377	335	0.9	3.9	5"	$26
	10mm Automatic	170	1340	1165	1145	680	510	415	0.7	3.2	5"	$31
	10mm Automatic	175	1290	1140	1035	650	505	420	0.7	3.3	5.5"	$11**
	10mm Auto. (FBI)	180	950	905	865	361	327	299	1.5	5.4	4"	$16**
	10mm Automatic	180	1030	970	920	425	375	340	1.1	4.7	5"	$16**
	10mm Auto H.V.	180†	1240	1124	1037	618	504	430	0.8	3.4	5"	$27
	10mm Automatic	200	1160	1070	1010	495	510	430	0.9	3.8	5"	$14**
	10.4mm Italian	177	950	NA	NA	360	NA	NA	NA	NA	NA	NEW
	41 Action Exp.	180	1000	947	903	400	359	326	0.5	4.2	5"	$13**
	41 Rem. Magnum	170	1420	1165	1015	760	515	390	0.7	3.2	4"V	$33
	41 Rem. Magnum	175	1250	1120	1030	605	490	410	0.8	3.4	4"V	$14**
	41 (Med. Vel.)	210	965	900	840	435	375	330	1.3	5.4	4"V	$30
	41 Rem. Magnum	210	1300	1160	1060	790	630	535	0.7	3.2	4"V	$33
	41 Rem. Magnum	240	1250	1151	1075	833	706	616	0.8	3.3	6.5V	NA

Notes: Blanks are available in 32 S&W, 38 S&W and 38 Special. "V" after barrel length indicates test barrel was vented to produce ballistics similar to a revolver with a normal barrel-to-cylinder gap. Ammo prices are per 50 rounds except when marked with an ** which signifies a 20 round box; *** signifies a 25-round box. Not all loads are available from all ammo manufacturers. Listed loads are those made by Remington, Winchester, Federal, and others. DISC. is a discontinued load. Prices are rounded to nearest whole dollar and will vary with brand and retail outlet. † = new bullet weight this year; "c" indicates a change in data.

Cartridge	Bullet Wgt. Grs.	VELOCITY (fps)			ENERGY (ft. lbs.)			Mid-Range Traj. (in.)		Bbl. Lgth. (in).	Est. Price/ box
		Muzzle	50 yds.	100 yds.	Muzzle	50 yds.	100 yds.	50 yds.	100 yds.		
44 S&W Russian	247	780	NA	NA	335	NA	NA	NA	NA	NA	NA
44 S&W Special	180	980	NA	NA	383	NA	NA	NA	NA	6.5"	NA
44 S&W Special	180	1000	935	882	400	350	311	NA	NA	7.5"V	NA
44 S&W Special	200†	875	825	780	340	302	270	1.2	6.0	6"	$13**
44 S&W Special	200	1035	940	865	475	390	335	1.1	4.9	6.5"	$13**
44 S&W Special	240/246	755	725	695	310	285	265	2.0	8.3	6.5"	$26
44-40 Win. Cowboy	225	750	723	695	281	261	242				NA
44 Rem. Magnum	180	1610	1365	1175	1035	745	550	0.5	2.3	4"V	$18**
44 Rem. Magnum	200	1400	1192	1053	870	630	492	0.6	NA	6.5"	$20
44 Rem. Magnum	210	1495	1310	1165	1040	805	635	0.6	2.5	6.5"	$18**
44 (Med. Vel.)	240	1000	945	900	535	475	435	1.1	4.8	6.5"	$17
44 R.M. (Jacketed)	240	1180	1080	1010	740	625	545	0.9	3.7	4"V	$18**
44 R.M. (Lead)	240	1350	1185	1070	970	750	610	0.7	3.1	4"V	$29
44 Rem. Magnum	250	1180	1100	1040	775	670	600	0.8	3.6	6.5"V	$21
44 Rem. Magnum	250	1250	1148	1070	867	732	635	0.8	3.3	6.5"V	NA
44 Rem. Magnum	275	1235	1142	1070	931	797	699	0.8	3.3	6.5"	NA
44 Rem. Magnum	300	1200	1100	1026	959	806	702	NA	NA	7.5"	$17
44 Rem. Magnum	330	1385	1297	1220	1406	1234	1090	1.83	0.00	NA	NA
440 CorBon	260	1700	1544	1403	1669	1377	1136	1.58	NA	10"	NA
450 Short Colt/450 Revolver	226	830	NA	NA	350	NA	NA	NA	NA	NA	NEW
45 S&W Schofield	180	730	NA	NA	213	NA	NA	NA	NA	NA	NA
45 S&W Schofield	230	730	NA	NA	272	NA	NA	NA	NA	NA	NA
45 G.A.P.	185	1090	970	890	490	385	320	1	4.7	5	NA
45 G.A.P.	230	880	842	NA	396	363	NA	NA	NA	NA	NA
45 Automatic	165	1030	930	NA	385	315	NA	1.2	NA	5"	NA
45 Automatic	185	1000	940	890	410	360	325	1.1	4.9	5"	$28
45 Auto. (Match)	185	770	705	650	245	204	175	2.0	8.7	5"	$28
45 Auto. (Match)	200	940	890	840	392	352	312	2.0	8.6	5"	$20
45 Automatic	200	975	917	860	421	372	328	1.4	5.0	5"	$18
45 Automatic	230	830	800	675	355	325	300	1.6	6.8	5"	$27
45 Automatic	230	880	846	816	396	366	340	1.5	6.1	5"	NA
45 Automatic +P	165	1250	NA	NA	573	NA	NA	NA	NA	NA	NA
45 Automatic +P	185	1140	1040	970	535	445	385	0.9	4.0	5"	$31
45 Automatic +P	200	1055	982	925	494	428	380	NA	NA	5"	NA
45 Super	185	1300	1190	1108	694	582	504	NA	NA	5"	NA
45 Win. Magnum	230	1400	1230	1105	1000	775	635	0.6	2.8	5"	$14**
45 Win. Magnum	260	1250	1137	1053	902	746	640	0.8	3.3	5"	$16**
45 Win. Mag. CorBon	320	1150	1080	1025	940	830	747	3.47			NA
455 Webley MKII	262	850	NA	NA	420	NA	NA	NA	NA	NA	NA
45 Colt	200	1000	938	889	444	391	351	1.3	4.8	5.5"	$21
45 Colt	225	960	890	830	460	395	345	1.3	5.5	5.5"	$22
45 Colt + P CorBon	265	1350	1225	1126	1073	884	746	2.65	0.0		NA
45 Colt + P CorBon	300	1300	1197	1114	1126	956	827	2.78	0.0		NA
45 Colt	250/255	860	820	780	410	375	340	1.6	6.6	5.5"	$27
454 Casull	250	1300	1151	1047	938	735	608	0.7	3.2	7.5"V	NA
454 Casull	260	1800	1577	1381	1871	1436	1101	0.4	1.8	7.5"V	NA
454 Casull	300	1625	1451	1308	1759	1413	1141	0.5	2.0	7.5"V	NA
454 Casull CorBon	360	1500	1387	1286	1800	1640	1323	2.01	0.0		NA
475 Linebaugh	400	1350	1217	1119	1618	1315	1112	NA	NA	NA	NA
480 Ruger	325	1350	1191	1076	1315	1023	835	2.6	0.0	7.5"	NA
50 Action Exp.	325	1400	1209	1075	1414	1055	835	0.2	2.3	6"	$24**
500 S&W	275	1665	1392	1183	1693	1184	854	1.5	NA	8.375	NA
500 S&W	400	1675	1472	1299	2493	1926	1499	1.3	NA	8.375	NA
500 S&W	440	1625	1367	1169	2581	1825	1337	1.6	NA	8.375	NA

Rimfire Ammunition — Ballistics & Prices

Note: The actual ballistics obtained with your firearm can vary considerably from the advertised ballistics. Also, ballistics can vary from lot to lot with the same brand and type load.

Cartridge	Bullet Wt. Grs.	Velocity (fps) 22-1/2" Bbl.		Energy (ft. lbs.) 22-1/2" Bbl.		Mid-Range Traj. (in.)	Muzzle Velocity
		Muzzle	100 yds.	Muzzle	100 yds.	100 yds.	6" Bbl.
17 Aguila	20	1850	1267	NA	NA	NA	NA
17 Hornady Mach 2	17	2100	1530	166	88	0.7	NA
17 Aguila	20	1850	NA	NA	NA	NA	NA
17 HMR	17	2550	1902	245	136	NA	NA
22 Short Blank	—	—	—	—	—	—	—
22 Short CB	29	727	610	33	24	NA	706
22 Short Target	29	830	695	44	31	6.8	786
22 Short HP	27	1164	920	81	50	4.3	1077
22 Colibri	20	375	183	6	1	NA	NA
22 Super Colibri	20	500	441	11	9	NA	NA
22 Long CB	29	727	610	33	24	NA	706
22 Long HV	29	1180	946	90	57	4.1	1031
22 LR Ballistician	25	1100	760	65	30	NA	NA
22 LR Pistol Match	40	1070	890	100	70	4.6	940
22 LR Sub Sonic HP	38	1050	901	93	69	4.7	NA
22 LR Standard Velocity	40	1070	890	100	70	4.6	940
22 LR HV	40	1255	1016	140	92	3.6	1060
22 LR Silhoutte	42	1220	1003	139	94	3.6	1025
22 SSS	60	950	802	120	86	NA	NA
22 LR HV HP	40	1280	1001	146	89	3.5	1085
22 Velocitor GDHP	40	1435	0	0	0	NA	NA
22 LR Hyper HP	32/33/34	1500	1075	165	85	2.8	NA
22 LR Stinger HP	32	1640	1132	191	91	2.6	1395
22 LR Hyper Vel	30	1750	1191	204	93	NA	NA
22 LR Shot #12	31	950	NA	NA	NA	NA	NA
22 WRF LFN	45	1300	1015	169	103	3	NA
22 Win. Mag.	30	2200	1373	322	127	1.4	1610
22 Win. Mag. V-Max BT	33	2000	1495	293	164	0.60	NA
22 Win. Mag. JHP	34	2120	1435	338	155	1.4	NA
22 Win. Mag. JHP	40	1910	1326	324	156	1.7	1480
22 Win. Mag. FMJ	40	1910	1326	324	156	1.7	1480
22 Win. Mag. Dyna Point	45	1550	1147	240	131	2.60	NA
22 Win. Mag. JHP	50	1650	1280	300	180	1.3	NA
22 Win. Mag. Shot #11	52	1000	—	NA	—	—	NA

Handloading 2004

by Charles Petty

TO BE BLUNT there haven't been too many things in handloading over the last few years that have made a lasting impression on my loading habits. New cartridges come along and I almost always work with them for a while, but the guns normally end up in the back corner of the safe or, more commonly, being returned to the manufacturer. Somehow I always end up with time-tested guns and cartridges.

One area where new products have truly, permanently, changed the way I do things is in the powders I use all the time. When I learned how to reload there weren't very many choices. Handguns were loaded with Bullseye, Unique and 2400 and shotguns used Red Dot. Rifles were a bit more complex but whenever possible I used surplus Hodgdon 4831 or IMR 4895.

Today I rarely use any of those. Hodgdon Varget is very similar to 4895 and is useful in a wide range of cartridges. It's not the only rifle powder I use but is often the starting point when I work up loads for moderate-size cases.

Almost every handgun cartridge that I shoot regularly with cast bullets is loaded with Hodgdon Titegroup. Those cartridges include: 32 S&W Long, 32-20, 38-40, 44-40, 44 Special and 45 Colt. Jacketed bullets in either 45 ACP or 9mm Luger get Alliant Power Pistol. I got to this point over a long period of time based upon two basic criteria: accuracy and consistent velocity. Some folks think those two are closely related. I don't, for I have seen superb accuracy with loads that had velocity spreads of 100 fps or more. It is obviously desirable to have things as consistent as possible, but that alone does not guarantee accuracy.

Hodgdon Titegroup and Varget.

Titegroup and Power Pistol are different as night and day. Titegroup is a fast-burning powder that is a bit slower than Bullseye in burning rate although it is, by Hodgdon's nomenclature, a "Spherical" powder it looks suspiciously like powders sold by Winchester. It should. It is made in the same place. Olin Corporation sold their St. Marks, Florida plant and it is now known as St. Marks Powder Co. and the identifier begins with, "SMP" followed by some numbers. They make many commercial powders used throughout the industry in addition to the canister powders sold by Winchester and Hodgdon.

Alliant Power Pistol is an extruded, small-grain powder that is a little slower than Unique. It began life as a commercial powder called Bullseye 84. Commercial powders are sold within the industry and are a bit different from the canister powders you and I can buy. The ammo factories routinely do pressure and velocity testing during the day and, when they open a new can of powder, test and make adjustments–if they need to. If there is a little variation from one batch to the next it's no big deal for them, but we don't have that facility so the stuff we buy needs to be very consistent so we can use standard loading data.

One event of last year could either pass unnoticed or produce sweeping change in the way we think of powders. "IMR" stands for improved military rifle and for generations if you said "IMR" everyone knew you were getting a powder made by the legendary DuPont family of companies that, of course, also included Remington Arms. It was completely logical for DuPont to make powder since it was a core business dating back to 1802 and a little powder mill on Brandywine Creek near Wilmington, Delaware. In the shadow of the Great Depression, Remington was purchased and operated until 1993. DuPont had begun, in what some called a move toward political correctness, to distance themselves from things that

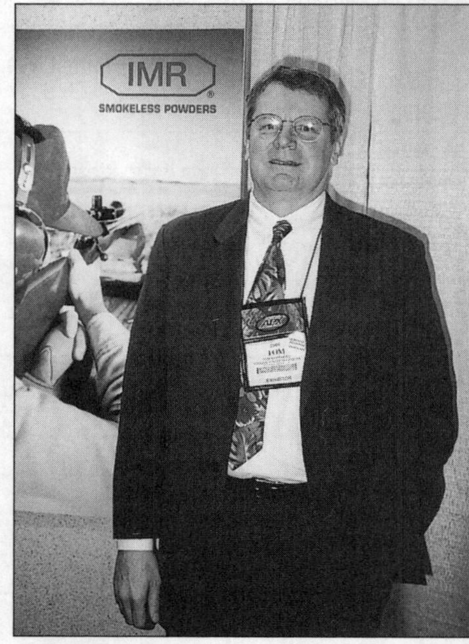

Tom Shepherd of Hodgdon introduces IMR powder.

went *bang* or *boom*. Most folks didn't know that the manufacture of IMR powder had moved to Canada, at least partly because of an explosion at the U.S. plant. IMR Powder Co. was formed but manufacturing was done by Expro-Tec in Valley Field Canada, a suburb of Montreal. It has been that way for a long time and consumers who weren't paying attention might have missed it because all the packaging was exactly the same—except for the company name, and that was in small print.

In late 2003 Hodgdon purchased the IMR Powder Company. This is one of those deals that hadn't generated any rumors until one day a press release came out announcing the purchase. Hodgdon has purchased the IMR trademark, powder formulas and intellectual property—and has exclusive marketing rights for the states. All packaging has moved to Kansas. Hodgdon did not buy as much as a brick, and manufacturing will continue in Canada. Hodgdon will be able to tweak powder specifications, and there are hints that we'll see some new powders in the future.

According to Hodgdon president Tom Shepherd the only change the consumer will notice will be a shift from the metal cans we're so used to, to the plastic containers Hodgdon is

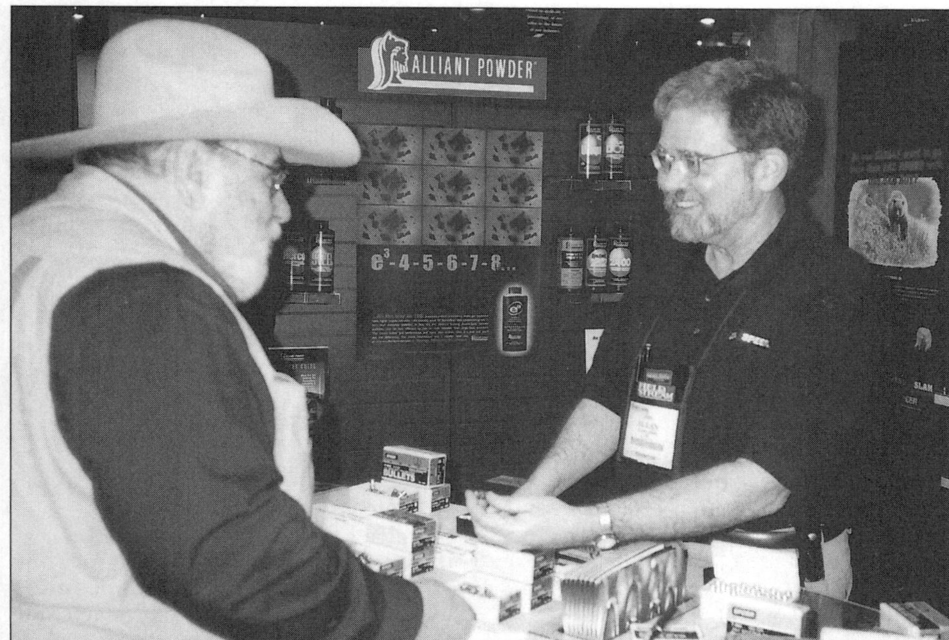

Allan Jones of Speer shows the new 38 Special bullet to John Taffin.

already using. The labeling will be the same and the color scheme will be preserved. One of the best things about DuPont and IMR powders was that each had a distinctive color all its own. I always liked that because one quickly learned the color of the powders used most often and I could grab them off the shelf without having to sort through a bunch of similar-looking cans.

There are a few new powders intended for some specialized niches within the broad spectrum of canister powders. **Alliant** has two shotgun powders that will almost surely find a place in handgun loads as well. First is "410" designed specifically for the .410-bore shotgun. If this works as well in small cases like the 221 Fireball, as does Hodgdon's competing "Lil'Gun," it is going to be lots of fun. The other has a name that will need explanation. It is called "e3" and is a faster-burning propellant intended for 12-gauge target loads. The name is derived from characteristics of "energy, efficiency and excellence". Alliant reports it should do very well in target-level handgun loads, too.

Western Powder is introducing Ramshot Hunter, an imported ball-type powder. It is geared toward the assorted short, and super short, magnum cartridges and should also do nicely in medium-size cases, up to and including 280 Remington and 30-06 Springfield.

Bullet Stuff

Everyone who sells component bullets always has "new" offerings-usually just a different weight of the same bullet types-but there are some innovations to report.

One of the real gaps in the bullet market is for a 38 Special bullet that will perform well from the 2-inch barrels that almost everyone uses for small carry guns. The "good ole boys" at **Speer** have three of their Gold Dot bullets crafted especially for the snubguns. There are 110-, 135- and 147-grain offerings, but Speer seems to be most proud of the 135. Samples loaded to +P levels fired from a 2-inch barrel are reported to penetrate the magic 12" and expand to over 50-caliber.

The Gold Dot is one of the best of the premium hollowpoints and takes advantage of Speer's ability to plate lots of copper onto a swaged lead core. This is exactly the same process they use to make their TMJ *(totally metal jacketed)* bullets—but then they poke a hole in the nose to create a hollowpoint. The Gold Dot is actually the remnant of the plating that is driven to the bottom of the hollowpoint.

The other hot topic in bullets is the growth in the class of "bonded" bullets. Everybody has some now and there is a definite appeal to this type of construction. The idea is to bond the lead core to the bullet jacket so the two will not separate as the bullet penetrates and expands in game. The process for making most of them is described as "proprietary" but there are only so many ways it can be done.

Some might call Speer's Hot-Cor process a form of bonding because they pour molten lead right into the bullet jacket on the machine. Actually, it's very clever because there is a lead pot which is triggered to pour a fixed amount every time a jacket comes by. Technically speaking, it is not bonding but the procedure does reduce what is called "slippage" between core and jacket.

Another variation is in the manufacture of **"Trophy Bonded Bear Claw"** bullets. In this one a bit of flux and a lead core are inserted in jackets arranged in a plate with lots of holes. Then the entire unit goes into a furnace and is heated almost red-hot. This "solders" the lead to the jacket and makes a strong physical bond. The bullet then goes through traditional forming operations. The

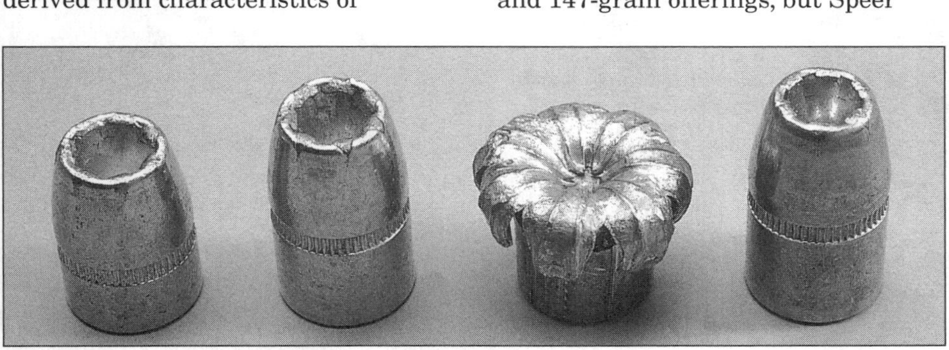
Speer Gold Dot 38 Special bullets in 110-, 135- and 147-grain weights. The expanded bullet is the new 135-grain Gold Dot fired from a 2-inch barrel.

RCBS Charge Master electronic scale and powder dispenser.

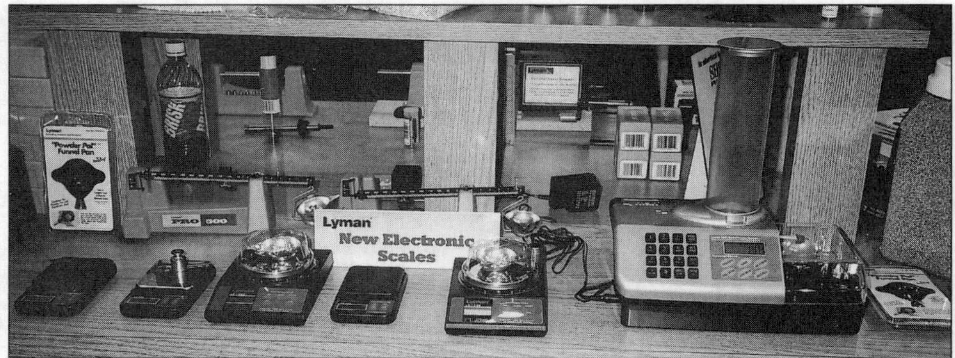

Lyman's array of scales with the Powder Pal combination weighing pan/powder funnel.

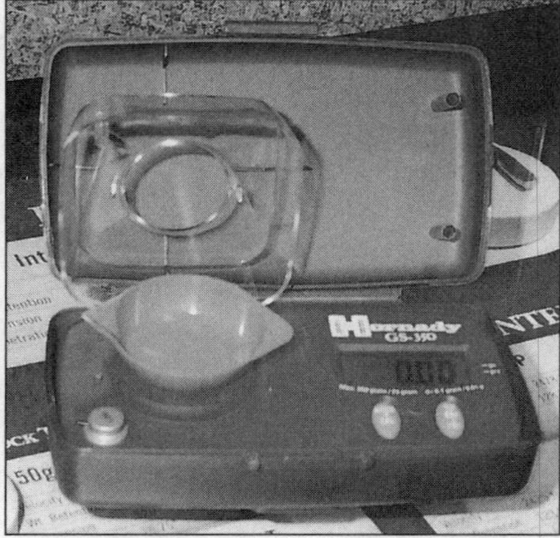

Hornady's new scale.

appeal of bonded bullets is that they lose very little weight as they expand and penetrate.

The **Barnes X-bullet** has always been a great game bullet, but sometimes was a challenge because of the large bearing surface. Barnes has now introduced the "Triple-shock X-bullet" that has three grooves in the shank of the solid copper bullet. This doesn't seem to change the way the bullet expands but has significantly reduced the bearing surface to allow for higher velocities at standard pressures. The grooves also appear to be beneficial in the accuracy department for some limited shooting I've done found them to be very accurate.

The Year of the Scale

Digital electronic scales are one of the best things to happen to reloaders in a long time. At first they were terribly expensive, but as it is with all electronic gadgets the price has been cut in half–and then half again–to the point where some cost very little more than a good-quality beam balance.

This year Lyman, Hornady and RCBS all have at least one addition, and Lyman has two. Most of these are relatively small units that have the advantage of portability. The idea of being able to take one to the range with you is surely appealing but requires considerable care to have everything come out right. First of all is the great sensitivity of the electronic scales that makes them subject to wild swings with just a little breeze. It is surely possible to shield them from wind, but that's a bit troublesome. Another issue is that electronic scales can be caused to drift by changes in temperature. This doesn't mean that you can't use them outdoors, for you surely can, but it does mean it is a very good idea to check the calibration frequently.

Last year we saw Lyman enter the digital powder dispenser market with their 1200 Digital Powder System to compete with units sold by RCBS and PACT. The only difference between them was the color of the box—both were made by PACT. Now RCBS is showing a unit of their own, called the Charge Master, which is being made offshore. The only criticism I ever had with the original was that it seemed to be pretty slow. PACT has gone through a complete re-design to produce a unit that is twice as fast. It's in the same box as the original but all the innards are new. I'm not sure that we really need to weigh each and every powder charge, but the improved speed makes it much more convenient to do so if you wish.

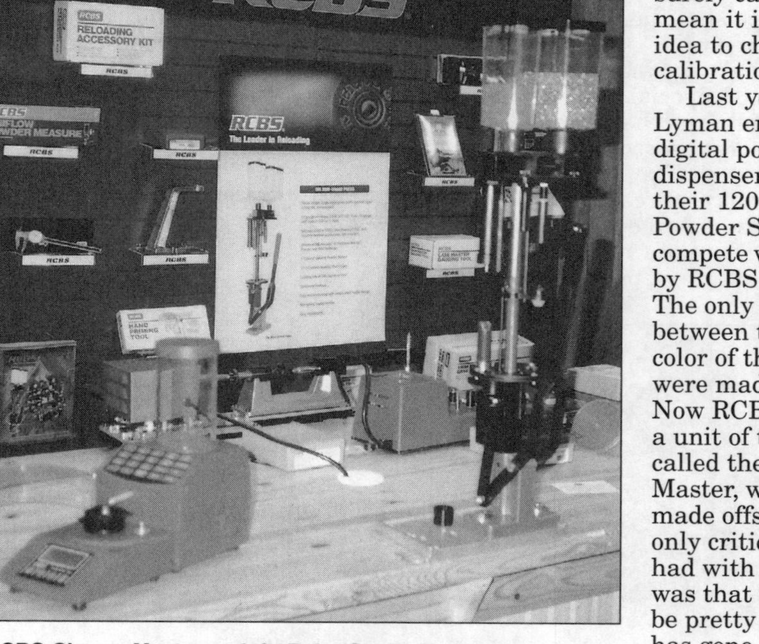

RCBS Charge Master on left; Baby Grand shotshell press on right.

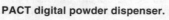

New Cartridges and Dies

We've got at least three new cartridges that were shown at the SHOT Show in February. Hornady is making the 204 Ruger and Winchester has the latest addition to the WSSM family, a 25-caliber that looks just like the others. And then there is the 50GI, a proprietary 50-caliber cartridge designed to work in a Government Model-size pistol that looks exactly like the old 45 we know and love. Guncrafter Industries is offering the gun, ammo, brass and loading dies. There are two factory loads at this writing, both using Speer's 300-grain TMJ bullet. One is loaded to around 700 fps, with recoil comparable to 45 ACP ball ammo; another at around 900 fps that feels a lot like the early 10mm Auto ammo. Neither is as severe in recoil as the

PACT digital powder dispenser.

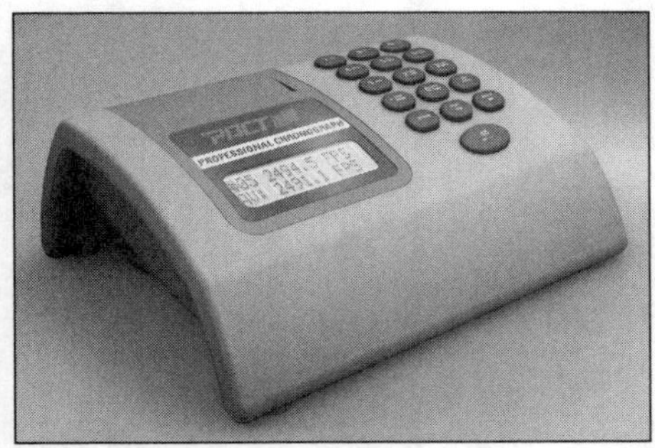

Re-designed PACT Professional Chronograph.

bigger 50s. It is an interesting concept, but very early in the process right now.

Of course, the 500 S&W is still getting lots of interest. The latest wrinkle is the availability of carbide sizing dies from RCBS. I'm sure the carbide is going to be an improvement, but the case is so big and has so much area to size that RCBS recommends lubricant still be applied to the case, anyhow. They also offer carbide sizing dies for the 480 Ruger and 475 Linebaugh cartridges. Redding has added steel dies, as has Lyman.

We've got new .500" jacketed bullets from Hornady (350-grain XTP) and Sierra (400-grain JSP and 350-grain JHP), and Barnes has added to their solid copper offerings with 325- and 385-grain spitzer styles. The big .50 also lends itself very well to big, fat lead bullets and **Cast Performance Bullet Company,** the original supplier for factory ammo, has 370-, 400- and 440-grain in the LBT style with gas checks. **Liberty Shooting Supplies** also offers a 430-grain flatnose with a plain base. These things really don't need to be driven flat-out to be effective hunting loads for most anything in North America, and I found the 400-grain offering to be super-accurate and easy to shoot at around 1100 fps.

25 WSSM

Everyone seems to have dies for the WSSM family of cartridges and Hornady showed the new 204 Ruger. It's funny how things catch your eye sometimes and that's what happened at the **Forster** booth. They've always had super dies and now they've really improved the box they come in.

This isn't really new, and in fact is so old odds are good that the current generation of reloaders have never heard of it. The product is Imperial Sizing Die Wax and it is now being manufactured and sold by **Redding Reloading Equipment.** We've got umpteen various case-sizing lubricants—and for general purpose use most work just fine, but if you're going to do any aggressive case-forming or have something that, for some reason, is hard to size, this is the stuff to use. It comes in a small tin that is probably a lifetime supply for most users and the only thing different is that it is green now. *(I'm sure you've noticed that manufacturers of reloading stuff are incredibly color conscious)* The best way to use it is to just smear a little on your fingers and then rub the case. It doesn't take much and it's pretty hard to over-lube with it, although I'm sure you can. With liquid lubricants it is easy to leave too much on the case and end up with a dimple at the bottleneck. I found that a rag dampened with rubbing alcohol easily takes off the lube.

Another gadget that isn't new but is so handy that it deserves more mention is **Lyman's "Powder Pal"** scale pan and powder funnel. This is only for digital scales. One side has a funnel that seems to fit just about everything *(I've used it for 45-70)* and all you do is dispense the charge into the pan and then go straight to the case. It's one of those inexpensive little things that helps a bunch and makes you wonder why nobody thought of it before.

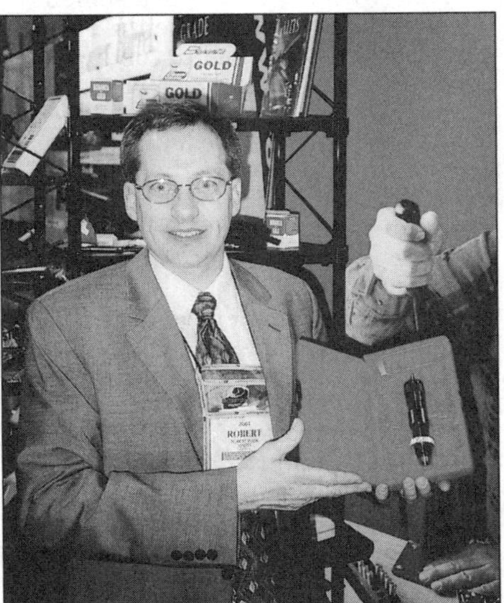

Robert Ruch of Forster, with their new die box.

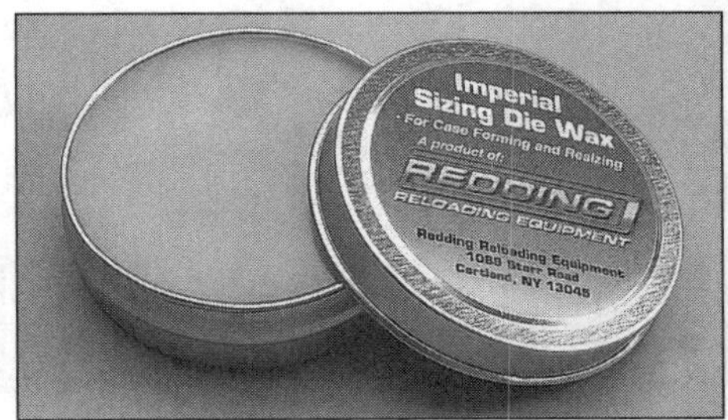

Redding's Imperial Sizing Die Wax.

It seems as if this is a year with something for everyone. We've got a couple of new cartridges from Winchester and Hornady that will keep folks like me off the streets but probably the most important news is that we've got lots of stuff to make the job of loading a little easier. I really do like electronic scales and powder dispensers. Only a prototype of RCBS's new Charge Master was available at the SHOT Show but I've been using the improved PACT model for awhile and find it to be much improved.

Rest Well, Old Friend

Any of you who called the RCBS customer service line over the last 20-30 years probably spoke to Jay Postman. He was the voice of RCBS to generations of reloaders... myself included... and the guy with the Santa Claus beard that was in RCBS print ads for years. Never have I known anyone with such an encyclopedic memory. Even after I became reasonably proficient at this stuff, tough questions were often most easily answered by getting Jay on the phone. He delighted in telling me where to find answers in GUN DIGEST or *The American Rifleman* —right down to the issue and even page number. Never once was he wrong. Jay died unexpectedly not long ago and there's a little empty space in the world now that will never be filled. •

Reference

Guncrafter Industries
171 Madison 1510
Huntsville, AR 72740
(479)-665-2466
www.guncrafterindustries.com

The Special Operations 45 ACP

The Heckler & Koch MK 23/Mark 23 USSOCOM

by Christopher R. Bartocci

ON JANUARY 14,1985, the 45 ACP model M1911A1 pistol was replaced by the 9mm NATO Beretta M9 as the standard sidearm for all U.S. forces. There was much bitterness throughout the branches of the U.S. military of the adoption of the perceived inferior 9mm cartridge. The resentful feelings ran very deep, so deep that some would accept nothing in 9mm, regardless of how good the pistol was. The Navy stopped procurement of the M9 in 1987 due to "durability" problems and purchased 1500 SIG Sauer model P226s until a suitable 45 ACP handgun could be produced. However no such pistol ever came, well not for general issue anyways!

In 1986, the United States Special Operations Command (USSOCOM) was established. What this did was to put all of the U.S. Special Operations Forces under one command. This would include the Navy SEALS and Special Boat Units, Army Green Berets, Operational Detachment Delta, and 75th Ranger Regiment, Air Force Special Operations Wing, Combat Control Teams and Para-Rescue. These units were unified into the Navy Special Warfare Command (WARCOM), U.S. Army Special Operations Command (USASOC), and Air Force Special Operations Command (AFSOC), all becoming separate components commands under USSOCOM.

In 1989 it was realized the majority of future military engagements would be with Special Operation Forces. The battle would be brought up very close and personal. With the establishment of USSOCOM, they would have the freedom to procure special weapons outside the normal unilateral procurement process. General Lindsey, the first Commander In Chief (CINC) of USSOCOM, mandated that the multitude of different small arms in the various special ops units be studied, with a view toward someday unifying future requirements. Major Gus Taylor was tasked to conduct this study. He was a member of General Lindsey's staff, Special Forces officer as well as a seasoned combat veteran. The findings were that there were more than 120 different variations of small arms that were in use by Army, Navy and Air Force Special Operations units.

The large number of non-standardized, unsupported small arms disturbed General Lindsey. He tasked Major Taylor to work with his counterparts in the USSOCOM components command to develop a unified plan to replace this wide variety of odd small arms with the development of joint standardized weapons for use by all Special Operations Forces (SOF)

One of the new special handgun requirements was to produce an Offensive Handgun Weapon System (OHWS). The basis of the OHWS requirement was the operational deficiencies (for special ops) found in the service 9mm NATO handguns. The M9, M12 and other handguns in the inventory were intended to be used as defensive weapons only and filled this role well. They were easy to handle, had little recoil and were easy to train the average soldier on. The 9mms, however, were less than adequate for the face-to-face offensive gunfights that were the norm in special ops Close Quarter Battle (CQB).

In CQB, the operator does not often have the option of defending himself and escaping. For an operator engaged in CQB, the handgun is his alternative offensive weapon in the case of his carbine or submachine gun malfunctions or runs out of ammunition. This is often in the middle of a close-range gunfight. The operator cannot clear his weapon under these circumstances, because his adversaries will most certainly shoot him at extremely short ranges if he tries. Rather the operator must quickly transition to his handgun and continue the offensive engagement.

General Lindsey decided the OHWS would be the first joint Special Operations weapon. He did so not because it was the most important, but because it was the most controversial. If consensus could be made on the OHWS, it would pave the way for agreement on other, more important weapons.

The first issue to be dealt with was what caliber cartridge the OHWS would fire. Certainly the 9mm NATO cartridge was ruled out based on poor combat/CQB performance. The first chambering looked at was the 10mm. However, it was quickly ruled out due to the few guns that fired it and their extremely short service life. The 45 ACP cartridge had an excellent record as a man-stopper. However, it did not always put an adversary down with one shot. The solution to the incapacitation problem was a newer high-velocity 45 ACP +P round. The next issue was the handgun. There was discussion of the feasibility of using a M1911 pistol as a baseline weapon; however, several problems arose. The M1911 could not handle the new high-velocity "+P" loads when firing many thousands of rounds per month as occurs in ops training. The OHWS was primarily to be designed to fire the high-velocity ammunition. Also the M1911 was–at the time–technically unable to use a suppressor, while still maintaining the semi-automatic function. Finally, if an M1911 was so thoroughly worked over that it met most of the requirements, it would be more expensive than a new weapon. For these reasons, it was decided to procure an entirely new weapon.

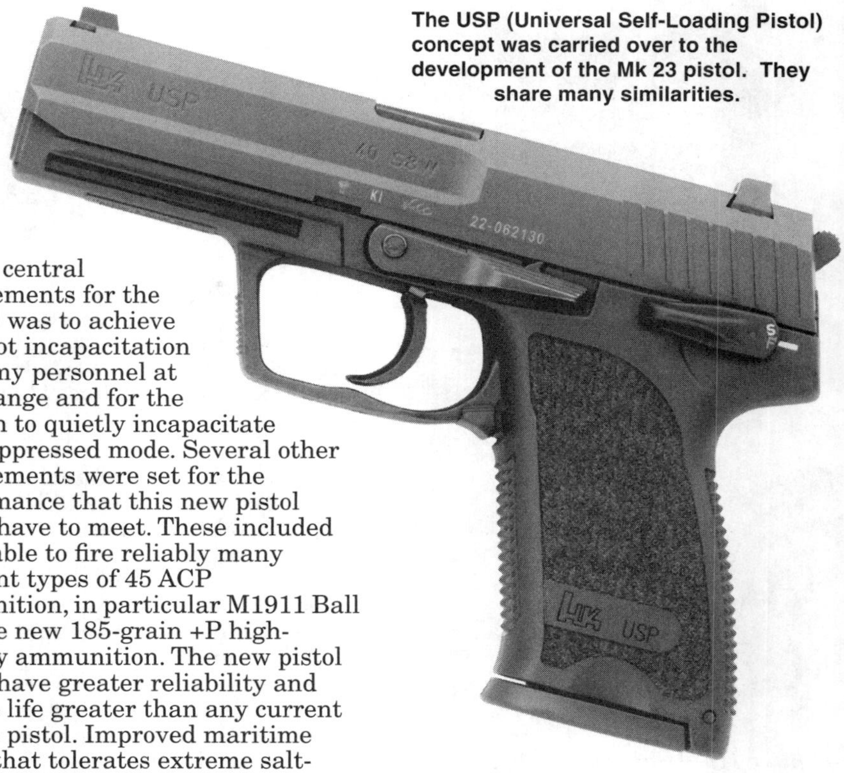

The USP (Universal Self-Loading Pistol) concept was carried over to the development of the Mk 23 pistol. They share many similarities.

The central requirements for the OHWS was to achieve one-shot incapacitation to enemy personnel at close range and for the weapon to quietly incapacitate in a suppressed mode. Several other requirements were set for the performance that this new pistol would have to meet. These included being able to fire reliably many different types of 45 ACP ammunition, in particular M1911 Ball and the new 185-grain +P high-velocity ammunition. The new pistol would have greater reliability and service life greater than any current service pistol. Improved maritime finish that tolerates extreme salt-water conditions. Greater mean-round-between-failure than any existing service pistol was also required. The pistol also would be adapted to a Laser Aiming Module (LAM) which will provide both laser and infrared capabilities as well as a white light source.

In August 1991 only two manufacturers were awarded developmental contracts for the new OHWS pistol: Colt's Manufacturing Company and Heckler & Koch. Both renowned manufacturers set out to develop the most advanced semi-automatic pistol the world has known.

The development stages would be broken up the three phases:

Phase I: **Development-** Developmental contracts were awarded to Colt and Heckler & Koch. Both companies were to supply 30 prototype pistols along with silencers and laser aiming modules. Colt's pistol was eliminated and Heckler & Koch's entry went on to Phase II.

The OHWS would be comprised of a 45 ACP semi-automatic pistol, silencer/suppressor and Laser Aiming Module (LAM). This would not be a sidearm but a primary weapon ideal for silent sentry incapacitation and Close Quarter Battle (CQB) scenarios. The Navy Program Executive Office for Expeditionary Warfare, and their Weapons Department at Crane, Indiana would be confirmed as the lead agency to solicit, develop, test and procure this new weapon system in December 1989. Mr. Chuck Zeller was appointed the OHWS Program Manager, responsible to USSOCOM for the research, development, testing, procurement and life-cycle sustainment of the system.

The complete Phase I OHWS (Offensive Handgun Weapon System) from Heckler & Koch. Notice the slide lock mechanism above the serial number, this was later omitted on the Phase II pistol.

The right side view of Colt's entry into the Offensive Handgun competition. Notice the similarity to the Colt Double Eagle pistol. Note the ambidextrous safety that will only engage if the hammer is in the cocked position. Also, the pistol has tritium night sights, as well as a muzzle brake that the Knight's Armament silencer attaches to. ***(photo courtesy Colt Defense LLC)***

- ***Phase II:*** **Refinement**- The Heckler & Koch pistol was subjected to numerous testing procedures of durability, reliability and accuracy. There were 30 additional weapons systems delivered with silencers only. The Laser Aiming Module design was delayed. Final part of Phase II was the production decision.
- ***Phase III:*** **Production**- June 28, 1995 the production contract was awarded to Heckler & Koch for 1,950 weapon systems at a cost of $1,186.00 per unit. Pistol was type-classified as the MK 23, MOD 0.

The design of the MK 23 began in July of 1989 when Heckler & Koch Germany did a market study of the United States of desirable characteristics for an entirely new family of weapons based on a new design. These criteria would include a conventional design, innovative features, reliability, durability, safety, accuracy, high quality, advanced materials, low recoil, single/double action and affordability. With this in mind, H&K engineers went to work on this new pistol in the fall of 1989. Simultaneously, in February of 1991 the OHWS proposal was submitted to H&K by USSOCOM. In August of 1991 OHWS developmental contract was awarded to H&K. In September of 1991 the new family of H&K pistols was given the acronym USP (**U**niversal **S**elf-loading **P**istol). The USP was designed for the new 40 S&W cartridge as well as the 9mm NATO cartridge. Later (1995) the USP would be chambered for the 45 ACP cartridge.

The USP was a truly innovative design. It used a polymer frame with a conventional short-recoil operation utilizing a modified Browning-type linkless system. The pistol was a light 27.86 oz. Unlike other trademark H&K pistols, the USP would use standard lands and grooves instead of H&K's traditional polygonal rifling. However, due to demand, H&K later changed back to the polygonal rifling. Unlike the Glock family of pistols, the USP utilized a conventional double/single action design with a exposed hammer.

There are 10 variants. The Variant 1 is SA/DA with a decocking lever on the left side. When safety lever is in the upward position the pistol can be carried "cocked and locked" or decocked with the safety on. The Variant 2 is identical but the lever is on the right side. The Variant 3 is also SA/DA but is decock only. Variant 4 is decocking lever on right side. Variant 5 is DA only with a manual safety on left side. Variant 6 is the same with the lever on the right side. Variant 7 is DAO with no manual safety. Variant 8 is not available in the United States. Variant 9 is DA/SA with a safety, no decock so pistol can be carried in the "cocked & locked" position with lever on left side. Variant 10 is the same with lever on right side.

Perhaps the most innovative aspect of this new USP pistol would be the patented recoil reduction mechanism built into the spring guide. Basically, it is a two-spring buffer mechanism that accomplishes a couple things. It decreases wear on the pistol, thus increasing the life of the frame. Also it reduces felt recoil by as much as 30 percent. This would be carried over to the MK 23 and would prove to be a

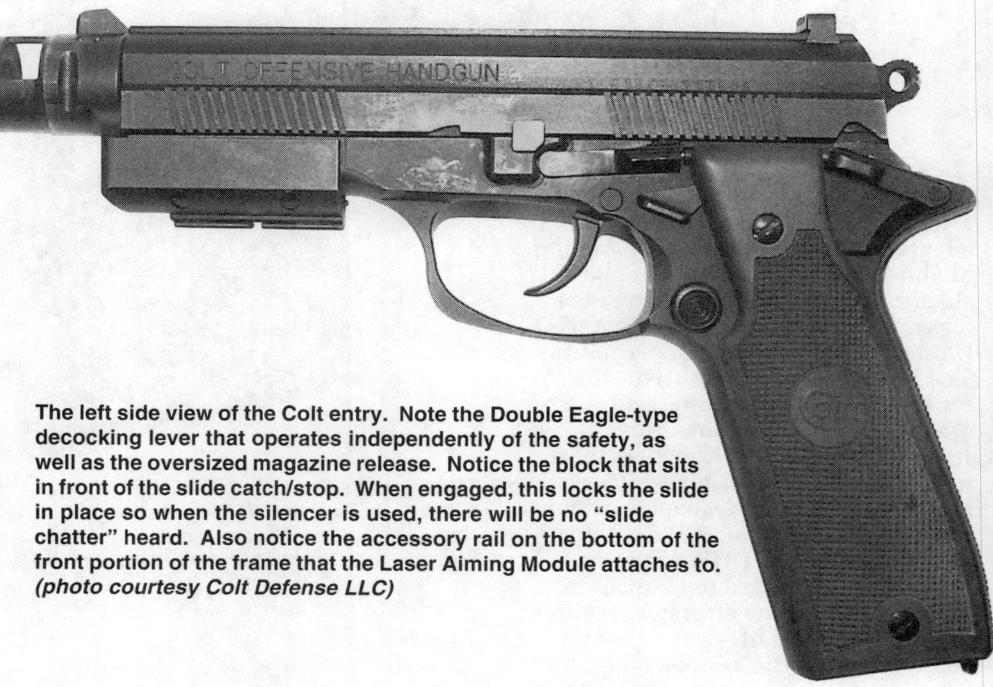

The left side view of the Colt entry. Note the Double Eagle-type decocking lever that operates independently of the safety, as well as the oversized magazine release. Notice the block that sits in front of the slide catch/stop. When engaged, this locks the slide in place so when the silencer is used, there will be no "slide chatter" heard. Also notice the accessory rail on the bottom of the front portion of the frame that the Laser Aiming Module attaches to. ***(photo courtesy Colt Defense LLC)***

The Phase II MK 23 pistol. Note the checkered front- and backstrap, as well as the removal of the slide lock mechanism.

crucial part in the extended durability of the pistol.

What does this have to do with the MK 23? How about everything! When H&K developed the MK 23, they started with the USP concept. The guns look very similar, in fact. Mechanically the USP and the MK 23 are identical with the exception of the different safety mechanism. The MK 23 utilizes the same firing pin block mechanism as the USP. The trigger must be pulled to the rear for the firing pin block to be disengaged. The overall length of the MK 23 pistol is 9.65 inches. Again, this is not a sidearm! This is a primary weapon. The barrel length is 5.87 inches. Unloaded with an empty magazine the MK 23 weighs 2.66 pounds. The magazine holds 12 rounds of potent 45 ACP ammunition.

The MK 23 uses the same high-strength polymer (called polyamide) for its frame as does the USP. Major difference being there is an oversized trigger guard, since Special Operation Forces operators often wear gloves. There is an accessory rail on the front of the frame for attaching the laser aiming module. The rear of the trigger guard is flared to protect the ambidextrous magazine release from accidental release. The front strap and back strap of the Phase I pistol were longitudinally serrated; the Phase II and Phase III pistols have a rather sharp checkering. This aids gripping when in adverse conditions such as water, mud and sweat.

The Phase I pistol is very similar to the final production with one major change. The Phase I pistol incorporated a slide lock mechanism. The purpose of this was when the silencer was in use, it would prevent the pistol from cycling, thus eliminating slide "chatter." This concept was abandoned early on for a couple of reasons. First the "chatter" was really not a large concern and the second was it was too risky. There was a great possibility of user confusion during stressful situations where a quick follow-up shot would be required and the slide being locked would prevent this.

Unlike the USP, the MK 23 has two separate levers instead of one. The decocking lever is on the left side and functions extremely quietly compared to the USP. Behind that is the ambidextrous safety lever. This enables the MK 23 to be carried in the "cocked & locked" fashion. The USP uses a single lever for both the safety and decocker. The single-action trigger pull is approximately 4.85 pounds and the double-action trigger pull is approximately12.13 pounds.

The slide of the MK 23 is machined from a single piece of steel. On the Phase I and II models there were gripping groves in the front of both sides of the slide as well as gripping grooves on the rear of the slide. On the Phase III and current production pistols, the forward gripping grooves were omitted. The adjustable front and rear sights sit up higher than other pistols since they must clear the silencer when installed. Both tritium nights sights as well as standard white dot sights are available. Most issue MK 23 pistols utilize night sights.

The finish of the slide is not pretty but it is highly effective against corrosion. The finish is designed to prevent corrosion when the pistol is exposed to prolonged salt/surf water conditions often encountered by Navy SEALS. Part of the testing the MK 23 went through was a 96-hour exposure in a salt/fog chamber. When removed the pistol was virtually corrosion-free. An H&K proprietary "Maritime" three-step finishing process protects the external surfaces. First the bare metal is nitrocarborised; second, it is phosphated; third, it receives a coating of black lacquer. The primary purpose of the lacquer is to give the pistol a dark non-glare finish. Even when the lacquer is scratched off, the slide is still protected from corrosion.

The barrel uses the same locking mechanism and recoil reduction mechanism as the USP. However, many modifications and enhancements would be made for the special requirements. The barrel was threaded at the end to accept the silencer. The barrel utilizes six land-and-groove chrome- lined polygonal rifling–basically the best of both worlds. Polygonal rifling provides better bullet-to-barrel fit for a tighter gas seal. Also, since there are no sharp edges to wear, the barrel life is significantly increased, which also makes the barrel easier to clean. Chrome lining gives three main benefits: First it is harder than standard barrel steel, increasing life. Second it is corrosion resistant. Third, when the barrel heats up, chrome has a self -lubricating property, increasing reliability of extraction.

The MK 23 pistol had to serve two purposes: it must have the durability and reliability of a combat pistol and second, have the accuracy of a match-grade pistol. USSOCOM required

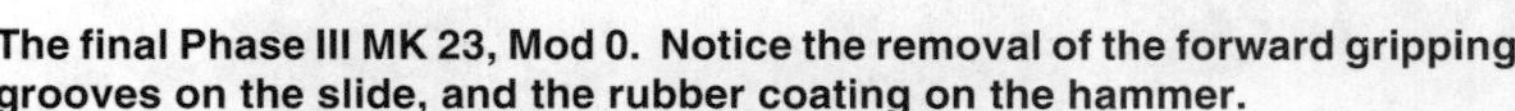

The final Phase III MK 23, Mod 0. Notice the removal of the forward gripping grooves on the slide, and the rubber coating on the hammer.

2 1/2-minute of angle groups at 25 meters. The MK 23 pistol far exceeded that, averaging 1.44 inches, with many grouping under 1 MOA. This was made possible by another innovative design in the barrel. H&K developed a rubber "O" ring. This established an extremely tight barrel-to-slide fit approximately 1/2-inch from the muzzle. This accomplishes two main things: one, it keeps a tight fit between the barrel and slide without the use of a conventional barrel bushing; two, it caused the slide-to-barrel fit to index repeatably from one round to the next, giving consistency in shot placement.

Operational Requirements and Endurance Testing

The MK 23 pistol was put through the most grueling and stringent testing of any known handgun. Due to the special requirements put forth by USSOCOM, a new standard for reliability, durability and accuracy was to be set.

During the Phase II testing, a reliability test was conducted. One of the criterions set forth by USSOCOM was that the pistol must not fall below 2000 mean rounds between failure/stoppages. The MK 23 pistol far surpassed that with a minimum of 6027 mean rounds between stoppages and a maximum of 15,122 mean rounds between stoppages.

During testing there were three pistols submitted for barrel life/accuracy testing after firing a total of 30,000 rounds. All three still held the USSOCOM standard of 2 1/2-MOA at 25 meters. The rubber O-ring that contributes significantly to this match-grade accuracy has a service life of more than 20,000 rounds. The O-ring requires no special installation and can be replaced in the field.

Several environmental tests were conducted to see the durability in adverse conditions. The pistol was subjected to a -25°F to +140°F. The pistol was exposed to maritime conditions such as being immersed in salt water, exposed to surf and salt fog testing. Also there was mud and sand-dust testing, and the gun was frozen in ice as well. Testing was also conducted with the pistol in a dry unlubricated state.

Knight's Armament Company Suppressor

During Phase I, the suppressor used by Heckler & Koch was designed and produced by them. Upon moving to Phase II, Heckler & Koch teamed up with Knight's Armament Company as it was deemed their silencer/suppressor was superior to the Heckler & Koch design. Knight's Armament was to adapt its suppressor for the Colt version of the OHWS to the Heckler & Koch version and manufacture the sound/flash suppressor. Knight's Armament is a sole proprietorship owned by C. Reed Knight Jr. They manufacture the 7.62 NATO-chambered SR-25 series rifles, recently adopted by Special Operations Command as the new Mk 11 Mod 0. This was adopted as a full weapon system including the rifle, Leupold scope, back-up pop-up iron sights and a sound suppressor. This is a modified SR-25 Match rifle, difference being it has a 20-inch barrel instead of 24 inches. Following this sale to the Navy SEALs, there was a sale to the U.S. Army Rangers.

Knight's is also a manufacturer of some of the finest suppressors in the world. The KAC OHG (Knight's Armament Company Offensive HandGun) suppressor designed by Doug Olson, is made of stainless steel with a Moly resin finish. The suppressor is approximately 1.37

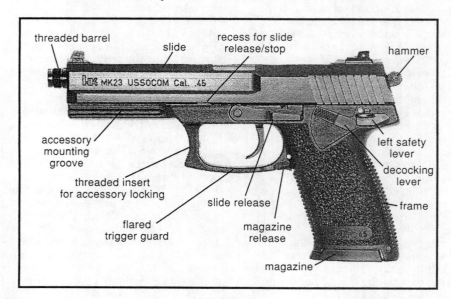

The anatomy of the MK 23 is very similar to that of the USP, the main difference being the decocking/safety mechanism.

inches in diameter with a 15,000 round service life. The use of robotic welding and the wired EDM process delivers gun-bore-to-baffle alignment, then the suppressors are heat-treated and stress-relieved. The suppressor serves a couple purposes. First and foremost it is a silencer, which due to its superior design does not affect the reliability of the pistol–even with the additional weight of the suppressor on the barrel. The suppressor does not have any adverse effect on the accuracy of the pistol and it functions wet; in fact, it functions better wet. The silencer also functions as a flash suppressor, reducing muzzle flash by 90 percent using M1911 230-grain ball ammunition.

One of the main issues that comes up when a silencer is added to a semi-automatic short-recoil operated pistol is that the additional weight of the silencer reduces the speed of the recoil. The process is slowed down, causing failure of the slide to fully recoil. Normally, during firing the slide is held closed due to it's mass, aided by the recoil spring and the hammer mainspring, until the pressure has dropped. Due to the requirement that the silencer must not compromise the integrity and reliability of this pistol, Knight's Armament had to come up with a solution for this, which they did.

Knight's manufactured a hollow piston that is in the rear of the silencer where the silencer is screwed onto the threaded barrel. There is a heavy captive coiled spring surrounding the piston. The piston is held in place with the suppressor by a threaded retaining ring. The suppressor body itself contains the baffles that muffle the shot.

The purpose of this spring-loaded piston is when the pistol is fired the expanding gasses that drive the bullet enters the suppressor and cause over-pressure in the suppressor. The over-pressure forces the suppressor body forward and drives the piston rearward. Due to the fact that the piston itself is screwed into the barrel

The MK 23 disassembled. Notice the recoil reduction mechanism on the rear of the spring guide and the rubber "O" ring approximately 1/2-inch from the rear of the muzzle. The MK 23 disassembles the same way as does the USP.

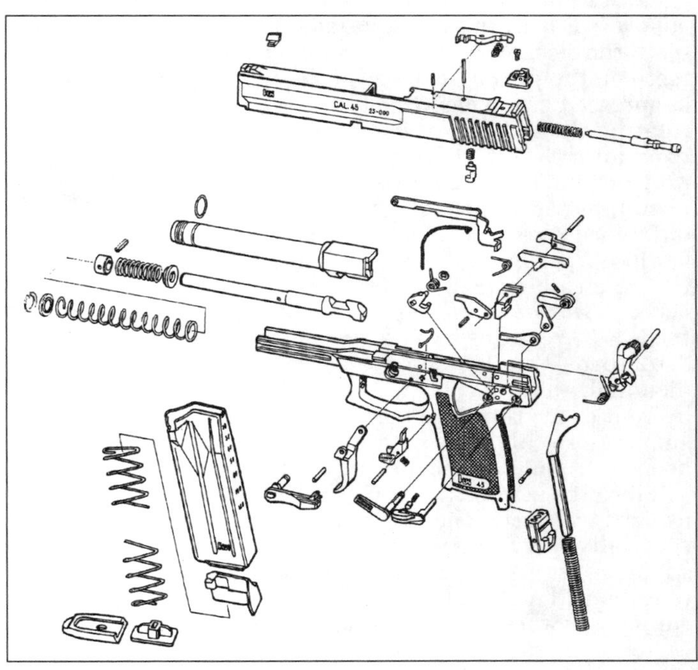

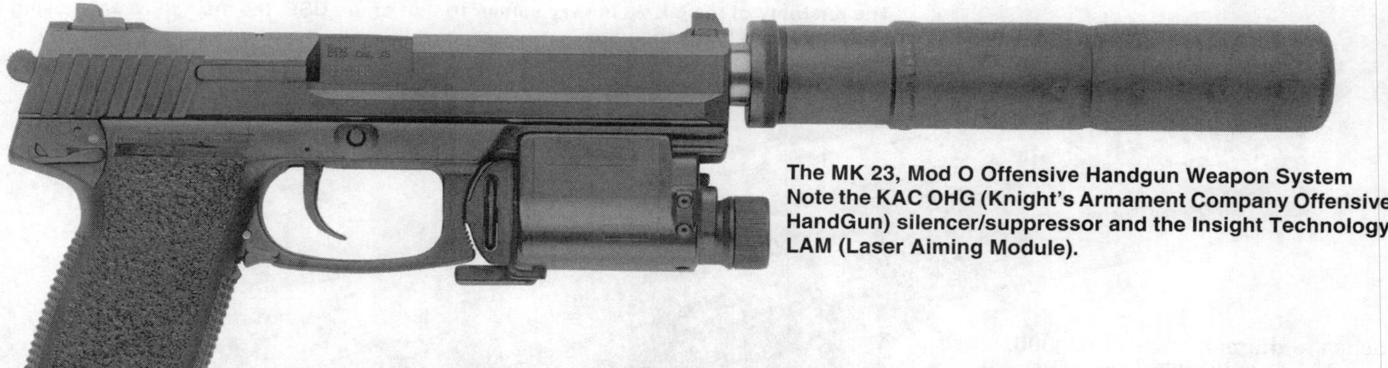

The MK 23, Mod O Offensive Handgun Weapon System Note the KAC OHG (Knight's Armament Company Offensive HandGun) silencer/suppressor and the Insight Technology LAM (Laser Aiming Module).

of the pistol, it gives the barrel an extra jolt to the rear. This totally alleviates any issue with the slide decelerating, causing failure of the slide to unlock and perform a full rearward cycle. After the bullet has left the barrel and the slide has made its full rearward motion the spring on the piston pulls the suppressor body and the piston back together. The design of the piston enhances compactness since the piston creates a separate expansion chamber.

Along with the requirement for reliability and sound reduction, there was a requirement for accuracy. Suppressed firearms are not known for uniform point of impact with and without the suppressor. This is because the added weight on the barrel changes the way the pistol recoils. When Knight's manufactured their OHG, they designed it so the suppressed point of impact could be moved to overlay the unsuppressed point of impact. At the rear of the suppressor body are ten squared-off teeth that lock in with squared-off teeth on the piston's cap spring. The suppressed group is moved by rotating the suppressor body one tooth after the other. The position that provides the least suppressed to unsuppressed point of impact difference is recorded. Once this is set, it will never have to be reset again for that particular MK 23 pistol and shooter. To mount the suppressor on the MK 23 requires it to be screwed on 3-1/2 turns. Once the suppressor is mounted, another rubber O-ring just in front of the threaded portion of the suppressor seals the suppressor and keeps it from loosening during firing.

Since the suppressor will be utilized by special operations units, especially Navy SEALs, the suppressor must function in wet conditions. The Knight's OHG suppressor works better wet than dry!

The MK 23 surpassed the most stringent accuracy requirements. These are 25-yard groups fired by the MK 23 pistol.

The OHG sound level is reduced by 26 dbs dry, with the addition of only 5 cc of water it is 36 dbs using standard M1911 230-grain ball ammunition. It should be noted that the suppressor will still dampen the blast of a 185-grain +P cartridge: however, there will still a supersonic crack when it passes through the atmosphere. For optimal use of the suppressor, only sub-sonic ammunition should be used. By cupping the end of the suppressor and submerging it in a stream–or any other water source–the baffles will fill

Laser Aiming Module (LAM) Technical Data

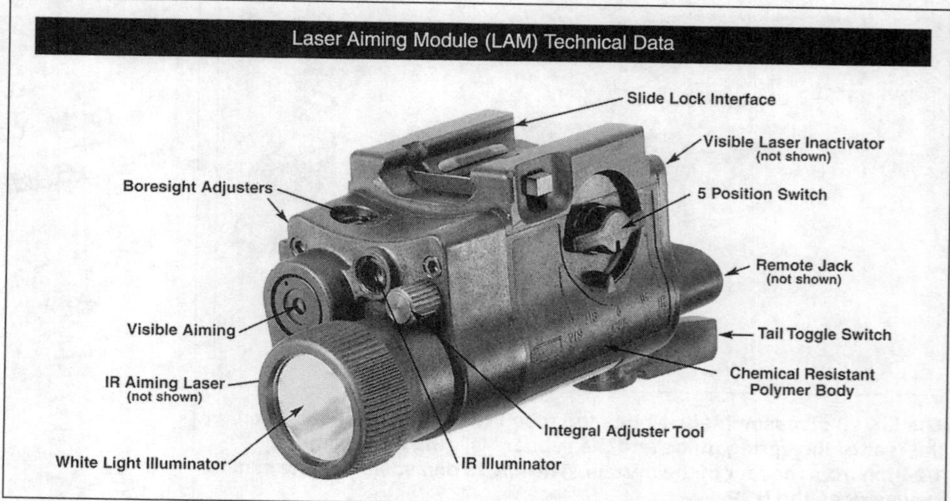

with water. When the pistol is fired with a wet suppressor the water retards the flow of propellant gas through the suppressor by lowering the temperature and reducing the expansion/pressure. As the water turns to steam, it adds to the weight of the expanding gas, creating additional turbulence further restricting gas flow, which in turn muffles the sound even more than when the suppressor is dry.

Insight Technology's LAM (Laser Aiming Module)

The third component of the MK 23 weapon system is the Laser Aiming Module (LAM) manufactured by Insight Technology. This was designed for special operation use in conjunction with night vision glasses. The LAM secures to the accessory rail on the front of the frame by screwing it into the front of the trigger guard. The LAM weighs approximately 5 ounces with the battery. The selector switch allows the LAM to be used in one of four of the capabilities of the LAM.

The first capability of the LAM is the standard visible laser sight. This 620-650nm laser can be manually adjusted to the proper zero. The range of the visible laser is approximately 50 meters in daylight and 700 meters at night, The second is a 6 volt Tungsten Halogen bulb with 70 lumens of white light (Flash Light) with a range of 25 meters. The third is an invisible infrared laser for use with night vision glasses. This aids in precision use of sentry removal in low light to night conditions. The range of this 810-850nm infrared laser is 200 meters. The fourth and final capability is an infrared light source to target and identify targets out to 50 meters with the use of night vision.

The LAM is operated by two DL123A 3V lithium batteries and activated by an ambidextrous toggle switch that extends back below the trigger guard. The center position is the *OFF* position. With a partial push in either direction there will be a momentary *ON* and when released it will spring back to the *OFF* position. When pushed to its farthest position on either side the LAM will remain in the *ON* position until manually put back to the *OFF* position. On the LAM as infrared laser, it is adjustable for beam size as well as windage and elevation.

Conclusions

After all the testing was said and done, on June 28, 1995, Heckler & Koch was awarded the contract for the United States Special Operation Command's new Offensive Handgun Weapon System (OHWS), now type-classified as the MK 23, Mod 0 (NSN 1005-01-426-8951). Heckler & Koch in Germany manufactured all MK 23 pistols. On May 1, 1996, the first MK 23 pistols were delivered to SOCOM for deployment. It is the first U.S. issue 45 ACP pistol since the old warhorse M1911/M1911A1 Government model. To some disappointment I am sure, it was only for special operations use.

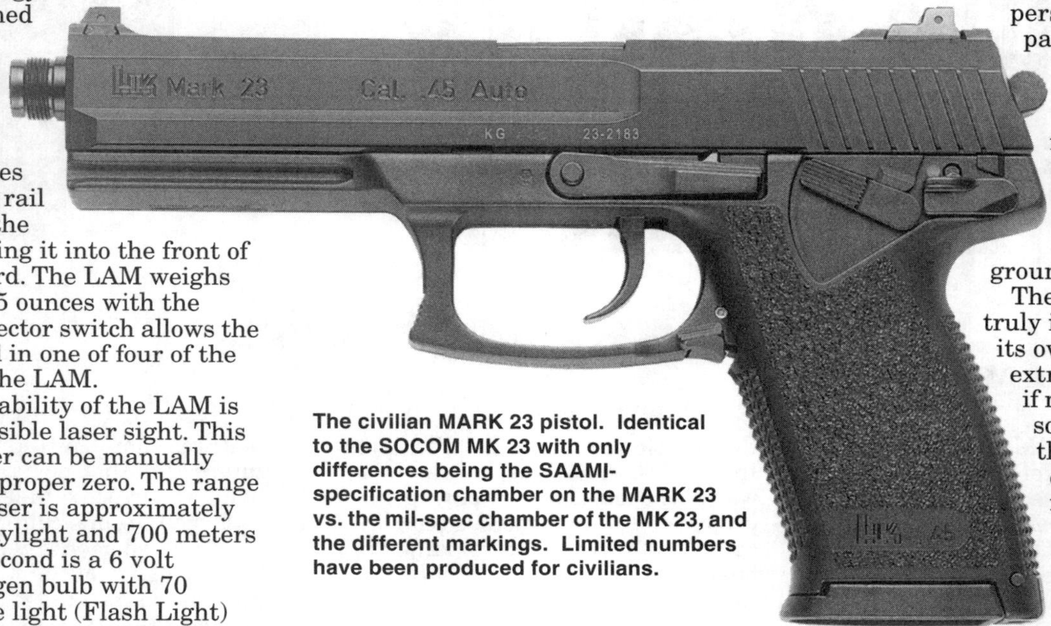

The civilian MARK 23 pistol. Identical to the SOCOM MK 23 with only differences being the SAAMI-specification chamber on the MARK 23 vs. the mil-spec chamber of the MK 23, and the different markings. Limited numbers have been produced for civilians.

Ironically, when the MK 23 was introduced to SOF operators in 1996, the weapon suffered from several non-mechanical problems. First, a new generation of shooters had grown up training with the 9mm and the double-tap mentality. Their extensive peacetime training on the lighter 9mm handguns, combined with a relative lack of combat experience with handguns, led the average SOF operator to reject the MK 23 in favor of the smaller and lighter 9mm NATO handguns. Second, the military budgets, even for USSOCOM, were cut in the mid 1990s, making General Lindsey's vision of joint special operations weapons a largely unaffordable proposition. Third, in the course of development of the MK 23, H&K also developed the USP 45, which held many of the advancements of the MK 23, but in a lighter, smaller, handier package. Finally, strong political pressure inside the services at the time worked against the fielding of the weapon to the Army and Air Force operators. These four factors combined to limit the production and fielding of the MK 23 and its +P ammunition to only Navy SOF units. The USP 45, however, is issued to a certain few special operators.

Complaints of poor lethality of the 9mm NATO handguns came in regularly from Enduring Freedom operations in Afghanistan during the winter of 2001. Complaints continued in 2002, as special operations shooters are once again calling for the 45 ACP pistol. The century-old lessons of handgun requirements for combat against enemy personnel were painfully re-learned. The MK 23 and the USP 45 may still prevail as the dominant handguns for the SOF and ground combat units.

The MK 23 pistol is truly in a category of its own. Often it is extremely difficult–if not impossible–to so closely bridge the worlds of combat reliability and match-grade accuracy. Under normal conditions you sacrifice one for the other. The MK 23 was able to accomplish both goals. The MK 23 truly represents the state-of-the-art in handgun development. Certainly our best of the best special operations forces received the best of the best in handgun technology. The quality and effectiveness of both complement each other. Currently there are a limited number of MARK 23 pistols available for civilian sales. The only difference between the military MK 23 and the civilian MARK 23 are the markings and the chamber on the MARK 23 is manufactured to SAAMI specifications, rather than military specifications of the MK 23. •

Acknowledgements

I would like to thank Jennifer Golisch from Heckler & Koch, Doug Olson of Knight's Manufacturing and Samantha Millett of Insight Technology for their technical assistance with this article. Photography provided by Heckler & Koch and Insight Technology.

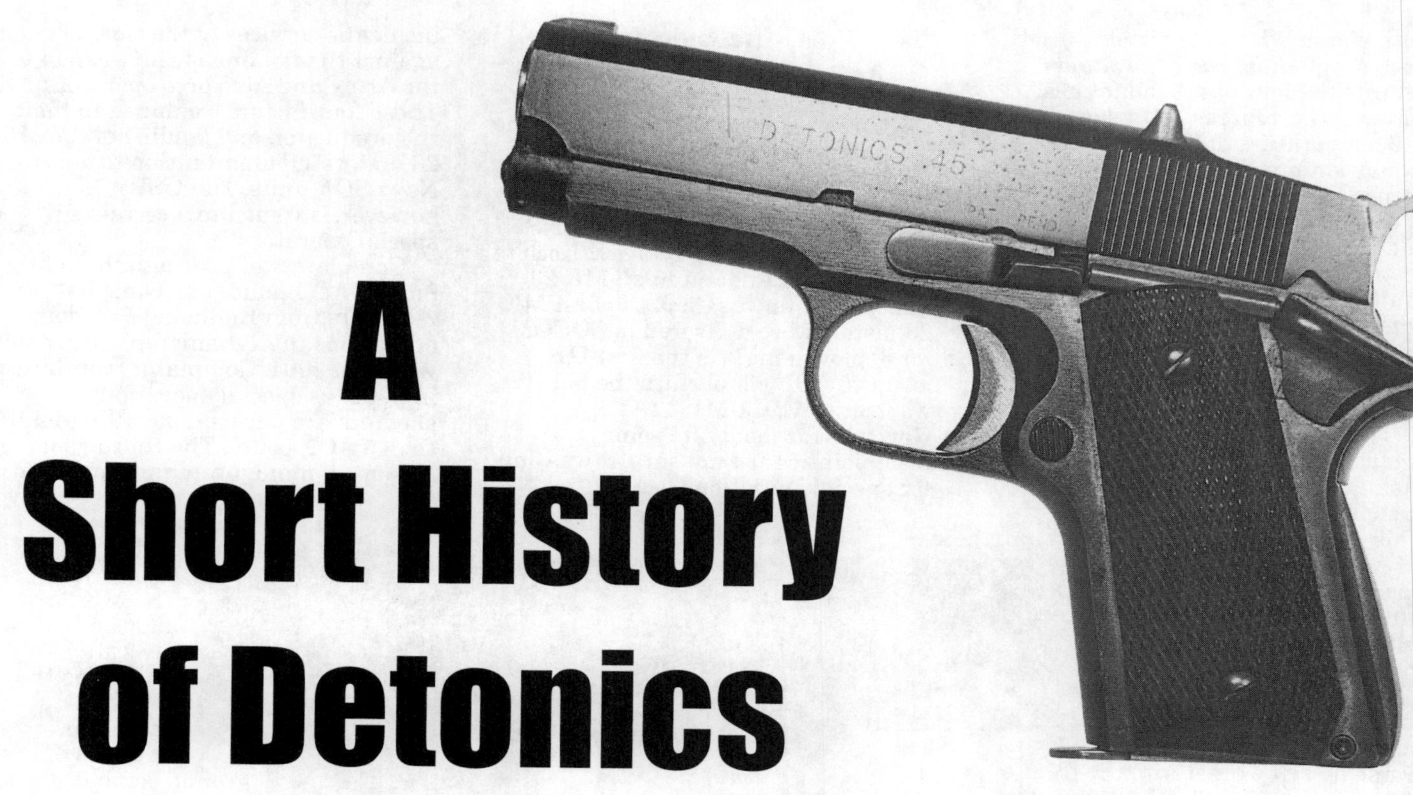

A Short History of Detonics

by John Malloy

TODAY, A NUMBER of handgun manufacturers offer compact 45-caliber pistols based on the Colt/Browning design of 1911. It is almost hard to remember a time when such small 45s were not available.

However, of course, there had to be a first one. It was the Detonics 45.

The Detonics story began officially in 1976, with the commercial introduction of a small 45-caliber pistol, originally simply designated as the "Detonics 45."

The actual beginning of the story, naturally, began some time before that. Sid Woodcock, a man with a background in explosives, had been intrigued with the idea of the package of compact power that would be available for personal protection and law enforcement backup if the reliable 1911 design could be scaled down substantially.

Woodcock eventually accomplished this. A company was formed for the new pistol's production. The pistol itself, at first, was simply called the Detonics 45. The term "Detonics" relates to the art and science of explosives. The company was first called Detonics 45 Associates, with a Seattle, WA, address. However, the company also did business under the names Detonics Manufacturing Corporation and Detonics Firearms Industries. A Bellvue, WA, address was also used. The company grew, produced different models and calibers of pistols, and remained in business until 1988. Another company, named New Detonics, took over production and continued until about 1992. Then came a hiatus in which no Detonics pistols were produced for a dozen years. But, in February 2004, a new company, Detonics USA, began business to produce the original design. In spite of the availability of other small 45s, there appears to be a continuing interest in the Detonics.

There is timelessness to the original compact Detonics design. The method of miniaturizing the 1911 was not an obvious one, nor was it easy to accomplish. The unique and innovative design of 1976 has lived on, and many companies use the features that it introduced. It is interesting that now the design is being resurrected in its original form.

The original Detonics pistols were lightly stenciled on the left side of the slide, "DETONICS .45" and "PAT. PEND." This specimen has "Detonics Associates" on the right frame side. Colt parts were used in these early pistols, and this hammer is a Colt Commander burr hammer with the bottom of the loop removed.

Of course, one cannot just take a 1911 and shorten some of the parts. The geometry of the working mechanism precludes this. The 1911 required the parts to be at the right place at the right time, and did not allow room for much change. Colt felt they had been pushing the limit with their Commander Model of the 1950s, made by shortening the slide and barrel of the 1911 by three-quarters of an inch.

The 1911 locking design requires the lugs on the top of the barrel to be locked into recesses inside the top of the slide during the time of highest pressure. As the slide and barrel recoil together, the barrel begins to tilt downward at the rear, unlocking the slide. The slide continues rearward, and the empty case is ejected at the rearmost position. Then, under the force of the compressed recoil spring below the barrel, the slide pushes a round from the magazine into the chamber and everything returns to the original position.

Trying to keep the tilting-barrel system functioning while radically shortening the barrel posed a number of problems. A 3 1/2-inch barrel (the length chosen for the production Detonics pistol) would substantially change the angle that the barrel assumed when the slide was back. A barrel bushing that would allow such increased movement would then no longer properly support the barrel at the muzzle end.

The problem was solved by eliminating the bushing completely. A cone shape, wider at the front than at the rear, was added to the barrel contour. The wide muzzle fitted directly to the open front of the slide when the parts were in battery.

The recoil spring was another problem. A certain spring strength was necessary to control the slide's rearward movement and return it forward. If the original spring were used with a shorter slide, the coils would compress until they contacted each other. At such a point, the slide would no longer be able to continue to move rearward. In addition, the shorter slide would be lighter, and would conceivably require more spring strength for recoil control.

These problems were solved by the use of multiple coil springs, of different diameters, placed around a common guide rod. The springs were counterwound—that is, the spiral of each spring turned in the direction opposite to that of the adjacent spring. The springs were held captive on the guide rod, making disassembly and reassembly of the pistol actually quicker and easier than the original 1911 system.

The shorter barrel and its modified angle also changed the point at which ejection of the fired case occurred. Lowering and reshaping of the ejection port on the right side of the slide took care of this situation.

Shortening of the grip frame also involved changing of other parts. The magazine, obviously, had to be shortened. Simply shortening a standard magazine would decrease capacity to an unacceptable level. With a redesigned follower, however, the rear part of the follower could protrude through a slot in the magazine base when fully loaded. This redesigned magazine was more than three-quarters of an inch shorter than the Colt design, but allowed a capacity of six rounds, only one less than the original. A perhaps unplanned advantage of this system was that the protruding follower served as a "fully-loaded" magazine indicator when it was inserted into the pistol.

Shortening the grip frame would obviously not leave enough room for both the original grip safety and the original mainspring housing. The

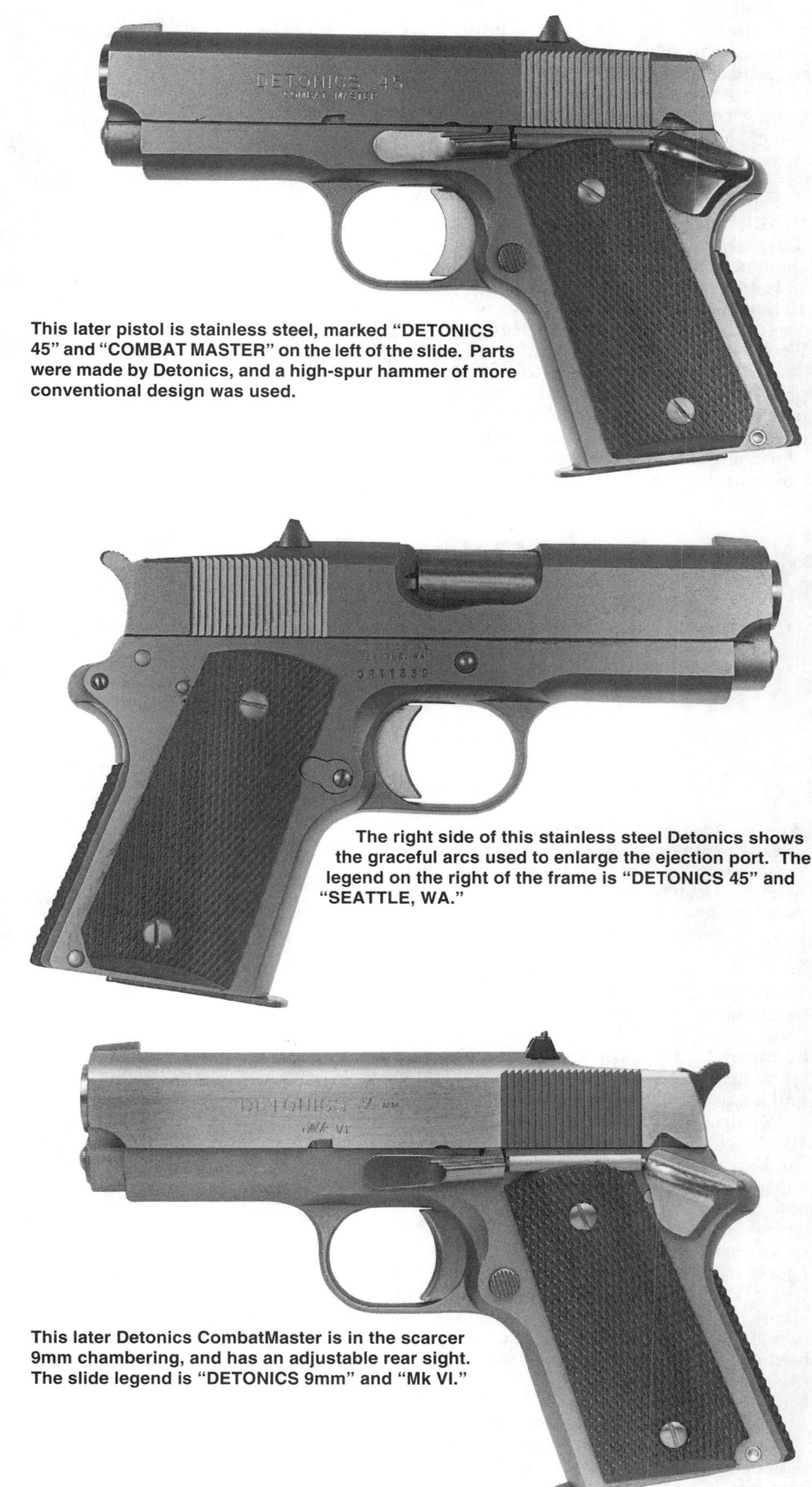

This later pistol is stainless steel, marked "DETONICS 45" and "COMBAT MASTER" on the left of the slide. Parts were made by Detonics, and a high-spur hammer of more conventional design was used.

The right side of this stainless steel Detonics shows the graceful arcs used to enlarge the ejection port. The legend on the right of the frame is "DETONICS 45" and "SEATTLE, WA."

This later Detonics CombatMaster is in the scarcer 9mm chambering, and has an adjustable rear sight. The slide legend is "DETONICS 9mm" and "Mk VI."

original style of mainspring housing was retained in general shape and size, but the grip safety was reduced to a small non-moving part that provided a very short, rounded tang. The rounded tang became one of the features that added to the Detonics 45's compactness and easy concealability.

However, a short tang had traditionally been associated with "hammer bite" of the fleshy web of the shooter's hand. (The original short 1911 tang had been lengthened in 1923 as part of the modification to create the 1911A1 variant.) Here, Woodcock was shortening the tang even further than the original. The problem of hammer bite was solved by using a high-spur hammer, one that could not contact the shooter's hand. The original hammers were Colt Commander "burr" hammers with the lower part of the loop removed.

The CombatMaster's short grip does not provide room for all the fingers of a large hand, but felt recoil seems the same as with a full-size 45, and the little gun is controllable.

With its slide back, the Detonics CombatMaster shows the forward-enlarged cone barrel and the recoil spring guide rod. These were some of the innovative features that made the compact Detonics pistol design possible.

These gave the early Detonics pistols' hammers an unusual hook shape. Soon, specially-made high-spur hammers with a more conventional spur shape were manufactured and used.

Woodcock retained the original 1911-style manual safety for use with the Detonics pistol. However, some shooters preferred to carry a 1911-style pistol hammer-down on a loaded chamber, thumbing the hammer back when ready to shoot. To permit this usage, the rear of the Detonics slide was flattened for over an inch, sloping slightly rearward. This modification (which also reduced weight) allowed the thumb to sweep along the top of the slide to rock the hammer back to the full-cock position.

The rear sight was mounted ahead of the slide flat. The rear sight was made a large one, with a wide notch. The matching front sight was also wide, providing prominent sights that allowed quick sight alignment.

Stripped for cleaning, the Detonics CombatMaster shows the cone barrel, bushingless slide and captive counterwound recoil springs. These features were introduced by the Detonics and are now used by other manufacturers.

The earliest Detonics pistols were made largely of original and modified Colt parts. Soon, Detonics-made parts were used. The compact pistols were well-received by those looking for such a gun for personal protection or as a law-enforcement backup. Initial concern about potential heavy recoil faded as the guns were used. Perhaps the multiple spring system, or possibly other factors, made the recoil seem no more than that of a heavier full-size pistol. Although most shooters, especially those with large hands, shot with their pinky fingers below the Detonics frame, there was still adequate frame for a firm grip.

The company grew. The Detonics company was one of the early users of stainless steel as a suitable material for autoloading pistols, introducing stainless versions in 1979; just three years after the first guns had been marketed.

With several variations in production, Detonics began calling their compact pistol the CombatMaster, and identified the variations as "Marks." Marks I through IV were of 4140 chrome moly steel, with either blue, nickel or chrome finishes. Marks V through VII were of stainless steel. After a few years, all Detonics pistols were of stainless steel. Soon, versions in 9mm and 38 Super were offered.

In 1982, Detonics introduced a powerful new cartridge, the 451 Detonics Magnum. Using a case slightly longer than that of the 45 ACP case, and reinforced internally, the 451 was capable of surpassing 45 ACP ballistics. Company literature claimed velocities up to 1240 feet per second from the 3 1/2-inch barrel, with unspecified types of bullets. Detonics provided the CombatMaster 451 pistols, and also offered 451 conversion kits for 1911-type pistols. The company offered 451 Detonics Magnum brass cartridge cases, loading data, and also a Forster reamer that allowed converting 30-06 and similar rifle brass into 451 cases. Though the case was longer, the overall length of the loaded 451 cartridge was the same as that of the 45 ACP, so the same magazine could be used.

In addition to the conversion kits, Detonics offered 1911 magazines with their special followers, which increased capacity to eight rounds. Also offered were counterwound recoil spring units for full-size 1911s.

Already making some of the parts, it seemed logical for the company to bring out larger-size pistols to expand their product line. In 1982, the full-size Detonics ScoreMaster, in 45 ACP and 451 Detonics Magnum chamberings, was introduced. In 1985, the ServiceMaster pistol, a 45 ACP commander-size pistol with a 4 1/4-inch barrel, was added. Detonics used its novel bushingless cone-barrel system in these full-size and mid-size pistols.

Beginning at least by 1982, and continuing during most of the 1980s, the company began offering commemorative and custom pistols.

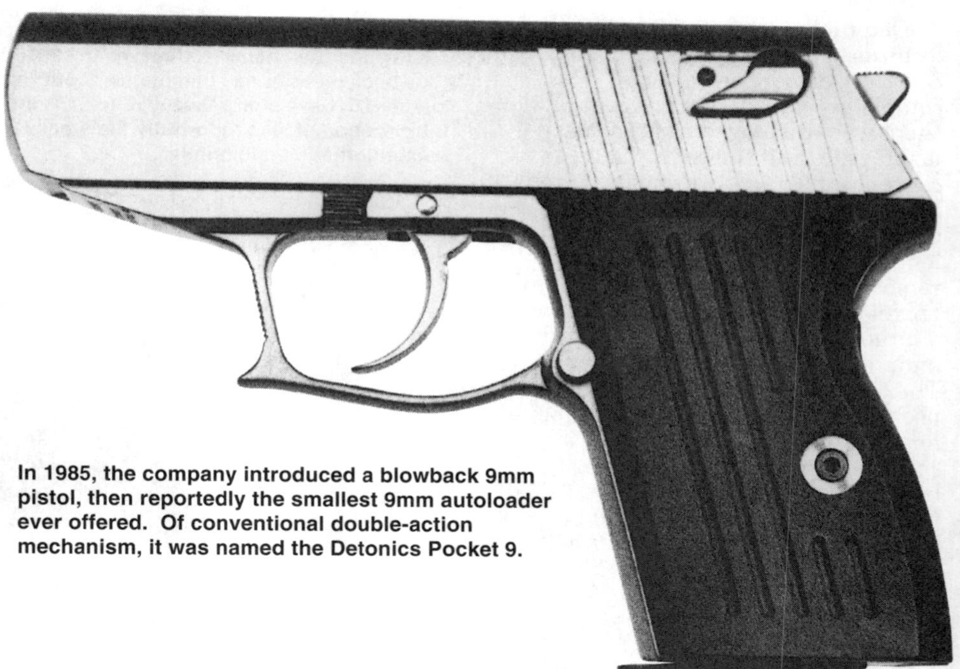

In 1985, the company introduced a blowback 9mm pistol, then reportedly the smallest 9mm autoloader ever offered. Of conventional double-action mechanism, it was named the Detonics Pocket 9.

Gunsmith Peter Dunn became head of the Detonics custom shop.

Detonics popularity was promoted by print, television and motion-picture action stories. Author Jerry Ahern, in his *The Survivalist* series of novels, had his hero, John Rourke, carry "twin stainless Detonics 45s." Detonics pistols appeared with Tom Selleck in the TV series *Magnum, P.I.,* and with Don Johnson in *Miami Vice.* In the Tom Selleck science-fiction motion picture *Runaway* (1984), Detonics pistols were featured, and later, in *Terminator 2* (1991), actress Linda Hamilton used a Detonics.

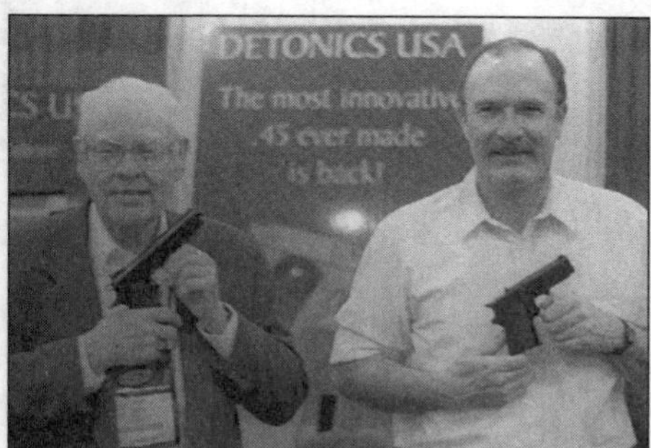

Principals of the original Detonics company are associated with Detonics USA. Sid Woodcock, left, was the original designer, and gunsmith Peter Dunn was the head of the Detonics custom shop. The Combat Master held by Dunn will be the first product of the new company, and the ScoreMaster, held by Woodcock, will be offered later.

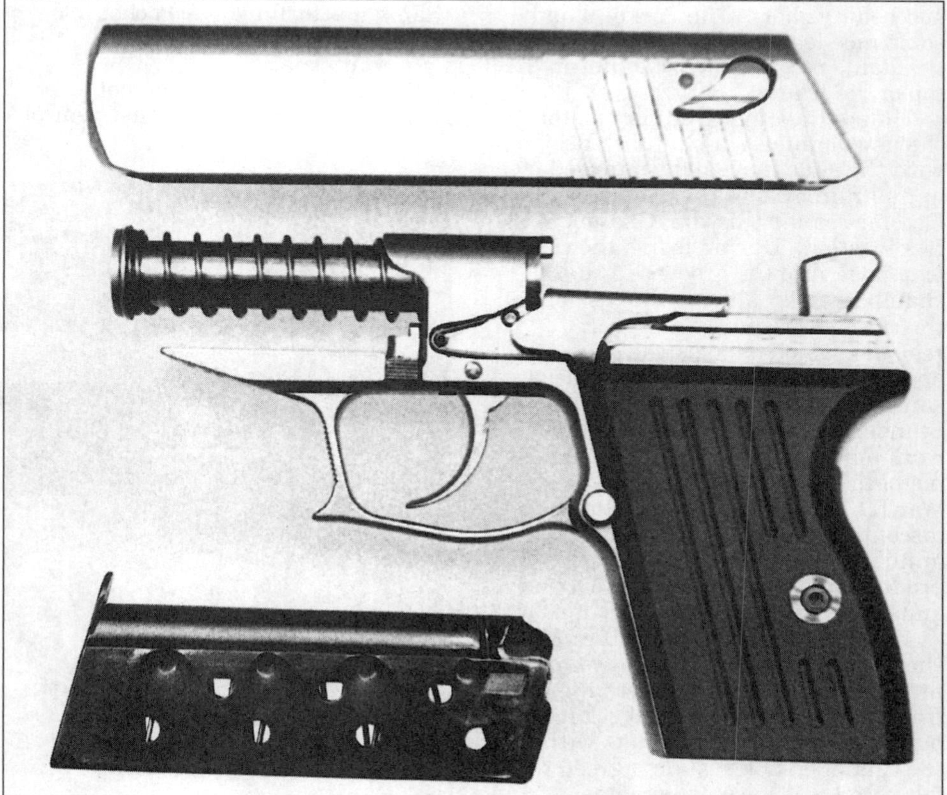

The Pocket 9 pistol was very different from previous Detonics offerings. Of blowback operation, it had a fixed barrel and a single recoil spring.

The Detonics Pocket 9 was already out of production when Malloy had the chance to fire one in 1991. He found the blowback pistol (this specimen without the Chamber-Lok system) to have sharp, heavy recoil. At the time of its introduction, it was reportedly the smallest 9mm semiautomatic pistol made.

Detonics seemed to be in the forefront of handgun trends. The company developed several completely new designs. Three of them were displayed at firearms displays during the early 1980s as concept guns. One was a strong top-break revolver, a 7-shot version, which could be changed to other barrel lengths or other calibers by simply removing one screw and replacing the barrel/cylinder unit. The second was a large-frame double-action 45 with ambidextrous manual safety levers. The third was a small, double-action, pocket-pistol-size handgun chambered for the 9mm Luger (9x19) cartridge.

Although the CombatMaster had been made in 9mm, the 9mm CombatMaster pistol had still been the same size and weight as the 45, and offered few advantages. The company decided to produce the new 9mm design, which was then the smallest pistol chambered for that cartridge. In 1983, a "Name the 9mm" contest was initiated, inviting people to think up a name for the new pistol. The new little gun was introduced in 1985 as the "Pocket 9." The standard version was a stainless-steel pistol with a matte finish, a 3-inch barrel, and a weight of 26 ounces. The trigger mechanism was what is now called conventional double-action. The pistol could be fired double-action for the first shot, and single-action for succeeding shots. The Pocket 9 had some nice features, including having the sights recessed in a channel on the top of the frame.

Unlike the other Detonics pistols, the new 9mm was a blowback design, with the slide movement retarded by annular grooves in the chamber. Detonics called this the "Chamber-Lok" system. During firing, the case expanded into the grooves in the chamber walls. Moving the case out of the chamber required a slight resizing, which delayed the slide opening. This was essentially the same method employed by High Standard during the development work on the experimental T3 9mm pistol in the period following World War II. For some reason, Detonics discontinued the "Chamber-Lok" annular grooves during the production of the Pocket 9. Early guns have them; later ones do not.

Production of the Pocket 9 was short-lived. 1986, its second year of production, was also its last. Reports from people who used the Pocket 9 pistols (especially those guns without the Chamber-Lok system) agreed that felt recoil was very heavy. One description was that the pistol delivered a sharp, hard blow to the hand with each shot. The recoil seemed not to bother the gun. However, unpleasant felt recoil was not a good selling point, and may have been a factor in the pistol's being discontinued.

Interestingly, three other variants of the Pocket 9 were also offered in 1986. The Pocket 9 LS (Long Slide) had a longer 4-inch barrel and a correspondingly longer slide and recoil spring. The Power 9 was essentially a standard Pocket 9, but differed in having a polished, rather than a matte, finish. A Pocket 380 was also offered, as a slimmer, lighter alternative.

The Pocket 9 series was not successful. 1986 was the last year of production for all Pocket 9 variations, most of which are now rarely seen. The 1987 Detonics catalog featured the CombatMaster in a Mark I variant (now matte stainless steel, not blued) and MarkVI version (polished stainless). The ServiceMaster and ScoreMaster pistols were available, but only the ScoreMaster was offered in 451. Parts and accessories were also offered, as in past years. However, the next year, 1988, was to be the original company's last year.

The original Detonics company had stayed in business until 1988. After

At the 1983 National Rifle Association annual meetings, Detonics displayed all the parts that went into making a stainless-steel CombatMaster. At that time, the company had been in business for less than seven years.

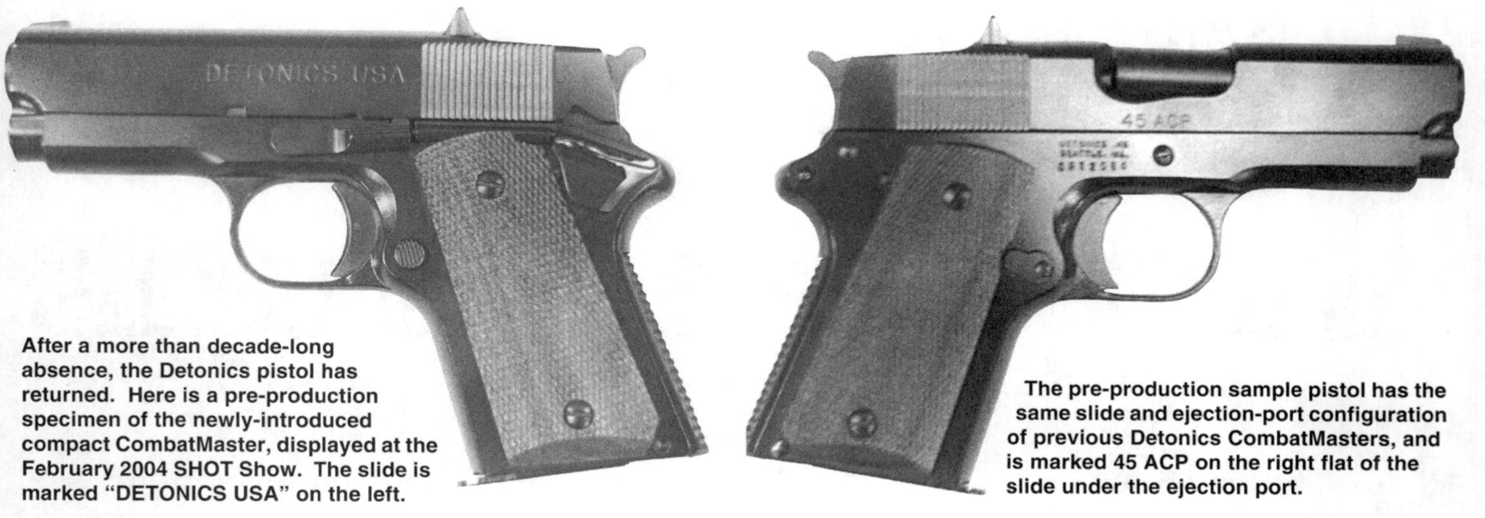

After a more than decade-long absence, the Detonics pistol has returned. Here is a pre-production specimen of the newly-introduced compact CombatMaster, displayed at the February 2004 SHOT Show. The slide is marked "DETONICS USA" on the left.

The pre-production sample pistol has the same slide and ejection-port configuration of previous Detonics CombatMasters, and is marked 45 ACP on the right flat of the slide under the ejection port.

that, the company was sold to another group, which began business in Phoenix, AZ, in 1989. Operating under the name New Detonics Manufacturing Corporation, the new company's key product was the compact CombatMaster pistol, slightly modified. The flat on the top rear of the slide was made minimal, and appeared more-or-less just a symbolic representation of the flat of the original. Beavertail tang grip safeties were coming into vogue, so the CombatMaster (which had had essentially no tang since its origin) was made with a beavertail tang. The value of such a change was questioned by those who liked the original design.

Along with the CombatMaster, the New Detonics product line also included the mid-size ServiceMaster and the full-size ScoreMaster, all in 45 ACP caliber. Practical and Action pistol shooting had increased in popularity, and a new version of the ScoreMaster, called the CompetitionMaster, was added. The new pistol had a 5 7/8-inch barrel with a dual-port compensator.

Here, Malloy shoots one of the earliest Detonics pistols. Now, a new company, Detonics USA, has been formed to once again offer newly-made Detonics pistols of the original design.

All the New Detonics pistols could be differentiated from their predecessors by a number of new features, most of which were related to the options preferred by competition shooters: angled slide grasping grooves were placed both front and rear on the slide, triggers were ventilated, manual safety controls were lowered and extended, and grip safeties were of the beavertail type.

A special variant of the New Detonics compact CombatMaster is of interest. To appeal to knowledgeable women shooters, a modified version to fit a smaller hand was made. The new variation had a reduced frame size (in width and girth) at the grip, thinner grip panels and a shorter trigger. Called the "Ladies Escort," the pistol was available in several special finishes. The Midnight Escort had a satin stainless frame with a black slide and smooth black grips. The Royal Escort had a black frame; its slide and grips were iridescent purple, and the hammer and trigger were gold plated. A Jade Escort, similar to the Royal Escort, but with iridescent jade-colored slide and grips, was also announced. These were extremely limited-production pistols then, and are rarely seen today. Reportedly, fewer than 25 or 30 specimens each of the Midnight and Royal Escorts were made. The Jade version was probably represented by fewer than 10 pistols.

By 1992, the New Detonics Manufacturing Corporation had also ceased to do business.

Then, a 12-year period went by when no pistols bearing the Detonics name were produced.

Now, it seems as if that gap has ended. At the February 2004 Shooting, Hunting Outdoor Trade Show (SHOT Show) in Las Vegas, NV, a new company, Detonics USA, was introduced. At the introduction of the new company, some of the principals of the original Detonics company were again involved. Designer Sid Woodcock and gunsmith Peter Dunn were on hand to display the latest incarnations of the Detonics pistols. Headquartered in Atlanta, GA, the new company has author Jerry Ahern, an early proponent of the Detonics design, as its president. Detonics USA plans to make all three sizes of the original pistols, but will offer the compact CombatMaster first. As Sid Woodcock explained it, "That is the Detonics that people remember."

Initial production of the CombatMaster was scheduled for October 2004. The mid-size ServiceMaster and full-size ScoreMaster pistols were planned to be offered later.

The Detonics design was an innovative one. Detonics pistols offered many features that were "firsts" in the firearms world. Many of these features have been used by other manufacturers now, and have been with us so long we may tend to forget their introduction.

The bushingless cone barrel, beveled magazine well, thumb relief on the slide, enlarged ejection port, large, wide sights, full-magazine indicator, compact rounded tang, high-spur hammer, counter-wound recoil springs, with the springs held captive on a guide rod—all these things were introduced simultaneously with the original Detonics pistol three decades ago. From the standpoint of shooters, collectors, and students of firearms, it seems a good thing that the history of the Detonics design will continue on. •

Wheel-Guns and Steel Guns

by Paul Scarlata

Photos by James Walters & Yousef Sansour

MOST READERS WHO are familiar with my writings know that I have no hesitation whatsoever about expressing my preferences. In fact, on occasion I have been known to vocalize my likes and dislikes to such a degree as to cause anger among certain acquaintances. But, as my former wife could vouch, that's just my nature—and there ain't much I can do about it!

One of the aforementioned strongly held beliefs is my continuing championship of the revolver.

I am well aware the majority of handgun *aficionados*—including most of my fellow pundits—consider this the "age of the semiauto pistol." Next time you are at your local newsstand, peruse the magazine racks and see how many firearm-related publications have revolvers on their covers. I'm willing to predict there will be damn few—if any at all. It's a fact of life that the self-loading pistol gets the vast majority of the ink nowadays.

Now, I am in no way attempting to denigrate the semiauto pistol. I readily admit the present generation of pistols probably represents the zenith of the genre's development. Modern pistols provide reliability, ruggedness, excellent ergonomics, high tech materials, are capable of resistance to abuse and environmental extremes, and display a level of quality control in their manufacture that was wishful thinking only two decades ago. There are dozens of models suitable for military/police service, home/personal defense, competition, and plinking. It's probably fair to say they are everything one could wish for—and I don't really see much room for improvement. I own close to two dozen semiauto pistols and use them for everything from hunting small game, to IPSC competition and concealed carry.

Then we have the revolver...

While the revolver *(a.k.a. wheel-gun, round-gun, six-shooter)* has been around since the 1830s, the modern double-action (DA) revolver as we know it was perfected in the late 1890s. For well over one hundred and sixty years, the revolver represented the handgun of choice of most civilian shooters, hunters, competitors, law enforcement professionals, and many knowledgeable military personnel.

Besides being the first truly practical repeating handgun, the DA revolver had much to recommend it:

1. Simplicity of operation - there is no slide to retract or levers and buttons to pull, push or squeeze. One merely aims the revolver and pulls the trigger.
2. Reliability - unlike the semiauto pistol, the revolver is not dependent on the energy of a cartridge to function—nor recoil and magazine springs to ensure reliable feeding and functioning. As long as the shooter's trigger finger continues to work, the revolver will fire.
3. Ammunition tolerance - unlike the pistol, the round-gun displays an ammunition tolerance approaching 110 percent. Light loads, heavy loads, bullet configuration, etc. have no effect on it.
4. Safety - to make a DA revolver safe, one merely removes the second digit of the shooting hand from inside the trigger guard. Unlike semiauto pistols, you can ascertain visually whether or not the cylinder is loaded. Lastly, unloading is fast and foolproof.

I still use a revolver as my home defense gun and one of my regular carry guns. In the past, I have used them extensively for action pistol shooting, usually for IPSC/USPSA and bowling pin matches. But the popularity of pin shooting has declined in my area over the last few

This photo shows the seven- and six-round cylinders of the 686 revolvers. You also get a good idea of the sighting arrangement on my 686-Plus.

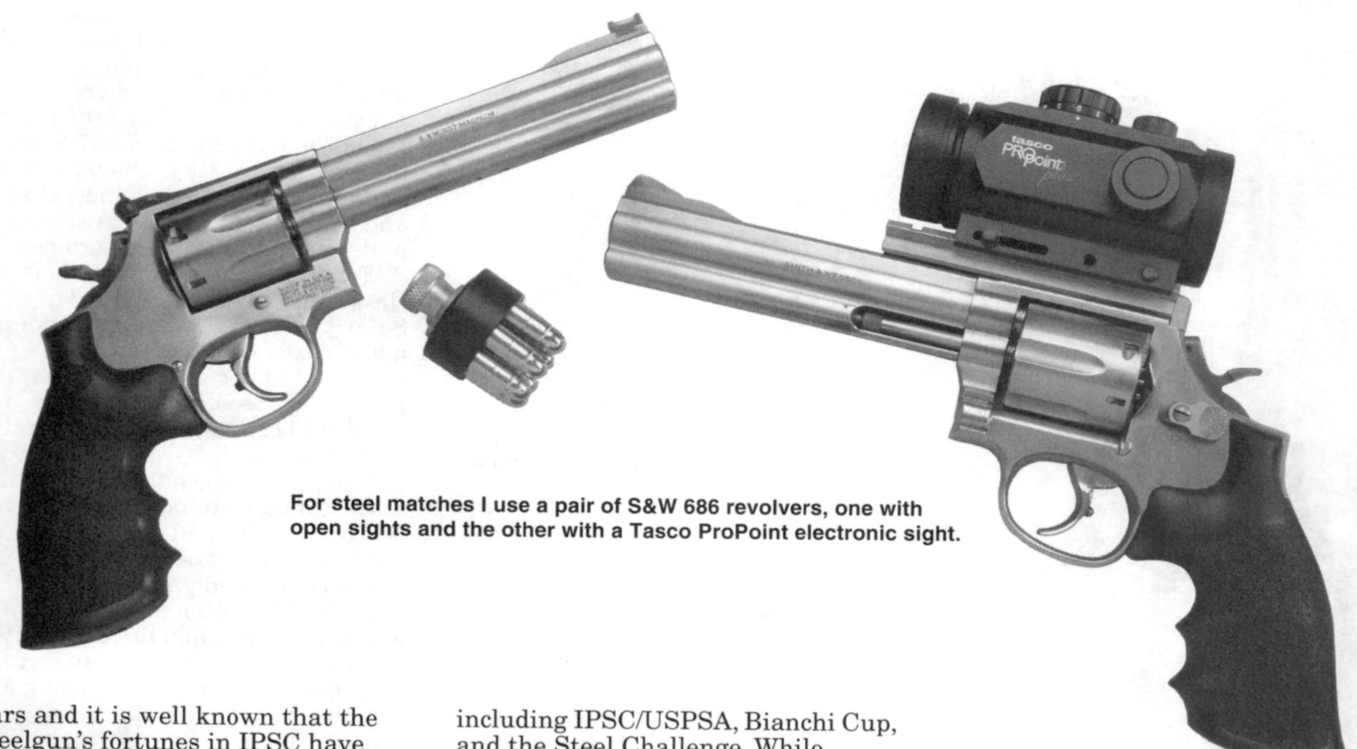

For steel matches I use a pair of S&W 686 revolvers, one with open sights and the other with a Tasco ProPoint electronic sight.

years and it is well known that the wheelgun's fortunes in IPSC have been in descent for well over two decades. In the last few years, when I ventured forth in an attempt to win the acclaim of my peers *(yeah, right!)*, a semiauto pistol of some type resided in my gun bag. But this has begun to change.

About a year ago I began attending a monthly steel match sponsored by the Piedmont Handgun Association of Lexington, North Carolina. PHA's match combines features of various disciplines, including IPSC/USPSA, Bianchi Cup, and the Steel Challenge. While cardboard targets are used on occasion, the vast majority of targets are of the steel variety, including static, swinging, plates, and Pepper Poppers. Except for the Poppers, which must to be knocked over, all other steel targets need only be "rung"— hit with a bullet—to score. Because of this, match rules state the minimum handgun caliber allowed is 9mm/38 Special. And while no power factor is specified, the Poppers are calibrated to fall over when hit by a standard velocity 115-grain 9mm bullet.

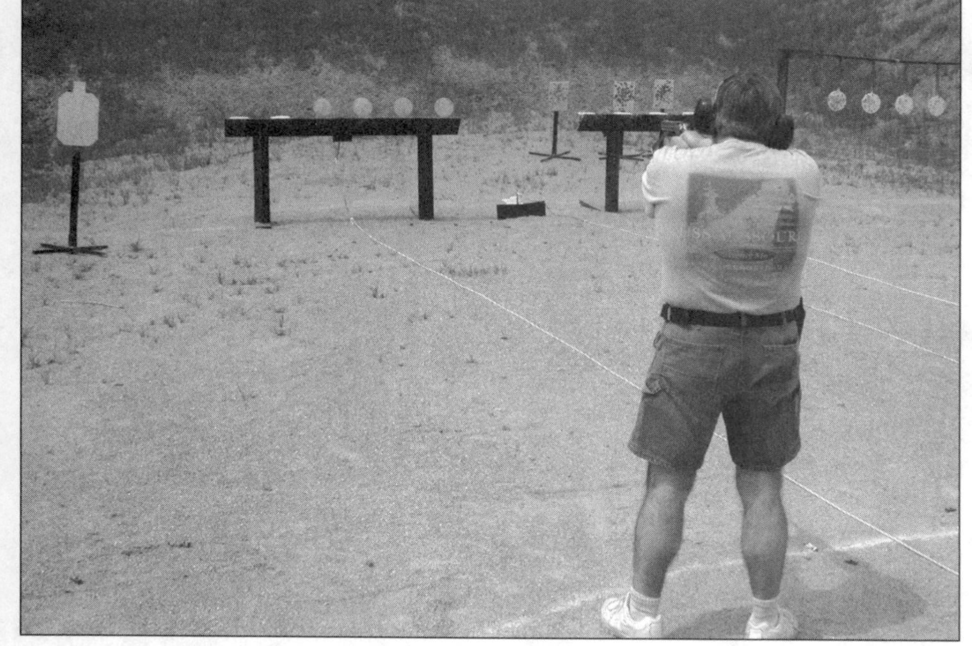
Here I am shooting PHA's monthly steel match. Note the variety of target styles that are used.

PHA recognizes four classes:

Open Pistol - any pistol equipped with an electronic sight and/or recoil-reducing device *(ported barrel, compensator, etc.)*. There are no limits on magazine capacity.

Limited Ten - the pistol must fit within USPSA's rules for Limited 10 Division. Magazines cannot be loaded with more than ten rounds.

Stock Revolver - any revolver of 38-caliber or larger. High-capacity revolvers are permitted as are those that can be loaded with full-moon clips.

Open Revolver - any revolver equipped with an electronic sight and/or recoil-reducing device. High-capacity revolvers are permitted as are those that can be loaded with full-moon clips.

Most stages require no more than 18 rounds to complete and all are "revolver neutral." In other words, no more than six shots are required *(although more may be fired)* from any one shooting position, before a mandatory reload or movement is called for. When I began shooting this match I used the same pistol I use when I compete in USPSA Production Division – a Para-Ordnance LDA 18.9 Limited. But, after a few months, I

My Bianchi revolver is a S&W 686 with a Tasco ProPoint Plus dot sight. Note the Hogue rubber grips and smooth trigger with overtravel stop.

began to notice that revolver shooters rarely showed up at the match. In fact, I can only recall two of them in the last year.

While preparing for the November match I realized that my supply cabinet contained an inordinate quantity of 38 Special reloads—about 500 rounds to be exact. Examining the dates on the boxes, I saw that some of them were over eight years old. Obviously, I had done very little revolver shooting that required 38 target loads, and I said to myself "…. this situation should not be allowed to continue." I reopened my gun safe, returned the Para LDA to its slot, and began digging around in the darker recesses for my bowling pin revolvers.

These consist of a pair of S&W Model 686 revolvers chambered for the 357 Magnum cartridge. One is a standard six-shot 686, while the other is a seven-shot 686-Plus. Both feature six-inch barrels, Hogue finger groove grips, and fiber optic front sights. As it was allowed by Second Chance bowling pin rules, I had my gunsmith modify both revolvers by drilling a series of five ports on the top rear half of the barrel that increase in size towards the muzzle. It was a relatively simple modification, and proved very effective at holding down the muzzle flip of the hot 180-grain 357 loads I used for pin-busting. The pair then had all internal parts hand-polished and fitted, resulting in DA trigger pulls that are a joy to experience.

Further exploration of various closets and cabinets revealed a Safariland Cup Challenge holster and a half dozen CD-2 speedloader holders. As I possessed a greater number of speedloaders for it, I decided to use the six-shot 686 in the upcoming match.

Being I was the only wheelgunner at the event, I can make no claim to "victory"—but I had one heck of a good time. It had been so long since I had used a round-gun in competition, that I had forgotten how much fun it was to perform rapid fire drills with a fine-handling DA revolver. In fact, the only disadvantage I saw to using a revolver was that it's six-round capacity did not leave any room for operator error. If a target was not hit, I was forced to either accept a "miss" or perform an extra reload while standing—something no action pistol shooter wants to do as it wastes too much precious time.

After studying the results of this foray into steel shooting I decided I could give myself a bit of an edge by using my seven-shot 686-Plus in the next match. All that was necessary was a quick call to HKS Products to obtain additional seven-round Model 587A speedloaders for the "hi-cap" S&W. As the body of these loaders are

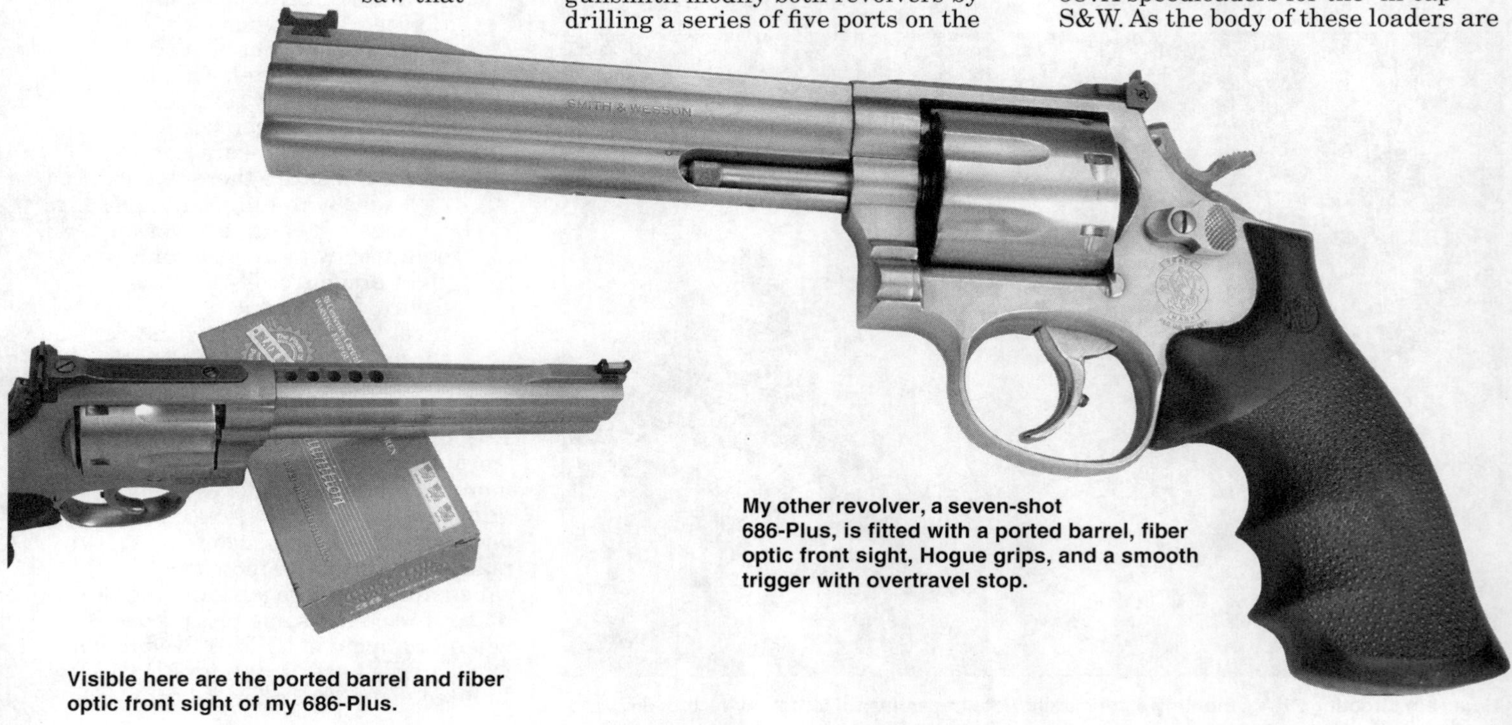

My other revolver, a seven-shot 686-Plus, is fitted with a ported barrel, fiber optic front sight, Hogue grips, and a smooth trigger with overtravel stop.

Visible here are the ported barrel and fiber optic front sight of my 686-Plus.

a bit wider then the six-round variety, over the next week I spent several hours practicing my reloads *(with dummy cartridges)* until I felt I could perform them just as smoothly as with the six-round revolver.

At PHA's next match, my scores improved noticeably. In fact, I beat several of my erstwhile pistol-armed companions. While some of the credit must go to that seventh round of ammunition, I believe it was more a matter that I had had an additional month of practice.

Another gun club in my area sponsors a monthly Bianchi Cup-style match and, as in this discipline all strings of fire are limited to six rounds, my 686 would not be at a disadvantage. As I began planning to attend this new match I said to myself, "Why not mount an electronic sight on the 686 and play with that?" Hey, it sounded like fun to me. In fact, a Tasco ProPoint Plus 5 red-dot sight had been residing (unused) in my storage closet for several years. As the top straps of late model S&W revolvers came from the factory drilled and tapped, mounting a Weaver-type rail on the 686 took a matter of minutes and the ProPoint was ready to sight in.

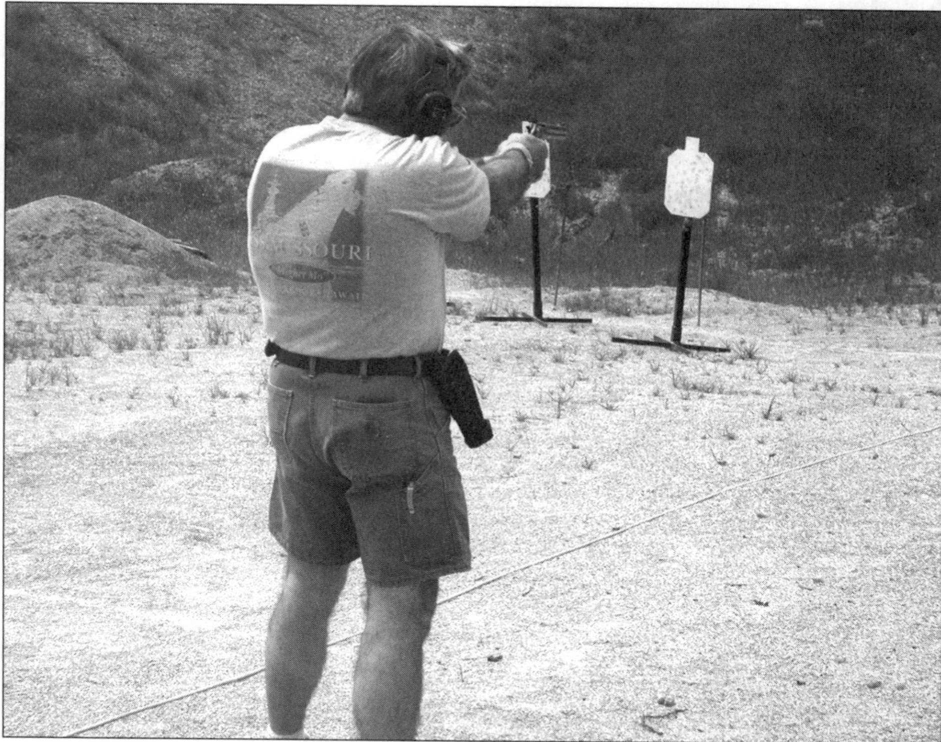

My 686-Plus has proven to be a fine-handling, fast-shooting, accurate steel gun. Note how the Safariland Cup Challenge holster holds the revolver out from the body and angled for a fast purchase and smooth presentation.

While performing said task at my gun club, a problem came to the fore. The ported barrel blew gas and lead particles on the front lens of the sight, requiring me to clean it every dozen rounds or so. Not wanting to degrade the lens in this manner, I took the revolver to Pat Linthicum of Woods & Wetlands, the gunsmith who had ported and performed the action jobs on my two 686s. After explaining the problem to him, Pat said the simplest way to correct the problem would be to install an un-ported barrel. He added that with the light 38 loads I would be shooting, he doubted recoil would present a problem, especially with the additional weight provided by the ProPoint sight.

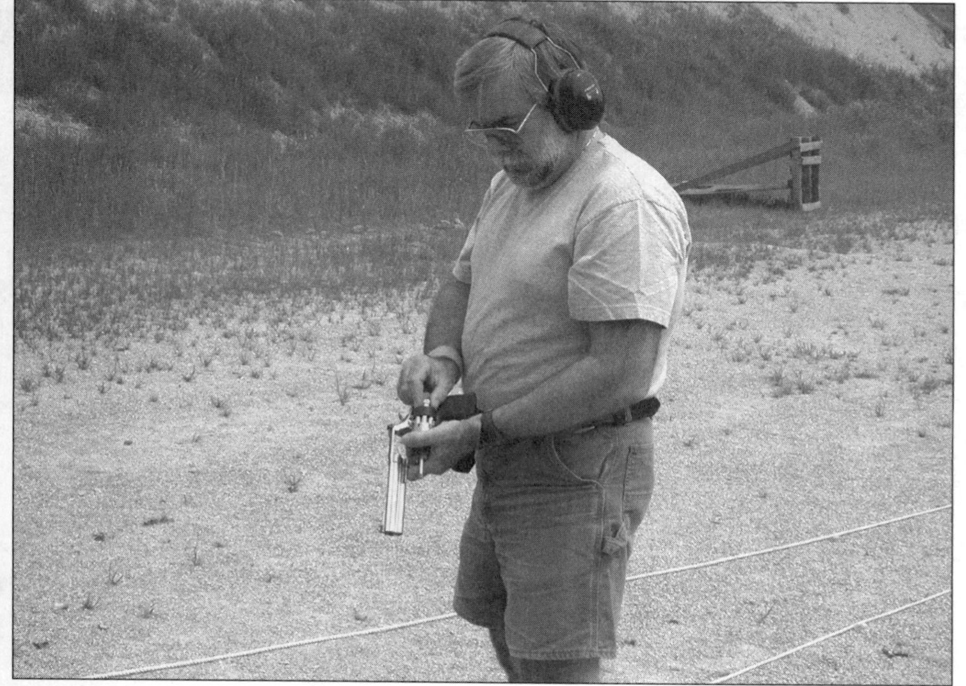

Here I am fumbling...uh, I mean performing a fast reload.

The following weekend I attended a local gun show and, as luck would have it, found a used 686 barrel in perfect condition which, being the seller was asking a mere $65, I scooped up without the usual dickering over price. The following Monday, it took Pat less than a half-hour to fit the new barrel to my revolver. Later that week, at the range, I zeroed in the Tasco sight from a rest at 25 yards. Once this chore was accomplished I put six rounds into a ragged, two-hole, figure 8-shaped group. "Yup..," I said to myself, "...that ought to do it." And Pat was right, with the extra mass of the ProPoint sight, I could not discern any difference in the degree of muzzle flip generated by the un-ported 686 as compared to its ported compatriot.

I then proceeded to burn up a couple of boxes of 38s on my club's plate rack, with very pleasing results. In fact, from the 15-yard line, I went six for six on the majority of my runs. There can be no denying that as my eyes get.... *ahem*, "more experienced"... the electronic dot sight provides a definite advantage.

For match ammo I have settled on two different 38 Special loads. When speed reloading is not a consideration I charge the cylinder with Black Hills

Here I have just cleaned the plate rack and am moving to engage the swinging plates.

For matches I use 38 Special ammo from Black Hills and Federal loaded with 148-grain wadcutter and 130-grain FMJ bullets. HKS speedloaders ensure fast, fumble-free reloads.

148-grain wadcutters. For those matches where fast reloads are a major factor, Federal's American Eagle ammo with round-nosed, 130-grain FMJ bullets ensure smooth, fumble-free reloading. Both types have proven accurate in my 686s and, while they provide more then sufficient power to take down the various types of steel targets I might encounter, recoil is minimal; permitting fast, accurate, follow-up shots.

My first foray into Bianchi-type shooting was what one might euphemistically refer to as a "learning experience." While I shot decently on the paper target stage, the only steel targets were eight-inch plates—unlike the steel matches I was used to shooting, with their generously sized targets. Normally I would not consider this a problem, but they are shot at distances ranging from 10 to 25 yards, and at the latter distance they appeared to be the size of aspirin tablets! In addition, all strings of fire are par time. In other words you will draw your handgun and engage the targets with a required number of rounds in a certain amount of time—any shots fired after the time expires count as penalties, while targets hit are scored as misses. While I always managed to get my shots off within the time limit I'm afraid that, as the shooting distances increased, a distressingly smaller number of my bullets impacted on the plates. Oh well, to paraphrase the well-known joke, "...practice, Man, practice!"

I will be the first to admit that shooting a revolver fast and accurately requires more practice, concentration, self-control, and hand-eye coordination then does a semiauto pistol. For these reasons, it is my firm belief that one acquires the basics of handgun shooting far better with a revolver than with a pistol. I'm sure most of you reading this article have a wheelgun or two gathering dust in the back of your gun safe. Do yourself a favor, dig it out and start experiencing just how much fun shooting a *REAL* handgun is again. You won't be sorry. Hell, you might just end up being downright ecstatic! •

For further information:

HKS Products - 7841 Foundation Dr., Florence, KY 41042. Tel. 606-342-7841.

Safariland, Ltd. - 3120 E. Mission Blvd., Ontario, CA 91761.

Smith & Wesson - PO Box 2208, Springfield, MA 01102.

Tasco Sales - 9200 Cody, Overland Park, KS 66214.

Woods & Wetlands - 334 N. Main St., Randleman, NC 27317. Tel. 336-495-5042.

Despite its large size, the ProPoint dot sight is light and does not adversely affect the handling of the revolver. And it sure makes it easy on my 50-something eyes!

Rare, Original Weapons From the British Empire

Atlanta Cutlery Corporation and International Military Antiques of New Jersey are pleased to announce the procurement of these **rare Antique British Victorian Weapons** from the Royal Nepalese Armoury.

These weapons were supplied to Nepal when it was allied with the British Crown after the signing of the Treaty of Sagauli in 1815. Stored in the 16th century ancestral palace of the Thapa family (whose most famous member, Bhimsen Thapa, was Nepal's first Prime Minister). These weapons have laid undisturbed for **over 100 years**.

This find is a time capsule. These weapons were put away after they were used and basically forgotten. They were truly filthy when we acquired them from Nepal. Each has undergone a rudimentary cleaning, but still displays the blemishes of old age.

These old, genuine firearms are marvelous historic artifacts with an impeccable provenance and make for impressive display pieces.

Removing antique guns from Lagan Silekhana Palace

The Gurkha Warrior

Brave, loyal and cheerful even under the most adverse circumstances, this wiry and tough little warrior from the Himalayan Mountains knows no peer when the battle starts. The Gurkha warrior has long been recognized as one of the finest mercenaries in the history of warfare, and also one of the most ferocious. The kukri has been his hand weapon of choice for hundreds of years. The combination of Gurkha and kukri has thrown fear into the toughest soldiers.

(A) British P-1841 Smooth-bored Brunswick Rifle–conceivably made for comparison testing against the rifled-barrel version that had already been in use since 1837. This experimental model was soon abandoned. Distinctive for the omission of the traditional brass patchbox. Bayonet bar on right side of barrel. Gurkha regimental markings enhance the mystery of how this unique rifle ended up in Nepal. **#600454...$695**

(B) P-1864 .577 Calibre Snider Breech Loading Rifle–utilized the breech loading system originally developed for the P-1853 Enfield (which was the most prolific imported percussion rifle used in the Civil War) by New Yorker Jacob Snider. Condition fair to good. **#600424...$495**

(C) British P-1871 Short Lever Rifle–probably the most famous military rifle of the Victorian era. The first manufactured breech loader issued by the British Army. Known for its role in the movies "Zulu" and "Zulu Dawn".

Dates 1870's–**#600410...$795**

Dates 1880's–**#600428...$595**

(D) British P-1885 Long Lever Rifle–developed to provide better leverage for case extraction than the P-1871 Short Lever, which occasionally had trouble ejecting spent cartridges because of powder residue clogging the chamber. **#600406...$595**

Traditional Bhojpure Kukri

Approx. 17" long, 2½" wide, ⅜" thick. Made prior to 1890. Some were made much earlier, but it's difficult to determine the exact date. This large kukri's blade was made for war. As spears and the Kora sword were being replaced by firearms, this was the weapon of choice for hand-to-hand combat. In the skilled hands of the Gurkha, it was a frightening weapon indeed. These have all seen service with both the Nepali military and the British Army. Many of the blades are marked in Devangari script with the date of manufacture. ***Limited quantity available.***

With original scabbard and 2 small kukri knives. Original scabbard not sold separately. **#401166...$189**

Without scabbard–**#401126...$129**

New Scabbard–**#800882...$35**

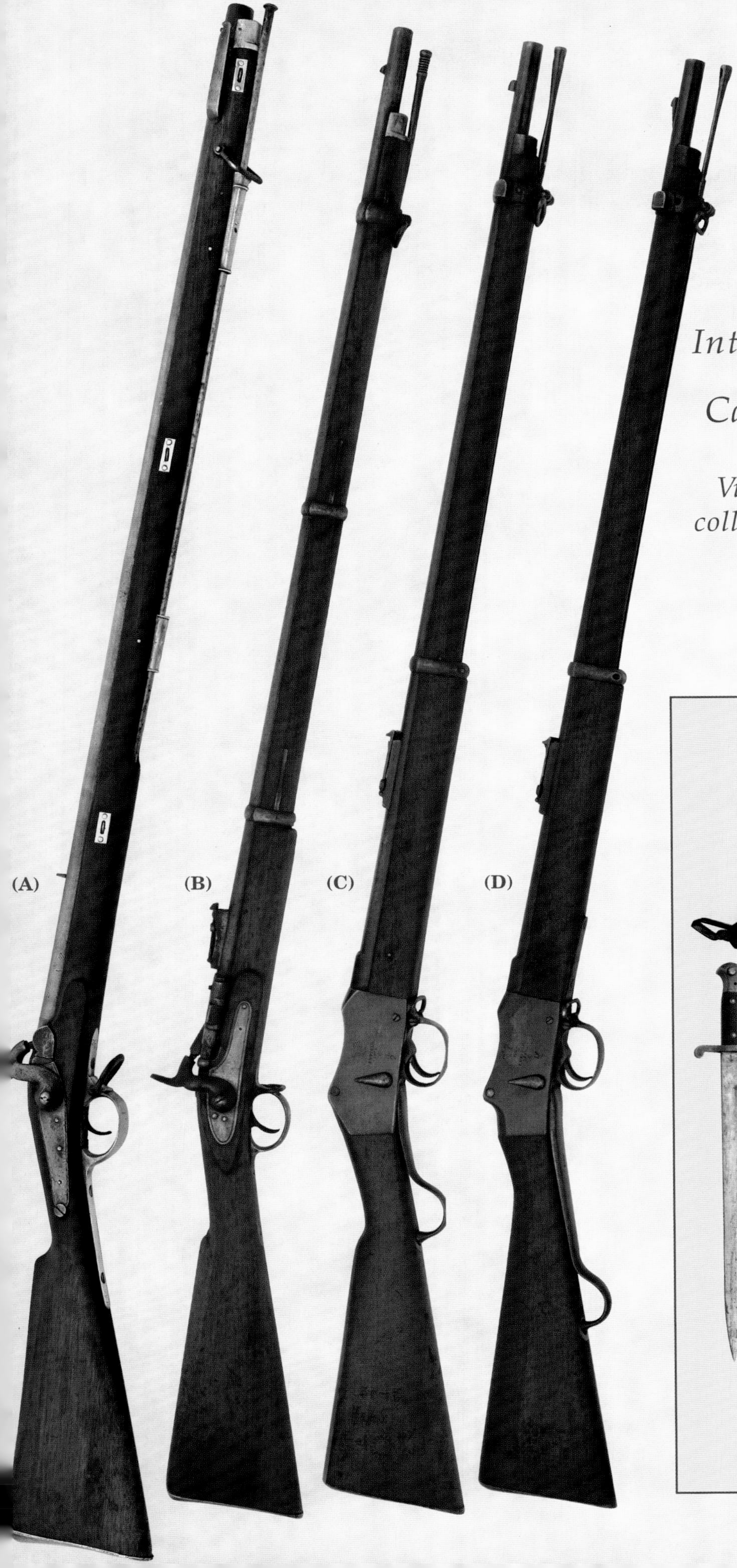

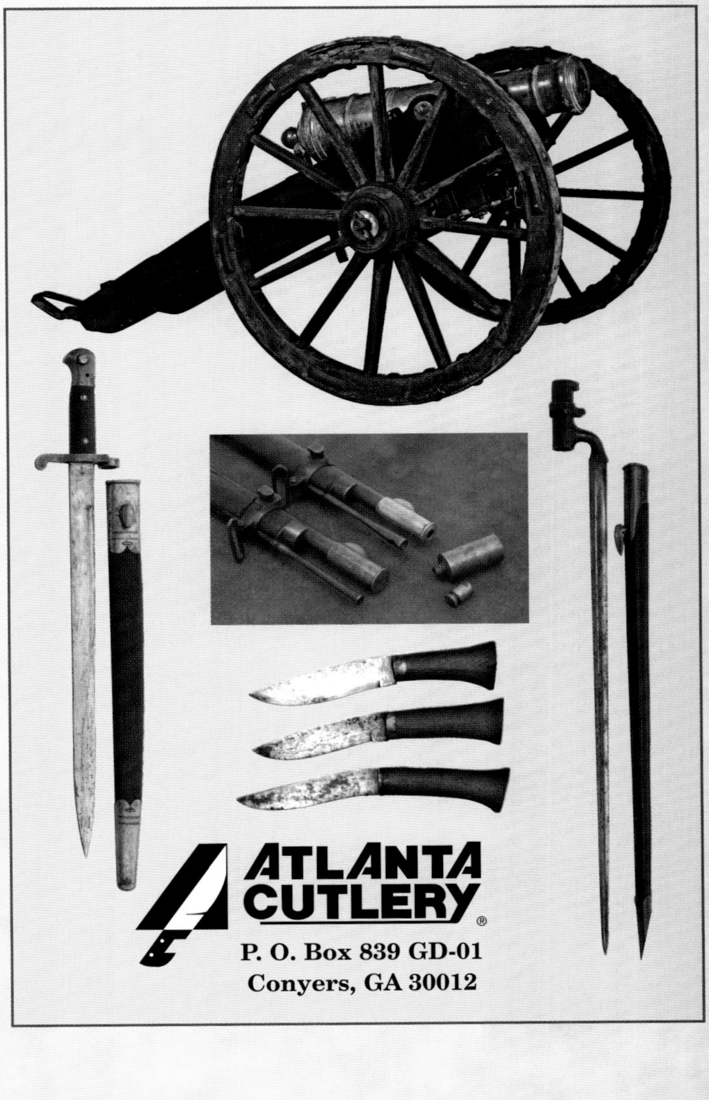

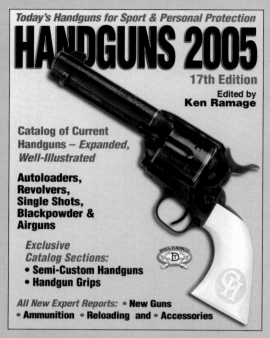

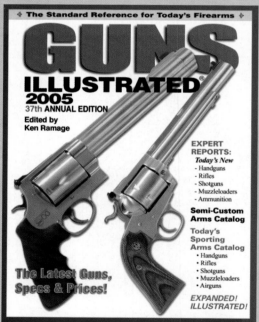

Zeroing Handguns

Different Techniques Mean Different Points of Impact

by Mike Thomas

MOST SERIOUS HANDGUN enthusiasts use a steady rest of some sort when evaluating various loads for accuracy and when adjusting sights for a desired setting, or "zero". The actual device used may be anything from a roll of paper towels to an elaborate and expensive shooting rest. Obviously, to evaluate any firearm purely for accuracy potential, a rest is necessary because our unrested shooting skill *(steadiness)* is somewhat less than perfect.

Following the discovery of a satisfactory load, the handgunner may fire several groups to confirm consistent accuracy, bullet drop at various ranges, terminal bullet performance, etc. At that point, the non-handloader may purchase a quantity of the identical commercially manufactured ammunition and precisely adjust the sights for the desired zero. The handloader will go through the same routine except for a handloaded duplication of the appropriate load.

Next trip to the range, some offhand shooting may be done with the handgun that was so painstakingly sighted-in. Much to the dismay of the shooter, it is quickly discovered that the point of impact is different. In fact, the difference is a significant one compared to the zero obtained by sighting from the bench rest. How could that be? Many shooters, author included, have learned this same lesson the hard way.

Perhaps some insight *(pun intended)* regarding the basics of zeroing handguns will save others the frustration of a task improperly performed. For the purpose of comparison and to illustrate how different zeroing techniques affect bullet impact versus point of aim, I selected four handguns. Three have adjustable rear sights while one is equipped with a fixed sight. Why use a fixed sight, since such a setup is not readily adjustable? It was included here to make light of a particular point, one that may be less than obvious to many at this stage but will blend with our topic as we continue. Some shooters often complain that a fixed rear sight will provide a group point of impact at a given distance that is, for example, eight inches high and six inches to the left. Granted, heavier bullets will often strike considerably higher on a target than lighter bullets. Experimentation in this area might prove successful for elevation adjustment. Depending on the particular gun, perhaps the rear sight can be drifted, via trial-and-error, for windage correction. A revolver or pistol that has nothing more than a groove down the topstrap for a rear sight complicates matters considerably, But, it is best not to do anything until several groups are fired in the position that will be most used. More than one surprised shooter has ultimately found sights believed to be "way off" were just fine, or at least close enough to live with. Perhaps handgun manufacturers know a bit more about sight regulation than we credit them for! One cannot beat the simplicity and reliability of a fixed sight despite the versatility offered by an adjustable rear sight. For a fixed-sight gun that just will not shoot close to the mark, there is still hope. Mechanical regulation, however, is best left to a competent gunsmith.

I'll describe the positions / techniques I employed. Two-handed holds were used throughout, except for position #7. Handgun butts did not touch the sandbag, with the exception of position #2.

1. With steel handgun rest – rear portion of barrel forward of trigger guard on padded rest cradle, hands rested on sandbag (with SIG Sauer auto, frame forward of trigger guard on padded rest cradle).
2. With steel handgun rest – rear portion of barrel forward of trigger guard on padded rest cradle, handgun butt on sandbag (with SIG Sauer auto, frame forward of trigger guard on padded rest cradle).
3. Hands rested on sandbag.
4. Hands ahead of sandbag; shooter's wrists rested on sandbag.
5. Sitting position with back against solid object, arms extended with elbows rested on knees.
6. Standing, "Weaver" stance.
7. Standing, strong hand only.

While admittedly subjective, I used what I consider a moderate grip *(defining firmness of hold)* during all firing. One 10-shot group was fired at 25 yards with each handgun using each of the seven described positions. For establishing a practical standard from which to measure any point of impact shift resulting from the use of the different methods, position #1 was employed. In the interest of keeping everything simple, this is referred to as the "zero group" in the accompanying chart. Consequently, all measurements obtained in positions #2 through #7 are variances from the center of the group to the center of the zero group. If eight rounds clustered into an obvious three-inch group, for example, and two rounds were four inches to the right and left of the main group respectively, the two rounds were discounted as part of the group. Measurements were recorded by first determining the approximate center of each group. Once found, horizontal and vertical deviations were measured. Accuracy histories of the handguns used in this trial were known and all guns were well broken-in. Ammunition consisted of cast bullet handloads, with the exception of 22 rimfire ammo for the Ruger pistol.

The reader must keep some important factors in mind if the information in the table is to be useful. It is unlikely any two people who participate in the exercise outlined in the text will have identical results. Why? The many variables involved have great effect on the outcome. Fundamentals of basic shooting skill such as proper sight picture, breathing control, uniformity and firmness of grip, and trigger release must be considered. Also included are factors like

Position #1- Rear of barrel forward of trigger guard rested on padded rest cradle, hands rested on sandbag.

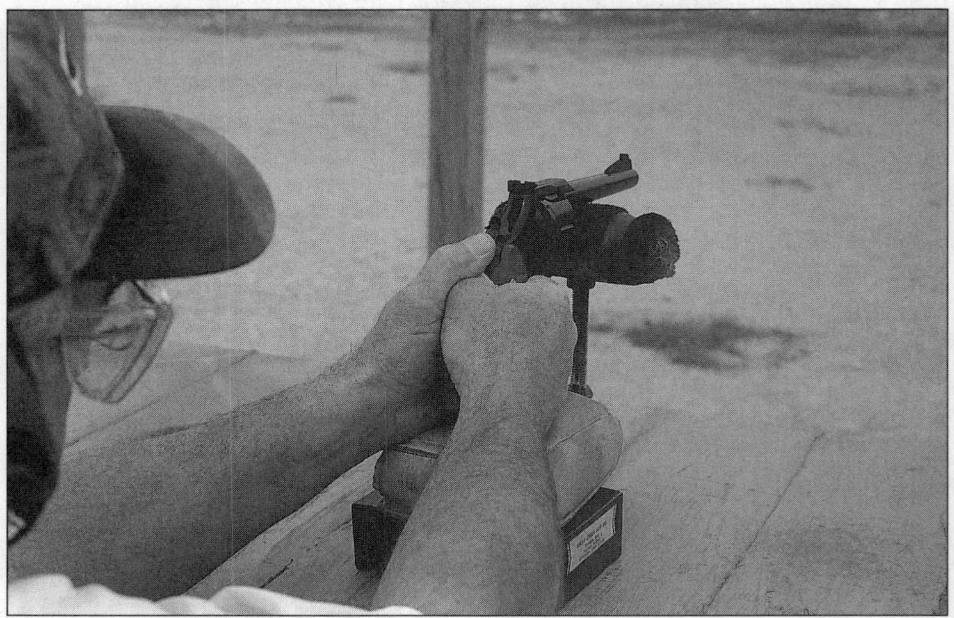

Position #2- Rear of barrel forward of trigger guard rested on padded rest cradle, handgun butt rested on sandbag.

Handguns used in zeroing project: *(from top)* Smith & Wesson Model 625, 45 ACP, Colt's Officers Model Match, 38 Special, Ruger Mark I, 22 LR, SIG Sauer P226, 9mm Luger.

tendency to flinch, eyesight, age, general physical condition, and fatigue. None can be overlooked.

Handguns are particularly sensitive to changes in grip, some more so than others. While a generalization, many find a heavier handgun more forgiving and easier to shoot accurately than a lightweight one. The shooter who never grips a handgun the same way twice will not be pleased with the poor results. Neither will the one who grips the gun in identical fashion for each shot, but varies the firmness of grip from shot-to-shot, or locks elbows for some rounds and relaxes them for others. These are prime examples of inconsistency and such haphazard shooting practices are worthless for learning and / or evaluation. As with any aspect of shooting or handloading, consistency leads to uniformity and these are of utmost importance.

While long barrels are no more accurate than short ones, increased sight radius provided by a longer barrel is a huge help for many. Sighting errors can be minimized considerably.

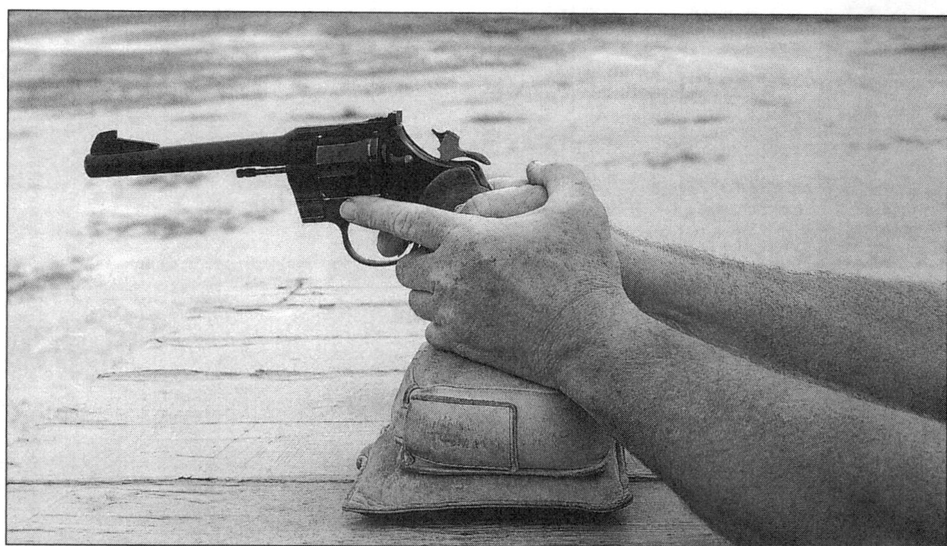

Position #3- Hands rested on sandbag.

Position #4- Hands ahead of sandbag; wrists rested on sandbag.

Front sights and glare

Sunlight glare on a front sight can play havoc with windage and elevation. I can handle about any front sight configuration as long as it does not reflect light. Personal preference for #1 best front sight always leads me in the direction of a dull, matte-finish Patridge type, though this style may not be practical on some handguns. A dull, non-reflective finish on a ramp-type front sight also works well.

Red ramp inserts? I use handguns that are so equipped, but I have always felt that any good shooting I do with such a gun is despite the red insert. Same goes for white outline rear sights. Perhaps these gizmos were designed for combat-type shooting where accuracy is secondary to speed.

Shooting from a bench rest conceals many faults – just as intended. An ample amount of non-bench shooting, however, plainly sheds light on weaknesses. Should a shooter consistently pull to the right ever so slightly when firing a handgun offhand, that is a weakness the shooter can live with and it is not necessarily a bad one. While adjustable sights will not eliminate the shortcoming, the weakness can be effectively dealt with by proper regulation of the rear sight.

Again, while my test results and the test results of others will vary, the point is made: different shooting

Position #5- Sitting with back against solid object; arms extended with elbows rested on knees.

Smith & Wesson Model 625, 45 ACP

Position #1	"Zero" group	
#2	windage, okay	elevation, okay
#3	windage, 1-1/2" left	elevation, 1/2" low
#4	windage, 2" right	elevation, okay
#5	windage, 1-1/2" left	elevation, 3/4" high
#6	windage, 1-1/4" left	elevation, 2-3/4" low
#7	windage, 2-1/4" right	elevation, 1-3/4" low

Colt's Officers Model Match, 38 Special

Position #1	"Zero" group	
#2	windage, okay	elevation, okay
#3	windage, 2 -1/2" left	elevation, 1" low
#4	windage, 1" left	elevation, 1/2" high
#5	windage, 2-3/4" left	elevation, 1-1/4" low
#6	windage, 2-1/2" left	elevation, 2-1/4" low
#7	windage, 2-1/4" left	elevation, 1" high

Ruger Mark I, bull barrel, 22 LR

Position #1	"Zero" group	
#2	windage, 1-1/4" right	elevation, 2-1/2" high
#3	windage, 1" left	elevation, 1/2" high
#4	windage, 1/4" right	elevation, 2" high
#5	windage, 1/4" right	elevation, 3/4" high
#6	windage, 3/4" left	elevation, okay
#7	windage, 1-1/2" left	elevation, 3/4" high

SigSauer P226, 9mm Luger

Position #1	"Zero" group	
#2	windage, 3-1/2" right	elevation, okay
#3	windage, 1/2" right	elevation , 2" low
#4	windage, okay	elevation, okay
#5	windage, 1/2" left	elevation, 1/2" low
#6	windage, 2-3/4" left	elevation, 5" low
#7	windage, 3/4" left	elevation, 2" high

Position #6- Standing, "Weaver" stance with feet apart.

positions / techniques do cause different points of impact. There are, of course, other shooting attitudes that could be used for comparative purposes in addition to those mentioned here.

For years, I knew of and actually observed a few shooters who sighted in handguns without the benefit of a steady rest. I wondered in amazement why anyone would attempt to sight-in a handgun in such a manner. It took a while to sink in, but I eventually developed an understanding of this method. These persons were excellent handgunners all; their shooting faults were few. Shooting from a rest reveals nothing more than the accuracy level of a particular load in a particular handgun. *Period.* Many of us began using a rest when testing handloads. Over time, we became increasingly dependent on the rest. This dependency developed in such a way that our shooting skills, modest as they may have been, suffered serious deterioration.

Back to the heavy-vs.-light handgun concept again, but this time we will focus on barrel weight. Heavy- or bull-barreled handguns are somewhat more forgiving in terms of overcoming *(concealing?)* shooters' weaknesses than are lighter-barreled counterparts.

Position #7- Standing, strong hand only.

These handguns were used for compiling data:

1. Smith & Wesson Model 625 revolver, 45 ACP, stainless steel, 5-inch barrel, adjustable rear sight.
2. Colt's Officers Model Match revolver, 38 Special, blue, 6-inch barrel, adjustable rear sight.
3. Ruger Mark I semi-automatic pistol, 22 LR, 5 1/2-inch bull barrel, blue, adjustable rear sight.
4. SIG Sauer P226 semi-automatic pistol, 9mm Luger, 4.4-inch barrel, matte finish, fixed rear sight.

Comparison of factory Smith & Wesson grip sizes on N-frame revolvers: *(top)* Model 29 44 Magnum, Model 25-5 45 Colt.

Colt's factory grip size comparison: *(top)* '357' Model 357 Magnum, Army Special 32-20 Winchester.

This would lead us to believe, perhaps, that the added weight would provide a reduction in point-of-impact vs. point-of-aim variances when firing a gun using different techniques. Yes and no. While such reduction is possible, it may be far less than anticipated.

Handgun stocks or grips are too often overlooked as a potentially problematic area when one attempts to improve shooting skills. As they should be, factory-installed grips on most handguns are a compromise fit, but for many of us, that compromise is just fine. In such a case, aftermarket grips that also fit offer nothing more than cosmetic appeal. Grips must fit one's hand comfortably. Should they not fit, a consistent shot-to-shot hold will be virtually unattainable.

There is an element of good shooting skill that most shooters are aware of yet make subconscious efforts to ignore, and that is fatigue. Proper concentration, muscle use, and breathing control are far easier when the shooter is rested. It is a total wasted effort in terms of time, ammunition cost, and firearm wear-and-tear to shoot when exhausted. It is true for most of us that time spent on the range is indeed precious. We too often hurry to get there, hurry to finish, and hurry to leave to do something else or fulfill some obligation. That is characteristic of our lifestyle these days. I have become very much aware of this in the last several years. While it varies from person to person, I have found that about thirty minutes of non-stop handgun shooting is my maximum without some sort of break. Some days more, some less, but shooting when tired increases group sizes and precludes the effective zeroing of a handgun. Be content with firing 50 or 60 rounds in a rested state as opposed to wasting that many more rounds in a worn-out condition. Take that break or come back another day.

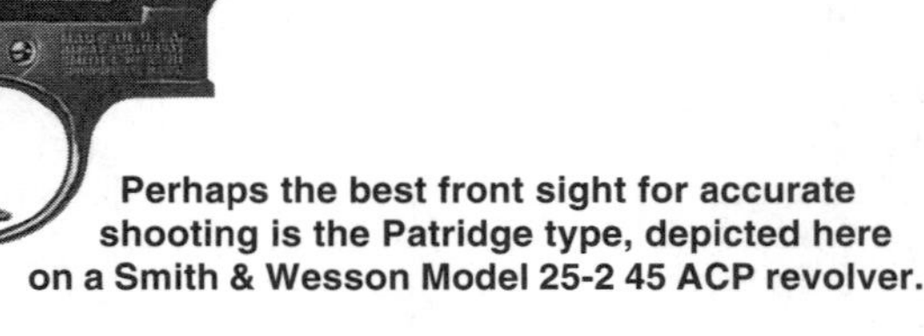

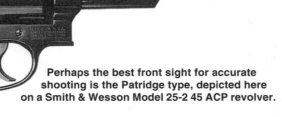

Perhaps the best front sight for accurate shooting is the Patridge type, depicted here on a Smith & Wesson Model 25-2 45 ACP revolver.

A few final notes…Regarding the use of positions #3 *(hands rested on sandbag)* and #4 *(handgun positioned forward of sandbag but not touching it, both wrists rested on bag)*. I have heard each of these positions touted as being the best way of sighting in a handgun. By "best" is meant that the zero will remain mostly true when some other position is employed. Based on my results, I have difficulty agreeing with such a premise. However, another shooter may have altogether different findings.

I discovered it surprising that position #2 *(barrel on rest cradle, handgun butt directly on sandbag)* delivered an insignificant amount of windage and elevation variance, in comparison to the "zero" group, with both revolvers—but not with the pistols. I seem to recall hearing that the butt of a handgun should never be allowed to touch the sandbag. From my limited testing, it appears that the two handgun types react quite differently to this method.

While this article is not intended to transform poor shooters into highly skilled marksmen, it was put together to point out factors that many simply overlook, or are unaware of when zeroing handguns. I suspect the interested reader will find that experimentation similar to that outlined here is a worthwhile endeavor. It takes little in the way of time or ammunition expense to achieve lasting benefits. As a bonus, such work may also starkly expose some handgunning weaknesses that need correction. •

A Little-Known Handgun:

The Wamo Powermaster Pistol

by John Malloy

TO MOST YOUNG boys in the period following World War II, the name Wamo was associated with slingshots. To kids of later generations, the name *(by then with the spelling changed to Wham-O)* was associated with hula hoops and other recreational items.

Few handgun enthusiasts know, however, that the Wamo Manufacturing Company marketed a low-priced 22-caliber single-shot pistol. This pistol was designed and manufactured by Wamo in the last half of the 1950s, when the company was located in San Gabriel, CA. The unique pistol, marketed for several years as the Wamo Powermaster, had a number of interesting features. It appeared at a time that allowed it to take advantage of the tremendous interest in shooting in post-WWII America.

For almost two decades after World War II, the shooting sports grew at a rapid rate in the United States. The Second World War and the following Korean Conflict had proved that people trained in marksmanship were an advantage to our country. Almost everyone was in favor of guns and shooting, and large numbers of people were participating in various shooting sports. Inexpensive firearms were in great demand. Traditional American firearms makers were sometimes hard put to meet the demand for new guns. Manufacturers of items other than firearms, such as Wamo, thus saw an opportunity to enter the firearms field. In those carefree days, firearms were considered as ordinary sporting equipment, and were bought and sold without today's restrictions.

The niche of low-priced single-shot plinking pistols came alive. Sheridan, a long-time maker of pneumatic air guns, brought out a compact single-shot 22-caliber pistol called the Sheridan Knockabout. The little Sheridan 22, a top-break design with a solid frame, was made during the period from 1953 into the 1960s. Before it was discontinued, Savage had introduced, in 1959, its inexpensive Model 101 single-shot 22 pistol. Because of the influence of TV and motion-picture "Westerns," the single-shot Savage was shaped like a single-action revolver. The 101 was produced until the Gun Control Act of 1968 came into being.

Still, Savage was already a large maker of firearms, and Sheridan was known as a pneumatic gunmaker. One pistol of the period, the Wamo, came from a manufacturer with no previous background in gun manufacture. Wamo designers simply offered something they thought Americans would like.

The Wamo Powermaster was introduced early in 1956. Looking like a sleek semiautomatic pistol, it was actually a blowback single-shot. However, the grip angle was similar to that of the contemporary Colt Woodsman autoloader. Retailing for $19.95, it was two dollars more expensive than the Sheridan, but was aimed at the same low-price market.

The Wamo Powermaster 22-caliber single-shot pistol was a good-looking pistol styled somewhat after the shape of the Colt Woodsman. Made for only four years, from 1956 to 1959, it is little-known to most of today's shooters.

The action was cleverly conceived. It consists of a reciprocating bolt, a striker-type firing pin, a trigger mechanism, and a curved flat spring that serves several functions. The action is opened by grasping a cocking handle, which is mounted at the left front portion of the bolt. Drawing the bolt back cocks the action and exposes the chamber. The bolt has no return spring, and so it remains open. The rear portion of the striker protrudes through the rear of the frame. With the bolt open, a cartridge can be loaded directly into the chamber. The flat spring at the bottom of the action rises behind the rim to hold the cartridge in place.

When the shooter is ready to fire the cartridge, the bolt is closed. The flat spring is pushed down and holds the bolt in the closed position by friction. The striker will fall when the trigger is pressed.

When the gun is fired, the fired case—in true blowback fashion—moves the bolt rearward, pushed by pressure of the propelling powder gases. The case itself moves out of the

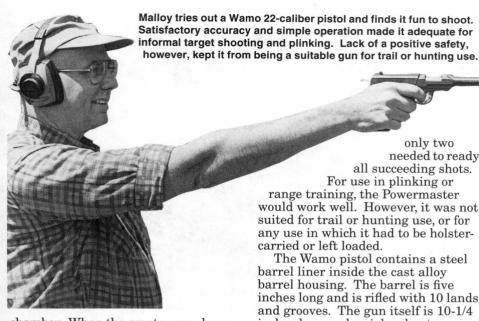

Malloy tries out a Wamo 22-caliber pistol and finds it fun to shoot. Satisfactory accuracy and simple operation made it adequate for informal target shooting and plinking. Lack of a positive safety, however, kept it from being a suitable gun for trail or hunting use.

chamber. When the empty case clears the chamber, the flat spring rises beneath it, flipping it upward and ejecting it from the pistol. There is no actual extractor or ejector in the pistol's mechanism.

The force of the case blowing backwards pushes the bolt to its rearward position. It stays back, and the chamber is exposed, ready to load again.

The pistol shoots almost any 22-caliber ammunition—Shorts, Longs or Long Rifles, and would even operate with the 22 CB Caps made by several ammunition companies during the 1950s.

There is no safety mechanism as such. However, Wamo advertised the open-bolt position as a safety. Actually, if the trigger is pressed with the bolt open, the bolt and striker will sluggishly run forward to contact the rim of the chambered cartridge. A number of trials were made under safe conditions to see if the pistol could be made to discharge this way. It never fired, but there was a slight indentation from the firing pin on the rim of the case. The obvious conclusion is that there is really no completely safe way to leave the pistol loaded. It should be loaded only when the shooter is actually ready to fire.

The Wamo, however, was an easy pistol to use. To load it, the bolt was pulled back, a cartridge inserted, and the bolt pushed forward again. Held in the right hand, a shot could be fired. The empty case would eject and the bolt would remain open. The left hand could then insert a new cartridge into the exposed chamber and push the bolt handle forward. These two operations would be the only two needed to ready all succeeding shots.

For use in plinking or range training, the Powermaster would work well. However, it was not suited for trail or hunting use, or for any use in which it had to be holster-carried or left loaded.

The Wamo pistol contains a steel barrel liner inside the cast alloy barrel housing. The barrel is five inches long and is rifled with 10 lands and grooves. The gun itself is 10-1/4 inches long and weighs about two pounds.

For informal target shooting, the sights were adequate, and were certainly better than most sights found on inexpensive pistols of the period. The front sight was an undercut square blade, a part of the barrel casting. The rear sight blade is mounted in a slotted projection at the upper rear of the gun. The sight blade is held in place by friction, and can simply be pried vertically or horizontally to provide elevation and windage adjustments.

Such a method of adjustment may seem crude. However, remember that most handguns of the period had no provision at all for sight adjustment. Those others with adjustable sights were the more expensive models of the major manufacturers. The Wamo thus provided adjustable sights with a good sight picture in the low-price category.

Although the firing pin fall was long and slow, the Wamo Powermaster was capable of decent accuracy. To verify this, I was fortunate to be able to use a Powermaster to shoot a series of groups on the NRA's B32 10-meter air pistol target.

I decided to use the types of ammunition most commonly available when the Wamo was made. Thus, groups were fired with 22 Short, 22 Long, 22 Long Rifle Standard Velocity and 22 Long Rifle High Velocity loads. The hand-held pistol fired average respective groups of 1-3/4", 1-1/2", 1-3/8" and 1-3/8". Although the two Long Rifle loadings produced the best groups, with any of these loads, the Wamo would certainly be suitable for informal target shooting and plinking.

Perhaps because of its unusual design, or the lack of a known firearms brand name, the Wamo Powermaster was not a big seller. It stayed in production only four years, from 1956 to 1959.

In 1960, Daisy acquired the rights to the Wamo pistol. Rather than continue its manufacture as a 22 rimfire pistol, the company extensively redesigned it. It was introduced as the Daisy Model 100, a CO2-powered repeating BB pistol. The "Powermaster" name, at least unofficially, was often associated with the new Daisy pistol. Although the inner workings were very different, Daisy kept the original shape and outward appearance.

The Powermaster pistol was an attractive design. Proof of this was its selection for use in a poster for one of the series of James Bond spy movies, which were popular in the 1960s. The pistol, in either its 22 or BB form, would have been completely inappropriate, but it looked good.

The Wamo 22 pistol offered a low-price choice for shooters in the 1950s who were looking for a pistol for plinking or informal target shooting. It is little remembered today, but it was an interesting gun. ●

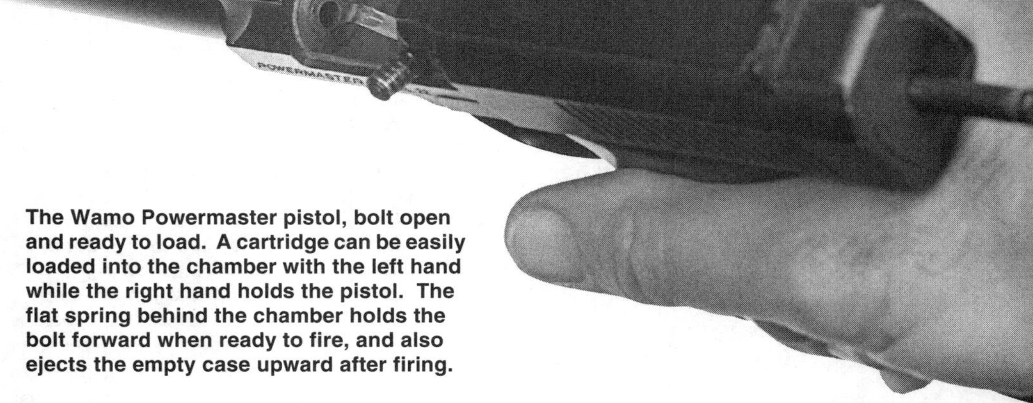

The Wamo Powermaster pistol, bolt open and ready to load. A cartridge can be easily loaded into the chamber with the left hand while the right hand holds the pistol. The flat spring behind the chamber holds the bolt forward when ready to fire, and also ejects the empty case upward after firing.

The

British Bulldog...

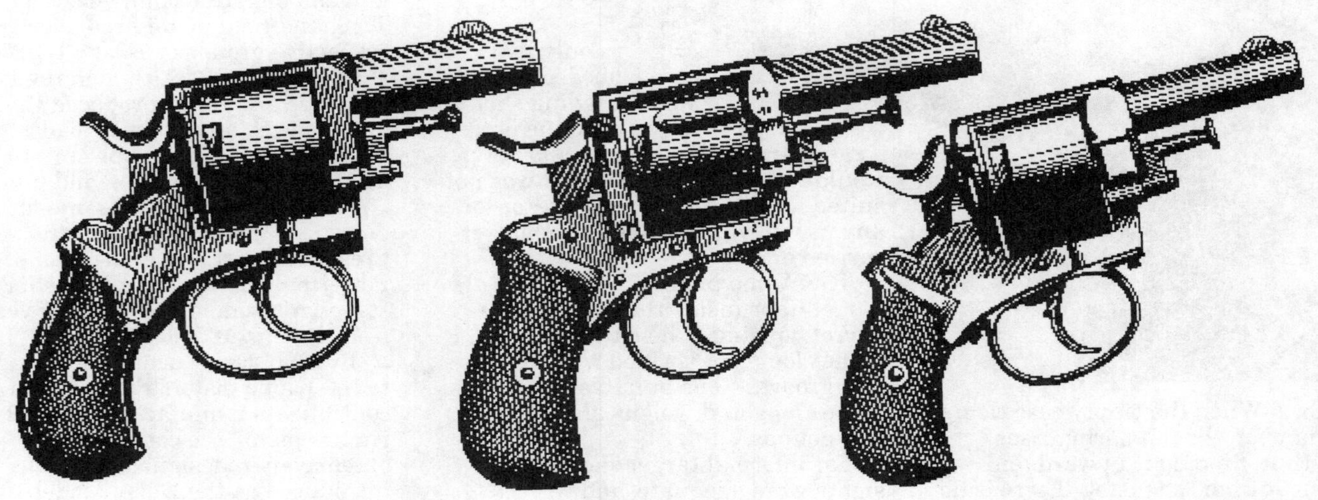

The World's First Mass-Produced Reproduction Revolver

by George J. Layman

NO ONE TODAY would ever think that the first replica of an original blackpowder wheel-gun would have made its debut in the 19th century. Before the modern Italian reproductions of 1957 to the present, the mid-1870s saw one of the greatest handgun legends of the day quickly become the world's most well-known and replicated revolver, copied by over a hundred manufacturers around the globe!

Reproductions of original firearms have become one of today's greatest success stories in the firearms manufacturing industry. From the late 1950s up to this moment, there are *(in some cases)* more replica units of the various models in existence than were produced by their original makers. In these modern times, with the resurgence of blackpowder cartridge and muzzleloading shooting, almost all of the major original arms models of the past two centuries have made an unprecedented comeback. With each new year, new additions have been introduced.

In the 1870s, these blackpowder cartridge revolvers that have become replica arms we shoot for pleasure, were utilized for far more serious purposes. Around 1869-71, a new double-action big-bore pocket revolver made its debut in Great Britain. The Birmingham, England, firm of Philip Webley & Son introduced a scaled-down version of their famous larger Royal Irish Constabulary Model that would probably become the most well-received and popular revolver the entire world would get to know.

The Webley Bulldog was unveiled to the public at a time when many needed a concealable, powerful, quick firing self-cocker at an affordable price. This sturdy little five-shot revolver had an aesthetically pleasing design with a short but peculiar shaped 2 1/2-inch oblong barrel, a bird's head grip and eventually a choice of different chamberings that were smaller than the standard 44 Webley. When production and export had reached full capacity by 1872, it was fast becoming a best seller worldwide. Not only did customers find it a high-quality pocket revolver at nominal cost, but other gun manufacturers on both sides of the Atlantic were also quick to notice and set their sights on similar profitable ventures in the near future involving a near-identical quality and at a far lower price than Webley's $9.50 for a plain no-frills version. Thus the die was cast, the gun which was becoming a legend in England, the British Colonies, and the American West would soon find itself with stiff competition coming at first from its own region of the world, the European continent.

By 1875, the first faithful reproduction of the Webley Bulldog had commenced production in one of western Europe's most prolific arms-making centers; Belgium. In the Liege-Herstal region several small and larger factories had begun to copy the Webley with near-perfect recreation. The quality of the steels and overall finish may not have been up to par with the English product, but none the less, it was beginning to be advertised and exported. In an additional effort to promote sales, it was the Belgians who began stamping the trendy logo of "British Bulldog" on each of their copies. The reason most

These three catalog line drawings are all Belgian reproductions of the Webley British Bulldog, each produced by a different manufacturer. It is simple to distinguish how much variance in design is present. Interestingly, the center example has a loading latch that pulls to the rear as opposed to the more conventional right swing latch of the others. Belgian British Bulldog copies with this unique pull-type latch are quite rare and highly desirable to the serious British Bulldog collector.

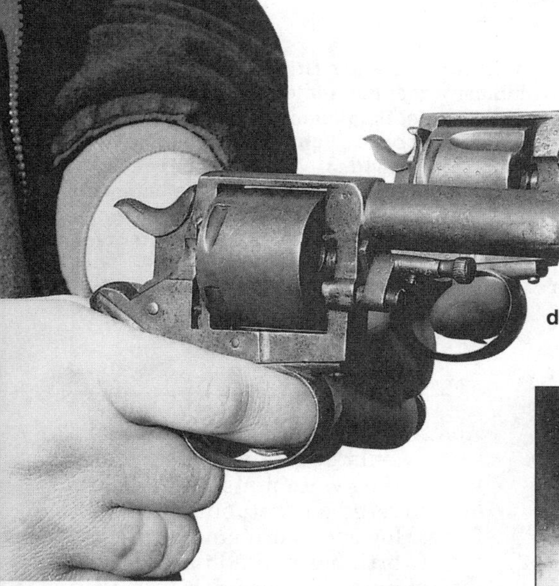

Armed with a pair of 44-caliber British Bulldogs, a pistolero of the 19th century was a formidable opponent despite their smaller pocket gun size.

think that it was a ploy to hoodwink the buyer into thinking they were purchasing a genuine British-made Bulldog, thus simultaneously boosting popularity of their own product. This tactic worked quite well. The trouble was, the English caught on to this and Webley, too, began stamping their products with the British Bulldog logo. Thus if a revolver did not have the Webley "flying bullet" cartouche, or Birmingham proof marks, the smart customer could discern whether he was purchasing the genuine article, or a Belgian reproduction. In time this began to have little effect, as long as the magic words over the frame said British Bulldog, this is all the customer actually cared about. In the United States this was true even more so; a Belgian copy sold over here for $2.93 to $3.25 on average. Thus by 1877, Belgian gun makers in the British Bulldog "manufacturing business," jumped up to a 100 or more in total, and it seemed that Belgium was about to capture the market worldwide. By now, there were other British gunmakers who were producing copies of the No.1 Model of the British Bulldog, but it is fairly certain they were paying Webley a small royalty as well.

In the United States, the overwhelming popularity of the British Bulldog was fast becoming a household word in both the tame East and the "Wild" West. The latter geographical location seemed to have the lion's share of action involving the handy little British double-action. Because many towns and

The bulldog head trademark was almost always stamped on Forehand and Wadsworth British Bulldogs. The author however, has some F&W specimens that lack this, usually in the high serial number range of 85,000 and beyond. This 32 S&W Forehand and Wadsworth is in the 49,000 range. Many European copies also have the Bulldog head logo, usually on the right side of frame.

settlements had laws and ordinances against the open carrying of firearms, the British Bulldog was perfectly suited to this type of environment. People were purchasing the original Webley and reproduction lower-priced Belgian British Bulldogs in amazing quantities from gun shops or mail-order houses. When the first of the Webley Bulldogs reached the United States in substantial quantities in early 1874, American arms companies were aghast that such a popular little product from abroad would sweep the U.S. so quickly. Nothing domestic arms makers had to offer–up to that time–could match the Bulldog in price and simple efficiency and the Bulldog took away quite a number of sales from the more popular American firearms companies.

In 1877, the Worcester, Massachusetts-based Forehand and Wadsworth Arms Co. applied for and received a patent for an "improved Bulldog" design. Thus, in 1878, the very first Forehand and Wadsworth British Bulldogs made their showing, devoid of any factory markings up to the first 1000 pieces, due to concerns similar to those of the Belgians some years earlier, that using the word "Bulldog" would possibly lead to a patent infringement case. As it stood, the original Webley was clearly a model or a pattern title and made no mention of the Webley name. After the Belgians added "British" to "Bulldog," there was even less worry because as mentioned earlier, Webley themselves began marking their own product "British Bulldog!" The Forehand and Wadsworth reproduction of the Webley actually exceeded its English counterpart in popularity.

Another reproduction of the Bulldog made in the United States was from Iver Johnson Company, also of Worcester, Massachusetts. Iver Johnson, however, deviated from the basic Webley design by incorporating features of its own. The original British Bulldog had a rod extractor that was pulled out of the hollow cylinder pin and rotated to the left in order to extract spent cases. At the same time the rod was removed, the cylinder pin could be pulled out, allowing the cylinder to fall free of the

Grip styles and sizes differ greatly on Belgian-made British Bulldog copies. These big-bore specimens show that some are short and sharply curved, with others longer with a less pronounced "parrot's beak."

This pair of Belgian British Bulldogs is another indicator that parts interchangeability among the different Belgian makers was non-existent. The lower copy is lightly engraved and has a much longer and straighter grip than the version above it. Furthermore, the hammer spurs show marked differences; one being an upswept style compared to a straighter type. Also, note the fluted versus non-fluted cylinders. Note the frames are visibly different, as well.

frame. Thus, cleaning and basic maintenance could be accomplished when the arm was stripped down to three components. The Iver Johnson, on the other hand, had a latch-retained cylinder pin that was simple to remove; however, spent cases had to be knocked out of the cylinder by a rod–or even the cylinder pin itself. The Iver Johnson Bulldogs were produced in three basic models: one bird's-head-gripped version marked British Bulldog, and two flat-butt variations marked American Bulldog and Boston Bulldog. The American Bulldog, though made in three variants, did not really copy the Webley British Bulldog in any sense of the word, nor did Iver Johnson's British and Boston Bulldogs.

It appears the first real "blackpowder" reproduction was copied to a "T", both in Belgium and the United States, by Forehand and Wadsworth. The Belgian replicas are an enigma among British Bulldogs as no two ever seem alike! After having examined and collected well over 350 British Bulldogs over a 30-year span, I have never observed any two Belgian copies to have an *EXACT* reflection. With over 100 makers exporting to the United States, South America, Middle East, India, and Australia, I suppose finding two of the same would be merely a coincidence unless they were matching sets or a lot delivered a constabulary or police force. However, Forehand and Wadsworth boasted all parts were interchangeable, indicating F&W British Bulldogs were apparently quite uniform in production. Along with the F&W, the various British-made copies of the Webley could be called the best repli-guns this side of their original English cousins. The author has owned several of the English-made Model No.1 and No.2 copies and found that they are as well constructed and finished with a high quality equal to-or at times even better than–that of a Webley! In the author's collection is a No.2 British Bulldog manufactured by F. Madeley

The 1883 1st Model Iver Johnson American Bulldog *(top)* and the earlier 1878-81 Iver Johnson British Bulldog *(bottom)* show a marked similarity with the latch retained cylinder pin. The primary physical difference is the American version had a saw-handle flat butt compared to the bird's-head grip of the British version. Both were sold for less than four dollars in 1884 by numerous mail-order gun dealers of the day.

of London and so marked on the lower rear sight groove flat. The upper flat is simply marked "The Bulldog." Having Birmingham proof marks on the cylinder and barrel, this specimen is as finely constructed as they get, and is in 100 percent functioning order, with the only detraction being that the extractor rod is missing. This 450 Webley-chambered No. 2 Bulldog is the first and only example I've ever observed with this makers address. The serial number is 1598, thus many more must be in circulation, but may have been exported to foreign countries in out-of-the-way places.

Regarding the Belgian copies of the British Bulldogs, many can be found with a few variables of their own in the area of sizes, grip design—to include some which are not even marked "British Bulldog" at all. There exists in my own collection what *might* be one of the most famous British Bulldogs of the old American West: an engraved Belgian copy purchased from an old ranch sale in New Mexico. Ten years later–quite by accident–after removing the grips I discovered the name of John H. Tunstall NM lightly penciled inside the smooth, worn checkered grips. To the historically informed, John H. Tunstall was a wealthy young rancher in Lincoln County, New Mexico who befriended William Bonney or, if you wish, Henry McCarty—alias Billy the Kid. Bonney became quite close to Tunstall after he began working for him and was fiercely loyal to him. When Tunstall was shot in 1878 by jealous rivals of the Murphy-Dolan faction while driving cattle into Lincoln, the Kid swore revenge. This act of violence kicked off the Lincoln County Range War that was responsible for turning Billy the Kid into an outlaw. When Billy knelt down beside Tunstall's body, there is a possibility he took Tunstall's Bulldog as a keepsake of his dear friend. There is also a chance it could well have been the self-cocker that Pat Garrett saw at the Maxwell ranch the night Billy was killed. Garrett thought it was a Colt Lightning double action, but no one ever verified the "self-cocker's" identification. The author stumbled upon this revolver when a gentleman happened to notice my "Wanted British Bulldog Revolvers" advertisement in one of the blackpowder magazines that I wrote for several years ago. The man said he was liquidating a quantity of old cowboy equipment that had lain in a ranch barn in New Mexico for over 50 years, much of it Old West memorabilia such as ledgers, tintypes, quirts, saddles—and one British Bulldog revolver wrapped in a musty cloth inside a dry-rotted leather saddle bag.

After purchasing the revolver for the going price of Bulldogs at the time, this find was truly one of those cases where something hidden for decades suddenly re-appears without warning. Few British Bulldog copies made in Belgium have been discovered with a promising, although circumstantial, provenance connecting them to the Old West, but at least one confirmed copy has. The surprise of this find which, through research not reported here, has proven to be a genuinely important piece of 19th century Western Americana, has entranced me since its discovery.

Shown are right and left views of what is possibly John H. Tunstall's engraved Belgian-made 44-caliber British Bulldog. Lying in obscurity for nearly 124 years without being identified, it took a simple operation of removing its grips to find the Tunstall name–a discovery of historical significance if true.

All British Bulldogs should probably be given the title "Unknown Gun that Won the West." Between the 1870s and 1900, more people—good and bad, and on both sides of the law––were probably killed or wounded by British Bulldogs than by any other type of handgun. The distribution of the Webley British Bulldog and its reproductions could well number a million and a half or more…or even quite a lot more. Few will dispute that in the United States, the small revolvers were literally everywhere,

Close-up of scroll engraving on the right frame of the Tunstall Belgian Bulldog. Note the fish design on the cylinder.

To the prospective British Bulldog buyer of old, the magic words over the frame said it all. Whether British-, Belgian- or American-made, a British Bulldog was a British Bulldog to most!

hidden out of sight in many a pocket and vest. This is precisely the reason they had lost out in popularity to the Colt or Smith & Wesson revolvers. It is these big six-guns that we have always seen in Old West cabinet and tintype photos of the 19th and early 20th centuries. The tucked-away Bulldog was thus rarely seen on the old-time photo plate.

On a further historical note concerning "Eastern" use of the British Bulldog, there was a New York City group of scalawags known as the "British Bulldog Gang" which operated in the city's roughhewn Five Points district between 1882 and 1894. All members carried Bulldog revolvers used for robberies, murders, and other dubious activities. It was recorded that after the gang's complete breakup in the mid-1890s, that all 80-plus members–when hauled in–carried British Bulldogs revolvers and other lethal instruments to ply their trade. All in all, it seemed the British Bulldog was in nationwide usage.

Both the 38 and 32 S&W cartridges are in current factory production. British Bulldogs chambered for either of these numbers should *never* be used with modern smokeless ammunition. Cases must be reloaded with blackpowder, or an approved substitute. This is due to the nature of pre-smokeless-era metallurgy.

Shown *(from left)* are modern-made 44 Bulldog and 44 Webley cartridges formed from 44 Special cases. At far right is an original UMC-made 450 Webley cartridge; brass for it can be made from 45 Colt cases.

One of the saddest incidents that occurred on the East Coast concerning the British Bulldog in a violent act was the assassination of President James A. Garfield on July 2,1881. Shot in the back and arm at the Baltimore and Potomac railroad station by one Charles J. Guiteau, a crazed attorney, it took Garfield several months to succumb to his wound. Guiteau used a 44-caliber British Bulldog that was officially reported by the Smithsonian Museum to be a Forehand and Wadsworth. The revolver, stolen from the museum in the early 1950s, has become something of an enigma. Right after the assassination–and for years after– it was reported to be a Webley, an F&W, a Belgian-made British Bulldog—its actual identification has become an ongoing debate. The ignorance of past media reporting on firearms is quite similar to today's lack of technical firearms expertise by modern-day news people. Details were seemingly guessed upon. The author has viewed the sole photograph in possession of the Smithsonian and by my own professional judgment, the revolver is *NOT* a Forehand and Wadsworth, due to several physical details uncharacteristic to the F&W. The Guiteau Bulldog is either a Webley or an excellent Belgian copy. As the photo is of the left side where markings were not stamped, it can not be positively identified and, since it has vanished forever, we'll never know the truth.

The British Bulldog in reproduction form, far out-produced its original Webley ancestor in total numbers, and in reality, the continental European copies lasted longer to production. The 1911 Adolph Frank Alpha catalog from Germany advertised well over a dozen British Bulldog-style revolvers this late in time. Most were probably Belgian, French, or German-made copies–with possibly only one English copy being a No.2 listed as "a British Bulldog of best quality." In fact, many of the British Bulldogs listed in the catalog even had improvements such as sliding or push-button safeties on the rear of the frame.

Today's collector and blackpowder cartridge shooters have made a drastic turn-around in this once highly neglected area of antique firearms. At one time during the 1970s and 80s, British Bulldogs wouldn't bring more than \$25 to \$40 and were classified with the generic

The 45/450 Webley cartridge was the largest caliber chambered for all British Bulldogs. When making up modern ammunition caliber from 45 Colt cases, reduction of rim thickness will often be required. At close to moderate ranges, it is a deadly number.

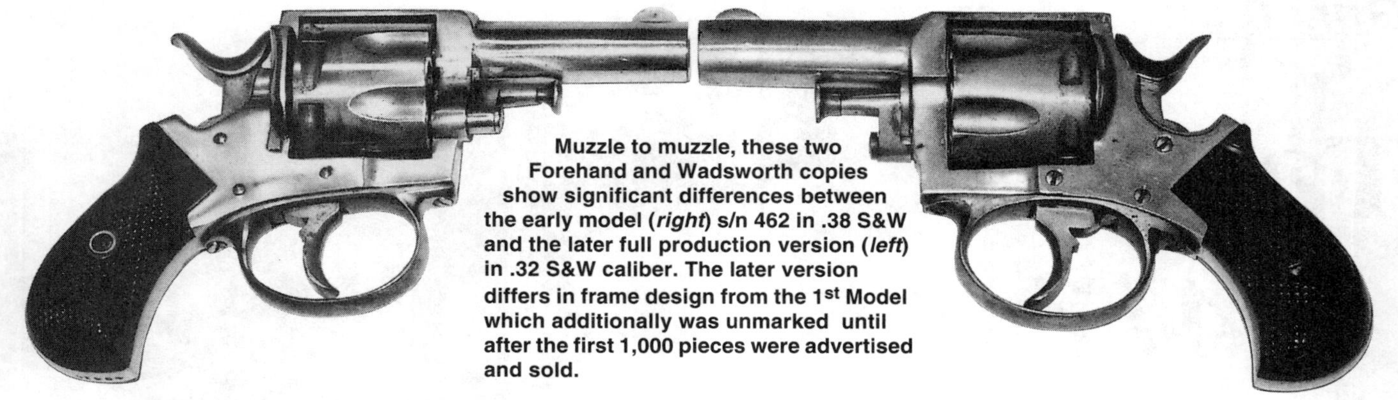

Muzzle to muzzle, these two Forehand and Wadsworth copies show significant differences between the early model (*right*) s/n 462 in .38 S&W and the later full production version (*left*) in .32 S&W caliber. The later version differs in frame design from the 1st Model which additionally was unmarked until after the first 1,000 pieces were advertised and sold.

turn-of-the-century and earlier cheap pocket revolvers. However, the British Bulldog actually was, and is, in a class of its own since the majority are indeed *true* reproductions of an original that became an overnight sensation and an immediate money-maker. It nearly started a production frenzy worldwide for manufacturers who had the expertise and knowledge of firearms manufacture. Had Colt or one of the large American firms brought out the first successful "Bulldog," infringement lawsuits would have been initiated in short order since, rest-assured, Colt or Smith & Wesson would have patented the Bulldog logo as their own. Though Colt brought out their 1877 double-action Thunderer and Lightning: when purchased with the short 2-inch barrel, it could be hidden away almost as compactly as a British Bulldog. This is likely the reason Colt rushed the 1877 double action into production, jealous they were losing money to the foreign-designed little big-bore British Bulldog self-cockers. The only shrewd American manufacturer who jumped feet first into the British Bulldog manufacturing business was Forehand and Wadsworth. Even today, they are among the more popular choices of cowboy action shooters who require a well-made Bulldog for pocket gun side matches. Collectors, on the other hand, who have well-rounded collections of British Bulldog revolvers, always seem to buy them up as quickly as they are advertised, to include the higher-quality Belgian copies—and the Webleys, too, if they can be routed from hiding.

It should be kept in mind that the reproductions of the British Bulldog put Webley in the back seat by 1880 for one reason…price. Webley never seemed to have a price reduction until the mid-1890s when overall popularity began to wane. It is for this reason that, in the United States, the British Bulldog reproductions are normally the easiest to find. In Europe, however, it may be a different story with more Webleys in circulation.

Those who contemplate shooting their British Bulldog should always remember that the metallurgy of the time was of the blackpowder era and due to the respect of this, either blackpowder or an approved substitute *MUST* always be used when gearing up the Bulldog for shooting. The chamberings of the British Bulldog ranged from 32 and 38 S&W to 44 Bulldog, and 44 and 450 Webley. Though the first two cartridges are still factory loaded, under *NO* circumstance should modern smokeless loadings of the 32 and 38 S&W be used in any of the British or American Bulldog revolvers of these chamberings. Either they must be reloaded from scratch, or factory loads must have their bullets pulled and, after discarding the smokeless powder, be reloaded with blackpowder or Pyrodex. Most often the Forehand and Wadsworth and several of the later No. 2 Webleys–or their European copies–will be found in these calibers. In Europe they are coined the 320 and 380, respectively.

Forming brass for the larger 44-caliber Bulldog and Webley cartridges can be accomplished quite easily by shortening 44 Special or 44 Magnum cases. Case length for the 44 Bulldog is 0.067-inch, and 0.095-inch for the 44 Webley. Cases for the 450 Webley can be formed from 45 Colt brass. It may be best to chamber-cast the cylinders, as many of the Belgian-made versions show a degree of variance, and tolerances may differ from the accepted standard. Prior to obtaining a bullet mould for any of the big-bore Webley 44 or 45 British Bulldogs made in Belgium or the United States, bores should be slugged. The 44s have been found to vary from 0.441-inch to 0.446-inch and the 45/450 Webley bullet diameters vary from 0.449-inch to 0.458-inch— especially on those Belgian copies with offset bores that are not concentric.

It is important to note the British Bulldog, whether a genuine Webley or a 19th century clone, is usually found with mechanical problems ranging from weak trigger springs, to being completely out of time. Before getting ready for the range, always have your Bulldog checked by a gunsmith for timing, proper indexing, and cylinder play. These faults can be remedied in spite of the tiny internal parts of the British Bulldog. In this day and age of renewed interest in the not-so-interesting ordnance of the past, the British Bulldog in any of its dozens upon dozens of replicated configurations were never actually neglected until after the First World War. After all, this was the era of the swing-out cylinder revolver and the automatic pistol, thus putting the Bulldogs into obsolescence. Because they were always known for their inexpensive cost and considered among the lower category of handguns, many were dry-fired like toys and given to kids to play with during the Depression years; subsequently, a great number broke down. Now that all of this has changed, the respect for what was once the world's most popular revolver has risen to the level of serious collection and shooting status. One fact remains–the British Bulldog may forever be considered the first real reproduction of the blackpowder era, and the tradition it started has made the modern replica a cornerstone of the American firearms industry. •

Gun Test:

Taurus 24/7

This is a semi-auto pistol that's ready to rock, 365 days a year!

by Dave Workman

FRONT SIGHT, REAR sight, press.

Anybody familiar with defensive pistol shooting knows the drill. And when it all comes together, if everything goes according to plan, there's a hole in the target where you meant it to be. If it happens time after time, you're a pretty reliable shooter and the pistol in your hand is probably better than that.

Which brings us around the new Taurus 24/7, a striker-fired semiauto pistol with some very good design features that – despite its long trigger stroke – is just plain impressive. I had fired only about 15 rounds at a target set downrange about 15 yards when I was reminded of a story about the Alamo. After the battle was over and the smoke cleared away, according to this tale, a Mexican soldier was said to have commented about the marksmanship skills of the Texan defenders. "If they put their sights on you," this fellow allegedly remarked, "you were dead."

Despite my fundamental dislike for striker-fired *pistols (never cared for the long double-action-only trigger stroke, I guess)*, the 24/7 is one more example, perhaps the best so far, of a continuing string of Taurus semi-autos that have just flat impressed me in the accuracy department. First off a sandbag rest, and then off-hand—once I got a feel for the trigger pull and let-off, this new Taurus did not seem capable of throwing an errant shot. After my less-than-stellar experiences now and then with other such handguns, that just didn't seem possible.

After I'd finished putting enough holes in a B-27 overlay Shoot-N-C target from Birchwood Casey that it started to actually become boring, I turned my attention to a tin can. If a person can repeatedly hit such a target that moves to a new position every time someone conks it, thus changing the distance from the muzzle to the target, it means that the firearm is up to the demand of hitting what it is aimed at. Sure, you can give credit to the person behind the gun, but in the final analysis, if a pistol or revolver–or any firearm for that matter–is a lemon, even Wyatt Earp or Jeff Cooper won't be able to make it perform like a peach.

Not that Taurus is going to change my opinion entirely about long trigger strokes on striker-fired pistols. But I might just soften up a bit thanks to the experience I've had with the 24/7.

Truth be known, Taurus may have arrived at something it seems to have been working toward for quite some time, through a series of handguns in the more compact PT series. The 24/7 has the size, heft and feel of an absolute "serious business" sidearm, one that rivals anything I've seen in the genre from anybody who builds them.

Featuring an almost featherweight polymer frame under a stainless steel slide and barrel assembly, the 24/7 is chambered in 9mm and 40 S&W. Barrel length is 4 inches, and the sight radius is 6 inches. The slide has a large ejection port, and the controls are located on the left side of the frame: positive thumb safety, slide stop, takedown lever and magazine release.

That frame, and especially the grip, requires some attention in this narrative. It features a molded accessory rail up front, for tactical lights, lasers or other accessories. The trigger guard is large enough to use with a gloved finger. But it is the grip, itself, that I believe will soon be earning accolades as one of the smartest design moves Taurus ever made.

Featuring a full wraparound surface of soft rubber, the front of the grip has finger grooves, and they are designed with a "ribber-type" surface that Taurus is using on some of its big-bore revolver grips. This is one incredibly comfortable grip, and this writer has strongly encouraged

Specifications

Manufacturer: Taurus International, 16175 NW 49th Ave., Miami, FL 33014-6314 / (305) 624-1115 / www.taurususa.com

Model: 24/7

Finish: Blue or stainless slide, black polymer frame

Barrel length: 4 inches

Caliber: 9mm or 40 S&W

Capacity: Ten rounds

Grips: Rubber overlay with "ribber" surface on front strap

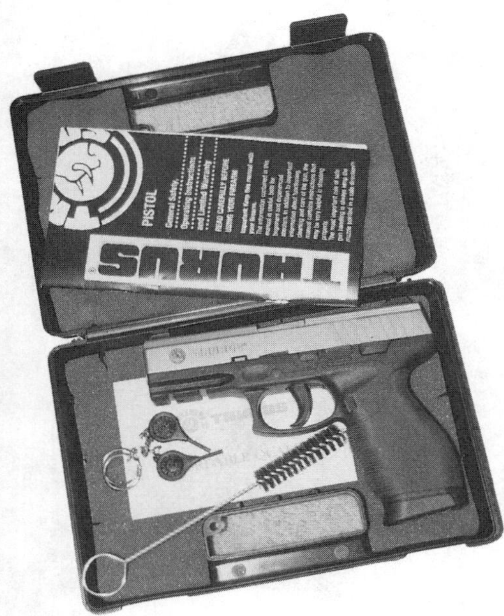
Taurus packages the 24/7 neatly in a lockable hard-sided box with two keys for the internal safety, a cleaning brush and owner's manual.

Taurus to use this kind of grip on all of its big-bore wheelguns.

At the 2004 SHOT Show in Las Vegas, I had the opportunity to accompany a lady friend of mine who works for one of the major optics companies. She was looking for her first handgun, something with which she might hunt, target shoot and, should the occasion arise, defend herself. We visited several different handgun makers' exhibits, but she came away extremely impressed with a Taurus 357 Magnum revolver, and primarily because of that Ribber grip.

On each side, the flats are also grooved to enhance the hold, and these grooves are set diagonally. In the rainy weather under which my initial range test was conducted, I'll say this for the record: That grip design greatly enhanced my ability to hold this pistol during recoil.

At the bottom rear of the grip, the polymer projects downward about a half-inch, matching up almost perfectly with the thick polymer base of the magazine. The overall result is an appearance that has smooth lines and feels very good in hand.

Cocking serrations on the slide are wide and found only on the rear. I've got one pistol with cocking serrations at both the front and rear of the slide, and some gunnies of my acquaintance say front serrations are a very bad idea, because they suggest that it's okay to be putting your hand anywhere near the muzzle. I'm not sure I agree with this, but everyone has an opinion.

As on other Taurus striker-fired pistols, the extractor is external, with an integral loaded chamber indicator. When a round is chambered, a flat "arm" on the extractor pivots outward, exposing a red mark visible to the eye. The fixed sights are held on with screws, not pins or via dovetails. This system doesn't seem to have any drawbacks, as I have yet to hear of a sight coming loose, even under the kind of heavy shooting one does during a test and evaluation.

My 9mm test pistol *(S/N TWL 32440)* was an eye-catcher right out of the lockable, hard plastic shipping box that Taurus has been using for quite some time on all of its handguns. The stainless slide had what I would describe as a bead-blasted, non-glare finish. Contrasted against the black frame, it gives this pistol a two-tone presentation that is hard to resist. This is one of two finishes available. The 24/7 also comes with a blued slide, in both calibers.

Whoever said "beauty is only skin deep" never wrapped his paw around the 24/7. This self-loader is quality through and through. After removing the ten-round magazine and racking the slide to confirm the chamber is clear, lock the slide back and rotate the takedown lever clockwise until the lever is vertical. Withdraw the pin and release the slide. I found that I had to squeeze the trigger to get the slide to move forward and come free from the rails.

Rear sight on the Taurus test pistol had two high-visibility white dots on either side of the notch.

Inside, you'll find a full-length guide rod with a flat-coil recoil spring. The frame rails appear to be an alloy to keep down weight, but to provide a metal-against-metal surface for the slide rails. That alloy skeleton is held firmly in the polymer frame, and try as I might, I could find no sloppiness in the fit; the assembly is as tight as I've ever seen on a pistol of this type, and that's saying a lot. This certainly contributes to what seems to be the 24/7's inherent accuracy.

One other thing that contributes to this tight lockup seems to be the slight "bell" at the muzzle end of the barrel.

Workman rounded up a variety of 9mm ammunition to put the new Taurus through its paces. The pistol functioned flawlessly with everything from hardball to Federal Hydra-Shok hollowpoints.

This is a bushingless design, and the barrel has about a quarter-inch swell that locks right up to the slide.

Taurus includes its integral safety-locking feature in the slide. Engaged by the turn of a small key *(two are included with the 24/7, same as with any of the company's handguns incorporating this mechanism)* and when it is in the "on" position, this pistol cannot be fired. This is about as fail-safe as it gets, because the "gun lock" never leaves the firearm. Say what you want about trigger locks and cable locks and any of a number of different kinds of "feel-good" safety locking devices upon which anti-gunners have long insisted; this one from Taurus is arguably the best of the bunch–simply because it is always there instead of gathering dust in a kitchen drawer.

One more thing about that slide, while we're on the subject. Taurus designers obviously have an eye for aesthetics. Instead of cursing this gun with a blocky, square-looking slide, Taurus has given the 24/7's top side something of a graceful "taper" that has the actual top 3/8-inch being narrower than the overall slide width. The slide on my test gun was 1-inch wide, but the top surface is but 5/8-inch wide. There is no better word for this than "graceful." It is, perhaps, a deceiving appearance, but so what? It looks good.

And a note here: The widest part of the frame is 1-1/8 inches, at the trigger and along the grip. This still does not appear to be too wide for a service pistol, though it is wider than a 1911 frame; the standard against what all such pistols seem to be measured, for better or worse. It is certainly no more bulky than any number of modern service pistols, from Glock, Smith & Wesson or Heckler & Koch, for example.

Controls are on the left side of the frame, and they include *(l-r)* takedown lever, magazine release and thumb safety. That safety functions the same way as that of a 1911-type pistol...

...Pressed to its upward position, it is engaged and the handgun will not fire.

One secret of the 24/7 is this ribbed grip front strap, which allows for a comfortable hold and does seem to help soak up recoil.

One thing I discovered about the grip frame is that on either side, behind the trigger, the frame is slightly recessed, with a flare that allows the trigger finger on either the right or left hand to index correctly on the trigger. This indentation reduces just slightly the circumference of the grip at the critical point where the thumb and finger constrict, improving what is called the "functional dimension" of the pistol. This dimension is the measurement around the grip and trigger. The smaller that measurement, the greater a pistol's functional dimension; that is, the more readily it fits the human hand, and contributes to the pistol's overall fit and comfort.

Workman turned his attention to a tin can, and blasted it across the range without missing a beat.

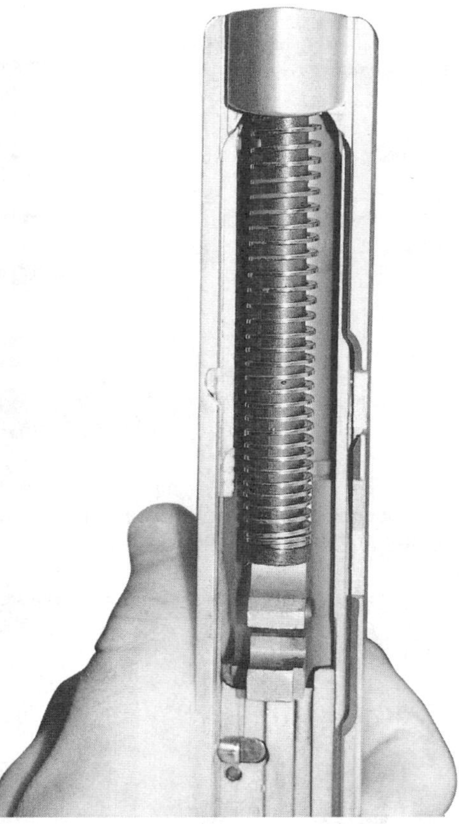
Recoil spring features flat coils on full-length guide rod.

Author's first off-hand group showed a nice tight pattern. He's convinced the 24/7 would make a terrific carry piece.

My test gun was fitted with three-dot sights, and the front white dot was very large and easy to acquire, even in the less-than-perfect Pacific Northwest light available on the cloudy day that I made my initial range visit. I dug into my ammunition stores and pulled what I figured would be a representative sampling of commercial ammunition, and found plenty to like, with bullet weights of 115, 124 and 147 grains. There were rounds from Federal, Black Hills, Hornady and Winchester, including *(dare I admit this?)* a handful of old Black Talons that I had lying around gathering dust. In all, I had seven different ammo choices for this evaluation, and every one of them turned in the kind of performance one expects from this cartridge.

I got the highest velocity, but just barely, from a 124-grain Black Hills round loaded with a Hornady XTP bullet, at 1249 fps, with the Chrony Delta chronograph set ten feet from the muzzle. To my surprise, the next-fastest round was a 115-grain USA ball, streaking across the screens at 1248 fps. My slowest recorded chronograph reading came from the 124-grain Winchester Black Talon/SXT loads, moving at a still-respectable 1118 fps.

All things considered, a hit from any of these rounds is going to carry with it what some folks like to call "a discouraging turn of events" for the target. My guess is that the careful handloader who invests the time to come up with an accurate load will wring the most out of this pistol.

All that shooting of various ammunition–most of it hollowpoint–demonstrated that the 24/7 feeds everything very well. While the 9mm round is not as prone to having the kind of wide mouth on a hollowpoint projectile as larger-caliber pistols, and thus suffer from ramping problems with those particular bullets, there is still an opportunity for a poorly-designed 9mm handgun to give someone fits if they use anything but, say ball ammo or a hollowpoint on the order of the XTP, which has a dandy taper.

The double-stack magazine in my test pistol was a ten-rounder, with a pretty healthy polymer base, and a synthetic follower housed in a metal body. It seemed tough enough, and was the only magazine that came with the pistol. Spares are, of course, available from Taurus.

Recoil is entirely manageable on the 24/7, though I'd hazard a guess that for smaller shooters, with smaller hands that don't wrap too well around the grip, it might feel a bit stouter. One feature that offsets this effect a bit is

In keeping with a current fad, the 24/7 features a grooved front end to accommodate tactical lights or laser sight.

Compared to Workman's Commander-size, customized Auto Ordnance 45 ACP, the 24/7 stacked up well. It's a little shorter OAL, and carries three more rounds.

Stripped for cleaning, the Taurus 24/7 is a study in simplicity. Barrel, slide, magazine, recoil spring and guide rod and frame.

the rear of the frame. It sweeps in from the butt and then back out to the rear to join the back end of the slide. It's as comfortable as–perhaps even more so–a typical beavertail on a Model 1911, and the surface is wide enough to effectively distribute effects of recoil over a wider area of the web between the thumb and index finger.

For concealed carry, the Taurus 24/7 is sized right. Overall, it's about the same size as a Colt Commander. Under a proper cover garment, this pistol disappears, whether carried in a belt holster or a shoulder rig.

If Taurus designers set out to develop a gun with good safety features, modern design, comfortable form and top quality materials that is capable of very good accuracy, they scored on all counts. ●

Work the takedown lever clockwise, and remove it. Slide will move forward and off the rails.

Taurus scores points with author for its key-activated integral locking system that never leaves the handgun.

BALLISTICS

Cartridge	*Bullet Weight/Type*	*Velocity (fps)*
Federal Hydra Shok	124 / JHP	1174
Winchester SXT (Black Talon)	124 / JHP	1118
Black Hills	124 / JHP/XTP	1249
Federal Hydra Shok	147 / JHP	1134
USA	115 / FMJ	1248
Federal Match	124 / FMJ	1200
Hornady Vector	115 / FMJ	1138

Gun Test:

Hamilton Bowen's Custom Ruger Redhawk

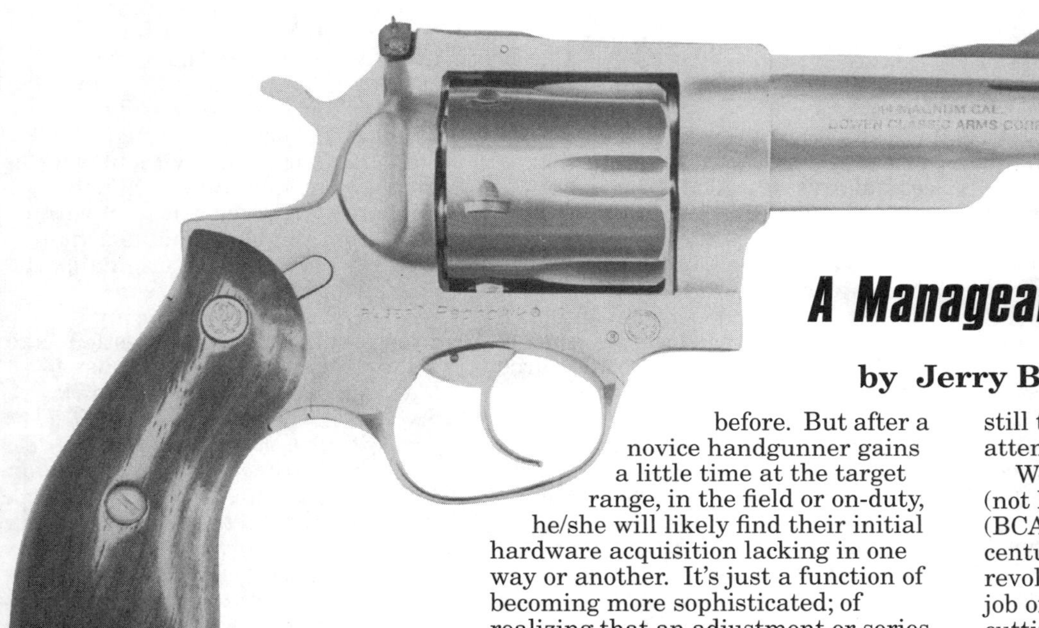

A Manageable Powerhouse!

by Jerry Burke

IF BOWEN CLASSIC Arms needed a corporate slogan, I'd suggest… "Making Great Revolvers Even Greater!" But the firm's founder and president, Hamilton Bowen, needs no fancy words. His reputation as a master pistolsmith is world-renowned, based on many hundreds of specially crafted custom revolver conversions since he turned pro in 1980. His customers are discriminating *pistoleros* with needs… both practical and aesthetic… not being met by available factory products. After all, it should come as no surprise that handguns, like most consumer products, are designed and marketed to appeal to the broadest possible base of potential buyers. And that's a role the American firearms industry fills better today than ever before. But after a novice handgunner gains a little time at the target range, in the field or on-duty, he/she will likely find their initial hardware acquisition lacking in one way or another. It's just a function of becoming more sophisticated; of realizing that an adjustment or series of changes in that factory shootin' iron could lead to better performance. It's a mild version of the relentless lifelong equipment quest from which every dedicated golfer suffers.

And Hamilton Bowen was no different as a novice handgunner decades ago. Skilled and schooled in machine work and the other talents required for first-rate gunsmithing, Hamilton took to tinkering continuously with every available factory product and developing solutions to improve his own shooting abilities. Having a preference for big-bore handguns with plenty of power, and with men like the legendary Elmer Keith to fuel the fire, Hamilton Bowen became a resolute revolver man. Can't say as I blame him. It's still the revolver that gets most of my attention for serious tasks.

A great handgun made greater! Bowen Classic Arms' Custom Ruger Redhawk.

Working from Louisville, Tennessee (not Kentucky) Bowen Classic Arms (BCA) has spent the past quarter century catering to the special-needs revolver crowd, and doing a masterful job of it. Mr. Bowen has been on the cutting edge of developments for conversions in the super-magnum cartridge category… the 454 Casull, 475 Linebaugh and 50-calibers… the 50 Special and 50 Action Express. While I enjoy testing such "outside-the-box" big-bores, they don't fill a vital niche in my handgunning lifestyle. My need for maximum handgun power stops with the 44 Remington Magnum. Thus, my own interest in the talents of Hamilton Bowen was for a practical "working gun"; a handgun not available from an original manufacturer's product line. One that would serve multiple purposes based on more than a half century of handgunning experience.

I've been a fan of the late Bill Ruger's products since the very early days of his brilliant career. My first 44 Magnum was a Ruger flattop single-action, acquired used but as-new in 1961. Happily, I developed experience with milder 44 Special cartridges before venturing very far

Just a sample of the cartridges used for range-testing Hamilton Bowen's custom Ruger Redhawk conversion. Twenty-five-yard results were excellent.

into the then-new world of the 44 Magnum. For those new to handgunning, the legendary Elmer Keith of Idaho experimented with every available handgun caliber and gunpowder known to mankind, starting well before WWI and continuing virtually nonstop until his death in 1984. Ever the beltgun innovator, he was seeking the most accurate and powerful handgun/cartridge combinations possible. In the 1950s, Elmer lobbied and bullied one ammunition manufacturer (Remington) into producing his 44 Magnum cartridge. Both Ruger and Smith & Wesson rushed to field new products accommodating the upsized 44 Special chambering.

While that's all "ancient" handgun history, I'm still not one to argue with Elmer. I knew the 44 Magnum was the first stop in my search for a custom big-bore handgun. For my project, I wanted a solid, hefty double-action revolver that could take plenty of shooting with a wide variety of loads, yet compact enough to make it easy carrying. I wanted a clean, crisp light trigger pull in single-action mode and an exceptionally smooth double-action function. I prefer a tight barrel-to-cylinder fit even on a production gun, and wanted the minimal practical clearance on my custom six-shooter. I required enough barrel length to gain a respectable amount of muzzle velocity, but no more than necessary. A compact grip was needed, making the final custom product not only handy on a gunbelt, but also usable for concealed carry if the occasion arose. Facing a heavy dose of regular humidity in the Texas coastal area, I needed a corrosion-resistant sidearm that didn't require continual maintenance. I also wanted to reduce felt recoil, especially when shooting heavy hunting loads. Finally, I had to have a front sight tall enough to allow the elevation needed for effective shooting out to 100 yards and more... just in case.

After examining several examples of Hamilton Bowen's craftsmanship and talking with some very satisfied owners, I knew where to go for this special-needs handgun. After developing the above list of what I wanted in the finished product... but keeping an open mind... the next step was to visit the Bowen Classic Arms website (www.bowenclassicarms.com). There, you can view every available custom revolver feature, their cost, estimated completion time, shipping instructions, and more. Some features are requested often enough that BCA offers them as a custom package. If you want a traditional printed catalog to review, just ask them to mail you one; price: $5.00 (BCA Corporation, 3512 Old Lowes Ferry Road, Louisville, TN 37777). And finally, if you're still not sure which features will create what you desire in the finished product, just give Hamilton Bowen a call 9 a.m. to 5 p.m. Eastern Standard Time (865.984.3583).

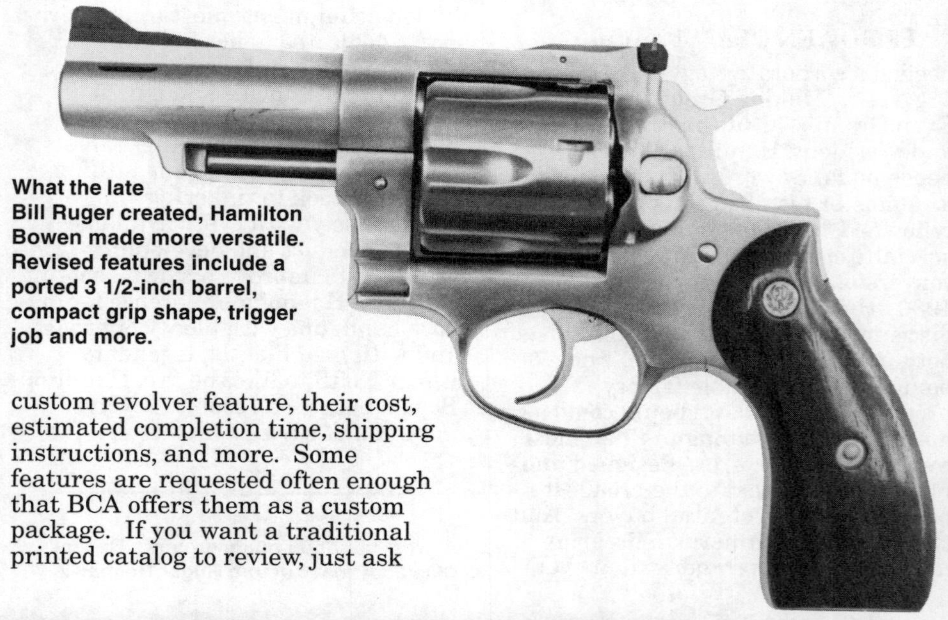

What the late Bill Ruger created, Hamilton Bowen made more versatile. Revised features include a ported 3 1/2-inch barrel, compact grip shape, trigger job and more.

By the way, Hamilton Bowen isn't just a master custom revolversmith, he's an accomplished published author. I probably have 200 firearms books in my personal library, including most of the classics dating back to the early days of such publications in the U.S. However, I was most pleased to add Hamilton Bowen's fine *The Custom Revolver* to my collection. Full of excellent photos and detailed-but-easy-reading text on the subject, Mr. Bowen's unique insight into the ins-and-outs of the custom revolver brings the topic to life. It's hard to imagine any handgunner pouring through the 300+ hardback pages without wanting their own custom Bowen classic.

Hamilton Bowen can start with any sound single- or double-action revolver as long as the original parts needed for the project are in serviceable condition. For my situation, there was no question as to where to start... Ruger's robust 44 Magnum double-action Redhawk revolver in stainless steel. *[FYI: The firm of Sturm, Ruger & Company does not in any way condone the alteration of any of their products after they leave their factories. At the very least, doing so will void the factory warranty. Any and all risks associated with the alteration of their products are borne by other parties].* While the single- and double-action trigger pulls on the original Redhawk were quite acceptable for a standard production gun, that was the obvious place to start the customization process. Hamilton Bowen offers a crisp 3-1/2 to 4 lb. single-action trigger pull that is creep-free, as well as a glassy-smooth DA trigger cycle with reduced trigger/main spring pressure. Custom alterations were also made to maximize firing pin protrusion for increased ignition reliability.

The forward edge of the standard Ruger Redhawk cylinder is efficiently squared-off. Nothing critically wrong with that, but this makes the revolver harder to holster and increases holster wear. One of the more subtle touches offered by Hamilton Bowen is beveling or "rounding-off" the outside leading edges of the cylinder as found on pre-war Colt Single Action Army revolvers. The chamfering may be more aesthetic than essential, but I knew it was a feature I wanted on my custom Bowen Redhawk. I also had the headspace and cylinder "endshake" set to minimum tolerances on the revised Redhawk, and the barrel-to-cylinder gap minimized to boost performance.

Next up was needed attention to the barrel. Standard Ruger Redhawk barrel lengths are 5-1/2 and 7-1/2 inches. The shorter of the two provides an excellent all-round length with excellent balance. The 7 1/2-inch tube makes for a fine primary hunting handgun, especially effective when mounted with a handgun scope. The shortest barrel BCA recommends for the Redhawk is 3-1/2 inches; that solved that. A 2-vent Mag-Na-Port recoil reduction system was applied to the business end of the barrel, greatly dampening felt recoil and allowing swifter follow-up shots. If you've never tried the Mag-Na-Port system, you should. The more powerful the load you shoot, and the more often you shoot it, the more you'll appreciate this little invention. Still concentrating on the barrel, a custom ramp front sight with extra height (.040) was installed, which can be removed/replaced with an Allen wrench. Finally, a roll stamp was added to the right side of the barrel below the caliber designation… "BOWEN CLASSIC ARMS CORP".

With all the above custom touches expertly applied, the "remodeled" Redhawk would represent a fine piece of heavy-duty, big-bore hardware. But, there was still too much bulk for my taste. The Redhawk's large, square-butt gripframe needed work. So, Hamilton Bowen creatively turned the square-butt frame into a compact, efficient round-butt. Not only was the metal gripframe altered, but the handsome original Brazilian rosewood grip panels were also custom-fitted to the gripframe, making the match an exact one. And whether firing heavy loads or enjoying an extended shooting session, you'll quickly appreciate a perfect grip-to-gripframe fit!

Next up, it was time to test fire the new creation. Quite honestly, I was so pleased with my Bowen Classic Arms Ruger Redhawk conversion I gathered-up every brand and type of 44 Special and 44 Magnum ammunition I had on-hand. Among the test products were the following, as reflected in the accompanying chart. Working through the alphabet, included were two Black Hills 44 Magnum cartridges utilizing jacketed hollowpoint (JHP) bullets; one 240 grains and the other a 300-grain product. CCI/Blazer rounds included a 200-grain 44 Special and a

Performance Chart

Brand	Ctg.	Bullet Wt (gr.)/Type	Velocity (Fps.)*	Group Size (Ins.)**
Black Hills	44 Mag.	240/JHP	1110	1.47
Black Hills	44 Mag.	300/JHP	1008	1.25
CCI/Blazer	44 Spl.	200/JHP	775	1.56
CCI/Blazer	44 Mag.	240/JHP	1095	1.8
CCI/ShotShell	44 Spl/ 44 Mag.	140 pellets/ #9 shot	1000***	56 hits/ 8" circle****
Federal/Power-Shok	44 Mag.	180 /JHP	1460	2.02
Remington/Core-Lokt	44 Mag.	275/JHP	1065	1.7
SPEER/GoldDot	44 Spl.	200/ JHP	822	2.3
SPEER/GoldDot	44 Mag.	210/JHP	1250	2.0
Winchester/Super-X	44 Spl.	200/STHP	799	1.5
Winchester/Super-X	44 Mag.	210/STHP	1293	1.62
Winchester/USA	44 Mag.	240/JSP	1033	1.53
Winchester/Supreme	44 Mag.	250/JHP	1006	1.41

JHP = Jacketed hollowpoint
STHP = SilverTip hollowpoint
JSP = Jacketed soft point

* Shooting Chrony chronograph used to determine velocity. Equipment placed 8 feet from revolver muzzle.
** Average of 5, 5-shot groups fired at 25 yards from solid rest. Group size measured from center-to-center of two widest shots.
*** Factory data. Don't try this at home!
**** Fired 8 feet from target

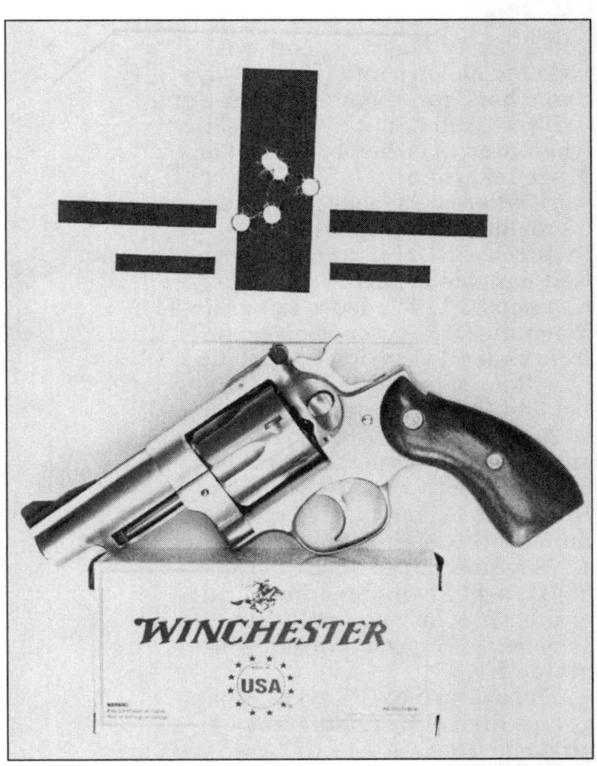

At 25 yards from a solid rest, the Bowen-converted Ruger Redhawk is an excellent performer. Best performing 44 Magnum cartridges tested were Black Hills' jacketed 300-grain jacketed hollowpoints.

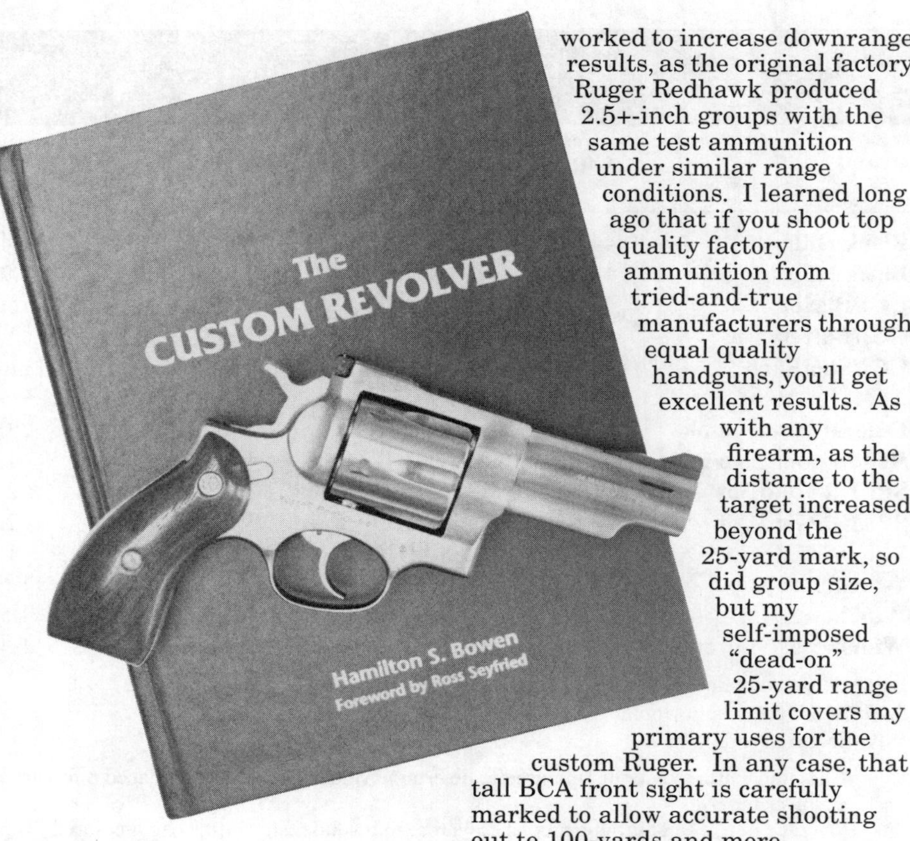

Hamilton Bowen's book on custom revolvers is a mouth-watering look at all aspects of the subject. Both color and b&w photos abound.

worked to increase downrange results, as the original factory Ruger Redhawk produced 2.5+-inch groups with the same test ammunition under similar range conditions. I learned long ago that if you shoot top quality factory ammunition from tried-and-true manufacturers through equal quality handguns, you'll get excellent results. As with any firearm, as the distance to the target increased beyond the 25-yard mark, so did group size, but my self-imposed "dead-on" 25-yard range limit covers my primary uses for the custom Ruger. In any case, that tall BCA front sight is carefully marked to allow accurate shooting out to 100-yards and more.

Thoroughly pleased with my Bowen Classic Arms Ruger Redhawk 44 Magnum conversion, I needed a top quality custom belt holster to comfortably carry the stubby sidearm, which weighs a stout 3 pounds loaded. William T. Tucker, owner of Tucker Gunleather, started making fine working leather long ago for fellow lawmen who weren't satisfied with available factory leathergoods. Today, Tucker's Houston-based shop creates a wide range of models hand-crafted from the best materials. For my custom Ruger Redhawk, I wanted enough leather to effectively cover the working parts of the big sixgun, an important feature when navigating the rough thorny terrain of south or west Texas. For comfort, I needed something to distribute the heavy load and keep it from shifting on the belt. Finally, I appreciate a new holster I can use almost immediately. Far too many leathergoods I receive require stuffing with shop rags for weeks just to break them in enough to even start working the gun fully into the holster, much less putting them to serious use.

I selected a "pancake-style" Tucker holster for my project. The results were all I'd hoped for, and what I've come to expect from every Tucker-made piece of leather. A tension screw behind the triggerguard, adjusted

240-grain 44 Magnum, both with jacketed hollowpoints. I've always found handgun shotshells useful, and CCI's 44-caliber offering is effective when used in either 44 Special or 44 Magnum cylinders. If you live or work where poisonous snakes can be a problem to your health or your livestock, CCI's ShotShells are the best possible medicine *(beware of ricochets!)*. I included a 180-grain 44 Magnum JHP Power-Shok round from Federal Cartridge Company plus Remington's 275-grain Core-Lokt 44 Magnum round. Next up were SPEER/GoldDot shells… a 200-grain 44 Special and 210-grain 44 Magnum, both with JHP bullets. From Winchester, I tested a 200-grain Super-X SilverTip hollowpoint, their 44 Magnum Super-X® 210-grain STHP, a 44 Magnum jacketed 240-grain soft point and finally, the Winchester Supreme with a 250-grain JHP.

The average-of-the-average of all groups fired with 12 different *products (leaving the CCI ShotShells out of the mix)* could be covered with the blunt end of a Mexican lime… 1.68 inches. The custom features applied by Bowen Classic Arms

A great custom handgun deserves the best in custom leather… a natural tan Tucker Gunleather pancake-style belt model with its own custom features.

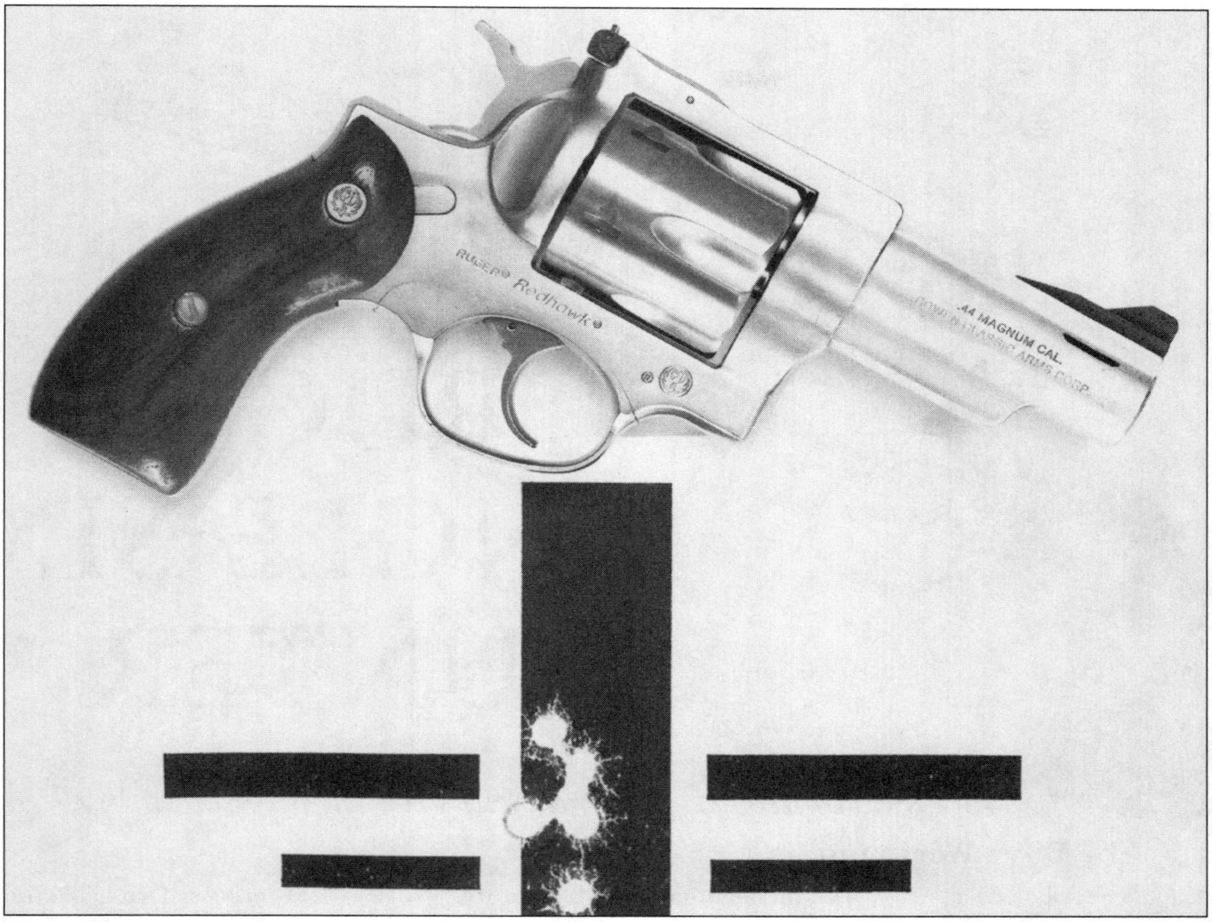

As a home defense and/or car gun, the Bowen Ruger Redhawk Conversion performed best with Winchester hollowpoint SilverTip 44 Special cartridges.

with the small provided Allen wrench, allows me to keep the big Ruger secure but readily available when needed. This is especially important as a handgun settles-in with regular use. And when that hunting expedition finds you needing to go to town for supplies, the Tucker pancake holster makes it possible to effectively conceal the largest of beltguns. Whether you need a practical Texas-style holster/belt/magazine carrier for your pet full-size 45 auto or something smaller, Terry Tucker will provide you with practical designs developed from decades of hands-on experience. You can find Tucker products on the worldwide web, at: www.TuckerGunleather.com. When you're ready to place your order you can do so directly through the website or by phone: (1.800.308.6628).

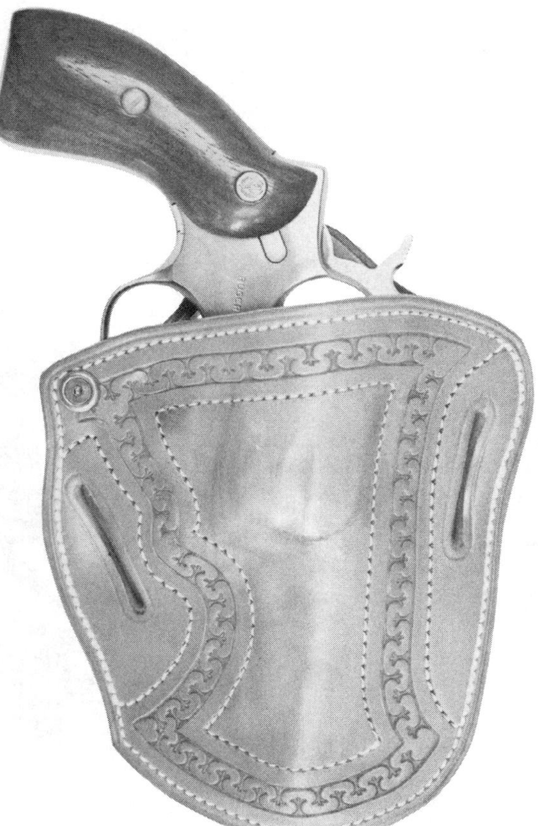

Custom Tucker pancake-style holster with special features to match Hamilton Bowen's custom Ruger Redhawk conversion.

When this project started, I was looking for a heavy-duty sixgun for farm and ranch carry, whether bouncing around in a Jeep or on foot in rough terrain where working cowboys still wear chaps to protect against thorny Texas terrain. Lots of things can happen out there, some good and some bad. A top quality heavy-duty handgun, customized for your specific needs, can be a great tool and comfort. I couldn't be happier with the Bowen Classic Arms Ruger Redhawk conversion or my one-of-a-kind custom Tucker pancake holster. But my BCA Ruger Redhawk conversion doesn't just get belt carry in the great outdoors. It has since become my "house gun" and my primary "car gun" when traveling, in both cases loaded with Winchester 44 Special SilverTip hollowpoints. So if your handgunning palate demands the sophistication of a custom-crafted revolver, you won't go wrong with the services of Hamilton Bowen and Bowen Classic Arms. •

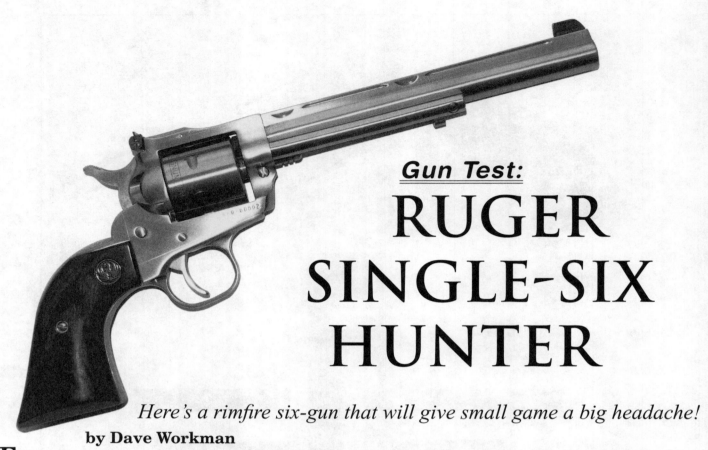

Gun Test:

RUGER SINGLE-SIX HUNTER

Here's a rimfire six-gun that will give small game a big headache!

by Dave Workman

From the moment I advised HANDGUNS Editor Ken Ramage that I would be securing one of the first available working models of the new Ruger Single-Six Hunter revolver, he began sort of an Internet drool, and in retrospect, he had every right to do so.

Ramage confided to me that he was seriously considering acquiring one of these new guns after having examined it at the 2004 Shooting, Hunting and Outdoor Trade (SHOT) Show in Las Vegas. One look at it and a handgun-hunting devotee will immediately figure out why.

This handsome stainless steel single-action wheelgun – available in either 17 HMR (Hornady Magnum Rimfire) or as a convertible in 22LR/22WMR – is a winner. One cannot help but gaze slowly over this new Ruger rimfire: from the muzzle with its recessed crown, back along that heavier 7 1/2-inch barrel with its front sight blade sporting a brass bead, to the adjustable rear sight, and down along the beautifully contrasting, smooth hardwood laminated grips. It is simply impressive, one of those "love at first sight" kinds of things.

My test model *(SN 880-00862)* came in a rush from the Ruger factory in New Hampshire, where it had been somewhat speedily put in running order because of a rather tight deadline I was facing. My biggest fear was that the well-balanced sixgun would arrive during a period of torrential Pacific Northwest rain, thus making it pretty tough for outdoor testing. Not to worry. While the Sun gods didn't necessarily shine down upon my shooting pit at the Snoqualmie Valley Rifle Club range about 30 miles east of Seattle, neither did the Rain gods provide one of their seasonal deluges to muck up my evaluation.

Give the folks at Ruger their due. This is *NOT* just another Single Six. The Hunter fully deserves its "handle," because it is an accurate instrument, well-balanced and rugged. That much I established by running quite a bit of 22 LR ammunition down the bore, while sticking to Winchester 22 Magnums to see just what this firearm can do when charged with full-house loads. I was not disappointed.

While the 22-caliber entry is rifled with a 1:14-inch twist, that 17 HMR version is cut with a 1:7-inch twist. The Single-Six Hunter hits the scale at about 44 ounces empty.

Of course the Hunter features Ruger's time-proven transfer bar firing pin mechanism. Its stainless finish is offset by the dark gloss black rear adjustable sight and front sight, which is set into the top rib not by a lateral dovetail, but rather from the muzzle back about 3/4-inch, and held in with what appears to be a detent pin. Those gray-black grips also provide an eye-catching

Top of frame is inscribed with the "Single-Six Hunter" logo just ahead of the adjustable rear sight.

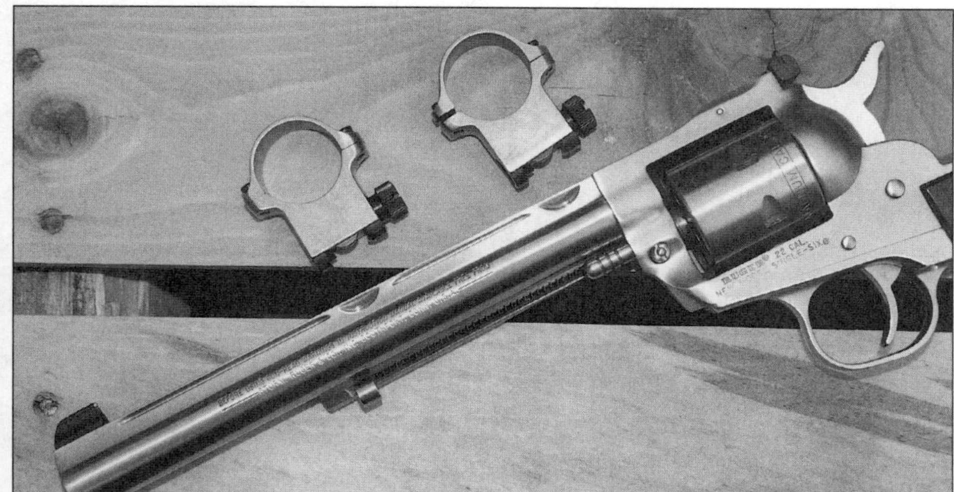

Each Single-Six Hunter comes with scope rings, and the solid rib along the barrel is notched to accept these rings.

contrast, and they are nicely finished and, in my case at least, they seemed to "marry" quickly with the palm of my gun hand.

A quick word about that rear sight. Unlike my two Blackhawks with their square notch rear sights, this one features a V-notch with a vertical white line centered at the bottom. This is designed to immediately bring the eye to focus and center the front bead right at the top of that vertical line at the point of the notch. It seems to naturally draw your eye to the sight.

This new Single-Six wears a brushed non-glare finish, and the barrel has a solid rib along the entire top, which adds critical weight, giving this gun a very solid feel in the hand. The rib is grooved to eliminate any glare when using the metallic sights, and there are slots for Ruger rings, so that scopes may be mounted. More about that in a minute. Ruger, incidentally, supplies medium rings with this revolver.

As on previous Single-Six convertible models, on which the traditional barrel length has stretched to only 6-1/2 inches, the 22 LR cylinder is fluted, while the 22 Magnum cylinder is unfluted and etched around the entire rear with the notation: "22 Win. Magnum Cal."

Out of the box, the action on my test piece was smooth, with the typical two clicks to reach full cock. There was the slightest bit of creep before the trigger letoff, but not enough to throw the sight picture awry. I found that the revolver, thanks to its weight-forward feel with that long barrel, came back on target quickly, and re-cocking for follow-up shots was fast.

The trigger is smooth, while the hammer is grooved but not checkered. This made cocking for quick second shots easy on the trigger finger and thumb.

Overall fit, finish and function were what one would expect from a working handgun, and whatever else the Single-Six Hunter happens to be, it is most assuredly a workhorse.

My test piece shot low out of the box with Long Rifles, and I found I had to elevate the rear sight considerably to bring the front sight up to where I could put them in the black consistently. The Hunter also shot to the right initially, so I moved the sight over several clicks. This pattern continued when I changed cylinders and shifted to magnums, and I wound up the first part of the test with the rear sight cranked up pretty far, and left of center.

But once the sights were adjusted, accuracy settled in to the point where I am confident this six-shooter would work magic on rabbits, squirrels, raccoons, coyotes: any game, predator or varmint you might want to tackle. It strikes me that the Single-Six Hunter might serve Alaska grouse hunters well, or those in any other state that allows fool hens to be taken with rifles or handguns. I've run across people who hunt blue grouse – called "hooters" in southeast Alaska – with a scoped 22 pistol, typically a Ruger semi-auto. They like the challenge of popping a grouse in the head with a rimfire, and no revolver is any more suited to that game than the new Ruger Hunter.

In my home state of Washington, shooting grouse in this manner is also legal, and something of a tradition. Alas, the test occurred at the wrong time of year to allow me a quick trek into the nearby hills to try the Hunter out on live game.

Compared to author's Blackhawk, the Single-Six hunter is a dandy hunting handgun.

Specifications:

Manufacturer: Sturm Ruger, 200 Ruger Road, Prescott, AZ 86301, (520) 541-8820 / www.ruger-firearms.com
Model: Single-Six Hunter
Finish: Non-glare stainless steel
Barrel length: 7-1/2 inches
Caliber: 22 LR / 22 WMR or 17 HMR
Capacity: Six rounds
Weight: 40 oz. (approx.)
Grips: Smooth gray-black laminated hardwood
Suggested Retail: $599 for the 17 HMR, $650 for the 22 LR/22WMR

None of the Long Rifle rounds I tried shot better than any of the others, which is neither good nor bad. That 7 1/2-inch barrel seems to wring the most out of a rimfire, leaving me favorably impressed. I loaded up with CCI Sub-Sonic loads using 40-grain lead bullets, which turned in the slowest speed of all at 982.3 fps with the Chrony Delta chronograph set eight feet from the muzzle.

I had a handful of Winchester Long Rifles, also topped with 40-grain lead pills, and they clocked an average of 1019 fps, with a top velocity of 1050 fps, and that's nothing to frown about. It is more than enough to put meat in the bag, or take care of some predator.

However, the best velocity I got from the 22 LR ammo was with the Federal lead hollowpoints. They turned in a very respectable 1228 fps average velocity over the screens, with a high speed of 1251 fps. Admittedly, that got my undivided attention, especially since shot after shot landed in the black.

Considering that the 22-caliber Long Rifle cartridge is pretty predictable from one to the other, and even from one brand to another, there is every reason to expect that whatever brand one selects, be it Federal, Winchester, Remington, CCI or something else, he or she will be satisfied with the performance.

When I started sailing magnum hollowpoints over the Chrony, they scooted out at an eyebrow-raising 1742 fps on the average, with the highest speed recorded at an impressive 1778 fps. Here, again, there really is nothing unique about one brand of magnums over another. I've never found one brand to be a worse performer than another. They all shoot very well from any firearm I've ever used that is chambered for the cartridge. Unless the barrel is bent or a sight is loose or out of alignment, the 22 WMR is a flat-shooting, straight-shooting cartridge that gets the job done. It will get the job done in the Single-Six Hunter, too.

Workman's selection of test ammunition was deliberately limited, but representative of the kinds of choices most small game handgunners will pick. Ammo from CCI, Winchester and Federal all performed superbly.

While shooting the Long Rifle rounds was almost a non-event in the recoil and muzzle blast department, that changed when I switched cylinders and started capping off magnums. The report was noticeably louder, and there was a genuine snap to the recoil, though hardly in the realm of unmanageable or uncomfortable. As I noted earlier, the barrel on the Hunter is heavier because of the solid rib along the top, and the additional length. Those factors combined to tame the recoil and make this sixgun a real pleasure to shoot.

Accuracy was maintained when I started shooting at Birchwood Casey Shoot-N-C targets for photographs.

Front sight blade features a brass bead that really shows up.

Rear sight notch is a "V"-cut with a white post. Notice Ruger's transfer bar firing pin.

Ballistics:

Cartridge	Bullet Weight/Type	Velocity/fps
Federal 22 Long Rifle High Velocity	40 RNL	1228
CCI Sub Sonic	40 RNL	982.3
Winchester	40 RNL	1019
Winchester 22 WMR	34 JHP	1742

These targets don't lie. The shooter with plenty of time to practice with this new Ruger model should be able to narrow his groups quite well. With an 8 5/8-inch sight radius on my test revolver, measured from the rear sight to the front bead, accuracy can only be enhanced.

To prove the point, I tossed out an empty soda pop can and started plinking away at it. Having done this over the years just for fun, a long time ago it occurred to me that any handgun with which I could consistently punch holes in a can would definitely serve me well when applied to a bigger target.

Loading and unloading is the same as with any other "new" model Single-Six. Just open the loading gate and the cylinder will rotate. Cases are ejected with a push on the ejector rod, which is long enough to fully kick out magnum-length empties.

One thing I noticed after firing less than a half-box of the magnums was that a couple of the chambers began fouling pretty badly, to the point where it was tough to chamber those long cartridges. This did not happen when I was using the Long Rifle cylinder, and from one loading to the next, live ones went in easily and the empty cases ejected just as smoothly.

This is important, because of the cartridges do not go all the way into the chamber, the cylinder will not

Ruger stood up to Workman's "acid test," bonking a tin can at various ranges as it bounced around the range. Author figures if you can hit a target that size on the move, you can plug anything bigger!

turn because of the tight tolerances between the frame and the rear of the cylinder, even though the chamber is recessed to allow the case rim to seat flush. There is no reason to despair, of course. Just keep the cylinder clean, and the Hunter should run perfectly.

I also discovered that the breech end of the barrel got fouled after barely more than 50 rounds, but here, again, that's nothing to be concerned with. It did not worry me, because I just kept on shooting. My strong recommendation is to take this revolver out of the box brand new, give it a bath in Hoppe's No. 9, wipe it down clean and shoot it. Then shoot it some more.

Taking this revolver apart for cleaning is a cinch. Clear all the chambers to make certain the cylinder is empty, then release the cylinder pin by pressing the retaining cross pin to the right. The cylinder pin comes all the way out, and the cylinder will literally roll out into your hand when the loading gate is open. Thanks to today's abundance of aerosol solvents, cleanup will go fast.

While aerosols are adequate, I still prefer getting into the tight little places with a small nylon bristle brush. These things really take away the fouling. And make no mistake, any stainless steel handgun, be it a revolver like the Hunter, or a semi-auto, needs some maintenance. This new Ruger model is a quality piece of equipment, and it should last a couple of lifetimes with proper maintenance. Clean off the crud after a shooting session, add a drop of oil here and there, store it properly, and your investment will pay off when you need it the most.

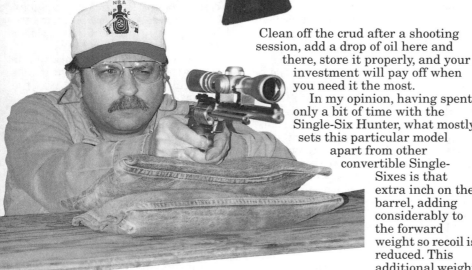

Ahhh, now *THIS* is a smallbore hunting handgun! Workman topped the Single-Six Hunter with what he considers a superb scope, the 2-6x32mm long eye-relief model from Bushnell.

Workman concentrates on those crosshairs while banging away off a sandbag rest. He found the Ruger, topped with the Bushnell scope, to be remarkably accurate at 25 yards.

In my opinion, having spent only a bit of time with the Single-Six Hunter, what mostly sets this particular model apart from other convertible Single-Sixes is that extra inch on the barrel, adding considerably to the forward weight so recoil is reduced. This additional weight also enables a shooter to hold the gun more steadily, and that improves the ability to stay on target.

While the Single-Six Hunter is longer than standard models, it would not be out of place in a belt holster. It is not too heavy to be packing around on your hip. For those who mount a scope on this gun, a shoulder holster is probably the best bet.

The addition of a long eye-relief pistol scope to this handgun will make it even heftier, thus counteracting any recoil one might expect from the magnums. When I knew the gun was in transit, I contacted Barbara Skinner at Bushnell and had quick delivery of a 2-6x32mm handgun scope, the Elite 3200 with a satin nickel finish that matches up quite well with the Ruger's stainless steel. Having had some experience over the years with scopes on handguns, it is my opinion that Bushnells are superb. I had used one earlier on a big Taurus 44 Magnum Silhouette revolver, and it took the heavy recoil in stride. Any scope that can stand up to round after punishing round from a big-bore magnum will handle the comparatively mild jolt of a 22 WMR or even lesser 22 LR.

A second visit to the range proved that Ruger's Single-Six Hunter reaches its full potential with a scope on top. Once the glass is adjusted and the gun is zeroed, there is nothing holding the Ruger six-gun back. It positively shines.

I sighted the revolver in at 25 yards late one afternoon, and after about a dozen rounds to click the crosshairs into zero, I began punching holes. Pretty soon, I was perforating the X-ring steadily. I happened to have a Shoot-N-C prairie dog target and I put a dozen rounds through one ragged hole.

The added weight of that scope removed any semblance of recoil, making this one incredibly comfortable handgun to shoot. Off a sandbag rest using a two-hand hold, I simply could not miss. I am convinced that this revolver-scope combination would be the ultimate bad nightmare for rabbits in my neighborhood.

My advice to anyone who buys a Single-Six Hunter is to plink with it using iron sights if you prefer, but for get-down-to-it serious hunting, buy a good quality scope and spend the range time to zero this revolver. You will wind up with a handgun that lives up to its name. This new Ruger is every bit a hunter, as people who buy it will learn in a hurry. ●

Cast Bullet Accuracy

in Production 45 ACP Handguns

by Mike Thomas

MANY CUSTOM GUNSMITHS and small shops devote considerable time to building, modifying, refining, customizing, and accurizing handguns chambered for the 45 ACP cartridge. Some revolver work is performed, but most endeavors are centered around John Browning's original 1911 semi-automatic pistol design. Upon completion, it is a reasonable expectation that such handguns should be *(and likely are)* quite accurate.

Despite the popularity of highly modified 45s, there are many shooters that use otherwise plain factory models straight from the box. These individuals may not shoot in formal competition, but many are serious enthusiasts and handloaders with a distinct penchant for accuracy. In the gun press, "plain" guns often take a back seat in comparison to more glamorous and expensive custom counterparts. That need not be the case since many out-of-the-box factory 45s are quite accurate and function reliably "as-is." There are published reports to the contrary. Some indeed have factual basis while others are too often merely armchair conjecture. Summarily, the entire issue is clouded despite the fact that the truth is probably buried in there someplace. It makes useful interpretation decidedly difficult.

Handguns used in cast bullet accuracy evaluation: *(clockwise from top left)* Colt Series 70, Colt Custom, Springfield Armory, Springfield Armory, Smith & Wesson Model 625 *(center)*.

A large percentage of serious 45 ACP enthusiasts use cast bullets. I have no idea what that percentage might be and neither does anyone else. Talk to handloaders who make up their own 45 ACP cartridges, however, and more than a few will admit to using cast bullets. There are several reasons for this, most of them being the ones so often cited by those who shoot cast bullets regularly. In my opinion, the most important reason for cast bullet use in the 45 ACP cartridge is the reason that receives the least mention, and that is total compatibility. Now what sort of double talk is that?

From the handloader's standpoint, the cartridge is one of the most forgiving rounds available for use in any handgun, be it pistol or revolver. A high velocity 45 ACP cast bullet load may be quite accurate simply because "high velocity" with this cartridge is seldom more than 1000 feet-per-second (fps), even with the lighter bullets. Leading is rarely a problem at such velocities unless bullet alloy is incredibly soft or bullet fit is extremely bad. Fortunately, such problems are encountered infrequently. Bullet lubricants are not a critical factor. Practically any lube will provide satisfactory performance. I've tried many different bullets, loads and lubricants. If I have ever run across a lube that did not work well in the 45 ACP, I don't recall what it was. Another aspect of compatibility is the fact that cast bullets will at least equal–and often exceed–the accuracy level of similar jacketed bullets. Sure, it takes some developmental work to achieve this but not nearly what is required with other handgun rounds capable of higher velocities.

There is a long list of cast bullet designs from which one may choose. If not a bullet caster also, the 45 ACP handloader can select from a variety of commercially cast bullets. These are available at prices often substantially below those of jacketed bullets. I do not use the commercial bullets, preferring to cast my own. I have read that some commercially cast bullets are much harder than need be for the 45 ACP. In defense of the commercial casters, a harder bullet will often feed more reliably than a soft one when used in a semi-automatic handgun. Accuracy may or may not suffer from using a bullet harder than necessary. It depends on the gun, the load, and that myriad of variables that handloaders are so often confronted with. I have tried my own hard bullets on a very limited basis. My conclusion is that they often work well and are accurate. Overall, however, bullets cast of wheelweight alloy work well and are accurate more often.

Most bullets intended for use in a 45 ACP firearm are sized to around .452-inch diameter, regardless of whether they are commercial bullets or of the homemade variety. I tried .454-inch bullets a number of years ago. From what I recall, there was little or no difference, accuracy-wise. However, a 45 ACP cartridge loaded with a .454-inch bullet may be too large in diameter to reliably chamber in some guns. Practical handloading wisdom would suggest that chamber pressure must be higher also, certainly a safety consideration with a near-maximum or maximum load.

After making claims as to the attributes of box-stock 45s and cast bullets, I suppose I should provide supporting testimony. For the results of this project to have any credence and real meaning for the author and readers, I felt it necessary to use a representative group of test pieces that included more than just one or two 45s. The following handguns were selected:

1. Colt Government Model, Series 70, blue, fixed sights.
2. Colt Custom, Series 80, stainless steel, adjustable rear sight *(limited edition model, virtually same gun as Gold Cup)*.
3. Springfield Armory 1911-A1 *(military specifications government model)*, Parkerized finish, fixed sights.
4. Springfield Armory 1911-A1, stainless steel, adjustable rear sight.
5. Smith & Wesson Model 625 double-action revolver, 3-inch barrel, stainless steel, adjustable rear sight.

The four 1911-type pistols all have standard 5-inch barrels.

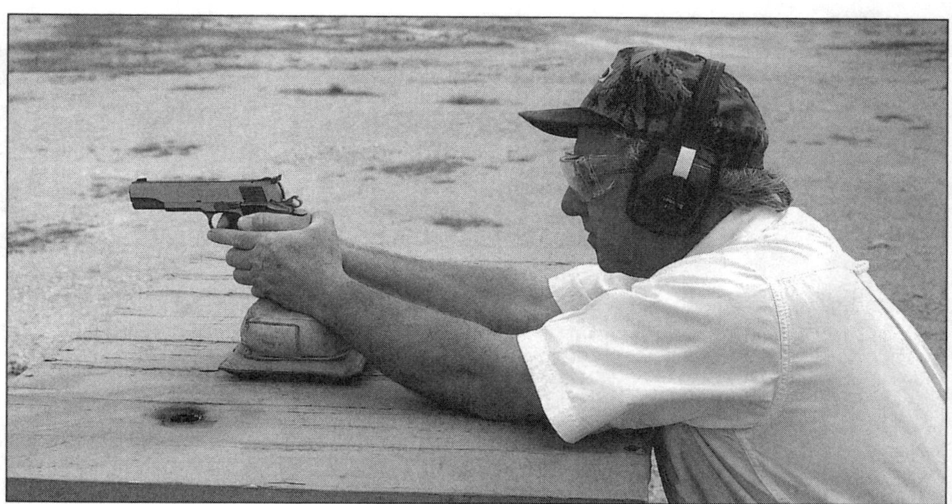

Five groups of five shots each were fired from a sandbag rest at 25 yards with each of the five handguns. Author is firing the Colt Custom, a Gold Cup equivalent.

Handloads

Working up individual "accuracy" loads for the guns was not done for several reasons. Such an undertaking would have consumed a great deal of time despite the fact that average group size figures would have been smaller than the actual figures obtained. Secondly, the purpose of this piece was not to develop 45 ACP load data. I have done that in the past, and many other writers have done the same. There is simply an abundance of data available from many sources, not the least of which are several currently published handloading manuals and brochures available from powder suppliers. No need *(or room)* to repeat all that here. As a matter of curiosity, I looked through the index card file where I have condensed my range notes for years. While I did not count the exact number of loads, it approaches *(or may exceed)* 150, using many powders and cast bullet designs ranging in weight from approximately 185 grains to 230 grains. As someone who cannot leave well enough alone, I am quite sure the list will be expanded in coming years. Lastly, a more stringent means of testing would insure an overall measure of objectivity that might be diluted if individual loads were developed for each handgun.

Loaded rounds: *(l-r)* Redding / SAECO #130, Redding / SAECO #069, RCBS 45-200-SWC, each loaded with 5 grains Winchester 231 powder.

Toward the end of this article, I will give brief descriptions of additional cast bullet designs that I have had ample experience with. Every design will shoot well. In fact, I have yet to find one 45 ACP cast bullet that could not be referred to as accurate, given proper load developmental work.

For the formal testing phase, three cast bullets with proven accuracy reputations were used. Of plain-base design, they were cast of wheelweight alloy from these moulds: Redding/SAECO #130, Redding/SAECO #069, and RCBS 45-200-SWC. In the author's experience, these bullets feed well in unmodified 1911s. Moreover, the styles are available from other mould manufacturers and commercial bullet casters.

Redding/SAECO #130 casts a short-nosed semi-wadcutter bullet of 189 grains. The bullet has a single wide lubrication groove. Overall cartridge length with this bullet was 1.190 inches. Redding/SAECO #069 is a very popular semi-wadcutter cone-nose design that is a virtual duplication of the original Hensley & Gibbs #68 design. Bullet weight is 203 grains. It has one wide lube groove. OAL with #069 was 1.25 inches. RCBS 45-200-SWC, another semi-wadcutter form, has two narrow lubrication grooves and nominally weighs in at 205 grains. The OAL with

Cast bullets used in evaluation: *(l-r)* Redding / SAECO #130, 189 grains, Redding / SAECO #069, 203 grains, RCBS 45-200-SWC, 205 grains.

Colt Gold Cup with custom work performed by Clark Custom Guns. A very accurate 45 for the shooter who demands an accuracy level greater than that provided by a production gun. Quite often, however, as pointed out in text, production handguns will satisfy the requirements of most shooters.

this bullet was 1.190 inches. I have included the overall cartridge lengths for the three bullets as a reference point. These could be varied slightly for whatever valid reason, but the OALs as listed work fine in a variety of 45 ACP handguns, not just the ones used for this article.

The author sized bullets to .452-inch using a Redding/SAECO lubricator-sizer. Two lubricants were used: NRA half-and-half formula Alox / beeswax *(as made and distributed by GAR for reloading)*, and Lyman Super Moly. Each was satisfactory and there was no discernible performance difference between the two. Handloads were assembled on an RCBS PRO 2000 progressive press using a Redding die set that included a taper crimp die. This die was adjusted to give a final crimp diameter in the .470/.471-inch range which works fine for the author. Some recommend a tighter crimp while others go to the max of .473-inch.

Loads with all bullets used 5 grains of Winchester 231 powder. Such loads are in the mild "target" realm, providing muzzle velocities in the 750-800 fps range. Winchester standard large pistol primers were used throughout testing, however, substituting CCI-300 (standard large pistol) primers seems to make no difference with these loads. Brass was mixed, though mostly Winchester, and all of it had been used for one or more firings.

Test firing was performed on the author's 25-yard range using a two-handed hold over a sandbag rest. Five groups of five rounds each were fired through each handgun with each of the three loads; 75 rounds per gun. Group size figures were averaged for every load in every gun. That information appears in the tables. During the firing sequence, any group affected by obvious shooter error *("pulling" a shot, for example)* was re-fired. All guns had clean bores at the commencement of testing. Light and normal powder fouling was removed with a dry bronze bore brush after about every 15 or 20 rounds. In retrospect, however, this procedure was unnecessary.

Test Results

What does an average group size tell us? It is an indication that the five test guns are relatively accurate, just as they are. That might surprise some, particularly persons who have been led to believe otherwise. For those who are accuracy-oriented, yet do not shoot in formal competition, the accuracy levels discussed herein may be perfectly adequate. An overall average group size of 2.93 inches is nothing to be sneered at. While it is basically a true statement that five custom 45s would be capable of better accuracy than the author's guns, the difference may not be all that much. With serious load development tailored for a particular

45 ACP Data Table

All loads: 5 grains Winchester 231 powder

	SAECO #130 189 grains/1.190"	SAECO #069 203 grains/1.25"	RCBS 45-200-SWC 205 grains/1.190"	Average each gun
1. Colt Gov't., Series 70	2.31"	2.50"	2.93"	2.58"
2. Colt Custom, Series 80	3.43"	2.43"	2.68"	2.85"
3. Spfld. Armory, 1911-A1	2.93"	3.00"	3.12"	3.02"
4. Spfld. Armory, 1911-A1	3.37"	3.06"	3.25"	3.23"
5. S&W Model 625 revolver	3.18"	3.31"	2.43"	2.97"
Average, each load	3.04"	2.86"	2.88"	

NOTES: All bullets cast of wheelweight alloy, sized to .452-inch diameter. Winchester Large Pistol primers. Mixed *(mostly Winchester)* brass had been fired at least once. Figures to right of bullet grain weights are overall cartridge lengths. Numbers in table represent the average of five groups of five shots each fired from a benchrest at 25 yards. All loads were safe in test guns. Common and accepted handloading safety practices are recommended for the duplication of loads. Refer to text material for additional information and specifications on firearms.

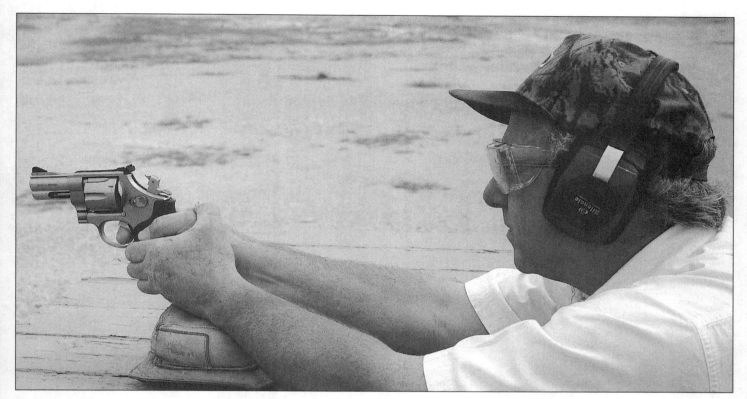

Author fires the Smith & Wesson Model 625 for group from the bench at 25 yards.

gun in the test bunch, average group size may shrink in the neighborhood of 10 to 15 percent. Little things like using one lot of one manufacturer's brass may make a difference as well. The key point to remember here is that we are referring to an accuracy improvement requiring no tuning or modification of the handgun.

There are 45 ACP handguns that, when bench-rested at 25 yards, will not group inside of six inches with the best of loads. At least, that is what I hear. Autoloader or revolver, these guns need work, perhaps major work. Fortunately, firearms such as these are not nearly as common as some would have us believe.

More 45 ACP Cast Bullet Designs

I have not tried them all and I doubt anyone else has. It is not my intention to slight any mould makers, but I can vouch only for the moulds I have used. There are other good mould designs not tested here that may be worth trying.

LEE #452-190-SWC makes a 192-grain semi-wadcutter with two lube grooves. Very little development work for accurate loads. Two lube grooves.

REDDING / SAECO #265 casts a 216-grain "hybrid" bullet with a semi-wadcutter body and round nose. One lube groove.

LYMAN #452374 weighs 220 grains and duplicates design features of the traditional and original "hardball" round-nose jacketed 45 ACP bullet. A longtime favorite and not generally considered a target bullet, it is quite accurate in many guns. One lube groove.

REDDING / SAECO #067 is a 230-grain truncated nose style. Feeds well in most guns. One lube groove.

RCBS #45-225-CAV weighs 233 grains. A truncated nose-style bullet, it will feed well in most guns. Manufacturer also recommends this bullet for the 45 Colt cartridge. Works well in that one, also. Two lube grooves. This is the heaviest bullet the author has used in the 45 ACP chambering.

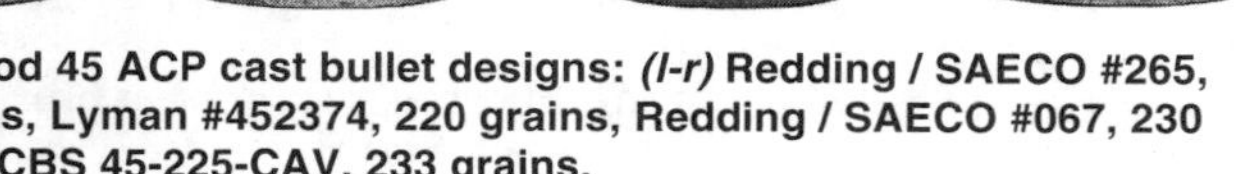

Other good 45 ACP cast bullet designs: ***(l-r)*** **Redding / SAECO #265, 216 grains, Lyman #452374, 220 grains, Redding / SAECO #067, 230 grains, RCBS 45-225-CAV, 233 grains.**

I'll mention a final observation that originates from both bewilderment and caution regarding cast bullet use in the 45 ACP cartridge. It may also apply to jacketed bullets, but my experience with them has been minimal. I have not found a slow-burning powder to date that provides consistently fine accuracy in this cartridge. There are several I have yet to try and I suppose that should be on my list of future projects. Many of us use progressive presses these days. With reasonable attention to safety, the chance of double-charging a case with a fast-burning powder is extremely remote. However, the possibility exists. An adequately slow-burning powder, in a charge weight of eight to ten grains, would eliminate the chance of an accidental overcharge. Something to consider… For the 45 ACP accuracy enthusiast, the use of cast bullet loads for target use *(and perhaps some types of hunting)* is a worthwhile endeavor that will provide lasting benefits far greater than the time and effort required for the initial load development work. At the very least, it is a practical alternative worth trying before going the "custom" route. •

Reliability Enhancements for the 1911

by Bob Campbell

SOME FEEL HANDGUN selection is an art, others a science. We realize handguns are individuals in performance and what pleases one shooter may not please the other. Just the same, a number of handguns give top-flight service and are capable of good performance in the hands of well-trained individuals. We all wish to have a reliable handgun, but there are those who play for high stakes on a weekly basis. These men and women take extraordinary care in selecting survival equipment. It behooves us to follow their lead in amount of testing and knowledge in order to make a trustworthy choice. We can look to the various law enforcement acquisition programs for help. A set of specifications is usually set up, that may read as follows:

Caliber	40 or larger
Action Type	Double-action only
Size	Mid-size frame, weighing no more than 35 ounces
Finish	Non-reflective corrosion resistant

(A western agency may not be so concerned with corrosion and, instead, concentrate on wear resistance. An agency with more training time may ignore the DAO.)

Maintaining reliability is fairly simple. Birchwood Casey is a major force in the author's toolbox.

The agencies then invite bids from the companies offering a handgun fitting the specifications.

Civilians have more choices. We can make both good and bad choices, and have only ourselves to answer to. My choice is the 1911 pistol. It may be a Colt or a Kimber—but it will be a 1911. I am satisfied with the reliability of the type, but I realize that some effort is required to maintain the degree of reliability I am happy with. Like many professionals, I would not give holster room to a handgun that would not go 500 trouble-free rounds without cleaning. On the other hand, a maintenance schedule that keeps the weapon clean and lubricated is important. With that in mind, I recently took a hard look at my pistols and the reason they are so reliable. My regimen has served me well for over 20 years.

As for my 1911s, it is no secret these pistols are the hands-down choice of professional handgunners. Our high-speed low-drag class seems to have rediscovered the 1911 after a brief flirtation with other types. I think it has something to do with actually needing and using the handgun…

My comments on maintaining the reliability of the 1911 can apply to most handguns, especially other Browning variants such as the High Power, CZ 75 and the Tokarev. These procedures are simple but vital. The 1911–as issued–is often reliable with any type of ammunition, but some demand hardball or round-nose ammunition only. Others can work well with slight modification. It is important to remember we tailor the ammunition to the gun, not vise-versa. You must decide whether you fight with the gun or the ammunition. Only complete reliability is acceptable.

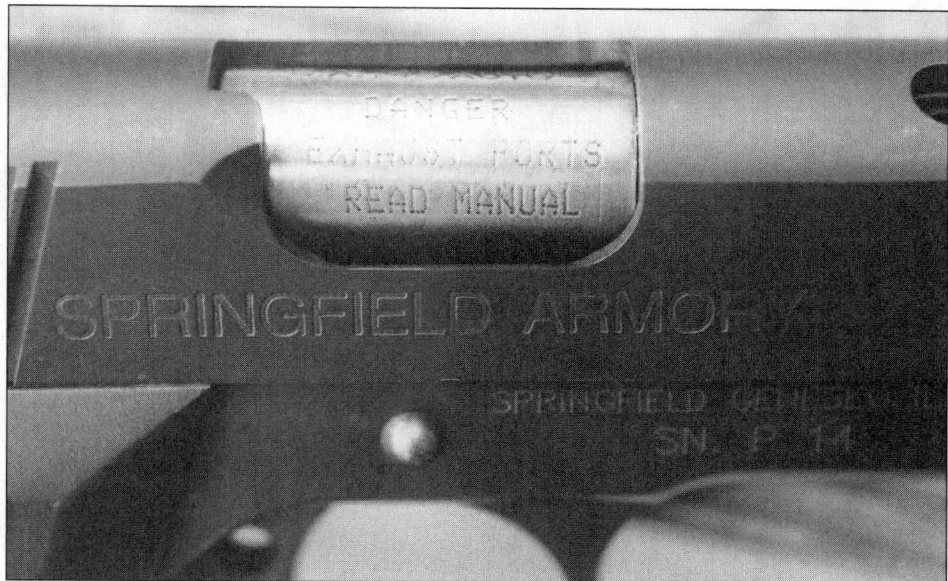

This Springfield exhibits a larger lowered ejection port, a considerable improvement over old production weapons.

Feed Reliability

I have a Mark IV Series 70 Colt that has always fed any bullet style. Others would not, and even Series 80 Colts sometimes choke on particularly odd bullet styles. Do not assume a small successful test with a bullet known for hanging on the feed ramp ensures the gun is reliable with all bullet styles. 1911s are too individualistic for that. I have seen a 45 Auto that fed short 200-grain JHPs *(notorious for feed difficulties)* brilliantly. But the gun jammed with Federal Hydra Shock bullets. Let reality be your guide. Most modern 1911s have a carefully radiused and polished feed ramp, and a smooth chamber. Narrower barrel ramps will feed hardball and nothing else with complete reliability. The original-type 1911 bumps the bullet nose across the feed ramp and into the chamber. A simple tactic is to change to Wilson Combat magazines. These magazines present the bullet in a different attitude, moving the bullet nose more directly into the chamber. Often, this is all that is needed to enhance feed reliability with hollow-point bullets. This more or less eliminates the problems caused by the bump between the feed ramp and the chamber. Still, a good polishing of the feed ramp, with care not to change the feed angle itself, is good insurance. It is important to carefully polish the upper barrel hood as well, as this ledge can capture the sharp edge of a flat-nose bullet.

When polishing the feed ramp, keep in mind that the lower case head of the 45 ACP cartridge is unsupported. This is not normally a problem with the relatively low pressures exhibited by the 45 ACP, but could become a problem if too much of the barrel is relieved.

The same is true of polishing the chamber. The bullet takes a bit of a bump in the top of the chamber before chambering, so the chamber, as well as the feed ramp, should be smooth. As is often the case, less is more, so polish in moderation. I have several 1911s with feed ramps as smooth and polished as quicksilver. You can do it quite nicely with time and care, or a custom pistol shop can do the work.

Author has used clean, reliable hardball ammunition, such as this type from Magtech, for reliability testing.

When a gunsmith such as Don Williams of the Action Works does a reliability package, he is not performing magic but instead painstaking labor well worth the modest tariff. A trick I have learned is to polish the locking lugs of the barrel for smooth function. Not normally considered part of feed reliability, this is simply another component of the big picture.

With all due respect to the various craftsmen, some of the Norinco guns and various foreign-produced copies were once pretty rugged to say the least, while a couple of United States-produced clones would have shamed Yankee factories. Some pistols have tool marks too deep for a complete mirror polish, and are too rough for reliability with anything but hardball or hardball-like ammunition.

When moving to the slide, I am glad to find almost all new production 1911s have a scalloped, wide, or lowered ejection port. My Rock Island Armory 45 is true GI with a small slide window, the 38 Super from the same maker has a wide ejection port. This port makes for much easier administrative handling. The original slide window is adequate for ejection but made unloading the weapon clumsy.

The breechface in most Colts is well polished, with little need for attention. Some pistols have a rougher breechface that can grab the cartridge head and result in a failure to feed. I worked on a "Frankenstein" gun of mismatched parts not long ago that suffered from a combination of a rough breechface and a weak extractor. It was a bear to repair but I

This Rock Island Armory 45 is a GI-type 1911A1 with many good features.

was able to do so. Please note that many of the problems we are discussing will never arise with a new Colt, Kimber or Springfield—but are within the realm of problems that can be encountered in any brand of old, worn 1911.

The extractor is a point of extraordinary significance in the 1911. The extractor controls feeding, chambering, and extraction. It is a piece of strong spring steel that must be of top quality. The 45 ACP does not headspace on the extractor as is sometimes stated; the 45 ACP headspaces correctly on the case mouth. However, ammunition that is too short or of poor quality will headspace only on the extractor and poor accuracy is normally the result. There are several steps in polishing and beveling the extractor that were once widely used by pistolsmiths. They work well, but in the last ten years or so my course of action has been to replace the extractor with a high-quality unit from Wilson Combat or Ed Brown. This is good, but when the 1911 gives up on Friday and the match is Saturday–and the parts bag does not contain an extractor–you have to repair your own. It is sometimes necessary to modify an extractor. An example is modifying an extractor to work with both 9mm Luger and 38 Super brass. The difference in dimensions (.405-inch breechface versus .386-inch for the 9mm) makes the extractor's ability to work with either cartridge problematical. But fitting a 9mm barrel to the 38 Super is commonly undertaken for economy. It is possible to modify the extractor to produce reliable function with both cartridges.

This extractor tool has proven a Godsend in many of the author's home repairs.

Yet another problem reared its head of late. I was working with a compact version of the Charles Daly 45 when the extractor proved incompatible with a certain cartridge case. Since I have a few thousand of these cases, the gun had to work with them! The extractor was worn and I would have replaced it–but it was not standard 1911. It was shorter than anything I had in stock. KBI has a good service department and they offered to repair the gun at no charge. Still, time is valuable. I was happy to have a Weigand extractor tool on hand. I placed the extractor in the tool, applied proper tension, and the part was good as new. I also recut the claw for sharper function.

A number of new 1911 designs have an external extractor. This is supposed to be the superior design, and the claw types are certainly strong. But they have more parts–extractor, spring, and retaining pin on most designs. The jury is out on that one but we will have standard internal extractors for some time. With care, they will last a lifetime but should be inspected for wear at least once every year, or every 5000 rounds. My Weigand tool has a small gauge, used with an RCBS trigger-pull weight scale, which measures extractor tension. This is an invaluable tool that allows checking the extractor without removing it from the gun.

While working in the slide, we consider the most overlooked problem source of all, the firing pin channel and spring. I have never broken a 1911 firing pin but it can happen.

The firing pin channel can become clogged with powder residue, or even small brass shavings.

The firing pin spring of the 1911 is an important safety component. In pre-firing pin block 1911 pistols, this spring prevents the firing pin from running forward and striking the cartridge primer if the hammer of the gun is struck. Hammer down on a live chamber is a more common carry than we like to admit, and the firing pin spring keeps us safe. The firing pin spring is easily overcome by the force of a flying hammer, but not if the gun is dropped. Tests show that a 1911 dropped muzzle down just might allow the firing pin to take a forward run against the firing pin spring, firing the gun. Extra-strength firing pin springs prevent this problem. However, in certain examples of the 1911 at least, I have found these springs can cause the firing pin to stick forward in "dry-fire." In other words, when firing the firing pin is rammed back in place when the gun goes off but in dry-fire it can stick forward. I am not confident with guns exhibiting this trait, but they seem functionally reliable.

Jeff Cooper remarked it was S.O.P. with the 1911 to peen the firing pin stop in order to retain the stop in the slide. Some were known to fall out or work out, allowing the firing pin to fly to the rear. I have never personally experienced this problem, but Cooper saw more older 1911s in hard use than I ever will. For peace of mind, I have often performed this operation on my 1911s.

The slide stop is overlooked but can be a source of aggravation. The oversize slide stops used in competition should never be used on a carry gun. The things will often be bumped by the weak-hand thumb in recoil, tying up the gun. However, I purchased a used 1911 with a large slide stop that tied the gun up in one-hand fire. After the gun locked to the rear, I did not believe I had allowed my thumb to contact the slide stop. Besides, I was firing Federal USA ball ammo, not noted for heavy recoil. Firing with one hand, I experienced the same malfunction on the fifth round. The weight of the slide stop was producing enough inertia to allow the gun to lock open. It was trashed. *(We are beginning to see the 1911 is fine as long as we don't attempt to fix what ain't broke----)* I learned a lot about slide stops when converting my High Power to 41 Action Express. Quite a few handloads caught on the inner lip of the slide stop. I polished away until the gun functioned. On one occasion, I did the same when converting a 1943 Remington Rand to 400 Cor Bon. All went well. Today, I plug in a Wilson Combat slide stop in standard configuration at the first sign of trouble.

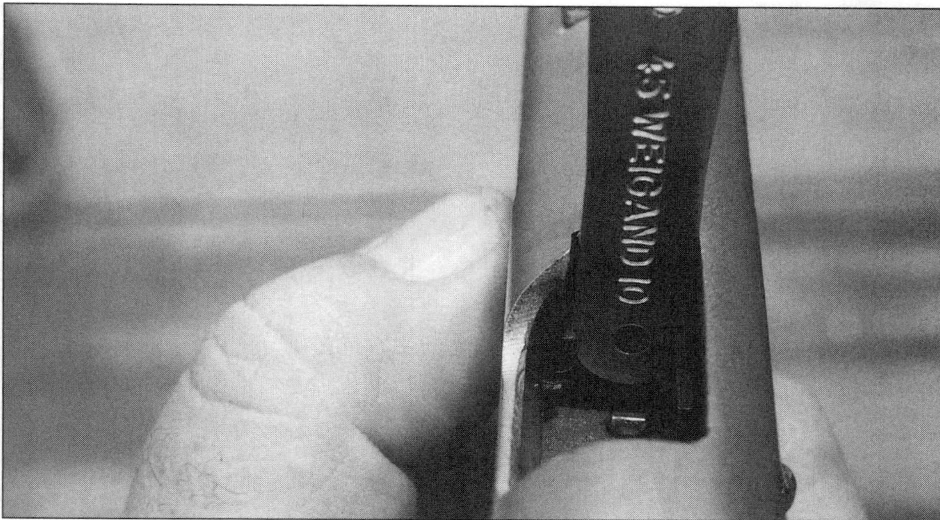

Simply press this gauge over the extractor and pull with a trigger pull gauge and you have your extractor tension.

Recoil spring rates are expertly covered in the W. C. Wolff catalog, which is well worth obtaining. Most factory springs are right on the money for use with a variety of loads. If you are into 'softball' competition using light loads, then a lighter poundage is desirable. I recently had the chance to fire a quantity of Michigan Ammunition's 185-grain lead semi-wadcutter hollowpoint loads, and used a 12-pound W. C. Wolff unit. Function was fine. However, when using Texas Ammuniton's +Ps –actually a sightly reduced 45 Super–I fitted an 18-pound unit. The rule is that 16 pounds works for most loads. With heavy loads slide velocity can be increased, outstripping the ability of the magazine to feed properly. Recoil springs lose free length with wear. Recommenced replacement is every 3000 rounds. Springs are inexpensive, and I always have a half-dozen on hand.

Full-length guide rods are controversial. The best comment I have from a reputable gunsmith comes from Jim Clark, Jr. He says the full-length guide rod is great for using heavy loads when the spring begins to "kink up and sound like a buzz saw." I have tested several pistols by using a normal spring setup, then dropping in a full-length guide rod, and seen little difference. My stock Kimbers

The author wringing out a 45 on the range. Off-hand fire tells the truth of the matter. This is a Wilson Combat Close Quarters Battle, among the top 1911s ever produced.

Firing from below eye level, a single case is almost out of the ejection port, during a test program.

and Action Work Custom Guns behaved the same. Then, on a whim, I dropped a Clark's full-length guide rod in a WWII 1911A1. The improvement was noticeable. The rod really seems to help well-worn guns the most: tightening up operation, while it may not be as noticeable in first rate 1911s. It is an added complication, increasing time in field stripping. But the most accurate 1911s I have fired incorporated full-length guide rods into the package. They clearly do not create a problem in reliability.

When it comes to magazines, the watchword is quality. Wilson Combat and Metalform are my top choices. A new brand I have used with satisfaction is Chip McCormick, and even my old standby W. C. Wolff now offers high-quality magazines. You will never be sorry for purchasing quality. These magazines are of a superior design, presenting the bullet more directly into the chamber than GI-type magazines. Magazines seem to last forever, but it is asking a lot for a device to feed from maximum compression *(fully loaded)* to minimum compression *(the last round)*. I prefer standard seven-round magazines for utmost reliability. Just the same, I have had excellent service with top quality eight-round magazines–loaded with seven rounds.

Once we have established a concern for reliability, we have to have a means to test for it. This means field-testing, firing the handgun with the service load. The only acceptable criteria is one 100 percent function. It is true that some 1911s have a break-in period, but most new 1911s come out of the box firing. After the initial 100 full-power rounds, the link and the slide should be settled in for good function.

It is important that we are able to isolate problems that occur in testing. If the fault is with the ammunition or the shooter we need to understand this. Failures to feed, chamber fire and eject are cause for concern. Operator error is always a possibility. I do not own a machine rest, preferring to keep in touch with reality. Machine-rest testing tells nothing of the pistol's reliability in human hands. The pistol may have a weak spring that does not perform well when held and fired, but which can operate against a machine rest. A too-large slide stop can interfere with operation in offhand firing. A problem in the shooter's grip will never be discovered in firing from a machine rest.

Prior to test-firing the handgun, it should be lubricated properly. This means placing a bead of oil on the slide rails *(the long bearing surfaces)* and, in the case of the 1911, on the barrel in front of the barrel bushing. Remember, WD 40 and certain other aerosol sprays do strip grime and powder away quickly, but they are not lubricants. They evaporate quickly, and can remove needed lubrication. Worse, they can intrude into ammunition, producing a failure to fire. Best to let the gun set and thoroughly dry after using such a cleaner.

When assessing reliability, it is important to perform a simple function check before engaging in live fire. This simple check, if conducted before the pistol is purchased, can save much trouble afterwards. I have found quite a few butchered 1911s in the shop and was able to avoid them.

Check Procedure

1 - Triple-check the pistol to be certain it is unloaded.

2 - Remove the magazine. Be certain the magazine release does not drag.

3 - Rack the slide. Be certain the gun cocks.

4 - Move the slide lock safety to 'on'.

5 - Press the trigger–it should not fall.

6 - Release the safety–the hammer should not fall

7 - Cock the hammer and press the trigger, verifying the gun performs correctly.

8 - While maintaining pressure on the trigger rack the slide to be certain the disconnection works properly–the hammer should not fall.

9 - Moving the slide to the rear slightly, press the trigger–the

Weigand extractor tension gauges for the 38 Super and 45 ACP.

Routine field stripping for maintenance is required of any self-defense handgun. The Colt Commander is simpler than others.

hammer should not fall while the gun is out of battery.

10 - Attempt to move the hammer forward with only finger pressure from the rear–it should not fall.

11 - Be certain the slide locks to the rear on an empty magazine.

12 - Remove the magazine and allow the slide to slam forward. The hammer should not fall.

(Do not allow the salesman to demonstrate this with his finger on the trigger–the disconnector will not allow the hammer to fall. A too-light hammer may fall. This is abuse and should not be done on a regular basis, but a single check is acceptable.)

When test firing the handgun, there are four possible sources of trouble:

Faulty ammunition or ammunition that is not suited to the individual pistol.

Shooter-induced malfunction. Usually related to an improper grip. The shooting hand may be placed wrong or insufficient gripping force is used to allow the handgun to recoil properly. The thumb riding against the slide is a common problem.

Lubrication problems. The gun could be dirty, or insufficiently or improperly lubricated.

Handgun-related problems

When you observe a problem, immediately stop firing and carefully study the problem. Keep the weapon pointed downrange. The magazine should be removed and the slide racked to clear the weapon. Often simple changes, such as holding the gun firmly or changing ammunition or the magazine, will solve the problem.

An important part of reliability is the ammunition itself. Ammunition integrity is more important than any perceived ballistic advantage. Ammunition that exhibits good primer and case mouth seal, which fires with little muzzle flash and leaves little unburned powder, shows a high degree of integrity. Ammunition should survive overnight soaks in solvent and repeated chambering in the weapon. Too many types will not survive this simple test. Among the 45 ACP loads that show good feed reliability are the various 230-grain hollowpoint loads from Remington, Federal, Winchester, Black Hills, Hornady and Speer. If you want a faster bullet, the Remington 185-grain JHP has a good reputation for feed reliability even in military-type 1911s due to a rounded ogive similar to ball ammunition. A number of short wide mouth hollowpoints are too far away from the hardball feed profile for complete reliability in a 1911. While I prefer a modern 230-grain hollowpoint as a carry load, I often load the Hornady 230-grain flat point bullet for general-purpose use. I would not feel undergunned with hardball or a good hard cast semi-wadcutter bulleted load. The point is, feed reliability cannot be compromised. Shot placement means much more than a theoretical advantage in a 'trick' loading. A balance of expansion and penetration is found in the top JHP loads. As an example, LAPD SWAT recently chose the Winchester SXT as a duty load. This is a feed-reliable loading with excellent accuracy, a full powder burn in five-inch barrels, and low muzzle signature. I would not second-guess our premier tactical unit. This is a good load. A lot of what is written about ammunition is suitable for use as fertilizer and would cover the entire Back Forty. Load selection is important, but feed reliability and cartridge integrity are a thousand times more important. •

The Glock 17 9mm pistol was the most influential design of the 1980s, and today the Glock is the most popular police handgun. The Glock 22, identical to this pistol but a 16-shot 40-caliber, is the single best-selling law enforcement pistol.

TRENDS In Law Enforcement Handguns And Training

by Massad Ayoob

AT THE LAST SHOT Show, attendees unanimously noted the most jam-packed booths were those in the law enforcement section of the firearms industry's premier trade show. Within two weeks of that event, the ASLET (American Society of Law Enforcement Trainers) national conference approached record numbers of attendees, and individual training workshops there showed that dynamic trends were afoot in the software as well as the hardware.

Powering up

One unmistakable trend has been away from 38s and 9mms to more powerful cartridges. A decade ago, our three biggest municipal police departments (those of New York City, Chicago, and Los Angeles) all issued 9mm autos to new recruits and allowed veteran officers to still carry "grandfathered" 38 Special revolvers, with more powerful sidearms prohibited. Today, only NYPD holds to that paradigm. Chicago PD has long since authorized double-action-only 45 autos by Beretta, Ruger, SIG, and Smith & Wesson. LAPD authorized personally-owned 45 autos for duty in 1998, allowing the two already approved brands, Beretta and S&W. By 2004, the department had authorized Glock pistols in 45 ACP, 40 S&W, and 9mm. A huge percentage of cops in the City Of Angels have taken advantage of the new policy. The single most popular of the newly-optionalized guns is the Glock 21, a fourteen-shot 45.

Fifteen years ago, the joint introduction of the 40 Smith & Wesson cartridge by S&W and Winchester rocked the police handgun world. Never before had a new handgun caliber been so swiftly and universally adopted by American law enforcement. The South Carolina Law Enforcement Division instantly adopted the Glock 22 in that chambering, and California Highway Patrol announced their adoption of the 40 Smith & Wesson Model 4006. For each, it was the first time any handgun but a revolver had been issued to the rank and file and, significantly, each still uses the same gun today. The trend to the 40-caliber service pistol had begun.

Numerous state police agencies (Mississippi, Missouri, and Iowa, to name three) transitioned directly from the service revolver to the 40 S&W pistol with no intermediate flirtation with the 9mm. Even more upgraded from 9mm to 40, including the state patrols of Florida, Michigan, Oregon, Washington and more. City police forces did the same. Milwaukee switched from Ruger GP100 revolvers directly to Glock 22 pistols. Municipalities unsatisfied with the stopping power of the 9mm swapped to the 40 and solved the problem. The latter included the city forces of Boston, Indianapolis, Miami, New Orleans and St. Louis among many others.

The state troopers of the six New England states were a microcosmic example of the trend. In 1995, all six issued 9mm semiautomatics: the S&W 5906 in New Hampshire, the SIG P226 in Massachusetts and P228 in Vermont, and the Beretta 92 in Connecticut, Maine, and Rhode Island. Today, however, there is not a 9mm to be found in a trooper's holster in the six-state region. Forty-fives had been adopted by New Hampshire (S&W 4566) and Maine (HK USP), and Connecticut, Massachusetts, and Vermont had all re-outfitted with 40-caliber SIGs. Rhode Island had chosen the SIG also, the 357 SIG.

Introduced in 1993, the 357 SIG cartridge could be defined with a bit of oversimplification as a 40 S&W cartridge necked down to 9mm. It launched a 125-grain jacketed hollow-point bullet at 1350 fps, approximating the ballistics of the old 125-grain 357 Magnum revolver round out of a three-inch barrel. It was adopted by Delaware State Police, followed by the troopers of Virginia and Texas and finally Rhode Island (all SIGs) as well as the New Mexico State Patrol (Glock 31) and North Carolina (Beretta Cougar). These agencies without exception reported a dramatic increase in stopping power, with a concomitant reductions in the number of times violent men or vicious animals had to be shot before they stopped attacking.

Meanwhile, Federal law enforcement was not exempt from this trend. The FBI had authorized 9mm SIG and S&W pistols for rank and file agents in 1988, with 45s by the same makers approved shortly thereafter. Their 10mm Auto project was well underway in 1990 when the 40 S&W came out, but in the end, the 10mm ran out of steam. The first 40 approved by the Bureau was Smith & Wesson's Sigma. In the late 1990s, the FBI adopted the 40-caliber Glock as standard issue for new agents, a practice that continues today.

The largest uniformed Federal agency, the Border Patrol, adopted the Beretta 96 in the mid-1990s, choosing the heavy-duty Brigadier variation with double action only mechanism. A 155-grain JHP at 1200 fps velocity was the issue cartridge for this 40-caliber pistol from the beginning, and the Border Patrol – with a high number of gunfights – has reported great success with both the ammunition and the gun.

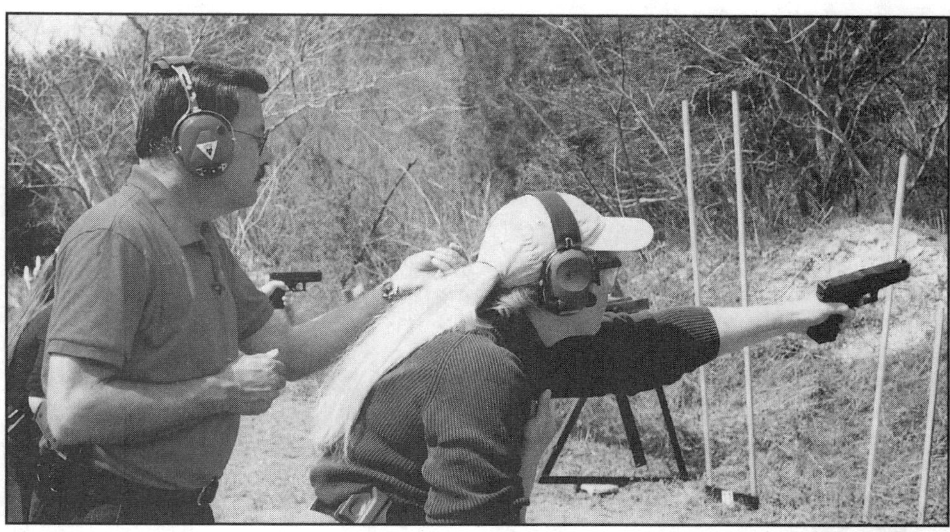

Above: Author times a female shooter weak hand-only with her Glock 19 9mm. There is more emphasis today on gun designs that work well for female officers.

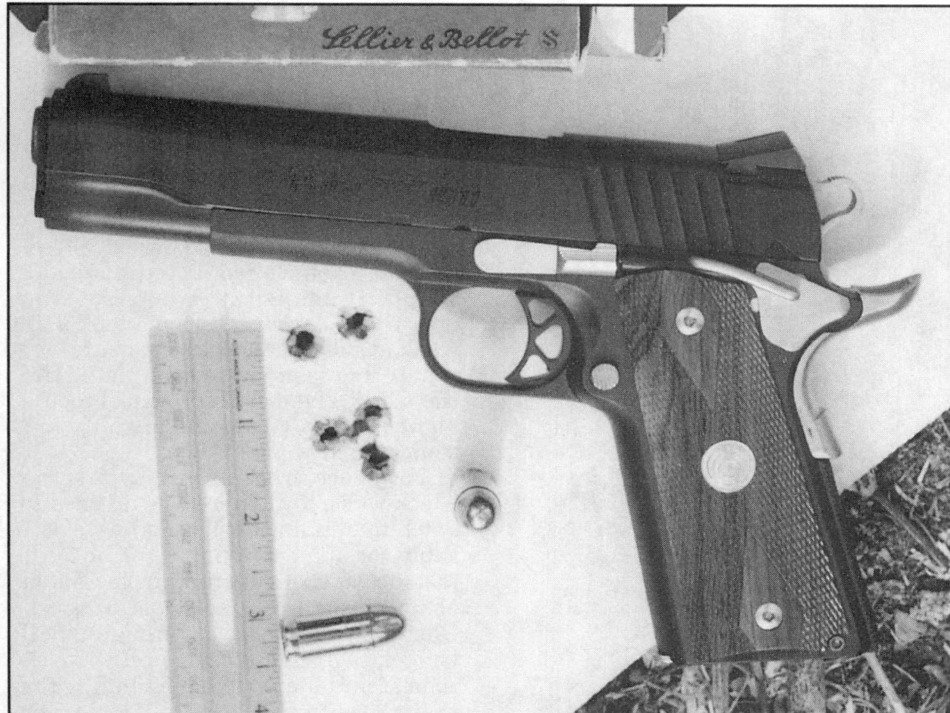

Left: 1911 pistols are experiencing something of a renaissance in law enforcement. This is a ParaOrdnance 45, with 2-inch group fired with inexpensive S&B training ammo from 25 yards.

Duty belt worn by a young deputy today shows use of force options. *From left:* M26 Taser, telescoping baton, high intensity flashlight, pepper spray, Glock 21 45 auto in security holster, spare ammo.

The 357 SIG cartridge has also found approval with the Feds. The SIG P229 pistol in that chambering is the choice of both the United States Secret Service and the Air Marshals, in both cases replacing the 9mm P228 by the same manufacturer.

Today, the 40 S&W is the overwhelmingly-favored chambering in American law enforcement.

Dumbing Down

The KISS principle ("Keep It Simple, Stupid") had long been a byword in police training, but seemed to become an overwhelming priority in the mid-1990s and has held sway ever since. This theory holds that under stress an officer will not be able to remember to flick off a safety catch, or transition effectively from a double-action first shot to single-action follow-up rounds. It was this thinking that led to "decocker-only" modifications of Beretta, Ruger, and S&W pistols originally designed with combination safety/decock levers. The KISS concept is a major reason why the Glock pistol is dominant in American law enforcement today.

Seen as a strange anomaly when it first appeared on the American scene in the early 1980s, the "plastic pistol from Austria" quickly won favor with the law enforcement sector. BATF defined the Glock as a double-action-only semiautomatic pistol. Meanwhile, in Miami, the chief had ordered all revolvers rendered double-action-only to prevent accidental discharges due to thumb-cocking. When the union came to him asking for high-capacity 9mm pistols, he initially placated them by saying, sure, so long as the guns were double-action-only. This seemed safe for a chief who wanted to keep revolvers, since there were no DAO auto pistols on the market. The Miami union approached Beretta, SIG, and S&W, who all blew them off.

BATF's designation of the Glock as DAO changed all that. The Glock 17 9mm passed a series of brutal torture tests and became the issue weapon of Miami PD, which in turn became the flagship of a burgeoning fleet of departments that switched to Glock pistols. Soon Glocks were accounting for half of the new handguns sold to police departments. Then 60 percent. Today's estimate of Glock domination of the domestic law enforcement market is in the 70th percentile. A broadening array of calibers helped; Miami was among the many that upgraded to the 40-caliber Glock 22.

Other factors in the Glock's ascendancy included its mechanical simplicity and ergonomic ease of operation. Armorer's school took a week at most factories to learn to repair their semiautomatic pistols; for the Glock, the armorer's school took all of one day. The pistol had only some 34 parts.

For police firearms instructors, the Glock was a joy. There was no need to teach manipulation of a manual safety, or of a decocking lever, or to instruct in the transition from double action to single action. Operating a Glock was as simple as "aim gun, pull trigger," with the trigger pull consistent for every shot including the first. An optimum grip-to-barrel angle made it point naturally. When departments switched from traditional double-action autos to Glocks, the scores on the range usually went up.

Moreover, the Glock pistols proved to be extremely reliable and durable. Concerns about the five-pound trigger pull being too light were answered by Glock with their

***Above*: Beretta duty pistols in three variations. 92FS (*top)*, has safety/decock lever. 92G *(center)* has lever that decocks only. 92D Centurion *(below)* is DAO. Middle gun has been customized by Ernest Langdon.**

***Right*: Some instructors feared that a safety/decock lever was too complicated for rank-and-file cops to master.**

optional New York Trigger, developed for the NY State Police. Keeping the trigger pull resistance firm from the first pressure applied to the moment the shot broke, the New York Trigger increased pull weight to approximately eight pounds, without any loss in real-world "shootability."

Perhaps too late, other manufacturers jumped onto the DAO bandwagon. However, their conventional pistols were more difficult to shoot well with longer, heavier pulls than the Glock. S&W came up with a new mechanism with a shorter, lighter pull for every shot. Many departments did go with these older-style guns in the DAO format, as Border Patrol did with their Beretta 40s. Troopers in Pennsylvania (Beretta 40s), Idaho (S&W 45s), and Ohio (SIG 40s) all proved that the DAO concept could work.

Above: Police training scenarios are more dynamic today. Capt. Ayoob begins in "execution position" with hands on top of head, armed hostile targets behind him...

Top Right: ... and when police instructor Ed Sevetz gives the signal, he begins to draw...

Bottom Right: ... and engages targets with his 40 Glock. Scene is an IDPA match, which has inspired in-house law enforcement training drills.

Most Recent Trends

Companies have rushed to create double-action-only mechanisms that are more user-friendly. Two spectacularly effective examples are the DAK option on the SIG and the LEM option on the HK USP.

However, another trend has come from an opposite direction. For decades, the cocked and locked single-action 1911-type pistol had been on the edge of extinction in police patrol, banned by more and more departments whose chiefs feared that short trigger pulls would lead to accidental discharges. In the early 21st century, this trend began reversing itself. Noticing that FBI had adopted single-action 45s for its most elite units *(customized Para-Ordnance 1911s for its Hostage Rescue Team and Springfield Armory 1911s for its scattered SWAT Teams),* some other agencies got into the act. Tacoma, Washington received heavy national publicity when it approved the Kimber 1911 pistol for rank and file patrol officers and detectives.

San Diego Police Department got even more attention when a new chief broadened weapons policy. Prior to his arrival in late 2003, only traditional style double-action auto pistols were allowed, and only in 9mm. He expanded the options to embrace 40- and 45-caliber weapons, and to include Glocks and such cocked and locked 1911s as the Kimber. A huge wave of SDPD officers "voted with their feet" and bought new guns out of their own pockets.

At the 2004 ASLET conference this writer coordinated the Panel of Experts on firearms issues with more than a hundred police instructors present. One thing that became clear in the subsequent interchange of information between many departments represented was that a growing number of agencies were giving their officers broader ranges of options as to firearms. Big departments still allowing cocked and locked guns included Las Vegas Metro and Denver PD. Fewer and fewer departments were issuing 9mm pistols without at least giving

Firing ten rounds of 40 S&W, the subcompact Glock 27 offers many advantages over the snub-nose detective revolvers of yesteryear.

their officers the option of more powerful handguns.

One law enforcement advantage of the cocked and locked pistol is the "locked" element. We are seeing another upsurge in officers being killed with their own weapons and weapons snatched from their partners. The "point gun, pull trigger" design is as user-friendly to a cop-killer who has grabbed a police gun as it is to the officer himself. There have been numerous incidents in which a suspect has grabbed an on-safe police pistol, attempted to kill a cop, and failed because he couldn't find the lever that "turns on" the gun.

This is also true with some traditional double-action auto designs. Several well respected police departments at the municipal, county, and state level mandate that their officers carry double-action autos on-safe. These include the Syracuse (NY) Police Department (S&W 45s), the Los Angeles County Sheriff's Department (9mm Berettas issued, 45-caliber Beretta, HK, Ruger and S&W pistols authorized), and the North Carolina Highway Patrol (Beretta pistols in 357 SIG). All report spectacular success in averting cases of personnel killed with their own weapons. Military police who are required to carry their Beretta M9 pistols on safe (Army, Marine Corps) likewise have a negligible rate of personnel shot with their own guns by offenders.

"Have it your way," most handgun makers said to cops, offering them options. These are Berettas. *Clockwise from top*: "F" series with safety/decock lever; "G" series with lever that decocks only; and DAO "D" series which doesn't need a lever for either purpose.

Reality-based Training

Perhaps more important than hardware upgrades have been "software" changes, new trends in training. The use of simulators pioneered by the FATS machine and now produced by many other companies raise the reality level of training to new heights. The officer faces a situation unfolding on the screen. His opponents are interactive. If he fires at them with his laser-equipped pistol and misses, they keep trying to kill him. If he wounds them, they may fall to their knees but keep shooting. If he scores a center hit, they fall, neutralized. The computer will record the exact times and hit locations of each shot fired by the officer.

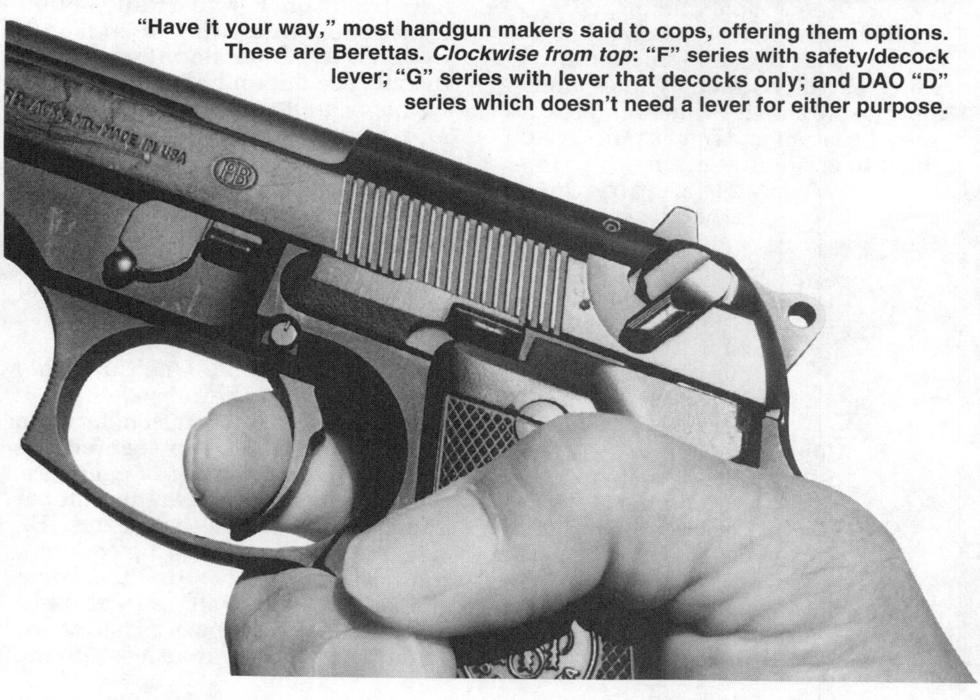

What's wrong with this picture? Unauthorized hand is pulling the trigger, but hammer will not move and gun will not fire. Reason: the pistol is still "on safe." Pistols so constructed can give officers a survival edge in disarming situations.

Improved training saves lives. Here police instructor Thelma Edwards of the St. Tammany Parish, Louisiana Sheriff's Dept., demonstrates a counter to a gun grab...

...locking the hand of a much larger Deputy Patrick Washington as he attempts the snatch...

... and neatly peeling him off with a technique developed by Jim Lindell of the National Law Enforcement Training Center in Kansas City, MO.

Even more realistic is "force on force" training enhanced by the use of Simunitions, paint-ball cartridges that fire only in modified service pistols, which can no longer accept live cartridges. The Simunitions projectiles sting sharply, reinforcing the officer's training experience when he makes a mistake and gets himself shot by a "bad guy" role-player. There is no better way to get movie fantasies of "kick in the door and shoot it out with the bad guy" out of a cop's system than to nail him with a hail of Simunitions rounds.

Once, this sort of training was the exclusive province of the richest and best-budgeted police departments. Today, even Mayberry RFD has access to such training through state and regional law enforcement training academies. Fred Mabardy in Massachusetts constructed a CAPS simulator complete with indoor range bullet trap inside a tractor-trailer, allowing the use of the officer's duty weapon with live service ammunition. He trucks the portable simulator around the country to give smaller departments an affordable taste of extremely realistic gunfight simulation

Integrated Use of Force

It used to be said, "there is a large, gray area between a kind word and a bullet." Today, that large gray area has been effectively filled in by extensive options in police use of force.

On the lowest end, the "Verbal Judo" concept originally popularized in California is widely taught throughout the United States, giving officers proven verbal crisis intervention skills that help them to de-escalate hostile situations without any physical use of force. Also popular is the MOAB (Management of Aggressive Behavior) program developed by retired Connecticut state trooper Roland Ouellette.

When force must be applied, modern pepper spray formulae, dispensers, and training have proven to be far more effective than the tear gas sprays of the old days. Minimum likelihood of injury plus street-proven effectiveness have made OC (oleoresin capsicum) spray acceptable at lower levels of the force continuum, and they are almost universally issued to patrol officers these days.

Batons are still essential, since they alone give the officer a tool that can physically block an opponent's strike. Properly managed baton blows can effectively end a fight with minimum likelihood of death or crippling injury to the suspect, and advanced techniques can swiftly put the suspect into a baton-reinforced wrist-lock or arm-lock, subduing him with maximum speed and minimum injury.

The Advanced Taser concept is perhaps the fastest growing and most dramatically effective element in the new spectrum of police use of force options. A five-second "ride" with the Advanced Taser M26 electronic stun gun quickly drops most opponents no matter how large, strong, or violent they may be. Departments that have made these devices standard issue have seen a dramatic reduction in injuries to police officers and suspects alike.

"Less-lethal" impact munitions, usually in the form of what are colloquially called "beanbag rounds," can be fired from 12-gauge shotguns to knock down violent offenders from a safe distance. Because some deaths have occurred with them, they are used only in situations where deadly force is warranted, but there is time to attempt a resolution that will be less likely to cause death.

Despite all the advances that have been made with intermediate weaponry, the handgun at the officer's hip remains the first line of protection of the public from violent criminals armed with lethal weapons. Advancement in both training and equipment over the last few years have given American citizens the best armed and best trained police who have ever stood on the Thin Blue Line to protect them. ●

The Model "Eden" P 210 is part of a four-pistol set intended to symbolize the transitions one makes through life. Illustrated above is the first model in the set, representing creation. The other three pistols in the set trace life through adolescence, adulthood and old age/death.

The Infinite Varieties of the SIG P 210

by Bob Hausman

LITTLE DID ANYONE know back in 1949 that the *"Pistole 49"* (thus designated when adopted as the service pistol of the Swiss Army) would enjoy 50 years of service, or that it would earn a prominent place on the "wish lists" of handgun aficionados around the world. Nor did the pistol's designers envision that one day it would become an icon of quality Swiss manufacturing, alongside the products of the great Swiss watchmakers. Finally, no one could foresee that what was conceived as a utilitarian military pistol would become the chosen platform for some of the most artistic embellishments of firearms anywhere in the world.

Swiss Arms Background

Swiss Arms, the producer of the SIG P210, is the oldest arms manufacturer in Switzerland. Formerly known as SIG Arms AG, a subsidiary of SIG (*Schweizer Industrie Gesellschaft,* or Swiss Industrial Company), the firm's name was changed to Swiss Arms in mid-2000 when two German investors, both gun enthusiasts, acquired it.

An important part of the new company's philosophy is to build on its foundation of tried and true designs and production technologies. A classic example of this is the P 210 pistol. Originally developed as a military pistol, its enduring quality has made it a status symbol recognized throughout the world.

In keeping with tradition, Swiss Arms still mills each P 210 from one solid piece of high-grade steel; the final components are synchronized and surface-treated by hand. The P 210's legendary accuracy is largely due to its close tolerances and its internally-riding slide—that is, the slide rides on rails in the interior of the frame, rather than on the outer edges. This method of manufacture is much more expensive than the conventional outside slide-mounting method, but it produces a much tighter-shooting pistol.

Engraver's Background

Many of the engraved SIG pistols the collector will see bear the signature of the engraver, appearing as simply "MM" in a circle, usually on or near the trigger guard. This symbol stands for the firm of Mueller Murgenthal AG of Murgenthal, Switzerland.

Founded in 1980 by silversmith Vivian Mueller, the firm initially began as an engraver of high-end Swiss watches made by such makers as IWC, and Rolex. Since 1982, when he began to branch out in his work beyond just watches, Mueller has produced more than 580 objects of art, primarily composed of gold and silver for the likes of sultans, sheiks, and various other royalty—as well as jewelers, such as Asprey of London.

In 1991 Mueller began to produce work for SIG—or today's SAN Swiss Arms—and has since engraved more than 2800 pistols. There are now four people working in the firm: Mueller, his wife Arlette, and daughters Audrey and Maureen, who also engrave. During 2004 Mueller

The Model Pistole 49 commemorates the 50 years of service the P 210 gave the Swiss Army from 1949 to 1999.

acquired the Swiss rifle and pistol maker Wuethrich, and has begun to produce highly ornamented examples of long- and handguns from that firm's production. In addition to his own designs, he can produce individual models to order if the customer so desires.

Individual Model Descriptions

There is a near infinite variety of engraved SIG pistols available, most of which are imported to order from Europe. Here is a run-down on some of the more interesting models:

The P 210 50 Years Jubilee model–Celebrating the 50 years of dependable service the SIG P 210 pistol provided the Swiss Army, this set consists of a special army edition of the "9mm pistole 49" as it was designated by the Swiss government. Limited to 250 pieces worldwide, it has gold scroll engraving on each side of the slide, with a commemorative medallion set in its wooden grips. It is supplied in a fitted, glass-topped wooden box with an illustration of two Pistole 49-equipped officers in battle, a reproduction of the original German language SIG field manual for the gun, and a certificate of authenticity. The green fabric lining the case's lid is actual surplus Swiss Army uniform material. Production is limited to 300 pieces worldwide. Retail price is about $4,995.

The P 210 is not the only embellished design available. The P 226 is the chosen platform for a limited edition commemorating the freedoms and traditions of America.

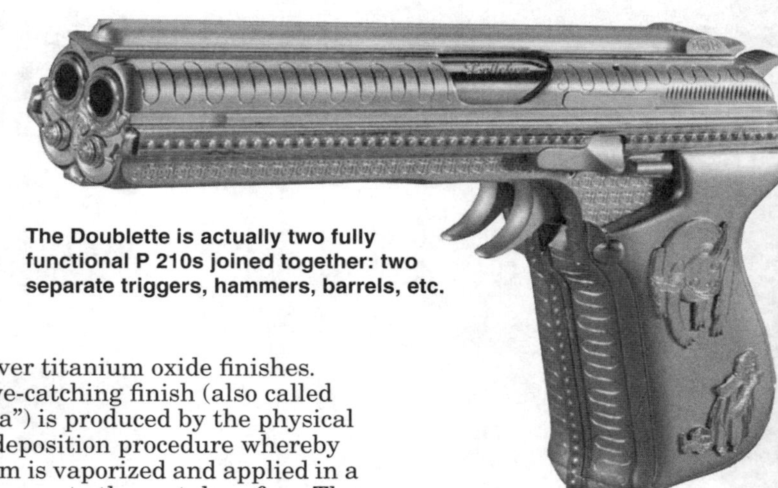

The Doublette is actually two fully functional P 210s joined together: two separate triggers, hammers, barrels, etc.

A slightly more expensive version of the 50-Year Jubilee (or *50 Jahre Jubilaeumsmodell* in German) is available in unique black, blue, gold and silver titanium oxide finishes. This eye-catching finish (also called "plasma") is produced by the physical vapor deposition procedure whereby titanium is vaporized and applied in a thin layer onto the metal surface. The result is a thin but highly scratch-resistant metal surface, greatly resistant to corrosion. The titanium oxide application process was first developed in the machine tool industry as a way of extending the life of expensive cutting tools.

Further, this 50-year Jubilee model also has golden script engraving on both sides of the slide, gold-filled markings and other details. It is stocked with maple wood grips with a unique white finish that is a dead ringer for elephant ivory. Produced by Nil Grips of Germany, these grips offer all the beauty of ivory without ivory's main drawback – fragility. In addition, the innovative mounting method of these special grips is accomplished with no visible outside grip screw. The pistol is supplied in a wooden display box with a certificate of authenticity. Suggested retail is $5,999.

Closer to home, there are two SIG pistol models that celebrate the United States of America.

The "United We Stand" model is a limited edition of the P 210 meant to celebrate the freedoms and traditions of America. Gold engravings adorn the slide's gold-inlayed motto "United We Stand." Additional details are gold-plated hammer, trigger, safety and slide stop levers, front and rear sights, magazine catch and magazine floorplate. Highly-polished white maple wood grips *(with no visible grip screw)* contain a golden American star. Finished in plasma blue, the pistol is supplied in a wooden box with a certificate of authenticity. Suggested retail is $7995.

The P 226 "America" is a limited edition of the classic German-made Sauer P 226 designed to

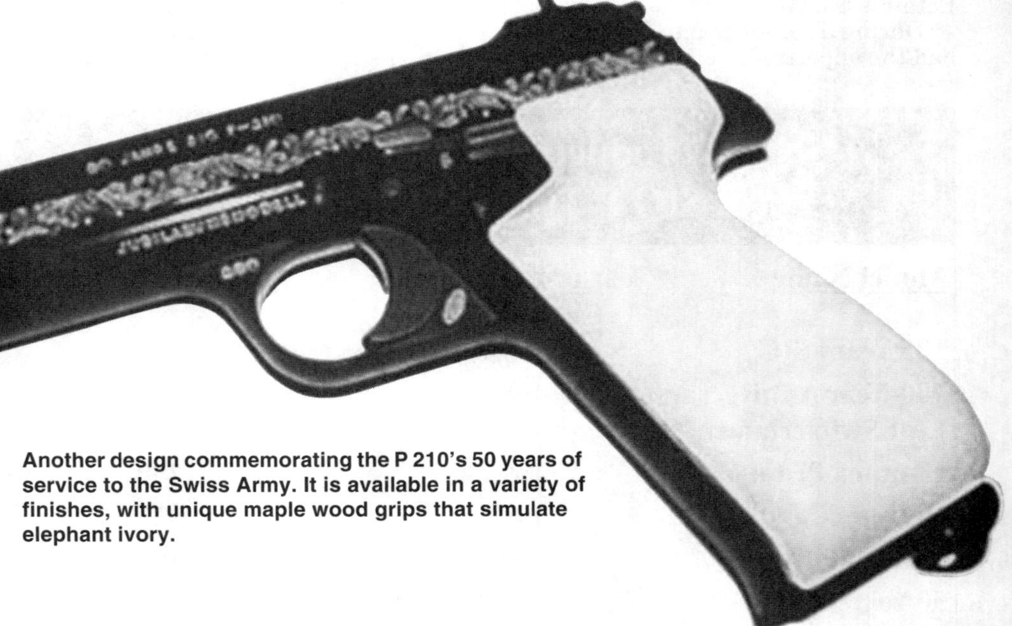

Another design commemorating the P 210's 50 years of service to the Swiss Army. It is available in a variety of finishes, with unique maple wood grips that simulate elephant ivory.

The Skeleton Model P 210 is a fully functioning cutaway with a racy appearance.

commemorate American solidarity. Characterized by a combination of gold and blue titanium and aluminum oxide coatings simulating the stripes of the American flag in gold, it is equipped with smooth white maple wood grips. It is furnished complete with a wooden storage box and a certificate of authenticity. Retail is $8990.

During a recent trip to Europe, I had the opportunity of visiting Mueller's shop. When asked why he made the transition from working on fine watches and designing objects of art *(high-end jewelry, water fountains constructed of precious materials, etc.)*, Mueller responded, "A firearm is by itself fascinating; an object of cult interest. For one who has a ripe imagination, a gun is a source of eternal potency. From catapult to cannons, the principle is the same: the human gives the order to the machine, which is actually a small power station that decides for life or death. The unique shape of a firearm tells all: fascination, danger, fear, and hope are all expressed by–and associated with–the form of a firearm."

The answer Mueller gave when asked why he chose the SIG P 210 as the platform for many of his creations may surprise many die-hard fans of this pistol: he considers it, despite its military origins, to be effeminate. "I see the SIG P 210 as embodying female grace. It is not masculine at all when one considers its large grip angle, and its slim and fine parts machined to close tolerances."

He also is impressed by the genius of the P 210's engineering design. "Most of the individual parts of the gun also perform multiple functions, thus making it kind of a Zen construction. A reduction to the essential is how I view the pistol's design philosophy. The SIG P 210 also embodies the best Swiss virtues of exactness, diligence and precision in everything a man does. The SIG P 210 is incomparably Swiss," he concludes.

More information on engraved SIG pistols can be obtained by sending an e-mail inquiry to: intlft@verizon.net.

Production Chronology of SIG P 210 Jubilee Editions

Model Name	Year of Production	Quantity Produced
125 Years SIG	1978	500
700-Year Anniversary of Switzerland	1991	2000
Cantons Pistol	1995	200
Helvetia	1998	25
Model 49 (Army)	1999	300
50 Years P 210	2002	200

Concealed-Carry Handguns and Holsters

There's more to it than one might think.

by Gary Paul Johnston

WHEN I BECAME a police officer in 1963, many of us with the LAPD carried what was called simply a second gun. Most often a 2-inch (snubnose) barrel double-action revolver in the same chambering as our issue 6-inch barrel 38 Special Colt or Smith & Wesson duty revolver, these smaller guns were often our primary defensive weapon. I carried a Colt Detective Special revolver in the right pocket of my duty jacket. A hole cut inside the pocket allowed me to shoot the gun without removing it from the pocket if necessary.

When approaching any situation, such as a traffic stop, I simply gripped my second gun in my pocket with my right hand and could hold a flashlight in my left. When necessary, I simply removed my right hand to accept identification or take field notes. Although thousands of people never knew it, or were offended by it, they were always covered.

Emerging a short time later were the terms *backup* gun and *hideout* gun. The difference was that a backup gun was one that was immediately accessible, or nearly so, while a hideout gun was one that was secreted somewhere to be used in case the officer was kidnapped. Such an event was heavy on the minds of LAPD officers in the wake of the kidnapping of LAPD Metro Officers Bob Hettinger and Ian Campbell *(who was murdered)* whose story inspired the book and movie, *The Onion Field*. Hettinger escaped and said that during the drive to rural Bakersfield he and Campbell had numerous opportunities to use a weapon if either of them had had one. This incident prompted the LAPD to encourage its officers to carry such weapons concealed.

Shown above are a variety of concealment holsters from different makers, in styles for various pistols.

With the second, or backup gun usually in the same caliber as the duty sidearm, the hideout gun was more than likely of a smaller caliber. The hideout gun was also often a pocket-size semi-automatic pistol or a derringer that was more easily hidden than a wider revolver. With the backup gun normally capable of combat accuracy out to 10 to 25 yards, the hideout gun is just as often limited to no more than a few yards and sometimes much less. I've seen tiny hideout guns carried in boots or ankle holsters, hung around the neck, in the back pocket and in the groin, and don't to anxious to scoff at such pistols chambered for 22 LR, 22 Magnum, or the like. I've seen as many people killed or instantly disabled by this caliber as any other. The reason for this is that these small bullets often bounce around inside the body instead of traveling in a straight line. However, I still prefer to carry a gun in a heavier caliber.

Concealed MEANS Concealed!

Not too long ago I saw a man come into a restaurant with his wife and kids. Although he was well dressed, he wasn't wearing a jacket even though it was a chilly day, and in plain view on his hip was a pistol. He had "cop" written all over him as he was waiting to be seated, and when he turned to follow the hostess I saw a badge, handcuffs and a spare magazine pouch on his belt. What's wrong with this picture? Everything.

When a uniformed officer stops to eat on duty there is usually a marked patrol car parked nearby. This signals any would-be perpetrator that, at least for the time being, this is a "no robbery zone," but when a plainclothes officer stops for dinner it's a different story, and he or she must never flaunt their identity. This particular officer was at least risking catching a cold, but if a robbery went down and his cover was blown, he could have been risking catching a bullet—not to mention putting his family in jeopardy. We'll probably never know his motive for doing what he did, but it was a stupid move.

Para-Ordnance makes a variety of 45 ACP caliber single- and double-action compact pistols, such as the P-13, 7.45, and Tac-Four.

What one calls his or her concealed carry gun is less important than how the weapon is thought of. The operator must have a clear understanding of the gun's role and effectiveness, and decide whether it will be readily accessible or carried covertly. Although I prefer at least a medium-size revolver or auto-pistol, others feel comfortable with small pistols, including derringers, and it's difficult to argue with success.

Whether you're a law enforcement officer or a private citizen, if you use a concealed-carry handgun for personal protection you must not only be properly trained in its use, but also in the legal requirements that go with it. You must also practice and/or qualify with your handgun as often as possible. Your life could depend on it.

Kimber's new 45 ACP compact Tactical Pro II and full-size Tactical Elite both have a lightweight alloy frame.

Skin Your Pistol!

Dating back more than a century, the old phrase, "Skin your pistol," means to draw your gun in a hurry. When I think back on how many times I skinned my pistol in the line of duty, there were more incidents than I could count, although I only used it against individuals on two occasions. The often-repeated adage of drawing your gun only when you're going to shoot someone, or, "every time I drew my gun someone died," is pure BS! The truth is that every time a law enforcement officer draws his or her gun, he or she is prepared to use it.

Then again, we're by no means only talking about uniformed duty when we talk about holsters. To try to count the holsters I've made and owned during my life would be almost impossible. However, having owned well over 100 handguns, concealable and otherwise, I would put the holster tally at about three times that number, and that has included holsters of all kinds. Today I still own about 50 holsters. Starting at the top, let's take a look at some holster types and modes of carry.

Shoulder Holsters

Having been around in some form for about as long as there have been handguns, the shoulder holster was one of my favorite carry rigs in plain clothes on special security details, or otherwise off duty. The advantages of this type of rig are good control of the pistol with fast access, not to mention that few will detect that you are armed. You can also use the old Bill Hickok trick of having your hand secretly on your pistol with your arms crossed in the folded position.

Shoulder rigs come in three basic styles: vertical, horizontal, and upside-down. Each has its advantage depending on how you are built. Retention should be a big concern and most shoulder rigs have good retention systems, but the upside-down shoulder rig needs good retention more than any other type. Murphy is always along for the ride and he owns gravity.

The Strong Side

Descending the torso, we come to pretty much the most popular place to hang a pistol for most: the waist. This carry location offers a variety of positions; most common of these is the strong-side (on the right side for right-handers and on the left side for "southpaws"). Here things can get confusing, especially for the new gun owner, but the selection often leaves even those with more experience scratching their heads over what type of strong-side holster to select.

Whether or not the pistol is to be worn concealed, as with the shoulder rig, I prefer a strong side-holster with some type of retention capability. This can be simply a good fit, extra tension provided by tightening the belt, a top strap, a spring-like mechanical retention, or an actual locking mechanism, such as is popular with uniform duty holsters. Holsters allowing the pistol to be removed with total freedom will allow it to fall out, and if your pistol can fall out of its holster, it will.

The Cross-Draw

Similar to the conventional vertical shoulder holster, the cross-draw operates in pretty much the same way, but is simply worn lower. Those who like a should rig, but suffer back or shoulder pain, may find the cross-draw is the answer. A disadvantage is that an assailant may be able to take the pistol away in a frontal attack. An advantage of the cross-draw is that the pistol is usually readily accessible by either hand.

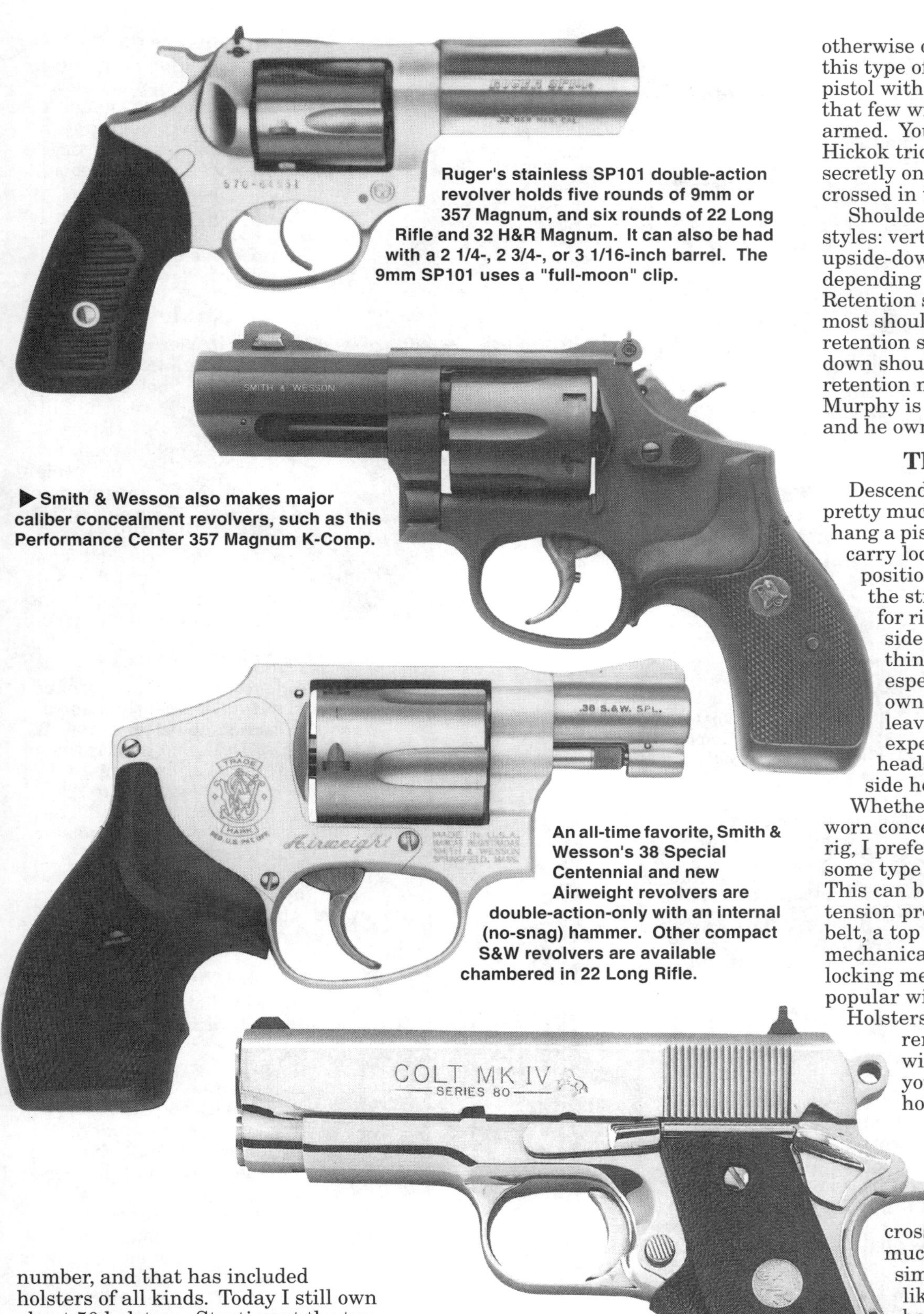

Ruger's stainless SP101 double-action revolver holds five rounds of 9mm or 357 Magnum, and six rounds of 22 Long Rifle and 32 H&R Magnum. It can also be had with a 2 1/4-, 2 3/4-, or 3 1/16-inch barrel. The 9mm SP101 uses a "full-moon" clip.

▶ Smith & Wesson also makes major caliber concealment revolvers, such as this Performance Center 357 Magnum K-Comp.

An all-time favorite, Smith & Wesson's 38 Special Centennial and new Airweight revolvers are double-action-only with an internal (no-snag) hammer. Other compact S&W revolvers are available chambered in 22 Long Rifle.

One of the large-caliber pocket pistols that started it all is the 45-caliber Colt Officer's ACP offered both in all stainless steel and a lightweight blued version. The Officer's ACP is a smaller version of the compact Colt Commander.

One of the smallest 45 ACP pistols made is Kimber's Ultra Carry II, a 1911-type auto-pistol with a lightweight alloy frame offered in blue or stainless steel.

Kahr makes a variety of superb double-action-only "pocket" pistols chambered in 9mm and 40 S&W.

Lightweight, reliable, and affordable, KEL-TEC's P-11 double-action pocket pistol carries a total of 11 rounds of 9mm. Models in 380 ACP and 32 ACP are also offered.

The Behind-The-Back Holster

This type of holster evolved from some users, such as undercover officers, simply putting their strong-side holsters in the middle, or small, of their backs for better concealment. Holster makers soon offered such holsters, often in the form of inside-the-waistband (IWB) models. Although this holster originated using a palm-inward draw, variations of it soon required the hand to draw the pistol with the palm outward, much like a reverse draw with the pistol's butt forward. Drawing the pistol in this way makes it easy to sweep one's own body, and under stress this could have disastrous results. Even under the best circumstances, the pistol, when worn behind the back, is not under control, leaving it vulnerable to "gun grab."

Inside-The-Waist-Band

Offering excellent concealment and good retention, IWB holsters come in a myriad of styles. No holster holds the pistol closer to the body than the IWB, and the gun can be worn either strong-side or cross-draw.

However, as popular as the IWB rig is, it isn't for everyone, as there is a comfort factor that is dependent on one's build. If you're not sure the IWB holster is for you, it's probably not. Even if it feels good at first, check again after wearing it for eight hours. Some IWB rigs can also be worn between the belt and the trousers.

Ankle Holsters

Worn around the ankle, this type of holster is pretty much limited to very small and lightweight pistols and revolvers. Like the IWB, the ankle rig isn't for everyone, but it has its advantages for carrying a "hideout" gun.

Pocket Holsters

Pocket holsters have been around for years, but have recently made a comeback thanks to better materials and designs. Designed to fit rather tightly in the pocket and remain there, this rig is also meant to stay put when the gun is drawn. The advantages of the pocket holster are obvious in terms of concealment, security, and easy access. Its disadvantage is that it only accommodates small-frame handguns.

Purse Holsters

Along with ladies' holster purses, we'll include the little zipper bags worn on the belt of your Levis *(sorry, fellas)*. Holster purses have become popular with female investigative and undercover officers who usually have a partner close by. Whether or not they are to be recommended for an unescorted woman who is not a law enforcement officer depends on how much training she has had. Since a purse is often the object of crimes against women, carrying your pistol in it might be a bad idea. The waist purse with a fast access feature is probably a better solution.

These are the most common holster styles available; their many makers and variations number in the hundreds. There is almost certainly a good holster-maker near you. ●

Manipulating the Single-Action Revolver

by Massad Ayoob

"Buckskin Kay," a.k.a. Kathy Larney, demonstrates the most efficient two-handed method of firing the single action. It's the off-hand thumb that cocks the hammer. Revolver is a 5 1/2-inch Ruger Bisley Vaquero firing 38 Special cowboy loads.

FOR MAXIMUM PERFORMANCE, there's a lot more to it than just cocking the hammer before each shot.

The single-action revolver – the "Peacemaker" and its predecessors and sisters and clones – is a timeless piece of American firearms history. I shouldn't wonder that Colt, AWA, Freedom Arms, US Firearms, Armi San Marco, Uberti, Ruger and others are selling more of them today than were sold in the nineteenth century. Back then, these guns were simply state-of-the-art tools. Today, they are touchstones of the past.

To see these six-guns truly sing, you need to watch today's masters of CAS, cowboy action shooting, in action. If you go to a Buckmasters shoot and watch the awesome Blackie Sleeva unerringly place 100-yard shots with surgical precision on three-dimensional deer targets that are exposed for only seconds at a time, you'll also have a sense of why, from working ranchers to handgun hunters, single-action revolvers are popular among a cadre of handgunners who are looking for modern performance instead of a blast from the past.

With any tool, the more efficiently we manipulate it, the better we'll perform with it. This is as true of the single-action revolver as of anything else.

Two-Handed Stances

The shape of the frontier-style revolver is distinctly different from that of the double-action wheelgun or the semiautomatic pistol. The web of the hand drops lower from the plane of the hammer spur. The trigger guard is normally much smaller and set further back.

For one thing, this makes a grasp with the forefinger of the support hand wrapped around the front of the trigger guard much more practical than with the DA revolver or the autoloader. Try this with a modern-style gun, and you'll find the finger is extended to the point where it can't really exert much rearward pressure to stabilize the gun against the pull of

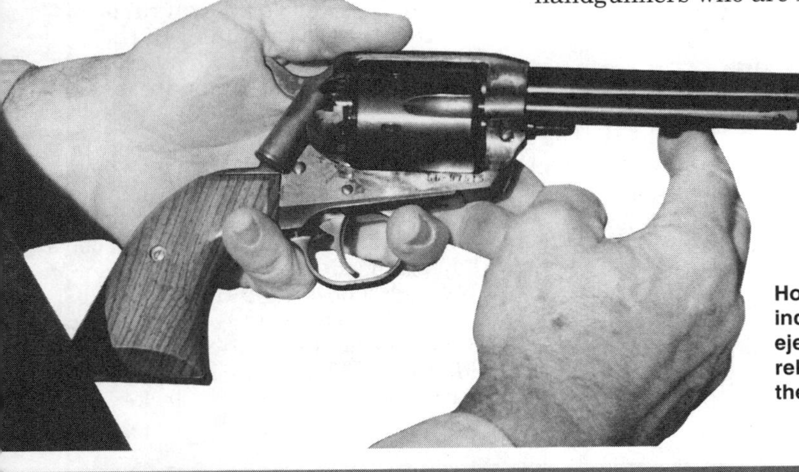

Holding the Peacemaker-style gun in the left hand, left thumb or index finger turns the cylinder while right index finger activates ejector rod and punches spent casings clear. The fastest way to reload one of these? That's definitely a "three-beer argument" after the match!

the trigger. Moreover, due to a sympathetic muscle reaction known as *interlimb response*, when the trigger finger pulls the trigger, the index finger of the support hand will instinctively pull with it, possibly tugging the muzzle off target at the worst possible moment.

None of this happens with the Peacemaker-style revolver, nor with the S&W Schofield-style single action, nor with Colt or Remington cap & ball designs. The forward part of their trigger guards is straight up and down for the most part, not curved as on most modern guns. This means that the finger is less likely to slip down during recoil, requiring readjustment before you're ready for the follow-up shot. Moreover, since the guard is smaller and placed relatively more rearward, you can wrap a lot more finger around it. This is stronger. The more deeply flexed support hand index finger not only exerts more force, but is now placed somewhere between the median joint and the distal joint, instead of out toward the finger tip. Already pulling tight, it can't pull tighter when the trigger finger does its thing, as can happen with more modern handgun designs. All things considered, it makes for a markedly stronger hold. While virtually all the handgun champions of IDPA, IPSC, and PPC have gotten away from the finger-forward grasp in two-hand shooting of their modern guns, that grasp is the choice of champions in cowboy action. You've just learned the reason.

One-handed cocking. Here, the shooter has enough range of movement that he can use the ball of the thumb to catch the hammer spur...

...and after hammer reaches full cock, thumb slides down to reinforce grasp as index finger only now contacts trigger...

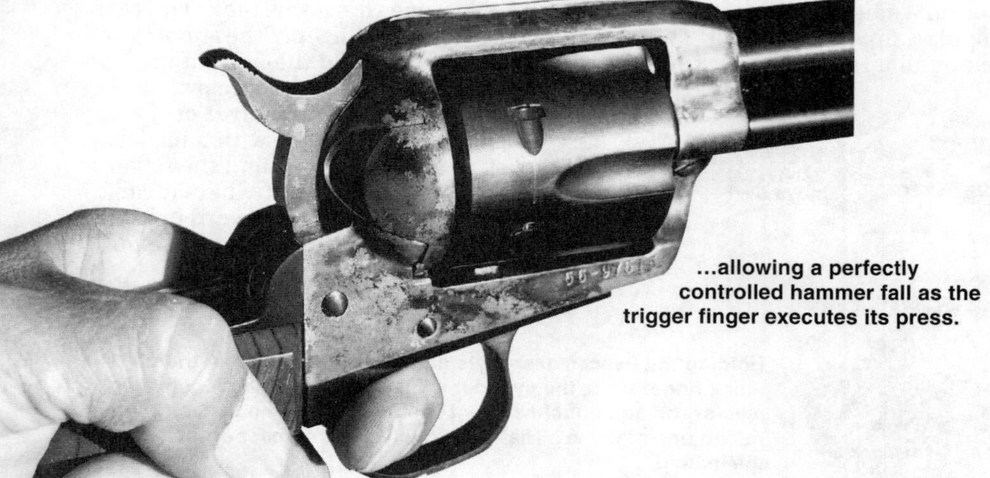

...allowing a perfectly controlled hammer fall as the trigger finger executes its press.

Of course, if you do a lot of work with modern handguns and have become habituated to the two-hand grasp which places the support hand index finger under the trigger guard, it is not compellingly necessary to change when you switch to a "hog-leg." The added advantage of the finger-forward grasp with the SA is not a huge one. This writer, who works primarily with modern service handguns, shoots SAs with the support forefinger under the guard and still wins his share of awards in Single Action Shooting Society matches.

Thumb placement is also handled differently with a single-action six-shooter. On the DA revolver, the thumb of the firing hand is normally curled down, to give maximum strength for the primary hold or "master grip." The thumb of the support hand will be curled down over it. The reason this added strength is important is that the DA revolver has to be stabilized against a rearward trigger pressure much greater than the gun's weight for every double-action shot. An autoloader will be held in similar fashion, or with both thumbs on the same side of the gun and pointing toward the target.

The SA revolver is another matter. That hammer has to be manually cocked to fire every shot. In a two-hand hold, the support hand thumb is the logical choice for this job. It has an easier and more natural range of movement than the thumb of the firing hand because of its placement, and it is the logical candidate for the task. Using the off-side thumb to manipulate the hammer is the unanimous choice of all the cowboy winners who fire with both hands on the gun, whether in Traditional class (fixed-sight revolvers) or Modern class (adjustable-sight guns).

Watch a dozen top shooters in these categories, and you'll see that almost without exception, their weak-side thumb "floats" during the firing sequence. That is, it's not locked onto

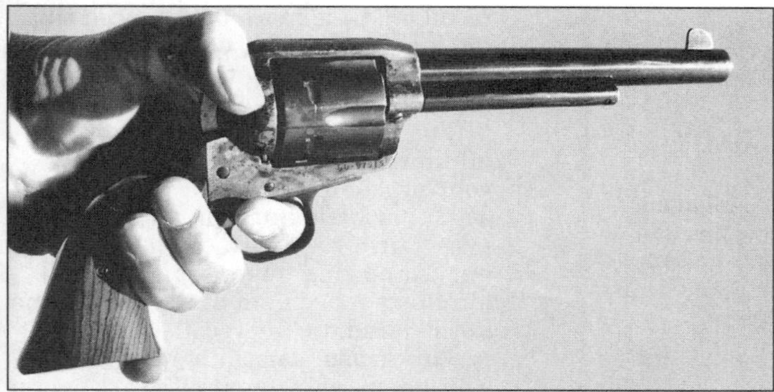

Flashy but inefficient, this method is best left to actors with blanks. As gun rolls up on recoil, thumb curls over hammer...

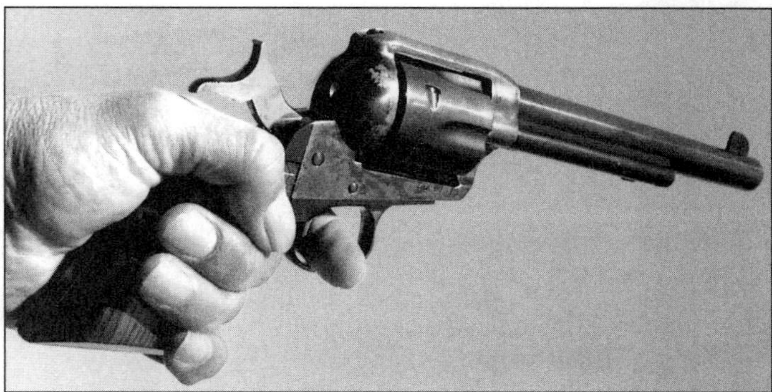

...and a flick of the wrist snaps the gun's weight forward, literally cocking the hammer against the thumb, which then curls down for the shot. This tends to throw hits low, and is not particularly fast.

either the firing hand or the frame of the revolver. The sequence will go like this.

At the signal, the gun is drawn with the firing hand and brought up on target, the support hand coming in from the side and from behind the muzzle to take its hold. The support thumb immediately goes to the hammer, rolling it straight back with a crisp, clean movement. As the trigger finger does its work, the cocking thumb appears to drift back forward along the left side of the hammer if the gun is being fired by the right hand. As that big hammer falls and the shot is fired, the support thumb by now is already forward and in position to repeat the cocking process.

It can be a mistake to cock the hammer with the support thumb and then leave that thumb across the back of the firing hand. If you're shooting a 44 Magnum, a 454 Casull, or a 475 Linebaugh, the violent upward-and-back roll of the gun upon recoil can bring the hammer crashing down upon that thumb. This may be why the term "thumb-buster" came to be applied to the single-action revolver.

In terms of body position, the shooter will always be stronger if the weak-side foot is forward and the feet are at least shoulder width apart. This is the same "pyramidal base" that combat shooters use with modern handguns. Some sixgunners like the Weaver stance with both arms bent, the gun hand pushing and the support hand pulling isometrically with equal and opposite pressure. This should be done very firmly with the big magnum hunting six-guns, but a more relaxed pressure is usually applied with the mild loads popular in cowboy action. The Isosceles hold, with both arms locked straight out, can of course be used, too. However, one sees more shooters with bent elbows at cowboy matches.

One-Hand Stances

The Duelist category of SASS requires that the revolver be fired one-handed. The Gunfighter category has one gun in each hand simultaneously. In either case, with only one hand to stabilize *and* manipulate the big revolver, subtleties of grasp become much more critical.

The plow-handle grip shape of the classic cowboy revolver causes the gun to roll back into the hand and pivot its muzzle upward. The more potent the cartridge, the more powerful the

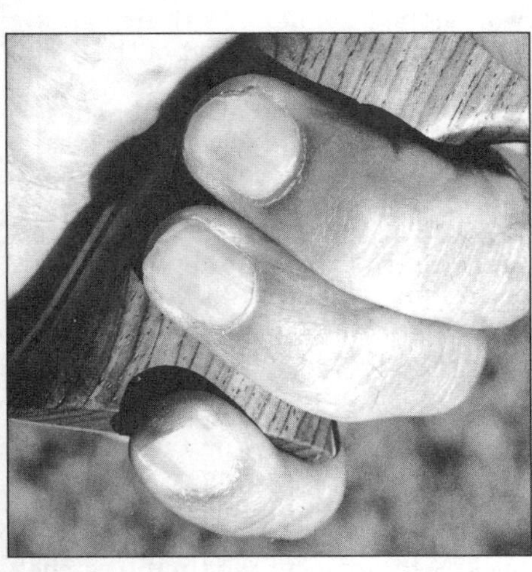

Tucking the pinkie finger under the forward edge of the grip, like this, is important. The reason is...

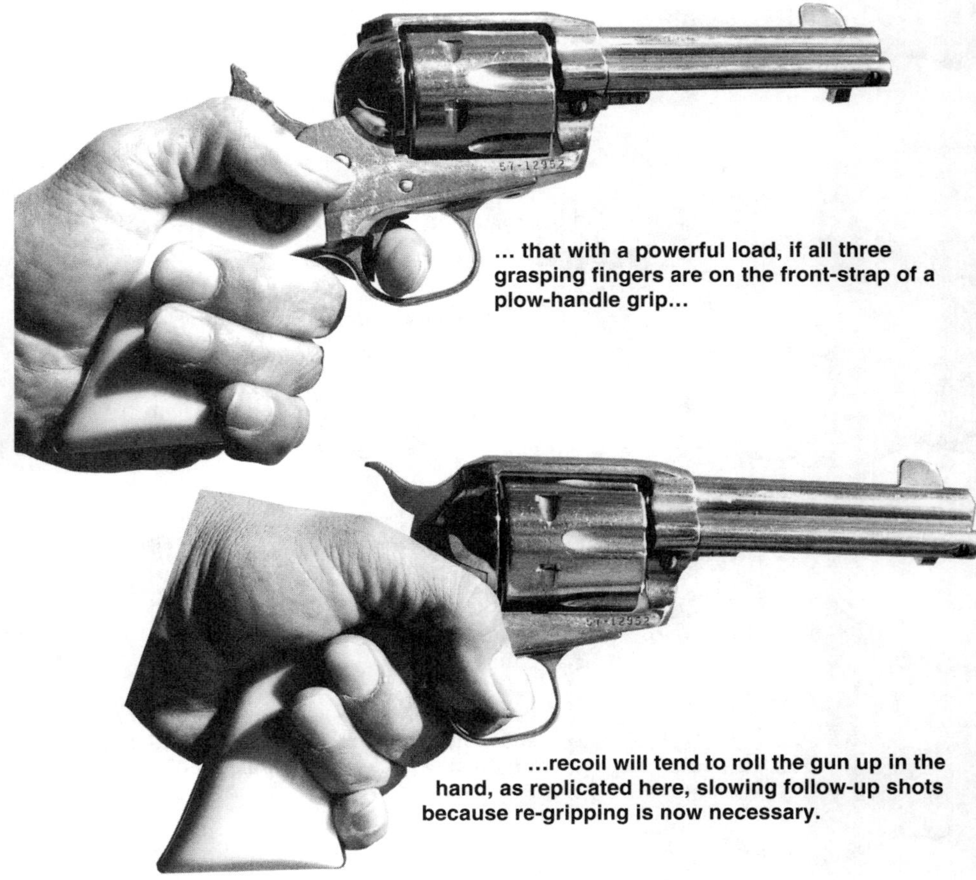

... that with a powerful load, if all three grasping fingers are on the front-strap of a plow-handle grip...

...recoil will tend to roll the gun up in the hand, as replicated here, slowing follow-up shots because re-gripping is now necessary.

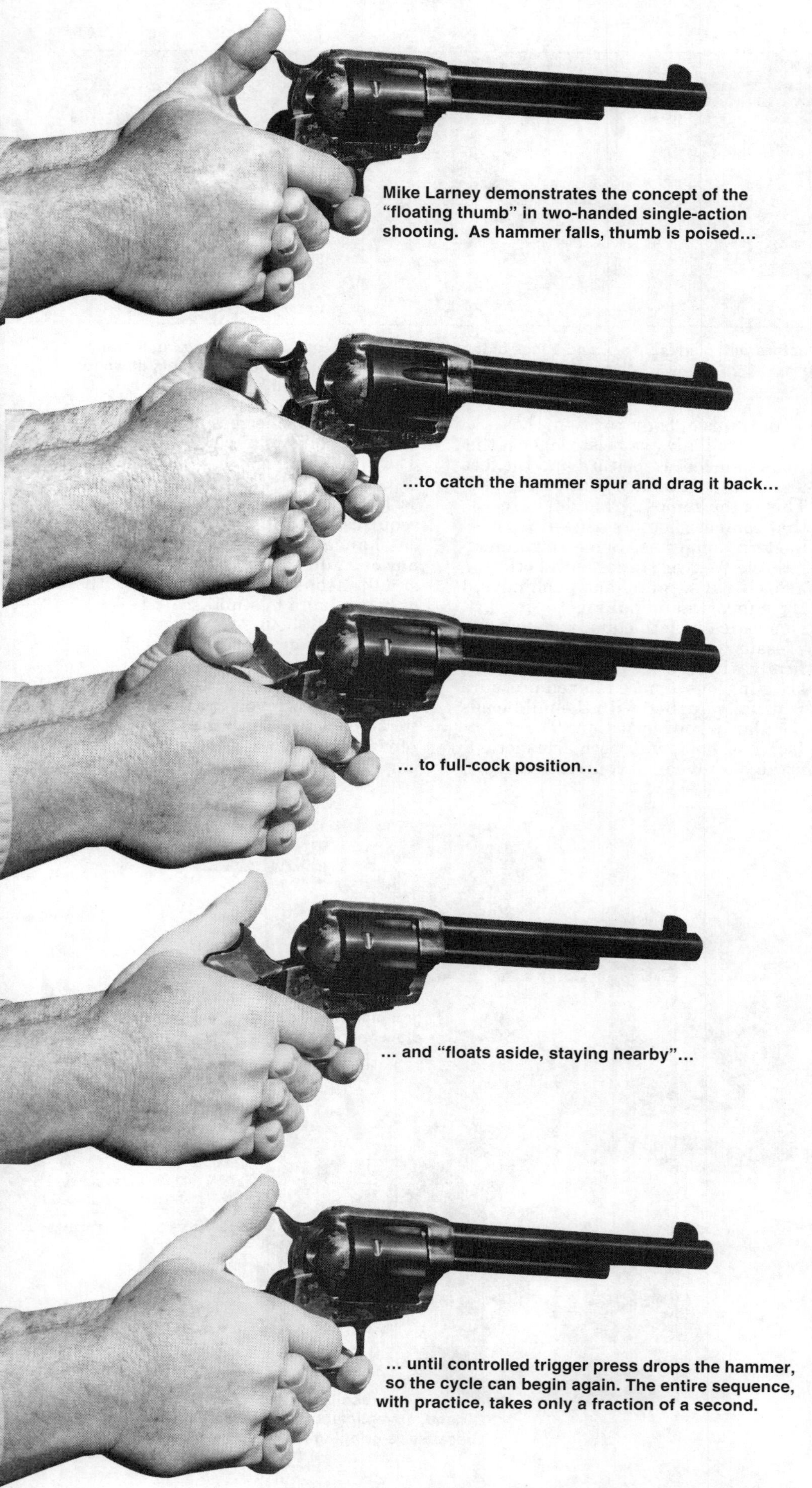

Mike Larney demonstrates the concept of the "floating thumb" in two-handed single-action shooting. As hammer falls, thumb is poised...

...to catch the hammer spur and drag it back...

... to full-cock position...

... and "floats aside, staying nearby"...

... until controlled trigger press drops the hammer, so the cycle can begin again. The entire sequence, with practice, takes only a fraction of a second.

recoil, and the more pronounced this tendency will be. It will require a distinct re-gripping to bring the muzzle back down on target.

The first thing you can do to minimize this movement is to tuck your pinkie finger under the butt. Curl that little finger in tight, and take a firm hold with the middle finger and ring finger too. This will minimize movement of the grip-frame in the hand during recoil.

This grasp is nothing new. Elmer Keith demonstrated it 50 years ago in "*Sixguns by Keith*." He, in turn, probably learned it from old cowboys who actually slung their guns back in the nineteenth century. It worked then, and it works now. The late, great Charles "Skeeter" Skelton, an adept with both single- and double-action revolvers, recommended the same grasp for modern snub-nose 38s that didn't have grip adapters or custom stocks.

One-handed, there's only one thumb available to cock the hammer. It can't do that and firmly grip the revolver at the same time, so if you want maximum speed of fire, that thumb too will be "floating" during a rapid-fire sequence. There are several ways to manipulate the hammer. The technique that works best for you will depend on the length and shape of the hammer spur, the length and range of movement of your thumb, and the shape of the backstrap of your shootin' iron's grip-frame.

The most popular grip shape, of course, is the Single Action Army (SAA) style. Some shooters like to let the revolver roll back into the hand upon recoil, lay the thumb over the hammer spur, and then flick the wrist and snap the gun back on target. The forward weight of the gun literally cocks the hammer against the resistance of the thumb. In other words, the hammer and thumb stay constant, and it's the rest of the revolver that moves.

This looks flashy and will bring the practitioner back to his days of watching B-movie cowboy matinees, but it's not a terribly efficient way to shoot. The violent movement of the main body of the six-gun with this technique is not conducive to bringing the muzzle back on target with maximum economy of time and movement.

It makes more sense to keep a firm hold so the gun stays on target as much as possible during recoil, and let the thumb do the hammer-cocking job. You want the thumb to pull straight back. As the pad of the thumb catches the checkered or serrated surface on the hammer spur, the tip of the thumb and the thumbnail should be pointed toward the front sight. This will align the bones of the thumb and allow a straight-back pull which ears the hammer back to the full-cock position without deviating the muzzle from the target. Depending on hammer shape and thumb size, you may have to use the tip of the thumb instead of the ball of the thumb to do this.

The proportionally smaller, more forward-sitting hammer of my old S&W #3 or the Schofield style requires, for my hand, distinctly more forward reach and I just can't cock it nearly as fast as I can my Peacemaker. I'm not the only one. While the S&W guns and their clones are very popular among the traditionalists who shoot cowboy action for fun, you seldom see them in the hands of the consistent overall winners.

The higher, flatter back-strap of the Bisley-style frame, particularly the Ruger interpretation of the Bisley, is less conducive to that *"roll up in the hand upon recoil"* effect. Many find them more comfortable to shoot with the most powerful loads – John Taffin and Ross Seyfried, to name two nationally recognized experts – and because the thumb is closer to an often-broader hammer spur, many shooters find them faster to manipulate at high speed irrespective of recoil level.

One-handed cocking of the Peacemaker-style revolver requires considerable flexibility of the median joint of the thumb. If injury or arthritis have limited you in this respect, take a look at a Bisley. Another option is the SASS-approved Ruger Single-Six revolver in 32 H&R Magnum. Built on a frame originally designed for 22s, this scaled-down six-gun has a distinctly shorter length of hammer movement in cocking than the full-size Colt and clones, or the bigger Rugers.

Drawing and Holstering

Half a century ago, during the first big "single action craze" of the twentieth century, fast-draw was the predominant game. Shooters tried to cock their guns in the holsters to shave time. If anything went wrong, the gun went off in the leather. Enough would-be cowboys blew their feet and legs away that holster-makers started putting in steel bullet deflector shields, and the fast-draw game became limited to blanks and wax bullets, rules that hold to this very day.

I suppose that's one way of treating the problem, but the best way is, *never so much as begin to cock the hammer until the muzzle of the gun is already clear of the holster and safely downrange!* In one-handed firing, the thumb begins to bring the hammer back as the muzzle is coming up on target. With practice, the movement becomes sufficiently coordinated that the muzzle is on target and ready for the shot by the time the hammer is at full cock.

Adapt your grasp to the grip shape. The classic plow-handle configuration of this standard Vaquero...

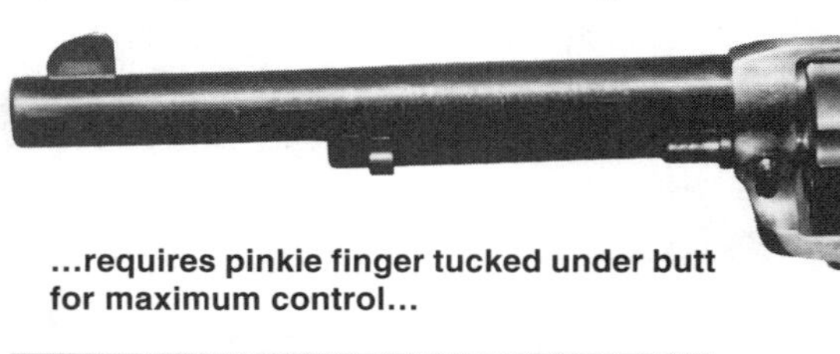

...requires pinkie finger tucked under butt for maximum control...

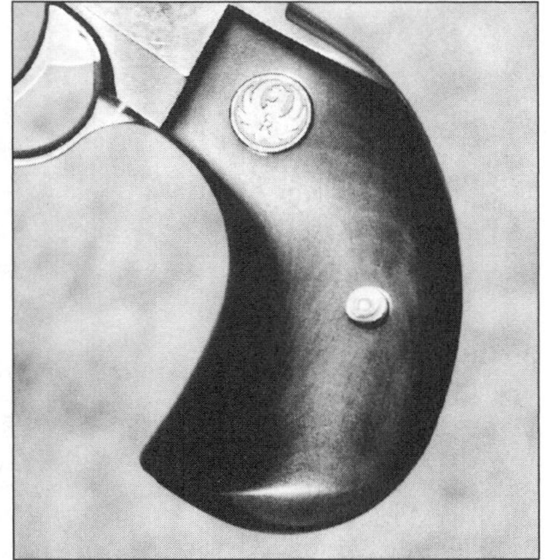

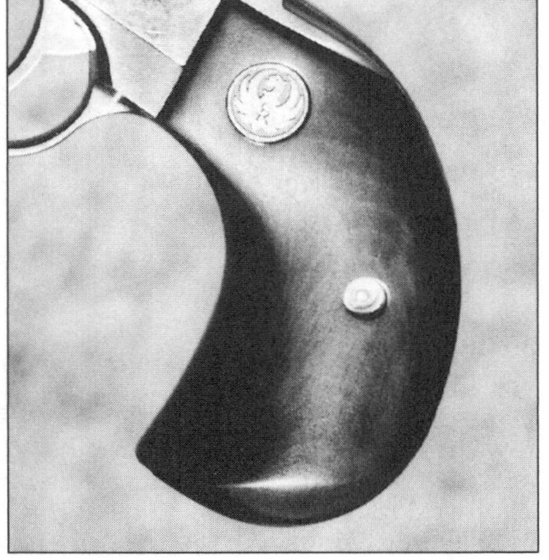

... and this currently popular bird's head Vaquero...

In two-handed firing, the muzzle should already be downrange when the gun hand is met by the support hand, which will immediately perform the cocking movement. Because the support hand has more range of thumb movement than the grasping hand, it will quickly catch up and have the hammer eared back for you in ample time.

When holstering any firearm, you want to have the trigger finger outside the guard and pointing parallel to the muzzle, and you want to have the thumb on the hammer holding it in its proper place. In a SASS match, almost every stage will require you to employ two six-guns. If you're shooting them one at a time, you have to get the first back into the holster before you can draw the second.

The pointing finger will help to "point" the revolver back into the holster by feel, smoothing and speeding up the movement. Remember the dictum of the first

... requires the same...

world combat pistol champion, Ray Chapman, a man who started his career with Colt Single Action Army revolvers: "Smoothness is five-sixths of speed." The thumb on the hammer, when holstering one of these old-style cowboy guns, is one more palpable verification the hammer is down on an empty chamber or a fired casing before it goes into the leather.

Many cowboy competitors in all but Gunfighter category choose to put their second six-shooter cross-draw on the point of *(or more efficiently, in front of)* the weak-side hip. To draw without breaking the 180-degree safety plane and sweeping the range officer and fellow competitors with your muzzle, turn the holster-side hip edgeways toward the target when making the draw. Now you just pull the gun out across your belly, and it's already pointed safely downrange, waiting for you to punch it forward to engage the targets.

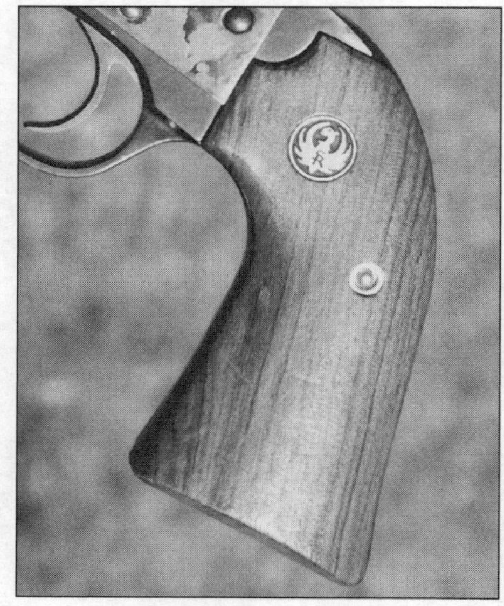

... but this Bisley style Vaquero has a higher backstrap that won't roll up in the hand so much, plus a longer frontstrap...

... and will survive this conventional grasp with all three support fingers at the front of the grip-frame.

The author wishes to thank Kathy and Mike Larney ("Buckskin Kay" and "Roland Darktower") for illustrating the techniques above.

When re-holstering cross draw, you likewise want to make that edgeways turn to keep the muzzle toward the berm. If you've carried a gun for years, holstering strong-side is a natural movement easy to perform by feel, but doing so cross-draw may not be so ingrained and natural a habit. If that's the case, it's a good idea to look downward and watch what you're doing as you holster. This won't slow you down as much as you think. By visually indexing the gun into the scabbard, you can prevent fumbles and actually speed up your overall time.

Some shooters harken back to the twin cap pistol rigs of their youth and wear one revolver on each hip, both butts pointing to the rear. This is how it's done in Gunfighter category, where both guns are drawn simultaneously and fired in turn. If you're shooting in Duelist, Traditional, or Modern class, there are other options.

One is to simply fire right-handed with the gun in the right-side holster, and left-handed with the one in the southpaw scabbard. However, most people shoot their best with their dominant hand controlling the frame and trigger. If this is the case, and you carry both guns with butts rearward, the sequence to follow is this:

Draw the gun from your strong-side holster and go to work. When the last shot is fired, leave the hammer down and holster it as outlined above. Now, with your weak side hand, draw the gun in a scooping movement, holding it with the index finger under or in front of the trigger guard, the thumb at the back of the frame just in front of the hammer, and the other three fingers supporting the front of the grip frame like a shelf. Bring the muzzle immediately downrange and sweep the gun in front of you toward the strong hand, which by now is coming across and reaching for it. As your dominant hand takes its firing hold, the support hand thumb and index finger are already in position to do their respective jobs, and the other three fingers of that hand are in position to wrap supportively around the fingers of the firing hand after the latter have closed on the gun.

Loading and Reloading

Even if you have New Model Rugers like those illustrating this article, or other single actions which can safely be carried with a live round under the hammer, it is a rigid rule among professional gunners to always leave an empty chamber under an SA's hammer. This is because habits acquired with one model transfer to another. Older designs can accidentally discharge with a live cartridge under the firing pin, which even Wyatt Earp is said to have discovered to his embarrassment.

The original users of these guns on the old Frontier learned to load them in this sequence. Load one, then skip an empty chamber, then load the next four. Logical rotation should automatically bring the empty chamber under the hammer when the last live round is in place. Even so, glance in at the back of the cylinder from the side and double-check.

The single-action revolver is a part of every American's heritage, and an avatar of the heritage of the gun enthusiast. The more safely and efficiently you operate them, the more enjoyment they will give you. •

Massad Ayoob began shooting single actions more than forty years ago with a mint, original Colt Frontier Six Shooter in 44/40. Today, he competes whenever possible in SASS matches under the monicker "Camelback Kid."

The 270 Winchester & 270 WSM Compared in Handguns

by Dr. George E. Dvorchak, Jr.

AS A YOUNGSTER hunting in my native state of Pennsylvania, it seemed that all my friends and their fathers had a rifle either in 30-30 Winchester, 30-06 Springfield or 270 Winchester. Also back in the 60s, I looked forward to read hunting stories by Jack O'Connor, who, when posing with a mountain sheep or goat seemed to always have a 270 Winchester in his hand. While he talked about the gun, chambering and loads, by the photos of the scenery you knew that this cartridge had to shoot flat at long ranges to anchor whatever Jack was hunting.

Today, although the 27-caliber has lost a little notoriety to the newer magnums, it is still sufficiently popular that Winchester added a new 27-caliber to their line of high-intensity short magnum cartridges. The big advantage of this new cartridge, dubbed the WSM or Winchester Short Magnum, is that being much shorter than the original 270, it can be chambered in a shorter–and therefore lighter–rifle action. According to what I was told about these cartridges at SHOT Show 2000, the efficiency of the powder burn is increased—which delivers bullet velocities equal to those of a regular-length cartridge of the same caliber. Here is where being short and fat is not a problem for cartridges as it is for us humans.

Handgun Adaptability

Being curious about the full range of potential of these new cartridges, specifically the 270 WSM and 300 WSM, I contacted various firearms companies to see if they were doing any work with these cartridges—specifically, were they adapting the WSM cartridges to their handguns.

The Winchester 270s: both new and old. The tall cartridge *(left)* is the 270 Winchester, which needs a long action; the newer 270 WSM *(right)* can operate through a shorter one. Of the two, the WSM operates under much higher pressures, which is why the Savage Striker is the only handgun capable of handling this cartridge.

At first I got answers such as "we are working on it," which was to me a promising step in the right direction–"right" if you are a handgun hunter. Then, finally after testing and the results having been evaluated by their experts, I was told that due to the excessive pressures of such cartridges, none of these companies would be chambering these cartridges in their handguns—no one except Savage. This progressive company was in a unique position, having the only bolt-action handgun commercially available. Since the action was designed for bolt-action rifles, the Savage bolt-action Striker *(which uses a rifle action)* should handle everything quite well. After speaking with Ron Coburn, CEO and President of Savage, my hunting partner on a few bear hunts *(during which the Striker and these new chamberings were a topic of mutual interest)* Ron told me that when a test gun was available, he would let me know. When he did, I got the ball rolling and, shortly afterwards, I had a production Striker in 270 WSM to evaluate in the field.

With this new 270, and for those who like this caliber, it will be interesting to compare the old with the new—especially out of handgun-length barrels, which are usually 12, 14, or 16 inches long. I knew the first 270 Winchester, dating back to 1925, would work fine since I have used this cartridge in an Encore and Competitor. After reading first reports on the new 270 WSM *(introduced 2002)*, it seemed everyone who reviewed it stated it needed those long rifle barrels to be an effective cartridge; which is true—but not totally. If that was the only application for this cartridge, there should not be any need to go on—except for my experience with the 300 WSM in a Striker the year before, wherein I found it shot incredibly well out of a 14-inch barrel. Therefore, why should the 270 be any different? Clearly, it was time to test the new 270 WSM and the original 270 Winchester—in handguns.

To add a control, I also brought out my Thompson/Center Encore rifle with its 24-inch barrel in 270 Winchester. This I would also chronograph to compare how some ammo would perform out of a short (Competitor) and long barrel of this rifle in the original chambering: 270 Winchester.

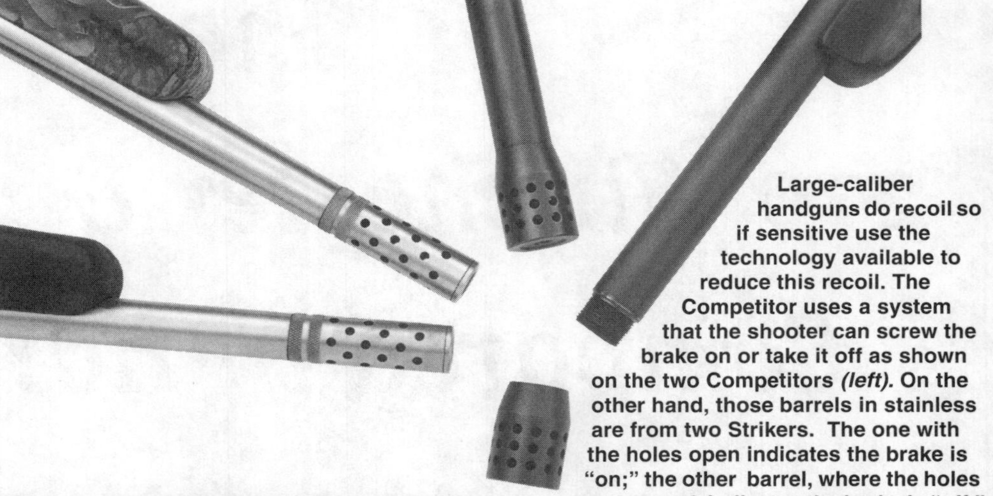

Large-caliber handguns do recoil so if sensitive use the technology available to reduce this recoil. The Competitor uses a system that the shooter can screw the brake on or take it off as shown on the two Competitors *(left)*. On the other hand, those barrels in stainless are from two Strikers. The one with the holes open indicates the brake is "on;" the other barrel, where the holes are covered, indicates the brake is "off."

Handgun: Savage Striker in 270 WSM

Accuracy at 100 yards; muzzle velocity of the ammunition tested. Chronograph: Oehler 35-P, Temperature: 60 degrees F, 100 percent humidity. Groups: 3 shots @ 100yards.

Ammo	Muzzle Velocity (fps): Brake Off/Brake On	Group (in.)
Speer 90-gr. HP TNT; 72.0-gr. H 4831; CCI 250	—/2680	0.80
Sierra 90-gr. HP; 60.0-gr. Varget; CCI 250	—/2901	0.55
Speer 100-gr. HP; 65.0-gr. H 4350; CCI 250	—/2533	0.55
Hornady 100-gr. SP; 58.0-gr. RL 15; CCI 250	—/2853	1.10
Sierra 110 Spitzer; 64.2-gr. XMR 4350; CCI 250	—/2875	0.75
Hornady 110 HP; 59.8-gr. H 4350; CCI 250	—/2403	0.95
Speer 130 -gr. SBT; 72.5-gr. H 1000; CCI 250	—/2596	1.75
Hornady 130 -gr. Interbond; 62.0-gr. H 4831; CCI 250	—/2381	0.70
Sierra 130 Spitzer; 60.7-gr. IMR 4350; CCI 250	—/2496	0.60
Hornady 130 -gr. SP; 60.4-gr. RL 19; CCI 250	—/2383	1.00
Sierra 130 BT; 61.0-gr. H 414; CCI 250	—/2624	1.45
Winchester 130-gr. Ballistic Silvertip	2613/2590	1.20
Hornady 130-gr. Interbond; 68.8-gr. WMR; CCI 250	—/2645	1.20
Winchester 140-gr. Fail Safe	2573/2566	1.35
Sierra 140-gr. Spitzer; 63.1-gr. RE-19; CCI 250	—/2497	0.60
Winchester 150-gr. Power Point	2501/2504	1.10
Winchester 150-gr. Ballistic Silvertip	—/2484	1.50
Speer Grand Slam 150-gr.; 57.4-gr. H 414; CCI 250	—/2520	0.75
Speer Spitzer SP 150-gr.; 59.4-gr. AA 3100; CCI 200	—/2437	1.10
Speer BT 150-gr.; 58.0-gr. H 4831; CCI 250	—/2320	2.0
Hornady 150-gr. SP; 58.4-gr. H-4350; CCI 250	—/2417	1.30

Savage Striker Specifications/Data:

Manufacturer and Contact Information: Savage Arms Inc. 118 Mountain Road, Suffield, CT 06078; 413-568-7001, www.savagearms.com

Model: 516FSAK

Action: Short with left-hand bolt and right side case ejection

Safety: Mechanical 3 position that is easily operated with the thumb of the right hand

Trigger Pull: 4.25 pounds with a little slack

Caliber: 270 WSM

Rifling Rate of Twist: 1 in 11 inches

Shot Capacity: 2, 1 in chamber and 1 in magazine

Barrel Length including muzzle brake: 14 inches of which 2.3 inches is unrifled barrel

Overall Length: 22.5 inches

Weight without scope: Around 88 ounces

Metal Finish: Stainless barrel and action

Stock: Black ambidextrous synthetic

Sights from the Factory: None but scope base installed at Savage

Suggested Retail Price: $ 562.00

Scope: Burris 2-7X: 970-356-1670, www.burrisoptics.com

Handgun: Competitor in 270 Winchester

Accuracy at 100 yards; muzzle velocity of the ammunition tested. Chronograph: Oehler 35-P, Temperature: 60 degrees F, 100 percent humidity. Groups: 3 shots @ 100yards.

Ammo	Muzzle Velocity (fps):	Group (in.)
Winchester 130-gr. Silvertip	2654	1.40
Winchester 130-gr. Power Point Plus	2746	0.60
Winchester 130-gr. Power-Point	2642	1.25
Hornady 130-gr. SST Light Magnum	2777	2.00
Hornady 130-gr. SP Interlock	2647	1.10
Federal 130-gr. Hi-Shok SP	2642	1.00
Federal 130-gr. Nosler BT	2672	0.65
Speer Nitrex 130-gr. Grand Slam	2788	0.85
Hornady 130-gr, Interbond; 58.8-gr. RL-19; WRL Primer	2696	2.0
Speer 130-gr. Spitzer BT; 53.0-gr. Win. 760; CCI 250	2700	1.10
Sierra 130-gr. Spitzer BT; 52.0-gr. Win. 760; WLR	2643	1.75
Hornady 140-gr. BTSP Interlok Bullet	2581	2.0
Winchester 140-gr. Fail Safe	2545	0.60
Speer 150-gr. BT; 52.2-gr. Win. 760; CCI 250	2613	0.60
Speer 150-gr. SP; 56.2-gr. AA 3100; CCI 200	2510	1.75
Remington 150-gr. Nosler Partition	2306	1.25

Firearms used in the ammo evaluation. Top, the Savage Striker in 270 WSM with its Burris scope in 2-7X power. Center, the Thompson/Center Encore 270 Winchester rifle with its Realtree stock and Bausch & Lomb Elite 4200 in 2.5-10X power. On the bottom, the Competitor in 270 Winchester with its laminated wood stock and Bushnell Elite 3200 2-6X power scope.

Competitor Specifications/Data:

Manufacturer and Contact Information: Competitor, Inc.
26 Knight St.,Unit 3
P.O. Box 352
Jaffrey, NH 03452-0352
603-532-9483/ e-mail: competitorcorp@aol.com
www.competitor-pistol.com

Model: Competitor Single Shot Pistol

Action: Rotary cannon, self-cocking on opening

Safety: Dual; sliding thumb on rear breech cap locks the sear. The second is located in the trigger

Trigger Pull: Adjustable from 2-7 pounds, mine was set to 2.75 pounds, there was no slack

Chamberings: 450-plus—wildcat and commercial cartridges

Rifling rate of twist: 1 in 10 inches

Shot Capacity: 1

Barrel Length with screw on/off muzzle brake: 16 inches.

Overall Length: 17-1/8 inches, with a 16-inch barrel.

Weight with 14-inch barrel and without scope: 71 ounces (with laminated wood stock)

Metal Finish: Matte blue is standard with electroless nickel optional

Stock Options: Ambidextrous laminate, synthetic or natural wood

Sights: Depends on what you order, scope base is included if no sights are ordered

Suggested Retail Price: Varies with options: 14/16-inch barrel and synthetic grip is $460.

Scope: Bushnell Elite 3200 2-6 X. 800-423-3537; www.bushnell.com

T/C Encore Specifications/Data:

Manufacturer and Contact Information: Thompson/Center Arms
P.O. Box 5002
Rochester, NH 03867
603-332-2333.
www.tcarms.com

Action: Single shot, break-open design

Safety: Automatic hammer block with bolt interlock

Chambering: 270 Winchester

Stock: American Walnut or Composite in black or Realtree camo

Trigger Pull: Crisp 3.5 pounds adjustable for over-travel

Barrel Length: 22 inches, with front and rear sight standard

Overall length: 38.5 inches

Weight without scope: Seven pounds

Suggested Retail Price: $582

Scope: Bausch & Lomb Elite 4200 2.5-10X; 800-423-3537, www.bushnell.com

Rifle: T/C Encore in 270 Winchester

Accuracy at 100 yards; muzzle velocity of the ammunition tested. Chronograph: Oehler 35-P, Temperature: 60 degrees F, 100 percent humidity. Groups: 3 shots @ 100yards.

Ammo	Muzzle Velocity (fps):	Group (in.)
Winchester 130-gr. Silvertip	2987	0.75
Winchester 130-gr. Power-Point Plus	3081	1.10
Winchester 130-gr. Power-Point	2965	1.25
Hornady 130-gr. SST Light Magnum	3128	1.75
Hornady 130-gr. SP Interlock	2955	0.60
Speer Nitrex 130-gr. Grand Slam	3122	0.70
Federal 130-gr. Hi-Shok SP	2942	0.90
Federal 130-gr. Nosler BT	2989	0.75
Winchester 140-gr. Fail Safe	2779	0.75

From the three tables of loads and muzzle velocities, one result we all expected is that the longer barrel of the rifle is needed to get the best velocity from a "rifle" cartridge. When it comes to accuracy, the load is the deciding factor. Here, shorter barrels do not always take a back seat to longer ones and, although velocities are not up there with rifle-length barrels, they are not bad out of the smaller gun.

If I wanted a 27-caliber handgun, then I would purchase either of these—with the determining factor being the handgun design I preferred. Safe Hunting! •

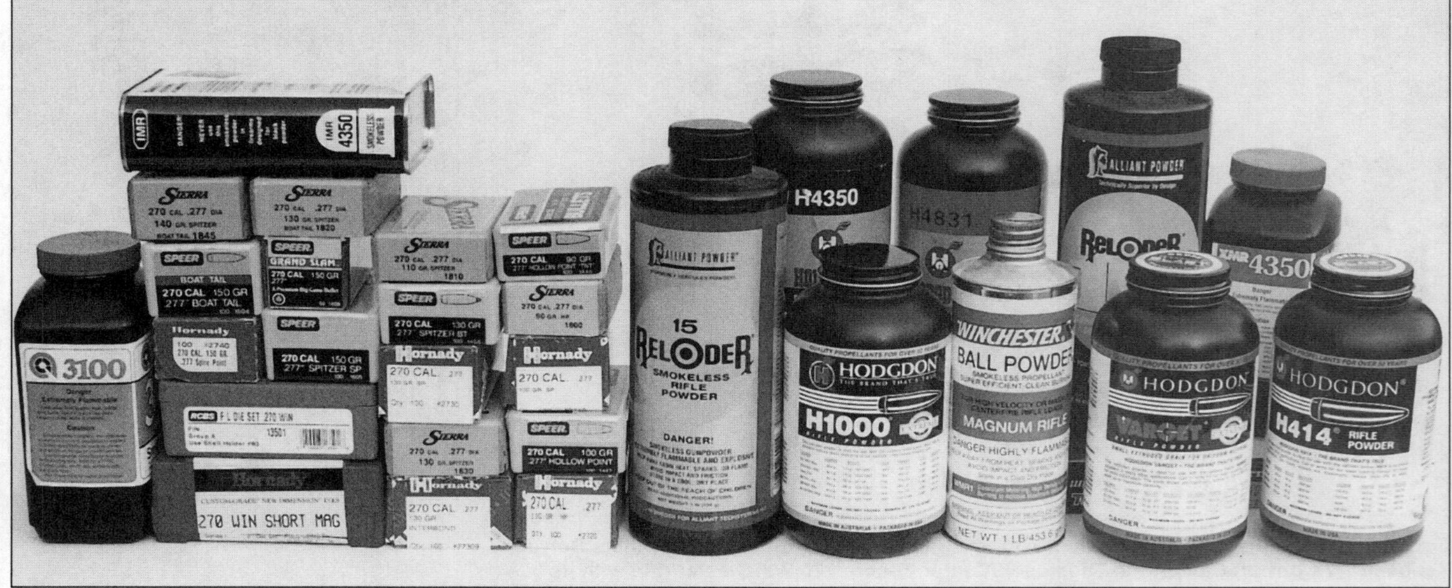

When loading for both cartridges, I used a variety of bullets and powders in my quest for good groups.

INTERESTING PRODUCT NEWS FOR THE ACTIVE SHOOTING SPORTSMAN

The companies represented on the following pages will be happy to provide additional information – feel free to contact them.

Doug Turnbull Restoration
Big Bore Classics
Turnbull Restoration Big Bore Classics Rifles are constructed using original and new manufactured Model 1886 Winchester & Browning Rifles. Available in calibers: 45-70, 45-90 & 50-110 (50 Express). For more information contact us at:
6680 Route 5 & 20, P.O. Box 471 Bloomfield, NY 14469
Phone: 585-657-6338 Email: turnbullrest@mindspring.com Website:www.turnbullrestoration.com

HIGH QUALITY OPTICS

One of the best indicators of quality is a scope's resolution number. The smaller the number, the better. Our scope has a resolution number of 2.8 seconds of angle. This number is about 20% smaller (better) than other well-known scopes costing much more. It means that two .22 caliber bullets can be a hair's breadth apart and edges of each still be clearly seen. With a Shepherd at 800 yards, you will be able to tell a four inch antler from a four inch ear and a burrowing owl from a prairie dog. Bird watchers will be able to distinguish a Tufted Titmouse from a Ticked-Off Field Mouse. Send for free catalog.

SHEPHERD ENTERPRISES, INC.

Box 189, Waterloo, NE 68069
Phone: 402-779-2424 • Fax: 402-779-4010
E-mail: shepherd@shepherdscopes.com • Web: www.shepherdscopes.com

BEAR TRACK CASES

Designed by an Alaskan bush pilot! Polyurethane coated, zinc plated corners and feet, zinc plated—spring loaded steel handles, stainless steel hinges, high density urethane foam inside with a neoprene seal. Aluminum walls are standard at .070 with riveted ends. Committed to quality that will protect your valuables regardless of the transportation method you use. Exterior coating also protects other items from acquiring "aluminum black."

Many styles, colors and sizes available. Wheels come on large cases and special orders can be accommodated. Call for a brochure or visit online.

Bear Track Cases when top quality protection is a must.

BEAR TRACK CASES

314 Highway 239, Freedom, WY 83120
Phone: 307-883-2468 • Fax: 307-883-2005
Web: www.beartrackcases.com

NYLON COATED GUN CLEANING RODS

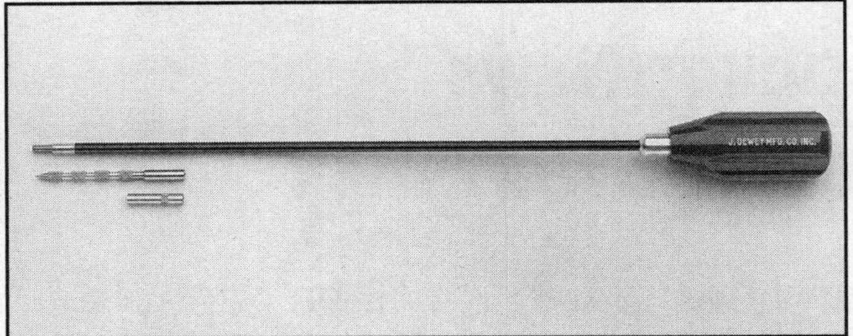

J. Dewey cleaning rods have been used by the U.S. Olympic shooting team and the benchrest community for over 20 years. These one-piece, spring-tempered, steel-base rods will not gall delicate rifling or damage the muzzle area of front-cleaned firearms. The nylon coating elminінates the problem of abrasives adhering to the rod during the cleaning operation. Each rod comes with a hard non-breakable plastic handle supported by ball-bearings, top and bottom, for ease of cleaning.

The brass cleaning jags are designed to pierce the center of the cleaning patch or wrap around the knurled end to keep the patch centered in the bore.

Coated rods are available from 17-caliber to shotgun bore size in several lengths to meet the needs of any shooter. Write for more information.

J. DEWEY MFG. CO., INC.

P.O. Box 2014, Southbury, CT 06488

Phone: 203-264-3064 • Fax: 203-262-6907

Web: www.deweyrods.com

ULTIMATE 500

Gary Reeder Custom Guns, builder of full custom guns for over 25 years, and with over 50 different series of custom hunting handguns, cowboy guns, custom Encores and large caliber hunting rifles, has a free brochure for you. Or visit their website. One of the most popular is their Ultimate 500, chambered in the 500 S&W Magnum. This beefy 5-shot revolver is for the serious handgun hunter and is one of several series of large caliber handguns, such as 475 Linebaugh and 475 Maximum, 500 Linebaugh and 500 Maximum. For more information, contact:

GARY REEDER CUSTOM GUNS

2601 E. 7th Avenue, Flagstaff, AZ 86004

Phone: 928-527-4100 or 928-526-3313

Website: www.reedercustomguns.com

FINE GUN STOCKS

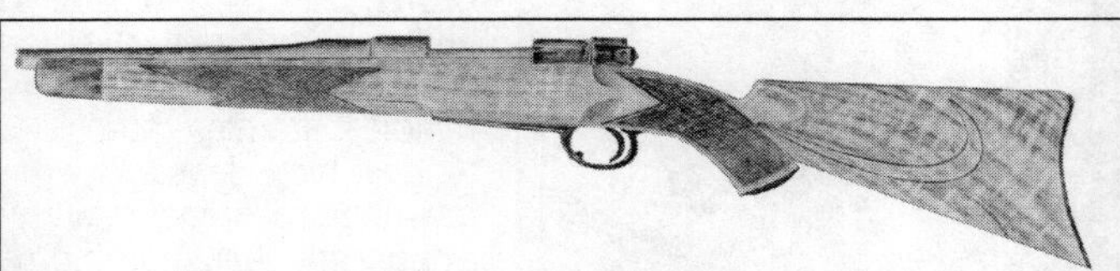

Manufacturing custom and production gunstocks for hundreds of models of rifles and shotguns—made from the finest stock woods and available in all stages of completion.

Visit www.gunstocks.com to view their bargain list of fine custom gunstocks. Each displayed in full color.

GREAT AMERICAN GUNSTOCK COMPANY

3420 Industrial Drive

Yuba City, CA 95993

Phone: 530-671-4570

Fax: 530-671-3906

Gunstock Hotline: 800-784-GUNS (4867)

Web: www.gunstocks.com

E-mail: gunstox@syix.com

COMBINATION RIFLE AND OPTICS REST

The Magna-Pod weighs less than two pounds, yet firmly supports more than most expensive tripods. It will hold 50 pounds at its low 9-inch height and over 10 pounds extended to 17 inches. It sets up in seconds where there is neither time nor space for a tripod and keeps your expensive equipment safe from knock-overs by kids, pets, pedestrians, or even high winds. It makes a great mono-pod for camcorders, etc., and its carrying box is less than 13" x 13" x 3 1/4" high for easy storage and access.

Attached to its triangle base it becomes an extremely stable table pod or rifle bench rest. The rifle yoke pictured in photo is included.

It's 5 pods in 1: Magna-Pod, Mono-Pod, Table-Pod, Shoulder-Pod and Rifle Rest. Send for free catalog.

SHEPHERD ENTERPRISES, INC.

Box 189, Waterloo, NE 68069

Phone: 402-779-2424 • Fax: 402-779-4010

E-mail: shepherd@shepherdscopes.com • Web: www.shepherdscopes.com

SHOOTER'S MARKETPLACE

BORDER CLASSIC

Gary Reeder Custom Guns, builder of full custom guns including hunting handguns, custom Encores, large caliber hunting rifles and over 20 different series of cowboy guns, including our Border Classic, shown. This beauty is the first ever snubbie Schofield, and can be built on any current Schofield. Fully engraved, round butted, with their Black Chromex finish and a solid silver Mexican coin for the front sight, this one is truly a masterpiece. See them all at their website, or call for a brochure.

GARY REEDER CUSTOM GUNS

2601 E. 7th Avenue, Flagstaff, AZ 86004
Phone: 928-527-4100 or 928-526-3313
Website: www.reedercustomguns.com

GARY LEVINE FINE KNIVES
A DEALER OF HANDMADE KNIVES

Gary's goal is to offer the collector the best custom knives available, in stock and ready for delivery. He has the best makers as well as the rising stars at fair prices. Gary enjoys working with collectors who want to enhance their collections, as well as someone who just wants a great knife to carry. Gary is also always on the lookout for collections, as well as single custom knives to purchase. Please stop by his website.

GARY LEVINE FINE KNIVES

P.O. Box 382, Chappaqua, NY 10514
Phone: 914-238-5748 • Fax: 914-238-6524
Web: http://www.levineknives.com
Email: gary@levineknives.com

QUALITY GUNSTOCK BLANKS

Cali'co Hardwoods has been cutting superior-quality shotgun and rifle blanks for more than 31 years. Cali'co supplies blanks to many of the major manufacturers—Browning, Weatherby, Ruger, Holland & Holland, to name a few—as well as custom gunsmiths the world over.

Profiled rifle blanks are available, ready for inletting and sanding. Cali'co sells superior California hardwoods in Claro walnut, French walnut, Bastogne, maple and myrtle.

Cali'co offers good, serviceable blanks and some of the finest exhibition blanks available. Satisfaction guaranteed.

Color catalog, retail and dealer price list (FFL required) free upon request.

CALI'CO HARDWOODS, INC.

3580 Westwind Blvd., Santa Rosa, CA 95403
Phone: 707-546-4045 • Fax: 707-546-4027

BLACK HILLS GOLD AMMUNITION

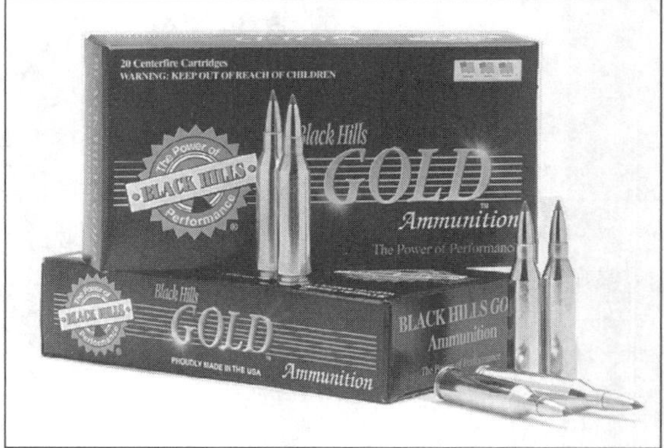

Black Hills Ammunition has introduced a new line of premium performance rifle ammunition. Calibers available in the Black Hills Gold Line are .243, .270, .308, .30-06, and .300 Win Mag. This line is designed for top performance in a wide range of hunting situations. Bullets used in this ammunition are the Barnes X-Bullet with XLC coating and the highly accurate Nosler Ballistic-Tip™.

Black Hills Ammunition is sold dealer direct. The Gold line is packaged in 20 rounds per box, 10 boxes per case. Black Hills pays all freight to dealers in the continental United States. Minimum dealer order is only one case.

BLACK HILLS AMMUNITION

P.O. Box 3090, Rapid City, SD 57709
Phone: 1-605-348-5150 • Fax: 1-605-348-9827
Web: www.black-hills.com

FOLDING BIPODS

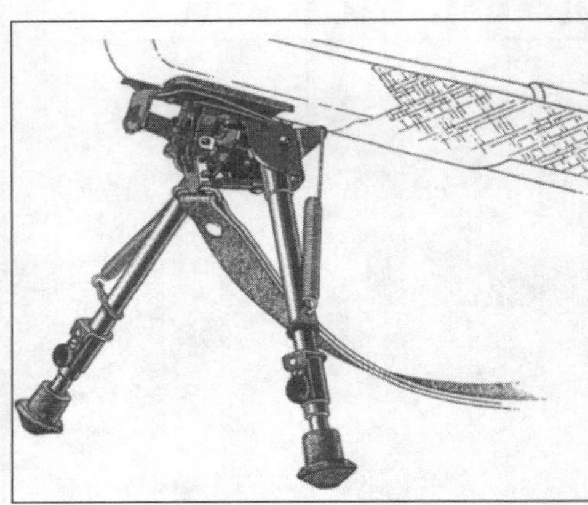

Harris Bipods clamp securely to most stud-equipped bolt-action rifles and are quick-detachable. With adapters, they will fit some other guns. On all models except the Model LM, folding legs have completely adjustable spring-return extensions. The sling swivel attaches to the clamp. This time-proven design is manufactured with heat-treated steel and hard alloys and has a black anodized finish.

Series S Bipods rotate 35° for instant leveling on uneven ground. Hinged base has tension adjustment and buffer springs to eliminate tremor or looseness in crotch area of bipod. They are otherwise similar to non-rotating Series 1A2.

Thirteen models are available from Harris Engineering; literature is free.

HARRIS ENGINEERING INC.

Dept: GD54, Barlow, KY 42024

Phone: 270-334-3633 • Fax: 270-334-3000

PRECISION RIFLE REST

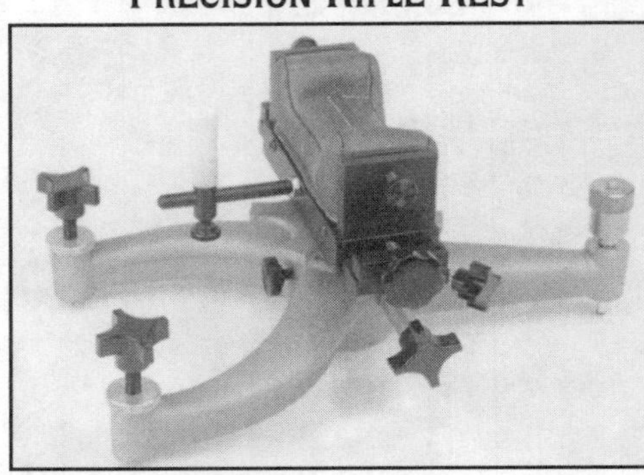

Bald Eagle Precision Machine Co. offers a rifle rest perfect for the serious benchrester or dedicated varminter.

"The Slingshot" or Next Generation has 60° front legs. The rest is constructed of aircraft-quality aluminum or fine grain cast iron and weighs 12 to 20 lbs. The finish is 3 coats of Imron clear. Primary height adjustments are made with a rack and pinion gear. Secondary adjustment uses a mariner wheel with thrust bearings for smooth operation. A hidden fourth leg allows for lateral movement on the bench.

Bald Eagle offers approximately 150 rest combinations to choose from, including windage adjustable, right or left hand, cast aluminum or cast iron.

Prices: $175.00 to $345.00

BALD EAGLE PRECISION MACHINE CO.

101-K Allison Street, Lock Haven, PA 17745

Phone: 570-748-6772 — Fax: 570-748-4443

Web: www.baldeaglemachine.com

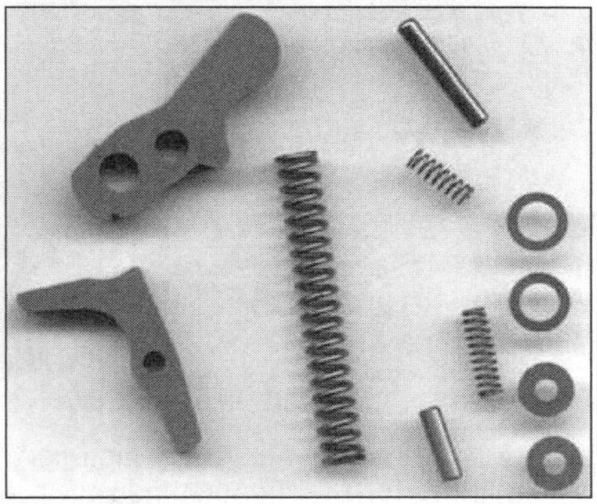

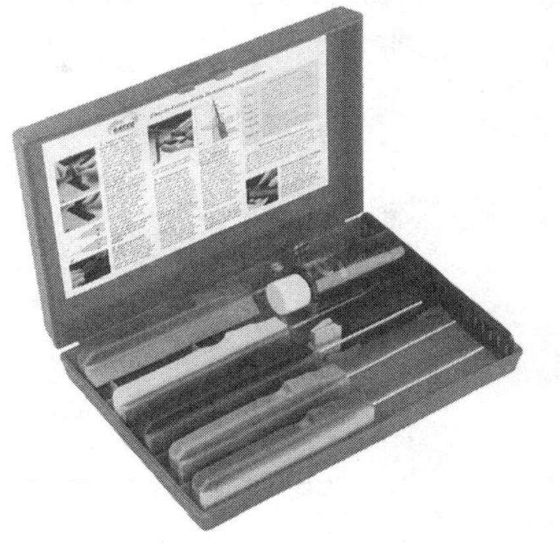

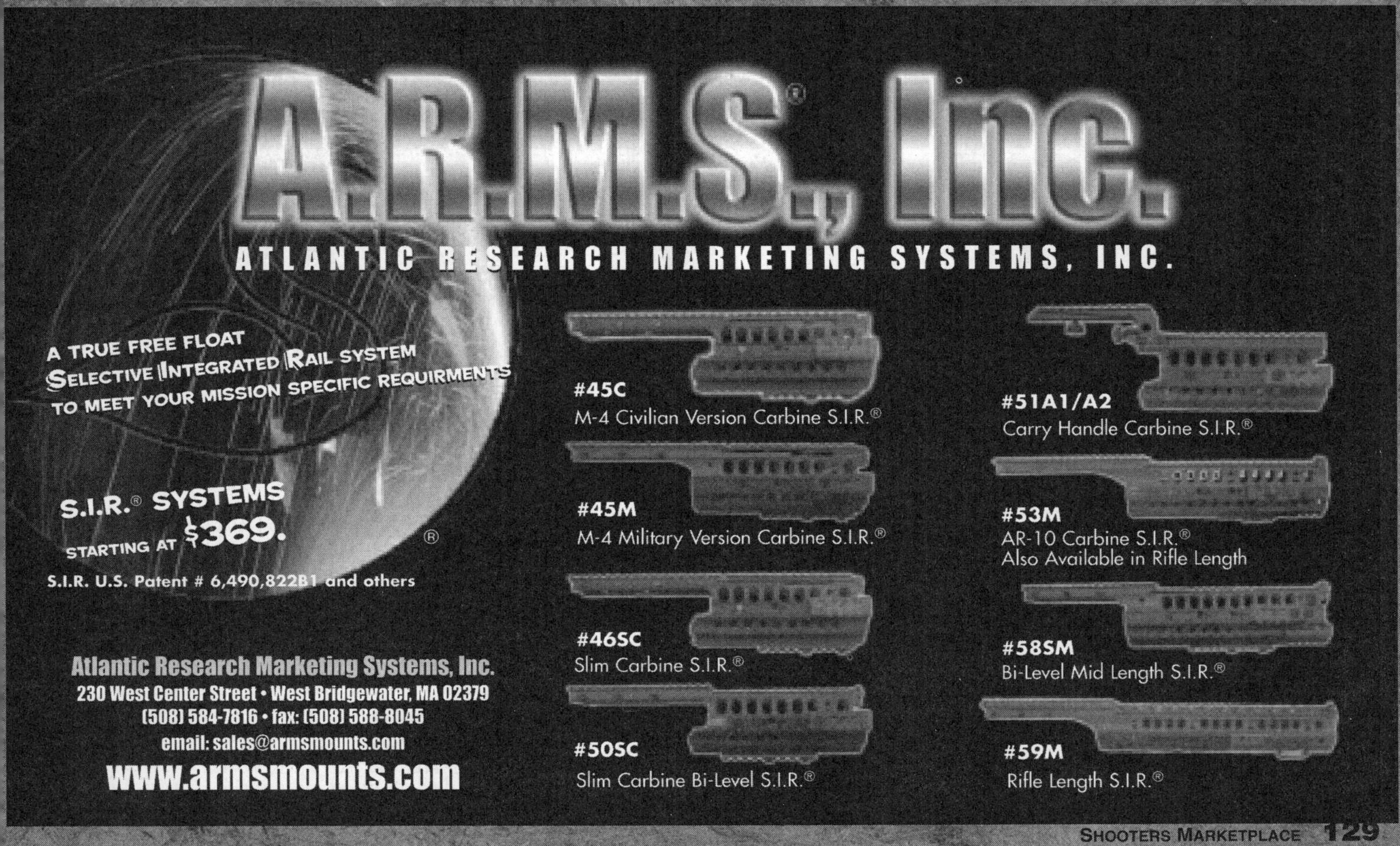

SHOOTER'S MARKETPLACE

SHOOTER'S MARKETPLACE

COMPLETE COMPACT CATALOG

HANDGUNS 2005

GUNDEX

NUMBERS

A

B

GUNDEX

C

GUNDEX

GUNDEX

D

E

F

GUNDEX

G

H

I

K

L

M

N

GUNDEX

GUNDEX

GUNDEX

SEMI-CUSTOM HANDGUNS — AUTOLOADERS

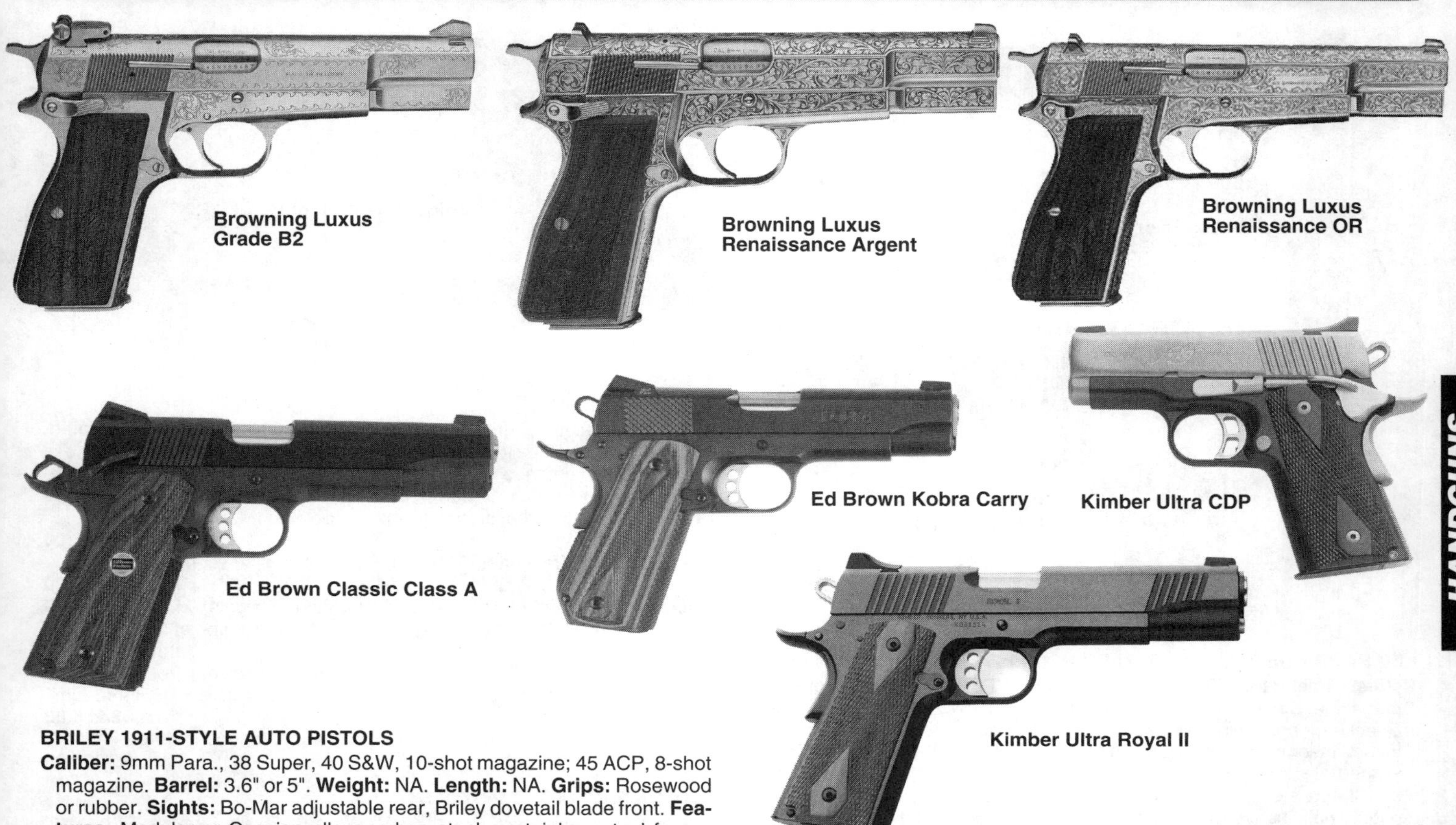

Browning Luxus Grade B2

Browning Luxus Renaissance Argent

Browning Luxus Renaissance OR

Ed Brown Classic Class A

Ed Brown Kobra Carry

Kimber Ultra CDP

Kimber Ultra Royal II

BRILEY 1911-STYLE AUTO PISTOLS

Caliber: 9mm Para., 38 Super, 40 S&W, 10-shot magazine; 45 ACP, 8-shot magazine. **Barrel:** 3.6" or 5". **Weight:** NA. **Length:** NA. **Grips:** Rosewood or rubber. **Sights:** Bo-Mar adjustable rear, Briley dovetail blade front. **Features:** Modular or Caspian alloy, carbon steel or stainless steel frame; match barrel and trigger group; lowered and flared ejection port; front and rear serrations on slide; beavertail grip safety; hot blue, hard chrome or stainless steel finish. Introduced 2000. Made in U.S. From Briley Manufacturing Inc.

Price: Fantom (3.6" bbl., fixed low-mount rear sight, armor coated lower receiver) . . . . from **$1,900.00**
Price: Fantom with two-port compensator . . . . from **$2,245.00**
Price: Advantage (5" bbl., adj. low-mount rear sight, checkered mainspring housing) . . . . from **$1,650.00**
Price: Versatility Plus (5" bbl., adj. low-mount rear sight, modular or Caspian frame) . . . . from **$1,850.00**
Price: Signature Series (5" bbl., adj. low-mount rear sight, 40 S&W only) . . . . from **$2,250.00**
Price: Plate Master (5" bbl. with compensator, lightened slide, Briley scope mount). . . . . from **$1,895.00**
Price: El Presidente (5" bbl. with Briley quad compensator, Briley scope mount). . . . . from **$2,550.00**

BROWNING HI-POWER LUXUS

The legendary Browning Hi-Power pistol still produced in Belgium is available in four grades in the Luxus series: Grade II, Renaissance Argent, Grade B2 and the gold-finished Renaissance OR. Other specifications NA.

Price: . . . . **NA**

ED BROWN CLASSIC CUSTOM AND CLASS A LIMITED 1911-STYLE AUTO PISTOLS

Caliber: 45 ACP; 7-shot magazine; 40 S&W, 400 Cor-Bon, 38 Super, 9x23, 9mm Para. **Barrel:** 4.25", 5", 6". **Weight:** NA. **Length:** NA. **Grips:** Hogue exotic checkered wood. **Sights:** Bo-Mar or Novak rear, blade front. **Features:** Blued or stainless steel frame; ambidextrous safety; beavertail grip safety; checkered forestrap and mainspring housing; match-grade barrel; slotted hammer; long lightweight or Videki short steel trigger. Many options offered. Made in U.S. by Ed Brown Products.

Price: Classic Custom (45 ACP, 5" barrel) . . . . from **$2,895.00**
Price: Class A Limited (all calibers; several bbl. lengths in competition and carry forms). . . . . from **$2,250.00**
Price: Commander Bobtail (most calibers, 4.25" bbl., has "bobtail" modification to reduce overall length). . . . . from **$2,300.00**
Price: Kobra (45 ACP only, 5" bbl., completely hand-fitted with heavy dehorning). . . . . from **$1,795.00**
Price: Kobra Carry (45 ACP only, 4.25" bbl., has exclusive snakeskin pattern on frame, top portion of mainspring housing and slide) . . . . from **$1,995.00**

KIMBER CUSTOM II 1911-STYLE AUTO PISTOLS

Caliber: 9mm Para., 38 Super, 9-shot magazines; 40 S&W, 8-shot magazine; 45 ACP, 7-shot magazine. **Barrel:** 5". **Weight:** 38 oz. **Length:** 8.7" overall. **Grips:** Black synthetic, smooth or double-diamond checkered rosewood, or double-diamond checkered walnut. **Sights:** McCormick low profile or Kimber adjustable rear, blade front. **Features:** Machined steel slide, frame and barrel; front and rear beveled slide serrations; cut and button-rifled, match-grade barrel; adjustable aluminum trigger; full-length guide rod; Commander-style hammer; high-ride beavertail safety; beveled magazine well. Other models available. Made in U.S. by Kimber Mfg. Inc.

Price: Custom II (black matte finish). **$730.00**
Price: Custom Royal II (polished blue finish, checkered rosewood grips) **$886.00**
Price: Custom Stainless II (satin-finished stainless steel frame and slide) **$832.00**
Price: Custom Target II (matte black or stainless finish, Kimber adj. sight) **$945.00**
Price: Custom Compact CDP II (4" bbl., alum. frame, tritium three-dot sights, 28 oz.) **$1,141.00**
Price: Custom Pro CDP II (4" bbl., alum. frame, tritium sights, full-length grip, 28 oz.) **$1,141.00**
Price: Ultra CDP II (3" bbl., aluminum frame, tritium sights, 25 oz.) **$1,141.00**
Price: Gold Match II (polished blue finish, hand-fitted barrel, ambid. safety) . . . . from **$1,168.00**
Price: Stainless Gold Match II (stainless steel frame and slide, hand-fitted bbl., amb. safety) . . . . **$1,315.00 to $1,345.00**

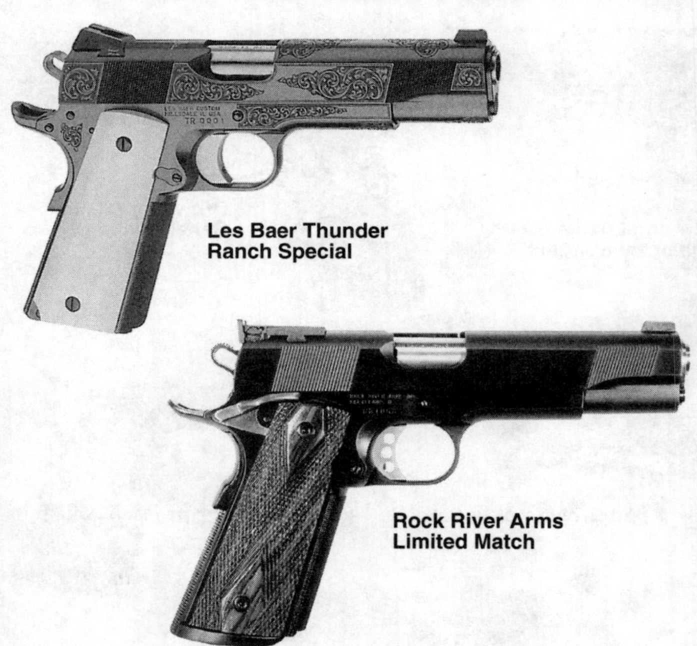

Les Baer Thunder Ranch Special

Rock River Arms Limited Match

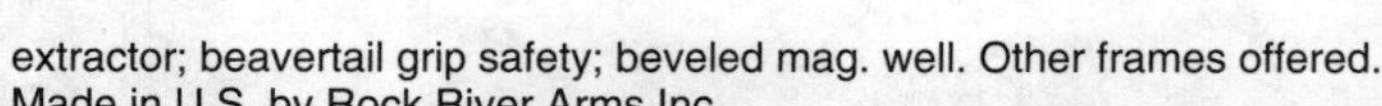

Volquartsen Stingray

LES BAER CUSTOM 1911-STYLE AUTO PISTOLS

Caliber: 9mm Para., 38 Super, 40 S&W, 45 ACP, 400 Cor-Bon; 7- or 8-shot magazine. **Barrel:** 4-1/4", 5", 6". **Weight:** 28 to 40 oz. **Length:** NA. **Grips:** Checkered cocobolo. **Sights:** Low-mount combat fixed, combat fixed with tritium inserts or low-mount adjustable rear, dovetail front. **Features:** Forged steel or aluminum frame; slide serrated front and rear; lowered and flared ejection port; beveled magazine well; speed trigger with 4-pound pull; beavertail grip safety; ambidextrous safety. Other models available. Made in U.S. by Les Baer Custom.

Price: Baer 1911 Premier II 5" Model (5" bbl., optional stainless steel frame and slide) . . . . from **$1,498.00**
Price: Premier II 6" Model (6" barrel) . . . . from **$1,675.00**
Price: Premier II LW1 (forged aluminum frame, steel slide and barrel) . . . . from **$1,835.00**
Price: Custom Carry (4" or 5" barrel, steel frame) . . . . from **$1,728.00**
Price: Custom Carry (4" barrel, aluminum frame). . . . . from **$2,039.00**
Price: Swift Response Pistol (fixed tritium sights, Bear Coat finish) . . . . from **$2,339.00**
Price: Monolith (5" barrel and slide with extra-long dust cover) . . . . from **$1,660.00**
Price: Stinger (4-1/4" barrel, steel or aluminum frame). . . . from **$1,552.00**
Price: Thunder Ranch Special (tritium fixed combat sight, Thunder Ranch logo) . . . . from **$1,685.00**
Price: National Match Hardball (low-mount adj. sight; meets DCM rules) . . . . from **$1,425.00**
Price: Bullseye Wadcutter Pistol (Bo-Mar rib w/ adj. sight, guar. 2-1/2" groups) . . . . from **$1,560.00**
Price: Ultimate Master Combat (5" or 6" bbl., adj. sights, checkered front strap). . . . . from **$2,530.00**
Price: Ultimate Master Combat Compensated (four-port compensator, adj. sights) . . . . from **$2,558.00**

ROCK RIVER ARMS 1911-STYLE AUTO PISTOLS

Caliber: 9mm Para., 38 Super, 40 S&W, 45 ACP. **Barrel:** 4" or 5". **Weight:** NA. **Length:** NA. **Grips:** Double-diamond, checkered cocobolo or black synthetic. **Sights:** Bo-Mar low-mount adjustable, Novak fixed with tritium inserts, Heine fixed or Rock River scope mount; dovetail front blade. **Features:** Chrome-moly, machined steel frame and slide; slide serrated front and rear; aluminum speed trigger with 3.5-4 lb. pull; national match KART barrel; lowered and flared ejection port; tuned and polished extractor; beavertail grip safety; beveled mag. well. Other frames offered. Made in U.S. by Rock River Arms Inc.

Price: Elite Commando (4" barrel, Novak tritium sights). **$1,395.00**
Price: Standard Match (5" barrel, Heine fixed sights) **$1,150.00**
Price: National Match Hardball (5" barrel, Bo-Mar adj. sights) . . . . from **$1,275.00**
Price: Bullseye Wadcutter (5" barrel, Rock River slide scope mount) . . . . from **$1,380.00**
Price: Basic Limited Match (5" barrel, Bo-Mar adj. sights) . from **$1,395.00**
Price: Limited Match (5" barrel, guaranteed 1-1/2" groups at 50 yards) . . . . from **$1,795.00**
Price: Hi-Cap Basic Limited (5" barrel, four frame choices) from **$1,895.00**
Price: Ultimate Match Achiever (5" bbl. with compensator, mount and Aimpoint). . . . . from **$2,255.00**
Price: Match Master Steel (5" bbl. with compensator, mount and Aimpoint) **$5,000.00**

STI COMPACT AUTO PISTOLS

Caliber: 9mm, 40 S&W. **Barrel:** 3.4". **Weight:** 28 oz. **Length:** 7" overall. **Grips:** Checkered double-diamond rosewood. **Sights:** Heine Low Mount fixed rear, slide integral front. **Features:** Similar to STI 2011 models except has compact frame, 7-shot magazine in 9mm (6-shot in 40 cal.), single-sided thumb safety, linkless barrel lockup system, matte blue finish. From STI International.

Price: (9mm or 40 S&W). . . . . from **$746.50**

VOLQUARTSEN CUSTOM 22 CALIBER AUTO PISTOLS

Caliber: 22 LR; 10-shot magazine. **Barrel:** 3.5" to 10"; stainless steel air gauge. **Weight:** 2-1/2 to 3 lbs. 10 oz. **Length:** NA. **Grips:** Finger-grooved plastic or walnut. **Sights:** Adjustable rear and blade front or Weaver-style scope mount. **Features:** Conversions of Ruger Mk. II Auto pistol. Variety of configurations featuring compensators, underlug barrels, etc. Stainless steel finish; black Teflon finish available for additional $85; target hammer, trigger. Made in U.S. by Volquartsen Custom.

Price: 3.5 Compact (3.5" barrel, T/L adjustable rear sight, scope base optional) **$640.00**
Price: Deluxe (barrel to 10", T/L adjustable rear sight) **$675.00**
Price: Deluxe with compensator **$745.00**
Price: Masters (6.5" barrel, finned underlug, T/L adjustable rear sight, compensator) **$950.00**
Price: Olympic (7" barrel, recoil-reducing gas chamber, T/L adjustable rear sight) **$870.00**
Price: Stingray (7.5" ribbed, ported barrel; red-dot sight) **$995.00**
Price: Terminator (7.5" ported barrel, grooved receiver, scope rings) **$730.00**
Price: Ultra-Light Match (6" tensioned barrel, Weaver mount, weighs 2-1/2 lbs.) **$885.00**
Price: V-6 (6", triangular, ventilated barrel with underlug, T/L adj. sight) **$1,030.00**
Price: V-2000 (6" barrel with finned underlug, T/L adj. sight) . . . **$1,095.00**
Price: V-Magic II (7.5" barrel, red-dot sight) **$1,055.00**

SEMI-CUSTOM HANDGUNS — REVOLVERS

Gary Reeder
Doc Holiday Classic

Gary Reeder
Ultimate 41

Gary Reeder
Black Widow

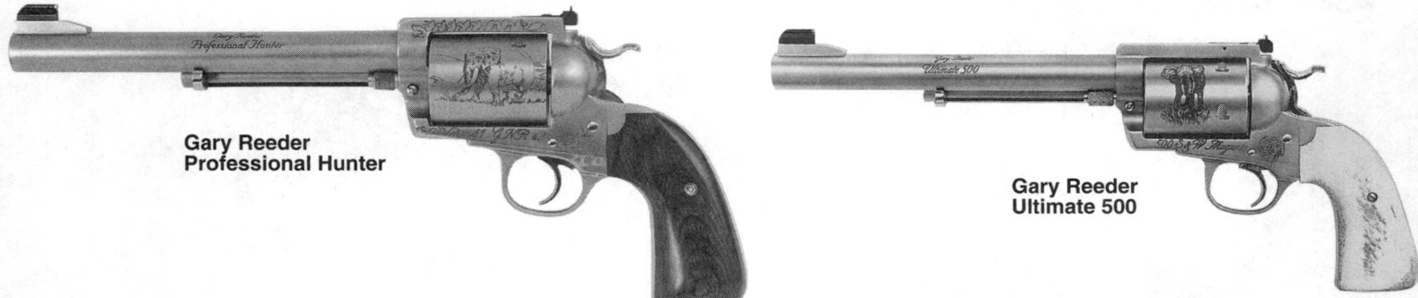

Gary Reeder
Professional Hunter

Gary Reeder
Ultimate 500

GARY REEDER CUSTOM GUNS REVOLVERS

Caliber: 22 WMR, 22 Hornet, 218 Bee, 356 GMR, 41 GNR, 410 GNR, 510 GNR, 357 Magnum, 45 Colt, 44-40, 41 Magnum, 44 Magnum, 454 Casull, 475 Linebaugh, 500 Linebaugh. **Barrel:** 2-1/2" to 12". **Weight:** Varies by model. **Length:** Varies by model. **Grips:** Black Cape buffalo horn, laminated walnut, simulated pearl, black and ivory micarta, others. **Sights:** Notch fixed or adjustable rear, blade or ramp front. **Features:** Custom conversions of Ruger Vaquero, Blackhawk Bisley and Super Blackhawk frames. Jeweled hammer and trigger, tuned action, model name engraved on barrel, additional engraving on frame and cylinder, integral muzzle brake, finish available in high-polish or satin stainless steel or black Chromex finish. Also available on customer's gun at reduced cost. Other models available. Made in U.S. by Gary Reeder Custom Guns.

Price: Gamblers Classic (2-1/2" bbl., engraved cards and dice, no ejector rod housing). . . . . from **$995.00**

Price: Tombstone Classic (3-1/2" bbl. with gold bands, notch sight, birdshead grips). . . . . from **$995.00**

Price: Doc Holliday Classic (3-1/2" bbl., engraved cards and dice, white pearl grips). . . . . from **$995.00**

Price: Border Classic (Built on customer furnished Schofield; 3" bbl., full scroll engraving, solid silver Mexican coin front sight, custom grips) . . . . from **$1,095.00**

Price: Cowboy Classic (stainless finish, cattle brand engraved, limited to 100 guns). . . . . from **$995.00**

Price: Lawman Classic (Full custom Vaquero, two-tone finish, Lawman-style engraving, special Lawman gripframe with lanyard ring. . . . . from **$1,295.00**

Price: Classic 45 (shoots 45 Colt, 45 ACP or 45 Schofield without moon clips, built to customer specs on customer furnished Ruger frame) . . . . from **$1,295.00**

Price: Classic 475 (Built on customer furnished base gun. 475 Linebaugh, 5 shot; satin black finish, gunfighter grip, set-back trigger. from **$1,295.00**

Price: Coyote Classic (chambered in 22 Hornet, 22 K-Hornet, 218 Bee, 218 Mashburn Bee, 17 Ackley Bee, 17 Ackley Hornet, 256 Winchester, 25-20, 6-shot unfluted cylinder, heavy 8" barrel, Super Blackhawk gripframe, finish of satin stainless, satin Black Chromex or high polished, comes with laminated cherry grips and Gunfighter grip). . . . from **$995.00**

Price: Black Widow (4-5/8" bbl., black Chromex finish, black widow spider engraving). . . . . from **$1,095.00**

Price: Alaskan Survivalist (3" bbl., Redhawk frame, engraved bear, 45 Colt or 44 Magnum). . . . . from **$1,095.00**

Price: Ultimate Backup (3-1/2" bbl., fixed sights, choice of animal engraving, 475 Linebaugh, 500 Linebaugh built on customer's gun.) . . . . from **$1,295.00**

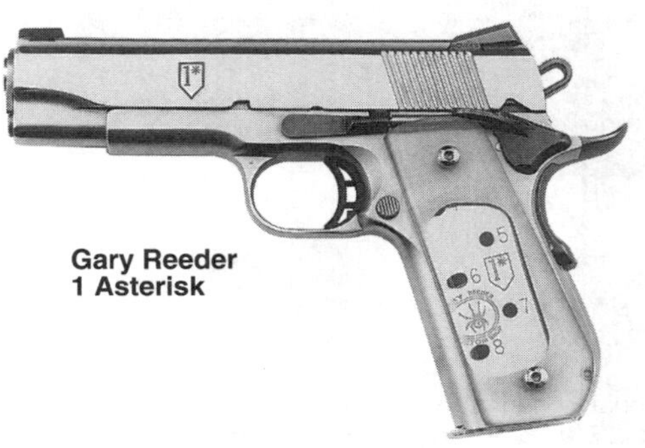

Gary Reeder
1 Asterisk

Price: Ultimate Vaquero (engraved barrel, frame and cylinder, made to customer specs) . . . . from **$995.00**

Price: Ultimate 41 (410 GNR 5-shot, built on customer furnished Ruger frame) . . . . from **$1,295.00**

Price: Ultimate 44 (ported, special recoil-taming grip frame, sling swivels, 44 Mag. 5-shot, built on customer furnished Ruger Hunter) . . . . from **$1,295.00**

Price: Ultimate 480 (choice of barrel lengths in any caliber, full vapor honed stainless steel, satin finish Black Chromex or two-toned finish, 5 shot cylinder, heavy barrel, Gunfighter grip, full action job, custom laminated grips, freewheeling cylinder, Belt Mountain base pin) . . . . from **$995.00**

Price: Ultimate Long Colt (Built on customer-furnished 45 Long Colt Vaquero. 5 shot. Satin black finish, gunfighter grip. . . . . . . from **$1,295.00**

Price: Ultimate 50 (choice of barrel lengths in any centerfire caliber, 5 shot stainless steel 50 Action Express, freewheeling cylinder) from **$1,195.00**

Price: Ultimate 500 (built on stretch frame in 500 S&W. Five shot. Choice of bbl. lengths, gunfigher grip, set-back trigger. . . . . from **$2,495.00**

Price: Ultimate Black Widow (475 Linebaugh or 500 Linebaugh, heavy duty 5 shot cylinder, heavy high grade barrel, Gunfighter Grip with black Micarta grips, Belt Mountain base pin) . . . . from **$1,295.00**

Price: 1 Asterisk (Full custom M1911. Stainless or blued finish. Full combat features including see-thru Lexan grip panel. . . . . . . from **$1,095.00**

Price: Double Deuce (8" heavy bbl., adjustable sights, laminated grips, 22 WMR 8-shot). . . . . from **$1,195.00**

Price: 510 Hunter (octagonal bbl., set back trigger, adjustable sights, 510 GNR 5-shot, built on customer furnished Ruger frame) . . from **$1,495.00**

Price: American Hunter (475 Linebaugh or 500 Linebaugh, built to customers specs on furnished Ruger frame).. . . . . from **$1,295.00**

Price: African Hunter (6" bbl., with or without muzzle brake, 475 or 500 Linebaugh. Built on customer's gun). . . . . from **$1,295.00**

SEMI-CUSTOM HANDGUNS — REVOLVERS

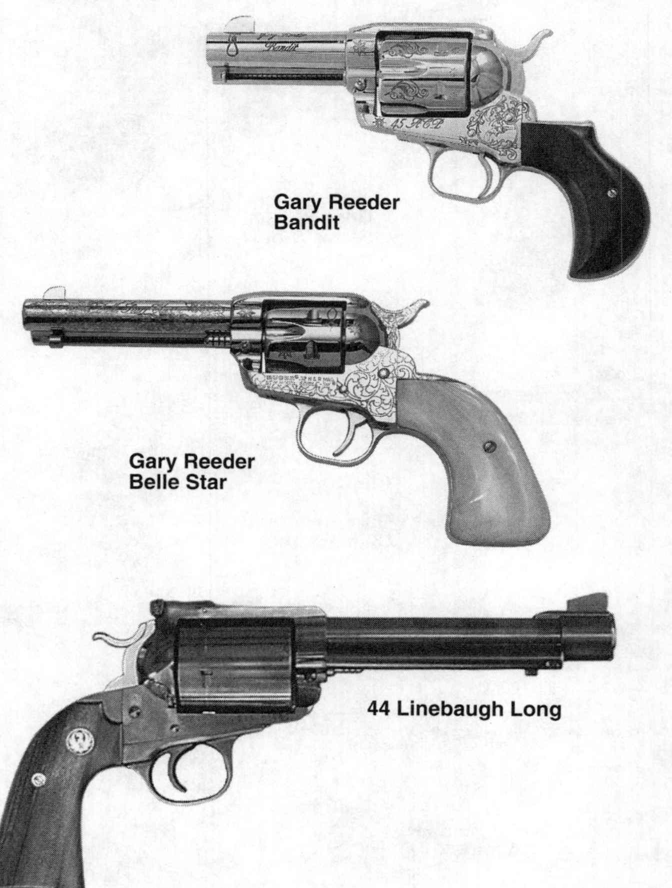

Gary Reeder Bandit

Gary Reeder Belle Star

44 Linebaugh Long

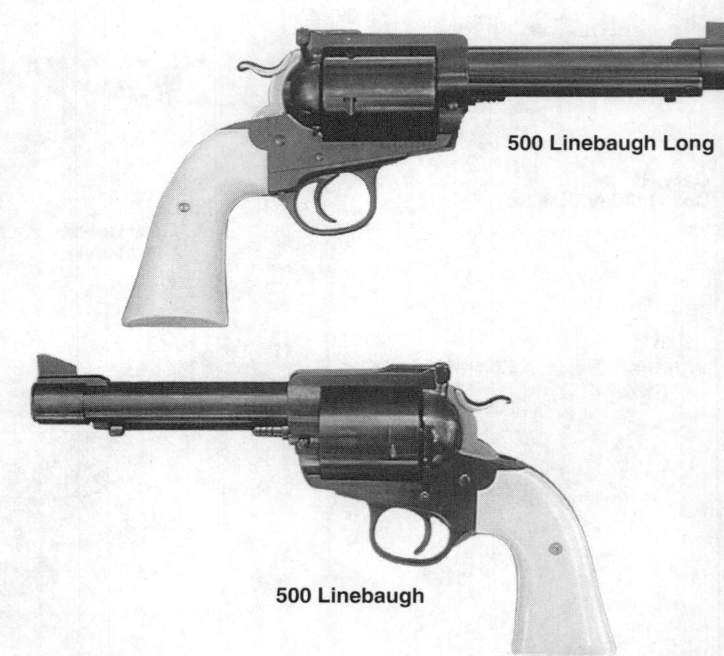

500 Linebaugh Long

500 Linebaugh

Price: Professional Hunter (stretch frame stainless 5-shot available in calibers including 475 Maximum and 500 Maximum). . . . . . . from **$2,395.00**
Price: Belle Starr Classic (engraved with gunfighter grip, 32 H&R) . . . . from **$1,095.00**
Price: Bandit (3-1/2" bbl., special Lightning style grip frame built on a Ruger Vaquero frame, engraved, set back trigger, Colt-style hammer) . . . . from **$1,095.00**
Price: Southern Comfort (5 shot cylinder, heavy duty base pin, tear drop hammer, special set back trigger, interchangeable blade system, special gripframe, satin Vapor Honed finish). . . . . from **$1,095.00**
Price: 45 Backpacker (weighs 28 oz., comes in 45 Long Colt, all stainless except for lightweight aircraft aluminum gripframe, black Micarta grips, not recommended for Plus P ammo). . . . . from **$995.00**
Price: Rio Grande Classic (built on any caliber Vaquero in barrel length of choice, Gunfighter grip, engraving is old southwest type with a few western features, specially designed base pin, long tapered hammer. . . . . from **$995.00**
Price: Enforcer (Full custom combat shotgun. 8 shot. Includes sling, sidesaddle magazine; buttstock holds 25 rounds; includes optical sight or flashlight. . . . . from **$1,295.00**

LINEBAUGH CUSTOM SIXGUNS REVOLVERS

Caliber: 45 Colt, 44 Linebaugh Long, 458 Linebaugh, 475 Linebaugh, 500 Linebaugh, 500 Linebaugh Long, 445 Super Mag. **Barrel:** 4-3/4", 5-1/2", 6", 7- 1/2"; other lengths available. **Weight:** NA. **Length:** NA. **Grips:** Dustin Linebaugh Custom made to customer's specs. **Sights:** Bowen steel rear or factory Ruger; blade front. **Features:** Conversions using customer's Ruger Blackhawk Bisley and Vaquero Bisley frames. Made in U.S. by Linebaugh Custom Sixguns.
Price: Small 45 Colt conversion (rechambered cyl., new barrel) . . . . from **$1,200.00**
Price: Large 45 Colt conversion (oversized cyl., new barrel, 5- or 6- shot) . . . . from **$1,800.00**
Price: 475 Linebaugh, 500 Linebaugh conversions . . . . . . from **$1,800.00**
Price: Linebaugh and 445 Super Mag calibers on 357 Maximum frame . . . . from **$3,000.00**

CONSULT
SHOOTER'S MARKETPLACE
Page 125, This Issue

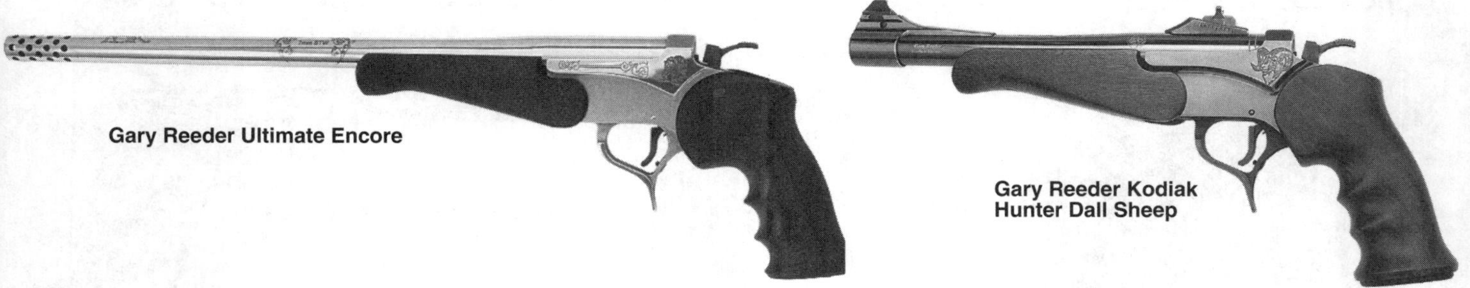

Gary Reeder Ultimate Encore

Gary Reeder Kodiak Hunter Dall Sheep

GARY REEDER CUSTOM GUNS CONTENDER AND ENCORE PISTOLS

Caliber: 22 Cheetah, 218 Bee, 22 K-Hornet, 22 Hornet, 218 Mashburn Bee, 22-250 Improved, 6mm/284, 7mm STW, 7mm GNR, 30 GNR, 338 GNR, 300 Win. Magnum, 338 Win. Magnum, 350 Rem. Magnum, 358 STA, 375 H&H, 378 GNR, 416 Remington, 416 GNR, 450 GNR, 475 Linebaugh, 500 Linebaugh, 50 Alaskan, 50 AE, 454 Casull; others available. **Barrel:** 8" to 15" (others available). **Weight:** NA. **Length:** Varies with barrel length. **Grips:** Walnut fingergroove. **Sights:** Express-style adjustable rear and barrel band front (Kodiak Hunter); none furnished most models. **Features:** Offers complete guns and barrels in the T/C Contender and Encore. Integral muzzle brake, engraved animals and model name, tuned action, high-polish or satin stainless steel or black Chromex finish. Made in U.S. by Gary Reeder Custom Guns.

Price: Kodiak Hunter (50 AE, 475 Linebaugh, 500 Linebaugh, 510 GNR, or 454 Casull, Kodiak bear and Dall sheep engravings) . . . . from **$1,195.00**

Price: Ultimate Encore (15" bbl. with muzzle brake, custom engraving). . . . . from **$1,095.00**

SSK Industries Contender

SSK INDUSTRIES CONTENDER AND ENCORE PISTOLS

Caliber: More than 200, including most standard pistol and rifle calibers, as well as 226 JDJ, 6mm JDJ, 257 JDJ, 6.5mm JDJ, 7mm JDJ, 6.5mm Mini-Dreadnaught, 30-06 JDJ, 280 JDJ, 375 JDJ, 6mm Whisper, 300 Whisper and 338 Whisper. **Barrel:** 10" to 26"; blued or stainless; variety of configurations. **Weight:** Varies with barrel length and features. **Length:** Varies with barrel length. **Grips:** Pachmayr, wood models available. **Features:** Offers frames, barrels and complete guns in the T/C Contender and Encore. Fluted, diamond, octagon and round barrels; flatside Contender frames; chrome-plating; muzzle brakes; trigger jobs; variety of stocks and forends; sights and optics. Made in U.S. by SSK Industries.

Price: Blued Contender frame . . . . .from **$390.00**

Price: Stainless Contender frame. . . . . from **$390.00**

Price: Blued Encore frame . . . . from **$290.00**

Price: Stainless Encore frame . . . . from **$318.00**

Price: Contender barrels. . . . . from **$315.00**

Price: Encore barrels . . . . from **$340.00**

HANDGUNS — AUTOLOADERS, SERVICE & SPORT

Includes models suitable for several forms of competition and other sporting purposes.

Accu-Tek HC-380

Accu-Tek XL-9

Auto-Ordnance 1911A1 Standard

Baer Custom Carry

Baer Premium II

Auto-Ordnance Deluxe

ACCU-TEK MODEL HC-380 AUTO PISTOL

Caliber: 380 ACP, 10-shot magazine. **Barrel:** 2.75". **Weight:** 26 oz. **Length:** 6" overall. **Grips:** Checkered black composition. **Sights:** Blade front, rear adjustable for windage. **Features:** External hammer; manual thumb safety with firing pin and trigger disconnect; bottom magazine release. Stainless steel construction. Introduced 1993. Price includes cleaning kit and gun lock. Made in U.S.A. by Accu-Tek.

Price: Satin stainless **$249.00**

ACCU-TEK XL-9 AUTO PISTOL

Caliber: 9mm Para., 5-shot magazine. **Barrel:** 3". **Weight:** 24 oz. **Length:** 5.6" overall. **Grips:** Black pebble composition. **Sights:** Three-dot system; rear adjustable for windage. **Features:** Stainless steel construction; double-action-only mechanism. Introduced 1999. Price includes cleaning kit and gun lock, two magazines. Made in U.S.A. by Accu-Tek.

Price: **$267.00**

AMERICAN DERRINGER LM-5 AUTOMATIC PISTOL

Caliber: 25 ACP, 5-shot magazine. **Barrel:** 2-1/4". **Weight:** 15 oz. **Length:** NA. **Grips:** Wood. **Sights:** Fixed. **Features:** Compact, stainless, semi-auto, single-action hammerless design. Hand assembled and fitted.

Price: **$425.00**

AUTO-ORDNANCE 1911A1 AUTOMATIC PISTOL

Caliber: 45 ACP, 7-shot magazine. **Barrel:** 5". **Weight:** 39 oz. **Length:** 8-1/2" overall. **Grips:** Checkered plastic with medallion. **Sights:** Blade front, rear adjustable for windage. **Features:** Same specs as 1911A1 military guns-parts interchangeable. Frame and slide blued; each radius has non-glare finish. Made in U.S.A. by Auto-Ordnance Corp.

Price: 45 ACP, blue **$511.00**

Price: 45 ACP, Parkerized **$515.00**

Price: 45 ACP Deluxe (three-dot sights, textured rubber wraparound grips) **$525.00**

AUTAUGA 32 AUTO PISTOL

Caliber: 32 ACP, 6-shot magazine. **Barrel:** 2". **Weight:** 11.3 oz. **Length:** 4.3" overall. **Grips:** Black polymer. **Sights:** Fixed. **Features:** Double-action-only mechanism. Stainless steel construction. Uses Winchester Silver Tip ammunition.

Price: .... **NA**

BAER 1911 CUSTOM CARRY AUTO PISTOL

Caliber: 45 ACP, 7- or 10-shot magazine. **Barrel:** 5". **Weight:** 37 oz. **Length:** 8.5" overall. **Grips:** Checkered walnut. **Sights:** Baer improved ramp-style dovetailed front, Novak low-mount rear. **Features:** Baer forged NM frame, slide and barrel with stainless bushing; fitted slide to frame; double serrated slide (full-size only); Baer speed trigger with 4-lb. pull; Baer deluxe hammer and sear, tactical-style extended ambidextrous safety, beveled magazine well; polished feed ramp and throated barrel; tuned extractor; Baer extended ejector, checkered slide stop; lowered and flared ejection port, full-length recoil guide rod; recoil buff. Partial listing shown. Made in U.S.A. by Les Baer Custom, Inc.

Price: Standard size, blued **$1,640.00**

Price: Standard size, stainless **$1,690.00**

Price: Comanche size, blued **$1,640.00**

Price: Comanche size, stainless **$1,690.00**

Price: Comanche size, aluminum frame, blued slide **$1,923.00**

Price: Comanche size, aluminum frame, stainless slide **$1,995.00**

BAER 1911 PREMIER II AUTO PISTOL

Caliber: 9x23, 38 Super, 400 Cor-Bon, 45 ACP, 7- or 10-shot magazine. **Barrel:** 5". **Weight:** 37 oz. **Length:** 8.5" overall. **Grips:** Checkered rosewood, double diamond pattern. **Sights:** Baer dovetailed front, low-mount Bo-Mar rear with hidden leaf. **Features:** Baer NM forged steel frame and barrel with stainless bushing; slide fitted to frame; double serrated slide; lowered, flared ejection port; tuned, polished extractor; Baer extended ejector, checkered slide stop, aluminum speed trigger with 4-lb. pull, deluxe Commander hammer and sear, beavertail grip safety with pad, beveled magazine well, extended ambidextrous safety; flat mainspring housing; polished feed ramp and throated barrel; 30 lpi checkered front strap. Made in U.S.A. by Les Baer Custom, Inc.

Price: Blued **$1,428.00**

Price: Stainless **$1,558.00**

Price: 6" model, blued, from **$1,595.00**

BAER 1911 S.R.P. PISTOL

Caliber: 45 ACP. **Barrel:** 5". **Weight:** 37 oz. **Length:** 8.5" overall. **Grips:** Checkered walnut. **Sights:** Trijicon night sights. **Features:** Similar to the F.B.I. contract gun except uses Baer forged steel frame. Has Baer match barrel with supported chamber, Wolff springs, complete tactical action job. All parts Mag-na-fluxed; deburred for tactical carry. Has Baer Ultra Coat finish. Tuned for reliability. Contact Baer for complete details. Introduced 1996. Made in U.S.A. by Les Baer Custom, Inc.

Price: Government or Comanche length **$2,240.00**

Beretta M8000/8040 Cougar

Beretta 96

Beretta U22 Neos

Bersa Thunder 380

BERETTA MODEL 92FS PISTOL

Caliber: 9mm Para., 10-shot magazine. **Barrel:** 4.9". **Weight:** 34 oz. **Length:** 8.5" overall. **Grips:** Checkered black plastic. **Sights:** Blade front, rear adjustable for windage. Tritium night sights available. **Features:** Double action. Extractor acts as chamber loaded indicator, squared trigger guard, grooved front and backstraps, inertia firing pin. Matte or blued finish. Introduced 1977. Made in U.S.A. and imported from Italy by Beretta U.S.A.

Price: With plastic grips **$712.00**
Price: Vertec with access rail **$751.00**
Price: Vertec Inox **$801.00**

Beretta Model 92FS/96 Brigadier Pistols

Similar to the Model 92FS/96 except with a heavier slide to reduce felt recoil and allow mounting removable front sight. Wrap-around rubber grips. Three-dot sights dovetailed to the slide, adjustable for windage. Weighs 35.3 oz. Introduced 1999.

Price: 9mm or 40 S&W, 10-shot **$772.00**
Price: Inox models (stainless steel) **$822.00**

Beretta Model 96 Pistol

Same as the Model 92FS except chambered for 40 S&W. Ambidextrous safety mechanism with passive firing pin catch, slide safety/decocking lever, trigger bar disconnect. Has 10-shot magazine. Available with three-dot sights. Introduced 1992.

Price: Model 96, plastic grips **$712.00**
Price: Stainless, rubber grips **$772.00**
Price: Vertec with access rail **$751.00**
Price: Vertec Inox **$801.00**

BERETTA MODEL 80 CHEETAH SERIES DA PISTOLS

Caliber: 380 ACP, 10-shot magazine (M84); 8-shot (M85); 22 LR, 7-shot (M87). **Barrel:** 3.82". **Weight:** About 23 oz. (M84/85); 20.8 oz. (M87). **Length:** 6.8" overall. **Grips:** Glossy black plastic (wood optional at extra cost). **Sights:** Fixed front, drift-adjustable rear. **Features:** Double action, quick takedown, convenient magazine release. Introduced 1977. Imported from Italy by Beretta U.S.A.

Price: Model 84 Cheetah, plastic grips **$615.00**
Price: Model 85 Cheetah, plastic grips, 8-shot **$579.00**
Price: Model 87 Cheetah, wood, 22 LR, 7-shot **$615.00**
Price: Model 87 Target, plastic grips **$708.00**

Beretta Model 86 Cheetah

Similar to the 380-caliber Model 85 except has tip-up barrel for first-round loading. Barrel length is 4.4", overall length of 7.33". Has 8-shot magazine, walnut grips. Introduced 1989.

Price: **$615.00**

Beretta Model 21 Bobcat Pistol

Similar to the Model 950 BS. Chambered for 22 LR or 25 ACP. Both double action. Has 2.4" barrel, 4.9" overall length; 7-round magazine on 22 cal.; 8 rounds in 25 ACP, 9.9 oz., available in nickel, matte, engraved or blue finish. Plastic grips. Introduced in 1985.

Price: Bobcat, 22 or 25, blue **$300.00**
Price: Bobcat, 22, stainless **$329.00**
Price: Bobcat, 22 or 25, matte **$265.00**

BERETTA MODEL 3032 TOMCAT PISTOL

Caliber: 32 ACP, 7-shot magazine. **Barrel:** 2.45". **Weight:** 14.5 oz. **Length:** 5" overall. **Grips:** Checkered black plastic. **Sights:** Blade front, drift-adjustable rear. **Features:** Double action with exposed hammer; tip-up barrel for direct loading/unloading; thumb safety; polished or matte blue finish. Imported from Italy by Beretta U.S.A. Introduced 1996.

Price: Blue **$393.00**
Price: Matte **$358.00**
Price: Stainless **$443.00**
Price: With Tritium sights **$436.00**

BERETTA MODEL 8000/8040/8045 COUGAR PISTOL

Caliber: 9mm Para., 10-shot, 40 S&W, 10-shot magazine; 45 ACP, 8-shot. **Barrel:** 3.6". **Weight:** 33.5 oz. **Length:** 7" overall. **Grips:** Checkered plastic. **Sights:** Blade front, rear drift adjustable for windage. **Features:** Slide-mounted safety; rotating barrel; exposed hammer. Matte black Bruniton finish. Announced 1994. Imported from Italy by Beretta U.S.A.

Price: 8000 and 8000L **$729.00**
Price: D model, 9mm, 40 S&W **$729.00**
Price: D model, 45 ACP **$779.00**
Price: Inox **$794.00**

BERETTA MODEL 9000S COMPACT PISTOL

Caliber: 9mm Para., 40 S&W; 10-shot magazine. **Barrel:** 3.4". **Weight:** 26.8 oz. **Length:** 6.6". **Grips:** Soft polymer. **Sights:** Windage-adjustable white-dot rear, white-dot blade front. **Features:** Glass-reinforced polymer frame; patented tilt-barrel, open-slide locking system; chrome-lined barrel; external serrated hammer; automatic firing pin and manual safeties. Introduced 2000. Imported from Italy by Beretta U.S.A.

Price: 9000S Type F (single and double action, external hammer) **$472.00**

BERETTA MODEL U22 NEOS

Caliber: 22 LR, 10-shot magazine. **Barrel:** 4.2"; 6". **Weight:** 32 oz.; 36 oz. **Length:** 8.8"; 10.3". **Sights:** Target. **Features:** Integral rail for standard scope mounts, light, perfectly weighted, 100% American-made by Beretta.

Price: **$265.00**
Price: Inox **$315.00**
Price: DLX **$336.00**
Price: Inox **$386.00**

BERSA THUNDER LITE 380 AUTO PISTOLS

Caliber: 380 ACP, 7-shot (Thunder 380 Lite), 9-shot magazine (Thunder 380 DLX). **Barrel:** 3.5". **Weight:** 23 oz. **Length:** 6.6" overall. **Grips:** Black polymer. **Sights:** Blade front, notch rear adjustable for windage; three-dot system. **Features:** Double action; firing pin and magazine safeties. Available in blue, nickel, or duo tone. Introduced 1995. Distributed by Eagle Imports, Inc.

Price: Thunder 380, 7-shot, deep blue finish **$266.95**
Price: Thunder 380 Deluxe, 9-shot, satin nickel **$299.95**
Price: Thunder 380 Gold, 7-shot **$299.95**

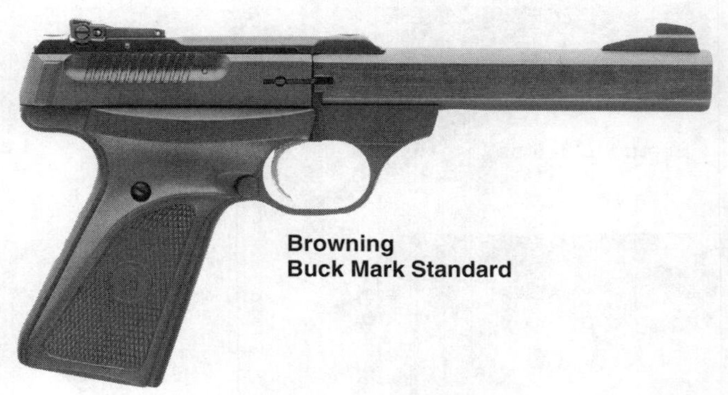
Browning Buck Mark Standard

Browning Buck Mark Challenge

Bersa Thunder 45 Ultra Compact Pistol

Similar to the Bersa Thunder 380 except in 45 ACP. Available in three finishes. Introduced 2003. Imported from Argentina by Eagle Imports, Inc.

Price: Thunder 45, matte blue **$400.95**
Price: Thunder 45, Duotone **$424.95**
Price: Thunder 45, Satin nickel **$441.95**

BLUE THUNDER/COMMODORE 1911-STYLE AUTO PISTOLS

Caliber: 45 ACP, 7-shot magazine. **Barrel:** 4-1/4", 5". **Weight:** NA. **Length:** NA. **Grips:** Checkered hardwood. **Sights:** Blade front, drift-adjustable rear. **Features:** Extended slide release and safety, spring guide rod, skeletonized hammer and trigger, magazine bumper, beavertail grip safety. Imported from the Philippines by Century International Arms Inc.

Price: . . . . **$464.80 to $484.80**

AUTOBOND 450

Caliber: 450 Autobond (also 45 ACP). Model 1911-style. **Barrel:** 5".

Price: **$1150.00**

BROWNING HI-POWER 9mm AUTOMATIC PISTOL

Caliber: 9mm Para.,10-shot magazine. **Barrel:** 4-21/32". **Weight:** 32 oz. **Length:** 7-3/4" overall. **Grips:** Walnut, hand checkered, or black Polyamide. **Sights:** 1/8" blade front; rear screw-adjustable for windage and elevation. Also available with fixed rear (drift-adjustable for windage). **Features:** External hammer with half-cock and thumb safeties. A blow on the hammer cannot discharge a cartridge; cannot be fired with magazine removed. Fixed rear sight model available. Includes gun lock. Imported from Belgium by Browning.

Price: Fixed sight model, walnut grips **$680.00**
Price: Fully adjustable rear sight, walnut grips **$730.00**
Price: Mark III, standard matte black finish, fixed sight, moulded grips, ambidextrous safety **$662.00**

Browning Hi-Power Practical Pistol

Similar to the standard Hi-Power except has silver-chromed frame with blued slide, wrap-around Pachmayr rubber grips, round-style serrated hammer and removable front sight, fixed rear (drift-adjustable for windage). Available in 9mm Para. Includes gun lock. Introduced 1991.

Price: **$717.00**

BROWNING BUCK MARK STANDARD 22 PISTOL

Caliber: 22 LR, 10-shot magazine. **Barrel:** 5-1/2". **Weight:** 32 oz. **Length:** 9-1/2" overall. **Grips:** Black moulded composite with checkering. **Sights:** Ramp front, Browning Pro Target rear adjustable for windage and elevation. **Features:** All steel, matte blue finish or nickel, gold-colored trigger. Buck Mark Plus has laminated wood grips. Includes gun lock. Made in U.S.A. Introduced 1985. From Browning.

Price: Buck Mark Standard, blue **$310.00**
Price: Buck Mark Nickel, nickel finish with contoured rubber grips **$366.00**
Price: Buck Mark Plus, matte blue with laminated wood grips . . . **$379.00**
Price: Buck Mark Plus Nickel, nickel finish, laminated wood grips **$415.00**

Browning Buck Mark Camper

Similar to the Buck Mark except 5-1/2" bull barrel. Weight is 34 oz. Matte blue finish, molded composite grips. Introduced 1999. From Browning.

Price: **$279.00**
Price: Camper Nickel, nickel finish, molded composite grips **$311.00**

Browning Buck Mark Challenge

Similar to the Buck Mark except has a lightweight barrel and smaller grip diameter. Barrel length is 5-1/2", weight is 25 oz. Introduced 1999. From Browning.

Price: **$346.00**

Browning Buck Mark Micro

Same as the Buck Mark Standard and Buck Mark Plus except has 4" barrel. Available in blue or nickel. Has 16-click Pro Target rear sight. Introduced 1992.

Price: Micro Standard, matte blue finish **$310.00**
Price: Micro Nickel, nickel finish **$366.00**
Price: Buck Mark Micro Plus Nickel **$415.00**

Browning Buck Mark Bullseye

Same as the Buck Mark Standard except has 7-1/4" fluted barrel, matte blue finish. Weighs 36 oz.

Price: Bullseye Standard, molded composite grips **$420.00**
Price: Bullseye Target, contoured rosewood grips **$541.00**

Browning Buck Mark 5.5

Same as the Buck Mark Standard except has a 5-1/2" bull barrel with integral scope mount, matte blue finish.

Price: 5.5 Field, Pro-Target adj. rear sight, contoured walnut grips . **$459.00**
Price: 5.5 Target, hooded adj. target sights, contoured walnut grips **$459.00**

BROWNING PRO-9

Caliber: 9mm Luger, 10-round magazine. **Barrel:** 4". **Weight:** 30 oz. **Length:** 7-1/4" overall. **Features:** Double-action, ambidextrous decocker and safety. Fixed, three-dot-style sights, 6" sight radius. Molded composite grips with interchangeable backstrap inserts.

Price: **$628.00**

BROWNING HI-POWER

Caliber: 9mm, 40 S&W. **Barrel:** 4-3/4". **Weight:** 32 to 35 oz. **Length:** 7-3/4" overall. **Features:** Blued, matte, polymer or silver-chromed frame; molded, wraparound Pachmayr or walnut grips; Commander-style or spur-type hammer.

Price: Practical model, fixed sights **$791.00**
Price: Mark II model, epoxy finish **$730.00**
Price: HP Standard, blued, fixed sights, walnut grips **$751.00**
Price: HP Standard, blued, adj. sights **$805.00**

CHARLES DALY M-1911-A1P AUTOLOADING PISTOL

Caliber: 45 ACP, 7- or 10-shot magazine. **Barrel:** 5". **Weight:** 38 oz. **Length:** 8-3/4" overall. **Grips:** Checkered. **Sights:** Blade front, rear drift adjustable for windage; three-dot system. **Features:** Skeletonized combat hammer and trigger; beavertail grip safety; extended slide release; oversize thumb safety; Parkerized finish. Introduced 1996. Imported from the Philippines by K.B.I., Inc.

Price: **$469.95**

Charles Daly M-1911-A1P

Cobra FS380

Cobra CA32

Colt 1991 Model O

Colt 1991 Model O Commander

Colt XSE Model O Commander

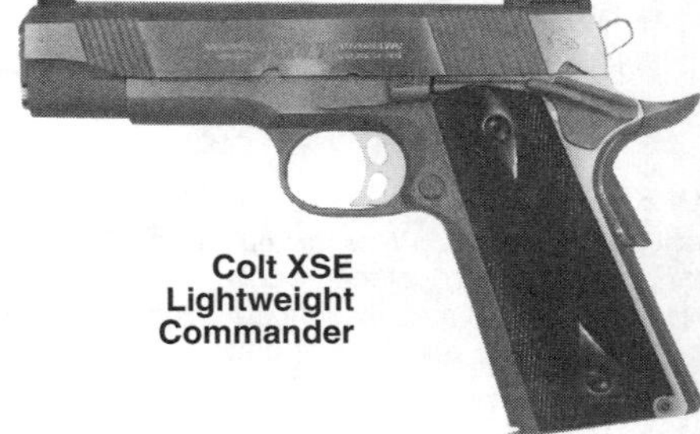
Colt XSE Lightweight Commander

COBRA ENTERPRISES FS380 AUTO PISTOL

Caliber: 380 ACP, 7-shot magazine. **Barrel:** 3.5". **Weight:** 2.1 lbs. **Length:** 6-3/8" overall. **Grips:** Black composition. **Sights:** Fixed. **Features:** Choice of bright chrome, satin nickel or black finish. Introduced 2002. Made in U.S.A. by Cobra Enterprises.

Price: **$130.00**

COBRA ENTERPRISES FS32 AUTO PISTOL

Caliber: 32 ACP, 8-shot magazine. **Barrel:** 3.5". **Weight:** 2.1 lbs. **Length:** 6-3/8" overall. **Grips:** Black composition. **Sights:** Fixed. **Features:** Choice of black, satin nickel or bright chrome finish. Introduced 2002. Made in U.S.A. by Cobra Enterprises.

Price: **$130.00**

COBRA INDUSTRIES PATRIOT PISTOL

Caliber: 380ACP, 9mm Luger, 10-shot magazine. **Barrel:** 3.3". **Weight:** 20 oz. **Length:** 6" overall. **Grips:** Checkered polymer. **Sights:** Fixed. **Features:** Stainless steel slide with load indicator; double-action-only trigger system. Introduced 2002. Made in U.S.A. by Cobra Enterprises, Inc.

Price: **$279.00**

COBRA INDUSTRIES CA32, CA380

Caliber: 32 ACP, 380 ACP. **Barrel:** 2.8" **Weight:** 22 oz. **Length:** 5.4". **Grips:** Laminated wood (CA32); Black molded synthetic (CA380). **Sights:** Fixed. **Features:** True pocket pistol size and styling without bulk. Made in U.S.A. by Cobra Enterprises.

Price: .... **NA**

COLT MODEL 1991 MODEL O AUTO PISTOL

Caliber: 45 ACP, 7-shot magazine. **Barrel:** 5". **Weight:** 38 oz. **Length:** 8.5" overall. **Grips:** Checkered black composition. **Sights:** Ramped blade front, fixed square notch rear, high profile. **Features:** Matte finish. Continuation of serial number range used on original G.I. 1911 A1 guns. Comes with one magazine and moulded carrying case. Introduced 1991.

Price: **$645.00**

Price: Stainless.... **$800.00**

Colt Model 1991 Model O Commander Auto Pistol

Similar to the Model 1991 A1 except has 4-1/4" barrel. Overall length is 7-3/4". Comes with one 7-shot magazine, molded case.

Price: Blue **$645.00**

Price: Stainless steel **$800.00**

COLT XSE SERIES MODEL O AUTO PISTOLS

Caliber: 45 ACP, 8-shot magazine. **Barrel:** 4-1/4", 5". **Grips:** Checkered, double diamond rosewood. **Sights:** Drift-adjustable three-dot combat. **Features:** Brushed stainless finish; adjustable, two-cut aluminum trigger; extended ambidextrous thumb safety; upswept beavertail with palm swell; elongated slot hammer; beveled magazine well. Introduced 1999. From Colt's Manufacturing Co., Inc.

Price: XSE Government (5" barrel) **$950.00**

Price: XSE Commander (4.25" barrel) **$950.00**

COLT XSE LIGHTWEIGHT COMMANDER AUTO PISTOL

Caliber: 45 ACP, 8-shot. **Barrel:** 4-1/4". **Weight:** 26 oz. **Length:** 7-3/4" overall. **Grips:** Double diamond checkered rosewood. **Sights:** Fixed, glare-proofed blade front, square notch rear; three-dot system. **Features:** Brushed stainless slide, nickeled aluminum frame; McCormick elongated-slot enhanced hammer, McCormick two-cut adjustable aluminum hammer. Made in U.S.A. by Colt's Mfg. Co., Inc.

Price: 45, stainless **$950.00**

COLT DEFENDER

Caliber: 40 S&W, 45 ACP, 7-shot magazine. **Barrel:** 3". **Weight:** 22-1/2 oz. **Length:** 6-3/4" overall. **Grips:** Pebble-finish rubber wraparound with finger grooves. **Sights:** White dot front, snag-free Colt competition rear. **Features:** Stainless finish; aluminum frame; combat-style hammer; Hi Ride grip safety, extended manual safety, disconnect safety. Introduced 1998. Made in U.S.A. by Colt's Mfg. Co.

Price: **$773.00**

Price: 41 Magnum Model, from **$825.00**

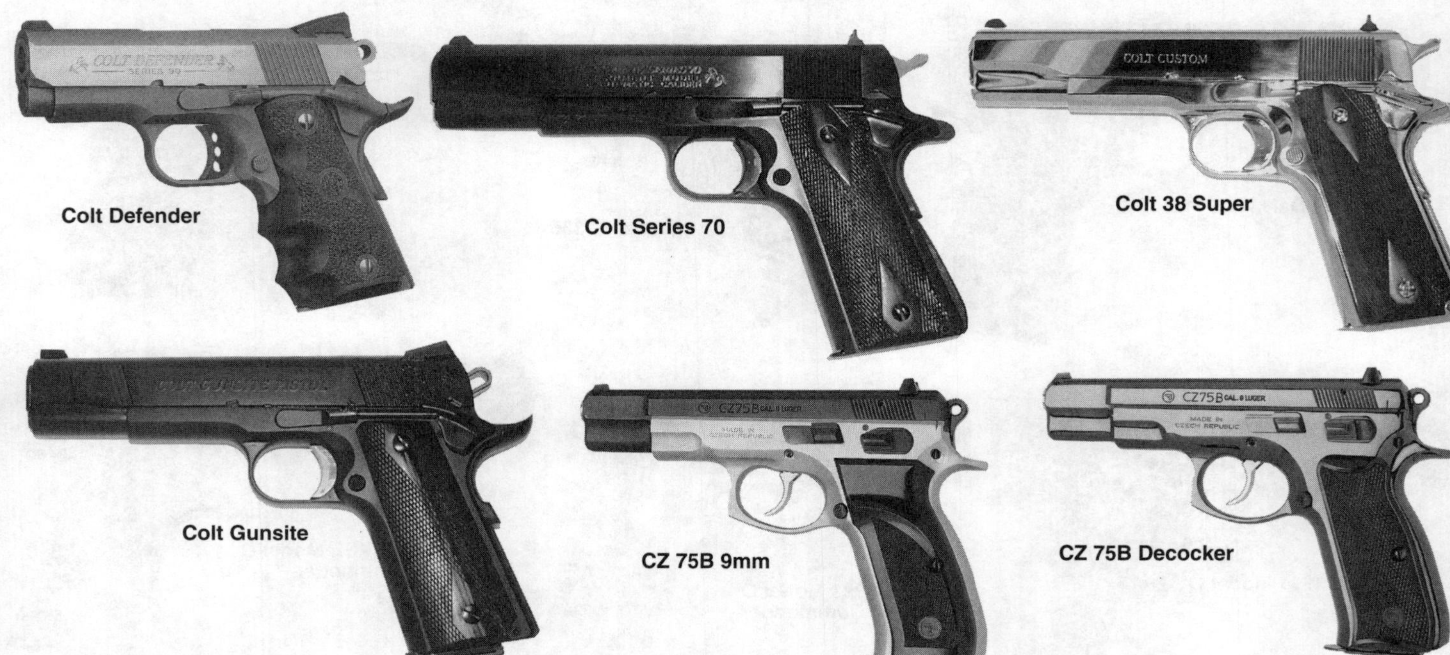

Colt Defender

Colt Series 70

Colt 38 Super

Colt Gunsite

CZ 75B 9mm

CZ 75B Decocker

CZ 85

COLT SERIES 70

Caliber: 45 ACP. **Barrel:** 5". **Weight:** NA **Length:** NA **Grips:** Rosewood with double diamond checkering pattern. **Sights:** Fixed. **Features:** A custom replica of the Original Series 70 pistol with a Series 70 firing system, original rollmarks. Introduced 2002. Made in U.S.A. by Colt's Manufacturing.

Price: . . . . **NA**

COLT 38 SUPER

Caliber: 38 Super. **Barrel:** 5". **Weight:** NA. **Length:** 8-1/2" **Grips:** Checkered rubber (stainless and blue models); Wood with double diamond checkering pattern (bright stainless model). **Sights:** Three-dot. **Features:** Beveled magazine well, standard thumb safety and service-style grip safety. Introduced 2003. Made in U.S.A. by Colt's Mfg. Co.

Price: . . . . . . (blue) **$864.00** (stainless steel) **$943.00**

Price: . . . . . . (bright stainless steel) **$1,152.00**

COLT GUNSITE PISTOL

Caliber: 45 ACP. **Barrel:** 5". **Weight:** NA. **Length:** NA. **Grips:** Rosewood. **Sights**: Heinie, front; Novak, rear. **Features:** Contains most all of the Gunsite school recommended features such as Series 70 firing system, Smith & Alexander metal grip safety w/palm swell, serrated flat mainspring housing, dehorned all around. Available in blue or stainless steel. Introduced 2003. Made in U.S.A. by Colt's Mfg. Co.

Price: . . . . **NA**

CZ 75B AUTO PISTOL

Caliber: 9mm Para., 40 S&W, 10-shot magazine. **Barrel:** 4.7". **Weight:** 34.3 oz. **Length:** 8.1" overall. **Grips:** High impact checkered plastic. **Sights:** Square post front, rear adjustable for windage; three-dot system. **Features:** Single action/double action design; firing pin block safety; choice of black polymer, matte or high-polish blue finishes. All-steel frame. Imported from the Czech Republic by CZ-USA.

Price: Black polymer. **$529.00**

Price: Glossy blue. **$559.00**

Price: Dual tone or satin nickel **$559.00**

Price: 22 LR conversion unit. **$399.00**

CZ 75B Decocker

Similar to the CZ 75B except has a decocking lever in place of the safety lever. All other specifications are the same. Introduced 1999. Imported from the Czech Republic by CZ-USA.

Price: 9mm, black polymer **$559.00**

Price: 40 S&W **$569.00**

CZ 75B Compact Auto Pistol

Similar to the CZ 75 except has 10-shot magazine, 3.9" barrel and weighs 32 oz. Has removable front sight, non-glare ribbed slide top. Trigger guard is squared and serrated; combat hammer. Introduced 1993. Imported from the Czech Republic by CZ-USA.

Price: 9mm, black polymer **$559.00**

Price: Dual tone or satin nickel **$569.00**

Price: D Compact, black polymer **$569.00**

Price: CZ2075 Sub-compact RAMI **$559.00**

CZ 75M IPSC Auto Pistol

Similar to the CZ 75B except has a longer frame and slide, slightly larger grip to accommodate new heavy-duty magazine. Ambidextrous thumb safety, safety notch on hammer; two-port in-frame compensator; slide racker; frame-mounted Firepoint red dot sight. Introduced 2001. Imported from the Czech Republic by CZ USA.

Price: 40 S&W, 10-shot mag. **$1,551.00**

Price: CZ 75 Standard IPSC (40 S&W, adj. sights) **$1,038.00**

CZ 85B Auto Pistol

Same gun as the CZ 75 except has ambidextrous slide release and safety-levers; non-glare, ribbed slide top; squared, serrated trigger guard; trigger stop to prevent overtravel. Introduced 1986. Imported from the Czech Republic by CZ-USA.

Price: Black polymer. **$483.00**

Price: Combat, black polymer. **$540.00**

Price: Combat, dual tone **$487.00**

Price: Combat, glossy blue. **$499.00**

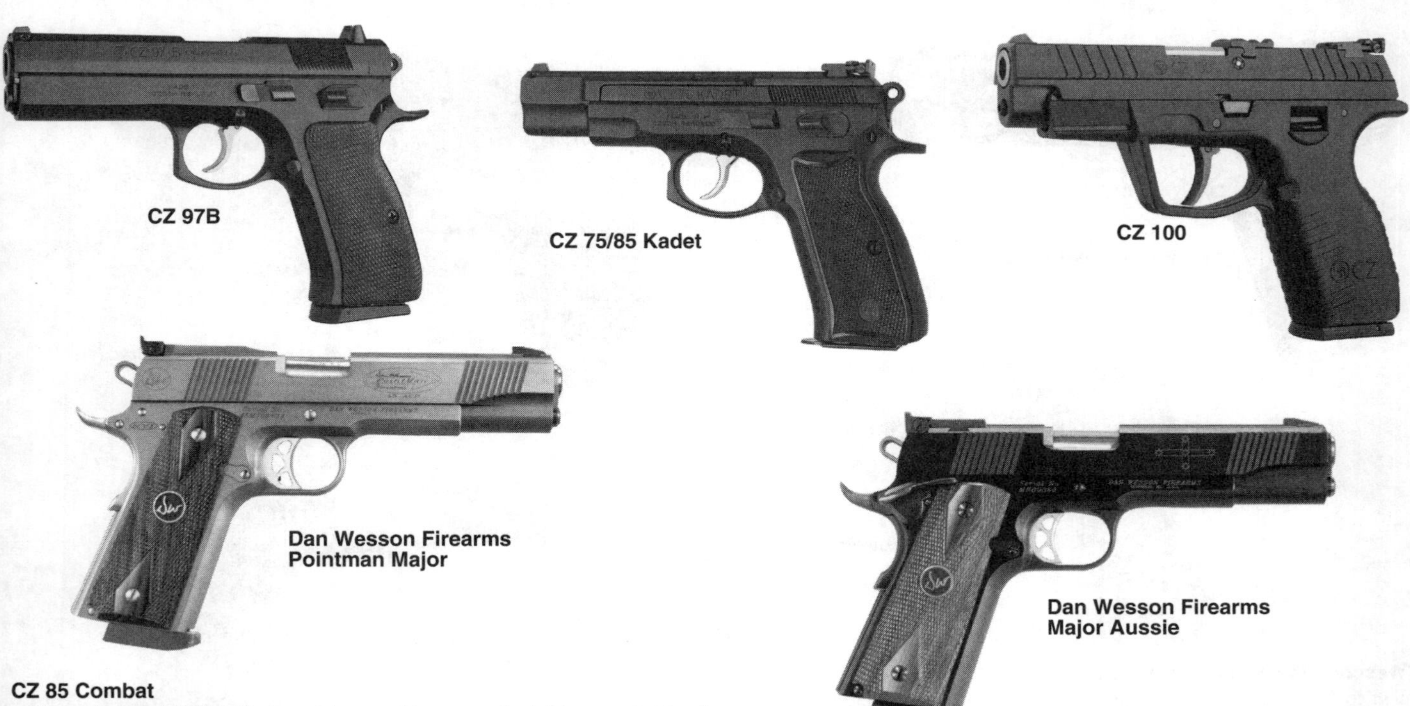

CZ 97B

CZ 75/85 Kadet

CZ 100

Dan Wesson Firearms Pointman Major

Dan Wesson Firearms Major Aussie

CZ 85 Combat

Similar to the CZ 85B (9mm only) except has an adjustable rear sight, adjustable trigger for overtravel, free-fall magazine, extended magazine catch. Does not have the firing pin block safety. Introduced 1999. Imported from the Czech Republic by CZ-USA.

Price: 9mm, black polymer **$540.00**
Price: 9mm, glossy blue **$566.00**
Price: 9mm, dual tone or satin nickel **$586.00**

CZ 83B DOUBLE-ACTION PISTOL

Caliber: 9mm Makarov, 32 ACP, 380 ACP, 10-shot magazine. **Barrel:** 3.8". **Weight:** 26.2 oz. **Length:** 6.8" overall. **Grips:** High impact checkered plastic. **Sights:** Removable square post front, rear adjustable for windage; three-dot system. **Features:** Single action/double action; ambidextrous magazine release and safety. Blue finish; non-glare ribbed slide top. Imported from the Czech Republic by CZ-USA.

Price: Blue **$378.00**
Price: Nickel **$397.00**

CZ 97B AUTO PISTOL

Caliber: 45 ACP, 10-shot magazine. **Barrel:** 4.85". **Weight:** 40 oz. **Length:** 8.34" overall. **Grips:** Checkered walnut. **Sights:** Fixed. **Features:** Single action/double action; full-length slide rails; screw-in barrel bushing; linkless barrel; all-steel construction; chamber loaded indicator; dual transfer bars. Introduced 1999. Imported from the Czech Republic by CZ-USA.

Price: Black polymer. **$625.00**
Price: Glossy blue. **$641.00**

CZ 75/85 KADET AUTO PISTOL

Caliber: 22 LR, 10-shot magazine. **Barrel:** 4.88". **Weight:** 36 oz. **Grips:** High impact checkered plastic. **Sights:** Blade front, fully adjustable rear. **Features:** Single action/double action mechanism; all-steel construction. Duplicates weight, balance and function of the CZ 75 pistol. Introduced 1999. Imported from the Czech Republic by CZ-USA.

Price: Black polymer. **$486.00**

CZ 100 AUTO PISTOL

Caliber: 9mm Para., 40 S&W, 10-shot magazine. **Barrel:** 3.7". **Weight:** 24 oz. **Length:** 6.9" overall. **Grips:** Grooved polymer. **Sights:** Blade front with dot, white outline rear drift adjustable for windage. **Features:** Double action only with firing pin block; polymer frame, steel slide; has laser sight mount. Introduced 1996. Imported from the Czech Republic by CZ-USA.

Price: 9mm Para. **$405.00**
Price: 40 S&W **$424.00**

DAN WESSON FIREARMS POINTMAN MAJOR AUTO PISTOL

Caliber: 45 ACP. **Barrel:** 5". **Grips:** Rosewood checkered. **Features:** Blued or stainless steel frame and serrated slide; Chip McCormick match-grade trigger group, sear and disconnect; match-grade barrel; high-ride beavertail safety; checkered slide release; **Sights:** High rib; interchangeable sight system; laser engraved. Introduced 2000. Made in U.S.A. by Dan Wesson Firearms.

Price: Model PM1-B (blued) **$799.00**
Price: Model PM1-S (stainless) **$699.00**

Dan Wesson Firearms Pointman Seven Auto Pistols

Similar to Pointman Major, dovetail adjustable target rear sight and dovetail target front sight. Available in blued or stainless finish. Introduced 2000. Made in U.S.A. by Dan Wesson Firearms.

Price: PM7 (blued frame and slide) **$999.00**
Price: PM7S (stainless finish). **$799.00**

Dan Wesson Firearms Pointman Guardian Auto Pistols

Similar to Pointman Major, more compact frame with 4.25" barrel. Available in blued or stainless finish with fixed or adjustable sights. Introduced 2000. Made in U.S.A. by Dan Wesson Firearms.

Price: PMG-FS, all new frame (fixed sights). **$769.00**
Price: PMG-AS (blued frame and slide, adjustable sights). **$799.00**
Price: PMGD-FS Guardian Duce, all new frame (stainless frame and blued slide, fixed sights) **$829.00**
Price: PMGD-AS Guardian Duce (stainless frame and blued slide, adj. sights) **$799.00**

Dan Wesson Firearms Major Tri-Ops Packs

Similar to Pointman Major. Complete frame assembly fitted to 3 match grade complete slide assemblied (9mm, 10mm, 40 S&W). Includes recoil springs and magazines that come in hard cases fashioned after high-grade European rifle case. Constructed of navy blue cordura stretched over hardwood with black leather trim and comfortable black leather-wrapped handle. Brass corner protectors, dual combination locks, engraved presentation plate on the lid. Inside, the Tri-Ops Pack components are nested in precision die-cut closed cell foam and held sercurely in place by convoluted foam in the inside of the lid. Introduced 2002. Made in U.S.A. by Dan Wesson Firearms.

Price: TOP1B (blued), TOP1-S (stainless) **$2,459.00**

Dan Wesson Firearms Patriot Marksman

Desert Eagle Mark XIX

Desert Baby Eagle

EAA Witness

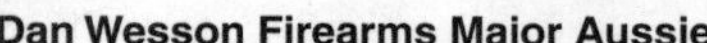

Dan Wesson Firearms Major Aussie

Similar to Pointman Major. Available in 45 ACP. Features Bo-Mar-style adjustable rear target sight, unique slide top configuration exclusive to this model (features radius from the flat side surfaces of the slide to a narrow flat on top and then a small redius and reveal ending in a flat, low (1/16" high) sight rib 3/8" wide with lengthwise serrations). Clearly identified by the Southern Cross flag emblem laser engraved on the sides of the slide (available in 45 ACP only). Introduced 2002. Made in U.S.A. by Dan Wesson Firearms.

Price: PMA-B (blued) **$799.00**
Price: PMA-S (stainless). **$799.00**

Dan Wesson Firearms Pointman Minor Auto Pistol

Similar to Pointman Major. Full size (5") entry level IDPA or action pistol model with blued carbon alloy frame and round top slide, bead blast matte finish on frame and slide top and radius, satin-brushed polished finish on sides of slide, chromed barrel, dovetail mount fixed rear target sight and tactical/target ramp front sight, match trigger, skeletonized target hammer, high ride beavertail, fitted extractor, serrations on thumb safety, slide release and mag release, lowered and relieved ejection port, beveled mag well, exotic hardwood grips, serrated mainspring housing, laser engraved. Introduced 2000. Made in U.S.A. by Dan Wesson Firearms.

Price: Model PM2-P **$599.00**

Dan Wesson Firearms Pointman Hi-Cap Auto Pistol

Similar to Pointman Minor, full-size high-capacity (10-shot) magazine with 5" chromed barrel, blued finish and dovetail fixed rear sight. Match adjustable trigger, ambidextrous extended thumb safety, beavertail safety. Introduced 2001. From Dan Wesson Firearms.

Price: PMHC (Pointman High-Cap) **$689.00**

Dan Wesson Firearms Pointman Dave Pruitt Signature Series

Similar to other full-sized Pointman models, customized by Master Pistolsmith and IDPA Grand Master Dave Pruitt. Alloy carbon-steel with black oxide bluing and bead-blast matte finish. Front and rear chevron cocking serrations, dovetail mount fixed rear target sight and tactical/target ramp front sight, ramped match barrel with fitted match bushing and link, Chip McCormick (or equivalent) match grade trigger group, serrated ambidextrous tactical/carry thumb safety, high ride beavertail, serrated slide release and checkered mag release, match grade sear and hammer, fitted extractor, lowered and relieved ejection port, beveled mag well, full length two-piece recoil spring guide rod, cocobolo double diamond checkered grips, serrated steel mainspring housing, special laser engraving. Introduced 2001. From Dan Wesson Firearms.

Price: PMDP (Pointman Dave Pruitt) **$899.00**

DAN WESSON FIREARMS PATRIOT 1911 PISTOL

Caliber: 45 ACP. **Grips:** Exotic exhibition grade cocobolo, double diamond hand cut checkering. **Sights:** New innovative combat/carry rear sight that completely encloses the dovetail. **Features:** The new Patriot Expert and Patriot Marksman are full size match grade series 70 1911s machined from steel forgings. Available in blued chome moly steel or stainless steel. Beveled mag well, lowered and flared ejection port, high sweep beavertail safety. Introduced June 2002.

Price: Model PTM-B (blued) **$797.00**
Price: Model PTM-S (stainless) **$898.00**
Price: Model PTE-B (blued) **$864.00**
Price: Model PTE-S (stainless). **$971.00**

DESERT EAGLE MARK XIX PISTOL

Caliber: 357 Mag., 9-shot; 44 Mag., 8-shot; 50 AE, 7-shot. **Barrel:** 6", 10", interchangeable. **Weight:** 357 Mag.-62 oz.; 44 Mag.-69 oz.; 50 AE-72 oz. **Length:** 10-1/4" overall (6" bbl.). **Grips:** Polymer; rubber available. **Sights:** Blade on ramp front, combat-style rear. Adjustable available. **Features:** Interchangeable barrels; rotating three-lug bolt; ambidextrous safety; adjustable trigger. Military epoxy finish. Satin, bright nickel, chrome, brushed, matte or black finishes available. 10" barrel extra. Imported from Israel by Magnum Research, Inc.

Price: 357, 6" bbl., standard pistol **$1,249.00**
Price: 44 Mag., 6", standard pistol **$1,249.00**
Price: 50 Magnum, 6" bbl., standard pistol. **$1,249.00**

DESERT BABY EAGLE PISTOLS

Caliber: 9mm Para., 40 S&W, 45 ACP, 10-round magazine. **Barrel:** 3.5", 3.7", 4.72". **Weight:** 26.8 - 39.8 oz. **Length:** 7.25" to 8.25" overall. **Grips:** Polymer. **Sights:** Drift-adjustable rear, blade front. **Features:** Steel frame and slide; polygonal rifling to reduce barrel wear; slide safety; decocker. Reintroduced in 1999. Imported from Israel by Magnum Research Inc.

Price: Standard (9mm or 40 cal.; 4.72" barrel, 8.25" overall) **$499.00**
Price: Semi-Compact (9mm, 40 or 45 cal.; 3.7" barrel, 7.75" overall) **$499.00**
Price: Compact (9mm or 40 cal.; 3.5" barrel, 7.25" overall) **$499.00**
Price: Polymer (9mm or 40 cal; polymer frame; 3.25" barrel, 7.25" overall) **$499.00**

Ed Brown Commander Bobtail

Ed Brown Kobra Carry

Entréprise Elite P500

Entréprise Boxer P500

Entréprise Tactical 500

EAA WITNESS DA AUTO PISTOL

Caliber: 9mm Para., 10-shot magazine; 38 Super, 40 S&W, 10-shot magazine; 45 ACP, 10-shot magazine. **Barrel:** 4.50". **Weight:** 35.33 oz. **Length:** 8.10" overall. **Grips:** Checkered rubber. **Sights:** Undercut blade front, open rear adjustable for windage. **Features:** Double-action trigger system; round trigger guard; frame-mounted safety. Introduced 1991. Imported from Italy by European American Armory.

Price: 9mm, blue **$449.00**
Price: 9mm, Wonder finish **$459.00**
Price: 9mm Compact, blue, 10-shot **$449.00**
Price: As above, Wonder finish. **$459.00**
Price: 38 Super, blue **$449.00**
Price: 38 Super, Wonder finish **$459.00**
Price: 40 S&W, blue **$449.00**
Price: As above, Wonder finish. **$459.00**
Price: 40 S&W Compact, 9-shot, blue **$449.00**
Price: As above, Wonder finish. **$459.00**
Price: 45 ACP, blue. **$449.00**
Price: As above, Wonder finish. **$459.00**
Price: 45 ACP Compact, 8-shot, blue. **$449.00**
Price: As above, Wonder finish. **$459.00**

ED BROWN CLASSIC CUSTOM

Caliber: 45 ACP, 7 shots. **Barrel:** 5". **Weight:** 39 oz. **Stocks:** Cocobolo wood. **Sights:** Bo-Mar adjustable rear, dovetail front. **Features:** Single-action, M1911 style, custom made to order, stainless frame and slide available.

Price: **$2,895.00**

ED BROWN COMMANDER BOBTAIL

Caliber: 45 ACP, 400 Cor-Bon, 40 S&W, 357 SIG, 38 Super, 9mm Luger, 7-shot magazine. **Barrel:** 4.25". **Weight:** 34 oz. **Grips:** Hogue exotic wood. **Sights:** Customer preference front; fixed Novak low-mount, rear. Optional night inserts available. **Features:** Checkered forestrap and bob-tailed mainspring housing. Other options available.

Price: Executive Carry **$2,295.00**
Price: Executive Elite **$2,195.00**

ED BROWN KOBRA

Caliber: 45 ACP, 7-shot magazine. **Barrel:** 5" (Kobra); 4.25" (Kobra Carry). **Weight:** 39 oz. (Kobra); 34 oz. (Kobra Carry). **Grips:** Hogue exotic wood. **Sights:** Ramp, front; fixed Novak low-mount night sights, rear. **Features:** Has snakeskin pattern serrations on forestrap and mainspring housing, dehorned edges, beavertail grip safety.

Price: Kobra **$1,895.00**
Price: Kobra Carry **$1,995.00**

ENTRÉPRISE ELITE P500 AUTO PISTOL

Caliber: 45 ACP, 10-shot magazine. **Barrel:** 5". **Weight:** 40 oz. **Length:** 8.5" overall. **Grips:** Black ultra-slim, double diamond, checkered synthetic. **Sights:** Dovetailed blade front, rear adjustable for windage; three-dot system. **Features:** Reinforced dust cover; lowered and flared ejection port; squared trigger guard; adjustable match trigger; bolstered front strap; high grip cut; high ride beavertail grip safety; steel flat mainspring housing; extended thumb lock; skeletonized hammer, match grade sear, disconnector; Wolff springs. Introduced 1998. Made in U.S.A. by Entréprise Arms.

Price: **$739.90**

Entréprise Boxer P500 Auto Pistol

Similar to the Medalist model except has adjustable Competizione "melded" rear sight with dovetailed Patridge front; high mass chiseled slide with sweep cut; machined slide parallel rails; polished breech face and barrel channel. Introduced 1998. Made in U.S.A. by Entréprise Arms.

Price: **$1,399.00**

Entréprise Medalist P500 Auto Pistol

Similar to the Elite model except has adjustable Competizione "melded" rear sight with dovetailed Patridge front; machined slide parallel rails with polished breech face and barrel channel; front and rear slide serrations; lowered and flared ejection port; full-length one-piece guide rod with plug; National Match barrel and bushing; stainless firing pin; tuned match extractor; oversize firing pin stop; throated barrel and polished ramp; slide lapped to frame. Introduced 1998. Made in U.S.A. by Entréprise Arms.

Price: 45 ACP **$979.00**
Price: 40 S&W **$1,099.00**

Entréprise Tactical P500 Auto Pistol

Similar to the Elite model except has Tactical2 Ghost Ring sight or Novak lo-mount sight; ambidextrous thumb safety; front and rear slide serrations; full-length guide rod; throated barrel, polished ramp; tuned match extractor; fitted barrel and bushing; stainless firing pin; slide lapped to frame; dehorned. Introduced 1998. Made in U.S.A. by Entréprise Arms.

Price: **$979.90**
Price: Tactical Plus (full-size frame, Officer's slide). **$1,049.00**

ERMA KGP68 AUTO PISTOL

Caliber: 32 ACP, 6-shot, 380 ACP, 5-shot. **Barrel:** 4". **Weight:** 22-1/2 oz. **Length:** 7-3/8" overall. **Grips:** Checkered plastic. **Sights:** Fixed. **Features:** Toggle action similar to original "Luger" pistol. Action stays open after last shot. Has magazine and sear disconnect safety systems.

Price: **$499.95**

HANDGUNS — AUTOLOADERS, SERVICE & SPORT

FEG PJK-9HP

Felk MTF 450

Firestorm Mini

Firestorm 45 Gov't

Glock 17C

Glock 22

FEG PJK-9HP AUTO PISTOL

Caliber: 9mm Para., 10-shot magazine. **Barrel:** 4.75". **Weight:** 32 oz. **Length:** 8" overall. **Grips:** Hand-checkered walnut. **Sights:** Blade front, rear adjustable for windage; three-dot system. **Features:** Single action; polished blue or hard chrome finish; rounded combat-style serrated hammer. Comes with two magazines and cleaning rod. Imported from Hungary by K.B.I., Inc.

Price: Blue **$259.95**

Price: Hard chrome. **$259.95**

FEG SMC-380 AUTO PISTOL

Caliber: 380 ACP, 6-shot magazine. **Barrel:** 3.5". **Weight:** 18.5 oz. **Length:** 6.1" overall. **Grips:** Checkered composition with thumbrest. **Sights:** Blade front, rear adjustable for windage. **Features:** Patterned after the PPK pistol. Alloy frame, steel slide; double action. Blue finish. Comes with two magazines, cleaning rod. Imported from Hungary by K.B.I., Inc.

Price: **$224.95**

FELK MTF 450 AUTO PISTOL

Caliber: 9mm Para. (10-shot); 40 S&W (8-shot); .357 Mag, 45 ACP (9-shot magazine). **Barrel:** 3.5". **Weight:** 19.9 oz. **Length:** 6.4" overall. **Grips:** Checkered. **Sights:** Blade front; adjustable rear. **Features:** Double-action-only trigger, striker fired; polymer frame; trigger safety, firing pin safety, trigger bar safety; adjustable trigger weight; fully interchangeable slide/barrel to change calibers. Introduced 1998. Imported by Felk Inc.

Price: **$395.00**

Price: 45 ACP pistol with 9mm and 40 S&W slide/barrel assemblies **$999.00**

FIRESTORM AUTO PISTOL

Features: 7 or 10 rd. double action pistols with matte, duotone or nickel finish. Distributed by SGS Importers International.

Price: 22 LR 10 rd, 380 7 rd. matte. **$264.95**

Price: Duotone **$274.95**

Price: Mini 9mm, 40 S&W, 10 rd. matte **$383.95**

Price: Duotone **$391.95**

Price: Nickel **$408.95**

Price: Mini 45, 7 rd. matte. **$383.95**

Price: Duotone 45. . . . . **$399.95**

Price: Nickel 45. . . . . **$416.95**

Price: 45 Government, Compact, 7 rd. matte **$324.95**

Price: Duotone **$333.95**

Price: Extra magazines **$29.95-49.95**

GLOCK 17 AUTO PISTOL

Caliber: 9mm Para., 10-shot magazine. **Barrel:** 4.49". **Weight:** 22.04 oz. (without magazine). **Length:** 7.32" overall. **Grips:** Black polymer. **Sights:** Dot on front blade, white outline rear adjustable for windage. **Features:** Polymer frame, steel slide; double-action trigger with "Safe Action" system; mechanical firing pin safety, drop safety; simple takedown without tools; locked breech, recoil operated action. Adopted by Austrian armed forces 1983. NATO approved 1984. Imported from Austria by Glock, Inc.

Price: Fixed sight, extra magazine, magazine loader, cleaning kit. . **$641.00**

Price: Adjustable sight **$671.00**

Price: Model 17L (6" barrel) **$800.00**

Price: Model 17C, ported barrel (compensated) **$646.00**

Glock 19 Auto Pistol

Similar to the Glock 17 except has a 4" barrel, giving an overall length of 6.85" and weight of 20.99 oz. Magazine capacity is 10 rounds. Fixed or adjustable rear sight. Introduced 1988.

Price: Fixed sight **$641.00**

Price: Adjustable sight **$671.00**

Price: Model 19C, ported barrel **$646.00**

Glock 20 10mm Auto Pistol

Similar to the Glock Model 17 except chambered for 10mm automatic cartridge. Barrel length is 4.60", overall length is 7.59", and weight is 26.3 oz. (without magazine). Magazine capacity is 10 rounds. Fixed or adjustable rear sight. Comes with an extra magazine, magazine loader, cleaning rod and brush. Introduced 1990. Imported from Austria by Glock, Inc.

Price: Fixed sight **$700.00**

Price: Adjustable sight **$730.00**

Glock 21 Auto Pistol

Similar to the Glock 17 except chambered for 45 ACP, 10-shot magazine. Overall length is 7.59", weight is 25.2 oz. (without magazine). Fixed or adjustable rear sight. Introduced 1991.

Price: Fixed sight **$700.00**

Price: Adjustable sight **$730.00**

Glock 22 Auto Pistol

Similar to the Glock 17 except chambered for 40 S&W, 10-shot magazine. Overall length is 7.28", weight is 22.3 oz. (without magazine). Fixed or adjustable rear sight. Introduced 1990.

Price: Fixed sight **$641.00**

Price: Adjustable sight **$671.00**

Price: Model 22C, ported barrel **$646.00**

HANDGUNS — AUTOLOADERS, SERVICE & SPORT

Glock 26

Glock 30

Glock 31

Glock 35

Hammerli Trailside

Glock 23 Auto Pistol

Similar to the Glock 19 except chambered for 40 S&W, 10-shot magazine. Overall length is 6.85", weight is 20.6 oz. (without magazine). Fixed or adjustable rear sight. Introduced 1990.

Price: Fixed sight **$641.00**
Price: Model 23C, ported barrel **$646.00**
Price: Adjustable sight **$671.00**

GLOCK 26, 27 AUTO PISTOLS

Caliber: 9mm Para. (M26), 10-shot magazine; 40 S&W (M27), 9-shot magazine. **Barrel:** 3.46". **Weight:** 21.75 oz. **Length:** 6.29" overall. **Grips:** Integral. Stippled polymer. **Sights:** Dot on front blade, fixed or fully adjustable white outline rear. **Features:** Subcompact size. Polymer frame, steel slide; double-action trigger with "Safe Action" system, three safeties. Matte black Tenifer finish. Hammer-forged barrel. Imported from Austria by Glock, Inc. Introduced 1996.

Price: Fixed sight **$641.00**
Price: Adjustable sight **$671.00**

GLOCK 29, 30 AUTO PISTOLS

Caliber: 10mm (M29), 45 ACP (M30), 10-shot magazine. **Barrel:** 3.78". **Weight:** 24 oz. **Length:** 6.7" overall. **Grips:** Integral. Stippled polymer. **Sights:** Dot on front, fixed or fully adjustable white outline rear. **Features:** Compact size. Polymer frame steel slide; double-recoil spring reduces recoil; Safe Action system with three safeties; Tenifer finish. Two magazines supplied. Introduced 1997. Imported from Austria by Glock, Inc.

Price: Fixed sight **$700.00**
Price: Adjustable sight **$730.00**

Glock 31/31C Auto Pistols

Similar to the Glock 17 except chambered for 357 Auto cartridge; 10-shot magazine. Overall length is 7.32", weight is 23.28 oz. (without magazine). Fixed or adjustable sight. Imported from Austria by Glock, Inc.

Price: Fixed sight **$641.00**
Price: Adjustable sight **$671.00**
Price: Model 31C, ported barrel **$646.00**

Glock 32/32C Auto Pistols

Similar to the Glock 19 except chambered for the 357 Auto cartridge; 10-shot magazine. Overall length is 6.85", weight is 21.52 oz. (without magazine). Fixed or adjustable sight. Imported from Austria by Glock, Inc.

Price: Fixed sight **$616.00**
Price: Adjustable sight **$644.00**
Price: Model 32C, ported barrel **$646.00**

Glock 33 Auto Pistol

Similar to the Glock 26 except chambered for the 357 Auto cartridge; 9-shot magazine. Overall length is 6.29", weight is 19.75 oz. (without magazine). Fixed or adjustable sight. Imported from Austria by Glock, Inc.

Price: Fixed sight **$641.00**
Price: Adjustable sight **$671.00**

GLOCK 34, 35 AUTO PISTOLS

Caliber: 9mm Para. (M34), 40 S&W (M35), 10-shot magazine. **Barrel:** 5.32". **Weight:** 22.9 oz. **Length:** 8.15" overall. **Grips:** Integral. Stippled polymer. **Sights:** Dot on front, fully adjustable white outline rear. **Features:** Polymer frame, steel slide; double-action trigger with "Safe Action" system; three safeties; Tenifer finish. Imported from Austria by Glock, Inc.

Price: Model 34, 9mm. **$770.00**
Price: Model 35, 40 S&W **$770.00**

GLOCK 36 AUTO PISTOL

Caliber: 45 ACP, 6-shot magazine. **Barrel:** 3.78". **Weight:** 20.11 oz. **Length:** 6.77" overall. **Grips:** Integral. Stippled polymer. **Sights:** Dot on front, fully adjustable white outline rear. **Features:** Polymer frame, steel slide; double-action trigger with "Safe Action" system; three safeties; Tenifer finish. Imported from Austria by Glock, Inc.

Price: Fixed sight **$700.00**
Price: Adj. sight **$730.00**

HAMMERLI "TRAILSIDE" TARGET PISTOL

Caliber: 22 LR. **Barrel:** 4.5", 6". **Weight:** 28 oz. **Grips:** Synthetic. **Sights:** Fixed. **Features:** 10-shot magazine. Imported from Switzerland by SIGARMS. Distributed by Hammerli U.S.A.

Price: **$579.00**

HECKLER & KOCH USP AUTO PISTOL

Caliber: 9mm Para., 10-shot magazine, 40 S&W, 10-shot magazine, 357 Mag. **Barrel:** 4.25". **Weight:** 28 oz. (USP40). **Length:** 6.9" overall. **Grips:** Non-slip stippled black polymer. **Sights:** Blade front, rear adjustable for windage. **Features:** New HK design with polymer frame, modified Browning action with recoil reduction system, single control lever. Special "hostile environment" finish on all metal parts. Available in SA/DA, DAO, left- and right-hand versions. Introduced 1993. Imported from Germany by Heckler & Koch, Inc.

Price: Right-hand **$769.00**
Price: Left-hand **$794.00**

Heckler & Koch USP Compact Auto Pistol

Similar to the USP except has 3.58" barrel, measures 6.81" overall, and weighs 1.60 lbs. (9mm). Available in 9mm Para. 357 SIG or 40 S&W with 10-shot magazine. Introduced 1996. Imported from Germany by Heckler & Koch, Inc.

Price: Blue **$799.00**
Price: Blue with control lever on right **$824.00**
Price: Same as USP Compact DAO, enhanced trigger performance **$799.00**

Heckler & Koch USP Compact

Heckler & Koch USP45

Heckler & Koch USP45 Compact

Heckler & Koch USP45 Tactical

Heckler & Koch Elite

Heckler & Koch Mark 23 Special Operations

Heckler & Koch P7M8

Heckler & Koch USP45 Auto Pistol

Similar to the 9mm and 40 S&W USP except chambered for 45 ACP, 10-shot magazine. Has 4.13" barrel, overall length of 7.87" and weighs 30.4 oz. Has adjustable three-dot sight system. Available in SA/DA, DAO, left- and right-hand versions. Introduced 1995. Imported from Germany by Heckler & Koch, Inc.

Price: Right-hand **$839.00**
Price: Left-hand **$864.00**

Heckler & Koch USP45 Compact

Similar to the USP45 except has stainless slide; 8-shot magazine; modified and contoured slide and frame; extended slide release; 3.80" barrel, 7.09" overall length, weighs 1.75 lbs.; adjustable three-dot sights. Introduced 1998. Imported from Germany by Heckler & Koch, Inc.

Price: With control lever on left, stainless **$909.00**
Price: As above, blue **$857.00**
Price: With control lever on right, stainless **$944.00**
Price: As above, blue **$892.00**

HECKLER & KOCH USP45 TACTICAL PISTOL

Caliber: 45 ACP, 10-shot magazine. **Barrel:** 4.92". **Weight:** 2.24 lbs. **Length:** 8.64" overall. **Grips:** Non-slip stippled polymer. **Sights:** Blade front, fully adjustable target rear. **Features:** Has extended threaded barrel with rubber O-ring; adjustable trigger; extended magazine floorplate; adjustable trigger stop; polymer frame. Introduced 1998. Imported from Germany by Heckler & Koch, Inc.

Price: **$1,115.00**

HECKLER & KOCH MARK 23 SPECIAL OPERATIONS PISTOL

Caliber: 45 ACP, 10-shot magazine. **Barrel:** 5.87". **Weight:** 43 oz. **Length:** 9.65" overall. **Grips:** Integral with frame; black polymer. **Sights:** Blade front, rear drift adjustable for windage; three-dot. **Features:** Polymer frame; double action; exposed hammer; short recoil, modified Browning action. Civilian version of the SOCOM pistol. Introduced 1996. Imported from Germany by Heckler & Koch, Inc.

Price: **$2,112.00**

Heckler & Koch USP Expert Pistol

Combines features of the USP Tactical and HK Mark 23 pistols with a new slide design. Chambered for 45 ACP, .40 S&W & 9mm; 10-shot magazine. Has adjustable target sights, 5.20" barrel, 8.74" overall length, weighs 1.87 lbs. Match-grade single- and double-action trigger pull with adjustable stop; ambidextrous control levers; elongated target slide; barrel O-ring that seals and centers barrel. Suited to IPSC competition. Introduced 1999. Imported from Germany by Heckler & Koch, Inc.

Price: **$1,869.00**

Heckler & Koch Elite

A long slide version of the USP combining features found on standard-sized and specialized models of the USP. Most noteworthy is the 6.2" barrel, making it the most accurate of the USP series. In 9mm and .45 ACP. Imported from Germany by Heckler & Koch, Inc. Introduced 2003.

Price: **$1,569.00**

HECKLER & KOCH P7M8 AUTO PISTOL

Caliber: 9mm Para., 8-shot magazine. **Barrel:** 4.13". **Weight:** 29 oz. **Length:** 6.73" overall. **Grips:** Stippled black plastic. **Sights:** Blade front, adjustable rear; three-dot system. **Features:** Unique "squeeze cocker" in frontstrap cocks the action. Gas-retarded action. Squared combat-type trigger guard. Blue finish. Compact size. Imported from Germany by Heckler & Koch, Inc.

Price: P7M8, blued **$1,515.00**

HECKLER & KOCH P2000 GPM PISTOL

Caliber: 9mmx19; 10-shot magazine. 13- or 16-round law enforcment/military magazines. **Barrel:** 3.62". **Weight:** 21.87 ozs. **Length:** 7". **Grips:** Interchangeable panels. **Sights:** Fixed Patridge style, drift adjustable for windage, standard three-dot. **Features:** German Pistol Model incorporating features of the HK USP Compact such as the pre-cocked hammer system which combines the advantages of a cocked striker with the double action hammer system. Introduced 2003. Imported from Germany by Heckler & Koch, Inc.

Price: **$887.00**

HECKLER & KOCK P2000SK SUBCOMPACT

Caliber: 9mm and 40 S&W. **Barrel:** 2.48". **Weight:** 1.49 lbs. (9mm) or 1.61 lbs. (40 S&W). **Sights:** Fixed Patridge style, drift adjustable. **Features:** Standard accessory rails, ambidextrous slide release, polymer frame, polygonal bore profile.

Price: **$887.00**

Hi-Point 9MM Comp

Kahr K9

Kahr MK40

Kel-Tec P-11

HI-POINT FIREARMS 9MM COMP PISTOL

Caliber: 9mm, Para., 10-shot magazine. **Barrel:** 4". **Weight:** 39 oz. **Length:** 7.72" overall. **Grips:** Textured acetal plastic. **Sights:** Adjustable; low profile. **Features:** Single-action design. Scratch-resistant, non-glare blue finish, alloy frame. Muzzle brake/compensator. Compensator is slotted for laser or flashlight mounting. Introduced 1998. From MKS Supply, Inc.

Price: Matte black **$159.00**

HI-POINT FIREARMS MODEL 9MM COMPACT PISTOL

Caliber: 9mm Para., 8-shot magazine. **Barrel:** 3.5". **Weight:** 29 oz. **Length:** 6.7" overall. **Grips:** Textured acetal plastic. **Sights:** Combat-style adjustable three-dot system; low profile. **Features:** Single-action design; frame-mounted magazine release; polymer or alloy frame. Scratch-resistant matte finish. Introduced 1993. Made in U.S.A. by MKS Supply, Inc.

Price: Black, alloy frame **$149.00**

Price: With polymer frame (29 oz.), non-slip grips **$149.00**

Price: Aluminum with polymer frame **$149.00**

Hi-Point Firearms Model 380 Polymer Pistol

Similar to the 9mm Compact model except chambered for 380 ACP, 8-shot magazine, adjustable three-dot sights. Weighs 29 oz. Polymer frame. Introduced 1998. Made in U.S.A. by MKS Supply.

Price: **$114.00**

Hi-Point Firearms 380 Comp Pistol

Similar to the 380 Polymer Pistol except has a 4" barrel with muzzle compensator; action locks open after last shot. Includes a 10-shot and an 8-shot magazine; trigger lock. Introduced 2001. Made in U.S.A. by MKS Supply Inc.

Price: **$135.00**

Price: With laser sight **$229.00**

HI-POINT FIREARMS 45 POLYMER FRAME

Caliber: 45 ACP, 9-shot, 40 S&W . **Barrel:** 4.5". **Weight:** 35 oz. **Sights:** Adjustable three-dot. **Features:** Last round lock-open, grip mounted magazine release, magazine disconnect safety, integrated accessory rail. Introduced 2002. Made in U.S.A. by MKS Supply Inc.

Price: **$179.00**

IAI M-2000 PISTOL

Caliber: 45 ACP, 8-shot. **Barrel:** 5", (Compact 4.25"). **Weight:** 36 oz. **Length:** 8.5", (6" Compact). **Grips:** Plastic or wood. **Sights:** Fixed. **Features:** 1911 Government U.S. Army-style. Steel frame and slide parkerized. GI grip safety. Beveled feed ramp barrel. By IAI, Inc.

Price: **$465.00**

KAHR K9, K40 DA AUTO PISTOLS

Caliber: 9mm Para., 7-shot, 40 S&W, 6-shot magazine. **Barrel:** 3.5". **Weight:** 25 oz. **Length:** 6" overall. **Grips:** Wrap-around textured soft polymer. **Sights:** Blade front, rear drift adjustable for windage; bar-dot combat style. **Features:** Trigger-cocking double-action mechanism with passive firing pin block. Made of 4140 ordnance steel with matte black finish. Contact maker for complete price list. Introduced 1994. Made in U.S.A. by Kahr Arms.

Price: E9, black matte finish **$425.00**

Price: Matte black, night sights 9mm **$668.00**

Price: Matte stainless steel, 9mm. . . **$638.00**

Price: 40 S&W, matte black **$580.00**

Price: 40 S&W, matte black, night sights **$668.00**

Price: 40 S&W, matte stainless **$638.00**

Price: K9 Elite 98 (high-polish stainless slide flats, Kahr combat trigger), from **$694.00**

Price: As above, MK9 Elite 98, from **$694.00**

Price: As above, K40 Elite 98, from **$694.00**

Price: Covert, black, stainless slide, short grip **$599.00**

Price: Covert, black, tritium nite sights **$689.00**

Kahr K9 9mm Compact Polymer Pistol

Similar to K9 steel frame pistol except has polymer frame, matte stainless steel slide. Barrel length 3.5"; overall length 6"; weighs 17.9 oz. Includes two 7-shot magazines, hard polymer case, trigger lock. Introduced 2000. Made in U.S.A. by Kahr Arms.

Price: **$599.00**

Kahr MK9/MK40 Micro Pistol

Similar to the K9/K40 except is 5.5" overall, 4" high, has a 3" barrel. Weighs 22 oz. Has snag-free bar-dot sights, polished feed ramp, dual recoil spring system, DA-only trigger. Comes with 6- and 7-shot magazines. Introduced 1998. Made in U.S.A. by Kahr Arms.

Price: Matte stainless **$638.00**

Price: Elite 98, polished stainless, tritium night sights **$791.00**

KAHR PM9 PISTOL

Caliber: 9x19. **Barrel:** 3", 1:10 twist. **Weight:** 15.9 oz. **Length:** 5.3" overall. **Features:** Lightweight black polymer frame, polygonal rifling, stainless steel slide, DAO with passive striker block, trigger lock, hard case, 6 and 7 rd. mags.

Price: Matte stainless slide **$622.00**

Price: Tritium night sights **$719.00**

KEL-TEC P-11 AUTO PISTOL

Caliber: 9mm Para., 10-shot magazine. **Barrel:** 3.1". **Weight:** 14 oz. **Length:** 5.6" overall. **Grips:** Checkered black polymer. **Sights:** Blade front, rear adjustable for windage. **Features:** Ordnance steel slide, aluminum frame. Double-action-only trigger mechanism. Introduced 1995. Made in U.S.A. by Kel-Tec CNC Industries, Inc.

Price: Blue **$314.00**

Price: Hard chrome. **$368.00**

Price: Parkerized **$355.00**

KEL-TEC P-32 AUTO PISTOL

Caliber: 32 ACP, 7-shot magazine. **Barrel:** 2.68". **Weight:** 6.6 oz. **Length:** 5.07" overall. **Grips:** Checkered composite. **Sights:** Fixed. **Features:** Double-action-only mechanism with 6-lb. pull; internal slide stop. Textured composite grip/frame. Now available in 380 ACP. Made in U.S.A. by Kel-Tec CNC Industries, Inc.

Price: Blue **$300.00**

Price: Hard chrome. **$340.00**

Price: Parkerized **$355.00**

KIMBER CUSTOM II AUTO PISTOL

Caliber: 45 ACP, 40 S&W, .38 Super, 9 mm. **Barrel:** 5", match grade; 9 mm, .40 S&W, .38 Super barrels ramped. **Weight:** 38 oz. **Length:** 8.7" overall. **Grips:** Checkered black rubber, walnut, rosewood. **Sights:** Dovetail front and rear, Kimber low profile adj. or fixed three-dot (green) Meprolight night sights. **Features:** Slide, frame and barrel machined from steel or stainless steel. Match grade barrel, chamber and trigger group. Extended thumb safety, beveled magazine well, beveled front and rear slide serrations, high ride beavertail grip safety, checkered flat mainspring housing, kidney cut under trigger guard, high cut grip, match grade stainless steel barrel bushing, polished breech face, Commander-style hammer, lowered and flared ejection port, Wolff springs, bead blasted black oxide finish. Introduced in 1996. Made in U.S.A. by Kimber Mfg., Inc.

Price: Custom **$745.00**
Price: Custom walnut (double-diamond walnut grips). **$767.00**
Price: Custom stainless **$848.00**
Price: Custom stainless 40 S&W **$799.00**
Price: Custom stainless Target 45 ACP (stainless, adj. sight) . . . **$989.00**
Price: Custom stainless Target 38 Super **$994.00**

Kimber Stainless II Auto Pistol

Similar to Custom II except has stainless steel frame, 4" bbl., grip is .400" shorter than standard, no front serrations. Weighs 34 oz. 45 ACP only. Introduced in 1998. Made in U.S.A. by Kimber Mfg., Inc.

Price: **$964.00**

Kimber Pro Carry II Auto Pistol

Similar to Custom II, has aluminum frame, 4" bull barrel fitted directly to the slide without bushing. HD with stainless steel frame. Introduced 1998. Made in U.S.A. by Kimber Mfg., Inc.

Price: Pro Carry **$789.00**
Price: Pro Carry w/night sights **$893.00**
Price: Pro Carry Stainless w/night sights **$862.00**
Price: Pro Carry HD II 38 Super **$936.00**

Kimber Ultra Carry II Auto Pistol

Similar to Compact Stainless II, lightweight aluminum frame, 3" match grade bull barrel fitted to slide without bushing. Grips .400" shorter. Special slide stop. Low effort recoil. Weighs 25 oz. Introduced in 1999. Made in U.S.A. by Kimber Mfg., Inc.

Price: **$783.00**
Price: Stainless. **$858.00**
Price: Stainless 40 S&W. **$903.00**

Kimber Ten II High Capacity Polymer Pistol

Similar to Custom II, Pro Carry II and Ultra Carry II depending on barrel length. Ten-round magazine capacity (double stack and flush fitting). Polymer grip frame molded over stainless steel or aluminum (BP Ten pistols only) frame insert. Checkered front strap and belly of trigger guard. All models have fixed sights except Gold Match Ten II, which has adjustable sight. Frame grip dimensions approximate that of the standard 1911 for natural aiming and better recoil control. **Weight:** 24 to 34 oz. Improved version of the Kimber Polymer series. Made in U.S.A. by Kimber Mfg., Inc.

Price: Pro Carry Ten II **$828.00**
Price: Stainless Ten II. **$812.00**

Kimber Gold Match II Auto Pistol

Similar to Custom II models. Includes stainless steel barrel with match grade chamber and barrel bushing, ambidextrous thumb safety, adjustable sight, premium aluminum trigger, hand-checkered double diamond rosewood grips. Barrel hand-fitted to bushing and slide for target accuracy. Made in U.S.A. by Kimber Mfg., Inc.

Price: Gold Match II **$1,192.00**
Price: Gold Match Stainless II 45 ACP. **$1,342.00**
Price: Gold Match Stainless II 40 S&W **$1,373.00**

Kimber Gold Match Ten II Polymer Auto Pistol

Similar to Stainless Gold Match II. High capacity polymer frame with 10-round magazine. No ambi thumb safety. Polished flats add elegant look. Introduced 1999. Made in U.S.A. by Kimber Mfg., Inc.

Price: **$1,373.00**

Kimber Gold Combat II Auto Pistol

Similar to Gold Match II except designed for concealed carry. Extended and beveled magazine well, Meprolight tritium night sights; premium aluminum trigger; 30 lpi front strap checkering; special Custom Shop markings; KimPro premium finish. Introduced 1999. Made in U.S.A. by Kimber Mfg., Inc.

Price: 45 ACP. **$1,716.00**
Price: Stainless (stainless frame and slide, special markings) . . **$1,657.00**

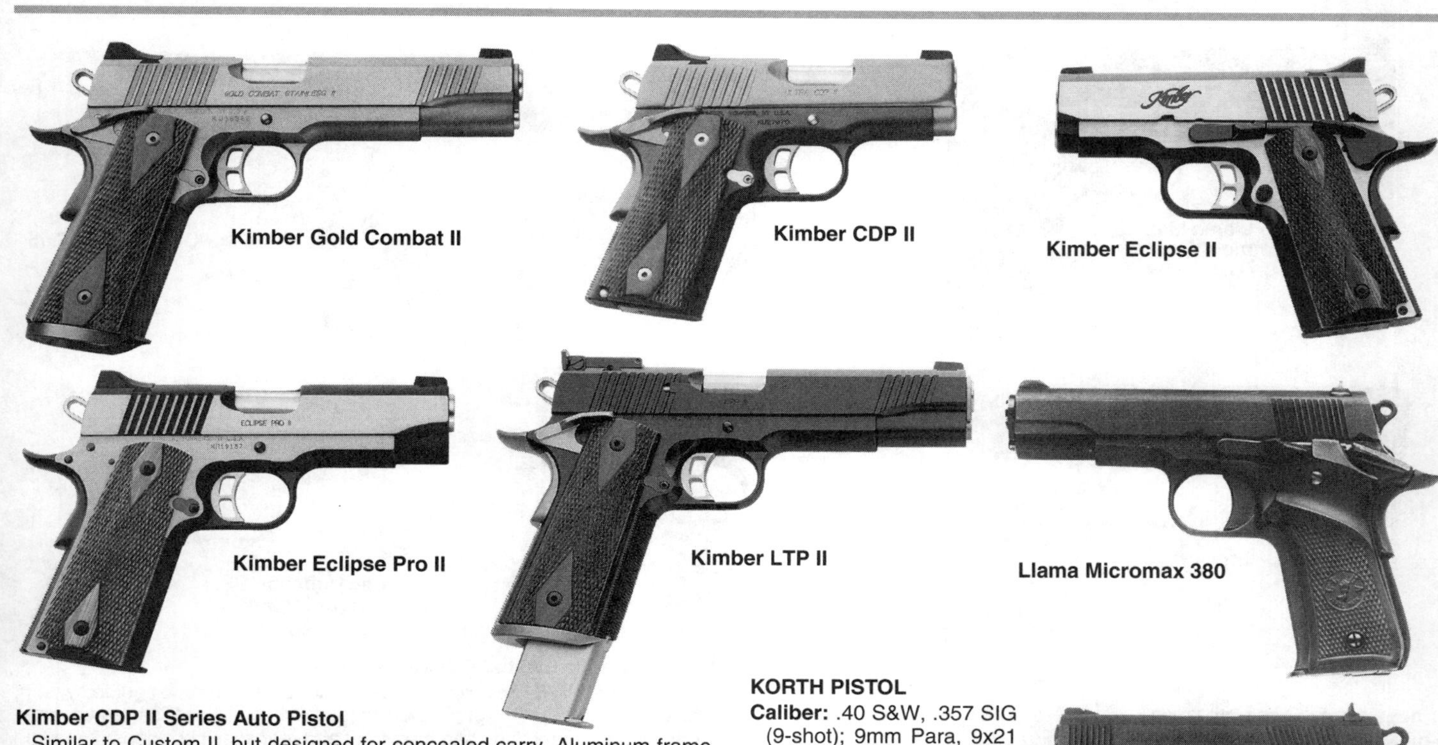

Kimber Gold Combat II

Kimber CDP II

Kimber Eclipse II

Kimber Eclipse Pro II

Kimber LTP II

Llama Micromax 380

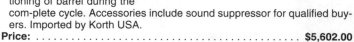

Kimber CDP II Series Auto Pistol

Similar to Custom II, but designed for concealed carry. Aluminum frame. Standard features include stainless steel slide, Meprolight tritium three-dot (green) dovetail-mounted night sights, match grade barrel and chamber, 30 lpi front strap checkering, two tone finish, ambidextrous thumb safety, hand-checkered double diamond rosewood grips. Introduced in 2000. Made in U.S.A. by Kimber Mfg., Inc.

Price: Ultra CDP II 40 S&W **$1,165.00**
Price: Ultra CDP II (3" barrel, short grip) **$1,165.00**
Price: Compact CDP II (4" barrel, short grip) **$1,165.00**
Price: Pro CDP II (4" barrel, full length grip) **$1,165.00**
Price: Custom CDP II (5" barrel, full length grip) **$1,203.00**

Kimber Eclipse II Series Auto Pistol

Similar to Custom II and other stainless Kimber pistols. Stainless slide and frame, black anodized, two tone finish. Gray/black laminated grips. 30 lpi front strap checkering. All have night sights, with Target versions having Meprolight adjustable Bar/Dot version. Made in U.S.A. by Kimber Mfg., Inc.

Price: Eclipse Ultra II (3" barrel, short grip) **$1,074.00**
Price: Eclipse Pro II (4" barrel, full length grip) **$1,074.00**
Price: Eclipse Pro Target II (4" barrel, full length grip, adjustable sight) **$1,177.00**
Price: Eclipse Custom II (5" barrel, full length grip) **$1,077.00**
Price: Eclipse Target II (5" barrel, full length grip, adjustable sight) **$1,177.00**

Kimber LTP II Auto Pistol

Similar to Gold Match II. Built for Limited Ten competition. First Kimber pistol with new, innovative Kimber external extractor. KimPro premium finish. Stainless steel match grade barrel. Extended and beveled magazine well. Checkered front strap and trigger guard belly. Tungsten full length guide rod. Premium aluminum trigger. Ten-round single stack magazine. Wide ambidextrous thumb safety. Made in U.S.A. by Kimber Mfg., Inc.

Price: **$2,078.00**

Kimber Super Match II Auto Pistol

Similar to Gold Match II. Built for target and action shotting competition. Tested for accuracy. Target included. Stainless steel barrel and chamber. KimPro finish on stainless steel slide. Stainless steel frame. 30 lpi checkered front strap, premium aluminum trigger, Kimber adjustable sight. Introduced in 1999.

Price: **$1,966.00**

KORTH PISTOL

Caliber: .40 S&W, .357 SIG (9-shot); 9mm Para, 9x21 (10-shot). **Barrel:** 4" (standard), 5" (optional). Trigger **Weight:** 3.3 lbs. (single action), 11 lbs. (double action). **Sights:** Fully adjustable. **Features:** All parts of surface-hardened steel; recoil-operated action, mechanically-locked via large pivoting bolt block maintaining parallel positioning of barrel during the com-plete cycle. Accessories include sound suppressor for qualified buyers. Imported by Korth USA.

Llama Minimax

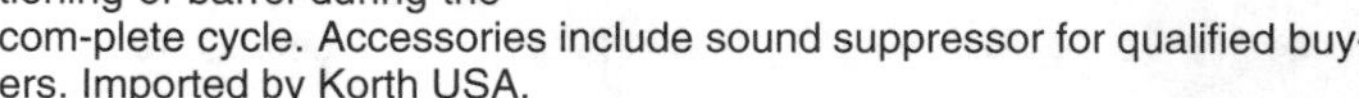

Price: **$5,602.00**

LLAMA MICROMAX 380 AUTO PISTOL

Caliber: 32 ACP, 8-shot, 380 ACP, 7-shot magazine. **Barrel:** 3-11/16". **Weight:** 23 oz. **Length:** 6-1/2" overall. **Grips:** Checkered high impact polymer. **Sights:** Three-dot combat. **Features:** Single-action design. Mini custom extended slide release; mini custom extended beavertail grip safety; combat-style hammer. Introduced 1997. Distributed by Import Sports, Inc.

Price: Matte blue **$291.95**
Price: Satin chrome (380 only) **$308.95**

LLAMA MINIMAX SERIES

Caliber: 40 S&W, 7-shot; 45 ACP, 6-shot magazine. **Barrel:** 3-1/2". **Weight:** 35 oz. **Length:** 7-1/3" overall. **Grips:** Checkered rubber. **Sights:** Three-dot combat. **Features:** Single action, skeletonized combat-style hammer, extended slide release, cone-style barrel, flared ejection port. Introduced 1996. Distributed by Import Sports, Inc.

Price: Blue **$341.95**
Price: Duo-Tone finish (45 only) **$349.95**
Price: Satin chrome **$358.95**

Llama Minimax Sub-Compact Auto Pistol

Similar to the Minimax except has 3.14" barrel, weighs 31 oz.; 6.8" overall length; has 10-shot magazine with finger extension; beavertail grip safety. Introduced 1999. Distributed by Import Sports, Inc.

Price: 45 ACP, matte blue **$358.95**
Price: As above, satin chrome **$374.95**
Price: Duo-Tone finish (45 only) **$366.95**

Llama Max-1 Government Deluxe

North American Arms Guardian

Para-Ordnance P12.45

Para-Ordnance LDA

Para-Ordnance C5 45 LDA Para Carry

Para-Ordnance C7 45 LDA Para Companion

LLAMA MAX-I AUTO PISTOLS

Caliber: 45 ACP, 7-shot. **Barrel:** 5-1/8". **Weight:** 36 oz. **Length:** 8-1/2" overall. **Grips:** Polymer. **Sights:** Blade front; three-dot system. **Features:** Single-action trigger; skeletonized combat-style hammer; steel frame; extended manual and grip safeties, matte finish. Introduced 1995. Distributed by Import Sports, Inc.

Price: 45 ACP, 7-shot, Government model **$358.95**

NORTH AMERICAN ARMS GUARDIAN PISTOL

Caliber: 32 ACP, 380 ACP, 32NAA, 6-shot magazine. **Barrel:** 2.1". **Weight:** 13.5 oz. **Length:** 4.36" overall. **Grips:** Black polymer. **Sights:** Fixed. **Features:** Double-action-only mechanism. All stainless steel construction; snag-free. Introduced 1998. Made in U.S.A. by North American Arms.

Price: . . . . **$402.00 to $479.00**

OLYMPIC ARMS OA-96 AR PISTOL

Caliber: 223. **Barrel:** 6", 8", 4140 chrome-moly steel. **Weight:** 5 lbs. **Length:** 15-3/4" overall. **Grips:** A2 stowaway pistol grip; no buttstock or receiver tube. **Sights:** Flat-top upper receiver, cut-down front sight base. **Features:** AR-15-type receivers with special bolt carrier; short aluminum hand guard; Vortex flash hider. Introduced 1996. Made in U.S.A. by Olympic Arms, Inc.

Price: **$858.00**

Olympic Arms OA-98 AR Pistol

Similar to the OA-93 except has removable 7-shot magazine, weighs 3 lbs. Introduced 1999. Made in U.S.A. by Olympic Arms, Inc.

Price: **$990.00**

PARA-ORDNANCE P-SERIES AUTO PISTOLS

Caliber: 9mm Para., 40 S&W, 45 ACP, 10-shot magazine. **Barrel:** 3", 3-1/2", 4-1/4", 5". **Weight:** From 24 oz. (alloy frame). **Length:** 8.5" overall. **Grips:** Textured composition. **Sights:** Blade front, rear adjustable for windage. High visibility three-dot system. **Features:** Available with alloy, steel or stainless steel frame with black finish (silver or stainless gun). Steel and stainless steel frame guns weigh 40 oz. (P14.45), 36 oz. (P13.45), 34 oz. (P12.45). Grooved match trigger, rounded combat-style hammer. Beveled magazine well. Manual thumb, grip and firing pin lock safeties. Solid barrel bushing. Contact maker for full details. Introduced 1990. Made in Canada by Para-Ordnance.

Price: Steel frame **$795.00**

Price: Alloy frame **$765.00**

Price: Stainless steel **$865.00**

Para-Ordnance Limited Pistols

Similar to the P-Series pistols except with full-length recoil guide system; fully adjustable rear sight; tuned trigger with overtravel stop; beavertail grip safety; competition hammer; front and rear slide serrations; ambidextrous safety; lowered ejection port; ramped match-grade barrel; dovetailed front sight. Introduced 1998. Made in Canada by Para-Ordnance.

Price: 9mm, 40 S&W, 45 ACP . . . . **$945.00 to $999.00**

Para-Ordnance LDA Auto Pistols

Similar to P-series except has double-action trigger mechanism. Steel frame with matte black finish, checkered composition grips. Available in 9mm Para., 40 S&W, 45 ACP. Introduced 1999. Made in Canada by Para-Ordnance.

Price: **$775.00**

Para-Ordnance LDA Limited Pistols

Similar to LDA, has ambidextrous safety, adjustable rear sight, front slide serrations and full-length recoil guide system. Made in Canada by Para-Ordnance.

Price: Black finish **$975.00**

Price: Stainless. **$1,049.00**

PARA-ORDNANCE C5 45 LDA PARA CARRY

Caliber: 45 ACP. **Barrel:** 3", 6+1 shot. **Weight:** 30 oz. **Length:** 6.5". **Grips:** Double diamond checkered Cocobolo. **Features:** Stainless finish and receiver, "world's smallest DAO 45 auto." Para LDA trigger system and safeties.

Price: **$899.00**

PARA-ORDNANCE C7 45 LDA PARA COMPANION

Caliber: 45 ACP. **Barrel:** 3.5", 7+1 shot. **Weight:** 32 oz. **Length:** 7". **Grips:** Double diamond checkered Cocobolo. **Features:** Para LDA trigger system with Para LDA 3 safeties (slide lock, firing pin block and grip safety). Lightning speed, full size capacity.

Price: **$899.00**

PETERS STAHL AUTOLOADING PISTOLS

Caliber: 9mm Para., 45 ACP. **Barrel:** 5" or 6". **Grips:** Walnut or walnut with rubber wrap. **Sights:** Fully adjustable rear, blade front. **Features:** Stainless steel extended slide stop, safety and extended magazine release button; speed trigger with stop and approx. 3-lb. pull; polished ramp. Introduced 2000. Imported from Germany by Phillips & Rogers.

Price: High Capacity (accepts 15-shot magazines in 45 cal.; includes 10-shot magazine) **$1,695.00**

Price: Trophy Master (blued or stainless, 7-shot in 45, 8-shot in 9mm) **$1,995.00**

Price: Millennium Model (titanium coating on receiver and slide) **$2,195.00**

Peters Stahl High Capacity

Peters Stahl Trophy Master

Peters Stahl Millennium

Phoenix Arms HP22

Ruger P89

Ruger P90

Rock River Standard Match

PHOENIX ARMS HP22, HP25 AUTO PISTOLS

Caliber: 22 LR, 10-shot (HP22), 25 ACP, 10-shot (HP25). **Barrel:** 3". **Weight:** 20 oz. **Length:** 5-1/2" overall. **Grips:** Checkered composition. **Sights:** Blade front, adjustable rear. **Features:** Single action, exposed hammer; manual hold-open; button magazine release. Available in satin nickel, polished blue finish. Introduced 1993. Made in U.S.A. by Phoenix Arms.

Price: With gun lock and cable lanyard **$130.00**

Price: HP Rangemaster kit with 5" bbl., locking case and assessories **$171.00**

Price: HP Deluxe Rangemaster kit with 3" and 5" bbls., 2 mags., case **$210.00**

ROCK RIVER ARMS STANDARD MATCH AUTO PISTOL

Caliber: 45 ACP. **Barrel:** NA. **Weight:** NA. **Length:** NA. **Grips:** Cocobolo, checkered. **Sights:** Heine fixed rear, blade front. **Features:** Chrome-moly steel frame and slide; beavertail grip safety with raised pad; checkered slide stop; ambidextrous safety; polished feed ramp and extractor; aluminum speed trigger with 3.5 lb. pull. Made in U.S.A. From Rock River Arms.

Price: **$1,025.00**

ROCKY MOUNTAIN ARMS PATRIOT PISTOL

Caliber: 223, 10-shot magazine. **Barrel:** 7", with muzzle brake. **Weight:** 5 lbs. **Length:** 20.5" overall. **Grips:** Black composition. **Sights:** None furnished. **Features:** Milled upper receiver with enhanced Weaver base; milled lower receiver from billet plate; machined aluminum National Match handguard. Finished in DuPont Teflon-S matte black or NATO green. Comes with black nylon case, one magazine. Introduced 1993. From Rocky Mountain Arms, Inc.

Price: With A-2 handle top . . . . **$2,500.00 to $2,800.00**

Price: Flat top model. **$3,000.00 to $3,500.00**

RUGER P89 AUTOLOADING PISTOL

Caliber: 9mm Para., 10-shot magazine. **Barrel:** 4.50". **Weight:** 32 oz. **Length:** 7.84" overall. **Grips:** Grooved black synthetic composition. **Sights:** Square post front, square notch rear adjustable for windage, both with white dot inserts. **Features:** Double action, ambidextrous slide-mounted safety levers. Slide 4140 chrome-moly steel or 400-series stainless steel, frame lightweight aluminum alloy. Ambidextrous magazine release. Blue, stainless steel. Introduced 1986; stainless 1990.

Price: P89, blue, extra mag and mag loader, plastic case locks . **$475.00**

Price: KP89, stainless, extra mag and mag loader, plastic case locks **$525.00**

Ruger P89D Decocker Autoloading Pistol

Similar to standard P89 except has ambidextrous decocking levers in place of regular slide-mounted safety. Decocking levers move firing pin inside slide where hammer cannot reach, while simultaneously blocking firing pin from forward movement; allows shooter to decock cocked pistol without manipulating trigger. Conventional thumb decocking procedures are therefore unnecessary. Blue, stainless steel. Introduced 1990.

Price: P89D, blue, extra mag and mag loader, plastic case locks **$475.00**

Price: KP89D, stainless, extra mag and mag loader, plastic case locks **$525.00**

Ruger P89 Double-Action-Only Autoloading Pistol

Same as KP89 except operates only in double-action mode. Has spurless hammer, gripping grooves on each side of rear slide; no external safety or decocking lever. Internal safety prevents forward movement of firing pin unless trigger is pulled. Available 9mm Para., stainless steel only. Introduced 1991.

Price: Lockable case, extra mag and mag loader. **$525.00**

RUGER P90 MANUAL SAFETY MODEL AUTOLOADING PISTOL

Caliber: 45 ACP, 8-shot magazine. **Barrel:** 4.50". **Weight:** 33.5 oz. **Length:** 7.75" overall. **Grips:** Grooved black synthetic composition. **Sights:** Square post front, square notch rear adjustable for windage, both with white dot. **Features:** Double action ambidextrous slide-mounted safety levers move firing pin inside slide where hammer cannot reach, simultaneously blocking firing pin from forward movement. Stainless steel only. Introduced 1991.

Price: KP90 with extra mag, loader, case and gunlock. **$565.00**

Price: P90 (blue). **$525.00**

Ruger P93D

Ruger KP94D

Ruger KP95DAO

Ruger KP90 Decocker Autoloading Pistol

Similar to the P90 except has a manual decocking system. The ambidextrous decocking levers move the firing pin inside the slide where the hammer cannot reach it, while simultaneously blocking the firing pin from forward movement; allows shooter to decock a cocked pistol without manipulating the trigger. Available only in stainless steel. Overall length 7.75", weighs 33.5 oz. Introduced 1991.

Price: KP90D with case, extra mag and mag loading tool **$565.00**

RUGER P93 COMPACT AUTOLOADING PISTOL

Caliber: 9mm Para., 10-shot magazine. **Barrel:** 3.9". **Weight:** 31 oz. **Length:** 7.25" overall. **Grips:** Grooved black synthetic composition. **Sights:** Square post front, square notch rear adjustable for windage. **Features:** Front of slide crowned with convex curve; slide has seven finger grooves; trigger guard bow higher for better grip; 400-series stainless slide, lightweight alloy frame; also blue. Decocker-only or DAO-only. Includes hard case and lock. Introduced 1993. Made in U.S.A. by Sturm, Ruger & Co.

Price: KP93DAO, double-action-only **$575.00**
Price: KP93D ambidextrous decocker, stainless **$575.00**
Price: P93D, ambidextrous decocker, blue **$495.00**

Ruger KP94 Autoloading Pistol

Sized midway between full-size P-Series and compact P93. 4.25" barrel, 7.5" overall length, weighs about 33 oz. KP94 manual safety model; KP94DAO double-action-only (both 9mm Para., 10-shot magazine); KP94D is decocker-only in 40-caliber with 10-shot magazine. Slide gripping grooves roll over top of slide. KP94 has ambidextrous safety levers; KP94DAO has no external safety, full-cock hammer position or decocking lever; KP94D has ambidextrous decocking levers. Matte finish stainless slide, barrel, alloy frame. Also blue. Includes hard case and lock. Introduced 1994. Made in U.S.A. by Sturm, Ruger & Co.

Price: P94, P944, blue (manual safety) **$495.00**
Price: KP94 (9mm), KP944 (40-caliber) (manual safety-stainless) **$575.00**
Price: KP94DAO (9mm), KP944DAO (40-caliber) **$575.00**
Price: KP94D (9mm), KP944D (40-caliber), decock only **$575.00**

RUGER P95 AUTOLOADING PISTOL

Caliber: 9mm Para., 10-shot magazine. **Barrel:** 3.9". **Weight:** 27 oz. **Length:** 7.25" overall. **Grips:** Grooved; integral with frame. **Sights:** Blade front, rear drift adjustable for windage; three-dot system. **Features:** Moulded polymer grip frame, stainless steel or chrome-moly slide. Suitable for +P+ ammunition. Safety model, decocker or DAO. Introduced 1996. Made in U.S.A. by Sturm, Ruger & Co. Comes with lockable plastic case, spare magazine, loader and lock.

Price: P95 DAO double-action-only **$425.00**
Price: P95D decocker only **$425.00**
Price: KP95D stainless steel decocker only **$475.00**
Price: KP95DAO double-action only, stainless steel.......... **$475.00**
Price: KP95 safety model, stainless steel................... **$475.00**
Price: P95 safety model, blued finish **$425.00**

RUGER P97 AUTOLOADING PISTOL

Caliber: 45 ACP 8-shot magazine. **Barrel:** 4-1/8". **Weight:** 30-1/2 oz. **Length:** 7-1/4" overall. Grooved: Integral with frame. **Sights:** Blade front, rear drift adjustable for windage; three-dot system. **Features:** Moulded polymer grip frame, stainless steel slide. Decocker or DAO. Introduced 1997. Made in U.S.A. by Sturm, Ruger & Co. Comes with lockable plastic case, spare magazine, loading tool.

Price: KP97D decocker only.................................. **$495.00**
Price: KP97DAO double-action-only **$495.00**
Price: P97D decocker only, blued **$460.00**

Ruger KMK 4

Ruger 22/45-P4

RUGER MARK II STANDARD AUTOLOADING PISTOL

Caliber: 22 LR, 10-shot magazine. **Barrel:** 4-3/4" or 6". **Weight:** 35 oz. (4-3/4" bbl.). **Length:** 8-5/16" (4-3/4" bbl.). **Grips:** Checkered composition grip panels. **Sights:** Fixed, wide blade front, fixed rear. **Features:** Updated design of original Standard Auto. New bolt hold-open latch. Ten-shot magazine, magazine catch, safety, trigger and new receiver contours. Introduced 1982.

Price: Blued (MK 4, MK 6) **$289.00**
Price: In stainless steel (KMK 4, KMK 6) **$379.00**

Ruger 22/45 Mark II Pistol

Similar to other 22 Mark II autos except has grip frame of Zytel that matches angle and magazine latch of Model 1911 45 ACP pistol. Available in 4" bull, 4-3/4" standard and 5-1/2" bull barrels. Comes with extra magazine, plastic case, lock. Introduced 1992.

Price: P4, 4" bull barrel, adjustable sights **$290.00**
Price: KP 4 (4-3/4" barrel), stainless steel, fixed sights **$315.00**
Price: KP512 (5-1/2" bull barrel), stainless steel, adj. sights **$380.00**
Price: P512 (5-1/2" bull barrel, all blue), adj. sights **$290.00**

HANDGUNS — AUTOLOADERS, SERVICE & SPORT

Ruger KP512

SIG-Sauer P220

SIG-Sauer P245 Compact

HANDGUNS

SAFARI ARMS ENFORCER PISTOL

Caliber: 45 ACP, 6-shot magazine. **Barrel:** 3.8", stainless. **Weight:** 36 oz. **Length:** 7.3" overall. **Grips:** Smooth walnut with etched black widow spider logo. **Sights:** Ramped blade front, LPA adjustable rear. **Features:** Extended safety, extended slide release; Commander-style hammer; beavertail grip safety; throated, polished, tuned. Parkerized matte black or satin stainless steel finishes. Made in U.S.A. by Safari Arms.

Price: **$630.00**

SAFARI ARMS GI SAFARI PISTOL

Caliber: 45 ACP, 7-shot magazine. **Barrel:** 5", 416 stainless. **Weight:** 39.9 oz. **Length:** 8.5" overall. **Grips:** Checkered walnut. **Sights:** G.I.-style blade front, drift-adjustable rear. **Features:** Beavertail grip safety; extended thumb safety and slide release; Commander-style hammer. Parkerized finish. Reintroduced 1996.

Price: **$439.00**

SAFARI ARMS CARRIER PISTOL

Caliber: 45 ACP, 7-shot magazine. **Barrel:** 6", 416 stainless steel. **Weight:** 30 oz. **Length:** 9.5" overall. **Grips:** Wood. **Sights:** Ramped blade front, LPA adjustable rear. **Features:** Beavertail grip safety; extended controls; full-length recoil spring guide; Commander-style hammer. Throated, polished and tuned. Satin stainless steel finish. Introduced 1999. Made in U.S.A. by Safari Arms, Inc.

Price: **$714.00**

SAFARI ARMS COHORT PISTOL

Caliber: 45 ACP, 7-shot magazine. **Barrel:** 3.8", 416 stainless. **Weight:** 37 oz. **Length:** 8.5" overall. **Grips:** Smooth walnut with laser-etched black widow logo. **Sights:** Ramped blade front, LPA adjustable rear. **Features:** Combines the Enforcer model, slide and MatchMaster frame. Beavertail grip safety; extended thumb safety and slide release; Commander-style hammer. Throated, polished and tuned. Satin stainless finish. Introduced 1996. Made in U.S.A. by Safari Arms, Inc.

Price: **$654.00**

SAFARI ARMS MATCHMASTER PISTOL

Caliber: 45 ACP, 7-shot. **Barrel:** 5" or 6", 416 stainless steel. **Weight:** 38 oz. (5" barrel). **Length:** 8.5" overall. **Grips:** Smooth walnut. **Sights:** Ramped blade, LPA adjustable rear. **Features:** Beavertail grip safety; extended controls; Commander-style hammer; throated, polished, tuned. Parkerized matte-black or satin stainless steel. Made in U.S.A. by Olympic Arms, Inc.

Price: 5" barrel **$594.00**
Price: 6" barrel **$654.00**

Safari Arms Carry Comp Pistol

Similar to the Matchmaster except has Wil Schueman-designed hybrid compensator system. Made in U.S.A. by Olympic Arms, Inc.

Price: **$1,067.00**

SEECAMP LWS 32 STAINLESS DA AUTO

Caliber: 32 ACP Win. Silvertip, 6-shot magazine. **Barrel:** 2", integral with frame. **Weight:** 10.5 oz. **Length:** 4-1/8" overall. **Grips:** Glass-filled nylon. **Sights:** Smooth, no-snag, contoured slide and barrel top. **Features:** Aircraft quality 17-4 PH stainless steel. Inertia-operated firing pin. Hammer fired double-action-only. Hammer automatically follows slide down to safety rest position after each shot; no manual safety needed. Magazine safety disconnector. Polished stainless. Introduced 1985. From L.W. Seecamp.

Price: **$425.00**

SEMMERLING LM-4 SLIDE-ACTION PISTOL

Caliber: 45 ACP, 4-shot magazine. **Barrel:** 2". **Weight:** 24 oz. **Length:** NA. **Grips:** NA. **Sights:** NA. **Features:** While outwardly appearing to be a semi-automatic, the Semmerling LM-4 is a unique and super compact pistol employing a thumb activated slide mechanism (the slide is manually retracted between shots). Hand-built and super reliable, it is intended for professionals in law enforcement and for concealed carry by licensed and firearms knowledgeable private citizens. From American Derringer Corp.

Price: **$2,635.00**

SIG-SAUER P220 SERVICE AUTO PISTOL

Caliber: 45 ACP, (7- or 8-shot magazine). **Barrel:** 4-3/8". **Weight:** 27.8 oz. **Length:** 7.8" overall. **Grips:** Checkered black plastic. **Sights:** Blade front, drift adjustable rear for windage. Optional Siglite nightsights. **Features:** Double action. Decocking lever permits lowering hammer onto locked firing pin. Squared combat-type trigger guard. Slide stays open after last shot. Imported from Germany by SIGARMS, Inc.

Price: Blue SA/DA or DAO **$790.00**
Price: Blue, Siglite night sights **$880.00**
Price: K-Kote or nickel slide **$830.00**
Price: K-Kote or nickel slide with Siglite night sights **$930.00**

SIG-Sauer P220 Sport Auto Pistol

Similar to the P220 except has 4.9" barrel, ported compensator, all-stainless steel frame and slide, factory-tuned trigger, adjustable sights, extended competition controls. Overall length is 9.9", weighs 43.5 oz. Introduced 1999. From SIGARMS, Inc.

Price: **$1,320.00**

SIG-Sauer P245 Compact Auto Pistol

Similar to the P220 except has 3.9" barrel, shorter grip, 6-shot magazine, 7.28" overall length, and weighs 27.5 oz. Introduced 1999. From SIGARMS, Inc.

Price: Blue **$780.00**
Price: Blue, with Siglite sights **$850.00**
Price: Two-tone **$830.00**
Price: Two-tone with Siglite sights **$930.00**
Price: With K-Kote finish **$830.00**
Price: K-Kote with Siglite sights **$930.00**

SIG-Sauer P229 DA Auto Pistol

Similar to the P228 except chambered for 9mm Para., 40 S&W, 357 SIG. Has 3.86" barrel, 7.08" overall length and 3.35" height. Weight is 30.5 oz. Introduced 1991. Frame made in Germany, stainless steel slide assembly made in U.S.; pistol assembled in U.S. From SIGARMS, Inc.

Price: **$795.00**
Price: With nickel slide **$890.00**
Price: Nickel slide Siglite night sights **$935.00**

HANDGUNS — AUTOLOADERS, SERVICE & SPORT

SIG-Sauer Pro 2009

SIG-Sauer P229 Sport

SIG-Sauer P232

Smith & Wesson 457 TDA

Smith & Wesson 908

Smith & Wesson 4013 TSW

SIG PRO AUTO PISTOL

Caliber: 9mm Para., 40 S&W, 10-shot magazine. **Barrel:** 3.86". **Weight:** 27.2 oz. **Length:** 7.36" overall. **Grips:** Composite and rubberized one-piece. **Sights:** Blade front, rear adjustable for windage. Optional Siglite night sights. **Features:** Polymer frame, stainless steel slide; integral frame accessory rail; replaceable steel frame rails; left- or right-handed magazine release. Introduced 1999. From SIGARMS, Inc.

Price: SP2340 (40 S&W) **$596.00**
Price: SP2009 (9mm Para.) **$596.00**
Price: As above with Siglite night sights **$655.00**

SIG-Sauer P226 Service Pistol

Similar to the P220 pistol except has 4.4" barrel, and weighs 28.3 oz. 357 SIG or 40 S&W. Imported from Germany by SIGARMS, Inc.

Price: Blue SA/DA or DAO **$830.00**
Price: With Siglite night sights **$930.00**
Price: Blue, SA/DA or DAO 357 SIG. **$830.00**
Price: With Siglite night sights **$930.00**
Price: K-Kote finish, 40 S&W only or nickel slide **$830.00**
Price: K-Kote or nickel slide Siglite night sights **$930.00**
Price: Nickel slide 357 SIG **$875.00**
Price: Nickel slide, Siglite night sights **$930.00**

SIG-Sauer P229 Sport Auto Pistol

Similar to the P229 except available in 357 SIG only; 4.8" heavy barrel; 8.6" overall length; weighs 40.6 oz.; vented compensator; adjustable target sights; rubber grips; extended slide latch and magazine release. Made of stainless steel. Introduced 1998. From SIGARMS, Inc.

Price: **$1,320.00**

SIG-SAUER P232 PERSONAL SIZE PISTOL

Caliber: 380 ACP, 7-shot. **Barrel:** 3-3/4". **Weight:** 16 oz. **Length:** 6-1/2" overall. **Grips:** Checkered black composite. **Sights:** Blade front, rear adjustable for windage. **Features:** Double action/single action or DAO. Blowback operation, stationary barrel. Introduced 1997. Imported from Germany by SIGARMS, Inc.

Price: Blue SA/DA or DAO **$505.00**
Price: In stainless steel. **$545.00**
Price: With stainless steel slide, blue frame **$525.00**
Price: Stainless steel, Siglite night sights, Hogue grips **$585.00**

SIG-SAUER P239 PISTOL

Caliber: 9mm Para., 8-shot, 357 SIG 40 S&W, 7-shot magazine. **Barrel:** 3.6". **Weight:** 25.2 oz. **Length:** 6.6" overall. **Grips:** Checkered black composite. **Sights:** Blade front, rear adjustable for windage. Optional Siglite night sights. **Features:** SA/DA or DAO; blackened stainless steel slide, aluminum alloy frame. Introduced 1996. Made in U.S.A. by SIGARMS, Inc.

Price: SA/DA or DAO **$620.00**
Price: SA/DA or DAO with Siglite night sights. **$720.00**
Price: Two-tone finish **$665.00**
Price: Two-tone finish, Siglite sights **$765.00**

SMITH & WESSON MODEL 22A SPORT PISTOL

Caliber: 22 LR, 10-shot magazine. **Barrel:** 4", 5-1/2", 7". **Weight:** 29 oz. **Length:** 8" overall. **Grips:** Two-piece polymer. **Sights:** Patridge front, fully adjustable rear. **Features:** Comes with a sight bridge with Weaver-style integral optics mount; alloy frame; .312" serrated trigger; stainless steel slide and barrel with matte blue finish. Introduced 1997. Made in U.S.A. by Smith & Wesson.

Price: 4" **$264.00**
Price: 5-1/2" **$292.00**
Price: 7" **$331.00**

SMITH & WESSON MODEL 457 TDA AUTO PISTOL

Caliber: 45 ACP, 7-shot magazine. **Barrel:** 3-3/4". **Weight:** 29 oz. **Length:** 7-1/4" overall. **Grips:** One-piece Xenoy, wrap-around with straight backstrap. **Sights:** Post front, fixed rear, three-dot system. **Features:** Aluminum alloy frame, matte blue carbon steel slide; bobbed hammer; smooth trigger. Introduced 1996. Made in U.S.A. by Smith & Wesson.

Price: **$591.00**

SMITH & WESSON MODEL 908 AUTO PISTOL

Caliber: 9mm Para., 8-shot magazine. **Barrel:** 3-1/2". **Weight:** 26 oz. **Length:** 6-13/16". **Grips:** One-piece Xenoy, wrap-around with straight backstrap. **Sights:** Post front, fixed rear, three-dot system. **Features:** Aluminum alloy frame, matte blue carbon steel slide; bobbed hammer; smooth trigger. Introduced 1996. Made in U.S.A. by Smith & Wesson.

Price: **$535.00**

SMITH & WESSON MODEL 4013, 4053 TSW AUTOS

Caliber: 40 S&W, 9-shot magazine. **Barrel:** 3-1/2". **Weight:** 26.4 oz. **Length:** 6-7/8" overall. **Grips:** Xenoy one-piece wrap-around. **Sights:** Novak three-dot system. **Features:** Traditional double-action system; stainless slide, alloy frame; fixed barrel bushing; ambidextrous decocker; reversible magazine catch, equipment rail. Introduced 1997. Made in U.S.A. by Smith & Wesson.

Price: Model 4013 TSW **$886.00**
Price: Model 4053 TSW, double-action-only. **$886.00**

Smith & Wesson 410 DA

Smith & Wesson 910 DA

Smith & Wesson 3913 LadySmith

Smith & Wesson 4006

Smith & Wesson 4566 TSW

SMITH & WESSON MODEL 22S SPORT PISTOLS

Similar to the Model 22A Sport except with stainless steel frame. Available only with 5-1/2" or 7" barrel. Introduced 1997. Made in U.S.A. by Smith & Wesson.

Price: 5-1/2" standard barrel **$358.00**
Price: 5-1/2" bull barrel, wood target stocks with thumbrest **$434.00**
Price: 7" standard barrel **$395.00**
Price: 5-1/2" bull barrel, two-piece target stocks with thumbrest . **$353.00**

SMITH & WESSON MODEL 410 DA AUTO PISTOL

Caliber: 40 S&W, 10-shot magazine. **Barrel:** 4". **Weight:** 28.5 oz. **Length:** 7.5 oz. **Grips:** One-piece Xenoy, wrap-around with straight backstrap. **Sights:** Post front, fixed rear; three-dot system. **Features:** Aluminum alloy frame; blued carbon steel slide; traditional double-action with left-side slide-mounted decocking lever. Introduced 1996. Made in U.S.A. by Smith & Wesson.

Price: Model 410 . . . . **$591.00**
Price: Model 410, HiViz front sight **$612.00**

SMITH & WESSON MODEL 910 DA AUTO PISTOL

Caliber: 9mm Para., 10-shot magazine. **Barrel:** 4". **Weight:** 28 oz. **Length:** 7-3/8" overall. **Grips:** One-piece Xenoy, wrap-around with straight backstrap. **Sights:** Post front with white dot, fixed two-dot rear. **Features:** Alloy frame, blue carbon steel slide. Slide-mounted decocking lever. Introduced 1995.

Price: Model 910 . . . . **$535.00**
Price: Model 410, HiViz front sight **$535.00**

SMITH & WESSON MODEL 3913 TRADITIONAL DOUBLE ACTION

Caliber: 9mm Para., 8-shot magazine. **Barrel:** 3-1/2". **Weight:** 26 oz. **Length:** 6-13/16" overall. **Grips:** One-piece Delrin wrap-around, textured surface. **Sights:** Post front with white dot, Novak LoMount Carry with two dots. **Features:** Aluminum alloy frame, stainless slide (M3913) or blue steel slide (M3914). Bobbed hammer with no half-cock notch; smooth .304" trigger with rounded edges. Straight backstrap. Equipment rail. Extra magazine included. Introduced 1989.

Price: **$760.00**

Smith & Wesson Model 3913-LS Ladysmith Auto

Similar to the standard Model 3913 except has frame that is upswept at the front, rounded trigger guard. Comes in frosted stainless steel with matching gray grips. Grips are ergonomically correct for a woman's hand. Novak LoMount Carry rear sight adjustable for windage, smooth edges for snag resistance. Extra magazine included. Introduced 1990.

Price: **$782.00**

Smith & Wesson Model 3953 DAO Pistol

Same as the Model 3913 except double-action-only. Model 3953 has stainless slide with alloy frame. Overall length 7"; weighs 25.5 oz. Extra magazine included. Equipment rail. Introduced 1990.

Price: **$760.00**

Smith & Wesson Model 3913TSW/3953TSW Auto Pistols

Similar to the Model 3913 and 3953 except TSW guns have tighter tolerances, ambidextrous manual safety/decocking lever, flush-fit magazine, delayed-unlock firing system; magazine disconnector. Compact alloy frame, stainless steel slide. Straight backstrap. Introduced 1998. Made in U.S.A. by Smith & Wesson.

Price: Single action/double action **$760.00**
Price: Double-action-only **$760.00**

SMITH & WESSON MODEL 4006 TDA AUTO

Caliber: 40 S&W, 10-shot magazine. **Barrel:** 4". **Weight:** 38.5 oz. **Length:** 7-7/8" overall. **Grips:** Xenoy wrap-around with checkered panels. **Sights:** Replaceable post front with white dot, Novak LoMount Carry fixed rear with two white dots, or micro click adjustable rear with two white dots. **Features:** Stainless steel construction with non-reflective finish. Straight backstrap, quipment rail. Extra magazine included. Introduced 1990.

Price: With adjustable sights **$944.00**
Price: With fixed sight **$907.00**
Price: With fixed night sights **$1,040.00**
Price: With Saf-T-Trigger, fixed sights **$927.00**

SMITH & WESSON MODEL 4006 TSW

Caliber: 40, 10-shot. **Barrel:** 4". **Grips:** Straight back strap grip. **Sights:** Fixed Novak LoMount Carry. **Features:** Traditional double action, ambidextrous safety, Saf-T-Trigger, equipment rail, satin stainless.

Price: **$927.00**

Smith & Wesson Model 4043, 4046 DA Pistols

Similar to the Model 4006 except is double-action-only. Has a semibobbed hammer, smooth trigger, 4" barrel; Novak LoMount Carry rear sight, post front with white dot. Overall length is 7-1/2", weighs 28 oz. Model 4043 has alloy frame, equipment rail. Extra magazine included. Introduced 1991.

Price: Model 4043 (alloy frame) **$886.00**
Price: Model 4046 (stainless frame) **$907.00**
Price: Model 4046 with fixed night sights **$1,040.00**

Smith & Wesson Sigma SW40V

Smith & Wesson 99

SMITH & WESSON MODEL 4500 SERIES AUTOS

Caliber: 45 ACP, 8-shot magazine. **Barrel:** 5" (M4506). **Weight:** 41 oz. (4506). **Length:** 8-1/2" overall. **Grips:** Xenoy one-piece wrap-around, arched or straight backstrap. **Sights:** Post front with white dot, adjustable or fixed Novak LoMount Carry on M4506. **Features:** M4506 has serrated hammer spur, equipment rail. All have two magazines. Contact Smith & Wesson for complete data. Introduced 1989.

Price: Model 4566 (stainless, 4-1/4", traditional DA, ambidextrous safety, fixed sight) **$942.00**
Price: Model 4586 (stainless, 4-1/4", DA only) **$942.00**
Price: Model 4566 (stainless, 4-1/4" with Saf-T-Trigger, fixed sight). . . . **$961.00**

SMITH & WESSON MODEL 4513TSW/4553TSW PISTOLS

Caliber: 45 ACP, 7-shot magazine. **Barrel:** 3-3/4". **Weight:** 28 oz. (M4513TSW). **Length:** 6-7/8 overall. **Grips:** Checkered Xenoy; straight backstrap. **Sights:** White dot front, Novak LoMount Carry 2-Dot rear. **Features:** Model 4513TSW is traditional double action, Model 4553TSW is double-action-only. TSW series has tighter tolerances, ambidextrous manual safety/decocking lever, flush-fit magazine, delayed-unlock firing system; magazine disconnector. Compact alloy frame, stainless steel slide, equipment rail. Introduced 1998. Made in U.S.A. by Smith & Wesson.

Price: Model 4513TSW. . . . **$924.00**
Price: Model 4553TSW. . . . **$924.00**

SMITH & WESSON MODEL 4566 TSW

Caliber: 45 ACP. **Barrel:** 4-1/4", 8-shot . **Grips:** Straight back strap grip. **Sights:** Fixed Novak LoMount Carry. **Features:** Ambidextrous safety, equipment rail, Saf-T-Trigger, satin stainless finish. Traditional double action.

Price: **$961.00**

SMITH & WESSON MODEL 5900 SERIES AUTO PISTOLS

Caliber: 9mm Para., 10-shot magazine. **Barrel:** 4". **Weight:** 28-1/2 to 37-1/2 oz. (fixed sight); 38 oz. (adjustable sight). **Length:** 7-1/2" overall. **Grips:** Xenoy wrap-around with curved backstrap. **Sights:** Post front with white dot, fixed or fully adjustable with two white dots. **Features:** All stainless, stainless and alloy or carbon steel and alloy construction. Smooth .304" trigger, .260" serrated hammer. Equipment rail. Introduced 1989.

Price: Model 5906 (stainless, traditional DA, adjustable sight, ambidextrous safety). . . . **$904.00**
Price: As above, fixed sight. . . . **$841.00**
Price: With fixed night sights. . . . **$995.00**
Price: With Saf-T-Trigger **$882.00**
Price: Model 5946 DAO (as above, stainless frame and slide) . . . **$863.00**

SMITH & WESSON ENHANCED SIGMA SERIES DAO PISTOLS

Caliber: 9mm Para., 40 S&W, 10-shot magazine. **Barrel:** 4". **Weight:** 26 oz. **Length:** 7.4" overall. **Grips:** Integral. **Sights:** White dot front, fixed rear; three-dot system. Tritium night sights available. **Features:** Ergonomic polymer frame; low barrel centerline; internal striker firing system; corrosion-resistant slide; Teflon-filled, electroless-nickel coated magazine, equipment rail. Introduced 1994. Made in U.S.A. by Smith & Wesson.

Price: SW9E, 9mm, 4" barrel, black finish, fixed sights **$447.00**
Price: SW9V, 9mm, 4" barrel, satin stainless, fixed night sights . . **$447.00**
Price: SW9VE, 4" barrel, satin stainless, Saf-T-Trigger, fixed sights **$466.00**
Price: SW40E, 40 S&W, 4" barrel, black finish, fixed sights **$657.00**
Price: SW40V, 40 S&W, 4" barrel, black polymer, fixed sights . . . **$447.00**
Price: SW40VE, 4" barrel, satin stainless, Saf-T-Trigger, fixed sights **$466.00**

SMITH & WESSON MODEL CS9 CHIEF'S SPECIAL AUTO

Caliber: 9mm Para., 7-shot magazine. **Barrel:** 3". **Weight:** 20.8 oz. **Length:** 6-1/4" overall. **Grips:** Hogue wrap-around rubber. **Sights:** White dot front, fixed two-dot rear. **Features:** Traditional double-action trigger mechanism. Alloy frame, stainless or blued slide. Ambidextrous safety. Introduced 1999. Made in U.S.A. by Smith & Wesson.

Price: Blue or stainless **$680.00**

Smith & Wesson Model CS40 Chief's Special Auto

Similar to CS9, chambered for 40 S&W (7-shot magazine), 3-1/4" barrel, weighs 24.2 oz., measures 6-1/2" overall. Introduced 1999. Made in U.S.A. by Smith & Wesson.

Price: Blue or stainless **$717.00**

Smith & Wesson Model CS45 Chief's Special Auto

Similar to CS40, chambered for 45 ACP, 6-shot magazine, weighs 23.9 oz. Introduced 1999. Made in U.S.A. by Smith & Wesson.

Price: Blue or stainless **$717.00**

SMITH & WESSON MODEL 99

Caliber: 9mm Para. 4" barrel; 40 S&W 4-1/8" barrel; 10-shot, adj. sights. **Features:** Traditional double action satin stainless, black polymer frame, equipment rail, Saf-T-Trigger.

Price: 4" barrel **$648.00**
Price: 4-1/8" barrel **$648.00**

SPRINGFIELD, INC. FULL-SIZE 1911A1 AUTO PISTOL

Caliber: 9mm Para., 9-shot; 38 Super, 9-shot; 40 S&W, 9-shot; 45 ACP, 7-shot. **Barrel:** 5". **Weight:** 35.6 oz. **Length:** 8-5/8" overall. **Grips:** Cocobolo. **Sights:** Fixed three-dot system. **Features:** Beveled magazine well; lowered and flared ejection port. All forged parts, including frame, barrel, slide. All new production. Introduced 1990. From Springfield, Inc.

Price: Mil-Spec 45 ACP, Parkerized **$559.00**
Price: Standard, 45 ACP, blued, Novak sights **$824.00**
Price: Standard, 45 ACP, stainless, Novak sights. . . . **$828.00**
Price: Lightweight 45 ACP (28.6 oz., matte finish, night sights) . . **$877.00**
Price: 40 S&W, stainless **$860.00**
Price: 9mm, stainless **$837.00**

Springfield, Inc. TRP Pistols

Similar to 1911A1 except 45 ACP only, checkered front strap and mainspring housing, Novak Night Sight combat rear sight and matching dovetailed front sight, tuned, polished extractor, oversize barrel link; lightweight speed trigger and combat action job, match barrel and bushing, extended ambidextrous thumb safety and fitted beavertail grip safety. Carry bevel on entire pistol; checkered cocobolo wood grips, comes with two Wilson 7-shot magazines. Frame is engraved "Tactical," both sides of frame with "TRP." Introduced 1998. From Springfield, Inc.

Price: Standard with Armory Kote finish **$1,395.00**
Price: Standard, stainless steel **$1,370.00**
Price: Standard with Operator Light Rail Armory Kote **$1,473.00**

HANDGUNS — AUTOLOADERS, SERVICE & SPORT

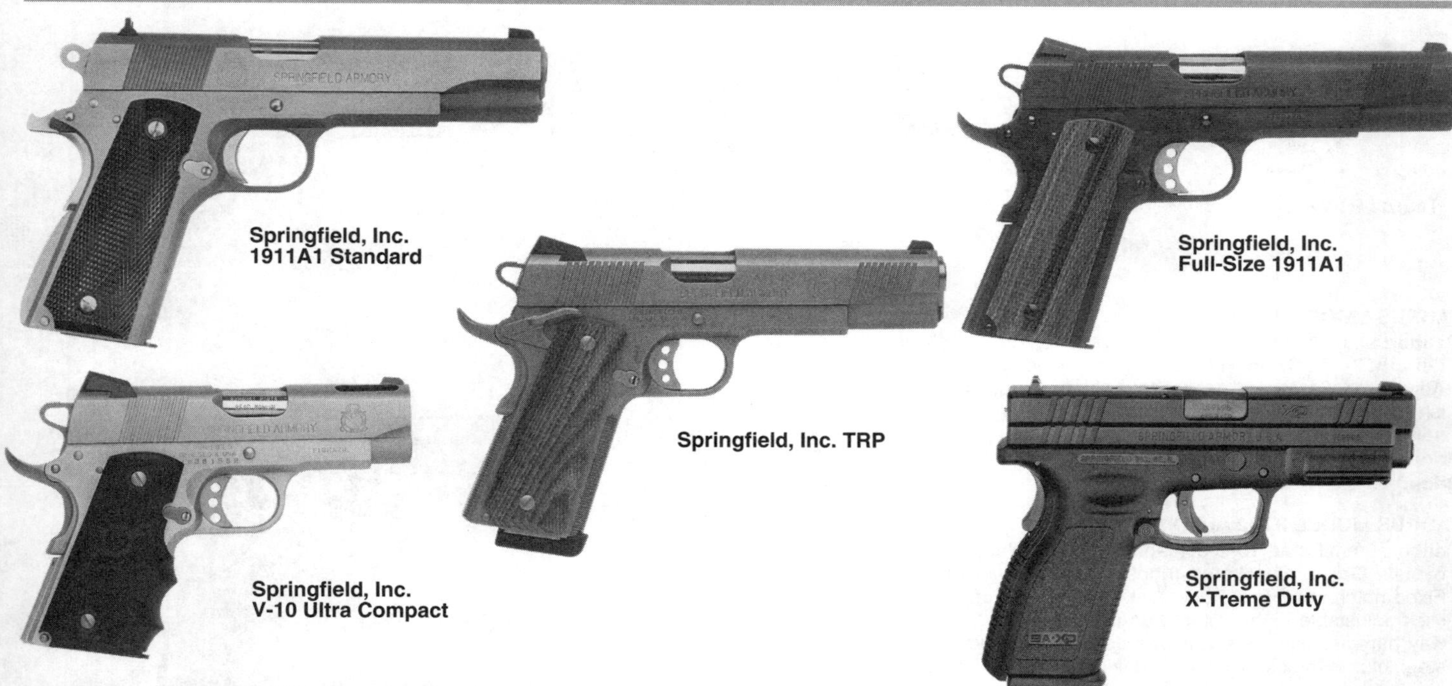

Springfield, Inc. 1911A1 Standard

Springfield, Inc. TRP

Springfield, Inc. Full-Size 1911A1

Springfield, Inc. V-10 Ultra Compact

Springfield, Inc. X-Treme Duty

HANDGUNS

Springfield, Inc. 1911A1 High Capacity Pistol

Similar to Standard 1911A1, available in 45 ACP with 10-shot magazine. Commander-style hammer, walnut grips, beveled magazine well, plastic carrying case. Can accept higher-capacity Para-Ordnance magazines. Introduced 1993. From Springfield, Inc.

Price: Mil-Spec 45 ACP **$756.00**
Price: 45 ACP Ultra Compact (3-1/2" bbl.) **$909.00**

Springfield, Inc. 1911A1 V-Series Ported Pistols

Similar to standard 1911A1, scalloped slides with 10, 12 or 16 matching barrel ports to redirect powder gasses and reduce recoil and muzzle flip. Adjustable rear sight, ambi thumb safety, Videki speed trigger, and beveled magazine well. Checkered walnut grips standard. Available in 45 ACP, stainless or bi-tone. Introduced 1992.

Price: V-16 Long Slide, stainless **$1,121.00**
Price: Target V-12, stainless **$878.00**
Price: V-10 (Ultra-Compact, bi-tone). **$853.00**
Price: V-10 stainless **$863.00**

Springfield, Inc. 1911A1 Champion Pistol

Similar to standard 1911A1, slide is 4". Novak Night Sights. Delta hammer and cocobolo grips. Available in 45 ACP only; Parkerized or stainless. Introduced 1989.

Price: Stainless. **$849.00**

Springfield, Inc. Ultra Compact Pistol

Similar to 1911A1 Compact, shorter slide, 3.5" barrel, beavertail grip safety, beveled magazine well, Novak Low Mount or Novak Night Sights, Videki speed trigger, flared ejection port, stainless steel frame, blued slide, match grade barrel, rubber grips. Introduced 1996. From Springfield, Inc.

Price: Parkerized 45 ACP, Night Sights **$589.00**
Price: Stainless 45 ACP, Night Sights. **$849.00**
Price: Lightweight, 9mm, stainless **$837.00**

Springfield, Inc. Compact Lightweight

Mates a Springfield Inc. Champion length slide with the shorter Ultra-Compact forged alloy frame for concealability. In 45 ACP.

Price: **$733.00**

Springfield, Inc. Long Slide 1911 A1 Pistol

Similar to Full Size model, 6" barrel and slide for increased sight radius and higher velocity, fully adjustable sights, muzzle-forward weight distribution for reduced recoil and quicker shot-to-shot recovery. From Springfield Inc.

Price: Target, 45 ACP, stainless with Night Sights **$1,049.00**
Price: Trophy Match, stainless with adj. sights **$1,452.00**
Price: V-16 stainless steel **$1,121.00**

SPRINGFIELD, INC. MICRO-COMPACT 1911A1 PISTOL

Caliber: 45 ACP, 40 S&W 6+1 capacity. **Barrel:** 3" 1:16 LH. **Weight:** 24 oz. **Length:** 5.7". **Sights:** Novak LoMount tritium. Dovetail front. **Features:** Forged frame and slide, ambi thumb safety, extreme carry bevel treatment, lockable plastic case, 2 magazines.

Price: . . . . **$993.00 to $1,021.00**

SPRINGFIELD, INC. X-TREME DUTY

Caliber: 9mm, 40 S&W, 357 Sig. **Barrel:** 4.08". **Weight:** 22.88 oz. **Length:** 7.2". **Sights:** Dovetail front and rear. **Features:** Lightweight, ultra high-impact polymer frame. Trigger, firing pin and grip safety. Two 10-rod steel easy glide magazines. Imported from Croatia.

Price: . . . . **$489.00 to $1,099.00**

STEYR M & S SERIES AUTO PISTOLS

Caliber: 9mm Para., 40 S&W, 357 SIG; 10-shot magazine. **Barrel:** 4" (3.58" for Model S). **Weight:** 28 oz. (22.5 oz. for Model S). **Length:** 7.05" overall (6.53" for Model S). **Grips:** Ultra-rigid polymer. **Sights:** Drift-adjustable, white-outline rear; white-triangle blade front. **Features:** Polymer frame; trigger-drop firing pin, manual and key-lock safeties; loaded chamber indicator; 5.5-lb. trigger pull; 111-degree grip angle enhances natural pointing. Introduced 2000. Imported from Austria by GSI Inc.

Price: Model M (full-sized frame with 4" barrel) **$609.95**
Price: Model S (compact frame with 3.58" barrel) **$609.95**
Price: Extra 10-shot magazines (Model M or S) **$39.00**

TAURUS MODEL PT 22/PT 25 AUTO PISTOLS

Caliber: 22 LR, 8-shot (PT 22); 25 ACP, 9-shot (PT 25). **Barrel:** 2.75". **Weight:** 12.3 oz. **Length:** 5.25" overall. **Grips:** Smooth rosewood or mother-of-pearl. **Sights:** Fixed. **Features:** Double action. Tip-up barrel for loading, cleaning. Blue, nickel, duotone or blue with gold accents. Introduced 1992. Made in U.S.A. by Taurus International.

Price: 22 LR, 25 ACP, blue, nickel or with duo-tone finish with rosewood grips **$219.00**
Price: 22 LR, 25 ACP, blue with gold trim, rosewood grips. **$234.00**
Price: 22 LR, 25 ACP, blue, nickel or duotone finish with checkered wood grips. **$219.00**
Price: 22 LR, 25 ACP, blue with gold trim, mother of pearl grips . **$250.00**

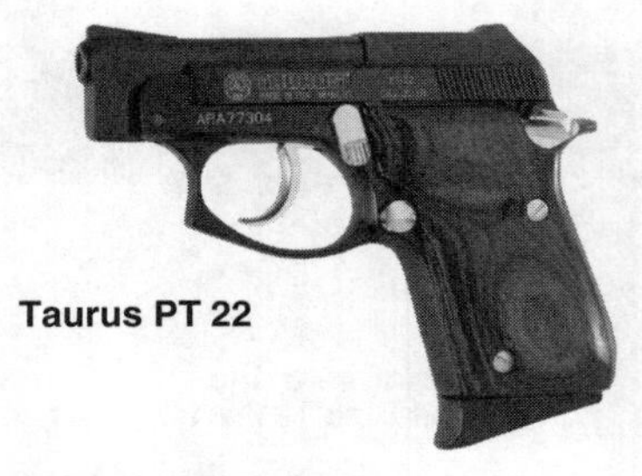

Taurus PT 22

Taurus PT-911

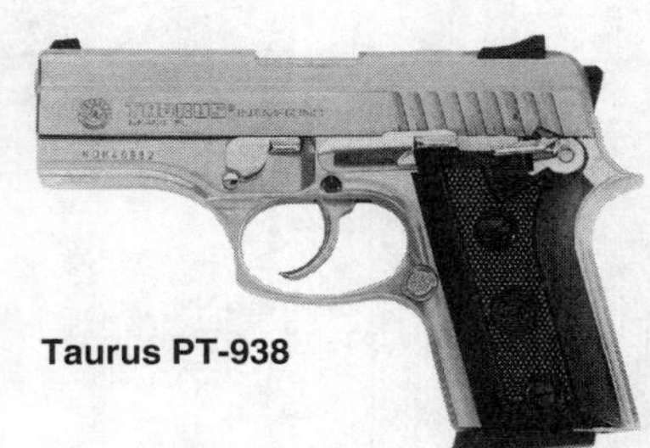

Taurus PT-938

TAURUS MODEL PT24/7

Caliber: 9mm, 10+1 shot; .40 Cal., 10+1 shot. **Barrel:** 4". **Weight:** 27.2 oz. **Length**: 7-18". **Grips:** RIBBER rubber-finned overlay on polymer. **Sights:** Adjustable. **Features:** Accessory rail, four safeties, blue or stainless finish, consistent trigger pull weight and travel. Introduced 2003. Imported from Brazil by Taurus International.

Price: 9mm **$578.00**
Price: .40 Cal. **$594.00**

TAURUS MODEL PT92 AUTO PISTOL

Caliber: 9mm Para., 10-shot mag. **Barrel:** 5". **Weight:** 34 oz. **Length:** 8.5" overall. **Grips:** Checkered rubber, rosewood, mother-of-pearl. **Sights:** Fixed notch rear. Three-dot sight system. Also offered with micrometer-click adjustable night sights. **Features:** Double action, ambidextrous 3-way hammer drop safety, allows cocked & locked carry. Blue, stainless steel, blue with gold highlights, stainless steel with gold highlights, forged aluminum frame, integral key-lock. .22 LR conversion kit available. Imported from Brazil by Taurus International.

Price: Blue . . . . **$578.00 to $672.00**

Taurus Model PT99 Auto Pistol

Similar to PT92, fully adjustable rear sight.

Price: Blue . . . . **$575.00 to $670.00**
Price: 22 Conversion kit for PT 92 and PT99 (includes barrel and slide) **$266.00**

TAURUS MODEL PT-100/101 AUTO PISTOL

Caliber: 40 S&W, 10-shot mag. **Barrel:** 5". **Weight:** 34 oz. **Length:** 8-1/2". **Grips:** Checkered rubber, rosewood, mother-of-pearl. **Sights:** Three-dot fixed or adjustable; night sights available. **Features:** Single/double action with three-position safety/decocker. Re-introduced in 2001. Imported by Tau-rus International.

Price: PT100. . . . . **$578.00 to $672.00**
Price: PT101. . . . . **$594.00 to $617.00**

TAURUS MODEL PT-111 MILLENNIUM PRO AUTO PISTOL

Caliber: 9mm Para., 10-shot mag. **Barrel:** 3.25". **Weight:** 18.7 oz. **Length:** 6-1/8" overall. **Grips:** Polymer. **Sights:** Three-dot fixed; night sights available. Low profile, three-dot combat. **Features:** Double-action-only, polymer frame, matte stainless or blue steel slide, manual safety, integral key-lock. Deluxe models with wood grip inserts. Now issued in a third generation series with many cosmetic and internal improvements.

Price: . . . . **$445.00 to $539.00**

Taurus Model PT-111 Millennium Titanium Pistol

Similar to PT-111, titanium slide, night sights.

Price: **$586.00**

TAURUS PT-132 MILLENIUM PRO AUTO PISTOL

Caliber: 32 ACP, 10-shot mag. **Barrel:** 3.25". **Weight:** 18.7 oz. **Grips:** Polymer. **Sights:** Three-dot fixed; night sights available. **Features:** Double-action-only, polymer frame, matte stainless or blue steel slide, manual safety, integral key-lock action. Introduced 2001.

Price: . . . . **$445.00 to $461.00**

TAURUS PT-138 MILLENIUM PRO SERIES

Caliber: 380 ACP, 10-shot mag. **Barrel:** 3.25". **Weight:** 18.7 oz. **Grips:** Polymer. **Sights:** Fixed three-dot. **Features:** Double action only, polymer frame, matte stainless or blue steel slide, manual safety, integral key-lock.

Price: . . . . **$445.00 to $461.00**

Taurus PT-940

TAURUS PT-140 MILLENIUM PRO AUTO PISTOL

Caliber: 40 S&W, 10-shot mag. **Barrel:** 3.25". **Weight:** 18.7 oz. **Grips:** Checkered polymer. **Sights:** Three-dot fixed; night sights available. **Features:** Double-action-only; matte stainless or blue steel slide, black polymer frame, manual safety, integral key-lock action. From Taurus International.

Price: . . . . **$484.00 to $578.00**

TAURUS PT-145 MILLENIUM AUTO PISTOL

Caliber: 45 ACP, 10-shot mag. **Barrel:** 3.27". **Weight:** 23 oz. **Stock:** Checkered polymer. **Sights:** Three-dot fixed; night sights available. **Features:** Double-action-only, matte stainless or blue steel slide, black polymer frame, manual safety, integral key-lock. From Taurus International.

Price: . . . . **$484.00 to $578.00**

TAURUS MODEL PT-911 AUTO PISTOL

Caliber: 9mm Para., 10-shot mag. **Barrel:** 4". **Weight:** 28.2 oz. **Length:** 7" overall. **Grips:** Checkered rubber, rosewood, mother-of-pearl. **Sights:** Fixed, three-dot blue or stainless; night sights optional. **Features:** Double action, semi-auto ambidextrous 3-way hammer drop safety, allows cocked and locked carry. Blue, stainless steel, blue with gold highlights, or stainless steel with gold highlights, forged aluminum frame, integral key-lock.

Price: . . . . **$523.00 to $617.00**

TAURUS MODEL PT-938 AUTO PISTOL

Caliber: 380 ACP, 10-shot mag. **Barrel:** 3.72". **Weight:** 27 oz. **Length:** 6.5" overall. **Grips:** Checkered rubber. **Sights:** Fixed, three-dot. **Features:** Double action, ambidextrous 3-way hammer drop allows cocked & locked carry. Forged aluminum frame. Integral key-lock. Imported by Taurus International.

Price: Blue **$516.00**
Price: Stainless. **$531.00**

TAURUS MODEL PT-940 AUTO PISTOL

Caliber: 40 S&W, 10-shot mag. **Barrel:** 3-5/8". **Weight:** 28.2 oz. **Length:** 7" overall. **Grips:** Checkered rubber, rosewood or mother-of-pearl. **Sights:** Fixed, three-dot blue or stainless; night sights optional. **Features:** Double action, semi-auto ambidextrous 3-way hammer drop safety, allows cocked & locked carry. Blue, stainless steel, blue with gold highlights, or stainless steel with gold hightlights, forged aluminum frame, integral key-lock.

Price: . . . . **$523.00 to $617.00**

Taurus PT-945

Taurus PT-957

Walther PPK/S

Walther P22

Walther P99

Walther PPK

Wilkinson Sherry

TAURUS MODEL PT-945 SERIES

Caliber: 45 ACP, 8-shot mag. **Barrel:** 4.25". **Weight:** 28.2/29.5 oz. **Length:** 7.48" overall. **Grips:** Checkered rubber, rosewood or mother-of-pearl. **Sights:** Fixed, three-dot; night sights optional. **Features:** Double-action with ambidextrous 3-way hammer drop safety allows cocked & locked carry. Forged aluminum frame, PT-945C has ported barrel/slide. Blue, stainless, blue with gold highlights, stainless with gold highlights, integral key-lock. Introduced 1995. Imported by Taurus International.

Price: . . . . **$563.00 to $641.00**

TAURUS MODEL PT-957 AUTO PISTOL

Caliber: 357 SIG, 10-shot mag. **Barrel:** 4". **Weight:** 28 oz. **Length:** 7" overall. **Grips:** Checkered rubber, rosewood or mother-of-pearl. **Sights:** Fixed, three-dot blue or stainless; night sights optional. **Features:** Double-action, blue, stainless steel, blue with gold accents or stainless with gold accents, ported barrel/slide, three-position safety with decocking lever and ambidextrous safety. Forged aluminum frame, integral key-lock. Introduced 1999. Imported by Taurus International.

Price: . . . . **$525.00 to $620.00**

Price: Non-ported . . . . **$525.00 to $535.00**

TAURUS MODEL 922 SPORT PISTOL

Caliber: .22 LR, 10-shot magazine. **Barrel:** 6". **Weight:** 24.8 oz. **Length:** 9-1/8". **Grips:** Polymer. **Sights:** Adjustable. **Features:** Matte blue steel finish, machined target crown, polymer frame, single and double action, easy disassembly for cleaning.

Price: (blue) **$310.00**

Price: (stainless) **$328.00**

WALTHER PPK/S AMERICAN AUTO PISTOL

Caliber: 380 ACP, 7-shot magazine. **Barrel:** 3.27". **Weight:** 23-1/2 oz. **Length:** 6.1" overall. **Stocks:** Checkered plastic. **Sights:** Fixed, white markings. **Features:** Double-action; manual safety blocks firing pin and drops hammer; chamber loaded indicator on 32 and 380; extra finger rest magazine provided. Made entirely in the United States. Introduced 1980.

Price: 380 ACP only, blue **$540.00**

Price: As above, 32 ACP or 380 ACP, stainless **$540.00**

Walther PPK American Auto Pistol

Similar to Walther PPK/S except weighs 21 oz., has 6-shot capacity. Made in the U.S. Introduced 1986.

Price: Stainless, 32 ACP or 380 ACP **$540.00**

Price: Blue, 380 ACP only **$540.00**

WALTHER P99 AUTO PISTOL

Caliber: 9mm Para., 9x21, 40 S&W,10-shot magazine. **Barrel:** 4". **Weight:** 25 oz. **Length:** 7" overall. **Grips:** Textured polymer. **Sights:** Blade front (comes with three interchangeable blades for elevation adjustment), micrometer rear adjustable for windage. **Features:** Double-action mechanism with trigger safety, decock safety, internal striker safety; chamber loaded indicator; ambidextrous magazine release levers; polymer frame with interchangeable backstrap inserts. Comes with two magazines. Introduced 1997. Imported from Germany by Carl Walther USA.

Price: **$799.00**

Walther P990 Auto Pistol

Similar to the P99 except is double-action-only. Available in blue or silver tenifer finish. Introduced 1999. Imported from Germany by Carl Walther USA.

Price: **$749.00**

WALTHER P22 PISTOL

Caliber: 22 LR. **Barrel:** 3.4", 5". **Weight:** 19.6 oz. (3.4"), 20.3 oz. (5"). **Length:** 6.26", 7.83". **Grips:** NA. **Sights:** Interchangeable white dot, front, two-dot adjustable, rear. **Features:** Rimfire version of the Walther P99 pistol, available in nickel slide with black frame, or green frame with black slide versions. Made in Germany and distributed in the U.S. by Smith & Wesson.

Price: . . . . **NA**

WILKINSON SHERRY AUTO PISTOL

Caliber: 22 LR, 8-shot magazine. **Barrel:** 2-1/8". **Weight:** 9-1/4 oz. **Length:** 4-3/8" overall. **Grips:** Checkered black plastic. **Sights:** Fixed, groove. **Features:** Cross-bolt safety locks the sear into the hammer. Available in all blue finish or blue slide and trigger with gold frame. Introduced 1985.

Price: **$280.00**

WILKINSON LINDA AUTO PISTOL

Caliber: 9mm Para. **Barrel:** 8-5/16". **Weight:** 4 lbs., 13 oz. **Length:** 12-1/4" overall. **Grips:** Checkered black plastic pistol grip, walnut forend. **Sights:** Protected blade front, aperture rear. **Features:** Fires from closed bolt. Semi-auto only. Straight blowback action. Cross-bolt safety. Removable barrel. From Wilkinson Arms.

Price: **$675.00**

Includes models suitable for several forms of competition and other sporting purposes.

Baer 1911 Ultimate Master

Baer 1911 Bullseye Wadcutter

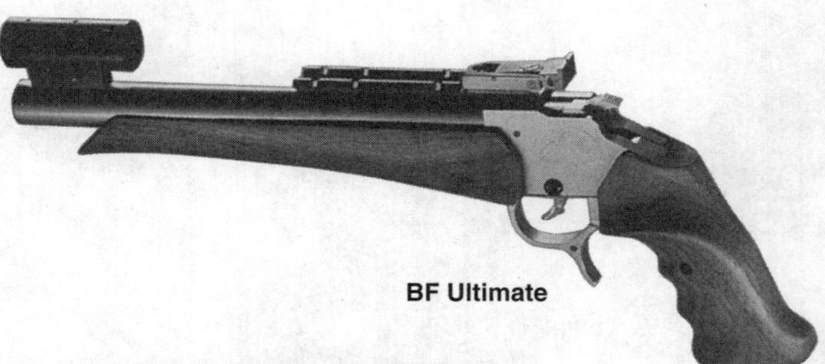
BF Ultimate

Browning Buck Mark Target 5.5

BAER 1911 ULTIMATE MASTER COMBAT PISTOL

Caliber: 9x23, 38 Super, 400 Cor-Bon 45 ACP (others available), 10-shot magazine. **Barrel:** 5", 6"; Baer NM. **Weight:** 37 oz. **Length:** 8.5" overall. **Grips:** Checkered rosewood. **Sights:** Baer dovetail front, low-mount Bo-Mar rear with hidden leaf. **Features:** Full-house competition gun. Baer forged NM blued steel frame and double serrated slide; Baer triple port, tapered cone compensator; fitted slide to frame; lowered, flared ejection port; Baer reverse recoil plug; full-length guide rod; recoil buff; beveled magazine well; Baer Commander hammer, sear; Baer extended ambidextrous safety, extended ejector, checkered slide stop, beavertail grip safety with pad, extended magazine release button; Baer speed trigger. Made in U.S.A. by Les Baer Custom, Inc.

Price: Compensated, open sights **$2,476.00**
Price: 6" Model 400 Cor-Bon **$2,541.00**

BAER 1911 NATIONAL MATCH HARDBALL PISTOL

Caliber: 45 ACP, 7-shot magazine. **Barrel:** 5". **Weight:** 37 oz. **Length:** 8.5" overall. **Grips:** Checkered walnut. **Sights:** Baer dovetail front with undercut post, low-mount Bo-Mar rear with hidden leaf. **Features:** Baer NM forged steel frame, double serrated slide and barrel with stainless bushing; slide fitted to frame; Baer match trigger with 4-lb. pull; polished feed ramp, throated barrel; checkered front strap, arched mainspring housing; Baer beveled magazine well; lowered, flared ejection port; tuned extractor; Baer extended ejector, checkered slide stop; recoil buff. Made in U.S.A. by Les Baer Custom, Inc.

Price: **$1,335.00**

Baer 1911 Bullseye Wadcutter Pistol

Similar to National Match Hardball except designed for wadcutter loads only. Polished feed ramp and barrel throat; Bo-Mar rib on slide; full-length recoil rod; Baer speed trigger with 3-1/2-lb. pull; Baer deluxe hammer and sear; Baer beavertail grip safety with pad; flat mainspring housing checkered 20 lpi. Blue finish; checkered walnut grips. Made in U.S.A. by Les Baer Custom, Inc.

Price: From **$1,495.00**
Price: With 6" barrel, from. **$1,690.00**

BF ULTIMATE SILHOUETTE HB SINGLE SHOT PISTOL

Caliber: 7mm U.S., 22 LR Match and 100 other chamberings. **Barrel:** 10.75" Heavy Match Grade with 11-degree target crown. **Weight:** 3 lbs., 15 oz. **Length:** 16" overall. **Grips:** Thumbrest target style. **Sights:** Bo-Mar/Bond ScopeRib I Combo with hooded post front adjustable for height and width, rear notch available in .032", .062", .080" and .100" widths; 1/2-MOA clicks. **Features:** Designed to meet maximum rules for IHMSA Production Gun. Falling block action gives rigid barrel-receiver mating. Hand fitted and headspaced. Etched receiver; gold-colored trigger. Introduced 1988. Made in U.S.A. by E. Arthur Brown Co. Inc.

Price: **$669.00**

BF Classic Hunting Pistol

Similar to BF Ultimate Silhouette HB Single Shot Pistol, except no sights; drilled and tapped for scope mount. Barrels from 8" to 15". Variety of options offered. Made in U.S.A. by E. Arthur Brown Co. Inc.

Price: **$599.00**

BROWNING BUCK MARK TARGET 5.5

Caliber: 22 LR, 10-shot magazine. **Barrel:** 5-1/2" barrel with .900" diameter. **Weight:** 35-1/2 oz. **Length:** 9-5/8" overall. **Grips:** Contoured walnut grips with thumbrest, or finger-groove walnut. **Sights:** Hooded sights mounted on scope base that accepts optical or reflex sight. Rear sight is Browning fully adjustable Pro Target, front sight is adjustable post that customizes to different widths, can be adjusted for height. **Features:** Matte blue finish. Introduced 1990. From Browning.

Price: **$496.00**

BROWNING BUCK MARK FIELD 5.5

Same as Target 5.5, hoodless ramp-style front sight and low profile rear sight. Matte blue finish, contoured or finger-groove walnut stocks. Introduced 1991.

Price: **$496.00**

BROWNING BUCK MARK BULLSEYE

Similar to Buck Mark Silhouette, 7-1/4" heavy barrel with three flutes per side; trigger adjusts from 2-1/2 to 5 lbs.; specially designed rosewood target or three-finger-groove stocks with competition-style heel rest, or with contoured rubber grip. Overall length 11-5/16", weighs 36 oz. Introduced 1996. Made in U.S.A. From Browning.

Price: With ambidextrous moulded composite stocks. **$454.00**
Price: With rosewood stocks, or wrap-around finger groove. **$586.00**

Browning Buck Mark Bullseye

Colt Special Combat

Competitor Single Shot

EAA Witness Gold Team

COLT GOLD CUP MODEL O PISTOL

Caliber: 45 ACP, 8-shot magazine. **Barrel:** 5", with new design bushing. **Weight:** 39 oz. **Length:** 8-1/2". **Grips:** Checkered rubber composite with silver-plated medallion. **Sights:** Patridge-style front, Bo-Mar-style rear adjustable for windage and elevation, sight radius 6-3/4". **Features:** Arched or flat housing; wide, grooved trigger with adjustable stop; ribbed-top slide, hand fitted, with improved ejection port.

Price: Blue **$1,050.00**

Price: Stainless **$1,116.00**

COLT SPECIAL COMBAT GOVERNMENT

Caliber: 45 ACP. **Barrel:** 5" **Weight:** NA. **Length:** 8-1/2" **Grips:** Rosewood w/double diamond checkering pattern. **Sights:** Clark dovetail, front; Bo-Mar adjustable, rear. **Features:** Competition-ready pistol with enhancements such as skeletonized trigger, upswept grip safety, custom tuned action, polished feed ramp. Blue or satin nickel finish. Introduced 2003. Made in U.S.A. by Colt's Mfg. Co.

Price: **$1,640.00**

COMPETITOR SINGLE SHOT PISTOL

Caliber: 22 LR through 50 Action Express, including belted magnums. **Barrel:** 14" standard; 10.5" silhouette; 16" optional. **Weight:** About 59 oz. (14" bbl.). **Length:** 15.12" overall. **Grips:** Ambidextrous; synthetic (standard) or laminated or natural wood. **Sights:** Ramp front, adjustable rear. **Features:** Rotary canon-type action cocks on opening; cammed ejector; interchangeable barrels, ejectors. Adjustable single stage trigger, sliding thumb safety and trigger safety. Matte blue finish. Introduced 1988. From Competitor Corp., Inc.

Price: 14", standard calibers, synthetic grip **$414.95**

Price: Extra barrels, from **$159.95**

CZ 75 CHAMPION COMPETITION PISTOL

Caliber: 9mm Para., 9x21, 40 S&W, 10-shot mag. **Barrel:** 4.49". **Weight:** 35 oz. **Length:** 9.44" overall. **Grips:** Black rubber. **Sights:** Blade front, fully adjustable rear. **Features:** Single-action trigger mechanism; three-port compensator (40 S&W, 9mm have two port) full-length guide rod; extended magazine release; ambidextrous safety; flared magazine well; fully adjustable match trigger. Introduced 1999. Imported from the Czech Republic by CZ USA.

Price: 9mm Para., 9x21, 40 S&W, dual-tone finish **$1,551.00**

CZ 75 ST IPSC AUTO PISTOL

Caliber: 40 S&W, 10-shot magazine. **Barrel:** 5.12". **Weight:** 2.9 lbs. **Length:** 8.86" overall. **Grips:** Checkered walnut. **Sights:** Fully adjustable rear. **Features:** Single-action mechanism; extended slide release and ambidextrous safety; full-length slide rail; double slide serrations. Introduced 1999. Imported from the Czech Republic by CZ-USA.

Price: Dual-tone finish **$1,038.00**

EAA/BAIKAL IZH35 AUTO PISTOL

Caliber: 22 LR, 5-shot mag. **Barrel:** 6". **Grips:** Walnut; fully adjustable right-hand target-style. **Sights:** Fully adjustable rear, blade front; detachable scope mount. **Features:** Hammer-forged target barrel; machined steel receiver; adjustable trigger; manual slide hold back, grip and manual trigger-bar disconnect safeties; cocking indicator. Introduced 2000. Imported from Russia by European American Armory.

Price: Blued finish **$489.00**

EAA WITNESS GOLD TEAM AUTO

Caliber: 9mm Para., 9x21, 38 Super, 40 S&W, 45 ACP. **Barrel:** 5.1". **Weight:** 44 oz. **Length:** 10.5" overall. **Grips:** Checkered walnut, competition style. **Sights:** Square post front, fully adjustable rear. **Features:** Triple-chamber cone compensator; competition SA trigger; extended safety and magazine release; competition hammer; beveled magazine well; beavertail grip. Hand-fitted major components. Hard chrome finish. Match-grade barrel. From E.A.A. Custom Shop. Introduced 1992. From European American Armory.

Price: **$1,699.00**

EAA Witness Silver Team Auto

Similar to Witness Gold Team, double-chamber compensator, oval magazine release, black rubber grips, double-dip blue finish. Super Sight and drilled and tapped for scope mount. Built for the intermediate competition shooter. Introduced 1992. From European American Armory Custom Shop.

Price: 9mm Para., 9x21, 38 Super, 40 S&W, 45 ACP. **$968.00**

ED BROWN CLASSIC CUSTOM PISTOL

Caliber: 45 ACP. **Barrel:** 5". **Weight:** 39 oz. **Grips:** Hogue exotic wood. **Sights:** Modified ramp or post, front; fully-adjustable Bo-Mar, rear. **Features:** Highly-polished slide, two-piece guide rod, oversize mag release, ambidextrous safety.

Price: **$2,895.00**

Freedom Arms 83 22 Silhouette Class

Hammerli SP 20

ED BROWN CLASS A LIMITED

Caliber: 45 ACP, 400 Cor-Bon, 10mm, 40 S&W, 357 SIG, 38 Super, 9x23, 9mm Luger, 7-shot magazine. **Barrel:** 4.25", 5". **Weight:** 34 to 39 oz. **Grips:** Hogue exotic wood. **Sights:** Customer preference, front; fixed Novak low-mount or fully-adjustable Bo-Mar, rear. **Features:** Checkered forestrap and mainspring housing, matte finished top sighting surface. Many options available.

Price: **$2,250.00**

ENTRÉPRISE TOURNAMENT SHOOTER MODEL I

Caliber: 45 ACP, 10-shot mag. **Barrel:** 6". **Weight:** 40 oz. **Length:** 8.5" overall. **Grips:** Black ultra-slim double diamond checkered synthetic. **Sights:** Dovetailed Patridge front, adjustable Competizione "melded" rear. **Features:** Oversized magazine release button; flared magazine well; fully machined parallel slide rails; front and rear slide serrations; serrated top of slide; stainless ramped bull barrel with fully supported chamber; full-length guide rod with plug; stainless firing pin; match extractor; polished ramp; tuned match extractor; black oxide. Introduced 1998. Made in U.S.A. by Entréprise Arms.

Price: **$2,300.00**

Price: TSMIII (Satin chrome finish, two-piece guide rod) **$2,700.00**

EXCEL INDUSTRIES CP-45, XP-45 AUTO PISTOL

Caliber: 45 ACP, 6-shot & 10-shot mags. **Barrel:** 3-1/4". **Weight:** 31 oz. & 25 oz. **Length:** 6-3/8" overall. **Grips:** Checkered black nylon. **Sights:** Fully adjustable rear. **Features:** Stainless steel frame and slide; single action with external hammer and firing pin block, manual thumb safety; last-shot hold open. Includes gun lock and cleaning kit. Introduced 2001. Made in U.S.A. by Excel Industries Inc.

Price: CP-45 .... **$425.00**

Price: XP-45 .... **$465.00**

FEINWERKEBAU AW93 TARGET PISTOL

Caliber: 22. **Barrel:** 6". **Grips:** Fully adjustable orthopaedic. **Sights:** Fully adjustable micrometer. **Features:** Advanced Russian design with German craftmanship. Imported from Germany by Nygord Precision Products.

Price: **$1,495.00**

FREEDOM ARMS MODEL 83 22 FIELD GRADE SILHOUETTE CLASS

Caliber: 22 LR, 5-shot cylinder. **Barrel:** 10". **Weight:** 63 oz. **Length:** 15.5" overall. **Grips:** Black Micarta. **Sights:** Removable patridge front blade; Iron Sight Gun Works silhouette rear, click adjustable for windage and elevation (optional adj. front sight and hood). **Features:** Stainless steel, matte finish, manual sliding-bar safety system; dual firing pins, lightened hammer for fast lock time, pre-set trigger stop. Introduced 1991. Made in U.S.A. by Freedom Arms.

Price: Silhouette Class **$1,901.75**

Price: Extra fitted 22 WMR cylinder **$264.00**

FREEDOM ARMS MODEL 83 CENTERFIRE SILHOUETTE MODELS

Caliber: 357 Mag., 41 Mag., 44 Mag.; 5-shot cylinder. **Barrel:** 10", 9" (357 Mag. only). **Weight:** 63 oz. (41 Mag.). **Length:** 15.5", 14-1/2" (357 only). **Grips:** Pachmayr Presentation. **Sights:** Iron Sight Gun Works silhouette rear sight, replaceable adjustable front sight blade with hood. **Features:** Stainless steel, matte finish, manual sliding-bar safety system. Made in U.S.A. by Freedom Arms.

Price: Silhouette Models **$1,634.85**

High Standard Trophy

GAUCHER GP SILHOUETTE PISTOL

Caliber: 22 LR, single shot. **Barrel:** 10". **Weight:** 42.3 oz. **Length:** 15.5" overall. **Grips:** Stained hardwood. **Sights:** Hooded post on ramp front, open rear adjustable for windage and elevation. **Features:** Matte chrome barrel, blued bolt and sights. Other barrel lengths available on special order. Introduced 1991. Imported by Mandall Shooting Supplies.

Price: **$425.00**

HAMMERLI SP 20 TARGET PISTOL

Caliber: 22 LR, 32 S&W. **Barrel:** 4.6". **Weight:** 34.6-41.8 oz. **Length:** 11.8" overall. **Grips:** Anatomically shaped synthetic Hi-Grip available in five sizes. **Sights:** Integral front in three widths, adjustable rear with changeable notch widths. **Features:** Extremely low-level sight line; anatomically shaped trigger; adjustable JPS buffer system for different recoil characteristics. Receiver available in red, blue, gold, violet or black. Introduced 1998. Imported from Switzerland by SIGARMS, Inc and Hammerli Pistols USA.

Price: Hammerli 22 LR **$1,668.00**

Price: Hammerli 32 S&W **$1,743.00**

HAMMERLI X-ESSE SPORT PISTOL

An all-steel .22 LR target pistol with a Hi-Grip in new anatomical shape and adjustable hand rest. Made in Switzerland. Introduced 2003.

Price: **$710.00**

HARRIS GUNWORKS SIGNATURE JR. LONG RANGE PISTOL

Caliber: Any suitable caliber. **Barrel:** To customer specs. **Weight:** 5 lbs. **Stock:** Gunworks fiberglass. **Sights:** None furnished; comes with scope rings. **Features:** Right- or left-hand benchrest action of titanium or stainless steel; single shot or repeater. Comes with bipod. Introduced 1992. Made in U.S.A. by Harris Gunworks, Inc.

Price: **$2,700.00**

HIGH STANDARD TROPHY TARGET PISTOL

Caliber: 22 LR, 10-shot mag. **Barrel:** 5-1/2" bull or 7-1/4" fluted. **Weight:** 44 oz. **Length:** 9.5" overall. **Stock:** Checkered hardwood with thumbrest. **Sights:** Undercut ramp front, frame-mounted micro-click rear adjustable for windage and elevation; drilled and tapped for scope mounting. **Features:** Gold-plated trigger, slide lock, safety-lever and magazine release; stippled front grip and backstrap; adjustable trigger and sear. Barrel weights optional. From High Standard Manufacturing Co., Inc.

Price: 5-1/2", scope base **$540.00**

Price: 7.25" **$689.00**

Price: 7.25", scope base **$625.00**

High Standard Victor

Ruger Mark II Target

Ruger Mark II Government Target

HIGH STANDARD VICTOR TARGET PISTOL

Caliber: 22 LR, 10-shot magazine. **Barrel:** 4-1/2" or 5-1/2"; push-button takedown. **Weight:** 46 oz. **Length:** 9.5" overall. **Stock:** Checkered hardwood with thumbrest. **Sights:** Undercut ramp front, micro-click rear adjustable for windage and elevation. Also available with scope mount, rings, no sights. **Features:** Stainless steel construction. Full-length vent rib. Gold-plated trigger, slide lock, safety-lever and magazine release; stippled front grip and backstrap; polished slide; adjustable trigger and sear. Comes with barrel weight. From High Standard Manufacturing Co., Inc.

Price: 4-1/2" scope base **$564.00**
Price: 5-1/2", sights **$625.00**
Price: 5-1/2" scope base **$564.00**

KIMBER SUPER MATCH II

Caliber: 45 ACP, 7-shot magazine. **Barrel:** 5". **Weight:** 38 oz. **Length:** 18.7" overall. **Sights:** Blade front, Kimber fully adjustable rear. **Features:** Guaranteed to have shot 3" group at 50 yards. Stainless steel frame, black KimPro slide; two-piece magazine well; premium aluminum match-grade trigger; 30 lpi front strap checkering; stainless match-grade barrel; ambidextrous safety; special Custom Shop markings. Introduced 1999. Made in U.S.A. by Kimber Mfg., Inc.

Price: **$1,927.00**

KORTH MATCH REVOLVER

Caliber: 357 Mag., 38 Special, 32 S&W Long, 9mm Para., 22 WMR, 22 LR. **Barrel:** 5-1/4", 6". **Grips:** Adjustable match of oiled walnut with matte finish. **Sights:** Fully adjustable with rear sight leaves (wide th of sight notch: 3.4mm, 3.5mm, 3.6mm), rear; undercut partridge, front. **Trigger:** Equipped with completely machined trigger shoe. Interchangeable caliber cylinders available as well as a variety of finishes. Made in Germany.

Price: . . . . From **$5,632.00**

MORINI MODEL 84E FREE PISTOL

Caliber: 22 LR, single shot. **Barrel:** 11.4". **Weight:** 43.7 oz. **Length:** 19.4" overall. **Grips:** Adjustable match type with stippled surfaces. **Sights:** Interchangeable blade front, match-type fully adjustable rear. **Features:** Fully adjustable electronic trigger. Introduced 1995. Imported from Switzerland by Nygord Precision Products.

Price: **$1,450.00**

PARDINI MODEL SP, HP TARGET PISTOLS

Caliber: 22 LR, 32 S&W, 5-shot magazine. **Barrel:** 4.7". **Weight:** 38.9 oz. **Length:** 11.6" overall. **Grips:** Adjustable; stippled walnut; match type. **Sights:** Interchangeable blade front, interchangeable, fully adjustable rear. **Features:** Fully adjustable match trigger. Introduced 1995. Imported from Italy by Nygord Precision Products.

Price: Model SP (22 LR) **$995.00**
Price: Model HP (32 S&W) **$1,095.00**

PARDINI GP RAPID FIRE MATCH PISTOL

Caliber: 22 Short, 5-shot magazine. **Barrel:** 4.6". **Weight:** 43.3 oz. **Length:** 11.6" overall. **Grips:** Wrap-around stippled walnut. **Sights:** Interchangeable post front, fully adjustable match rear. Introduced 1995. Imported from Italy by Nygord Precision Products.

Price: Model GP **$1,095.00**
Price: Model GP-E Electronic, has special parts **$1,595.00**

PARDINI K22 FREE PISTOL

Caliber: 22 LR, single shot. **Barrel:** 9.8". **Weight:** 34.6 oz. **Length:** 18.7" overall. **Grips:** Wrap-around walnut; adjustable match type. **Sights:** Interchangeable post front, fully adjustable match open rear. **Features:** Removable, adjustable match trigger. Toggle bolt pushes cartridge into chamber. Barrel weights mount above the barrel. New upgraded model introduced in 2002. Imported from Italy by Nygord Precision Products.

Price: **$1,295.00**

PARDINI GT45 TARGET PISTOL

Caliber: 45, 9mm, 40 S&W. **Barrel:** 5", 6". **Grips:** Checkered fore strap. **Sights:** Interchangeable post front, fully adjustable match open rear. **Features:** Ambi-safeties, trigger pull adjustable. Fits Helweg Glock holsters for defense shooters. Imported from Italy by Nygord Precision Products.

Price: 5" **$1,050.00**
Price: 6" **$1,125.00**
Price: Frame mount available . . . . **$75.00 extra**
Price: Slide mount available . . . . **$35.00 extra**

PARDINI/NYGORD "MASTER" TARGET PISTOL

Caliber: 22 cal. **Barrel:** 5-1/2". **Grips:** Semi-wrap-around. **Sights:** Micrometer rear and red dot. **Features:** Elegant NRA "Bullseye" pistol. Superior balance of Pardini pistols. Revolutionary recipricating internal weight barrel shroud. Imported from Italy by Nygord Precision Products.

Price: **$1,145.00**

RUGER MARK II TARGET MODEL AUTOLOADING PISTOL

Caliber: 22 LR, 10-shot magazine. **Barrel:** 6-7/8". **Weight:** 42 oz. **Length:** 11-1/8" overall. **Grips:** Checkered composition grip panels. **Sights:** .125" blade front, micro-click rear, adjustable for windage and elevation. Sight radius 9-3/8". **Features:** Plastic case with lock included. Introduced 1982.

Price: Blued (MK-678) **$349.00**
Price: Stainless (KMK-678) **$439.00**

Ruger Mark II Government Target Model

Same gun as Mark II Target Model except has 6-7/8" barrel, higher sights and is roll marked "Government Target Model" on right side of receiver below rear sight. Identical in all aspects to military model used for training U.S. Armed Forces except for markings. Comes with factory test target, also lockable plastic case. Introduced 1987.

Price: Blued (MK-678G) **$425.00**
Price: Stainless (KMK-678G) **$509.00**

Ruger Mark II Bull Barrel - MK10

Safari Arms Big Deuce

Smith & Wesson Model 41

Springfield, Inc. 1911A1 Bullseye Wadcutter

Ruger Stainless Competition Model Pistol

Similar to Mark II Government Target Model stainless pistol, 6-7/8" slab-sided barrel; receiver top is fitted with Ruger scope base of blued, chrome moly steel; has Ruger 1" stainless scope rings for mounting variety of optical sights; checkered laminated grip panels with right-hand thumbrest. Blued open sights with 9-1/4" radius. Overall length 11-1/8", weight 45 oz. Case and lock included. Introduced 1991.

Price: KMK-678GC **$529.00**

Ruger Mark II Bull Barrel

Same gun as Target Model except has 5-1/2" or 10" heavy barrel (10" meets all IHMSA regulations). Weight with 5-1/2" barrel is 42 oz., with 10" barrel, 51 oz. Case with lock included.

Price: Blued (MK-512) **$349.00**
Price: Blued (MK-10) **$357.00**
Price: Stainless (KMK-10) **$445.00**
Price: Stainless (KMK-512) **$439.00**

SAFARI ARMS BIG DEUCE PISTOL

Caliber: 45 ACP, 7-shot magazine. **Barrel:** 6", 416 stainless steel. **Weight:** 40.3 oz. **Length:** 9.5" overall. **Grips:** Smooth walnut. **Sights:** Ramped blade front, LPA adjustable rear. **Features:** Beavertail grip safety; extended thumb safety and slide release; Commander-style hammer. Throated, polished and tuned. Parkerized matte black slide with satin stainless steel frame. Introduced 1995. Made in U.S.A. by Safari Arms, Inc.

Price: **$714.00**

SMITH & WESSON MODEL 41 TARGET

Caliber: 22 LR, 10-shot clip. **Barrel:** 5-1/2", 7". **Weight:** 44 oz. (5-1/2" barrel). **Length:** 9" overall (5-1/2" barrel). **Grips:** Checkered walnut with modified thumbrest, usable with either hand. **Sights:** 1/8" Patridge on ramp base; micro-click rear adjustable for windage and elevation. **Features:** 3/8" wide, grooved trigger; adjustable trigger stop drilled and tapped.

Price: S&W Bright Blue, either barrel **$958.00**

SMITH & WESSON MODEL 22A TARGET PISTOL

Caliber: 22 LR, 10-shot magazine. **Barrel:** 5-1/2" bull. **Weight:** 38.5 oz. **Length:** 9-1/2" overall. **Grips:** Dymondwood with ambidextrous thumbrests and flared bottom or rubber soft touch with thumbrest. **Sights:** Patridge front, fully adjustable rear. **Features:** Sight bridge with Weaver-style integral optics mount; alloy frame, stainless barrel and slide; blue finish. Introduced 1997. Made in U.S.A. by Smith & Wesson.

Price: **$367.00**
Price: HiViz front sight **$387.00**
Price: Camo model **$355.00**

Smith & Wesson Model 22S Target Pistol

Similar to the Model 22A except has stainless steel frame. Introduced 1997. Made in U.S.A. by Smith & Wesson.

Price: **$434.00**
Price: HiViz front sight **$453.00**

SPRINGFIELD, INC. 1911A1 BULLSEYE WADCUTTER PISTOL

Caliber: 38 Super, 45 ACP. **Barrel:** 5". **Weight:** 45 oz. **Length:** 8.59" overall (5" barrel). **Grips:** Checkered walnut. **Sights:** Bo-Mar rib with undercut blade front, fully adjustable rear. **Features:** Built for wadcutter loads only. Has full-length recoil spring guide rod, fitted Videki speed trigger with 3.5-lb. pull; match Commander hammer and sear; beavertail grip safety; lowered and flared ejection port; tuned extractor; fitted slide to frame; recoil buffer system; beveled and polished magazine well; checkered front strap and steel mainspring housing (flat housing standard); polished and throated National Match barrel and bushing. Comes with two magazines with slam pads, plastic carrying case, test target. Introduced 1992. From Springfield, Inc.

Price: **$1,499.00**
Price: Adj. Target **$1,049.00**
Price: M1911SC, Commander style **$1,029.00**

Springfield, Inc. Basic Competition Pistol

Has low-mounted Bo-Mar adjustable rear sight, undercut blade front; match throated barrel and bushing; polished feed ramp; lowered and flared ejection port; fitted Videki speed trigger with tuned 3.5-lb. pull; fitted slide to frame; recoil buffer system; checkered walnut grips; serrated, arched mainspring housing. Comes with two magazines with slam pads, plastic carrying case. Introduced 1992. From Springfield, Inc.

Price: 45 ACP, blue, 5" only **$1,295.00**

Springfield, Inc. Expert

Springfield, Inc. N.M. Hardball

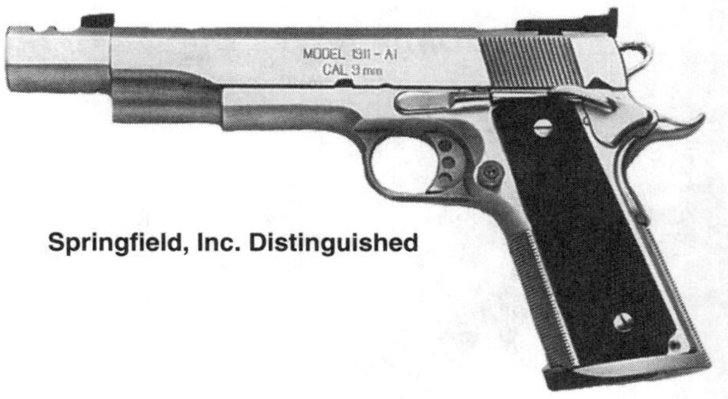

Springfield, Inc. Distinguished

Springfield, Inc. 1911A1 Trophy Match

Springfield, Inc. Expert Pistol

Similar to the Competition Pistol except has triple-chamber tapered cone compensator on match barrel with dovetailed front sight; lowered and flared ejection port; fully tuned for reliability; fitted slide to frame; extended ambidextrous thumb safety, extended magazine release button; beavertail grip safety; Pachmayr wrap-around grips. Comes with two magazines, plastic carrying case. Introduced 1992. From Springfield, Inc.

Price: 45 ACP, Duotone finish **$1,724.00**
Price: Expert Ltd. (non-compensated) **$1,624.00**

Springfield, Inc. Distinguished Pistol

Has all the features of the 1911A1 Expert except is full-house pistol with deluxe Bo-Mar low-mounted adjustable rear sight; full-length recoil spring guide rod and recoil spring retainer; checkered frontstrap; S&A magazine well; walnut grips. Hard chrome finish. Comes with two magazines with slam pads, plastic carrying case. From Springfield, Inc.

Price: 45 ACP **$2,445.00**
Price: Distinguished Limited (non-compensated) **$2,345.00**

Springfield, Inc. 1911A1 N.M. Hardball Pistol

Has Bo-Mar adjustable rear sight with undercut front blade; fitted match Videki trigger with 4-lb. pull; fitted slide to frame; throated National Match barrel and bushing, polished feed ramp; recoil buffer system; tuned extractor; Herrett walnut grips. Comes with two magazines, plastic carrying case, test target. Introduced 1992. From Springfield, Inc.

Price: 45 ACP, blue **$1,336.00**

Springfield, Inc. Leatham Legend TGO Series Pistols

Three models of 5" barrel, 45 ACP 1911 pistols built for serious competition. TGO 1 has deluxe low mount Bo-Mar rear sight, Dawson fiber optics front sight, 3.5 lb. trigger pull. TGO 2 has Bo-Mar low mount adjustable rear sight, Dawson fiber optic front sight, 4.5 to 5 lb. trigger pull. TGO 3 has Springfield Armory fully adjustable rear sight with low mount Bo-Mar cut Dawson fiber optic front sight, 4.5 to 5 lb. trigger.

Price: TGO 1 .... **$2,999.00**
Price: TGO 2 .... **$1,899.00**
Price: TGO 3 .... **$1,295.00**

Springfield, Inc. Trophy Match Pistol

Similar to Springfield, Inc.'s Full Size model, but designed for bullseye and action shooting competition. Available with a Service Model 5" frame with matching slide and barrel in 5" and 6" lengths. Fully adjustable sights, checkered frame front strap, match barrel and bushing. In 45 ACP only. From Springfield Inc.

Price: **$1,248.00**

STI EAGLE 5.0, 6.0 PISTOL

Caliber: 9mm, 9x21, 38 & 40 Super, 40 S&W, 10mm, 45 ACP, 10-shot magazine. **Barrel:** 5", 6" bull. **Weight:** 34.5 oz. **Length:** 8.62" overall. **Grips:** Checkered polymer. **Sights:** STI front, Novak or Heine rear. **Features:** Standard frames plus 7 others; adjustable match trigger; skeletonized hammer; extended grip safety with locator pad; match-grade fit of all parts. Many options available. Introduced 1994. Made in U.S.A. by STI International.

Price: .... (5.0 Eagle) **$1,794.00**, (6.0 Eagle) **$1,894.00**

STI EXECUTIVE PISTOL

Caliber: 40 S&W. **Barrel:** 5" bull. **Weight:** 39 oz. **Length:** 8-5/8". **Grips:** Gray polymer. **Sights:** Dawson fiber optic, front; STI adjustable rear. **Features:** Stainless mag. well, front and rear serrations on slide. Made in U.S.A. by STI.

Price: **$2,389.00**

STI TROJAN

Caliber: 9mm, 38 Super, 40S&W, 45 ACP. **Barrel:** 5", 6". **Weight:** 36 oz. **Length:** 8.5". **Grips:** Rosewood. **Sights:** STI front with STI adjustable rear. **Features:** Stippled front strap, flat top slide, one-piece steel guide rod.

Price: (Trojan 5") **$1,024.00**
Price: (Trojan 6", not available in 38 Super) **$1,232.50**

WALTHER GSP MATCH PISTOL

Caliber: 22 LR, 32 S&W Long (GSP-C), 5-shot magazine. **Barrel:** 4.22". **Weight:** 44.8 oz. (22 LR), 49.4 oz. (32). **Length:** 11.8" overall. **Grips:** Walnut. **Sights:** Post front, match rear adjustable for windage and elevation. **Features:** Available with either 2.2-lb. (1000 gm) or 3-lb. (1360 gm) trigger. Spare magazine, barrel weight, tools supplied. Imported from Germany by Nygord Precision Products.

Price: GSP, with case **$1,495.00**
Price: GSP-C, with case **$1,595.00**

Includes models suitable for hunting and competitive courses of fire, both police and international.

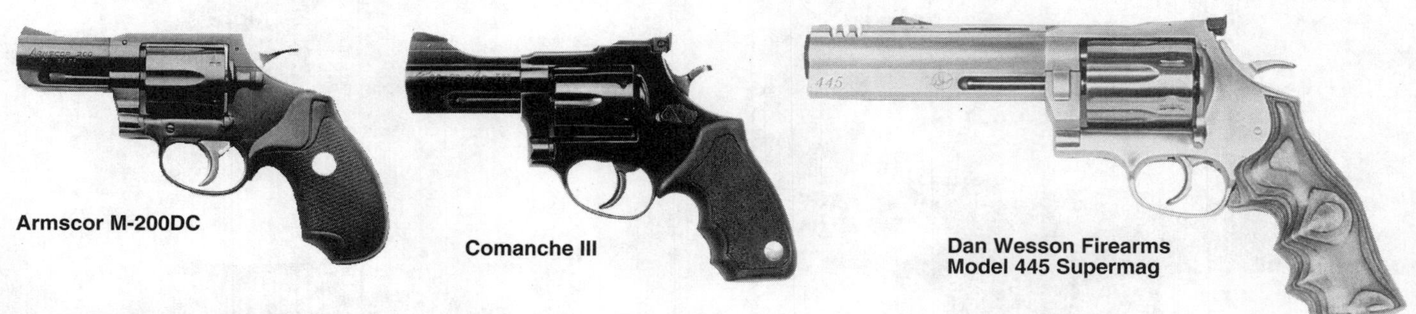

Armscor M-200DC

Comanche III

Dan Wesson Firearms Model 445 Supermag

ARMSCOR M-200DC REVOLVER

Caliber: 38 Spec., 6-shot cylinder. **Barrel:** 2-1/2", 4". **Weight:** 22 oz. (2-1/2" barrel). **Length:** 7-3/8" overall (2-1/2" barrel). **Grips:** Checkered rubber. **Sights:** Blade front, fixed notch rear. **Features:** All-steel construction; floating firing pin, transfer bar ignition; shrouded ejector rod; blue finish. Reintroduced 1996. Imported from the Philippines by K.B.I., Inc.

Price: 2-1/2" **$199.99**
Price: 4" **$205.00**

ARMSPORT MODEL 4540 REVOLVER

Caliber: 38 Special. **Barrel:** 4". **Weight:** 32 oz **Length:** 9" overall. **Sights:** Fixed rear, blade front. **Features:** Ventilated rib; blued finish. Imported from Argentina by Armsport Inc.

Price: **$140.00**

COMANCHE I, II, III DA REVOLVERS

Features: Adjustable sights. Blue or stainless finish. Distributed by SGS Importers.

Price: I 22 LR, 6" bbl, 9-shot, blue **$236.95**
Price: I 22LR, 6" bbl, 9-shot, stainless **$258.95**
Price: II 38 Special, 3", 4" bbl, 6-shot, blue **$219.95**
Price: II 38 Special, 4" bbl, 6-shot, stainless **$236.95**
Price: III 357 Mag, 3", 4", 6" bbl, 6-shot, blue **$253.95**
Price: III 357 Mag, 3", 4", 6" bbl, 6-shot, stainless **$274.95**
Price: II 38 Special, 3" bbl, 6-shot, stainless steel **$236.95**

DAN WESSON FIREARMS MODEL 722 SILHOUETTE REVOLVER

Caliber: 22 LR, 6-shot. **Barrel:** 10", vent heavy. **Weight:** 53 oz. **Grips:** Combat style. **Sights:** Patridge-style front, .080" narrow notch rear. **Features:** Single-action-only. Satin brushed stainless finish. Reintroduced 1997. Made in U.S.A. by Dan Wesson Firearms.

Price: 722 VH10 (vent heavy 10" bbl.) **$888.00**
Price: 722 VH10 SRS1 (Super Ram Silhouette, Bo-Mar sights, front hood, trigger job) **$1,164.00**

DAN WESSON FIREARMS MODEL 3220/73220 TARGET REVOLVER

Caliber: 32-20, 6-shot. **Barrel:** 2.5", 4", 6", 8", 10" standard vent, vent heavy. **Weight:** 47 oz. (6" VH). **Length:** 11.25" overall. **Grips:** Hogue Gripper rubber (walnut, exotic hardwoods optional). **Sights:** Red ramp interchangeable front, fully adjustable rear. **Features:** Bright blue (3220) or stainless (73220). Reintroduced 1997. Made in U.S.A. by Dan Wesson Firearms.

Price: 3220 VH2.5 (blued, 2.5" vent heavy bbl.) **$643.00**
Price: 73220 VH10 (stainless 10" vent heavy bbl.) **$873.00**

DAN WESSON FIREARMS MODEL 40/740 REVOLVERS

Caliber: 357 Maximum, 6-shot. **Barrel:** 4", 6", 8", 10". **Weight:** 72 oz. (8" bbl.). **Length:** 14.3" overall (8" bbl.). **Grips:** Hogue Gripper rubber (walnut or exotic hardwood optional). **Sights:** 1/8" serrated front, fully adjustable rear. **Features:** Blue or stainless steel. Made in U.S.A. by Dan Wesson Firearms.

Price: Blue, 4" **$702.00**
Price: Blue, 6" **$749.00**
Price: Blue, 8" **$795.00**
Price: Blue, 10" **$858.00**
Price: Stainless, 4" **$834.00**
Price: Stainless, 6" **$892.00**
Price: Stainless, 8" slotted **$1,024.00**
Price: Stainless, 10" **$998.00**
Price: 4", 6", 8" Compensated, blue . . . . **$749.00 to $885.00**
Price: As above, stainless . . . . **$893.00 to $1,061.00**

Dan Wesson Firearms Model 414/7414 and 445/7445 SuperMag Revolvers

Similar size and weight as Model 40 revolvers. Chambered for 414 SuperMag or 445 SuperMag cartridge. Barrel lengths of 4", 6", 8", 10". Contact maker for complete price list. Reintroduced 1997. Made in the U.S. by Dan Wesson Firearms.

Price: 4", vent heavy, blue or stainless **$904.00**
Price: 8", vent heavy, blue or stainless **$1,026.00**
Price: 10", vent heavy, blue or stainless **$1,103.00**
Price: Compensated models . . . . **$965.00 to $1,149.00**

DAN WESSON FIREARMS MODEL 22/722 REVOLVERS

Caliber: 22 LR, 22 WMR, 6-shot. **Barrel:** 2-1/2", 4", 6", 8" or 10"; interchangeable. **Weight:** 36 oz. (2-1/2"), 44 oz. (6"). **Length:** 9-1/4" overall (4" barrel). **Grips:** Hogue Gripper rubber (walnut, exotic woods optional). **Sights:** 1/8" serrated, interchangeable front, white outline rear adjustable for windage and elevation. **Features:** Built on the same frame as the Wesson 357; smooth, wide trigger with over-travel adjustment, wide spur hammer, with short double-action travel. Available in blue or stainless steel. Reintroduced 1997. Contact Dan Wesson Firearms for complete price list.

Price: 22 VH2.5/722 VH2.5 (blued or stainless 2-1/2" bbl.) **$551.00**
Price: 22VH10/722 VH10 (blued or stainless 10" bbl.) **$750.00**

Dan Wesson 722M Small Frame Revolver

Similar to Model 22/722 except chambered for 22 WMR. Blued or stainless finish, 2-1/2", 4", 6", 8" or 10" barrels.

Price: Blued or stainless finish . . . . **$643.00 to $873.00**

DAN WESSON FIREARMS MODEL 15/715 and 32/732 REVOLVERS

Caliber: 32-20, 32 H&R Mag. (Model 32), 357 Mag. (Model 15). **Barrel:** 2-1/2", 4", 6", 8" (M32), 2-1/2", 4", 6", 8", 10" (M15); vent heavy. **Weight:** 36 oz. (2-1/2" barrel). **Length:** 9-1/4" overall (4" barrel). **Grips:** Checkered, interchangeable. **Sights:** 1/8" serrated front, fully adjustable rear. **Features:** New Generation Series. Interchangeable barrels; wide, smooth trigger, wide hammer spur; short double-action travel. Available in blue or stainless. Reintroduced 1997. Made in U.S.A. by Dan Wesson Firearms. Contact maker for full list of models.

Price: Model 15/715, 2-1/2" (blue or stainless) **$551.00**
Price: Model 15/715, 8" (blue or stainless) **$612.00**
Price: Model 15/715, compensated . . . . **$704.00 to $827.00**
Price: Model 32/732, 4" (blue or stainless) **$674.00**
Price: Model 32/732, 8" (blue or stainless) **$766.00**

Handguns — Double Action Revolvers, Service & Sport

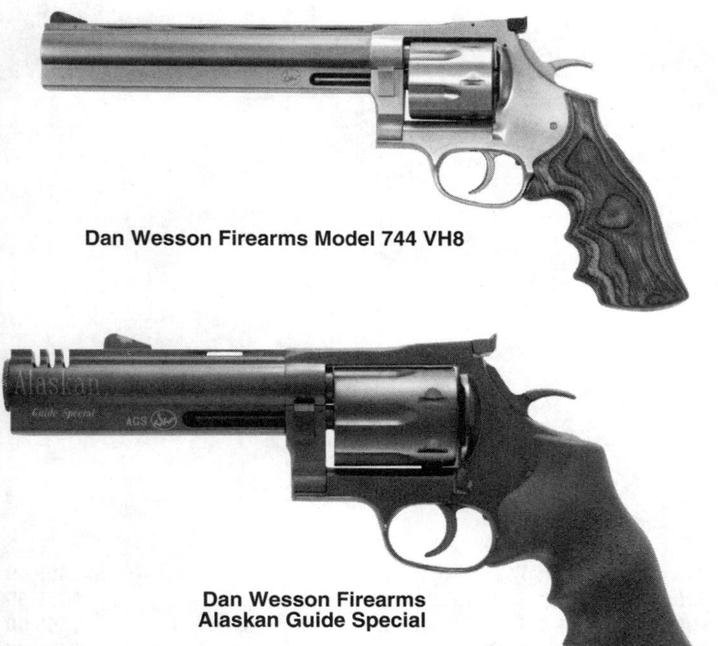

Dan Wesson Firearms Model 744 VH8

Dan Wesson Firearms
Super Ram Silhouette

Dan Wesson Firearms
Alaskan Guide Special

DAN WESSON FIREARMS MODEL 41/741, 44/744 and 45/745 REVOLVERS

Caliber: 41 Mag., 44 Mag., 45 Colt, 6-shot. **Barrel:** 4", 6", 8", 10"; interchangeable; 4", 6", 8" Compensated. **Weight:** 48 oz. (4"). **Length:** 12" overall (6" bbl.) **Grips:** Smooth. **Sights:** 1/8" serrated front, white outline rear adjustable for windage and elevation. **Features:** Available in blue or stainless steel. Smooth, wide trigger with adjustable over-travel, wide hammer spur. Available in Pistol Pac set also. Reintroduced 1997. Contact Dan Wesson Firearms for complete price list.

Price: 41 Mag., 4", vent heavy (blue or stainless). **$643.00**
Price: 44 Mag., 6", vent heavy (blue or stainless). **$689.00**
Price: 45 Colt, 8", vent heavy (blue or stainless) **$766.00**
Price: Compensated models (all calibers) . . . . **$812.00 to $934.00**

DAN WESSON FIREARMS LARGE FRAME SERIES REVOLVERS

Caliber: 41, 741/41 Magnum; 44, 744/44 Magnum; 45, 745/45 Long Colt; 360, 7360/357; 460, 7460/45. **Barrel:** 2"-10". **Weight:** 49 oz.-69 oz. **Grips:** Standard, Hogue rubber Gripper Grips. **Sights:** Standard front, serrated ramp with color insert. Standard rear, adustable wide notch. Other sight options available. **Features:** Available in blue or stainless steel. Smooth, wide trigger with overtravel, wide hammer spur. Double- and single-action.

Price: . . . . **$769.00 to $889.00**

DAN WESSON FIREARMS MODEL 360/7360 REVOLVERS

Caliber: 357 Mag. **Barrel:** 4", 6", 8", 10"; vent heavy. **Weight:** 64 oz. (8" barrel). **Grips:** Hogue rubber finger groove. **Sights:** Interchangeable ramp or Patridge front, fully adjustable rear. **Features:** New Generation Large Frame Series. Interchangeable barrels and grips; smooth trigger, wide hammer spur. Blue (360) or stainless (7360). Introduced 1999. Made in U.S.A. by Dan Wesson Firearms.

Price: 4" bbl., blue or stainless **$735.00**
Price: 10" bbl., blue or stainless **$873.00**
Price: Compensated models . . . . **$858.00 to $980.00**

DAN WESSON FIREARMS MODEL 460/7460 REVOLVERS

Caliber: 45 ACP, 45 Auto Rim, 45 Super, 45 Winchester Magnum and 460 Rowland. **Barrel:** 4", 6", 8", 10"; vent heavy. **Weight:** 49 oz. (4" barrel). **Grips:** Hogue rubber finger groove; interchangeable. **Sights:** Interchangeable ramp or Patridge front, fully adjustable rear. **Features:** New Generation Large Frame Series. Shoots five cartridges (45 ACP, 45 Auto Rim, 45 Super, 45 Winchester Magnum and 460 Rowland; six half-moon clips for auto cartridges included). Interchangeable barrels and grips. Available with non-fluted cylinder and Slotted Lightweight barrel shroud. Introduced 1999. Made in U.S.A. by Dan Wesson Firearms.

Price: 4" bbl., blue or stainless **$735.00**
Price: 10" bbl., blue or stainless **$888.00**
Price: Compensated models . . . . **$919.00 to $1,042.00**

DAN WESSON FIREARMS STANDARD SILHOUETTE REVOLVERS

Caliber: 357 SuperMag/Maxi, 41 Mag., 414 SuperMag, 445 SuperMag. **Barrel:** 8", 10". **Weight:** 64 oz. (8" barrel). **Length:** 14.3" overall (8" barrel). **Grips:** Hogue rubber finger groove; interchangeable. **Sights:** Patridge front, fully adjustable rear. **Features:** Interchangeable barrels and grips, fluted or non-fluted cylinder, satin brushed stainless finish. Introduced 1999. Made in U.S.A. by Dan Wesson Firearms.

Price: 357 SuperMag/Maxi, 8" **$1,057.00**
Price: 41 Mag., 10" **$888.00**
Price: 414 SuperMag., 8" **$1,057.00**
Price: 445 SuperMag., 8" **$1,057.00**

Dan Wesson Firearms Super Ram Silhouette Revolver

Similar to Standard Silhouette except has 10 land and groove Laser Coat barrel, Bo-Mar target sights with hooded front, special laser engraving. Fluted or non-fluted cylinder. Introduced 1999. Made in U.S.A. by Dan Wesson Firearms.

Price: 357 SuperMag/Maxi, 414 SuperMag., 445 SuperMag., 8", blue or stainless **$1,364.00**
Price: 41 Magnum, 44 Magnum, 8", blue or stainless **$1,241.00**
Price: 41 Magnum, 44 Magnum, 10", blue or stainless **$1,333.00**

DAN WESSON FIREARMS ALASKAN GUIDE SPECIAL

Caliber: 445 SuperMag, 44 Magnum. **Barrel:** Compensated 4" vent heavy barrel assembly. **Features:** Stainless steel with baked on, non-glare, matte black coating, special laser engraving.

Price: Model 7445 VH4C AGS **$995.00**
Price: Model 744 VH4C AGS **$855.00**

EAA WINDICATOR REVOLVERS

Caliber: 38 Spec., 6-shot; 357 magnum, 6-shot. **Barrel:** 2", 4". **Weight:** 38 oz. (22 rimfire, 4"). **Length:** 8.5" overall (4" bbl.). **Grips:** Rubber with finger grooves. **Sights:** Blade front, fixed or adjustable on rimfires; fixed only on 32, 38. **Features:** Swing-out cylinder; hammer block safety; blue finish. Introduced 1991. Imported from Germany by European American Armory.

Price: 38 Special 2" **$249.00**
Price: 38 Special, 4" **$259.00**
Price: 357 Magnum, 2" **$259.00**
Price: 357 Magnum, 4" **$279.00**

KORTH COMBAT REVOLVER

Caliber: .357 Mag., .32 S&W Long, 9mm Para., .22 WMR, .22 LR. **Barrel:** 3", 4", 5-1/4", 6", 8". **Sights:** Fully-adjustable, rear; Baughman ramp, front. **Grips:** Walnut (checkered or smooth). Also available as a Target model in .22 LR, .38 Spl., .32 S&W Long, .357 Mag. with undercut partridge front sight; fully-adjustable rear. Made in Germany. Imported by Korth USA.

Price: . . . . From **$5,442.00**

HANDGUNS — DOUBLE ACTION REVOLVERS, SERVICE & SPORT

Medusa Model 47

Ruger GP-161

Ruger KGP-141

HANDGUNS

KORTH TROJA REVOLVER

Caliber: .357 Mag. **Barrel:** 6". **Finish:** Matte blue. **Grips:** Smooth, oversized finger contoured walnut. **Features:** Maintaining all of the precision German craftsmanship that has made this line famous, the final surface finish is not as finely polished as the firm's other products; thus the lower price. Introduced 2003. Imported from Germany by Korth USA.

Price: . . . . From **$3,995.00**

MEDUSA MODEL 47 REVOLVER

Caliber: Most 9mm, 38 and 357 caliber cartridges; 6-shot cylinder. **Barrel:** 2-1/2", 3", 4", 5", 6"; fluted. **Weight:** 39 oz. **Length:** 10" overall (4" barrel). **Grips:** Gripper-style rubber. **Sights:** Changeable front blades, fully adjustable rear. **Features:** Patented extractor allows gun to chamber, fire and extract over 25 different cartridges in the .355 to .357 range, without half-moon clips. Steel frame and cylinder; match quality barrel. Matte blue finish. Introduced 1996. Made in U.S.A. by Phillips & Rogers, Inc.

Price: **$899.00**

ROSSI MODEL 351/352 REVOLVERS

Caliber: 38 Special +P, 5-shot. **Barrel:** 2". **Weight:** 24 oz. **Length:** 6-1/2" overall. **Grips:** Rubber. **Sights:** Blade front, fixed rear. **Features:** Patented key-lock Taurus Security System; forged steel frame handles +P ammunition. Introduced 2001. Imported by BrazTech/Taurus.

Price: Model 351 (blued finish) **$298.00**
Price: Model 352 (stainless finish) **$345.00**

ROSSI MODEL 461/462 REVOLVERS

Caliber: 357 Magnum +P, 6-shot. **Barrel:** 2". **Weight:** 26 oz. **Length:** 6-1/2" overall. **Grips:** Rubber. **Sights:** Fixed. **Features:** Single/double action. Patented key-lock Taurus Security System; forged steel frame handles +P ammunition. Introduced 2001. Imported by BrazTech/Taurus.

Price: Model 461 (blued finish) **$298.00**
Price: Model 462 (stainless finish) **$345.00**

ROSSI MODEL 971/972 REVOLVERS

Caliber: 357 Magnum +P, 6-shot. **Barrel:** 4", 6". **Weight:** 40-44 oz. **Length:** 8-1/2" or 10-1/2" overall. **Grips:** Rubber. **Sights:** Fully adjustable. **Features:** Single/double action. Patented key-lock Taurus Security System; forged steel frame handles +P ammunition. Introduced 2001. Imported by BrazTech/Taurus.

Price: Model 971 (blued finish, 4" barrel) **$345.00**
Price: Model 972 (stainless steel finish, 6" barrel) **$391.00**

Rossi Model 851

Similar to Model 971/972, chambered for 38 Special +P. Blued finish, 4" barrel. Introduced 2001. From BrazTech/Taurus.

Price: **$298.00**

RUGER GP-100 REVOLVERS

Caliber: 38 Spec., 357 Mag., 6-shot. **Barrel:** 3", 3" full shroud, 4", 4" full shroud, 6", 6" full shroud. **Weight:** 3" barrel-35 oz., 3" full shroud-36 oz., 4" barrel-37 oz., 4" full shroud-38 oz. **Sights:** Fixed; adjustable on 4" full shroud, all 6" barrels. **Grips:** Ruger Santoprene Cushioned Grip with Goncalo Alves inserts. **Features:** Uses action, frame incorporating improvements and features of both the Security-Six and Redhawk revolvers. Full length, short ejector shroud. Satin blue and stainless steel.

Price: GP-141 (357, 4" full shroud, adj. sights, blue) **$499.00**
Price: GP-160 (357, 6", adj. sights, blue) **$499.00**
Price: GP-161 (357, 6" full shroud, adj. sights, blue), 46 oz. **$499.00**
Price: GPF-331 (357, 3" full shroud) **$495.00**

Ruger KSP-331X

Price: GPF-340 (357, 4") **$495.00**
Price: GPF-341 (357, 4" full shroud) **$495.00**
Price: KGP-141 (357, 4" full shroud, adj. sights, stainless) **$555.00**
Price: KGP-160 (357, 6", adj. sights, stainless), 43 oz. **$555.00**
Price: KGP-161 (357, 6" full shroud, adj. sights, stainless) 46 oz. **$555.00**
Price: KGPF-330 (357, 3", stainless) **$555.00**
Price: KGPF-331 (357, 3" full shroud, stainless) **$555.00**
Price: KGPF-340 (357, 4", stainless), KGPF-840 (38 Special). . . **$555.00**
Price: KGPF-341 (357, 4" full shroud, stainless) **$555.00**
Price: KGPF-840 (38 Special, 4", stainless) **$555.00**

Ruger SP101 Double-Action-Only Revolver

Similar to standard SP101 except double-action-only with no single-action sear notch. Spurless hammer for snag-free handling, floating firing pin and Ruger's patented transfer bar safety system. Available with 2-1/4" barrel in 357 Magnum. Weighs 25 oz., overall length 7.06". Natural brushed satin, high-polish stainless steel. Introduced 1993.

Price: KSP321XL (357 Mag.) **$495.00**

RUGER SP101 REVOLVERS

Caliber: 22 LR, 32 H&R Mag., 6-shot; 38 Spec. +P, 357 Mag., 5-shot. **Barrel:** 2-1/4", 3-1/16", 4". **Weight:** (38 & 357 mag models) 2-1/4"-25 oz.; 3-1/16"-27 oz. **Sights:** Adjustable on 22, 32, fixed on others. **Grips:** Ruger Cushioned Grip with inserts. **Features:** Incorporates improvements and features found in the GP-100 revolvers into a compact, small frame, double-action revolver. Full-length ejector shroud. Stainless steel only. Introduced 1988.

Price: KSP-821X (2-1/4", 38 Spec.) **$495.00**
Price: KSP-831X (3-1/16", 38 Spec.) **$495.00**
Price: KSP-241X (4" heavy bbl., 22 LR), 34 oz. **$495.00**
Price: KSP-3231X (3-1/16", 32 H&R), 30 oz. **$495.00**
Price: KSP-321X (2-1/4", 357 Mag.) **$495.00**
Price: KSP-331X (3-1/16", 357 Mag.) **$495.00**
Price: KSP-3241X (32 Mag., 4" bbl) **$495.00**

CONSULT
SHOOTER'S MARKETPLACE
Page 125, This Edition

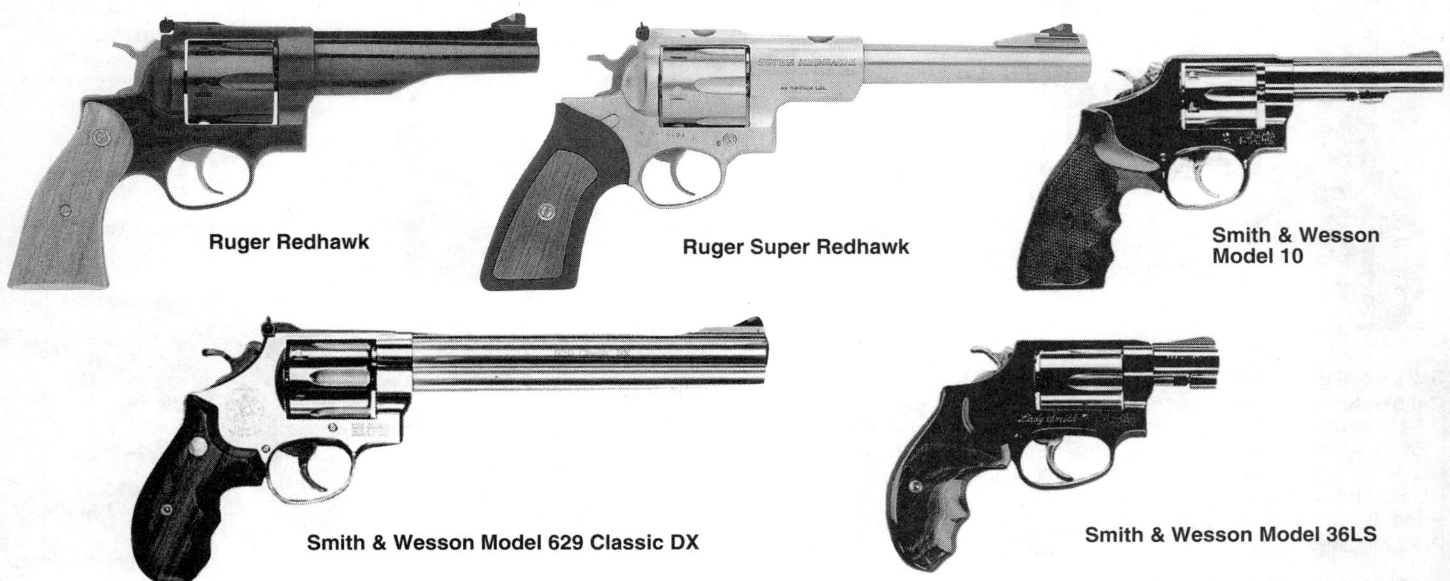

Ruger Redhawk

Ruger Super Redhawk

Smith & Wesson Model 10

Smith & Wesson Model 629 Classic DX

Smith & Wesson Model 36LS

RUGER REDHAWK

Caliber: 44 Rem. Mag., 45 Colt, 6-shot. **Barrel:** 5-1/2", 7-1/2". **Weight:** About 54 oz. (7-1/2" bbl.). **Length:** 13" overall (7-1/2" barrel). **Grips:** Square butt cushioned grip panels. **Sights:** Interchangeable Patridge-type front, rear adjustable for windage and elevation. **Features:** Stainless steel, brushed satin finish, blued ordnance steel. 9-1/2" sight radius. Introduced 1979.

Price: Blued, 44 Mag., 5-1/2" RH-445, 7-1/2" RH-44 .... **$585.00**
Price: Blued, 44 Mag., 7-1/2" RH44R, with scope mount, rings .. **$625.00**
Price: Stainless, 44 Mag., KRH445, 5-1/2", 7-1/2" KRH-44 ..... **$645.00**
Price: Stainless, 44 Mag., 7-1/2", with scope mount, rings KRH-44R.......... **$685.00**
Price: Stainless, 45 Colt, KRH455, 5-1/2", 7-1/2" KRH-45 ...... **$645.00**
Price: Stainless, 45 Colt, 7-1/2", with scope mount and rings KRH-45R.......... **$685.00**

Ruger Super Redhawk Revolver

Similar to standard Redhawk except has heavy extended frame with Ruger Integral Scope Mounting System on wide topstrap. Also available 454 Casull and 480 Ruger. Wide hammer spur lowered for better scope clearance. Incorporates mechanical design features and improvements of GP-100. Choice of 7-1/2" or 9-1/2" barrel, both ramp front sight base with Redhawk-style Interchangeable Insert sight blades, adjustable rear sight. Comes with Ruger "Cushioned Grip" panels with wood panels. Target gray stainless steel. Introduced 1987.

Price: KSRH-7 (7-1/2"), KSRH-9 (9-1/2"), 44 Mag **$685.00**
Price: KSRH-7454 (7-1/2") 454 Casull, 9-1/2 KSRH-9454 ...... **$775.00**
Price: KSRH-7480 (7-1/2") 480 Ruger **$775.00**
Price: KSRH-9480 (9-1/2") 480 Ruger **$775.00**

SMITH & WESSON MODEL 10 M&P HB REVOLVER

Caliber: 38 Spec., 6-shot. **Barrel:** 4". **Weight:** 33.5 oz. **Length:** 9-5/16" overall. **Grips:** Uncle Mike's Combat soft rubber; square butt. **Sights:** Fixed; ramp front, square notch rear.

Price: Blue **$496.00**

SMITH & WESSON COMMEMORATIVE MODEL 29

Features: Reflects original Model 29: 6-1/2" barrel, four-screw side plate, over-sized target grips, red vamp front and black blade rear sights, 150th Anniversary logo, engraved, gold-plated, blue, in wood presentation case. Limited.

Price: .... **NA**

SMITH & WESSON MODEL 629 REVOLVERS

Caliber: 44 Magnum, 44 S&W Special, 6-shot. **Barrel:** 5", 6", 8-3/8". **Weight:** 47 oz. (6" bbl.). **Length:** 11-3/8" overall (6" bbl.). **Grips:** Soft rubber; wood optional. **Sights:** 1/8" red ramp front, white outline rear, internal lock, adjustable for windage and elevation.

Price: Model 629, 4" **$717.00**
Price: Model 629, 6" **$739.00**
Price: Model 629, 8-3/8" barrel **$756.00**

Smith & Wesson Model 629 Classic Revolver

Similar to standard Model 629, full-lug 5", 6-1/2" or 8-3/8" barrel, chamfered front of cylinder, interchangeable red ramp front sight with adjustable white outline rear, Hogue grips with S&W monogram, frame is drilled and tapped for scope mounting. Factory accurizing and endurance packages. Overall length with 5" barrel is 10-1/2"; weighs 51 oz. Introduced 1990.

Price: Model 629 Classic (stainless), 5", 6-1/2" **$768.00**
Price: As above, 8-3/8" **$793.00**
Price: Model 629 with HiViz front sight.................... **$814.00**

Smith & Wesson Model 629 Classic DX Revolver

Similar to Model 629 Classic, offered only with 6-1/2" or 8-3/8" full-lug barrel, five front sights: red ramp, black Patridge, black Patridge with gold bead, black ramp, black Patridge with white dot, white outline rear sight, adjustable sight, internal lock. Hogue combat-style and wood round butt grip. Introduced 1991.

Price: Model 629 Classic DX, 6-1/2"....................... **$986.00**
Price: As above, 8-3/8" **$1,018.00**

SMITH & WESSON MODEL 37 CHIEF'S SPECIAL & AIRWEIGHT

Caliber: 38 Spec. +P, 5-shot. **Barrel:** 1-7/8". **Weight:** 19-1/2 oz. (2" bbl.); 13-1/2 oz. (Airweight). **Length:** 6-1/2" (round butt). **Grips:** Round butt soft rubber. **Sights:** Fixed, serrated ramp front, square notch rear. Glass beaded finish.

Price: Model 37... **$523.00**

Smith & Wesson Model 637 Airweight Revolver

Similar to the Model 37 Airweight except has alloy frame, stainless steel barrel, cylinder and yoke; rated for 38 Spec. +P; Uncle Mike's Boot Grip. Weighs 15 oz. Introduced 1996. Made in U.S.A. by Smith & Wesson.

Price: **$548.00**

SMITH & WESSON MODEL 36LS, 60LS LADYSMITH

Caliber: .38 S&W Special +P, 5-shot. **Barrel:** 1-7/8". **Weight:** 20 oz. **Length:** 6-5/16 overall (1-7/8" barrel). **Grips:** Combat Dymondwood® grips with S&W monogram. **Sights:** Serrated ramp front, fixed notch rear. **Features:** Speedloader cutout. Comes in a fitted carry/storage case. Introduced 1989.

Price: Model 36LS **$518.00**
Price: Model 60LS, 2-1/8" barrel stainless, 357 Magnum....... **$566.00**

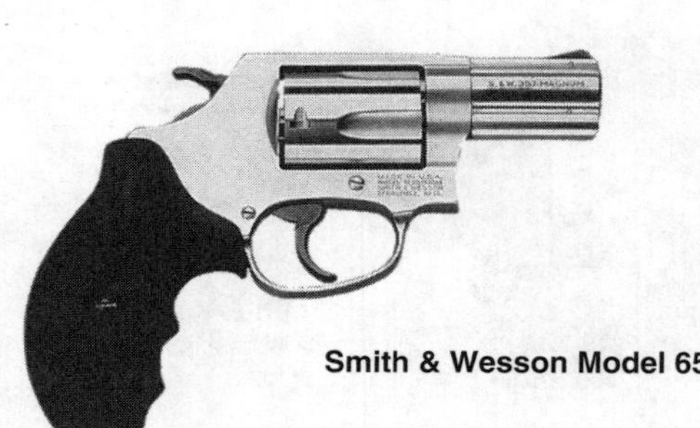

Smith & Wesson Model 65LS

Smith & Wesson Model 317 AirLite

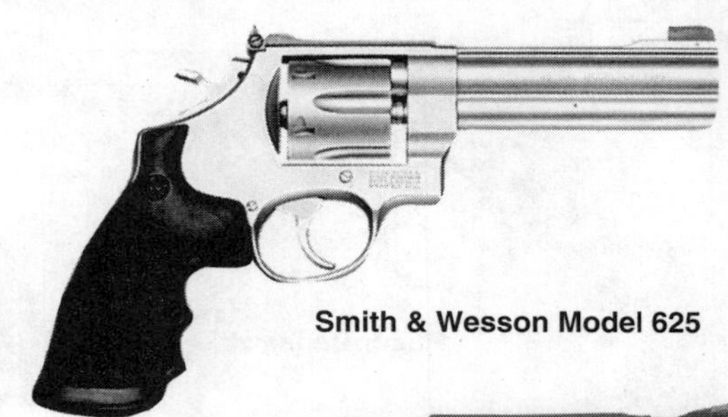

Smith & Wesson Model 625

SMITH & WESSON MODEL 60 CHIEF'S SPECIAL

Caliber: 357 Magnum, 5-shot. **Barrel:** 2-1/8" or 3". **Weight:** 24 oz. **Length:** 7-1/2 overall (3" barrel). **Grips:** Rounded butt synthetic grips. **Sights:** Fixed, serrated ramp front, square notch rear. **Features:** Stainless steel construction, 3" full lug barrel, adjustable sights, internal lock. Made in U.S.A. by Smith & Wesson.

Price: 2-1/8" barrel **$541.00**
Price: 3" barrel **$574.00**

SMITH & WESSON MODEL 65

Caliber: 357 Mag. and 38 Spec., 6-shot. **Barrel:** 4". **Weight:** 34 oz. **Length:** 9-5/16" overall (4" bbl.). **Grips:** Uncle Mike's Combat. **Sights:** 1/8" serrated ramp front, fixed square notch rear. **Features:** Heavy barrel. Stainless steel construction. Internal lock.

Price: **$531.00**

SMITH & WESSON MODEL 317 AIRLITE, 317 LADYSMITH REVOLVERS

Caliber: 22 LR, 8-shot. **Barrel:** 1-7/8" 3". **Weight:** 9.9 oz. **Length:** 6-3/16" overall. **Grips:** Dymondwood Boot or Uncle Mike's Boot. **Sights:** Serrated ramp front, fixed notch rear. **Features:** Aluminum alloy, carbon and stainless steels, and titanium construction. Short spur hammer, smooth combat trigger. Clear Cote finish. Introduced 1997. Made in U.S.A. by Smith & Wesson.

Price: With Uncle Mike's Boot grip **$550.00**
Price: With DymondWood Boot grip, 3" barrel, HiViz front sight, internal lock................ **$600.00**
Price: Model 317 LadySmith (DymondWood only, comes with display case) **$596.00**

SMITH & WESSON MODEL 351PD

Caliber: 22 Mag. **Barrel:** 2". **Features:** Seven-shot, Scandium alloy.

Price: **$625.00**

SMITH & WESSON MODEL 64 STAINLESS M&P

Caliber: 38 Spec. +P, 6-shot. **Barrel:** 2", 3", 4". **Weight:** 34 oz. **Length:** 9-5/16" overall. **Grips:** Soft rubber. **Sights:** Fixed, 1/8" serrated ramp front, square notch rear. **Features:** Satin finished stainless steel, square butt.

Price: 2" **$522.00**
Price: 3", 4"................ **$532.00**

SMITH & WESSON MODEL 65LS LADYSMITH

Caliber: 357 Magnum, 38 Spec. +P, 6-shot. **Barrel:** 3". **Weight:** 31 oz. **Length:** 7.94" overall. **Grips:** Rosewood, round butt. **Sights:** Serrated ramp front, fixed notch rear. **Features:** Stainless steel with frosted finish. Smooth combat trigger, service hammer, shrouded ejector rod. Comes with case. Introduced 1992.

Price: **$584.00**

SMITH & WESSON MODEL 66 STAINLESS COMBAT MAGNUM

Caliber: 357 Mag. and 38 Spec. +P, 6-shot. **Barrel:** 2-1/2", 4", 6". **Weight:** 36 oz. (4" barrel). **Length:** 9-9/16" overall. **Grips:** Soft rubber. **Sights:** Red ramp front, micro-click rear adjustable for windage and elevation. **Features:** Satin finish stainless steel. Internal lock.

Price: 2-1/2" **$590.00**
Price: 4" **$579.00**
Price: 6" **$608.00**

Smith & Wesson Model 340 PD Airlite Sc

SMITH & WESSON MODEL 67 COMBAT MASTERPIECE

Caliber: 38 Special, 6-shot. **Barrel:** 4". **Weight:** 32 oz. **Length:** 9-5/16" overall. **Grips:** Soft rubber. **Sights:** Red ramp front, micro-click rear adjustable for windage and elevation. **Features:** Stainless steel with satin finish. Smooth combat trigger, semi-target hammer. Introduced 1994.

Price: **$585.00**

Smith & Wesson Model 686 Magnum PLUS Revolver

Similar to the Model 686 except has 7-shot cylinder, 2-1/2", 4" or 6" barrel. Weighs 34-1/2 oz., overall length 7-1/2" (2-1/2" barrel). Hogue rubber grips. Internal lock. Introduced 1996. Made in U.S.A. by Smith & Wesson.

Price: 2-1/2" barrel **$631.00**
Price: 4" barrel **$653.00**
Price: 6" barrel **$663.00**

SMITH & WESSON MODEL 625 REVOLVER

Caliber: 45 ACP, 6-shot. **Barrel:** 5". **Weight:** 46 oz. **Length:** 11.375" overall. **Grips:** Soft rubber; wood optional. **Sights:** Patridge front on ramp, S&W micrometer click rear adjustable for windage and elevation. **Features:** Stainless steel construction with .400" semi-target hammer, .312" smooth combat trigger; full lug barrel. Glass beaded finish. Introduced 1989.

Price: 5" **$745.00**
Price: 4" with internal lock................ **$745.00**

SMITH & WESSON MODEL 640 CENTENNIAL DA ONLY

Caliber: 357 Mag., 38 Spec. +P, 5-shot. **Barrel:** 2-1/8". **Weight:** 25 oz. **Length:** 6-3/4" overall. **Grips:** Uncle Mike's Boot Grip. **Sights:** Serrated ramp front, fixed notch rear. **Features:** Stainless steel. Fully concealed hammer, snag-proof smooth edges. Internal lock. Introduced 1995 in 357 Magnum.

Price: **$599.00**

SMITH & WESSON MODEL 617 K-22 MASTERPIECE

Caliber: 22 LR, 6- or 10-shot. **Barrel:** 4", 6", 8-3/8". **Weight:** 42 oz. (4" barrel). **Length:** NA. **Grips:** Soft rubber. **Sights:** Patridge front, adjustable rear. Drilled and tapped for scope mount. **Features:** Stainless steel with satin finish; 4" has .312" smooth trigger, .375" semi-target hammer; 6" has either .312" combat or .400" serrated trigger, .375" semi-target or .500" target hammer; 8-3/8" with .400" serrated trigger, .500" target hammer. Introduced 1990.

Price: 4" **$644.00**
Price: 6", target hammer, target trigger **$625.00**
Price: 6", 10-shot **$669.00**
Price: 8-3/8", 10 shot **$679.00**

SMITH & WESSON MODEL 610 CLASSIC HUNTER REVOLVER

Caliber: 10mm, 40 S&W, 6-shot cylinder. **Barrel:** 6-1/2" full lug. **Weight:** 52 oz. **Length:** 12" overall. **Grips:** Hogue rubber combat. **Sights:** Interchangeable blade front, micro-click rear adjustable for windage and elevation. **Features:** Stainless steel construction; target hammer, target trigger; unfluted cylinder; drilled and tapped for scope mounting. Introduced 1998.

Price: **$785.00**

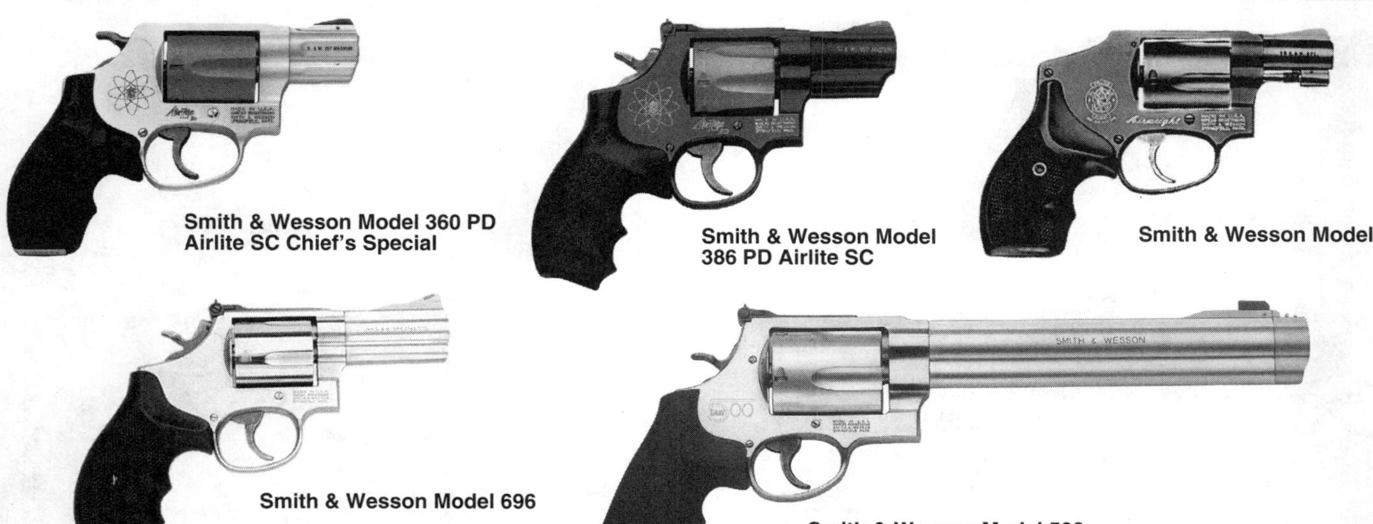

Smith & Wesson Model 360 PD Airlite SC Chief's Special

Smith & Wesson Model 386 PD Airlite SC

Smith & Wesson Model 442

Smith & Wesson Model 696

Smith & Wesson Model 500

SMITH & WESSON MODEL 340 PD AIRLITE Sc CENTENNIAL

Caliber: 357 Magnum, 38 Spec. +P, 5-shot. **Barrel:** 1-7/8". **Grips:** Round-ed butt grip. **Sights:** HiViz front. **Features:** Synthetic grip, internal lock. Blue.

Price: **$799.00**

SMITH & WESSON MODEL 360 PD AIRLITE Sc CHIEF'S SPECIAL

Caliber: 357 Magnum, 38 Spec. +P, 5-shot. **Barrel:** 1-7/8". **Grips:** Round-ed butt grip. **Sights:** Fixed. **Features:** Synthetic grip, internal lock. Stainless.

Price: Red ramp front **$767.00**
Price: HiViz front. **$781.00**

SMITH & WESSON MODEL 386 PD AIRLITE Sc

Caliber: 357 Magnum, 38 Spec. +P, 7-shot. **Barrel:** 2-1/2". **Grips:** Round-ed butt grip. **Sights:** Adjustable, HiViz front. **Features:** Synthetic grip, internal lock.

Price: Blue **$815.00**

SMITH & WESSON MODEL 331, 332 AIRLITE Ti REVOLVERS

Caliber: 32 H&R Mag., 6-shot. **Barrel:** 1-7/8". **Weight:** 11.2 oz. (with wood grip). **Length:** 6-15/16" overall. **Grips:** Uncle Mike's Boot or Dymondwood Boot. **Sights:** Black serrated ramp front, fixed notch rear. **Features:** Aluminum alloy frame, barrel shroud and yoke; titanium cylinder; stainless steel barrel liner. Matte finish. Introduced 1999. Made in U.S.A. by Smith & Wesson.

Price: Model 331 Chiefs **$716.00**
Price: Model 332, internal lock **$734.00**

SMITH & WESSON MODEL 337 CHIEF'S SPECIAL AIRLITE Ti

Caliber: 38 Spec. +P, 5-shot. **Barrel:** 1-7/8". **Weight:** 11.2 oz. (Dymondwood grips). **Length:** 6-5/16" overall. **Grips:** Uncle Mike's Boot or Dymondwood Boot. **Sights:** Black serrated front, fixed notch rear. **Features:** Aluminum alloy frame, barrel shroud and yoke; titanium cylinder; stainless steel barrel liner. Matte finish. Introduced 1999. Made in U.S.A. by Smith & Wesson.

Price: **$716.00**

SMITH & WESSON MODEL 342 CENTENNIAL AIRLITE Ti

Caliber: 38 Spec. +P, 5-shot. **Barrel:** 1-7/8". **Weight:** 11.3 oz. (Dymondwood stocks). **Length:** 6-15/16" overall. **Grips:** Uncle Mike's Boot or Dymondwood Boot. **Sights:** Black serrated ramp front, fixed notch rear. **Features:** Aluminum alloy frame, barrel shroud and yoke; titanium cylinder; stainless steel barrel liner. Shrouded hammer. Matte finish. Internal lock. Introduced 1999. Made in U.S.A. by Smith & Wesson.

Price: **$734.00**

Smith & Wesson Model 442 Centennial Airweight

Similar to Model 640 Centennial, alloy frame giving weighs 15.8 oz. Chambered for 38 Special +P, 1-7/8" carbon steel barrel; carbon steel cylinder; concealed hammer; Uncle Mike's Boot grip. Fixed square notch rear sight, serrated ramp front. DA only, glass beaded finish. Introduced 1993.

Price: Blue **$547.00**

SMITH & WESSON MODEL 638 AIRWEIGHT BODYGUARD

Caliber: 38 Spec. +P, 5-shot. **Barrel:** 1-7/8". **Weight:** 15 oz. **Length:** 6-15/16" overall. **Grips:** Uncle Mike's Boot grip. **Sights:** Serrated ramp front, fixed notch rear. **Features:** Alloy frame, stainless cylinder and barrel; shrouded hammer. Glass beaded finish. Introduced 1997. Made in U.S.A. by Smith & Wesson.

Price: With Uncle Mike's Boot grip **$564.00**

Smith & Wesson Model 642 Airweight Revolver

Similar to Model 442 Centennial Airweight, stainless steel barrel, cylinder and yoke with matte finish; Uncle Mike's Boot Grip; DA only; weighs 15.8 oz. Introduced 1996. Made in U.S.A. by Smith & Wesson.

Price: **$571.00**

Smith & Wesson Model 642LS Ladysmith Revolver

Same as Model 642 except has smooth combat wood grips, comes with deluxe soft case; Dymondwood grip; aluminum alloy frame, stainless cylinder, barrel and yoke; frosted matte finish. Weighs 15.8 oz. Introduced 1996. Made in U.S.A. by Smith & Wesson.

Price: 1-7/8" **$597.00**

SMITH & WESSON MODEL 649 BODYGUARD REVOLVER

Caliber: 357 Mag., 38 Spec. +P, 5-shot. **Barrel:** 2-1/8". **Weight:** 20 oz. **Length:** 6-5/16" overall. **Grips:** Uncle Mike's Combat. **Sights:** Black pinned ramp front, fixed notch rear. **Features:** Stainless steel construction; shrouded hammer; smooth combat trigger. Internal lock. Made in U.S.A. by Smith & Wesson.

Price: **$594.00**

SMITH & WESSON MODEL 657 REVOLVER

Caliber: 41 Mag., 6-shot. **Barrel:** 7-1/2" full lug. **Weight:** 48 oz. **Grips:** Soft rubber. **Sights:** Pinned 1/8" red ramp front, micro-click rear adjustable for windage and elevation. Target hammer, drilled and tapped, unfluted cylinder. **Features:** Stainless steel construction.

Price: **$706.00**

SMITH & WESSON MODEL 696 REVOLVER

Caliber: 44 Spec., 5-shot. **Barrel:** 3". **Weight:** 35.5 oz. **Length:** 8-1/4" overall. **Grips:** Uncle Mike's Combat. **Sights:** Red ramp front, click adjustable white outline rear. **Features:** Stainless steel construction; round butt frame; satin finish. Introduced 1997. Made in U.S.A. by Smith & Wesson.

Price: **$620.00**

Taurus Model 82

Taurus Model 85

Taurus Model 94 UL

Taurus Model 22H Raging Hornet

Taurus Model 44

SMITH & WESSON MODEL 500

Caliber: 50. **Barrel:** 4 and 8-3/8". **Weight:** 72.5 oz. **Length:** NA. **Grips:** Rubber. **Sights:** Interchangeable blade, front, adjustable rear. **Features:** Built on the massive, new X-Frame, recoil compensator, ball detent cylinder latch. Made in U.S.A. by Smith & Wesson.

Price: **$1,150.00**

Taurus Silhouette Revolvers

Available in calibers from 22 LR through 454 Casull, the common trait is a 12" vent rib barrel. An optional arm support that wraps around the forearm is available.

Price: . . . . **$414.00 to $859.00**

TAURUS MODEL 17 "TRACKER"

Caliber: 17 HMR, 7-shot. **Barrel:** 6-1/2". **Weight:** 45.8 oz. **Grips:** Rubber. **Sights:** Adjustable. **Features:** Double-action, matte stainless, integral key-lock.

Price: . . . . **$430.00 to $438.00**

TAURUS MODEL 17-12 TARGET "SILHOUETTE"

Caliber: 17 HMR, 7-shot. **Barrel:** 12". **Weight:** 57.8 oz. **Grips:** Rubber. **Sights:** Adjustable. **Features:** Vent rib, double-action, adjustable main spring and trigger stop. Matte stainless, integral key-lock.

Price: **$430.00**

Taurus Model 17-C Series

Similar to the Models 17 Tracker and Silhouette series but 8-shot cylinder, 2", 4" or 5" barrel, blue or stainless finish and regular (24 oz.) or UltraLite (18.5 oz.) versions available. All models have target crown for enhanced accuracy.

Price: . . . . **$359.00 to $391.00**

TAURUS MODEL 63

Caliber: 22 LR, 10 + 1 shot. **Barrel:** 23". **Weight:** 97.9 oz. **Grips:** Premium hardwood. **Sights:** Adjustable. **Features:** Auto loading action, round barrel, manual firing pin block, integral security system lock, trigger guard mounted safety, blue or stainless finish.

Price: . . . . **$295.00 to $310.00**

TAURUS MODEL 65 REVOLVER

Caliber: 357 Mag., 6-shot. **Barrel:** 4". **Weight:** 38 oz. **Length:** 10-1/2" overall. **Grips:** Soft rubber. **Sights:** Fixed. **Features:** Double-action, integral key-lock. Imported by Taurus International.

Price: Blue or matte stainless . . . . **$375.00 to $422.00**

Taurus Model 66 Revolver

Similar to Model 65, 4" or 6" barrel, 7-shot cylinder, adjustable rear sight. Integral key-lock action. Imported by Taurus International.

Price: Blue or matte stainless . . . . **$422.00 to $469.00**

Taurus Model 66 Silhouette Revolver

Similar to Model 6, 12" barrel, 7-shot cylinder, adjustable sight. Integral key-lock action, blue or matte stainless steel finish, rubber grips. Introduced 2001. Imported by Taurus International.

Price: . . . . **$414.00 to $461.00**

TAURUS MODEL 82 HEAVY BARREL REVOLVER

Caliber: 38 Spec., 6-shot. **Barrel:** 4", heavy. **Weight:** 36.5 oz. **Length:** 9-1/4" overall (4" bbl.). **Grips:** Soft black rubber. **Sights:** Serrated ramp front, square notch rear. **Features:** Double-action, solid rib, integral key-lock. Imported by Taurus International.

Price: Blue or matte stainless . . . . **$352.00 to $398.00**

TAURUS MODEL 85 REVOLVER

Caliber: 38 Spec., 5-shot. **Barrel:** 2". **Weight:** 17-24.5 oz., titanium 13.5-15.4 oz. **Grips:** Rubber, rosewood or mother-of-pearl. **Sights:** Ramp front, square notch rear. **Features:** Blue, matte stainless, blue with gold accents, stainless with gold accents; rated for +P ammo. Integral key-lock. Introduced 1980. Imported by Taurus International.

Price: . . . . **$375.00 to $547.00**

Price: Total Titanium **$531.00**

TAURUS MODEL 94 REVOLVER

Caliber: 22 LR, 9-shot cylinder. **Barrel:** 2", 4", 5". **Weight:** 18.5-27.5 oz. **Grips:** Soft black rubber. **Sights:** Serrated ramp front, click-adjustable rear. **Features:** Double-action, integral key-lock. Introduced 1989. Imported by Taurus International.

Price: Blue **$325.00**

Price: Matte stainless **$375.00**

Price: Model 94 UL, forged aluminum alloy, 18-18.5 oz. **$365.00**

Price: As above, stainless. **$410.00**

TAURUS MODEL 22H RAGING HORNET REVOLVER

Caliber: 22 Hornet, 8-shot. **Barrel:** 10". **Weight:** 50 oz. **Length:** 6.5" overall. **Grips:** Soft black rubber. **Sights:** Fully adjustable, scope mount base included. **Features:** Ventilated rib, stainless steel construction with matte finish. Double action, integral key-lock. Introduced 1999. Imported by Taurus International.

Price: **$898.00**

TAURUS MODEL 30C RAGING THIRTY

Caliber: 30 Carbine, 8-shot. **Barrel:** 10". **Weight:** 72.3 oz. **Grips:** Soft black rubber. **Sights:** Adjustable. **Features:** Double-action, ventilated rib, matte stainless, comes with five "Stellar" full-moon clips, integral key-lock.

Price: **$898.00**

TAURUS MODEL 44 REVOLVER

Caliber: 44 Mag., 6-shot. **Barrel:** 4", 6-1/2", 8-3/8". **Weight:** 44-3/4 oz. **Grips:** Rubber. **Sights:** Adjustable. **Features:** Double-action. Integral key-lock. Introduced 1994. New Model 44S12 has 12" vent rib barrel. Imported from Brazil by Taurus International Manufacturing, Inc.

Price: Blue or stainless steel . . . . **$445.00 to $602.00**

Taurus Model 415

Taurus Model 608

Taurus Model 450

TAURUS MODEL 217 TARGET "SILHOUETTE"

Caliber: 218 Bee, 8-shot. **Barrel:** 12". **Weight:** 52.3 oz. **Grips:** Rubber. **Sights:** Adjustable. **Features:** Double-action, ventilated rib, adjustable mainspring and trigger stop, matte stainless, integral key-lock.

Price: **$461.00**

TAURUS MODEL 218 RAGING BEE

Caliber: 218 Bee, 7-shot. **Barrel:** 10". **Weight:** 74.9 oz. **Grips:** Rubber. **Sights:** Adjustable rear. **Features:** Ventilated rib, adjustable action, matte stainless, integral key-lock. Also Available as Model 218SS6 Tracker with 6-1/2" vent rib barrel.

Price: . . . . . (Raging Bee) **$898.00**

Price: . . . . . (Tracker) **$406.00**

TAURUS MODEL 415 REVOLVER

Caliber: 41 Mag., 5-shot. **Barrel:** 2-1/2". **Weight:** 30 oz. **Length:** 7-1/8" overall. **Grips:** Rubber. **Sights:** Fixed. **Features:** Stainless steel construction; matte finish; ported barrel. Double-action. Integral key-lock. Introduced 1999. Imported by Taurus International.

Price: **$508.00**

Price: Total Titanium **$602.00**

TAURUS MODEL 425/627 TRACKER REVOLVERS

Caliber: 357 Mag., 7-shot; 41 Mag., 5-shot. **Barrel:** 4" and 6". **Weight:** 28.8-40 oz. (titanium) 24.3-28. (6"). **Grips:** Rubber. **Sights:** Fixed front, adjustable rear. **Features:** Double-action stainless steel, Shadow Gray or Total Titanium; vent rib (steel models only); integral key-lock action. Imported by Taurus International.

Price: . . . . . **$508.00 to $516.00**

Price: Total Titanium **$688.00**

TAURUS MODEL 445

Caliber: 44 Special, 5-shot. **Barrel:** 2". **Weight:** 20.3-28.25 oz. **Length:** 6-3/4" overall. **Grips:** Rubber. **Sights:** Ramp front, notch rear. **Features:** Blue or stainless steel. Standard or DAO concealed hammer, optional porting. Introduced 1997. Imported by Taurus International.

Price: . . . . . **$345.00 to $500.00**

Price: Total Titanium 19.8 oz. **$600.00**

TAURUS MODEL 455 "STELLAR TRACKER"

Caliber: 45 ACP, 5-shot. **Barrel:** 2", 4", 6". **Weight:** 28/33/38.4 oz. **Grips:** Rubber. **Sights:** Adjustable. **Features:** Double-action, matte stainless, includes five "Stellar" full-moon clips, integral key-lock.

Price: **$523.00**

TAURUS MODEL 460 "TRACKER"

Caliber: 45 Colt, 5-shot. **Barrel:** 4" or 6". **Weight:** 33/38.4 oz. **Grips:** Rubber. **Sights:** Adjustable. **Features:** Double-action, ventilated rib, matte stainless steel, comes with five "Stellar" full-moon clips.

Price: **$516.00**

Price: (Shadow gray, Total Titanium) **$688.00**

TAURUS MODEL 605 REVOLVER

Caliber: 357 Mag., 5-shot. **Barrel:** 2". **Weight:** 24 oz. **Grips:** Rubber. **Sights:** Fixed. **Features:** Double-action, blue or stainless, concealed hammer models DAO, porting optional, integral key-lock. Introduced 1995. Imported by Taurus International.

Price: . . . . . **$375.00 to $438.00**

Taurus Model 731 Revolver

Similar to the Taurus Model 605, except in .32 Magnum.

Price: . . . . . **$438.00 to $531.00**

Taurus Model 454 Raging Bull

TAURUS MODEL 608 REVOLVER

Caliber: 357 Mag. 38 Spec., 8-shot. **Barrel:** 4", 6-1/2", 8-3/8". **Weight:** 44-57 oz. **Length:** 9-3/8" overall. **Grips:** Soft black rubber. **Sights:** Adjustable. **Features:** Double-action, integral key-lock action. Available in blue or stainless. Introduced 1995. Imported by Taurus International.

Price: . . . . . **$469.00 to $547.00**

Taurus Model 44 Series Revolver

Similar to Taurus Model 60 series, but in .44 Rem. Mag. With six-shot cylinder, blue and matte stainless finishes.

Price: . . . . . **$500.00 to $578.00**

TAURUS MODEL 650CIA REVOLVER

Caliber: 357 Magnum, 5-shot. **Barrel:** 2". **Weight:** 24.5 oz. **Grips:** Rubber. **Sights:** Ramp front, square notch rear. **Features:** Double-action-only, blue or matte stainless steel, integral key-lock, internal hammer. Introduced 2001. From Taurus International.

Price: . . . . . **$406.00 to $453.00**

TAURUS MODEL 651 CIA REVOLVER

Caliber: 357 Magnum, 5-shot. **Barrel:** 2". **Weight:** 17-24.5 oz. **Grips:** Rubber. **Sights:** Fixed. **Features:** Concealed single-action/double-action design. Shrouded cockable hammer, blue, matte stainless, Shadow Gray, Total Titanium, integral key-lock. Made in Brazil. Imported by Taurus International Manufacturing, Inc.

Price: . . . . . **$406.00 to $578.00**

TAURUS MODEL 450 REVOLVER

Caliber: 45 Colt, 5-shot. **Barrel:** 2". **Weight:** 21.2-22.3 oz. **Length:** 6-5/8" overall. **Grips:** Rubber. **Sights:** Ramp front, notch rear. **Features:** Double-action, blue or stainless, ported, integral key-lock. Introduced 1999. Im-ported from Brazil by Taurus International.

Price: **$492.00**

Price: Ultra-Lite (alloy frame) **$523.00**

Price: Total Titanium, 19.2 oz. **$600.00**

TAURUS MODEL 444/454/480 RAGING BULL REVOLVERS

Caliber: 44 Mag., 45 LC, 454 Casull, 480 Ruger, 5-shot. **Barrel:** 5", 6-1/2", 8-3/8". **Weight:** 53-63 oz. **Length:** 12" overall (6-1/2" barrel). **Grips:** Soft black rubber. **Sights:** Patridge front, adjustable rear. **Features:** Double-action, ventilated rib, ported, integral key-lock. Introduced 1997. Imported by Taurus International.

Price: Blue . . . . . **$578.00 to $797.00**

Price: Matte stainless . . . . . **$641.00 to $859.00**

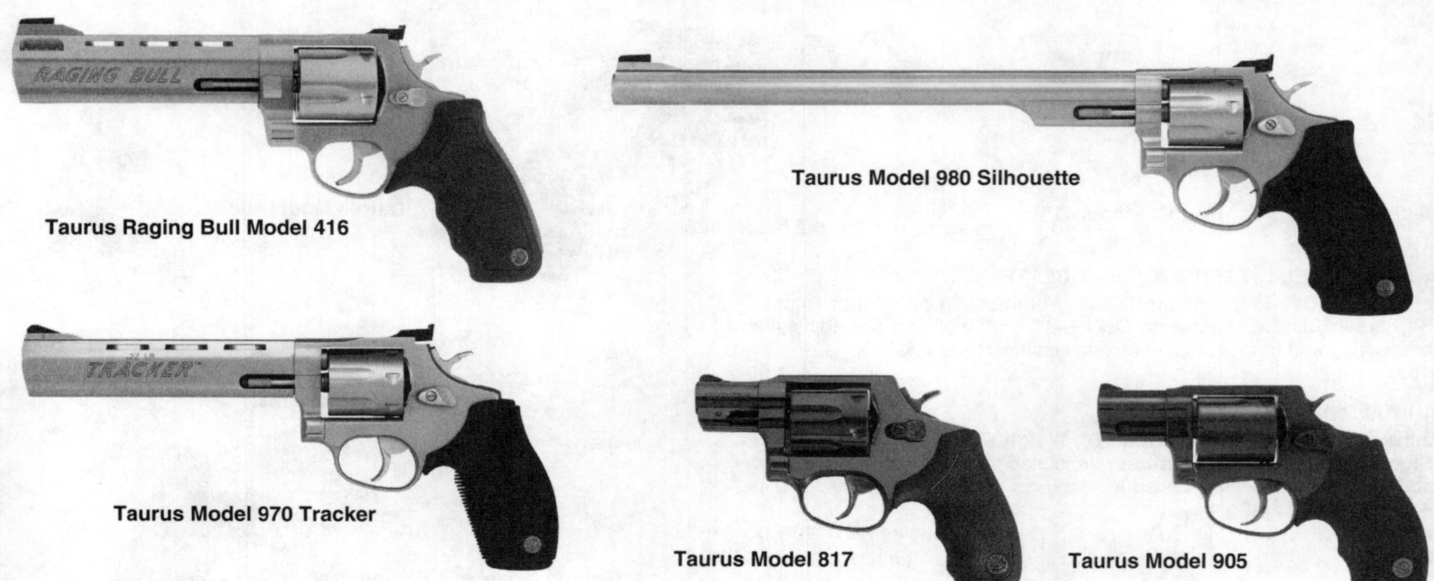

Taurus Raging Bull Model 416

Taurus Model 980 Silhouette

Taurus Model 970 Tracker

Taurus Model 817

Taurus Model 905

TAURUS RAGING BULL MODEL 416

Caliber: 41 Magnum, 6-shot. **Barrel:** 6-1/2". **Weight:** 61.9 oz. **Grips:** Rubber. **Sights:** Adjustable. **Features:** Double-action, ported, ventilated rib, matte stainless, integral key-lock.

Price: **$641.00**

TAURUS MODEL 617 REVOLVER

Caliber: 357 Magnum, 7-shot. **Barrel:** 2". **Weight:** 28.3 oz. **Length:** 6-3/4" overall. **Grips:** Soft black rubber. **Sights:** Fixed. **Features:** Double-action, blue, shadow gray, bright spectrum blue or matte stainless steel, integral key-lock. Available with porting, concealed hammer. Introduced 1998. Imported by Taurus International.

Price: . . . . **$391.00 to $453.00**

Price: Total Titanium, 19.9 oz. **$602.00**

Taurus Model 445 Series Revolver

Similar to Taurus Model 617 series except in .44 Spl. with 5-shot cylinder.

Price: . . . . **$389.00 to $422.00**

Taurus Model 617ULT Revolver

Similar to Model 617 except aluminum alloy and titanium components, matte stainless finish, integral key-lock action. Weighs 18.5 oz. Available ported or non-ported. Introduced 2001. Imported by Taurus International.

Price: (5-shot cylinder) . . . . **$530.00 to $545.00**

TAURUS MODEL 817 ULTRA-LITE REVOLVER

Caliber: 38 Spec., 7-shot. **Barrel:** 2". **Weight:** 21 oz. **Length:** 6-1/2" overall. **Grips:** Soft rubber. **Sights:** Fixed. **Features:** Double-action, integral key-lock. Rated for +P ammo. Introduced 1999. Imported from Brazil by Taurus International.

Price: Blue **$375.00**

Price: Blue, ported **$395.00**

Price: Matte, stainless. **$420.00**

Price: Matte, stainless, ported **$440.00**

TAURUS MODEL 850CIA REVOLVER

Caliber: 38 Special, 5-shot. **Barrel:** 2". **Weight:** 17-24.5 oz. **Grips:** Rubber. **Sights:** Ramp front, square notch rear. **Features:** Double-action-only, blue or matte stainless steel, rated for +P ammo, integral key-lock, internal hammer. Introduced 2001. From Taurus International.

Price: . . . . **$406.00 to $453.00**

Price: Total Titanium **$578.00**

TAURUS MODEL 851CIA REVOLVER

Caliber: 38 Spec., 5-shot. **Barrel:** 2". **Weight:** 17-24.5 oz. **Grips:** Rubber. **Sights:** Fixed-UL/ULT adjustable. **Features:** Concealed single-action/double-action design. Shrouded cockable hammer, blue, matte stainless, Total Titanium, blue or stainless UL and ULT, integral key-lock. Rated for +P ammo.

Price: . . . . **$406.00 to $578.00**

TAURUS MODEL 94, 941 REVOLVER

Caliber: 22 LR (Mod. 94), 22 WMR (Mod. 941), 8-shot. **Barrel:** 2", 4", 5". **Weight:** 27.5 oz. (4" barrel). **Grips:** Soft black rubber. **Sights:** Serrated ramp front, rear adjustable. **Features:** Double-action, integral key-lock. Introduced 1992. Imported by Taurus International.

Price: Blue . . . . **$328.00 to $344.00**

Price: Stainless (matte) . . . . **$375.00 to $391.00**

Price: Model 941 Ultra Lite,
forged aluminum alloy, 2" . . . . **$359.00 to $375.00**

Price: As above, stainless. . . . . **$406.00 to $422.00**

TAURUS MODEL 970/971 TRACKER REVOLVERS

Caliber: 22 LR (Model 970), 22 Magnum (Model 971); 7-shot. **Barrel:** 6". **Weight:** 53.6 oz. **Grips:** Rubber. **Sights:** Adjustable. **Features:** Double barrel, heavy barrel with ventilated rib; matte stainless finish, integral key-lock. Introduced 2001. From Taurus International.

Price: . . . . **$391.00 to $406.00**

TAURUS MODEL 980/981 SILHOUETTE REVOLVERS

Caliber: 22 LR (Model 980), 22 Magnum (Model 981); 7-shot. **Barrel:** 12". **Weight:** 68 oz. **Grips:** Rubber. **Sights:** Adjustable. **Features:** Double-action, heavy barrel with ventilated rib and scope mount, matte stainless finish, integral key-lock. Introduced 2001. From Taurus International.

Price: (Model 980) **$398.00**

Price: (Model 981) **$414.00**

TAURUS MODEL 905, 405, 455 PISTOL CALIBER REVOLVERS

Caliber: 9mm, .40, .45 ACP, 5-shot. **Barrel:** 2", 4", 6-1/2". **Weight:** 21 oz. to 40.8 oz. **Grips:** Rubber. **Sights:** Fixed, adjustable on Model 455SS6 in .45 ACP. **Features:** Produced as a backup gun for law enforcement officers who desire to carry the same caliber ammunition in their back-up revolver as they do in their service sidearm. Introduced 2003. Imported from Brazil by Taurus International Manufacturing, Inc.

Price: . . . . **$383.00 to $523.00**

HANDGUNS — SINGLE ACTION REVOLVERS

Both classic six-shooters and modern adaptations for hunting and sport.

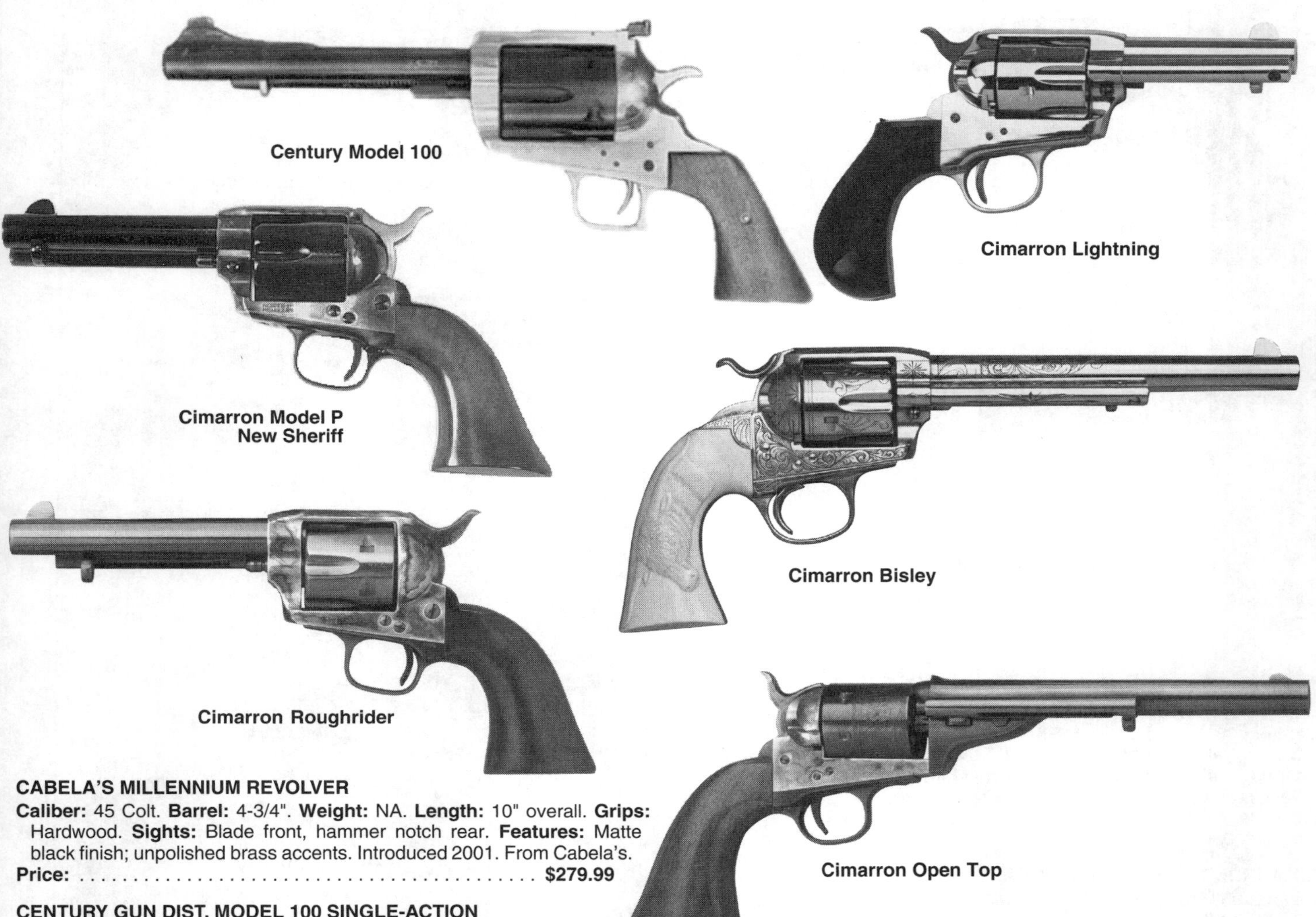

Century Model 100

Cimarron Lightning

Cimarron Model P New Sheriff

Cimarron Bisley

Cimarron Roughrider

Cimarron Open Top

HANDGUNS

CABELA'S MILLENNIUM REVOLVER

Caliber: 45 Colt. **Barrel:** 4-3/4". **Weight:** NA. **Length:** 10" overall. **Grips:** Hardwood. **Sights:** Blade front, hammer notch rear. **Features:** Matte black finish; unpolished brass accents. Introduced 2001. From Cabela's.

Price: **$279.99**

CENTURY GUN DIST. MODEL 100 SINGLE-ACTION

Caliber: 30-30, 375 Win., 444 Marlin, 45-70, 50-70. **Barrel:** 6-1/2" (standard), 8", 10". **Weight:** 6 lbs. (loaded). **Length:** 15" overall (8" bbl.). **Grips:** Smooth walnut. **Sights:** Ramp front, Millett adjustable square notch rear. **Features:** Highly polished high tensile strength manganese bronze frame, blue cylinder and barrel; coil spring trigger mechanism. Contact maker for full price information. Introduced 1975. Made in U.S.A. From Century Gun Dist., Inc.

Price: 6-1/2" barrel, 45-70. . . . . **$2,000.00**

CIMARRON LIGHTNING SA

Caliber: 38 Colt, 38 Special. **Barrel:** 3-1/2", 4-3/4", 5-1/2". **Grips:** Smooth or checkered walnut. **Sights:** Blade front. **Features:** Replica of the Colt 1877 Lightning DA. Similar to Cimarron Thunderer™, except smaller grip frame to fit smaller hands. Standard blue, charcoal blue or nickel finish with forged, old model, or color case hardened frame. Introduced 2001. From Cimarron F.A. Co.

Price: . . . . **$499.00 to $559.00**

CIMARRON MODEL P

Caliber: 32 WCF, 38 WCF, 357 Mag., 44 WCF, 44 Spec., 45 Colt. **Barrel:** 4-3/4", 5-1/2", 7-1/2". **Weight:** 39 oz. **Length:** 10" overall (4" barrel). **Grips:** Walnut. **Sights:** Blade front, fixed or adjustable rear. **Features:** Uses "old model" blackpowder frame with "Bullseye" ejector or New Model frame. Imported by Cimarron F.A. Co.

Price: . . . . **$489.00 to $549.00**

Price: New Sheriff . . . . **$489.00 to $564.00**

Cimarron Bisley Model Single-Action Revolvers

Similar to 1873 Model P, special grip frame and trigger guard, knurled wide-spur hammer, curved trigger. Available in 357 Mag., 44 WCF, 44 Spl., 45 Colt. Introduced 1999. Imported by Cimarron F.A. Co.

Price: **$525.00**

Cimarron Flat-Top Single-Action Revolvers

Similar to 1873 Model P, flat top strap with windage-adjustable rear sight, elevation-adjustable front sight. Available in 44 WCF, 45 Colt; 7-1/2" barrel. Introduced 1999. Imported by Cimarron F.A. Co.

Price: **$525.00**

CIMARRON MODEL "P" JR.

Caliber: 38 Special. **Barrel:** 3-1/2", 4-3/4", 5-1/2". **Grips:** Checkered walnut. **Sights:** Blade front. **Features:** Styled after 1873 Colt Peacemaker, except 20 percent smaller. Blue finish with color-case hardened frame; Cowboy Comp® action. Introduced 2001. From Cimarron F.A. Co.

Price: . . . . **$419.00 to $479.00**

CIMARRON ROUGHRIDER ARTILLERY MODEL SINGLE-ACTION

Caliber: 45 Colt. **Barrel:** 5-1/2". **Weight:** 39 oz. **Length:** 11-1/2" overall. **Grips:** Walnut. **Sights:** Fixed. **Features:** U.S. markings and cartouche, case-hardened frame and hammer; 45 Colt only. Imported by Cimarron F.A. Co.

Price: . . . . **$549.00 to $599.00**

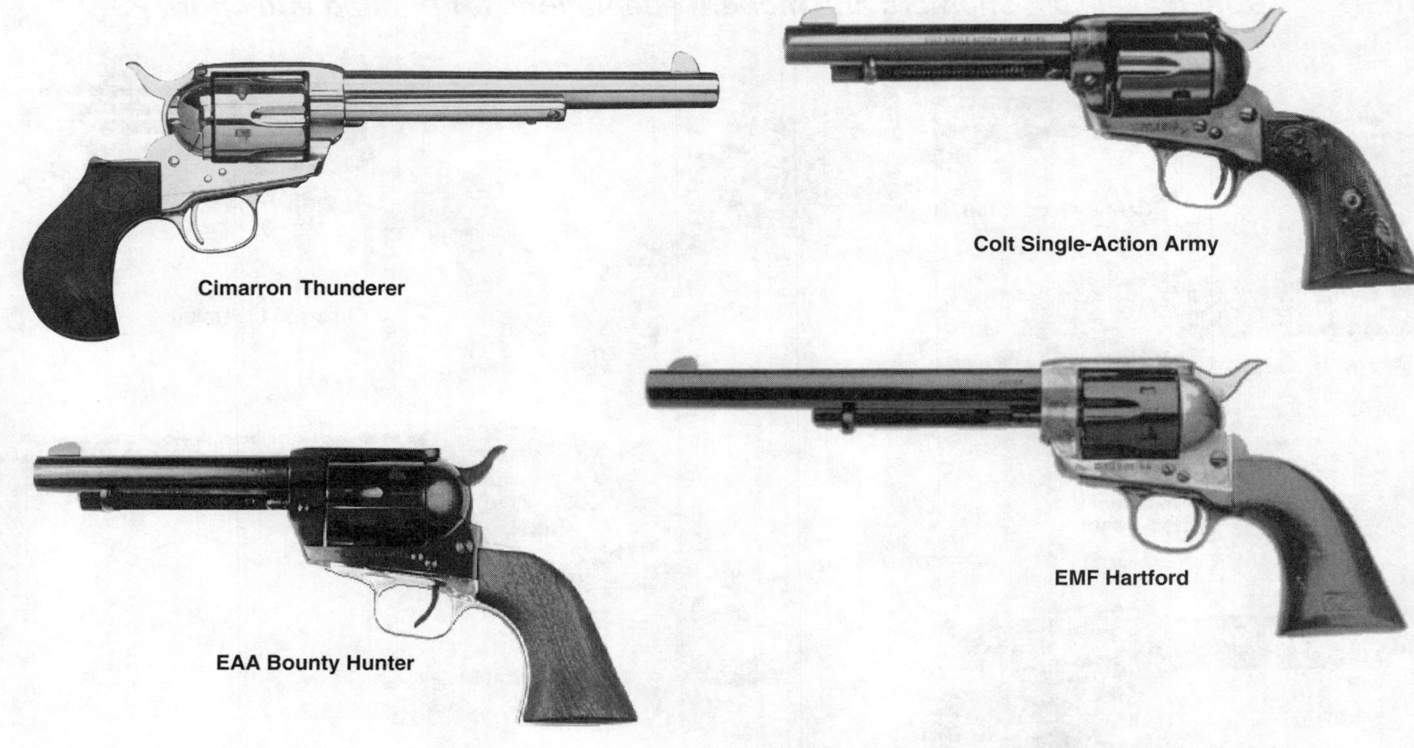

Cimarron Thunderer

Colt Single-Action Army

EAA Bounty Hunter

EMF Hartford

CIMARRON 1872 OPEN TOP REVOLVER

Caliber: 38, 44 Special, 45 S&W Schofield. **Barrel:** 5-1/2" and 7-1/2". **Grips:** Walnut. **Sights:** Blade front, fixed rear. **Features:** Replica of first cartridge-firing revolver. Blue, charcoal blue, nickel or Original® finish; Navy-style brass or steel Army-style frame. Introduced 2001 by Cimarron F.A. Co.

Price: . . . . **$529.00 to $599.00**

CIMARRON THUNDERER REVOLVER

Caliber: 357 Mag., 44 WCF, 44 Spl, 45 Colt, 6-shot. **Barrel:** 3-1/2", 4-3/4", 5-1/2", 7-1/2", with ejector. **Weight:** 38 oz. (3-1/2" barrel). **Grips:** Smooth walnut. **Sights:** Blade front, notch rear. **Features:** Thunderer grip; color case-hardened frame with balance blued. Introduced 1993. Imported by Cimarron F.A. Co.

Price: 3-1/2", 4-3/4", smooth grips . . . . . **$519.00 to $549.00**
Price: As above, checkered grips . . . . . **$564.00 to $584.00**
Price: 5-1/2", 7-1/2", smooth grips . . . . . **$519.00 to $549.00**
Price: As above, checkered grips . . . . . **$564.00 to $584.00**

COLT SINGLE-ACTION ARMY REVOLVER

Caliber: 357 Mag., 38 Special, .32/20, 44-40, 45 Colt, 6-shot. **Barrel:** 4-3/4", 5-1/2", 7-1/2". **Weight:** 40 oz. (4-3/4" barrel). **Length:** 10-1/4" overall (4-3/4" barrel). **Grips:** Black Eagle composite. **Sights:** Blade front, notch rear. **Features:** Available in full nickel finish with nickel grip medallions, or Royal Blue with color case-hardened frame. Reintroduced 1992.

Price: **$1,380.00**

EAA BOUNTY HUNTER SA REVOLVERS

Caliber: 22 LR/22 WMR, 357 Mag., 44 Mag., 45 Colt, 6-shot. **Barrel:** 4-1/2", 7-1/2". **Weight:** 2.5 lbs. **Length:** 11" overall (4-5/8" barrel). **Grips:** Smooth walnut. **Sights:** Blade front, grooved topstrap rear. **Features:** Transfer bar safety; three position hammer; hammer forged barrel. Introduced 1992. Imported by European American Armory.

Price: Blue or case-hardened **$369.00**
Price: Nickel **$399.00**
Price: 22LR/22WMR, blue **$269.00**
Price: As above, nickel **$299.00**

EMF 1894 Bisley

EMF HARTFORD SINGLE-ACTION REVOLVERS

Caliber: 357 Mag., 32-20, 38-40, 44-40, 44 Spec., 45 Colt. **Barrel:** 4-3/4", 5-1/2", 7-1/2". **Weight:** 45 oz. **Length:** 13" overall (7-1/2" barrel). **Grips:** Smooth walnut. **Sights:** Blade front, fixed rear. **Features:** Identical to the original Colts with inspector cartouche on left grip, original patent dates and U.S. markings. All major parts serial numbered using original Colt-style lettering, numbering. Bullseye ejector head and color case-hardening on frame and hammer. Introduced 1990. From E.M.F.

Price: **$500.00**
Price: Cavalry or Artillery **$390.00**
Price: Nickel plated, add **$125.00**
Price: Casehardened New Model frame **$365.00**

EMF 1894 Bisley Revolver

Similar to the Hartford single-action revolver except has special grip frame and trigger guard, wide spur hammer; available in 38-40 or 45 Colt, 4-3/4", 5-1/2" or 7-1/2" barrel. Introduced 1995. Imported by E.M.F.

Price: Casehardened/blue **$400.00**
Price: Nickel **$525.00**

EMF Hartford Pinkerton Single-Action Revolver

Same as the regular Hartford except has 4" barrel with ejector tube and bird's-head grip. Calibers: 357 Mag., 45 Colt. Introduced 1997. Imported by E.M.F.

Price: **$375.00**

HANDGUNS — SINGLE ACTION REVOLVERS

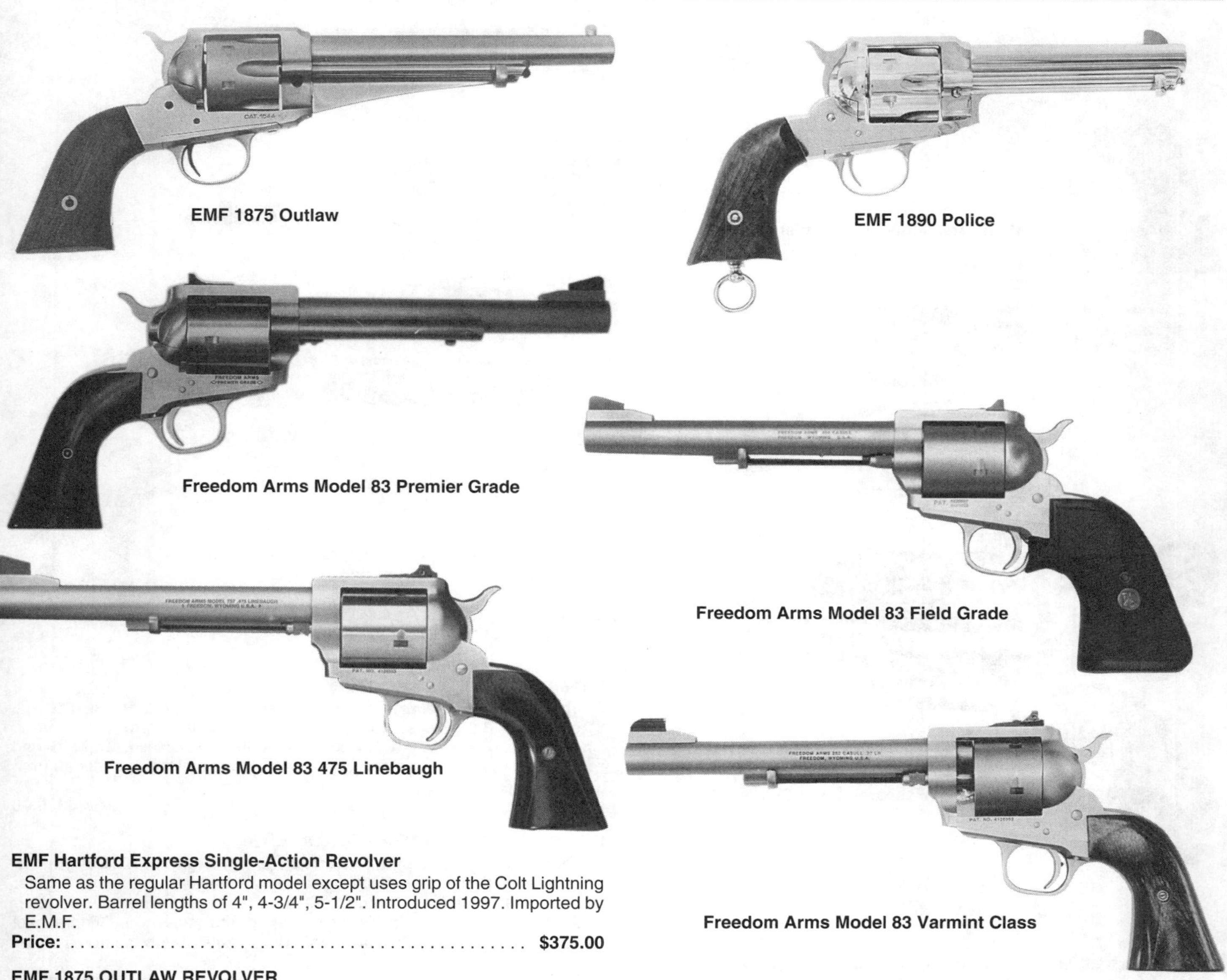

EMF 1875 Outlaw

EMF 1890 Police

Freedom Arms Model 83 Premier Grade

Freedom Arms Model 83 Field Grade

Freedom Arms Model 83 475 Linebaugh

Freedom Arms Model 83 Varmint Class

EMF Hartford Express Single-Action Revolver

Same as the regular Hartford model except uses grip of the Colt Lightning revolver. Barrel lengths of 4", 4-3/4", 5-1/2". Introduced 1997. Imported by E.M.F.

Price: **$375.00**

EMF 1875 OUTLAW REVOLVER

Caliber: 357 Mag., 44-40, 45 Colt. **Barrel:** 7-1/2". **Weight:** 46 oz. **Length:** 13-1/2" overall. **Grips:** Smooth walnut. **Sights:** Blade front, fixed groove rear. **Features:** Authentic copy of 1875 Remington with firing pin in hammer; color case-hardened frame, blue cylinder, barrel, steel backstrap and brass trigger guard. Also available in nickel, factory engraved. Imported by E.M.F.

Price: All calibers **$575.00**
Price: Nickel **$735.00**

EMF 1890 Police Revolver

Similar to the 1875 Outlaw except has 5-1/2" barrel, weighs 40 oz., with 12-1/2" overall length. Has lanyard ring in butt. No web under barrel. Calibers 357, 44-40, 45 Colt. Imported by E.M.F.

Price: All calibers **$590.00**
Price: Nickel **$750.00**

FREEDOM ARMS MODEL 83 PREMIER GRADE REVOLVER

Caliber: 357 Mag., 41 Mag., 44 Mag., 454 Casull, 475 Linebaugh, 50 AE, 5-shot. **Barrel:** 4-3/4", 6", 7-1/2", 9" (357 Mag. only), 10". **Weight:** 52.8 oz. **Length:** 13" (7-1/2" bbl.). **Grips:** Impregnated hardwood. **Sights:** Blade front, notch or adjustable rear. **Features:** All stainless steel construction; sliding bar safety system. Lifetime warranty. Made in U.S.A. by Freedom Arms, Inc.

Price: 454 Casull, 475 Linebaugh, 50 AE. **$2,058.00**
Price: 454 Casull, fixed sight **$1,979.00**
Price: 357 Mag., 41 Mag., 44 Mag. **$1,976.00**
Price: 44 Mag., fixed sight **$1,911.00**

Freedom Arms Model 83 Field Grade Revolver

Model 83 frame. Weighs 52-56 oz. Adjustable rear sight, replaceable front blade, matte finish, Pachmayr grips. All stainless steel. Introduced 1988. Made in U.S.A. by Freedom Arms Inc.

Price: 454 Casull, 475 Linebaugh, 50 AE, adj. sights. **$1,591.00**
Price: 454 Casull, fixed sights. **$1,553.00**
Price: 357 Mag., 41 Mag., 44 Mag. **$1,527.00**

FREEDOM ARMS MODEL 83 VARMINT CLASS REVOLVERS

Caliber: 22 LR, 5-shot. **Barrel:** 5-1/8, 7-1/2". **Weight:** 58 oz. (7-1/2" bbl.). **Length:** 11-1/2" (7-1/2" bbl.). **Grips:** Impregnated hardwood. **Sights:** Steel base adjustable "V" notch rear sight and replaceable brass bead front sight. **Features:** Stainless steel, matte finish, manual sliding-bar system, dual firing pins, pre-set trigger stop. One year limited wararanty to original owner. Made in U.S.A. by Freedom Arms, Inc.

Price: Varmint Class **$1,828.00**
Price: Extra fitted 22 WMR cylinder **$264.00**

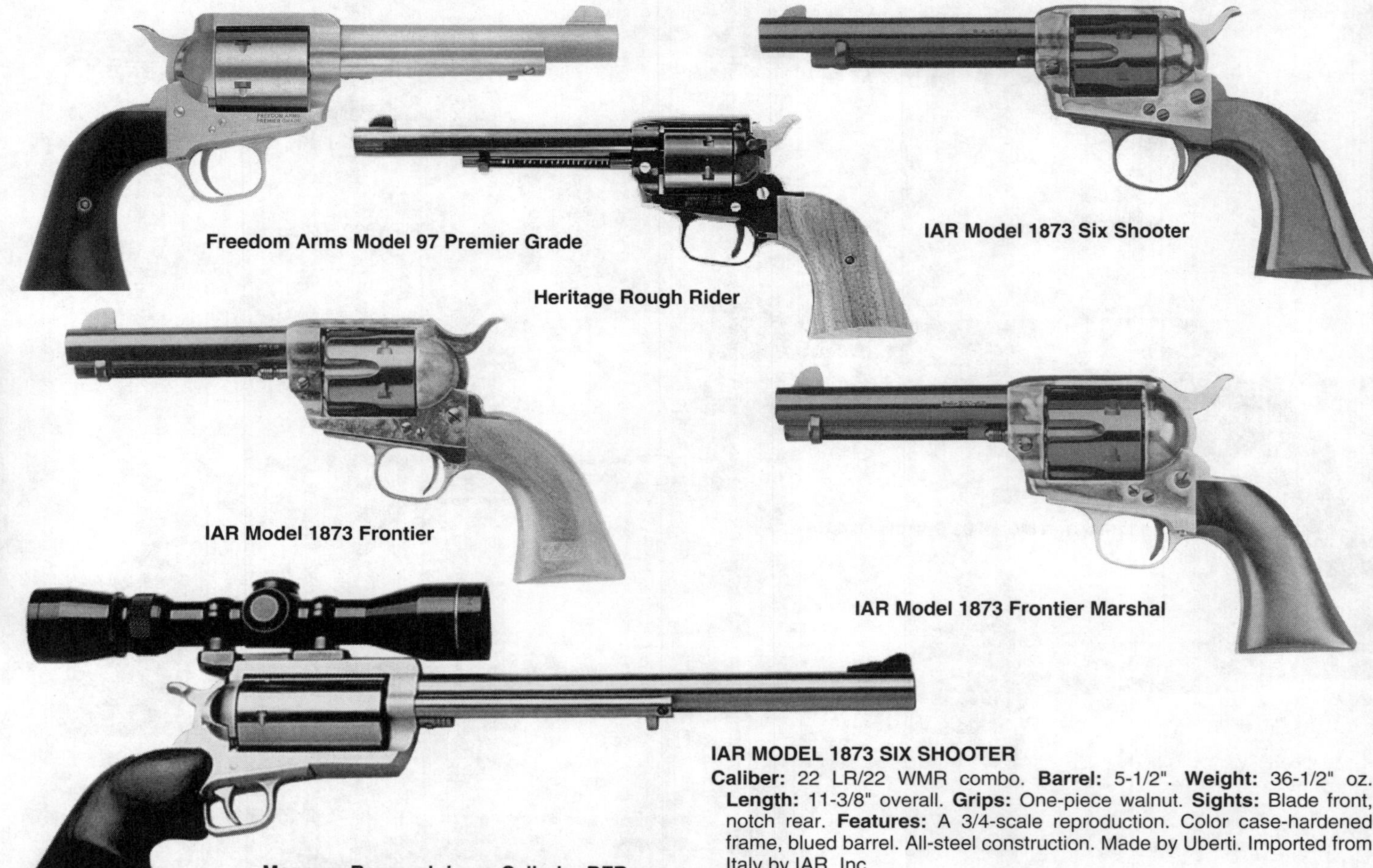
Freedom Arms Model 97 Premier Grade
Heritage Rough Rider
IAR Model 1873 Six Shooter
IAR Model 1873 Frontier
IAR Model 1873 Frontier Marshal
Magnum Research Long Cylinder BFR

FREEDOM ARMS MODEL 97 PREMIER GRADE REVOLVER

Caliber: 22 LR, 357 Mag., 41 Mag., 44 Special, 45 Colt, 5-shot. **Barrel:** 4-1/2", 5-1/2", 7-1/2", 10". **Weight:** 37 oz. (45 Colt 5-1/2"). **Length:** 10-3/4" (5-1/2" bbl.). **Grips:** Impregnated hardwood. **Sights:** Adjustable rear, replaceable blade front. **Features:** Stainless steel, brushed finish, automatic transfer bar safety system. Introduced in 1997. Made in U.S.A. by Freedom Arms.

Price: 357 Mag., 41 Mag., 45 Colt **$1,668.00**
Price: 357 Mag., 45 Colt, fixed sight **$1,576.00**
Price: Extra fitted cylinders 38 Special, 45 ACP **$264.00**
Price: 22 LR with sporting chambers **$1,732.00**
Price: Extra fitted 22 WMR cylinder **$264.00**
Price: Extra fitted 22 LR match grade cylinder **$476.00**
Price: 22 match grade chamber instead of 22 LR sport chamber **$214.00**

HERITAGE ROUGH RIDER REVOLVER

Caliber: 22 LR, 22 LR/22 WMR combo, 6-shot. **Barrel:** 2-3/4", 3-1/2", 4-3/4", 6-1/2", 9". **Weight:** 31 to 38 oz. **Length:** NA. **Grips:** Exotic hardwood, laminated wood or mother-of-pearl; bird's-head models offered. **Sights:** Blade front, fixed rear. Adjustable sight on 6-1/2" only. **Features:** Hammer block safety. High polish blue or nickel finish. Introduced 1993. Made in U.S.A. by Heritage Mfg., Inc.

Price: . . . . **$184.95 to $239.95**

IAR MODEL 1873 SIX SHOOTER

Caliber: 22 LR/22 WMR combo. **Barrel:** 5-1/2". **Weight:** 36-1/2" oz. **Length:** 11-3/8" overall. **Grips:** One-piece walnut. **Sights:** Blade front, notch rear. **Features:** A 3/4-scale reproduction. Color case-hardened frame, blued barrel. All-steel construction. Made by Uberti. Imported from Italy by IAR, Inc.

Price: **$360.00**

IAR MODEL 1873 FRONTIER REVOLVER

Caliber: 22 RL, 22 LR/22 WMR. **Barrel:** 4-3/4". **Weight:** 45 oz. **Length:** 10-1/2" overall. **Grips:** One-piece walnut with inspector's cartouche. **Sights:** Blade front, notch rear. **Features:** Color case-hardened frame, blued barrel, black nickel-plated brass trigger guard and backstrap. Bright nickel and engraved versions available. Introduced 1997. Imported from Italy by IAR, Inc.

Price: **$380.00**
Price: Nickel-plated **$425.00**
Price: 22 LR/22WMR combo **$420.00**

IAR MODEL 1873 FRONTIER MARSHAL

Caliber: 357 Mag., 45 Colt. **Barrel:** 4-3/4", 5-1/2, 7-1/2". **Weight:** 39 oz. **Length:** 10-1/2" overall. **Grips:** One-piece walnut. **Sights:** Blade front, notch rear. **Features:** Bright brass trigger guard and backstrap, color case-hardened frame, blued barrel and cylinder. Introduced 1998. Imported from Italy by IAR, Inc.

Price: **$395.00**

MAGNUM RESEARCH BFR SINGLE-ACTION REVOLVER

(Long cylinder) Caliber: 30/30, 45/70 Government, 444 Marlin, 45 LC/410, 450 Marlin, 50 AE, .500 S&W. **Barrel:** 7.5", 10". **Weight:** 4 lbs., 4.36 lbs. **Length:** 15", 17.5".

(Short cylinder) Caliber: 454 Casull, 22 Hornet, BFR 480/475. **Barrel:** 6.5", 7.5", 10". **Weight:** 3.2 lbs, 3.5 lbs., 4.36 lbs. (10"). **Length:** 12.75 (6"), 13.75", 16.25"

Sights: All have fully adjustable rear, black blade ramp front. **Features:** Stainless steel construction, rubber grips, all 5-shot capacity. Barrels are stress-relieved and cut rifled. Made in U.S.A. From Magnum Research, Inc.

Price: **$999.00**

Handguns — Single Action Revolvers

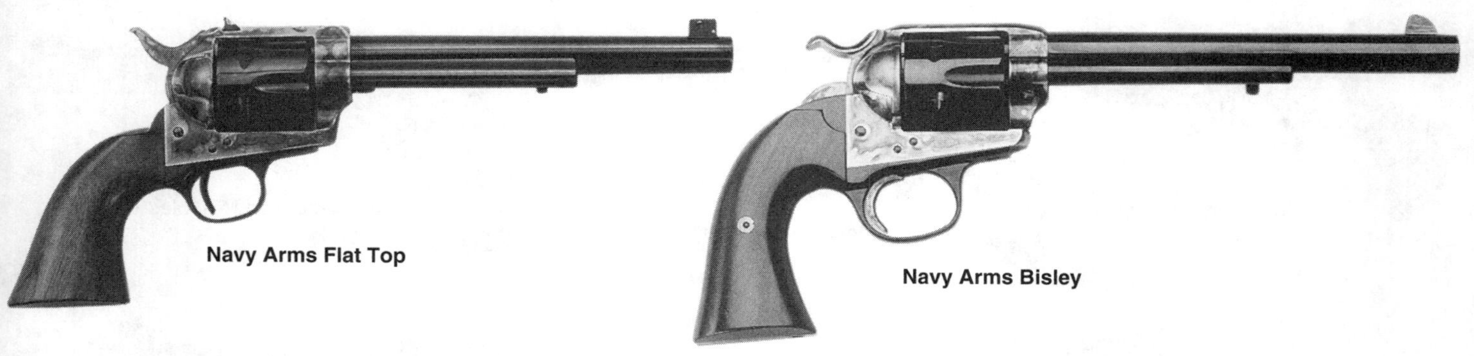

Navy Arms Flat Top

Navy Arms Bisley

Navy Arms 1873

Navy Arms New Model Russian

NAVY ARMS FLAT TOP TARGET MODEL REVOLVER

Caliber: 45 Colt, 6-shot cylinder. **Barrel:** 7-1/2". **Weight:** 40 oz. **Length:** 13-1/4" overall. **Grips:** Smooth walnut. **Sights:** Spring-loaded German silver front, rear adjustable for windage. **Features:** Replica of Colt's Flat Top Frontier target revolver made from 1888 to 1896. Blue with color case-hardened frame. Introduced 1997. Imported by Navy Arms.

Price: **$450.00**

NAVY ARMS BISLEY MODEL SINGLE-ACTION REVOLVER

Caliber: 44-40 or 45 Colt, 6-shot cylinder. **Barrel:** 4-3/4", 5-1/2", 7-1/2". **Weight:** 40 oz. **Length:** 12-1/2" overall (7-1/2" barrel). **Grips:** Smooth walnut. **Sights:** Blade front, notch rear. **Features:** Replica of Colt's Bisley Model. Polished blue finish, color case-hardened frame. Introduced 1997. Imported by Navy Arms.

Price: . . . . **$425.00 to $460.00**

NAVY ARMS 1873 SINGLE-ACTION REVOLVER

Caliber: 357 Mag., 44-40, 45 Colt, 6-shot cylinder. **Barrel:** 4-3/4", 5-1/2", 7-1/2". **Weight:** 36 oz. **Length:** 10-3/4" overall (5-1/2" barrel). **Grips:** Smooth walnut. **Sights:** Blade front, notch rear. **Features:** Blue with color case-hardened frame. Introduced 1991. Imported by Navy Arms.

Price: **$405.00**

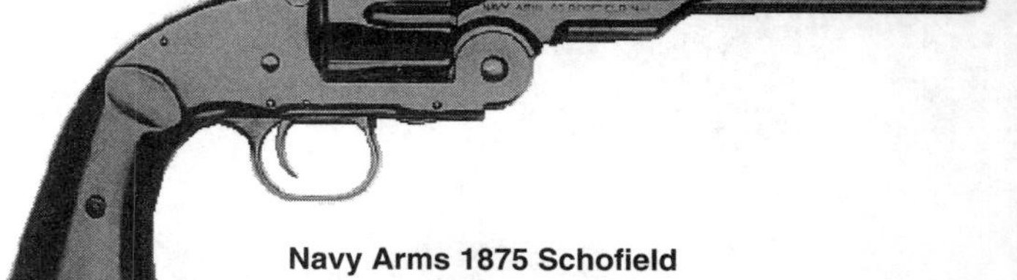

Navy Arms 1875 Schofield

NAVY ARMS 1875 SCHOFIELD REVOLVER

Caliber: 44-40, 45 Colt, 6-shot cylinder. **Barrel:** 3-1/2", 5", 7". **Weight:** 39 oz. **Length:** 10-3/4" overall (5" barrel). **Grips:** Smooth walnut. **Sights:** Blade front, notch rear. **Features:** Replica of Smith & Wesson Model 3 Schofield. Single-action, top-break with automatic ejection. Polished blue finish. Introduced 1994. Imported by Navy Arms.

Price: Hideout Model, 3-1/2" barrel. **$695.00**
Price: Wells Fargo, 5" barrel **$695.00**
Price: U.S. Cavalry model, 7" barrel, military markings **$695.00**

NAVY ARMS NEW MODEL RUSSIAN REVOLVER

Caliber: 44 Russian, 6-shot cylinder. **Barrel:** 6-1/2". **Weight:** 40 oz. **Length:** 12" overall. **Grips:** Smooth walnut. **Sights:** Blade front, notch rear. **Features:** Replica of the S&W Model 3 Russian Third Model revolver. Spur trigger guard, polished blue finish. Introduced 1999. Imported by Navy Arms.

Price: **$769.00**

NAVY ARMS 1851 NAVY CONVERSION REVOLVER

Caliber: 38 Spec., 38 Long Colt. **Barrel:** 5-1/2", 7-1/2". **Weight:** 44 oz. **Length:** 14" overall (7-1/2" barrel). **Grips:** Smooth walnut. **Sights:** Bead front, notch rear. **Features:** Replica of Colt's cartridge conversion revolver. Polished blue finish with color case-hardened frame, silver plated trigger guard and backstrap. Introduced 1999. Imported by Navy Arms.

Price: **$165.00**

NAVY ARMS 1860 ARMY CONVERSION REVOLVER

Caliber: 38 Spec., 38 Long Colt. **Barrel:** 5-1/2", 7-1/2". **Weight:** 44 oz. **Length:** 13-1/2" overall (7-1/2" barrel). **Grips:** Smooth walnut. **Sights:** Blade front, notch rear. **Features:** Replica of Colt's conversion revolver. Polished blue finish with color case-hardened frame, full-size 1860 Army grip with blued steel backstrap. Introduced 1999. Imported by Navy Arms.

Price: **$190.00**

NORTH AMERICAN MINI REVOLVERS

Caliber: 22 Short, 22 LR, 22 WMR, 5-shot. **Barrel:** 1-1/8", 1-5/8". **Weight:** 4 to 6.6 oz. **Length:** 3-5/8" to 6-1/8" overall. **Grips:** Laminated wood. **Sights:** Blade front, notch fixed rear. **Features:** All stainless steel construction. Polished satin and matte finish. Engraved models available. From North American Arms.

Price: 22 Short, 22 LR **$193.00**
Price: 22 WMR, 1-1/8" or 1-5/8" bbl. **$193.00**
Price: 22 WMR, 1-1/8" or 1-5/8" bbl. with extra 22 LR cylinder. . . **$193.00**

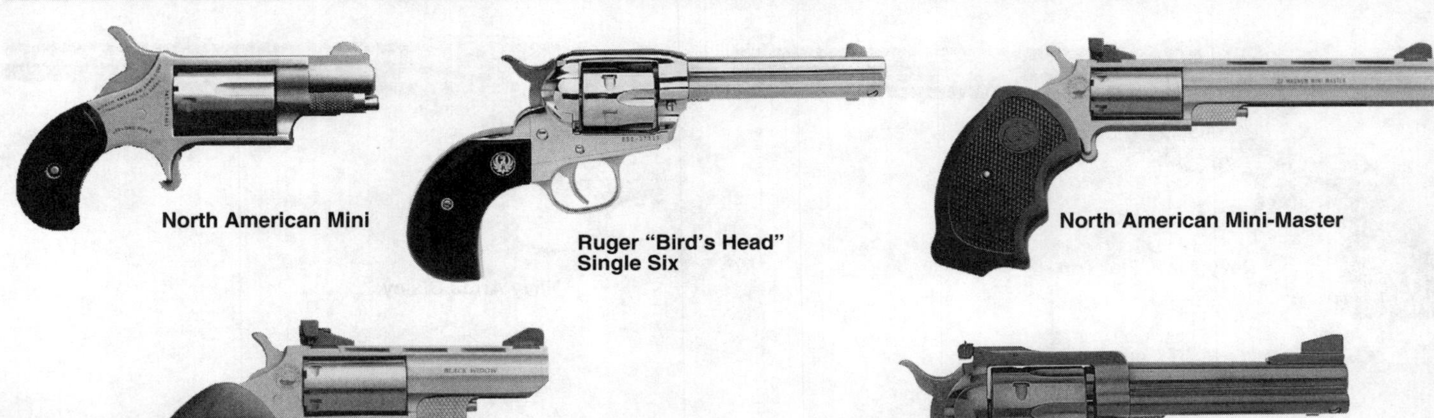

North American Mini

Ruger "Bird's Head" Single Six

North American Mini-Master

North American Black Widow

Ruger Blackhawk

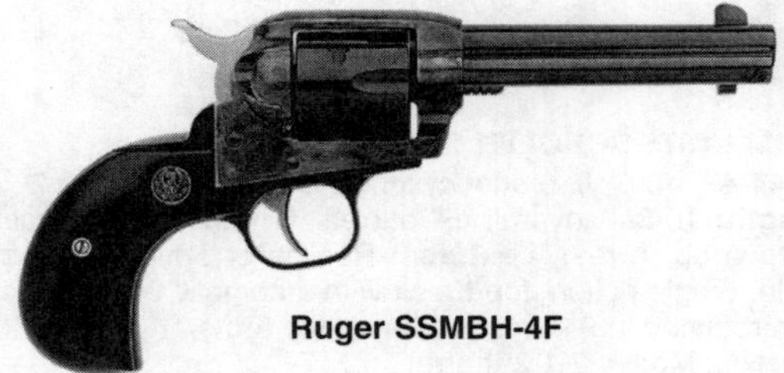

Ruger SSMBH-4F

Ruger Bisley Single-Action

NORTH AMERICAN MINI-MASTER

Caliber: 22 LR, 22 WMR, 17 HMR, 5-shot cylinder. **Barrel:** 4". **Weight:** 10.7 oz. **Length:** 7.75" overall. **Grips:** Checkered hard black rubber. **Sights:** Blade front, white outline rear adjustable for elevation, or fixed. **Features:** Heavy vent barrel; full-size grips. Non-fluted cylinder. Introduced 1989.

Price: Adjustable sight, 22 WMR, 17 HMR or 22 LR **$301.00**
Price: As above with extra WMR/LR cylinder **$330.00**
Price: Fixed sight, 22 WMR, 17 HMR or 22 LR **$272.00**
Price: As above with extra WMR/LR cylinder **$330.00**

North American Black Widow Revolver

Similar to Mini-Master, 2" heavy vent barrel. Built on 22 WMR frame. Non-fluted cylinder, black rubber grips. Available with Millett Low Profile fixed sights or Millett sight adjustable for elevation only. Overall length 5-7/8", weighs 8.8 oz. From North American Arms.

Price: Adjustable sight, 22 LR, 17 HMR or 22 WMR **$287.00**
Price: As above with extra WMR/LR cylinder **$316.00**
Price: Fixed sight, 22 LR, 17 HMR or 22 WMR **$287.00**
Price: As above with extra WMR/LR cylinder **$287.00**

RUGER NEW MODEL SINGLE SIX REVOLVER

Caliber: 32 H&R. **Barrel:** 4-5/8", 6-shot. **Grips:** Black Micarta "bird's-head", rosewood with color case. **Sights:** Fixed. **Features:** Instruction manual, high impact case, gun lock standard.

Price: Stainless, KSSMBH-4F, bird's-head **$576.00**
Price: Color case, SSMBH-4F, bird's-head **$576.00**
Price: Color case, SSM-4F-S, rosewood **$576.00**

RUGER NEW MODEL BLACKHAWK AND BLACKHAWK CONVERTIBLE

Caliber: 30 Carbine, 357 Mag./38 Spec., 41 Mag., 45 Colt, 6-shot. **Barrel:** 4-5/8" or 5-1/2", either caliber; 7-1/2" (30 Carbine and 45 Colt). **Weight:** 42 oz. (6-1/2" bbl.). **Length:** 12-1/4" overall (5-1/2" bbl.). **Grips:** American walnut. **Sights:** 1/8" ramp front, micro-click rear adjustable for windage and elevation. **Features:** Ruger transfer bar safety system, independent firing pin, hardened chrome-moly steel frame, music wire springs throughout. Case and lock included.

Price: Blue 30 Carbine, 7-1/2" (BN31) **$435.00**
Price: Blue, 357 Mag., 4-5/8", 6-1/2" (BN34, BN36) **$435.00**
Price: As above, stainless (KBN34, KBN36) **$530.00**
Price: Blue, 357 Mag./9mm Convertible, 4-5/8", 6-1/2" (BN34X, BN36X) includes extra cylinder **$489.00**
Price: Blue, 41 Mag., 4-5/8", 6-1/2" (BN41, BN42) **$435.00**
Price: Blue, 45 Colt, 4-5/8", 5-1/2", 7-1/2" (BN44, BN455, BN45) **$435.00**
Price: Stainless, 45 Colt, 4-5/8", 7-1/2" (KBN44, KBN45) **$530.00**
Price: Blue, 45 Colt/45 ACP Convertible, 4-5/8", 5-1/2" (BN44X, BN455X) includes extra cylinder **$489.00**

Ruger Bisley Single-Action Revolver

Similar to standard Blackhawk, hammer is lower with smoothly curved, deeply checkered wide spur. The trigger is strongly curved with wide smooth surface. Longer grip frame has hand-filling shape. Adjustable rear sight, ramp-style front. Unfluted cylinder and roll engraving, adjustable sights. Chambered for 357, 44 Mags. and 45 Colt; 7-1/2" barrel; overall length of 13"; weighs 48 oz. Plastic lockable case. Introduced 1985.

Price: RB-35W, 357Mag, RBD-44W, 44Mag, RB-45W, 45 Colt . . **$535.00**

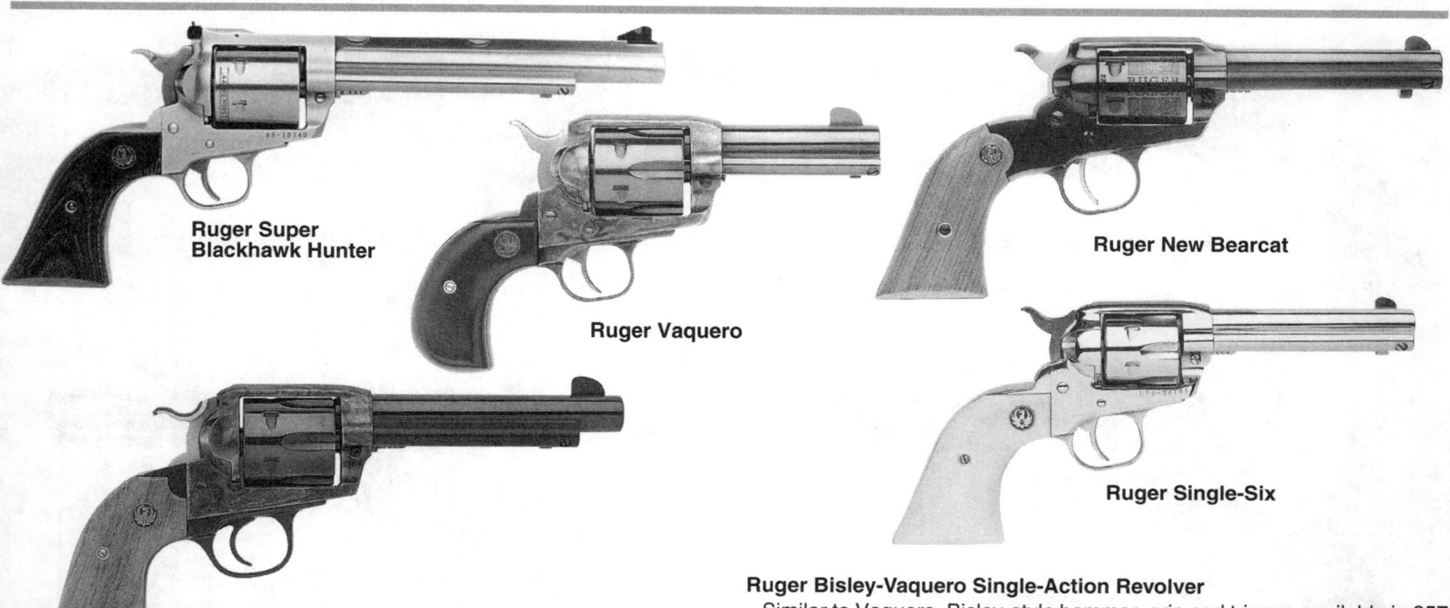

Ruger Super Blackhawk Hunter

Ruger Vaquero

Ruger New Bearcat

Ruger Single-Six

Ruger Bisley-Vaquero

RUGER NEW MODEL SUPER BLACKHAWK

Caliber: 44 Mag., 6-shot. Also fires 44 Spec. **Barrel:** 4-5/8", 5-1/2", 7-1/2", 10-1/2" bull. **Weight:** 48 oz. (7-1/2" bbl.), 51 oz. (10-1/2" bbl.). **Length:** 13-3/8" overall (7-1/2" bbl.). **Grips:** American walnut. **Sights:** 1/8" ramp front, micro-click rear adjustable for windage and elevation. **Features:** Ruger transfer bar safety system, fluted or unfluted cylinder, steel grip and cylinder frame, round or square back trigger guard, wide serrated trigger, wide spur hammer. With case and lock.

Price: Blue, 4-5/8", 5-1/2", 7-1/2" (S458N, S45N, S47N) **$519.00**
Price: Blue, 10-1/2" bull barrel (S411N) **$529.00**
Price: Stainless, 4-5/8", 5-1/2", 7-1/2" (KS458N, KS45N, KS47N) **$535.00**
Price: Stainless, 10-1/2" bull barrel (KS411N) **$545.00**

RUGER NEW MODEL SUPER BLACKHAWK HUNTER

Caliber: 44 Mag., 6-shot. **Barrel:** 7-1/2", full-length solid rib, unfluted cylinder. **Weight:** 52 oz. **Length:** 13-5/8". **Grips:** Black laminated wood. **Sights:** Adjustable rear, replaceable front blade. **Features:** Reintroduced Ultimate SA revolver. Includes instruction manual, high-impact case, set 1" medium scope rings, gun lock, ejector rod as standard.

Price: **$639.00**

RUGER VAQUERO SINGLE-ACTION REVOLVER

Caliber: 357 Mag., 44-40, 44 Mag., 45 LC, 6-shot. **Barrel:** 4-5/8", 5-1/2", 7-1/2". **Weight:** 38-41 oz. **Length:** 13-1/8" overall (7-1/2" barrel). **Grips:** Smooth rosewood with Ruger medallion. **Sights:** Blade front, fixed notch rear. **Features:** Uses Ruger's patented transfer bar safety system and loading gate interlock with classic styling. Blued model color case-hardened finish on frame, rest polished and blued. Stainless has high-gloss. Introduced 1993. From Sturm, Ruger & Co.

Price: 357 Mag. BNV34, KBNV34 (4-5/8"), BNV35, KBNV35 (5-1/2") **$535.00**
Price: 44-40 BNV40, KBNV40 (4-5/8"). BNV405, KBNV405 (5-1/2"). BNV407, KBNV407 (7-1/2") **$535.00**
Price: 44 Mag., BNV474, KBNV474 (4-5/8"). BNV475, KBNV475 (5-1/2"). BNV477, KBNV477 (7-1/2") **$535.00**
Price: 45 LC, BN444, KBNV44 (4-5/8"). BNV455, KBNV455 (5-1/2"). BNV45, KBNV45 (7-1/2") **$535.00**
Price: 45 LC, BNVBH453, KBNVBH453 3-3/4" with "bird's-head" grip **$576.00**
Price: 357 Mag., RBNV35 (5-1/2") **$535.00**; KRBNV35 (5-1/2") . **$555.00**
Price: 45 LC, RBNV44 (4-5/8"), RBNV455 (5-1/2") **$535.00**
Price: 45 LC, KRBNV44 (4-5/8"), KRBNV455 (5-1/2") **$555.00**

Ruger Bisley-Vaquero Single-Action Revolver

Similar to Vaquero, Bisley-style hammer, grip and trigger, available in 357 Magnum, 44 Magnum and 45 LC only, 4-5/8" or 5-1/2" barrel. Smooth rosewood grips with Ruger medallion. Roll-engraved, unfluted cylinder. Introduced 1997. From Sturm, Ruger & Co.

Price: Color case-hardened frame, blue grip frame, barrel and cylinder, RBNV-475, RBNV-474, 44 Mag. **$535.00**
Price: High-gloss stainless steel, KRBNV-475, KRBNV-474 . . . . **$555.00**
Price: For simulated ivory grips add . . . . **$41.00 to $44.00**

RUGER NEW BEARCAT SINGLE-ACTION

Caliber: 22 LR, 6-shot. **Barrel:** 4". **Weight:** 24 oz. **Length:** 8-7/8" overall. **Grips:** Smooth rosewood with Ruger medallion. **Sights:** Blade front, fixed notch rear. **Features:** Reintroduction of the Ruger Bearcat with slightly lengthened frame, Ruger patented transfer bar safety system. Available in blue only. Introduced 1993. With case and lock. From Sturm, Ruger & Co.

Price: SBC4, blue **$379.00**
Price: KSBC-4, SS **$429.00**

RUGER MODEL SINGLE-SIX REVOLVER

Caliber: 32 H&R Magnum. **Barrel:** 4-5/8", 6-shot. **Weight:** 33 oz. **Length:** 10-1/8". **Grips:** Blue, rosewood, stainless, simulated ivory. **Sights:** Blade front, notch rear fixed. **Features:** Transfer bar and loading gate interlock safety, instruction manual, high impact case and gun lock.

Price: **$576.00**
Price: Blue, SSM4FS **$576.00**
Price: SS, KSSM4FSI **$576.00**

RUGER SINGLE-SIX AND SUPER SINGLE-SIX CONVERTIBLE

Caliber: 22 LR, 6-shot; 22 WMR in extra cylinder; 17 HMR. **Barrel:** 4-5/8", 5-1/2", 6-1/2", 9-1/2" (6-groove). **Weight:** 35 oz. (6-1/2" bbl.). **Length:** 11-13/16" overall (6-1/2" bbl.). **Grips:** Smooth American walnut. **Sights:** Improved Patridge front on ramp, fully adjustable rear protected by integral frame ribs (super single-six); or fixed sight (single six). **Features:** Ruger transfer bar safety system, loading gate interlock, hardened chrome-moly steel frame, wide trigger, music wire springs throughout, independent firing pin.

Price: 4-5/8", 5-1/2", 6-1/2", 9-1/2" barrel, blue, adjustable sight NR4, NR5, NR6, NR9 . . . . **$399.00**
Price: 5-1/2", 6-1/2" bbl. only, stainless steel, adjustable sight KNR5, KNR6. . . . . **$485.00**
Price: 5-1/2", 6-1/2" barrel, blue fixed sights **$399.00**
Price: 6-1/2" barrel, NR 617, 17 HMR **$399.00**
Price: Ruger 50th Anniversary Single Six, 4-5/8" barrel, gold-colored rollmark "50 years of Single Six 1953 to 2003," blued steel finish, Cocobolo wood grips with red Ruger medallions, both .22 LR and .22 WMR cylinders **$599.00**
Price: Stainless Hunter. **$650.00**

HANDGUNS — SINGLE ACTION REVOLVERS

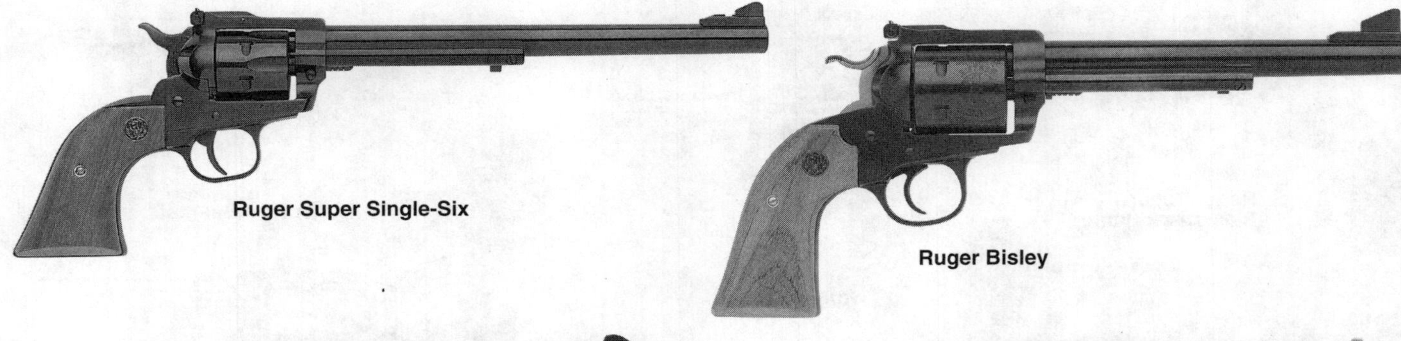

Ruger Super Single-Six

Ruger Bisley

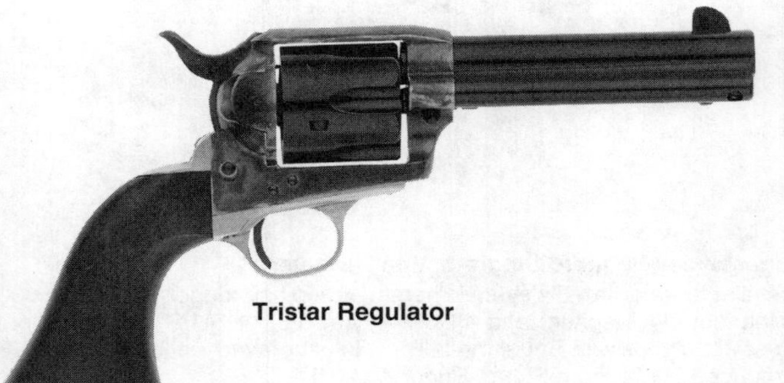

Tristar Regulator

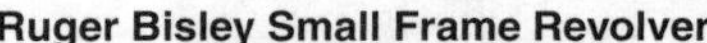

Uberti 1873 Cattleman

Ruger Bisley Small Frame Revolver

Similar to Single-Six, frame is styled after classic Bisley "flat-top." Most mechanical parts are unchanged. Hammer is lower and smoothly curved with deeply checkered spur. Trigger is strongly curved with wide smooth surface. Longer grip frame designed with hand-filling shape, and trigger guard is a large oval. Adjustable dovetail rear sight; front sight base accepts interchangeable square blades of various heights and styles. Unfluted cylinder and roll engraving. Weighs 41 oz. Chambered for 22 LR, 6-1/2" barrel only. Plastic lockable case. Introduced 1985.

Price: RB-22AW **$422.00**

SMITH & WESSON COMMEMORATIVE MODEL 2000

Caliber: 45 S&W Schofield. **Barrel:** 7". **Features:** 150th Anniversary logo, engraved, gold-plated, walnut grips, blue, original style hammer, trigger, and barrel latch. Wood presentation case. Limited.

Price: . . . . **NA**

TRISTAR/UBERTI REGULATOR REVOLVER

Caliber: 45 Colt. **Barrel:** 4-3/4", 5-1/2". **Weight:** 32-38 oz. **Length:** 8-1/4" overall (4-3/4" bbl.) **Grips:** One-piece walnut. **Sights:** Blade front, notch rear. **Features:** Uberti replica of 1873 Colt Model "P" revolver. Color-case hardened steel frame, brass backstrap and trigger guard, hammer-block safety. Imported from Italy by Tristar Sporting Arms.

Price: Regulator **$335.00**

Price: Regulator Deluxe (blued backstrap, trigger guard). **$367.00**

UBERTI 1873 CATTLEMAN SINGLE-ACTION

Caliber: 22 LR/22 WMR, 38 Spec., 357 Mag., 44 Spec., 44-40, 45 Colt/45 ACP, 6-shot. **Barrel:** 4-3/4", 5-1/2", 7-1/2"; 44-40, 45 Colt also with 3", 3-1/2", 4". **Weight:** 38 oz. (5-1/2" bbl.). **Length:** 10-3/4" overall (5-1/2" bbl.). **Grips:** One-piece smooth walnut. **Sights:** Blade front, groove rear; fully adjustable rear available. **Features:** Steel or brass backstrap, trigger guard; color case-hardened frame, blued barrel, cylinder. Imported from Italy by Uberti U.S.A.

Price: Steel backstrap, trigger guard, fixed sights. **$410.00**

Price: Brass backstrap, trigger guard, fixed sights **$359.00**

Price: Bisley model **$435.00**

Uberti 1873 Buckhorn Single-Action

A slightly larger version of the Cattleman revolver. Available in 44 Magnum or 44 Magnum/44-40 convertible, otherwise has same specs.

Price: Steel backstrap, trigger guard, fixed sights. **$410.00**

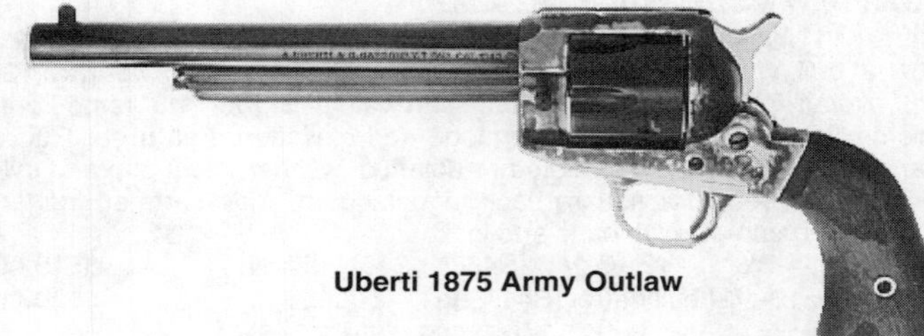

Uberti 1875 Army Outlaw

UBERTI 1875 SA ARMY OUTLAW REVOLVER

Caliber: 357 Mag., 44-40, 45 Colt, 45 Colt/45 ACP convertible, 6-shot. **Barrel:** 5-1/2", 7-1/2". **Weight:** 44 oz. **Length:** 13-3/4" overall. **Grips:** Smooth walnut. **Sights:** Blade front, notch rear. **Features:** Replica of the 1875 Remington S.A. Army revolver. Brass trigger guard, color case-hardened frame, rest blued. Imported by Uberti U.S.A.

Price: **$483.00**

Price: 45 Colt/45 ACP convertible **$525.00**

UBERTI 1890 ARMY OUTLAW REVOLVER

Caliber: 357 Mag., 44-40, 45 Colt, 45 Colt/45 ACP convertible, 6-shot. **Barrel:** 5-1/2", 7-1/2". **Weight:** 37 oz. **Length:** 12-1/2" overall. **Grips:** American walnut. **Sights:** Blade front, groove rear. **Features:** Replica of the 1890 Remington single-action. Brass trigger guard, rest is blued. Imported by Uberti U.S.A.

Price: **$483.00**

UBERTI NEW MODEL RUSSIAN REVOLVER

Caliber: 44 Russian, 6-shot cylinder. **Barrel:** 6-1/2". **Weight:** 40 oz. **Length:** 12" overall. **Grips:** Smooth walnut. **Sights:** Blade front, notch rear. **Features:** Repica of the S&W Model 3 Russian Third Model revolver. Spur trigger guard, polished blue finish. Introduced 1999. Imported by Uberti USA.

Price: **$800.00**

UBERTI 1875 SCHOFIELD-STYLE BREAK-TOP REVOLVER

Caliber: 44-40, 45 Colt, 6-shot cylinder. **Barrel:** 5", 7". **Weight:** 39 oz. **Length:** 10-3/4" overall (5" barrel). **Grips:** Smooth walnut. **Sights:** Blade front, notch rear. **Features:** Replica of Smith & Wesson Model 3 Schofield. Single-action, top-break with automatic ejection. Polished blue finish. Introduced 1994. Imported by Uberti USA.

Price: **$750.00**

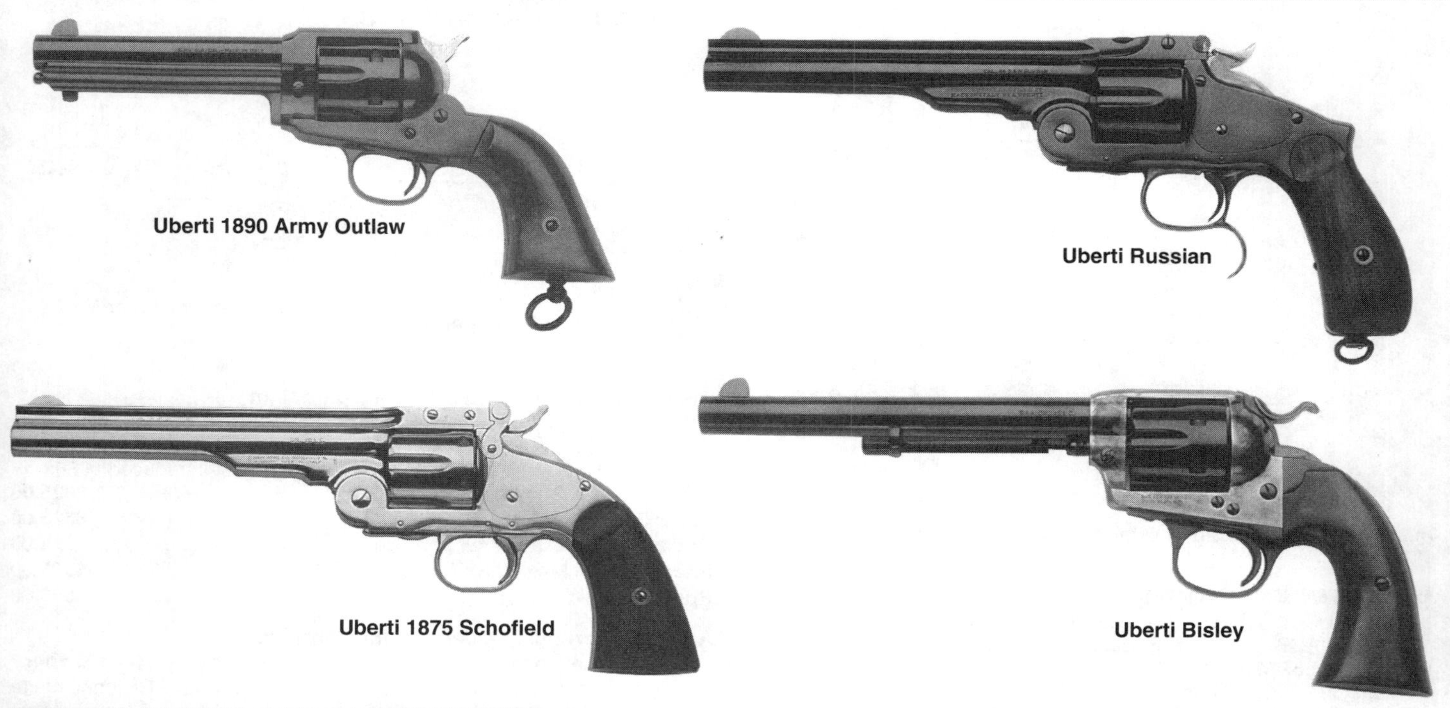

Uberti 1890 Army Outlaw

Uberti Russian

Uberti 1875 Schofield

Uberti Bisley

UBERTI BISLEY MODEL SINGLE-ACTION REVOLVER

Caliber: 38-40, 357 Mag., 44 Spec., 44-40 or 45 Colt, 6-shot cylinder. **Barrel:** 4-3/4", 5-1/2", 7-1/2". **Weight:** 40 oz. **Length:** 12-1/2" overall (7-1/2" barrel). **Grips:** Smooth walnut. **Sights:** Blade front, notch rear. **Features:** Replica of Colt's Bisley Model. Polished blue finish, color case-hardened frame. Introduced 1997. Imported by Uberti USA.

Price: **$435.00**

Uberti Bisley Model Flat Top Target Revolver

Similar to standard Bisley model, flat top strap, 7-1/2" barrel only, spring-loaded German silver front sight blade, standing leaf rear sight adjustable for windage. Polished blue finish, color case-hardened frame. Introduced 1998. Imported by Uberti USA.

Price: **$435.00**

U.S. FIRE ARMS SINGLE ACTION ARMY REVOLVER

Caliber: 45 Colt (standard); 32 WCF, 38 WCF, 38 S&W, 41 Colt, 44WCF, 44 S&W (optional, additional charge), 6-shot cylinder. **Barrel:** 4-3/4", 5-1/2", 7-1/2". **Weight:** 37 oz. **Length:** NA. **Grips:** Hard rubber. **Sights:** Blade front, notch rear. **Features:** Recreation of original guns; 3" and 4" have no ejector. Available with all-blue, blue with color case-hardening, or full nickel-plate finish. Made in U.S.A. by United States Fire Arms Mfg. Co.

Price: Blue/cased-colors **$949.00**

Price: Nickel **$1220.00**

CONSULT
SHOOTER'S MARKETPLACE
Page 125, This Edition

Uberti Bisley Flat Top

U. S. FIRE ARMS NETTLETON CAVALRY

Caliber: 45 Colt, 6-shot cylinder. **Barrel:** 5-1/2 (Artillery model), 7-1/2". **Grips:** One-piece walnut. **Features:** Military armory blue and bone case finish. Made in U. S. by Fire Arms Mfg. Co.

Price: Blued finish **$1,265.00**

Price: Nickel finish **$1,380.00**

U.S. FIRE ARMS RODEO COWBOY ACTION REVOLVER

Caliber: 45 Colt. **Barrel:** 4-3/4", 5-1/2". **Grips:** Rubber. **Features:** Historically correct armory bone case hammer, blue satin finish, transfer bar safety system, correct solid firing pin. Entry level basic cowboy SASS gun for beginner or expert.

Price: **$649.00**

U.S. FIRE ARMS UNITED STATES PRE-WAR

Caliber: 45 Colt, other caliber available. **Barrel:** 4-3/4", 5-1/2", 7-1/2". **Grips:** Hard rubber. **Features:** Armory bone case/Armory blue finish standard, cross-pin or black powder frame. Introduced 2002. Made in U.S.A. by United States Firearms Manufacturing Co.

Price: **$1,195.00**

HANDGUNS — MISCELLANEOUS

Specially adapted single-shot and multi-barrel arms.

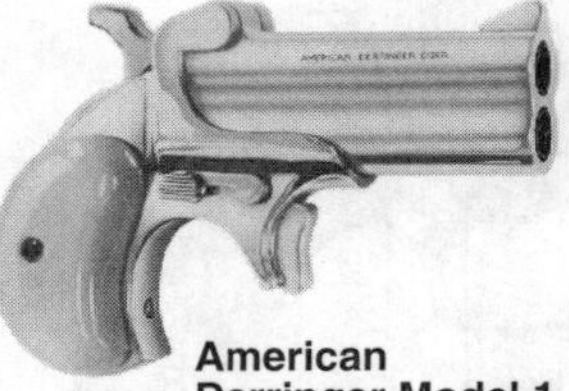

American Derringer Model 1

American Derringer Model 4

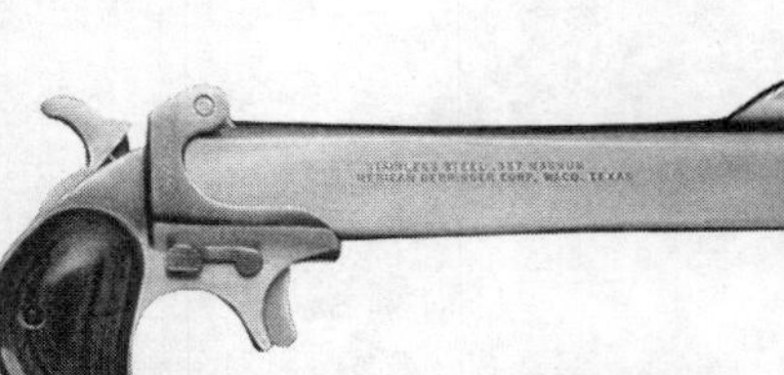

American Derringer Model 6

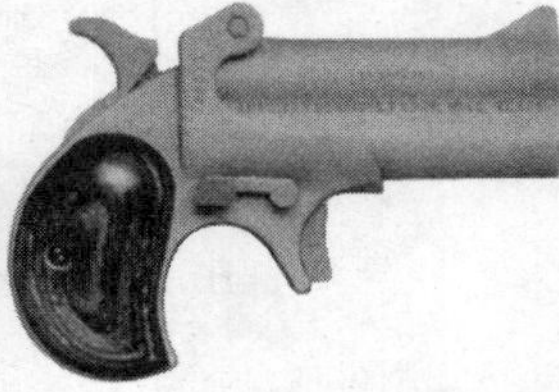

American Derringer Model 7

American Derringer Lady Derringer

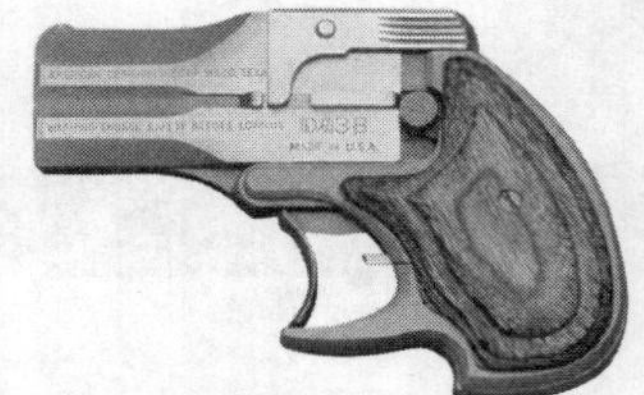

American Derringer DA 38

AMERICAN DERRINGER MODEL 1

Caliber: 22 LR, 22 WMR, 30 Carbine, 30 Luger, 30-30 Win., 32 H&R Mag., 32-20, 380 ACP, 38 Super, 38 Spec., 38 Spec. shotshell, 38 Spec. +P, 9mm Para., 357 Mag., 357 Mag./45/410, 357 Maximum, 10mm, 40 S&W, 41 Mag., 38-40, 44-40 Win., 44 Spec., 44 Mag., 45 Colt, 45 Win. Mag., 45 ACP, 45 Colt/410, 45-70 single shot. **Barrel:** 3". **Weight:** 15-1/2 oz. (38 Spec.). **Length:** 4.82" overall. **Grips:** Rosewood, Zebra wood. **Sights:** Blade front. **Features:** Made of stainless steel with high-polish or satin finish. Two-shot capacity. Manual hammer block safety. Introduced 1980. Available in almost any pistol caliber. Contact the factory for complete list of available calibers and prices. From American Derringer Corp.

Price: 22 LR . . . . **NA**
Price: 38 Spec. . . . . **NA**
Price: 357 Maximum . . . . **NA**
Price: 357 Mag. . . . . **NA**
Price: 9mm, 380 . . . . **NA**
Price: 40 S&W . . . . **NA**
Price: 44 Spec. . . . . **NA**
Price: 44-40 Win. . . . . **NA**
Price: 45 Colt . . . . **NA**
Price: 30-30, 45 Win. Mag. . . . . **NA**
Price: 41, 44 Mags. . . . . **NA**
Price: 45-70, single shot . . . . **NA**
Price: 45 Colt, 410, 2-1/2" . . . . **NA**
Price: 45 ACP, 10mm Auto . . . . **NA**

American Derringer Model 4

Similar to the Model 1 except has 4.1" barrel, overall length of 6", and weighs 16-1/2 oz.; chambered for 357 Mag., 357 Maximum, 45-70, 3" 410-bore shotshells or 45 Colt or 44 Mag. Made of stainless steel. Manual hammer block safety. Introduced 1980.

Price: 3" 410/45 Colt **$425.00**
Price: 45-70 . . . . **$560.00**
Price: 44 Mag. with oversize grips **$515.00**
Price: Alaskan Survival model (45-70 upper barrel, 410 or 45 Colt lower) **$475.00**

American Derringer Model 6

Similar to the Model 1 except has 6" barrel chambered for 3" 410 shotshells or 22 WMR, 357 Mag., 45 ACP, 45 Colt; rosewood stocks; 8.2" o.a.l. and weighs 21 oz. Shoots either round for each barrel. Manual ham-mer block safety. Introduced 1980.

Price: 22 WMR **$440.00**
Price: 357 Mag. **$440.00**
Price: 45 Colt/410 . . . . **$450.00**
Price: 45 ACP **$440.00**

American Derringer Model 7 Ultra Lightweight

Similar to Model 1 except made of high strength aircraft aluminum. Weighs 7-1/2 oz., 4.82" o.a.l., rosewood stocks. Available in 22 LR, 22 WMR, 32 H&R Mag., 380 ACP, 38 Spec., 44 Spec. Introduced 1980.

Price: 22 LR, WMR **$325.00**
Price: 38 Spec. **$325.00**
Price: 380 ACP **$325.00**
Price: 32 H&R Mag/32 S&W Long **$325.00**
Price: 44 Spec. **$565.00**

American Derringer Model 10 Ultra Lightweight

Similar to the Model 1 except frame is aluminum, giving weight of 10 oz. Stainless barrels. Available in 38 Spec., 45 Colt or 45 ACP only. Matte gray finish. Introduced 1980.

Price: 45 Colt **$385.00**
Price: 45 ACP **$330.00**
Price: 38 Spec. **$305.00**

American Derringer Lady Derringer

Same as the Model 1 except has tuned action, fitted with scrimshawed synthetic ivory grips; chambered for 32 H&R Mag. and 38 Spec.; 357 Mag., 45 Colt, 45/410. Deluxe Grade is highly polished; Deluxe Engraved is engraved in a pattern similar to that used on 1880s derringers. All come in a French-fitted jewelry box. Introduced 1989.

Price: 32 H&R Mag. **$375.00**
Price: 357 Mag. **$405.00**
Price: 38 Spec. **$360.00**
Price: 45 Colt, 45/410 . . . . **$435.00**

American Derringer Texas Commemorative

A Model 1 Derringer with solid brass frame, stainless steel barrel and rosewood grips. Available in 38 Spec., 44-40 Win., or 45 Colt. Introduced 1980.

Price: 38 Spec. **$365.00**
Price: 44-40 . . . . **$420.00**
Price: Brass frame, 45 Colt **$450.00**

AMERICAN DERRINGER DA 38 MODEL

Caliber: 22 LR, 9mm Para., 38 Spec., 357 Mag., 40 S&W. **Barrel:** 3". **Weight:** 14.5 oz. **Length:** 4.8" overall. **Grips:** Rosewood, walnut or other hardwoods. **Sights:** Fixed. **Features:** Double-action only; two-shots. Manual safety. Made of satin-finished stainless steel and aluminum. Introduced 1989. From American Derringer Corp.

Price: 22 LR **$435.00**
Price: 38 Spec. **$460.00**
Price: 9mm Para. **$445.00**
Price: 357 Mag. **$450.00**
Price: 40 S&W **$475.00**

ANSCHUTZ MODEL 64P SPORT/TARGET PISTOL

Caliber: 22 LR, 22 WMR, 5-shot magazine. **Barrel:** 10". **Weight:** 3 lbs., 8 oz. **Length:** 18-1/2" overall. **Stock:** Choate Rynite. **Sights:** None furnished; grooved for scope mounting. **Features:** Right-hand bolt; polished blue finish. Introduced 1998. Imported from Germany by AcuSport.

Price: 22 LR **$455.95**
Price: 22 WMR **$479.95**

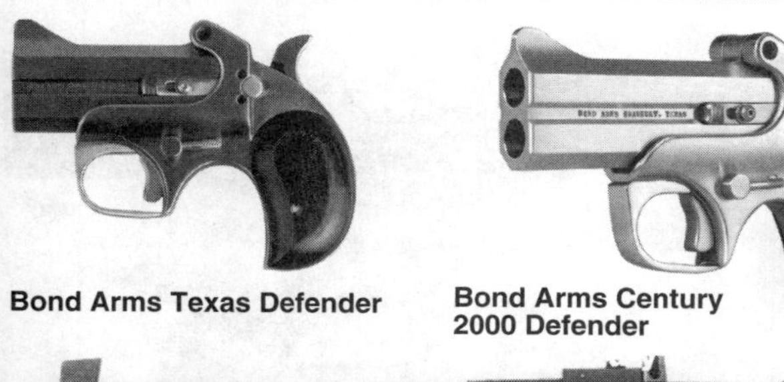

Bond Arms Texas Defender

Bond Arms Century 2000 Defender

Cobra Big Bore

Cobra D-Series

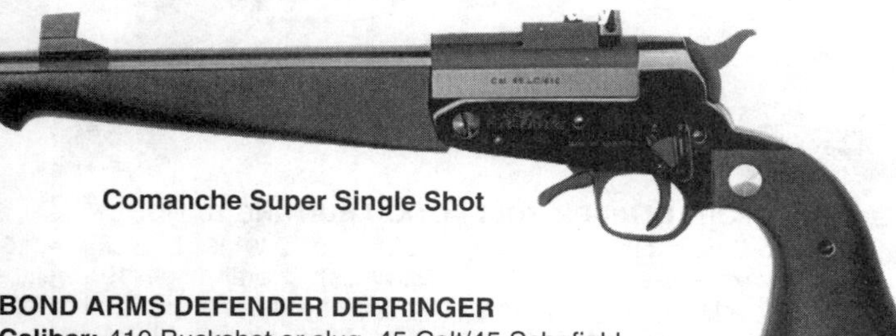

Comanche Super Single Shot

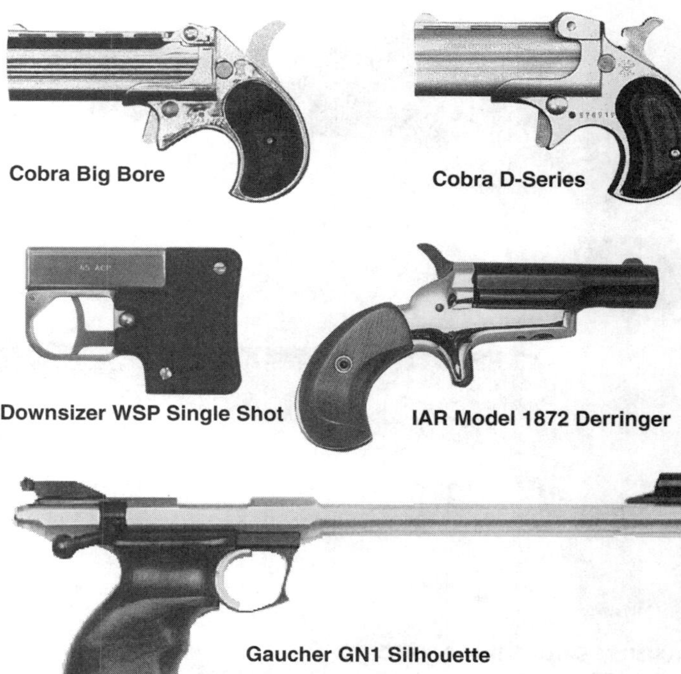

Downsizer WSP Single Shot

IAR Model 1872 Derringer

Gaucher GN1 Silhouette

BOND ARMS DEFENDER DERRINGER

Caliber: 410 Buckshot or slug, 45 Colt/45 Schofield (2.5" chamber), 45 Colt (only), 450 Bond Super/45 ACP/45 Super, 44 Mag./44 Special/44 Russian, 10mm, 40 S&W, 357 SIG, 357 Maxi-mum/357 Mag./38 Special, 357 Mag/38 Special & 38 Long Colt, 38 Short Colt, 9mm Luger (9x19), 32 H&R Mag./38 S&W Long/32 Colt New Police, 22 Mag., 22 LR., 38-40, 44-40. **Barrel:** 3", 3-1/2". **Weight:** 20-21 oz. **Length:** 5"-5-1/2". **Grips:** Exotic woods or animal horn. **Sights:** Blade front, fixed rear. **Features:** Interchangeable barrels, retracting and rebounding firing pins, cross-bolt safety, automatic extractor for rimmed calibers. Stainless steel construction. Right or left hand.

Price: Texas (with TG) 3" bbl. **$379.00**
Price: Super (with TG) 3" bbl., 450 Bond Super and 45 ACP . . . **$379.00**
Price: Cowboy (no TG) **$379.00**
Price: Century 2000 (with TG), Cowboy Century 2000 (no TG), 3-1/2" bbls., 410/45 Colt **$394.00**
Price: Additional calibers - available separately

BROWN CLASSIC SINGLE SHOT PISTOL

Caliber: 17 Ackley Hornet through 375x444. **Barrel:** 15" airgauged match grade. **Weight:** About 3 lbs., 7 oz. **Grips:** Walnut; thumbrest target style. **Sights:** None furnished; drilled and tapped for scope mounting. **Features:** Falling block action gives rigid barrel-receiver mating; hand-fitted and headspaced. Introduced 1998. Made in U.S.A. by E.A. Brown Mfg.

Price: **$589.00**

COBRA BIG BORE DERRINGERS

Caliber: 22 WMR, 32 H&R Mag, 38 Spec., 9mm Para. **Barrel:** 2.75". **Weight:** 11.5 oz. **Length:** 4.65" overall. **Grips:** Textured black synthetic. **Sights:** Blade front, fixed notch rear. **Features:** Alloy frame, steel-lined barrels, steel breech block. Plunger-type safety with integral hammer block. Chrome or black Teflon finish. Introduced 2002. Made in U.S.A. by Cobra Enterprises.

Price: **$98.00**
Price: 9mm Para **$136.00**

COBRA LONG-BORE DERRINGERS

Caliber: 22 WMR, 38 Spec., 9mm Para. **Barrel:** 3.5". **Weight:** 13 oz. **Length**: 5.65" overall. **Grips:** Textured black synthetic. **Sights:** Fixed. **Features:** Chrome or black Teflon finish. Larger than Davis D-Series models. Introduced 2002. Made in U.S.A. by Cobra Enterprises.

Price: **$136.00**
Price: 9mm Para. **$136.00**
Price: Big-Bore models (same calibers, 3/4" shorter barrels). . . . **$136.00**

COBRA STARBIRD-SERIES DERRINGERS

Caliber: 22 LR, 22 WMR, 25 ACP, 32 ACP. **Barrel:** 2.4". **Weight:** 9.5 oz. **Length**: 4" overall. **Grips:** Laminated wood or pearl. **Sights:** Blade front, fixed notch rear. **Features:** Choice of black powder coat, satin nickel or chrome finish; spur trigger. Introduced 2002. Made in U.S.A. by Cobra Enterprises.

Price: **$112.00**

COMANCHE SUPER SINGLE SHOT PISTOL

Caliber: 45 LC, 410 ga. **Barrel:** 10." **Sights:** Adjustable. **Features:** Blue finish, not available for sale in CA, MA. Distributed by SGS Importers International, Inc.

Price: **$174.95**
Price: Satin nickel **$191.95**
Price: Duo tone **$185.95**

DOWNSIZER WSP SINGLE SHOT PISTOL

Caliber: 357 Magnum, 45 ACP, 38 Special. **Barrel:** 2.10." **Weight:** 11 oz. **Length:** 3.25" overall. **Grips:** Black polymer. **Sights:** None. **Features:** Single shot, tip-up barrel. Double-action-only. Stainless steel construction. Measures .900" thick. Introduced 1997. From Downsizer Corp.

Price: **$499.00**

GAUCHER GN1 SILHOUETTE PISTOL

Caliber: 22 LR, single-shot. **Barrel:** 10". **Weight:** 2.4 lbs. **Length:** 15.5" overall. **Grips:** European hardwood. **Sights:** Blade front, open adjustable rear. **Features:** Bolt action, adjustable trigger. Introduced 1990. Imported from France by Mandall Shooting Supplies.

Price: About **$525.00**
Price: Model GP Silhouette **$425.00**

IAR MODEL 1872 DERRINGER

Caliber: 22 Short. **Barrel:** 2-3/8". **Weight:** 7 oz. **Length:** 5-1/8" overall. **Grips:** Smooth walnut. **Sights:** Blade front, notch rear. **Features:** Gold or nickel frame with blue barrel. Reintroduced 1996 using original Colt designs and tooling for the Colt Model 4 Derringer. Made in U.S.A. by IAR, Inc.

Price: **$109.00**
Price: Single cased gun **$125.00**
Price: Double cased set **$215.00**

IAR MODEL 1866 DOUBLE DERRINGER

Caliber: 38 Special. **Barrel:** 2-3/4". **Weight:** 16 oz. **Grips:** Smooth walnut. **Sights:** Blade front, notch rear. **Features:** All steel construction. Blue barrel, color case-hardened frame. Uses original designs and tooling for the Uberti New Maverick Derringer. Introduced 1999. Made in U.S.A. by IAR, Inc.

Price: **$395.00**

HANDGUNS — MISCELLANEOUS

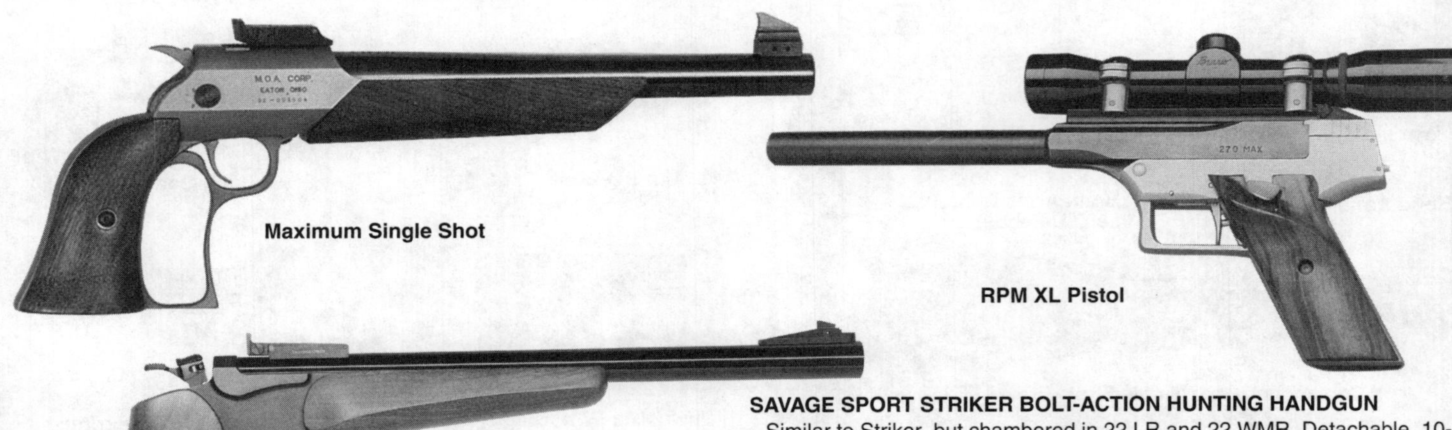

Maximum Single Shot

RPM XL Pistol

Thompson/Center G2 Contender

MAXIMUM SINGLE SHOT PISTOL

Caliber: 22 LR, 22 Hornet, 22 BR, 22 PPC, 223 Rem., 22-250, 6mm BR, 6mm PPC, 243, 250 Savage, 6.5mm-35M, 270 MAX, 270 Win., 7mm TCU, 7mm BR, 7mm-35, 7mm INT-R, 7mm-08, 7mm Rocket, 7mm Super-Mag., 30 Herrett, 30 Carbine, 30-30, 308 Win., 30x39, 32-20, 350 Rem. Mag., 357 Mag., 357 Maximum, 358 Win., 375 H&H, 44 Mag., 454 Casull. **Barrel:** 8-3/4", 10-1/2", 14". **Weight:** 61 oz. (10-1/2" bbl.); 78 oz. (14" bbl.). **Length:** 15", 18-1/2" overall (with 10-1/2" and 14" bbl., respectively). **Grips:** Smooth walnut stocks and forend. Also available with 17" finger groove grip. **Sights:** Ramp front, fully adjustable open rear. **Features:** Falling block action; drilled and tapped for M.O.A. scope mounts; integral grip frame/receiver; adjustable trigger; Douglas barrel (interchangeable). Introduced 1983. Made in U.S.A. by M.O.A. Corp.

Price: Stainless receiver, blue barrel **$799.00**
Price: Stainless receiver, stainless barrel **$883.00**
Price: Extra blued barrel **$254.00**
Price: Extra stainless barrel **$317.00**
Price: Scope mount **$60.00**

RPM XL SINGLE SHOT PISTOL

Caliber: 22 LR through 45-70. **Barrel:** 8", 10-3/4", 12", 14". **Weight:** About 60 oz. **Grips:** Smooth Goncalo Alves with thumb and heel rests. **Sights:** Hooded front with interchangeable post, or Patridge; ISGW rear adjustable for windage and elevation. **Features:** Barrel drilled and tapped for scope mount. Visible cocking indicator. Spring-loaded barrel lock, positive hammer-block safety. Trigger adjustable for weight of pull and over-travel. Contact maker for complete price list. Made in U.S.A. by RPM.

Price: XL Hunter model (action only) **$1,045.00**
Price: Extra barrel, 8" through 10-3/4" **$407.50**
Price: Extra barrel, 12" through 14" **$547.50**
Price: Muzzle brake **$160.00**
Price: Left hand action, add **$50.00**

SAVAGE STRIKER BOLT-ACTION HUNTING HANDGUN

Caliber: 223, 243, 7mm-08, 308, 300 WSM 2-shot mag. **Barrel:** 14". **Weight:** About 5 lbs. **Length:** 22-1/2" overall. **Stock:** Black composite ambidextrous mid-grip; grooved forend; "Dual Pillar" bedding. **Sights:** None furnished; drilled and tapped for scope mounting. **Features:** Short left-hand bolt with right-hand ejection; free-floated barrel; uses Savage Model 110 rifle scope rings/bases. Introduced 1998. Made in U.S.A. by Savage Arms, Inc.

Price: Model 503 (blued barrel and action). **$285.00**
Price: Model 503 R17FSS (stainless barrel and action). **$281.00**
Price: Model 516FSAK black stock (SS, AMB, 300WSM) **$260.00**

SAVAGE SPORT STRIKER BOLT-ACTION HUNTING HANDGUN

Similar to Striker, but chambered in 22 LR and 22 WMR. Detachable, 10-shot magazine (5-shot magazine for 22 WMR). Overall length 19", weighs 4 lbs. Ambidextrous fiberglass/graphite composite rear grip. Drilled and tapped, scope mount installed. Introduced 2000. Made in U.S.A. by Savage Arms Inc.

Price: Model 501F (blue finish, 22LR) **$236.00**
Price: Model 501FXP with soft case, 1.25-4x28 scope **$258.00**
Price: Model 502F (blue finish, 22 WMR). **$238.00**

SPRINGFIELD M6 SCOUT PISTOL

Caliber: 22 LR/45 LC/.410, 22 Hornet, 45 LC/.410. **Barrel:** 10". **Weight:** NA. **Length:** NA. **Grips:** NA. **Sights:** NA. **Features:** Adapted from the U.S. Air Force M6 Survival Rifle, it is also available as a carbine with 16" barrel.

Price: . . . . **$169.00 to $197.00**
Price: Pistol/Carbine . . . . **$183.00 to $209.00**

THOMPSON/CENTER ENCORE PISTOL

Caliber: 22-250, 223, 260 Rem., 7mm-08, 243, 308, 270, 30-06, 375 JDJ, 204 Ruger, 44 Mag., 454 Casull, 480 Ruger, 444 Marlin single shot, 450 Marlin with muzzle tamer, no sights. **Barrel:** 12", 15", tapered round. **Weight:** NA. **Length:** 21" overall with 12" barrel. **Grips:** American walnut with finger grooves, walnut forend. **Sights:** Blade on ramp front, adjustable rear, or none. **Features:** Interchangeable barrels; action opens by squeezing the trigger guard; drilled and tapped for scope mounting; blue finish. Announced 1996. Made in U.S.A. by Thompson/Center Arms.

Price: . . . . **$578.00 to $641.00**
Price: Extra 12" barrels. **$260.00**
Price: Extra 15" barrels. **$267.00**
Price: 45 Colt/410 barrel, 12" **$289.00**
Price: 45 Colt/410 barrel, 15" **$297.00**

Thompson/Center Stainless Encore Pistol

Similar to blued Encore, made of stainless steel, available with 15" barrel in 223, 22-250, 243 Win., 7mm-08, 308, 30/06 Sprgfld., 45/70 Gov't., 45/410 VR. With black rubber grip and forend. Made in U.S.A. by Thompson/Center Arms.

Price: . . . . **$633.00 to $670.00**

Thompson/Center G2 Contender Pistol

A second generation Contender pistol maintaining the same barrel interchangeability with older Contender barrels and their corresponding forends (except Herrett forend). The G2 frame will not accept old-style grips due to the change in grip angle. Incorporates an automatic hammer block safety with built-in interlock. Features include trigger adjustable for overtravel, adjustable rear sight; ramp front sight blade, blued steel finish.

Price: **$566.75**

UBERTI ROLLING BLOCK TARGET PISTOL

Caliber: 22 LR, 22 WMR, 22 Hornet, 357 Mag., 45 Colt, single shot. **Barrel:** 9-7/8", half-round, half-octagon. **Weight:** 44 oz. **Length:** 14" overall. **Stock:** Walnut grip and forend. **Sights:** Blade front, fully adjustable rear. **Features:** Replica of the 1871 rolling block target pistol. Brass trigger guard, color case-hardened frame, blue barrel. Imported by Uberti U.S.A.

Price: **$410.00**

Dixie Pennsylvania Harper's Ferry Kentucky Le Page Lyman Plains Pistol

DIXIE PENNSYLVANIA PISTOL

Caliber: 44 (.430" round ball). **Barrel:** 10", (7/8" octagon). **Weight:** 2-1/2 labs. **Stocks:** Walnut-stained hardwood. **Sights:** Blade front, open rear drift-adjustable for windage; brass. **Features:** Available in flint only. Brass trigger guard, thimbles, instep, wedge plates; high-luster blue barrel. Imported from Italy by Dixie Gun Works.

Price: Finished **$215.00**

Price: Kit **$195.00**

FRENCH-STYLE DUELING PISTOL

Caliber: 44. **Barrel:** 10". **Weight:** 35 oz. **Length:** 15-3/4" overall. **Stocks:** Carved walnut. **Sights:** Fixed. **Features:** Comes with velvet-lined case and accessories. Imported by Mandall Shooting Supplies.

Price: **$295.00**

HARPER'S FERRY 1806 PISTOL

Caliber: 58 (.570" round ball). **Barrel:** 10". **Weight:** 40 oz. **Length:** 16" overall. **Stocks:** Walnut. **Sights:** Fixed. **Features:** Case-hardened lock, brass-mounted browned barrel. Replica of the first U.S. Gov't.-made flintlock pistol. Imported by Navy Arms, Dixie Gun Works.

Price: . . . . **$275.00 to $405.00**

Price: Kit (Dixie) **$250.00**

KENTUCKY FLINTLOCK PISTOL

Caliber: 44, 45. **Barrel:** 10-1/8". **Weight:** 32 oz. **Length:** 15-1/2" overall. **Stocks:** Walnut. **Sights:** Fixed. **Features:** Specifications, including caliber, weight and length may vary with importer. Case-hardened lock, blued barrel; available also as brass barrel flint Model 1821. Imported by Navy Arms, The Armoury, Dixie Gun Works.

Price: **$300.00**

Price: In kit form, from. . . . . **$90.00 to $112.00**

Price: Single cased set (Navy Arms) **$360.00**

Price: Double cased set (Navy Arms). **$590.00**

Kentucky Percussion Pistol

Similar to flint version but percussion lock. Imported by The Armoury, Navy Arms, CVA (50-cal.).

Price: . . . . **$129.95 to $225.00**

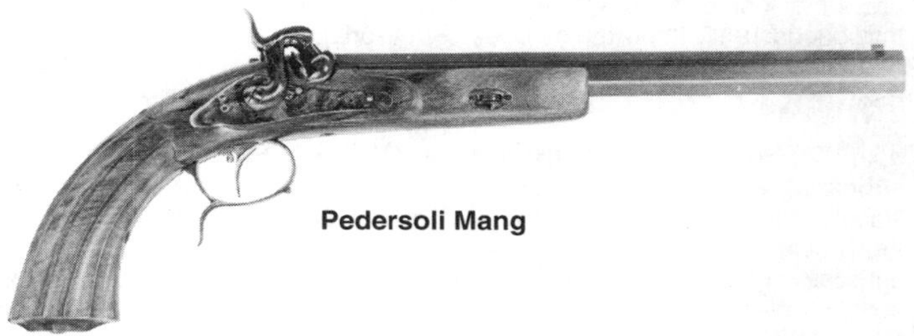

Pedersoli Mang

Price: Steel barrel (Armoury) **$179.00**

Price: Single cased set (Navy Arms) **$355.00**

Price: Double cased set (Navy Arms). **$600.00**

LE PAGE PERCUSSION DUELING PISTOL

Caliber: 44. **Barrel:** 10", rifled. **Weight:** 40 oz. **Length:** 16" overall. **Stocks:** Walnut, fluted butt. **Sights:** Blade front, notch rear. **Features:** Double-set triggers. Blued barrel; trigger guard and buttcap are polished silver. Imported by Dixie Gun Works.

Price: **$545.00**

LYMAN PLAINS PISTOL

Caliber: 50 or 54. **Barrel:** 8"; 1:30" twist, both calibers. **Weight:** 50 oz. **Length:** 15" overall. **Stocks:** Walnut half-stock. **Sights:** Blade front, square notch rear adjustable for windage. **Features:** Polished brass trigger guard and ramrod tip, color case-hardened coil spring lock, spring- loaded trigger, stainless steel nipple, blackened iron furniture. Hooked patent breech, detachable belt hook. Introduced 1981. From Lyman Products.

Price: Finished **$244.95**

Price: Kit **$189.95**

PEDERSOLI MANG TARGET PISTOL

Caliber: 38. **Barrel:** 10.5", octagonal; 1:15" twist, **Weight:** 2.5 lbs. **Length:** 17.25" overall. **Stocks:** Walnut with fluted grip. **Sights:** Blade front, open rear adjustable for windage. **Features:** Browned barrel, polished breech plug, rest color case-hardened. Imported from Italy by Dixie Gun Works.

Price: **$925.00**

BLACKPOWDER SINGLE SHOT PISTOLS — FLINT & PERCUSSION

Queen Anne   Thompson/Center Encore   Traditions Pioneer   Traditions William Parker

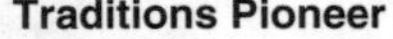

QUEEN ANNE FLINTLOCK PISTOL

Caliber: 50 (.490" round ball). **Barrel:** 7-1/2", smoothbore. **Stocks:** Walnut. **Sights:** None. **Features:** Browned steel barrel, fluted brass trigger guard, brass mask on butt. Lockplate left in the white. Made by Pedersoli in Italy. Introduced 1983. Imported by Dixie Gun Works.

Price: **$275.00**
Price: Kit **$195.00**

THOMPSON/CENTER ENCORE 209x50 MAGNUM PISTOL

Caliber: 50. **Barrel:** 15"; 1:20" twist. **Weight:** About 4 lbs. Grips: American walnut grip and forend. **Sights:** Click-adjustable, steel rear, ramp front. **Features:** Uses 209 shotgun primer for closed-breech ignition; accepts charges up to 110 grains of FFg black powder or two, 50-grain Pyrodex pellets. Introduced 2000.

Price: **$611.00**
Price: (barrel only) **$325.00**

TRADITIONS BUCKHUNTER PRO IN-LINE PISTOL

Caliber: 50. **Barrel:** 9-1/2", round. **Weight:** 48 oz. **Length:** 14" overall. **Stocks:** Smooth walnut or black epoxy-coated hardwood grip and forend. **Sights:** Beaded blade front, folding adjustable rear. **Features:** Thumb safety; removable stainless steel breech plug; adjustable trigger, barrel drilled and tapped for scope mounting. From Traditions.

Price: With walnut grip **$229.00**
Price: Nickel with black grip **$239.00**
Price: With walnut grip and 12-1/2" barrel **$239.00**
Price: Nickel with black grip, muzzle brake and 14-3/4" fluted barrel **$289.00**
Price: 45 cal. nickel w/bl. grip, muzzlebrake and 14-3/4" fluted bbl. **$289.00**

TRADITIONS KENTUCKY PISTOL

Caliber: 50. **Barrel:** 10"; octagon with 7/8" flats; 1:20" twist. **Weight:** 40 oz. **Length:** 15" overall. **Stocks:** Stained beech. **Sights:** Blade front, fixed rear. **Features:** Birds-head grip; brass thimbles; color case-hardened lock. Percussion only. Introduced 1995. From Traditions.

Price: Finished **$139.00**
Price: Kit **$109.00**

TRADITIONS PIONEER PISTOL

Caliber: 45. **Barrel:** 9-5/8"; 13/16" flats, 1:16" twist. **Weight:** 31 oz. **Length:** 15" overall. **Stocks:** Beech. **Sights:** Blade front, fixed rear. **Features:** V-

Traditions Buckhunter Pro

type mainspring. Single trigger. German silver furniture, blackened hardware. From Traditions.

Price: **$139.00**
Price: Kit **$119.00**

TRADITIONS TRAPPER PISTOL

Caliber: 50. **Barrel:** 9-3/4"; 7/8" flats; 1:20" twist. **Weight:** 2-3/4 lbs. **Length:** 16" overall. **Stocks:** Beech. **Sights:** Blade front, adjustable rear. **Features:** Double-set triggers; brass buttcap, trigger guard, wedge plate, forend tip, thimble. From Traditions.

Price: Percussion **$189.00**
Price: Flintlock **$209.00**
Price: Kit **$149.00**

TRADITIONS VEST-POCKET DERRINGER

Caliber: 31. **Barrel:** 2-1/4"; brass. **Weight:** 8 oz. **Length:** 4-3/4" overall. **Stocks:** Simulated ivory. **Sights:** Beed front. **Features:** Replica of riverboat gamblers' derringer; authentic spur trigger. From Traditions.

Price: **$109.00**

TRADITIONS WILLIAM PARKER PISTOL

Caliber: 50. **Barrel:** 10-3/8"; 15/16" flats; polished steel. **Weight:** 37 oz. **Length:** 17-1/2" overall. **Stocks:** Walnut with checkered grip. **Sights:** Brass blade front, fixed rear. **Features:** Replica dueling pistol with 1:20" twist, hooked breech. Brass wedge plate, trigger guard, cap guard; separate ramrod. Double-set triggers. Polished steel barrel, lock. Imported by Traditions.

Price: **$269.00**

Army 1860

Baby Dragoon 1848

Dixie Wyatt Earp

Le Mat Revolver

Navy Arms 1836 Paterson

ARMY 1860 PERCUSSION REVOLVER

Caliber: 44, 6-shot. **Barrel:** 8". **Weight:** 40 oz. **Length:** 13-5/8" overall. **Stocks:** Walnut. **Sights:** Fixed. **Features:** Engraved Navy scene on cylinder; brass trigger guard; case-hardened frame, loading lever and hammer. Some importers supply pistol cut for detachable shoulder stock, have accessory stock available. Imported by Cabela's (1860 Lawman), E.M.F., Navy Arms, The Armoury, Cimarron, Dixie Gun Works (half-fluted cylinder, not roll engraved), Euroarms of America (brass or steel model), Armsport, Traditions (brass or steel), Uberti U.S.A. Inc., United States Patent Fire-Arms.

Price: About **$195.00**

Price: Hartford model, steel frame, German silver trim, cartouches (E.M.F.) **$215.00**

Price: Single cased set (Navy Arms) **$300.00**

Price: Double cased set (Navy Arms) **$490.00**

Price: 1861 Navy: Same as Army except 36-cal., 7-1/2" bbl., weighs 41 oz., cut for shoulder stock; round cylinder (fluted available), from Cabela's, CVA (brass frame, 44-cal.), United States Patent Fire-Arms . . . . **$99.95 to $385.00**

Price: Steel frame kit (E.M.F., Euroarms) . . . . **$125.00 to $216.25**

Price: Colt Army Police, fluted cyl., 5-1/2", 36-cal. (Cabela's) **$124.95**

Price: With nickeled frame, barrel and backstrap, gold-tone fluted cylinder, trigger and hammer, simulated ivory grips (Traditions) **$199.00**

BABY DRAGOON 1848, 1849 POCKET, WELLS FARGO

Caliber: 31. **Barrel:** 3", 4", 5", 6"; seven-groove; RH twist. **Weight:** About 21 oz. **Stocks:** Varnished walnut. **Sights:** Brass pin front, hammer notch rear. **Features:** No loading lever on Baby Dragoon or Wells Fargo models. Unfluted cylinder with stagecoach holdup scene; cupped cylinder pin; no grease grooves; one safety pin on cylinder and slot in hammer face; straight (flat) mainspring. From Armsport, Cimarron F.A. Co., Dixie Gun Works, Uberti U.S.A. Inc.

Price: 6" barrel, with loading lever (Dixie Gun Works) **$275.00**

Price: 4" (Uberti USA Inc.) **$335.00**

CABELA'S 1860 ARMY SNUBNOSE REVOLVER

Caliber: .44. **Barrel:** 3". **Weight:** 2 lbs., 3 oz. **Length:** 9" overall. **Grips:** Hardwood. **Sights:** Blade front, hammer notch near. **Features:** Shortened barrels w/o loading lever. Separate brass loading tool included.

Price: Revolver only **$189.99**

Price: W/starter kit **$289.99**

CABELA'S 1862 POLICE SNUBNOSE REVOLVER

Caliber: .36. **Barrel:** 3". **Weight:** 2 lbs., 3 oz. **Length:** 8.5" overall. **Grips:** Hardwood. **Sights:** Blade front, hammer notch rear. **Features:** Shortened barrel, removed loading lever. Separate brass loading tool included.

Price: . . . . **$169.99** (revolver only); **$209.99** (with starter kit).

DIXIE WYATT EARP REVOLVER

Caliber: 44. **Barrel:** 12", octagon. **Weight:** 46 oz. **Length:** 18" overall. **Stocks:** Two-piece walnut. **Sights:** Fixed. **Features:** Highly polished brass frame, backstrap and trigger guard; blued barrel and cylinder; case-hardened hammer, trigger and loading lever. Navy-size shoulder stock ($45) will fit with minor fitting. From Dixie Gun Works.

Price: **$160.00**

LE MAT REVOLVER

Caliber: 44/65. **Barrel:** 6-3/4" (revolver); 4-7/8" (single shot). **Weight:** 3 lbs., 7 oz. **Stocks:** Hand-checkered walnut. **Sights:** Post front, hammer notch rear. **Features:** Exact reproduction with all-steel construction; 44-cal. 9-shot cylinder, 65-cal. single barrel; color case-hardened hammer with selector; spur trigger guard; ring at butt; lever-type barrel release. From Navy Arms.

Price: Cavalry model (lanyard ring, spur trigger guard) **$595.00**

Price: Army model (round trigger guard, pin-type barrel release) **$595.00**

Price: Naval-style (thumb selector on hammer) **$595.00**

NAVY ARMS NEW MODEL POCKET REVOLVER

Caliber: 31, 5-shot. **Barrel:** 3-1/2", octagon. **Weight:** 15 oz. **Length:** 7-3/4". **Stocks:** Two-piece walnut. **Sights:** Fixed. **Features:** Replica of the Remington New Model Pocket. Available with polisehd brass frame or nickel plated finish. Introduced 2000. Imported by Navy Arms.

Price: **$300.00**

NAVY ARMS 1836 PATERSON REVOLVER

Features: Hidden trigger, 36 cal., blued barrel, replica of 5-shooter, roll-engraved with stagecoach hold-up.

Price: . . . . **$340.00 to $499.00**

BLACKPOWDER REVOLVERS

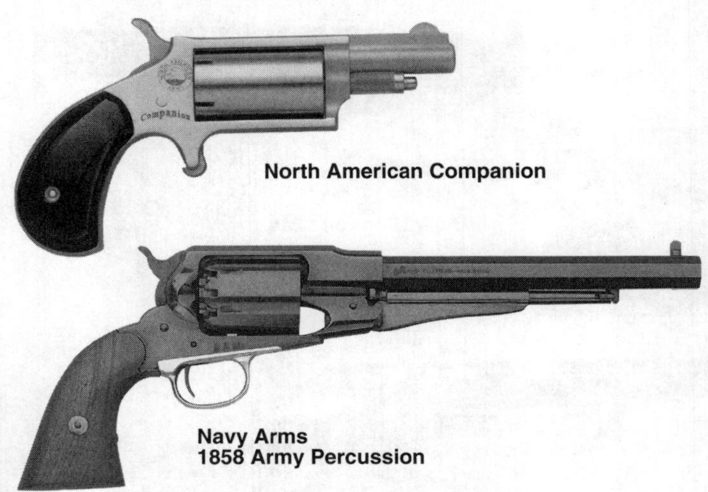

North American Companion

Navy Arms
1858 Army Percussion

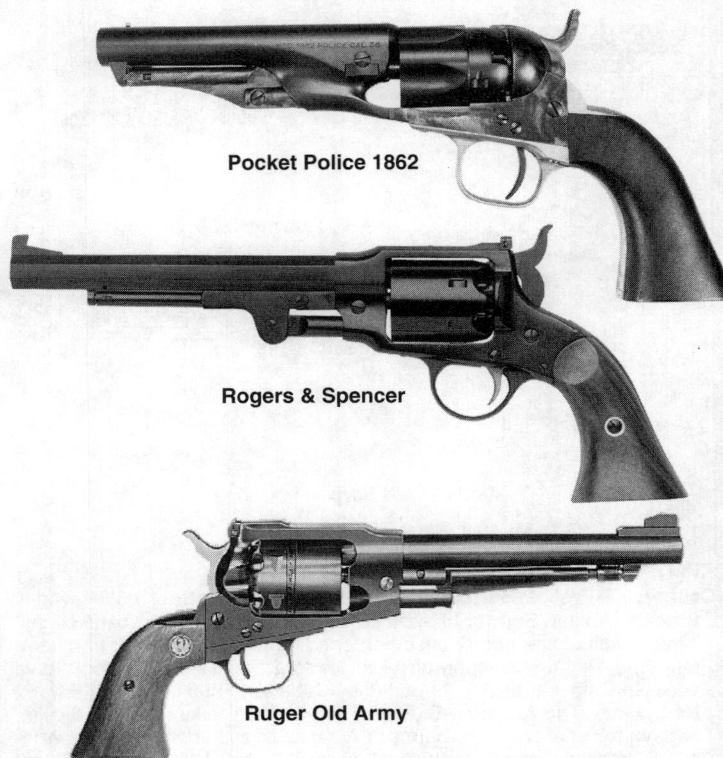

Pocket Police 1862

Rogers & Spencer

Ruger Old Army

NAVY MODEL 1851 PERCUSSION REVOLVER

Caliber: 36, 44, 6-shot. **Barrel:** 7-1/2". **Weight:** 44 oz. **Length:** 13" overall. **Stocks:** Walnut finish. **Sights:** Post front, hammer notch rear. **Features:** Brass backstrap and trigger guard; some have 1st Model squareback trigger guard, engraved cylinder with navy battle scene; case-hardened frame, hammer, loading lever. Imported by The Armoury, Cabela's, Cimarron F.A. Co., Navy Arms, E.M.F., Dixie Gun Works, Euroarms of America, Armsport, CVA (44-cal. only), Traditions (44 only), Uberti U.S.A. Inc., United States Patent Fire-Arms.

Price: Brass frame . . . . **$99.95 to $385.00**
Price: Steel frame . . . . **$130.00 to $285.00**
Price: Kit form . . . . **$110.00 to $123.95**
Price: Engraved model (Dixie Gun Works) **$182.50**
Price: Single cased set, steel frame (Navy Arms) **$280.00**
Price: Double cased set, steel frame (Navy Arms) **$455.00**
Price: Confederate Navy (Cabela's) **$89.99**
Price: Hartford model, steel frame, German silver trim, cartouche (E.M.F.) **$190.00**

NEW MODEL 1858 ARMY PERCUSSION REVOLVER

Caliber: 36 or 44, 6-shot. **Barrel:** 6-1/2" or 8". **Weight:** 38 oz. **Length:** 13-1/2" overall. **Stocks:** Walnut. **Sights:** Blade front, groove-in-frame rear. **Features:** Replica of Remington Model 1858. Also available from some importers as Army Model Belt Revolver in 36-cal., a shortened and light-ened version of the 44. Target Model (Uberti U.S.A. Inc., Navy Arms) has fully adjustable target rear sight, target front, 36 or 44. Imported by Cabe-la's, Cimarron F.A. Co., CVA (as 1858 Army, brass frame, 44 only), Dixie Gun Works, Navy Arms, The Armoury, E.M.F., Euroarms of America (engraved, stainless and plain), Armsport, Traditions (44 only), Uberti U.S.A. Inc.

Price: Steel frame, about . . . . **$99.95 to $280.00**
Price: Steel frame kit (Euroarms, Navy Arms) . . . . . . **$115.95 to $150.00**
Price: Single cased set (Navy Arms) **$290.00**
Price: Double cased set (Navy Arms) **$480.00**
Price: Stainless steel Model 1858 (Euroarms, Uberti U.S.A. Inc., Cabela's, Navy Arms, Armsport, Traditions) . . . . . . **$169.95 to $380.00**
Price: Target Model, adjustable rear sight (Cabela's, Euroarms, Uberti U.S.A. Inc., Stone Mountain Arms) . . . . . . **$95.95 to $399.00**
Price: Brass frame (CVA, Cabela's, Traditions, Navy Arms) . . . . **$79.95 to $159.95**
Price: As above, kit (Dixie Gun Works, Navy Arms) . . **$145.00 to $188.95**
Price: Buffalo model, 44-cal. (Cabela's) **$119.99**
Price: Hartford model, steel frame, German silver trim, cartouche (E.M.F.) **$215.00**

NORTH AMERICAN COMPANION PERCUSSION REVOLVER

Caliber: 22. **Barrel:** 1-1/8". **Weight:** 5.1 oz. **Length:** 4-5/10" overall. **Stocks:** Laminated wood. **Sights:** Blade front, notch fixed rear. **Features:** All stainless steel construction. Uses standard #11 percussion caps. Comes with bullets, powder measure, bullet seater, leather clip holster, gun rug. Long Rifle or Magnum frame size. Introduced 1996. Made in U.S. by North American Arms.

Price: Long Rifle frame **$156.00**

North American Magnum Companion Percussion Revolver

Similar to the Companion except has larger frame. Weighs 7.2 oz., has 1-5/8" barrel, measures 5-7/16" overall. Comes with bullets, powder measure, bullet seater, leather clip holster, gun rag. Introduced 1996. Made in U.S. by North American Arms.

Price: **$215.00**

POCKET POLICE 1862 PERCUSSION REVOLVER

Caliber: 36, 5-shot. **Barrel:** 4-1/2", 5-1/2", 6-1/2", 7-1/2". **Weight:** 26 oz. **Length:** 12" overall (6-1/2" bbl.). **Stocks:** Walnut. **Sights:** Fixed. **Features:** Round tapered barrel; half-fluted and rebated cylinder; case-hardened frame, loading lever and hammer; silver or brass trigger guard and backstrap. Imported by Dixie Gun Works, Navy Arms (5-1/2" only), Uberti U.S.A. Inc. (5-1/2", 6-1/2" only), United States Patent Fire-Arms and Cimarron F.A. Co.

Price: About . . . . **$139.95 to $335.00**
Price: Single cased set with accessories (Navy Arms) **$365.00**
Price: Hartford model, steel frame, German silver trim, cartouche (E.M.F.) **$215.00**

ROGERS & SPENCER PERCUSSION REVOLVER

Caliber: 44. **Barrel:** 7-1/2". **Weight:** 47 oz. **Length:** 13-3/4" overall. **Stocks:** Walnut. **Sights:** Cone front, integral groove in frame for rear. **Features:** Accurate reproduction of a Civil War design. Solid frame; extra large nipple cut-out on rear of cylinder; loading lever and cylinder easily removed for cleaning. From Dixie Gun Works, Euroarms of America (standard blue, engraved, burnished, target models), Navy Arms.

Price: . . . . **$160.00 to $299.95**
Price: Nickel-plated **$215.00**
Price: Engraved (Euroarms) **$287.00**
Price: Kit version . . . . **$245.00 to $252.00**
Price: Target version (Euroarms) . . . . **$239.00 to $270.00**
Price: Burnished London Gray (Euroarms) . . . . . . **$245.00 to $270.00**

BLACKPOWDER REVOLVERS

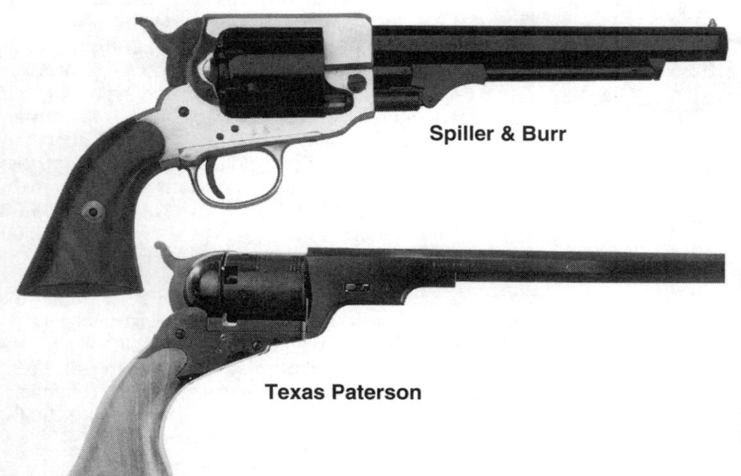

Spiller & Burr

Texas Paterson

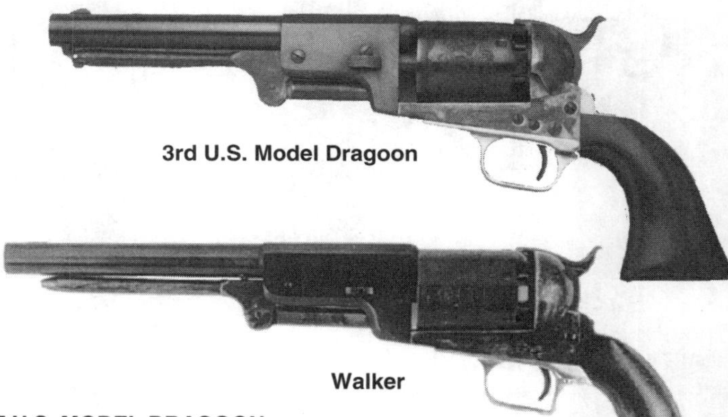

3rd U.S. Model Dragoon

Walker

RUGER OLD ARMY PERCUSSION REVOLVER

Caliber: 45, 6-shot. Uses .457" dia. lead bullets or 454 conical. **Barrel:** 7-1/2" (6-groove; 1:16" twist). **Weight:** 2-7/8 lbs. **Length:** 13-1/2" overall. **Stocks:** Rosewood. **Sights:** Ramp front, rear adjustable for windage and elevation; or fixed (groove). **Features:** Stainless steel; standard size nipples, chrome-moly steel cylinder and frame, same lockwork as original Super Blackhawk. Also stainless steel. Includes hard case and lock. Made in USA. From Sturm, Ruger & Co.

Price: Blued steel, fixed sight (Model BP-5F) **$499.00**
Price: Stainless steel, fixed sight (Model KBP-5F-I) **$576.00**
Price: Stainless steel (Model KBP-7) **$535.00**
Price: Blued steel (Model BP-7) **$499.00**
Price: Blued steel, fixed sight (BP-7F) **$499.00**
Price: Stainless steel, fixed sight (KBP-7F) **$535.00**

SHERIFF MODEL 1851 PERCUSSION REVOLVER

Caliber: 36, 44, 6-shot. **Barrel:** 5". **Weight:** 40 oz. **Length:** 10-1/2" overall. **Stocks:** Walnut. **Sights:** Fixed. **Features:** Brass backstrap and trigger guard; engraved navy scene; case-hardened frame, hammer, loading lever. Imported by E.M.F.

Price: Steel frame **$169.95**
Price: Brass frame **$140.00**

SPILLER & BURR REVOLVER

Caliber: 36 (.375" round ball). **Barrel:** 7", octagon. **Weight:** 2-1/2 lbs. **Length:** 12-1/2" overall. **Stocks:** Two-piece walnut. **Sights:** Fixed. **Features:** Reproduction of the C.S.A. revolver. Brass frame and trigger guard. Also available as a kit. From Dixie Gun Works, Navy Arms.

Price: **$150.00**
Price: Kit form (Dixie) **$125.00**
Price: Single cased set (Navy Arms) **$270.00**
Price: Double cased set (Navy Arms) **$430.00**

TEXAS PATERSON 1836 REVOLVER

Caliber: 36 (.375" round ball). **Barrel:** 7-1/2". **Weight:** 42 oz. **Stocks:** One-piece walnut. **Sights:** Fixed. **Features:** Copy of Sam Colt's first commercially-made revolving pistol. Has no loading lever but comes with loading tool. From Cimarron F.A. Co., Dixie Gun Works, Navy Arms, Uber-ti U.S.A. Inc.

Price: About **$495.00**
Price: With loading lever (Uberti U.S.A. Inc.) **$450.00**
Price: Engraved (Navy Arms) **$485.00**

UBERTI 1861 NAVY PERCUSSION REVOLVER

Caliber: 36. **Barrel:** 7-1/2", round. **Weight:** 40-1/2 oz. **Stocks:** One-piece oiled American walnut. **Sights:** Brass pin front, hammer notch rear. **Features:** Rounded trigger guard, German silver blade front sight, "creeping" loading lever. Available with fluted or round cylinder. Imported by Uberti U.S.A. Inc.

Price: Steel backstrap, trigger guard, cut for stock **$265.00**

1ST U.S. MODEL DRAGOON

Caliber: 44. **Barrel:** 7-1/2", part round, part octagon. **Weight:** 64 oz. **Stocks:** One-piece walnut. **Sights:** German silver blade front, hammer notch rear. **Features:** First model has oval bolt cuts in cylinder, square- back flared trigger guard, V-type mainspring, short trigger. Ranger and Indian scene roll-engraved on cylinder. Color case-hardened frame, loading lever, plunger and hammer; blue barrel, cylinder, trigger and wedge. Available with old-time charcoal blue or standard blue-black finish. Polished brass backstrap and trigger guard. From Cimarron F.A. Co., Dixie Gun Works, Uberti U.S.A. Inc., Navy Arms.

Price: . . . . **$295.00 to $435.00**

2nd U.S. Model Dragoon Revolver

Similar to the 1st Model except distinguished by rectangular bolt cuts in the cylinder. From Cimarron F.A. Co., Uberti U.S.A. Inc., United States Patent Fire-Arms, Navy Arms, Dixie Gunworks.

Price: . . . . **$295.00 to $435.00**

3rd U.S. Model Dragoon Revolver

Similar to the 2nd Model except for oval trigger guard, long trigger, modifications to the loading lever and latch. Imported by Cimarron F.A. Co., Uberti U.S.A. Inc., United States Patent Fire-Arms, Dixie Gunworks.

Price: Military model (frame cut for shoulder stock, steel backstrap) . . . . **$295.00 to $435.00**
Price: Civilian (brass backstrap, trigger guard) . . . . . . **$295.00 to $325.00**

1862 POCKET NAVY PERCUSSION REVOLVER

Caliber: 36, 5-shot. **Barrel:** 5-1/2", 6-1/2", octagonal, 7-groove, LH twist. **Weight:** 27 oz. (5-1/2" barrel). **Length:** 10-1/2" overall (5-1/2" bbl.). **Stocks:** One-piece varnished walnut. **Sights:** Brass pin front, hammer notch rear. **Features:** Rebated cylinder, hinged loading lever, brass or silver-plated backstrap and trigger guard, color-cased frame, hammer, loading lever, plunger and latch, rest blued. Has original-type markings. From Cimarron F.A. Co., Uberti U.S.A. Inc., Dixie Gunworks.

Price: With brass backstrap, trigger guard . . . . **$260.00 to $310.00**

1861 Navy Percussion Revolver

Similar to Colt 1851 Navy except has round 7-1/2" barrel, rounded trigger guard, German silver blade front sight, "creeping" loading lever. Fluted or round cylinder. Imported by Cimarron F.A. Co., Uberti U.S.A. Inc., Dixie Gunworks.

Price: Steel backstrap, trigger guard, cut for stock . . . **$255.00 to $300.00**

WALKER 1847 PERCUSSION REVOLVER

Caliber: 44, 6-shot. **Barrel:** 9". **Weight:** 84 oz. **Length:** 15-1/2" overall. **Stocks:** Walnut. **Sights:** Fixed. **Features:** Case-hardened frame, loading lever and hammer; iron backstrap; brass trigger guard; engraved cylinder. Imported by Cabela's, Cimarron F.A. Co., Navy Arms, Dixie Gun Works, Uberti U.S.A. Inc., E.M.F., Cimarron, Traditions, United States Patent Fire-Arms.

Price: About . . . . **$225.00 to $445.00**
Price: Single cased set (Navy Arms) **$405.00**
Price: Deluxe Walker with French fitted case (Navy Arms) **$540.00**
Price: Hartford model, steel frame, German silver trim, cartouche (E.M.F.) **$295.00**

Gamo PT-80

Daisy 662X

AIR FORCE CONDOR

Caliber: 177, 22. **Barrel:** 24" rifled. **Weight:** 6.5 lbs. **Overall length:** 38.75". **Sights:** None, integral mount supplied. **Features:** 600-1,300 fps. 3,000 psi fill pressure. Automatic safety. Air tank volume: 490cc.

Price: 22 w/refill clamp and open sights **$649.95**
Price: 177 w/refill clamp and open sights **$599.95**
Price: Gun only (22 or 177) **$549.95**

AIR FORCE TALON SS

Caliber: 177, 22. **Barrel:** 12". **Weight:** 5.25 lbs. **Overall length:** 32.75". **Sights:** None, integral mount supplied. **Features:** 400-1000 fps. Fill pressure: 3000 psi. Air tank volume: 490cc.

Price: 22 w/refill clamp, open sights **$559.95**
Price: 177 w/refill clamp, open sights **$559.95**
Price: Gun only (22 or 177) **$459.95**

AIR FORCE TALON

Same as Talon SS but 32.6" long, weight: 5.5 lbs.

Price: 22 w/refill clamp, open sights **$539.95**
Price: 177 w/refill clamp, open sights **$539.95**
Price: Gun only **$439.95**

ARS HUNTING MASTER AR6 PISTOL

Caliber: 22 (177 +20 special order). **Barrel:** 12" rifled. **Weight:** 3 lbs. **Length:** 18.25 overall. **Stock:** Indonesian walnut with checkered grip. **Sights:** Adjustable rear, blade front. **Features:** 6 shot repeater with rotary magazine, single or double action, receiver grooved for scope, hammer block and trigger block safeties.

Price: . . . . **NA**

BEEMAN P1 MAGNUM AIR PISTOL

Caliber: 177, 5mm, single shot. **Barrel:** 8.4". **Weight:** 2.5 lbs. **Length:** 11" overall. **Power:** Top lever cocking; spring-piston. **Stocks:** Checkered walnut. **Sights:** Blade front, square notch rear with click micrometer adjustments for windage and elevation. Grooved for scope mounting. **Features:** Dual power for 177 and 20-cal.: low setting gives 350-400 fps; high setting 500-600 fps. Rearward expanding mainspring simulates firearm recoil. All Colt 45 auto grips fit gun. Dry-firing feature for practice. Optional wooden shoulder stock. Imported by Beeman.

Price: 177, 5mm **$440.00**

BEEMAN P3 AIR PISTOL

Caliber: 177 pellet, single shot. **Barrel:** N/A. **Weight:** 1.7 lbs. **Length:** 9.6" overall. **Power:** Single-stroke pneumatic; overlever barrel cocking. **Grips:** Reinforced polymer. **Sights:** Adjustable rear, blade front. **Features:** Velocity 410 fps. Polymer frame; automatic safety; two-stage trigger; built-in muzzle brake.

Price: **$180.00**
Price: Combo **$285.00**

BEEMAN/FEINWERKBAU 103 PISTOL

Caliber: 177, single shot. **Barrel:** 10.1", 12-groove rifling. **Weight:** 2.5 lbs. **Length:** 16.5" overall. **Power:** Single-stroke pneumatic, underlever cocking. **Stocks:** Stippled walnut with adjustable palm shelf. **Sights:** Blade front, open rear adjustable for windage and elevation. Notch size adjustable for width. Interchangeable front blades. **Features:** Velocity 510 fps. Fully adjustable trigger. Cocking effort of 2 lbs. Imported by Beeman.

Price: Right-hand **$1,236.00**
Price: Left-hand **$1,275.00**

BEEMAN/FWB P34 MATCH AIR PISTOL

Caliber: 177, single shot. **Barrel:** 10-5/16", with muzzlebrake. **Weight:** 2.4 lbs. **Length:** 16.5" overall. **Power:** Pre-charged pneumatic. **Stocks:** Stippled walnut; adjustable match type. **Sights:** Undercut blade front, fully adjustable match rear. **Features:** Velocity to 525 fps; up to 200 shots per CO2 cartridge. Fully adjustable trigger; built-in muzzlebrake. Imported from Germany by Beeman.

Price: Right-hand **$1,395.00**
Price: Left-hand **$1,440.00**

BEEMAN HW70A AIR PISTOL

Caliber: 177, single shot. **Barrel:** 6-1/4", rifled. **Weight:** 38 oz. **Length:** 12-3/4" overall. **Power:** Spring, barrel cocking. **Stocks:** Plastic, with thumbrest. **Sights:** Hooded post front, square notch rear adjustable for windage and elevation. Comes with scope base. **Features:** Adjustable trigger, 31-lb. cocking effort, 440 fps MV; automatic barrel safety. Imported by Beeman.

Price: **$190.00**

BEEMAN/WEBLEY TEMPEST AIR PISTOL

Caliber: 177, 22, single shot. **Barrel:** 6-7/8". **Weight:** 32 oz. **Length:** 8.9" overall. **Power:** Spring-piston, break barrel. **Stocks:** Checkered black plastic with thumbrest. **Sights:** Blade front, adjustable rear. **Features:** Velocity to 500 fps (177), 400 fps (22). Aluminum frame; black epoxy finish; manual safety. Imported from England by Beeman.

Price: **$205.00**

Beeman/Webley Hurricane Air Pistol

Similar to the Tempest except has extended frame in the rear for a click-adjustable rear sight; hooded front sight; comes with scope mount. Imported from England by Beeman.

Price: **$255.00**

BENJAMIN SHERIDAN CO2 PELLET PISTOLS

Caliber: 177, 20, 22, single shot. **Barrel:** 6-3/8", rifled brass. **Weight:** 29 oz. **Length:** 9.8" overall. **Power:** 12-gram CO2 cylinder. **Stocks:** Walnut. **Sights:** High ramp front, fully adjustable notch rear. **Features:** Velocity to 500 fps. Turnbolt action with cross-bolt safety. Gives about 40 shots per CO2 cylinder. Black or nickel finish. Made in U.S. by Benjamin Sheridan Co.

Price: Black finish, EB17 (177), EB20 (20), ... **$190.00**

BENJAMIN SHERIDAN PNEUMATIC PELLET PISTOLS

Caliber: 177, 20, 22, single shot. **Barrel:** 9-3/8", rifled brass. **Weight:** 38 oz. **Length:**13-1/8" overall. **Power:** Underlever pnuematic, hand pumped. **Stocks:** Walnut stocks and pump handle. **Sights:** High ramp front, fully adjustable notch rear. **Features:** Velocity to 525 fps (variable). Bolt action with cross-bolt safety. Choice of black or nickel finish. Made in U.S. by Benjamin Sheridan Co.

Price: Black finish, HB17 (177), HB20 (20) **$190.00**
Price: HB22 (22) **$199.00**

BRNO TAU-7 CO2 MATCH PISTOL

Caliber: 177. **Barrel:** 10.24". **Weight:** 37 oz. **Length:** 15.75" overall. **Power:** 12.5-gram CO2 cartridge. **Stocks:** Stippled hardwood with adjustable palm rest. **Sights:** Blade front, open fully adjustable rear. **Features:** Comes with extra seals and counterweight. Blue finish. Imported by Great Lakes Airguns.

Price: **$299.50**

CROSMAN BLACK VENOM PISTOL

Caliber: 177 pellets, BB, 17-shot magazine; darts, single shot. **Barrel:** 4.75" smooth-bore. **Weight:** 16 oz. **Length:** 10.8" overall. **Power:** Spring. **Sights:** Blade front, adjustable rear. **Features:** Velocity to 270 fps (BBs), 250 fps (pellets). Spring-fed magazine; cross-bolt safety. Made in U.S.A. by Crosman Corp.

Price: **$60.00**

CROSMAN MODEL 1377 AIR PISTOLS

Caliber: 177, single shot. **Barrel:** 8", rifled steel. **Weight:** 39 oz. **Length:** 13-5/8". **Power:** Hand pumped. **Sights:** Blade front, rear adjustable for windage and elevation. **Features:** Bolt action moulded plastic grip, hand size pump forearm. Cross-bolt safety. From Crosman.

Price: **$60.00**

CROSMAN AUTO AIR II PISTOL

Caliber: BB, 17-shot magazine, 177 pellet, single shot. **Barrel:** 8-5/8" steel, smooth-bore. **Weight:** 13 oz. **Length:** 10-3/4" overall. **Power:** CO2 Powerlet. **Sights:** Blade front, adjustable rear; highlighted system. **Features:** Velocity to 480 fps (BBs), 430 fps (pellets). Semi-automatic action with BBs, single shot with pellets. Black. From Crosman.

Price: AAIIB **$38.00**
Price: AAIIBRD . . . . **NA**

CROSMAN MODEL 1008 REPEAT AIR

Caliber: 177, 8-shot pellet clip. **Barrel:** 4.25", rifled steel. **Weight:** 17 oz. **Length:** 8.625" overall. **Power:** CO2 Powerlet. **Stocks:** Checkered black plastic. **Sights:** Post front, adjustable rear. **Features:** Velocity about 430 fps. Break-open barrel for easy loading; single or double semi-automatic action; two 8-shot clips included. Optional carrying case available. From Crosman.

Price: **$60.00**
Price: Model 1008SB (silver and black finish), about **$60.00**

CROSMAN SEMI AUTO AIR PISTOL

Caliber: 177, pellets. **Barrel:** Rifled steel. **Weight:** 40 oz. **Length:** 8.63". **Power:** CO2. **Sights:** Blade front, rear adjustable. **Features:** Velocity up to 430 fps. Synthetic grips, zinc alloy frame. From Crosman.

Price: C40 . . . . **NA**

CROSMAN MAGNUM AIR PISTOLS

Caliber: 177, pellets. **Barrel:** Rifled steel. **Weight:** 27 oz. **Length:** 9.38". **Power:** CO2. **Sights:** Blade front, rear adjustable. **Features:** Single/double action accepts sights and scopes with standard 3/8" dovetail mount. Model 3576W features 6" barrel for increased accuracy. From Crosman.

Price: 3574W . . . . **NA**
Price: 3576W . . . . **NA**

DAISY/POWERLINE MODEL 15XT AIR PISTOL

Caliber: 177 BB, 15-shot built-in magazine. **Barrel:** NA. **Weight:** NA. **Length:** 7.21". **Power:** CO2. **Stocks:** NA. **Sights:** NA. **Features:** Velocity 425 fps. Made in the U.S.A. by Daisy Mfg. Co.

Price: **$36.95**
New! Price: 15XK Shooting Kit **$59.95**

DAISY/POWERLINE 717 PELLET PISTOL

Caliber: 177, single shot. **Barrel:** 9.61". **Weight:** 2.25 lbs. **Length:** 13-1/2" overall. **Stocks:** Moulded wood-grain plastic, with thumbrest. **Sights:** Blade and ramp front, micro-adjustable notch rear. **Features:** Single pump pneumatic pistol. Rifled steel barrel. Cross-bolt trigger block. Muzzle velocity 385 fps. From Daisy Mfg. Co.

Price: **$71.95**

DAISY/POWERLINE 1270 CO2 AIR PISTOL

Caliber: BB, 60-shot magazine. **Barrel:** Smoothbore steel. **Weight:** 17 oz. **Length:** 11.1" overall. **Power:** CO2 pump action. **Stocks:** Moulded black polymer. **Sights:** Blade on ramp front, adjustable rear. **Features:** Velocity to 420 fps. Crossbolt trigger block safety; plated finish. Made in U.S. by Daisy Mfg. Co.

Price: **$39.95**

DAISY/POWERLINE 93 AIR PISTOL

Caliber: BB, 15-shot magazine. **Barrel:** Smoothbore steel. **Weight:** 1.1 lbs. **Length:** 7.9" overall. **Power:** CO2 powered semi-auto. **Stocks:** Moulded brown checkered. **Sights:** Blade on ramp front, fixed open rear. **Features:** Velocity to 400 fps. Manual trigger block. Made in U.S.A. by Daisy Mfg. Co.

Price: **$48.95**

Daisy/Powerline 693 Air Pistol

Similar to Model 93 except has velocity to 235 fps.

Price: **$52.95**

DAISY/POWERLINE 622X PELLET PISTOL

Caliber: 22 (5.5mm), 6-shot. **Barrel:** Rifled steel. **Weight:** 1.3 lbs. **Length:** 8.5". **Power:** CO2. **Grips:** Molded black checkered. **Sights:** Fiber optic front, fixed open rear. **Features:** Velocity 225 fps. Rotary hammer block. Made by Daisy Mfg. Co.

Price: **$69.95**

DAISY/POWERLINE 45 AIR PISTOL

Caliber: BB, 13-shot magazine. **Barrel:** Rifled steel. **Weight:** 1.25 lbs. **Length:** 8.5" overall. **Power:** CO2 powered semi-auto. **Stocks:** Moulded black checkered. **Sights:** TRUGLO® fiber optic front, fixed open rear. **Features:** Velocity to 224 fps. Manual trigger block. Made in U.S.A. by Daisy Mfg. Co.

Price: **$54.95**

EAA MP651K

Daisy/Powerline 645 Air Pistol

Similar to Model 93 except has distinctive black and nickel-finish.

Price: **$59.95**

EAA/BAIKAL IZH-M46 TARGET AIR PISTOL

Caliber: 177, single shot. **Barrel:** 10". **Weight:** 2.4 lbs. **Length:** 16.8" overall. **Power:** Underlever single-stroke pneumatic. **Grips:** Adjustable wooden target. **Sights:** Micrometer fully adjustable rear, blade front. **Features:** Velocity about 420 fps. Hammer-forged, rifled barrel. Imported from Russia by European American Armory.

Price: **$349.00**

GAMO AUTO 45

Caliber: .177 (12-shot). **Barrel:** 4.25". **Weight:** 1.10 lbs. **Length:** 7.50". **Power:** CO2 cartridge, semi-automatic, 410 fps. **Stock:** Plastic. **Sights:** Rear sights adjusts for windage. **Features:** Looking very much like a Glock cartridge pistol, it fires in the double-action model and has a manual safety. Imported from Spain by Gamo.

Price: **$99.95**

GAMO COMPACT TARGET PISTOL

Caliber: .177, single shot. **Barrel:** 8.26". **Weight:** 1.95 lbs. **Length:** 12.60. **Power:** Spring-piston, 400 fps. **Stock:** Walnut. **Sights:** Micro-adjustable. **Features:** Rifle steel barrel, adjustable match trigger, recoil and vibration-free. Imported from Spain by Gamo.

Price: **$229.95**

GAMO P-23, P-23 LASER PISTOL

Caliber: .177 (12-shot). **Barrel:** 4.25". **Weight:** 1 lb. **Length:** 7.5". **Power:** CO2 cartridge, semi-automatic, 410 fps. **Stock:** Plastic. **Sights:** NA. **Features:** Style somewhat like a Walther PPK cartridge pistol, an optional laser allows fast sight acquisition. Imported from Spain by Gamo.

Price: . . . . **$89.95**, (with laser) **$129.95**

GAMO PT-80, PT-80 LASER PISTOL

Caliber: .177 (8-shot). **Barrel:** 4.25". **Weight:** 1.2 lbs. **Length:** 7.2". **Power:** CO2 cartridge, semi-automatic, 410 fps. **Stock:** Plastic. **Sights:** 3-dot. **Features:** Available with optional laser sight and with optional walnut grips. Imported from Spain by Gamo.

Price: . . . . **$108.95,** (with laser) **$129.95**, (with walnut grip) **$119.95**

"GAT" AIR PISTOL

Caliber: 177, single shot. **Barrel:** 7-1/2" cocked, 9-1/2" extended. **Weight:** 22 oz. **Power:** Spring-piston. **Stocks:** Cast checkered metal. **Sights:** Fixed. **Features:** Shoots pellets, corks or darts. Matte black finish. Imported from England by Stone Enterprises, Inc.

Price: **$24.95**

HAMMERLI AP40 AIR PISTOL

Caliber: 177. **Barrel:** 10". **Stocks:** Adjustable orthopaedic. **Sights:** Fully adjustable micrometer. **Features:** Sleek, light, well balanced and accurate. Imported from Switzerland by Nygord Precision Products.

Price: **$1,195.00**

MARKSMAN 2000 REPEATER PISTOL

Caliber: 177, 18-shot BB repeater. **Barrel:** 2-1/2", smoothbore. **Weight:** 24 oz. **Length:** 8-1/4" overall. **Power:** Spring. **Features:** Velocity to 200 fps. Thumb safety. Uses BBs, darts, bolts or pellets. Repeats with BBs only. From Marksman Products.

Price: **$27.00**

MARKSMAN 2005 LASERHAWK SPECIAL EDITION AIR PISTOL

Caliber: 177, 24-shot magazine. **Barrel:** 3.8", smoothbore. **Weight:** 22 oz. **Length:** 10.3" overall. **Power:** Spring-air. **Stocks:** Checkered. **Sights:** Fixed fiber optic front sight. **Features:** Velocity to 300 fps with Hyper-Velocity pellets. Square trigger guard with skeletonized trigger; extended barrel for greater velocity and accuracy. Shoots BBs, pellets, darts or bolts. Made in the U.S. From Marksman Products.

Price: **$32.00**

MORINI 162E MATCH AIR PISTOL

Caliber: 177, single shot. **Barrel:** 9.4". **Weight:** 32 oz. **Length:** 16.1" overall. **Power:** Scuba air. **Stocks:** Adjustable match type. **Sights:** Interchangeable blade front, fully adjustable match-type rear. **Features:** Power mechanism shuts down when pressure drops to a preset level. Adjustable electronic trigger. Imported from Switzerland by Nygord Precision Products.

Price: **$825.00**
Price: 162 EI **$1,075.00**

MORINI SAM K-11 AIR PISTOL

Caliber: 177. **Barrel:** 10". **Weight:** 38 oz. **Stocks:** Fully adjustable. **Sights:** Fully adjustable. **Features:** Improved trigger, more angle adjustment on grip. Sophisticated counter balance system. Deluxe aluminum case, two cylinders and manometer. Imported from Switzerland by Nygord Precision Products.

Price: **$975.00**

PARDINI K58 MATCH AIR PISTOL

Caliber: 177, single shot. **Barrel:** 9". **Weight:** 37.7 oz. **Length:** 15.5" overall. **Power:** Precharged compressed air; single-stroke cocking. **Stocks:** Adjustable match type; stippled walnut. **Sights:** Interchangeable post front, fully adjustable match rear. **Features:** Fully adjustable trigger. Short version K-2 available. Imported from Italy by Nygord Precision Products.

Price: **$795.00**
Price: K2S model, precharged air pistol, introduced in 1998 . . . . **$945.00**

RWS 9B/9N AIR PISTOLS

Caliber: 177, single shot. **Grips:** Plastic with thumbrest. **Sights:** Adjustable. **Features:** Spring-piston powered; 550 fps. Black or nickel finish. Imported from Spain by Dynamit Nobel-RWS.

Price: 9B **$169.00**
Price: 9N **$185.00**

STEYR LP 5CP MATCH AIR PISTOL

Caliber: 177, 5-shot magazine. **Weight:** 40.7 oz. **Length:** 15.2" overall. **Power:** Precharged air cylinder. **Stocks:** Adjustable match type. **Sights:** Interchangeable blade front, fully adjustable match rear. **Features:** Adjustable sight radius; fully adjustable trigger. Barrel compensator. One-shot magazine available. Imported from Austria by Nygord Precision Products.

Price: **$1,100.00**

STEYR LP10P MATCH PISTOL

Caliber: 177, single shot. **Barrel:** 9". **Weight:** 38.7 oz. **Length:** 15.3" overall. **Power:** Scuba air. **Stocks:** Fully adjustable Morini match, palm shelf, stippled walnut. **Sights:** Interchangeable blade in 4mm, 4.5mm or 5mm widths, fully adjustable open rear, interchangeable 3.5mm or 4mm leaves. **Features:** Velocity about 500 fps. Adjustable trigger, adjustable sight radius from 12.4" to 13.2". With compensator. New "absorber" eliminates recoil. Imported from Austria by Nygord Precision Products.

Price: **$1,175.00**

TECH FORCE SS2 OLYMPIC COMPETITION AIR PISTOL

Caliber: 177 pellet, single shot. **Barrel:** 7.4". **Weight:** 2.8 lbs. **Length:** 16.5" overall. **Power:** Spring piston, sidelever. **Grips:** Hardwood. **Sights:** Extended adjustable rear, blade front accepts inserts. **Features:** Velocity 520 fps. Recoilless design; adjustments allow duplication of a firearm's feel. Match-grade, adjustable trigger; includes carrying case. Imported from China by Compasseco Inc.

Price: **$295.00**

TECH FORCE 35 AIR PISTOL

Caliber: 177 pellet, single shot. **Weight:** 2.86 lbs. **Length:** 14.9" overall. **Power:** Spring piston, underlever. **Grips:** Hardwood. **Sights:** Micrometer adjustable rear, blade front. **Features:** Velocity 400 fps. Grooved for scope mount; trigger safety. Imported from China by Compasseco Inc.

Price: **$39.95**

Tech Force 8 Air Pistol

Similar to Tech Force 35, but with break-barrel action, ambidextrous polymer grips.

Price: **$59.95**

Tech Force S2-1 Air Pistol

Similar to Tech Force 8, more basic grips and sights for plinking.

Price: **$29.95**

WALTHER LP300 MATCH PISTOL

Caliber: 177. **Barrel:** 236mm. **Weight:** 1.018g. **Length:** NA. **Power:** NA. **Stocks:** NA. **Sights:** Integrated front with three different widths, adjustable rear. **Features:** Adjustable grip and trigger. Imported from Germany by Nygord Precision Products.

Price: **$1,095.00**

CONSULT
SHOOTER'S MARKETPLACE
Page 125, This Edition

AJAX

Grip materials include genuine stag, buffalo horn, ivory polymer, white and black Pearlite, exotic woods, buffalo polymer, pewter, genuine ivory and Staglite (imitation stag horn). Available for most single- and double-action revolvers and semi-automatic pistols. Custom fittings are available.

Prices: Genuine stag . . . . **$199.95 to $249.95**
Prices: Genuine buffalo horn . . . . **$60.00 to $80.00**
Prices: Ivory polymer . . . . **$35.00 to $90.00**
Prices: Pearlite . . . . **$35.00 to $90.00**
Prices: Exotic woods (super walnut, cherrywood, black Silverwood) . . . . **$14.95 to $50.00**
Prices: Buffalo polymer. . . . . **$35.00 to $45.00**
Prices: Pewter . . . . **$50.00 to $60.00**
Prices: Genuine ivory . . . . **$325.00 to $350.00**
Prices: Staglite . . . . **$49.95 to $59.95**

Textured decal grips in various textures also available from Ajax for many semi-automatic pistols.

Prices: **$9.95**

ALUMNA GRIPS

Aluminum handgun grips available in several configurations including checkered, UltraLight, ThinLine, olive gray finish, laser engraved and Custom Deluxe with up to 3 engraved initials. Anodized aluminum colors also available.

Prices: .... **$39.95 to $44.95**

BLU MAGNUM GRIPS

Makers of double- and single-action style grips in Skeeter Skelton, Sheriff Wilson and other styles, made of maple and exotic woods, ivory, stag, and Micarta.

Prices: .... **N/A**

BROWNELLS

Not a manufacturer, but an on-line and catalog retailer, supplying gunsmiths and retailers, as well as the shooting public. Many of the products shown in this section are also available from Brownells.

BUTLER CREEK (UNCLE MIKE'S)

Designed by handgun stock designer and craftsman Craig Spegel, revolver and pistol grips made of polymer are available for a wide range of handgun models. Revolver grips are made to be hand-filling, but not oversize. Finger grooves are provided on double-action revolver grips for good control. Revolver boot grips are designed not to "print" when used on concealed-carry revolvers, yet allow a controlled rapid draw. Pistol grips are specifically designed to maintain the original stock dimensions. Slip-on grips are offered in three sizes. Medium and large versions have finger grooves.

Prices: Revolver and handgun grips. **$20.95**
Prices: Slip-on pistol grips **$10.95**

COAST IVORY

Offers handguns grips of elephant ivory, stag, California buckeye burl and other exotic woods, as well as polyester pearl.

Prices: Custom-fitted elephant ivory for 1911-style pistols. **$450.00**
Prices: Custom-fitted ivory grips for Colt single-action revolvers . . . . **$500.00 and up**
Prices: Custom-fitted Derringer pistol ivory grips . . . . **$200.00 and up**
Prices: Custom-fitted genuine stag grips for Colt single-action revolvers. **$190.00**
Prices: Polyester pearl grips. . . . . **$60.00 to $85.00**

CRIMSON TRACE

Makers of special grip replacements for many popular revolvers and pistols, including Lasergrip sighting systems. Lasergrips are intended for police agencies and military armed citizens.

Prices: . . . . **N/A**

GRIPS

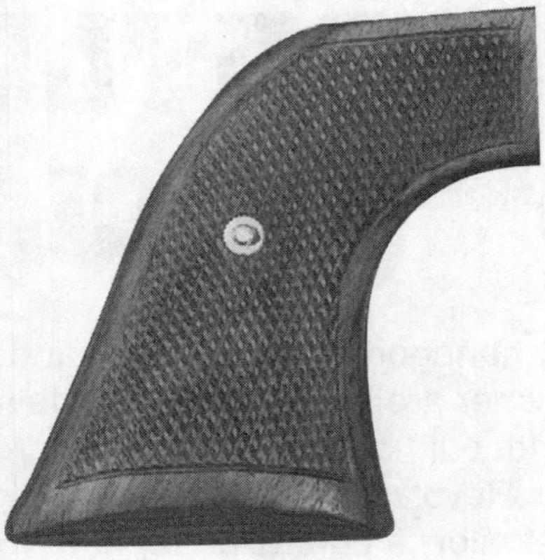

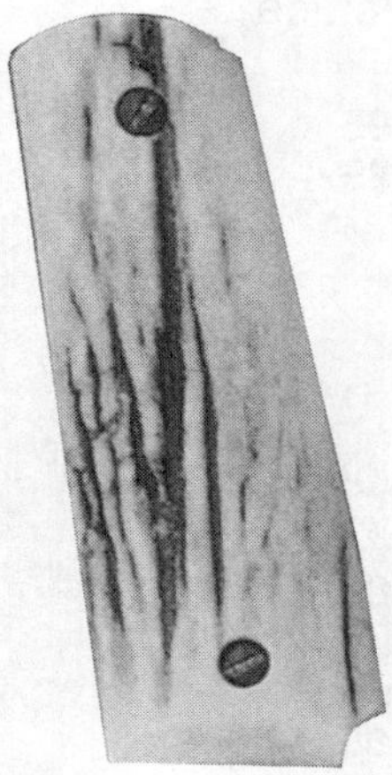

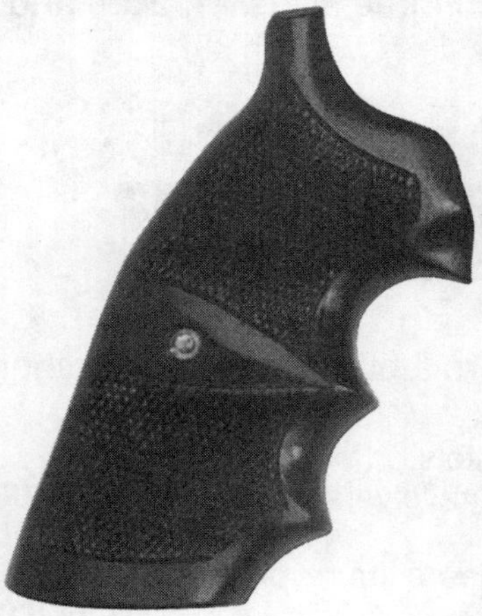

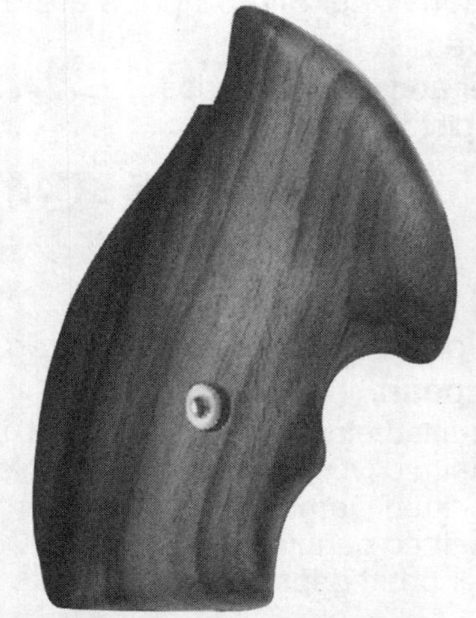

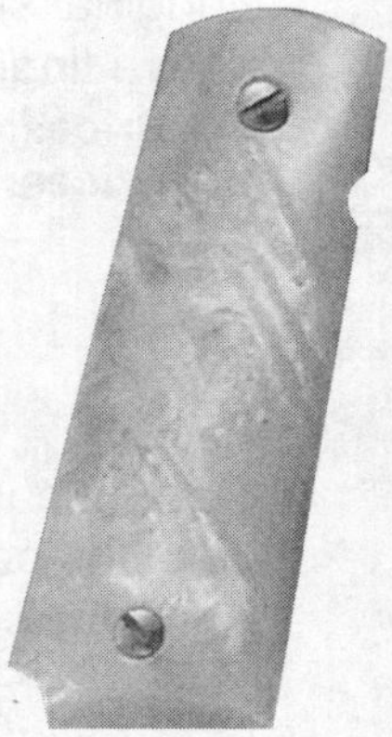

EAGLE GRIPS

Available grip materials include an extensive variety of rosewood, buffalo horn, ebony, mother-of-pearl, American elk, polymer and Ultra ivory (imitation of elephant ivory). Can produce grips for virtually any handgun. Custom-fittings available.

Prices: Rosewood or ebony handgun grips **$39.95 to $59.95**
Prices: Compact revolver Secret Service grips **$59.95 to $125.95**
Prices: Rosewood handgun thumb-rest grips (smooth finish) **$59.95**
Prices: Single-action revolver grips **$59.95 to $99.95**

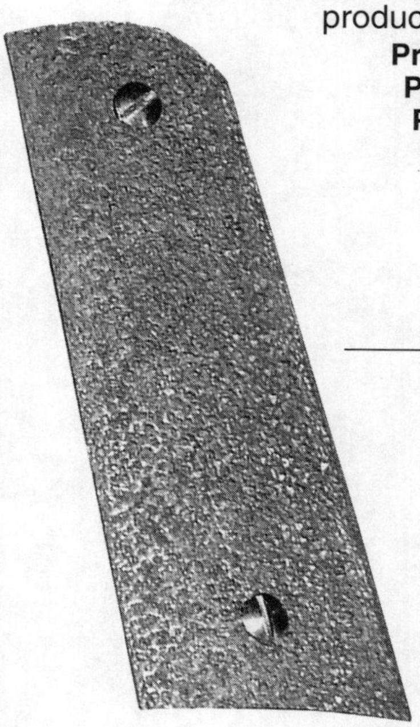

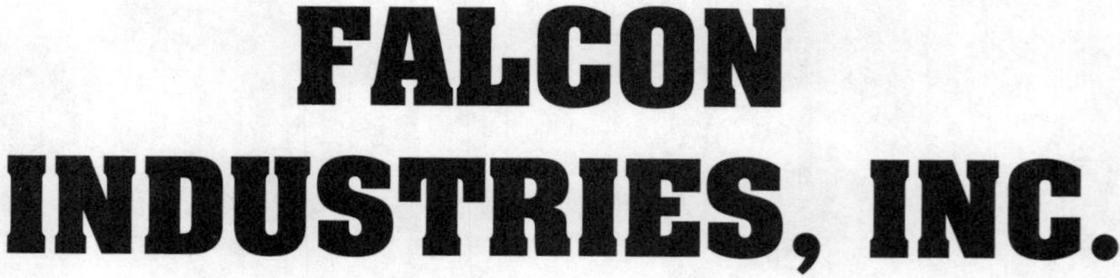

Producer of the Ergo Grip XT for 1911-type Government and Colt Commander-size frames. Made of textured nylon-based rigid polymer with pebble grain grip surface.

Price: $22.00

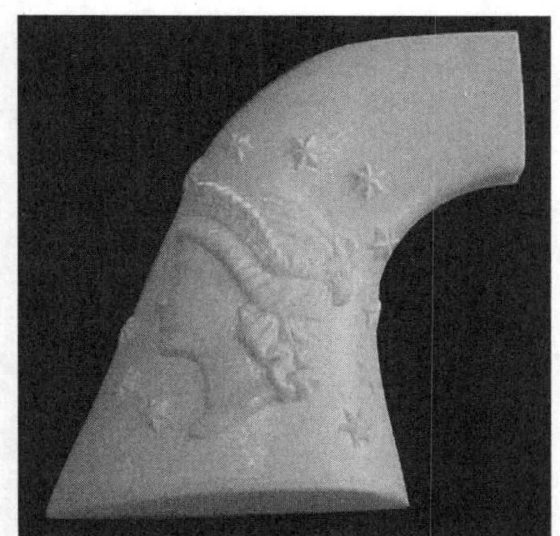

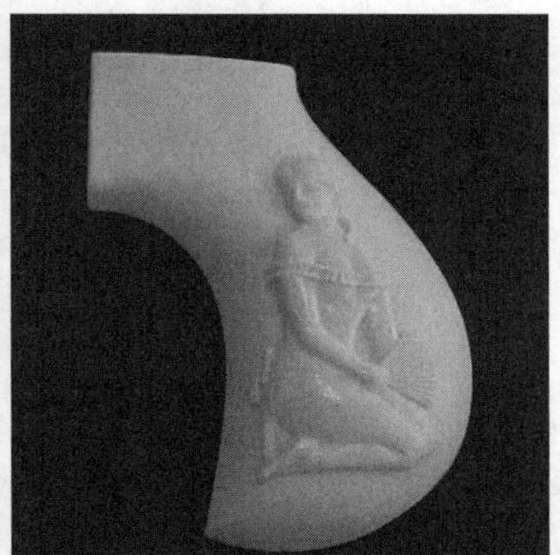
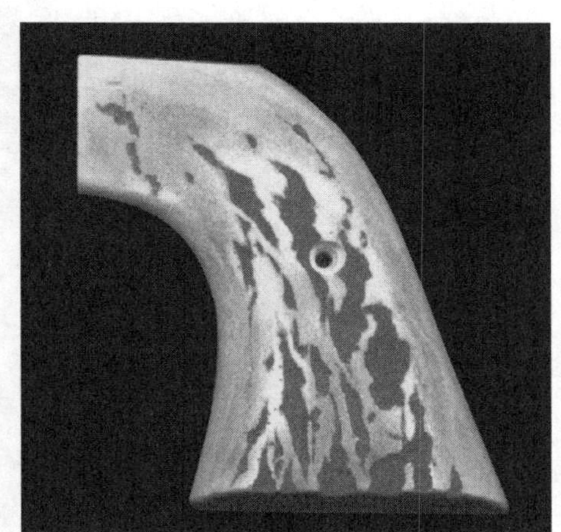
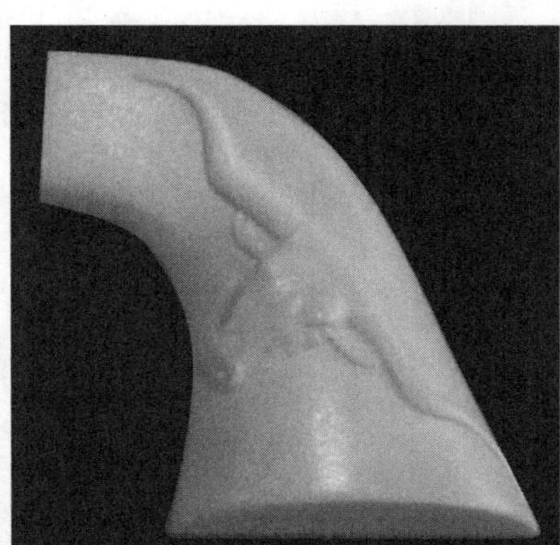

GRIPMAKER

Specializing in the production of original and authentic single-action revolver grip designs from the 1850s to 1890s. Made of white urethane which ages (yellows) like real ivory; also available in stag. Models available to fit Colt Single-Action Army and similar models, blackpowder revolvers (1851 and 1861 Navy, 1860 Army), Ruger single-actions, Smith & Wesson Schofield, #1 & #3 American and Model #3 Russian, and Derringers.

Prices: Revolvers (urethane) .... **$40.00 to $50.00;** stag **$60.00 to $70.00**
Prices: Derringers (urethane)..**$20.00;** stag **$30.00**

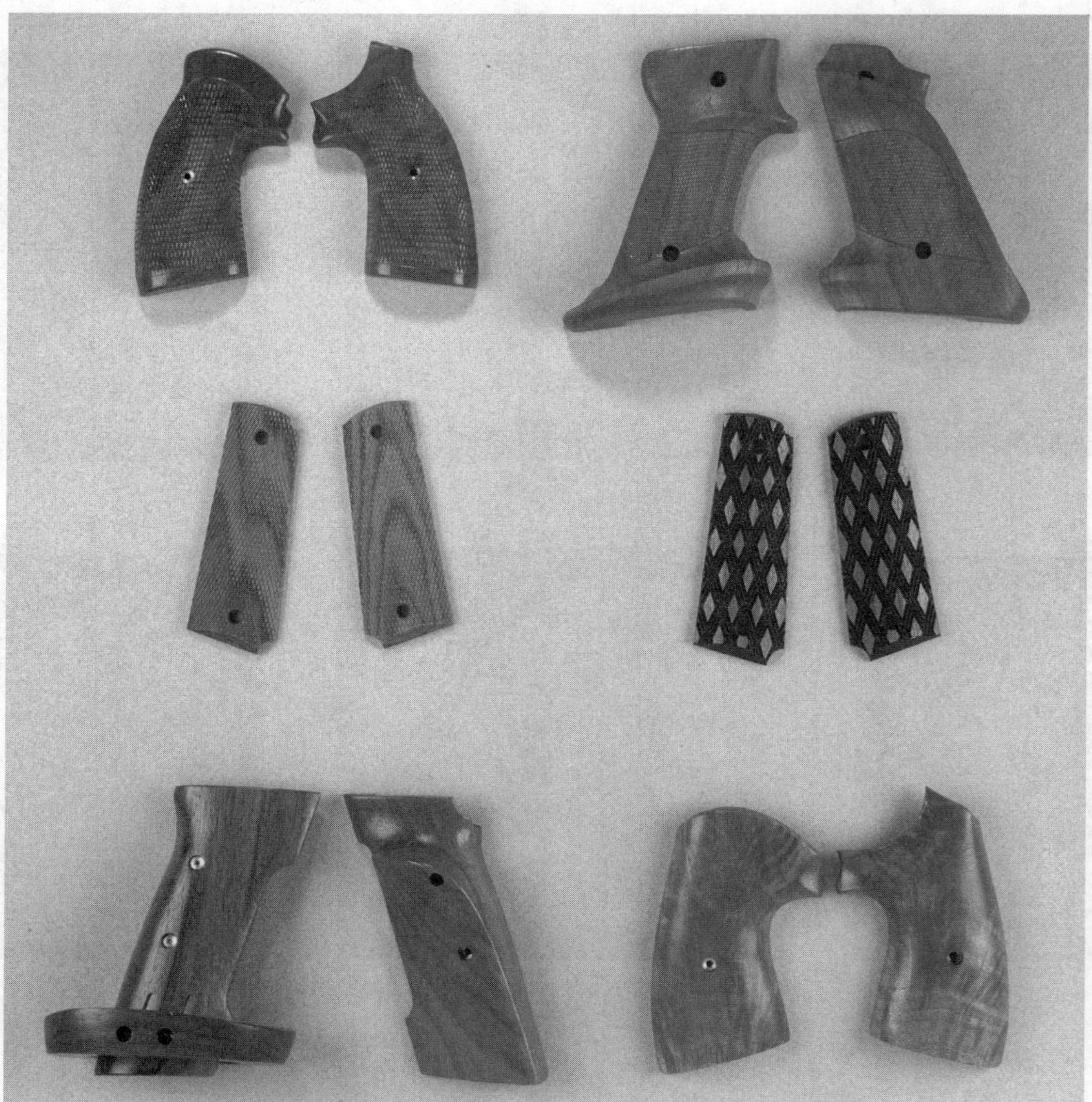

HERRETT'S STOCKS, INC.

Standard and custom hand-fitted grips made of American walnut. Exotic woods such as cocobolo and bubinga are available on request. Grips are available in configurations including target, Camp Perry, combat, field, Jordan trooper, detective, and others. Offered in a variety of checkering patterns, or smooth finish.

Prices: .... $19.95 to $329.95

HOGUE, INC.

Producer of a wide range of grips including the Monogrip, a one-piece design that slides on revolver frames from the bottom. Hand-All grip sleeves fit over the original grips of over 50 handgun models. Grip materials include soft rubber, nylon, laminated hardwoods and fancy hardwoods such as cocobolo, goncalo alves, pau ferro, and kingwood. Single-action revolver grips are available in materials such as white and black Micarta, white and black pearlized polymer, ebony, fancy walnut, ivory polymer and exotic hardwoods.

Prices: Revolver & pistol grips of rubber or nylon. . . . . **$14.95 to $22.95**
Prices: Revolver & pistol grips of goncalo alves or pau ferro . . . . **$24.95 to $59.95**
Prices: Revolver & pistol grips of laminated or fancy woods . . . . **$24.95 to $69.95**
Prices: Revolver & pistol grips of Kingwood, tulipwood or rosewood . . . . **$24.95 to $79.95**
Prices: Single-action revolver grips wood, polymer or Micarta. . . . . **$39.95 to $79.95**

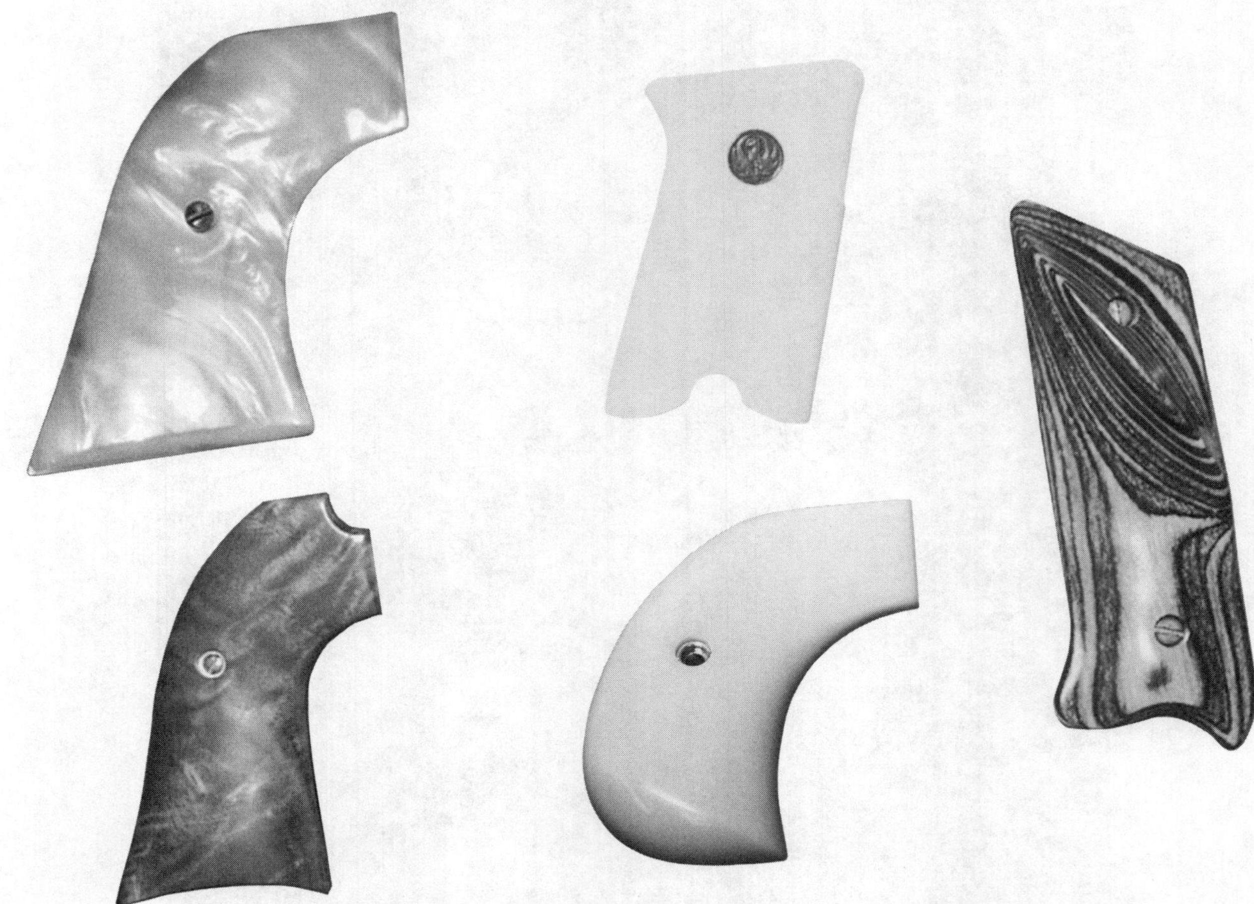

LETT CUSTOM GRIPS

Established in 1940, W.F. Lett Mfg., Inc. has been the principal OEM grip manufacturer for Sturm, Ruger & Co., Inc. since 1955. Grip materials include fancy hardwoods, such as Bolivian rosewood, zebrawood, bocote, goncalo alves and cocobola. Laminated grips are made of hardwood veneers impregnated with plastic resins. Other materials include black or ivory Micarta, buffalo horn, simulated ivory, and pearl-LETT, a synthetic material offering the fiery beauty of genuine mother-of-pearl. Hand-checkering is available on many models.

Prices: Available for most Ruger handguns and Colt 1911 A1-style pistols **. . . $19.95 to $98.50**

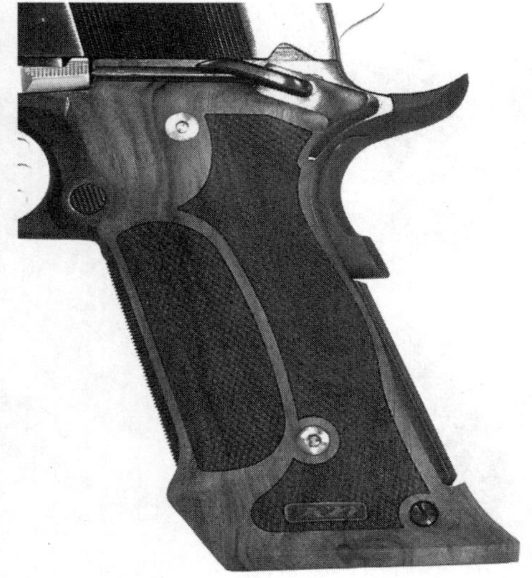

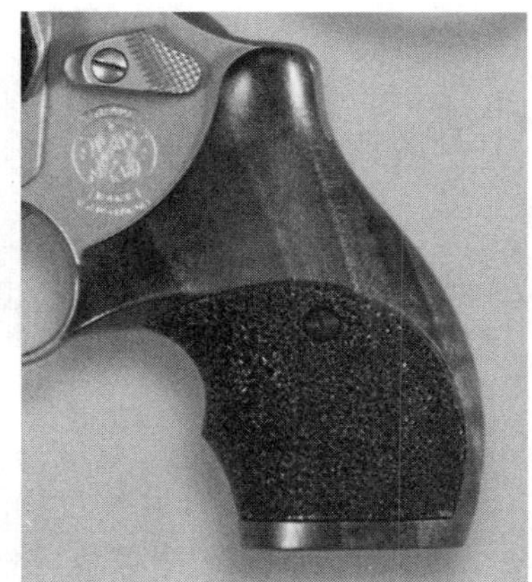

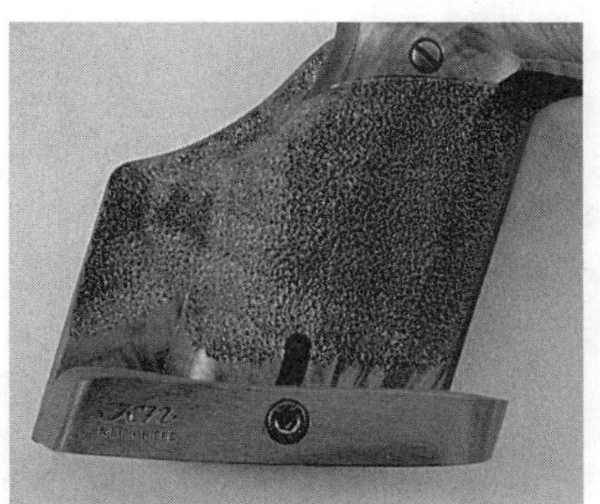

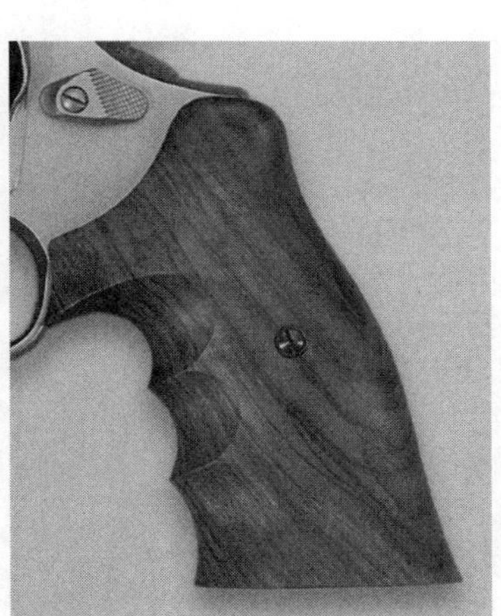

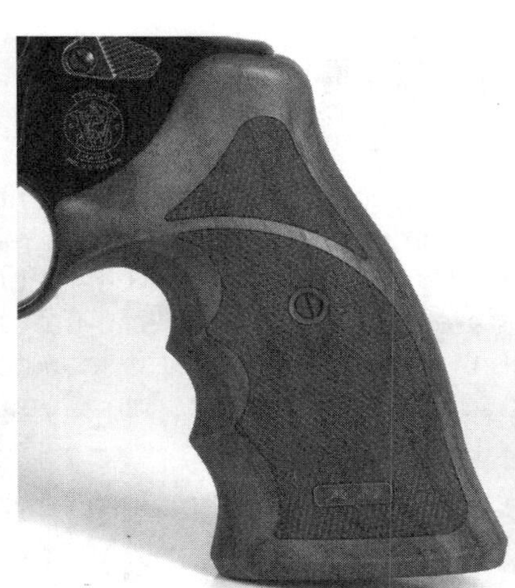

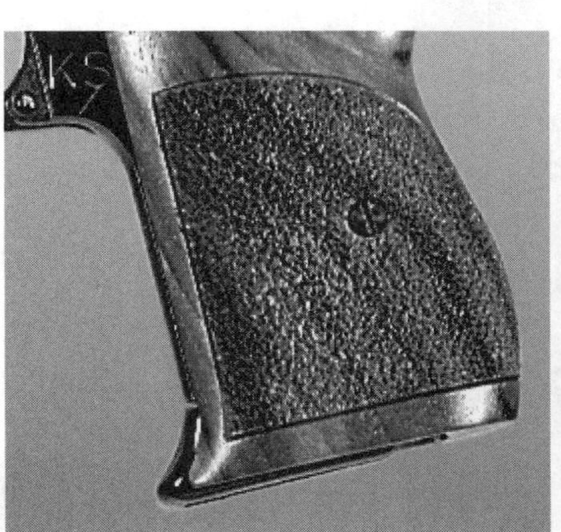

NILL GRIPS

Double-action revolver grips are available with closed or open backstrap area in walnut with smooth, stippled, checkered or Rhomlas finishes, with or without finger grooves in a variety of styles. Anatomical match grips with or without adjustable palm rest are available for standard cartridge handguns and air pistols, as are match grips for Olympic rapid-fire and free pistols.

Prices: Closed back revolver combat-style grips . . . . **$67.90 to $116.00**
Prices: Open back revolver combat-style grips . . . . **$62.90 to $88.90**
Prices: Combat-style grips for pistols . . . . **$54.90 to $137.50**
Prices: Palm rest grips for revolvers . . . . **$109.90 to $164.50**
Prices: Anatomical match grips with adjustable palm rest . . . . **$137.50 to $155.00**

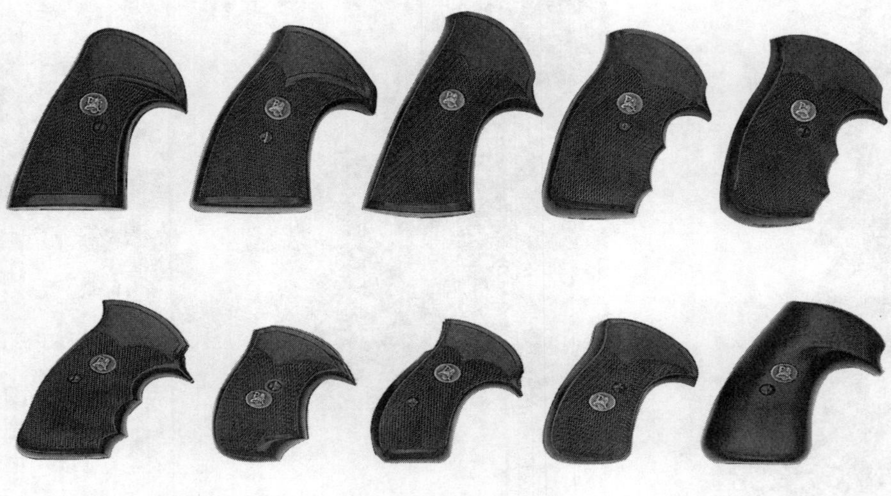

PACHMAYR

Models available in rubber, combination wood and rubber (American Legend Series), and slip-on variations. Some have steel inserts to improve function and finger grooves and/or a palm swell is available on some models. Decelerator rubber grips are designed to dampen recoil on heavy-kicking handguns. Signature grips are available in full wrap-around or without coverage of the pistol backstrap for use on handguns such as the 1911-style pistols with grip safety mechanisms. Slip-on grips come in five sizes to fit virtually any handgun. Compact grips are for small, concealed carry handguns.

PEARCE GRIP

Producer of rubber grips for handgun models including those produced by Glock, Beretta, Colt, Makarov, Kahr Arms, Taurus and Para Ordnance. Highly contoured grips with palm swells, finger grooves and ultra-thin grip panels are available, depending on model.

Prices: .... **$9.95 to $24.95**

WILSON COMBAT

Grips for 1911-A1 style pistols in a variety of woods. Full-checkered models available in cocobolo and Diamondwood. Slim Line grips are laminated from cocobolo or Diamondwood and are 1/3 the thickness of standard 1911-style grips. Exotic wood 1911 grips are offered in cocobolo, Kingwood and Diamondwood and have a double-diamond checkering pattern.

Price: .... **$49.95 to $59.95**

METALLIC CARTRIDGE PRESSES

CH4D Heavyduty Champion

Frame: Cast iron
Frame Type: O-frame
Die Thread: 7/8-14 or 1-14
Avg. Rounds Per Hour: NA
Ram Stroke: 3-1/4"
Weight: 26 lbs.
Features: 1.185" diameter ram with 16 square inches of bearing surface; ram drilled to allow passage of spent primers; solid steel handle; toggle that slightly breaks over the top dead center. Includes universal primer arm with large and small punches. From CH Tool & Die/4D Custom Die.
Price: **$220.00**

CH4D No. 444 4-Station "H" Press

Frame: Aluminum alloy
Frame Type: H-frame
Die Thread: 7/8-14
Avg. Rounds Per Hour: 200
Ram Stroke: 3-3/4"
Weight: 12 lbs.
Features: Two 7/8" solid steel shaft "H" supports; platen rides on permanently lubed bronze bushings; loads smallest pistol to largest magnum rifle cases and has strength to full-length resize. Includes four rams, large and small primer arm and primer catcher. From CH Tool & Die/4D Custom Die, Co.
Price: **$195.00**

CH4D No. 444-X Pistol Champ

Frame: Aluminum alloy
Frame Type: H-frame
Die Thread: 7/8-14
Avg. Rounds Per Hour: 200
Ram Stroke: 3-3/4"
Weight: 12 lbs.
Features: Tungsten carbide sizing die; Speed Seater seating die with tapered entrance to automatically align bullet on case mouth; automatic primer feed for large or small primers; push-button powder measure with easily changed bushings for 215 powder/load combinations; taper crimp die. Conversion kit for caliber changeover available. From CH Tool & Die/4D Custom Die, Co.
Price: .... **$292.00-$316.50**

CORBIN CSP-2 MEGA MITE

Frame: N/A
Frame Type: N/A
Die Thread: 1-1/2 x 12
Avg. Rounds Per Hour: N/A
Ram Stroke: 6"
Weight: 70 lbs.
Features: Roller bearing linkage, hardened tool steel pivots, precision bush bushings glide on polished steel guide rods. Made for use with -H type (hydraulic) swage dies, it is capable of swaging rifle calibers up to .600 Nitro, lead shotgun slugs up to 12 gauge and the reloading of .50 BMG ammo. From Corbin Manufacturing.
Price: **$750.00**

FORSTER Co-Ax Press B-2

Frame: Cast iron
Frame Type: Modified O-frame
Die Thread: 7/8-14
Avg. Rounds Per Hour: 120
Ram Stroke: 4"
Weight: 18 lbs.
Features: Snap in/snap out die change; spent primer catcher with drop tube threaded into carrier below shellholder; automatic, handle-activated, cammed shellholder with opposing spring-loaded jaws to contact extractor groove; floating guide rods for alignment and reduced friction; no torque on the head due to design of linkage and pivots; shellholder jaws that float with die permitting case to center in the die; right- or left-hand operation; priming device for seating to factory specifications. "S" shellholder jaws included. From Forster Products.
Price: **$318.30**
Price: Extra LS shellholder jaws **$27.80**

HOLLYWOOD Senior Press

Frame: Ductile iron
Frame Type: O-frame
Die Thread: 7/8-14
Avg. Rounds Per Hour: 50-100
Ram Stroke: 6-1/2"
Weight: 50 lbs.
Features: Leverage and bearing surfaces ample for reloading cartridges or swaging bullets. Precision ground one-piece 2-1/2" pillar with base; operating handle of 3/4" steel and 15" long; 5/8" steel tie-down rod fro added strength when swaging; heavy steel toggle and camming arms held by 1/2" steel pins in reamed holes. The 1-1/2" steel die bushing takes standard threaded dies; removed, it allows use of Hollywood shotshell dies. From Hollywood Engineering.
Price: **$600.00**

HOLLYWOOD Senior Turret Press

Frame: Ductile iron
Frame Type: H-frame
Die Thread: 7/8-14
Avg. Rounds Per Hour: 50-100
Ram Stroke: 6-1/2"
Weight: 50 lbs.
Features: Same features as Senior press except has three-position turret head; holes in turret may be tapped 1-1/2" or 7/8" or four of each. Height, 15". Comes complete with one turret indexing handle; one operating handle and three turret indexing handles; one 5/8" tie down bar for swaging. From Hollywood Engineering.
Price: **$700.00**

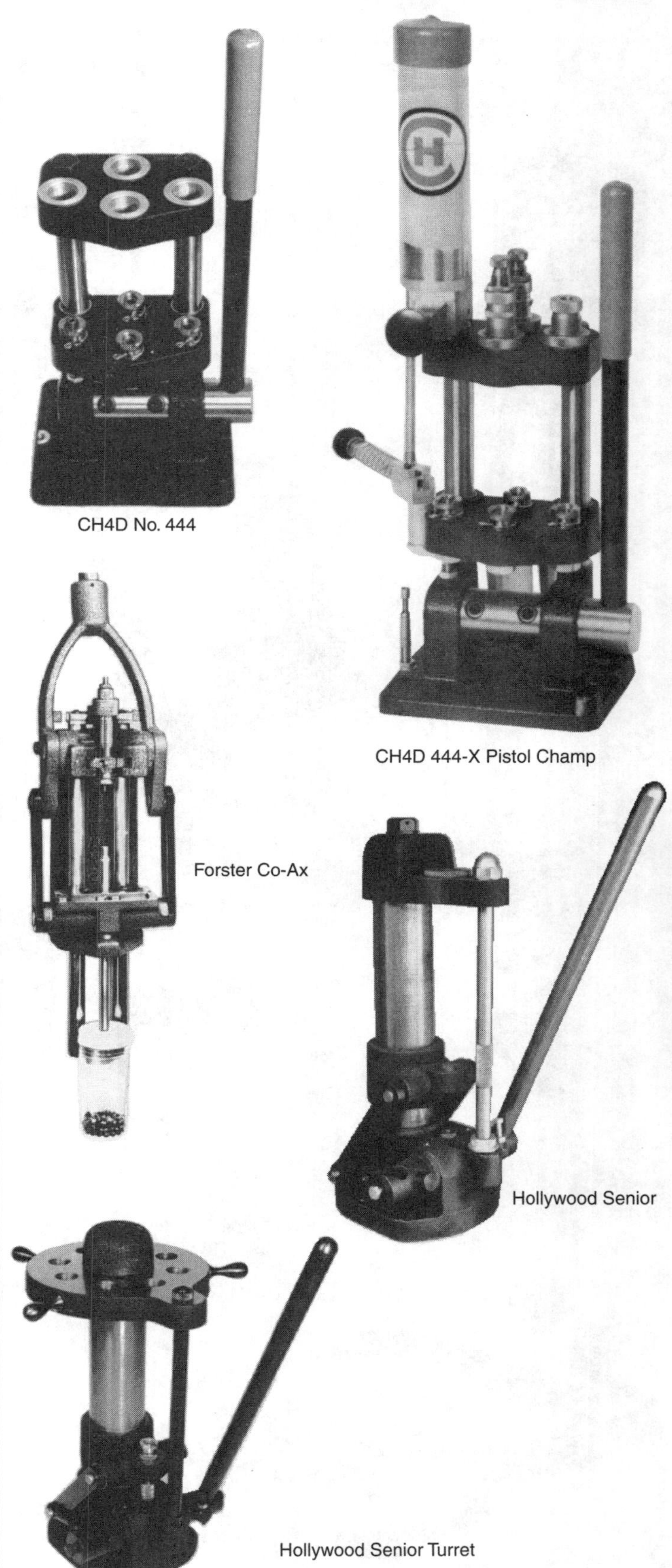

CH4D No. 444

CH4D 444-X Pistol Champ

Forster Co-Ax

Hollywood Senior

Hollywood Senior Turret

ACCESSORIES

Metallic Cartridge Presses

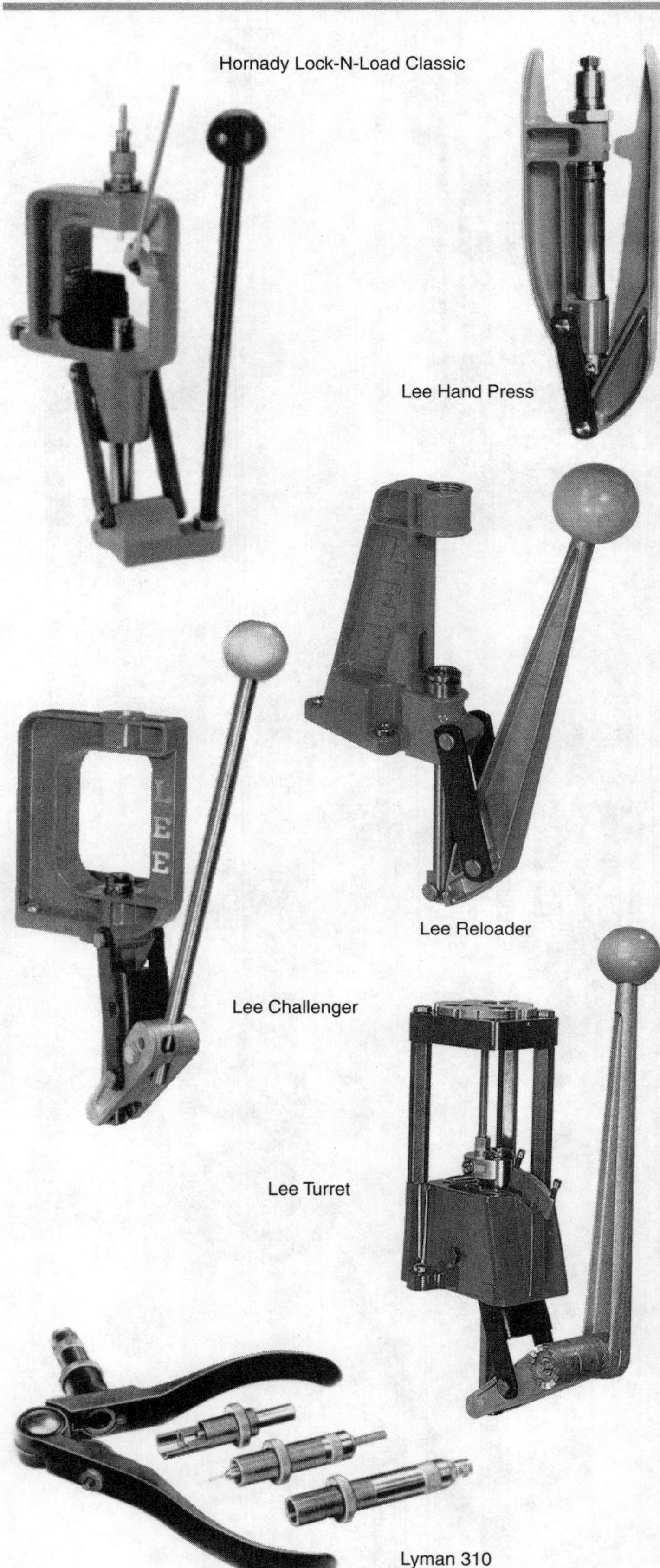

Hornady Lock-N-Load Classic

Lee Hand Press

Lee Reloader

Lee Challenger

Lee Turret

Lyman 310

HORNADY Lock-N-Load Classic

Frame: Die cast heat-treated aluminum alloy
Frame Type: O-frame
Die Thread: 7/8-14
Avg. Rounds Per Hour: NA
Ram Stroke: 3-5/8"
Weight: 14 lbs.
Features: Features Lock-N-Load bushing system that allows instant die changeovers. Solid steel linkage arms that rotate on steel pins; 30° angled frame design for improved visibility and accessibility; primer arm automatically moves in and out of ram for primer pickup and solid seating; two primer arms for large and small primers; long offset handle for increased leverage and unobstructed reloading; lifetime warranty. Comes as a package with primer catcher, PPS automatic primer feed and three Lock-N-Load die bushings. Dies and shellholder available separately or as a kit with primer catcher, positive priming system, automatic primer feed, three die bushings and reloading accessories. From Hornady Mfg. Co.
Price: Press and Three Die Bushings $99.95
Price: Classic Reloading Kit $259.95

LEE Hand Press

Frame: ASTM 380 aluminum
Frame Type: NA
Die Thread: 7/8-14
Avg. Rounds Per Hour: 100
Ram Stroke: 3-1/4"
Weight: 1 lb., 8 oz.
Features: Small and lightweight for portability; compound linkage for handling up to 375 H&H and case forming. Dies and shellholder not included. From Lee Precision, Inc.
Price: $26.98

LEE Challenger Press

Frame: ASTM 380 aluminum
Frame Type: O-frame
Die Thread: 7/8-14
Avg. Rounds Per Hour: 100
Ram Stroke: 3-1/2"
Weight: 4 lbs., 1 oz.
Features: Larger than average opening with 30° offset for maximum hand clearance; steel connecting pins; spent primer catcher; handle adjustable for start and stop positions; handle repositions for left- or right-hand use; shortened handle travel to prevent springing the frame from alignment. Dies and shellholders not included. From Lee Precision, Inc.
Price: $45.00

LEE Classic Cast

Features: Cast iron, O-type. Adjustable handle moves from right to left, start and stop position is adjustable. Large 1 1/8" diameter hollow ram catches primers for disposal. Automatic primer arm with bottom of stroke priming. Two assembled primer arms included. From Lee Precision, Inc.
Price: $90.00

LEE Reloader Press

Frame: ASTM 380 aluminum
Frame Type: C-frame
Die Thread: 7/8-14
Avg. Rounds Per Hour: 100
Ram Stroke: 3"
Weight: 1 lb., 12 oz.
Features: Balanced lever to prevent pinching fingers; unlimited hand clearance; left- or right-hand use. Dies and shellholders not included. From Lee Precision, Inc.
Price: $26.98

LEE Turret Press

Frame: ASTM 380 aluminum
Frame Type: O-frame
Die Thread: 7/8-14
Avg. Rounds Per Hour: 300
Ram Stroke: 3"
Weight: 7 lbs., 2 oz.
Features: Replaceable turret lifts out by rotating 30°; T-primer arm reverses for large or small primers; built-in primer catcher; adjustable handle for right- or left-hand use or changing angle of down stroke; accessory mounting hole for Lee Auto-Disk powder measure. Optional Auto-Index rotates die turret to next station for semi-progressive use. Safety override prevents overstressing should turret not turn. From Lee Precision, Inc.
Price: $69.98
Price: With Auto-Index $83.98
Price: Four-Hole Turret with Auto-Index $85.98

LYMAN 310 Tool

Frame: Stainless steel
Frame Type: NA
Die Thread: 7/8-14
Avg. Rounds Per Hour: NA
Ram Stroke: NA
Weight: 10 oz.
Features: Compact, portable reloading tool for pistol or rifle cartridges. Adapter allows loading rimmed or rimless cases. Die set includes neck resizing/decapping die, primer seating chamber; neck expanding die; bullet seating die; and case head adapter. From Lyman Products Corp.
Price: Dies $45.00
Price: Handles $47.50
Price: Carrying pouch $9.95

METALLIC CARTRIDGE PRESSES

LYMAN AccuPress

Frame: Die cast
Frame Type: C-frame
Die Thread: 7/8-14
Avg. Rounds Per Hour: 75
Ram Stroke: 3.4"
Weight: 4 lbs.
Features: Reversible, contoured handle for bench mount or hand-held use; for rifle or pistol; compound leverage; Delta frame design. Accepts all standard powder measures. From Lyman Products Corp.
Price: **$34.95**

LYMAN Crusher II

Frame: Cast iron
Frame Type: O-frame
Die Thread: 7/8-14
Avg. Rounds Per Hour: 75
Ram Stroke: 3-7/8"
Weight: 19 lbs.
Features: Reloads both pistol and rifle cartridges; 1" diameter ram; 4-1/2" press opening for loading magnum cartridges; direct torque design; right- or left-hand use. New base design with 14 square inches of flat mounting surface with three bolt holes. Comes with priming arm and primer catcher. Dies and shellholders not included. From Lyman Products Corp.
Price: **$116.50**

LYMAN T-Mag II

Frame: Cast iron with silver metalflake powder finish
Frame Type: Turret
Die Thread: 7/8-14
Avg. Rounds Per Hour: 125
Ram Stroke: 3-13/16"
Weight: 18 lbs.
Features: Reengineered and upgraded with new turret system for ease of indexing and tool-free turret removal for caliber changeover; new flat machined base for bench mounting; new nickel-plated non-rust handle and links; and new silver hammertone powder coat finish for durability. Right- or left-hand operation; handles all rifle or pistol dies. Comes with priming arm and primer catcher. Dies and shellholders not included. From Lyman Products Corp.
Price: **$164.95**
Price: Extra turret **$37.50**

MEACHAM ANYWHERE PORTABLE RELOADING PRESS

Frame: Anodized 6061 T6 aircraft aluminum
Frame Type: Cylindrical
Die Thread: 7/8-14
Avg. Rounds Per Hour: N/A
Ram Stroke: 2.7"
Weight: 2 lbs. (hand held); 5 lbs. (with docking kit)
Features: A light weight, portable press that can be used hand-held (or with a docking kit) can be clamped to a table top up to 9.75" thick. Docking kit includes a threaded powder measure mount and holder for the other die. Designed for neck sizing abd bullet seating of short action cartridges, it can be used for long action cartridges with the addition of an Easy Seater straight line seating die. Dies not included.
Price: **$99.95**
Price: (with docking kit) **$144.95**
Price: Easy Seater **$114.95**
Price: Re-De-Capper .... **N/A**

PONSNESS/WARREN Metal-Matic P-200

Frame: Die cast aluminum
Frame Type: Unconventional
Die Thread: 7/8-14
Avg. Rounds Per Hour: 200+
Weight: 18 lbs.
Features: Designed for straight-wall cartridges; die head with 10 tapped holes for holding dies and accessories for two calibers at one time; removable spent primer box; pivoting arm moves case from station to station. Comes with large and small primer tool. Optional accessories include primer feed, extra die head, primer speed feeder, powder measure extension and dust cover. Dies, powder measure and shellholder not included. From Ponsness/Warren.
Price: **$215.00**
Price: Extra die head **$44.95**
Price: Powder measure extension **$29.95**
Price: Primer feed **$44.95**
Price: Primer speed feed **$14.50**
Price: Dust cover **$21.95**

RCBS Partner

Frame: Aluminum
Frame Type: O-frame
Die Thread: 7/8-14
Avg. Rounds Per Hour: 50-60
Ram Stroke: 3-5/8"
Weight: 5 lbs.
Features: Designed for the beginning reloader. Comes with primer arm equipped with interchangeable primer plugs and sleeves for seating large and small primers. Shellholder and dies not included. Available in kit form (see Metallic Presses-Accessories). From RCBS.
Price: **$69.95**

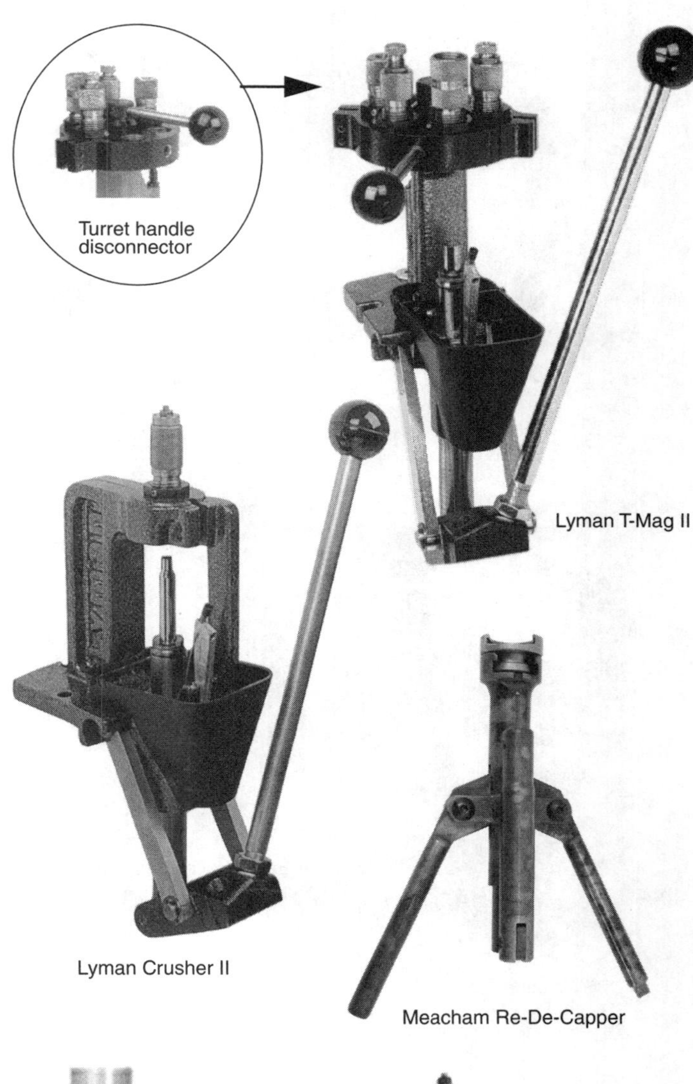

Turret handle disconnector

Lyman T-Mag II

Lyman Crusher II

Meacham Re-De-Capper

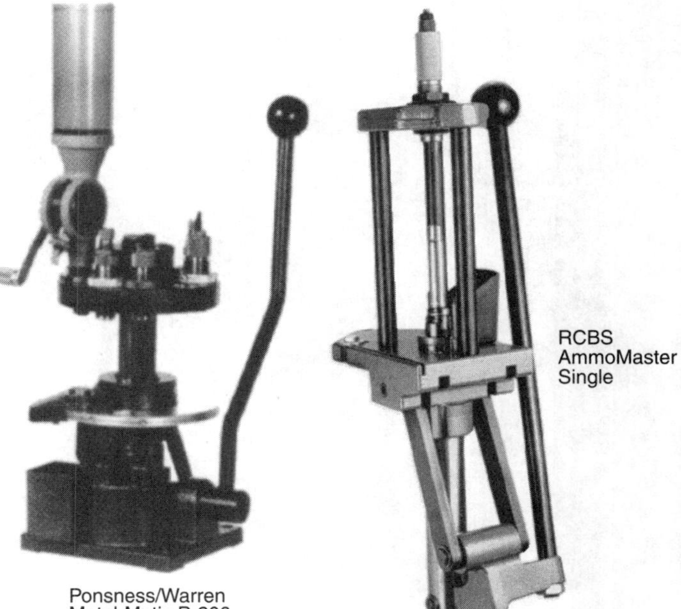

RCBS AmmoMaster Single

Ponsness/Warren Metal-Matic P-200

ACCESSORIES

METALLIC CARTRIDGE PRESSES

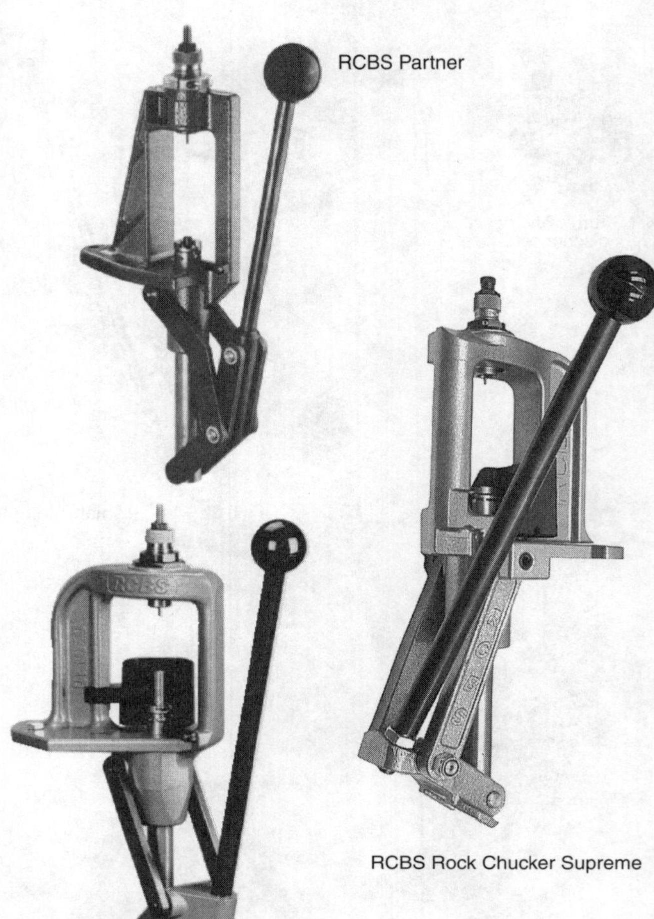

RCBS Partner

RCBS Rock Chucker Supreme

RCBS Reloader Special-5

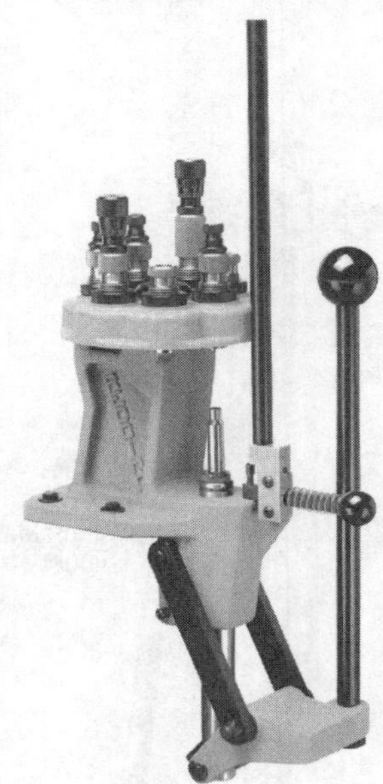

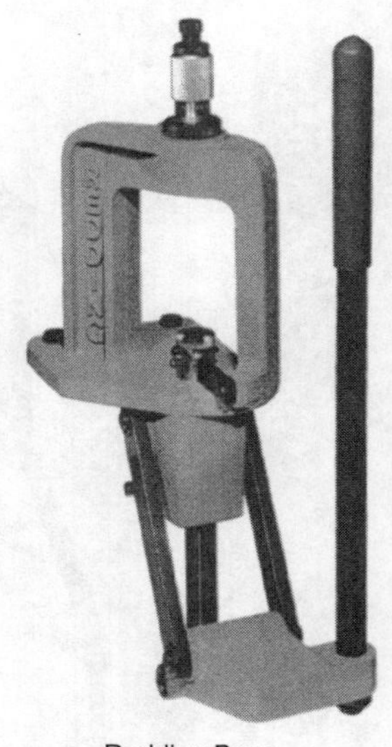

Redding Boss

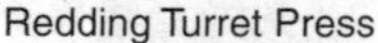

Redding Turret Press

RCBS AmmoMaster Single

Frame: Aluminum base; cast iron top plate connected by three steel posts.
Frame Type: NA
Die Thread: 1-1/4"-12 bushing; 7/8-14 threads
Avg. Rounds Per Hour: 50-60
Ram Stroke: 5-1/4"
Weight: 19 lbs.
Features: Single-stage press convertible to progressive. Will form cases or swage bullets. Case detection system to disengage powder measure when no case is present in powder charging station; five-station shellplate; Uniflow Powder measure with clear powder measure adaptor to make bridged powders visible and correctable. 50-cal. conversion kit allows reloading 50 BMG. Kit includes top plate to accommodate either 1-3/8" x 12 or 1-1/2" x 12 reloading dies. Piggyback die plate for quick caliber change-overs available. Reloading dies not included. From RCBS.
Price: **$229.95**
Price: 50 conversion kit **$109.95**
Price: Piggyback/AmmoMaster die plate **$23.95**
Price: Piggyback/AmmoMaster shellplate **$31.95**
Price: Press cover **$13.95**

RCBS Reloader Special-5

Frame: Aluminum
Frame Type: 30˚ offset O-frame
Die Thread: 1-1/4"-12 bushing; 7/8-14 threads
Avg. Rounds Per Hour: 50-60
Ram Stroke: 3-1/16"
Weight: 7.5 lbs.
Features: Single-stage press convertible to progressive with RCBS Piggyback II. Primes cases during resizing operation. Will accept RCBS shotshell dies. From RCBS.
Price: **$123.95**

RCBS Rock Chucker Supreme

Frame: Cast iron
Frame Type: O-frame
Die Thread: 1-1/4"-12 bushing; 7/8-14 threads
Avg. Rounds Per Hour: 50-60
Ram Stroke: 3-1/16"
Weight: 17 lbs.
Features: Redesigned to allow loading of longer cartridge cases. Made for heavy-duty reloading, case forming and bullet swaging. Provides 4" of ram-bearing surface to support 1" ram and ensure alignment; ductile iron toggle blocks; hardened steel pins. Comes standard with Universal Primer Arm and primer catcher. Can be converted from single-stage to progressive with Piggyback II conversion unit. From RCBS.
Price: **$155.95**

REDDING T-7 Turret Press

Frame: Cast iron
Frame Type: Turret
Die Thread: 7/8-14
Avg. Rounds Per Hour: NA
Ram Stroke: 3.4"
Weight: 23 lbs., 2 oz.
Features: Strength to reload pistol and magnum rifle, case form and bullet swage; linkage pins heat-treated, precision ground and in double shear; hollow ram to collect spent primers; removable turret head for caliber changes; progressive linkage for increased power as ram nears die; rear turret support for stability and precise alignment; 7-station turret head; priming arm for both large and small primers. Also available in kit form with shellholder and one die set. From Redding Reloading Equipment.
Price: **$298.50**
Price: Kit **$336.00**

REDDING Boss

Frame: Cast iron
Frame Type: O-frame
Die Thread: 7/8-14
Avg. Rounds Per Hour: NA
Ram Stroke: 3.4"
Weight: 11 lbs., 8 oz.
Features: 36˚ frame offset for visibility and accessibility; primer arm positioned at bottom ram travel; positive ram travel stop machined to hit exactly top-dead-center. Also available in kit form with shellholder and set of Redding A dies. From Redding Reloading Equipment.
Price: **$142.50**
Price: Kit **$189.00**

REDDING Ultramag

Frame: Cast iron
Frame Type: Non-conventional
Die Thread: 7/8-14
Avg. Rounds Per Hour: NA
Ram Stroke: 4-1/8"
Weight: 23 lbs., 6 oz.
Features: Unique compound leverage system connected to top of press for tons of ram pressure; large 4-3/4" frame opening for loading outsized cartridges; hollow ram for spent primers. Kit available with shellholder and one set Redding A dies. From Redding Reloading Equipment.
Price: **$321.00**
Price: Kit **$363.00**

METALLIC CARTRIDGE PRESSES

ROCK CRUSHER Press

Frame: Cast iron
Frame Type: O-frame
Die Thread: 2-3/4"-12 with bushing reduced to 1-1/2"-12
Avg. Rounds Per Hour: 50
Ram Stroke: 6"
Weight: 67 lbs.

Features: Designed to load and form ammunition from 50 BMG up to 23x115 Soviet. Frame opening of 8-1/2"x3-1/2"; 1-1/2"x12"; bushing can be removed and bushings of any size substituted; ram pressure can exceed 10,000 lbs. with normal body weight; 40mm diameter ram. Angle block for bench mounting and reduction bushing for RCBS dies available. Accessories for Rock Crusher include powder measure, dies, shellholder, bullet puller, priming tool, case gauge and other accessories found elsewhere in this catalog. From The Old Western Scrounger.

Price: **$795.00**
Price: Angle block **$57.95**
Price: Reduction bushing **$21.00**
Price: Shellholder **$47.25**
Price: Priming tool, 50 BMG, 20 Lahti **$65.10**

PROGRESSIVE PRESSES

CORBIN BENCHREST S-PRESS

Frame: All steel
Frame Type: O-Frame
Die Thread: 7/8-14 and T-slot adapter
Avg. Rounds Per Hour: NA
Ram Stroke: 4"
Weight: 22 lbs.

Features: Roller bearing linkage, removeable head, right- or left-hand mount.

Price: **$298.00**

DILLON AT 500

Frame: Aluminum alloy
Frame Type: NA
Die Thread: 7/8-14
Avg. Rounds Per Hour: 200-300
Ram Stroke: 3-7/8"
Weight: NA

Features: Four stations; removable tool head to hold dies in alignment and allow caliber changes without die adjustment; manual indexing; capacity to be upgraded to progressive RL 550B. Comes with universal shellplate to accept 223, 22-250, 243, 30-06, 9mm, 38/357, 40 S&W, 45 ACP. Dies not included. From Dillon Precision Products.

Price: **$193.95**

DILLON RL 550B

Frame: Aluminum alloy
Frame Type: NA
Die Thread: 7/8-14
Avg. Rounds Per Hour: 500-600
Ram Stroke: 3-7/8"
Weight: 25 lbs.

Features: Four stations; removable tool head to hold dies in alignment and allow caliber changes without die adjustment; auto priming system that emits audible warning when primer tube is low; a 100-primer capacity magazine contained in DOM steel tube for protection; new auto powder measure system with simple mechanical connection between measure and loading platform for positive powder bar return; a separate station for crimping with star-indexing system; 220 ejected-round capacity bin; 3/4-lb. capacity powder measure. Height above bench, 35"; requires 3/4" bench overhang. Will reload 120 different rifle and pistol calibers. Comes with one caliber conversion kit. Dies not included. From Dillon Precision Products, Inc.

Price: **$329.95**

DILLON Super 1050

Frame: Ductile iron
Frame Type: Platform type
Die Thread: 7/8-14
Avg. Rounds Per Hour: 1000-1200
Ram Stroke: 2-5/16"
Weight: 62 lbs.

Features: Eight stations; auto case feed; primer pocket swager for military cartridge cases; auto indexing; removable tool head; auto prime system with 100-primer capacity; low primer supply alarm; positive powder bar return; auto powder measure; 515 ejected round bin capacity; 500-600 case feed capacity; 3/4-lb. capacity powder measure. Has lengthened frame and short-stroke crank to accommodate long calibers. Loads all pistol rounds as well as 30 M1 Carbine, 223, and 7.62x39 rifle rounds. Height above the bench, 43". Dies not included. From Dillon Precision Products, Inc.

Price: **$1,399.95**

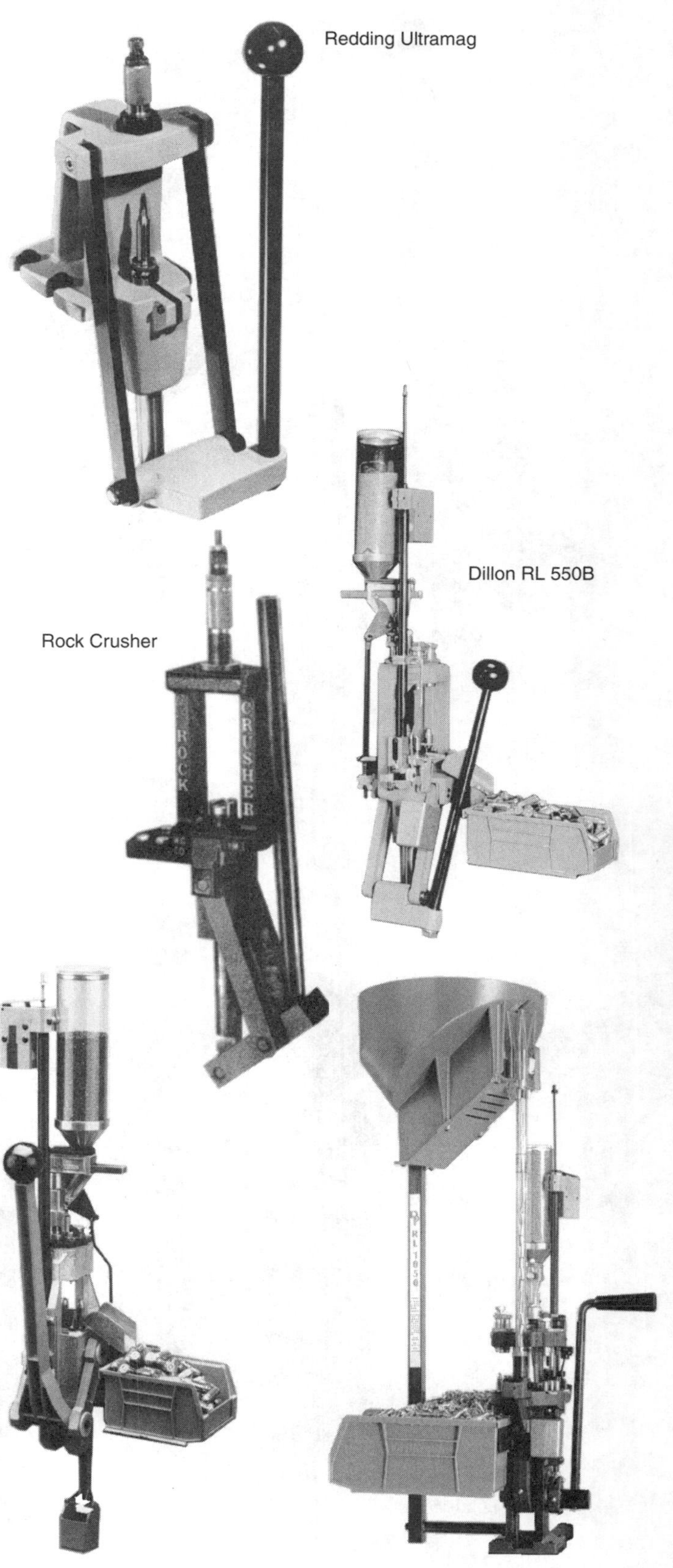

Redding Ultramag

Rock Crusher

Dillon RL 550B

Dillon Square Deal B

Dillon RL 1050

ACCESSORIES

METALLIC CARTRIDGE PRESSES

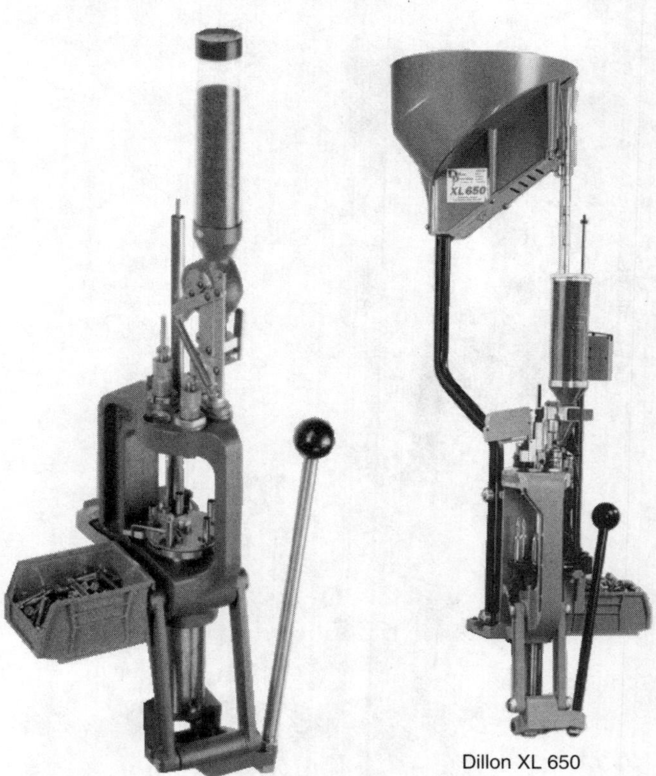

Hornady Lock-N-Load AP

Dillon XL 650

Lee Load-Master

DILLON Square Deal B

Frame: Zinc alloy
Frame Type: NA
Die Thread: None (unique Dillon design)
Avg. Rounds Per Hour: 400-500
Ram Stroke: 2-5/16"
Weight: 17 lbs.
Features: Four stations; auto indexing; removable tool head; auto prime system with 100-primer capacity; low primer supply alarm; auto powder measure; positive powder bar return; 170 ejected round capacity bin; 3/4-lb. capacity powder measure. Height above the bench, 34". Comes complete with factory adjusted carbide die set. From Dillon Precision Products, Inc.
Price: **$252.95**

DILLON XL 650

Frame: Aluminum alloy
Frame Type: NA
Die Thread: 7/8-14
Avg. Rounds Per Hour: 800-1000
Ram Stroke: 4-9/16"
Weight: 46 lbs.
Features: Five stations; auto indexing; auto case feed; removable tool head; auto prime system with 100-primer capacity; low primer supply alarm; auto powder measure; positive powder bar return; 220 ejected round capacity bin; 3/4-lb. capacity powder measure. 500-600 case feed capacity with optional auto case feed. Loads all pistol/rifle calibers less than 3-1/2" in length. Height above the bench, 44"; 3/4" bench overhang required. From Dillon Precision Products, Inc.
Price: Less dies **$443.95**

HORNADY Lock-N-Load AP

Frame: Die cast heat-treated aluminum alloy
Frame Type: O-frame
Die Thread: 7/8-14
Avg. Rounds Per Hour: NA
Ram Stroke: 3-3/4"
Weight: 26 lbs.
Features: Features Lock-N-Load bushing system that allows instant die changeovers; five-station die platform with option of seating and crimping separately or adding taper-crimp die; auto prime with large and small primer tubes with 100-primer capacity and protective housing; brass kicker to eject loaded rounds into 80-round capacity cartridge catcher; offset operating handle for leverage and unobstructed operation; 2" diameter ram driven by heavy-duty cast linkage arms rotating on steel pins. Comes with five Lock-N-Load die bushings, shellplate, deluxe powder measure, auto powder drop, and auto primer feed and shut-off, brass kicker and primer catcher. Lifetime warranty. From Hornady Mfg. Co.
Price: **$367.65**

LEE Load-Master

Frame: ASTM 380 aluminum
Frame Type: O-frame
Die Thread: 7/8-14
Avg. Rounds Per Hour: 600
Ram Stroke: 3-1/4"
Weight: 8 lbs., 4 oz.
Features: Available in kit form only. A 1-3/4" diameter hard chrome ram for han-dling largest magnum cases; loads rifle or pistol rounds; five station press to fac-tory crimp and post size; auto indexing with wedge lock mechanism to hold one ton; auto priming; removable turrets; four- tube case feeder with optional case collator and bullet feeder (late 1995); loaded round ejector with chute to optional loaded round catcher; quick change shellplate; primer catcher. Dies and shell-holder for one caliber included. From Lee Precision, Inc.
Price: Rifle **$320.00**
Price: Pistol **$330.00**
Price: Extra turret **$14.98**
Price: Adjustable charge bar **$9.98**

LEE Pro 1000

Frame: ASTM 380 aluminum and steel
Frame Type: O-frame
Die Thread: 7/8-14
Avg. Rounds Per Hour: 600
Ram Stroke: 3-1/4"
Weight: 8 lbs., 7 oz.
Features: Optional transparent large/small or rifle case feeder; deluxe auto-disk case-activated powder measure; case sensor for primer feed. Comes complete with carbide die set (steel dies for rifle) for one caliber. Optional accessories include: case feeder for large/small pistol cases or rifle cases; shell plate carrier with auto prime, case ejector, auto-index and spare parts; case collator for case feeder. From Lee Precision, Inc.
Price: **$199.98**

METALLIC CARTRIDGE PRESSES

PONSNESS/WARREN Metallic II

Frame: Die cast aluminum
Frame Type: H-frame
Die Thread: 7/8-14
Avg. Rounds Per Hour: 150+
Ram Stroke: NA
Weight: 32 lbs.
Features: Die head with five tapped 7/8-14 holes for dies, powder measure or other accessories; pivoting die arm moves case from station to station; depriming tube for removal of spent primers; auto primer feed; interchangeable die head. Optional accessories include additional die heads, powder measure extension tube to accommodate any standard powder measure, primer speed feeder to feed press primer tube without disassembly. Comes with small and large primer seating tools. Dies, powder measure and shellholder not included. From Ponsness/ Warren.
Price: **$375.00**
Price: Extra die head **$56.95**
Price: Primer speed feeder **$14.50**
Price: Powder measure extension **$29.95**
Price: Dust cover **$27.95**

RCBS Pro 2000™

Frame: Cast iron
Frame Type: H-Frame
Die Thread: 7/8 x 14
Avg. Rounds Per Hour: 500-600
Ram Stroke: NA
Weight: NA
Features: Five-station manual indexing; full-length sizing; removable die plate; fast caliber conversion. Uses APS Priming System. From RCBS.
Price: **$42.95**

RCBS Turret Press

Frame: Cast iron
Frame Type: NA
Die Thread: 7/8x14
Avg. Rounds Per Hour: 50 to 200
Ram Stroke: NA
Weight: NA
Features: Six-station turret head; positive alignment; on-press priming.
Price: **$214.95**

STAR Universal Pistol Press

Frame: Cast iron with aluminum base
Frame Type: Unconventional
Die Thread: 11/16-24 or 7/8-14
Avg. Rounds Per Hour: 300
Ram Stroke: NA
Weight: 27 lbs.
Features: Four or five-station press depending on need to taper crimp; handles all popular handgun calibers from 32 Long to 45 Colt. Comes completely assembled and adjusted with carbide dies (except 30 Carbine) and shellholder to load one caliber. Prices slightly higher for 9mm and 30 Carbine. From Star Machine Works.
Price: With taper crimp **$1,055.00**
Price: Without taper crimp **$1,025.00**
Price: Extra tool head, taper crimp **$425.00**
Price: Extra tool head, w/o taper crimp **$395.00**

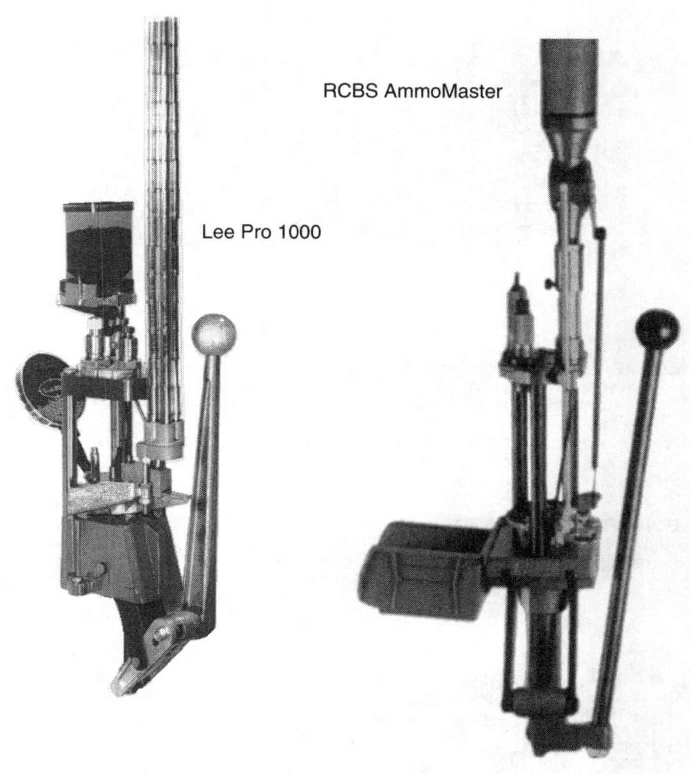

Lee Pro 1000

RCBS AmmoMaster

Fully-automated Star Universal

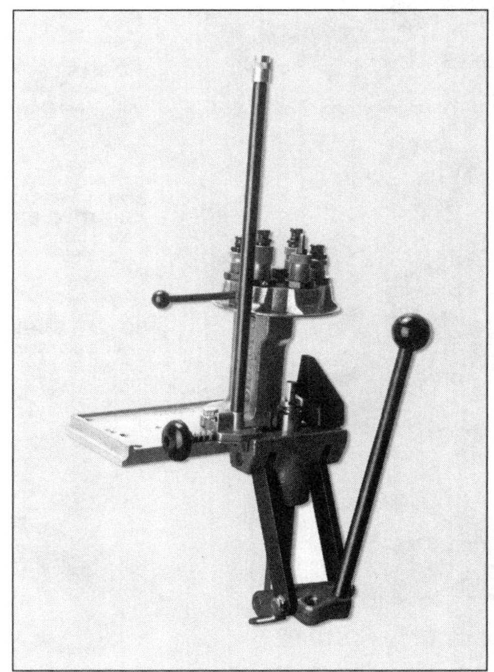

RCBS Turret

METALLIC SIGHTS

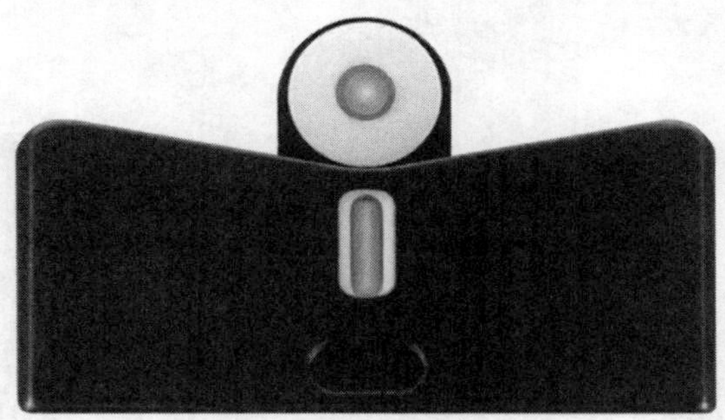

AO Express

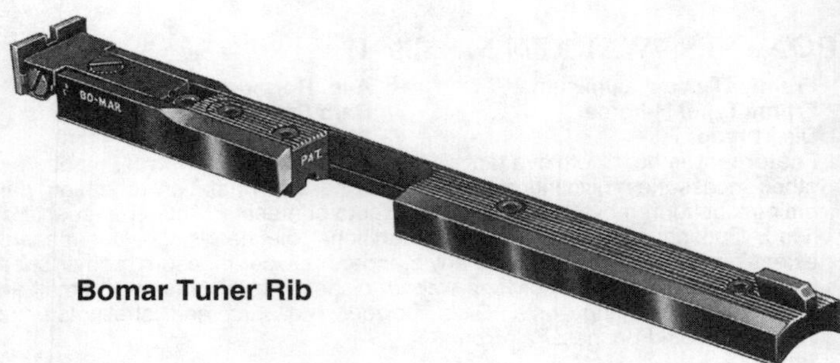

Bomar Tuner Rib

Handgun Sights

AO EXPRESS SIGHTS Low-profile, snag-free express-type sights. Shallow V rear with white vertical line, white dot front. All-steel, matte black finish. Rear is available in different heights. Made for most pistols, many with double set-screws. From AO Sight Systems, Inc.
Price: Standard Set, front and rear. **$60.00**
Price: Big Dot Set, front and rear. **$60.00**
Price: Tritium Set, Standard or Big Dot. **$90.00**
Price: 24/7 Pro Express, Std. or Big Dot Tritium **$120.00**

BO-MAR DELUXE BMCS Gives 3/8" windage and elevation adjustment at 50 yards on Colt Gov't 45; sight radius under 7". For GM and Commander models only. Uses existing dovetail slot. Has shield-type rear blade.
Price: **$65.95**
Price: BMCS-2 (for GM and 9mm). **$68.95**
Price: Flat bottom. . . **$65.95**
Price: BMGC (for Colt Gold Cup), angled serrated blade, rear. **$68.95**
Price: BMGC front sight. **$12.95**
Price: BMCZ-75 (for CZ-75,TZ-75, P-9 and most clones). Works with factory front. **$68.95**

Bomar BMGS

BO-MAR FRONT SIGHTS Dovetail style for S&W 4506, 4516, 1076; undercut style (.250", .280", 5/16" high); Fast Draw style (.210", .250", .230" high).
Price:. **$12.95**

BO-MAR BMU XP-100/T/C CONTENDER No gunsmithing required; has .080" notch.
Price:. **$77.00**

BO-MAR BMML For muzzleloaders; has .062" notch, flat bottom.
Price:. **$65.95**
Price: With 3/8" dovetail. **$65.95**

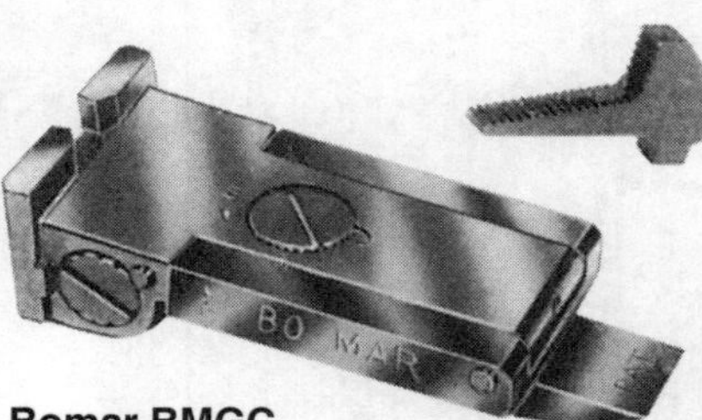

Bomar BMGC

Bomar BMU XP-100

Bomar BMML

Bomar BMR

BO-MAR RUGER "P" ADJUSTABLE SIGHT Replaces factory front and rear sights.
Price: Rear sight. **$65.95**
Price: Front sight. **$12.00**

BO-MAR BMR Fully adjustable rear sight for Ruger MKI, MKII Bull barrel autos.
Price: Rear. **$65.95**
Price: Undercut front sight. **$12.00**

BO-MAR GLOCK Fully adjustable, all-steel replacement sights. Sight fits factory dovetail. Longer sight radius. Uses Novak Glock .275" high, .135" wide front, or similar.
Price: Rear sight. **$68.95**
Price: Front sight. **$20.95**

BO-MAR LOW PROFILE RIB & ACCURACY TUNER Streamlined rib with front and rear sights; 7 1/8" sight radius. Brings sight line closer to the bore than standard or extended sight and ramp. Weight 5 oz. Made for Colt Gov't 45, Super 38, and Gold Cup 45 and 38.
Price:. **$140.00**

Bomar Combat Rib

BO-MAR COMBAT RIB For S&W Model 19 revolver with 4" barrel. Sight radius 5 3/4", weight 5 1/2 oz.
Price:. **$127.00**

Bomar Winged Rib

BO-MAR WINGED RIB For S&W 4" and 6" length barrels-K-38, M10, HB 14 and 19. Weight for the 6" model is about 7 1/4 oz.
Price:. **$140.00**

Bomar Cover-Up Rib

BO-MAR COVER-UP RIB Adjustable rear sight, winged front guards. Fits right over revolver's original front sight. For S&W 4" M-10HB, M-13, M-58, M-64 & 65, Ruger 4" models SDA-34, SDA-84, SS-34, SS-84, GF-34, GF-84.
Price:. **$130.00**

METALLIC SIGHTS

Chip McCormick "Drop In"

CHIP MCCORMICK "DROP-IN" A low mount sight that fits any 1911-style slide with a standard military-type dovetail sight cut (60x.290"). Dovetail front sights also available. From Chip McCormick Corp.
Price: **$47.95**

CHIP MCCORMICK FIXED SIGHTS Same sight picture (.110" rear - .110" front) that's become the standard for pro combat shooters. Low mount design with rounded edges. For 1911-style pistols. May require slide machining for installation. From Chip McCormick Corp.
Price: **$24.95**

Chip McCormick Fixed Sight

C-MORE SIGHTS Replacement front sight blades offered in two types and five styles. Made of Du Pont Acetal, they come in a set of five high-contrast colors: blue, green, pink, red and yellow. Easy to install. Patridge style for Colt Python (all barrels), Ruger Super Blackhawk (7 1/2"), Ruger Blackhawk (4 5/8"); ramp style for Python (all barrels), Blackhawk (4 5/8"), Super Blackhawk (7 1/2" and 10 1/2"). From C-More Systems.
Price: Per set. **$19.95**

G.G. & G. GHOST RINGS Replaces the factory rear sight without gunsmithing. Black phosphate finish. Available for Colt M1911 and Commander, Beretta M92F, Glock, S&W, SIG Sauer.
Price:. **$65.00**

Heinie Slant Pro

HEINIE SLANT PRO Made with a slight forward slant, the unique design of these rear sights is snag free for unimpeded draw from concealment. The combination of the slant and the rear serrations virtually eliminates glare. Made for most popular handguns. From Heinie Specialty Products.
Price: . . . . **$50.35 to $122.80**

HEINIE STRAIGHT EIGHT SIGHTS Consists of one tritium dot in the front sight and a slightly smaller Tritium dot in the rear sight. When aligned correctly, an elongated 'eight' is created. The Tritium dots are green in color. Designed with the belief that the human eye can correct vertical alignment faster than horizontal. Available for most popular handguns. From Heinie Specialty Products.
Price: . . . . **$104.95 to $122.80**

HEINIE CROSS DOVETAIL FRONT SIGHTS Made in a variety of heights, the standard dovetail is 60 degrees x .305" x .062" with a .002 taper. From Heinie Specialty Products.
Price:. . . . . **$20.95 to $47.20**

JP GHOST RING Replacement bead front, ghost ring rear for Glock and M1911 pistols. From JP Enterprises.
Price:. **$79.95**
Price: Bo-Mar replacement leaf with JP dovetail front bead. **$99.95**

LES BAER CUSTOM ADJUSTABLE LOW MOUNT REAR SIGHT Considered one of the top adjustable sights in the world for target shooting with 1911-style pistols. Available with Tritium inserts. From Les Baer Custom.
Price:. . . . . **$49.00** (standard); **$99.00** (tritium)

LES BAER DELUXE FIXED COMBAT SIGHT A tactical-style sight with a very low profile. Incorporates a no-snag design and has serrations on sides. For 1911-style pistols. Available with Tritium inserts for night shooting. From Les Baer Custom.
Price:. . . . . **$26.00** (standard); **$67.00** (with Tritium)

LES BAER DOVETAIL FRONT SIGHT Blank dovetail sight machined from bar stock. Can be contoured to many different configurations to meet user's needs. Available with Tritium insert. From Les Baer Custom.
Price:. . . . . **$17.00** (standard); **$47.00** (with Tritium insert)

LES BAER FIBER OPTIC FRONT SIGHT Dovetail .330x65 degrees, .125" wide post, .185" high, .060" diameter. Red and green fiber optic. From Les Baer Custom.
Price: **$24.00**

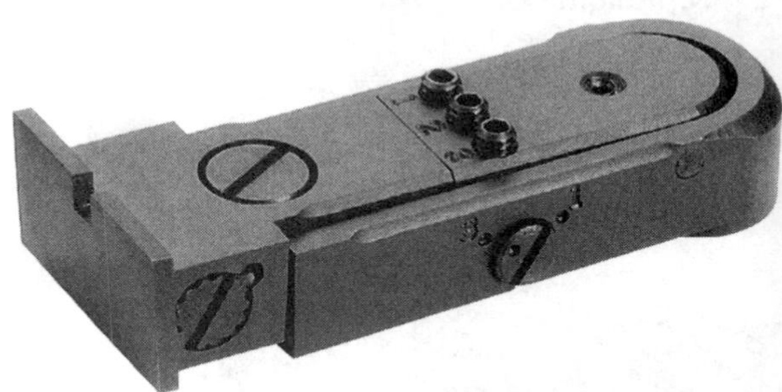

Les Baer PPC-Style Adjustable Rear Sight

LES BAER PPC-STYLE ADJUSTABLE REAR SIGHT Made for use with custom built 1911-style pistols, allows the user to preset three elevation adjustments for PPC-style shooting. Milling required for installation. Made from 4140 steel. From Les Baer Custom.
Price: **$120.00**

Les Baer Dovetail

LES BAER DOVETAIL FRONT SIGHT WITH TRITIUM INSERT This fully contoured and finished front sight comes ready for gunsmith installation. From Les Baer Custom.
Price: **$47.00**

MMC TACTICAL ADJUSTABLE SIGHTS Low-profile, snag free design. Twenty-two click positions for elevation, drift adjustable for windage. Machined from 4140 steel and heat treated to 40 RC. Tritium and non-tritium. Ten different configurations and colors. Three different finishes. For 1911s, all Glock, HK USP, S&W, Browning Hi-Power.
Price: Sight set, tritium. **$144.92**
Price: Sight set, white outline or white dot. **$99.90**
Price: Sight set, black. **$93.90**

MEPROLIGHT TRITIUM NIGHT SIGHTS Replacement sight assemblies for low-light conditions. Available for pistols (fixed and adj.),rifles, shotguns. 12-year warranty for useable illumination, while non-TRU-DOT have a 5-year warranty. Distributed in American by Kimber.

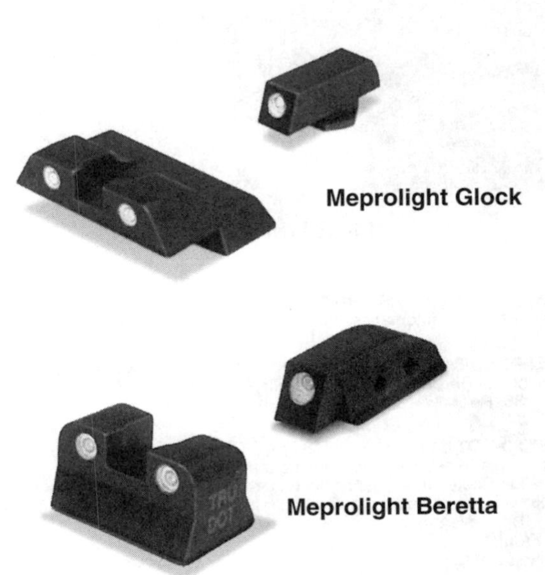

Meprolight Glock

Meprolight Beretta

METALLIC SIGHTS

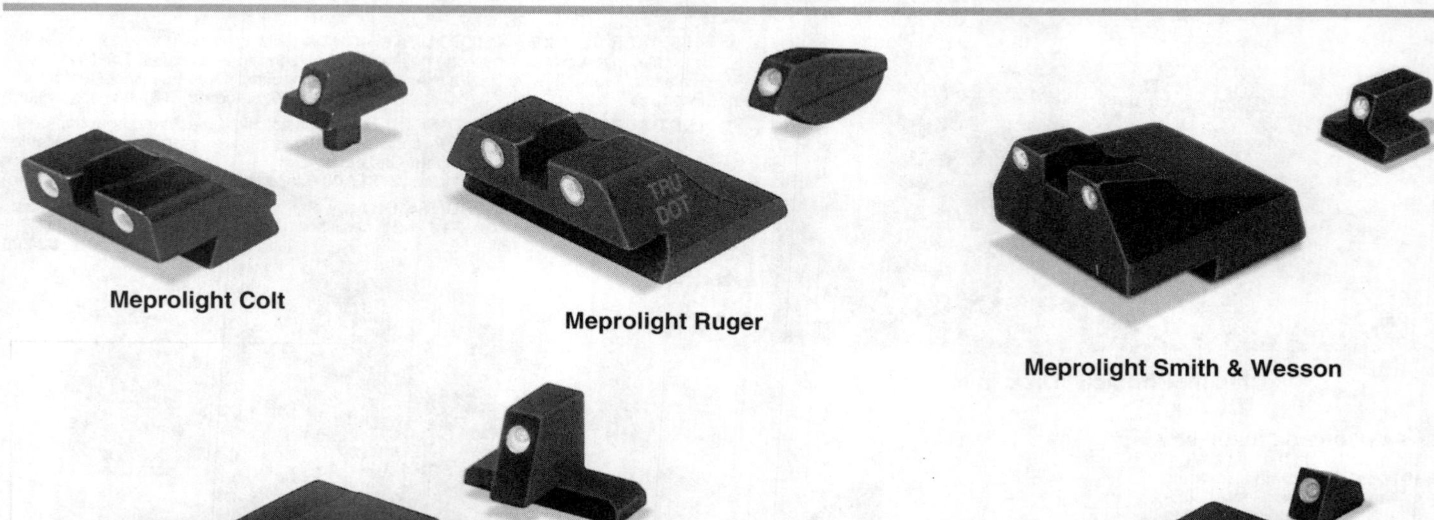

Meprolight Colt

Meprolight Ruger

Meprolight Smith & Wesson

Meprolight H&K

Meprolight Taurus

Price: Kahr K9, K40, fixed, TRU-DOT. **$100.00**
Price: Ruger P85, P89, P94, adjustable, TRU-DOT. **$156.00**
Price: Ruger Mini-14R sights. **$140.00**
Price: SIG Sauer P220, P225, P226, P228, adjustable, TRU-DOT. **$156.00**
Price: Smith&Wesson autos, fixed or adjustable, TRU-DOT. **$100.00**
Price: Taurus PT92, PT100, adjustable, TRU-DOT. **$156.00**
Price: Walther P-99, fixed, TRU-DOT. **$100.00**
Price: Shotgun bead. **$32.00**
Price: Beretta M92, Cougar, Brigadier, fixed, TRU-DOT. **$100.00**
Price: Browning Hi-Power, adjustable, TRU-DOT. **$156.00**
Price: Colt M1911 Govt., adjustable, TRU-DOT. **$156.00**

MILLETT SERIES 100 REAR SIGHTS All-steel highly visible, click adjustable. Blades in white outline, target black, silhouette, 3-dot. Fit most popular revolvers and autos.
Price:. . . . . **$51.77 to $84.00**

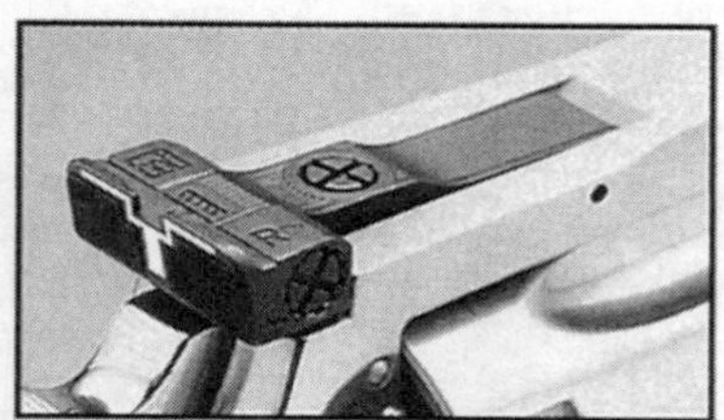

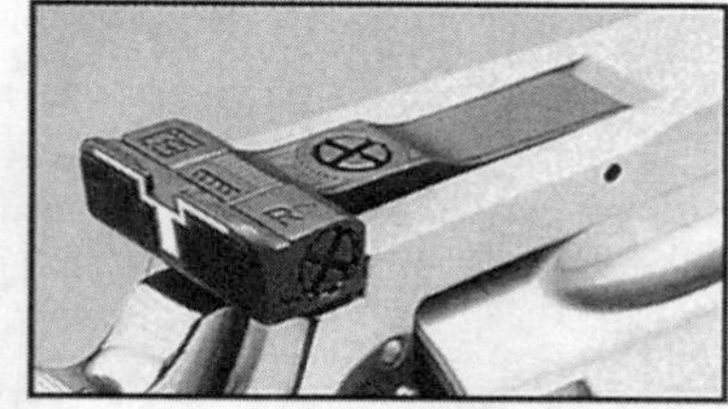

Millett Colt

Millett Tritium Night Sight

Millett Ruger

MILLETT BAR-DOT-BAR TRITIUM NIGHT SIGHTS Replacement front and rear combos fit most automatics. Horizontal tritium bars on rear, dot front sight.
Price:. **$152.25**

MILLETT BAR/DOT Made with orange or white bar or dot for increased visibility. Available for Beretta 84, 85, 92S, 92SB, Browning, Colt Python & Trooper, Ruger GP 100, P85, Redhawk, Security Six.
Price:. . . . . **$14.99 to $24.99**

MILLETT 3-DOT SYSTEM SIGHTS The 3-Dot System sights use a single white dot on the front blade and two dots flanking the rear notch. Fronts available in Dual-Crimp and Wide Stake-On styles, as well as special applications. Adjustable rear sight available for most popular auto pistols and revolvers including Browning Hi-Power, Colt 1911 Government and Ruger P85.
Price: Front, from. **$16.80**
Price: Adjustable rear.. . . . . **$55.60**

MILLETT REVOLVER FRONT SIGHTS All-steel replacement front sights with either white or orange bar. Easy to install. For Ruger GP-100, Redhawk, Security-Six, Police- Six, Speed-Six, Colt Trooper, Diamondback, King Cobra, Peacemaker, Python, Dan Wesson 22 and 15-2.
Price:. . . . . **$13.60 to $16.00**

MILLETT DUAL-CRIMP FRONT SIGHT Replacement front sight for automatic pistols. Dual-Crimp uses an all-steel two-point hollow rivet system. Available in eight heights and four styles. Has a skirted base that covers the front sight pad. Easily installed with the Millett Installation Tool Set. Available in Blaze Orange Bar, White Bar, Serrated Ramp, Plain Post. Available in heights of .185", .200", .225", .275", .312", .340" and .410".
Price:. **$16.80**

MILLETT STAKE-ON FRONT SIGHT Replacement front sight for automatic pistols. Stake-On sights have skirted base that covers the front sight pad. Easily installed with the Millet Installation Tool Set. Available in seven heights and four styles-Blaze Orange Bar, White Bar, Serrated Ramp, Plain Post. Available for Glock 17L and 24, others.
Price:. **$16.80**

METALLIC SIGHTS

MILLETT ADJUSTABLE TARGET Positive light-deflection serration and slant to eliminate glare and sharp edge sight notch. Audible "click" adjustments. For AMT Hardballer, Beretta 84, 85, 92S, 92SB, Browning Hi-Power, Colt 1911 Government and Gold Cup, Colt revolvers, Dan Wesson 15, 41, 44, Ruger revolvers, Glock 17, 17L, 19, 20, 21, 22, 23.
Price:. **$44.99**

MILLETT ADJUSTABLE WHITE OUTLINE Similar to the Target sight, except has a white outline on the blade to increase visibility. Available for the same handguns as the Target model, plus BRNO CZ-75/TZ-75/TA-90 without pin on front sight, and Ruger P85.
Price:. . . . . **$44.99 to $49.99**

OMEGA OUTLINE SIGHT BLADES Replacement rear sight blades for Colt and Ruger single action guns and the Interarms Virginian Dragoon. Standard Outline available in gold or white notch outline on blue metal. From Omega Sales, Inc.
Price:. **$10.00**

OMEGA MAVERICK SIGHT BLADES Replacement "peep-sight" blades for Colt, Ruger SAs, Virginian Dragoon. Three models available-No. 1, Plain; No. 2, Single Bar; No. 3, Double Bar Rangefinder. From Omega Sales, Inc.
Price: Each.. . . . . **$10.00**

ONE RAGGED HOLE Replacement rear sight ghost ring sight for Ruger handguns. Fits Blackhawks, Redhawks, Super Blackhawks, GP series and Mk. II target pistols with adjustable sights. From One Ragged Hole, Tallahassee, Florida.
Price:. . . . . **NA**

Pachmayr Accu-Set

PACHMAYR ACCU-SET Low-profile, fully adjustable rear sight to be used with existing front sight. Available with target, white outline or 3-dot blade. Blue finish. Uses factory dovetail and locking screw. For Browning, Colt, Glock, SIG Sauer, S&W and Ruger autos. From Pachmayr.
Price:. **$59.98**

P-T TRITIUM NIGHT SIGHTS Self-luminous tritium sights for most popular handguns, Colt AR-15, H&K rifles and shotguns. Replacement handgun sight sets available in 3- Dot style (green/green, green/yellow, green/orange) with bold outlines around inserts; Bar-Dot available in green/green with or without white outline rear sight. Functional life exceeds 15 years. From Innovative Weaponry, Inc.
Price: Handgun sight sets. **$99.95**
Price: Rifle sight sets. **$99.95**
Price: Rifle, front only. **$49.95**
Price: Shotgun, front only.. . . . . **$49.95**

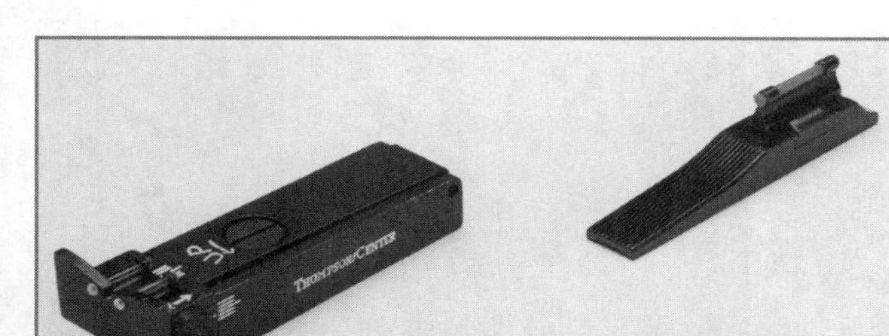

T/C Encore Fiber Optic Sight Set

T/C ENCORE FIBER OPTIC SIGHT SETS Click adjustable, steel rear sight and ramp-style front sight, both fitted with Tru-GloTM fiber optics. Specifically-designed for the T/C Encore pistol series. From Thompson/Center Arms.
Price:. **$49.35**

T/C ENCORE TARGET REAR SIGHT Precision, steel construction with click adjustments (via knurled knobs) for windage and elevation. Models available with low, medium and high blades. From Thompson/Center Arms.
Price:' **$54.00**

T/C Encore Target Rear Sight

Trijicon Night Sight

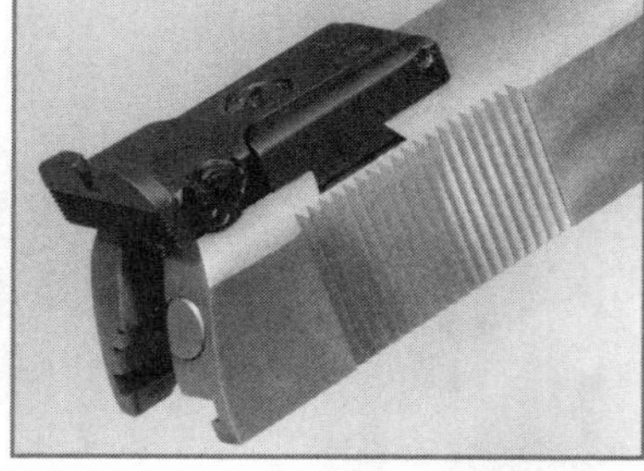

Wichita Series 70/80 Sight

TRIJICON NIGHT SIGHTS Three-dot night sight system uses tritium lamps in the front and rear sights. Tritium "lamps" are mounted in silicone rubber inside a metal cylinder. A polished crystal sapphire provides protection and clarity. Inlaid white outlines provide 3-dot aiming in daylight also. Available for most popular handguns including Glock 17, 19, 20, 21, 23, 24, 25, 26, 29, 30, H&K USP, Ruger P94, SIG P220, P225, 226, Colt 1911. Front and rear sets available. From Trijicon, Inc.
Price:. . . . . **$80.00 to $299.00**

TRIJICON 3-DOT Self-luminous front iron night sight for the Ruger SP101.
Price:. **$50.00**

WICHITA SERIES 70/80 SIGHT Provides click windage and elevation adjustments with precise repeatability of settings. Sight blade is grooved and angled back at the top to reduce glare. Available in Low Mount Combat or Low Mount Target styles for Colt 45s and their copies, S&W 645, Hi-Power, CZ 75 and others.
Price: Rear sight, target or combat. **$75.00**
Price: Front sight, Patridge or ramp. **$18.00**

WICHITA GRAND MASTER DELUXE RIBS Ventilated rib has wings machined into it for better sight acquisition and is relieved for Mag-Na-Porting. Milled to accept Weaver see-thru-style rings. Made of stainless; front and rear sights blued. Has Wichita Multi-Range rear sight system, adjustable front sight. Made for revolvers with 6" barrel.
Price: Model 301S, 301B (adj. sight K frames with custom bbl. of 1" to 1.032" dia. L and N frame with 1.062" to 1.100" dia. bbl.). **$225.00**
Price: Model 303S, 303B (adj. sight K, L, N frames with factory barrel). **$225.00**

WICHITA MULTI-RANGE QUICK CHANGE SIGHTING SYSTEM Multi-range rear sight can be pre-set to four positive repeatable range settings. Adjustable front sight allows compensation for changing lighting and weather conditions with just one front sight adjustment. Front sight comes with Lyman 17A Globe and set of apertures.
Price: Rear sight **$125.00**
Price: Front, sight **$95.00**

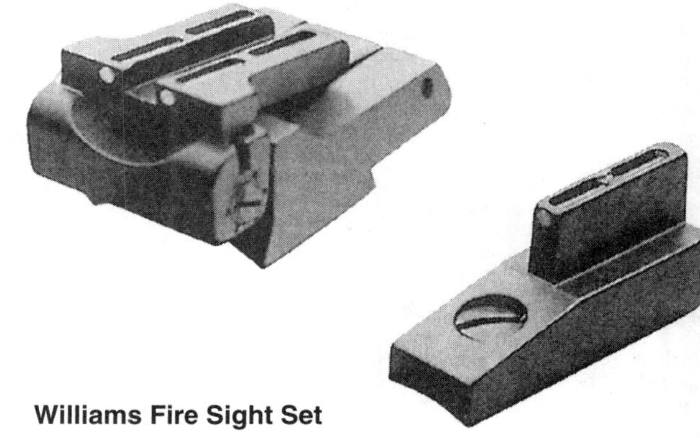

Williams Fire Sight Set

WILLIAMS FIRE SIGHT SETS Red fiber optic metallic sight replaces the original. Rear sight has two green fiber optic elements. Made of CNC-machined aluminum. Fits all Glocks, Ruger P-Series (except P-85), S&W 910, Colt Gov't. Model Series 80, Ruger GP 100 and Redhawk, and SIG Sauer (front only).
Price: Front and rear set **$39.95**
Price: SIG Sauer front. **$22.95**
Price: Browning BuckMark sight set **$44.95**
Price: Taurus PT111,PT140, PT145, PT1232, PT138 . . . .**$44.95**
Price: Ruger P Series, Glock, S&W 910, Colt Gov't. Series 80, Springfield XD .**$44.95**

WILSON ADJUSTABLE REAR SIGHTS Machined from steel, the click adjustment design requires simple cuts and no dovetails for installation. Available in several configurations: matte black standard blade with .128" notch; with .110" notch; with Tritium dots and .128" square or "U" shaped notch; and Combat Pyramid. From Wilson Combat.
Price:. . . . . **$24.95 to $69.95**

METALLIC SIGHTS

Wilson Nite-Eyes

WILSON NITE-EYES SIGHTS Low-profile, snag free design with green and yellow Tritium inserts. For 1911-style pistols. From Wilson Combat.
Price: $119.95

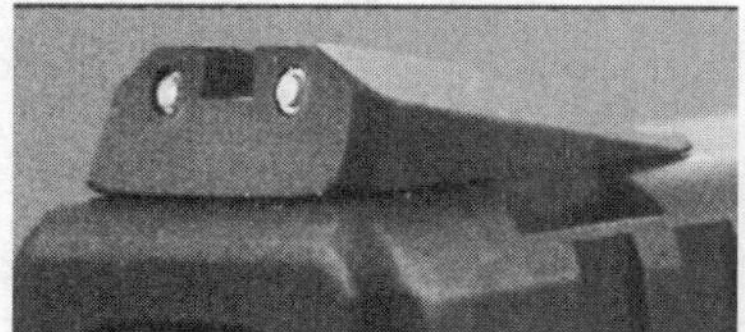

WILSON TACTICAL COMBAT SIGHTS Low-profile and snag-free in design, the sight employs the Combat Pyramid shape. For many 1911-style pistols and some Glock models. From Wilson Combat.
Price: $139.95

Sight Attachments

MERIT OPTICAL ATTACHMENT For iron sight shooting with handgun or rifle. Instantly attached by rubber suction cup to prescription or shooting glasses. Swings aside. Aperture adjustable from .020" to .156".
Price: $65.00

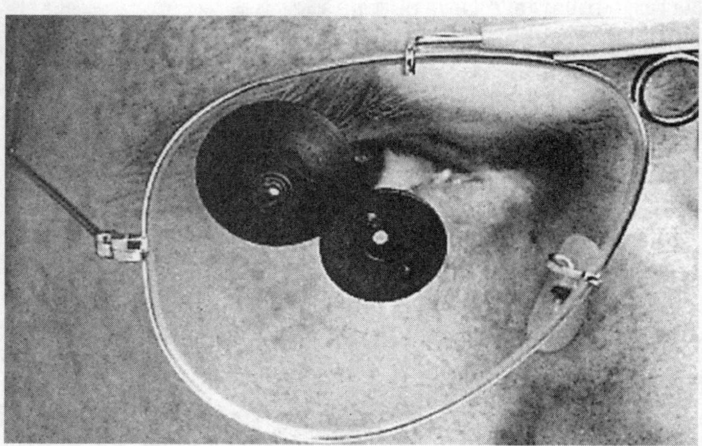
Merit Optical Attachment

MUZZLE BRAKES

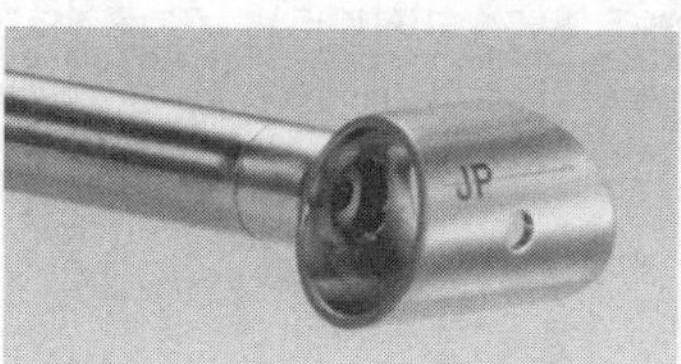

JP Muzzle Brake

JP Muzzle Brake

Designed for single shot handguns, AR-15, Ruger Mini-14, Ruger Mini Thirty and other sporting rifles, the JP Muzzle Brake redirects high pressure gases against a large frontal surface which applies forward thrust to the gun. All gases are directed up, rearward and to the sides. Priced at **$79.95** (AR-15 or sporting rifles), **$89.95** (bull barrel and SKS, AK models), **$89.95** (Ruger Minis), Dual Chamber model **$79.95.** From JP Enterprises, Inc.

Laseraim

Simple, no-gunsmithing compensator reduces felt recoil and muzzle flip by up to 30 percent. Machined from single piece of Stainless Steel (Beretta/Taurus model made of aircraft aluminum). In black and polished finish. For Colt Government/Commander and Beretta/Taurus full-size pistols. Weighs 1 ounce. **$49.00.** From Laseraim Arms Inc.

Mag-Na-Port

Electrical Discharge Machining works on any firearm except those having non-conductive shrouded barrels. EDM is a metal erosion technique using carbon electrodes that control the area to be processed. The Mag-Na-Port venting process utilizes small trapezoidal openings to direct powder gases upward and outward to reduce recoil. No effect is had on bluing or nickeling outside the Mag-Na-Port area so no refinishing is needed. Rifle-style porting on single shot or large caliber handguns with barrels 7 1/2″ or longer is **$115.00**; Dual Trapezoidal porting on most handguns with minimum barrel length of 3″, **$115.00**; standard revolver porting, **$88.50**; porting through the slide and barrel for semi-autos, **$129.50**; traditional rifle porting, **$135.00.** Prices do not include shipping, handling and insurance. From Mag-Na-Port International.

Mag-Na-Brake

A screw-on brake under 2″ long with progressive integrated exhaust chambers to neutralize expanding gases. Gases dissipate with an opposite twist to prevent the brake from unscrewing, and with a 5-degree forward angle to minimize sound pressure level. Available in blue, satin blue, bright or satin stainless. Standard and Light Contour installation cost **$195.00** for bolt-action rifles, many single action and single shot handguns. A knurled thread protector supplied at extra cost. Also available in Varmint style with exhaust chambers covering 220 degrees for prone-position shooters. From Mag-Na-Port International.

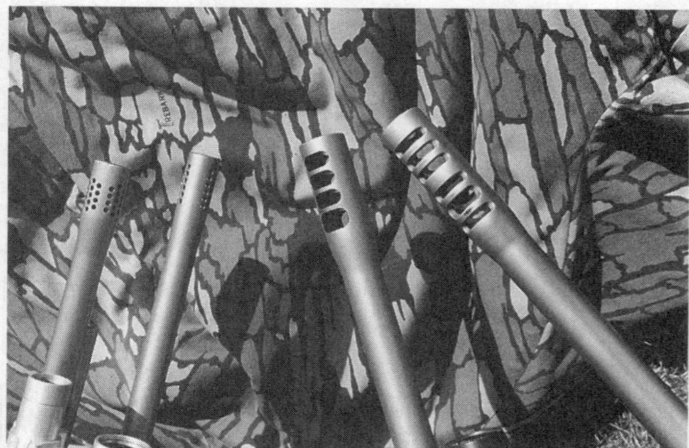

SSK Arrestor Brake

This is a true muzzle brake with an expansion chamber. It takes up about 1″ of barrel and reduces velocity accordingly. Some Arrestors are added to a barrel, increasing its length. Said to reduce the felt recoil of a 458 to that approaching a 30-06. Can be set up to give zero muzzle rise in any caliber, and can be added to most guns. For handgun or rifle. Prices start at **$95.00.** Contact SSK Industries for full data.

Maker and Model	Magn.	Field at 100 Yds. (feet)	Eye Relief (in.)	Length (in.)	Tube Dia. (in.)	W & E Adjustments	Weight (ozs.)	Price	Other Data
ADCO									
Magnum 50 mm[5]	0			4.1	45 mm	Int.	6.8	**$269.00**	[1]Multi-Color Dot system changes from red to green. [2]For airguns, paint ball, rimfires. Uses common lithium water battery. [3]Comes with standard dovetail mount. [4].75" dovetail mount; poly body; adj. intensity diode. [5]10 MOA dot; black or nickel. [6]Square format; with mount battery. From ADCO Sales.
MIRAGE Ranger 1"	0			5.2	1	Int.	3.9	**159.00**	
MIRAGE Ranger 30mm	0			5.5	30mm	Int.	5	**159.00**	
MIRAGE Competitor	0			5.5	30mm	Int.	5.5	**229.00**	
IMP Sight[2]	0			4.5		Int.	1.3	**17.95**	
Square Shooter 2[3]	0			5		Int.	5	**99.00**	
MIRAGE Eclipse[1]	0			5.5	30mm	Int.	5.5	**229.00**	
Champ Red Dot	0			4.5		Int.	2	**33.95**	
Vantage 1"	0			3.9	1	Int.	3.9	**129.00**	
Vantage 30mm	0			4.2	30mm	Int.	4.9	**159.00**	
Vision 2000[6]	0	60		4.7		Int.	6.2	**79.00**	
e-dot ESB[1]	0			4.12	1	Int.	3.7	**139.00**	
e-dot E1B	0			4.12	1	Int.	3.7	**99.00**	
e-dot ECB	0			3.8	30mm	Int.	6.4	**99.00**	
e-dot E30B	0			4.3	30mm	Int.	4.6	**99.00**	
AIMPOINT									
Comp	0			4.6	30mm	Int.	4.3	**331.00**	Illuminates red dot in field of view. Noparallax (dot does not need to be centered). Unlimited field of view and eye relief. On/off, adj. intensity. Dot covers 3" @100 yds. [1]Comes with 30mm rings, battery, lense cloth. [2]Requires 1" rings. Black finish. AP Comp avail. in black, blue, SS, camo. [3]Black finish (AP 5000-B) ; avail. with regular 3-min. or 10-min. Mag Dot as B2 or S2. [4]Band pass reflection coating for compatibility with night vision equipment; U.S. Army contract model; with anti-reflex coated lenses (Comp ML), **$359.00**. From Aimpoint U.S.A.
Comp M[4]	0			5	30mm	Int.	6.1	**409.00**	
Series 5000[3]	0			6	30mm	Int.	6	**297.00**	
Series 3000 Universal[2]	0			6.25	1	Int.	6	**232.00**	
Series 5000/2x[1]	2			7	30mm	Int.	9	**388.00**	
ARMSON O.E.G.									
Standard	0			5.125	1	Int.	4.3	**202.00**	Shown red dot aiming point. No batteries needed. Standard model fits 1" ring mounts (not incl.). Other O.E.G. models for shotguns and rifles can be special ordered. [1]Daylight Only Sight with .375" dovetail mount for 22s. Does not contain tritium. From Trijicon, Inc.
22 DOS[1]	0			3.75		Int.	3	**127.00**	
22 Day/Night	0			3.75		Int.	3	**169.00**	
M16/AR-15	0			5.125		Int.	5.5	**226.00**	
BEEMAN									
Pistol Scopes									
5021	2	19	10-24	9.1	1	Int.	7.4	**85.50**	All scopes have 5 point reticle, all glass fully coated lenses. [1]Parallel adjustable. [2]Reticle lighted by ambient light. [3]Available with lighted Electro-Dot reticle. Imported by Beeman.
5020	1.5	14	11-16	8.3	.75	Int.	3.6	**NA**	
BSA									
Pistol									
P52x20	2	N/A	N/A	N/A	N/A	Int.	N/A	**89.95**	[1]Red dot sights also available in 42mm and 50mm versions. [2]Includes Universal Bow Mount. From BSA.
Red Dot									
RD30[1]	0			3.8	30mm	Int.	5	**59.95**	
PB30[1]	0			3.8	30mm	Int.	4.5	**79.95**	
Bow30[2]	0			N/A	30mm	Int.	5	**89.95**	
BURRIS									
Speeddot 135[7]									
Red Dot	1			4.85	35mm	Int.	5	**291.00**	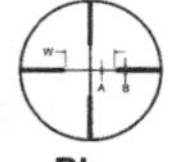 Plex. **Black Diamond & Fullfield:** All scopes avail. with Plex reticle. Steel-on- steel click adjustments. [1]Dot reticle on some models. [2]Matte satin finish. [3]Available with parallax adjustment (standard on 10x, 12x, 4-12x, 6-12x, 6-18x, 6x HBR and 3-12x Signature). [4]Silver matte finish extra. [5]Target knobs extra, standard on silhouette models. LER and XER with P.A., 6x HBR. [6]Available with Posi-Lock. **Signature Series:** LER=Long Eye Relief; IER=Intermediate Eye Relief; XER=Extra Eye Relief. **Speeddot 135:** [7]Waterproof, fogproof, coated lenses, 11 bright ness set tings; 3-MOA or 11-MOA dot size; includes Weaver-style rings and battery. **Partial listing shown.** Contact Burris for complete details.
Handgun									
1.50-4x LER[1,4,6]	1.6-3	16-11	11-25	10.25	1	Int.	11	**411.00**	
2-7x LER[2,3,4,6]	2-6.5	21-7	7-27	9.5	1	Int.	12.6	**458.00**	
2x LER[3,4,5]	1.7	21	10-24	8.75	1	Int.	6.8	**286.00**	
4x LER[1,3,4,5,6]	3.7	11	10-22	9.625	1	Int.	9	**338.00**	
3x12x LER[1,3,5]	9.5	4	8-12	13.5	1	Int.	14	**558.00**	

SCOPES / HUNTING, TARGET & VARMINT

Maker and Model	Magn.	Field at 100 Yds. (feet)	Eye Relief (in.)	Length (in.)	Tube Dia. (in.)	W & E Adjustments	Weight (ozs.)	Price	Other Data
BUSHNELL (Bausch & Lomb Elite rifle scopes now sold under Bushnell brand)									
Elite 3200 Handgun RainGuard									
32-2632M[1]	2-6	10-4	20	9	1	Int.	10	**389.95**	[1]Also in silver finish. **Partial listings shown. Contact Bushnell Performance Optics for details.**
32-2636[10]	2-6	10-4	20	9	1	Int.	10	**431.95**	
Trophy Handgun									
73-2632[3]	2-6	21-7	9-26	9.1	1	Int.	10.9	**251.95**	
SIGHTRON									
Pistol									
SII 1x28P[1]	1	30	9-24	9.49	1	Int.	8.46	**212.95**	[1]Satin black; also stainless. Pistol scopes have aluminum tubes, Exac Trak adjustments. Lifetime warranty. From Sightron, Inc.
SII 2x28P[1]	2	16-10	9-24	9.49	1	Int.	8.28	**212.95**	
SIMMONS									
Prohunter Handgun									
7732[2]	2	22	9-17	8.75	1	Int.	7	**109.99**	[1]Black matte finish; also available in silver. [2]With 3V lithium battery, extension tube, polarizing filter, Weaver rings. **Only selected models shown.** Contact Simmons Outdoor Corp. for complete details.
7738[2]	4	15	11.8- 17.6	8.5	1	Int.	8	**129.99**	
82200[1]	2-6							**159.99**	

Truplex™

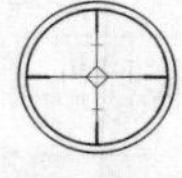
Smart

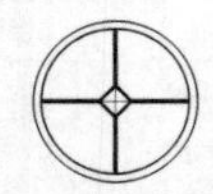
ProDiamond®

Crossbow

Maker and Model	Magn.	Field at 100 Yds. (feet)	Eye Relief (in.)	Length (in.)	Tube Dia. (in.)	W & E Adjustments	Weight (ozs.)	Price	Other Data
THOMPSON/CENTER RECOIL PROOF SERIES									
Pistol Scopes									
8315[2]	2.5-7	15-5	8-21, 8-11	9.25	1	Int.	9.2	**349.00**	[1]Black finish; silver optional. [2]Black; lighted reticle. From Thompson/ Center Arms.
8326[4]	2.5-7	15-5	8-21, 8-11	9.25	1	Int.	10.5	**416.00**	
ULTRA DOT									
Ultra-Dot Sights[1]									
Ultra-Dot 25[2]	1			5.1	1	Int.	3.9	**159.00**	[1]Ultra Dot sights include rings, battery, polarized filter, and 5-year warranty. All models available in black or satin finish. [2]Illuminated red dot has eleven brightness settings. Shock-proof aluminum tube. From Ultra Dot Distribution.
Ultra-Dot 30[2]	1			5.1	30mm	Int.	4	**179.00**	
WEAVER									
Handgun									
H2[1-3]	2	21	4-29	8.5	1	Int.	6.7	**161.43**	[1]Gloss black. [2]Matte black. [3]Silver. All scopes are shock-proof, waterproof, and fogproof. Dual-X reticle available. From Weaver Products.
H4[1-3]	4	18	11.5-18	8.5	1	Int.	6.7	**175.00**	
VH4[1-3]	1.5-4	13.6-5.8	11-17	8.6	1	Int.	8.1	**215.71**	
VH8[1-3]	2.5-8	8.5-3.7	12.16	9.3	1	Int.	8.3	**228.57**	

Hunting scopes in general are furnished with a choice of reticlecrosshairs, post with crosshairs, tapered or blunt post, or dot crosshairs, etc. The great majority of target and varmint scopes have medium or fine crosshairs but post or dot reticles may be ordered. Wwindage EElevation MOAMinute of Angle or 1" (approx.) at 100 yards.

Laser Sights

Alpec Mini Shot

Laseraim LA5X

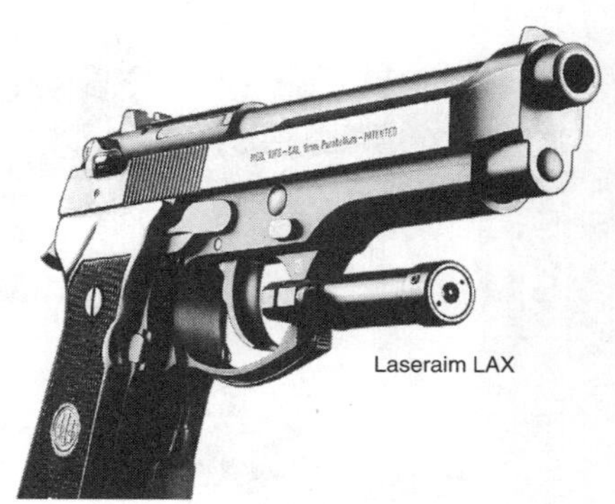
Laseraim LAX

Maker and Model	Wave length (nm)	Beam Color	Lens	Operating Temp. (degrees F.)	Weight (ozs.)	Price	Other Data
ALPEC							[1]Range 1000 yards. [2]Range 300 yards. Mini Shot II range 500 yards, output 650mm, **$129.95**. [3]Range 300 yards; Laser Shot II 500 yards; Super Laser Shot 1000 yards. Black or stainless finish aluminum; removable pressure or push-button switch. Mounts for most handguns, many rifles and shotguns. From Alpec Team, Inc.
Power Shot[1]	635	Red	Glass	NA	2.5	**$199.95**	
Mini Shot[2]	670	Red	Glass	NA	2.5	**99.95**	
Laser Shot[3]	670	Red	Glass	NA	3.0	**99.95**	
BEAMSHOT							[1]Black or silver finish; adj. for windage and elevation; 300-yd. range; also M1000/S (500-yd. range), M1000/u (800-yd.). [2]Black finish; 300-, 500-, 800-yd. models. All come with removable touch pad switch, 5" cable. Mounts to fit virtually any firearm. From Quarton USA Co.
1000[1]	670	Red	Glass		3.8	**NA**	
3000[2]	635/670	Red	Glass		2	**NA**	
1001/u	635	Red	Glass		3.8	**NA**	
780	780	Red	Glass		3.8	**NA**	
BSA							[1]Comes with mounts for 22/air rifle and Weaver-style bases.
LS650[1]	N/A	Red	NA	NA	NA	**49.95**	
LASERAIM							[1]Red dot/laser combo; 300-yd. range: LA3xHD Hotdot has 500-yd. range **$249.00**; [4] MOA dot size, laser gives 2" dot size at 100 yds. 230mm obj. lens: [4]MOA dot at 100 yds: fits Weaver base. 3300-yd range; 2" dot at 100 yds.; rechargeable Nicad battery 41.5-mile range; 1" dot at 100 yds.; 20+ hrs. batt. life. [5]1.5-mile range; 1" dot at 100 yds; rechargeable Nicad battery (comes with in-field charger); [6]Black or satin finish. With mount, **$169.00.** [7]Laser projects 2" dot at 100 yds.: with rotary switch; with Hotdot **$237.00**; with Hotdot touch switch **$357.00.** [8]For Glock 17-27; G1 Hotdot **$299.00**; price installed. 10Fits std. Weaver base, no rings required; 6-MOA dot; seven brightness settings. All have w&e adj.; black or satin silver finish. From Laser aim Technologies, Inc.
LA10 Hotdot[4]					NA	**199.00**	
Lasers							
MA-35RB Mini Aimer[7]					1.0	**129.00**	
G1 Laser[8]					2.0	**229.00**	
LASER DEVICES							[1]For S&W P99 semi-auto pistols; also BA-2, 5 oz., **$339.00**. [2]For revolvers. [3]For HK, Walther P99. [4]For semi-autos. [5]For rifles; also FA-4/ULS, 2.5 oz., **$325.00.** [6]For HK sub guns. [7]For military rifles. [8]For shotguns. [9]For SIG-Pro pistol. [10]Universal, semi-autos. [11]For AR-15 variants. All avail. with Magnum Power Point (650nM) or daytime-visible Super Power Point (632nM) diode. Infrared diodes avail. for law enforcement. From Laser Devices, Inc.
BA-1[1]	632	Red	Glass		2.4	**372.00**	
BA-3[2]	632	Red	Glass		3.3	**332.50**	
BA-5[3]	632	Red	Glass		3.2	**372.00**	
Duty-Grade[4]	632	Red	Glass		3.5	**372.00**	
FA-4[5]	632	Red	Glass		2.6	**358.00**	
LasTac[1]	632	Red	Glass		5.5	**298.00 to 477.00**	

ACCESSORIES

LASER SIGHTS

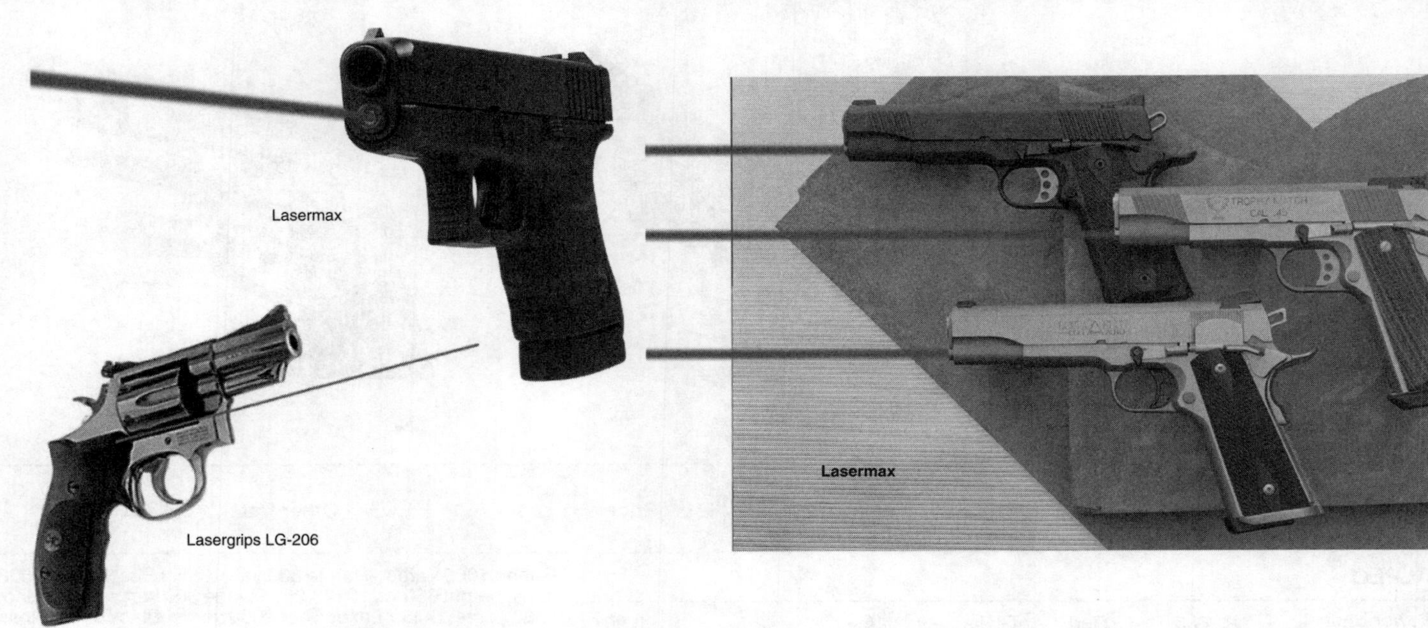
Lasermax

Lasergrips LG-206

Lasermax

Maker and Model	Wave length (nm)	Beam Color	Lens	Operating Temp. (degrees F.)	Weight (ozs.)	Price	Other Data
LASER DEVICES *(cont.)*							
MP-5[6]	632	Red	Glass		2.2	**495.00**	
MR-2[7]	632	Red	Glass		6.3	**485.00**	
SA-2[8]	632	Red	Glass		3.0	**360.00**	
SIG-Pro[9]	632	Red	Glass		2.6	**372.00**	
ULS-2001[10]	632	Red	Glass		4.5	**210.95**	
Universal AR-2A	632	Red	Glass		4.5	**445.00**	
LASERGRIPS							Replaces existing grips with built-in laser high in the right grip panel. Integrated pressure sensi tive pad in grip activates the laser. Also has master on/off switch. [1]For Colt 1911/Commander. [2]For all Glock models. Option on/off switch. Requires factory installation. [3]For S&W K, L, N frames, round or square butt (LG-207); [4]For Taurus small-frame revolvers. [5]For Ruger SP-101. [6]For SIG Sauer P226. From Crimson Trace Corp. [7]For Beretta 92/96. [8]For Ruger MK II. [9]For S&W J-frame. [10]For Sig Sauer P228/229. [11]For Colt 1911 full size, wraparound. [12]For Beretta 92/96, wraparound. [13]For Colt 1911 compact, wraparound. [14]For S&W J-frame, rubber.
LG-201[1]	633	Red-Orange	Glass	NA		**299.00**	
LG-206[3]	633	Red-Orange	Glass	NA		**229.00**	
LG-085[4]	633	Red-Orange	Glass	NA		**229.00**	
LG-101[5]	633	Red-Orange	Glass	NA		**229.00**	
LG-226[6]	633	Red-Orange	Glass	NA		**229.00**	
GLS-630[2]	633	Red-Orange	Glass	NA		**595.00**	
LG202[7]	633	Red-Orange	Glass	NA		**299.00**	
LG203[8]	633	Red-Orange	Glass	NA		**299.00**	
LG205[9]	633	Red-Orange	Glass	NA		**299.00**	

ACCESSORIES

LASER SIGHTS

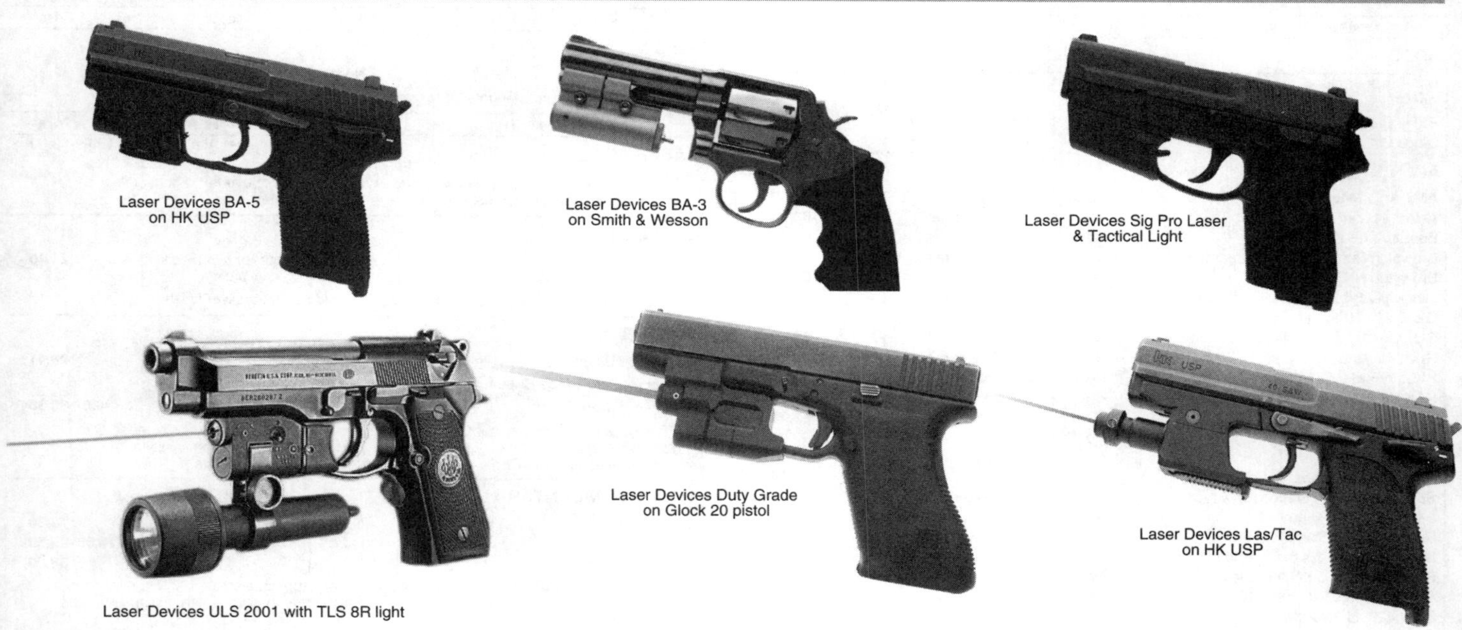

Laser Devices BA-5 on HK USP

Laser Devices BA-3 on Smith & Wesson

Laser Devices Sig Pro Laser & Tactical Light

Laser Devices ULS 2001 with TLS 8R light

Laser Devices Duty Grade on Glock 20 pistol

Laser Devices Las/Tac on HK USP

Maker and Model	Wave length (nm)	Beam Color	Lens	Operating Temp. (degrees F.)	Weight (ozs.)	Price	Other Data
LASERGRIPS *(cont.)*							
LG229[10]	633	Red-Orange	Glass	NA		**299.00**	
LG301[11]	633	Red-Orange	Glass	NA		**329.00**	
LG302[12]	633	Red-Orange	Glass	NA		**329.00**	
LG304[13]	633	Red-Orange	Glass	NA		**329.00**	
LG305[14]	633	Red-Orange	Glass	NA		**299.00**	
LASERLYTE							[1]Dot/circle or dot/crosshair projection; black or stainless. [2]Also 635/645mm model. From Tac Star Laserlyte. in grip activates the laser. Also has master on/off switch.
LLX-0006-140/090[1]	635/645	Red			1.4	**159.95**	
WPL-0004-140/090[2]	670	Red			1.2	**109.95**	
TPL-0004-140/090[2]	670	Red			1.2	**109.95**	
T7S-0004-140[2]	670	Red			0.8	**109.95**	
LASERMAX							Replaces the recoil spring guide rod; includes a customized takedown lever that serves as the laser's insta in grip activates the laser. Also has master on/off switch. [1]For Colt 1911/Commant on/off switch. For Glock, Smith & Wesson, Sigarms, Beretta, Colt, Kimber, Springfield Gov't. Model 1911, Heckler & Koch and select Taurus models. Installs in most pistols without gunsmithing. Battery life 1/2 hour to 2 hours in continuous use. From Laser Max.
LMS-1000 Internal Guide Rod	635	Red-Orange	Glass	40-120	.25	**389.00**	
NIGHT STALKER							Waterproof; LCD panel displays power remaining; programmable blink rate; con stant or memory on. From Wilcox Industri in grip activates the laser. Also has master on/off switch. [1]For Colt 1911/Commaes Corp.
S0 Smart	635	Red	NA	NA	2.46	**515.00**	

Scope Rings & Bases

Maker, Model, Type	Adjust.	Scopes	Price
ADCO			
Std. Black or nickel		1"	$13.95
Std. Black or nickel		30mm	13.95
Rings Black or nickel		30mm w/ 3/8" grv.	13.95
Rings Black or nickel		1" raised 3/8" grv.	13.95
AIMTECH			
AMT Auto Mag II .22 Mag.	No	Weaver rail	$56.99
Astra .44 Mag Revolver	No	Weaver rail	63.25
Beretta/Taurus 92/99	No	Weaver rail	63.25
Browning Buckmark/Challenger II	No	Weaver rail	56.99
Browning Hi-Power	No	Weaver rail	63.25
Glock 17, 17L, 19, 23, 24 etc. no rail	No	Weaver rail	63.25
Glock 20, 21 no rail	No	Weaver rail	63.25
Glock 9mm and .40 with access. rail	No	Weaver rail	74.95
Govt. 45 Auto/.38 Super	No	Weaver rail	63.25
Hi-Standard (Mitchell version) 107	No	Weaver rail	63.25
H&K USP 9mm/40 rail mount	No	Weaver rail	74.95
Rossi 85/851/951 Revolvers	No	Weaver rail	63.25
Ruger Mk I, Mk II	No	Weaver rail	49.95
Ruger P85/P89	No	Weaver rail	63.25
S&W K, L, N frames	No	Weaver rail	63.25
S&W K. L, N with tapped top strap*	No	Weaver rail	69.95
S&W Model 41 Target 22	No	Weaver rail	63.25
S&W Model 52 Target 38	No	Weaver rail	63.25
S&W Model 99 Walther frame rail mount	No	Weaver rail	74.95
S&W 2nd Gen. 59/459/659 etc.	No	Weaver rail	56.99
S&W 3rd Gen. full size 5906 etc.	No	Weaver rail	69.95
S&W 422, 622, 2206	No	Weaver rail	56.99
S&W 645/745	No	Weaver rail	56.99
S&W Sigma	No	Weaver rail	64.95
Taurus PT908	No	Weaver rail	63.25
Taurus 44 6.5" bbl.	No	Weaver rail	69.95
Walther 99	No	Weaver rail	74.95

All mounts no-gunsmithing, iron sight usable. Rifle mounts are solid see-through bases. All mounts accommodate standard Weaver-style rings of all makers. From Aimtech division, L&S Technologies, Inc. *3-blade sight mount combination.

Maker, Model, Type	Adjust.	Scopes	Price
B-SQUARE			
Pistols (centerfire)			
Beretta 92, 96/Taurus 99	No	Weaver rail	69.95
Colt M1911	E only	Weaver rail	69.95
Desert Eagle	No	Weaver rail	69.95
Glock	No	Weaver rail	69.95
H&K USP, 9mm and 40 S&W	No	Weaver rail	69.95
Ruger P85/89	E only	Weaver rail	69.95
SIG Sauer P226	E only	Weaver rail	69.95
Pistols (rimfire)			
Browning Buck Mark	No	Weaver rail	32.95
Colt 22	No	Weaver rail	49.95
Ruger Mk I/II, bull or taper	No	Weaver rail	32.95-49.95
Smith & Wesson 41, 2206	No	Weaver rail	36.95-49.95
Revolvers			
Colt Anaconda/Python	No	Weaver rail	35.95-74.95
Ruger Single-Six	No	Weaver rail	64.95
Ruger GP-100	No	Weaver rail	64.95
Ruger Blackhawk, Super	No	Weaver rail	64.95
Ruger Redhawk, Super	No	Weaver rail	64.95
Smith & Wesson K, L, N	No	Weaver rail	36.95-74.95
Taurus 66, 669, 607, 608	No	Weaver rail	64.95

Prices shown for anodized black finish; add $10 for stainless finish. Partial listing of mounts shown here. Contact B-Square for complete listing and details.

Maker, Model, Type	Adjust.	Scopes	Price
BURRIS			
L.E.R. (LU) Mount Bases[1]	W only	1" split rings	24.00-52.00
L.E.R. No Drill-No Tap Bases[1,2,3]	W only	1" split rings	48.00-52.00

[1]Universal dovetail; accepts Burris, Universal, Redfield, Leupold rings. For Dan Wesson, S&W, Virginian, Ruger Blackhawk, Win. 94. [2]Selected rings and bases available with matte Safari or silver finish. [3]For S&W K, L, N frames, Colt Python, Dan Wesson with 6" or longer barrels.

Maker, Model, Type	Adjust.	Scopes	Price
CONETROL			
Pistol Bases, 2-or 3-ring[6]	W only		
Metric Rings[8]	W only	26mm, 26.5mm, 30mm	99.96-149.88

[1]For XP-100, T/C Contender, Colt SAA, Ruger Blackhawk, S&W and others. [2]26mm, 26.5mm, and 30mm rings made in projectionless style, in three heights. Three-ring mount for T/C Contender and other pistols in Conetrol's three grades. Any Conetrol mount available in stainless steel add 50 percent.

Maker, Model, Type	Adjust.	Scopes	Price
KRIS MOUNTS			
One Piece (T)[1]	No	1", 26mm split rings	12.98

[13]Blackhawk revolver. Mounts have oval hole to permit use of iron sights.

Maker, Model, Type	Adjust.	Scopes	Price
LASER AIM	No	Laser Aim	19.99-69.00

Mounts Laser Aim above or below barrel. Avail. for most popular hand guns, rifles, shotguns, including militaries. From Laser Aim Technologies, Inc.

Maker, Model, Type	Adjust.	Scopes	Price
LEUPOLD			
STD Bases[1]	W only	One- or two-piece bases	25.40

[1]Base and two rings; Casull, Ruger, S&W, T/C; add $5.00 for silver finish.

Maker, Model, Type	Adjust.	Scopes	Price
MILLETT			
One-Piece Bases[6]	Yes	1"	26.41
Universal Two-Piece Bases			
Handgun Bases, Rings[1]		1"	36.07-80.38

[1]Two- and three-ring sets for Colt Python, Trooper, Diamondback, Peacekeeper, Dan Wesson, Ruger Redhawk, Super Redhawk. [2]Turn-in bases and Weaver-style for most popular rifles and T/C Contender, XP-100 pistols. From Millett Sights.

Maker, Model, Type	Adjust.	Scopes	Price
THOMPSON/CENTER			
Duo-Ring Mount[1]	No	1"	73.80
Weaver-Style Bases	No		13.00–42.50
Weaver-Style Rings[2]	No	1"	36.00

[1]Attaches directly to T/C Contender bbl., no drilling/tapping; also for T/C M/L rifles, needs base adapter; blue or stainless. [2]Medium and high; blue or silver finish. From Thompson/Center.

Maker, Model, Type	Adjust.	Scopes	Price
WARNE			
Premier Series (all steel)			
T.P.A. (Permanently Attached)	No	1", 4 heights 30mm, 2 heights	87.75-98.55
Premier Series Rings fit Premier Series Bases			
Premier Series (all-steel Q.D. rings)			
Premier Series (all steel) Quick detachable lever	No	1", 4 heights 26mm, 2 heights 30mm, 3 heights	131.25-129.95 142.00
All-Steel One-Piece Base, ea.			38.50
All-Steel Two-Piece Base, ea.			14.00
Maxima Series (fits all Weaver-style bases)			
Permanently Attached[1]	No	1", 3 heights 30mm, 3 heights	25.50 36.00
Adjustable Double Lever[2]	No	1", 3 heights 30mm, 3 heights	72.60 80.75
Thumb Knob	No	1", 3 heights 30mm, 3 heights	59.95 68.25
Stainless-Steel Two-Piece Base, ea.			15.25

Vertically split rings with dovetail clamp, precise return to zero. Fit most popular rifles, handguns. Regular blue, matte blue, silver finish. [1]All-Steel, non-Q.D. rings. [2]All-steel, Q.D. rings. From Warne Mfg. Co.

Maker, Model, Type	Adjust.	Scopes	Price
WEAVER			
Complete Mount Systems			
Pistol	No	1"	75.00-105.00

No Drill & Tap Pistol systems in gloss or silver for: Colt Python, Trooper, 357, Officer's Model; Ruger Single-Six, Security- Six (gloss finish only), Blackhawk, Super Blackhawk, Blackhawk SRM 357, Redhawk, Mini-14 Series (not Ranch), Ruger 22 Auto Pistols, Mark II; Smith & Wesson I- and current K-frames with adj. rear sights. From Weaver.

Maker, Model, Type	Adjust.	Scopes	Price
WEIGAND			
Browning Buck Mark[1]	No		29.95
Integra Mounts[2]	No		39.95-69.00
S&W Revolver[3]	No		29.95
Ruger 10/22[4]	No		14.95-39.95
Ruger Revolver[5]	No		29.95
Taurus Revolver[4]	No		29.95-65.00
Lightweight Rings	No	1", 30mm	29.95-39.95
1911			
SM3[6]	No	Weaver rail	99.95
APCMNT[7]	No		69.95

[1]No gunsmithing. [2]S&W K, L, N frames; Taurus vent rib models; Colt Anaconda/ Python; Ruger Redhawk; Ruger 10/22. [3]K, L, N frames. [4]Three models. [5]Redhawk, Blackhawk, GP-100. [6]3rd Gen.; drill and tap; without slots **$59.95**. [7]For Aimpoint Comp. Red Dot scope, silver only. From Weigand Combat Handguns, Inc.

Maker, Model, Type	Adjust.	Scopes	Price
WIDEVIEW			
Desert Eagle Pistol Mount	No	1", 30mm	34.95-44.95

From Wideview Scope Mount Corp.

NOTES

(S) — Side Mount; (T) — Top Mount; 22mm = .866", 25.4mm = 1.024"; 26.5mm = 1.045"; 30mm = 1.81".

Bushnell Collapsible Spotting Scope

BROWNING 15-45x zoom, 65mm objective lens. Weight: 48 oz. Waterproof, fogproof. Tripod, soft and hard cases included.
Price:. $559.95

BUSHNELL DISCOVERER 15x to 60x zoom, 60mm objective. Constant focus throughout range. Field at 1000 yds. 38 ft (60x), 150 ft. (15x). Comes with lens caps. Length 17 1/2"; weight 48.5 oz.
Price:. $342.95

BUSHNELL ELITE 15x to 45x zoom, 60mm objective. Field at 1000 yds., 125-65 ft. Length is 12.2"; weight, 26.5 oz. Waterproof, armored. Tripod mount. Comes with black case.
Price:. $559.95

BUSHNELL ELITE ZOOM 20x-60x, 70mm objective. Roof prism. Field at 1000 yds. 90-50 ft. Length is 16"; weight 40 oz. Waterproof, armored. Tripod mount. Comes with black case.
Price: $769.95

BUSHNELL 80MM ELITE 20x-60x zoom, 80mm objective. Field of view at 1000 yds. 98-50 ft. (zoom). Weight 51 oz. (20x, 30x), 54 oz. (zoom); length 17". Interchangeable bayonet-style eyepieces. Built-in peep sight.
Price: With EDPrime Glass $1,119.95

BUSHNELL TROPHY 65mm objective, 20x-60x zoom. Field at 1000 yds. 90ft. (20x), 45 ft. (60x). Length 12.7"; weight 20 oz. Black rubber armored, waterproof. Case included.
Price: $297.95

BUSHNELL COMPACT TROPHY 50mm objective, 20x-50x zoom. Field at 1000 yds. 92 ft. (20x), 52 ft. (50x). Length 12.2"; weight 17 oz. Black rubber armored, waterproof. Case included.
Price:. $257.95

BUSHNELL SENTRY 16-32 zoom, 50mm objective. Field at 1000 yds. 140-65 ft. Length 8.7", weight 21.5 oz. Black rubber armored. Built-in peep sight. Comes with tripod and hardcase.
Price:. $199.95

BUSHNELL SPACEMASTER 20x-45x zoom. Long eye relief. Rubber armored, prismatic. 60mm objective. Field at 1000 yds. 90-58 ft. Minimum focus 20 ft. Length 12.7"; weight 43 oz.
Price: With tripod, carrying case and 20x-45x LER eyepiece. $491.95

BUSHNELL SPACEMASTER COLLAPSIBLE 15-45x zoom, 50mm objective lens. Field of view at 1000 yds., 113 ft. (15x) 52 ft. (45x). Length: 8". Weight: 22.8 oz. Comes with tripod, window mount and case.
Price:. $209.95

BUSHNELL SPORTVIEW 15x-45x zoom, 50mm objective. Field at 100 yds. 103 ft. (15x), 35 ft. (45x). Length 17.4"; weight 34.4 oz.
Price: With tripod and carrying case $91.95

HERMES 1 70mm objective, 16x, 25x, 40x. Field at 1000 meters 160 ft. (16x), 75ft. (40x). Length 12.2"; weight 33 oz. From CZ-USA.
Price: Body. $359.00
Price: 25x eyepiece $86.00
Price: 40x eyepiece $128.00

KOWA TS-500 SERIES Offset 45° or straight body. Comes with 20-40x zoom eyepiece or 20x fixed eyepiece. 50mm obj. Field of view at 1000 yds.: 171 ft. (20x fixed), 132-74 ft. (20-40x zoom). Length 8.9-10.4", weight 13.4-14.8 oz.
Price: TS-501 (offset 45° body w/20x fixed eyepiece) $258.00
Price: TS-502 (straight body w/20x fixed eyepiece) $231.00
Price: TS-501Z (offset 45° body w/20-40x zoom eyepiece). $321.00
Price: TS-502Z (straight body w/20-40x zoom eyepiece). $290.00

KOWA TS-660 SERIES Offset 45° or straight body. Fully waterproof. Available with ED lens.Sunshade and rotating tripod mount. 66mm obj. Field of view at 1000 yds.: 177 ft. (20xW), 154 ft. (27xW), 131 ft. (30xW), 102 ft. (25x), 92 ft. (25xLER), 108-79 ft. (20-40x multi-coated zoom), 98-62 ft. (20-60x high grade zoom). Length 12.3"; weight 34.9-36.7 oz. Note: Eyepieces for TSN 77mm series, TSN-660 series, 661 body (45° offset) **$660.00**
Price: TSN-662 body (straight). $610.00
Price: TSN-663 body (45 offset, ED lens) $1,070.00
Price: TSN-664 body (straight, ED lens) $1,010.00
Price: TSE-Z6 (20-40x multi-coatedzoom eyepiece). $378.00
Price: TSE-17HB (25x long eye relief eyepiece) $240.00
Price: TSE-14W (30x wide angle high-grade eyepiece) $288.00
Price: TSE-21WB (20x wide-angle eyepiece) $230.00
Price: TSE-15 WM (27x wide-angle eyepiece) $182.00
Price: TSE-16 PM (25x eyepiece). $108.00
Price: TSN-DA1 digital photo adapter $105.00
Price: DA1 adapter rings. $43.00
Price: TSN-PA2 (800mm photo adapter). $269.00
Price: TSN-PA4 (1200mm photo adapter). $330,00
Price: Camera mounts (for use with photo adapter) $30.00

KOWA TSN-660 SERIES Offset 45° or straight body. Fully waterproof. Available with fluorite lens. Sunshade and rotating tripod mount. 66mm obj., field of view at 1000 yds: 177 ft. (20x@), 154 ft. (27xW), 131 ft. (30xW), 102 ft. (25x), 92 ft. (25xLER), 62 ft. (40x), 108-79 ft. (20-40x Multi-Coated Zoom), 102-56 ft. (20-60x Zoom), 98-62 ft. (20-60x High Grade Zoom). Length 12.3"; weight 34.9-36.7 oz. Note: Eyepieces for TSN 77mm Series, TSN-660 Series, and TSN610 Series are interchangeable.
Price: TSN-661 body (45° offset) $660.00
Price: TSN-662 body (straight). $610.00
Price: TSN-663 body (45° offset, fluorite lens). $1,070.00
Price: TSN-664 body (straight, fluorite lens) $1,010.00
Price: TSE-Z4 (20-60x high-grade zoom eyepiece) $378.00
Price: TSE-Z6 (20-40x multi-coated zoom eyepiece) $250.00
Price: TSE-17HB (25x long eye relief eyepiece) $240.00
Price: TSE-14W (30x wide angle eyepiece) $288.00
Price: TSE-21WB (20x wide angle eyepiece) $230.00
Price: TSE-15PM (27x wide angle eyepiece) $182.00
Price: TSE-10PM (40x eyepiece). $108.00
Price: TSE-16PM (25x eyepiece) $105.00
Price: TSN-DA1 (digital photo adapter) $105.00
Price: Adapter rings for DA1. . . . . $43.00
Price: TSN-PA2 (800mm photo adapter). $269.00
Price: TSN-PA4 (1200mm photo adapter). $330.00
Price: Camera mounts (for use with photo adapter) $30.00

KOWA TSN-820M SERIES Offset 45° or straight body. Fully waterproof. Available with fluorite lens. Sunshade and rotating tripod mount. 82mm obj., field of view at 1000 yds: 75 ft (27xLER, 50xW), 126 ft. (32xW), 115-58 ft. (20-60xZoom). Length 15"; weight 49.4-52.2 oz.
Price: TSN-821M body (45° offset) $850.00
Price: TSN-822M body (straight) $770.00
Price: TSN-823M body (45° offset, fluorite lens) $1,850.00
Price: TSN-824M body (straight, fluorite lens). $1,730.00
Price: TSE-Z7 (20-60x zoom eyepiece). $433.00
Price: TSE-9W (50x wide angle eyepiece) $345.00
Price: TSE-14WB (32x wide angle eyepiece) $366.00
Price: TSE-17HC (27x long eye relief eyepiece) $248.00
Price: TSN-DA1 (digital photo adapter) $105.00
Price: Adapter rings for DA1. . . . . $43.00
Price: TSN-PA2C (850mm photo adapter) $300.00
Price: Camera mounts (for use with photo adapter) $30.00

LEUPOLD 10-20x40mm COMPACT 40mm objective, 10-20x. Field at 100 yds. 19.9-13.6ft.; eye relief 18.5mm (10x). Overall length 7.5", weight 15.8 oz. Rubber armored.
Price:. $439.95

LEUPOLD 55-30x50 COMPACT 50mm objective, 15-30x. Field at 100 yds. 13.6ft.; eye relief 17.5mm; length overall 11"; weight 1.5 oz.
Price: $564.99

LEUPOLD Wind River Sequoia 15-30x60mm, 60mm objective, 15-30x. Field at 100 yards: 13.1 ft.; eye relief: 16.5mm. Overall length: 13 inches. Weight: 35.1 oz.
Price: $294.99

LEUPOLD Wind River Sequoia 15-45x60mm Angled. Armored, 15-45x. Field at 100 yards: 13.1-6.3 ft.; eye relief: 16.5-13.0. Overall length: 12.5". Weight: 35.1 oz.
Price: $309.99

LEUPOLD Golden Ring 12-40x60mm; 12.7x38.1x. Field at 100 yards: 16.8-5.2 ft.; eye relief: 30.0; Overall length: 12.4". Weight: 37.0 oz.
Price: $1,124.99

LEUPOLD Golden Ring15-30x50mm Compact Armored; 15.2-30.4x; field at 100 yards: 13.6-8.9; eye relief: 17.5-17.1; overall length: 11.0". Weight: 21.5 oz.
Price:. $564.99

MIRADOR TTB SERIES Draw tube armored spotting scopes. Available with 75mm or 80mm objective. Zoom model (28x-62x, 80mm) is 11 7/8" (closed), weighs 50 oz. Field at 1000 yds. 70-42 ft. Comes with lens covers.
Price: 28-62x80mm. $1,133.95
Price: 32x80mm $971.95
Price: 26-58x75mm. $989.95
Price: 30x75mm $827.95

SPOTTING SCOPES

MIRADOR SSD SPOTTING SCOPES 60mm objective, 15x, 20x, 22x, 25x, 40x, 60x, 20-60x; field at 1000 yds. 37 ft.; length 10 1/4"; weight 33 oz.
Price: 25x **$575.95**
Price: 22x Wide Angle **$593.95**
Price: 20-60x Zoom **$746.95**
Price: As above, with tripod, case **$944.95**

MIRADOR SIA SPOTTING SCOPES Similar to the SSD scopes except with 45° eyepiece. Length 12 1/4"; weight 39 oz.
Price: 25x **$809.95**
Price: 22x Wide Angle **$827.95**
Price: 20-60x Zoom **$980.95**

MIRADOR SSR SPOTTING SCOPES 50mm or 60mm objective. Similar to SSD except rubber armored in black or camouflage. Length 11 1/8"; weight 31 oz.
Price: Black, 20x. **$521.95**
Price: Black, 18x Wide Angle. **$539.95**
Price: Black, 16-48x Zoom. **$692.95**
Price: Black, 20x, 60mm, EER **$692.95**
Price: Black, 22x Wide Angle, 60mm **$701.95**
Price: Black, 20-60x Zoom. **$854.95**

MIRADOR SSF FIELD SCOPES Fixed or variable power, choice of 50mm, 60mm, 75mm objective lens. Length 9 3/4"; weight 20 oz. (15-32x50).
Price: 20x50mm. **$359.95**
Price: 25x60mm. **$440.95**
Price: 30x75mm. **$584.95**
Price: 15-32x50mm Zoom **$548.95**
Price: 18-40x60mm Zoom **$629.95**
Price: 22-47x75mm Zoom **$773.95**

MIRADOR SRA MULTI ANGLE SCOPES Similar to SSF Series except eyepiece head rotates for viewing from any angle.
Price: 20x50mm. **$503.95**
Price: 25x60mm. **$647.95**
Price: 30x75mm. **$764.95**
Price: 15-32x50mm Zoom **$692.95**
Price: 18-40x60mm Zoom **$836.95**
Price: 22-47x75mm Zoom **$953.95**

MIRADOR SIB FIELD SCOPES Short-tube, 45° scopes with porro prism design. 50mm and 60mm objective. Length 10 1/4"; weight 18.5 oz. (15-32x50mm); field at 1000 yds. 129-81 ft.
Price: 20x50mm. **$386.95**
Price: 25x60mm. **$449.95**
Price: 15-32x50mm Zoom **$575.95**
Price: 18-40x60mm Zoom **$638.95**

NIKON FIELDSCOPES 60mm and 78mm lens. Field at 1000 yds. 105 ft. (60mm, 20x), 126 ft. (78mm, 25x). Length 12.8" (straight 60mm), 12.6" (straight 78mm); weight 34.5- 47.5 oz. Eyepieces available separately.
Price: 60mm straight body. **$499.99**
Price: 60mm angled body **$519.99**
Price: 60mm straight ED body. **$779.99**
Price: 60mm angled ED body **$849.99**
Price: 78mm straight ED body. **$899.99**
Price: 78mm angled ED body **$999.99**
Price: Eyepieces (15x to 60x) . . . . **$146.95 to $324.95**
Price: 20-45x eyepiece (25-56x for 78mm). **$320.55**

NIKON SPOTTING SCOPE 60mm objective, 20x fixed power or 15-45x zoom. Field at 1000 yds. 145 ft. (20x). Gray rubber armored. Straight or angled eyepiece. Weighs 44.2 oz., length 12.1" (20x).
Price: 20x60 fixed (with eyepiece). **$290.95**
Price: 15-45x zoom (with case, tripod, eyepiece) **$578.95**

PENTAX PF-80ED spotting scope 80mm objective lens available in 18x, 24x, 36x, 48x, 72x and 20-60x. Length 15.6", weight 11.9 to 19.2 oz.
Price: **$1,320.00**

SIGHTRON SII 2050X63 63mm objective lens, 20x-50x zoom. Field at 1000 yds 91.9 ft. (20x), 52.5 ft. (50x). Length 14"; weight 30.8 oz. Black rubber finish. Also available with 80mm objective lens.
Price: 63mm or 80mm **$339.95**

SIMMONS 1280 50mm objective, 15-45x zoom. Black matte finish. Ocular focus. Peep finder sight. Waterproof. FOV 95-51 ft. @ 1000 yards. Wgt. 33.5 oz., length 12".
Price: With tripod **$189.99**

SIMMONS 1281 60mm objective, 20-60x zoom. Black matte finish. Ocular focus. Peep finder sight. Waterproof. FOV 78-43 ft. @ 1000 yards. Wgt. 34.5 oz. Length 12".
Price: With tripod **$209.99**

SIMMONS 77206 PROHUNTER 50mm objectives, 25x fixed power. Field at 1000 yds. 113 ft.; length 10.25"; weighs 33.25 oz. Black rubber armored.
Price: With tripod case. **$160.60**

SIMMONS 41200 REDLINE 50mm objective, 15x-45x zoom. Field at 1000 yds. 104-41 ft.; length 16.75"; weighs 32.75 oz.
Price: With hard case and tripod **$74.99**
Price: 20-60x, 60mm objective **$99.99**

SWAROVSKI CTC and **CTS EXTENDIBLE SCOPES**. 30x75 mm or 85mm objective, 20-60x zoom or fixed 20x, 30x or 45x eyepieces. Field at 1000 yards: 180 ft. (20xSW), 126 ft. (30xSW), 84 ft. (45xSW), 108-60 ft. (20-60xS) for zoom. Length 12.2" (closed), 19.3" (open) for the CTC; 9.7"/17.2" for theCTS. Weight 42.3 oz. (CTC), 49.4 oz. (CTS). Green rubber armored.
Price: CTC 30x75 body. **$1,032.22**
Price: CTS-85 body. **$1,298.89**

SWAROVSKI ATS-65 SCOPES. 65mm or 80mm objective, 20-60x zoom, or fixed 20x, 30x 45x eyepieces. Field at 1000 yds. 180 ft.(20xSW). 126 ft. (30xSW), 84 ft. (45xSW), 108-60 ft. (20-60xS) for zoom. Length: 13.98" (ATS/STS 80), 12.8" (ATS/STS 65); weight: 45.93 oz. (ATS 80), 47.70 oz. (ATS 80HD), 45.23 oz., (STS 80), 46.9 oz. (STS 80 HD), 38.3 oz. (ATS 65), 39.9 oz. (ATS 65HD) 38.1 oz. (STS 65), 39.2 oz. (STS 65 HD). Available with HD (high density) glass add approximately **$450**.
Price: ATS65 (angled eyepiece) **$1,087.78**
Price: STS 65 (straight eyepiece). **$1,087.78**
Price: ATS-80 (angled eyepiece) **$1,321.11**
Price: ATS-80 (straight eyepiece) **$1,321.11**
Price: 20xSW **$310.00**
Price: 30xSW **$310.00**
Price: 45xSW **$376.67**

SWIFT LYNX M836 15x-45x zoom, 60mm objective. Weight 7 lbs., length 14". Has 45° eyepiece, sunshade.
Price: **$315.00**

SWIFT NIGHTHAWK M849U 80mm objective, 20x-60x zoom, or fixed 19, 25x, 31x, 50x, 75x eyepieces. Has rubber armored body, 1.8x optical finder, retractable lens hood, 45° eyepiece. Field at 1000 yds. 60 ft. (28x), 41 ft. (75x). Length 13.4 oz.; weight 39 oz.
Price: Body only **$870.00**
Price: 20-68x eyepiece **$370.00**
Price: Fixed eyepieces . . . . **$130.00 to $240.00**
Price: Model 849 (straight) body. **$795.00**

SWIFT LYNX 60mm objective, 15-45X zoom, 45-degree inclined roof prism, magenta coated on all air-to-glass surfaces, rubber armored body, length 14 inches, weighs 30 ounces. Equipped with sun shade, threaded dust covers and low level tripod.
Price: complete **$330.00**

SWIFT TELEMASTER M841 60mm objective. 15x to 60x variable power. Field at 1000 yds. 160 feet (15x) to 40 feet (60x). Weight 3.25 lbs.; length 18" overall.
Price: **$399.50**

SWIFT PANTHER M844 15x-45x zoom or 22x WA, 15x, 20x, 40x. 60mm objective. Field at 1000 yds. 141 ft. (15x), 68 ft. (40x), 95-58 ft. (20x-45x).
Price: Body only **$380.00**
Price: 15x-45x zoom eyepiece **$120.00**
Price: 20x-45x zoom (long eye relief) eyepiece **$140.00**
Price: 15x, 40x eyepiece. **$65.00**
Price: 22x WA eyepiece **$80.00**

SWIFT M700T 12x-36x, 50mm objective. Field of view at 100 yds. 16 ft. (12x), 9 ft. (36x). Length 14"; weight with tripod 3.22 lbs.
Price: **$30.00**

TASCO 15-45x Zoom, 50mm objective lens, 20x-60x zoom. Field of view at 100 yds. 19 ft (15x) Length: 16". Weight: 19 oz. Matte black finish.
Price: **$67.95**

TASCO 20-60x zoom, 60mm objective, 12-36x zoom. Field of view at 100 yds. 12 ft. (20x). Length: 20". Weight: 50 oz. Black finish.
Price: **$95.95**

TASCO 18-36x zoom 50mm objective. Field of view at 100 yds. 12 ft. (18x). Length: 14.5". Weight: 31 oz. Camo or black rubber armor. Includes carrying case.
Price: **$131.95**

UNERTL "FORTY-FIVE" 54mm objective. 20x (single fixed power). Field at 100 yds. 10',10"; eye relief 1"; focusing range infinity to 33 ft. Weight about 32 oz.; overall length 15 3/4". With lens covers.
Price: With mono-layer magnesium coating **$810.00**

UNERTL STRAIGHT PRISMATIC 24x63. 63.5mm objective, 24x. Field at 100 yds., 7 ft. Relative brightness, 6.96. Eye relief 1/2". Weight 40 oz.; length closed 19". Push-pull and screw-focus eyepiece. 16x and 32x eyepieces **$125.00 each.**
Price: **$786.00**

UNERTL 20x STRAIGHT PRISMATIC 54mm objective, 20x. Field at 100 yds. 8.5 ft. Relative brightness 6.1. Eye relief 1/2". Weight 36 oz.; length closed 13 1/2". Complete with lens covers.
Price: **$695.00**

UNERTL TEAM SCOPE 100mm objective. 15x, 24x, 32x eyepieces. Field at 100 yds. 13 to 7.5 ft. Relative brightness, 39.06 to 9.79. Eye relief 2" to 1 1/2". Weight 13 lbs.; length 29 7/8" overall. Metal tripod, yoke and wood carrying case furnished (total weight 80 lbs.).
Price: **$3,624.50**

WEAVER 20x50 50mm objective. Field of view 124 ft. at 100 yds. Eye relief .85"; weighs 21 oz.; overall length 10". Waterproof, armored.
Price: **$249.99**

WEAVER 15-40x60 ZOOM 60mm objective. 15x-40x zoom. Field at 100 yds. 119 ft. (15x), 66 ft. (60x). Overall length 12.5", weighs 26 oz. Waterproof, armored.
Price: **$399.99**

Compendium of State Laws Governing Firearms

The following chart lists the main provisions of state firearms laws as of the date of publication. In addition to the state provisions, the purchase, sale, and, in certain circumstances, the possession and interstate transportation of firearms are regulated by the Federal Gun Control Act of 1968 as amended by the Firearms Owners' Protection Act of 1986. Also, cities and localities may have their own gun ordinances in addition to federal and state restrictions. Details may be obtained by contacting local law enforcement authorities or by consulting your state's firearms law digest compiled by the NRA Institute for Legislative Action.

STATE	GUN BAN	EXEMPTIONS TO NICS$_2$	STATE WAITING PERIOD - NUMBER OF DAYS		LICENSE OR PERMIT TO PURCHASE or other prerequesite		REGISTRATION		RECORD OF SALE REPORTED TO STATE OR LOCAL GOVT.
			HANDGUNS	LONG GUNS	HANDGUNS	LONG GUNS	HANDGUNS	LONG GUNS	
Alabama	—	—	—	—	—	—	—	—	—
Alaska	—	RTC	—	—	—	—	—	—	—
Arizona	—	RTC	—	—	—	—	—	—	—
Arkansas	—	RTC$_3$	—	—	—	—	—	—	—
California	X_{20}	—	10_{14}	$10_{14,15}$	8, 23	—	X	24	X
Colorado	—	—	—	—	—	—	—	—	—
Connecticut	X_{20}	—	$14_{14,15}$	$14_{14,15}$	$X_{16,23}$	—	—	24	X
Delaware	—	—	—	—	—	—	—	—	—
Florida	—	GRTC	$3_{14,15}$	—	—	—	—	—	—
Georgia	—	RTC	—	—	—	—	—	—	—
Hawaii	X_{20}	L, RTC	—	—	$X_{16,23}$	X_{16}	X_{12}	X_{12}	X
Idaho	—	RTC	—	—	—	—	—	—	—
Illinois	20	—	3	2	X_{16}	X_{16}	4	4	X
Indiana	—	RTC, O$_3$	—	—	—	—	—	—	X
Iowa	—	L, RTC	—	—	X_{16}	—	—	—	—
Kansas	—	—	1	—	1	—	1	—	1
Kentucky	—	RTC$_3$	—	—	—	—	—	—	—
Louisiana	—	GRTC	—	—	—	—	—	—	—
Maine	—	—	—	—	—	—	—	—	—
Maryland	X_{20}	O$_3$	7_{14}	$7_{9,14}$	8, 23	—	—	—	X
Massachusetts	X_{20}	GRTC	—	—	X_{16}	X_{16}	—	—	X
Michigan	—	O$_3$	—	—	$X_{16,23}$	—	X	—	X
Minnesota	—	—	7_{16}	16	X_{16}	X_{16}	—	—	—
Mississippi	—	RTC$_3$	—	—	—	—	—	—	—
Missouri	—	—	—	—	X_{16}	—	—	—	X
Montana	—	RTC	—	—	—	—	—	—	—
Nebraska	—	L	—	—	X	—	—	—	—
Nevada	—	RTC	1	—	—	—	1	—	—
New Hampshire	—	—	—	—	—	—	—	—	—
New Jersey	X_{20}	—	—	—	X_{16}	X_{16}	—	24	X
New Mexico	—	—	—	—	—	—	—	—	—
New York	X_{20}	L, RTC	—	—	$X_{16,23}$	16	X	7	X
North Carolina	—	L, RTC	—	—	X_{16}	—	—	—	X
North Dakota	—	RTC	—	—	—	—	—	—	—
Ohio	20	—	1	—	16	—	1	—	1
Oklahoma	—	—	—	—	—	—	—	—	—
Oregon	—	GRTC	—	—	—	—	—	—	X
Pennsylvania	—	—	—	—	—	—	—	—	X
Rhode Island	—	—	7	7	23	—	—	—	X
South Carolina	—	RTC	8	—	8	—	—	—	X
South Dakota	—	GRTC	2	—	—	—	—	—	X
Tennessee	—	—	—	—	—	—	—	—	—
Texas	—	RTC$_3$	—	—	—	—	—	—	—
Utah	—	RTC	—	—	—	—	—	—	—
Vermont	—	—	—	—	—	—	—	—	—
Virginia	X_{20}	—	1,8	—	1,8	—	—	—	1
Washington	—	O$_3$	5_{10}	—	—	—	—	—	X
West Virginia	—	—	—	—	—	—	—	—	—
Wisconsin	—	—	2	—	—	—	—	—	—
Wyoming	—	RTC	—	—	—	—	—	—	—
District of Columbia	X_{20}	L	—	—	X_{16}	X_{16}	X_{16}	X	X

REFERENCE

COMPENDIUM OF STATE LAWS GOVERNING FIREARMS

Since state laws are subject to frequent change, this chart is not to be considered legal advice or a restatement of the law.

All fifty states have sportsmen's protections laws to halt harrassment.

STATE	STATE PROVISION FOR RIGHT-TO-CARRY CONCEALED	CARRYING OPENLY PROHIBITED	OWNER ID CARDS OR LICENSING	FIREARM RIGHTS CONSTITUTIONAL PROVISION	STATE FIREARMS PREEMPTION LAWS	RANGE PROTECTION LAW
Alabama	R	X_{11}	—	X	X	X
Alaska	R_{19}	—	—	X	—	X
Arizona	R	—	—	X	X	X
Arkansas	R	X_{5}	—	X	X	X
California	L	X_{6}	—	—	X	X
Colorado	R	25	—	X	X_{25}	X
Connecticut	R	X	—	X	X_{17}	X
Delaware	L	—	—	X	X	—
Florida	R	X	—	X	X	X
Georgia	R	X	—	X	X	X
Hawaii	L	X	X	X	—	—
Idaho	R	—	—	X	X	X
Illinois	D	X	X	X	—	X
Indiana	R	X	—	X	X_{18}	X
Iowa	L	X	—	—	X	X
Kansas	D	1	—	X	—	X
Kentucky	R	—	—	X	X	X
Louisiana	R	—	—	X	X	X
Maine	R	—	—	X	X	X
Maryland	L	X	—	—	X	X
Massachusetts	L	X	X	X	X_{17}	X
Michigan	R	X_{11}	—	X	X	X
Minnesota	R	X	—	—	X	—
Mississippi	R	—	—	X	X	X
Missouri	R	—	—	X	X	X
Montana	R	—	—	X	X	X
Nebraska	D	—	—	X	—	—
Nevada	R	—	—	X	X	X
New Hampshire	R	—	—	X	X	X
New Jersey	L	X	X	—	X_{17}	X
New Mexico	R	—	—	X	X	X
New York	L	X	X	—	X_{22}	X
North Carolina	R	—	—	X	X	X
North Dakota	R	X_{6}	—	X	X	X
Ohio	D	1	16	X	—	X
Oklahoma	R	X_{6}	—	X	X	X
Oregon	R	—	—	X	X	X
Pennsylvania	R	X_{11}	—	X	X	X
Rhode Island	L	X	—	X	X	X
South Carolina	R	X	—	X	X	X
South Dakota	R	—	—	X	X	X
Tennessee	R	X_{5}	—	X	X	X
Texas	R	X	—	X	X	X
Utah	R	X_{6}	—	X	X	X
Vermont	R_{19}	X_{5}	—	X	X	X
Virginia	R	—	—	X	X	X
Washington	R	X_{21}	—	X	X	—
West Virginia	R	—	—	X	X	X
Wisconsin	D	—	—	X	X	X
Wyoming	R	—	—	X	X	X
District of Columbia	D	X	X	NA	—	—

Compendium of State Laws Governing Firearms

With over 20,000 "gun control" laws on the books in America, there are two challenges facing every gun owner. First, you owe it to yourself to become familiar with the federal laws on gun ownership. Only by knowing the laws can you avoid innocently breaking one.

Second, while federal legislation receives much more media attention, state legislatures and city councils make many more decisions regarding your right to own and carry firearms. NRA members and all gun owners must take extra care to be aware of anti-gun laws and ordinances at the state and local levels.

Notes:

1. In certain cities or counties.

2. **National Instant Check System (NICS) exemption codes:**
RTC-Carry Permit Holders Exempt From NICS
GRTC-Holders of RTC Permits issued before November 30, 1998 exempt from NICS. Holders of more recent permits are not exempt.
L-Holders of state licenses to possess or purchase or firearms ID cards exempt from NICS.
O-Other, See Note 3.

3. **NICS exemption notes**: **Arkansas**: RTC permits issued prior to 11/30/98 and those issued on and after 4/1/99 qualify. Those issued between 11/1/98 and 3/31/99 do not qualify. **Indiana**: Personal protection, hunting and target permits all qualify for exemptions. **Kentucky**: RTC permits issued after July 15, 1998 and prior to November 30, 1998 are exempt. **Maryland:** There are no exemptions for handgun purchases. For long gun purchases, those holding RTC permits issued before November 30, 1998 are exempt. **Michigan:** No exemptions for handguns, license for long guns. **Mississippi**: Permits issued to security guards do not qualify. **Texas**: Texas Peace Officer License, TCLEOSE Card, is valid only if issued prior to November 30, 1998. **Washington**: RTC permits issued after July 1, 1996 and prior to November 30, 1998 are exempt.

4. Chicago only. No handgun not already registered may be possessed.

5. **Arkansas** prohibits carrying a firearm "with a purpose to employ it as a weapon against a person." **Tennessee** prohibits carrying "with the intent to go armed." **Vermont** prohibits carrying a firearm "with the intent or purpose of injuring another."

6. Loaded.

7. New York City only.

8. A permit is required to acquire another handgun before 30 days have elapsed following the acquisition of a handgun.

9. **Maryland** subjects purchases of "assault weapons" to a 7-day waiting period.

10. May be extended by police to 30 days in some circumstances. An individual not holding a driver's license must wait 90 days.

11. Carrying a handgun openly in a motor vehicle requires a license.

12. Every person arriving in **Hawaii** is required to register any firearm(s) brought into the State within 3 days of arrival of the person or firearm(s), whichever occurs later. Handguns purchased from licensed dealers must be registered within 5 days.

13. Concealed carry laws vary significantly between the states. Ratings reflect the real effect a state's particular laws have on the ability of citizens to carry firearms for self-defense.

14. Purchases from dealers only. **Maryland**: 7 business days. Purchasers of regulated firearms must undergo background checks performed by the State Police, either through a dealer or directly through the State Police.

15. The waiting period does not apply to a person holding a valid permit or license to carry a firearm. In **Connecticut**, a hunting license also exempts the holder for long gun purchasers. **California**: transfers of a long gun to a person's parent, child or grandparent are exempt from the waiting period.

16. **Connecticut:** A certificate of eligibility or a carry permit is required to obtain a handgun and a carry permit is required to transport a handgun outside your home. **District of Columbia:** No handgun may be possessed unless it was registered prior to Sept. 23, 1976 and re-registered by Feb. 5, 1977. A permit to purchase is required for a rifle or shotgun. **Hawaii:** Purchase permits, required for all firearms, may not be issued until 14 days after application. A handgun purchase permit is valid for 10 days, for one handgun; a long gun permit is valid for one year, for multiple long guns. **Illinois:** A Firearm Owner's Identification Card (FOI) is required to possess or purchase a firearm, must be issued to qualified applicants within 30 days, and is valid for 5 years. **Iowa:** A purchase permit is required for handguns, and is valid for one year, beginning three days after issuance. **Massachusetts:** Firearms and feeding devices for firearms are divided into classes. Depending on the class, a firearm identification card (FID) or class A license or class B license is required to possess, purchase, or carry a firearm, ammunition thereof, or firearm feeding device, or "large capacity feeding device." **Michigan:** A handgun purchaser must obtain a license to purchase from local law enforcement, and within 10 days present the license and handgun to obtain a certificate of inspection. **Minnesota:** A handgun transfer or carrying permit, or a 7-day waiting period and handgun transfer report, is required to purchase handguns or "assault weapons" from a dealer. A permit or transfer report must be issued to qualified applicants within 7 days. A permit is valid for one year, a transfer report for 30 days. **Missouri:** A purchase permit is required for a handgun, must be issued to qualified applicants within 7 days, and is valid for 30 days. **New Jersey:** Firearm owners must possess a FID, which must be issued to qualified applicants within 30 days. To purchase a handgun, a purchase permit, which must be issued within 30 days to qualified applicants and is valid for 90 days, is required. An FID is required to purchase long guns. **New York:** Purchase, possession and/or carrying of a handgun require a single license, which includes any restrictions made upon the bearer. New York City also requires a license for long guns. **North Carolina:** To purchase a handgun, a license or permit is required, which must be issued to qualified applicants within 30 days. **Ohio**: Some cities require a permit-to-purchase or firearm owner ID card.

17. Preemption through judicial ruling. Local regulation may be instituted in **Massachusetts** if ratified by the legislature.

18. Except Gary and East Chicago and local laws enacted before January, 1994.

19. **Vermont and Alaska** law respect your right to carry without a permit. Alaska also has a permit to carry system to establish reciprocity with other states.

20. "Assault weapons" are prohibited in **California, Connecticut, New Jersey** and **New York.** Some local jurisdictions in **Ohio** also ban "assault weapons." **Hawaii** prohibits "assault pistols." **California** bans "unsafe handguns." **Illinois:** Chicago, Evanston, Oak Park, Morton Grove, Winnetka, Wilmette, and Highland Park prohibit handguns; some cities prohibit other kinds of firearms. **Maryland** prohibits "assault pistols" and the sale or manufacture of any handgun manufactured after Jan. 1, 1985, that appears on the Handgun Roster. **Massachusetts:** It is unlawful to sell, transfer or possess "any assault weapon or large capacity feeding device" [more than 10 rounds] that was not legally possessed on September 13, 1994. **Ohio:** some cities prohibit handguns of certain magazine capacities." **Virginia** prohibits "Street Sweeper" shotguns. The **District of Columbia** prohibits new acquisition of handguns and any semi-automatic firearm capable of using a detachable ammunition magazine of more than 12 rounds capacity. (With respect to some of these laws and ordinances, individuals may retain prohibited firearms owned previously, with certain restrictions.)

21. Local jurisdictions may opt out of prohibition.

22. Preemption only applies to handguns.

23. Requires proof of safety training for purchase. **California**: Must have Handgun Safety Certificate receipt which is valid for five years. **Connecticut:** To receive certificate of eligibility, must complete a handgun safety course approved by the Commissioner of Public Safety. **Hawaii:** Must have completed an approved handgun safety course. **Maryland:** Must complete an approved handgun safety course. **Michigan**: A person must correctly answer 70% of the questions on a basic safety review questionnaire in order to obtain a license to purchase. **New York:** Some counties require a handgun safety training course to receive a license. **Rhode Island**: Must receive a state-issued handgun safety card.

24. "Assault weapon" registration. **California** had two dates by which assault weapons had to be registered or possession after such date would be considered a felony: March 31, 1992 for the named make and model firearms banned in the 1989 legislation and December 31, 2000 for the firearms meeting the definition of the "assault weapons in the 1999 legislation. In **Connecticut**, those firearms banned by specific make and model in the 1993 law had to be registered by October 1, 1994 or possession would be considered a felony. A recent law requires registration of additional guns by October 1, 2003. In **New Jersey**, any "assault weapon" not registered, licensed, or rendered inoperable pursuant to a state police certificate by May 1, 1991, is considered contraband.

25. Local governments cannot enact ordinances that prohibit the sale, purchase, or possession of a firearm. Municipalities cannot restrict a person's ability to travel into, through, or within their jurisdiction for hunting or personal protection. Local governments, including law enforcement agencies, cannot maintain a database of guns or gun owners. Municipalities may prohibit open carry in government buildings if such prohibition is clearly posted.

Concealed carry codes:

R: Right-to-Carry "Shall issue" or less restrictive discretionary permit system (Ala., Conn.) (See also note #21.)
L: Right-to-Carry Limited by local authority's discretion over permit issuance.
D: Right-to-Carry Denied, no permit system exists; concealed carry is prohibited.

NL 00930 Rev. 9/2003 10m

REFERENCE

Guide to Right-to-Carry Reciprocity and Recognition

- **The right to self-defense neither begins nor ends at a state border.**
- **A law-abiding citizen does not suffer a character change by crossing a state line.**
- **An "unalienable right" is not determined by geographical boundaries.**
- **A patchwork of state laws regarding the carrying of firearms can make criminals out of honest folks, especially those who frequently must travel the states to earn a living.**
- **Using data for all 3,054 U.S. counties from 1977 to 1994, University of Chicago Prof. John Lott finds that for each additional year a concealed handgun law is in effect the murder rate declines by 3%, robberies by over 2%, and the rape rate by 2%.**

In spite of the truth of these statements and the fact that nearly half of all Americans live in states that allow a law-abiding citizen to carry a firearm concealed for personal protection, it has not been commonplace that these same citizens could carry their firearm across states lines. NRA-ILA is working to pass right-to-carry reciprocity laws granting permit holders the ability to carry their firearms legally while visiting or traveling beyond their home state.

In order to assist NRA Members in determining which states recognize their permits, NRA-ILA has created this guide. This guide is not to be considered as legal advice or a restatement of the law. It is important to remember that state carry laws vary considerably. Be sure to check with state and local authorities outside your home state for a complete listing of restrictions on carrying concealed in that state. Many states restrict carrying in bars, restaurants (where alcohol is served), establishments where packaged alcohol is sold, schools, colleges, universities, churches, parks, sporting events, correctional facilities, courthouses, federal and state government offices/buildings, banks, airport terminals, police stations, polling places, any posted private property restricting the carrying of concealed firearms, etc. In addition to state restrictions, federal law prohibits carrying on military bases, in national parks and the sterile area of airports. National Forests usually follow laws of the state wherein the forest is located.

NOTE: Alaska and Vermont allow the concealed carry of firearms without a permit. Vermont residents traveling to other states must first obtain a non-resident permit from that state—if available—prior to carrying concealed. Alaska still issues permits to those who want them, allowing them to benefit by recognition and reciprocity laws.

NOTE TO READERS: Right To Carry reciprocity and recognition between the various states is subject to frequent change through legislative action and regulatory interpretation. This information is the best available at the time of publication. This summary is not intended as legal advice or restatement of law.

Rev. 3/2004

Alabama

Right-To-Carry Law Type: Reasonable May Issue

Issuing Authority:	County Sheriff	
Contact agency for out of state permits:	Permits not granted.	
These states recognize your permit:	Alaska, Colorado, Florida, Georgia, Idaho, Indiana, Kentucky, Michigan, Mississippi, Missouri, New Hampshire, North Carolina, North Dakota, Oklahoma, Utah, Tennessee, Vermont, Wyoming	
This state recognizes permits from the following states:	Alaska, Colorado, Florida, Georgia, Idaho, Indiana, Kentucky, Michigan, Mississippi, New Hampshire, North Carolina, North Dakota, Oklahoma, Utah, Tennessee, Wyoming	
Cost & Term of Permit:	$10	1 year
Key Government Offices:	Alabama Dept. of Public Safety 500 Dexter Ave. Montgomery, Alabama 36130 Phone: (334)242-4392 Email: info@dps.state.al.us	Attorney General Alabama State House 11 South Union Street, 3rd Floor Montgomery, Alabama 36130 Phone: 334-242-7300
	http://www.dps.state.al.us	

Alaska

Right-To-Carry Law Type: Shall Issue

Issuing Authority:	State Trooper	
Contact agency for out of state permits:	Permits not granted.	
These states recognize your permit:	Alabama, Arizona, Colorado, Delaware, Florida, Idaho, Indiana, Kentucky, Michigan, Missouri, Montana, New Hampshire, North Carolina, North Dakota, Oklahoma, South Dakota, Utah, Vermont, Virginia, Wyoming	
This state recognizes permits from the following states:	No permit required to carry concealed in Alaska.	
Cost & Term of Permit:	$99	5 years
Key Government Offices:	Alaska Concealed Handgun Permit Program 5700 East Tudor Road Anchorage, Alaska 99507 Phone: (907) 269-0392	
	http://www.dps.state.ak.us/ast/achp/	

Arizona

Right-To-Carry Law Type: Shall Issue

Issuing Authority:	Arizona Department of Public Safety	
Contact agency for out of state permits:	Arizona Department of Public Safety	
These states recognize your permit:	Alaska, Arkansas, Colorado, Delaware, Florida, Idaho, Indiana, Kentucky, Michigan, Missouri, Montana, North Carolina, North Dakota, Oklahoma, Tennessee, Texas, Utah, Vermont, Virginia	
This state recognizes permits from the following states:	Alaska, Arkansas, California, Colorado ,Connecticut, Deleware, Florida, Iowa, Kentucky, Louisiana, Maryland, Massachusetts, Michigan, Minnesota, Missouri, Montana, Nevada, New Mexico, North Carolina, North Dakota, Oklahoma, Oregon, South Carolina, Tennessee, Texas, Utah, West Virginia, Wyoming	
Cost & Term of Permit:	$50	4 years
Key Government Offices:	Arizona Department of Public Safety Attn: Concealed Weapons Permit Unit P.O. Box 6488 Phoenix, Arizona 85005 Phone: (602) 256-6280 and (800) 256-6280 Fax: (602) 223-2928 Email: ccw@dps.state.az.us	Arizona Attorney General 1275 W. Washington Street Phoenix, Arizona 85007 Phone: (602) 542-4266 and (888) 377-6108
	http://www.dps.state.az.us/ccw/default.asp	

REFERENCE

Right-to-Carry Reciprocity and Recognition, cont.

Connecticut

Right-To-Carry Law Type: Reasonable May Issue

Issuing Authority:	Department of Public Safety, Special Licenses & Firearms Unit	
Contact agency for out of state permits:	Department of Public Safety, Special Licenses & Firearms Unit	
These states recognize your permit:	Alaska, Arizona, Idaho, Indiana, Kentucky, Michigan, Missouri, Montana, Oklahoma, Tennessee, Utah, Vermont	
This state recognizes permits from the following states:	none	
Cost & Term of Permit:	$35.00 plus $24.00 fingerprint processing fee	5 years
Key Government Offices:	Department of Public Safety 1111 Country Club Road Middletown, Connecticut 06450-9294 Phone: (860) 685-8000 Fax: (860) 685-8354 Email: DPS.Feedback@po.state.ct.us	Attorney General 55 Elm Street Hartford, Connecticut 06106 Phone: 860-808-5318 Fax: 860 808-5387 Email: Attorney.General@po.state.ct.us
	http://www.state.ct.us/dps/slfu/index.html	

Delaware

Right-To-Carry Law Type: Restrictive May Issue

Issuing Authority:	Prothonotary of Superior Court	
Contact agency for out of state permits:	Permits not granted.	
These states recognize your permit:	Alaska, Arizona, Florida, Idaho, Indiana, Kentucky, Michigan, Missouri, Montana, North Carolina, Oklahoma, Tennessee, Utah, Vermont	
This state recognizes permits from the following states:	Alaska, Arizona, Colorado, Florida, Michigan, North Carolina, North Dakota, Oklahoma, Tennessee, Utah	
Cost & Term of Permit:	$34.50 plus other fees	Initially 2 years, renewal for 3 years.
Key Government Offices:	Delaware State Police P.O. Box 430 Dover, Delaware 9903-0430 Phone: (302) 739-5900	Attorney General Carvel State Office Building 820 N. French Street Wilmington, Delaware 19801 Email: Attorney.General@State.DE.US
	http://www.state.de.us/dsp/	

Florida

Right-To-Carry Law Type: Shall Issue

Issuing Authority:	Department of Agriculture and Consumer Services, Division of Licensing	
Contact agency for out of state permits:	Department of Agriculture and Consumer Services, Division of Licensing	
These states recognize your permit:	Alabama, Alaska, Arizona, Arkansas, Colorado, Delaware, Georgia, Idaho, Indiana, Kentucky, Louisiana, Michigan, Mississippi, Missouri, Montana, New Hampshire, North Carolina, North Dakota, Oklahoma, Pennsylvania, South Dakota, Tennessee, Texas, Utah, Vermont, Wyoming	
This state recognizes permits from the following states:	Alabama, Alaska, Arizona, Arkansas, Colorado, Delaware, Georgia, Idaho, Indiana, Kentucky, Louisiana, Michigan, Mississippi, Montana, New Hampshire, North Carolina, North Dakota*, Oklahoma, Pennsylvania, South Dakota*, Tennessee, Texas, Utah, Wyoming *must be 21	
Cost & Term of Permit:	Residents: $75 plus fingerprinting fee, Renewal: $65	5 years
Key Government Offices:	Florida Dept. of Agriculture and Consumer Services, Division of Licensing P.O. Box 6687 Tallahassee, Florida 32314-6687 Phone: (850) 488-5381 email: springb@doacs.state.fl.us	Office of Attorney General State of Florida The Capital Tallahasse, Florida 32399-1050 Phone: 850-414-3300 Fax: 850-410-1630 email: ag@oag.state.fl.us
	http://licgweb.doacs.state.fl.us/	

REFERENCE

Right-to-Carry Reciprocity and Recognition, cont.

Arkansas

Right-To-Carry Law Type: Shall Issue

Issuing Authority:	State Police	
Contact agency for out of state permits:	Permits not granted.	
These states recognize your permit:	Alaska, Arizona, Florida, Idaho, Indiana, Kentucky, Michigan, Missouri, Montana, North Carolina, Oklahoma, South Carolina, South Dakota, Tennessee, Texas, Utah, Vermont	
This state recognizes permits from the following states:	Arizona, Florida, Kentucky, North Carolina, Oklahoma, South Carolina, Tennessee, Texas, Utah	
Cost & Term of Permit:	$115	4 Years
Key Government Offices:	Regulatory Services Division Attn: Arkansas State Police #1 State Police Plaza Drive Little Rock, Arkansas 72209-2971 Phone: 501-618-8627 Fax: 501-618-8647	Office of the Attorney General 200 Catlett-Prien Tower 323 Center Street Little Rock, Arkansas 72201 Phone: 501-682-1323 (1-800-448-3014) Email: oag@ag.state.ar.us
	www.state.ar.us/chl/chl.html	

California

Right-To-Carry Law Type: Restrictive May Issue

Issuing Authority:	County Sheriff	
Contact agency for out of state permits:	Permits not granted.	
These states recognize your permit:	Alaska, Arizona, Idaho, Indiana, Kentucky, Michigan, Missouri, Montana, Oklahoma, Tennessee, Utah, Vermont	
This state recognizes permits from the following states:	none	
Cost & Term of Permit:	varies	2 years maximum
Key Government Offices:	California Attorney General Attn: Department of Justice P.O. Box 944255 Sacramento, California 94244-2550 Phone: (916) 445-9555	
	http://caag.state.ca.us/	

Colorado

Right-To-Carry Law Type: Shall Issue

Issuing Authority:	County Sheriff	
Contact agency for out of state permits:	Permits not granted.	
These states recognize your permit:	Alabama, Alaska, Arizona, Florida, Georgia, Idaho, Indiana, Kentucky, Michigan, Missouri, Montana, New Hampshire, North Carolina, Oklahoma, South Dakota, Tennessee, Utah, Vermont, Wyoming	
This state recognizes permits from the following states:	Alabama, Alaska, Arizona, Florida, Georgia, Idaho, Iowa, Indiana, Kentucky, Michigan, Montana, New Hampshire, North Carolina, Oklahoma, South Dakota, Tennessee, Utah, Wyoming	
Cost & Term of Permit:	No more than $100	5 years
Key Government Offices:	Attorney General 1525 Sherman 5th Floor Denver, Colorado 80203 Phone: (303) 866-4500 Fax: (303) 866-5691 Email: attorney.general@state.co.us	Colorado Bureau of Investigation 690 Kipling St. Suite 3000 Denver, Colorado 80215 Phone: (303) 239-5850 Email: james.spoden@cdps.state.co.us
	http://cbi.state.co.us/ccw/reciprocity.asp	

Right-to-Carry Reciprocity and Recognition, cont.

Georgia

Right-To-Carry Law Type: Shall Issue

Issuing Authority:	County Probate Judge	
Contact agency for out of state permits:	Permits not granted.	
These states recognize your permit:	Alabama, Alaska, Arizona, Colorado, Florida, Idaho, Indiana, Kentucky, Michigan, Missouri, Montana, New Hampshire, North Caolina, Oklahoma, Pennsylvania, South Dakota, Tennessee, Utah, Vermont, Wyoming	
This state recognizes permits from the following states:	Alabama, Colorado, Florida, Idaho, Indiana, Kentucky, Michigan, Montana, New Hampshire, North Carolina, Pennsylvania, South Dakota, Tennessee, Wyoming	
Cost & Term of Permit:	$24 to GBI and additional fee set by County.	5 years
Key Government Offices:	Georgia Bureau of Investigation P.O. Box 370748 Decatur, Georgia 30037-0748 Phone: (404) 244-2501	Georgia Attorney General 40 Capitol Square, SW Atlanta, Georgia 30334-1300 Phone: 404-656-3300
	http://www.ganet.org/ago/	

Hawaii

Right-To-Carry Law Type: Restrictive May Issue

Issuing Authority:	Chief of Police	
Contact agency for out of state permits:	Permits not granted.	
These states recognize your permit:	Alaska, Idaho, Indiana, Kentucky, Michigan, Missouri, Montana, Oklahoma, Tennessee, Utah, Vermont	
This state recognizes permits from the following states:	none	
Cost & Term of Permit:	varies	varies
Key Government Offices:	Honolulu Police Department Attn: Firearms Division 801 S. Beretania Honolulu, Hawaii Phone: 808-529-3371, Fax: 808-529-3525 hpd@honolulupd.org http://www.honolulupd.org/service/gunlaw/htm	Attorney General Department of the Attorney General 425 Queen Street Honolulu, Hawaii 96813
	http://www.hawaii.gov/ag/index.html	

Idaho

Right-To-Carry Law Type: Shall Issue

Issuing Authority:	County Sheriff	
Contact agency for out of state permits:	Any Sheriffs' Department	
These states recognize your permit:	Alabama, Alaska, Colorado, Florida, Georgia, Indiana, Kentucky, Michigan, Missouri, Montana, New Hampshire, North Carolina, North Dakota, Oklahoma, Tennessee, Utah, Vermont, Virginia, Wyoming	
This state recognizes permits from the following states:	All state permits	
Cost & Term of Permit:	$20 plus fingerprinting fee	4 years
Key Government Offices:	Idaho Department of Law Enforcement 700 S. Stratford Dr P.O. Box 700 Meridian, Idaho 83680-0700 Phone: (208)884-7000	Idaho Attorney General 700 W. Jefferson Street P.O. Box 83720 Boise, Idaho 83720-0010 Phone: (208) 334-2400 Fax: (208) 334-2530
	http://www.state.id.us/dle/dle.htm	

Illinois

Right-To-Carry Law Type: Non-Issue

Issuing Authority:	Permits Not Available	
Contact agency for out of state permits:	Permits not granted.	
These states recognize your permit:	none	
This state recognizes permits from the following states:	none	
Cost & Term of Permit:	n/a	n/a
Key Government Offices:	Illinois State Police P.O. Box 19461 Springfield, Illinois 62794-9461 Phone: 217-782-7263 Fax: 217-785-2821	Attorney General 500 South Second St. Springfield, Illinois 62706 Phone: (217) 782-1090 Email: attorney_general@state.il.us
	http://www.state.il.us/isp/isphpage.htm	

Indiana

Right-To-Carry Law Type: Shall Issue

Issuing Authority:	State Police through Chief Law Enforcement Officer of Municipality	
Contact agency for out of state permits:	Permits not granted.	
These states recognize your permit:	Alabama, Alaska, Colorado, Florida, Georgia, Idaho, Kentucky, Michigan, Missouri, Montana, New Hampshire, North Carolina, North Dakota, Oklahoma, South Dakota, Tennessee, Utah, Vermont, Wyoming	
This state recognizes permits from the following states:	All state permits recognized for non-Indiana residents.	
Cost & Term of Permit:	$30	4 years
Key Government Offices:	State Police 100 North Senate Avenue Indiana Government Center North, 3rd Floor Indianapolis, Indiana 46204-2259 Phone: (317) 232-8200	Indiana Attorney General State House, Room 219 Indianapolis, Indiana 46204 Phone: (317) 232 - 6201
	http://www.state.in.us/isp/	

Iowa

Right-To-Carry Law Type: Reasonable May Issue

Issuing Authority:	Sheriff for residents, Commissioner of Public Safety for non residents	
Contact agency for out of state permits:	Commissioner of Public Safety	
These states recognize your permit:	Alaska, Arizona, Idaho, Indiana, Kentucky, Michigan, Missouri, Montana, Oklahoma, Tennessee, Utah, Vermont	
This state recognizes permits from the following states:	none	
Cost & Term of Permit:	$10 for permit	1 year
Key Government Offices:	Iowa Department of Public Safety Wallace State Office Building Des Moines, Iowa 50319 Phone: (515) 281-3211 Email: webteam@dps.state.ia.us	Attorney General 1305 E. Walnut Street Des Moines, Iowa 50319 Phone: 515-281-5164 Fax: 515-281-4209 Email: webteam@ag.state.ia.us
	http://www.state.ia.us/government/dps/index.html	

Right-to-Carry Reciprocity and Recognition, cont.

Kansas

Right-To-Carry Law Type: Non-Issue

Issuing Authority:	Permits Not Available	
Contact agency for out of state permits:	Permits Not Granted.	
These states recognize your permit:	none	
This state recognizes permits from the following states:	none	
Cost & Term of Permit:	n/a	n/a
Key Government Offices:	Attorney General 301 S.W. 10th Avenue Topeka, Kansas 66612-1597 Phone: (785) 296-2215 Fax: (785) 296-6296 Email: GENERAL@at01po.wpo.state.ks.us	Highway Patrol General Headquarters 122 SW 7th Street Topeka, Kansas 66603-3847 Phone: 785-296-6800 Fax: 785-296-3049
	http://www.ink.org/public/ksag/	

Kentucky

Right-To-Carry Law Type: Shall Issue

Issuing Authority:	State Police	
Contact agency for out of state permits:	Permits not granted.	
These states recognize your permit:	Alabama, Alaska, Arizona, Arkansas, Colorado, Florida, Georgia, Idaho, Indiana, Louisiana, Michigan, Mississippi, Missouri, Montana, New Hampshire, North Carolina, North Dakota, Oklahoma, South Dakota, Pennsylvania, Tennessee, Texas, Utah, West Virginia, Vermont, Wyoming	
This state recognizes permits from the following states:	All state permits recognized.	
Cost & Term of Permit:	$60	5 years
Key Government Offices:	Kentucky State Police 919 Versailles Road Frankfort, Kentucky 40601 Phone: (502) 227-8725	Office of the Kentucky Attorney General Frankfort, Kentucky 40601 Phone: (502) 696-5300
	http://www.kentuckystatepolice.org/conceal.htm#recip	

Louisiana

Right-To-Carry Law Type: Shall Issue

Issuing Authority:	Department of Public Safety & Corrections	
Contact agency for out of state permits:	Permits not granted.	
These states recognize your permit:	Alaska, Arizona, Florida, Idaho, Indiana, Kentucky, Michigan, Minnesota, Missouri, Montana, Oklahoma, Tennessee, Texas, Utah, Vermont, Virginia, Wyoming	
This state recognizes permits from the following states:	Florida, Kentucky, Tennessee, Texas, Wyoming	
Cost & Term of Permit:	$50 for 2 year permit, $100 for 4 year permit.	2 years or 4 years
Key Government Offices:	Louisiana State Police/Department of Public Safety P.O. Box 66614 Baton Rouge, Louisiana 70896-6614 Phone: 225-925-4239 Fax: 225-925-3717 Email: concealed-handguns@dps.state.la.us	Louisiana Attorney General State Capitol, 22nd Floor P.O. Bos 940005 Baton Rouge, Louisiana 70804-9005 Phone: (225) 342-7013 Fax: (225) 342-7335 http://www.ag.state.la.us
	http://www.lsp.org/handguns	

Right-to-Carry Reciprocity and Recognition, cont.

Maine

Right-To-Carry Law Type: Shall Issue

Issuing Authority:	Dept of Public Safety, Maine State Police, Licensing Division	
Contact agency for out of state permits:	Chief of State Police	
These states recognize your permit:	Alaska, Idaho, Indiana, Kentucky, Michigan, Missouri, Oklahoma, Tennessee, Utah, Vermont	
This state recognizes permits from the following states:	none	
Cost & Term of Permit:	Residents: new $35. renewal $20. Non residents: new & renewal $60.	4 years
Key Government Offices:	Department of Public Safety Maine State Police, Licensing Division 164 State House Station Augusta, Maine 043333-0164 Phone: (207) 624-8775	Attorney General 6 State House Station Augusta, Maine 04333 Phone: (207) 626-8800 http://www.me.state.us.ag/homepage.htm
	http://www.state.me.us.dps/msp	

Maryland

Right-To-Carry Law Type: Restrictive May Issue

Issuing Authority:	Superintendent of State Police	
Contact agency for out of state permits:	Superintendent of State Police	
These states recognize your permit:	Alaska, Arizona, Idaho, Indiana, Kentucky, Michigan, Missouri, Montana, Oklahoma, Tennessee, Utah, Vermont	
This state recognizes permits from the following states:	none	
Cost & Term of Permit:	New $117 Renewal $74	2 years
Key Government Offices:	Maryland State Police Attn: Handgun Permit Section 7751 Washington Blvd Jessup, Maryland 20794 Phone: (410) 79-0191, (800) 525-5555	Attorney General 200 St. Paul Place Baltimore, Maryland 21202 Phone: (410) 576-6300 Fax: (410) 576-6447
	http://www.mdsp.maryland.gov/mdsp/downloads/licensingapplications	

Massachusetts

Right-To-Carry Law Type: Restrictive May Issue

Issuing Authority:	Department of State Police, Firearms Record Bureau	
Contact agency for out of state permits:	Permits are technically available for non-residents, but are rarely granted.	
These states recognize your permit:	Alaska, Arizona, Idaho, Indiana, Kentucky, Michigan, Missouri, Montana, Oklahoma, Tennessee, Utah, Vermont	
This state recognizes permits from the following states:	none	
Cost & Term of Permit:	Residents and Non-Residents: $100.	Residents: 4 years. Non res.: 1 year.
Key Government Offices:	Firearms Records Bureau Attn: Firearms License 200 Arlington Street Suite 2200 Chelsea, Massachusetts 02150 Phone: (617) 660-4780	Massachusetts State Police 470 Worcester Road Framingham, Massachusetts 01702 Phone: (508) 820-2300 Email: msp.webmaster@pol.state.ma.us
	http://www.state.ma.us/msp/firearms/index.htm	

REFERENCE

Right-to-Carry Reciprocity and Recognition, cont.

Michigan	Right-To-Carry Law Type: Shall Issue	
Issuing Authority:	County Gun Board/Sheriff	
Contact agency for out of state permits:	Permits not granted.	
These states recognize your permit:	Alabama, Alaska, Arizona, Colorado, Delaware, Florida, Georgia, Idaho, Indiana, Kentucky, Minnesota, Montana, Missouri, New Hampshire, North Carolina, North Dakota, Oklahoma, Pennsylvania, South Dakota, Tennessee, Utah, Vermont, Virginia, Wyoming	
This state recognizes permits from the following states:	All state permits recognized, as long as permit holder is resident of issuing state.	
Cost & Term of Permit:	$105 New and renewal.	5 years
Key Government Offices:	Michigan Department of State Police 714 S. Harrison Road East Lansing, Michigan 48823 Phone: (517) 332-2521	Michigan Attorney General P.O. Box 30212 Lansing, Michigan 48909 Phone: (517) 373-1110 Fax: (517) 241-1850 http://www.ag.state.mi.us
	http://www.michigan.gov/msp	

Minnesota	Right-To-Carry Law Type: Shall Issue	
Issuing Authority:	Chief of Police/County Sheriff	
Contact agency for out of state permits:	Any Minnesota County Sheriff	
These states recognize your permit:	Alaska, Arizona, Idaho, Indiana, Kentucky, Michigan, Missouri, Montana, Oklahoma, Tennessee, Utah, Vermont	
This state recognizes permits from the following states:	Michigan, Louisiana, Wyoming	
Cost & Term of Permit:	Not to exceed $100.	5 years
Key Government Offices:	Minnesota Department of Public Safety 444 Cedar Street Saint Paul, Minnesota 55101 Phone: (651) 282-6565 bca.permitstocarry@state.mn.us	Minnesota Attorney General 102 State Capitol St. Paul, Minnesota 55155 Phone: (651) 296-6196 Fax: (651) 297-4193 http://www.ag.state.mn.us
	http://www.dps.state.mn.us/bca/CJIS/documents/carrypermits/states.html	

Mississippi	Right-To-Carry Law Type: Shall Issue	
Issuing Authority:	Department of Public Safety/Highway Patrol	
Contact agency for out of state permits:	Permits not granted.	
These states recognize your permit:	Alabama, Alaska, Florida, Idaho, Indiana, Kentucky, Michigan, Missouri, Montana, Oklahoma, Tennessee, Utah, Vermont, Wyoming	
This state recognizes permits from the following states:	Alabama, Florida, Kentucky, Tennessee, Wyoming	
Cost & Term of Permit:	New: $100. Renewal: $50.	4 years
Key Government Offices:	Mississippi State Police P. O. Box 958 Jackson, Mississippi 39205-0958 Phone: (601) 987-1586 Email: jtucker@dps.state.ms.us	Attorney General P.O. Box 220 Jackson, Mississippi 39205-0220 Phone: (601) 359-3680 http://www.ago.state.ms.us
	http://www.dps.state.ms.us/dps/dps.nsf	

Right-to-Carry Reciprocity and Recognition, cont.

Missouri	Right-To-Carry Law Type: Shall Issue	
Issuing Authority:	County Sheriff	
Contact agency for out of state permits:	Permits not granted.	
These states recognize your permit:	Alaska, Arizona, Idaho, Indiana, Kentucky, Michigan, New Hampshire, Oklahoma, Tennessee, Utah, Vermont	
This state recognizes permits from the following states:	All state permits are recognized.	
Cost & Term of Permit:	$100	3 years
Key Government Offices:	Deparment of Public Safety P.O. Box 749 Jefferson City, Missouri 65102-0749 Phone: (573) 751-4905 Fax: (573) 751-5399	Attorney General Supreme Court Building 207 W. High St. P.O. Box 899 Jefferson City, Missouri 65102 Phone: (573) 751-3321 Fax: (573) 751-0774
	http://www.dps.state.mo.us	

Montana	Right-To-Carry Law Type: Shall Issue	
Issuing Authority:	County Sheriff	
Contact agency for out of state permits:	Permits not granted.	
These states recognize your permit:	Alaska, Arizona, Colorado, Florida, Idaho, Indiana, Kentucky, Michigan, Missouri, North Carolina, North Dakota, Oklahoma, South Carolina, Tennessee, Utah, Vermont, Wyoming	
This state recognizes permits from the following states:	Alaska, Arizona, Arkansas, California, Colorado, Connecticut, Florida, Georgia, Idaho, Indiana, Iowa, Kentucky, Louisiana, Maryland, Massachusetts, Michigan, Minnesota, Mississippi, Nevada, New Jersey, New Mexico, New York, North Carolina, North Dakota, Oklahoma, Oregon, Pennsylvania, South Carolina, South Dakota, Tennessee, Texas, Utah, Virginia, Washington, West Virginia, Wyoming	
Cost & Term of Permit:	New: $50. Renewal: $25.	4 years
Key Government Offices:	Montana Highway Patrol 2550 Prospect Ave. P.O. Box 201419 Helena, Montana 59620-1419 Phone: (406) 444-3780 Fax: (406) 444-4169	Montana Attorney General P.O. Box 201401 Helena, Montana 59620-1401 Phone: 406-444-2026 Fax: 406-444-3549 contact:doj@state.mt.us
	http://www.doj.state.mt.us/enforcement/concealedweapons.asp	

Nebraska	Right-To-Carry Law Type: Non-Issue	
Issuing Authority:	Permits not available	
Contact agency for out of state permits:	Permits not granted.	
These states recognize your permit:	none	
This state recognizes permits from the following states:	none	
Cost & Term of Permit:	n.a	n.a
Key Government Offices:	Nebraska State Patrol P.O. Box 94907 Lincoln, Nebraska 68509 Phone: 402-471-4545	Attorney General 2115 State Capitol P.O. Box 98920 Lincoln, Nebraska 68509-8920 Phone: 402-471-2682 Fax: 402-471-3297
	http://www.nsp.state.ne.us	

Right-to-Carry Reciprocity and Recognition, cont.

Nevada	Right-To-Carry Law Type: Shall Issue	
Issuing Authority:	County Sheriff	
Contact agency for out of state permits:	In person with any County Sheriff	
These states recognize your permit:	Alaska, Arizona, Idaho, Indiana, Kentucky, Michigan, Missouri, Montana, Oklahoma, Tennessee, Utah, Vermont	
This state recognizes permits from the following states:	none	
Cost & Term of Permit:	New $60. Renewal $25	5 years; 3 years non-resident
Key Government Offices:		Office of the Attorney General 100 N. Carson Street Carson City, Nevada 89701-4717 Phone: (775)684-1100 Fax: (775) 684-1108 Email: aginfo@ag.state.nv.us
	http://www.ag.state.nv.us	

New Hampshire	Right-To-Carry Law Type: Shall Issue	
Issuing Authority:	Selectman/Mayor or Chief of Police	
Contact agency for out of state permits:	Director of State Police	
These states recognize your permit:	Alabama, Alaska, Colorado, Florida, Georgia, Idaho, Indiana, Kentucky, Michigan, Missouri, North Carolina, North Dakota, Oklahoma, Tennessee, Utah, Vermont, Wyoming	
This state recognizes permits from the following states:	Alabama, Alaska, Colorado, Florida, Georgia, Idaho, Indiana, Kentucky, Michigan, North Carolina, North Dakota, Oklahoma, Tennesse, Wyoming	
Cost & Term of Permit:	Residents: $10. Non Residents: $20.	4 years
Key Government Offices:	Director of State Police Permits and Licensing Unit 10 Hazen Drive Concord, New Hampshire 03301 Phone: (603) 271-3575 Fax: (603) 271-1153	
	http://www.state.nh.us/safety/nhsp/plupr.html	

New Jersey	Right-To-Carry Law Type: Restrictive May Issue	
Issuing Authority:	Chief of Police/Superintendent of State Police	
Contact agency for out of state permits:	Superintendent of State Police--Permits are technically available for non-residents, but are rarely granted.	
These states recognize your permit:	Alaska, Idaho, Indiana, Kentucky, Michigan, Missouri, Montana, Oklahoma, Tennessee, Utah, Vermont	
This state recognizes permits from the following states:	none	
Cost & Term of Permit:	$20	2 years
Key Government Offices:	New Jersey State Police Firearms Investigation Unit PO Box 7068 West Trenton, NJ 08628-0068 609-882-2000 ext. 2664	Office of the Attorney General Dept. of Law & Public Safety P.O. Box 080 Trenton, New Jersey 08625-0080 Phone: (609) 292-4925, Fax: (609) 292-3508 http://www.njpublicsafety.com
	http://www.njsp.org/faq.html#firearms	

REFERENCE

Right-to-Carry Reciprocity and Recognition, cont.

New Mexico

Right-To-Carry Law Type: Shall Issue

Issuing Authority:	Department of Public Safety	
Contact agency for out of state permits:	Permits not granted.	
These states recognize your permit:	Alaska, Arizona, Colorado, Idaho, Indiana, Kentucky, Michigan, Missouri, Oklahoma, Tennessee, Utah, Vermont	
This state recognizes permits from the following states:	A list of reciprocal states is not available at this time, since New Mexico's new law was implemented 1/1/2004.	
Cost & Term of Permit:	$100 for initial permit plus fingerprint fee. $50 for renewal.	2 years
Key Government Offices:	Department of Public Safety P.O. Box 1628 Santa Fe, New Mexico 87504 Phone: (505) 827-3370 or (505) 827-9000	Attorney General 407 Galisteo Street Bataan Memorial Building, Rm 260 Santa Fe, New Mexico 87501 Phone: (505) 827-6000, Fax: (505) 827-5826 http://www.ago.state.nm.us
	http://www.dps.nm.org/	

New York

Right-To-Carry Law Type: Restrictive May Issue

Issuing Authority:	Varies by county	
Contact agency for out of state permits:	Permits not granted.	
These states recognize your permit:	Alaska, Idaho, Indiana, Kentucky, Michigan, Missouri, Montana, Oklahoma, Tennessee, Utah, Vermont	
This state recognizes permits from the following states:	none	
Cost & Term of Permit:	Varies by county	Varies, 2 years to lifetime
Key Government Offices:	State Police Counsel's Office Bldg. 22, 1220 Washington Ave. Albany, New York 12226 Phone: (518) 457-6811	Attorney General 120 Broadway New York, New York 10271-0332 Phone: (212)416-8050 http://www.oag.state.ny.us
	http://www.troopers.state.ny.us/firearms/firearmsindex.html	

North Carolina

Right-To-Carry Law Type: Shall Issue

Issuing Authority:	County Sheriff	
Contact agency for out of state permits:	Permits not granted.	
These states recognize your permit:	Alabama, Alaska, Arizona, Colorado, Delaware, Florida, Georgia, Idaho, Indiana, Kentucky, Michigan, Missouri, Montana, New Hampshire, Oklahoma, Pennsylvania, South Carolina, South Dakota, Tennessee, Utah, Vermont, Virginia	
This state recognizes permits from the following states:	Alabama, Alaska, Arkansas, Arizona, Colorado, Delaware, Florida, Georgia, Idaho, Indiana, Kentucky, Michigan, Montana, New Hampshire, Oklahoma, Pennsylvania, South Carolina, South Dakota, Tennessee, Utah, Virginia, Wyoming	
Cost & Term of Permit:	$80 permit fee	5 years
Key Government Offices:	North Carolina Highway Partol 512 N. Salisbury Street 4702 Mail Service Center Raleigh, North Carolina 27699-4702 Phone: (919) 733-7952 Email: Webmaster@ncshp.org	Attorney General North Carolina Department of Justice P.O. Box 629 Raleigh, North Carolina 27602-0629 Phone: 919-716-6400 Fax: 919-716-6750 Email: agjus@mail.jus.state.nc.us
	http://www.jus.state.nc.us/	

Right-to-Carry Reciprocity and Recognition, cont.

North Dakota

Right-To-Carry Law Type: Shall Issue

Issuing Authority:	Chief of the Bureau of Criminal Investigation	
Contact agency for out of state permits:	Chief of the Bureau of Criminal Investigation	
These states recognize your permit:	Alabama, Alaska*, Arizona, Delaware, Florida*, Idaho, Indiana, Kentucky, Michigan, Missouri, Montana, New Hampshire, Oklahoma, South Dakota, Tennessee, Utah, Vermont, Wyoming *Must be 21 years old	
This state recognizes permits from the following states:	Alabama, Alaska*, Arizona, Florida*, Indiana, Kentucky, Michigan, Montana, New Hampshire, Oklahoma, South Dakota, Tennessee**, Utah, Wyoming *Must be 21 years old **Handguns only	
Cost & Term of Permit:	$25	3 years
Key Government Offices:	North Dakota Office of Attorney General Bureau of Criminal Investigation Bismarck, North Dakota 58502-1054 Phone: (701) 328-5500 Fax: (701) 328-5510 Email: bciinfo@state.nd.us	Office of Attorney General State Capitol 600 E Boulevard Ave. Dept 125 Bismarck, North Dakota 58505-0040 Phone: (701) 328-2210 Fax: (701) 328-2226 Email: ndag@state.nd.us
	http://www.ag.state.nd.us/BCI/reciprocity.htm	

Ohio

Right-To-Carry Law Type: Shall Issue

Issuing Authority:	County Sheriff	
Contact agency for out of state permits:	Permits not granted.	
These states recognize your permit:	Many states will recognize Ohio permits, once Ohio begins issuing them and the Attorney General has reciprocal agreements in place.	
This state recognizes permits from the following states:	HB 12, which gave Ohio citizens the right to carry a firearm concealed, become law in January, 2004. The Attorney General must now negotiate reciprocal agreements with other states.	
Cost & Term of Permit:	$45 new and renewal	4 years
Key Government Offices:	Ohio Highway Patrol P O Box 182074 Columbus, Ohio 43232 http://www.state.oh.us/ohiostatepatrol	Attorney General 30 E. Broad Street 17th Floor Columbus, Ohio 43215-3420 Phone: (614) 466-4320 Fax: (614) 466-5057
	http://www.ag.state.oh.us/	

Oklahoma

Right-To-Carry Law Type: Shall Issue

Issuing Authority:	State Bureau of Investigation	
Contact agency for out of state permits:	Permits not granted.	
These states recognize your permit:	Alabama, Alaska, Arkansas, Arizona, Colorado, Delaware, Florida. Idaho, Indiana, Kentucky, Michigan, Missouri, Montana, New Hampshire, North Carolina, North Dakota, Tennessee, Texas, Utah, Virginia, Vermont, Wyoming	
This state recognizes permits from the following states:	All state permits recognized.	
Cost & Term of Permit:	New $100, Renewal $85.	5 years
Key Government Offices:	Oklahoma State Bureau of Investigation 6600 N. Harvey Suite 300 Oklahoma City, Oklahoma 73116 Phone: (405) 848-6724 or (800)207-6724 outside OK City sda@osbi.state.ok.us	Attorney General 112 State Capitol 2300 N. Lincoln Blvd. Oklahoma City, Oklahoma 73105 Phone: (405) 521-3921, Fax: (405) 521-6246 http://www.oag.state.of.us
	http://www.osbi.state.ok.us/sda.htm	

Oregon

Right-To-Carry Law Type: Shall Issue

Issuing Authority:	County Sheriff	
Contact agency for out of state permits:	Discretionary to residents of contiguous states only	
These states recognize your permit:	Alaska, Arizona, Idaho, Indiana, Kentucky, Michigan, Missouri, Montana, Oklahoma, Tennessee, Utah, Vermont	
This state recognizes permits from the following states:	none	
Cost & Term of Permit:	New: $65. Renewal $50.	4 years
Key Government Offices:	State Police 400 Public Service Bldg. 255 Capitol St. N.E. Salem, Oregon 97310 Phone: (503) 378-3720 Fax: (503) 378-8282 http://www.osp.state.or.us	Attorney General Justice Department 1162 Court St. NE Salem Oregon, 97310 Phone: (503) 378-4400, Fax: (503) 378-5938 http://www.doj.state.or.us
	http://www.osp.state.or.us	

Pennsylvania

Right-To-Carry Law Type: Shall Issue

Issuing Authority:	County Sheriff or Chief of Police	
Contact agency for out of state permits:	Any Sheriff's Department	
These states recognize your permit:	Alaska, Florida, Georgia, Idaho, Indiana, Kentucky, Michigan, Missouri, Montana, North Carolina, Oklahoma, Tennessee, Utah, Vermont, Wyoming	
This state recognizes permits from the following states:	Florida, Georgia, Kentucky, Michigan, North Carolina, Wyoming	
Cost & Term of Permit:	$19	5 years
Key Government Offices:	State Police 1800 Elmerton Avenue Harrisburg, Pennsylvania 17110-9758 Phone: (717) 783-5599 Fax: (717) 787-2948	Attorney General 16th Floor, Strawberry Square Harrisburg, Pennsylvania 17120 Phone: 717-787-3391 Fax: (717) 787-8242 http://www.attorneygeneral.gov
	http://www.psp.state.pa.us	

Rhode Island

Right-To-Carry Law Type: Restrictive May Issue

Issuing Authority:	Attorney General	
Contact agency for out of state permits:	Attorney General by mail only. Permits are technically available for non-residents, but are rarely granted.	
These states recognize your permit:	Alaska, Idaho, Indiana, Kentucky, Michigan, Missouri, Oklahoma, Tennessee, Utah, Vermont	
This state recognizes permits from the following states:	none	
Cost & Term of Permit:	$40	4 years
Key Government Offices:	State Police 311 Danielson Pike North Scituate, Rhode Island 02857 Phone: (401) 444-1000 Fax: (401) 444-1105 http://www.risp.state.ri.us	Attorney General 150 South Main Street Providence, Rhode Island 02903 Phone: (401) 274-4400 Fax: (401) 222-1331 http://www.riag.state.ri.us
	http://www.riag.state.ri.us/	

Right-to-Carry Reciprocity and Recognition, cont.

South Carolina

Right-To-Carry Law Type: Shall Issue

Issuing Authority:	S.C. Law Enforcement Division	
Contact agency for out of state permits:	Permits not granted.	
These states recognize your permit:	Alaska, Arizona, Arkansas, Idaho, Indiana, Kentucky, Michigan, Missouri, Montana, North Carolina, Oklahoma, Tennessee, Utah, Vermont, Virginia, Wyoming	
This state recognizes permits from the following states:	Arkansas, North Carolina, Tennessee, Wyoming	
Cost & Term of Permit:	$50	4 years
Key Government Offices:	South Carolina Law Enforcement Division Attn: Regulatory Services Unit P.O. Box 21398 Columbia, South Carolina 29221 Phone: 803-896-7014	Attorney General Box 11549 Columbia, South Carolina 29211 Phone: (803) 734-3970 Fax: (803) 253-6283 http://www.scattorneygeneral.org
	http://www.sled.state.sc.us	

South Dakota

Right-To-Carry Law Type: Shall Issue

Issuing Authority:	Chief of Police/County Sheriff	
Contact agency for out of state permits:	Permits not granted.	
These states recognize your permit:	Alaska, Colorado, Florida*, Georgia, Idaho, Indiana, Kentucky, Michigan, Missouri, Montana, North Carolina, North Dakota, Oklahoma, Tennessee, Utah, Vermont, Wyoming *must be 21	
This state recognizes permits from the following states:	Alaska, Colorado*, Florida, Georgia, Indiana, Kentucky, Michigan, Montana, North Carolina, North Dakota, Tennessee, Utah, Wyoming *must be 21	
Cost & Term of Permit:	$10	4 years
Key Government Offices:	Highway Patrol 118 West Capitol Pierre, South Dakota 57501 Phone: (605) 773-3105 Fax: (605) 773-6046 http://hp.state.sd.us/information.htm	Attorney General 500 East Capitol Ave. Pierre, South Dakota 57501-5070 Phone: (605)-773-3215 Fax: 605)773-4106 http://www.state.sd.attorney/office/news/concealed.asp
	http://sdsos.gov/firearms	

Tennessee

Right-To-Carry Law Type: Shall Issue

Issuing Authority:	Department of Public Safety	
Contact agency for out of state permits:	Permits not granted.	
These states recognize your permit:	Alaska, Arizona, Arkansas, Colorado, Delaware, Florida, Georgia, Idaho, Indiana, Kentucky, Louisiana, Michigan, Mississippi, Missouri, Montana, New Hampshire, North Carolina, North Dakota, Oklahoma, South Carolina, South Dakota, Texas, Utah, Virginia, Vermont, Wyoming	
This state recognizes permits from the following states:	All state permits recognized.	
Cost & Term of Permit:	New: $115; Renewal: $50	4 years
Key Government Offices:	Tennessee Department of Safety Attn: Handgun Carry Permit Office 1150 Foster Ave Nashville, Tennessee 37249-1000 Phone: (615) 251-8590	Attorney General P.O. Box 20207 Nashville, Tennessee 37202 Phone: (615) 741-3491 Fax: (615) 741-2009 http://www.attorneygeneral.state.tn.us
	http://www.state.tn.us/safety/	

Texas

Right-To-Carry Law Type: Shall Issue

Issuing Authority:	Department of Public Safety	
Contact agency for out of state permits:	Department of Public Safety	
These states recognize your permit:	Alaska, Arizona, Arkansas, Florida, Idaho, Indiana, Kentucky, Louisiana, Michigan, Missouri, Montana, Oklahoma, Tennessee, Utah, Virginia, Vermont, Wyoming	
This state recognizes permits from the following states:	Arizona, Arkansas, Florida, Kentucky, Louisiana, Oklahoma, Tennessee. Wyoming	
Cost & Term of Permit:	$140 ($70 for seniors)	4 years
Key Government Offices:	Texas Department of Public Safety Concealed Handgun Licensing Section P O Box 4143 Austin, Texas 78791-4143 Phone: (512) 424-7293 or (800) 224-5744 http://www.txdps.state.tx.us	Attorney General P. O. Box 12548 Austin, Texas 78711-2548 Phone: (512) 463-2100 Fax: (512) 463-2063 http://www.oag.state.tx.us
	http://www.txdps.state.tx.us/administration/crime_records/chl/reciprocity.htm	

Utah

Right-To-Carry Law Type: Shall Issue

Issuing Authority:	Department of Public Safety	
Contact agency for out of state permits:	Department of Public Safety	
These states recognize your permit:	Alabama, Alaska, Arizona, Arkansas, Delaware, Florida, Idaho, Indiana, Kentucky, Michigan, Missouri, Montana, North Carolina, North Dakota, Oklahoma, South Dakota, Vermont, Wyoming	
This state recognizes permits from the following states:	All state permits recognized.	
Cost & Term of Permit:	New $35, $10 Renewal	5 years
Key Government Offices:	Utah Department of Public Safety Bureau of Criminal Identification 3888 W. 5400 S. P.O. Box 148280 Salt Lake City, Utah 84114-8280 Phone: (801) 965-4445	Utah Attorney General 236 State Capitol Salt Lake City, Utah 84114 Phone: (801) 366-0260 Fax: (801) 538-1121 http://www.attorneygeneral.utah.gov
	http://bci.utah.gov/cfp/cfphome.html	

Vermont

Right-To-Carry Law Type: Permits Not Required

Issuing Authority:	Permits Not Required	
Contact agency for out of state permits:	Permits Not Required	
These states recognize your permit:	none	
This state recognizes permits from the following states:	Permits Not Required	
Cost & Term of Permit:	n/a	n/a
Key Government Offices:		Attorney General 109 State Street Montpelier, Vermont 05609-1001 Phone: (802) 828 3171 Fax: (802) 828 2154
	http://www.state.vt.us/atg/	

Right-to-Carry Reciprocity and Recognition, cont.

Virginia

Right-To-Carry Law Type: Shall Issue

Issuing Authority:	State Circuit Court of residence	
Contact agency for out of state permits:	Permits not granted.	
These states recognize your permit:	Alaska, Idaho, Indiana, Kentucky, Michigan, Missouri, Montana, North Carolina, Oklahoma, Tennessee, Utah, West Virginia, Vermont	
This state recognizes permits from the following states:	Alaska, Arizona, Arkansas, Idaho, Louisiana, Michigan, North Carolina, Oklahoma, South Carolina, Tennessee, Texas, Utah, Washington, West Virginia	
Cost & Term of Permit:	no more than $50	5 years
Key Government Offices:	Virginia State Police P.O. Box 27472 Richmond, Virginia 23261 Phone: (804) 674-2000	Attorney General 900 East Main Street Richmond, Virginia 23219 Phone: (804) 786-2071 Fax: (804) 786-1991 http://www.oag.state.va.us
	http://www.vsp.state.va.us/vsp.html	

Washington

Right-To-Carry Law Type: Shall Issue

Issuing Authority:	Chief of Police/Sheriff	
Contact agency for out of state permits:	Permits not granted.	
These states recognize your permit:	Alaska, Idaho, Indiana, Kentucky, Michigan, Missouri, Montana, Oklahoma, Tennessee, Utah, Vermont, Virginia	
This state recognizes permits from the following states:	none	
Cost & Term of Permit:	New: $36; Renewal: $32	5 years
Key Government Offices:	Washington State Patrol General Administration Building PO Box 42600 Olympia, Washington 98504-2600 Phone: (360) 753-6540 Fax: (360) 753-2492	Attorney General 1125 Washington St. SE Olympia, Washington 98504-0100 Phone: (360) 753-6200 Fax: (360) 664-0988 http://www.atg.wa.gov
	http://www.wsp.wa.gov/newsfaqs/answers.htm#weapons	

West Virginia

Right-To-Carry Law Type: Shall Issue

Issuing Authority:	County Sheriff	
Contact agency for out of state permits:	Permits not granted.	
These states recognize your permit:	Alaska, Arizona, Idaho, Indiana, Kentucky, Michigan, Missouri, Montana, Oklahoma, Tennessee, Utah, Vermont, Virginia	
This state recognizes permits from the following states:	Kentucky, Virginia	
Cost & Term of Permit:	$60	5 years
Key Government Offices:	West Virginia State Police 725 Jefferson Road South Charleston, West Virginia 25309 Phone: (304) 746-2100 Fax: (304) 746-2246	Attorney General State Capitol, Room 26-E 1900 Kanawha Blvd. East Charleston, West Virginia 25305-0220 Phone: (304) 558-2021 Fax: (304) 558-0140
	http://www.wvstatepolice.com/legal/legal.shtml	

Right-to-Carry Reciprocity and Recognition, cont.

Wisconsin

Right-To-Carry Law Type: Non-Issue

Issuing Authority:	Permits not available	
Contact agency for out of state permits:	Permits not granted.	
These states recognize your permit:	none	
This state recognizes permits from the following states:	none	
Cost & Term of Permit:	n/a	n/a
Key Government Offices:		Attorney General 123 West Washington Ave. PO Box 7857 Madison, Wisconsin 53707-7857 Phone: 608-266-1221 Fax: 608-267-2779
	http://www.doj.state.wi.us/	

Wyoming

Right-To-Carry Law Type: Shall Issue

Issuing Authority:	Attorney General	
Contact agency for out of state permits:	Permits not granted.	
These states recognize your permit:	Alabama, Alaska, Arizona, Colorado, Florida, Georgia, Idaho, Indiana, Kentucky, Louisiana, Michigan, Minnesota, Mississippi, Missouri, Montana, New Hampshire, North Carolina, North Dakota, Oklahoma, Pennsylvania, South Carolina, South Dakota, Tennessee, Texas, Utah, Vermont	
This state recognizes permits from the following states:	Alabama, Alaska, Colorado, Florida, Georgia, Idaho, Indiana, Kentucky, Louisiana, Michigan, Mississippi, Montana, New Hampshire, North Carolina, North Dakota, Oklahoma, Pennsylvania, South Carolina, South Dakota, Tennessee, Texas, Utah	
Cost & Term of Permit:	$74	5 years
Key Government Offices:		Wyoming Attorney General's Office 123 Capitol Building 200 W. 24th Street Cheyenne, Wyoming 82002 Phone: (307) 777-7841 Fax: (307) 777-6869
	http://attorneygeneral.state.dci.cwp.html	

REFERENCE

ARMS ASSOCIATIONS

UNITED STATES

ALABAMA

Alabama Gun Collectors Assn.
Secretary, P.O. Box 70965, Tuscaloosa, AL 35407

ALASKA

Alaska Gun Collectors Assn., Inc.
C.W. Floyd, Pres., 5240 Little Tree, Anchorage, AK 99507

ARIZONA

Arizona Arms Assn.
Don DeBusk, President, 4837 Bryce Ave., Glendale, AZ 85301

CALIFORNIA

California Cartridge Collectors Assn.
Rick Montgomery, 1729 Christina, Stockton, CA 95204/209-463-7216 evs.

California Waterfowl Assn.
4630 Northgate Blvd., #150, Sacramento, CA 95834

Greater Calif. Arms & Collectors Assn.
Donald L. Bullock, 8291 Carburton St., Long Beach, CA 90808-3302

Los Angeles Gun Ctg. Collectors Assn.
F.H. Ruffra, 20810 Amie Ave., Apt. #9, Torrance, CA 90503

Stock Gun Players Assn.
6038 Appian Way, Long Beach, CA, 90803

COLORADO

Colorado Gun Collectors Assn.
L.E.(Bud) Greenwald, 2553 S. Quitman St., Denver, CO 80219/303-935-3850

Rocky Mountain Cartridge Collectors Assn.
John Roth, P.O. Box 757, Conifer, CO 80433

CONNECTICUT

Ye Connecticut Gun Guild, Inc.
Dick Fraser, P.O. Box 425, Windsor, CT 06095

FLORIDA

Unified Sportsmen of Florida
P.O. Box 6565, Tallahassee, FL 32314

GEORGIA

Georgia Arms Collectors Assn., Inc.
Michael Kindberg, President, P.O. Box 277, Alpharetta, GA 30239-0277

ILLINOIS

Illinois State Rifle Assn.
P.O. Box 637, Chatsworth, IL 60921

Mississippi Valley Gun & Cartridge Coll. Assn.
Bob Filbert, P.O. Box 61, Port Byron, IL 61275/309-523-2593

Sauk Trail Gun Collectors
Gordell M. Matson, P.O. Box 1113, Milan, IL 61264

Wabash Valley Gun Collectors Assn., Inc.
Roger L. Dorsett, 2601 Willow Rd., Urbana, IL 61801/217-384-7302

INDIANA

Indiana State Rifle & Pistol Assn.
Thos. Glancy, P.O. Box 552, Chesterton, IN 46304

Southern Indiana Gun Collectors Assn., Inc.
Sheila McClary, 309 W. Monroe St., Boonville, IN 47601/812-897-3742

IOWA

Beaver Creek Plainsmen Inc.
Steve Murphy, Secy., P.O. Box 298, Bondurant, IA 50035

Central States Gun Collectors Assn.
Dennis Greischar, Box 841, Mason City, IA 50402-0841

KANSAS

Kansas Cartridge Collectors Assn.
Bob Linder, Box 84, Plainville, KS 67663

KENTUCKY

Kentuckiana Arms Collectors Assn.
Charles Billips, President, Box 1776, Louisville, KY 40201

Kentucky Gun Collectors Assn., Inc.
Ruth Johnson, Box 64, Owensboro, KY 42302/502-729-4197

LOUISIANA

Washitaw River Renegades
Sandra Rushing, P.O. Box 256, Main St., Grayson, LA 71435

MARYLAND

Baltimore Antique Arms Assn.
Mr. Cillo, 1034 Main St., Darlington, MD 21304

MASSACHUSETTS

Bay Colony Weapons Collectors, Inc.
John Brandt, Box 111, Hingham, MA 02043

Massachusetts Arms Collectors
Bruce E. Skinner, P.O. Box 31, No. Carver, MA 02355/508-866-5259

MICHIGAN

Association for the Study and Research of .22 Caliber Rimfire Cartridges
George Kass, 4512 Nakoma Dr., Okemos, MI 48864

MINNESOTA

Sioux Empire Cartridge Collectors Assn.
Bob Cameron, 14597 Glendale Ave. SE, Prior Lake, MN 55372

MISSISSIPPI

Mississippi Gun Collectors Assn.
Jack E. Swinney, P.O. Box 16323, Hattiesburg, MS 39402

MISSOURI

Greater St. Louis Cartridge Collectors Assn.
Don MacChesney, 634 Scottsdale Rd., Kirkwood, MO 63122-1109

Mineral Belt Gun Collectors Assn.
D.F. Saunders, 1110 Cleveland Ave., Monett, MO 65708

Missouri Valley Arms Collectors Assn., Inc.
L.P Brammer II, Membership Secy., P.O. Box 33033, Kansas City, MO 64114

MONTANA

Montana Arms Collectors Assn.
Dean E. Yearout, Sr., Exec. Secy., 1516 21st Ave. S., Great Falls, MT 59405

Weapons Collectors Society of Montana
R.G. Schipf, Ex. Secy., 3100 Bancroft St., Missoula, MT 59801/406-728-2995

NEBRASKA

Nebraska Cartridge Collectors Club
Gary Muckel, P.O. Box 84442, Lincoln, NE 68501

NEW HAMPSHIRE

New Hampshire Arms Collectors, Inc.
James Stamatelos, Secy., P.O. Box 5, Cambridge, MA 02139

NEW JERSEY

Englishtown Benchrest Shooters Assn.
Michael Toth, 64 Cooke Ave., Carteret, NJ 07008

Jersey Shore Antique Arms Collectors
Joe Sisia, P.O. Box 100, Bayville, NJ 08721-0100

New Jersey Arms Collectors Club, Inc.
Angus Laidlaw, Vice President, 230 Valley Rd., Montclair, NJ 07042/201-746-0939; e-mail: acclaidlaw@juno.com

NEW YORK

Iroquois Arms Collectors Assn.
Bonnie Robinson, Show Secy., P.O. Box 142, Ransomville, NY 14131/716-791-4096

Mid-State Arms Coll. & Shooters Club
Jack Ackerman, 24 S. Mountain Terr., Binghamton, NY 13903

NORTH CAROLINA

North Carolina Gun Collectors Assn.
Jerry Ledford, 3231-7th St. Dr. NE, Hickory, NC 28601

OHIO

Ohio Gun Collectors Assn.
P.O. Box 9007, Maumee, OH 43537-9007/419-897-0861; Fax:419-897-0860

Shotshell Historical and Collectors Society
Madeline Bruemmer, 3886 Dawley Rd., Ravenna, OH 44266

The Stark Gun Collectors, Inc.
William I. Gann, 5666 Waynesburg Dr., Waynesburg, OH 44688

OREGON

Oregon Arms Collectors Assn., Inc.
Phil Bailey, P.O. Box 13000-A, Portland, OR 97213-0017/503-281-6864; off.:503-281-0918

Oregon Cartridge Collectors Assn.
Boyd Northrup, P.O. Box 285, Rhododendron, OR 97049

PENNSYLVANIA

Presque Isle Gun Collectors Assn.
James Welch, 156 E. 37 St., Erie, PA 16504

SOUTH CAROLINA

Belton Gun Club, Inc.
Attn. Secretary, P.O. Box 126, Belton, SC 29627/864-369-6767

Gun Owners of South Carolina
Membership Div.: William Strozier, Secretary, P.O. Box 70, Johns Island, SC 29457-0070/803-762-3240; Fax:803-795-0711; e-mail:76053.222@compuserve.com

SOUTH DAKOTA

Dakota Territory Gun Coll. Assn., Inc.
Curt Carter, Castlewood, SD 57223

TENNESSEE

Smoky Mountain Gun Coll. Assn., Inc.
Hugh W. Yabro, President, P.O. Box 23225, Knoxville, TN 37933

Tennessee Gun Collectors Assn., Inc.
M.H. Parks, 3556 Pleasant Valley Rd., Nashville, TN 37204-3419

TEXAS

Houston Gun Collectors Assn., Inc.
P.O. Box 741429, Houston, TX 77274-1429

Texas Gun Collectors Assn.
Bob Eder, Pres., P.O. Box 12067, El Paso, TX 79913/915-584-8183

Texas State Rifle Assn.
1131 Rockingham Dr., Suite 101, Richardson, TX 75080-4326

VIRGINIA

Virginia Gun Collectors Assn., Inc.
Addison Hurst, Secy., 38802 Charlestown Height, Waterford, VA 20197/540-882-3543

WASHINGTON

Association of Cartridge Collectors on the Pacific Northwest
Robert Jardin, 14214 Meadowlark Drive KPN, Gig Harbor, WA 98329

Washington Arms Collectors, Inc.
Joyce Boss, P.O. Box 389, Renton, WA, 98057-0389/206-255-8410

WISCONSIN

Great Lakes Arms Collectors Assn., Inc.
Edward C. Warnke, 2913 Woodridge Lane, Waukesha, WI 53188

Wisconsin Gun Collectors Assn., Inc.
Lulita Zellmer, P.O. Box 181, Sussex, WI 53089

WYOMING

Wyoming Weapons Collectors
P.O. Box 284, Laramie, WY 82073/307-745-4652 or 745-9530

NATIONAL ORGANIZATIONS

Amateur Trapshooting Assn.
David D. Bopp, Exec. Director, 601 W. National Rd., Vandalia, OH 45377/937-898-4638; Fax:937-898-5472

American Airgun Field Target Assn.
5911 Cherokee Ave., Tampa, FL 33604

American Coon Hunters Assn.
Opal Johnston, P.O. Cadet, Route 1, Box 492, Old Mines, MO 63630

American Custom Gunmakers Guild
Jan Billeb, Exec. Director, 22 Vista View Drive, Cody, WY 82414-9606 (307) 587-4297 (phone/fax). Email: acgg@acgg.org Website: www.acgg.org

American Defense Preparedness Assn.
Two Colonial Place, 2101 Wilson Blvd., Suite 400, Arlington, VA 22201-3061

American Paintball League
P.O. Box 3561, Johnson City, TN 37602/800-541-9169

American Pistolsmiths Guild
Alex B. Hamilton, Pres., 1449 Blue Crest Lane, San Antonio, TX 78232/210-494-3063

American Police Pistol & Rifle Assn.
3801 Biscayne Blvd., Miami, FL 33137

American Single Shot Rifle Assn.
Gary Staup, Secy., 709 Carolyn Dr., Delphos, OH 45833/419-692-3866. Website: www.assra.com

American Society of Arms Collectors
George E. Weatherly, P.O. Box 2567, Waxahachie, TX 75165

American Tactical Shooting Assn.(A.T.S.A.)
c/o Skip Gochenour, 2600 N. Third St., Harrisburg, PA 17110/717-233-0402; Fax:717-233-5340

Association of Firearm and Tool Mark Examiners
Lannie G. Emanuel, Secy., Southwest Institute of Forensic Sciences, P.O. Box 35728, Dallas, TX 75235/214-920-5979; Fax:214-920-5928; Membership Secy., Ann D. Jones, VA Div. of Forensic Science, P.O. Box 999, Richmond, VA 23208/804-786-4706; Fax:804-371-8328

Boone & Crockett Club
250 Station Dr., Missoula, MT 59801-2753

Browning Collectors Assn.
Secretary:Scherrie L. Brennac, 2749 Keith Dr., Villa Ridge, MO 63089/314-742-0571

The Cast Bullet Assn., Inc.
Ralland J. Fortier, Editor, 4103 Foxcraft Dr., Traverse City, MI 49684

Citizens Committee for the Right to Keep and Bear Arms
Natl. Hq., Liberty Park, 12500 NE Tenth Pl., Bellevue, WA 98005

Colt Collectors Assn.
25000 Highland Way, Los Gatos, CA 95030/408-353-2658.

Contemporary Longrifle Association
P.O. Box 2097, Staunton, VA 24402/540-886-6189. Website: www.CLA@longrifle.ws

Ducks Unlimited, Inc.
Natl. Headquarters, One Waterfowl Way, Memphis, TN 38120/901-758-3937

Fifty Caliber Shooters Assn.
PO Box 111, Monroe UT 84754-0111

Firearms Coalition/Neal Knox Associates
Box 6537, Silver Spring, MD 20906/301-871-3006

Firearms Engravers Guild of America
Rex C. Pedersen, Secy., 511 N. Rath Ave., Lundington, MI 49431/616-845-7695(Phone and Fax)

Foundation for North American Wild Sheep
720 Allen Ave., Cody, WY 82414-3402/web site: http://iigi.com/os/non/fnaws/fnaws.htm; e-mail: fnaws@wyoming.com

Freedom Arms Collectors Assn.
P.O. Box 160302, Miami, FL 33116-0302

Garand Collectors Assn.
P.O. Box 181, Richmond, KY 40475

Glock Collectors Association
P.O. Box 1063, Maryland Heights, MO 63043/314-878-2061 phone/FAX.

Glock Shooting Sports Foundation
BO Box 309, Smyrna GA 30081 770-432-1202 Website: www.gssfonline.com

Golden Eagle Collectors Assn. (G.E.C.A.)
Chris Showler, 11144 Slate Creek Rd., Grass Valley, CA 95945

REFERENCE

ARMS ASSOCIATIONS

Gun Owners of America
8001 Forbes Place, Suite 102, Springfield, VA 22151/703-321-8585

Handgun Hunters International
J.D. Jones, Director, P.O. Box 357 MAG, Bloomingdale, OH 43910

Harrington & Richardson Gun Coll. Assn.
George L. Cardet, 330 S.W. 27th Ave., Suite 603, Miami, FL 33135

High Standard Collectors' Assn.
John J. Stimson, Jr., Pres., 540 W. 92nd St., Indianapolis, IN 46260 Website: www.highstandard.org

Hopkins & Allen Arms & Memorabilia Society (HAAMS)
P.O. Box 187, 1309 Pamela Circle, Delphos, OH 45833

International Ammunition Association, Inc.
C.R. Punnett, Secy., 8 Hillock Lane, Chadds Ford, PA 19317/610-358-1285;Fax:610-358-1560

International Benchrest Shooters
Joan Borden, RR1, Box 250BB, Springville, PA 18844/717-965-2366

International Blackpowder Hunting Assn.
P.O. Box 1180, Glenrock, WY 82637/307-436-9817

IHMSA (Intl. Handgun Metallic Silhouette Assn.)
PO Box 368, Burlington, IA 52601 Website: www.ihmsa.org

International Society of Mauser Arms Collectors
Michael Kindberg, Pres., P.O. Box 277, Alpharetta, GA 30239-0277

Jews for the Preservation of Firearms Ownership (JPFO) 501(c)(3)
2872 S. Wentworth Ave., Milwaukee, WI 53207/414-769-0760; Fax:414-483-8435

The Mannlicher Collectors Assn.
Membership Office: P.O. Box1249, The Dalles, Oregon 97058

Marlin Firearms Collectors Assn., Ltd.
Dick Paterson, Secy., 407 Lincoln Bldg., 44 Main St., Champaign, IL 61820

Merwin Hulbert Association,
2503 Kentwood Ct., High Point, NC 27265

Miniature Arms Collectors/Makers Society, Ltd.
Ralph Koebbeman, Pres., 4910 Kilburn Ave., Rockford, IL 61101/815-964-2569

M1 Carbine Collectors Assn. (M1-CCA)
623 Apaloosa Ln., Gardnerville, NV 89410-7840

National Association of Buckskinners (NAB)
Territorial Dispatch—1800s Historical Publication, 4701 Marion St., Suite 324, Livestock Exchange Bldg., Denver, CO 80216/303-297-9671

The National Association of Derringer Collectors
P.O. Box 20572, San Jose, CA 95160

National Assn. of Federally Licensed Firearms Dealers
Andrew Molchan, 2455 E. Sunrise, Ft. Lauderdale, FL 33304

National Association to Keep and Bear Arms
P.O. Box 78336, Seattle, WA 98178

National Automatic Pistol Collectors Assn.
Tom Knox, P.O. Box 15738, Tower Grove Station, St. Louis, MO 63163

National Bench Rest Shooters Assn., Inc.
Pat Ferrell, 2835 Guilford Lane, Oklahoma City, OK 73120-4404/405-842-9585; Fax: 405-842-9575

National Muzzle Loading Rifle Assn.
Box 67, Friendship, IN 47021 / 812-667-5131. Website: www.nmlra@nmlra.org

National Professional Paintball League (NPPL)
540 Main St., Mount Kisco, NY 10549/914-241-7400

National Reloading Manufacturers Assn.
One Centerpointe Dr., Suite 300, Lake Oswego, OR 97035

National Rifle Assn. of America
11250 Waples Mill Rd., Fairfax, VA 22030 / 703-267-1000. Website: www.nra.org

National Shooting Sports Foundation, Inc.
Doug Painter, President, Flintlock Ridge Office Center, 11 Mile Hill Rd., Newtown, CT 06470-2359/203-426-1320; FAX: 203-426-1087

National Skeet Shooting Assn.
Dan Snyuder, Director, 5931 Roft Road, San Antonio, TX 78253-9261/800-877-5338. Website: nssa-nsca.com

National Sporting Clays Association
Ann Myers, Director, 5931 Roft Road, San Antonio, TX 78253-9261/800-877-5338. Website: nssa-nsca.com

National Wild Turkey Federation, Inc.
P.O. Box 530, 770 Augusta Rd., Edgefield, SC 29824

North American Hunting Club
P.O. Box 3401, Minnetonka, MN 55343/612-936-9333; Fax: 612-936-9755

North American Paintball Referees Association (NAPRA)
584 Cestaric Dr., Milpitas, CA 95035

North-South Skirmish Assn., Inc.
Stevan F. Meserve, Exec. Secretary, 507 N. Brighton Court, Sterling, VA 20164-3919
Old West Shooter's Association
712 James Street, Hazel TX 76020 817-444-2049

Remington Society of America
Gordon Fosburg, Secretary, 11900 North Brinton Road, Lake, MI 48623

Rocky Mountain Elk Foundation
P.O. Box 8249, Missoula, MT 59807-8249/406-523-4500;Fax: 406-523-4581
Website: www.rmef.org

Ruger Collector's Assn., Inc.
P.O. Box 240, Greens Farms, CT 06436

Safari Club International
4800 W. Gates Pass Rd., Tucson, AZ 85745/520-620-1220

Sako Collectors Assn., Inc.
Jim Lutes, 202 N. Locust, Whitewater, KS 67154

Second Amendment Foundation
James Madison Building, 12500 NE 10th Pl., Bellevue, WA 98005

Single Action Shooting Society (SASS)
23255-A La Palma Avenue, Yorba Linda, CA 92887/714-694-1800; FAX: 714-694-1815/email: sasseot@aol.com Website: www.sassnet.com

Smith & Wesson Collectors Assn.
Cally Pletl, Admin. Asst.,PO Box 444, Afton, NY 13730

The Society of American Bayonet Collectors
P.O. Box 234, East Islip, NY 11730-0234

Southern California Schuetzen Society
Dean Lillard, 34657 Ave. E., Yucaipa, CA 92399

Sporting Arms and Ammunition Manufacturers' Institute (SAAMI)
Flintlock Ridge Office Center, 11 Mile Hill Rd., Newtown, CT 06470-2359/203-426-4358; FAX: 203-426-1087

Sporting Clays of America (SCA)
Ron L. Blosser, Pres., 9257 Buckeye Rd., Sugar Grove, OH 43155-9632/614-746-8334; Fax: 614-746-8605
Steel Challenge
23234 Via Barra, Valencia CA 91355 Website: www.steelchallenge.com

The Thompson/Center Assn.
Joe Wright, President, Box 792, Northboro, MA 01532/508-845-6960

U.S. Practical Shooting Assn./IPSC
Dave Thomas, P.O. Box 811, Sedro Woolley, WA 98284/360-855-2245 Website: www.uspsa.org

U.S. Revolver Assn.
Brian J. Barer, 40 Larchmont Ave., Taunton, MA 02780/508-824-4836

U.S.A. Shooting
U.S. Olympic Shooting Center, One Olympic Plaza, Colorado Springs, CO 80909/719-578-4670. Website: wwwusashooting.org

The Varmint Hunters Assn., Inc.
Box 759, Pierre, SD 57501/Member Services 800-528-4868

Weatherby Collectors Assn., Inc.
P.O. Box 478, Pacific, MO 63069 Website: www.weatherbycollectors.com Email: WCAsecretary@aol.com

The Wildcatters
P.O. Box 170, Greenville, WI 54942

Winchester Arms Collectors Assn.
P.O. Box 230, Brownsboro, TX 75756/903-852-4027

The Women's Shooting Sports Foundation (WSSF)
4620 Edison Avenue, Ste. C, Colorado Springs, CO 80915/719-638-1299; FAX: 719-638-1271/email: wssf@worldnet.att.net

ARGENTINA

Asociacion Argentina de Coleccionistas de Armes y Municiones
Castilla de Correos No. 28, Succursal I B, 1401 Buenos Aires, Republica Argentina

AUSTRALIA

Antique & Historical Arms Collectors of Australia
P.O. Box 5654, GCMC Queensland 9726, Australia

The Arms Collector's Guild of Queensland, Inc.
Ian Skennerton, P.O. Box 433, Ashmore City 4214, Queensland, Australia

Australian Cartridge Collectors Assn., Inc.
Bob Bennett, 126 Landscape Dr., E. Doncaster 3109, Victoria, Australia

Sporting Shooters Assn. of Australia, Inc.
P.O. Box 2066, Kent Town, SA 5071, Australia

BRAZIL

Associaçao de Armaria Coleçao e Tiro (ACOLTI)
Rua do Senado, 258 - 2 andar, Centro, Rio de Janeiro - RJ - 20231-002 Brazil / tel: 0055-21-31817989

CANADA

ALBERTA

Canadian Historical Arms Society
P.O. Box 901, Edmonton, Alb., Canada T5J 2L8

National Firearms Assn.
Natl. Hq: P.O. Box 1779, Edmonton, Alb., Canada T5J 2P1

BRITISH COLUMBIA

The Historical Arms Collectors of B.C. (Canada)
Harry Moon, Pres., P.O. Box 50117, South Slope RPO, Burnaby, BC V5J 5G3, Canada/604-438-0950; Fax:604-277-3646

ONTARIO

Association of Canadian Cartridge Collectors
Monica Wright, RR 1, Millgrove, ON, LOR IVO, Canada

Tri-County Antique Arms Fair
P.O. Box 122, RR #1, North Lancaster, Ont., Canada K0C 1Z0

EUROPE

BELGIUM

European Cartridge Research Assn.
Graham Irving, 21 Rue Schaltin, 4900 Spa, Belgium/32.87.77.43.40; Fax:32.87.77.27.51

CZECHOSLOVAKIA

Spolecnost Pro Studium Naboju (Czech Cartridge Research Assn.)
JUDr. Jaroslav Bubak, Pod Homolko 1439, 26601 Beroun 2, Czech Republic

DENMARK

Aquila Dansk Jagtpatron Historic Forening (Danish Historical Cartridge Collectors Club)
Steen Elgaard Møller, Ulriksdalsvej 7, 4840 Nr. Alslev, Denmark 10045-53846218;Fax:00455384 6209

ENGLAND

Arms and Armour Society
Hon. Secretary A. Dove, P.O. Box 10232, London, 5W19 2ZD, England

Dutch Paintball Federation
Aceville Publ., Castle House 97 High Street, Colchester, Essex C01 1TH, England/011-44-206-564840

European Paintball Sports Foundation
c/o Aceville Publ., Castle House 97 High St., Colchester, Essex, C01 1TH, England

Historical Breechloading Smallarms Assn.
D.J. Penn M.A., Secy., P.O. Box 12778, London SE1 6BX, England.
Journal and newsletter are $23 a yr., including airmail.

National Rifle Assn.
(Great Britain) Bisley Camp, Brookwood, Woking Surrey GU24 OPB, England/01483.797777; Fax: 014730686275

United Kingdom Cartridge Club
Ian Southgate, 20 Millfield, Elmley Castle, Nr. Pershore, Worcestershire, WR10 3HR, England

FRANCE

STAC-Western Co.
3 Ave. Paul Doumer (N.311); 78360 Montesson, France/01.30.53-43-65; Fax: 01.30.53.19.10

GERMANY

Bund Deutscher Sportschützen e.v. (BDS)
Borsigallee 10, 53125 Bonn 1, Germany

Deutscher Schützenbund
Lahnstrasse 120, 65195 Wiesbaden, Germany

NORWAY

Scandinavian Ammunition Research Assn.
c/o Morten Stoen, Annerudstubben 3, N-1383 Asker, Norway

NEW ZEALAND

New Zealand Cartridge Collectors Club
Terry Castle, 70 Tiraumea Dr., Pakuranga, Auckland, New Zealand

New Zealand Deerstalkers Assn.
P.O. Box 6514 TE ARO, Wellington, New Zealand

SOUTH AFRICA

Historical Firearms Soc. of South Africa
P.O. Box 145, 7725 Newlands, Republic of South Africa

Republic of South Africa Cartridge Collectors Assn.
Arno Klee, 20 Eugene St., Malanshof Randburg, Gauteng 2194, Republic of South Africa

S.A.A.C.A. (Southern Africa Arms and Ammunition Assn.)
Gauteng office:
P.O. Box 7597, Weltevreden Park, 1715, Republic of South Africa/011-679-1151; Fax: 011-679-1131;
e-mail: saaaca@iafrica.com.
Kwa-Zulu Natal office:
P.O. Box 4065, Northway, Kwazulu-Natal 4065, Republic of South Africa

SAGA (S.A. Gunowners' Assn.)
P.O. Box 35203, Northway, Kwazulu-Natal 4065, Republic of South Africa

SPAIN

Asociacion Espanola de Colleccionistas de Cartuchos (A.E.C.C.)
Secretary: Apdo. Correos No. 1086, 2880-Alcala de Henares (Madrid), Spain. President: Apdo. Correos No. 682, 50080 Zaragoza, Spain

Periodical Publications

AAFTA News (M)
5911 Cherokee Ave., Tampa, FL 33604. Official newsletter of the American Airgun Field Target Assn.

The Accurate Rifle
Precisions Shooting, Inc., 222 Mckee Street, Manchester CT 06040. $37 yr. Dedicated to the rifle accuracy enthusiast.

Action Pursuit Games Magazine (M)
CFW Enterprises, Inc., 4201 W. Vanowen Pl., Burbank, CA 91505 818-845-2656. $4.99 single copy U.S., $5.50 Canada. Editor: Dan Reeves. World's leading magazine of paintball sports.

Air Gunner Magazine
4 The Courtyard, Denmark St., Wokingham, Berkshire RG11 2AZ, England/011-44-734-771677. $U.S. $44 for 1 yr. Leading monthly airgun magazine in U.K.

Airgun Ads
Box 33, Hamilton, MT 59840/406-363-3805; Fax: 406-363-4117. $35 1 yr. (for first mailing; $20 for second mailing; $35 for Canada and foreign orders.) Monthly tabloid with extensive For Sale and Wanted airgun listings.

The Airgun Letter
Gapp, Inc., 4614 Woodland Rd., Ellicott City, MD 21042-6329/410-730-5496; Fax: 410-730-9544; e-mail: staff@airgnltr.net; http://www.airgunletter.com. $21 U.S., $24 Canada, $27 Mexico and $33 other foreign orders, 1 yr. Monthly newsletter for airgun users and collectors.

Airgun World
4 The Courtyard, Denmark St., Wokingham, Berkshire RG40 2AZ, England/011-44-734-771677. Call for subscription rates. Oldest monthly airgun magazine in the U.K., now a sister publication to *Air Gunner.*

Alaska Magazine
Morris Communications, 735 Broad Street, Augusta, GA 30901/706-722-6060. Hunting, Fishing and Life on the Last Frontier articles of Alaska and western Canada.

American Firearms Industry
Nat'l. Assn. of Federally Licensed Firearms Dealers, 2455 E. Sunrise Blvd., Suite 916, Ft. Lauderdale, FL 33304. $35.00 yr. For firearms retailers, distributors and manufacturers.

American Guardian
NRA, 11250 Waples Mill Rd., Fairfax, VA 22030. Publications division. $15.00 1 yr. Magazine features personal protection; home-self-defense; family recreation shooting; women's issues; etc.

American Gunsmith
Belvoir Publications, Inc., 75 Holly Hill Lane, Greenwich, CT 06836-2626/203-661-6111. $49.00 (12 issues). Technical journal of firearms repair and maintenance.

American Handgunner*
Publisher's Development Corp., 591 Camino de la Reina, Suite 200, San Diego, CA 92108/800-537-3006 $16.95 yr. Articles for handgun enthusiasts, competitors, police and hunters.

American Hunter (M)
National Rifle Assn., 11250 Waples Mill Rd., Fairfax, VA 22030 (Same address for both.) Publications Div. $35.00 yr. Wide scope of hunting articles.

American Rifleman (M)
National Rifle Assn., 11250 Waples Mill Rd., Fairfax, VA 22030 (Same address for both). Publications Div. $35.00 yr. Firearms articles of all kinds.

American Survival Guide
McMullen Angus Publishing, Inc., 774 S. Placentia Ave., Placentia, CA 92670-6846. 12 issues $19.95/714-572-2255; FAX: 714-572-1864.

Armes & Tir*
c/o FABECO, 38, rue de Trévise 75009 Paris, France. Articles for hunters, collectors, and shooters. French text.

Arms Collecting (Q)
Museum Restoration Service, P.O. Box 70, Alexandria Bay, NY 13607-0070. $22.00 yr.; $62.00 3 yrs.; $112.00 5 yrs.
Australian Shooter *(formerly Australian Shooters Journal)*
Sporting Shooters' Assn. of Australia, Inc., P.O. Box 2066, Kent Town SA 5071, Australia. $60.00 yr. locally; $65.00 yr. overseas surface mail. Hunting and shooting articles.

The Backwoodsman Magazine
P.O. Box 627, Westcliffe, CO 81252. $16.00 for 6 issues per yr.; $30.00 for 2 yrs.; sample copy $2.75. Subjects include muzzle-loading, woodslore, primitive survival, trapping, homesteading, blackpowder cartridge guns, 19th century how-to.

Black Powder Cartridge News (Q)
SPG, Inc., P.O. Box 761, Livingston, MT 59047/Phone/Fax: 406-222-8416. $17 yr. (4 issues) ($6 extra 1st class mailing). For the blackpowder cartridge enthusiast.

Blackpowder Hunting (M)
Intl. Blackpowder Hunting Assn., P.O. Box 1180Z, Glenrock, WY 82637/307-436-9817. $20.00 1 yr., $36.00 2 yrs. How-to and where-to features by experts on hunting; shooting; ballistics; traditional and modern blackpowder rifles, shotguns, pistols and cartridges.

Black Powder Times
P.O. Box 234, Lake Stevens, WA 98258. $20.00 yr.; add $5 per year for Canada, $10 per year other foreign. Tabloid newspaper for blackpowder activities; test reports.

Blade Magazine
Krause Publications, 700 East State St., Iola, WI 54990-0001. $25.98 for 12 issues. Foreign price (including Canada-Mexico) $50.00. A magazine for all enthusiasts of handmade, factory and antique knives.

Caliber
GFI-Verlag, Theodor-Heuss Ring 62, 50668 Koln, Germany. For hunters, target shooters and reloaders.

The Caller (Q) (M)
National Wild Turkey Federation, P.O. Box 530, Edgefield, SC 29824. Tabloid newspaper for members; 4 issues per yr. (membership fee $25.00)

Cartridge Journal (M)
Robert Mellichamp, 907 Shirkmere, Houston, TX 77008/713-869-0558. Dues $12 for U.S. and Canadian members (includes the newsletter); 6 issues.

The Cast Bullet*(M)
Official journal of The Cast Bullet Assn. Director of Membership, 203 E. 2nd St., Muscatine, IA 52761. Annual membership dues $14, includes 6 issues.

Cibles
14, rue du Patronage-Laique, BP 2057, 52902 Chaumont, cedex 9, France. French-language arms magazine also carries a small amount of arms-related and historical content. 12 issues per year. Tel/03-25-03-87-47/Email cibeles@graphycom.com; Website: www.graphycom.com

COLTELLI, che Passione (Q)
Casella postale N.519, 20101 Milano, Italy/Fax:02-48402857. $15 1 yr., $27 2 yrs. Covers all types of knives—collecting, combat, historical. Italian text.

Combat Handguns*
Harris Publications, Inc., 1115 Broadway, New York, NY 10010.

Deer & Deer Hunting Magazine
Krause Publications, 700 E. State St., Iola, WI 54990-0001. $19.95 yr. (9 issues). For the serious deer hunter. Website: www.krause.com

The Derringer Peanut (M)
The National Association of Derringer Collectors, P.O. Box 20572, San Jose, CA 95160. A newsletter dedicated to developing the best derringer information. Write for details.

Deutsches Waffen Journal
Journal-Verlag Schwend GmbH, Postfach 100340, D-74503 Schwäbisch Hall, Germany/0791-404-500; FAX:0791-404-505 and 404-424. DM102 p. yr. (interior); DM125.30 (abroad), postage included. Antique and modern arms and equipment. German text.

Double Gun Journal
P.O. Box 550, East Jordan, MI 49727/800-447-1658. $35 for 4 issues.

Ducks Unlimited, Inc. (M)
1 Waterfowl Way, Memphis, TN 38120

The Engraver (M) (Q)
P.O. Box 4365, Estes Park, CO 80517/970-586-2388; Fax: 970-586-0394. Mike Dubber, editor. The journal of firearms engraving.

The Field
King's Reach Tower, Stamford St., London SE1 9LS England. £36.40 U.K. 1 yr.; 49.90 (overseas, surface mail) yr.; £82.00 (overseas, air mail) yr. Hunting and shooting articles, and all country sports.

Field & Stream
Time4 Media, Two Park Ave., New York, NY 10016/212-779-5000. 12 issues/$19.97. Monthly shooting column. Articles on hunting and fishing.

Field Tests
Belvoir Publications, Inc., 75 Holly Hill Lane; P.O. Box 2626, Greenwich, CT 06836-2626/203-661-6111; 800-829-3361 (subscription line). U.S. & Canada $29 1 yr., $58 2 yrs.; all other countries $45 1 yr., $90 2 yrs. (air).

Fur-Fish-Game
A.R. Harding Pub. Co., 2878 E. Main St., Columbus, OH 43209. $15.95 yr. Practical guidance regarding trapping, fishing and hunting.

The Gottlieb-Tartaro Report
Second Amendment Foundation, James Madison Bldg., 12500 NE 10th Pl., Bellevue, WA 98005/206-454-7012;Fax:206-451-3959. $30 for 12 issues. An insiders guide for gun owners.

Gray's Sporting Journal
Gray's Sporting Journal, P.O. Box 1207, Augusta, GA 30903. $36.95 per yr. for 6 issues. Hunting and fishing journals. Expeditions and Guides Book (Annual Travel Guide).

Gun List†
700 E. State St., Iola, WI 54990. $37.98 yr. (26 issues); $66.98 2 yrs. (52 issues). Indexed market publication for firearms collectors and active shooters; guns, supplies and services. Website: www.krause.com

Gun News Digest (Q)
Second Amendment Fdn., P.O. Box 488, Station C, Buffalo, NY 14209/716-885-6408; Fax:716-884-4471. $10 U.S.; $20 foreign.

The Gun Report
World Wide Gun Report, Inc., Box 38, Aledo, IL 61231-0038. $33.00 yr. For the antique and collectable gun dealer and collector.

Gunmaker (M) (Q)
ACGG, P.O. Box 812, Burlington, IA 52601-0812. The journal of custom gunmaking.

The Gunrunner
Div. of Kexco Publ. Co. Ltd., Box 565G, Lethbridge, Alb., Canada T1J 3Z4. $23.00 yr., sample $2.00. Monthly newspaper, listing everything from antiques to artillery.

Gun Show Calendar (Q)
700 E. State St., Iola, WI 54990. $14.95 yr. (4 issues). Gun shows listed; chronologically and by state. Website: www.krause.com

Gun Tests
11 Commerce Blvd., Palm Coast, FL 32142. The consumer resource for the serious shooter. Write for information.

Gun Trade News
Bruce Publishing Ltd., P.O. Box 82, Wantage, Ozon OX12 7A8, England/44-1-235-771770; Fax: 44-1-235-771848. Britain's only "trade only" magazine exclusive to the gun trade.

Gun Week†
Second Amendment Foundation, P.O. Box 488, Station C, Buffalo, NY 14209. $35.00 yr. U.S. and possessions; $45.00 yr. other countries. Tabloid paper on guns, hunting, shooting and collecting (36 issues).

Gun World
Y-Visionary Publishing, LP 265 South Anita Drive, Ste. 120, Orange, CA 92868. $21.97 yr.; $34.97 2 yrs. For the hunting, reloading and shooting enthusiast.

Guns & Ammo
Primedia, 6420 Wilshire Blvd., Los Angeles, CA 90048/213-782-2780. $23.94 yr. Guns, shooting, and technical articles.

Guns
Publishers Development Corporation, P.O. Box 85201, San Diego, CA 92138/800-537-3006. $19.95 yr. In-depth articles on a wide range of guns, shooting equipment and related accessories for gun collectors, hunters and shooters.

Guns Review
Ravenhill Publishing Co. Ltd., Box 35, Standard House, Bonhill St., London EC 2A 4DA, England. £20.00 sterling (approx. U.S. $38 USA & Canada) yr. For collectors and shooters.

H.A.C.S. Newsletter (M)
Harry Moon, Pres., P.O. Box 50117, South Slope RPO, Burnaby BC, V5J 5G3, Canada/604-438-0950; Fax:604-277-3646. $25 p. yr. U.S. and Canada. Official newsletter of The Historical Arms Collectors of B.C. (Canada).

Handgunner*
Richard A.J. Munday, Seychelles house, Brightlingsen, Essex CO7 ONN, England/012063-305201. £18.00 (sterling).

Handguns*
Primedia, 6420 Wilshire Blvd., Los Angeles, CA 90048/323-782-2868. For the handgunning and shooting enthusiast.

Handloader*
Wolfe Publishing Co., 2626 Stearman Road, Ste. A, Prescott, AZ 86301/520-445-7810;Fax:520-778-5124. $22.00 yr. The journal of ammunition reloading.

INSIGHTS*
NRA, 11250 Waples Mill Rd., Fairfax, VA 22030. Editor, John E. Robbins. $15.00 yr., which includes NRA junior membership; $10.00 for adult subscriptions (12 issues). Plenty of details for the young hunter and target shooter; emphasizes gun safety, marksmanship training, hunting skills.

International Arms & Militaria Collector (Q)
Arms & Militaria Press, P.O. Box 80, Labrador, Qld. 4215, Australia. A$39.50 yr. (U.S. & Canada), 2 yrs. A$77.50; A$37.50 (others), 1 yr., 2 yrs. $73.50 all air express mail; surface mail is less. Editor: Ian D. Skennerton.

International Shooting Sport*/UIT Journal
International Shooting Union (UIT), Bavariaring 21, D-80336 Munich, Germany. Europe: (Deutsche Mark) DM44.00 yr., 2 yrs. DM83.00; outside Europe: DM50.00 yr., 2 yrs. DM95.00 (air mail postage included.) For international sport shooting.

Internationales Waffen-Magazin
Habegger-Verlag Zürich, Postfach 9230, CH-8036 Zürich, Switzerland. SF 105.00 (approx. U.S. $73.00) surface mail for 10 issues. Modern and antique arms, self-defense. German text; English summary of contents.

The Journal of the Arms & Armour Society (M)
A. Dove, P.O. Box 10232, London, SW19 2ZD England. £15.00 surface mail; £20.00 airmail sterling only yr. Articles for the historian and collector.

Journal of the Historical Breechloading Smallarms Assn.
Published annually. P.O. Box 12778, London, SE1 6XB, England. $21.00 yr. Articles for the collector plus mailings of short articles on specific arms, reprints, newsletters, etc.

Knife World
Knife World Publications, P.O. Box 3395, Knoxville, TN 37927. $15.00 yr.; $25.00 2 yrs. Published monthly for knife enthusiasts and collectors. Articles on custom and factory knives; other knife-related interests, monthly column on knife identification, military knives.

Man At Arms*
P.O. Box 460, Lincoln, RI 02865. $27.00 yr., $52.00 2 yrs. plus $8.00 for foreign subscribers. The N.R.A. magazine of arms collecting-investing, with excellent articles for the collector of antique arms and militaria.

The Mannlicher Collector (Q)(M)
Mannlicher Collectors Assn., Inc., P.O. Box 7144, Salem Oregon 97303. $20/ yr. subscription included in membership.

MAGNUM
Rua Madre Rita Amada de Jesus, 182 , Granja Julieta, Sao Paulo – SP – 04721-050 Brazil. No details.

---

*Published bi-monthly
† Published weekly
‡Published three times per month. All others are published monthly.

M=Membership requirements; write for details.
Q=Published Quarterly.

PERIODICAL PUBLICATIONS

MAN/MAGNUM
S.A. Man (Pty) Ltd., P.O. Box 35204, Northway, Durban 4065, Republic of South Africa. SA Rand 200.00 for 12 issues. Africa's only publication on hunting, shooting, firearms, bushcraft, knives, etc.

The Marlin Collector (M)
R.W. Paterson, 407 Lincoln Bldg., 44 Main St., Champaign, IL 61820.

Muzzle Blasts (M)
National Muzzle Loading Rifle Assn., P.O. Box 67, Friendship, IN 47021/812-667-5131. $35.00 yr. annual membership. For the blackpowder shooter.

Muzzleloader Magazine*
Scurlock Publishing Co., Inc., Dept. Gun, Route 5, Box 347-M, Texarkana, TX 75501. $18.00 U.S.; $22.50 U.S./yr. for foreign subscribers. The publication for blackpowder shooters.

National Defense (M)*
American Defense Preparedness Assn., Two Colonial Place, Suite 400, 2101 Wilson Blvd., Arlington, VA 22201-3061/703-522-1820; FAX: 703-522-1885. $35.00 yr. Articles on both military and civil defense field, including weapons, materials technology, management.

National Knife Magazine (M)
Natl. Knife Coll. Assn., 7201 Shallowford Rd., P.O. Box 21070, Chattanooga, TN 37424-0070. Membership $35 yr.; $65.00 International yr.

National Rifle Assn. Journal (British) (Q)
Natl. Rifle Assn. (BR.), Bisley Camp, Brookwood, Woking, Surrey, England. GU24, OPB. £24.00 Sterling including postage.

National Wildlife*
Natl. Wildlife Fed., 1400 16th St. NW, Washington, DC 20036, $16.00 yr. (6 issues); *International Wildlife*, 6 issues, $16.00 yr. Both, $22.00 yr., includes all membership benefits. Write attn.: Membership Services Dept., for more information.

New Zealand GUNS*
Waitekauri Publishing, P.O. 45, Waikino 3060, New Zealand. $NZ90.00 (6 issues) yr. Covers the hunting and firearms scene in New Zealand.

New Zealand Wildlife (Q)
New Zealand Deerstalkers Assoc., Inc., P.O. Box 6514, Wellington, N.Z. $30.00 (N.Z.). Hunting, shooting and firearms/game research articles.

North American Hunter* (M)
P.O. Box 3401, Minnetonka, MN 55343/612-936-9333; e-mail: huntingclub@pclink.com. $18.00 yr. (7 issues). Articles on all types of North American hunting.

Outdoor Life
Time4 Media, Two Park Ave., New York, NY 10016. $14.97/10 issues. Extensive coverage of hunting and shooting. Shooting column by Jim Carmichel.

La Passion des Courteaux (Q)
Phenix Editions, 25 rue Mademoiselle, 75015 Paris, France. French text.

Paintball Games International Magazine
Aceville Publications, Castle House, 97 High St., Colchester, Essex, England CO1 1TH/011-44-206-564840. Write for subscription rates. Leading magazine in the U.K. covering competitive paintball activities.

Paintball News
PBN Publishing, P.O. Box 1608, 24 Henniker St., Hillsboro, NH 03244/603-464-6080. $35 U.S. 1 yr. Bi-weekly. Newspaper covering the sport of paintball, new product reviews and industry features.

Paintball Sports (Q)
Paintball Publications, Inc., 540 Main St., Mount Kisco, NY 10549/941-241-7400. $24.75 U.S. 1 yr., $32.75 foreign. Covering the competitive paintball scene.

Performance Shooter
Belvoir Publications, Inc., 75 Holly Hill Lane, Greenwich, CT 06836-2626/203-661-6111. $45.00 yr. (12 issues). Techniques and technology for improved rifle and pistol accuracy.

Petersen's HUNTING Magazine
Primedia, 6420 Wilshire Blvd., Los Angeles, CA 90048. $19.94 yr.; Canada $29.34 yr.; foreign countries $29.94 yr. Hunting articles for all game; test reports.

P.I. Magazine
America's Private Investigation Journal, 755 Bronx Dr., Toledo, OH 43609. Chuck Klein, firearms editor with column about handguns.

Pirsch
BLV Verlagsgesellschaft GmbH, Postfach 400320, 80703 Munich, Germany/089-12704-0;Fax:089-12705-354. German text.

Point Blank
Citizens Committee for the Right to Keep and Bear Arms (sent to contributors), Liberty Park, 12500 NE 10th Pl., Bellevue, WA 98005

POINTBLANK (M)
Natl. Firearms Assn., Box 4384 Stn. C, Calgary, AB T2T 5N2, Canada. Official publication of the NFA.

The Police Marksman*
6000 E. Shirley Lane, Montgomery, AL 36117. $17.95 yr. For law enforcement personnel.

Police Times (M)
3801 Biscayne Blvd., Miami, FL 33137/305-573-0070.

Popular Mechanics
Hearst Corp., 224 W. 57th St., New York, NY 10019. Firearms, camping, outdoor oriented articles.

Precision Shooting
Precision Shooting, Inc., 222 McKee St., Manchester, CT 06040. $37.00 yr. U.S. Journal of the International Benchrest Shooters, and target shooting in general. Also considerable coverage of varmint shooting, as well as big bore, small bore, schuetzen, lead bullet, wildcats and precision reloading.

Rifle*
Wolfe Publishing Co., 2626 Stearman Road, Ste. A, Prescott, AZ 86301/520-445-7810; Fax: 520-778-5124. $19.00 yr. The sporting firearms journal.

Rifle's Hunting Annual
Wolfe Publishing Co., 2626 Stearman Road, Ste. A, Prescott, AZ 86301/520-445-7810; Fax: 520-778-5124. $4.99 Annual. Dedicated to the finest pursuit of the hunt.

Rod & Rifle Magazine
Lithographic Serv. Ltd., P.O. Box 38-138, Wellington, New Zealand. $50.00 yr. (6 issues). Hunting, shooting and fishing articles.

Safari* (M)
Safari Magazine, 4800 W. Gates Pass Rd., Tucson, AZ 85745/602-620-1220. $55.00 (6 times). The journal of big game hunting, published by Safari Club International. Also publish *Safari Times*, a monthly newspaper, included in price of $55.00 national membership.

Second Amendment Reporter
Second Amendment Foundation, James Madison Bldg., 12500 NE 10th Pl., Bellevue, WA 98005. $15.00 yr. (non-contributors).

Shoot! Magazine*
Shoot! Magazine Corp., 1770 West State Stret PMB 340, Boise ID 83702/208-368-9920; Fax: 208-338-8428. Website: www.shootmagazine.com; $32.95 (6 times/yr.). Articles of interest to the cowboy action shooter, or others interested the Western-era firearms and ammunition.

Shooter's News
23146 Lorain Rd., Box 349, North Olmsted, OH 44070/216-979-5258;Fax:216-979-5259. $29 U.S. 1 yr., $54 2 yrs.; $52 foreign surface. A journal dedicated to precision riflery.

Shooting Industry
Publisher's Dev. Corp., 591 Camino de la Reina, Suite 200, San Diego, CA 92108. $50.00 yr. To the trade. $25.00.

Shooting Sports USA
National Rifle Assn. of America, 11250 Waples Mill Road, Fairfax, VA 22030. Annual subscriptions for NRA members are $5 for classified shooters and $10 for non-classified shooters. Non-NRA member subscriptions are $15. Covering events, techniques and personalities in competitive shooting.

Shooting Sportsman*
P.O. Box 11282, Des Moines, IA 50340/800-666-4955 (for subscriptions). Editorial: P.O. Box 1357, Camden, ME 04843. $19.95 for six issues. The magazine of wingshooting and fine guns.

The Shooting Times & Country Magazine (England)†
IPC Magazines Ltd., King's Reach Tower, Stamford St, 1 London SE1 9LS, England/0171-261-6180;Fax:0171-261-7179. £65 (approx. $98.00) yr.; £79 yr. overseas (52 issues). Game shooting, wild fowling, hunting, game fishing and firearms articles. Britain's best selling field sports magazine.

Shooting Times
Primedia, 2 News Plaza, P.O. Box 1790, Peoria, IL 61656/309-682-6626. $16.97 yr. Guns, shooting, reloading; articles on every gun activity.

The Shotgun News‡
Primedia, 2 News Plaza, P.O. Box 1790, Peoria, IL 61656/800-495-8362. 36 issues/ yr. @ $28.95; 12 issues/yr. @ $19.95. foreign subscription call for rates. Sample copy $4.00. Gun ads of all kinds.

SHOT Business
National Shooting Sports Foundation, Flintlock Ridge Office Center, 11 Mile Hill Rd., Newtown, CT 06470-2359/203-426-1320; FAX: 203-426-1087. For the shooting, hunting and outdoor trade retailer.

Shotgun Sports
P.O. Box 6810, Auburn, CA 95604/916-889-2220; FAX:916-889-9106. $31.00 yr. Trapshooting how-to's, shotshell reloading, shotgun patterning, shotgun tests and evaluations, Sporting Clays action, waterfowl/upland hunting. Call 1-800-676-8920 for a free sample copy.

The Single Shot Exhange Magazine
PO box 1055, York SC 29745/803-628-5326 phone/fax. $31.50/yr., monthly. Articles of interest to the blackpowder cartridge shooter and antique arms collector.

Single Shot Rifle Journal* (M)
Editor John Campbell, PO Box 595, Bloomfield Hills, MI 48303/248-458-8415. Email: jcampbel@dmbb.com Annual dues $35 for 6 issues. Journal of the American Single Shot Rifle Assn.

The Sixgunner (M)
Handgun Hunters International, P.O. Box 357, MAG, Bloomingdale, OH 43910

The Skeet Shooting Review
National Skeet Shooting Assn., 5931 Roft Rd., San Antonio, TX 78253. $20.00 yr. (Assn. membership includes mag.) Competition results, personality profiles of top Skeet shooters, how-to articles, technical, reloading information.

Soldier of Fortune
Subscription Dept., P.O. Box 348, Mt. Morris, IL 61054. $29.95 yr.; $39.95 Canada; $50.95 foreign.
Sporting Classics

Sporting Classics, Inc.
PO Box 23707, Columbia, SC 29223/1-800-849-1004. 1 yr./6 issues/$23.95; 2 yrs./12 issues/$38.95; 3 yrs./18 issues/$47.95. Firearms & outdoor articles and columns.

Sporting Clays Magazine
Patch Communications, 5211 South Washington Ave., Titusville, FL 32780/407-268-5010; FAX: 407-267-7216. $29.95 yr. (12 issues). Official publication of the National Sporting Clays Association.

Sporting Goods Business
Miller Freeman, Inc., One Penn Plaza, 10th Fl., New York, NY 10119-0004. Trade journal.

Sporting Goods Dealer
Two Park Ave., New York, NY 10016. $100.00 yr. Sporting goods trade journal.

Sporting Gun
Bretton Court, Bretton, Peterborough PE3 8DZ, England. £27.00 (approx. U.S. $36.00), airmail £35.50 yr. For the game and clay enthusiasts.

Sports Afield
15621 Chemical Lane, Huntington Beach CA 92648. U.S./800-234-3537. International/714-894-9080. Nine issues for $29.97. Website: www.sportsafield.com. America's oldest outdoor publication is now devoted to high-end sporting pursuits, especially in North America and Africa.

The Squirrel Hunter
P.O. Box 368, Chireno, TX 75937. $14.00 yr. Articles about squirrel hunting.

Stott's Creek Calendar
Stott's Creek Printers, 2526 S 475 W, Morgantown, IN 46160/317-878-5489. 1 yr (3 issues) $11.50; 2 yrs. (6 issues) $20.00. Lists all gun shows everywhere in convenient calendar form; call for information.

Super Outdoors
2695 Aiken Road, Shelbyville, KY 40065/502-722-9463; 800-404-6064; Fax: 502-722-8093. Mark Edwards, publisher. Contact for details.

TACARMI
Via E. De Amicis, 25; 20123 Milano, Italy. $100.00 yr. approx. Antique and modern guns. (Italian text.)

Territorial Dispatch—1800s Historical Publication (M)
National Assn. of Buckskinners, 4701 Marion St., Suite 324, Livestock Exchange Bldg., Denver, CO 80216. Michael A. Nester & Barbara Wyckoff, editors. 303-297-9671.

Trap & Field
1000 Waterway Blvd., Indianapolis, IN 46202. $25.00 yr. Official publ. Amateur Trapshooting Assn. Scores, averages, trapshooting articles.

Turkey Call* (M)
Natl. Wild Turkey Federation, Inc., P.O. Box 530, Edgefield, SC 29824. $25.00 with membership (6 issues per yr.)

Turkey & Turkey Hunting*
Krause Publications, 700 E. State St., Iola, WI 54990-0001. $13.95 (6 issue p. yr.). Magazine with leading-edge articles on all aspects of wild turkey behavior, biology and the successful ways to hunt better with that info. Learn the proper techniques to calling, the right equipment, and more.

The U.S. Handgunner* (M)
U.S. Revolver Assn., 40 Larchmont Ave., Taunton, MA 02780. $10.00 yr. General handgun and competition articles. Bi-monthly sent to members.

U.S. Airgun Magazine
P.O. Box 2021, Benton, AR 72018/800-247-4867; Fax: 501-316-8549. 10 issues a yr. Cover the sport from hunting, 10-meter, field target and collecting. Write for details.

The Varmint Hunter Magazine (Q)
The Varmint Hunters Assn., Box 759, Pierre, SD 57501/800-528-4868. $24.00 yr.

Waffenmarkt-Intern
GFI-Verlag, Theodor-Heuss Ring 62, 50668 K"ln, Germany. Only for gunsmiths, licensed firearms dealers and their suppliers in Germany, Austria and Switzerland.

Wild Sheep (M) (Q)
Foundation for North American Wild Sheep, 720 Allen Ave., Cody, WY 82414. Website: http://iigi.com/os/non/fnaws/fnaws.htm; e-mail: fnaws@wyoming.com. Official journal of the foundation.

Wisconsin Outdoor Journal
Krause Publications, 700 E. State St., Iola, WI 54990-0001. $17.97 yr. (8 issues). For Wisconsin's avid hunters and fishermen, with features from all over that state with regional reports, legislative updates, etc. Website: www.krause.com

Women & Guns
P.O. Box 488, Sta. C, Buffalo, NY 14209. $24.00 yr. U.S.; $72.00 foreign (12 issues). Only magazine edited by and for women gun owners.

World War II*
Cowles History Group, 741 Miller Dr. SE, Suite D-2, Leesburg, VA 20175-8920. Annual subscriptions $19.95 U.S.; $25.95 Canada; 43.95 foreign. The title says it—WWII; good articles, ads, etc.

*Published bi-monthly
† Published weekly
‡Published three times per month. All others are published monthly.

M=Membership requirements; write for details.
Q=Published Quarterly.

REFERENCE

THE HANDGUNNER'S LIBRARY

FOR COLLECTOR ◆ HUNTER ◆ SHOOTER ◆ OUTDOORSMAN

IMPORTANT NOTICE TO BOOK BUYERS

Books listed here may be bought from Ray Riling Arms Books Co., 6844 Gorsten St., P.O. Box 18925, Philadelphia, PA 19119, Phone 215/438-2456; FAX: 215-438-5395. E-Mail: sales@rayrilingarmsbooks.com. Larry Riling is the researcher and compiler of "The Arms Library" and a seller of gun books for over 32 years. The Riling stock includes books classic and modern, many hard-to-find items, and many not obtainable elsewhere. These pages list a portion of the current stock. They offer prompt, complete service, with delayed shipments occurring only on out-of-print or out-of-stock books.

Visit our web site at **www.rayrilingarmsbooks.com** and order all of your favorite titles on line from our secure site.

NOTICE FOR ALL CUSTOMERS: Remittance in U.S. funds must accompany all orders. For your convenience we now accept VISA, MasterCard & American Express. For shipments in the U.S. add $7.00 for the 1st book and $2.00 for each additional book for postage and insurance. Minimum order $10.00. International Orders add $13.00 for the 1st book and $5.00 for each additional book. All International orders are shipped at the buyer's risk unless an additional $5 for insurance is included. USPS does not offer insurance to all countries unless shipped Air-Mail please e-mail or call for pricing.

Payments in excess of order or for "Backorders" are credited or fully refunded at request. Books "As-Ordered" are not returnable except by permission and a handling charge on these of 10% or $2.00 per book which ever is greater is deducted from refund or credit. Only Pennsylvania customers must include current sales tax.

A full variety of arms books also available from Rutgers Book Center, 127 Raritan Ave., Highland Park, NJ 08904/908-545-4344; FAX: 908-545-6686 or I.D.S.A. Books, 1324 Stratford Drive, Piqua, OH 45356/937-773-4203; FAX: 937-778-1922.

BALLISTICS AND HANDLOADING

ABC's of Reloading, 6th Edition, by C. Rodney James and the editors of Handloader's Digest, DBI Books, a division of Krause Publications, Iola, WI, 1997. 288 pp., illus. Paper covers. $21.95

The definitive guide to every facet of cartridge and shotshell reloading.

Accurate Arms Loading Guide Number 2, by Accurate Arms. McEwen, TN: Accurate Arms Company, Inc., 2000. Paper Covers. $18.95

Includes new data on smokeless powders XMR4064 and XMP5744 as well as a special section on Cowboy Action Shooting. The new manual includes 50 new pages of data. An appendix includes nominal rotor charge weights, bullet diameters.

American Cartridge, The, by Charles Suydam, Borden Publishing Co. Alhambra, CA, 1986. 184 pp., illus. Softcover $24.95

An illustrated study of the rimfire cartridge in the United States.

Ammo and Ballistics, by Robert W. Forker, Safari Press, Inc., Huntington Beach, CA., 1999. 252 pp., illustrated. Paper covers. $18.95

Ballistic data on 125 calibers and 1,400 loads out to 500 yards.

Ammunition: Grenades and Projectile Munitions, by Ian V. Hogg, Stackpole Books, Mechanicsburg, PA, 1998. 144 pp., illus. $22.95

Concise guide to modern ammunition. International coverage with detailed specifications and illustrations.

Barnes Reloading Manual #2, Barnes Bullets, American Fork, UT, 1999. 668 pp., illus. $24.95

Features data and trajectories on the new weight X, XBT and Solids in calibers from .22 to .50 BMG.

Black Powder Guide, 2nd Edition, by George C. Nonte, Jr., Stoeger Publishing Co., So. Hackensack, NJ, 1991. 288 pp., illus. Paper covers. $14.95

How-to instructions for selection, repair and maintenance of muzzleloaders, making your own bullets, restoring and refinishing, shooting techniques.

Blackpowder Loading Manual, 3rd Edition, by Sam Fadala, DBI Books, a division of Krause Publications, Iola, WI, 1995. 368 pp., illus. Paper covers. $20.95

Revised and expanded edition of this landmark blackpowder loading book. Covers hundreds of loads for most of the popular blackpowder rifles, handguns and shotguns.

Cartridges of the World, 9th Edition, by Frank Barnes, Krause Publications, Iola, WI, 2000. 512 pp., illus. Paper covers. $27.95

Completely revised edition of the general purpose reference work for which collectors, police, scientists and laymen reach first for answers to cartridge identification questions.

Cartridge Reloading Tools of the Past, by R.H. Chamberlain and Tom Quigley, Tom Quigley, Castle Rock, WA, 1998. 167 pp., illustrated. Paper covers. $25.00

A detailed treatment of the extensive Winchester and Ideal line of handloading tools and bullet molds, plus Remington, Marlin, Ballard, Browning, Maynard, and many others.

Cast Bullets for the Black Powder Rifle, by Paul A. Matthews, Wolfe Publishing Co., Prescott, AZ, 1996. 133 pp., illus. Paper covers. $22.50

The tools and techniques used to make your cast bullet shooting a success.

Complete Blackpowder Handbook, 4th Edition, by Sam Fadala, DBI Books, a division of Krause Publications, Iola, WI, 2001. 400 pp., illus. Paper covers. $22.95

Expanded and completely rewritten edition of the definitive book on the subject of blackpowder.

Complete Reloading Manual, One Book / One Caliber. California: Load Books USA, 2000. $7.95 each

Containing unabridged information from U. S. Bullet and Powder Makers. With thousands of proven and tested loads, plus dozens of various bullet designs and different powders. Spiral bound. Available in all Calibers.

Designing and Forming Custom Cartridges for Rifles and Handguns, by Ken Howell. Precision Shooting, Manchester, CT. 2002. 600 pages, illus. $59.95

The classic work in its field, out of print for the last few years, and virtually unobtainable on the used book market, now returns in an exact reprint of the original. Some 600 pages, full size (8 1/2" x 11"), hard covers. Dozens of cartridge drawings never published anywhere before-dozens you've never heard of (guaranteed!). Precisely drawn to the dimensions specified by men who designed them, the factories that made them, and the authorities that set the standards. All drawn to the same format and scale (1.5x)-for most, how to form them from brass. Some 450 pages of them, two to a page. Plus other practical information.

Early Loading Tools & Bullet Molds, Pioneer Press, 1988. 88 pages, illustrated. Softcover. $7.50

Handbook for Shooters and Reloaders, by P.O. Ackley, Salt Lake City, UT, 1998, (Vol. I), 567 pp., illus. Includes a separate exterior ballistics chart. $21.95 (Vol. II), a new printing with specific new material. 495 pp., illus. $20.95

Handgun Stopping Power; The Definitive Study, by Marshall & Sandow. Boulder, CO: Paladin Press, 1992. 240 pages. $45.00

Offers accurate predictions of the stopping power of specific loads in calibers from .380 Auto to .45 ACP, as well as such specialty rounds as the Glaser Safety Slug, Federal Hydra-Shok, MagSafe, etc. This is the definitive methodology for predicting the stopping power of handgun loads, the first to take into account what really happens when a bullet meets a man.

Handloader's Manual of Cartridge Conversions, 2nd Revised Edition by John J. Donnelly, Stoeger Publishing Co., So. Hackensack, NJ, 2002. Unpaginated. $39.95

From 14 Jones to 70-150 Winchester in English and American cartridges, and from 4.85 U.K. to 15.2x28R Gevelot in metric cartridges. Over 900 cartridges described in detail.

Hatcher's Notebook, by S. Julian Hatcher, Stackpole Books, Harrisburg, PA, 1992. 488 pp., illus. $39.95

A reference work for shooters, gunsmiths, ballisticians, historians, hunters and collectors.

History and Development of Small Arms Ammunition; Volume 2 Centerfire: Primitive, and Martial Long Arms. by George A. Hoyem. Oceanside, CA: Armory Publications, 1991. 303 pages, illustrated. $60.00

Covers the blackpowder military centerfire rifle, carbine, machine gun and volley gun ammunition used in 28 nations and dominions, together with the firearms that chambered them.

THE HANDGUNNER'S LIBRARY

History and Development of Small Arms Ammunition; Volume 4, American Military Rifle Cartridges. Oceanside, CA: Armory Publications, 1998. 244pp., illus. $60.00

Carries on what Vol. 2 began with American military rifle cartridges. Now the sporting rifle cartridges are at last organized by their originators-235 individual case types designed by eight makers of single shot rifles and four of magazine rifles from .50-140 Winchester Express to .22-15-60 Stevens. plus experimentals from .70-150 to .32-80. American Civil War enthusiasts and European collectors will find over 150 primitives in Appendix A to add to those in Volumes One and Two. There are 16 pages in full color of 54 box labels for Sharps, Remington and Ballard cartridges. There are large photographs with descriptions of 15 Maynard, Sharps, Winchester, Browning, Freund, Remington-Hepburn, Farrow and other single shot rifles, some of them rare one of a kind specimens.

Hodgdon Powder Data Manual #27, Hodgdon Powder Co., Shawnee Mission, KS, 1999. 800 pp. $27.95

Reloading data for rifle and pistol loads.

Hodgdon Shotshell Data Manual, Hodgdon Powder Co., Shawnee Mission, KS, 1999. 208 pp. $19.95

Contains hundreds of loads for lead shot, buck shot, slugs, bismuth shot and steel shot plus articles on ballistics, patterning, special reloads and much more.

Home Guide to Cartridge Conversions, by Maj. George C. Nonte Jr., The Gun Room Press, Highland Park, NJ, 1976. 404 pp., illus. $24.95

Revised and updated version of Nonte's definitive work on the alteration of cartridge cases for use in guns for which they were not intended.

Hornady Handbook of Cartridge Reloading, 5th Edition, Vol. I and II, Edited by Larry Steadman, Hornady Mfg. Co., Grand Island, NE, 2000., illus. $49.95

2 Volumes; Volume 1, 773 pp.; Volume 2, 717 pp. New edition of this famous reloading handbook covers rifle and handgun reloading data and ballistic tables.

Latest loads, ballistic information, etc.

How-To's for the Black Powder Cartridge Rifle Shooter, by Paul A. Matthews, Wolfe Publishing Co., Prescott, AZ, 1995. 45 pp. Paper covers. $22.50

Covers lube recipes, good bore cleaners and over-powder wads. Tips include compressing powder charges, combating wind resistance, improving ignition and much more.

Illustrated Reference of Cartridge Dimensions, The, edited by Dave Scovill, Wolfe Publishing Co., Prescott, AZ, 1994. 343 pp., illus. Paper covers. $19.00

A comprehensive volume with over 300 cartridges. Standard and metric dimensions have been taken from SAAMI drawings and/or fired cartridges.

Lee Modern Reloading, by Richard Lee, 350 pp. of charts and data and 85 illustrations. 512 pp. $24.95

Bullet casting, lubricating and author's formula for calculating proper charges for cast bullets. Includes virtually all current load data published by the powder suppliers. Exclusive source of volume measured loads.

Loading the Black Powder Rifle Cartridge, by Paul A Matthews, Wolfe Publishing Co., Prescott, AZ, 1993. 121 pp., illus. Paper covers. $22.50

Author Matthews brings the blackpowder cartridge shooter valuable information on the basics, including cartridge care, lubes and moulds, powder charges and developing and testing loads in his usual authoritative style.

Loading the Peacemaker—Colt's Model P, by Dave Scovill, Wolfe Publishing Co., Prescott, AZ, 1996. 227 pp., illus. $24.95

A comprehensive work about the history, maintenance and repair of the most famous revolver ever made, including the most extensive load data ever published.

Lyman Cast Bullet Handbook, 3rd Edition, edited by C. Kenneth Ramage, Lyman Publications, Middlefield, CT, 1980. 416 pp., illus. Paper covers. $19.95

Information on more than 5000 tested cast bullet loads and 19 pages of trajectory and wind drift tables for cast bullets.

Lyman Black Powder Handbook, 2nd Edition, edited by C. Kenneth Ramage, Lyman Products for Shooters, Middlefield, CT, 2000. 239 pp., illus. Paper covers. $19.95

Comprehensive load information for the modern blackpowder shooter.

Lyman Pistol & Revolver Handbook, 2nd Edition, edited by Thomas J. Griffin, Lyman Products Co., Middlefield, CT, 1996. 287 pp., illus. Paper covers. $18.95

The most up-to-date loading data available including the hottest new calibers, like 40 S&W, 9x21, 9mm Makarov, 9x25 Dillon and 454 Casull.

Lyman Reloading Handbook No. 48, edited by Edward A. Matunas, Lyman Publications, Middlefield, CT, 2003. 480 pp., illus. Paper covers. $24.95

A comprehensive reloading manual complete with "How to Reload" information. Expanded data section with all the newest rifle and pistol calibers.

Lyman Shotshell Handbook, 4th Edition, edited by Edward A. Matunas, Lyman Products Co., Middlefield, CT, 1996. 330 pp., illus. Paper covers. $24.95

Has 9000 loads, including slugs and buckshot, plus feature articles and a full color I.D. section.

Lyman's Guide to Big Game Cartridges & Rifles, by Edward Matunas, Lyman Publishing Corporation, Middlefield, CT, 1994. 287 pp., illus. Paper covers. $17.95

A selection guide to cartridges and rifles for big game—antelope to elephant.

Military Rifle and Machine Gun Cartridges, by Jean Huon, Alexandria, VA: Ironside International, 1995. 1st edition. 378 pages, over 1,000 photos. $34.95

Superb reference text.

Modern Combat Ammunition, by Duncan Long, Paladin Press, Boulder, CO, 1997, soft cover, photos, illus., 216 pp. $34.00

Now, Paladin's leading weapons author presents his exhaustive evaluation of the stopping power of modern rifle, pistol, shotgun and machine gun rounds based on actual case studies of shooting incidents. He looks at the hot new cartridges that promise to dominate well into the next century .40 S&W, 10mm auto, sub-sonic 9mm's - as well as the trusted standbys. Find out how to make your own exotic tracers, fléchette and sabot rounds, caseless ammo and fragmenting bullets.

Modern Exterior Ballistics, by Robert L. McCoy, Schiffer Publishing Co., Atglen, PA, 1999. 128 pp. $95.00

Advanced students of exterior ballistics and flight dynamics will find this comprehensive textbook on the subject a useful addition to their libraries.

Modern Reloading, by Richard Lee, Inland Press, 1996. 510 pp., illus. $24.98

The how-to's of rifle, pistol and shotgun reloading plus load data for rifle and pistol calibers.

Modern Reloading 2nd Edition, by Richard Lee, Inland Press, 2003. 623 pp., illus. $29.95

The how-to's of rifle, pistol and shotgun reloading plus load data for rifle and pistol calibers.

Modern Sporting Rifle Cartridges, by Wayne van Zwoll, Stoeger Publishing Co., Wayne, NJ, 1998. 310 pp., illustrated. Paper covers. $21.95

Illustrated with hundreds of photos and backed up by dozens of tables and schematic drawings, this four-part book tells the story of how rifle bullets and cartridges were developed and, in some cases, discarded.

Mr. Single Shot's Cartridge Handbook, by Frank de Haas, Mark de Haas, Orange City, IA, 1996. 116 pp., illus. Paper covers. $21.50

This book covers most of the cartridges, both commercial and wildcat, that the author has known and used.

Nosler Reloading Manual #5, edited by Gail Root, Nosler Bullets, Inc., Bend, OR, 2002. 516 pp., illus. $29.99

Combines information on their Ballistic Tip, Partition and Handgun bullets with traditional powders and new powders never before used, plus trajectory information from 100 to 500 yards.

Paper Jacket, The, by Paul Matthews, Wolfe Publishing Co., Prescott, AZ, 1991. Paper covers. $14.50

Up-to-date and accurate information about paper-patched bullets.

Reloading Tools, Sights and Telescopes for S/S Rifles, by Gerald O. Kelver, Brighton, CO, 1982. 163 pp., illus. Softcover. $15.00

A listing of most of the famous makers of reloading tools, sights and telescopes with a brief description of the products they manufactured.

Reloading for Shotgunners, 4th Edition, by Kurt D. Fackler and M.L. McPherson, DBI Books, a division of Krause Publications, Iola, WI, 1997. 320 pp., illus. Paper covers. $19.95

Expanded reloading tables with over 11,000 loads. Bushing charts for every major press and component maker. All new presentation on all aspects of shotshell reloading by two of the top experts in the field.

Rimfire Cartridge in the United States and Canada, The, Illustrated history of rimfire cartridges, manufacturers, and the products made from 1857-1984. by John L. Barber, Thomas Publications, Gettysburg, PA 2000. 1st edition. Profusely illustrated. 221 pages. $50.00

The author has written an encyclopedia of rimfire cartridges from the .22 to the massive 1.00 in. Gatling. Fourteen chapters, six appendices and an excellent bibliography make up a reference volume that all cartridge collectors should aquire.

Shotshells & Ballistics. Long Beach, CA: Safari Press, 2002. 275pp, photos. Softcover. $19.95

There is a bewildering array of commercially loaded shotgun shells for sale, from the .410 to the 10-gauge. In fact, there are more types of shells and shot sizes on the market now than ever before. With this overwhelming selection of shells available, here, finally, is a practical, reasonably priced book that makes sense of it all. It lists commercially available shotshell loads from the .410-bore to the 10-gauge, in all shot sizes available, different shot types (lead, steel, bismuth, tungsten, and others) so that the shooter or hunter can quickly find what will be best for the gun he has and the game or targets he wants to shoot. Each shotgun shell with each loading has its own table--over 1,600 tables!!--showing shot size; weight of shot; recoil; average number of pellets in the shell; manufacturer's order number; shell length and type of hull; type of wad; and whether the shot is buffered or not. In addition, each table contains data that details velocity (in 10-yard intervals from 0 to 70 yards); average pellet energy; and time of flight in seconds. This book includes complete listings and tables of every load made from the following manufacturers: Aguilla, Armscorp, ARMUSA, Baschieri & Pellagri, Bismuth Cartridge Company, Clever, Dionisi, Dynamit Nobel, Eley Hawk, Federal, Fiocchi, Hevi-Shot (now loaded exclusively by Remington), Kent, Lightfield, Nobel

Sport, PMC, RIO, Remington, Rotweil, Sellier & Bellot, RST, RWS, and Winchester. In addition, this informative reference contains authoritative articles on the history and development of shotshells, the components and technical data that govern production of shotshells, what load and shot size to use for what type of game or target, and much more. Never before has so much information on shotshells and ballistics been placed in a single book. Accentuated with photos from the field and the range, this is a reference book unlike any other.

Sierra Reloading Manual, 5th Edition: Rifle and Handgun Manual of Reloading Data. Sedalia, MO: Sierra Bullets, 2003. 5th edition. Hardcover. $39.95

This 1152 page manual retains the popular three-ring binder format and has been modernized with new cartridge information, histories and reloading recommendations. New bullets, new cartridges and new powders make this manual a necessity in every reloader's library.

Sixgun Cartridges and Loads, by Elmer Keith, The Gun Room Press, Highland Park, NJ, 1986. 151 pp., illus. $24.95

A manual covering the selection, uses and loading of the most suitable and popular revolver cartridges. Originally published in 1936. Reprint.

Speer Reloading Manual No. 13, edited by members of the Speer research staff, Omark Industries, Lewiston, ID, 1999. 621 pp., illustrated. $24.95

With thirteen new sections containing the latest technical information and reloading trends for both novice and expert in this latest edition. More than 9,300 loads are listed, including new propellant powders from Accurate Arms, Alliant, Hodgdon and Vihtavuori.

Stopping Power: A Practical Analysis of the Latest Handgun Ammunition, by Marshall & Sanow. Boulder, CO: Paladin Press, 2002. 1st edition. 600+ photos, 360 pp. Softcover. $49.95

If you want to know how handgun ammunition will work against human targets in the future, you must look at how similar ammo has worked against human targets in the past. Stopping Power bases its conclusions on real-world facts from real-world gunfights. It provides the latest street results of actual police and civilian shootings in all of the major handgun calibers, from .22 LR to .45 ACP, plus more than 30 chapters of vital interest to all gun owners. The only thing worse than being involved in a gunfight is losing one. The info. in this book will help you choose the right bullets for your gun so you don't lose.

Street Stoppers, The Latest Handgun Stopping Power Street Results, by Marshall & Lanow. Boulder, CO, Paladin Press, 1996. 374 pages, illus. Softcover. $42.95

Street Stoppers is the long-awaited sequel to Handgun Stopping Power. It provides the latest results of real-life shootings in all of the major handgun calibers, plus more than 25 thought-provoking chapters that are vital to anyone interested in firearms, would ballistics, and combat shooting. This book also covers the street results of the hottest new caliber to hit the shooting world in years, the .40 Smith & Wesson. Updated street results of the latest exotic ammunition including Remington Golden Saber and CCI-Speer Gold Dot, plus the venerable offerings from MagSafe, Glaser, Cor-Bon and others. A fascinating look at the development of Hydra-Shok ammunition is included.

Understanding Ballistics, Revised 2nd Edition by Robert A. Rinker, Mulberry House Publishing Co., Corydon, IN, 2000. 430 pp., illus Paper covers. New, Revised and Expanded. 2nd Edition. $24.95

Explains basic to advanced firearm ballistics in understandable terms.

Why Not Load Your Own?, by Col. T. Whelen, Gun Room Press, Highland Park, NJ 1996, 4th ed., rev. 237 pp., illus. $20.00

A basic reference on handloading, describing each step, materials and equipment. Includes loads for popular cartridges.

Wildcat Cartridges Volumes 1 & 2 Combination, by the editors of Handloaders magazine, Wolfe Publishing Co., Prescott, AZ, 1997. 350 pp., illus. Paper covers. $39.95

A profile of the most popular information on wildcat cartridges that appeared in the Handloader magazine.

COLLECTORS

18th Century Weapons of the Royal Welsh Fuziliers from Flixton Hall, by Goldstein, Erik. Thomas Publications, Gettysburg, PA: 2002. 1st edition. 126 pages, illustrated with B & W photos. Softcover. $19.95

Ackermann Military Prints: Uniforms of the British and Indian Armies 1840-1855, The, by Carman, William Y. with Robert W. Kenny Jr. Schiffer Publications, Atglen, PA: 2002. 1st edition. 176 pages, with over 160 color images. $69.95

Accoutrements of the United States Infantry, Riflemen, and Dragoons 1834-1839. by R.T. Huntington, Historical Arms Series No. 20. Canada: Museum Restoration. 58 pp. illus. Softcover. $8.95

Although the 1841 edition of the U.S. Ordnance Manual provides ample information on the equipment that was in use during the 1840s, it is evident that the patterns of equipment that it describes were not introduced until 1838 or 1839. This guide is intended to fill this gap in our knowledge by providing an overview of what we now know about the accoutrements that were issued to the regular infantryman, rifleman, and dragoon, in the 1830's with excursions into earlier and later years.

Age of the Gunfighter; Men and Weapons on the Frontier 1840-1900, by Joseph G. Rosa, University of Oklahoma Press, Norman, OK, 1999. 192 pp., illustrated. Paper covers. $21.95

Stories of gunfighters and their encounters and detailed descriptions of virtually every firearm used in the old West.

Air Guns, by Eldon G. Wolff, Duckett's Publishing Co., Tempe, AZ, 1997. 204 pp., illus Paper covers. $35.00

Historical reference covering many makers, European and American guns, canes and more.

Allied and Enemy Aircraft: May 1918; Not to be Taken from the Front Lines, Historical Arms Series No. 27. Canada: Museum Restoration. Softcover. $8.95

The basis for this title is a very rare identification manual published by the French government in 1918 that illustrated 60 aircraft with three or more views: French, English American, German, Italian, and Belgian, which might have been seen over the trenches ofFrance. Each is describe in a text translated from the original French. This is probably the most complete collection of illustrations of WW1 aircraft which has survived.

American Military and Naval Belts, 1812-1902, by Dorsey, R. Stephen. Eugene, OR: Collectors Library, 2002. 1st edition. Hardcover. $80.00

With introduction by Norm Flayderman, this massive work is the NEW key reference on Sword Belts, Waist Belts, Sabre Belts, Shoulder Belts and Cartridge Belts (looped and non-looped). At over 460 pages, this 8.5x 11 inch book offers over 840 photos (primarily in colour) and original period drawings. In addition, this work offers the first, comprehensive research on the Anson Mills Woven Cartridge Belts: the man, the company and its personalities, the belt-related patents and the government contracts from 1880 through 1902. This book is a "must" for all accoutrements collectors, military historians and museums.

American Military Belt Plates, by O'Donnell, Michael J. and J. Duncan Campbell. Alexandria, VA: O'Donnell Publishing, 2000. 2nd edition. 614 pages, illus. Hardcover $49.00

At last available and well worth the wait! This massive study encompasses all the known plates from the Revolutionary War through the Spanish-American conflict. A sweeping, handsomely presented study that covers 1776 through 1910. Over 1,025 specimens are illustrated front and back along with many images of soldiers wearing various plates.

American Military Saddle, 1776-1945, The, by R. Stephen Dorsey & Kenneth L. McPheeters, Collector's Library, Eugene, OR, 1999. 400 pp., illustrated. $59.95

The most complete coverage of the subject ever writeen on the American Military Saddle. Nearly 1000 actual photos and official drawings, from the major public and private collections in the U.S. and Great Britain.

American Police Collectibles; Dark Lanterns and Other Curious Devices, by Matthew G. Forte, Turn of the Century Publishers, Upper Montclair, NJ, 1999. 248 pp., illustrated. $24.95

For collectors of police memorabilia (handcuffs, police dark lanterns, mechanical and chain nippers, rattles, billy clubs and nightsticks) and police historians.

Ammunition; Small Arms, Grenades, and Projected Munitions, by Greenhill Publishing. 144 pp., Illustrated. $22.95

The best concise guide to modern ammunition available today. Covers ammo for small arms, grenades, and projected munitions. 144 pp., Illustrated. As New – Hardcover.

Antique Guns, the Collector's Guide, 2nd Edition, edited by John Traister, Stoeger Publishing Co., So. Hackensack, NJ, 1994. 320 pp., illus. Paper covers. $19.95

Covers a vast spectrum of pre-1900 firearms: those manufactured by U.S. gunmakers as well as Canadian, French, German, Belgian, Spanish and other foreign firms.

Arming the Glorious Cause; Weapons of the Second War for Independence, by James B. Whisker, Daniel D. Hartzler and Larry W. Tantz, Old Bedford Village Press, Bedford, PA., 1998. 175 pp., illustrated. $45.00

A photographic study of Confederate weapons.

Arms & Accoutrements of the Mounted Police 1873-1973, by Roger F. Phillips and Donald J. Klancher, Museum Restoration Service, Ont., Canada, 1982. 224 pp., illus. $49.95

A definitive history of the revolvers, rifles, machine guns, cannons, ammunition, swords, etc. used by the NWMP, the RNWMP and the RCMP during the first 100 years of the Force.

Arms and Armor in the Art Institute of Chicago. By Waltler J. Karcheski, Bulfinch, New York 1999. 128 pp., 103 color photos, 12 black & white illustrations. $50.00

The George F. Harding Collection of arms and armor is the most visited installation at the Art Institute of Chicago - a testament to the enduring appeal of swords, muskets and the other paraphernalia of medieval and early modern war. Organized both chronologically and by type of weapon, this book captures the best of this astonishing collection in 115 striking photographs - most in color - accompanied by illuminating text. Here are intricately filigreed breastplates and ivory-handled crossbows, samurai katana and Toledo-steel scimitars, elaborately decorated maces and beautifully carved flintlocks - a treat for anyone who has ever been beguiled by arms, armor and the age of chivalry.

Arms and Armor in Colonial America 1526-1783. by Harold Peterson, Dover Publishing, New York, 2000. 350 pages with over 300 illustrations, index, bibliography & appendix. Softcover. $34.95

Over 200 years of firearms, ammunition, equipment & edged weapons.

Arms and Armor: The Cleveland Museum of Art. By Stephen N. Fliegel, Abrams, New York, 1998. 172 color photos, 17 halftones. 181 pages. $49.50

Intense look at the culture of the warrior and hunter, with an intriguing discussion of the decorative arts found on weapons and armor, set against the background of political and social history. Also provides information on the evolution of armor, together with manufacture and decoration, and weapons as technology and art.

Arms Makers of Maryland, by Daniel D. Hartzler, George Shumway, York, PA, 1975. 200 pp., illus. $50.00

A thorough study of the gunsmiths of Maryland who worked during the late 18th and early 19th centuries.

Arms Makers of Pennsylvania, by James B. Whisker, Selinsgrove, PA, Susquehanna Univ. Press, 1990. 1st edition. 218 pages, illustrated in black and white and color. $50.00

Concentrates primarily on the cottage industry gunsmiths & gun makers who worked in the Keystone State from it's early years through 1900.

Arms Makers of Western Pennsylvania, by James B. Whisker, Old Bedford Village Press. 1st edition. This deluxe hard bound edition has 176 pages, $50.00

Printed on fine coated paper, with many large photographs, and detailed text describing the period, lives, tools, and artistry of the Arms Makers of Western Pennsylvania.

Arsenal Of Freedom: The Springfield Armory 1890-1948, by Lt. Col. William Brophy, Andrew Mowbray, Inc., Lincoln, RI,1997. 20 pgs. of photos. 400 pages. As new — Softcover. $29.95

A year by year account drawn from offical records. Packed with reports, charts, tables, line drawings, and 20 page photo section.

Artistic Ingredients of the Longrifle, by George Shumway Publisher, 1989 102 pp., with 94 illus. $20.00

After a brief review of Pennsylvania-German folk art and architecture, to establish the artistic enviroment in which the longrifle was made, the author demonstrates that the sophisticated rococo decoration on the many of the finer longrifles is comparable to the best rococo work of Philadelphia cabinet makers and silversmiths.

Art of Miniature Firearms: Centuries of Craftsmanship, The, by Miniature Arms Society. Plainfield, IL: MAS Publications, 1999. 1st edition. Hardcover. $100.00

This volume of miniature arms includes some of the finest collector's items in existence, from antique replicas to contemporary pieces made by premium craftsmen working today, many of whom are members of the Miniature Arms Society. Beautiful color photographs highlight details of miniature firearms, including handguns, shoulder guns, and machine guns; cannon weaponry; weapons systems such as suits of armor, crossbows, and Gatling guns; and hand weapons, which include bows and arrows, daggers, knives, swords, maces, and spears. Also featured are exquisite replicas of accessories, from gun cases to cavalry saddles. 335 pages, full color photos.

Art of Gun Engraving, The, by Claude Gaier and Pietro Sabatti, Knickerbocker Press, N.Y., 1999. 160 pp., illustrated. $34.95

The richness and detail lavished on early firearms represents a craftmanship nearly vanished. Beginning with crossbows in the 100's, hunting scenes, portraits, or mythological themes are intricately depicted within a few square inches of etched metal. The full-color photos contained herein recaptures this lost art with exquisite detail.

Artillery Fuses of the Civil War, by Jones, Charles H., O'Donnell Publishing, Alexandria, VA: 2001. 1st edition. Hardcover. $34.00

Chuck Jones has been recognized as the leading authority on Civil War fuses for decades. Over the course of "Artillery Fuses" 167 pages Mr. Jones imparts the reader with the culmination of his life-long study of the subject with well-researched text and hundreds of photographs of every type of Civil War fuse known. The book is hardbound, color cover format, printed on lustrous glossy paper. A valuable reference for every serious Civil War collector.

Astra Automatic Pistols, by Leonardo M. Antaris, FIRAC Publishing Co., Sterling, CO, 1989. 248 pp., illus. $55.00

Charts, tables, serial ranges, etc. The definitive work on Astra pistols.

Ballard: The Great American Single Shot Rifle, by John T. Dutcher. Denver, CO: Privately Printed, 2002. 1st edition. 380 pages, illustrated with black & white photos, with 8-page color insert. Hardcover. New in New Dust Jacket. $79.95

Basic Documents on U.S. Martial Arms, commentary by Col. B. R. Lewis, reissue by Ray Riling, Phila., PA, 1956 and 1960. *Rifle Musket Model 1855.*

The first issue rifle of musket caliber, a muzzle loader equipped with the Maynard Primer, 32 pp. *Rifle Musket Model 1863.* The typical Union muzzle-loader of the Civil War, 26 pp. *Breech-Loading Rifle Musket Model 1866.* The first of our 50-caliber breechloading rifles, 12 pp. *Remington Navy Rifle Model 1870.* A commercial type breech-loader made at Springfield, 16 pp. *Lee Straight Pull Navy Rifle Model 1895.* A magazine cartridge arm of 6mm caliber. 23 pp. *Breech-Loading Arms* (five models) 27 pp. *Ward-Burton Rifle Musket 1871*-16 pp. Each $10.00

Battle Weapons of the American Revolution, by George C. Neuman, Scurlock Publishing Co., Texarkana, TX, 2001. 400 pp. Illus. Softcovers. $34.95

The most extensive photographic collection of Revolutionary War weapons ever in one volume. More than 1,600 photos of over 500 muskets, rifles, swords, bayonets, knives and other arms used by both sides in America's War for Independence.

Bedford County Rifle and Its Makers, The, by George Shumway. 40pp. illustrated, Softcover. $10.00

The authors study of the graceful and distinctive muzzle-loading rifles made in Bedford County, Pennsylvania. Stands as a milestone on the long path to the understanding of America's longrifles.

Belgian Rattlesnake; The Lewis Automatic Machine Gun, The, by William M. Easterly, Collector Grade Publications, Cobourg, Ontario, Canada, 1998. 584 pp., illustrated. $79.95

The most complete account ever published on the life and times of Colonel Isaac Newton Lewis and his crowning invention, the Lewis Automatic machine gun.

Beretta Automatic Pistols, by J.B. Wood, Stackpole Books, Harrisburg, PA, 1985. 192 pp., illus. $24.95

Only English-language book devoted to the Beretta line. Includes all important models.

Best of Holland & Holland, England's Premier Gunmaker, The, by McIntosh, Michael & Roosenburg, Jan G. Safari Press, Inc., Long Beach, CA: 2002. 1st edition. 298 pages. Profuse color illustrations. $69.95

Holland & Holland has had a long history of not only building London's "best" guns but also providing superior guns--the ultimate gun in finish, engraving, and embellishment. From the days of old in which a maharaja would order 100 fancifully engraved H&H shotguns for his guests to use at his duck shoot to the recent elaborately decorated sets depicting the Apollo 11 moon landing or the history of the British Empire, all of these guns represent the zenith in the art and craft of gunmaking and engraving. These and other H&H guns in the series named "Products of Excellence" are a cut above the ordinary H&H gun and hark back to a time when the British Empire ruled over one-third of the globe--a time when rulers, royalty, and the rich worldwide came to H&H for a gun that would elevate them above the crowd. In this book master gunwriter and acknowledged English gun expert Michael McIntosh and former H&H director Jan Roosenburg show us in words and pictures the finest products ever produced by H&H and, many would argue, by any gun company on earth. From a dainty and elegant .410 shotgun with gold relief engraving of scenes from Greek and Roman antiquity to the massive .700 Nitro Express double rifle, some of the most expensive and opulent guns ever produced on earth parade through these pages. An overview of the Products of Excellence series is given as well as a description and history of these special H&H guns. Never before have so many superlative guns from H&H--or any other maker for that manner--been displayed in one book. Many photos shown are firearms from private collections, which cannot be seen publicly anywhere except in this book. In addition, many interesting details and a general history of H&H are provided.

Big Guns, Civil War Siege, Seacoast, and Naval Cannon, The, by Edwin Olmstead, Wayne E. Stark, and Spencer C. Tucker, Museum Restoration Service, Bloomfield, Ontario, Canada, 1997. 360 pp., illustrated. $80.00

This book is designed to identify and record the heavy guns available to both sides by the end of the Civil War.

Blue Book of Air Guns, 2nd Edition, edited by S.P. Fjestad, Blue Book Publications, Inc. Minneapolis, MN 2002. $14.95

This new 2nd edition simply contains more airgun values and information than any other single publication.

Blue Book of Gun Values, 23rd Edition, edited by S.P. Fjestad, Blue Book Publications, Inc. Minneapolis, MN 2003. $39.95

This new 23rd edition simply contains more firearms values and information than any other single publication. Expanded to over 1,600 pages featuring over 100,000 firearms prices, the new Blue Book of Gun Values also contains over Ω million words of text – no other book is even close! Most of the information contained in this publication is simply not available anywhere else, for any price!

Blue Book of Modern Black Powder Values, 2nd Edtion by Dennis Adler, Blue Book Publications, Inc. Minneapolis, MN 2002. 200 pp., illustrated. 41 color photos. Softcover. $17.95

This new title contains more up-to-date black powder values and related information than any other single publication. With 163 pages, this new book will keep you up to date on modern black powder models and prices, including most makes & models introduced this year! .

Blunderbuss 1500-1900, The, by James D. Forman, Historical Arms Series No. 32. Canada: Museum Restoration, 1994. An excellent and authoritative booklet giving tons of information on the Blunderbuss, a very neglected subject. 40 pages, illustrated. Softcover. $8.95

REFERENCE

THE HANDGUNNER'S LIBRARY

Boarders Away I: With Steel-Edged Weapons & Polearms, by William Gilkerson, Andrew Mowbray, Inc. Publishers, Lincoln, RI, 1993. 331 pages. $48.00

Contains the essential 24 page chapter 'War at Sea' which sets the historical and practical context for the arms discussed. Includeds chapters on, Early Naval Weapons, Boarding Axes, Cutlasses, Officers Fighting Swords and Dirks, and weapons at hand of Random Mayhem.

Boarders Away, Volume II: Firearms of the Age of Fighting Sail, by William Gilkerson, Andrew Mowbray, Inc. Publishers, Lincoln, RI, 1993. 331 pp., illus. $65.00

Covers the pistols, muskets, combustibles and small cannon used aboard American and European fighting ships, 1626-1826.

Boston's Gun Bible, by Boston T. Party, Ignacio, CO: Javelin Press, August 2000. Expanded Edition. Softcover. $28.00

This mammoth guide for gun owners everywhere is a completely updated and expanded edition (more than 500 new pages!) of Boston T. Party's classic Boston on Guns and Courage. Pulling no punches, Boston gives new advice on which shoulder weapons and handguns to buy and why before exploring such topics as why you should consider not getting a concealed carry permit, what guns and gear will likely be outlawed next, how to spend within your budget, why you should go to a quality defensive shooting academy now, which guns and gadgets are inferior and why, how to stay off illegal government gun registration lists, how to spot an undercover agent trying to entrap law-abiding gun owners and much more.

Breech-Loading Carbines of the United States Civil War Period, by Brig. Gen. John Pitman, Armory Publications, Tacoma, WA, 1987. 94 pp., illus. $29.95

The first in a series of previously unpublished manuscripts originated by the late Brigadier General John Putnam. Exploded drawings showing parts actual size follow each sectioned illustration.

Breech-Loading Single-Shot Rifle, The, by Major Ned H. Roberts and Kenneth L. Waters, Wolfe Publishing Co., Prescott, AZ, 1995. 333 pp., illus. $28.50

A comprehensive and complete history of the evolution of the Schutzen and single-shot rifle.

Bren Gun Saga, The, by Thomas B. Dugelby, Collector Grade Publications, Cobourg, Ontario, Canada, 1999, revised and expanded edition. 406 pp., illustrated. $65.95

A modern, definitive book on the Bren in this revised expanded edition, which in terms of numbers of pages and illustrations is nearly twice the size of the original.

British Board of Ordnance Small Arms Contractors 1689-1840, by De Witt Bailey, Rhyl, England: W. S. Curtis, 2000. 150 pp. $18.00

Thirty years of research in the Archives of the Ordnance Board in London has identified more than 600 of these suppliers. The names of many can be found marking the regulation firearms of the period. In the study, the contractors are identified both alphabetically and under a combination of their date period together with their specialist trade.

British Enfield Rifles, The, Volume 1, The SMLE Mk I and Mk III Rifles, by Charles R. Stratton, North Cape Pub. Tustin, CA, 1997. 150 pp., illus. Paper covers. $16.95

A systematic and thorough examination on a part-by-part basis of the famous British battle rifle that endured for nearly 70 years as the British Army's number one battle rifle.

British Enfield Rifles, Volume 2, No.4 and No.5 Rifles, by Charles R. Stratton, North Cape Publications, Tustin, CA, 1999. 150 pp., illustrated. Paper covers. $16.95

The historical background for the development of both rifles describing each variation and an explanation of all the "marks", "numbers" and codes found on most parts.

British Enfield Rifles, Volume 4, The Pattern 1914 and U. S. Model 1917 Rifles, by Charles R. Stratton, North Cape Publications, Tustin, CA, 2000. Paper covers. $16.95

One of the lease know American and British collectible military rifles is analyzed on a part by part basis. All markings and codes, refurbishment procedures and WW 2 upgrade are included as are the varios sniper rifle versions.

British Falling Block Breechloading Rifle from 1865, The, by Jonathan Kirton, Tom Rowe Books, Maynardsville, TN, 2nd edition, 1997. 380 pp., illus. $70.00

Expanded 2nd edition of a comprehensive work on the British falling block rifle.

British Gun Engraving, by Douglas Tate, Safari Press, Inc., Huntington Beach, CA, 1999. 240 pp., illustrated. Limited, signed and numbered edition, in a slipcase. $80.00

A historic and photographic record of the last two centuries.

British Military Flintlock Rifles 1740-1840. 264 pages with over 320 photographs. Hardcover. $47.95

With a remarkable weath of data about the Rifleman and Regiments that carried these weapons, by Bailey, De Witt. Andrew Mowbray, Inc. Lincoln, RI:, 2002. 1st edition. Pattern 1776 Rifles, The Ferguson Breechloader, The Famous Baker Rifle, Rifles of the Hessians and other German Mercenaries, American Loylist Rifles, Rifles given to indians, Cavalry Rifles and Rifled Carbines, Bayonets, Accoutrements, Ammunition and more.

British Service Rifles and Carbines 1888-1900, by Alan M. Petrillo, Excaliber Publications, Latham, NY, 1994. 72 pp., illus, Paper covers. $11.95

A complete review of the Lee-Metford and Lee-Enfield rifles and carbines.

British Single Shot Rifles, Volume 1, Alexander Henry, by Wal Winfer, Tom Rowe, Maynardsville, TN, 1998, 200 pp., illus. $50.00

Detailed Study of the single shot rifles made by Henry. Illustrated with hundreds of photographs and drawings.

British Single Shot Rifles Volume 2, George Gibbs, by Wal Winfer, Tom Rowe, Maynardsville, TN, 1998. 177 pp., illus. $50.00

Detailed study of the Farquharson as made by Gibbs. Hundreds of photos.

British Single Shot Rifles, Volume 3, Jeffery, by Wal Winfer, Rowe Publications, Rochester, N.Y., 1999. 260 pp., illustrated. $60.00

The Farquharsen as made by Jeffery and his competitors, Holland & Holland, Bland, Westley, Manton, etc. Large section on the development of nitro cartridges including the .600.

British Single Shot Rifles, Vol. 4; Westley Richards, by Wal Winfer, Rowe Publications, Rochester, N.Y., 2000. 265 pages, illustrated, photos. $60.00

In his 4th volume Winfer covers a detailed study of the Westley Richards single shot rifles, including Monkey Tails, Improved Martini, 1872,1873, 1878,1881, 1897 Falling Blocks. He also covers Westley Richards Cartridges, History and Reloading information.

British Small Arms Ammunition, 1864-1938 (Other than .303 inch), by Peter Labbett, Armory Publications, Seattle, WA. 1993, 358 pages, illus. Four-color dust jacket. $79.00

A study of British military rifle, handgun, machine gun, and aiming tube ammunition through 1 inch from 1864 to 1938. Photo-illustrated including the firearms that chambered the cartridges.

British Soldier's Firearms from Smoothbore to Rifled Arms, The, 1850-1864, by Dr. C.H. Roads, R&R Books, Livonia, NY, 1994. 332 pp., illus. $49.00

A reprint of the classic text covering the development of British military hand and shoulder firearms in the crucial years between 1850 and 1864.

British Sporting Guns & Rifles, compiled by George Hoyem, Armory Publications, Coeur d'Alene, ID, 1997. 1024 pp., illus. In two volumes. $250.00

Eighteen old sporting firearms trade catalogs and a rare book reproduced with their color covers in a limited, signed and numbered edition.

Browning Dates of Manufacture, compiled by George Madis, Art and Reference House, Brownsboro, TX, 1989. 48 pp. $10.00

Gives the date codes and product codes for all models from 1824 to the present.

Buffalo Bill's Wild West: An American Legend, by R.L. Wilson and Greg Martine, Random House, N.Y., 1999. 3,167 pp., illustrated. $60.00

Over 225 color plates and 160 black-and-white illustrations, with in-depth text and captions, the colorful arms, posters, photos, costumes, saddles, accoutrement are brought to life.

Bullard Firearms, by Jamieson, G. Scott, Schiffer Publications, Atglen, PA 2002. 1st edition. 400 pages, with over 1100 color and b/w photographs, charts, diagrams. Hardcover. $100.00

Bullard Firearms is the story of a mechanical genius whose rifles and cartridges were the equal of any made in America in the 1880s, yet little of substance had been written about James H. Bullard or his arms prior to 1988 when the first edition called Bullard Arms was published. This greatly expanded volume with over 1,000 black and white and 150 color plates, most not previously published answers many of the questions posed in the first edition. The book is divided into eleven chapters each covering a different aspect of the Bullard story. For example, chapter two discusses Bullard's pioneering automotive work for the Overman Automobile Company (he was probably first to use a metal body on a production automobile (1899). Chapters four through eight outline in detail the large-frame repeaters, the small-frame repeaters, the solid-frame single-shot rifles, the detachable-interchangeable barrel model single-shots and lastly the very rare military and experimental models. Each model is covered in depth with many detailed photographs of the interior parts and workings of the repeaters. Chapter nine covers the fascinating and equally unknown world of Bullard cartridges and reloading tools. The final chapter outlines in chart form almost 500 Bullard rifles by serial number, caliber and type. Quick and easy to use, this book is a real benefit for collectors and dealers alike.

Burning Powder, compiled by Major D.B. Wesson, Wolfe Publishing Company, Prescott, AZ, 1992. 110 pp. Soft cover. $10.95

A rare booklet from 1932 for Smith & Wesson collectors.

Burnside Breech Loading Carbines, The, by Edward A. Hull, Andrew Mowbray, Inc., Lincoln, RI, 1986. 95 pp., illus. $16.00

No. 1 in the "Man at Arms Monograph Series." A model-by-model historical/technical examination of one of the most widely used cavalry weapons of the American Civil War based upon important and previously unpublished research.

THE HANDGUNNER'S LIBRARY

Camouflage Uniforms of European and NATO Armies; 1945 to the Present, by J. F. Borsarello, Atglen, PA: Schiffer Publications. Over 290 color and b/w photographs, 120 pages. Softcover. $29.95

This full-color book covers nearly all of the NATO, and other European armies' camouflaged uniforms, and not only shows and explains the many patterns, but also their efficacy of design. Described and illustrated are the variety of materials tested in over forty different armies, and includes the history of obsolete trial tests from 1945 to the present time. More than two hundred patterns have been manufactured since World War II using various landscapes and seasonal colors for their look. The Vietnam and Gulf Wars, African or South American events, as well as recent Yugoslavian independence wars have been used as experimental terrains to test a variety of patterns. This book provides a superb reference for the historian, reenactor, designer, and modeler.

Camouflage Uniforms of the Waffen-SS A Photographic Reference, by Michael Beaver, Schiffer Publishing, Atglen, PA. Over 1,000 color and b/w photographs and illustrations, 296 pages. $69.95

Finally a book that unveils the shroud of mystery surrounding Waffen-SS camouflage clothing. Illustrated here, both in full color and in contemporary black and white photographs, this unparalleled look at Waffen-SS combat troops and their camouflage clothing will benefit both the historian and collector.

Canadian Gunsmiths from 1608: A Checklist of Tradesmen, by John Belton, Historical Arms Series No. 29. Canada: Museum Restoration, 1992. 40 pp., 17 illustrations. Softcover. $8.95

This Checklist is a greatly expanded version of HAS No. 14, listing the names, occupation, location, and dates of more than 1,500 men and women who worked as gunmakers, gunsmiths, armorers, gun merchants, gun patent holders, and a few other gun related trades. A collection of contemporary gunsmiths' letterhead have been provided to add color and depth to the study.

Cap Guns, by James Dundas, Schiffer Publishing, Atglen, PA, 1996. 160 pp., illus. Paper covers. $29.95

Over 600 full-color photos of cap guns and gun accessories with a current value guide.

Carbines of the Civil War, by John D. McAulay, Pioneer Press, Union City, TN, 1981. 123 pp., illus. Paper covers. $12.95

A guide for the student and collector of the colorful arms used by the Federal cavalry.

Carbines of the U.S. Cavalry 1861-1905, by John D. McAulay, Andrew Mowbray Publishers, Lincoln, RI, 1996. $35.00

Covers the crucial use of carbines from the beginning of the Civil War to the end of the cavalry carbine era in 1905.

Cartridge Carbines of the British Army, by Alan M. Petrillo, Excalibur Publications, Latham, NY, 1998. 72 pp., illustrated. Paper covers. $11.95

Begins with the Snider-Enfield which was the first regulation cartridge carbine introduced in 1866 and ends with the .303 caliber No.5, Mark 1 Enfield.

Cartridge Catalogues, compiled by George Hoyem, Armory Publications, Coeur d'Alene, ID., 1997. 504 pp., illus. $125.00

Fourteen old ammunition makers' and designers' catalogs reproduced with their color covers in a limited, signed and numbered edition. Completely revised edition of the general purpose reference work for which collectors, police, scientists and laymen reach first for answers to cartridge identification questions.

Cartridge Reloading Tools of the Past, by R.H. Chamberlain and Tom Quigley, Tom Quigley, Castle Rock, WA, 1998. 167 pp., illustrated. Paper covers. $25.00

A detailed treatment of the extensive Winchester and Ideal lines of handloading tools and bulletmolds plus Remington, Marlin, Ballard, Browning and many others.

Cartridges for Collectors, by Fred Datig, Pioneer Press, Union City, TN, 1999. In three volumes of 176 pp. each. Vol.1 (Centerfire); Vol.2 (Rimfire and Misc.) types; Vol.3 (Additional Rimfire, Centerfire, and Plastic.). All illustrations are shown in full-scale drawings. Volume 1, softcover only, $19.95. Volumes 2 & 3, Hardcover $19.95

Civil War Arms Makers and Their Contracts, edited by Stuart C. Mowbray and Jennifer Heroux, Andrew Mowbray Publishing, Lincoln, RI, 1998. 595 pp. $39.50

A facsimile reprint of the Report by the Commissioner of Ordnance and Ordnance Stores, 1862.

Civil War Arms Purchases and Deliveries, edited by Stuart C. Mowbray, Andrew Mowbray Publishing, Lincoln, RI, 1998. 300pp., illus. $39.50

A facsimile reprint of the master list of Civil War weapons purchases and deliveries including Small Arms, Cannon, Ordnance and Projectiles.

Civil War Breech Loading Rifles, by John D. McAulay, Andrew Mowbray, Inc., Lincoln, RI, 1991. 144 pp., illus. Paper covers. $15.00

All the major breech-loading rifles of the Civil War and most, if not all, of the obscure types are detailed, illustrated and set in their historical context.

Civil War Cartridge Boxes of the Union Infantryman, by Paul Johnson, Andrew Mowbray, Inc., Lincoln, RI, 1998. 352 pp., illustrated. $45.00

There were four patterns of infantry cartridge boxes used by Union forces during the Civil War. The author describes the development and subsequent pattern changes to these cartridge boxes.

Civil War Collector's Price Guide; Expanded Millennium Edition, by North South Trader. Orange, VA: Publisher's Press, 2000. 9th edition. 260 pps., illus. Softcover. $29.95

All updated prices, scores of new listings, and hundreds of new pictures! It's the one reference work no collector should be without. An absolute must.

Civil War Commanders, by Dean Thomas, Thomas Publications, Gettysburg, PA. 1998. 72 pages, illustrated, photos. Paper Covers. $9.95

138 photographs and capsule biographies of Union and Confederate officers. A convenient personalities reference guide.

Civil War Guns, by William B. Edwards, Thomas Publications, Gettysburg, PA, 1997. 444 pp., illus. $40.00

The complete story of Federal and Confederate small arms; design, manufacture, identifications, procurement issue, employment, effectiveness, and postwar disposal by the recognized expert.

Civil War Infantryman: In Camp, On the March, And in Battle, by Dean Thomas, Thomas Publications, Gettysburg, PA. 1998. 72 pages, illustrated, Softcovers. $12.95

Uses first-hand accounts to shed some light on the "common soldier" of the Civil War from enlistment to muster-out, including camp, marching, rations, equipment, fighting, and more.

Civil War Pistols, by John D. McAulay, Andrew Mowbray Inc., Lincoln, RI, 1992. 166 pp., illus. $38.50

A survey of the handguns used during the American Civil War.

Civil War Projectiles II; Small Arms & Field Artillery, With Supplement, by McKee, W. Reid, and M. E. Mason, Jr. Orange, VA: Publisher's Press, 2001. 202 pages, illus. Hardcover. $40.00

The standard reference work is now available. Essential for every Civil War bullet collector.

Civil War Sharps Carbines and Rifles, by Earl J. Coates and John D. McAulay, Thomas Publications, Gettysburg, PA, 1996. 108 pp., illus. Paper covers. $12.95

Traces the history and development of the firearms including short histories of specific serial numbers and the soldiers who received them.

Civil War Small Arms of the U.S. Navy and Marine Corps, by John D. McAulay, Mowbray Publishing, Lincoln, RI, 1999. 186 pp., illustrated. $39.00

The first reliable and comprehensive guide to the firearms and edged weapons of the Civil War Navy and Marine Corps.

Cody Buffalo Bill Collector's Guide with Values, The W.F., by James W. Wojtowicz, Collector Books, Paducah, KY, 1998. 271 pp., illustrated. $24.95

A profusion of colorful collectibles including lithographs, programs, photographs, books, medals, sheet music, guns, etc. and today's values.

Col. Burton's Spiller & Burr Revolver, by Matthew W. Norman, Mercer University Press, Macon, GA, 1997. 152 pp., illus. $22.95

A remarkable archival research project on the arm together with a comprehensive story of the establishment and running of the factory.

Collector's Guide to United States Combat Shotguns, A, by Bruce N. Canfield, Andrew Mowbray Inc., Lincoln, RI, 1992. 184 pp., illus. Paper covers. $24.00

This book provides full coverage of combat shotguns, from the earliest examples right up to the Gulf War and beyond.

Collector's Guide to Winchester in the Service, A, by Bruce N. Canfield, Andrew Mowbray, Inc., Lincoln, RI, 1991. 192 pp., illus. Paper covers. $22.00

The firearms produced by Winchester for the national defense. From Hotchkiss to the M14, each firearm is examined and illustrated.

Collector's Guide to the '03 Springfield, A, by Bruce N. Canfield, Andrew Mowbray Inc., Lincoln, RI, 1989. 160 pp., illus. Paper covers. $22.00

A comprehensive guide follows the '03 through its unparalleled tenure of service. Covers all of the interesting variations, modifications and accessories of this highly collectible military rifle.

Collector's Illustrated Encyclopedia of the American Revolution, by George C. Neumann and Frank J. Kravic, Rebel Publishing Co., Inc., Texarkana, TX, 1989. 286 pp., illus. $36.95

A showcase of more than 2,300 artifacts made, worn, and used by those who fought in the War for Independence.

Colonial Frontier Guns, by T.M. Hamilton, Pioneer Press, Union City, TN, 1988. 176 pp., illus. Paper covers. $17.50

A complete study of early flint muskets of this country.

Colt: An American Legend, by R.L. Wilson, Artabras, New York, 1997. 406 pages, fully illustrated, most in color. $35.00

A reprint of the commemorative album celebrates 150 years of the guns of Samuel Colt and the manufacturing empire he built, with expert discussion of every model ever produced, the innovations of each model and variants, updated model and serial number charts and magnificent photographic showcases of the weapons.

Colt Engraving Book, The, Volumes I & II, by R. L. Wilson. Privately printed, 2001. Each volume is approximately 500 pages, with 650 illustrations, most in color. $390.00

This third edition from the original texts of 1974 and 1982 has been fine-tuned and dramatically expanded, and is by far the most illuminating and complete. With over 1,200 illustrations, more than 2/3 of which are in color, this book joins

REFERENCE

the author's The Book of Colt Firearms, and Fine Colts as companion volumes. Approximately 1,000 pages in two volumes, each signed by the author, serial numbered, and strictly limited to 3000 copies. Volume I covers from the Paterson and pre-Paterson period through c.1921 (end of the Helfricht period). Volume II commences with Kornbrath, and Glahn, and covers Colt embellished arms from c.1919 through 2000.

Colt Model 1905 Automatic Pistol, The, by John Potocki, Andrew Mowbray Publishing, Lincoln, RI, 1998. 191 pp., illus. $28.00

Covers all aspects of the Colt Model 1905 Automatic Pistol, from its invention by the legendary John Browning to its numerous production variations.

Colt Peacemaker British Model, by Keith Cochran, Cochran Publishing Co., Rapid City, SD, 1989. 160 pp., illus. $35.00

Covers those revolvers Colt squeezed in while completing a large order of revolvers for the U.S. Cavalry in early 1874, to those magnificent cased target revolvers used in the pistol competitions at Bisley Commons in the 1890s.

Colt Peacemaker Encyclopedia, by Keith Cochran, Keith Cochran, Rapid City, SD, 1986. 434 pp., illus. $60.00

A must book for the Peacemaker collector.

Colt Peacemaker Encyclopedia, Volume 2, by Keith Cochran, Cochran Publishing Co., SD, 1992. 416 pp., illus. $60.00

Included in this volume are extensive notes on engraved, inscribed, historical and noted revolvers, as well as those revolvers used by outlaws, lawmen, movie and television stars.

Colt Presentations: From The Factory Ledgers 1856-1869, by Herbert G. Houze. Lincoln, RI: Andrew Mowbray, Inc., 2003. 112 pages, 45 b&w photos. Softcover. $21.95

Samuel Colt was a generous man. He also used gifts to influence government decision makers. But after Congress investigated him in 1854, Colt needed to hide the gifts from prying eyes, which makes it very difficult for today's collectors to document the many revolvers presented by Colt and the factory. Using the original account journals of the Colt's Patent Fire Arms Manufacturing Co., renowned arms authority Herbert G. Houze finally gives us the full details behind hundreds of the most exciting Colts ever made.

Colt Revolvers and the Tower of London, by Joseph G. Rosa, Royal Armouries of the Tower of London, London, England, 1988. 72 pp., illus. Soft covers. $15.00

Details the story of Colt in London through the early cartridge period.

Colt's SAA Post War Models, by George Garton, The Gun Room Press, Highland Park, NJ, 1995. 166 pp., illus. $39.95

Complete facts on the post-war Single Action Army revolvers. Information on calibers, production numbers and variations taken from factory records.

Colt Single Action Army Revolvers: The Legend, the Romance and the Rivals, by "Doc" O'Meara, Krause Publications, Iola, WI, 2000. 160 pp., illustrated with 250 photos in b&w and a 16 page color section. $34.95

Production figures, serial numbers by year, and rarities.

Colt Single Action Army Revolvers and Alterations, by C. Kenneth Moore, Mowbray Publishers, Lincoln, RI, 1999. 112 pp., illustrated. $35.00

A comprehensive history of the revolvers that collectors call "Artillery Models." These are the most historical of all S.A.A. Colts, and this new book covers all the details.

Colt Single Action Army Revolvers and the London Agency, by C. Kenneth Moore, Andrew Mowbray Publishers, Lincoln, RI, 1990. 144 pp., illus. $35.00

Drawing on vast documentary sources, this work chronicles the relationship between the London Agency and the Hartford home office.

Colt U.S. General Officers' Pistols, The, by Horace Greeley IV, Andrew Mowbray Inc., Lincoln, RI, 1990. 199 pp., illus. $38.00

These unique weapons, issued as a badge of rank to General Officers in the U.S. Army from WWII onward, remain highly personal artifacts of the military leaders who carried them. Includes serial numbers and dates of issue.

Colts from the William M. Locke Collection, by Frank Sellers, Andrew Mowbray Publishers, Lincoln, RI, 1996. 192 pp., illus. $55.00

This important book illustrates all of the famous Locke Colts, with captions by arms authority Frank Sellers.

Colt's Dates of Manufacture 1837-1978, by R.L. Wilson, published by Maurie Albert, Coburg, Australia; N.A. distributor Madis Books, TX, 1997. 61 pp. $7.50

An invaluable pocket guide to the dates of manufacture of Colt firearms up to 1978.

Colt's Pocket '49: Its Evolution Including the Baby Dragoon and Wells Fargo, by Robert Jordan and Darrow Watt, privately printed, Loma Mar, CA 2000. 304 pages, with 984 color photos, illus. Beautifully bound in a deep blue leather like case. $125.00

Detailed information on all models and covers engaving, cases, accoutrements, holsters, fakes, and much more. Included is a summary booklet containing information such as serial numbers, production ranges & identifing photos. This book is a masterpiece on its subject.

Complete Guide to all United States Military Medals 1939 to Present, by Colonel Frank C. Foster, Medals of America Press, Fountain Inn, SC, 2000. 121 pp,.illustrated, photos. $29.95

Complete criteria for every Army, Navy, Marines, Air Force, Coast Guard, and Merchant Marine awards since 1939. All decorations, service medals, and ribbons shown in full-color and accompanied by dates and campaigns as well as detailed descriptions on proper wear and display.

Complete Guide to the M1 Garand and the M1 Carbine, by Bruce N. Canfield, 2nd printing, Andrew Mowbray Inc., Lincoln, RI, 1999. 296 pp., illus. $39.50

Expanded and updated coverage of both the M1 Garand and the M1 Carbine, with more than twice as much information as the author's previous book on this topic.

Complete Guide to U.S. Infantry Weapons of the First War, The, by Bruce Canfield, Andrew Mowbray, Publisher, Lincoln, RI, 2000. 304 pp., illus. $39.95

The definitive study of the U.S. Infantry weapons used in WWI.

Complete Guide to U.S. Infantry Weapons of World War Two, The, by Bruce Canfield, Andrew Mowbray, Publisher, Lincoln, RI, 1995. 303 pp., illus. $39.95

A definitive work on the weapons used by the United States Armed Forces in WWII.

Confederate Belt Buckles & Plates, by Mullinax, Steve E. O'Donnell Publishing, Alexandria, VA: 1999. Expanded edition. Hardbound, 247 pages, illus. Hardcover. $34.00

Hundreds of crisp photographs augment this classic study of Confederate accoutrement plates.

Confederate Carbines & Musketoons Cavalry Small Arms manufactured in and for the Southern Confederacy 1861-1865, by Murphy, John M. Santa Ana, CA: Privately Printed, 2002. Reprint. 320 pages, illustrated with B & W drawings and photos. Color Frontis by Don Troiani. Hardcover. $79.95

This is Dr. Murphy's first work on Confederate arms. See also "Confederate Rifles & Muskets". Exceptional photography compliments the text. John Murphy has one of the finest collections of Confederate arms known.

Confederate Rifles & Muskets Infantry Small Arms Manufactured in the Southern Confederacy 1861-1865, by Murphy, John M. Santa Ana, CA: Privately Printed, 1996. Reprint. 768pp, 8pp color plates, profusely illustrated. Hardcover. $119.95

The first in-depth and academic analysis and discussion of the "long" longarms produced in the South by and for the Confederacy during the American Civil War. The collection of Dr. Murphy is doubtless the largest and finest grouping of Confederate longarms in private hands today.

Confederate Saddles & Horse Equipment, by Knopp, Ken R. Orange, VA: Publisher's Press, 2002. 194 pps., illus. Hardcover. $39.95

Confederate Saddles & Horse Equipment is a pioneer work on the subject. After ten years of research Ken Knopp has compiled a thorough and fascinating study of the little-known field of Confederate saddlery and equipment. His analysis of ordnance operations coupled with his visual presentation of surviving examples offers an indispensable source for collectors and historians.

Concise Guide to the Artillery at Gettysburg, A, by Gregory Coco, Thomas Publications, Gettysburg, PA, 1998. 96 pp., illus. Paper Covers. $10.00

Coco's tenth book on Gettysburg is a beginner's guide to artillery and its use at the battle. It covers the artillery batteries describing the types of cannons, shells, fuses, etc.using interesting narrative and human interest stories.

Cooey Firearms, Made in Canada 1919-1979, by John A. Belton, Museum Restoration, Canada, 1998. 36pp., with 46 illus. Paper Covers. $8.95

More than 6 million rifles and at least 67 models, were made by this small Canadian riflemaker. They have been identified from the first 'Cooey Canuck' through the last variations made by the 'Winchester-Cooey'. Each is descibed and most are illustrated in this first book on The Cooey.

Cowboy Collectibles and Western Memorabilia, by Bob Bell and Edward Vebell, Schiffer Publishing, Atglen, PA, 1992. 160 pp., illus. Paper covers. $29.95

The exciting era of the cowboy and the wild west collectibles including rifles, pistols, gun rigs, etc.

Cowboy Culture: The Last Frontier of American Antiques, by Michael Friedman, Schiffer Publishing, Ltd., West Chester, PA, 1992. 300 pp., illustrated.

Covers the artful aspects of the old west, the antiques and collectibles. Illustrated with clear color plates of over 1,000 items such as spurs, boots, guns, saddles etc.

Cowboy and Gunfighter Collectible, by Bill Mackin, Mountain Press Publishing Co., Missoula, MT, 1995. 178 pp., illus. Paper covers. $25.00

A photographic encyclopedia with price guide and makers' index.

Cowboys and the Trappings of the Old West, by William Manns and Elizabeth Clair Flood, Zon International Publishing Co., Santa Fe, NM, 1997, 1st edition. 224 pp., illustrated. $45.00

A pictorial celebration of the cowboys dress and trappings.

Cowboy Hero Cap Pistols, by Rudy D'Angelo, Antique Trader Books, Dubuque, IA, 1998. 196 pp., illus. Paper covers. $34.95

Aimed at collectors of cap pistols created and named for famous film and television cowboy heros, this in-depth guide hits all the marks. Current values are given.

THE HANDGUNNER'S LIBRARY

Custom Firearms Engraving, by Tom Turpin, Krause Publications, Iola, WI, 1999. 208 pp., illustrated. $49.95

Over 200 four-color photos with more than 75 master engravers profiled. Engravers Directory with addresses in the U.S. and abroad.

Daisy Air Rifles & BB Guns: The First 100 Years, by Punchard, Neal. St. Paul, MN: Motorbooks, 2002. 1st edition. Hardcover, 10 x 10, 156 pp, 300 color. Hardcover. $29.95

Flash back to the days of your youth and recall fond memories of your Daisy. Daisy Air Rifles and BB Guns looks back fondly on the first 100 years of Daisy BB rifles and pistols, toy and cork guns, accessories, packaging, period advertising and literature. Wacky ads and catalogs conjure grins of pure nostalgia as chapters reveal how Daisy used a combination of savvy business sense and quality products to dominate the market.

Decorations, Medals, Ribbons, Badges and Insignia of the United States Army; World War 2 to Present, The, by Col. Frank C. Foster, Medals of America Press, Fountain Inn, SC. 2001. 145 pages, illustrated. $29.95

The most complete guide to United States Army medals, ribbons, rank, insignia nad patches from WWII to the present day. Each medal and insignia shown in full color. Includes listing of respective criteria and campaigns.

Decorations, Medals, Ribbons, Badges and Insignia of the United States Navy; World War 2 to Present, The, by James G. Thompson, Medals of America Press, Fountain Inn, SC. 2000. 123 pages, illustrated. $29.95

The most complete guide to United States Army medals, ribbons, rank, insignia nad patches from WWII to the present day. Each medal and insignia shown in full color. Includes listing of respective criteria and campaigns.

Derringer in America, The, Volume 1, The Percussion Period, by R.L. Wilson and L.D. Eberhart, Andrew Mowbray Inc., Lincoln, RI, 1985. 271 pp., illus. $48.00

A long awaited book on the American percussion deringer.

Derringer in America, The, Volume 2, The Cartridge Period, by L.D. Eberhart and R.L. Wilson, Andrew Mowbray Inc., Publishers, Lincoln, RI, 1993. 284 pp., illus. $65.00

Comprehensive coverage of cartridge deringers organized alphabetically by maker. Includes all types of deringers known by the authors to have been offered to the American market.

Devil's Paintbrush: Sir Hiram Maxim's Gun, The, by Dolf Goldsmith, 3rd Edition, expanded and revised, Collector Grade Publications, Toronto, Canada, 2002. 384 pp., illus. $79.95

The classic work on the world's first true automatic machine gun.

Dr. Josephus Requa Civil War Dentist and the Billinghurst-Requa Volley Gun, by John M. Hyson, Jr., & Margaret Requa DeFrancisco, Museum Restoration Service, Bloomfield, Ont., Canada, 1999. 36 pp., illus. Paper covers. $8.95

The story of the inventor of the first practical rapid-fire gun to be used during the American Civil War.

Dutch Luger (Parabellum) A Complete History, The, by Bas J. Martens and Guus de Vries, Ironside International Publishers, Inc., Alexandria, VA, 1995. 268 pp., illus. $49.95

The history of the Luger in the Netherlands. An extensive description of the Dutch pistol and trials and the different models of the Luger in the Dutch service.

Eagle on U.S. Firearms, The, by John W. Jordan, Pioneer Press, Union City, TN, 1992. 140 pp., illus. Paper covers. $17.50

Stylized eagles have been stamped on government owned or manufactured firearms in the U.S. since the beginning of our country. This book lists and illustrates these various eagles in an informative and refreshing manner.

Encyclopedia of Rifles & Handguns; A Comprehensive Guide to Firearms, edited by Sean Connolly, Chartwell Books, Inc., Edison, NJ., 1996. 160 pp., illustrated. $26.00

A lavishly illustrated book providing a comprehensive history of military and civilian personal firepower.

Eprouvettes: A Comprehensive Study of Early Devices for the Testing of Gunpowder, by R.T.W. Kempers, Royal Armouries Museum, Leeds, England, 1999. 352 pp., illustrated with 240 black & white and 28 color plates. $125.00

The first comprehensive study of eprouvettes ever attempted in a single volume.

European Firearms in Swedish Castles, by Kaa Wennberg, Bohuslaningens Boktryckeri AB, Uddevalla, Sweden, 1986. 156 pp., illus. $50.00

The famous collection of Count Keller, the Ettersburg Castle collection, and others. English text.

Fifteen Years in the Hawken Lode, by John D. Baird, The Gun Room Press, Highland Park, NJ, 1976. 120 pp., illus. $24.95

A collection of thoughts and observations gained from many years of intensive study of the guns from the shop of the Hawken brothers.

'51 Colt Navies, by Nathan L. Swayze, The Gun Room Press, Highland Park, NJ, 1993. 243 pp., illus. $59.95

The Model 1851 Colt Navy, its variations and markings.

Fighting Iron, by Art Gogan, Andrew Mowbray, Inc., Lincoln, R.I., 2002. 176 pp., illustrated. $28.00

It doesn't matter whether you collect guns, swords, bayonets or accountrement— sooner or later you realize that it all comes down to the metal. If you don't understand the metal you don't understand your collection.

Fine Colts, The Dr. Joseph A. Murphy Collection, by R.L. Wilson, Sheffield Marketing Associates, Inc., Doylestown, PA, 1999. 258 pp., illustrated. Limited edition signed and numbered. $99.00

This lavish new work covers exquisite, deluxe and rare Colt arms from Paterson and other percussion revolvers to the cartridge period and up through modern times.

Firearms, by Derek Avery, Desert Publications, El Dorado, AR, 1999. 95 pp., illustrated. $9.95

The firearms included in this book are by necessity only a selection, but nevertheless one that represents the best and most famous weapons seen since the Second World War.

Firearms and Tackle Memorabilia, by John Delph, Schiffer Publishing, Ltd., West Chester, PA, 1991. 124 pp., illus. $39.95

A collector's guide to signs and posters, calendars, trade cards, boxes, envelopes, and other highly sought after memorabilia. With a value guide.

Firearms of the American West 1803-1865, Volume 1, by Louis A. Garavaglia and Charles Worman, University of Colorado Press, Niwot, CO, 1998. 402 pp., illustrated. $59.95

Traces the development and uses of firearms on the frontier during this period.

Firearms of the American West 1866-1894, by Louis A. Garavaglia and Charles G. Worman, University of Colorado Press, Niwot, CO, 1998. 416 pp., illus. $59.95

A monumental work that offers both technical information on all of the important firearms used in the West during this period and a highly entertaining history of how they were used, who used them, and why.

Firearms from Europe, 2nd Edition, by David Noe, Larry W. Yantz, Dr. James B. Whisker, Rowe Publications, Rochester, N.Y., 2002. 192 pp., illustrated. $45.00

A history and description of firearms imported during the American Civil War by the United States of America and the Confederate States of America.

Firepower from Abroad, by Wiley Sword, Andrew Mowbray Publishing, Lincoln, R.I., 2000. 120 pp., illustrated. $23.00

The Confederate Enfield and the LeMat revolver and how they reached the Confederate market.

Flayderman's Guide to Antique American Firearms and Their Values, 8th Edition, edited by Norm Flayderman, Krause Publications, Iola, WI, 2001. 692 pp., illus. Paper covers. $34.95

A completely updated and new edition with more than 3,600 models and variants extensively described with all marks and specifications necessary for quick identification.

FN-FAL Rifle, et al, The, by Duncan Long, Paladin Press, Boulder, CO, 1999. 144 pp., illustrated. Paper covers. $18.95

Detailed descriptions of the basic models produced by Fabrique Nationale and the myriad variants that evolved as a result of the firearms universal acceptance.

.45-70 Springfield; Book 1, The, by Frasca, Albert and Robert Hill. Frasca, Albert and Robert Hill. Frasca Publishing, 2000. Memorial edition. Hardback with gold embossed cover and spine. $95.00

The Memorial Edition reprint of The .45-70 Springfield was done to honor Robert H. Hill who was an outstanding Springfield collector, historian, researcher, and gunsmith. Only 1000 of these highly regarded books were printed using the same binding and cover material as the original 1980 edition. The book is considered The Bible for .45-70 Springfield Trapdoor collectors.

.45-70 Springfield Book II 1865-1893, The, by Frasca, Albert. Frasca Publishing, Springfield, Ohio 1997 Hardback with gold embossed cover and spine. The book has 400+ pages and 400+ photographs which cover ALL the trapdoor Springfield models. A MUST for the trapdoor collector! Hardback with gold embossed cover and spine. $85.00

.45-70 Springfield, The, by Joe Poyer and Craig Riesch, North Cape Publications, Tustin, CA, 1996. 150 pp., illus. Paper covers. $16.95

A revised and expanded second edition of a best-selling reference work organized by serial number and date of production to aid the collector in identifying popular "Trapdoor" rifles and carbines.

The French 1935 Pistols, by Eugene Medlin and Colin Doane, Eugene Medlin, El Paso, TX, 1995. 172 pp., illus. Paper covers. $25.95

The development and identification of successive models, fakes and variants, holsters and accessories, and serial numbers by dates of production.

Freund & Bro. Pioneer Gunmakers to the West, by F.J. Pablo Balentine, Graphic Publishers, Newport Beach, CA, 1997. 380 pp., illustrated $69.95

The story of Frank W. and George Freund, skilled German gunsmiths who plied their trade on the Western American frontier during the final three decades of the nineteenth century.

THE HANDGUNNER'S LIBRARY

Fusil de Tulole in New France, 1691-1741, The, by Russel Bouchard, Museum Restorations Service, Bloomfield, Ontario, Canada, 1997. 36 pp., illus. Paper covers. $8.95

The development of the company and the identification of their arms.

Game Guns & Rifles: Percussion to Hammerless Ejector in Britain, by Richard Akehurst, Trafalgar Square, N. Pomfret, VT, 1993. 192 pp., illus. $39.95

Long considered a classic this important reprint covers the period of British gunmaking between 1830-1900.

Gas Trap Garand, The, by Billy Pyle, Collector Grade Publications, Cobourg, Ontario, Canada, 1999 316 pp., illustrated. $59.95

The in-depth story of the rarest Garands of them all, the initial 80 Model Shop rifles made under the personal supervision of John Garand himself in 1934 and 1935, and the first 50,000 plus production "gas trap" M1's manufactured at Springfield Armory between August, 1937 and August, 1940.

George Schreyer, Sr. and Jr., Gunmakers of Hanover, Pennsylvania, by George Shumway, George Shumway Publishers, York, PA, 1990. 160pp., illus. $50.00

This monograph is a detailed photographic study of almost all known surviving long rifles and smoothbore guns made by highly regarded gunsmiths George Schreyer, Sr. and Jr.

German Assault Rifle 1935-1945, The, by Peter R. Senich, Paladin Press, Boulder, CO, 1987. 328 pp., illus. $60.00

A complete review of machine carbines, machine pistols and assault rifles employed by Hitler's Wehrmacht during WWII.

German K98k Rifle, 1934-1945, The: The Backbone of the Wehrmacht, by Richard D. Law, Collector Grade Publications, Toronto, Canada, 1993. 336 pp., illus. $69.95

The most comprehensive study ever published on the 14,000,000 bolt-action K98k rifles produced in Germany between 1934 and 1945.

German Machine Guns, by Daniel D. Musgrave, revised edition, Ironside International Publishers, Inc. Alexandria, VA, 1992. 586 pp., 650 illus. $49.95

The most definitive book ever written on German machineguns. Covers the introduction and development of machineguns in Germany from 1899 to the rearmament period after WWII.

German Military Rifles and Machine Pistols, 1871-1945, by Hans Dieter Gotz, Schiffer Publishing Co., West Chester, PA, 1990. 245 pp., illus. $35.00

This book portrays in words and pictures the development of the modern German weapons and their ammunition including the scarcely known experimental types.

Glossary of the Construction, Decoration and Use of Arms and Armor in All Countries and in All Times, A, by George Cameron Stone., Dover Publishing, New York 1999. Softcover. $39.95

An exhaustive study of arms and armor in all countries through recorded history - from the stone age up to the second world war. With over 4500 Black & White Illustrations. This Dover edition is an unabridged republication of the work originally published in 1934 by the Southworth Press, Portland MA. A new Introduction has been specially prepared for this edition.

Government Models, The, by William H.D. Goddard, Andrew Mowbray Publishing, Lincoln, RI, 1998. 296 pp., illustrated. $58.50

The most authoritative source on the development of the Colt model of 1911.

Grasshoppers and Butterflies, by Adrian B. Caruana, Museum Restoration Service, Alexandria, Bay, N.Y., 1999. 32 pp., illustrated. Paper covers. $8.95

No.39 in the Historical Arms Series. The light 3 pounders of Pattison and Townsend.

Greener Story, The, by Graham Greener, Quiller Press, London, England, 2000. 256 pp., illustrated with 32 pages of color photos. $64.50

W.W. Greener, his family history, inventions, guns, patents, and more.

Greenhill Dictionary of Guns And Gunmakers: From Colt's First Patent to the Present Day, 1836-2001, The, by John Walter, Greenhill Publishing, 2001, 1st edition, 576 pages, illustrated with 200 photos, 190 trademarks and 40 line drawings, Hardcover: $59.95

Covers military small arms, sporting guns and rifles, air and gas guns, designers, inventors, patentees, trademarks, brand names and monograms.

Guide to American Trade Catalogs 1744-1900, A, by Lawrence B. Romaine, Dover Publications, New York, NY. 422 pp., illus. Paper covers. $12.95

Guide to Ballard Breechloaders, A, by George J. Layman, Pioneer Press, Union City, TN, 1997. 261 pp., illus. Paper covers. $19.95

Documents the saga of this fine rifle from the first models made by Ball & Williams of Worchester, to its production by the Marlin Firearms Co, to the cessation of 19th century manufacture in 1891, and finally to the modern reproductions made in the 1990's.

Guide to Civil War Artillery Projectiles, A, by Jack W. Melton, and Lawrence E. Pawl . Kennesaw, GA: Kennesaw Mounton Press, 1996

The concise pictorial study belongs on the shelf of every enthusiast. Hundreds of crisp photographs and a wealth of rich, well-researched information. 96 pps., illus. Softcover. $9.95

Guide to the Maynard Breechloader, A, by George J. Layman, George J. Layman, Ayer, MA, 1993. 125 pp., illus. Paper covers. $11.95

The first book dedicated entirely to the Maynard family of breech-loading firearms. Coverage of the arms is given from the 1850s through the 1880s.

Guide to U. S. Army Dress Helmets 1872-1904, A, by Kasal and Moore, North Cape Publications, 2000. 88 pp., illus. Paper covers. $15.95

This thorough study provides a complete description of the Model 1872 & 1881 dress helmets worn by the U.S. Army. Including all componets from bodies to plates to plumes & shoulder cords and tells how to differentiate the originals from reproductions. Extensively illustrated with photographs, '8 pages in full color' of complete helmets and their components.

The Gun and Its Development, by W.W. Greener, New York: Lyons Press, 2002. 9th edition. Rewritten, and with many additional illustrations. 804 pages plus advertising section. Contains over 700 illustrations plus many tables. Softcover. $19.95

A famed book of great value, truly encyclopedic in scope and sought after by firearms collectors.

Gun Collecting, by Geoffrey Boothroyd, Sportsman's Press, London, 1989. 208 pp., illus. $29.95

The most comprehensive list of 19th century British gunmakers and gunsmiths ever published.

Gunmakers of London 1350-1850 with Supplement, by Howard L. Blackmore, Museum Restoration Service, Alexandria Bay, NY, 1999. 222 pp., illus. $135.00

A listing of all the known workmen of gun making in the first 500 years, plus a history of the guilds, cutlers, armourers, founders, blacksmiths, etc. 260 gunmarks are illustrated. Supplement is 156 pages, and Begins with an introductory chapter on "foreighn" gunmakers followed by records of all the new information found about previously unidentified armourers, gunmakers and gunsmiths. 2 Volumes Slipcased

Guns that Won the West: Firearms of the American Frontier, 1865-1898, The, by John Walter, Stackpole Books, Inc., Mechanicsburg, PA.,1999. 256 pp., illustrated. $34.95

Here is the story of the wide range of firearms from pistols to rifles used by plainsmen and settlers, gamblers, native Americans and the U.S. Army.

Gunsmiths of Illinois, by Curtis L. Johnson, George Shumway Publishers, York, PA, 1995. 160 pp., illus. $50.00

Genealogical information is provided for nearly one thousand gunsmiths. Contains hundreds of illustrations of rifles and other guns, of handmade origin, from Illinois.

Gunsmiths of Manhattan, 1625-1900: A Checklist of Tradesmen, The, by Michael H. Lewis, Museum Restoration Service, Bloomfield, Ont., Canada, 1991. 40 pp., illus. Paper covers. $8.95

This listing of more than 700 men in the arms trade in New York City prior to about the end of the 19th century will provide a guide for identification and further research.

Guns of Dagenham: Lanchester, Patchett, Sterling, The, by Peter Laidler and David Howroyd, Collector Grade Publications, Inc., Cobourg, Ont., Canada, 1995. 310 pp., illus. $39.95

An in-depth history of the small arms made by the Sterling Company of Dagenham, Essex, England, from 1940 until Sterling was purchased by British Aerospace in 1989 and closed.

Guns of the Western Indian War, by R. Stephen Dorsey, Collector's Library, Eugene, OR, 1997. 220 pp., illus. Paper covers. $30.00

The full story of the guns and ammunition that made western history in the turbulent period of 1865-1890.

Gun Powder Cans & Kegs, by Ted & David Bacyk and Tom Rowe, Rowe Publications, Rochester, NY, 1999. 150 pp., illus. $65.00

The first book devoted to powder tins and kegs. All cans and kegs in full color. With a price guide and rarity scale.

Gun Tools, Their History and Identification by James B. Shaffer, Lee A. Rutledge and R. Stephen Dorsey, Collector's Library, Eugene, OR, 1992. 375 pp., illus. $30.00

Written history of foreign and domestic gun tools from the flintlock period to WWII.

Gun Tools, Their History and Identifications, Volume 2, by Stephen Dorsey and James B. Shaffer, Collectors' Library, Eugene, OR, 1997. 396 pp., illus. Paper covers. $30.00

Gun tools from the Royal Armouries Museum in England, Pattern Room, Royal Ordnance Reference Collection in Nottingham and from major private collections.

Gunsmiths of Maryland, by Daniel D. Hartzler and James B. Whisker, Old Bedford Village Press, Bedford, PA, 1998. 208 pp., illustrated. $40.00

Covers firelock Colonial period through the breech-loading patent models. Featuring longrifles.

Gunsmiths of Virginia, by Daniel D. Hartzler and James B. Whisker, Old Bedford Village Press, Bedford, PA, 1992. 206 pp., illustrated. $40.00

A photographic study of American longrifles.

Gunsmiths of West Virginia, by Daniel D. Hartzler and James B. Whisker, Old Bedford Village Press, Bedford, PA, 1998. 176 pp., illustrated. $40.00

A photographic study of American longrifles.

THE HANDGUNNER'S LIBRARY

Hall's Military Breechloaders, by Peter A. Schmidt, Andrew Mowbray Publishers, Lincoln, RI, 1996. 232 pp., illus. $55.00

The whole story behind these bold and innovative firearms.

Handgun, The, by Geoffrey Boothroyd, David and Charles, North Pomfret, VT, 1989. 566 pp., illus. $50.00

Every chapter deals with an important period in handgun history from the 14th century to the present.

Handguns & Rifles: The Finest Weapons from Around the World, by Ian Hogg, Random House Value Publishing, Inc., N.Y., 1999. 128 pp., illustrated. $18.98

The serious gun collector will welcome this fully illustrated examination of international handguns and rifles. Each entry covers the history of the weapon, what purpose it serves, and its advantages and disadvantages.

Hawken Rifle: Its Place in History, The, by Charles E. Hanson, Jr., The Fur Press, Chadron, NE, 1979. 104 pp., illus. Paper covers. $15.00

A definitive work on this famous rifle.

Hawken Rifles, The Mountain Man's Choice, by John D. Baird, The Gun Room Press, Highland Park, NJ, 1976. 95 pp., illus. $29.95

Covers the rifles developed for the Western fur trade. Numerous specimens are described and shown in photographs.

High Standard: A Collector's Guide to the Hamden & Hartford Target Pistols, by Tom Dance, Andrew Mowbray, Inc., Lincoln, RI, 1991. 192 pp., illus. Paper covers. $24.00

From Citation to Supermatic, all of the production models and specials made from 1951 to 1984 are covered according to model number or series.

Historical Hartford Hardware, by William W. Dalrymple, Colt Collector Press, Rapid City, SD, 1976. 42 pp., illus. Paper covers. $10.00

Historically associated Colt revolvers.

History and Development of Small Arms Ammunition, The, Volume 2, by George A. Hoyem, Armory Publications, Oceanside, CA, 1991. 303 pp., illus. $65.00

Covers the blackpowder military centerfire rifle, carbine, machine gun and volley gun ammunition used in 28 nations and dominions, together with the firearms that chambered them.

History and Development of Small Arms Ammunition, The, Volume 4, by George A. Hoyem, Armory Publications, Seattle, WA, 1998. 200 pp., illustrated $65.00

A comprehensive book on American black powder and early smokeless rifle cartridges.

History of Colt Firearms, The, by Dean Boorman, Lyons Press, New York, NY, 2001. 144 pp., illus. $29.95

Discover the fascinating story of the world's most famous revolver, complete with more than 150 stunning full-color photographs.

History of the German Steel Helmet: 1916-1945, by Ludwig Baer. Bender Publishing, San Jose, CA, 2001. 448 pages, nearly 1,000 photos & illustrations. $54.95

This publication is the most complete and detailed German steel helmet book ever produced, with in-depth documentated text and nearly 1,000 photographs and illustrations encompassing all German steel helmets from 1916 through 1945. The regulations, modifications and use of camouflage are carefully clarified for the Imperial Army, Reichswehr and the numerous 3rd Reich organizations.

History of Modern U.S. Military Small Arms Ammunition. Volume 1, 1880-1939, revised by F.W. Hackley, W.H. Woodin and E.L. Scranton, Thomas Publications, Gettysburg, PA, 1998. 328 pp., illus. $49.95

This revised edition incorporates all publicly available information concerning military small arms ammunition for the period 1880 through 1939 in a single volume.

History of Modern U.S. Military Small Arms Ammunition. Volume 2, 1940-1945 by F.W. Hackley, W.H. Woodin and E.L. Scranton. Gun Room Press, Highland Park, NJ. 300 + pages, illustrated. $39.95

Based on decades of original research conducted at the National Archives, numerous military, public and private museums and libraries, as well as individual collections, this edition incorporates all publicly available information concerning military small arms ammunition for the period 1940 through 1945.

The History of Smith & Wesson Firearms, by Dean Boorman, Lyons Press, New York, NY, 2002. 144 pp., illustrated in full color. Hardcover. New dust jacket. $29.95

The definitive guide to one of the world's best-known firearms makers. Takes the story through the years of the Military & Police .38 & of the Magnum cartridge, to today's wide range of products for law-enforcement customers.

The History of Winchester Rifles, by Dean Boorman, Lyons Press, New York, NY, 2001. 144 pp., illus. $29.95

A captivating and wonderfully photographed history of one of the most legendary names in gun lore. 150 full-color photos.

History of Winchester Firearms 1866-1992, The, sixth edition, updated, expanded, and revised by Thomas Henshaw, New Win Publishing, Clinton, NJ, 1993. 280 pp., illus. $27.95

This classic is the standard reference for all collectors and others seeking the facts about any Winchester firearm, old or new.

Honour Bound: The Chauchat Machine Rifle, by Gerard Demaison and Yves Buffetaut, Collector Grade Publications, Inc., Cobourg, Ont., Canada, 1995. $39.95.

The story of the CSRG (Chauchat) machine rifle, the most manufactured automatic weapon of World War One.

Hunting Weapons From the Middle Ages to the Twentieth Century, by Howard L. Blackmore, Dover Publications, Meneola, NY, 2000. 480 pp., illustrated. Paper covers. $16.95

Dealing mainly with the different classes of weapons used in sport—swords, spears, crossbows, guns, and rifles—from the Middle Ages until the present day.

Identification Manual on the .303 British Service Cartridge, No. 1-Ball Ammunition, by B.A. Temple, I.D.S.A. Books, Piqua, OH, 1986. 84 pp., 57 illus. $12.50

Identification Manual on the .303 British Service Cartridge, No. 2-Blank Ammunition, by B.A. Temple, I.D.S.A. Books, Piqua, OH, 1986. 95 pp., 59 illus. $12.50

Identification Manual on the .303 British Service Cartridge, No. 3-Special Purpose Ammunition, by B.A. Temple, I.D.S.A. Books, Piqua, OH, 1987. 82 pp., 49 illus. $12.50

Identification Manual on the .303 British Service Cartridge, No. 4-Dummy Cartridges Henry 1869-c.1900, by B.A. Temple, I.D.S.A. Books, Piqua, OH, 1988. 84 pp., 70 illus. $12.50

Identification Manual on the .303 British Service Cartridge, No. 5-Dummy Cartridges (2), by B.A. Temple, I.D.S.A. Books, Piqua, OH, 1994. 78 pp. $12.50

Illustrated Book of Guns, The, by David Miller, Salamander Books, N.Y., N.Y., 2000. 304 pp., illustrated in color. $34.95

An illustrated directory of over 1,000 military and sporting firearms.

Illustrated Encyclopedia of Civil War Collectibles, The, by Chuck Lawliss, Henry Holt and Co., New York, NY, 1997. 316 pp., illus. Paper covers. $22.95

A comprehensive guide to Union and Confederate arms, equipment, uniforms, and other memorabilia.

Illustrations of United States Military Arms 1776-1903 and Their Inspector's Marks, compiled by Turner Kirkland, Pioneer Press, Union City, TN, 1988. 37 pp., illus. Paper covers. $7.00

Reprinted from the 1949 Bannerman catalog. Valuable information for both the advanced and beginning collector.

Indian War Cartridge Pouches, Boxes and Carbine Boots, by R. Stephen Dorsey, Collector's Library, Eugene, OR, 1993. 156 pp., illus. Paper Covers. $20.00

The key reference work to the cartridge pouches, boxes, carbine sockets and boots of the Indian War period 1865-1890.

International Armament, with History, Data, Technical Information and Photographs of Over 800 Weapons, by George Johnson. Alexandria, VA: Ironside International, 2002. 2nd edition, new printing. Over 947 pages, illustrated with over 800 photos. Hardcover. $59.95

The development and progression of modern military small arms. All significant weapons have been included and examined in depth. Over 800 photographs and illustrations with both historical and technical data. Two volumes are now bound into one book.

Introduction to the Civil War Small Arms, An, by Earl J. Coates and Dean S. Thomas, Thomas Publishing Co., Gettysburg, PA, 1990. 96 pp., illus. Paper covers. $10.00

The small arms carried by the individual soldier during the Civil War.

Japanese Rifles of World War Two, by Duncan O. McCollum, Excalibur Publications, Latham, NY, 1996. 64 pp., illus. Paper covers. $18.95

A sweeping view of the rifles and carbines that made up Japan's arsenal during the conflict.

Kalashnikov "Machine Pistols, Assault Rifles, and Machine Guns, 1945 to the Present", by John Walter, Paladin Press, Boulder, CO, 1999, hardcover, photos, illus., 146 pp. $22.95

This exhaustive work published by Greenhill Military Manuals features a gun-by-gun directory of Kalashnikov variants. Technical specifications and illustrations are provided throughout, along with details of sights, bayonets, markings and ammunition. A must for the serious collector and historian.

Kentucky Pistol, The, by Roy Chandler and James Whisker, Old Bedford Village Press, Bedford, PA, 1997. 225 pp., illus. $60.00

A photographic study of Kentucky pistols from famous collections.

Kentucky Rifle, The, by Captain John G.W. Dillin, George Shumway Publisher, York, PA, 1993. 221 pp., illus. $50.00

This well-known book was the first attempt to tell the story of the American longrifle. This edition retains the original text and illustrations with supplemental footnotes provided by Dr. George Shumway.

Know Your Broomhandle Mausers, by R.J. Berger, Blacksmith Corp., Southport, CT, 1996. 96 pp., illus. Paper covers. $14.95

An interesting story on the big Mauser pistol and its variations.

THE HANDGUNNER'S LIBRARY

Law Enforcement Memorabilia Price and Identification Guide, by Monty McCord, DBI Books a division of Krause Publications, Inc. Iola, WI, 1999. 208 pp., illustrated. Paper covers. $19.95

An invaluable reference to the growing wave of law enforcement collectors. Hundreds of items are covered from miniature vehicles to clothes, patches, and restraints.

Legendary Sporting Guns, by Eric Joly, Abbeville Press, New York, N.Y., 1999. 228 pp., illustrated. $65.00

A survey of hunting through the ages and relates how many different types of firearms were created and refined for use afield.

Legends and Reality of the AK, by Val Shilin and Charlie Cutshaw, Paladen Press, Boulder, CO, 2000. 192 pp., illustrated. Paper covers. $35.00

A behind-the-scenes look at history, design and impact of the Kalashnikov family of weapons.

LeMat, the Man, the Gun, by Valmore J. Forgett and Alain F. and Marie-Antoinette Serpette, Navy Arms Co., Ridgefield, NJ, 1996. 218 pp., illus. $49.95

The first definitive study of the Confederate revolvers invention, development and delivery by Francois Alexandre LeMat.

Light 6-Pounder Battalion Gun of 1776, The, by Adrian Caruana, Museum Restoration Service, Bloomfield, Ontario, Canada, 2001. 76 pp., illus. Paper covers. $8.95

London Gun Trade, 1850-1920, The, by Joyce E. Gooding, Museum Restoration Service, Bloomfield, Ontario, Canada, 2001. 48 pp., illus. Paper covers. $8.95

Names, dates and locations of London gunmakers working between 1850 and 1920 are listed. Compiled from the original Kelly's Post Office Directories of the City of London.

London Gunmakers and the English Duelling Pistol, 1770-1830, The, by Keith R. Dill, Museum Restoration Service, Bloomfield, Ontario, Canada, 1997. 36 pp., illus. Paper covers. $8.95

Ten gunmakers made London one of the major gunmaking centers of the world. This book examines how the design and construction of their pistols contributed to that reputation and how these characteristics may be used to date flintlock arms.

Longrifles of Pennsylvania, Volume 1, Jefferson, Clarion & Elk Counties, by Russel H. Harringer, George Shumway Publisher, York, PA, 1984. 200 pp., illus. $50.00

First in series that will treat in great detail the longrifles and gunsmiths of Pennsylvania.

Luger Handbook, The, by Aarron Davis, Krause Publications, Iola, WI, 1997. 112 pp., illus. Paper covers. $9.95

Quick reference to classify Luger models and variations with complete details including proofmarks.

Lugers at Random, by Charles Kenyon, Jr., Handgun Press, Glenview, IL, 1990. 420 pp., illus. $59.95

A new printing of this classic, comprehensive reference for all Luger collectors.

Luger Story, The, by John Walter, Stackpole Books, Mechanicsburg, PA, 2001. 256 pp., illus. Paper Covers $19.95

The standard history of the world's most famous handgun.

M1 Carbine, by Larry Ruth, Gun room Press, Highland Park, NJ, 1987. 291 pp., illus. Paper $19.95

The origin, development, manufacture and use of this famous carbine of World War II.

M-1 Carbine—A Revolution in Gun-Stocking, The, by Grafton H. Cook II and Barbara W. Cook. Lincoln, RI: Andrew Mowbray, Inc., 2002. 1st edition. 208 pages, heavily illustrated with 157 rare photographs of the guns and the men and women who made them. Softcover. $29.95

Shows you, step by step, how M1 Carbine stocks were made, right through to assembly with the hardware. Learn about M1 Carbine development, and how the contracting and production process actually worked. Also contains lots of detailed information about other military weapons, like the M1A1, the M1 Garand, the M14 and much, much more. Includes more than 200 short biographies of the people who made M1 Carbines. The depth of this information will amaze you. Shows and explains the machinery used to make military rifle stocks during World War II, with photos of these remarkable machines and data about when they were invented and shipped. Explains why walnut gunstocks are so very difficult to make, and why even large gun manufacturers are usually unable to do this specialized work.

M1 Carbine: Owner's Guide, The by Scott A. Duff, Scott A. Duff, Export, PA, 1997. 126 pp., illus. Paper covers. $21.95

This book answers the questions M1 owners most often ask concerning maintenance activities not encounted by military users.

M1 Garand: Owner's Guide, The by Scott A. Duff, Scott A. Duff, Export, PA, 1998. 132 pp., illus. Paper covers. $21.95

This book answers the questions M1 owners most often ask concerning maintenance activities not encounted by military users.

M1 Garand Serial Numbers and Data Sheets, The by Scott A. Duff, Export, PA, 1995. 101 pp., illus. Paper covers. $11.95

Provides the reader with serial numbers related to dates of manufacture and a large sampling of data sheets to aid in identification or restoration.

M1 Garand 1936 to 1957, The by Joe Poyer and Craig Riesch, North Cape Publications, Tustin, CA, 1996. 216 pp., illus. Paper covers. $19.95

Describes the entire range of M1 Garand production in text and quick-scan charts.

M1 Garand: Post World War, The by Scott A. Duff, Scott A. Duff, Export, PA, 1990. 139 pp., illus. Soft covers. $21.95

A detailed account of the activities at Springfield Armory through this period. International Harvester, H&R, Korean War production and quantities delivered. Serial numbers.

M1 Garand: World War 2, The by Scott A. Duff, Scott A. Duff, Export, PA, 2001. 210 pp., illus. Paper covers. $34.95

The most comprehensive study available to the collector and historian on the M1 Garand of World War II.

Machine Guns, by Ian V. Hogg. Iola, WI: Krause Publications, 2002. 1st edition. 336 pages, illustrated with b & w photos with a 16 page color section. Softcover. $29.95

A detailed history of the rapid-fire gun, 14th century to present. Covers the development, history and specifications.

Maine Made Guns and Their Makers, by Dwight B. Demeritt Jr., Maine State Museum, Augusta, ME, 1998. 209 pp., illustrated. $55.00

An authoritative, biographical study of Maine gunsmiths.

Marlin Firearms: A History of the Guns and the Company That Made Them, by Lt. Col. William S. Brophy, USAR, Ret., Stackpole Books, Harrisburg, PA, 1989. 672 pp., illus. $80.00

The definitive book on the Marlin Firearms Co. and their products.

Martini-Henry .450 Rifles & Carbines, by Dennis Lewis, Excalibur Publications, Latham, NY, 1996. 72 pp., illus. Paper covers. $11.95

The stories of the rifles and carbines that were the mainstay of the British soldier through the Victorian wars.

Mauser Bolt Rifles, by Ludwig Olson, F. Brownell & Son, Inc., Montezuma, IA, 1999. 364 pp., illus. $59.95

The most complete, detailed, authoritative and comprehensive work ever done on Mauser bolt rifles. Completely revised deluxe 3rd edition.

Mauser Military Rifles of the World, 2nd Edition, by Robert Ball, Krause Publications, Iola, WI, 2000. 304 pp., illustrated with 1,000 b&w photos and a 48 page color section. $44.95

This 2nd edition brings more than 100 new photos of these historic rifles and the wars in which they were carried.

Mauser Military Rifle Markings, by Terence W. Lapin, Arlington, VA: Hyrax Publishers, LLC, 2001. 167 pages, illustrated. 2nd edition. Revised and expanded. Softcover. $22.95

A general guide to reading and understanding the often mystifying markings found on military Mauser Rifles. Includes German Regimental markings as well as German police markings and W.W. 2 German Mauser subcontractor codes. A handy reference to take to gun shows.

Mauser Smallbores Sporting, Target and Training Rifles, by Jon Speed, Collector Grade Publications, Cobourg, Ontario, Canada 1998. 349 pp., illustrated. $67.50

A history of all the smallbore sporting, target and training rifles produced by the legendary Mauser-Werke of Obendorf Am Neckar.

Military Holsters of World War 2, by Eugene J. Bender, Rowe Publications, Rochester, NY, 1998. 200 pp., illustrated. $45.00

A revised edition with a new price guide of the most definitive book on this subject.

Military Pistols of Japan, by Fred L. Honeycutt, Jr., Julin Books, Palm Beach Gardens, FL, 1997. 168 pp., illus. $42.00

Covers every aspect of military pistol production in Japan through WWII.

Military Remington Rolling Block Rifle, The, by George Layman, Pioneer Press, TN, 1998. 146 pp., illus. Paper covers. $24.95

A standard reference for those with an interest in the Remington rolling block family of firearms.

Military Rifles of Japan, 5th Edition, by F.L. Honeycutt, Julin Books, Lake Park, FL, 1999. 208 pp., illus. $42.00

A new revised and updated edition. Includes the early Murata-period markings, etc.

Military Small Arms Data Book, by Ian V. Hogg, Stackpole Books, Mechanicsburg, PA, 1999. $44.95. 336 pp., illustrated.

Data on more than 1,500 weapons. Covers a vast range of weapons from pistols to anti-tank rifles. Essential data, 1870-2000, in one volume.

MP38, 40, 40/1 & 41 Submachine Gun, The, by de Vries & Martens. Propaganda Photo Series, Volume II. Alexandria, VA: Ironside International, 2001. 1st edition. 150 pages, illustrated with 200 high quality black & white photos. Hardcover. $34.95

Covers all essential information on history and development, ammunition and accessories, codes and markings, and contains photos of nearly every model and accessory. Includes a unique selection of original German WWII propoganda photos, most never published before.

THE HANDGUNNER'S LIBRARY

Modern Beretta Firearms, by Gene Gangarosa, Jr., Stoeger Publishing Co., So. Hackensack, NJ, 1994. 288 pp., illus. Paper covers. $16.95

Traces all models of modern Beretta pistols, rifles, machine guns and combat shotguns.

Modern Gun Values, The Gun Digest Book of, 11th Edition, by the Editors of Gun Digest. Krause Publications, Iola, WI., 2002. 560 pp. illus. Paper covers. $21.95

Greatly updated and expanded edition describing and valuing over 7,000 firearms manufactured from 1900 to 1996. The standard for valuing modern firearms.

Modern Gun Identification & Value Guide, 13th Edition, by Russell and Steve Quertermous, Collector Books, Paducah, KY, 1998. 504 pp., illus. Paper covers. $14.95

Features current values for over 2,500 models of rifles, shotguns and handguns, with over 1,800 illustrations.

More Single Shot Rifles, by James C. Grant, The Gun Room Press, Highland Park, NJ, 1976. 324 pp., illus. $35.00

Details the guns made by Frank Wesson, Milt Farrow, Holden, Borchardt, Stevens, Remington, Winchester, Ballard and Peabody-Martini.

Mortimer, the Gunmakers, 1753-1923, by H. Lee Munson, Andrew Mowbray Inc., Lincoln, RI, 1992. 320 pp., illus. $65.00

Seen through a single, dominant, English gunmaking dynasty this fascinating study provides a window into the classical era of firearms artistry.

Mosin-Nagant Rifle, The, by Terence W. Lapin, North Cape Publications, Tustin, CA, 1998. 30 pp., illustrated. Paper covers. $19.95

The first ever complete book on the Mosin-Nagant rifle written in English. Covers every variation.

Navy Luger, The, by Joachim Gortz and John Walter, Handgun Press, Glenview, IL, 1988. 128 pp., illus. $24.95

The 9mm Pistole 1904 and the Imperial German Navy. A concise illustrated history.

New World of Russian Small Arms and Ammunition, The, by Charlie Cutshaw, Paladin Press, Boulder, CO, 1998. 160 pp., illustrated. $42.95

Detailed descriptions, specifications and first-class illustrations of the AN-94, PSS silent pistol, Bizon SMG, Saifa-12 tactical shotgun, the GP-25 grenade launcher and more cutting edge Russian weapons.

Number 5 Jungle Carbine, The, by Alan M. Petrillo, Excalibur Publications, Latham, NY, 1994. 32 pp., illus. Paper covers. $7.95

A comprehensive treatment of the rifle that collectors have come to call the "Jungle Carbine"—the Lee-Enfield Number 5, Mark 1.

Observations on Colt's Second Contract, November 2, 1847, by G. Maxwell Longfield and David T. Basnett, Museum Restoration Service, Bloomfield, Ontario, Canada, 1997. 36 pp., illus. Paper covers. $6.95

This study traces the history and the construction of the Second Model Colt Dragoon supplied in 1848 to the U.S. Cavalry.

Official Price Guide to Gun Collecting, by R.L. Wilson, Ballantine/House of Collectibles, New York, NY, 1998. 450 pp., illus. Paper covers. $21.50

Covers more than 30,000 prices from Colt revolvers to Winchester rifles and shotguns to German Lugers and British sporting rifles and game guns.

Official Price Guide to Military Collectibles, 6th edition, by Richard J. Austin, Random House, Inc., New York, NY, 1998. 200 pp., illus. Paper cover. $20.00

Covers weapons and other collectibles from wars of the distant and recent past. More than 4,000 prices are listed. Illustrated with 400 black & white photos plus a full-color insert.

Official Soviet SVD Manual, The, by Major James F. Gebhardt (Ret.) Paladin Press, Boulder, CO, 1999. 112 pp., illustrated. Paper covers. $15.00

Operating instructions for the 7.62mm Dragunov, the first Russian rifle developed from scratch specifically for sniping.

Old Gunsights: A Collector's Guide, 1850 to 2000, by Nicholas Stroebel, Krause Publications, Iola, WI, 1998. 320 pp., illus. Paper covers. $29.95

An in-depth and comprehensive examination of old gunsights and the rifles on which they were used to get accurate feel for prices in this expanding market.

Old Rifle Scopes, by Nicholas Stroebel, Krause Publications, Iola, WI, 2000. 400 pp., illustrated. Paper covers. $31.95

This comprehensive collector's guide takes aim at more than 120 scope makers and 60 mount makers and features photos and current market values for 300 scopes and mounts manufactured from 1950-1985.

Ordnance Tools, Accessories & Appendages of the M1 Rifle, by Billy Pyle. Houston, TX: Privately Printed, 2002. 2nd edition. 206 pages, illustrated with b & w photos. Softcover $40.00

This is the new updated second edition with over 350 pictures and drawings - 30 of which are new. Part I contains accessories, appendages, and equipment including such items as bayonets, blank firing attachments, cheek pads, cleaning equipment, clips, flash hiders, grenade launchers, scabbards, slings, telescopes and mounts, winter triggers, and much more. Part II covers ammunition, grenades, and pyrotechnics. Part III shows the inspection gages. Part IV presents the ordnance tools, fixtures, and assemblies. Part V contains miscellaneous items related to the M1 Rifle such as arms racks, rifle racks, clip loading machine, and other devices.

Orders, Decorations and Badges of the Socialist Republic of Vietnam and the National Front for the Liberation of South Vietnam, by Edward J. Emering. Schiffer Publications, Atglen, PA. 2000. 96 pages, 190 color and b/w photographs, line drawings. $24.95

The Orders and Decorations of the "enemy" during the Vietnam War have remained shrouded in mystery for many years. References to them are scarce and interrogations of captives during the war often led to the proliferation of misinformation concerning them. Includes value guide.

Packing Iron, by Richard C. Rattenbury, Zon International Publishing, Millwood, NY, 1993. 216 pp., illus. $45.00

The best book yet produced on pistol holsters and rifle scabbards. Over 300 variations of holster and scabbards are illustrated in large, clear plates.

Painted Steel, Steel Pots Volume 2, by Chris Armold. Bender Publishing, San Jose, CA, 2001. 384 pages - 1,053 photos (hundreds in color) $57.95

From the author of "Steel Pots: The History of America's Steel Combat Helmets" comes "Painted Steel: Steel Pots, Vol. II." This companion volume features detailed chapters on painted and unit marked helments of WWI and WWII, plus a variety of divisional, regimental and subordinate markings. Special full-color plates detail subordinate unit markings such as the tactical markings used by the U.S. 2nd Division in WWI. In addition, insignia and specialty markings such as USN beach battalion, Army engineers, medics, MP and airborne division tactical markings are examined. For those interested in American armored forces, a complete chapter is devoted to the history of the U.S. tank and combat vehicle crewman's helmet from WWI to present. Other chapters provide tips on reproductions and fake representations of U.S. helmets and accessories. With over 1,000 photos and images (many in color), "Painted Steel" will be a prized addition to any collector's reference bookshelf.

Parabellum: A Technical History of Swiss Lugers, by Vittorio Bobba, Priuli & Verlucca, Editori, Torino, Italy, 1996. Italian and English text. Illustrated. $100.00

Patents for Inventions, Class 119 (Small Arms), 1855-1930. British Patent Office, Armory Publications, Oceanside, CA, 1993. 7 volume set. $375.00

Contains 7980 abridged patent descriptions and their sectioned line drawings, plus a 37-page alphabetical index of the patentees.

Pattern Dates for British Ordnance Small Arms, 1718-1783, by DeWitt Bailey, Thomas Publications, Gettysburg, PA, 1997. 116 pp., illus. Paper covers. $20.00

The weapons discussed in this work are those carried by troops sent to North America between 1737 and 1783, or shipped to them as replacement arms while in America.

Peters & King, by Thomas D. Schiffer. Krause Publications, Iola, WI 2002. 1st edition. 256 pages, 200+ black & white photos with a 32 page color section. Hardcover. $44.95

Discover the history behind Peters Cartridge and King Powder and see how they shaped the arms industry into what it is today and why their products fetch hundreds and even thousands of dollars at auctions. Current values are provided for their highly collectible product packaging and promotional advertising premiums such as powder kegs, tins, cartridge boxes, and calendars.

Pitman Notes on U.S. Martial Small Arms and Ammunition, 1776-1933, Volume 2, Revolvers and Automatic Pistols, The, by Brig. Gen. John Pitman, Thomas Publications, Gettysburg, PA, 1990. 192 pp., illus. $29.95

A most important primary source of information on United States military small arms and ammunition.

Plates and Buckles of the American Military 1795-1874, by Sydney C. Kerksis, Orange, VA: Publisher's Press, 1998. 5th edition. 568 pages, illustrated with 100's of black and white photos. Hardcover. $39.00

The single most comprehensive reference for U.S. and Confederate plates.

Plains Rifle, The, by Charles Hanson, Gun Room Press, Highland Park, NJ, 1989. 169 pp., illus. $35.00

All rifles that were made with the plainsman in mind, including pistols.

Powder and Ball Small Arms, by Martin Pegler, Windrow & Green, London, 1998. 128 pp., illus. $39.95

Part of the new "Live Firing Classic Weapons" series featuring full color photos of experienced shooters dressed in authentic costumes handling, loading and firing historic weapons.

Powder Flask Book, The, by Ray Riling, R&R Books, Livonia, NY, 1993. 514 pp., illus. $69.95

The complete book on flasks of the 19th century. Exactly scaled pictures of 1,600 flasks are illustrated.

Proud Promise: French Autoloading Rifles, 1898-1979,by Jean Huon, Collector Grade Publications, Inc., Cobourg, Ont., Canada, 1995. 216 pp., illus. $39.95

The author has finally set the record straight about the importance of French contributions to modern arms design.

E. C. Prudhomme's Gun Engraving Review, by E. C. Prudhomme, R&R Books, Livonia, NY, 1994. 164 pp., illus. $60.00

As a source for engravers and collectors, this book is an indispensable guide to styles and techniques of the world's foremost engravers.

THE HANDGUNNER'S LIBRARY

Purdey Gun and Rifle Makers: The Definitive History, by Donald Dallas, Quiller Press, London, 2000. 245 pp., illus. Color throughout. $100.00

A limited edition of 3,000 copies. Signed and numbered. With a PURDEY book plate.

Queen Anne Pistol, 1660-1780: A History of the Turn-Off Pistol, The, by John W. Burgoyne, Bloomfield, Ont. CANADA: Museum Restoration Service, 2002. 1st edition — Historical Arms New Series No. 1. ISBN: 0-88855-0154. 120 pages. Pictorial Hardcover. $35.00

A detailed, fast moving, thoroughly researched text and almost 200 cross-referenced illustrations. This distinctive breech-loading arm was developed in the middle years of the 17th century but found popularity during the reign of the monarch (1702-1714), by whose name it is known.

Red Shines the Sun: A Pictorial History of the Fallschirm-Infantrie, by Eric Queen. San Jose, CA: R. James Bender Publishing, 2003. 1st edition. Hardcover. $69.95

A culmination of 12 years of research, this reference work traces the history of the Army paratroopers of the Fallschirm-Infanterie from their origins in 1937, to the expansion to battalion strength in 1938, then on through operations at Wola Gulowska (Poland), and Moerdijk (Holland). This 240 page comprehensive look at their history is supported by 600 images, many of which are in full color, and nearly 90% are previously unpublished. This work also features original examples of nearly all documents awarded to the Army paratroopers, as well as the most comprehensive study to date of the Army paratrooper badge or Fallschirmschützenabzeichen (Heer). Original examples of all known variations (silver, aluminum, cloth, feinzink) are pictured in full color. If you are interested in owning one of these badges, this book can literally save you from making a $2,000.00 mistake.

Reloading Tools, Sights and Telescopes for Single Shot Rifles, by Gerald O. Kelver, Brighton, CO, 1982. 163 pp., illus. Paper covers. $13.95

A listing of most of the famous makers of reloading tools, sights and telescopes with a brief description of the products they manufactured.

The Remington-Lee Rifle, by Eugene F. Myszkowski, Excalibur Publications, Latham, NY, 1995. 100 pp., illus. Paper covers. $22.50

Features detailed descriptions, including serial number ranges, of each model from the first Lee Magazine Rifle produced for the U.S. Navy to the last Remington-Lee Small Bores shipped to the Cuban Rural Guard.

Remington 'America's Oldest Gunmaker' The Official Authorized History Of The Remington Arms Company, by Roy Marcot. Madison, NC: Remington Arms Company, 1999. 1st edition. 312 pages, with 167 black & white illustrations, plus 291 color plates. $79.95

This is without a doubt the finest history of that firm ever to have been compiled. Based on firsthand research in the Remington companies archives, it is extremely well written.

Remington's Vest Pocket Pistols, by Hatfield, Robert E. Lincoln, RI: Andrew Mowbray, Inc., 2002. 117 pages. Hardcover. $29.95

While Remington Vest Pocket Pistols have always been popular with collectors, very little solid information has been available about them. Such simple questions such as "When were they made?"..."How many were produced?"...and "What calibers were they available in?" have all remained unanswered. This new book, based upon years of study and a major survey of surviving examples, attempts to answer these critical questions. Specifications, markings, mechanical design and patents are also presented here. Inside you will find 100+ photographs, serial number data, exploded views of all four Remington Vest Pocket Pistol sizes, component parts lists and a guide to disassembly and reassembly. Also includes a discussion of Vest Pocket Wire-Stocked Buggy/Bicycle rifles, plus the documented serial number story.

Revolvers of the British Services 1854-1954, by W.H.J. Chamberlain and A.W.F. Taylerson, Museum Restoration Service, Ottawa, Canada, 1989. 80 pp., illus. $27.50

Covers the types issued among many of the United Kingdom's naval, land or air services.

Rifles of the World, by Oliver Achard, Chartwell Books, Inc., Edison, NJ, 141 pp., illus. $24.95

A unique insight into the world of long guns, not just rifles, but also shotguns, carbines and all the usual multi-barreled guns that once were so popular with European hunters, especially in Germany and Austria.

Round Ball to Rimfire, Vol. 1, by Dean Thomas, Thomas Publications, Gettysburg, PA, 1997. 144 pp., illus. $49.95

The first of a two-volume set of the most complete history and guide for all small arms ammunition used in the Civil War. The information includes data from research and development to the arsenals that created it.

Round Ball to Rimfire: A History of Civil War Small Arms Ammunition, Vol. 2. by Dean Thomas, Thomas Publications, Gettysburg, PA 2002. 528 pages. Hardcover. $49.95

Completely discusses the ammunition for Federal Breechloading Carbines and Rifles. The seven chapters with eighteen appendices detailing the story of the twenty-seven or so different kinds of breechloaders actually purchased or ordered by the Ordnance Department during the Civil War. The book is conveniently divided by the type of priming — external or internal — and then alphabetically by maker or supplier. A wealth of new information and research has proven that these weapons either functioned properly or were inadequate relative to the design and ingenuity of the proprietary cartridges.

Russell M. Catron and His Pistols, by Warren H. Buxton, Ucross Books, Los Alamos, NM, 1998. 224 pp., illustrated. Paper covers. $49.50

An unknown American firearms inventor and manufacturer of the mid twentieth century. Military, commerical, ammunition.

SAFN-49 and The FAL, The, by Joe Poyer and Dr. Richard Feirman, North Cape Publications, Tustin, CA, 1998. 160 pp., illus. Paper covers. $14.95

The first complete overview of the SAFN-49 battle rifle, from its pre-World War 2 beginnings to its military service in countries as diverse as the Belgian Congo and Argentina. The FAL was "light" version of the SAFN-49 and it became the Free World's most adopted battle rifle.

Sauer & Sohn, Sauer "Dein Waffenkamerad" Volume 2, J. P., by Cate & Krause, Walsworth Publishing, Chattanooga, TN, 2000. 440 pp., illus. $69.95

A historical study of Sauer automatic pistols. This new volume includes a great deal of new knowledge that has surfaced about the firm J.P. Sauer. You will find new photos, documentation, serial number ranges and historial facts which will expand the knowledge and interest in the oldest and best of the German firearms companies.

Scottish Firearms, by Claude Blair and Robert Woosnam-Savage, Museum Restoration Service, Bloomfield, Ont., Canada, 1995. 52 pp., illus. Paper covers. $8.95

This revision of the first book devoted entirely to Scottish firearms is supplemented by a register of surviving Scottish long guns.

Scottish Pistol, The, by Martin Kelvin. Fairleigh Dickinson University Press, Dist. By Associated University Presses, Cranbury, NJ, 1997. 256 pp., illus. $49.50

The Scottish pistol, its history, manufacture and design.

Sharps Firearms, by Frank Seller, Frank M. Seller, Denver, CO, 1998. 358 pp., illus. $59.95

Traces the development of Sharps firearms with full range of guns made including all martial variations.

Simeon North: First Official Pistol Maker of the United States, by S. North and R. North, The Gun Room Press, Highland Park, NJ, 1972. 207 pp., illus. $15.95

Reprint of the rare first edition.

SKS Carbine, The, by Steve Kehaya and Joe Poyer, North Cape Publications, Tustin, CA, 1997. 150 pp., illus. Paper covers. $16.95

The first comprehensive examination of a major historical firearm used through the Vietnam conflict to the diamond fields of Angola.

SKS Type 45 Carbines, The, by Duncan Long, Desert Publications, El Dorado, AZ, 1992. 110 pp., illus. Paper covers. $19.95

Covers the history and practical aspects of operating, maintaining and modifying this abundantly available rifle.

Smith & Wesson 1857-1945, by Robert J. Neal and Roy G. Jinks, R&R Books, Livonia, NY, 1996. 434 pp., illus. $50.00

The bible for all existing and aspiring Smith & Wesson collectors.

Sniper Variations of the German K98k Rifle, by Richard D. Law, Collector Grade Publications, Ontario, Canada, 1997. 240 pp., illus. $47.50

Volume 2 of "Backbone of the Wehrmacht" the author's in-depth study of the German K98k rifle. This volume concentrates on the telescopic-sighted rifle of choice for most German snipers during World War 2.

Southern Derringers of the Mississippi Valley, by Turner Kirkland, Pioneer Press, Tenn., 1971. 80 pp., illus., paper covers. $4.00

A guide for the collector, and a much-needed study.

Soviet Russian Postwar Military Pistols and Cartridges, by Fred A. Datig, Handgun Press, Glenview, IL, 1988. 152 pp., illus. $29.95

Thoroughly researched, this definitive sourcebook covers the development and adoption of the Makarov, Stechkin and the new PSM pistols. Also included in this source book is coverage on Russian clandestine weapons and pistol cartridges.

Soviet Russian Tokarev "TT" Pistols and Cartridges 1929-1953, by Fred Datig, Graphic Publishers, Santa Ana, CA, 1993. 168 pp., illus. $39.95

Details of rare arms and their accessories are shown in hundreds of photos. It also contains a complete bibliography and index.

Spencer Repeating Firearms, by Roy M. Marcot. New York: Rowe Publications, 2002. 316 pages; numerous B&W photos & illustrations. Hardcover. $65.00

Sporting Collectibles, by Jim and Vivian Karsnitz, Schiffer Publishing Ltd., West Chester, PA, 1992. 160 pp., illus. Paper covers. $29.95.

The fascinating world of hunting related collectibles presented in an informative text.

Springfield 1903 Rifles, The, by Lt. Col. William S. Brophy, USAR, Ret., Stackpole Books Inc., Harrisburg, PA, 1985. 608 pp., illus. $75.00

The illustrated, documented story of the design, development, and production of all the models, appendages, and accessories.

Springfield Armory Shoulder Weapons 1795-1968, by Robert W.D. Ball, Antique Trader Books, Dubuque, IA, 1998. 264 pp., illus. $34.95

This book documents the 255 basic models of rifles, including test and trial rifles, produced by the Springfield Armory. It features the entire history of rifles and carbines manufactured at the Armory, the development of each weapon with specific operating characteristics and procedures.

THE HANDGUNNER'S LIBRARY

Springfield Model 1903 Service Rifle Production and Alteration, 1905-1910, by C.S. Ferris and John Beard, Arvada, CO, 1995. 66 pp., illus. Paper covers. $12.50

A highly recommended work for any serious student of the Springfield Model 1903 rifle.

Springfield Shoulder Arms 1795-1865, by Claud E. Fuller, S. & S. Firearms, Glendale, NY, 1996. 76 pp., illus. Paper covers. $14.95

Exact reprint of the scarce 1930 edition of one of the most definitive works on Springfield flintlock and percussion muskets ever published.

SS Headgear, by Kit Wilson. Johnson Reference Books, Fredericksburg, VA. 72 pages, 15 full-color plates and over 70 black and white photos. $16.50

An excellent source of information concerning all types of SS headgear, to include Allgemeine-SS, Waffen-SS, visor caps, helmets, overseas caps, M-43's and miscellaneous headgear. Also included is a guide on the availability and current values of SS headgear. This guide was compiled from auction catalogs, dealer price lists, and input from advanced collectors in the field.

SS Helmets: A Collector's Guide, Vol 1, by Kelly Hicks. Johnson Reference Books, Fredericksburg, VA. 96 pages, illustrated. $17.50

Deals only with SS helmets and features some very nice color close-up shots of the different SS decals used. Also, has some nice color shots of entire helmets. Over 85 photographs, 27 in color. The author has documented most of the known types of SS helmets, and describes in detail all of the vital things to look for in determining the originality, style type, and finish. Complete descriptions of each helmet are provided along with detailed close-ups of interior and exterior views of the markings and insignia. Also featured are several period photos of helmets in wear.

SS Helmets: A Collector's Guide, Vol 2, by Kelly Hicks. Johnson Reference Books, Fredericksburg, VA. 2000. 128 pages. 107 full-color photos, 14 period photos. $25.00

Volume II contains dozen of highly detailed, full-color photos of rare and original SS and Field Police helmets, featuring both sides as well as interior view. The very best graphics techniques ensure that these helmets are presented in such a way that the reader can 'almost feel' the different paint textures of the camo and factory finishes. The outstanding decal section offers detailed close-ups of original SS and Police decals, and in conjunction with Volume I, completes the documentation of virtually all types of original decal variations used between 1934 and 1945.

SS Uniforms, Insignia and Accoutrements, by A. Hayes. Schiffer Publications, Atglen, PA. 1996. 248 pages, with over 800 color and b/w photographs. $69.95

This new work explores in detailed color the complex subject of Allgemeine and Waffen-SS uniforms, insignia, and accoutrements. Hundreds of authentic items are extensively photographed in close-up to enable the reader to examine and study.

Steel Pots: The History of America's Steel Combat Helmets, by Chris Armold. Bender Publishing, San Jose, CA, 2000. $47.95

Packed with hundreds of color photographs, detailed specification diagrams and supported with meticulously researched data, this book takes the reader on a fascinating visual journey covering 80 years of American helmet design and development. From the classic Model 1917 "Doughboy" helmet to the distinctive ballistic "Kelvar" helmet, Steel Pots will introduce you to over 50 American helmet variations. Also, rare WWI experimental helmets to specialized WWII aircrew anti-flak helmets, plus liners, suspensions, chinstraps, camouflage covers, nets and even helmet radios!

Standard Catalog of Firearms, 13th Edition, by Ned Schwing, Krause Publications, Iola, WI, 2003.1382 Pages, illustrated. 6,000+ b&w photos plus a 16-page color section. Paper covers. $34.95

This is the largest, most comprehensive and best-selling firearm book of all time! And this year's edition is a blockbuster for both shooters and firearm collectors. More than 14,000 firearms are listed and priced in up to six grades of condition. That's almost 100,000 prices! Gun enthusiasts will love the new full-color section of photos highlighting the finest firearms sold at auction this past year.

Steel Canvas: The Art of American Arms, by R.L. Wilson, Random House, NY, 1995, 384 pp., illus. $65.00

Presented here for the first time is the breathtaking panorama of America's extraordinary engravers and embellishers of arms, from the 1700s to modern times.

Stevens Pistols & Pocket Rifles, by K.L. Cope, Museum Restoration Service, Alexandria Bay, NY, 1992. 114 pp., illus. $24.50

This is the story of the guns and the man who designed them and the company which he founded to make them.

Sumptuous Flaske, The, by Herbert G. Houze, Andrew Mowbray, Inc., Lincoln, RI, 1989. 158 pp., illus. Soft covers. $35.00

Catalog of a recent show at the Buffalo Bill Historical Center bringing together some of the finest European and American powder flasks of the 16th to 19th centuries.

Swedish Mauser Rifles, The, by Steve Kehaya and Joe Poyer, North Cape Publications, Tustin, CA, 1999. 267 pp., illustrated. Paper covers. $19.95

Every known variation of the Swedish Mauser carbine and rifle is described including all match and target rifles and all sniper fersions. Includes serial number and production data.

System Lefaucheaux, by Chris C. Curtis, with a Foreword by Norm Flayderman. Armslore Press, 2002. 312 pages, heavily illustrated with b & w photos. Hardcover. $44.95

The study of pinfire cartridge arms including their role in the American Civil War.

Televisions Cowboys, Gunfighters & Cap Pistols, by Rudy A. D'Angelo, Antique Trader Books, Norfolk, VA, 1999. 287 pp., illustrated in color and black and white. Paper covers. $31.95

Over 850 beautifully photographed color and black and white images of cap guns, actors, and the characters they portrayed in the "Golden Age of TV Westerns. With accurate descriptions and current values.

Thompson: The American Legend, by Tracie L. Hill, Collector Grade Publications, Ontario, Canada, 1996. 584 pp., illus. $85.00

The story of the first American submachine gun. All models are featured and discussed.

Thoughts on the Kentucky Rifle in its Golden Age by Kindig, Joe K. III. York, PA: George Shumway Publisher, 2002. Annotated Second Edition. 561pp; Illustrated. Hardcover. $85.00

The definitive book on the Kentucky Rifle, illustrating 266 of these guns in 856 detailed phototgraphs. This scarce title, long out of print, is once again available.

Toys that Shoot and other Neat Stuff, by James Dundas, Schiffer Books, Atglen, PA, 1999. 112 pp., illustrated. Paper covers. $24.95

Shooting toys from the twentieth century, especially 1920's to 1960's, in over 420 color photographs of BB guns, cap shooters, marble shooters, squirt guns and more. Complete with a price guide.

Trapdoor Springfield, The, by M.D. Waite and B.D. Ernst, The Gun Room Press, Highland Park, NJ, 1983. 250 pp., illus. $39.95

The first comprehensive book on the famous standard military rifle of the 1873-92 period.

Treasures of the Moscow Kremlin: Arsenal of the Russian Tsars, A Royal Armories and the Moscow Kremlin exhibition. HM Tower of London 13, June 1998 to 11 September, 1998. BAS Printers, Over Wallop, Hampshire, England. XXII plus 192 pp. over 180 color illustrations. Text in English and Russian. $65.00

For this exhibition catalog each of the 94 objects on display are photographed and described in detail to provide a most informative record of this important exhibition.

U.S. Army Headgear 1812-1872, by Langellier, John P. and C. Paul Loane. Atglen, PA: Schiffer Publications, 2002. 167 pages, with over 350 color and b/w photos. $69.95

This profusely illustrated volume represents more than three decades of research in public and private collections by military historian John P. Langellier and Civil War authority C. Paul Loane. Hardcover.

U.S. Army Rangers & Special Forces of World War II Their War in Photographs, by Robert Todd Ross. Atglen, PA: Schiffer Publications, 2002. 216 pages, over 250 b/w & color photographs. Hardcover. $59.95

Never before has such an expansive view of World War II elite forces been offered in one volume. An extensive search of public and private archives unearthed an astonishing number of rare and never before seen images, including color. Most notable are the nearly twenty exemplary photographs of Lieutenant Colonel William O. Darby's Ranger Force in Italy, taken by Robert Capa, considered by many to be the greatest combat photographer of all time. Complementing the period photographs are numerous color plates detailing the rare and often unique items of insignia, weapons, and equipment that marked the soldiers whose heavy task it was to Lead the Way. Includes rare, previously unpublished photographs by legendary combat photographer Robert Capa.

U.S. Breech-Loading Rifles and Carbines, Cal. 45, by Gen. John Pitman, Thomas Publications, Gettysburg, PA, 1992. 192 pp., illus. $29.95

The third volume in the Pitman Notes on U.S. Martial Small Arms and Ammunition, 1776-1933. This book centers on the "Trapdoor Springfield" models.

U.S. Handguns of World War 2: The Secondary Pistols and Revolvers, by Charles W. Pate, Andrew Mowbray, Inc., Lincoln, RI, 1998. 515 pp., illus. $39.00

This indispensable new book covers all of the American military handguns of World War 2 except for the M1911A1 Colt automatic.

United States Martial Flintlocks, by Robert M. Reilly, Mowbray Publishing Co., Lincoln, RI, 1997. 264 pp., illus. $40.00

A comprehensive history of American flintlock longarms and handguns (mostly military) c. 1775 to c. 1840.

U.S. Martial Single Shot Pistols, by Daniel D. Hartzler and James B. Whisker, Old Bedford Village Pess, Bedford, PA, 1998. 128 pp., illus. $45.00

A photographic chronicle of military and semi-martial pistols supplied to the U.S. Government and the several States.

U.S. Military Arms Dates of Manufacture from 1795, by George Madis, David Madis, Dallas, TX, 1995. 64 pp. Soft covers. $9.95

Lists all U.S. military arms of collector interest alphabetically, covering about 250 models.

THE HANDGUNNER'S LIBRARY

U.S. Military Small Arms 1816-1865, by Robert M. Reilly, The Gun Room Press, Highland Park, NJ, 1983. 270 pp., illus. $39.95

Covers every known type of primary and secondary martial firearms used by Federal forces.

U.S. M1 Carbines: Wartime Production, by Craig Riesch, North Cape Publications, Tustin, CA, 1994. 72 pp., illus. Paper covers. $16.95

Presents only verifiable and accurate information. Each part of the M1 Carbine is discussed fully in its own section; including markings and finishes.

U.S. Naval Handguns, 1808-1911, by Fredrick R. Winter, Andrew Mowbray Publishers, Lincoln, RI, 1990. 128 pp., illus. $26.00

The story of U.S. Naval Handguns spans an entire century—included are sections on each of the important naval handguns within the period.

Uniform and Dress Army and Navy of the Confederate States of America. (Official Regulations), by Confederate States of America. Ray Riling Arms Books, Philadelphia, PA. 1960. $20.00

A portfolio containing a complete set of nine color plates expecially prepared for framing Reproduced in exactly 200 sets from the very rare Richmond, VA., 1861 regulations.

Uniform Buttons of the United States 1776-1865, by Warren K. Tice. Thomas Publications, Gettysburg, PA. 1997. 520 pages over 3000 illustrations. $60.00

A timely work on US uniform buttons for a growing area of collecting. This work interrelates diverse topics such as manufacturing processes, history of manufacturing companies, known & recently discovered button patterns and the unist that wore them.

Uniforms & Equipment of the Imperial German Army 1900-1918: A Study in Period Photographs, by Charles Woolley. Schiffer Publications, Atglen, PA. 2000. 375 pages, over 500 b/w photographs and 50 color drawings. $69.95

Features formal studio portraits of pre-war dress and wartime uniforms of all arms. Also contains photo postal cards taken in the field of Infantry, Pionier, Telegraph-Signal, Landsturm, and Mountain Troops, vehicles, artillery, musicians, the Bavarian Leib Regiment, specialized uniforms and insignia, small arms close-ups, unmotorized transport, group shots and Balloon troops and includes a 60 page full-color uniform section reproduced from rare 1914 plates. Fully illustrated.

Uniforms & Equipment of the Imperial German Army 1900-1918: A Study in Period Photographs, Volume 2. by Charles Woolley. Schiffer Publications, Atglen, PA. 2000. 320 pages, over 500 b/w photographs and 50 color drawings. $69.95

Contains over 500 never before published photographic images of Imperial German military subjects. This initial volume, of a continuing study, features formal studio portraits of pre-war dress and wartime uniforms of all arms. It also contains photo postal cards taken in the field of Infantry, Pionier, Telegraph-Signal, Landsturm and Mountain Troops, Vehicles, Artillery, Musicians, the Bavarian Leib Regiment, specialized uniforms and insignia, small arms close-ups, unmotorized transport, group shots and Balloon troops.

Uniforms of the Third Reich: A Study in Photographs, by Maguire Hayes. Schiffer Publications, Atglen, PA. 1997. 200 pages, with over 400 color photographs. $69.95

This new book takes a close look at a variety of authentic World War II era German uniforms including examples from the Army, Luftwaffe, Kriegsmarine, Waffen-SS, Allgemeine-SS, Hitler Youth and Political Leaders. The pieces are shown in large full frame front and rear shots, and in painstaking detail to show tailors tags, buttons, insignia detail etc. and allow the reader to see what the genuine article looks like. Various accoutrements worn with the uniforms are also included to aid the collector.

Uniforms of The United States Army, 1774-1889, by Henry Alexander Ogden. Dover Publishing, Mineola, NY. 1998. 48 pages of text plus 44 color plates. Softcover. $9.95

A republication of the work published by the quarter-master general, United States army in 1890. A striking collection of lithographs and a marvelous archive of military, social, and costume history portraying the gamut of U.S. Army uniforms from fatigues to full dress, between 1774 and 1889.

Uniforms, Organization, and History of the NSKK/NSFK, by John R. Angolia & David Littlejohn. Bender Publishing, San Jose, CA, 2000. $44.95

This work is part of the on-going study of political organizations that formed the structure of the Hitler hierarchy, and is authored by two of the most prominent authorities on the subject of uniforms and insignia of the Third Reich. This comprehensive book covers details on the NSKK and NSFK such as history, organization, uniforms, insignia, special insignia, flags and standards, gorgets, daggers, awards, "day badges," and much more!

Uniforms of the Waffen-SS; Black Service Uniform —LAH Guard Uniform— SS Earth-Grey Service Uniform—Model 1936 Field Service Uniform— 1939-1940 —1941 Volume 1, by Michael D. Beaver. Schiffer Publications, Atglen, PA. 2002. 272 pages, with 500 color, and black and white photos. $79.95

This spectacular work is a heavily documented record of all major clothing articles of the Waffen-SS. Hundreds of unpublished photographs were used in production. Original and extremely rare SS uniforms of various types are carefully photographed and presented here. Among the subjects covered in this multi volume series are field-service uniforms, sports, drill, dress, armored personnel, tropical, and much more. A large updated chapter on SS camouflage clothing is also provided. Special chapters on the SD and concentration camp personnel assist the reader in differentiating these elements from combat units of the Waffen-SS. Difficult areas such as mountain and ski troops, plus ultra-rare pre-war uniforms are covered. Included are many striking and exquisite uniforms worn by such men as Himmler, Dietrich, Ribbentrop (father and son), Wolff, Demelhuber, and many others. From the enlisted man to the top of the SS empire, this book covers it all. This book is indispensable and an absolute must-have for any serious historian of World War II German uniforms.

Uniforms of the Waffen-SS; 1942-1943 — 1944-1945 — Ski Uniforms — Overcoats — White Service Uniforms — Tropical Clothing, Volume 2, by Michael D. Beaver. Schiffer Publications, Atglen, PA. 2002. 272 pages, with 500 color, and black and white photos. $79.95

Uniforms of the Waffen-SS; Sports and Drill Uniforms — Black Panzer Uniform — Camouflage — Concentration Camp Personnel-SD-SS Female Auxiliaries, Volume 3, by Michael D. Beaver. Schiffer Publications, Atglen, PA. 2002. 272 pages, with 500 color, and black and white photos. $79.95

U.S. Silent Service - Dolphins & Combat Insignia 1924-1945, by David Jones. Bender Publishing, San Jose, CA, 2001. 224 pages, 532 photos. (most in full color) $39.95

After eight years of extensive research, the publication of this book is a submarine buff and collector∂s dream come true. This beautiful full-color book chronicles, with period letters and sketches, the developmental history of US submarine insignia prior to 1945. It also contains many rare and never before published photographs, plus interviews with WWII submarine veterans, from enlisted men to famous skippers. Each insignia is photographed (obverse and reverse) and magnified in color. All known contractors are covered plus embroidered versions, mess dress variations, the Roll of Honor, submarine combat insignia, battleflags, launch memorabilia and related submarine collectibles (postal covers, match book covers, jewelry, posters, advertising art, postcards, etc.)

Variations of Colt's New Model Police and Pocket Breech Loading Pistols, by Breslin, John D., Pirie, William Q., & Price, David E.: Lincoln, RI: Andrew Mowbray Publishers, 2002. 1st edition. 158 pages, heavily illustrated with over 160 photographs and superb technical detailed drawings and diagrams. Pictorial Hardcover. $37.95

A type-by-type guide to what collectors call small frame conversions.

Walther: A German Legend, by Manfred Kersten, Safari Press, Inc., Huntington Beach, CA, 2000. 400 pp., illustrated. $85.00

This comprehensive book covers, in rich detail, all aspects of the company and its guns, including an illustrious and rich history, the WW2 years, all the pistols (models 1 through 9), the P-38, P-88, the long guns, .22 rifles, centerfires, Wehrmacht guns, and even a gun that could shoot around a corner.

Walther Pistols: Models 1 Through P99, Factory Variations and Copies, by Dieter H. Marschall, Ucross Books, Los Alamos, NM. 2000. 140 pages, with 140 b & w illustrations, index. Paper Covers. $19.95

This is the English translation, revised and updated, of the highly successful and widely acclaimed German language edition. This book provides the collector with a reference guide and overview of the entire line of the Walther military, police, and self-defense pistols from the very first to the very latest. Models 1-9, PP, PPK, MP, AP, HP, P.38, P1, P4, P38K, P5, P88, P99 and the Manurhin models. Variations, where issued, serial ranges, calibers, marks, proofs, logos, and design aspects in an astonishing quantity and variety are crammed into this very well researched and highly regarded work.

Walther Handgun Story: A Collector's and Shooter's Guide, The, by Gene Gangarosa, Steiger Publications, 1999. 300., illustrated. Paper covers. $21.95

Covers the entire history of the Walther empire. Illustrated with over 250 photos.

Walther P-38 Pistol, by Maj. George Nonte, Desert Publications, Cornville, AZ, 1982. 100 pp., illus. Paper covers. $12.95

Complete volume on one of the most famous handguns to come out of WWII. All models covered.

Walther Models PP & PPK, 1929-1945 – Volume 1, by James L. Rankin, Coral Gables, FL, 1974. 142 pp., illus. $40.00

Complete coverage on the subject as to finish, proofmarks and Nazi Party inscriptions.

Walther Volume II, Engraved, Presentation and Standard Models, by James L. Rankin, J.L. Rankin, Coral Gables, FL, 1977. 112 pp., illus. $40.00

The new Walther book on embellished versions and standard models. Has 88 photographs, including many color plates.

Walther, Volume III, 1908-1980, by James L. Rankin, Coral Gables, FL, 1981. 226 pp., illus. $40.00

Covers all models of Walther handguns from 1908 to date, includes holsters, grips and magazines.

Winchester Bolt Action Military & Sporting Rifles 1877 to 1937, by Herbert G. Houze, Andrew Mowbray Publishing, Lincoln, RI, 1998. 295 pp., illus. $45.00

Winchester was the first American arms maker to commercially manufacture a bolt action repeating rifle, and this book tells the exciting story of these Winchester bolt actions.

THE HANDGUNNER'S LIBRARY

Winchester Book, The, by George Madis, David Madis Gun Book Distributor, Dallas, TX, 2000. 650 pp., illus. $54.50

A new, revised 25th anniversary edition of this classic book on Winchester firearms. Complete serial ranges have been added.

Winchester Dates of Manufacture 1849-1984, by George Madis, Art & Reference House, Brownsboro, TX, 1984. 59 pp. $7.50

A most useful work, compiled from records of the Winchester factory.

Winchester Model 1876 "Centennial" Rifle, The, by Houze, Herbert G. Lincoln, RI: Andrew Mowbray, Inc., 2001. Illustrated with over 180 black and white photographs. 192 Pages. Hardcover. $45.00

The first authoritative study of the Winchester Model 1876 written using the company's own records. This book dispels the myth that the Model 1876 was merely a larger version of the Winchester company's famous Model 1873 and instead traces its true origins to designs developed immediately after the American Civil War. The specifics of the model-such as the numbers made in its standard calibers, barrel lengths, finishes and special order features-are fully listed here for the first time. In addition, the actual processes and production costs involved in its manufacture are also completely documented. For Winchester collectors, and those interested in the mechanics of the 19th-century arms industry, this book provides a wealth of previously unpublished information.

Winchester Engraving, by R.L. Wilson, Beinfeld Books, Springs, CA, 1989. 500 pp., illus. $135.00

A classic reference work of value to all arms collectors.

Winchester Handbook, The, by George Madis, Art & Reference House, Lancaster, TX, 1982. 287 pp., illus. $26.95

The complete line of Winchester guns, with dates of manufacture, serial numbers, etc.

Winchester-Lee Rifle, The, by Eugene Myszkowski, Excalibur Publications, Tucson, AZ 2000. 96 pp., illustrated. Paper Covers. $22.95

The development of the Lee Straight Pull, the cartridge and the approval for military use. Covers details of the inventor and memorabilia of Winchester-Lee related material.

Winchester Lever Action Repeating Firearms, Vol. 1, The Models of 1866, 1873 and 1876, by Arthur Pirkle, North Cape Publications, Tustin, CA, 1995. 112 pp., illus. Paper covers. $19.95

Complete, part-by-part description, including dimensions, finishes, markings and variations throughout the production run of these fine, collectible guns.

Winchester Lever Action Repeating Rifles, Vol. 2, The Models of 1886 and 1892, by Arthur Pirkle, North Cape Publications, Tustin, CA, 1996. 150 pp., illus. Paper covers. $19.95

Describes each model on a part-by-part basis by serial number range complete with finishes, markings and changes.

Winchester Lever Action Repeating Rifles, Volume 3, The Model of 1894, by Arthur Pirkle, North Cape Publications, Tustin, CA, 1998. 150 pp., illus. Paper covers. $19.95

The first book ever to provide a detailed description of the Model 1894 rifle and carbine.

Winchester Lever Legacy, The, by Clyde "Snooky" Williamson, Buffalo Press, Zachary, LA, 1988. 664 pp., illustrated. $75.00

A book on reloading for the different calibers of the Winchester lever action rifle.

Winchester Model 94: The First 100 Years, The, by Robert C. Renneberg, Krause Publications, Iola, WI, 1991. 208 pp., illus. $34.95

Covers the design and evolution from the early years up to the many different editions that exist today.

Winchester Rarities, by Webster, Krause Publications, Iola, WI, 2000. 208 pp., with over 800 color photos, illus. $49.95

This book details the rarest of the rare; the one-of-a-kind items and the advertising pieces from years gone by. With nearly 800 full color photos and detailed pricing provided by experts in the field, this book gives collectors and enthusiasts everything they need.

Winchester Shotguns and Shotshells, by Ronald W. Stadt, Krause Publications, Iola, WI, 1995. 256 pp., illus. $34.95

The definitive book on collectible Winchester shotguns and shotshells manufactured through 1961.

Winchester Single-Shot—Volume 1; A History and Analysis, The, by John Campbell, Andrew Mowbray, Inc., Lincoln RI, 1995. 272 pp., illus. $55.00

Covers every important aspect of this highly-collectible firearm.

Winchester Single-Shot—Volume 2; Old Secrets and New Discoveries, The, by John Campbell, Andrew Mowbray, Inc., Lincoln RI, 2000. 280 pp., illus. $55.00

An exciting follow-up to the classic first volume.

Winchester Slide-Action Rifles, Volume 1: Model 1890 & 1906, by Ned Schwing, Krause Publications, Iola, WI, 1992. 352 pp., illus. $39.95

First book length treatment of models 1890 & 1906 with over 50 charts and tables showing significant new information about caliber style and rarity.

Worldwide Webley and the Harrington and Richardson Connection, by Stephen Cuthbertson, Ballista Publishing and Distributing Ltd., Gabriola Island, Canada, 1999. 259 pp., illus. $50.00

A masterpiece of scholarship. Over 350 photographs plus 75 original documents, patent drawings, and advertisements accompany the text.

GENERAL

Action Shooting: Cowboy Style, by John Taffin, Krause Publications, Iola, WI, 1999. 320 pp., illustrated. $39.95

Details on the guns and ammunition. Explanations of the rules used for many events. The essential cowboy wardrobe.

Advanced Muzzleloader's Guide, by Toby Bridges, Stoeger Publishing Co., So. Hackensack, NJ, 1985. 256 pp., illus. Paper covers. $14.95

The complete guide to muzzle-loading rifles, pistols and shotguns—flintlock and percussion.

Aids to Musketry for Officers & NCOs, by Capt. B.J. Friend, Excalibur Publications, Latham, NY, 1996. 40 pp., illus. Paper covers. $7.95

A facsimile edition of a pre-WWI British manual filled with useful information for training the common soldier.

Air Gun Digest, 3rd Edition, by J.I. Galan, DBI Books, a division of Krause Publications, Iola, WI, 1995. 258 pp., illus. Paper covers. $19.95

Everything from A to Z on air gun history, trends and technology.

American Air Rifles, by House, James E. Krause Publications, Iola, WI. 2002. 1st edition. 208 pages, with 198 b&w photos. Softcover. $22.95

Air rifle ballistics, sights, pellets, games, and hunting caliber recommendations are thoroughly explained to help shooters get the most out of their American air rifles. Evaluation of more than a dozen American-made and American-imported air rifle models.

American B.B. Gun: A Collector's Guide, The, by Dunathan, Arni T. A.S. Barnes And Co., Inc., South Brunswick. 2001. 154 pages, illustrated with nearly 200 photographs, drawings and detailed diagrams. Hardcover. $35.00

American and Imported Arms, Ammunition and Shooting Accessories, Catalog No. 18 of the Shooter's Bible, Stoeger, Inc., reprinted by Fayette Arsenal, Fayetteville, NC, 1988. 142 pp., illus. Paper covers. $10.95

A facsimile reprint of the 1932 Stoeger's Shooter's Bible.

America's Great Gunmakers, by Wayne van Zwoll, Stoeger Publishing Co., So. Hackensack, NJ, 1992. 288 pp., illus. Paper covers. $16.95

This book traces in great detail the evolution of guns and ammunition in America and the men who formed the companies that produced them.

Armed and Female, by Paxton Quigley, E.P. Dutton, New York, NY, 1989. 237 pp., illus. $16.95

The first complete book on one of the hottest subjects in the media today, the arming of the American woman.

Arming the Glorious Cause: Weapons of the Second War for Independence, by James B. Whisker, Daniel D. Hartzler and Larry W. Yantz, R & R Books, Livonia, NY, 1998. 175 pp., illustrated. $45.00.

A photographic study of Confederate weapons.

Arms and Armour in Antiquity and the Middle Ages, by Charles Boutell, Stackpole Books, Mechanicsburg, PA, 1996. 352 pp., illus. $22.95

Detailed descriptions of arms and armor, the development of tactics and the outcome of specific battles.

Arms & Armor in the Art Institute of Chicago, by Walter J. Karcheski, Jr., Bulfinch Press, Boston, MA, 1995. 128 pp., illus. $35.00

Now, for the first time, the Art Institute of Chicago's arms and armor collection is presented in the visual delight of 103 color illustrations.

Arms for the Nation: Springfield Longarms, edited by David C. Clark, Scott A. Duff, Export, PA, 1994. 73 pp., illus. Paper covers. $9.95

A brief history of the Springfield Armory and the arms made there.

Arsenal of Freedom, The Springfield Armory, 1890-1948: A Year-by-Year Account Drawn from Official Records, compiled and edited by Lt. Col. William S. Brophy, USAR Ret., Andrew Mowbray, Inc., Lincoln, RI, 1991. 400 pp., illus. Soft covers. $29.95

A "must buy" for all students of American military weapons, equipment and accoutrements.

Assault Pistols, Rifles and Submachine Guns, by Duncan Long, Paladin Press, Boulder, CO, 1997, 8 1/2 x 11, soft cover, photos, illus. 152 pp. $21.95

This book offers up-to-date, practical information on how to operate and field-strip modern military, police and civilian combat weapons. Covers new developments and trends such as the use of fiber optics, liquid-recoil systems and lessening of barrel length are covered. Troubleshooting procedures, ballistic tables and a list of manufacturers and distributors are also included.

Assault Weapons, 5th Edition, The Gun Digest Book of, edited by Jack Lewis and David E. Steele, DBI Books, a division of Krause Publications, Iola, WI, 2000. 256 pp., illustrated. Paper covers. $21.95

This is the latest word on true assault weaponry in use today by international military and law enforcement organizations.

Benchrest Shooting Primer, The, by Brennan, Dave (Editor). Precision Shooting, Inc., Manchester, CT 2000. 2nd edition. 420 pages, illustrated with black and white photographs, drawings and detailed diagrams. Pictorial softcover. $24.95

The very best articles on shooting and reloading for the most challenging of all the rifle accuracy disciplines...benchrest shooting.

Black Powder, Pig Lead and Steel Silhouettes, by Matthews, Paul A. Wolfe Publishing, Prescott, AZ, 2002. 132 pages, illustrated with black and white photographs and detailed drawings and diagrams. Softcover. $16.95

Book of the Crossbow The, by Sir Ralph Payne-Gallwey, Dover Publications, Mineola, NY, 1996. 416 pp., illus. Paper covers. $14.95

Unabridged republication of the scarce 1907 London edition of the book on one of the most devastating hand weapons of the Middle Ages.

British Small Arms of World War 2, by Ian D. Skennerton, I.D.S.A. Books, Piqua, OH, 1988. 110 pp., 37 illus. $25.00

Carbine And Shotgun Speed Shooting: How To Hit Hard And Fast In Combat, by Moses, Steve. Paladin Press, Boulder, CO. 2002. 96 pages, illus. Softcover $18.00

In this groundbreaking book, he breaks down the mechanics of speed shooting these weapons, from stance and grip to sighting, trigger control and more, presenting them in a concise and easily understood manner. Whether you wish to further your defensive, competitive or recreational shooting skills, you will find this book a welcome resource for learning to shoot carbines and shotguns with the speed and accuracy that are so critical at short distances.

Combat Handgunnery, 5th Edition, The Gun Digest Book of, by Chuck Taylor, DBI Books, a division of Krause Publications, Iola, WI, 2002. 256 pp., illus. Paper covers. $21.95

This edition looks at real world combat handgunnery from three different perspectives—military, police and civilian.

Complete Blackpowder Handbook, 4th Edition, The, by Sam Fadala, DBI Books, a division of Krause Publications, Iola, WI, 2002. 400 pp., illus. Paper covers. $21.95

Expanded and completely rewritten edition of the definitive book on the subject of blackpowder.

Complete .50-caliber Sniper Course, The, by Dean Michaelis, Paladin Press, Boulder, CO, 2000. 576 pp, illustrated, $60.00

The history from German Mauser T-Gewehr of World War 1 to the Soviet PTRD and beyond. Includes the author's Program of Instruction for Special Operations Hard-Target Interdiction Course.

cowboy Action Shooting, by Charly Gullett, Wolfe Publishing Co., Prescott, AZ, 1995. 400 pp., illus. Paper covers. $24.50

The fast growing of the shooting sports is comprehensively covered in this text— the guns, loads, tactics and the fun and flavor of this Old West era competition.

Custom Firearms Engraving, by Tom Turpin, Krause Publications, Iola, WI, 1999. 208 pp., illustrated. $49.95

Provides a broad and comprehensive look at the world of firearms engraving. The exquisite styles of more than 75 master engravers are shown on beautiful examples of handguns, rifles, shotguns, and other firearms, as well as knives.

Dead On, by Tony Noblitt and Warren Gabrilska, Paladin Press, Boulder, CO, 1998. 176 pp., illustrated. Paper covers. $22.00

The long-range marksman's guide to extreme accuracy.

Elmer Keith: The Other Side of A Western Legend, by Gene Brown., Precision Shooting, Inc., Manchester, CT 2002. 1st edition. 168 pages, illustrated with black and white photographs. Softcover. $19.95

An updated and expanded edition of his original work, incorporating new tales and information that has come to light in the past six years. Additional photos have been added, and the expanded work has been professionally edited and formatted. Gene Brown was a long time friend of Keith, and today is unquestionably the leading authority on Keith's books. The chapter on the topic is worth the price of admission by itself.

Encyclopedia of Native American Bows, Arrows and Quivers, by Steve Allely and Jim Hamm, The Lyons Press, N.Y., 1999. 160 pp., illustrated. $29.95

A landmark book for anyone interested in archery history, or Native Americans.

Exercise of Armes, The, by Jacob de Gheyn, edited and with an introduction by Bas Kist, Dover Publications, Inc., Mineola, NY, 1999. 144 pp., illustrated. Paper covers. $14.95

Republications of all 117 engravings from the 1607 classic military manual. A meticulously accurate portrait of uniforms and weapons of the 17th century Netherlands.

Federal Civil War Shelter Tent, The, by Gaede, Frederick C., Alexandria, VA: O'Donnell Publishing, 2001. 1st edition. 134 pages, and illustrated. Softcover $20.00

This is a great monograph for all Civil War collectors. The text covers everything from government patents, records, and contract data to colorful soldier's descriptions. In addition, it is extensively illustrated with drawings and photos of over 30 known examples with close-ups of stitching, fastening buttons, and some that were decorated with soldier's art. This book is a well-presented study by a leading researcher, collector, and historian.

Fighting Iron; A Metals Handbook for Arms Collectors, by Art Gogan, Mowbray Publishers, Inc., Lincoln, RI, 2002. 176 pp., illustrated. $28.00

A guide that is easy to use, explains things in simple English and covers all of the different historical periods that we are interested in.

Fighting Submachine Gun, Machine Pistol, and Shotgun, a Hands-On Evaluation, The, by Timothy J. Mullin, Paladin Press, Boulder, CO, 1999. 224 pp., illustrated. Paper covers. $35.00

An invaluable reference for military, police and civilian shooters who may someday need to know how a specific weapon actually performs when the targets are shooting back and the margin of errors is measured in lives lost.

Fireworks: A Gunsight Anthology, by Jeff Cooper, Paladin Press, Boulder, CO, 1998. 192 pp., illus. Paper cover. $27.00

A collection of wild, hilarious, shocking and always meaningful tales from the remarkable life of an American firearms legend.

Frank Pachmayr: The Story of America's Master Gunsmith and his Guns, by John Lachuk, Safari Press, Huntington Beach, CA, 1996. 254 pp., illus. First edition, limited, signed and slipcased. $85.00; Second printing trade edition. $50.00

The colorful and historically significant biography of Frank A. Pachmayr, America's own gunsmith emeritus.

From a Stranger's Doorstep to the Kremlin Gate, by Mikhail Kalashnikov, Ironside International Publishers, Inc., Alexandria, VA, 1999. 460 pp., illustrated. $34.95

A biography of the most influential rifle designer of the 20th century. His AK-47 assault rifle has become the most widely used (and copied) assault rifle of this century.

Frontier Rifleman, The, by H.B. LaCrosse Jr., Pioneer Press, Union City, TN, 1989. 183 pp., illus. Soft covers. $17.50

The Frontier rifleman's clothing and equipment during the era of the American Revolution, 1760-1800.

Gatling Gun: 19th Century Machine Gun to 21st Century Vulcan, The, by Joseph Berk, Paladin Press, Boulder, CO, 1991. 136 pp., illus. $34.95

Here is the fascinating on-going story of a truly timeless weapon, from its beginnings during the Civil War to its current role as a state-of-the-art modern combat system.

German Artillery of World War Two, by Ian V. Hogg, Stackpole Books, Mechanicsburg, PA, 1997. 304 pp., illus. $44.95

Complete details of German artillery use in WWII.

Gone Diggin: Memoirs of A Civil War Relic Hunter, by Toby Law. Orange, VA: Publisher's Press, 2002. 1st edition signed. ISBN: 0942365138. 151 pages, illustrated with black & white photos. $24.95

The true story of one relic hunter's life - the author kept exacting records of every relic hunt and every relic hunter he was with working with.

Grand Old Lady of No Man's Land: The Vickers Machine Gun, by Dolf L. Goldsmith, Collector Grade Publications, Cobourg, Canada, 1994. 600 pp., illus. $79.95

Goldsmith brings his years of experience as a U.S. Army armourer, machine gun collector and shooter to bear on the Vickers, in a book sure to become a classic in its field.

Grenade Recognition Manual, Volume 1, U.S. Grenades & Accessories, The, by Darryl W. Lynn, Service Publications, Ottawa, Canada, 1998. 112 pp., illus. Paper covers. $29.95

This new book examines the hand grenades of the United States beginning with the hand grenades of the U.S. Civil War and continues through to the present.

Grenade Recognition Manual, Vol. 2, British and Commonwealth Grenades and Accessories, The, by Darryl W. Lynn, Printed by the Author, Ottawa, Canada, 2001. 201 pp., illustrated with over 200 photos and drawings. Paper covers. $40.00

Covers British, Australian, and Canadian Grenades. It has the complete British Numbered series, most of the L series as well as the Australian and Canadian grenades in use. Also covers Launchers, fuzes and lighters, launching cartridges, fillings, and markings.

Gun Digest 2003, 57th Edition, edited by Ken Ramage, DBI Books a division of Krause Publications, Iola, WI, 2002. 544 pp., illustrated. Paper covers. $27.95

This all new 56th edition continues the editorial excellence, quality, content and comprehensive cataloguing that firearms enthusiasts have come to know and expect. The most read gun book in the world for the last half century.

Gun Engraving, by C. Austyn, Safari Press Publication, Huntington Beach, CA, 1998. 128 pp., plus 24 pages of color photos. $50.00

A well-illustrated book on fine English and European gun engravers. Includes a fantastic pictorial section that lists types of engravings and prices.

Gun Notes, Volume 1, by Elmer Keith, Safari Press, Huntington Beach, CA, 2002. 219 pp., illustrated Softcover. $24.95

A collection of Elmer Keith's most interesting columns and feature stories that appeared in "Guns & Ammo" magazine from 1961 to the late 1970's.

Gun Notes, Volume 2, by Elmer Keith, Safari Press, Huntington Beach, CA, 2002. 292 pp., illustrated. Softcover. $24.95

THE HANDGUNNER'S LIBRARY

Covers articles from Keith's monthly column in "Guns & Ammo" magazine during the period from 1971 through Keith's passing in 1982.

Gun Talk, edited by Dave Moreton, Winchester Press, Piscataway, NJ, 1973. 256 pp., illus. $9.95

A treasury of original writing by the top gun writers and editors in America. Practical advice about every aspect of the shooting sports.

Gun That Made the Twenties Roar, The, by Wm. J. Helmer, rev. and enlarged by George C. Nonte, Jr., The Gun Room Press, Highland Park, NJ, 1977. Over 300 pp., illus. $24.95

Historical account of John T. Thompson and his invention, the infamous "Tommy Gun."

Gun Trader's Guide, 24th Edition, published by Stoeger Publishing Co., Wayne, NJ, 2002. 592 pp., illus. Paper covers. $23.95

Complete specifications and current prices for used guns. Prices of over 5,000 handguns, rifles and shotguns both foreign and domestic.

Gunfighter, Man or Myth?, The, by Joseph G. Rosa, Oklahoma Press, Norman, OK, 1969. 229 pp., illus. (including weapons). Paper covers. $14.95

A well-documented work on gunfights and gunfighters of the West and elsewhere. Great treat for all gunfighter buffs.

Guns Illustrated 2003, 23rd Edition, edited by Ken Ramage, DBI Books a division of Krause Publications, Iola, WI, 2003. 352 pp., illustrated. Softcovers. $22.95

Highly informative, technical articles on a wide range of shooting topics by some of the top writers in the industry. A catalog section lists more than 3,000 firearms currently manufactured in or imported to the U.S.

Guns Of The Old West, by Dean K. Boorman, New York: Lyons Press, 2002. Color & b&w illus, 144 pgs. Hardcover. $29.95

An illustrated history of the firearms used by pioneers, hunters, soldiers, lawmen, & the lawless.

Guns & Shooting: A Selected Bibliography, by Ray Riling, Ray Riling Arms Books Co., Phila., PA, 1982. 434 pp., illus. Limited, numbered edition. $75.00

A limited edition of this superb bibliographical work, the only modern listing of books devoted to guns and shooting.

Guns, Bullets, and Gunfighters, by Jim Cirillo, Paladin Press, Boulder, CO, 1996. 119 pp., illus. Paper covers. $16.00

Lessons and tales from a modern-day gunfighter.

Hidden in Plain Sight, "A Practical Guide to Concealed Handgun Carry" (Revised 2nd Edition), by Trey Bloodworth and Mike Raley, Paladin Press, Boulder, CO, 1997, 5 1/2 x 8 1/2, softcover, photos, 176 pp. $20.00

Concerned with how to comfortably, discreetly and safely exercise the privileges granted by a CCW permit? This invaluable guide offers the latest advice on what to look for when choosing a CCW, how to dress for comfortable, effective concealed carry, traditional and more unconventional carry modes, accessory holsters, customized clothing and accessories, accessibility data based on draw-time comparisons and new holsters on the market. Includes 40 new manufacturer listings.

HK Assault Rifle Systems, by Duncan Long, Paladin Press, Boulder, CO, 1995. 110 pp., illus. Paper covers. $27.95

The little known history behind this fascinating family of weapons tracing its beginnings from the ashes of World War Two to the present time.

Hunting Time: Adventures In Pursuit Of North American Big Game: A Forty Year Chronicle, The, by John E.Howard, Deforest, WI: Saint Huberts Press, 2002. 1st edition. ISBN: 0963309447. 537 pages, illustrated with drawings. Hardcover. $29.95

From a novice's first hunt for whitetailed deer in his native Wisconsin, to a seasoned hunter's pursuit of a Boone and Crockett Club record book caribou in the northwest territories, the author carries the reader along on his forty year journey through the big game fields of North America.

I Remember Skeeter, compiled by Sally Jim Skelton, Wolfe Publishing Co., Prescott, AZ, 1998. 401 pp., illus. Paper covers. $19.95

A collection of some of the beloved storyteller's famous works interspersed with anecdotes and tales from the people who knew best.

Indian Tomahawks and Frontiersmen Belt Axes, by Daniel Hartzler & James Knowles. New Windsor, MD: Privately Printed, 2002. 4th revised edition. 279 pages, illustrated with photos and drawings. Hardcover. $65.00

This fourth revised edition has over 160 new tomahawks and trade axes added since the first edition, also a list of 205 makers names. There are 15 chapters from the earliest known tomahawks to the present day. Some of the finest tomahawks in the country are shown in this book with 31 color plates. This comprehensive study is invaluable to any collector.

Jack O'Connor Catalogue of Letters, by Enzler-Herring, E. Cataloguer. Agoura CA: Trophy Room Books, 2002. 262 pages, 18 illustrations. Hardcover. $55.00

During a sixteen year period beginning in 1960, O'Connor exchanged many letters with his pal, John Jobson. Material from nearly three hundred of these has been assembled and edited by Ellen Enzler Herring and published in chronological order. A number of the letters have been reproduced in full or part. They offer considerable insight into the beloved gun editor and "Dean of Outdoor Writers"over and beyond what we know about him from his books.

Jack O'Connor — The Legendary Life of America's Greatest Gunwriter, by R. Anderson. Long Beach, CA: Safari Press, 2002. 1st edition. 240pp, profuse photos. Hardcover. $29.95

This is the book all hunters in North America have been waiting for—the long-awaited biography on Jack O'Connor! Jack O'Connor was the preeminent North American big-game hunter and gunwriter of the twentieth century, and Robert Anderson's masterfully written new work is a blockbuster filled with fascinating facts and stories about this controversial character. With the full cooperation of the O'Connor children, Anderson spent three years interviewing O'Connor's family and friends as well as delving into JOC's papers, photos, and letters, including the extensive correspondence between O'Connor and Bob Householder, and the O'Connor papers from Washington State University. O'Connor's lifelong friend Buck Buckner has contributed two chapters on his experiences with the master of North American hunting.

Kill or Get Killed, by Col. Rex Applegate, Paladin Press, Boulder, CO, 1996. 400 pp., illus. $49.95

The best and longest-selling book on close combat in history.

Long-Range War: Sniping in Vietnam, The, by Peter R. Senich, Paladin Press, Boulder, CO, 1999. 280 pp., illus. Softcover $59.95

The most complete report on Vietnam-era sniping ever documented.

Manual for H&R Reising Submachine Gun and Semi-Auto Rifle, edited by George P. Dillman, Desert Publications, El Dorado, AZ, 1994. 81 pp., illus. Paper covers. $12.95

A reprint of the Harrington & Richardson 1943 factory manual and the rare military manual on the H&R submachine gun and semi-auto rifle.

Manufacture of Gunflints, The, by Sydney B.J. Skertchly, facsimile reprint with new introduction by Seymour de Lotbiniere, Museum Restoration Service, Ontario, Canada, 1984. 90 pp., illus. $24.50

Limited edition reprinting of the very scarce London edition of 1879.

Master Tips, by J. Winokur, Potshot Press, Pacific Palisades, CA, 1985. 96 pp., illus. Paper covers. $11.95

Basics of practical shooting.

Military and Police Sniper, The, by Mike R. Lau, Precision Shooting, Inc., Manchester, CT, 1998. 352 pp., illustrated. Paper covers. $44.95

Advanced precision shooting for combat and law enforcement.

Military Rifle & Machine Gun Cartridges, by Jean Huon, Paladin Press, Boulder, CO, 1990. 392 pp., illus. $34.95

Describes the primary types of military cartridges and their principal loadings, as well as their characteristics, origin and use.

Military Small Arms of the 20th Century, 7th Edition, by Ian V. Hogg and John Weeks, DBI Books, a division of Krause Publications, Iola, WI, 2000. 416 pp., illustrated. Paper covers. $24.95

Cover small arms of 46 countries. Over 800 photographs and illustrations.

Modern Custom Guns, Walnut, Steel, and Uncommon Artistry, by Tom Turpin, Krause Publications, Iola, WI, 1997. 206 pp., illus. $49.95

From exquisite engraving to breathtaking exotic woods, the mystique of today's custom guns is expertly detailed in word and awe-inspiring color photos of rifles, shotguns and handguns.

Modern Law Enforcement Weapons & Tactics, 2nd Edition, by Tom Ferguson, DBI Books, a division of Krause Publications, Iola, WI, 1991. 256 pp., illus. Paper covers. $18.95

An in-depth look at the weapons and equipment used by law enforcement agencies of today.

Modern Machine Guns, by John Walter, Stackpole Books, Inc. Mechanicsburg, PA, 2000. 144 pp., with 146 illustrations. $22.95

A compact and authoritative guide to post-war machine-guns. A gun-by-gun directory identifying individual variants and types including detailed evaluations and technical data.

Modern Sporting Guns, by Christopher Austyn, Safari Press, Huntington Beach, CA, 1994. 128 pp., illus. $40.00

A discussion of the "best" English guns; round action, over-and-under, boxlocks, hammer guns, bolt action and double rifles as well as accessories.

More Complete Cannoneer, The, by M.C. Switlik, Museum & Collectors Specialties Co., Monroe, MI, 1990. 199 pp., illus. $19.95

Compiled agreeably to the regulations for the U.S. War Department, 1861, and containing current observations on the use of antique cannons.

MP-40 Machine Gun, The, Desert Publications, El Dorado, AZ, 1995. 32 pp., illus. Paper covers. $11.95

A reprint of the hard-to-find operating and maintenance manual for one of the most famous machine guns of World War II.

Naval Percussion Locks and Primers, by Lt. J. A. Dahlgren, Museum Restoration Service, Bloomfield, Canada, 1996. 140 pp., illus. $35.00

First published as an Ordnance Memoranda in 1853, this is the finest existing study of percussion locks and primers origin and development.

Official Soviet AKM Manual, The, translated by Maj. James F. Gebhardt (Ret.), Paladin Press, Boulder, CO, 1999. 120 pp., illustrated. Paper covers. $18.00

This official military manual, available in English for the first time, was originally published by the Soviet Ministry of Defence. Covers the history, function, maintenance, assembly and disassembly, etc. of the 7.62mm AKM assault rifle.

THE HANDGUNNER'S LIBRARY

One-Round War: U.S.M.C. Scout-Snipers in Vietnam, The, by Peter Senich, Paladin Press, Boulder, CO, 1996. 384 pp., illus. Paper covers $59.95

Sniping in Vietnam focusing specifically on the Marine Corps program.

Parker Brothers: Knight of the Trigger, by Ed Muderlak. A Fact-Based Historical Novel Describing the Life and Times of Captain Arthur William du Bray, 1848-1928. Davis, IL: Old Reliable Publishing, 2002. 223 pages. $25.00

Knight of the Trigger tells the story of the Old West when Parker's most famous gun saleman traveled the country by rail, competing in the pigeon ring, hunting with the rich and famous, and selling the "Old Reliable" Parker shotgun. The life and times of Captain Arthur William du Bray, Parker Brothers' on-the-road sales agent from 1884 to 1926, is described in a novelized version of his interesting life.

Powder Horns and Their Architecture and Decoration as Used by the Soldier, Indian, Sailor and Traders of the Era, by Madison Grant. York, PA: Privately Printed, 1987. 165 pages, profusely illustrated. Hardcover. $45.00

Covers homemade pieces from the late eighteenth and early nineteenth centuries.

Practically Speaking: An Illustrated Guide — The Game, Guns and Gear of the International Defensive Pistol Association, by Walt Rauch. Lafayette Hills, PA: Privately Printed, 2002. 1st edition. Softcover. $24.95

The game, guns and gear of the International Defensive Pistol Association with real-world applications. 79 pages, illustated with drawings and color photos.

Present Sabers: A Popular History of the U.S. Horse Cavalry, by Allan T. Heninger, Tucson, AZ: Excalibur Publications, 2002. 1st edition. 160 pages, with 148 photographs, 45 illustrations and 4 charts. Softcover. $24.95

An illustrated history of America's involvement with the horse cavalry, from its earliest beginnings during the Revolutionary War through it's demise in World War 2. The book also contains several appendices, as well as depictions of the regular insignia of all the U.S. Cavalry units.

Principles of Personal Defense, by Jeff Cooper, Paladin Press, Boulder, CO, 1999. 56 pp., illustrated. Paper covers. $14.00

This revised edition of Jeff Cooper's classic on personal defense offers great new illustrations and a new preface while retaining the timeliness theory of individual defense behavior presented in the original book.

Quotable Hunter, The, edited by Jay Cassell and Peter Fiduccia, The Lyons Press, N.Y., 1999. 224 pp., illustrated. $20.00

This collection of more than three hundred memorable quotes from hunters through the ages captures the essence of the sport, with all its joys idiosyncrasies, and challenges.

Rifleman Went to War, A, by H. W. McBride, Lancer Militaria, Mt. Ida, AR, 1987. 398 pp., illus. $29.95

The classic account of practical marksmanship on the battlefields of World War I.

Sharpshooting for Sport and War, by W.W. Greener, Wolfe Publishing Co., Prescott, AZ, 1995. 192 pp., illus. $30.00

This classic reprint explores the *first* expanding bullet; service rifles; shooting positions; trajectories; recoil; external ballistics; and other valuable information.

Shooter's Bible 2003, The, No. 94, edited by William S. Jarrett, Stoeger Publishing Co., Wayne, NJ, 2002. 576 pp., illustrated. Paper covers. $23.95

Over 3,000 firearms currently offered by major American and foreign gunmakers. Represented are handguns, rifles, shotguns and black powder arms with complete specifications and retail prices.

Shooting to Live, by Capt. W. E. Fairbairn & Capt. E. A. Sykes, Paladin Press, Boulder, CO, 1997, 4 1/2 x 7, soft cover, illus., 112 pp. $14.00

Shooting to Live is the product of Fairbairn's and Sykes' practical experience with the handgun. Hundreds of incidents provided the basis for the first true book on life-or-death shootouts with the pistol. Shooting to Live teaches all concepts, considerations and applications of combat pistol craft.

Shooting Buffalo Rifles of the Old West, by Mike Venturino, MLV Enterprises, Livingston, MT, 2002. 278 pages, illustrated with black and white photos. Softcover. $30.00

This tome will take you through the history, the usage, the many models, and the actual shooting (and how to's) of the many guns that saw service on the Frontier and are lovingly called "Buffalo Rifles" today. If you love to shoot your Sharps, Ballards, Remingtons, or Springfield "Trapdoors" for hunting or competition, or simply love Old West history, your library WILL NOT be complete without this latest book from Mike Venturino!

Shooting Colt Single Actions, by Mike Venturino, MLV Enterprises, Livingston, MT 1997. 205 pp., illus. Black and white photos throughout. Softcover. $25.00

A complete examination of the Colt Single Action including styles, calibers and generations.

Shooting Lever Guns Of The Old West, by Mike Venturino, MLV Enterprises, Livingston, MT, 1999. 300 pp., illustrated. Softcover. $27.95

Shooting the lever action type repeating rifles of our American West.

Shooting Sixguns of the Old West, by Mike Venturino, MLV Enterprises, Livingston, MT, 1997. 221 pp., illus. Paper covers. $26.50

A comprehensive look at the guns of the early West: Colts, Smith & Wesson and Remingtons, plus blackpowder and reloading specs.

Sniper Training, FM 23-10, Reprint of the U.S. Army field manual of August, 1994, Paladin Press, Boulder, CO, 1995. 352pp., illus. Paper covers. $30.00

The most up-to-date U.S. military sniping information and doctrine.

Sniping in France, by Major H. Hesketh-Prichard, Lancer Militaria, Mt. Ida, AR, 1993. 224 pp., illus. $24.95

The author was a well-known British adventurer and big game hunter. He was called upon in the early days of "The Great War" to develop a program to offset an initial German advantage in sniping. How the British forces came to overcome this advantage.

Special Warfare: Special Weapons, by Kevin Dockery, Emperor's Press, Chicago, IL, 1997. 192 pp., illus. $29.95

The arms and equipment of the UDT and SEALS from 1943 to the present.

Sporting Collectibles, by Dr. Stephen R. Irwin, Stoeger Publishing Co., Wayne, NJ, 1997. 256 pp., illus. Paper covers. $19.95

A must book for serious collectors and admirers of sporting collectibles.

Sporting Craftsmen: A Complete Guide to Contemporary Makers of Custom-Built Sporting Equipment, The, by Art Carter, Countrysport Press, Traverse City, MI, 1994. 240 pp., illus. $35.00

Profiles leading makers of centerfire rifles; muzzleloading rifles; bamboo fly rods; fly reels; flies; waterfowl calls; decoys; handmade knives; and traditional longbows and recurves.

Street Smart Gun Book, The, by John Farnam, Police Bookshelf, Concord, NH, 1986. 45 pp., illus. Paper covers. $11.95

Weapon selection, defensive shooting techniques, and gunfight-winning tactics from one of the world's leading authorities.

Stress Fire, Vol. 1: Stress Fighting for Police, by Massad Ayoob, Police Bookshelf, Concord, NH, 1984. 149 pp., illus. Paper covers. $11.95

Gunfighting for police, advanced tactics and techniques.

Survival Guns, by Mel Tappan, Desert Publications, El Dorado, AZ, 1993. 456 pp., illus. Paper covers. $25.00

Discusses in a frank and forthright manner which handguns, rifles and shotguns to buy for personal defense and securing food, and the ones to avoid.

Tactical Advantage, The, by Gabriel Suarez, Paladin Press, Boulder, CO, 1998. 216 pp., illustrated. Paper covers. $22.00

Learn combat tactics that have been tested in the world's toughest schools.

Tactical Marksman, by Dave M. Lauch, Paladin Press, Boulder, CO, 1996. 165 pp., illus. Paper covers. $35.00

A complete training manual for police and practical shooters.

Thompson Guns 1921-1945, Anubis Press, Houston, TX, 1980. 215 pp., illus. Paper covers. $15.95

Facsimile reprinting of five complete manuals on the Thompson submachine gun.

To Ride, Shoot Straight, and Speak the Truth, by Jeff Cooper, Paladin Press, Boulder, CO, 1997, 5 1/2 x 8 1/2, soft-cover, illus., 384 pp. $32.00

Combat mind-set, proper sighting, tactical residential architecture, nuclear war - these are some of the many subjects explored by Jeff Cooper in this illustrated anthology. The author discusses various arms, fighting skills and the importance of knowing how to defend oneself, and one's honor, in our rapidly changing world.

Trailriders Guide to Cowboy Action Shooting, by James W. Barnard, Pioneer Press, Union City, TN, 1998. 134 pp., plus 91 photos, drawings and charts. Paper covers. $24.95

Covers the complete spectrum of this shooting discipline, from how to dress to authentic leather goods, which guns are legal, calibers, loads and ballistics.

Ultimate Sniper, The, by Major John L. Plaster, Paladin Press, Boulder, CO, 1994. 464 pp., illus. Paper covers. $49.95

An advanced training manual for military and police snipers.

Uniforms and Equipment of the Imperial Japanese Army in World War 2, by Mike Hewitt. Atglen, PA: Schiffer Publications, 2002. 176 pages, with over 520 color and b/w photos. Hardcover. $59.95

Unrepentant Sinner, by Col. Charles Askins, Paladin Press, Boulder, CO, 2000. 322 pp., illustrated. $29.95

The autobiography of Colonel Charles Askins.

U.S. Marine Corp Rifle and Pistol Marksmanship, 1935, reprinting of a government publication, Lancer Militaria, Mt. Ida, AR, 1991. 99 pp., illus. Paper covers. $11.95

The old corps method of precision shooting.

U.S. Marine Corps Scout/Sniper Training Manual, Lancer Militaria, Mt. Ida, AR, 1989. Soft covers. $27.95

Reprint of the original sniper training manual used by the Marksmanship Training Unit of the Marine Corps Development and Education Command in Quantico, Virginia.

U.S. Marine Corps Scout-Sniper, World War II and Korea, by Peter R. Senich, Paladin Press, Boulder, CO, 1994. 236 pp., illus. $44.95

The most thorough and accurate account ever printed on the training, equipment and combat experiences of the U.S. Marine Corps Scout-Snipers.

U.S. Marine Corps Sniping, Lancer Militaria, Mt. Ida, AR, 1989. Irregular pagination. Soft covers. $18.95

A reprint of the official Marine Corps FMFM1-3B.

THE HANDGUNNER'S LIBRARY

U.S. Marine Uniforms—1912-1940, by Jim Moran. Williamstown, NJ: Phillips Publications, 2001. 174 pages, illustrated with black and white photographs. Hardcover. $49.95

Weapons of the Waffen-SS, by Bruce Quarrie, Sterling Publishing Co., Inc., 1991. 168 pp., illus. $24.95.

An in-depth look at the weapons that made Hitler's Waffen-SS the fearsome fighting machine it was.

Winchester Era, The, by David Madis, Art & Reference House, Brownsville, TX, 1984. 100 pp., illus. $19.95

Story of the Winchester company, management, employees, etc.

With British Snipers to the Reich, by Capt. C. Shore, Lander Militaria, Mt. Ida, AR, 1988. 420 pp., illus. $29.95

One of the greatest books ever written on the art of combat sniping.

World's Machine Pistols and Submachine Guns - Vol. 2a 1964 to 1980, The, by Nelson & Musgrave, Ironside International, Alexandria, VA, 2000. 673 pages, illustrated. $59.95

Containing data, history and photographs of over 200 weapons. With a special section covering shoulder stocked automatic pistols, 100 additional photos.

World's Sniping Rifles, The, by Ian V. Hogg, Paladin Press, Boulder, CO, 1998. 144 pp., illustrated. $22.95

A detailed manual with descriptions and illustrations of more than 50 high-precision rifles from 14 countries and a complete analysis of sights and systems.

GUNSMITHING

Accurizing the Factory Rifle, by M.L. McPhereson, Precision Shooting, Inc., Manchester, CT, 1999. 335 pp., illustrated. Paper covers. $44.95

A long-awaiting book, which bridges the gap between the rudimentary (mounting sling swivels, scope blocks and that general level of accomplishment) and the advanced (precision chambering, barrel fluting, and that general level of accomplishment) books that are currently available today.

Art of Engraving, The, by James B. Meek, F. Brownell & Son, Montezuma, IA, 1973. 196 pp., illus. $38.95

A complete, authoritative, imaginative and detailed study in training for gun engraving. The first book of its kind—and a great one.

Artistry in Arms, The R. W. Norton Gallery, Shreveport, LA, 1970. 42 pp., illus. Paper covers. $9.95.

The art of gunsmithing and engraving.

Checkering and Carving of Gun Stocks, by Monte Kennedy, Stackpole Books, Harrisburg, PA, 1962. 175 pp., illus. $39.95

Revised, enlarged cloth-bound edition of a much sought-after, dependable work.

Firearms Assembly/Disassembly, Part I: Automatic Pistols, 2nd Revised Edition, The Gun Digest Book of, by J.B. Wood, DBI Books, a division of Krause Publications, Iola, WI, 1999. 480 pp., illus. Paper covers. $24.95

Covers 58 popular autoloading pistols plus nearly 200 variants of those models integrated into the text and completely cross-referenced in the index.

Firearms Assembly/Disassembly Part II: Revolvers, Revised Edition, The Gun Digest Book of, by J.B. Wood, DBI Books, a division of Krause Publications, Iola, WI, 1990. 480 pp., illus. Paper covers. $19.95

Covers 49 popular revolvers plus 130 variants. The most comprehensive and professional presentation available to either hobbyist or gunsmith.

Firearms Assembly/Disassembly Part III: Rimfire Rifles, Revised Edition, The Gun Digest Book of, by J. B. Wood, DBI Books, a division of Krause Publications, Iola, WI., 1994. 480 pp., illus. Paper covers. $19.95

Greatly expanded edition covering 65 popular rimfire rifles plus over 100 variants all completely cross-referenced in the index.

Firearms Assembly/Disassembly Part IV: Centerfire Rifles, Revised Edition, The Gun Digest Book of, by J.B. Wood, DBI Books, a division of Krause Publications, Iola, WI, 1991. 480 pp., illus. Paper covers. $19.95

Covers 54 popular centerfire rifles plus 300 variants. The most comprehensive and professional presentation available to either hobbyist or gunsmith.

Firearms Assembly/Disassembly, Part V: Shotguns, Revised Edition, The Gun Digest Book of, by J.B. Wood, DBI Books, a division of Krause Publications, Iola, WI, 1992. 480 pp., illus. Paper covers. $19.95

Covers 46 popular shotguns plus over 250 variants with step-by-step instructions on how to dismantle and reassemble each. The most comprehensive and professional presentation available to either hobbyist or gunsmith.

Firearms Assembly/Disassembly Part VI: Law Enforcement Weapons, The Gun Digest Book of, by J.B. Wood, DBI Books, a division of Krause Publications, Iola, WI, 1981. 288 pp., illus. Paper covers. $16.95

Step-by-step instructions on how to completely dismantle and reassemble the most commonly used firearms found in law enforcement arsenals.

Firearms Assembly 3: The NRA Guide to Rifle and Shotguns, NRA Books, Wash., DC, 1980. 264 pp., illus. Paper covers. $13.95

Text and illustrations explaining the takedown of 125 rifles and shotguns, domestic and foreign.

Firearms Assembly 4: The NRA Guide to Pistols and Revolvers, NRA Books, Wash., DC, 1980. 253 pp., illus. Paper covers. $13.95

Text and illustrations explaining the takedown of 124 pistol and revolver models, domestic and foreign.

Firearms Bluing and Browning, By R.H. Angier, Stackpole Books, Harrisburg, PA. 151 pp., illus. $19.95

A world master gunsmith reveals his secrets of building, repairing and renewing a gun, quite literally, lock, stock and barrel. A useful, concise text on chemical coloring methods for the gunsmith and mechanic.

Firearms Disassembly—With Exploded Views, by John A. Karns & John E. Traister, Stoeger Publishing Co., S. Hackensack, NJ, 1995. 320 pp., illus. Paper covers. $19.95

Provides the do's and don'ts of firearms disassembly. Enables owners and gunsmiths to disassemble firearms in a professional manner.

Guns and Gunmaking Tools of Southern Appalachia, by John Rice Irwin, Schiffer Publishing Ltd., 1983. 118 pp., illus. Paper covers. $9.95

The story of the Kentucky rifle.

Gunsmith Of Grenville County: Building The American Longrifle, The, by Peter Alexander, Texarkana, TX: Scurlock Publishing Co., 2002. Stiff paper covers. $45.00

The most extensive how to book on building longrifles ever published. Takes you through every step of building your own longrifle, from shop set up and tools to engraving, carving and finishing. 400 pages, with hundreds of illustrations, and six color photos of original rifles. Wire O Bind spine will lay flat on the workbench.

Gunsmithing: Pistols & Revolvers, by Patrick Sweeney, DBI Books, a division of Krause Publications, Iola, WI, 1998. 352 pp., illus. Paper covers. $24.95

Do-it-Yourself projects, diagnosis and repair for pistols and revolvers.

Gunsmithing: Rifles, by Patrick Sweeney, Krause Publications, Iola, WI, 1999. 352 pp., illustrated. Paper covers. $24.95

Tips for lever-action rifles. Building a custom Ruger 10/22. Building a better hunting rifle.

Gunsmith Kinks, by F.R. (Bob) Brownell, F. Brownell & Son, Montezuma, IA, 1st ed., 1969. 496 pp., well illus. $22.98

A widely useful accumulation of shop kinks, short cuts, techniques and pertinent comments by practicing gunsmiths from all over the world.

Gunsmith Kinks 2, by Bob Brownell, F. Brownell & Son, Publishers, Montezuma, IA, 1983. 496 pp., illus. $22.95

A collection of gunsmithing knowledge, shop kinks, new and old techniques, shortcuts and general know-how straight from those who do them best—the gunsmiths.

Gunsmith Kinks 3, edited by Frank Brownell, Brownells Inc., Montezuma, IA, 1993. 504 pp., illus. $24.95

Tricks, knacks and "kinks" by professional gunsmiths and gun tinkerers. Hundreds of valuable ideas are given in this volume.

Gunsmith Kinks 4, edited by Frank Brownell, Brownells Inc., Montezuma, IA, 2001. 564 pp., illus. $27.75

332 detailed illustrations. 560+ pages with 706 separate subject headings and over 5000 cross-indexed entries. An incredible gold mine of information.

Gunsmithing, by Roy F. Dunlap, Stackpole Books, Harrisburg, PA, 1990. 742 pp., illus. $34.95

A manual of firearm design, construction, alteration and remodeling. For amateur and professional gunsmiths and users of modern firearms.

Gunsmithing at Home: Lock, Stock and Barrel, by John Traister, Stoeger Publishing Co., Wayne, NJ, 1997. 320 pp., illus. Paper covers. $19.95

A complete step-by-step fully illustrated guide to the art of gunsmithing.

Gunsmith's Manual, The, by J.P. Stelle and Wm. B. Harrison, The Gun Room Press, Highland Park, NJ, 1982. 376 pp., illus. $19.95

For the gunsmith in all branches of the trade.

Home Gunsmithing the Colt Single Action Revolvers, by Loren W. Smith, Ray Riling Arms Books, Co., Phila., PA, 2001. 119 pp., illus. $29.95

Affords the Colt Single Action owner detailed, pertinent information on the operating and servicing of this famous and historic handgun.

Mauser M98 & M96, by R.A. Walsh, Wolfe Publishing Co., Prescott, AR, 1998. 123 pp., illustrated. Paper covers. $32.50

How to build your own favorite custom Mauser rifle from two of the best bolt action rifle designs ever produced—the military Mauser Model 1898 and Model 1896 bolt rifles.

Mr. Single Shot's Gunsmithing-Idea-Book, by Frank de Haas, Mark de Haas, Orange City, IA, 1996. 168 pp., illus. Paper covers. $21.50

Offers easy to follow, step-by-step instructions for a wide variety of gunsmithing procedures all reinforced by plenty of photos.

Pistolsmithing, by George C. Nonte, Jr., Stackpole Books, Harrisburg, PA, 1974. 560 pp., illus. $34.95

A single source reference to handgun maintenance, repair, and modification at home, unequaled in value.

THE HANDGUNNER'S LIBRARY

Practical Gunsmithing, by the editors of American Gunsmith, DBI Books, a division of Krause Publications, Iola, WI, 1996. 256 pp., illus. Paper covers. $19.95

A book intended primarily for home gunsmithing, but one that will be extremely helpful to professionals as well.

Professional Stockmaking, by D. Wesbrook, Wolfe Publishing Co., Prescott AZ, 1995. 308 pp., illus. $54.00

A step-by-step how-to with complete photographic support for every detail of the art of working wood into riflestocks.

Recreating the American Longrifle, by William Buchele, et al, George Shumway Publisher, York, Pa, 5th edition, 1999. 175 pp., illustrated. $40.00

Includes full size plans for building a Kentucky rifle.

Story of Pope's Barrels, The, by Ray M. Smith, R&R Books, Livonia, NY, 1993. 203 pp., illus. $39.00

A reissue of a 1960 book whose author knew Pope personally. It will be of special interest to Schuetzen rifle fans, since Pope's greatest days were at the height of the Schuetzen-era before WWI.

Survival Gunsmithing, by J.B. Wood, Desert Publications, Cornville, AZ, 1986. 92 pp., illus. Paper covers. $11.95

A guide to repair and maintenance of the most popular rifles, shotguns and handguns.

Tactical 1911, The, by Dave Lauck, Paladin Press, Boulder, CO, 1998. 137 pp., illus. Paper covers. $20.00

Here is the only book you will ever need to teach you how to select, modify, employ and maintain your Colt.

HANDGUNS

Advanced Master Handgunning, by Charles Stephens, Paladin Press, Boulder, CO., 1994. 72 pp., illus. Paper covers. $14.00

Secrets and surefire techniques for winning handgun competitions.

Advanced Tactical Marksman More High Performance Techniques for Police, Military, and Practical Shooters, by Lauck, Dave M. Paladin Press, Boulder, CO 2002. 1st edition. 232 pages, photos, illus. Softcover. $35.00

Lauck, one of the most respected names in high-performance shooting and gunsmithing, refines and updates his 1st book . Dispensing with overcomplicated mil-dot formulas and minute-of-angle calculations, Lauck shows you how to achieve superior accuracy and figure out angle shots, streamline the zero process, hit targets at 2,000 yards, deal with dawn and dusk shoots, train for real-world scenarios, choose optics and accessories and create a mobile shooting platform. He also demonstrates the advantages of his custom reticle design and describes important advancements in the MR-30PG shooting system.

American Beauty: The Prewar Colt National Match Government Model Pistol, by Timothy Mullin, Collector Grade Publications, Canada, 1999. 72 pp., 69 illus. $34.95

69 illustrations, 20 in full color photos of factory engraved guns and other authenticated upgrades, including rare 'double-carved' ivory grips.

Ayoob Files: The Book, The, by Massad Ayoob, Police Bookshelf, Concord, NH, 1995. 223 pp., illus. Paper covers. $14.95

The best of Massad Ayoob's acclaimed series in American Handgunner magazine.

Belgian Browning Pistols 1889-1949, The, by Vanderlinden, Anthony. Wet Dog Publications, Geensboro, NC 2001. Limited edition of 2000 copies, signed by the author. 243 pages, plus index. Illustrated with black and white photos. Hardcover. $65.00

Includes the 1899 compact, 1899 Large, 1900,01903, Grand Browning, 1910, 1922 Grand Rendement and high power pistols. Also includes a chapter on holsters.

Big Bore Handguns, by Taffin, John, Krause Publishing, Iola, WI: 2002. 1st edition. 352 Pages, 320 b&w photos with a 16-page color section. Hardcover. $39.95

Gives honest reviews and an inside look at shooting, hunting, and competing with the biggest handguns around. Covers handguns from major gunmakers, as well as handgun customizing, accessories, reloading, and cowboy activities. Significant coverage is also given to handgun customizing, accessories, reloading, and popular shooting hobbies including hunting and cowboy activities. Accessories consist of stocks, handgun holster rigs, and much more. Firearms include single-shot pistols, revolvers, and semi-automatics.

Big Bore Sixguns, by John Taffin, Krause Publications, Iola, WI, 1997. 336 pp., illus. $39.95

The author takes aim on the entire range of big bores from .357 Magnums to .500 Maximums, single actions and cap-and-ball sixguns to custom touches for big bores.

Browning High Power Automatic Pistol (Expanded Edition), The, by Blake R. Stevens, Collector Grade Publications, Canada, 1996. 310 pages, with 313 illus. $49.95

An in-depth chronicle of seventy years of High Power history, from John M Browning's original 16-shot prototypes to the present. Profusely illustrated with rare original photos and drawings from the FN Archive to describe virtually every sporting and military version of the High Power. The numerous modifications made to the basic design over the years are, for the first time, accurately arranged in chronological order, thus permitting the dating of any High Power to within a few years of its production. Full details on the WWII Canadian-made Inglis Browning High Power pistol. The Expanded Edition contains 30 new pages on the interesting Argentine full-auto High Power, the latest FN 'MK3' and BDA9 pistols, plus FN's revolutionary P90 5.7x28mm Personal Defence Weapon, and more!

Browning Hi-Power Pistols, Desert Publications, Cornville, AZ, 1982. 20 pp., illus. Paper covers. $11.95

Covers all facets of the various military and civilian models of the Browning Hi-Power pistol.

Canadian Military Handguns 1855-1985, by Clive M. Law, Museum Restoration Service, Bloomfield, Ont. Canada, 1994. 130pp., illus. $40.00

A long-awaited and important history for arms historians and pistol collectors.

Collecting U.S. Pistols & Revolvers, 1909-1945, by J. C. Harrison. The Arms Chest, Okla. City, OK. 1999. 2nd edition (revised). 185 pages, illus. with pictures and drawings. Spiral bound. $35.00

Valuable and detailed reference book for the collector of U.S. Pistols & Revolvers. Identifies standard issue original military models of the M1911, M1911A1 and M1917Cal .45 Pistols and Revolvers as produced by all manufacturers from 1911 through 1945. Plus .22 ACE Models, National Match Models, and similar foreign military models produced by Colt or manufactured under Colt license. Plus Arsenal repair, refinish and Lend-Lease Models.

Colt .45 Auto Pistol, The, compiled from U.S. War Dept. Technical Manuals, and reprinted by Desert Publications, Cornville, AZ, 1978. 80 pp., illus. Paper covers. $11.95

Covers every facet of this famous pistol from mechanical training, manual of arms, disassembly, repair and replacement of parts.

Colt Automatic Pistols, by Donald B. Bady, Pioneer Press, Union City, TN, 1999. 368 pp., illustrated. Softcover. $19.95

A revised and enlarged edition of a key work on a fascinating subject. Complete information on every Colt automatic pistol.

Combat Handgunnery, 5th Edition, by Chuck Taylor, Krause Publications, Iola, WI, 2002. 256 pp., illus. Paper covers. $21.95

This all-new edition looks at real world combat handgunnery from three different perspectives—military, police and civilian.

Combat Revolvers, by Duncan Long, Paladin Press, Boulder, CO, 1999, 8 1/2 x 11, soft cover, 115 photos, 152 pp. $21.95

This is an uncompromising look at modern combat revolvers. All the major foreign and domestic guns are covered: the Colt Python, S&W Model 29, Ruger GP 100 and hundreds more. Know the gun that you may one day stake your life on.

Complete Guide to Compact Handguns, by Gene Gangarosa, Jr., Stoeger Publishing Co., Wayne, NJ, 1997. 228 pp., illus. Paper covers. $22.95

Includes hundreds of compact firearms, along with text results conducted by the author.

Complete Guide to Service Handguns, by Gene Gangarosa, Jr., Stoeger Publishing Co., Wayne, NJ, 1998. 320 pp., illus. Paper covers. $22.95

The author explores the revolvers and pistols that are used around the globe by military, law enforcement and civilians.

Concealable Pocket Pistols: How to Choose and Use Small-Caliber Handguns, McLeod, Terence. Paladin Press, 2001. 1st edition. 80 pages. Softcover. $14.00

Small-caliber handguns are often maligned as too puny for serious self-defense, but millions of Americans own and carry these guns and have used them successfully to stop violent assaults. This is the first book ever devoted to eliminating the many misconceptions about the usefulness of these popular guns. "Pocket pistols" are small, easily concealed, inexpensive semiautomatic handguns in .22, .25, .32 and .380 calibers. Their small size and hammerless design enable them to be easily concealed and carried so they are immediately accessible in an emergency. Their purpose is not to knock an assailant off his feet with fire-breathing power (which no handgun is capable of doing) but simply to deter or stop his assault by putting firepower in your hands when you need it most. Concealable Pocket Pistols addresses every aspect of owning, carrying and shooting small-caliber handguns in a realistic manner. It cuts right to the chase and recommends a handful of the best pistols on the market today as well as the best ammunition for them. It then gets into the real-world issues of how to carry a concealed pocket pistol, how to shoot it under stress and how to deal with malfunctions quickly and efficiently. In an emergency, a small-caliber pistol in the pocket is better than the .357 Magnum left at home. Find out what millions of Americans already know about these practical self-defense tools.

Custom Government Model Pistol, The, by Layne Simpson, Wolfe Publishing Co., Prescott, AZ, 1994. 639 pp., illus. Paper covers. $26.95

The book about one of the world's greatest firearms and the things pistolsmiths do to make it even greater.

CZ-75 Family: The Ultimate Combat Handgun, The, by J.M. Ramos, Paladin Press, Boulder, CO, 1990. 100 pp., illus. Soft covers. $25.00

An in-depth discussion of the early-and-late model CZ-75s, as well as the many newest additions to the Czech pistol family.

THE HANDGUNNER'S LIBRARY

Encyclopedia of Pistols & Revolvers, by A.E. Hartnik, Knickerbocker Press, New York, NY, 1997. 272 pp., illus. $19.95

A comprehensive encyclopedia specially written for collectors and owners of pistols and revolvers.

Engraved Handguns of .22 Calibre, by John S. Laidacker, Atglen, PA: Schiffer Publications, 2003. 1st edition. 192 pages, with over 400 color and b/w photos. $69.95

Experiments of a Handgunner, by Walter Roper, Wolfe Publishing Co., Prescott, AZ, 1989. 202 pp., illus. $37.00

A limited edition reprint. A listing of experiments with functioning parts of handguns, with targets, stocks, rests, handloading, etc.

Farnam Method of Defensive Handgunning, The, by John S. Farnam, Police Bookshelf, 1999. 191 pp., illus. Paper covers. $24.00

A book intended to not only educate the new shooter, but also to serve as a guide and textbook for his and his instructor's training courses.

Fast and Fancy Revolver Shooting, by Ed. McGivern, Anniversary Edition, Winchester Press, Piscataway, NJ, 1984. 484 pp., illus. $19.95

A fascinating volume, packed with handgun lore and solid information by the acknowledged dean of revolver shooters.

German Handguns: The Complete Book of the Pistols and Revolvers of Germany, 1869 To The Present, by Ian Hogg. Greenhill Publishing, 2001. 320 pages, 270 illustrations. Hardcover. $49.95

Ian Hogg examines the full range of handguns produced in Germany from such classics as the Luger M1908, Mauser HsC and Walther PPK, to more unusual types such as the Reichsrevolver M1879 and the Dreyse 9mm. He presents the key data (length, weight, muzzle velocity, and range) for each weapon discussed and also gives its date of introduction and service record, evaluates and discusses peculiarities, and examines in detail particular strengths and weaknesses.

Glock: The New Wave in Combat Handguns, by Peter Alan Kasler, Paladin Press, Boulder, CO, 1993. 304 pp., illus. $27.00

Kasler debunks the myths that surround what is the most innovative handgun to be introduced in some time.

Glock's Handguns, by Duncan Long, Desert Publications, El Dorado, AR, 1996. 180 pp., illus. Paper covers. $19.95

An outstanding volume on one of the world's newest and most successful firearms of the century.

Gun Digest Book of the 1911, The, by Patrick Sweeney. Krause Publications, Iola, WI, 2002. 336 pages, with 700 b&w photos. Softcover. $27.95

Compete guide of all models and variations of the Model 1911. The author also includes repair tips and information on buying a used 1911.

Hand Cannons: The World's Most Powerful Handguns, by Duncan Long, Paladin Press, Boulder, CO, 1995. 208 pp., illus. Paper covers. $22.00

Long describes and evaluates each powerful gun according to their features.

Handgun, The, by Geoffrey Boothroyd, Safari Press, Inc., Huntington Beach, CA, 1999. 566 pp., illustrated. $50.00

A very detailed history of the handgun. Now revised and a completely new chapter written to take account of developments since the 1970 edition.

Handguns 2003, 14th Edition, edited by Ken Ramage, DBI Books a division of Krause Publications, Iola, WI, 2002. 352 pp., illustrated. Paper covers. $22.95

Top writers in the handgun industry give you a complete report on new handgun developments, testfire reports on the newest introductions and previews on what's ahead.

Handgun Stopping Power "The Definitive Study", by Evan P. Marshall & Edwin J. Sanow, Paladin Press, Boulder, CO, 1997, soft cover, photos, 240 pp. $45.00

Dramatic first-hand accounts of the results of handgun rounds fired into criminals by cops, storeowners, cabbies and others are the heart and soul of this long-awaited book. This is the definitive methodology for predicting the stopping power of handgun loads, the first to take into account what really happens when a bullet meets a man.

Heckler & Koch's Handguns, by Duncan Long, Desert Publications, El Dorado, AR, 1996. 142 pp., illus. Paper covers. $19.95.

Traces the history and the evolution of H&K's pistols from the company's beginning at the end of WWII to the present.

Hidden in Plain Sight, by Trey Bloodworth & Mike Raley, Professional Press, Chapel Hill, NC, 1995. Paper covers. $19.95.

A practical guide to concealed handgun carry.

High Standard: A Collectors Guide to the Hamden & Hartford Target Pistols, Dance, Tom. Andrew Mowbray, Inc., Lincoln, RI: 1999. 192 pp., Heavily illustrated with black & white photographs and technical drawings. $24.00

From Citation to Supermatic, all of the production models and specials made from 1951 to 1984 are covered according to model number or series, making it easy to understand the evolution to this favorite of shooters and collectors.

High Standard Automatic Pistols 1932-1950, by Charles E. Petty, The Gunroom Press, Highland Park, NJ, 1989. 124 pp., illus. $14.95

A definitive source of information for the collector of High Standard arms.

Hi-Standard Pistols and Revolvers, 1951-1984, by James Spacek, James Spacek, Chesire, CT, 1998. 128 pp., illustrated. Paper covers. $12.50

Technical details, marketing features and instruction/parts manual of every model High Standard pistol and revolver made between 1951 and 1984. Most accurate serial number information available.

Hi-Standard Pistol Guide, The, by Burr Leyson, Duckett's Sporting Books, Tempe AZ, 1995. 128 pp., illus. Paper covers. $26.00

Complete information on selection, care and repair, ammunition, parts, and accessories.

How to Become a Master Handgunner: The Mechanics of X-Count Shooting, by Charles Stephens, Paladin Press, Boulder, CO, 1993. 64 pp., illus. Paper covers. $14.00

Offers a simple formula for success to the handgunner who strives to master the technique of shooting accurately.

Illustrated Encyclopedia of Handguns, by A.B. Zhuk, Stackpole Books, Mechanicsburg, PA, 2002. 256 pp., illus. Softcover, $24.95

Identifies more than 2,000 military and commercial pistols and revolvers with details of more than 100 popular handgun cartridges.

Inglis Diamond: The Canadian High Power Pistol, The, by Clive M. Law, Collector Grade Publications, Canada, 2001. 312 pp., illustrated. $49.95

This definitive work on Canada's first and indeed only mass produced handgun, in production for a very brief span of time and consequently made in relatively few numbers, the venerable Inglis-made Browning High Power covers the pistol's initial history, the story of Chinese and British adoption, use post-war by Holland, Australia, Greece, Belgium, New Zealand, Peru, Brasil and other countries. All new information on the famous light-weights and the Inglis Diamond variations. Completely researched through official archives in a dozen countries. Many of the bewildering variety of markings have never been satisfactorily explained until now. Also included are many photos of holsters and accessories.

Instinct Combat Shooting, by Chuck Klein, The Goose Creek, IN, 1989. 49 pp., illus. Paper covers. $12.00

Defensive handgunning for police.

Know Your 45 Auto Pistols—Models 1911 & A1, by E.J. Hoffschmidt, Blacksmith Corp., Southport, CT, 1974. 58 pp., illus. Paper covers. $14.95

A concise history of the gun with a wide variety of types and copies.

Know Your Ruger Single Actions: The Second Decade 1963-1973, by John C. Dougan. Blacksmith Corp., North Hampton, OH, 1994. 143 pp., illus. Paper covers. $19.95

Know Your Ruger S/A Revolvers 1953-1963 (Revised Edition), by John C. Dougan. Blacksmith Corp., North Hampton, OH, 2002. 191 pp., illus. Paper covers. $19.95

Know Your Walther P38 Pistols, by E.J. Hoffschmidt, Blacksmith Corp., Southport, CT, 1974. 77 pp., illus. Paper covers. $14.95

Covers the Walther models Armee, M.P., H.P., P.38—history and variations.

Know Your Walther PP & PPK Pistols, by E.J. Hoffschmidt, Blacksmith Corp., Southport, CT, 1975. 87 pp., illus. Paper covers. $14.95

A concise history of the guns with a guide to the variety and types.

La Connaissance du Luger, Tome 1, by Gerard Henrotin, H & L Publishing, Belguim, 1996. 144 pages, illustrated. $45.00

(The Knowledge of Luger, Volume 1, translated.) Black & white and color photos. French text.

Living with Glocks: The Complete Guide to the New Standard in Combat Handguns, by Robert H Boatman, Boulder, CO: Paladin Press, 2002. 1st edition. ISBN: 1581603401. 184 pages, illustrated. Hardcover. $29.95

In this book he explains why in no uncertain terms. In addition to demystifying the enigmatic Glock trigger, Boatman describes and critiques each Glock model in production. Separate chapters on the G36, the enhanced G20 and the full-auto G18 emphasize the job-specific talents of these standout models for those seeking insight on which Glock pistol might best meet their needs. And for those interested in optimizing their Glock's capabilities, this book addresses all the peripherals – holsters, ammo, accessories, silencers, modifications and conversions, training programs and more. Whether your focus is on concealed carry, home protection, hunting, competition, training or law enforcement.

Luger Handbook, The, by Aarron Davis, Krause Publications, Iola, WI, 1997. 112 pp., illus. Paper covers. $9.95

Now you can identify any of the legendary Luger variations using a simple decision tree. Each model and variation includes pricing information, proof marks and detailed attributes in a handy, user-friendly format. Plus, it's fully indexed. Instantly identify that Luger!

Lugers of Ralph Shattuck, by Ralph Shattuck, Peoria, AZ, 2000. 49 pages, illus. Hardcover. $29.95

49 pages, illustrated with maps and full color photos of here to now never before shown photos of some of the rarest lugers ever. Written by one of the world's renowned collectors. A MUST have book for any Luger collector.

Lugers at Random (Revised Format Edition), by Charles Kenyon, Jr., Handgun Press, Glenview, IL, 2000. 420 pp., illus. $59.95

A new printing of this classic, comprehensive reference for all Luger collectors.

Luger Story, The, by John Walter, Stackpole Books, Mechanicsburg, PA, 2001. 256 pp., illus. Paper Covers. $19.95

The standard history of the world's most famous handgun.

The Handgunner's Library

Mauser Self-Loading Pistol, The, by Belford & Dunlap, Borden Publ. Co., Alhambra, CA. Over 200 pp., 300 illus., large format. $29.95

The long-awaited book on the "Broom Handles," covering their inception in 1894 to the end of production. Complete and in detail: pocket pistols, Chinese and Spanish copies, etc.

Mental Mechanics of Shooting: How to Stay Calm at the Center, by Vishnu Karmakar and Thomas Whitney. Littleton, CO: Center Vision, Inc., 2001. 144 pages. Softcover. $19.95

Not only will this book help you stay free of trigger jerk, it will help you in all areas of your shooting.

9mm Parabellum; The History & Development of the World's 9mm Pistols & Ammunition, by Klaus-Peter Konig and Martin Hugo, Schiffer Publishing Ltd., Atglen, PA, 1993. 304 pp., illus. $39.95

Detailed history of 9mm weapons from Belguim, Italy, Germany, Israel, France, USA, Czechoslovakia, Hungary, Poland, Brazil, Finland and Spain.

Official 9mm Markarov Pistol Manual, The, translated into English by Major James Gebhardt, U.S. Army (Ret.), Desert Publications, El Dorado, AR, 1996. 84 pp., illus. Paper covers. $12.95

The information found in this book will be of enormous benefit and interest to the owner or a prospective owner of one of these pistols.

Official Soviet 7.62mm Handgun Manual, The, by Translation by Maj. James F. Gebhardt Ret.), Paladin Press, Boulder, CO, 1997, soft cover, illus., 104 pp. $20.00

This Soviet military manual, now available in English for the first time, covers instructions for use and maintenance of two side arms, the Nagant 7.62mm revolver, used by the Russian tsarist armed forces and later the Soviet armed forces, and the Tokarev7.62mm semi-auto pistol, which replaced the Nagant.

P-08 Parabellum Luger Automatic Pistol, The, edited by J. David McFarland, Desert Publications, Cornville, AZ, 1982. 20 pp., illus. Paper covers. $13.95

Covers every facet of the Luger, plus a listing of all known Luger models.

P08 Luger Pistol, The, by de Vries & Martens. Alexandria, VA: Ironside International, 2002. 152 pages, illustrated with 200 high quality black & white photos. Hardcover. $34.95

Covers all essential information on history and development, ammunition and accessories, codes and markings, and contains photos of nearly every model and accessory. Includes a unique selection of original German WWII propoganda photos, most never published before.

P-38 Automatic Pistol, by Gene Gangarosa, Jr., Stoeger Publishing Co., S. Hackensack, NJ, 1993. 272 pp., illus. Paper covers. $16.95

This book traces the origins and development of the P-38, including the momentous political forces of the World War II era that caused its near demise and, later, its rebirth.

P-38 Pistol: The Walther Pistols, 1930-1945. Volume 1, The, by Warren Buxton, Ucross Books, Los Alamos, MN 1999. $68.50

A limited run reprint of this scarce and sought-after work on the P-38 Pistol. 328 pp. with 160 illustrations.

P-38 Pistol: The Contract Pistols, 1940-1945. Volume 2, The, by Warren Buxton, Ucross Books, Los Alamos, MN 1999. 256 pp. with 237 illustrations. $68.50

P-38 Pistol: Postwar Distributions, 1945-1990. Volume 3, The, by Warren Buxton, Ucross Books, Los Alamos, MN 1999. $68.50

Plus an addendum to Volumes 1 & 2. 272 pp. with 342 illustrations.

Parabellum - A Technical History of Swiss Lugers, by V. Bobba, Italy.1998. 224pp, profuse color photos, large format. $100.00

The is the most beautifully illustrated and well-documented book on the Swiss Lugers yet produced. This splendidly produced book features magnificent images while giving an incredible amount of detail on the Swiss Luger. In-depth coverage of key issues include: the production process, pistol accessories, charts with serial numbers, production figures, variations, markings, patent drawings, etc. Covers the Swiss Luger story from 1894 when the first Bergmann-Schmeisser models were tested till the commercial model 1965. Shows every imaginable production variation in amazing detail and full color! A must for all Luger collectors. This work has been produced in an extremely attractive package using quality materials throughout and housed in a protective slipcase.

Report of Board on Tests of Revolvers and Automatic Pistols, From the Annual Report of the Chief of Ordnance, 1907. Reprinted by J.C. Tillinghast, Marlow, NH, 1969. 34 pp., 7 plates, paper covers. $9.95

A comparison of handguns, including Luger, Savage, Colt, Webley-Fosbery and other makes.

Ruger "P" Family of Handguns, The, by Duncan Long, Desert Publications, El Dorado, AZ, 1993. 128 pp., illus. Paper covers. $14.95

A full-fledged documentary on a remarkable series of Sturm Ruger handguns.

Ruger .22 Automatic Pistol, Standard/Mark I/Mark II Series, The, by Duncan Long, Paladin Press, Boulder, CO, 1989. 168 pp., illus. Paper covers. $16.00

The definitive book about the pistol that has served more than 1 million owners so well.

Semiautomatic Pistols in Police Service and Self Defense, The, by Massad Ayoob, Police Bookshelf, Concord, NH, 1990. 25 pp., illus. Soft covers. $11.95.

First quantitative, documented look at actual police experience with 9mm and 45 police service automatics.

Shooting Colt Single Actions, by Mike Venturino, Livingston, MT, 1997. 205 pp., illus. Paper covers. $25.00

A definitive work on the famous Colt SAA and the ammunition it shoots.

Sig Handguns, by Duncan Long, Desert Publications, El Dorado, AZ, 1995. 150 pp., illus. Paper covers. $19.95

The history of Sig/Sauer handguns, including Sig, Sig-Hammerli and Sig/Sauer variants.

Sixgun Cartridges and Loads, by Elmer Keith, reprint edition by The Gun Room Press, Highland Park, NJ, 1984. 151 pp., illus. $24.95

A manual covering the selection, use and loading of the most suitable and popular revolver cartridges.

Sixguns, by Elmer Keith, Wolfe Publishing Company, Prescott, AZ, 1992. 336 pp. Paper covers. $29.95. Hardcover $35.00

The history, selection, repair, care, loading, and use of this historic frontiersman's friend—the one-hand firearm.

Smith & Wesson's Automatics, by Larry Combs, Desert Publications, El Dorado, AZ, 1994. 143 pp., illus. Paper covers. $19.95

A must for every S&W auto owner or prospective owner.

Spanish Handguns: The History of Spanish Pistols and Revolvers, by Gene Gangarosa, Jr., Stoeger Publishing Co., Accokeek, MD, 2001. 320 pp., illustrated. B & W photos. Paper covers. $21.95

Standard Catalog of Smith & Wesson; 2nd Edition, by Jim Supica and Richard Nahas.Krause Publications, Iola, WI: 2001. 2nd edition. 272 Pages, 350 b&w photos, with a 16 page color section. Pictorial Hardcover. $34.95

Clearly details 775 Smith & Wesson models, knives, holsters, ammunition and police items with complete pricing information, illustrated glossary and index.

Star Firearms, by Leonardo M. Antaris, Davenport, IA: Firac Publications Co., 2002. 640 pages, with over 1,100 b/w photos, 47 pages in full color. Hardcover. $119.95

The definitive work on Star's many models with a historical context, with a review of their mechanical features, & details their development throughout production plus tables of proof marks & codes, serial numbers, annual summaries, procurements by Spanish Guardia Civil & Spanish Police, exports to Bulgaria, Germany, & Switzerland during WW2; text also covers Star's .22 rifles & submachine guns & includes a comprehensive list of Spanish trade names matched to manufacturer for arms made prior to the Spanish Civil War (1936-1939).

Street Stoppers: The Latest Handgun Stopping Power Street Results, by Evan P. Marshall & Edwin J. Sandow, Paladin Press, Boulder, CO, 1997. 392 pp., illus. Paper covers. $42.95

Compilation of the results of real-life shooting incidents involving every major handgun caliber.

Tactical 1911, The, by Dave Lauck, Paladin Press, Boulder, CO, 1999. 152 pp., illustrated. Paper covers. $22.00

The cop's and SWAT operator's guide to employment and maintenance.

Tactical Pistol, The, by Gabriel Suarez with a foreword by Jeff Cooper, Paladin Press, Boulder, CO, 1996. 216 pp., illus. Paper covers. $25.00

Advanced gunfighting concepts and techniques.

Thompson/Center Contender Pistol, The, by Charles Tephens, Paladin Press, Boulder, CO, 1997. 58 pp., illus. Paper covers. $14.00

How to tune and time, load and shoot accurately with the Contender pistol.

.380 Enfield No. 2 Revolver, The, by Mark Stamps and Ian Skennerton, I.D.S.A. Books, Piqua, OH, 1993. 124 pp., 80 illus. Paper covers. $19.95

Truth About Handguns, The, by Duane Thomas, Paladin Press, Boulder, CO, 1997. 136 pp., illus. Paper covers. $18.00

Exploding the myths, hype, and misinformation about handguns.

Walther Pistols: Models 1 Through P99, Factory Variations and Copies, by Dieter H. Marschall, Ucross Books, Los Alamos, NM. 2000. 140 pages, with 140 b & w illustrations, index. Paper Covers. $19.95

This is the English translation, revised and updated, of the highly successful and widely acclaimed German language edition. This book provides the collector with a reference guide and overview of the entire line of the Walther military, police, and self-defense pistols from the very first to the very latest. Models 1-9, PP, PPK, MP, AP, HP, P.38, P1, P4, P38K, P5, P88, P99 and the Manurhin models. Variations, where issued, serial ranges, calibers, marks, proofs, logos, and design aspects in an astonishing quantity and variety are crammed into this very well researched and highly regarded work.

U.S. Handguns of World War 2, The Secondary Pistols and Revolvers, by Charles W. Pate, Mowbray Publishers, Lincoln, RI, 1997. 368 pp., illus. $39.00

This indispensable new book covers all of the American military handguns of W.W.2 except for the M1911A1

DIRECTORY OF THE HANDGUNNING TRADE

HANDGUNS 2005

PRODUCT & SERVICE DIRECTORY

AMMUNITION COMPONENTS, SHOTSHELL

A.W. Peterson Gun Shop, Inc.
Ballistic Product, Inc.
Blount, Inc., Sporting Equipment Div.
CCI Ammunition ATK
Cheddite, France S.A.
Claybuster Wads & Harvester Bullets
Garcia National Gun Traders, Inc.
Peterson Gun Shop, Inc., A.W.
Precision Reloading, Inc.
Ravell Ltd.
Tar-Hunt Custom Rifles, Inc.
Vitt/Boos

AMMUNITION COMPONENTS--BULLETS, POWDER, PRIMERS, CASES

A.W. Peterson Gun Shop, Inc.
Acadian Ballistic Specialties
Accuracy Unlimited
Accurate Arms Co., Inc.
Action Bullets & Alloy Inc.
ADCO Sales, Inc.
Alaska Bullet Works, Inc.
Alliant Techsystems Smokeless Powder Group
Allred Bullet Co.
Alpha LaFranck Enterprises
American Products, Inc.
Arizona Ammunition, Inc.
Armfield Custom Bullets
A-Square Co.
Atlantic Rose, Inc.
Baer's Hollows
Ballard Rifle & Cartridge Co., LLC
Barnes
Barnes Bullets, Inc.
Beartooth Bullets
Bell Reloading, Inc.
Berger Bullets Ltd.
Berry's Mfg., Inc.
Big Bore Bullets of Alaska
Big Bore Express
Bitterroot Bullet Co.
Black Belt Bullets (See Big Bore Express)
Black Hills Shooters Supply
Black Powder Products
Blount, Inc., Sporting Equipment Div.
Blue Mountain Bullets
Brenneke GmbH
Briese Bullet Co., Inc.
Brown Co., E. Arthur
Brown Dog Ent.
BRP, Inc. High Performance Cast Bullets
Buck Stix-SOS Products Co.
Buckeye Custom Bullets
Buckskin Bullet Co.
Buffalo Arms Co.
Buffalo Bullet Co., Inc.
Buffalo Rock Shooters Supply
Bullseye Bullets
Bull-X, Inc.
Butler Enterprises
Cambos Outdoorsman
Canyon Cartridge Corp.
Cascade Bullet Co., Inc.
Cast Performance Bullet Company
Casull Arms Corp.
CCI Ammunition ATK
Champion's Choice, Inc.
Cheddite, France S.A.
CheVron Bullets
Chuck's Gun Shop
Clean Shot Technologies
Competitor Corp., Inc.
Cook Engineering Service
Corbin Mfg. & Supply, Inc.
Cummings Bullets
Curtis Cast Bullets
Curtis Gun Shop (See Curtis Cast Bullets)
Custom Bullets by Hoffman
Dakota Arms, Inc.
Davide Pedersoli and Co.
DKT, Inc.
Dohring Bullets
Eichelberger Bullets, Wm.
Federal Cartridge Co.
Fiocchi of America, Inc.
Forkin, Ben (See Belt MTN Arms)
Forkin Arms
Fowler Bullets
Fowler, Bob (See Black Powder Products)
Foy Custom Bullets
Freedom Arms, Inc.
Garcia National Gun Traders, Inc.
Gehmann, Walter (See Huntington Die Specialties)
GOEX, Inc.
Golden Bear Bullets
Gotz Bullets
Grayback Wildcats
Green Mountain Rifle Barrel Co., Inc.
Grier's Hard Cast Bullets
GTB
Gun City
Harris Enterprises
Harrison Bullets
Hart & Son, Inc.
Hawk Laboratories, Inc. (See Hawk, Inc.)
Hawk, Inc.
Haydon Shooters Supply, Russ
Heidenstrom Bullets
Hercules, Inc. (See Alliant Techsystems, Smokeless)
Hi-Performance Ammunition Company
Hirtenberger AG
Hobson Precision Mfg. Co.
Hodgdon Powder Co.
Hornady Mfg. Co.
HT Bullets
Hunters Supply, Inc.
Huntington Die Specialties
Impact Case & Container, Inc.
Imperial Magnum Corp.
IMR Powder Co.
Intercontinental Distributors, Ltd.
J&D Components
J&L Superior Bullets (See Huntington Die Special)
J.R. Williams Bullet Co.
James Calhoon Mfg.
James Calhoon Varmint Bullets
Jamison International
Jensen Bullets
Jensen's Firearms Academy
Jericho Tool & Die Co., Inc.
Jester Bullets
JLK Bullets
JRP Custom Bullets
Ka Pu Kapili
Kaswer Custom, Inc.
Keith's Bullets
Keng's Firearms Specialty, Inc./US Tactical Systems
Ken's Kustom Kartridges
Kent Cartridge Mfg. Co. Ltd.
KLA Enterprises
Knight Rifles
Knight Rifles (See Modern Muzzle Loading, Inc.)
Lapua Ltd.
Lawrence Brand Shot (See Precision Reloading)
Legend Products Corp.
Liberty Shooting Supplies
Lightning Performance Innovations, Inc.
Lindsley Arms Cartridge Co.
Littleton, J. F.
Lomont Precision Bullets
Lyman Products Corp.
Magnus Bullets
Maine Custom Bullets
Maionchi-L.M.I.
Marchmon Bullets
Markesbery Muzzle Loaders, Inc.
MarMik, Inc.
Marshall Fish Mfg. Gunsmith Sptg. Co.
MAST Technology, Inc.
McMurdo, Lynn (See Specialty Gunsmithing)
Meister Bullets (See Gander Mountain)
Men-Metallwerk Elisenhuette GmbH
Merkuria Ltd.
Michael's Antiques
Midway Arms, Inc.
Mitchell Bullets, R.F.
MI-TE Bullets
Montana Precision Swaging
Mountain State Muzzleloading Supplies, Inc.
Mulhern, Rick
Murmur Corp.
Nagel's Custom Bullets
National Bullet Co.
Naval Ordnance Works
North American Shooting Systems
North Devon Firearms Services
Northern Precision Custom Swaged Bullets
Nosler, Inc.
OK Weber, Inc.
Oklahoma Ammunition Co.
Old Wagon Bullets
Oregon Trail Bullet Company
Pacific Cartridge, Inc.
Pacific Rifle Co.
Page Custom Bullets
Pease Accuracy
Penn Bullets
Peterson Gun Shop, Inc., A.W.
Petro-Explo Inc.
Phillippi Custom Bullets, Justin
Pinetree Bullets
PMC/Eldorado Cartridge Corp.
Polywad, Inc.
Pony Express Reloaders
Power Plus Enterprises, Inc.
Precision Delta Corp.
Prescott Projectile Co.
Price Bullets, Patrick W.
PRL Bullets, c/o Blackburn Enterprises
Professional Hunter Supplies (See Star Custom Bullets)
Proofmark Corp.
R.I.S. Co., Inc.
Rainier Ballistics Corp.
Ramon B. Gonzalez Guns
Ravell Ltd.
Redwood Bullet Works
Reloading Specialties, Inc.
Remington Arms Co., Inc.
Rhino
Robinson H.V. Bullets
Rubright Bullets
Russ Haydon's Shooters' Supply
SAECO (See Redding Reloading Equipment)
Scharch Mfg., Inc.-Top Brass
Schneider Bullets
Schroeder Bullets
Schumakers Gun Shop
Scot Powder
Seebeck Assoc., R.E.
Shappy Bullets
Sharps Arms Co., Inc., C.
Shilen, Inc.
Sierra Bullets
SOS Products Co. (See Buck Stix-SOS Products Co.)
Southern Ammunition Co., Inc.
Specialty Gunsmithing
Speer Bullets
Spencer's Rifle Barrels, Inc.
SSK Industries
Stanley Bullets
Star Ammunition, Inc.
Star Custom Bullets
Starke Bullet Company
Starline, Inc.
Stewart's Gunsmithing
Swift Bullet Co.
T.F.C. S.p.A.
Taracorp Industries, Inc.
Tar-Hunt Custom Rifles, Inc.
TCCI
TCSR
The A.W. Peterson Gun Shop, Inc.
The Gun Works
The Ordnance Works
Thompson Bullet Lube Co.
Thompson Precision
TMI Products (See Haselbauer Products, Jerry)
Traditions Performance Firearms
Trico Plastics
True Flight Bullet Co.
Tucson Mold, Inc.
Unmussig Bullets, D. L.
USAC
Vann Custom Bullets
Vihtavuori Oy/Kaltron-Pettibone
Vincent's Shop
Viper Bullet and Brass Works
Walters Wads
Warren Muzzleloading Co., Inc.
Watson Trophy Match Bullets
Weatherby, Inc.
Western Nevada West Coast Bullets
Widener's Reloading & Shooting Supply, Inc.
Winchester Div. Olin Corp.
Winkle Bullets
Woodleigh (See Huntington Die Specialties)
Worthy Products, Inc.
Wyant Bullets
Wyoming Custom Bullets
Zero Ammunition Co., Inc.

AMMUNITION, COMMERCIAL

3-Ten Corp.
A.W. Peterson Gun Shop, Inc.
Ace Custom 45's, Inc.
Ad Hominem
Air Arms
American Ammunition
Arizona Ammunition, Inc.
Arms Corporation of the Philippines
Arundel Arms & Ammunition, Inc., A.
A-Square Co.
Atlantic Rose, Inc.
Badger Shooters Supply, Inc.
Ballistic Product, Inc.
Ben William's Gun Shop
Benjamin/Sheridan Co., Crosman
Big Bear Arms & Sporting Goods, Inc.
Black Hills Ammunition, Inc.
Blammo Ammo
Blount, Inc., Sporting Equipment Div.
Brenneke GmbH
Buffalo Bullet Co., Inc.
Bull-X, Inc.
Cabela's
Cambos Outdoorsman
Casull Arms Corp.
CBC
Champion's Choice, Inc.
Cor-Bon Inc./Glaser LLC
Crosman Airguns
Cubic Shot Shell Co., Inc.
Daisy Outdoor Products
Dead Eye's Sport Center
Delta Arms Ltd.
Delta Frangible Ammunition LLC
Dynamit Nobel-RWS, Inc.
Effebi SNC-Dr. Franco Beretta
Eley Ltd.
Elite Ammunition
Estate Cartridge, Inc.
Federal Cartridge Co.
Fiocchi of America, Inc.
Garcia National Gun Traders, Inc.
Garrett Cartridges, Inc.
Garthwaite Pistolsmith, Inc., Jim
Gibbs Rifle Co., Inc.
Gil Hebard Guns Inc.
Glaser LLC
Glaser Safety Slug, Inc.
GOEX, Inc.
Goodwin's Gun Shop
Gun City
Hansen & Co.
Hart & Son, Inc.
Hi-Performance Ammunition Company
Hirtenberger AG
Hornady Mfg. Co.
Hunters Supply, Inc.
Intercontinental Distributors, Ltd.
Ion Industries, Inc.
Keng's Firearms Specialty, Inc./US Tactical Systems
Kent Cartridge America, Inc.
Kent Cartridge Mfg. Co. Ltd.
Knight Rifles
Lapua Ltd.
Lethal Force Institute (See Police Bookshelf)
Lock's Philadelphia Gun Exchange
Magnum Research, Inc.
MagSafe Ammo Co.
Magtech Ammunition Co. Inc.
Maionchi-L.M.I.
Mandall Shooting Supplies Inc.
Markell,Inc.
Marshall Fish Mfg. Gunsmith Sptg. Co.
McBros Rifle Co.
Men-Metallwerk Elisenhuette GmbH
Mullins Ammunition
New England Ammunition Co.
Oklahoma Ammunition Co.
Omark Industries, Div. of Blount, Inc.
Outdoor Sports Headquarters, Inc.
P.S.M.G. Gun Co.
Pacific Cartridge, Inc.
Paragon Sales & Services, Inc.
Parker & Sons Shooting Supply
Parker Gun Finishes
Peterson Gun Shop, Inc., A.W.
PMC/Eldorado Cartridge Corp.
Police Bookshelf
Polywad, Inc.
Pony Express Reloaders
Precision Delta Corp.
Pro Load Ammunition, Inc.
R.E.I.
Ravell Ltd.
Remington Arms Co., Inc.
Rucker Dist. Inc.
RWS (See US Importer-Dynamit Nobel-RWS, Inc.)
Sellier & Bellot, USA Inc.
Southern Ammunition Co., Inc.
Speer Bullets
TCCI
The A.W. Peterson Gun Shop, Inc.
The BulletMakers Workshop
The Gun Room Press
The Gun Works
Thompson Bullet Lube Co.
USAC
VAM Distribution Co. LLC

Product & Service Directory

Victory USA
Vihtavuori Oy/Kaltron-Pettibone
Visible Impact Targets
Voere-KGH GmbH
Weatherby, Inc.
Westley Richards & Co.
Whitestone Lumber Corp.
Widener's Reloading & Shooting Supply, Inc.
William E. Phillips Firearms
Winchester Div. Olin Corp.
Zero Ammunition Co., Inc.

AMMUNITION, CUSTOM

3-Ten Corp.
A.W. Peterson Gun Shop, Inc.
Accuracy Unlimited
AFSCO Ammunition
Allred Bullet Co.
American Derringer Corp.
American Products, Inc.
Arizona Ammunition, Inc.
Arms Corporation of the Philippines
Atlantic Rose, Inc.
Ballard Rifle & Cartridge Co., LLC
Bear Arms
Belding's Custom Gun Shop
Berger Bullets Ltd.
Big Bore Bullets of Alaska
Black Hills Ammunition, Inc.
Blue Mountain Bullets
Brynin, Milton
Buckskin Bullet Co.
CBC
CFVentures
Champlin Firearms, Inc.
Cubic Shot Shell Co., Inc.
Custom Tackle and Ammo
Dakota Arms, Inc.
Dead Eye's Sport Center
Delta Frangible Ammunition LLC
DKT, Inc.
Elite Ammunition
Estate Cartridge, Inc.
GDL Enterprises
GOEX, Inc.
Grayback Wildcats
Hirtenberger AG
Hobson Precision Mfg. Co.
Horizons Unlimited
Hornady Mfg. Co.
Hunters Supply, Inc.
James Calhoon Mfg.
James Calhoon Varmint Bullets
Jensen Bullets
Jensen's Custom Ammunition
Jensen's Firearms Academy
Kaswer Custom, Inc.
Kent Cartridge Mfg. Co. Ltd.
L. E. Jurras & Assoc.
L.A.R. Mfg., Inc.
Lethal Force Institute (See Police Bookshelf)
Lindsley Arms Cartridge Co.
Linebaugh Custom Sixguns
Loch Leven Industries/Convert-A-Pell
MagSafe Ammo Co.
MAST Technology, Inc.
McBros Rifle Co.
McMurdo, Lynn (See Specialty Gunsmithing)
Men-Metallwerk Elisenhuette GmbH
Milstor Corp.
Mullins Ammunition
Oklahoma Ammunition Co.
P.S.M.G. Gun Co.
Peterson Gun Shop, Inc., A.W.
Phillippi Custom Bullets, Justin
Police Bookshelf
Power Plus Enterprises, Inc.
Precision Delta Corp.
Professional Hunter Supplies (See Star Custom Bullets)
R.E.I.
Ramon B. Gonzalez Guns
Sandia Die & Cartridge Co.
SOS Products Co. (See Buck Stix-SOS Products Co.)
Specialty Gunsmithing
Spencer's Rifle Barrels, Inc.
SSK Industries
Star Custom Bullets
Stewart's Gunsmithing
The A.W. Peterson Gun Shop, Inc.
The BulletMakers Workshop
The Country Armourer
Unmussig Bullets, D. L.
Vitt/Boos
Vulpes Ventures, Inc. Fox Cartridge Division
Warren Muzzleloading Co., Inc.
Watson Trophy Match Bullets
Worthy Products, Inc.
Zero Ammunition Co., Inc.

AMMUNITION, FOREIGN

A.W. Peterson Gun Shop, Inc.
Ad Hominem
AFSCO Ammunition
Armscorp USA, Inc.
Atlantic Rose, Inc.
B&P America
Beeman Precision Airguns
Cape Outfitters
CBC
Cheddite, France S.A.
Cubic Shot Shell Co., Inc.
Dead Eye's Sport Center
DKT, Inc.
Dynamit Nobel-RWS, Inc.
E. Arthur Brown Co.
Fiocchi of America, Inc.
First Inc., Jack
Gamebore Division, Polywad Inc.
Gibbs Rifle Co., Inc.
GOEX, Inc.
Goodwin's Gun Shop
Gunsmithing, Inc.
Hansen & Co.
Heidenstrom Bullets
Hirtenberger AG
Hornady Mfg. Co.
I.S.S.
Intrac Arms International
K.B.I. Inc.
MagSafe Ammo Co.
Maionchi-L.M.I.
Mandall Shooting Supplies Inc.
Marksman Products
MAST Technology, Inc.
Merkuria Ltd.
Mullins Ammunition
Navy Arms Company
Oklahoma Ammunition Co.
P.S.M.G. Gun Co.
Paragon Sales & Services, Inc.
Peterson Gun Shop, Inc., A.W.
Petro-Explo Inc.
Precision Delta Corp.
R.E.T. Enterprises
Ramon B. Gonzalez Guns
RWS (See US Importer-Dynamit Nobel-RWS, Inc.)
Samco Global Arms, Inc.
Sentinel Arms
Southern Ammunition Co., Inc.
Speer Bullets
Stratco, Inc.
T.F.C. S.p.A.
The A.W. Peterson Gun Shop, Inc.
The BulletMakers Workshop
The Paul Co.
Victory Ammunition
Vihtavuori Oy/Kaltron-Pettibone
Vulpes Ventures, Inc. Fox Cartridge Division
Wolf Performance Ammunition

ANTIQUE ARMS DEALER

Ackerman & Co.
Ad Hominem
Antique American Firearms
Antique Arms Co.
Aplan Antiques & Art, James O.
Armoury, Inc., The
Arundel Arms & Ammunition, Inc., A.
Ballard Rifle & Cartridge Co., LLC
Bear Mountain Gun & Tool
Bob's Tactical Indoor Shooting Range & Gun Shop
Buffalo Arms Co.
Cape Outfitters
Carlson, Douglas R, Antique American Firearms
CBC-BRAZIL
Chadick's Ltd.
Chambers Flintlocks Ltd., Jim
Champlin Firearms, Inc.
Chuck's Gun Shop
Clements' Custom Leathercraft, Chas
Cole's Gun Works
D&D Gunsmiths, Ltd.
David R. Chicoine
Dixie Gun Works
Dixon Muzzleloading Shop, Inc.
Duffy, Charles E (See Guns Antique & Modern DBA)
Ed's Gun House
Enguix Import-Export
Fagan & Co.Inc
Flayderman & Co., Inc.
Fulmer's Antique Firearms, Chet
George Madis Winchester Consultants
Getz Barrel Co.
Glass, Herb
Goergen's Gun Shop, Inc.
Golden Age Arms Co.
Goodwin's Gun Shop
Gun Hunter Books (See Gun Hunter Trading Co.)
Gun Hunter Trading Co.
Guns Antique & Modern DBA / Charles E. Duffy
Hallowell & Co.
Hammans, Charles E.
HandCrafts Unltd (See Clements' Custom Leather)
Handgun Press
Hansen & Co.
Hunkeler, A (See Buckskin Machine Works
Imperial Miniature Armory
James Wayne Firearms for Collectors and Investors
Kelley's
Knight's Mfg. Co.
Ledbetter Airguns, Riley
LeFever Arms Co., Inc.
Lever Arms Service Ltd.
Lock's Philadelphia Gun Exchange
Log Cabin Sport Shop
Logdewood Mfg.
Mandall Shooting Supplies Inc.
Marshall Fish Mfg. Gunsmith Sptg. Co.
Martin's Gun Shop
Michael's Antiques
Mid-America Recreation, Inc.
Montana Outfitters, Lewis E. Yearout
Muzzleloaders Etcetera, Inc.
Navy Arms Company
New England Arms Co.
Olathe Gun Shop
Peter Dyson & Son Ltd.
Pony Express Sport Shop
Powder Horn Ltd.
Ravell Ltd.
Reno, Wayne
Retting, Inc., Martin B
Robert Valade Engraving
Rutgers Book Center
Samco Global Arms, Inc.
Sarco, Inc.
Scott Fine Guns Inc., Thad
Shootin' Shack
Sportsmen's Exchange & Western Gun Traders, Inc.
Steves House of Guns
Stott's Creek Armory, Inc.
The Gun Room
The Gun Room Press
The Gun Works
Turnbull Restoration, Doug
Vic's Gun Refinishing
Vintage Arms, Inc.
Wallace, Terry
Westley Richards & Co.
Wild West Guns
William Fagan & Co.
Winchester Sutler, Inc., The
Wood, Frank (See Classic Guns, Inc.)
Yearout, Lewis E. (See Montana Outfitters)

APPRAISER - GUNS, ETC.

A.W. Peterson Gun Shop, Inc.
Ackerman & Co.
Antique Arms Co.
Armoury, Inc., The
Arundel Arms & Ammunition, Inc., A.
Barta's Gunsmithing
Beitzinger, George
Blue Book Publications, Inc.
Bob's Tactical Indoor Shooting Range & Gun Shop
Bullet N Press
Butterfield's
Cape Outfitters
Chadick's Ltd.
Champlin Firearms, Inc.
Christie's East
Chuilli, Stephen
Clark Firearms Engraving
Clements' Custom Leathercraft, Chas
Cole's Gun Works
Colonial Arms, Inc.
Colonial Repair
Corry, John
Custom Tackle and Ammo
D&D Gunsmiths, Ltd.
David R. Chicoine
DGR Custom Rifles
Dietz Gun Shop & Range, Inc.
Dixie Gun Works
Dixon Muzzleloading Shop, Inc.
Duane's Gun Repair (See DGR Custom Rifles)
Ed's Gun House
Eversull Co., Inc.
Fagan & Co.Inc
Ferris Firearms
Flayderman & Co., Inc.
Forty Five Ranch Enterprises
Francotte & Cie S.A. Auguste
Frontier Arms Co.,Inc.
Gene's Custom Guns
George E. Mathews & Son, Inc.
George Madis Winchester Consultants
Gerald Pettinger Books (See Pettinger Books)
Getz Barrel Co.
Gillmann, Edwin
Gilmore Sports Concepts
Goergen's Gun Shop, Inc.
Golden Age Arms Co.
Goodwin's Gun Shop
Griffin & Howe, Inc.
Groenewold, John
Gun City
Gun Hunter Books (See Gun Hunter Trading Co.)
Gun Hunter Trading Co.
Guncraft Books (See Guncraft Sports Inc.)
Guncraft Sports Inc.
Gunsmithing, Inc.
Hallowell & Co.
Hammans, Charles E.
HandCrafts Unltd (See Clements' Custom Leather)
Handgun Press
Hank's Gun Shop
Hansen & Co.
Irwin, Campbell H.
Island Pond Gun Shop
Ithaca Classic Doubles
Jackalope Gun Shop
James Wayne Firearms for Collectors and Investors
Jensen's Custom Ammunition
Kelley's
L.L. Bean, Inc.
Lampert, Ron
LaRocca Gun Works
Ledbetter Airguns, Riley
LeFever Arms Co., Inc.
Lock's Philadelphia Gun Exchange
Log Cabin Sport Shop
Logdewood Mfg.
Lomont Precision Bullets
Long, George F.
Mahony, Philip Bruce
Mandall Shooting Supplies Inc.
Marshall Fish Mfg. Gunsmith Sptg. Co.
Martin's Gun Shop
Mathews & Son, Inc., George E.
McCann Industries
McCann's Machine & Gun Shop
Mercer Custom Guns
Montana Outfitters, Lewis E. Yearout
Muzzleloaders Etcetera, Inc.
Navy Arms Company
New England Arms Co.
Nitex Gun Shop
Olathe Gun Shop
P&M Sales & Services, LLC
Pasadena Gun Center
Pentheny de Pentheny
Peterson Gun Shop, Inc., A.W.
Pettinger Books, Gerald
Pony Express Sport Shop
Powder Horn Ltd.
R.A. Wells Custom Gunsmith
R.E.T. Enterprises
Ramon B. Gonzalez Guns
Retting, Inc., Martin B
Robert Valade Engraving
Rutgers Book Center
Scott Fine Guns Inc., Thad
Shootin' Shack
Spencer Reblue Service
Sportsmen's Exchange & Western Gun Traders, Inc.
Steven Dodd Hughes
Stott's Creek Armory, Inc.
Stratco, Inc.
Ten-Ring Precision, Inc.
The A.W. Peterson Gun Shop, Inc.
The Gun Room Press
The Gun Shop
The Gun Works
The Orvis Co.
The Swampfire Shop (See Peterson Gun Shop, Inc.)
Thurston Sports, Inc.
Vic's Gun Refinishing
Walker Arms Co., Inc.
Wallace, Terry
Wasmundt, Jim

REFERENCE

Product & Service Directory

Weber & Markin Custom Gunsmiths
Werth, T. W.
Whildin & Sons Ltd, E.H.
Whitestone Lumber Corp.
Wichita Arms, Inc.
Wild West Guns
William Fagan & Co.
Williams Shootin' Iron Service, The Lynx-Line
Winchester Sutler, Inc., The
Wood, Frank (See Classic Guns, Inc.)
Yearout, Lewis E. (See Montana Outfitters)

AUCTIONEER - GUNS, ETC.

"Little John's" Antique Arms
Buck Stix-SOS Products Co.
Butterfield's
Christie's East
Fagan & Co.Inc
Sotheby's

BOOKS & MANUALS (PUBLISHERS & DEALERS)

"Su-Press-On", Inc.
Alpha 1 Drop Zone
American Handgunner Magazine
Armory Publications
Arms & Armour Press
Ballistic Product, Inc.
Ballistic Product, Inc.
Barnes Bullets, Inc.
Bauska Barrels
Beartooth Bullets
Beeman Precision Airguns
Blacksmith Corp.
Blacktail Mountain Books
Blue Book Publications, Inc.
Blue Ridge Machinery & Tools, Inc.
Boone's Custom Ivory Grips, Inc.
Brown Co., E. Arthur
Brownells, Inc.
Bullet N Press
C. Sharps Arms Co. Inc./Montana Armory
Cape Outfitters
Cheyenne Pioneer Products
Colonial Repair
Corbin Mfg. & Supply, Inc.
DBI Books Division of Krause Publications
deHaas Barrels
Dixon Muzzleloading Shop, Inc.
Excalibur Publications
Executive Protection Institute
Galati International
Gerald Pettinger Books (See Pettinger Books)
Golden Age Arms Co.
Gun City
Gun List (See Krause Publications)
Guncraft Books (See Guncraft Sports Inc.)
Guncraft Sports Inc.
Gunnerman Books
GUNS Magazine
Gunsmithing, Inc.
H&P Publishing
Handgun Press
Harris Publications
Hawk Laboratories, Inc. (See Hawk, Inc.)
Hawk, Inc.
Heritage/VSP Gun Books
Hodgdon Powder Co.
Home Shop Machinist, The Village Press Publications
Hornady Mfg. Co.
Huntington Die Specialties
I.D.S.A. Books
Info-Arm
Ironside International Publishers, Inc.
Jantz Supply
Kelley's
King & Co.
Koval Knives
Krause Publications, Inc.
L.B.T.
Lapua Ltd.
Lebeau-Courally
Lethal Force Institute (See Police Bookshelf)
Lyman Products Corp.
Madis Books
Magma Engineering Co.
Mandall Shooting Supplies Inc.
MarMik, Inc.
Montana Armory, Inc .(See C. Sharps Arms Co. Inc.)
Mountain South
Mountain State Muzzleloading Supplies, Inc.
Mulberry House Publishing
Navy Arms Company
Numrich Gun Parts Corporation
OK Weber, Inc.
Outdoor Sports Headquarters, Inc.
Paintball Games International Magazine Aceville
Pejsa Ballistics
Petersen Publishing Co.
Pettinger Books, Gerald
PFRB Co.
Police Bookshelf
Precision Shooting, Inc.
Professional Hunter Supplies (See Star Custom Bullets)
Ravell Ltd.
Ray Riling Arms Books Co.
Remington Double Shotguns
Russ Haydon's Shooters' Supply
Rutgers Book Center
S&S Firearms
Safari Press, Inc.
Saunders Gun & Machine Shop
Scharch Mfg., Inc.-Top Brass
Scharch Mfg., Inc.-Top Brass
Semmer, Charles (See Remington Double Shotguns)
Sharps Arms Co., Inc., C.
Shotgun Sports Magazine, dba Shootin' Accessories Ltd.
Sierra Bullets
Speer Bullets
SPG LLC
Stackpole Books
Star Custom Bullets
Stewart Game Calls, Inc., Johnny
Stoeger Industries
Stoeger Publishing Co. (See Stoeger Industries)
Swift Bullet Co.
The A.W. Peterson Gun Shop, Inc.
The Gun Room Press
The Gun Works
The NgraveR Co.
Thomas, Charles C.
Track of the Wolf, Inc.
Trafalgar Square
Trotman, Ken
Tru-Balance Knife Co.
Vega Tool Co.
Vintage Industries, Inc.
VSP Publishers (See Heritage/VSP Gun Books)
W.E. Brownell Checkering Tools
WAMCO-New Mexico
Wells Creek Knife & Gun Works
Wilderness Sound Products Ltd.
Williams Gun Sight Co.
Wolfe Publishing Co.
Wolf's Western Traders

BULLET CASTING, ACCESSORIES

Ballisti-Cast, Inc.
Buffalo Arms Co.
Bullet Metals
Cast Performance Bullet Company
CFVentures
Cooper-Woodward
Davide Pedersoli and Co.
Ferguson, Bill
Huntington Die Specialties
Lee Precision, Inc.
Lithi Bee Bullet Lube
Lyman Products Corp.
Magma Engineering Co.
Ox-Yoke Originals, Inc.
Rapine Bullet Mould Mfg. Co.
SPG LLC
The A.W. Peterson Gun Shop, Inc.
The Hanned Line
United States Products Co.

BULLET CASTING, FURNACES & POTS

Ballisti-Cast, Inc.
Buffalo Arms Co.
Bullet Metals
Ferguson, Bill
GAR
Lee Precision, Inc.
Lyman Products Corp.
Magma Engineering Co.
Rapine Bullet Mould Mfg. Co.
RCBS/ATK
The A.W. Peterson Gun Shop, Inc.
The Gun Works
Thompson Bullet Lube Co.

BULLET CASTING, LEAD

Action Bullets & Alloy Inc.
Ames Metal Products
Belltown Ltd.
Buckskin Bullet Co.
Buffalo Arms Co.
Bullet Metals
Bullseye Bullets
Hunters Supply, Inc.
Jericho Tool & Die Co., Inc.
Lee Precision, Inc.
Lithi Bee Bullet Lube
Magma Engineering Co.
Montana Precision Swaging
Ox-Yoke Originals, Inc.
Penn Bullets
Proofmark Corp.
SPG LLC
Splitfire Sporting Goods, L.L.C.
The A.W. Peterson Gun Shop, Inc.
The Gun Works
Walters Wads

BULLET PULLERS

Battenfeld Technologies
Davide Pedersoli and Co.
Hollywood Engineering
Huntington Die Specialties
Royal Arms Gunstocks
The A.W. Peterson Gun Shop, Inc.
The Gun Works

BULLET TOOLS

Brynin, Milton
Camdex, Inc.
Corbin Mfg. & Supply, Inc.
Cumberland Arms
Eagan, Donald V.
Holland's Gunsmithing
Hollywood Engineering
Lee Precision, Inc.
Niemi Engineering, W. B.
North Devon Firearms Services
Rorschach Precision Products
Sport Flite Manufacturing Co.
The A.W. Peterson Gun Shop, Inc.
The Hanned Line
WTA Manufacturing

BULLET, CASE & DIE LUBRICANTS

Beartooth Bullets
Bonanza (See Forster Products)
Brown Co., E. Arthur
Buckskin Bullet Co.
Buffalo Arms Co.
Camp-Cap Products
CFVentures
Cooper-Woodward
CVA
E-Z-Way Systems
Ferguson, Bill
Forster Products
GAR
Guardsman Products
Heidenstrom Bullets
Hollywood Engineering
Hornady Mfg. Co.
Imperial (See E-Z-Way Systems)
Knoell, Doug
L.B.T.
Le Clear Industries (See E-Z-Way Systems)
Lee Precision, Inc.
Lithi Bee Bullet Lube
MI-TE Bullets
Paco's (See Small Custom Mould & Bullet Co.)
RCBS Operations/ATK
Reardon Products
Rooster Laboratories
Shay's Gunsmithing
Small Custom Mould & Bullet Co.
Tamarack Products, Inc.
The Hanned Line
Uncle Mike's (See Michaels of Oregon Co.)
Warren Muzzleloading Co., Inc.
Widener's Reloading & Shooting Supply, Inc.
Young Country Arms

CARTRIDGES FOR COLLECTORS

Ackerman & Co.
Ad Hominem
Armory Publications
Cameron's
Campbell, Dick
Cartridge Transfer Group, Pete de Coux
Cherry Creek State Park Shooting Center
Cole's Gun Works
Colonial Repair
Cubic Shot Shell Co., Inc.
de Coux, Pete (See Cartridge Transfer Group)
Duane's Gun Repair (See DGR Custom Rifles)
Ed's Gun House
Ed's Gun House
Enguix Import-Export
Epps, Ellwood/Isabella
First Inc., Jack
Forty Five Ranch Enterprises
George Madis Winchester Consultants
Goergen's Gun Shop, Inc.
Goodwin's Gun Shop
Grayback Wildcats
Gun City
Gun Hunter Books (See Gun Hunter Trading Co.)
Gun Hunter Trading Co.
Jack First, Inc.
Kelley's
Liberty Shooting Supplies
Mandall Shooting Supplies Inc.
MAST Technology, Inc.
Michael's Antiques
Montana Outfitters, Lewis E. Yearout
Numrich Gun Parts Corporation
Pasadena Gun Center
Samco Global Arms, Inc.
SOS Products Co. (See Buck Stix-SOS Products Co.)
Stone Enterprises Ltd.
The Country Armourer
The Gun Room Press
Ward & Van Valkenburg
Yearout, Lewis E. (See Montana Outfitters)

CASE & AMMUNITION PROCESSORS, INSPECTORS, BOXERS

Ammo Load, Inc.
Ben's Machines
Hafner World Wide, Inc.
Scharch Mfg., Inc.-Top Brass
The A.W. Peterson Gun Shop, Inc.

CASE CLEANERS & POLISHING MEDIA

Battenfeld Technologies
Belltown Ltd.
Buffalo Arms Co.
G96 Products Co., Inc.
Huntington Die Specialties
Lee Precision, Inc.
Penn Bullets
The A.W. Peterson Gun Shop, Inc.
The Gun Works
Tru-Square Metal Products Inc.
VibraShine, Inc.

CASE PREPARATION TOOLS

Battenfeld Technologies
CONKKO
High Precision
Hoehn Sales, Inc.
Huntington Die Specialties
J. Dewey Mfg. Co., Inc.
K&M Services
Lee Precision, Inc.
Match Prep-Doyle Gracey
Plum City Ballistic Range
RCBS Operations/ATK
Russ Haydon's Shooters' Supply
Sinclair International, Inc.
Stoney Point Products, Inc.
The A.W. Peterson Gun Shop, Inc.

CASE TRIMMERS, TRIM DIES & ACCESSORIES

Buffalo Arms Co.
Creedmoor Sports, Inc.
Fremont Tool Works
Goodwin's Gun Shop
Hollywood Engineering
K&M Services
Lyman Products Corp.
Match Prep-Doyle Gracey
OK Weber, Inc.
Ozark Gun Works
RCBS/ATK
Redding Reloading Equipment
The A.W. Peterson Gun Shop, Inc.
Time Precision

PRODUCT & SERVICE DIRECTORY

CASE TUMBLERS, VIBRATORS, MEDIA & ACCESSORIES

4-D Custom Die Co.
Battenfeld Technologies
Berry's Mfg., Inc.
Dillon Precision Products, Inc.
Goodwin's Gun Shop
Penn Bullets
Raytech Div. of Lyman Products Corp.
The A.W. Peterson Gun Shop, Inc.
Tru-Square Metal Products Inc.
VibraShine, Inc.

CASES, CABINETS, RACKS & SAFES - GUN

All Rite Products, Inc.
Allen Co., Bob
Allen Co., Inc.
Allen Sportswear, Bob (See Allen Co., Bob)
Alumna Sport by Dee Zee
American Display Co.
American Security Products Co.
Americase
Art Jewel Enterprises Ltd.
Ashby Turkey Calls
Bagmaster Mfg., Inc.
Barramundi Corp.
Berry's Mfg., Inc.
Big Spring Enterprises "Bore Stores"
Bill's Custom Cases
Bison Studios
Black Sheep Brand
Brauer Bros.
Brown, H. R. (See Silhouette Leathers)
Browning Arms Co.
Bushmaster Hunting & Fishing
Cannon Safe, Inc.
Chipmunk (See Oregon Arms, Inc.)
Cobalt Mfg., Inc.
CONKKO
Connecticut Shotgun Mfg. Co.
D&L Industries (See D.J. Marketing)
D.J. Marketing
Dara-Nes, Inc. (See Nesci Enterprises, Inc.)
Deepeeka Exports Pvt. Ltd.
Doskocil Mfg. Co., Inc.
DTM International, Inc.
EMF Co., Inc.
English, Inc., A.G.
Enhanced Presentations, Inc.
Eversull Co., Inc.
Fort Knox Security Products
Freedom Arms, Inc.
Frontier Safe Co.
Galati International
GALCO International Ltd.
Gun-Ho Sports Cases
Hall Plastics, Inc., John
Hastings
Homak
Hoppe's Div. Penguin Industries, Inc.
Hunter Co., Inc.
Hydrosorbent Products
Impact Case & Container, Inc.
Johanssons Vapentillbehor, Bert
Johnston Bros. (See C&T Corp. TA Johnson Brothers)
Kalispel Case Line
Kane Products, Inc.
KK Air International (See Impact Case & Container Co.)
Knock on Wood Antiques
Kolpin Mfg., Inc.
Lakewood Products LLC
Liberty Safe
Mandall Shooting Supplies Inc.
Marsh, Mike
McWelco Products
Morton Booth Co.
MPC
MTM Molded Products Co., Inc.
Nalpak
Necessary Concepts, Inc.
Nesci Enterprises Inc.
Oregon Arms, Inc. (See Rogue Rifle Co., Inc.)
Outa-Site Gun Carriers
Pflumm Mfg. Co.
Poburka, Philip (See Bison Studios)
Powell & Son (Gunmakers) Ltd., William
Protektor Model
Prototech Industries, Inc.
Rogue Rifle Co., Inc.
Schulz Industries
Southern Security
Sportsman's Communicators
Sun Welding Safe Co.
Sweet Home, Inc.
Talmage, William G.
The Outdoor Connection, Inc.
The Surecase Co.
Tinks & Ben Lee Hunting Products (See Wellington)
Trulock Tool
Universal Sports
W. Waller & Son, Inc.
Whitestone Lumber Corp.
Wilson Case, Inc.
Woodstream
Zanotti Armor, Inc.
Ziegel Engineering

CHRONOGRAPHS & PRESSURE TOOLS

Air Rifle Specialists
Brown Co., E. Arthur
C.W. Erickson's L.L.C.
Canons Delcour
Clearview Products
Competition Electronics, Inc.
Custom Chronograph, Inc.
D&H Precision Tooling
Hege Jagd-u. Sporthandels GmbH
Hutton Rifle Ranch
Kent Cartridge Mfg. Co. Ltd.
Mac-1 Airgun Distributors
Oehler Research,Inc.
P.A.C.T., Inc.
Romain's Custom Guns, Inc.
Savage Arms, Inc.
Stratco, Inc.
Tepeco

CLEANERS & DEGREASERS

Barnes Bullets, Inc.
Belltown Ltd.
Camp-Cap Products
G96 Products Co., Inc.
Goodwin's Gun Shop
Hafner World Wide, Inc.
Half Moon Rifle Shop
Kleen-Bore,Inc.
LEM Gun Specialties, Inc. The Lewis Lead Remover
Modern Muzzleloading, Inc.
Northern Precision Custom Swaged Bullets
Parker & Sons Shooting Supply
Parker Gun Finishes
Perazone-Gunsmith, Brian
PrOlixr Lubricants
R&S Industries Corp.
Ramon B. Gonzalez Guns
Rusteprufe Laboratories
Sheffield Knifemakers Supply, Inc.
Shooter's Choice Gun Care
Sierra Specialty Prod. Co.
Spencer's Rifle Barrels, Inc.
The A.W. Peterson Gun Shop, Inc.
The Gun Works
United States Products Co.

CLEANING & REFINISHING SUPPLIES

AC Dyna-tite Corp.
Alpha 1 Drop Zone
American Gas & Chemical Co., Ltd
Answer Products Co.
Armite Laboratories
Atlantic Mills, Inc.
Atsko/Sno-Seal, Inc.
Barnes Bullets, Inc.
Battenfeld Technologies
Beeman Precision Airguns
Belltown Ltd.
Bill's Gun Repair
Birchwood Casey
Blount, Inc., Sporting Equipment Div.
Blount/Outers ATK
Blue and Gray Products Inc. (See Ox-Yoke Originals)
Break-Free, Inc.
Bridgers Best
Brown Co., E. Arthur
Brownells, Inc.
C.S. Van Gorden & Son, Inc.
Cambos Outdoorsman
Cambos Outdoorsman
Camp-Cap Products
CONKKO
Connecticut Shotgun Mfg. Co.
Creedmoor Sports, Inc.
CRR, Inc./Marble's Inc.
Custom Products (See Jones Custom Products)
Cylinder & Slide, Inc., William R. Laughridge
Dara-Nes, Inc. (See Nesci Enterprises, Inc.)
Deepeeka Exports Pvt. Ltd.
Desert Mountain Mfg.
Du-Lite Corp.
Dykstra, Doug
E&L Mfg., Inc.
Eezox, Inc.
Ekol Leather Care
Faith Associates
Flitz International Ltd.
Fluoramics, Inc.
Frontier Products Co.
G96 Products Co., Inc.
Golden Age Arms Co.
Guardsman Products
Gunsmithing, Inc.
Hafner World Wide, Inc.
Half Moon Rifle Shop
Heatbath Corp.
Hoppe's Div. Penguin Industries, Inc.
Hornady Mfg. Co.
Hydrosorbent Products
Iosso Products
J. Dewey Mfg. Co., Inc.
Jantz Supply
Jantz Supply
Johnston Bros. (See C&T Corp. TA Johnson Brothers)
Jonad Corp.
K&M Industries, Inc.
Kellogg's Professional Products
Kent Cartridge Mfg. Co. Ltd.
Kesselring Gun Shop
Kleen-Bore,Inc.
Knight Rifles
Laurel Mountain Forge
Lee Supplies, Mark
LEM Gun Specialties, Inc. The Lewis Lead Remover
List Precision Engineering
LPS Laboratories, Inc.
Lyman Products Corp.
Mac-1 Airgun Distributors
Mandall Shooting Supplies Inc.
Marble Arms (See CRR, Inc./Marble's Inc.)
Mark Lee Supplies
Micro Sight Co.
Minute Man High Tech Industries
Mountain State Muzzleloading Supplies, Inc.
MTM Molded Products Co., Inc.
Muscle Products Corp.
Nesci Enterprises Inc.
Northern Precision Custom Swaged Bullets
Now Products, Inc.
October Country Muzzleloading
Old World Oil Products
Omark Industries, Div. of Blount, Inc.
Original Mink Oil, Inc.
Otis Technology, Inc.
Outers Laboratories Div. of ATK
Ox-Yoke Originals, Inc.
Parker & Sons Shooting Supply
Parker Gun Finishes
Pendleton Royal, c/o Swingler Buckland Ltd.
Perazone-Gunsmith, Brian
Pete Rickard, Inc.
Peter Dyson & Son Ltd.
Precision Airgun Sales, Inc.
PrOlixr Lubricants
Pro-Shot Products, Inc.
R&S Industries Corp.
Radiator Specialty Co.
Rooster Laboratories
Russ Haydon's Shooters' Supply
Rusteprufe Laboratories
Rusty Duck Premium Gun Care Products
Saunders Gun & Machine Shop
Schumakers Gun Shop
Sheffield Knifemakers Supply, Inc.
Shooter's Choice Gun Care
Shotgun Sports Magazine, dba Shootin' Accessories Ltd.
Silencio/Safety Direct
Sinclair International, Inc.
Sno-Seal, Inc. (See Atsko/Sno-Seal, Inc.)
Southern Bloomer Mfg. Co.
Splitfire Sporting Goods, L.L.C.
Starr Trading Co., Jedediah
Stoney Point Products, Inc.
Svon Corp.
T.F.C. S.p.A.
TDP Industries, Inc.
Tetra Gun Care
Texas Platers Supply Co.
The A.W. Peterson Gun Shop, Inc.
The Dutchman's Firearms, Inc.
The Lewis Lead Remover (See LEM Gun Specialties)
The Paul Co.
Track of the Wolf, Inc.
United States Products Co.
Van Gorden & Son Inc., C. S.
Venco Industries, Inc. (See Shooter's Choice Gun Care)
VibraShine, Inc.
Volquartsen Custom Ltd.
Warren Muzzleloading Co., Inc.
Watson Trophy Match Bullets
WD-40 Co.
Wick, David E.
Willow Bend
Wolf's Western Traders
Young Country Arms

COMPUTER SOFTWARE - BALLISTICS

Action Target, Inc.
AmBr Software Group Ltd.
Arms Software
Arms, Programming Solutions (See Arms Software)
Barnes Bullets, Inc.
Canons Delcour
Corbin Mfg. & Supply, Inc.
Data Tech Software Systems
Hodgdon Powder Co.
J.I.T. Ltd.
Jensen Bullets
Kent Cartridge Mfg. Co. Ltd.
Maionchi-L.M.I.
Oehler Research,Inc.
Outdoor Sports Headquarters, Inc.
P.A.C.T., Inc.
Pejsa Ballistics
Powley Computer (See Hutton Rifle Ranch)
RCBS Operations/ATK
Sierra Bullets
The Ballistic Program Co., Inc.
The Country Armourer
The Gun Works
Tioga Engineering Co., Inc.
W. Square Enterprises

CUSTOM GUNSMITH

A&W Repair
A.A. Arms, Inc.
Acadian Ballistic Specialties
Accuracy Unlimited
Ace Custom 45's, Inc.
Acra-Bond Laminates
Adair Custom Shop, Bill
Ahlman Guns
Al Lind Custom Guns
Aldis Gunsmithing & Shooting Supply
Alpha Precision, Inc.
Alpine Indoor Shooting Range
Amrine's Gun Shop
Answer Products Co.
Antique Arms Co.
Armament Gunsmithing Co., Inc.
Arms Craft Gunsmithing
Arms Ingenuity Co.
Armscorp USA, Inc.
Artistry in Wood
Art's Gun & Sport Shop, Inc.
Arundel Arms & Ammunition, Inc., A.
Autauga Arms, Inc.
Badger Creek Studio
Baelder, Harry
Baer Custom Inc., Les
Bain & Davis, Inc.
Bansner's Ultimate Rifles, LLC
Barnes Bullets, Inc.
Baron Technology
Barta's Gunsmithing
Bear Arms
Bear Mountain Gun & Tool
Beaver Lodge (See Fellowes, Ted)
Behlert Precision, Inc.
Beitzinger, George
Belding's Custom Gun Shop
Ben William's Gun Shop
Bengtson Arms Co., L.
Bill Adair Custom Shop
Billings Gunsmiths
BlackStar AccuMax Barrels
BlackStar Barrel Accurizing (See BlackStar AccuMax)
Bob Rogers Gunsmithing
Bond Custom Firearms
Borden Ridges Rimrock Stocks
Borovnik KG, Ludwig
Bowen Classic Arms Corp.
Brace, Larry D.
Briese Bullet Co., Inc.
Briganti, A.J.
Briley Mfg. Inc.
Broad Creek Rifle Works, Ltd.
Brockman's Custom Gunsmithing
Broken Gun Ranch

REFERENCE

PRODUCT & SERVICE DIRECTORY

Brown Precision, Inc.
Brown Products, Inc., Ed
Buchsenmachermeister
Buckhorn Gun Works
Budin, Dave
Bull Mountain Rifle Co.
Bullberry Barrel Works, Ltd.
Burkhart Gunsmithing, Don
Cache La Poudre Rifleworks
Cambos Outdoorsman
Cambos Outdoorsman
Campbell, Dick
Carolina Precision Rifles
Carter's Gun Shop
Caywood, Shane J.
CBC-BRAZIL
Chambers Flintlocks Ltd., Jim
Champlin Firearms, Inc.
Chicasaw Gun Works
Chuck's Gun Shop
Chuilli, Stephen
Clark Custom Guns, Inc.
Clark Firearms Engraving
Classic Arms Company
Classic Arms Corp.
Clearview Products
Cleland's Outdoor World, Inc
Coffin, Charles H.
Cogar's Gunsmithing
Cole's Gun Works
Colonial Arms, Inc.
Colonial Repair
Colorado Gunsmithing Academy
Colorado School of Trades
Colt's Mfg. Co., Inc.
Conrad, C. A.
Corkys Gun Clinic
Cox, Ed. C.
Cullity Restoration
Custom Gun Stocks
Custom Single Shot Rifles
D&D Gunsmiths, Ltd.
Dangler, Homer L.
D'Arcy Echols & Co.
Darlington Gun Works, Inc.
Dave's Gun Shop
David Miller Co.
David R. Chicoine
David W. Schwartz Custom Guns
Davis, Don
Delorge, Ed
Del-Sports, Inc.
DGR Custom Rifles
DGS, Inc., Dale A. Storey
Dietz Gun Shop & Range, Inc.
Dilliott Gunsmithing, Inc.
Donnelly, C. P.
Duane A. Hobbie Gunsmithing
Duane's Gun Repair (See DGR Custom Rifles)
Duffy, Charles E (See Guns Antique & Modern DBA)
Duncan's Gun Works, Inc.
E. Arthur Brown Co.
Eckelman Gunsmithing
Ed Brown Products, Inc.
Eggleston, Jere D.
Entre`prise Arms, Inc.
Erhardt, Dennis
Eversull Co., Inc.
Evolution Gun Works Inc.
F.I., Inc. - High Standard Mfg. Co.
FERLIB
Ferris Firearms
Fisher, Jerry A.
Fisher Custom Firearms
Fleming Firearms
Flynn's Custom Guns
Forkin, Ben (See Belt MTN Arms)
Forkin Arms
Forster, Kathy (See Custom Checkering)
Forster, Larry L.
Forthofer's Gunsmithing & Knifemaking
Francesca, Inc.
Francotte & Cie S.A. Auguste
Fred F. Wells/Wells Sport Store
Frontier Arms Co.,Inc.
Fullmer, Geo. M.
G.G. & G.
Galaxy Imports Ltd., Inc.
Garthwaite Pistolsmith, Inc., Jim
Gary Reeder Custom Guns
Gator Guns & Repair
Genecco Gun Works
Gene's Custom Guns
Gentry Custom Gunmaker, David
George E. Mathews & Son, Inc.
George Hoenig, Inc.
Gillmann, Edwin
Gilman-Mayfield, Inc.
Gilmore Sports Concepts
Giron, Robert E.
Goens, Dale W.
Gonic Arms/North American Arm
Goodling's Gunsmithing
Goodwin's Gun Shop
Grace, Charles E.
Grayback Wildcats
Graybill's Gun Shop
Green, Roger M.
Greg Gunsmithing Repair
Gre-Tan Rifles
Griffin & Howe, Inc.
Griffin & Howe, Inc.
Griffin & Howe, Inc.
Gruning Precision Inc.
Guncraft Books (See Guncraft Sports Inc.)
Guncraft Sports Inc.
Guncraft Sports, Inc.
Guns Antique & Modern DBA / Charles E. Duffy
Gunsite Custom Shop
Gunsite Gunsmithy (See Gunsite Custom Shop)
Gunsite Training Center
Gunsmithing Ltd.
Hamilton, Alex B (See Ten-Ring Precision, Inc)
Hammans, Charles E.
Hammerli Service-Precision Mac
Hammond Custom Guns Ltd.
Hank's Gun Shop
Hanson's Gun Center, Dick
Harris Gunworks
Harry Lawson Co.
Hart & Son, Inc.
Hart Rifle Barrels,Inc.
Hartmann & Weiss GmbH
Harwood, Jack O.
Hawken Shop, The (See Dayton Traister)
Hecht, Hubert J, Waffen-Hecht
Heilmann, Stephen
Heinie Specialty Products
Hensley, Gunmaker, Darwin
High Bridge Arms, Inc
High Performance International
High Precision
Highline Machine Co.
Hill, Loring F.
Hiptmayer, Armurier
Hiptmayer, Klaus
Hoag, James W.
Hodgson, Richard
Hoehn Sales, Inc.
Hofer Jagdwaffen, P.
Holland's Gunsmithing
Huebner, Corey O.
Hunkeler, A (See Buckskin Machine Works
Imperial Magnum Corp.
Irwin, Campbell H.
Island Pond Gun Shop
Israel Arms International, Inc.
Ivanoff, Thomas G. (See Tom's Gun Repair)
J&S Heat Treat
J.J. Roberts / Engraver
Jack Dever Co.
Jackalope Gun Shop
James Calhoon Mfg.
James Calhoon Varmint Bullets
Jamison's Forge Works
Jarrett Rifles, Inc.
Jarvis, Inc.
Jay McCament Custom Gunmaker
Jeffredo Gunsight
Jensen's Custom Ammunition
Jim Norman Custom Gunstocks
Jim's Gun Shop (See Spradlin's)
Jim's Precision, Jim Ketchum
John Norrell Arms
John Rigby & Co.
Jones Custom Products, Neil A.
Juenke, Vern
K. Eversull Co., Inc.
KDF, Inc.
Keith's Custom Gunstocks
Ken Eyster Heritage Gunsmiths, Inc.
Ken Starnes Gunmaker
Ketchum, Jim (See Jim's Precision)
Kilham & Co.
King's Gun Works
KLA Enterprises
Klein Custom Guns, Don
Kleinendorst, K. W.
KOGOT
Korzinek Riflesmith, J.
L. E. Jurras & Assoc.
LaFrance Specialties
Lampert, Ron
LaRocca Gun Works
Larry Lyons Gunworks
Lathrop's, Inc.
Laughridge, William R (See Cylinder & Slide Inc)
Lawson Co., Harry
Lazzeroni Arms Co.
LeFever Arms Co., Inc.
Linebaugh Custom Sixguns
List Precision Engineering
Lock's Philadelphia Gun Exchange
Lone Star Rifle Company
Long, George F.
Mag-Na-Port International, Inc.
Mahony, Philip Bruce
Mahony, Philip Bruce
Mahovsky's Metalife
Makinson, Nicholas
Mandall Shooting Supplies Inc.
Marshall Fish Mfg. Gunsmith Sptg. Co.
Martin's Gun Shop
Martz, John V.
Mathews & Son, Inc., George E.
Mazur Restoration, Pete
McCann's Muzzle-Gun Works
McCluskey Precision Rifles
McGowen Rifle Barrels
McMillan Rifle Barrels
MCS, Inc.
Mercer Custom Guns
Michael's Antiques
Mid-America Recreation, Inc.
Middlebrooks Custom Shop
Miller Arms, Inc.
Miller Custom
Mills Jr., Hugh B.
Moeller, Steve
Monell Custom Guns
Montgomery Community College
Morrison Custom Rifles, J. W.
Morrow, Bud
Mo's Competitor Supplies (See MCS, Inc.)
Mowrey's Guns & Gunsmithing
Mullis Guncraft
Muzzleloaders Etcetera, Inc.
NCP Products, Inc.
Neil A. Jones Custom Products
Nelson's Custom Guns, Inc.
Nettestad Gun Works
New England Arms Co.
New England Custom Gun Service
Newman Gunshop
Nicholson Custom
Nickels, Paul R.
Nicklas, Ted
Nitex Gun Shop
North American Shooting Systems
Nu-Line Guns,Inc.
Old World Gunsmithing
Olson, Vic
Ottmar, Maurice
Ox-Yoke Originals, Inc.
Ozark Gun Works
P&M Sales & Services, LLC
P.S.M.G. Gun Co.
PAC-NOR Barreling
Pagel Gun Works, Inc.
Parker & Sons Shooting Supply
Parker Gun Finishes
Pasadena Gun Center
Paterson Gunsmithing
Paulsen Gunstocks
Peacemaker Specialists
PEM's Mfg. Co.
Pence Precision Barrels
Pennsylvania Gunsmith School
Penrod Precision
Pentheny de Pentheny
Performance Specialists
Pete Mazur Restoration
Peter Dyson & Son Ltd.
Peterson Gun Shop, Inc., A.W.
Piquette's Custom Engraving
Plum City Ballistic Range
Powell & Son (Gunmakers) Ltd., William
Power Custom, Inc.
Professional Hunter Supplies (See Star Custom Bullets)
Quality Custom Firearms
R&J Gun Shop
R.A. Wells Custom Gunsmith
Ramon B. Gonzalez Guns
Ray's Gunsmith Shop
Renfrew Guns & Supplies
Ridgetop Sporting Goods
Ries, Chuck
RMS Custom Gunsmithing
Robert Valade Engraving
Robinson, Don
Rocky Mountain Arms, Inc.
Romain's Custom Guns, Inc.
Ron Frank Custom Classic Arms
Ruger's Custom Guns
Rupert's Gun Shop
Savage Arms, Inc.
Schiffman, Mike
Schumakers Gun Shop
Score High Gunsmithing
Sharp Shooter Supply
Shaw, Inc., E. R. (See Small Arms Mfg. Co.)
Shay's Gunsmithing
Shockley, Harold H.
Shooters Supply
Shootin' Shack
Shooting Specialties (See Titus, Daniel)
Shotguns Unlimited
Silver Ridge Gun Shop (See Goodwin, Fred)
Simmons Gun Repair, Inc.
Singletary, Kent
Siskiyou Gun Works (See Donnelly, C. P.)
Skeoch, Brian R.
Sklany's Machine Shop
Slezak, Jerome F.
Small Arms Mfg. Co.
Small Arms Specialists
Smith, Art
Snapp's Gunshop
Sound Technology
Speiser, Fred D.
Spencer Reblue Service
Spencer's Rifle Barrels, Inc.
Splitfire Sporting Goods, L.L.C.
Sportsmen's Exchange & Western Gun Traders, Inc.
Springfield Armory
Springfield, Inc.
SSK Industries
Star Custom Bullets
Steelman's Gun Shop
Steffens, Ron
Steven Dodd Hughes
Stiles Custom Guns
Stott's Creek Armory, Inc.
Sturgeon Valley Sporters
Sullivan, David S .(See Westwind Rifles Inc.)
Swann, D. J.
Swenson's 45 Shop, A. D.
Swift River Gunworks
Szweda, Robert (See RMS Custom Gunsmithing)
Taconic Firearms Ltd., Perry Lane
Talmage, William G.
Tank's Rifle Shop
Tar-Hunt Custom Rifles, Inc.
Tarnhelm Supply Co., Inc.
Taylor & Robbins
Ten-Ring Precision, Inc.
Terry K. Kopp Professional Gunsmithing
The A.W. Peterson Gun Shop, Inc.
The Competitive Pistol Shop
The Custom Shop
The Gun Shop
The Gun Works
The Orvis Co.
The Robar Co.'s, Inc.
The Swampfire Shop (See Peterson Gun Shop, Inc.)
Theis, Terry
Thompson, Randall (See Highline Machine Co.)
Thurston Sports, Inc.
Time Precision
Tom's Gun Repair, Thomas G. Ivanoff
Tom's Gunshop
Trevallion Gunstocks
Trulock Tool
Tucker, James C.
Turnbull Restoration, Doug
Unmussig Bullets, D. L.
Upper Missouri Trading Co.
Van Horn, Gil
Van Patten, J. W.
Van's Gunsmith Service
Vest, John
Vic's Gun Refinishing
Vintage Arms, Inc.
Virgin Valley Custom Guns
Volquartsen Custom Ltd.
Walker Arms Co., Inc.
Wallace, Terry
Wasmundt, Jim
Wayne E. Schwartz Custom Guns
Weatherby, Inc.
Weber & Markin Custom Gunsmiths
Weems, Cecil
Werth, T. W.
Wessinger Custom Guns & Engraving
Western Design (See Alpha Gunsmith Division)
Westley Richards & Co.
Westwind Rifles, Inc., David S. Sullivan
White Barn Wor
White Rifles, Inc.
Wichita Arms, Inc.
Wiebe, Duane
Wild West Guns
William E. Phillips Firearms
Williams Gun Sight Co.
Williams Shootin' Iron Service, The Lynx-Line
Williamson Precision Gunsmithing
Wilsom Combat
Winter, Robert M.
Wise Guns, Dale
Wiseman and Co., Bill

REFERENCE

Wood, Frank (See Classic Guns, Inc.)
Working Guns
Wright's Gunstock Blanks
Yankee Gunsmith "Just Glocks"
Zeeryp, Russ

CUSTOM METALSMITH

A&W Repair
Ackerman & Co.
Ahlman Guns
Alaskan Silversmith, The
Aldis Gunsmithing & Shooting Supply
Alpha Precision, Inc.
Amrine's Gun Shop
Answer Products Co.
Antique Arms Co.
Artistry in Wood
Baer Custom Inc., Les
Baron Technology
Bear Mountain Gun & Tool
Behlert Precision, Inc.
Beitzinger, George
Bengtson Arms Co., L.
Bill Adair Custom Shop
Billings Gunsmiths
Billingsley & Brownell
Bob Rogers Gunsmithing
Bowen Classic Arms Corp.
Brace, Larry D.
Briganti, A.J.
Broad Creek Rifle Works, Ltd.
Brown Precision, Inc.
Buckhorn Gun Works
Bull Mountain Rifle Co.
Bullberry Barrel Works, Ltd.
Carter's Gun Shop
Caywood, Shane J.
Checkmate Refinishing
Cleland's Outdoor World, Inc
Colonial Repair
Colorado Gunsmithing Academy
Craftguard
Crandall Tool & Machine Co.
Cullity Restoration
Custom Single Shot Rifles
D&D Gunsmiths, Ltd.
D&H Precision Tooling
D'Arcy Echols & Co.
Dave's Gun Shop
Delorge, Ed
DGS, Inc., Dale A. Storey
Dietz Gun Shop & Range, Inc.
Dilliott Gunsmithing, Inc.
Duane's Gun Repair (See DGR Custom Rifles)
Duncan's Gun Works, Inc.
Erhardt, Dennis
Eversull Co., Inc.
Ferris Firearms
Fisher, Jerry A.
Forster, Larry L.
Forthofer's Gunsmithing & Knifemaking
Francesca, Inc.
Fred F. Wells/Wells Sport Store
Fullmer, Geo. M.
Genecco Gun Works
Gentry Custom Gunmaker, David
Grace, Charles E.
Grayback Wildcats
Graybill's Gun Shop
Green, Roger M.
Gunsmithing Ltd.
Hamilton, Alex B (See Ten-Ring Precision, Inc)
Harry Lawson Co.
Hartmann & Weiss GmbH
Harwood, Jack O.
Hecht, Hubert J, Waffen-Hecht
Heilmann, Stephen
Highline Machine Co.
Hiptmayer, Armurier
Hiptmayer, Klaus
Hoag, James W.
Holland's Gunsmithing
Island Pond Gun Shop
Ivanoff, Thomas G. (See Tom's Gun Repair)
J J Roberts Firearm Engraver
J&S Heat Treat
J.J. Roberts / Engraver
Jamison's Forge Works
Jay McCament Custom Gunmaker
Jeffredo Gunsight
KDF, Inc.
Ken Eyster Heritage Gunsmiths, Inc.
Ken Starnes Gunmaker
Kilham & Co.
Klein Custom Guns, Don
Kleinendorst, K. W.
Lampert, Ron
LaRocca Gun Works
Larry Lyons Gunworks
Lawson Co., Harry
List Precision Engineering
Mahovsky's Metalife
Makinson, Nicholas
Mandall Shooting Supplies Inc.
Mazur Restoration, Pete
McCann Industries
McCann's Machine & Gun Shop
Mid-America Recreation, Inc.
Miller Arms, Inc.
Montgomery Community College
Morrison Custom Rifles, J. W.
Morrow, Bud
Mullis Guncraft
Nelson's Custom Guns, Inc.
Nettestad Gun Works
New England Custom Gun Service
Nicholson Custom
Nitex Gun Shop
Noreen, Peter H.
Nu-Line Guns,Inc.
Olson, Vic
Ozark Gun Works
P.S.M.G. Gun Co.
Pagel Gun Works, Inc.
Parker & Sons Shooting Supply
Parker Gun Finishes
Pasadena Gun Center
Penrod Precision
Pete Mazur Restoration
Precision Specialties
Quality Custom Firearms
R.A. Wells Custom Gunsmith
Rice, Keith (See White Rock Tool & Die)
Robert Valade Engraving
Rocky Mountain Arms, Inc.
Romain's Custom Guns, Inc.
Ron Frank Custom Classic Arms
Score High Gunsmithing
Simmons Gun Repair, Inc.
Singletary, Kent
Skeoch, Brian R.
Sklany's Machine Shop
Small Arms Specialists
Smith, Art
Smith, Sharmon
Snapp's Gunshop
Spencer Reblue Service
Spencer's Rifle Barrels, Inc.
Sportsmen's Exchange & Western Gun Traders, Inc.
SSK Industries
Steffens, Ron
Stiles Custom Guns
Taylor & Robbins
Ten-Ring Precision, Inc.
The A.W. Peterson Gun Shop, Inc.
The Custom Shop
The Gun Shop
The Robar Co.'s, Inc.
Thompson, Randall (See Highline Machine Co.)
Tom's Gun Repair, Thomas G. Ivanoff
Turnbull Restoration, Doug
Van Horn, Gil
Van Patten, J. W.
Waldron, Herman
Wallace, Terry
Weber & Markin Custom Gunsmiths
Werth, T. W.
Wessinger Custom Guns & Engraving
White Rock Tool & Die
Wiebe, Duane
Wild West Guns
Williams Shootin' Iron Service, The Lynx-Line
Williamson Precision Gunsmithing
Winter, Robert M.
Wise Guns, Dale
Wood, Frank (See Classic Guns, Inc.)
Wright's Gunstock Blanks
Zufall, Joseph F.

DIE ACCESSORIES, METALLIC

High Precision
King & Co.
MarMik, Inc.
Rapine Bullet Mould Mfg. Co.
Redding Reloading Equipment
Royal Arms Gunstocks
Sport Flite Manufacturing Co.
The A.W. Peterson Gun Shop, Inc.
Wolf's Western Traders

DIES, METALLIC

4-D Custom Die Co.
Badger Creek Studio
Buffalo Arms Co.
Dakota Arms, Inc.
Dillon Precision Products, Inc.
Dixie Gun Works
Fremont Tool Works
Goodwin's Gun Shop
Gruning Precision Inc.
Jones Custom Products, Neil A.
King & Co.
Lee Precision, Inc.
Montana Precision Swaging
Neil A. Jones Custom Products
Ozark Gun Works
Rapine Bullet Mould Mfg. Co.
RCBS Operations/ATK
RCBS/ATK
Redding Reloading Equipment
Romain's Custom Guns, Inc.
Spencer's Rifle Barrels, Inc.
Sport Flite Manufacturing Co.
SSK Industries
The A.W. Peterson Gun Shop, Inc.
Vega Tool Co.
Wolf's Western Traders

DIES, SWAGE

4-D Custom Die Co.
Bullet Swaging Supply, Inc.
Goodwin's Gun Shop
Hollywood Engineering
Montana Precision Swaging
Sport Flite Manufacturing Co.
The A.W. Peterson Gun Shop, Inc.

ENGRAVER, ENGRAVING TOOLS

Ackerman & Co.
Adair Custom Shop, Bill
Ahlman Guns
Alaskan Silversmith, The
Alfano, Sam
Allard, Gary/Creek Side Metal & Woodcrafters
Allen Firearm Engraving
Altamont Co.
American Pioneer Video
Baron Technology
Barraclough, John K.
Bates Engraving, Billy
Bill Adair Custom Shop
Billy Bates Engraving
Boessler, Erich
Brooker, Dennis
Buchsenmachermeister
Churchill, Winston G.
Clark Firearms Engraving
Collings, Ronald
Creek Side Metal & Woodcrafters
Cullity Restoration
Cupp, Alana, Custom Engraver
Custom Single Shot Rifles
Dayton Traister
Delorge, Ed
Dolbare, Elizabeth
Drain, Mark
Dremel Mfg. Co.
Dubber, Michael W.
Engraving Artistry
Engraving Only
Evans Engraving, Robert
Eversull Co., Inc.
Firearms Engraver's Guild of America
Flannery Engraving Co., Jeff W
Forty Five Ranch Enterprises
Fountain Products
Francotte & Cie S.A. Auguste
Frank Knives
Fred F. Wells/Wells Sport Store
French, Artistic Engraving, J. R.
Gary Reeder Custom Guns
Gene's Custom Guns
George Madis Winchester Consultants
Glimm's Custom Gun Engraving
Golden Age Arms Co.
Gournet Artistic Engraving
Grant, Howard V.
GRS / Glendo Corp.
Gurney, F. R.
Half Moon Rifle Shop
Harris Gunworks
Harris Hand Engraving, Paul A.
Harwood, Jack O.
Hawken Shop, The (See Dayton Traister)
Hiptmayer, Armurier
Hiptmayer, Heidemarie
Hofer Jagdwaffen, P.
Ingle, Ralph W.
J J Roberts Firearm Engraver
J.J. Roberts / Engraver
Jantz Supply
Jeff W. Flannery Engraving Co.
Jim Blair Engraving
John J. Adams & Son Engravers
Kane, Edward
Kehr, Roger
Kelly, Lance
Ken Eyster Heritage Gunsmiths, Inc.
Kenneth W. Warren Engraver
Klingler Woodcarving
Larry Lyons Gunworks
LeFever Arms Co., Inc.
Leibowitz, Leonard
Lindsay Engraving & Tools
Little Trees Ramble (See Scott Pilkington)
McCombs, Leo
McDonald, Dennis
McKenzie, Lynton
Mele, Frank
Mid-America Recreation, Inc.
Mittermeier, Inc., Frank
Montgomery Community College
Nelson, Gary K.
New Orleans Jewelers Supply Co.
Pedersen, C. R.
Pedersen, Rex C.
Peter Hale/Engraver
Pilgrim Pewter,Inc. (See Bell Originals Inc. Sid)
Pilkington, Scott (See Little Trees Ramble)
Piquette's Custom Engraving
Potts, Wayne E.
Quality Custom Firearms
Rabeno, Martin
Ralph Bone Engraving
Reed, Dave
Reno, Wayne
Riggs, Jim
Robert Evans Engraving
Robert Valade Engraving
Rohner, Hans
Rohner, John
Rosser, Bob
Rundell's Gun Shop
Runge, Robert P.
Sam Welch Gun Engraving
Sampson, Roger
Schiffman, Mike
Sheffield Knifemakers Supply, Inc.
Sherwood, George
Singletary, Kent
Smith, Mark A.
Smith, Ron
Smokey Valley Rifles
SSK Industries
Steve Kamyk Engraver
Swanson, Mark
The Gun Room
The NgraveR Co.
Theis, Terry
Thiewes, George W.
Thirion Gun Engraving, Denise
Viramontez Engraving
Vorhes, David
W.E. Brownell Checkering Tools
Wagoner, Vernon G.
Wallace, Terry
Warenski, Julie
Weber & Markin Custom Gunsmiths
Wells, Rachel
Wessinger Custom Guns & Engraving
Ziegel Engineering

GAUGES, CALIPERS & MICROMETERS

Blue Ridge Machinery & Tools, Inc.
Goodwin's Gun Shop
Gruning Precision Inc.
Huntington Die Specialties
K&M Services
King & Co.
Spencer's Rifle Barrels, Inc.
Starrett Co., L. S.
Stoney Point Products, Inc.

GUN PARTS, U.S. & FOREIGN

"Su-Press-On", Inc.
A.A. Arms, Inc.
Ahlman Guns
Amherst Arms
Antique Arms Co.
Armscorp USA, Inc.
Auto-Ordnance Corp.
B.A.C.
Badger Shooters Supply, Inc.
Ballard Rifle & Cartridge Co., LLC
Bar-Sto Precision Machine
Bear Mountain Gun & Tool
Billings Gunsmiths
Bill's Gun Repair
Bob's Gun Shop
Briese Bullet Co., Inc.
Brown Products, Inc., Ed
Brownells, Inc.

PRODUCT & SERVICE DIRECTORY

Bryan & Assoc.
Buffer Technologies
Cambos Outdoorsman
Cambos Outdoorsman
Cape Outfitters
Caspian Arms, Ltd.
CBC-BRAZIL
Chicasaw Gun Works
Ciener Inc., Jonathan Arthur
Cole's Gun Works
Colonial Arms, Inc.
Colonial Repair
Colt's Mfg. Co., Inc.
Custom Riflestocks, Inc., Michael M. Kokolus
Cylinder & Slide, Inc., William R. Laughridge
David R. Chicoine
Delta Arms Ltd.
DGR Custom Rifles
Dibble, Derek A.
Dixie Gun Works
Duane's Gun Repair (See DGR Custom Rifles)
Duffy, Charles E (See Guns Antique & Modern DBA)
E.A.A. Corp.
Elliott Inc., G. W.
EMF Co., Inc.
Enguix Import-Export
Entre`prise Arms, Inc.
European American Armory Corp (See E.A.A. Corp)
Evolution Gun Works Inc.
F.I., Inc. - High Standard Mfg. Co.
Faloon Industries, Inc.
Federal Arms Corp. of America
Fleming Firearms
Forrest Inc., Tom
Gentry Custom Gunmaker, David
Glimm's Custom Gun Engraving
Goodwin's Gun Shop
Granite Mountain Arms, Inc.
Greider Precision
Gre-Tan Rifles
Groenewold, John
Gun Hunter Books (See Gun Hunter Trading Co.)
Gun Hunter Trading Co.
Guns Antique & Modern DBA / Charles E. Duffy
Gunsmithing, Inc.
Hastings
Hawken Shop, The (See Dayton Traister)
High Performance International
I.S.S.
Irwin, Campbell H.
Jack First, Inc.
Jamison's Forge Works
Jonathan Arthur Ciener, Inc.
Kimber of America, Inc.
Knight's Mfg. Co.
Krico Deutschland GmbH
LaFrance Specialties
Lampert, Ron
LaPrade
Laughridge, William R (See Cylinder & Slide Inc)
Leapers, Inc.
List Precision Engineering
Lodewick, Walter H.
Logdewood Mfg.
Long, George F.
Mandall Shooting Supplies Inc.
Markell,Inc.
Martin's Gun Shop
McCormick Corp., Chip
MCS, Inc.
Merkuria Ltd.
Mid-America Recreation, Inc.
Morrow, Bud
Mo's Competitor Supplies (See MCS, Inc.)
North Star West
Northwest Arms
Nu-Line Guns,Inc.
Numrich Gun Parts Corporation
Nygord Precision Products, Inc.
Olathe Gun Shop
Olympic Arms Inc.
P.S.M.G. Gun Co.
Pacific Armament Corp
Pennsylvania Gun Parts Inc
Performance Specialists
Peter Dyson & Son Ltd.
Peterson Gun Shop, Inc., A.W.
Ranch Products
Randco UK
Ravell Ltd.
Retting, Inc., Martin B
Romain's Custom Guns, Inc.
Ruger (See Sturm, Ruger & Co., Inc.)
Rutgers Book Center
S&S Firearms
Sabatti SPA
Samco Global Arms, Inc.
Sarco, Inc.
Shockley, Harold H.
Shootin' Shack
Silver Ridge Gun Shop (See Goodwin, Fred)
Simmons Gun Repair, Inc.
Smires, C. L.
Smith & Wesson
Southern Ammunition Co., Inc.
Sportsmen's Exchange & Western Gun Traders, Inc.
Springfield Sporters, Inc.
Springfield, Inc.
Steyr Mannlicher GmbH P Co KG
STI International
Strayer-Voigt, Inc.
Sturm Ruger & Co. Inc.
Sunny Hill Enterprises, Inc.
T&S Industries, Inc.
Tank's Rifle Shop
Tarnhelm Supply Co., Inc.
Terry K. Kopp Professional Gunsmithing
The A.W. Peterson Gun Shop, Inc.
The Gun Room Press
The Gun Shop
The Gun Works
The Southern Armory
The Swampfire Shop (See Peterson Gun Shop, Inc.)
VAM Distribution Co. LLC
Vektor USA
Vintage Arms, Inc.
W. Waller & Son, Inc.
W.C. Wolff Co.
Walker Arms Co., Inc.
Wescombe, Bill (See North Star West)
Whitestone Lumber Corp.
Wild West Guns
Williams Mfg. of Oregon
Winchester Sutler, Inc., The
Wise Guns, Dale
Wisners Inc/Twin Pine Armory

GUNS & GUN PARTS, REPLICA & ANTIQUE

Ackerman & Co.
Ahlman Guns
Armi San Paolo
Auto-Ordnance Corp.
Ballard Rifle & Cartridge Co., LLC
Bear Mountain Gun & Tool
Billings Gunsmiths
Bob's Gun Shop
Buffalo Arms Co.
Cache La Poudre Rifleworks
Campbell, Dick
Cash Mfg. Co., Inc.
CBC-BRAZIL
CCL Security Products
Chambers Flintlocks Ltd., Jim
Chicasaw Gun Works
Cimarron F.A. Co.
Cogar's Gunsmithing
Cole's Gun Works
Colonial Repair
Colt Blackpowder Arms Co.
Colt's Mfg. Co., Inc.
Custom Riflestocks, Inc., Michael M. Kokolus
Custom Single Shot Rifles
David R. Chicoine
Delhi Gun House
Delta Arms Ltd.
Dilliott Gunsmithing, Inc.
Dixie Gun Works
Dixon Muzzleloading Shop, Inc.
Ed's Gun House
Euroarms of America, Inc.
Flintlocks, Etc.
George E. Mathews & Son, Inc.
Getz Barrel Co.
Golden Age Arms Co.
Goodwin's Gun Shop
Groenewold, John
Gun Hunter Books (See Gun Hunter Trading Co.)
Gun Hunter Trading Co.
Hastings
Heidenstrom Bullets
Hunkeler, A (See Buckskin Machine Works)
IAR Inc.
Imperial Miniature Armory
Ithaca Classic Doubles
Jack First, Inc.
Ken Starnes Gunmaker
Kokolus, Michael M. (See Custom Riflestocks In)
L&R Lock Co.
Leonard Day
List Precision Engineering
Lock's Philadelphia Gun Exchange
Logdewood Mfg.
Lone Star Rifle Company
Lucas, Edward E
Mandall Shooting Supplies Inc.
Martin's Gun Shop
Mathews & Son, Inc., George E.
Mid-America Recreation, Inc.
Mountain State Muzzleloading Supplies, Inc.
Mowrey Gun Works
Navy Arms Company
Neumann GmbH
North Star West
Numrich Gun Parts Corporation
Olathe Gun Shop
Parker & Sons Shooting Supply
Pasadena Gun Center
Pecatonica River Longrifle
PEM's Mfg. Co.
Peter Dyson & Son Ltd.
Pony Express Sport Shop
R.A. Wells Custom Gunsmith
Randco UK
Ravell Ltd.
Retting, Inc., Martin B
Rutgers Book Center
S&S Firearms
Samco Global Arms, Inc.
Sarco, Inc.
Shootin' Shack
Silver Ridge Gun Shop (See Goodwin, Fred)
Simmons Gun Repair, Inc.
Sklany's Machine Shop
Southern Ammunition Co., Inc.
Starr Trading Co., Jedediah
Stott's Creek Armory, Inc.
Taylor's & Co., Inc.
Tennessee Valley Mfg.
The A.W. Peterson Gun Shop, Inc.
The Gun Room Press
The Gun Works
Tiger-Hunt Gunstocks
Turnbull Restoration, Doug
Upper Missouri Trading Co.
Vintage Industries, Inc.
Vortek Products, Inc.
VTI Gun Parts
Weber & Markin Custom Gunsmiths
Wescombe, Bill (See North Star West)
Whitestone Lumber Corp.
Winchester Sutler, Inc., The

GUNS, AIR

Air Arms
Air Rifle Specialists
Air Venture Airguns
AirForce Airguns
Airrow
Allred Bullet Co.
Arms Corporation of the Philippines
BEC, Inc.
Beeman Precision Airguns
Benjamin/Sheridan Co., Crosman
Brass Eagle, Inc.
Brocock Ltd.
Bryan & Assoc.
BSA Guns Ltd.
Compasseco, Ltd.
Component Concepts, Inc.
Conetrol Scope Mounts
Crosman Airguns
Daisy Outdoor Products
Daystate Ltd.
Domino
Dynamit Nobel-RWS, Inc.
European American Armory Corp (See E.A.A. Corp)
Feinwerkbau Westinger & Altenburger
Gamo USA, Inc.
Gaucher Armes, S.A.
Great Lakes Airguns
Groenewold, John
Hammerli Service-Precision Mac
I.S.S.
IAR Inc.
J.G. Anschutz GmbH & Co. KG
Labanu, Inc.
Leapers, Inc.
List Precision Engineering
Mac-1 Airgun Distributors
Marksman Products
Maryland Paintball Supply
Merkuria Ltd.
Nationwide Airgun Repair
Nygord Precision Products, Inc.
Olympic Arms Inc.
Pardini Armi Srl
Precision Airgun Sales, Inc.
Precision Sales International, Inc.
Ripley Rifles
Robinson, Don
RWS (See US Importer-Dynamit Nobel-RWS, Inc.)
S.G.S. Sporting Guns Srl.
Safari Arms/Schuetzen Pistol Works
Savage Arms, Inc.
Smart Parts
Smith & Wesson
Steyr Mannlicher GmbH P Co KG
Stone Enterprises Ltd.
The A.W. Peterson Gun Shop, Inc.
The Gun Room Press
The Park Rifle Co., Ltd.
Tippman Pneumatics, Inc.
Tristar Sporting Arms, Ltd.
Trooper Walsh
UltraSport Arms, Inc.
Visible Impact Targets
Vortek Products, Inc.
Walther GmbH, Carl
Webley and Scott Ltd.
Weihrauch KG, Hermann
Whiscombe (See U.S. Importer-Pelaire Products)

GUNS, FOREIGN MANUFACTURER U.S. IMPORTER

Accuracy Internationl Precision Rifles (See U.S.)
Accuracy Int'l. North America, Inc.
Ad Hominem
Air Arms
Armas Garbi, S.A.
Armas Kemen S. A. (See U.S. Importers)
Armi Perazzi S.p.A.
Armi San Marco (See U.S. Importers-Taylor's & Co I
Armi Sport (See U.S. Importers-Cape Outfitters)
Arms Corporation of the Philippines
Armscorp USA, Inc.
Arrieta S.L.
Astra Sport, S.A.
Atamec-Bretton
AYA (See U.S. Importer-New England Custom Gun Serv
B.A.C.
B.C. Outdoors
BEC, Inc.
Benelli Armi S.p.A.
Benelli USA Corp
Beretta S.p.A., Pietro
Beretta U.S.A. Corp.
Bernardelli S.p.A., Vincenzo
Bersa S.A.
Bertuzzi (See U.S. Importer-New England Arms Co)
Bill Hanus Birdguns
Blaser Jagdwaffen GmbH
Borovnik KG, Ludwig
Bosis (See U.S. Importer-New England Arms Co.)
Brenneke GmbH
Browning Arms Co.
Bryan & Assoc.
BSA Guns Ltd.
Cabanas (See U.S. Importer-Mandall Shooting Supply
Cabela's
Cape Outfitters
CBC
Chapuis Armes
Churchill (See U.S. Importer-Ellett Bros.)
Conetrol Scope Mounts
Cosmi Americo & Figlio s.n.c.
Crucelegui, Hermanos (See U.S. Importer-Mandall)
Cubic Shot Shell Co., Inc.
Daewoo Precision Industries Ltd.
Dakota (See U.S. Importer-EMF Co., Inc.)
Dakota Arms, Inc.
Daly, Charles (See U.S. Importer)
Davide Pedersoli and Co.
Domino
Dumoulin, Ernest
Eagle Imports, Inc.
EAW (See U.S. Importer-New England Custom Gun Serv
Ed's Gun House
Effebi SNC-Dr. Franco Beretta
EMF Co., Inc.
Eversull Co., Inc.
F.A.I.R.
Fabarm S.p.A.
FEG
Feinwerkbau Westinger & Altenburger
Felk Pistols Inc.
FERLIB
Fiocchi Munizioni S.p.A. (See U.S. Importer-Fiocch
Firearms Co Ltd. / Alpine (See U.S. Importer-Mandall
Firearms International
Flintlocks, Etc.

REFERENCE

PRODUCT & SERVICE DIRECTORY

Franchi S.p.A.
Galaxy Imports Ltd., Inc.
Gamba S.p.A. Societa Armi Bresciane Srl
Gamo (See U.S. Importers-Arms United Corp, Daisy M
Gaucher Armes, S.A.
Gibbs Rifle Co., Inc.
Glock GmbH
Goergen's Gun Shop, Inc.
Griffin & Howe, Inc.
Griffin & Howe, Inc.
Griffin & Howe, Inc.
Grulla Armes
Hammerli Ltd.
Hammerli USA
Hartford (See U.S. Importer-EMF Co. Inc.)
Hartmann & Weiss GmbH
Heckler & Koch, Inc.
Hege Jagd-u. Sporthandels GmbH
Helwan (See U.S. Importer-Interarms)
Holland & Holland Ltd.
Howa Machinery, Ltd.
I.A.B. (See U.S. Importer-Taylor's & Co. Inc.)
IAR Inc.
IGA (See U.S. Importer-Stoeger Industries)
Ignacio Ugartechea S.A.
Imperial Magnum Corp.
Imperial Miniature Armory
Import Sports Inc.
Inter Ordnance of America LP
Intrac Arms International
J.G. Anschutz GmbH & Co. KG
JSL Ltd (See U.S. Importer-Specialty Shooters)
K. Eversull Co., Inc.
Kimar (See U.S. Importer-IAR,Inc)
Korth Germany GmbH
Krico Deutschland GmbH
Krieghoff Gun Co., H.
Lakefield Arms Ltd. (See Savage Arms, Inc.)
Lapua Ltd.
Laurona Armas Eibar, S.A.L.
Lebeau-Courally
Lever Arms Service Ltd.
Llama Gabilondo Y Cia
London Guns Ltd.
M. Thys (See U.S. Importer-Champlin Firearms Inc)
Magtech Ammunition Co. Inc.
Mandall Shooting Supplies Inc.
Marocchi F.lli S.p.A
Mauser Werke Oberndorf Waffensysteme GmbH
McCann Industries
MEC-Gar S.R.L.
Merkel
Miltex, Inc
Morini (See U.S. Importers-Mandall Shooting Supply)
New England Custom Gun Service
New SKB Arms Co.
Norica, Avnda Otaola
Norinco
Norma Precision AB (See U.S. Importers-Dynamit)
Northwest Arms
Nygord Precision Products, Inc.
OK Weber, Inc.
Para-Ordnance Mfg., Inc.
Pardini Armi Srl
Perugini Visini & Co. S.r.l.
Peters Stahl GmbH
Pietta (See U.S. Importers-Navy Arms Co, Taylor's
Piotti (See U.S. Importer-Moore & Co, Wm. Larkin)
PMC/Eldorado Cartridge Corp.
Powell & Son (Gunmakers) Ltd., William
Prairie Gun Works
Ramon B. Gonzalez Guns
Rizzini F.lli (See U.S. Importers-Moore & C England)
Rizzini SNC
Robinson Armament Co.
Rossi Firearms
Rottweil Compe
Rutten (See U.S. Importer-Labanu Inc)
RWS (See US Importer-Dynamit Nobel-RWS, Inc.)
S.A.R.L. G. Granger
S.I.A.C.E. (See U.S. Importer-IAR Inc)
Sabatti SPA
Sako Ltd (See U.S. Importer-Stoeger Industries)
San Marco (See U.S. Importers-Cape Outfitters-EMF
Sarsilmaz Shotguns - Turkey (see B.C. Outdoors)
Sauer (See U.S. Importers-Paul Co., The, Sigarms I
Savage Arms (Canada), Inc.
SIG
Sigarms, Inc.
SIG-Sauer (See U.S. Importer-Sigarms Inc.)
SKB Shotguns
Small Arms Specialists
Societa Armi Bresciane Srl (See U.S. Importer-Cape
Sphinx Systems Ltd.
Springfield Armory
Springfield, Inc.
Starr Trading Co., Jedediah
Steyr Mannlicher GmbH P Co KG
T.F.C. S.p.A.
Tanfoglio Fratelli S.r.l.
Tanner (See U.S. Importer-Mandall Shooting Supply)
Tar-Hunt Custom Rifles, Inc.
Taurus International Firearms (See U.S. Importer)
Taurus S.A. Forjas
Taylor's & Co., Inc.
Techno Arms (See U.S. Importer-Auto-Ordnance Corp
The A.W. Peterson Gun Shop, Inc.
Tikka (See U.S. Importer-Stoeger Industries)
TOZ (See U.S. Importer-Nygord Precision Products)
Ugartechea S. A., Ignacio
Ultralux (See U.S. Importer-Keng's Firearms)
Unique/M.A.P.F.
Valtro USA, Inc
Verney-Carron
Voere-KGH GmbH
Walther GmbH, Carl
Weatherby, Inc.
Webley and Scott Ltd.
Weihrauch KG, Hermann
Westley Richards & Co.
Whiscombe (See U.S. Importer-Pelaire Products)
Wolf (See J.R. Distributing)
Yankee Gunsmith "Just Glocks"
Zabala Hermanos S.A.

GUNS, FOREIGN-IMPORTER

Accuracy International
AcuSport Corporation
Air Rifle Specialists
American Frontier Firearms Mfg., Inc
Auto-Ordnance Corp.
B.A.C.
B.C. Outdoors
Bell's Legendary Country Wear
Benelli USA Corp
Big Bear Arms & Sporting Goods, Inc.
Bill Hanus Birdguns
Bridgeman Products
British Sporting Arms
Browning Arms Co.
Cape Outfitters
Century International Arms, Inc.
Champion Shooters' Supply
Champion's Choice, Inc.
Chapuis USA
Cimarron F.A. Co.
CVA
CZ USA
Dixie Gun Works
Dynamit Nobel-RWS, Inc.
E&L Mfg., Inc.
E.A.A. Corp.
Eagle Imports, Inc.
Ellett Bros.
EMF Co., Inc.
Euroarms of America, Inc.
Eversull Co., Inc.
Fiocchi of America, Inc.
Flintlocks, Etc.
Franzen International,Inc (See U.S. Importer for)
G.U. Inc (See U.S. Importer for New SKB Arms Co.)
Galaxy Imports Ltd., Inc.
Gamba, USA
Gamo USA, Inc.
Giacomo Sporting USA
Glock, Inc.
Gremmel Enterprises
GSI, Inc.
Guncraft Books (See Guncraft Sports Inc.)
Guncraft Sports Inc.
Gunsite Custom Shop
Gunsite Training Center
Hammerli USA
I.S.S.
IAR Inc.
Imperial Magnum Corp.
Imperial Miniature Armory
Import Sports Inc.
Intrac Arms International
K. Eversull Co., Inc.
K.B.I. Inc.
Kemen America
Keng's Firearms Specialty, Inc./US Tactical Systems
Krieghoff International,Inc.
Labanu, Inc.
Legacy Sports International
Lion Country Supply
London Guns Ltd.
Magnum Research, Inc.
Marx, Harry (See U.S. Importer for FERLIB)
MCS, Inc.
MEC-Gar U.S.A., Inc.
Navy Arms Company
New England Arms Co.
Nygord Precision Products, Inc.
OK Weber, Inc.
P.S.M.G. Gun Co.
Para-Ordnance, Inc.
Parker Reproductions
Pelaire Products
Perazzi U.S.A. Inc.
Powell Agency, William
Precision Sales International, Inc.
Rocky Mountain Armoury
S.D. Meacham
Safari Arms/Schuetzen Pistol Works
Samco Global Arms, Inc.
Savage Arms, Inc.
Scott Fine Guns Inc., Thad
Sigarms, Inc.
SKB Shotguns
Small Arms Specialists
Southern Ammunition Co., Inc.
Specialty Shooters Supply, Inc.
Springfield, Inc.
Stoeger Industries
Stone Enterprises Ltd.
Swarovski Optik North America Ltd.
Tar-Hunt Custom Rifles, Inc.
Taurus Firearms, Inc.
Taylor's & Co., Inc.
The A.W. Peterson Gun Shop, Inc.
The Gun Shop
The Orvis Co.
The Paul Co.
Track of the Wolf, Inc.
Traditions Performance Firearms
Tristar Sporting Arms, Ltd.
Trooper Walsh
U.S. Importer-Wm. Larkin Moore
VAM Distribution Co. LLC
Vektor USA
Vintage Arms, Inc.
VTI Gun Parts
Westley Richards Agency USA (See U.S. Importer for
Wingshooting Adventures

GUNS, SURPLUS, PARTS & AMMUNITION

Ahlman Guns
Alpha 1 Drop Zone
Armscorp USA, Inc.
Arundel Arms & Ammunition, Inc., A.
B.A.C.
Bondini Paolo
Cambos Outdoorsman
Century International Arms, Inc.
Cole's Gun Works
Conetrol Scope Mounts
Delta Arms Ltd.
Ed's Gun House
First Inc., Jack
Fleming Firearms
Forrest Inc., Tom
Garcia National Gun Traders, Inc.
Goodwin's Gun Shop
Gun City
Gun Hunter Books (See Gun Hunter Trading Co.)
Gun Hunter Trading Co.
Hank's Gun Shop
Hege Jagd-u. Sporthandels GmbH
Jackalope Gun Shop
Ken Starnes Gunmaker
LaRocca Gun Works
Lever Arms Service Ltd.
Log Cabin Sport Shop
Martin's Gun Shop
Navy Arms Company
Nevada Pistol Academy, Inc.
Northwest Arms
Numrich Gun Parts Corporation
Oil Rod and Gun Shop
Olathe Gun Shop
Paragon Sales & Services, Inc.
Pasadena Gun Center
Power Plus Enterprises, Inc.
Ravell Ltd.
Retting, Inc., Martin B
Rutgers Book Center
Samco Global Arms, Inc.
Sarco, Inc.
Shootin' Shack
Silver Ridge Gun Shop (See Goodwin, Fred)
Simmons Gun Repair, Inc.
Sportsmen's Exchange & Western Gun Traders, Inc.
Springfield Sporters, Inc.
T.F.C. S.p.A.
Tarnhelm Supply Co., Inc.
The A.W. Peterson Gun Shop, Inc.
The Gun Room Press
Thurston Sports, Inc.
Williams Shootin' Iron Service, The Lynx-Line

GUNS, U.S. MADE

3-Ten Corp.
A.A. Arms, Inc.
Accu-Tek
Ace Custom 45's, Inc.
Acra-Bond Laminates
Ad Hominem
Airrow
Allred Bullet Co.
American Derringer Corp.
American Frontier Firearms Mfg., Inc
AR-7 Industries, LLC
ArmaLite, Inc.
Armscorp USA, Inc.
A-Square Co.
Austin & Halleck, Inc.
Autauga Arms, Inc.
Auto-Ordnance Corp.
Baer Custom Inc., Les
Ballard Rifle & Cartridge Co., LLC
Barrett Firearms Manufacturer, Inc.
Bar-Sto Precision Machine
Benjamin/Sheridan Co., Crosman
Beretta S.p.A., Pietro
Beretta U.S.A. Corp.
Big Bear Arms & Sporting Goods, Inc.
Bill Russ Trading Post
Bond Arms, Inc.
Borden Ridges Rimrock Stocks
Borden Rifles Inc.
Brockman's Custom Gunsmithing
Brown Co., E. Arthur
Brown Products, Inc., Ed
Browning Arms Co.
Bryan & Assoc.
Bushmaster Firearms
C. Sharps Arms Co. Inc./Montana Armory
Cabela's
Calico Light Weapon Systems
Cambos Outdoorsman
Cape Outfitters
Casull Arms Corp.
CCL Security Products
Century Gun Dist. Inc.
Champlin Firearms, Inc.
Charter 2000
Cobra Enterprises, Inc.
Colt's Mfg. Co., Inc.
Competitor Corp., Inc.
Conetrol Scope Mounts
Connecticut Shotgun Mfg. Co.
Connecticut Valley Classics (See CVC, BPI)
Cooper Arms
Crosman Airguns
Cumberland Arms
Cumberland Mountain Arms
CVA
Daisy Outdoor Products
Dakota Arms, Inc.
Dan Wesson Firearms
Dayton Traister
Dixie Gun Works
Downsizer Corp.
DS Arms, Inc.
DunLyon R&D Inc.
E&L Mfg., Inc.
E. Arthur Brown Co.
Eagle Arms, Inc. (See ArmaLite, Inc.)
Ed Brown Products, Inc.
Emerging Technologies, Inc. (See Laseraim Technologies, Inc.)
Entre`prise Arms, Inc.
Essex Arms
Excel Industries Inc.
F.I., Inc. - High Standard Mfg. Co.
Fletcher-Bidwell, LLC.
FN Manufacturing
Fort Worth Firearms
Freedom Arms, Inc.
Fulton Armory
Galena Industries AMT

REFERENCE

PRODUCT & SERVICE DIRECTORY

Garcia National Gun Traders, Inc.
Gary Reeder Custom Guns
Genecco Gun Works
Gentry Custom Gunmaker, David
George Hoenig, Inc.
George Madis Winchester Consultants
Gibbs Rifle Co., Inc.
Gil Hebard Guns Inc.
Gilbert Equipment Co., Inc.
Goergen's Gun Shop, Inc.
Goodwin's Gun Shop
Granite Mountain Arms, Inc.
Grayback Wildcats
Gunsite Custom Shop
Gunsite Gunsmithy (See Gunsite Custom Shop)
H&R 1871.LLC
Hammans, Charles E.
Hammerli USA
Harrington & Richardson (See H&R 1871, Inc.)
Harris Gunworks
Hart & Son, Inc.
Hatfield Gun
Hawken Shop, The (See Dayton Traister)
Heritage Firearms (See Heritage Mfg., Inc.)
Heritage Manufacturing, Inc.
Hesco-Meprolight
High Precision
Hi-Point Firearms/MKS Supply
HJS Arms, Inc.
H-S Precision, Inc.
Hutton Rifle Ranch
IAR Inc.
Imperial Miniature Armory
Israel Arms International, Inc.
Ithaca Classic Doubles
Ithaca Gun Company LLC
J.P. Enterprises Inc.
Jim Norman Custom Gunstocks
John Rigby & Co.
John's Custom Leather
K.B.I. Inc.
Kahr Arms
Kehr, Roger
Kelbly, Inc.
Kel-Tec CNC Industries, Inc.
Kimber of America, Inc.
Knight Rifles
Knight's Mfg. Co.
Kolar
L.A.R. Mfg., Inc.
L.W. Seecamp Co., Inc.
LaFrance Specialties
Lakefield Arms Ltd. (See Savage Arms, Inc.)
Laseraim Technologies, Inc.
Lever Arms Service Ltd.
Ljutic Industries, Inc.
Lock's Philadelphia Gun Exchange
Lomont Precision Bullets
Lone Star Rifle Company
Mag-Na-Port International, Inc.
Magnum Research, Inc.
Mandall Shooting Supplies Inc.
Marlin Firearms Co.
Maverick Arms, Inc.
McBros Rifle Co.
McCann Industries
Mid-America Recreation, Inc.
Miller Arms, Inc.
MKS Supply, Inc. (See Hi-Point Firearms)
MOA Corporation
Montana Armory, Inc .(See C. Sharps Arms Co. Inc.)
MPI Stocks
Navy Arms Company
NCP Products, Inc.
New Ultra Light Arms, LLC
Noreen, Peter H.
North American Arms, Inc.
North Star West
Northwest Arms
Nowlin Mfg. Co.
Olympic Arms Inc.
Oregon Arms, Inc. (See Rogue Rifle Co., Inc.)
P&M Sales & Services, LLC
Parker & Sons Shooting Supply
Parker Gun Finishes
Phillips & Rogers, Inc.
Phoenix Arms
Precision Small Arms Inc.
ProWare, Inc.
Ramon B. Gonzalez Guns
Rapine Bullet Mould Mfg. Co.
Remington Arms Co., Inc.
Robinson Armament Co.
Rock River Arms
Rocky Mountain Arms, Inc.
Rogue Rifle Co., Inc.
Rogue River Rifleworks
Rohrbaugh
Romain's Custom Guns, Inc.
RPM
Ruger (See Sturm, Ruger & Co., Inc.)
Safari Arms/Schuetzen Pistol Works
Savage Arms (Canada), Inc.
Searcy Enterprises
Sharps Arms Co., Inc., C.
Shiloh Rifle Mfg.
Sklany's Machine Shop
Small Arms Specialists
Smith & Wesson
Sound Technology
Spencer's Rifle Barrels, Inc.
Springfield Armory
Springfield, Inc.
SSK Industries
STI International
Stoeger Industries
Strayer-Voigt, Inc.
Sturm Ruger & Co. Inc.
Sunny Hill Enterprises, Inc.
T&S Industries, Inc.
Taconic Firearms Ltd., Perry Lane
Tank's Rifle Shop
Tar-Hunt Custom Rifles, Inc.
Taurus Firearms, Inc.
Texas Armory (See Bond Arms, Inc.)
The A.W. Peterson Gun Shop, Inc.
The Gun Room Press
The Gun Works
Thompson/Center Arms
Tristar Sporting Arms, Ltd.
U.S. Fire Arms Mfg. Co., Inc.
U.S. Repeating Arms Co., Inc.
Visible Impact Targets
Volquartsen Custom Ltd.
Wallace, Terry
Weatherby, Inc.
Wescombe, Bill (See North Star West)
Wessinger Custom Guns & Engraving
Whildin & Sons Ltd, E.H.
Whitestone Lumber Corp.
Wichita Arms, Inc.
Wichita Arms, Inc.
Wildey, Inc.
Wilsom Combat
Z-M Weapons

GUNSMITH SCHOOL

American Gunsmithing Institute
Bull Mountain Rifle Co.
Colorado Gunsmithing Academy
Colorado School of Trades
Cylinder & Slide, Inc., William R. Laughridge
Lassen Community College, Gunsmithing Dept.
Laughridge, William R (See Cylinder & Slide Inc)
Log Cabin Sport Shop
Modern Gun Repair School
Montgomery Community College
Murray State College
North American Correspondence Schools The Gun Pro
Nowlin Mfg. Co.
NRI Gunsmith School
Pennsylvania Gunsmith School
Piedmont Community College
Pine Technical College
Professional Gunsmiths of America
Smith & Wesson
Southeastern Community College
Spencer's Rifle Barrels, Inc.
Trinidad St. Jr. Col. Gunsmith Dept.
Wright's Gunstock Blanks
Yavapai College

GUNSMITH SUPPLIES, TOOLS & SERVICES

Ace Custom 45's, Inc.
Actions by "T" Teddy Jacobson
Alaskan Silversmith, The
Aldis Gunsmithing & Shooting Supply
Alley Supply Co.
Allred Bullet Co.
Alpec Team, Inc.
American Frontier Firearms Mfg., Inc
American Gunsmithing Institute
Baer Custom Inc., Les
Ballard Rifle & Cartridge Co., LLC
Bar-Sto Precision Machine
Bauska Barrels
Bear Mountain Gun & Tool
Bengtson Arms Co., L.
Bill's Gun Repair
Blue Ridge Machinery & Tools, Inc.
Boyds' Gunstock Industries, Inc.
Break-Free, Inc.
Briley Mfg. Inc.
Brockman's Custom Gunsmithing
Brown Products, Inc., Ed
Brownells, Inc.
Bryan & Assoc.
B-Square Company, Inc.
Buffer Technologies
Bull Mountain Rifle Co.
Bushmaster Firearms
C.S. Van Gorden & Son, Inc.
Carbide Checkering Tools (See J&R Engineering)
Carter's Gun Shop
Caywood, Shane J.
CBC-BRAZIL
Chapman Manufacturing Co.
Chicasaw Gun Works
Choate Machine & Tool Co., Inc.
Ciener Inc., Jonathan Arthur
Colonial Arms, Inc.
Colorado School of Trades
Colt's Mfg. Co., Inc.
Conetrol Scope Mounts
Corbin Mfg. & Supply, Inc.
CRR, Inc./Marble's Inc.
Cumberland Arms
Cumberland Mountain Arms
Custom Checkering Service, Kathy Forster
D'Arcy Echols & Co.
Dem-Bart Checkering Tools, Inc.
Dixie Gun Works
Dixie Gun Works
Dremel Mfg. Co.
Du-Lite Corp.
Efficient Machinery Co.
Entre`prise Arms, Inc.
Erhardt, Dennis
Evolution Gun Works Inc.
Faith Associates
Faloon Industries, Inc.
FERLIB
Fisher, Jerry A.
Forgreens Tool & Mfg., Inc.
Forkin, Ben (See Belt MTN Arms)
Forster, Kathy (See Custom Checkering)
Gentry Custom Gunmaker, David
Goodwin's Gun Shop
Grace Metal Products
Gre-Tan Rifles
Gruning Precision Inc.
Gunline Tools
Half Moon Rifle Shop
Hammond Custom Guns Ltd.
Hastings
Henriksen Tool Co., Inc.
High Performance International
High Precision
Holland's Gunsmithing
Ironsighter Co.
Israel Arms International, Inc.
Ivanoff, Thomas G. (See Tom's Gun Repair)
J&R Engineering
J&S Heat Treat
J. Dewey Mfg. Co., Inc.
Jantz Supply
Jenkins Recoil Pads, Inc.
JGS Precision Tool Mfg., LLC
Jonathan Arthur Ciener, Inc.
Jones Custom Products, Neil A.
Kailua Custom Guns Inc.
Kasenit Co., Inc.
Kleinendorst, K. W.
Korzinek Riflesmith, J.
LaBounty Precision Reboring, Inc
LaFrance Specialties
Laurel Mountain Forge
Lea Mfg. Co.
Lee Supplies, Mark
List Precision Engineering
Lock's Philadelphia Gun Exchange
London Guns Ltd.
Mahovsky's Metalife
Marble Arms (See CRR, Inc./Marble's Inc.)
Mark Lee Supplies
Marsh, Mike
Martin's Gun Shop
McFarland, Stan
Menck, Gunsmith Inc., T.W.
Metalife Industries (See Mahovsky's Metalife)
Michael's Antiques
Micro Sight Co.
Midway Arms, Inc.
MMC
Mo's Competitor Supplies (See MCS, Inc.)
Mowrey's Guns & Gunsmithing
Neil A. Jones Custom Products
New England Custom Gun Service
Ole Frontier Gunsmith Shop
Olympic Arms Inc.
Parker & Sons Shooting Supply
Parker Gun Finishes
Paulsen Gunstocks
PEM's Mfg. Co.
Perazone-Gunsmith, Brian
Peter Dyson & Son Ltd.
Power Custom, Inc.
Practical Tools, Inc.
Precision Specialties
R.A. Wells Custom Gunsmith
Ranch Products
Ransom International Corp.
Reardon Products
Rice, Keith (See White Rock Tool & Die)
Robert Valade Engraving
Rocky Mountain Arms, Inc.
Romain's Custom Guns, Inc.
Royal Arms Gunstocks
Rusteprufe Laboratories
Sharp Shooter Supply
Shooter's Choice Gun Care
Simmons Gun Repair, Inc.
Smith Abrasives, Inc.
Southern Bloomer Mfg. Co.
Spencer Reblue Service
Spencer's Rifle Barrels, Inc.
Spradlin's
Starr Trading Co., Jedediah
Starrett Co., L. S.
Stiles Custom Guns
Stoney Point Products, Inc.
Sullivan, David S .(See Westwind Rifles Inc.)
Sunny Hill Enterprises, Inc.
T&S Industries, Inc.
T.W. Menck Gunsmith Inc.
Tank's Rifle Shop
Texas Platers Supply Co.
The A.W. Peterson Gun Shop, Inc.
The Dutchman's Firearms, Inc.
The Gun Works
The NgraveR Co.
The Robar Co.'s, Inc.
Theis, Terry
Tom's Gun Repair, Thomas G. Ivanoff
Track of the Wolf, Inc.
Trinidad St. Jr. Col. Gunsmith Dept.
Trulock Tool
Turnbull Restoration, Doug
United States Products Co.
Van Gorden & Son Inc., C. S.
Venco Industries, Inc. (See Shooter's Choice Gun Care)
W.C. Wolff Co.
Warne Manufacturing Co.
Washita Mountain Whetstone Co.
Weigand Combat Handguns, Inc.
Wessinger Custom Guns & Engraving
White Rock Tool & Die
Wilcox All-Pro Tools & Supply
Wild West Guns
Will-Burt Co.
Williams Gun Sight Co.
Williams Shootin' Iron Service, The Lynx-Line
Willow Bend
Windish, Jim
Winter, Robert M.
Wise Guns, Dale
Wright's Gunstock Blanks
Yavapai College
Ziegel Engineering

HANDGUN ACCESSORIES

"Su-Press-On", Inc.
A.A. Arms, Inc.
Ace Custom 45's, Inc.
Action Direct, Inc.
ADCO Sales, Inc.
Aimtech Mount Systems
Ajax Custom Grips, Inc.
Alpha 1 Drop Zone
American Derringer Corp.
American Frontier Firearms Mfg., Inc
Arms Corporation of the Philippines
Astra Sport, S.A.
Autauga Arms, Inc.
Badger Creek Studio
Baer Custom Inc., Les
Bagmaster Mfg., Inc.
Bar-Sto Precision Machine
Behlert Precision, Inc.
Berry's Mfg., Inc.
Bill's Custom Cases
Blue and Gray Products Inc. (See Ox-Yoke Originals)
Bond Custom Firearms
Bowen Classic Arms Corp.
Bridgeman Products
Broken Gun Ranch
Brooks Tactical Systems-Agrip
Brown Products, Inc., Ed
Bushmaster Hunting & Fishing
Butler Creek Corp.
Cannon Safe, Inc.

Product & Service Directory

Centaur Systems, Inc.
Central Specialties Ltd (See Trigger Lock Division
Charter 2000
Cheyenne Pioneer Products
Chicasaw Gun Works
Ciener Inc., Jonathan Arthur
Clark Custom Guns, Inc.
Classic Arms Company
Conetrol Scope Mounts
Crimson Trace Lasers
CRR, Inc./Marble's Inc.
Cylinder & Slide, Inc., William R. Laughridge
D&L Industries (See D.J. Marketing)
D.J. Marketing
Dade Screw Machine Products
Delhi Gun House
DeSantis Holster & Leather Goods, Inc.
Dixie Gun Works
Doskocil Mfg. Co., Inc.
E&L Mfg., Inc.
E. Arthur Brown Co.
E.A.A. Corp.
Ed Brown Products, Inc.
Essex Arms
European American Armory Corp (See E.A.A. Corp)
Evolution Gun Works Inc.
F.I., Inc. - High Standard Mfg. Co.
Faloon Industries, Inc.
Federal Arms Corp. of America
Feinwerkbau Westinger & Altenburger
Fisher Custom Firearms
Fleming Firearms
Freedom Arms, Inc.
G.G. & G.
Galati International
GALCO International Ltd.
Garcia National Gun Traders, Inc.
Garthwaite Pistolsmith, Inc., Jim
Gil Hebard Guns Inc.
Gilmore Sports Concepts
Glock, Inc.
Goodwin's Gun Shop
Gould & Goodrich
Gremmel Enterprises
Gun-Alert
Gun-Ho Sports Cases
H.K.S. Products
Hafner World Wide, Inc.
Hammerli USA
Heinie Specialty Products
Henigson & Associates, Steve
Hill Speed Leather, Ernie
Hi-Point Firearms/MKS Supply
Hobson Precision Mfg. Co.
Hoppe's Div. Penguin Industries, Inc.
H-S Precision, Inc.
Hunter Co., Inc.
Impact Case & Container, Inc.
J.P. Enterprises Inc.
Jarvis, Inc.
JB Custom
Jeffredo Gunsight
Jim Noble Co.
John's Custom Leather
Jonathan Arthur Ciener, Inc.
Kalispel Case Line
KeeCo Impressions, Inc.
King's Gun Works
KK Air International (See Impact Case & Container Co.)
L&S Technologies Inc. (See Aimtech Mount Systems)
Lakewood Products LLC
LaserMax, Inc.
Loch Leven Industries/Convert-A-Pell
Lock's Philadelphia Gun Exchange
Lohman Mfg. Co., Inc.
Mag-Na-Port International, Inc.
Magnolia Sports,Inc.
Mag-Pack Corp.
Mahony, Philip Bruce
Mandall Shooting Supplies Inc.
Marble Arms (See CRR, Inc./Marble's Inc.)
Markell,Inc.
McCormick Corp., Chip
MEC-Gar S.R.L.
Menck, Gunsmith Inc., T.W.
Merkuria Ltd.
Middlebrooks Custom Shop
Millett Sights
Mogul Co./Life Jacket
MTM Molded Products Co., Inc.
No-Sho Mfg. Co.
Numrich Gun Parts Corporation
Omega Sales
Outdoor Sports Headquarters, Inc.
Ox-Yoke Originals, Inc.
Pachmayr Div. Lyman Products
Pager Pal
Palmer Security Products
Parker & Sons Shooting Supply
Pearce Grip, Inc.
Perazone-Gunsmith, Brian
Phoenix Arms
Practical Tools, Inc.
Precision Small Arms Inc.
Protektor Model
Ram-Line ATK
Ranch Products
Ransom International Corp.
Ringler Custom Leather Co.
RPM
Seecamp Co. Inc., L. W.
Simmons Gun Repair, Inc.
Sound Technology
Southern Bloomer Mfg. Co.
Springfield Armory
Springfield, Inc.
SSK Industries
Sturm Ruger & Co. Inc.
T.F.C. S.p.A.
Tactical Defense Institute
Tanfoglio Fratelli S.r.l.
The A.W. Peterson Gun Shop, Inc.
The Concealment Shop, Inc.
The Gun Works
The Keller Co.
The Protector Mfg. Co., Inc.
Thompson/Center Arms
Trigger Lock Division / Central Specialties Ltd.
Trijicon, Inc.
Triple-K Mfg. Co., Inc.
Truglo, Inc.
Tyler Manufacturing & Distributing
United States Products Co.
Universal Sports
Volquartsen Custom Ltd.
W. Waller & Son, Inc.
W.C. Wolff Co.
Warne Manufacturing Co.
Weigand Combat Handguns, Inc.
Wessinger Custom Guns & Engraving
Western Design (See Alpha Gunsmith Division)
Whitestone Lumber Corp.
Wild West Guns
Williams Gun Sight Co.
Wilsom Combat
Yankee Gunsmith "Just Glocks"
Ziegel Engineering

HANDGUN GRIPS

A.A. Arms, Inc.
African Import Co.
Ahrends, Kim (See Custom Firearms, Inc)
Ajax Custom Grips, Inc.
Altamont Co.
American Derringer Corp.
American Frontier Firearms Mfg., Inc
American Gripcraft
Arms Corporation of the Philippines
Art Jewel Enterprises Ltd.
Baelder, Harry
Baer Custom Inc., Les
Big Bear Arms & Sporting Goods, Inc.
Bob's Gun Shop
Boone Trading Co., Inc.
Boone's Custom Ivory Grips, Inc.
Boyds' Gunstock Industries, Inc.
Brooks Tactical Systems-Agrip
Brown Products, Inc., Ed
Clark Custom Guns, Inc.
Cole-Grip
Colonial Repair
Crimson Trace Lasers
Custom Firearms (See Ahrends, Kim)
Cylinder & Slide, Inc., William R. Laughridge
Dixie Gun Works
E.A.A. Corp.
EMF Co., Inc.
Essex Arms
European American Armory Corp (See E.A.A. Corp)
F.I., Inc. - High Standard Mfg. Co.
Faloon Industries, Inc.
Feinwerkbau Westinger & Altenburger
Fibron Products, Inc.
Fisher Custom Firearms
Forrest Inc., Tom
Garthwaite Pistolsmith, Inc., Jim
Goodwin's Gun Shop
Herrett's Stocks, Inc.
HIP-GRIP Barami Corp.
Hogue Grips
H-S Precision, Inc.
Huebner, Corey O.
I.S.S.
Israel Arms International, Inc.
John Masen Co. Inc.
KeeCo Impressions, Inc.
Kim Ahrends Custom Firearms, Inc.
Korth Germany GmbH
Lett Custom Grips
Linebaugh Custom Sixguns
Lyman Products Corp.
Mandall Shooting Supplies Inc.
Michaels Of Oregon, Co.
Millett Sights
N.C. Ordnance Co.
Newell, Robert H.
Northern Precision Custom Swaged Bullets
Pachmayr Div. Lyman Products
Pardini Armi Srl
Parker & Sons Shooting Supply
Perazone-Gunsmith, Brian
Pilgrim Pewter,Inc. (See Bell Originals Inc. Sid)
Precision Small Arms Inc.
Radical Concepts
Rosenberg & Son, Jack A
Roy's Custom Grips
Spegel, Craig
Stoeger Industries
Sturm Ruger & Co. Inc.
Sunny Hill Enterprises, Inc.
Tactical Defense Institute
Taurus Firearms, Inc.
The A.W. Peterson Gun Shop, Inc.
Tirelli
Triple-K Mfg. Co., Inc.
Tyler Manufacturing & Distributing
U.S. Fire Arms Mfg. Co., Inc.
Uncle Mike's (See Michaels of Oregon Co.)
Vintage Industries, Inc.
Volquartsen Custom Ltd.
Western Mfg. Co.
Whitestone Lumber Corp.
Wright's Gunstock Blanks

HEARING PROTECTORS

Aero Peltor
Ajax Custom Grips, Inc.
Brown Co., E. Arthur
Browning Arms Co.
Creedmoor Sports, Inc.
David Clark Co., Inc.
Dillon Precision Products, Inc.
Dixie Gun Works
E-A-R, Inc.
Electronic Shooters Protection, Inc.
Gentex Corp.
Goodwin's Gun Shop
Gunsmithing, Inc.
Hoppe's Div. Penguin Industries, Inc.
Kesselring Gun Shop
Mandall Shooting Supplies Inc.
North Specialty Products
Parker & Sons Shooting Supply
Paterson Gunsmithing
Peltor, Inc. (See Aero Peltor)
R.E.T. Enterprises
Ridgeline, Inc.
Rucker Dist. Inc.
Silencio/Safety Direct
Sound Technology
Tactical Defense Institute
The A.W. Peterson Gun Shop, Inc.
The Gun Room Press
Triple-K Mfg. Co., Inc.
Watson Trophy Match Bullets
Whitestone Lumber Corp.

HOLSTERS & LEATHER GOODS

A&B Industries,Inc (See Top-Line USA Inc)
A.A. Arms, Inc.
Action Direct, Inc.
Action Products, Inc.
Aker International, Inc.
AKJ Concealco
Alessi Holsters, Inc.
Arratoonian, Andy (See Horseshoe Leather Products)
Autauga Arms, Inc.
Bagmaster Mfg., Inc.
Baker's Leather Goods, Roy
Bandcor Industries, Div. of Man-Sew Corp.
Bang-Bang Boutique (See Holster Shop, The)
Beretta S.p.A., Pietro
Bianchi International, Inc.
Bond Arms, Inc.
Brocock Ltd.
Brooks Tactical Systems-Agrip
Brown, H. R. (See Silhouette Leathers)
Browning Arms Co.
Bull-X, Inc.
Cape Outfitters
Cathey Enterprises, Inc.
Chace Leather Products
Churchill Glove Co., James
Cimarron F.A. Co.
Classic Old West Styles
Clements' Custom Leathercraft, Chas
Cobra Sport S.r.l.
Colonial Repair
Counter Assault
Delhi Gun House
DeSantis Holster & Leather Goods, Inc.
Dillon Precision Products, Inc.
Dixie Gun Works
Ekol Leather Care
El Paso Saddlery Co.
EMF Co., Inc.
Faust Inc., T. G.
Freedom Arms, Inc.
Gage Manufacturing
GALCO International Ltd.
Garcia National Gun Traders, Inc.
Gil Hebard Guns Inc.
Gilmore Sports Concepts
GML Products, Inc.
Goodwin's Gun Shop
Gould & Goodrich
Gun Leather Limited
Gunfitters
Hafner World Wide, Inc.
HandCrafts Unltd (See Clements' Custom Leather)
Hank's Gun Shop
Heinie Specialty Products
Henigson & Associates, Steve
Hill Speed Leather, Ernie
HIP-GRIP Barami Corp.
Hobson Precision Mfg. Co.
Hogue Grips
Horseshoe Leather Products
Hume, Don
Hunter Co., Inc.
Jim Noble Co.
John's Custom Leather
K.L. Null Holsters Ltd.
Kane Products, Inc.
Kirkpatrick Leather Co.
Kolpin Mfg., Inc.
Korth Germany GmbH
Kramer Handgun Leather
L.A.R. Mfg., Inc.
Lawrence Leather Co.
Lock's Philadelphia Gun Exchange
Lone Star Gunleather
Magnolia Sports,Inc.
Mandall Shooting Supplies Inc.
Markell,Inc.
Marksman Products
Michaels Of Oregon, Co.
Minute Man High Tech Industries
Navy Arms Company
No-Sho Mfg. Co.
Null Holsters Ltd. K.L.
October Country Muzzleloading
Ojala Holsters, Arvo
Oklahoma Leather Products,Inc.
Old West Reproductions,Inc. R.M. Bachman
Pager Pal
Parker & Sons Shooting Supply
Pathfinder Sports Leather
Protektor Model
PWL Gunleather
Ramon B. Gonzalez Guns
Renegade
Ringler Custom Leather Co.
Rogue Rifle Co., Inc.
Safariland Ltd., Inc.
Safety Speed Holster, Inc.
Scharch Mfg., Inc.-Top Brass
Schulz Industries
Second Chance Body Armor
Silhouette Leathers
Smith Saddlery, Jesse W.
Sparks, Milt
Stalker, Inc.
Starr Trading Co., Jedediah
Strong Holster Co.
Stuart, V. Pat
Tabler Marketing
Tactical Defense Institute
Ted Blocker Holsters, Inc.
Tex Shoemaker & Sons, Inc.
Thad Rybka Custom Leather Equipment
The A.W. Peterson Gun Shop, Inc.
The Concealment Shop, Inc.
The Gun Works
The Keller Co.
The Outdoor Connection, Inc.
Torel, Inc.
Triple-K Mfg. Co., Inc.
Tristar Sporting Arms, Ltd.
Tyler Manufacturing & Distributing
Uncle Mike's (See Michaels of Oregon Co.)

Product & Service Directory

Venus Industries
Walt's Custom Leather, Walt Whinnery
Watson Trophy Match Bullets
Westley Richards & Co.
Whinnery, Walt (See Walt's Custom Leather)
Wild Bill's Originals
Wilson Combat

KNIVES & KNIFEMAKER'S SUPPLIES

A.G. Russell Knives, Inc.
Action Direct, Inc.
Adventure 16, Inc.
African Import Co.
Aitor-Cuchilleria Del Norte S.A.
American Target Knives
Art Jewel Enterprises Ltd.
Atlanta Cutlery Corp.
B&D Trading Co., Inc.
Barteaux Machete
Belltown Ltd.
Benchmark Knives (See Gerber Legendary Blades)
Beretta S.p.A., Pietro
Beretta U.S.A. Corp.
Big Bear Arms & Sporting Goods, Inc.
Bill Russ Trading Post
Bill's Custom Cases
Boker USA, Inc.
Boone Trading Co., Inc.
Boone's Custom Ivory Grips, Inc.
Bowen Knife Co., Inc.
Brooks Tactical Systems-Agrip
Browning Arms Co.
Buck Knives, Inc.
Buster's Custom Knives
Camillus Cutlery Co.
Campbell, Dick
Case & Sons Cutlery Co., W R
Chicago Cutlery Co.
Clements' Custom Leathercraft, Chas
Cold Steel Inc.
Coleman Co., Inc.
Compass Industries, Inc.
Crosman Blades (See Coleman Co., Inc.)
CRR, Inc./Marble's Inc.
Cutco Cutlery
damascususa@inteliport.com
Dan's Whetstone Co., Inc.
Deepeeka Exports Pvt. Ltd.
Degen Inc. (See Aristocrat Knives)
Delhi Gun House
DeSantis Holster & Leather Goods, Inc.
Diamond Machining Technology, Inc. (See DMT)
Dixie Gun Works
EdgeCraft Corp., S. Weiner
Empire Cutlery Corp.
Eze-Lap Diamond Prods.
Flitz International Ltd.
Forrest Tool Co.
Forthofer's Gunsmithing & Knifemaking
Fortune Products, Inc.
Frank Knives
Frost Cutlery Co.
Galati International
George Ibberson (Sheffield) Ltd.
Gerber Legendary Blades
Gibbs Rifle Co., Inc.
Glock, Inc.
Golden Age Arms Co.
H&B Forge Co.
Hafner World Wide, Inc.
Hammans, Charles E.
HandCrafts Unltd (See Clements' Custom Leather)
Harris Publications
High North Products, Inc.
Hoppe's Div. Penguin Industries, Inc.
Hunter Co., Inc.
Imperial Schrade Corp.
J.A. Blades, Inc. (See Christopher Firearms Co.)
J.A. Henckels Zwillingswerk Inc.
Jackalope Gun Shop
Jantz Supply
Jenco Sales, Inc.
Jim Blair Engraving
Johnson Wood Products
KA-BAR Knives
Kasenit Co., Inc.
Kershaw Knives
Knifeware, Inc.
Koval Knives
Lamson & Goodnow Mfg. Co.
Lansky Sharpeners
Leapers, Inc.
Leatherman Tool Group, Inc.
Lethal Force Institute (See Police Bookshelf)
Linder Solingen Knives
Mandall Shooting Supplies Inc.
Marble Arms (See CRR, Inc./Marble's Inc.)
Marshall Fish Mfg. Gunsmith Sptg. Co.
Matthews Cutlery
McCann Industries
McCann's Machine & Gun Shop
Molin Industries, Tru-Nord Division
Mountain State Muzzleloading Supplies, Inc.
Normark Corp.
October Country Muzzleloading
Outdoor Edge Cutlery Corp.
Pilgrim Pewter,Inc. (See Bell Originals Inc. Sid)
Plaza Cutlery, Inc.
Police Bookshelf
Queen Cutlery Co.
R&C Knives & Such
R. Murphy Co., Inc.
Randall-Made Knives
Ringler Custom Leather Co.
Robert Valade Engraving
Rodgers & Sons Ltd., Joseph (See George Ibberson)
Scansport, Inc.
Schiffman, Mike
Sheffield Knifemakers Supply, Inc.
Smith Saddlery, Jesse W.
Springfield Armory
Spyderco, Inc.
T.F.C. S.p.A.
The A.W. Peterson Gun Shop, Inc.
The Creative Craftsman, Inc.
The Gun Room
The Gun Works
Theis, Terry
Traditions Performance Firearms
Traditions Performance Firearms
Tru-Balance Knife Co.
United Cutlery Corp.
Utica Cutlery Co.
Venus Industries
W.R. Case & Sons Cutlery Co.
Washita Mountain Whetstone Co.
Weber Jr., Rudolf
Wells Creek Knife & Gun Works
Wenger North America/Precise Int'l
Western Cutlery (See Camillus Cutlery Co.)
Whinnery, Walt (See Walt's Custom Leather)
Wideview Scope Mount Corp.
Wostenholm (See Ibberson [Sheffield] Ltd., George)
Wyoming Knife Corp.

LABELS, BOXES & CARTRIDGE HOLDERS

Ballistic Product, Inc.
Berry's Mfg., Inc.
Brocock Ltd.
Brown Co., E. Arthur
Cabinet Mtn. Outfitters Scents & Lures
Cheyenne Pioneer Products
Del Rey Products
DeSantis Holster & Leather Goods, Inc.
Flambeau Products Corp.
Goodwin's Gun Shop
Hafner World Wide, Inc.
J&J Products, Inc.
Kolpin Mfg., Inc.
Liberty Shooting Supplies
Midway Arms, Inc.
MTM Molded Products Co., Inc.
Pendleton Royal, c/o Swingler Buckland Ltd.
Protektor Model
Ziegel Engineering

LEAD WIRES & WIRE CUTTERS

Ames Metal Products
Big Bore Express
Bullet Swaging Supply, Inc.
Goodwin's Gun Shop
Liberty Metals
Lightning Performance Innovations, Inc.
Montana Precision Swaging
Northern Precision Custom Swaged Bullets
Sport Flite Manufacturing Co.
Star Ammunition, Inc.
Unmussig Bullets, D. L.

LOAD TESTING & PRODUCT TESTING

Ballistic Research
Bitterroot Bullet Co.
Bridgeman Products
Briese Bullet Co., Inc.
Buckskin Bullet Co.
Bull Mountain Rifle Co.
CFVentures
Claybuster Wads & Harvester Bullets
Clearview Products
D&H Precision Tooling
Dead Eye's Sport Center
Defense Training International, Inc.
Duane's Gun Repair (See DGR Custom Rifles)
Gruning Precision Inc.
Gun Hunter Books (See Gun Hunter Trading Co.)
Gun Hunter Trading Co.
H.P. White Laboratory, Inc.
Hank's Gun Shop
Henigson & Associates, Steve
Hutton Rifle Ranch
J&J Sales
Jackalope Gun Shop
Jensen Bullets
L. E. Jurras & Assoc.
Liberty Shooting Supplies
Linebaugh Custom Sixguns
Lomont Precision Bullets
Maionchi-L.M.I.
MAST Technology, Inc.
McMurdo, Lynn (See Specialty Gunsmithing)
Middlebrooks Custom Shop
Modern Gun Repair School
Multiplex International
Northwest Arms
Oil Rod and Gun Shop
Plum City Ballistic Range
R.A. Wells Custom Gunsmith
Ramon B. Gonzalez Guns
Rupert's Gun Shop
Small Custom Mould & Bullet Co.
SOS Products Co. (See Buck Stix-SOS Products Co.)
Spencer's Rifle Barrels, Inc.
Tar-Hunt Custom Rifles, Inc.
Trinidad St. Jr. Col. Gunsmith Dept.
Vulpes Ventures, Inc. Fox Cartridge Division
W. Square Enterprises
X-Spand Target Systems

LOADING BLOCKS, METALLIC & SHOTSHELL

Battenfeld Technologies
Buffalo Arms Co.
Huntington Die Specialties
Jericho Tool & Die Co., Inc.
Sinclair International, Inc.
The A.W. Peterson Gun Shop, Inc.

LUBRISIZERS, DIES & ACCESSORIES

Ballisti-Cast, Inc.
Ben's Machines
Buffalo Arms Co.
Cast Performance Bullet Company
Cooper-Woodward
Corbin Mfg. & Supply, Inc.
GAR
Hart & Son, Inc.
Javelina Lube Products
Lee Precision, Inc.
Lithi Bee Bullet Lube
Lyman Products Corp.
Magma Engineering Co.
RCBS Operations/ATK
Redding Reloading Equipment
SPG LLC
The A.W. Peterson Gun Shop, Inc.
Thompson Bullet Lube Co.
United States Products Co.
WTA Manufacturing

MOULDS & MOULD ACCESSORIES

Ad Hominem
American Products, Inc.
Ballisti-Cast, Inc.
Buffalo Arms Co.
Bullet Swaging Supply, Inc.
Cast Performance Bullet Company
Corbin Mfg. & Supply, Inc.
Davide Pedersoli and Co.
GAR
Huntington Die Specialties
Lee Precision, Inc.
Lyman Products Corp.
Magma Engineering Co.
NEI Handtools, Inc.
Old West Bullet Moulds
Penn Bullets
Rapine Bullet Mould Mfg. Co.
RCBS Operations/ATK
Redding Reloading Equipment
S&S Firearms
Small Custom Mould & Bullet Co.
The A.W. Peterson Gun Shop, Inc.
The Gun Works
Wolf's Western Traders

MUZZLE-LOADING GUNS, BARRELS & EQUIPMENT

Accuracy Unlimited
Ackerman & Co.
Adkins, Luther
Allen Mfg.
Armi San Paolo
Armoury, Inc., The
Austin & Halleck, Inc.
Bauska Barrels
Beaver Lodge (See Fellowes, Ted)
Bentley, John
Big Bore Express
Birdsong & Assoc., W. E.
Black Powder Products
Blount/Outers ATK
Blue and Gray Products Inc. (See Ox-Yoke Originals)
Bridgers Best
Buckskin Bullet Co.
Bullberry Barrel Works, Ltd.
Butler Creek Corp.
Cabela's
Cache La Poudre Rifleworks
California Sights (See Fautheree, Andy)
Cash Mfg. Co., Inc.
Caywood Gunmakers
CBC-BRAZIL
Chambers Flintlocks Ltd., Jim
Chicasaw Gun Works
Cimarron F.A. Co.
Claybuster Wads & Harvester Bullets
Cogar's Gunsmithing
Colonial Repair
Colt Blackpowder Arms Co.
Conetrol Scope Mounts
Cousin Bob's Mountain Products
Cumberland Arms
Cumberland Mountain Arms
Curly Maple Stock Blanks (See Tiger-Hunt)
CVA
Dangler, Homer L.
Davide Pedersoli and Co.
Dayton Traister
deHaas Barrels
Delhi Gun House
Dixie Gun Works
Dixie Gun Works
Dixon Muzzleloading Shop, Inc.
EMF Co., Inc.
Euroarms of America, Inc.
Feken, Dennis
Fellowes, Ted
Flintlocks, Etc.
Fort Hill Gunstocks
Fowler, Bob (See Black Powder Products)
Frontier
Getz Barrel Co.
Goergen's Gun Shop, Inc.
Golden Age Arms Co.
Gonic Arms/North American Arm
Goodwin's Gun Shop
Green Mountain Rifle Barrel Co., Inc.
H&R 1871.LLC
Hastings
Hawken Shop, The (See Dayton Traister)
Hege Jagd-u. Sporthandels GmbH
Hodgdon Powder Co.
Hoppe's Div. Penguin Industries, Inc.
Hornady Mfg. Co.
House of Muskets, Inc., The
Hunkeler, A (See Buckskin Machine Works
IAR Inc.
Impact Case & Container, Inc.
Ironsighter Co.
J. Dewey Mfg. Co., Inc.
Jamison's Forge Works
Jones Co., Dale
K&M Industries, Inc.
Kalispel Case Line
Kennedy Firearms
Knight Rifles

REFERENCE

PRODUCT & SERVICE DIRECTORY

Knight Rifles (See Modern Muzzle Loading, Inc.)
Kolar
L&R Lock Co.
L&S Technologies Inc. (See Aimtech Mount Systems)
Lakewood Products LLC
Legend Products Corp.
Lodgewood Mfg.
Log Cabin Sport Shop
Lothar Walther Precision Tool Inc.
Lyman Products Corp.
Markesbery Muzzle Loaders, Inc.
Marlin Firearms Co.
McCann's Muzzle-Gun Works
Michaels Of Oregon, Co.
Millennium Designed Muzzleloaders
Modern Muzzleloading, Inc.
Mountain State Muzzleloading Supplies, Inc.
Mowrey Gun Works
Mt. Alto Outdoor Products
Navy Arms Company
Newman Gunshop
North Star West
October Country Muzzleloading
Oklahoma Leather Products,Inc.
Olson, Myron
Orion Rifle Barrel Co.
Ox-Yoke Originals, Inc.
Pacific Rifle Co.
Parker & Sons Shooting Supply
Parker Gun Finishes
Pecatonica River Longrifle
Peter Dyson & Son Ltd.
Pioneer Arms Co.
Prairie River Arms
Rusty Duck Premium Gun Care Products
S&S Firearms
Selsi Co., Inc.
Simmons Gun Repair, Inc.
Sklany's Machine Shop
Smokey Valley Rifles
South Bend Replicas, Inc.
Southern Bloomer Mfg. Co.
Splitfire Sporting Goods, L.L.C.
Starr Trading Co., Jedediah
Stone Mountain Arms
Sturm Ruger & Co. Inc.
Taylor's & Co., Inc.
Tennessee Valley Mfg.
The A.W. Peterson Gun Shop, Inc.
The Gun Works
The Hawken Shop
Thompson Bullet Lube Co.
Thompson/Center Arms
Tiger-Hunt Gunstocks
Track of the Wolf, Inc.
Traditions Performance Firearms
Truglo, Inc.
Uncle Mike's (See Michaels of Oregon Co.)
Universal Sports
Upper Missouri Trading Co.
Venco Industries, Inc. (See Shooter's Choice Gun Care)
Virgin Valley Custom Guns
Voere-KGH GmbH
W.E. Birdsong & Assoc.
Warne Manufacturing Co.
Warren Muzzleloading Co., Inc.
Wescombe, Bill (See North Star West)
White Rifles, Inc.
William E. Phillips Firearms
Woodworker's Supply
Wright's Gunstock Blanks
Young Country Arms
Ziegel Engineering

PISTOLSMITH

A.W. Peterson Gun Shop, Inc.
Acadian Ballistic Specialties
Accuracy Unlimited
Ace Custom 45's, Inc.
Actions by "T" Teddy Jacobson
Adair Custom Shop, Bill
Ahlman Guns
Ahrends, Kim (See Custom Firearms, Inc)
Aldis Gunsmithing & Shooting Supply
Alpha Precision, Inc.
Alpine Indoor Shooting Range
Armament Gunsmithing Co., Inc.
Arundel Arms & Ammunition, Inc., A.
Badger Creek Studio
Baer Custom Inc., Les
Bain & Davis, Inc.
Banks, Ed
Bar-Sto Precision Machine
Behlert Precision, Inc.
Ben William's Gun Shop
Bengtson Arms Co., L.
Bill Adair Custom Shop
Billings Gunsmiths
Bowen Classic Arms Corp.
Broken Gun Ranch
Caraville Manufacturing
Chicasaw Gun Works
Clark Custom Guns, Inc.
Cleland's Outdoor World, Inc
Colonial Repair
Colorado School of Trades
Colt's Mfg. Co., Inc.
Corkys Gun Clinic
Custom Firearms (See Ahrends, Kim)
Cylinder & Slide, Inc., William R. Laughridge
D&D Gunsmiths, Ltd.
D&L Sports
David R. Chicoine
Dayton Traister
Dilliott Gunsmithing, Inc.
Ellicott Arms, Inc. / Woods Pistolsmithing
Evolution Gun Works Inc.
F.I., Inc. - High Standard Mfg. Co.
Ferris Firearms
Fisher Custom Firearms
Forkin, Ben (See Belt MTN Arms)
Forkin Arms
Francesca, Inc.
G.G. & G.
Garthwaite Pistolsmith, Inc., Jim
Gary Reeder Custom Guns
Genecco Gun Works
Gentry Custom Gunmaker, David
George E. Mathews & Son, Inc.
Greider Precision
Guncraft Sports Inc.
Guncraft Sports, Inc.
Gunsite Custom Shop
Gunsite Gunsmithy (See Gunsite Custom Shop)
Gunsite Training Center
Hamilton, Alex B (See Ten-Ring Precision, Inc)
Hammerli Service-Precision Mac
Hammond Custom Guns Ltd.
Hank's Gun Shop
Hanson's Gun Center, Dick
Harris Gunworks
Harwood, Jack O.
Hawken Shop, The (See Dayton Traister)
Heinie Specialty Products
High Bridge Arms, Inc
Highline Machine Co.
Hoag, James W.
Irwin, Campbell H.
Island Pond Gun Shop
Ivanoff, Thomas G. (See Tom's Gun Repair)
J&S Heat Treat
Jarvis, Inc.
Jeffredo Gunsight
Jensen's Custom Ammunition
Jungkind, Reeves C.
Kaswer Custom, Inc.
Ken Starnes Gunmaker
Kilham & Co.
Kim Ahrends Custom Firearms, Inc.
King's Gun Works
La Clinique du .45
LaFrance Specialties
LaRocca Gun Works
Lathrop's, Inc.
Lawson, John G (See Sight Shop, The)
Leckie Professional Gunsmithing
Linebaugh Custom Sixguns
List Precision Engineering
Long, George F.
Mag-Na-Port International, Inc.
Mahony, Philip Bruce
Mahovsky's Metalife
Mandall Shooting Supplies Inc.
Marvel, Alan
Mathews & Son, Inc., George E.
McCann's Machine & Gun Shop
MCS, Inc.
Middlebrooks Custom Shop
Miller Custom
Mitchell's Accuracy Shop
MJK Gunsmithing, Inc.
Modern Gun Repair School
Montgomery Community College
Mo's Competitor Supplies (See MCS, Inc.)
Mowrey's Guns & Gunsmithing
Mullis Guncraft
NCP Products, Inc.
Novak's, Inc.
Nowlin Mfg. Co.
Olathe Gun Shop
Paris, Frank J.
Pasadena Gun Center
Peacemaker Specialists
PEM's Mfg. Co.
Performance Specialists
Peterson Gun Shop, Inc., A.W.
Pierce Pistols
Piquette's Custom Engraving
Power Custom, Inc.
Precision Specialties
Ramon B. Gonzalez Guns
Randco UK
Ries, Chuck
Rim Pac Sports, Inc.
Rocky Mountain Arms, Inc.
RPM
Ruger's Custom Guns
Score High Gunsmithing
Shooters Supply
Shootin' Shack
Singletary, Kent
Springfield, Inc.
SSK Industries
Swenson's 45 Shop, A. D.
Swift River Gunworks
Ten-Ring Precision, Inc.
Terry K. Kopp Professional Gunsmithing
The A.W. Peterson Gun Shop, Inc.
The Gun Works
The Robar Co.'s, Inc.
The Sight Shop
Thompson, Randall (See Highline Machine Co.)
Thurston Sports, Inc.
Tom's Gun Repair, Thomas G. Ivanoff
Turnbull Restoration, Doug
Vic's Gun Refinishing
Volquartsen Custom Ltd.
Walker Arms Co., Inc.
Walters Industries
Wardell Precision Handguns Ltd.
Wessinger Custom Guns & Engraving
White Barn Wor
Wichita Arms, Inc.
Wild West Guns
Williams Gun Sight Co.
Williamson Precision Gunsmithing
Wilsom Combat
Wright's Gunstock Blanks

POWDER MEASURES, SCALES, FUNNELS & ACCESSORIES

4-D Custom Die Co.
Battenfeld Technologies
Buffalo Arms Co.
Dillon Precision Products, Inc.
Fremont Tool Works
Frontier
GAR
High Precision
Hoehn Sales, Inc.
Jones Custom Products, Neil A.
Modern Muzzleloading, Inc.
Neil A. Jones Custom Products
Peter Dyson & Son Ltd.
Precision Reloading, Inc.
Ramon B. Gonzalez Guns
RCBS Operations/ATK
RCBS/ATK
Redding Reloading Equipment
Saunders Gun & Machine Shop
Spencer's Rifle Barrels, Inc.
The A.W. Peterson Gun Shop, Inc.
Vega Tool Co.
VibraShine, Inc.
VTI Gun Parts

PRESS ACCESSORIES, METALLIC

Buffalo Arms Co.
Corbin Mfg. & Supply, Inc.
Efficient Machinery Co.
Hollywood Engineering
Huntington Die Specialties
R.E.I.
Redding Reloading Equipment
The A.W. Peterson Gun Shop, Inc.
Thompson Tool Mount
Vega Tool Co.

PRESSES, METALLIC

4-D Custom Die Co.
Battenfeld Technologies
Dillon Precision Products, Inc.
Fremont Tool Works
Goodwin's Gun Shop
Hornady Mfg. Co.
Huntington Die Specialties
Lee Precision, Inc.
Midway Arms, Inc.
R.E.I.
Ramon B. Gonzalez Guns
RCBS Operations/ATK
RCBS/ATK
Redding Reloading Equipment
Spencer's Rifle Barrels, Inc.
The A.W. Peterson Gun Shop, Inc.

PRESSES, SWAGE

Bullet Swaging Supply, Inc.
The A.W. Peterson Gun Shop, Inc.

PRIMING TOOLS & ACCESSORIES

Goodwin's Gun Shop
Hart & Son, Inc.
Huntington Die Specialties
K&M Services
RCBS Operations/ATK
Simmons, Jerry
Sinclair International, Inc.
The A.W. Peterson Gun Shop, Inc.

REBORING & RERIFLING

Ahlman Guns
Bauska Barrels
BlackStar AccuMax Barrels
BlackStar Barrel Accurizing (See BlackStar AccuMax)
Buffalo Arms Co.
Champlin Firearms, Inc.
Ed's Gun House
Fred F. Wells/Wells Sport Store
H&S Liner Service
Ivanoff, Thomas G. (See Tom's Gun Repair)
Jackalope Gun Shop
LaBounty Precision Reboring, Inc
NCP Products, Inc.
Pence Precision Barrels
Redman's Rifling & Reboring
Rice, Keith (See White Rock Tool & Die)
Ridgetop Sporting Goods
Savage Arms, Inc.
Shaw, Inc., E. R. (See Small Arms Mfg. Co.)
Siegrist Gun Shop
Simmons Gun Repair, Inc.
Stratco, Inc.
Terry K. Kopp Professional Gunsmithing
The Gun Works
Time Precision
Tom's Gun Repair, Thomas G. Ivanoff
Turnbull Restoration, Doug
Van Patten, J. W.
White Rock Tool & Die
Zufall, Joseph F.

RELOADING TOOLS AND ACCESSORIES

4-D Custom Die Co.
Advance Car Mover Co., Rowell Div.
American Products, Inc.
Ammo Load, Inc.
Armfield Custom Bullets
Armite Laboratories
Arms Corporation of the Philippines
Atlantic Rose, Inc.
Atsko/Sno-Seal, Inc.
Bald Eagle Precision Machine Co.
Ballistic Product, Inc.
Belltown Ltd.
Ben William's Gun Shop
Ben's Machines
Berger Bullets Ltd.
Berry's Mfg., Inc.
Blount, Inc., Sporting Equipment Div.
Blue Mountain Bullets
Blue Ridge Machinery & Tools, Inc.
Bonanza (See Forster Products)
Break-Free, Inc.
Brown Co., E. Arthur
BRP, Inc. High Performance Cast Bullets
Brynin, Milton
B-Square Company, Inc.
Buck Stix-SOS Products Co.
Buffalo Arms Co.
Bull Mountain Rifle Co.
Bullseye Bullets
C&D Special Products (See Claybuster Wads & Harvester Bullets)
Camdex, Inc.
Camp-Cap Products
Canyon Cartridge Corp.
Case Sorting System
CH Tool & Die Co. (See 4-D Custom Die Co.)
CheVron Bullets

REFERENCE

PRODUCT & SERVICE DIRECTORY

Claybuster Wads & Harvester Bullets
CONKKO
Cook Engineering Service
Crouse's Country Cover
Cumberland Arms
Curtis Cast Bullets
Custom Products (See Jones Custom Products)
CVA
D.C.C. Enterprises
Davide Pedersoli and Co.
Davis, Don
Davis Products, Mike
Denver Instrument Co.
Dillon Precision Products, Inc.
Dropkick
E&L Mfg., Inc.
Eagan, Donald V.
Eezox, Inc.
Eichelberger Bullets, Wm.
Enguix Import-Export
Euroarms of America, Inc.
E-Z-Way Systems
Federated-Fry (See Fry Metals)
Feken, Dennis
Ferguson, Bill
First Inc., Jack
Fisher Custom Firearms
Flambeau Products Corp.
Flitz International Ltd.
Forster Products
Fremont Tool Works
Fry Metals
Gehmann, Walter (See Huntington Die Specialties)
Graf & Sons
Graphics Direct
Graves Co.
Green, Arthur S.
Greenwood Precision
GTB
Gun City
Hanned Precision (See The Hanned Line)
Harrell's Precision
Harris Enterprises
Harrison Bullets
Haydon Shooters Supply, Russ
Heidenstrom Bullets
High Precision
Hirtenberger AG
Hodgdon Powder Co.
Hoehn Sales, Inc.
Holland's Gunsmithing
Hondo Ind.
Hornady Mfg. Co.
Howell Machine
Hunters Supply, Inc.
Hutton Rifle Ranch
Image Ind. Inc.
Imperial Magnum Corp.
INTEC International, Inc.
Iosso Products
J&L Superior Bullets (See Huntington Die Special)
Javelina Lube Products
JGS Precision Tool Mfg., LLC
JLK Bullets
Jonad Corp.
Jones Custom Products, Neil A.
Jones Moulds, Paul
K&M Services
Kapro Mfg. Co. Inc. (See R.E.I.)
Knoell, Doug
Korzinek Riflesmith, J.
L.A.R. Mfg., Inc.
L.E. Wilson, Inc.
Lapua Ltd.
Le Clear Industries (See E-Z-Way Systems)
Lee Precision, Inc.
Legend Products Corp.
Liberty Metals
Liberty Shooting Supplies
Lightning Performance Innovations, Inc.
Lithi Bee Bullet Lube
Littleton, J. F.
Lock's Philadelphia Gun Exchange
Lortone Inc.
Lyman Instant Targets, Inc. (See Lyman Products)
Lyman Products Corp.
MA Systems
Magma Engineering Co.
MarMik, Inc.
Marquart Precision Co.
Match Prep-Doyle Gracey
Mayville Engineering Co. (See MEC, Inc.)
MCS, Inc.
MEC, Inc.
Midway Arms, Inc.
MI-TE Bullets
Montana Armory, Inc .(See C. Sharps Arms Co. Inc.)
Mo's Competitor Supplies (See MCS, Inc.)
Mountain South
Mountain State Muzzleloading Supplies, Inc.
MTM Molded Products Co., Inc.
Multi-Scale Charge Ltd.
MWG Co.
Navy Arms Company
Newman Gunshop
North Devon Firearms Services
Old West Bullet Moulds
Omark Industries, Div. of Blount, Inc.
Original Box, Inc.
Outdoor Sports Headquarters, Inc.
Paco's (See Small Custom Mould & Bullet Co.)
Paragon Sales & Services, Inc.
Pease Accuracy
Pinetree Bullets
Ponsness/Warren
Prairie River Arms
Prime Reloading
Professional Hunter Supplies (See Star Custom Bullets)
Pro-Shot Products, Inc.
R.A. Wells Custom Gunsmith
R.E.I.
R.I.S. Co., Inc.
Rapine Bullet Mould Mfg. Co.
Reloading Specialties, Inc.
Rice, Keith (See White Rock Tool & Die)
Rochester Lead Works
Rooster Laboratories
Rorschach Precision Products
SAECO (See Redding Reloading Equipment)
Sandia Die & Cartridge Co.
Saunders Gun & Machine Shop
Saville Iron Co. (See Greenwood Precision)
Seebeck Assoc., R.E.
Sharp Shooter Supply
Sharps Arms Co., Inc., C.
Shiloh Rifle Mfg.
Sierra Specialty Prod. Co.
Silver Eagle Machining
Skip's Machine
Small Custom Mould & Bullet Co.
Sno-Seal, Inc. (See Atsko/Sno-Seal, Inc.)
SOS Products Co. (See Buck Stix-SOS Products Co.)
Spencer's Rifle Barrels, Inc.
SPG LLC
SSK Industries
Stalwart Corporation
Star Custom Bullets
Starr Trading Co., Jedediah
Stillwell, Robert
Stoney Point Products, Inc.
Stratco, Inc.
Tamarack Products, Inc.
Taracorp Industries, Inc.
TCCI
TCSR
TDP Industries, Inc.
Tetra Gun Care
The Hanned Line
The Protector Mfg. Co., Inc.
Thompson/Center Arms
TMI Products (See Haselbauer Products, Jerry)
Vega Tool Co.
Venco Industries, Inc. (See Shooter's Choice Gun Care)
VibraShine, Inc.
Vibra-Tek Co.
Vihtavuori Oy/Kaltron-Pettibone
Vitt/Boos
W.B. Niemi Engineering
W.J. Riebe Co.
WD-40 Co.
Webster Scale Mfg. Co.
White Rock Tool & Die
Widener's Reloading & Shooting Supply, Inc.
Wise Custom Guns
Woodleigh (See Huntington Die Specialties)
Yesteryear Armory & Supply
Young Country Arms

RESTS BENCH, PORTABLE AND ACCESSORIES

Adventure 16, Inc.
Armor Metal Products
Bald Eagle Precision Machine Co.
Bartlett Engineering
Battenfeld Technologies
Blount/Outers ATK
Browning Arms Co.
B-Square Company, Inc.
Bull Mountain Rifle Co.
Canons Delcour
Clift Mfg., L. R.
Desert Mountain Mfg.
Efficient Machinery Co.
Greenwood Precision
Harris Engineering Inc.
Hidalgo, Tony
Hoehn Sales, Inc.
Hoppe's Div. Penguin Industries, Inc.
J&J Sales
Keng's Firearms Specialty, Inc./US Tactical Systems
Kolpin Mfg., Inc.
Kramer Designs
Midway Arms, Inc.
Millett Sights
Protektor Model
Ransom International Corp.
Russ Haydon's Shooters' Supply
Saville Iron Co. (See Greenwood Precision)
Sinclair International, Inc.
Stoney Point Products, Inc.
T.H.U. Enterprises, Inc.
The A.W. Peterson Gun Shop, Inc.
The Outdoor Connection, Inc.
Thompson Target Technology
Tonoloway Tack Drives
Varmint Masters, LLC
Wichita Arms, Inc.
Zanotti Armor, Inc.
Ziegel Engineering

SCOPES, MOUNTS, ACCESSORIES, OPTICAL EQUIPMENT

A.R.M.S., Inc.
Accu-Tek
Ackerman, Bill (See Optical Services Co.)
Action Direct, Inc.
ADCO Sales, Inc.
Aimtech Mount Systems
Air Rifle Specialists
Air Venture Airguns
All Rite Products, Inc.
Alley Supply Co.
Alpec Team, Inc.
Apel GmbH, Ernst
ArmaLite, Inc.
Arundel Arms & Ammunition, Inc., A.
B.A.C.
Badger Creek Studio
Baer Custom Inc., Les
Bansner's Ultimate Rifles, LLC
Barrett Firearms Manufacturer, Inc.
Beaver Park Product, Inc.
BEC, Inc.
Beeman Precision Airguns
Ben William's Gun Shop
Benjamin/Sheridan Co., Crosman
Bill Russ Trading Post
BKL Technologies
Blount, Inc., Sporting Equipment Div.
Blount/Outers ATK
Borden Rifles Inc.
Brockman's Custom Gunsmithing
Brocock Ltd.
Brown Co., E. Arthur
Brownells, Inc.
Brunton U.S.A.
BSA Optics
B-Square Company, Inc.
Bull Mountain Rifle Co.
Burris Co., Inc.
Bushmaster Firearms
Bushnell Sports Optics Worldwide
Butler Creek Corp.
Cabela's
Carl Zeiss Inc.
Center Lock Scope Rings
Chuck's Gun Shop
Clark Custom Guns, Inc.
Clearview Mfg. Co., Inc.
Compass Industries, Inc.
Compasseco, Ltd.
Concept Development Corp.
Conetrol Scope Mounts
Creedmoor Sports, Inc.
Crimson Trace Lasers
Crosman Airguns
Custom Quality Products, Inc.
D.C.C. Enterprises
Daisy Outdoor Products
Del-Sports, Inc.
DHB Products
E. Arthur Brown Co.
Eclectic Technologies, Inc.
Edmund Scientific Co.
Ednar, Inc.
Eggleston, Jere D.
Emerging Technologies, Inc. (See Laseraim Technologies, Inc.)
Entre`prise Arms, Inc.
Euro-Imports
Evolution Gun Works Inc.
Excalibur Electro Optics Inc.
Excel Industries Inc.
Faloon Industries, Inc.
Farr Studio, Inc.
Federal Arms Corp. of America
Freedom Arms, Inc.
Fujinon, Inc.
G.G. & G.
Galati International
Gentry Custom Gunmaker, David
Gil Hebard Guns Inc.
Gilmore Sports Concepts
Goodwin's Gun Shop
GSI, Inc.
Gun South, Inc. (See GSI, Inc.)
Guns Div. of D.C. Engineering, Inc.
Gunsmithing, Inc.
Hakko Co. Ltd.
Hammerli USA
Harris Gunworks
Harvey, Frank
Highwood Special Products
Hiptmayer, Armurier
Hiptmayer, Klaus
HiTek International
Holland's Gunsmithing
Impact Case & Container, Inc.
Ironsighter Co.
Jeffredo Gunsight
Jena Eur
Jerry Phillips Optics
Jewell Triggers, Inc.
John Masen Co. Inc.
John's Custom Leather
Kahles A. Swarovski Company
Kalispel Case Line
KDF, Inc.
Keng's Firearms Specialty, Inc./US Tactical Systems
Kesselring Gun Shop
Kimber of America, Inc.
Knight's Mfg. Co.
Kowa Optimed, Inc.
KVH Industries, Inc.
Kwik-Site Co.
L&S Technologies Inc. (See Aimtech Mount Systems)
L.A.R. Mfg., Inc.
Laser Devices, Inc.
Laseraim Technologies, Inc.
LaserMax, Inc.
Leapers, Inc.
Leica USA, Inc.
Leupold & Stevens, Inc.
List Precision Engineering
Lohman Mfg. Co., Inc.
Lomont Precision Bullets
London Guns Ltd.
Mac-1 Airgun Distributors
Mag-Na-Port International, Inc.
Mandall Shooting Supplies Inc.
Marksman Products
Maxi-Mount Inc.
McBros Rifle Co.
McCann's Machine & Gun Shop
McMillan Optical Gunsight Co.
MCS, Inc.
MDS
Merit Corp.
Military Armament Corp.
Millett Sights
Mirador Optical Corp.
Mitchell Optics, Inc.
MMC
Mo's Competitor Supplies (See MCS, Inc.)
MWG Co.
Navy Arms Company
New England Custom Gun Service
Nikon, Inc.
Norincoptics (See BEC, Inc.)
Olympic Optical Co.
Optical Services Co.
Orchard Park Enterprise
Oregon Arms, Inc. (See Rogue Rifle Co., Inc.)
Ozark Gun Works
Parker & Sons Shooting Supply
Parsons Optical Mfg. Co.
PECAR Herbert Schwarz GmbH
PEM's Mfg. Co.
Pentax Corp.
PMC/Eldorado Cartridge Corp.
Precision Sport Optics
Premier Reticles
R.A. Wells Custom Gunsmith
Ram-Line ATK
Ramon B. Gonzalez Guns
Ranch Products
Randolph Engineering Inc.
Rice, Keith (See White Rock Tool & Die)
Robinson Armament Co.
Rogue Rifle Co., Inc.
Romain's Custom Guns, Inc.
S&K Scope Mounts
Saunders Gun & Machine Shop
Schmidt & Bender, Inc.

REFERENCE

PRODUCT & SERVICE DIRECTORY

Schumakers Gun Shop
Scope Control, Inc.
Score High Gunsmithing
Seecamp Co. Inc., L. W.
Segway Industries
Selsi Co., Inc.
Sharp Shooter Supply
Shepherd Enterprises, Inc.
Sightron, Inc.
Simmons Outdoor Corp.
Six Enterprises
Southern Bloomer Mfg. Co.
Spencer's Rifle Barrels, Inc.
Splitfire Sporting Goods, L.L.C.
Sportsmatch U.K. Ltd.
Springfield Armory
Springfield, Inc.
SSK Industries
Stiles Custom Guns
Stoeger Industries
Stoney Point Products, Inc.
Sturm Ruger & Co. Inc.
Sunny Hill Enterprises, Inc.
Swarovski Optik North America Ltd.
Swift Instruments, Inc.
T.K. Lee Co.
Talley, Dave
Tasco Sales, Inc.
Tele-Optics
The A.W. Peterson Gun Shop, Inc.
The Outdoor Connection, Inc.
Thompson/Center Arms
Traditions Performance Firearms
Trijicon, Inc.
Truglo, Inc.
Ultra Dot Distribution
Uncle Mike's (See Michaels of Oregon Co.)
Unertl Optical Co., Inc.
United Binocular Co.
United States Optics Technologies, Inc.
Virgin Valley Custom Guns
Visible Impact Targets
Voere-KGH GmbH
Warne Manufacturing Co.
Warren Muzzleloading Co., Inc.
Watson Trophy Match Bullets
Weaver Products ATK
Weaver Scope Repair Service
Weigand Combat Handguns, Inc.
Wessinger Custom Guns & Engraving
Westley Richards & Co.
White Rifles, Inc.
White Rock Tool & Die
Whitestone Lumber Corp.
Wideview Scope Mount Corp.
Wilcox Industries Corp.
Wild West Guns
Williams Gun Sight Co.
York M-1 Conversions
Zanotti Armor, Inc.

SHELLHOLDERS

Corbin Mfg. & Supply, Inc.
Fremont Tool Works
Goodwin's Gun Shop
Hart & Son, Inc.
Hollywood Engineering
Huntington Die Specialties
K&M Services
King & Co.
RCBS Operations/ATK
Redding Reloading Equipment
The A.W. Peterson Gun Shop, Inc.
Vega Tool Co.

SHOOTING/TRAINING SCHOOL

Alpine Indoor Shooting Range
American Gunsmithing Institute
American Small Arms Academy
Auto Arms
Beretta U.S.A. Corp.
Bob's Tactical Indoor Shooting Range & Gun Shop
Bridgeman Products
Chapman Academy of Practical Shooting
Chelsea Gun Club of New York City Inc.
Cherry Creek State Park Shooting Center
CQB Training
Defense Training International, Inc.
Executive Protection Institute
Ferris Firearms
Front Sight Firearms Training Institute
G.H. Enterprises Ltd.
Gene's Custom Guns
Griffin & Howe, Inc.
Griffin & Howe, Inc.
Griffin & Howe, Inc.
Guncraft Books (See Guncraft Sports Inc.)
Guncraft Sports Inc.
Guncraft Sports, Inc.
Gunsite Training Center
Henigson & Associates, Steve
Jensen's Custom Ammunition
Jensen's Firearms Academy
Kemen America
L.L. Bean, Inc.
Lethal Force Institute (See Police Bookshelf)
Loch Leven Industries/Convert-A-Pell
Long, George F.
McMurdo, Lynn (See Specialty Gunsmithing)
Mendez, John A.
NCP Products, Inc.
Nevada Pistol Academy, Inc.
North American Shooting Systems
North Mountain Pine Training Center (See Executive
Nowlin Mfg. Co.
Paxton Quigley's Personal Protection Strategies
Pentheny de Pentheny
Performance Specialists
Police Bookshelf
SAFE
Shoot Where You Look
Shooter's World
Shooters, Inc.
Sigarms, Inc.
Smith & Wesson
Specialty Gunsmithing
Starlight Training Center, Inc.
Tactical Defense Institute
The Firearm Training Center
The Midwest Shooting School
The Shooting Gallery
Thunden Ranch
Western Missouri Shooters Alliance
Yankee Gunsmith "Just Glocks"
Yavapai Firearms Academy Ltd.

SIGHTS, METALLIC

100 Straight Products, Inc.
Accura-Site (See All's, The Jim Tembelis Co., Inc.)
Ad Hominem
Alley Supply Co.
All's, The Jim J. Tembelis Co., Inc.
Alpec Team, Inc.
Andela Tool & Machine, Inc.
AO Sight Systems
ArmaLite, Inc.
Ashley Outdoors, Inc.
Aspen Outfitting Co.
Axtell Rifle Co.
B.A.C.
Baer Custom Inc., Les
Ballard Rifle & Cartridge Co., LLC
BEC, Inc.
Bob's Gun Shop
Bo-Mar Tool & Mfg. Co.
Bond Custom Firearms
Bowen Classic Arms Corp.
Brockman's Custom Gunsmithing
Brooks Tactical Systems-Agrip
Brown Co., E. Arthur
Brown Dog Ent.
Brownells, Inc.
Buffalo Arms Co.
Bushmaster Firearms
C. Sharps Arms Co. Inc./Montana Armory
California Sights (See Fautheree, Andy)
Campbell, Dick
Cape Outfitters
Cape Outfitters
Cash Mfg. Co., Inc.
Center Lock Scope Rings
Champion's Choice, Inc.
C-More Systems
Colonial Repair
CRR, Inc./Marble's Inc.
Davide Pedersoli and Co.
DHB Products
Dixie Gun Works
DPMS (Defense Procurement Manufacturing Services, Inc.)
E. Arthur Brown Co.
Evolution Gun Works Inc.
Faloon Industries, Inc.
Farr Studio, Inc.
G.G. & G.
Garthwaite Pistolsmith, Inc., Jim
Goergen's Gun Shop, Inc.
Goodwin's Gun Shop
Guns Div. of D.C. Engineering, Inc.
Gunsmithing, Inc.
Hank's Gun Shop
Heidenstrom Bullets
Heinie Specialty Products
Hesco-Meprolight
Hiptmayer, Armurier
Hiptmayer, Klaus
I.S.S.
Innovative Weaponry Inc.
J.G. Anschutz GmbH & Co. KG
J.P. Enterprises Inc.
Keng's Firearms Specialty, Inc./US Tactical Systems
Knight Rifles
Knight's Mfg. Co.
L.P.A. Inc.
Leapers, Inc.
List Precision Engineering
London Guns Ltd.
Lyman Instant Targets, Inc. (See Lyman Products)
Mandall Shooting Supplies Inc.
Marble Arms (See CRR, Inc./Marble's Inc.)
MCS, Inc.
MEC-Gar S.R.L.
Meprolight (See Hesco-Meprolight)
Merit Corp.
Mid-America Recreation, Inc.
Middlebrooks Custom Shop
Millett Sights
MMC
Modern Muzzleloading, Inc.
Montana Armory, Inc .(See C. Sharps Arms Co. Inc.)
Montana Vintage Arms
Mo's Competitor Supplies (See MCS, Inc.)
Navy Arms Company
New England Custom Gun Service
Newman Gunshop
Novak's, Inc.
OK Weber, Inc.
One Ragged Hole
Parker & Sons Shooting Supply
PEM's Mfg. Co.
Perazone-Gunsmith, Brian
RPM
Sharps Arms Co., Inc., C.
Slug Site
STI International
T.F.C. S.p.A.
Talley, Dave
Tank's Rifle Shop
The A.W. Peterson Gun Shop, Inc.
The Gun Doctor
Trijicon, Inc.
Truglo, Inc.
United States Optics Technologies, Inc.
Warne Manufacturing Co.
Weigand Combat Handguns, Inc.
Wichita Arms, Inc.
Wild West Guns
Williams Gun Sight Co.
Wilson Combat
Wilson Combat

STUCK CASE REMOVERS

Goodwin's Gun Shop
Huntington Die Specialties
MarMik, Inc.
The A.W. Peterson Gun Shop, Inc.
Tom's Gun Repair, Thomas G. Ivanoff

TARGETS, BULLET & CLAYBIRD TRAPS

Action Target, Inc.
Air Arms
American Target
Autauga Arms, Inc.
Beeman Precision Airguns
Benjamin/Sheridan Co., Crosman
Beomat of America, Inc.
Birchwood Casey
Blount, Inc., Sporting Equipment Div.
Blount/Outers ATK
Blue and Gray Products Inc. (See Ox-Yoke Originals)
Brown Precision, Inc.
Bull-X, Inc.
Champion Target Co.
Creedmoor Sports, Inc.
Crosman Airguns
D.C.C. Enterprises
Daisy Outdoor Products
Detroit-Armor Corp.
Diamond Mfg. Co.
Federal Champion Target Co.
G.H. Enterprises Ltd.
Hiti-Schuch, Atelier Wilma
H-S Precision, Inc.
Hunterjohn
J.G. Dapkus Co., Inc.
Kennebec Journal
Kleen-Bore,Inc.
Lakefield Arms Ltd. (See Savage Arms, Inc.)
Leapers, Inc.
Littler Sales Co.
Lyman Instant Targets, Inc. (See Lyman Products)
Marksman Products
Mendez, John A.
Mountain Plains Industries
MSR Targets
Muscle Products Corp.
N.B.B., Inc.
National Target Co.
North American Shooting Systems
Outers Laboratories Div. of ATK
Ox-Yoke Originals, Inc.
Palsa Outdoor Products
Passive Bullet Traps, Inc. (See Savage Range Systems, Inc.)
PlumFire Press, Inc.
Precision Airgun Sales, Inc.
Protektor Model
Quack Decoy & Sporting Clays
Remington Arms Co., Inc.
Rockwood Corp.
Rocky Mountain Target Co.
Savage Range Systems, Inc.
Schaefer Shooting Sports
Seligman Shooting Products
Shooters Supply
Shoot-N-C Targets (See Birchwood Casey)
Target Shooting, Inc.
The A.W. Peterson Gun Shop, Inc.
Thompson Target Technology
Trius Traps, Inc.
Universal Sports
Visible Impact Targets
Watson Trophy Match Bullets
Woods Wise Products
World of Targets (See Birchwood Casey)
X-Spand Target Systems

TAXIDERMY

African Import Co.
Bill Russ Trading Post
Kulis Freeze Dry Taxidermy
Montgomery Community College
World Trek, Inc.

MANUFACTURER'S DIRECTORY

A

A Zone Bullets, 2039 Walter Rd., Billings, MT 59105 / 800-252-3111; FAX: 406-248-1961
A&B Industries, Inc (See Top-Line USA Inc.)
A&W Repair, 2930 Schneider Dr., Arnold, MO 63010 / 617-287-3725
A.A. Arms, Inc., 4811 Persimmont Ct., Monroe, NC 28110 / 704-289-5356; or 800-935-1119; FAX: 704-289-5859
A.B.S. III, 9238 St. Morritz Dr., Fern Creek, KY 40291
A.G. Russell Knives, Inc., 1920 North 26th Street, Springdale, AR 72764 / 479-751-7341; FAX: 479-751-4520 ag@agrussell.com agrussell.com
A.R.M.S., Inc., 230 W. Center St., West Bridgewater, MA 02379-1620 / 508-584-7816; FAX: 508-588-8045
A.W. Peterson Gun Shop, Inc., 4255 W. Old U.S. 441, Mt. Dora, FL 32757-3299 / 352-383-4258; FAX: 352-735-1001
AC Dyna-tite Corp., 155 Kelly St., P.O. Box 0984, Elk Grove Village, IL 60007 / 847-593-5566; FAX: 847-593-1304
Acadian Ballistic Specialties, P.O. Box 787, Folsom, LA 70437 / 504-796-0078 gunsmith@neasolft.com
Accuracy International, Foster, PO Box 111, Wilsall, MT 59086 / 406-587-7922; FAX: 406-585-9434
Accuracy Internationl Precision Rifles (See U.S.)
Accuracy Int'l. North America, Inc., PO Box 5267, Oak Ridge, TN 37831 / 423-482-0330; FAX: 423-482-0336
Accuracy Unlimited, 16036 N. 49 Ave., Glendale, AZ 85306 / 602-978-9089; FAX: 602-978-9089 fglenn@cox.net www.glenncustom.com
Accuracy Unlimited, 7479 S. DePew St., Littleton, CO 80123
Accura-Site (See All's, The Jim Tembelis Co., Inc.)
Accurate Arms Co., Inc., 5891 Hwy. 230 West, McEwen, TN 37101 / 931-729-4207; FAX: 931-729-4211 burrensburg@aac-ca.com www.accuratepowder.com
Accu-Tek, 4510 Carter Ct., Chino, CA 91710
Ace Custom 45's, Inc., 1880 1/2 Upper Turtle Creek Rd., Kerrville, TX 78028 / 830-257-4290; FAX: 830-257-5724 www.acecustom45.com
Ackerman & Co., Box 133 US Highway Rt. 7, Pownal, VT 05261 / 802-823-9874 muskets@togsther.net
Ackerman, Bill (See Optical Services Co.)
Acra-Bond Laminates, 134 Zimmerman Rd., Kalispell, MT 59901 / 406-257-9003; FAX: 406-257-9003 merlins@digisys.net www.acrabondlaminates.com
Action Bullets & Alloy Inc., RR 1, P.O. Box 189, Quinter, KS 67752 / 785-754-3609; FAX: 785-754-3629 bullets@ruraltel.net
Action Direct, Inc., P.O. Box 770400, Miami, FL 33177 / 305-969-0056; FAX: 305-256-3541 www.action-direct.com
Action Products, Inc., 22 N. Mulberry St., Hagerstown, MD 21740 / 301-797-1414; FAX: 301-733-2073
Action Target, Inc., PO Box 636, Provo, UT 84603 / 801-377-8033; FAX: 801-377-8096
Actions by "T" Teddy Jacobson, 16315 Redwood Forest Ct., Sugar Land, TX 77478 / 281-277-4008; FAX: 281-277-9112 tjacobson@houston.rr.com www.actionsbyt.us
AcuSport Corporation, 1 Hunter Place, Bellefontaine, OH 43311-3001 / 513-593-7010; FAX: 513-592-5625
Ad Hominem, 3130 Gun Club Lane, RR #3, Orillia, ON L3V 6H3 CANADA / 705-689-5303; FAX: 705-689-5303
Adair Custom Shop, Bill, 2886 Westridge, Carrollton, TX 75006
ADCO Sales, Inc., 4 Draper St. #A, Woburn, MA 01801 / 781-935-1799; FAX: 781-935-1011
Adkins, Luther, 1292 E. McKay Rd., Shelbyville, IN 46176-8706 / 317-392-3795
Advance Car Mover Co., Rowell Div., P.O. Box 1, 240 N. Depot St., Juneau, WI 53039 / 414-386-4464; FAX: 414-386-4416
Advantage Arms, Inc., 25163 W. Ave. Stanford, Valencia, CA 91355 / 661-257-2290
Adventure 16, Inc., 4620 Alvarado Canyon Rd., San Diego, CA 92120 / 619-283-6314
Aero Peltor, 90 Mechanic St., Southbridge, MA 01550 / 508-764-5500; FAX: 508-764-0188
African Import Co., 22 Goodwin Rd, Plymouth, MA 02360 / 508-746-8552; FAX: 508-746-0404 africanimport@aol.com
AFSCO Ammunition, 731 W. Third St., P.O. Box L, Owen, WI 54460 / 715-229-2516 sailers@webtv.net
Ahlman Guns, 9525 W. 230th St., Morristown, MN 55052 / 507-685-4243; FAX: 507-685-4280 www.ahlmans.com
Ahrends, Kim (See Custom Firearms, Inc), Box 203, Clarion, IA 50525 / 515-532-3449; FAX: 515-532-3926
Aimtech Mount Systems, P.O. Box 223, Thomasville, GA 31799 / 229-226-4313; FAX: 229-227-0222 mail@aimtech-mounts.com www.aimtech-mounts.com
Air Arms, Hailsham Industrial Park, Diplocks Way, Hailsham, E. Sussex, BN27 3JF ENGLAND / 011-0323-845853
Air Rifle Specialists, P.O. Box 138, 130 Holden Rd., Pine City, NY 14871-0138 / 607-734-7340; FAX: 607-733-3261 ars@stny.rr.com www.air-rifles.com
Air Venture Airguns, 9752 E. Flower St., Bellflower, CA 90706 / 562-867-6355
AirForce Airguns, P.O. Box 2478, Fort Worth, TX 76113 / 817-451-8966; FAX: 817-451-1613 www.airforceairguns.com
Airrow, 11 Monitor Hill Rd., Newtown, CT 06470 / 203-270-6343
Aitor-Cuchilleria Del Norte S.A., Izelaieta, 17, 48260, Ermua, S SPAIN / 43-17-08-50 info@aitor.com www.ailor.com
Ajax Custom Grips, Inc., 9130 Viscount Row, Dallas, TX 75247 / 214-630-8893; FAX: 214-630-4942
Aker International, Inc., 2248 Main St., Suite 6, Chula Vista, CA 91911 / 619-423-5182; FAX: 619-423-1363 aker@akerleather.com www.akerleather.com
AKJ Concealco, P.O. Box 871596, Vancouver, WA 98687-1596 / 360-891-8222; FAX: 360-891-8221 Concealco@aol.com www.greatholsters.com
Alana Cupp Custom Engraver, P.O. Box 207, Annabella, UT 84711 / 801-896-4834
Alaska Bullet Works, Inc., 9978 Crazy Horse Drive, Juneau, AK 99801 / 907-789-3834; FAX: 907-789-3433
Alaskan Silversmith, The, 2145 Wagner Hollow Rd., Fort Plain, NY 13339 / 518-993-3983 sidbell@capital.net www.sidbell.cizland.com
Aldis Gunsmithing & Shooting Supply, 502 S. Montezuma St., Prescott, AZ 86303 / 602-445-6723; FAX: 602-445-6763
Alessi Holsters, Inc., 2465 Niagara Falls Blvd., Amherst, NY 14228-3527 / 716-691-5615
Alex, Inc., 3420 Cameron Bridge Rd., Manhattan, MT 59741-8523 / 406-282-7396; FAX: 406-282-7396
Alfano, Sam, 36180 Henry Gaines Rd., Pearl River, LA 70452 / 504-863-3364; FAX: 504-863-7715
All American Lead Shot Corp., P.O. Box 224566, Dallas, TX 75062
All Rite Products, Inc., 9554 Wells Circle, Suite D, West Jordan, UT 84088-6226 / 800-771-8471; FAX: 801-280-8302 info@allriteproducts.com www.allriteproducts.com
Allard, Gary/Creek Side Metal & Woodcrafters, Fishers Hill, VA 22626 / 703-465-3903
Allen Co., Inc., 525 Burbank St., Broomfield, CO 80020 / 303-469-1857; or 800-876-8600; FAX: 303-466-7437
Allen Firearm Engraving, P.O. Box 155, Camp Verde, AZ 86322 / 928-567-6711 rosebudmukco@netzero.com
Allen Mfg., 6449 Hodgson Rd., Circle Pines, MN 55014 / 612-429-8231
Alley Supply Co., PO Box 848, Gardnerville, NV 89410 / 775-782-3800; FAX: 775-782-3827 jetalley@aol.com www.alleysupplyco.com
Alliant Techsystems Smokeless Powder Group, P.O. Box 6, Rt. 114, Bldg. 229, Radford, VA 24141-0096 www.alliantpowder.com
Allred Bullet Co., 932 Evergreen Drive, Logan, UT 84321 / 435-752-6983; FAX: 435-752-6983
All's, The Jim J. Tembelis Co., Inc., 216 Loper Ct., Neenah, WI 54956 / 920-725-5251; FAX: 920-725-5251
Alpec Team, Inc., 201 Ricken Backer Cir., Livermore, CA 94550 / 510-606-8245; FAX: 510-606-4279
Alpha 1 Drop Zone, 2121 N. Tyler, Wichita, KS 67212 / 316-729-0800; FAX: 316-729-4262 www.alpha1dropzone.com
Alpha LaFranck Enterprises, P.O. Box 81072, Lincoln, NE 68501 / 402-466-3193
Alpha Precision, Inc., 3238 Della Slaton Rd., Comer, GA 30629-2212 / 706-783-2131 jim@alphaprecisioninc.com www.alphaprecisioninc.com
Alpine Indoor Shooting Range, 2401 Government Way, Coeur d'Alene, ID 83814 / 208-676-8824; FAX: 208-676-8824
Altamont Co., 901 N. Church St., P.O. Box 309, Thomasboro, IL 61878 / 217-643-3125; or 800-626-5774; FAX: 217-643-7973
Alumna Sport by Dee Zee, 1572 NE 58th Ave., P.O. Box 3090, Des Moines, IA 50316 / 800-798-9899
Amadeo Rossi S.A., Rua: Amadeo Rossi, 143, Sao Leopoldo, RS 93030-220 BRAZIL / 051-592-5566
AmBr Software Group Ltd., P.O. Box 301, Reistertown, MD 21136-0301 / 800-888-1917; FAX: 410-526-7212
American Ammunition, 3545 NW 71st St., Miami, FL 33147 / 305-835-7400; FAX: 305-694-0037
American Derringer Corp., 127 N. Lacy Dr., Waco, TX 76705 / 800-642-7817; or 254-799-9111; FAX: 254-799-7935
American Display Co., 55 Cromwell St., Providence, RI 02907 / 401-331-2464; FAX: 401-421-1264
American Gas & Chemical Co., Ltd, 220 Pegasus Ave, Northvale, NJ 07647 / 201-767-7300
American Gripcraft, 3230 S Dodge 2, Tucson, AZ 85713 / 602-790-1222
American Gunsmithing Institute, 1325 Imola Ave #504, Napa, CA 94559 / 707-253-0462; FAX: 707-253-7149
American Handgunner Magazine, 591 Camino de la Reina, Ste. 200, San Diego, CA 92108 / 619-297-5350; FAX: 619-297-5353
American Pioneer Video, PO Box 50049, Bowling Green, KY 42102-2649 / 800-743-4675
American Products, Inc., 14729 Spring Valley Road, Morrison, IL 61270 / 815-772-3336; FAX: 815-772-8046
American Safe Arms, Inc., 1240 Riverview Dr., Garland, UT 84312 / 801-257-7472; FAX: 801-785-8156
American Security Products Co., 11925 Pacific Ave., Fontana, CA 92337 / 909-685-9680; or 800-421-6142; FAX: 909-685-9685
American Small Arms Academy, P.O. Box 12111, Prescott, AZ 86304 / 602-778-5623
American Target, 1328 S. Jason St., Denver, CO 80223 / 303-733-0433; FAX: 303-777-0311
American Target Knives, 1030 Brownwood NW, Grand Rapids, MI 49504 / 616-453-1998
Americase, P.O. Box 271, 1610 E. Main, Waxahachie, TX 75165 / 800-880-3629; FAX: 214-937-8373
Ames Metal Products, 4323 S. Western Blvd., Chicago, IL 60609 / 773-523-3230; or 800-255-6937; FAX: 773-523-3854
Amherst Arms, P.O. Box 1457, Englewood, FL 34295 / 941-475-2020; FAX: 941-473-1212
Ammo Load, Inc., 1560 E. Edinger, Suite G, Santa Ana, CA 92705 / 714-558-8858; FAX: 714-569-0319
Amrine's Gun Shop, 937 La Luna, Ojai, CA 93023 / 805-646-2376
Amsec, 11925 Pacific Ave., Fontana, CA 92337
Analog Devices, Box 9106, Norwood, MA 02062
Andela Tool & Machine, Inc., RD3, Box 246, Richfield Springs, NY 13439
Anderson Manufacturing Co., Inc., 22602 53rd Ave. SE, Bothell, WA 98021 / 206-481-1858; FAX: 206-481-7839
Andres & Dworsky KG, Bergstrasse 18, A-3822 Karlstein, Thaya, AUSTRIA / 0 28 44-285; FAX: 02844 28619 andres.dnorsky@wvnet.as
Angelo & Little Custom Gun Stock Blanks, P.O. Box 240046, Dell, MT 59724-0046
Answer Products Co., 1519 Westbury Drive, Davison, MI 48423 / 810-653-2911
Antique American Firearms, P.O. Box 71035, Dept. GD, Des Moines, IA 50325 / 515-224-6552
Antique Arms Co., 1110 Cleveland Ave., Monett, MO 65708 / 417-235-6501
AO Sight Systems, 2401 Ludelle St., Fort Worth, TX 76105 / 888-744-4880; or 817-536-0136; FAX: 817-536-3517
Apel GmbH, Ernst, Am Kirschberg 3, D-97218, Gerbrunn, GERMANY / 0 (931) 707192 info@eaw.de www.eaw.de
Aplan Antiques & Art, James O., James O., HC 80, Box 793-25, Piedmont, SD 57769 / 605-347-5016
AR-7 Industries, LLC, 998 N. Colony Rd., Meriden, CT 06450 / 203-630-3536; FAX: 203-630-3637

REFERENCE

MANUFACTURER'S DIRECTORY

Arizona Ammunition, Inc., 21421 No. 14th Ave., Suite E, Phoenix, AZ 85027 / 623-516-9004; FAX: 623-516-9012 www.azammo.com
ArmaLite, Inc., P.O. Box 299, Geneseo, IL 61254 / 800-336-0184; or 309-944-6939; FAX: 309-944-6949
Armament Gunsmithing Co., Inc., 525 Rt. 22, Hillside, NJ 07205 / 908-686-0960; FAX: 718-738-5019 armamentgunsmithing@worldnet.att.net
Armas Garbi, S.A., 12-14 20.600 Urki, 12, Eibar (Guipuzcoa), SPAIN / 943203873; FAX: 943203873 armosgarbi@euskalnet.n
Armas Kemen S. A. (See U.S. Importers)
Armfield Custom Bullets, 10584 County Road 100, Carthage, MO 64836 / 417-359-8480; FAX: 417-359-8497
Armi Perazzi S.P.A., Via Fontanelle 1/3, 1-25080, Botticino Mattina, ITALY / 030-2692591; FAX: 030 2692594
Armi San Marco (See U.S. Importers-Taylor's & Co.)
Armi San Paolo, 172-A, I-25062, via Europa, ITALY / 030-2751725
Armi Sport (See U.S. Importers-Cape Outfitters)
Armite Laboratories, 1560 Superior Ave., Costa Mesa, CA 92627 / 213-587-7768; FAX: 213-587-5075
Armoloy Co. of Ft. Worth, 204 E. Daggett St., Fort Worth, TX 76104 / 817-332-5604; FAX: 817-335-6517
Armor (See Buck Stop Lure Co., Inc.)
Armor Metal Products, P.O. Box 4609, Helena, MT 59604 / 406-442-5560; FAX: 406-442-5650
Armory Publications, 2120 S. Reserve St., PMB 253, Missoula, MT 59801 / 406-549-7670; FAX: 406-728-0597 armorypub@aol.com www.armorypub.com
Armoury, Inc., The, Rt. 202, Box 2340, New Preston, CT 06777 / 860-868-0001; FAX: 860-868-2919
Arms & Armour Press, Wellington House, 125 Strand, London, WC2R 0BB ENGLAND / 0171-420-5555; FAX: 0171-240-7265
Arms Corporation of the Philippines, Bo. Parang Marikina, Metro Manila, PHILIPPINES / 632-941-6243; or 632-941-6244; FAX: 632-942-0682
Arms Craft Gunsmithing, 1106 Linda Dr., Arroyo Grande, CA 93420 / 805-481-2830
Arms Software, 4851 SW Madrona St., Lake Oswego, OR 97035 / 800-366-5559; or 503-697-0533; FAX: 503-697-3337
Arms, Programming Solutions (See Arms Software)
Armscor Precision, 5740 S. Arville St. #219, Las Vegas, NV 89118 / 702-362-7750
Armscorp USA, Inc., 4424 John Ave., Baltimore, MD 21227 / 410-247-6200; FAX: 410-247-6205 info@armscorpusa.com www.armscorpusa.com
Arratoonian, Andy (See Horseshoe Leather Products)
Arrieta S.L., Morkaiko 5, 20870, Elgoibar, SPAIN / 34-43-743150; FAX: 34-43-743154
Art Jewel Enterprises Ltd., Eagle Business Ctr., 460 Randy Rd., Carol Stream, IL 60188 / 708-260-0400
Artistry in Wood, 134 Zimmerman Rd., Kalispell, MT 59901 / 406-257-9003; FAX: 406-257-9167 merlins@digisys.net www.acrabondlaminates.com
Art's Gun & Sport Shop, Inc., 6008 Hwy. Y, Hillsboro, MO 63050
Arundel Arms & Ammunition, Inc., A., 24A Defense St., Annapolis, MD 21401 / 410-224-8683
Ashley Outdoors, Inc., 2401 Ludelle St., Fort Worth, TX 76105 / 888-744-4880; FAX: 800-734-7939
Aspen Outfitting Co., Jon Hollinger, 9 Dean St., Aspen, CO 81611 / 970-925-3406
A-Square Co., 205 Fairfield Ave., Jeffersonville, IN 47130 / 812-283-0577; FAX: 812-283-0375
Astra Sport, S.A., Apartado 3, 48300 Guernica, Espagne, SPAIN / 34-4-6250100; FAX: 34-4-6255186
Atamec-Bretton, 19 rue Victor Grignard, F-42026, St.-Etienne (Cedex 1, FRANCE / 77-93-54-69; FAX: 33-77-93-57-98
Atlanta Cutlery Corp., 2143 Gees Mill Rd., Box 839 CIS, Conyers, GA 30207 / 800-883-0300; FAX: 404-388-0246
Atlantic Mills, Inc., 1295 Towbin Ave., Lakewood, NJ 08701-5934 / 800-242-7374
Atlantic Rose, Inc., P.O. Box 10717, Bradenton, FL 34282-0717
Atsko/Sno-Seal, Inc., 2664 Russell St., Orangeburg, SC 29115 / 803-531-1820; FAX: 803-531-2139 info@atsko.com www.atsko.com
Auguste Francotte & Cie S.A., rue du Trois Juin 109, 4400 Herstal-Liege, BELGIUM / 32-4-248-13-18; FAX: 32-4-948-11-79
Austin & Halleck, Inc., 2150 South 950 East, Provo, UT 84606-6285 / 877-543-3256; or 801-374-9990; FAX: 801-374-9998 www.austinhallek.com
Austin Sheridan USA, Inc., P.O. Box 577, 36 Haddam Quarter Rd., Durham, CT 06422 / 860-349-1772; FAX: 860-349-1771 swalzer@palm.net
Autauga Arms, Inc., Pratt Plaza Mall No. 13, Prattville, AL 36067 / 800-262-9563; FAX: 334-361-2961
Auto Arms, 738 Clearview, San Antonio, TX 78228 / 512-434-5450
Auto-Ordnance Corp., PO Box 220, Blauvelt, NY 10913 / 914-353-7770
Autumn Sales, Inc. (Blaser), 1320 Lake St., Fort Worth, TX 76102 / 817-335-1634; FAX: 817-338-0119
Avnda Otaola Norica, 16 Apartado 68, 20600, Eibar, SPAIN
AWC Systems Technology, P.O. Box 41938, Phoenix, AZ 85080-1938 / 623-780-1050; FAX: 623-780-2967 awc@awcsystech.com www.awcsystech.com
Axtell Rifle Co., 353 Mill Creek Road, Sheridan, MT 59749 / 406-842-5814
AYA (See U.S. Importer-New England Custom Gun Serv

B

B&D Trading Co., Inc., 3935 Fair Hill Rd., Fair Oaks, CA 95628 / 800-334-3790; or 916-967-9366; FAX: 916-967-4873
B&P America, 12321 Brittany Cir., Dallas, TX 75230 / 972-726-9069
B.A.C., 17101 Los Modelos St., Fountain Valley, CA 92708 / 435-586-3286
B.B. Walker Co., PO Box 1167, 414 E Dixie Dr, Asheboro, NC 27204 / 910-625-1380; FAX: 910-625-8125
B.C. Outdoors, Larry McGhee, PO Box 61497, Boulder City, NV 89006 / 702-294-3056; FAX: 702-294-0413 jdalton@pmcammo.com www.pmcammo.com
B.M.F. Activator, Inc., 12145 Mill Creek Run, Plantersville, TX 77363 / 936-894-2397; FAX: 936-894-2397 bmf25years@aol.com
Badger Creek Studio, 1629 Via Monserate, Fallbrook, CA 92028 / 760-723-9279; or 619-728-2663
Badger Shooters Supply, Inc., P.O. Box 397, Owen, WI 54460 / 800-424-9069; FAX: 715-229-2332
Baekgaard Ltd., 1855 Janke Dr., Northbrook, IL 60062 / 708-498-3040; FAX: 708-493-3106
Baelder, Harry, Alte Goennebeker Strasse 5, 24635, Rickling, GERMANY / 04328-722732; FAX: 04328-722733
Baer's Hollows, P.O. Box 284, Eads, CO 81036 / 719-438-5718
Bagmaster Mfg., Inc., 2731 Sutton Ave., St. Louis, MO 63143 / 314-781-8002; FAX: 314-781-3363 sales@bagmaster.com www.bagmaster.com
Bain & Davis, Inc., 307 E. Valley Blvd., San Gabriel, CA 91776-3522 / 626-573-4241 baindavis@aol.com
Baker, Stan. See: STAN BAKER SPORTS
Baker's Leather Goods, Roy, PO Box 893, Magnolia, AR 71754 / 870-234-0344 pholsters@ipa.net
Bald Eagle Precision Machine Co., 101-A Allison St., Lock Haven, PA 17745 / 570-748-6772; FAX: 570-748-4443
Balickie, Joe, 408 Trelawney Lane, Apex, NC 27502 / 919-362-5185
Ballard, Donald. See: BALLARD INDUSTRIES
Ballard Industries, Donald Ballard Sr., PO Box 2035, Arnold, CA 95223 / 408-996-0957; FAX: 408-257-6828
Ballard Rifle & Cartridge Co., LLC, 113 W. Yellowstone Ave., Cody, WY 82414 / 307-587-4914; FAX: 307-527-6097 ballard@wyoming.com www.ballardrifles.com
Ballistic Products, Inc., 20015 75th Ave. North, Corcoran, MN 55340-9456 / 763-494-9237; FAX: 763-494-9236 info@ballisticproducts.com www.ballisticproducts.com
Ballistic Research, 1108 W. May Ave., McHenry, IL 60050 / 815-385-0037
Ballisti-Cast, Inc., P.O. Box 1057, Minot, ND 58702-1057 / 701-497-3333; FAX: 701-497-3335
Bandcor Industries, Div. of Man-Sew Corp., 6108 Sherwin Dr., Port Richey, FL 34668 / 813-848-0432
Bang-Bang Boutique (See Holster Shop, The)
Bansner's Ultimate Rifles, LLC, P.O. Box 839, 261 E. Main St., Adamstown, PA 19501 / 717-484-2370; FAX: 717-484-0523 bansner@aol.com www.bansnersrifle.com
Barbour, Inc., 55 Meadowbrook Dr., Milford, NH 03055 / 603-673-1313; FAX: 603-673-6510
Barnes, 4347 Tweed Dr., Eau Claire, WI 54703-6302
Barnes Bullets, Inc., P.O. Box 215, American Fork, UT 84003 / 801-756-4222; or 800-574-9200; FAX: 801-756-2465 email@barnesbullets.com www.barnesbullets.com
Baron Technology, 62 Spring Hill Rd., Trumbull, CT 06611 / 203-452-0515; FAX: 203-452-0663 dbaron@baronengraving.com www.baronengraving.com
Barraclough, John K., 55 Merit Park Dr., Gardena, CA 90247 / 310-324-2574 johnbar120@aol.com
Barramundi Corp., P.O. Drawer 4259, Homosassa Springs, FL 32687 / 904-628-0200
Barrel & Gunworks, 2601 Lake Valley Rd., Prescott Valley, AZ 86314 / 928-772-4060 www.cutrifle.com
Barrett Firearms Manufacturer, Inc., P.O. Box 1077, Murfreesboro, TN 37133 / 615-896-2938; FAX: 615-896-7313
Bar-Sto Precision Machine, 73377 Sullivan Rd., PO Box 1838, Twentynine Palms, CA 92277 / 760-367-2747; FAX: 760-367-2407 barsto@eee.org www.barsto.com
Barta's Gunsmithing, 10231 US Hwy. 10, Cato, WI 54230 / 920-732-4472
Barteaux Machete, 1916 SE 50th Ave., Portland, OR 97215-3238 / 503-233-5880
Bartlett Engineering, 40 South 200 East, Smithfield, UT 84335-1645 / 801-563-5910
Bates Engraving, Billy, 2302 Winthrop Dr. SW, Decatur, AL 35603 / 256-355-3690 bbrn@aol.com
Battenfeld Technologies Inc., 5885 W. Van Horn Tavern Rd., Columbia, MO 65203 / 573-445-9200; FAX: 573-447-4158 battenfeldtechnologies.com
Bauer, Eddie, 15010 NE 36th St., Redmond, WA 98052
Baumgartner Bullets, 3011 S. Alane St., W. Valley City, UT 84120
Bauska Barrels, 105 9th Ave. W., Kalispell, MT 59901 / 406-752-7706
Bear Archery, RR 4, 4600 Southwest 41st Blvd., Gainesville, FL 32601 / 904-376-2327
Bear Arms, 374-A Carson Road, St. Mathews, SC 29135
Bear Mountain Gun & Tool, 120 N. Plymouth, New Plymouth, ID 83655 / 208-278-5221; FAX: 208-278-5221
Beartooth Bullets, PO Box 491, Dept. HLD, Dover, ID 83825-0491 / 208-448-1865 bullets@beartoothbullets.com beartoothbullets.com
Beaver Park Product, Inc., 840 J St., Penrose, CO 81240 / 719-372-6744
BEC, Inc., 1227 W. Valley Blvd., Suite 204, Alhambra, CA 91803 / 626-281-5751; FAX: 626-293-7073
Beeks, Mike. See: GRAYBACK WILDCATS
Beeman Precision Airguns, 5454 Argosy Dr., Huntington Beach, CA 92649 / 714-890-4808; FAX: 714-890-4808
Behlert Precision, Inc., P.O. Box 288, 7067 Easton Rd., Pipersville, PA 18947 / 215-766-8681; or 215-766-7301; FAX: 215-766-8681
Beitzinger, George, 116-20 Atlantic Ave., Richmond Hill, NY 11419 / 718-847-7661
Belding's Custom Gun Shop, 10691 Sayers Rd., Munith, MI 49259 / 517-596-2388
Bell & Carlson, Inc., Dodge City Industrial Park, 101 Allen Rd., Dodge City, KS 67801 / 800-634-8586; or 620-225-6688; FAX: 620-225-6688 email@bellandcarlson.com www.bellandcarlson.com
Bell Reloading, Inc., 1725 Harlin Lane Rd., Villa Rica, GA 30180
Bell's Gun & Sport Shop, 3309-19 Mannheim Rd, Franklin Park, IL 60131
Bell's Legendary Country Wear, 22 Circle Dr., Bellmore, NY 11710 / 516-679-1158
Benchmark Knives (See Gerber Legendary Blades)
Benelli Armi S.P.A., Via della Stazione, 61029, Urbino, ITALY / 39-722-307-1; FAX: 39-722-327427
Benelli USA Corp, 17603 Indian Head Hwy, Accokeek, MD 20607 / 301-283-6981; FAX: 301-283-6988 benelliusa.com

MANUFACTURER'S DIRECTORY

Bengtson Arms Co., L., 6345-B E. Akron St., Mesa, AZ 85205 / 602-981-6375

Benjamin/Sheridan Co., Crosman, Rts. 5 and 20, E. Bloomfield, NY 14443 / 716-657-6161; FAX: 716-657-5405 www.crosman.com

Bentley, John, 128-D Watson Dr., Turtle Creek, PA 15145

Beretta S.P.A., Pietro, Via Beretta, 18, 25063, Gardone Vae Trompia, ITALY / 39-30-8341-1 info@benetta.com www.benetta.com

Beretta U.S.A. Corp., 17601 Beretta Drive, Accokeek, MD 20607 / 301-283-2191; FAX: 301-283-0435

Berger Bullets Ltd., 5443 W. Westwind Dr., Glendale, AZ 85310 / 602-842-4001; FAX: 602-934-9083

Bernardelli, Vincenzo, P.O. Box 460243, Houston, TX 77056-8243 www.bernardelli.com

Bernardelli, Vincenzo, Via Grande, 10, Sede Legale Torbole Casaglia, Brescia, ITALY / 39-30-8912851-2-3; FAX: 39-030-2150963 bernardelli@bernardelli.com www.bernardelli.com

Berry's Mfg., Inc., 401 North 3050 East St., St. George, UT 84770 / 435-634-1682; FAX: 435-634-1683 sales@berrysmfg.com www.berrysmfg.com

Bersa S.A., Benso Bonadimani, Magallanes 775 B1704 FLC, Ramos Mejia, ARGENTINA / 011-4656-2377; FAX: 011-4656-2093+ info@bersa-sa.com.dr www.bersa-sa.com.ar

Bert Johanssons Vapentillbehor, S-430 20 Veddige, SWEDEN,

Bertuzzi (See U.S. Importer-New England Arms Co)

Better Concepts Co., 663 New Castle Rd., Butler, PA 16001 / 412-285-9000

Beverly, Mary, 3201 Horseshoe Trail, Tallahassee, FL 32312

Bianchi International, Inc., 100 Calle Cortez, Temecula, CA 92590 / 909-676-5621; FAX: 909-676-6777

Big Bear Arms & Sporting Goods, Inc., 1112 Milam Way, Carrollton, TX 75006 / 972-416-8051; or 800-400-BEAR; FAX: 972-416-0771

Big Bore Bullets of Alaska, PO Box 521455, Big Lake, AK 99652 / 907-373-2673; FAX: 907-373-2673 doug@mtaonline.net ww.awloo.com/bbb/index.

Big Bore Express, 16345 Midway Rd., Nampa, ID 83651 / 208-466-9975; FAX: 208-466-6927 bigbore.com

Big Spring Enterprises "Bore Stores", P.O. Box 1115, Big Spring Rd., Yellville, AR 72687 / 870-449-5297; FAX: 870-449-4446

Bilal, Mustafa. See: TURK'S HEAD PRODUCTIONS

Bilinski, Bryan. See: FIELDSPORT LTD.

Bill Adair Custom Shop, 2886 Westridge, Carrollton, TX 75006 / 972-418-0950

Bill Austin's Calls, Box 284, Kaycee, WY 82639 / 307-738-2552

Bill Hanus Birdguns, P.O. Box 533, Newport, OR 97365 / 541-265-7433; FAX: 541-265-7400 www.billhanusbirdguns.com

Bill Russ Trading Post, William A. Russ, 25 William St., Addison, NY 14801-1326 / 607-359-3896

Bill Wiseman and Co., P.O. Box 3427, Bryan, TX 77805 / 409-690-3456; FAX: 409-690-0156

Billeb, Stepehn. See: QUALITY CUSTOM FIREARMS

Billings Gunsmiths, 1841 Grand Ave., Billings, MT 59102 / 406-256-8390; FAX: 406-256-6530 blgsgunsmiths@msn.com www.billingsgunsmiths.net

Billingsley & Brownell, P.O. Box 25, Dayton, WY 82836 / 307-655-9344

Bill's Gun Repair, 1007 Burlington St., Mendota, IL 61342 / 815-539-5786

Billy Bates Engraving, 2302 Winthrop Dr. SW, Decatur, AL 35603 / 256-355-3690 bbrn@aol.com

Birchwood Casey, 7900 Fuller Rd., Eden Prairie, MN 55344 / 800-328-6156; or 612-937-7933; FAX: 612-937-7979

Birdsong & Assoc., W. E., 1435 Monterey Rd, Florence, MS 39073-9748 / 601-366-8270

Bismuth Cartridge Co., 3500 Maple Ave., Suite 1650, Dallas, TX 75219 / 214-521-5880; FAX: 214-521-9035

Bison Studios, 1409 South Commerce St., Las Vegas, NV 89102 / 702-388-2891; FAX: 702-383-9967

Bitterroot Bullet Co., 2001 Cedar Ave., Lewiston, ID 83501-0412 / 208-743-5635 brootbil@lewiston.com

BKL Technologies, PO Box 5237, Brownsville, TX 78523

Black Belt Bullets (See Big Bore Express)

Black Hills Ammunition, Inc., P.O. Box 3090, Rapid City, SD 57709-3090 / 605-348-5150; FAX: 605-348-9827

Black Hills Shooters Supply, P.O. Box 4220, Rapid City, SD 57709 / 800-289-2506

Black Powder Products, 67 Township Rd. 1411, Chesapeake, OH 45619 / 614-867-8047

Black Sheep Brand, 3220 W. Gentry Parkway, Tyler, TX 75702 / 903-592-3853; FAX: 903-592-0527

Blacksmith Corp., P.O. Box 280, North Hampton, OH 45349 / 937-969-8389; FAX: 937-969-8399 sales@blacksmithcorp.com www.blacksmithcorp.com

BlackStar AccuMax Barrels, 11501 Brittmoore Park Drive, Houston, TX 77041 / 281-721-6040; FAX: 281-721-6041

BlackStar Barrel Accurizing (See BlackStar AccuMax)

Blacktail Mountain Books, 42 First Ave. W., Kalispell, MT 59901 / 406-257-5573

Blammo Ammo, P.O. Box 1677, Seneca, SC 29679 / 803-882-1768

Blaser Jagdwaffen GmbH, D-88316, Isny Im Allgau, GERMANY

Blount, Inc., Sporting Equipment Div., 2299 Snake River Ave., P.O. Box 856, Lewiston, ID 83501 / 800-627-3640; or 208-746-2351; FAX: 208-799-3904

Blount/Outers ATK, P.O. Box 39, Onalaska, WI 54650 / 608-781-5800; FAX: 608-781-0368

Blue and Gray Products Inc. (See Ox-Yoke Originals)

Blue Book Publications, Inc., 8009 34th Ave. S., Ste. 175, Minneapolis, MN 55425 / 952-854-5229; FAX: 952-853-1486 bluebook@bluebookinc.com www.bluebookinc.com

Blue Mountain Bullets, 64146 Quail Ln., Box 231, John Day, OR 97845 / 541-820-4594; FAX: 541-820-4594

Blue Ridge Machinery & Tools, Inc., P.O. Box 536-GD, Hurricane, WV 25526 / 800-872-6500; FAX: 304-562-5311 blueridgemachine@worldnet.att.net www.blueridgemachinery.com

BMC Supply, Inc., 26051 - 179th Ave. S.E., Kent, WA 98042

Bob Allen Co., P.O. Box 477, 214 SW Jackson, Des Moines, IA 50315 / 800-685-7020; FAX: 515-283-0779

Bob Allen Sportswear, 220 S. Main St., Osceola, IA 50213 / 210-344-8531; FAX: 210-342-2703 sales@bob-allen.com www.bob-allen.com

Bob Rogers Gunsmithing, P.O. Box 305, 344 S. Walnut St., Franklin Grove, IL 61031 / 815-456-2685; FAX: 815-456-2685

Bob's Gun Shop, P.O. Box 200, Royal, AR 71968 / 501-767-1970; FAX: 501-767-1970 gunparts@hsnp.com www.gun-parts.com

Bob's Tactical Indoor Shooting Range & Gun Shop, 90 Lafayette Rd., Salisbury, MA 01952 / 508-465-5561

Boessler, Erich, Am Vogeltal 3, 97702, Munnerstadt, GERMANY

Boker USA, Inc., 1550 Balsam Street, Lakewood, CO 80214 / 303-462-0662; FAX: 303-462-0668 sales@bokerusa.com bokerusa.com

Boltin, John M., P.O. Box 644, Estill, SC 29918 / 803-625-2185

Bo-Mar Tool & Mfg. Co., 6136 State Hwy. 300, Longview, TX 75604 / 903-759-4784; FAX: 903-759-9141 marykor@earthlink.net bo-mar.com

Bonadimani, Benso. See: BERSA S.A.

Bonanza (See Forster Products), 310 E. Lanark Ave., Lanark, IL 61046 / 815-493-6360; FAX: 815-493-2371

Bond Arms, Inc., P.O. Box 1296, Granbury, TX 76048 / 817-573-4445; FAX: 817-573-5636

Bond Custom Firearms, 8954 N. Lewis Ln., Bloomington, IN 47408 / 812-332-4519

Bonham's & Butterfields, 220 San Bruno Ave., San Francisco, CA 94103 / 415-861-7500; FAX: 415-861-0183 arms@butterfields.com www.butterfields.com

Boone Trading Co., Inc., PO Box 669, Brinnon, WA 98320 / 800-423-1945; or 360-796-4330; FAX: 360-796-4511 sales@boonetrading.com boonetrading.com

Boone's Custom Ivory Grips, Inc., 562 Coyote Rd., Brinnon, WA 98320 / 206-796-4330

Boonie Packer Products, P.O. Box 12517, Salem, OR 97309-0517 / 800-477-3244; or 503-581-3244; FAX: 503-581-3191 booniepacker@aol.com www.booniepacker.com

Borden Ridges Rimrock Stocks, RR 1 Box 250 BC, Springville, PA 18844 / 570-965-2505; FAX: 570-965-2328

Borden Rifles Inc., RD 1, Box 250BC, Springville, PA 18844 / 717-965-2505; FAX: 717-965-2328

Border Barrels Ltd., Riccarton Farm, Newcastleton, SCOTLAND UK

Borovnik KG, Ludwig, 9170 Ferlach, Bahnhofstrasse 7, AUSTRIA / 042 27 24 42; FAX: 042 26 43 49

Bosis (See U.S. Importer-New England Arms Co.)

Boss Manufacturing Co., 221 W. First St., Kewanee, IL 61443 / 309-852-2131; or 800-447-4581; FAX: 309-852-0848

Bostick Wildlife Calls, Inc., P.O. Box 728, Estill, SC 29918 / 803-625-2210; or 803-625-4512

Bowen Classic Arms Corp., P.O. Box 67, Louisville, TN 37777 / 865-984-3583 www.bowenclassicarms.com

Bowen Knife Co., Inc., P.O. Box 590, Blackshear, GA 31516 / 912-449-4794

Bowerly, Kent, 710 Golden Pheasant Dr., Redmond, OR 97756 / 541-923-3501 jkbowerly@aol.com

Boyds' Gunstock Industries, Inc., 25376 403 Rd. Ave., Mitchell, SD 57301 / 605-996-5011; FAX: 605-996-9878

Brace, Larry D., 771 Blackfoot Ave., Eugene, OR 97404 / 541-688-1278; FAX: 541-607-5833

Brass Eagle, Inc., 7050A Bramalea Rd., Unit 19, Mississauga,, ON L4Z 1C7 CANADA / 416-848-4844

Brauer Bros., 1520 Washington Avenue., St. Louis, MO 63103 / 314-231-2864; FAX: 314-249-4952 www.brauerbros.com

Break-Free, Inc., 13386 International Parkway, Jacksonville, FL 32218 / 800-428-0588; FAX: 904-741-5407 contactus@armorholdings.com www.break-free.com

Brenneke GmbH, P.O. Box 1646, 30837 Langenhagen, Langenhagen, GERMANY / +49-511-97262-0; FAX: +49-511-97262-62 info@brenneke.de brenneke.com

Bridgeman Products, Harry Jaffin, 153 B Cross Slope Court, Englishtown, NJ 07726 / 732-536-3604; FAX: 732-972-1004

Bridgers Best, P.O. Box 1410, Berthoud, CO 80513

Briese Bullet Co., Inc., 3442 42nd Ave. SE, Tappen, ND 58487 / 701-327-4578; FAX: 701-327-4579

Brigade Quartermasters, 1025 Cobb International Blvd., Dept. VH, Kennesaw, GA 30144-4300 / 404-428-1248; or 800-241-3125; FAX: 404-426-7726

Briganti, A.J., 512 Rt. 32, Highland Mills, NY 10930 / 914-928-9573

Briley Mfg. Inc., 1230 Lumpkin, Houston, TX 77043 / 800-331-5718; or 713-932-6995; FAX: 713-932-1043

Brill, R. See: ROYAL ARMS INTERNATIONAL

British Sporting Arms, RR1, Box 130, Millbrook, NY 12545 / 914-677-8303

Broad Creek Rifle Works, Ltd., 120 Horsey Ave., Laurel, DE 19956 / 302-875-5446; FAX: 302-875-1448 bcrw4guns@aol.com

Brockman's Custom Gunsmithing, P.O. Box 357, Gooding, ID 83330 / 208-934-5050

Brocock Ltd., 43 River Street, Digbeth, Birmingham, B5 5SA ENGLAND / 011-021-773-1200; FAX: 011-021-773-1211 sales@brocock.co.un www.brocock.co.uk

Broken Gun Ranch, 10739 126 Rd., Spearville, KS 67876 / 316-385-2587; FAX: 316-385-2597 nbowlin@ucom.net www.brokengunranch

Brooker, Dennis, Rt. 1, Box 12A, Derby, IA 50068 / 515-533-2103

Brooks Tactical Systems-Agrip, 279-C Shorewood Ct., Fox Island, WA 98333 / 253-549-2866 FAX: 253-549-2703 brooks@brookstactical.com www.brookstactical.com

Brown Co., E. Arthur, 3404 Pawnee Dr., Alexandria, MN 56308 / 320-762-8847

Brown Dog Ent., 2200 Calle Camelia, 1000 Oaks, CA 91360 / 805-497-2318; FAX: 805-497-1618

Brown Precision, Inc., 7786 Molinos Ave., Los Molinos, CA 96055 / 530-384-2506; FAX: 916-384-1638 www.brownprecision.com

Brown Products, Inc., Ed, 43825 Muldrow Trail, Perry, MO 63462 / 573-565-3261; FAX: 573-565-2791 edbrown@edbrown.com www.edbrown.com

Brownells, Inc., 200 S. Front St., Montezuma, IA 50171 / 800-741-0015; FAX: 800-264-3068 orderdesk@brownells.com www.brownells.com

Browning Arms Co., One Browning Place, Morgan, UT 84050 / 801-876-2711; FAX: 801-876-3331 www.browning.com

Manufacturer's Directory

Browning Arms Co. (Parts & Service), 3005 Arnold Tenbrook Rd., Arnold, MO 63010 / 617-287-6800; FAX: 617-287-9751
BRP, Inc. High Performance Cast Bullets, 1210 Alexander Rd., Colorado Springs, CO 80909 / 719-633-0658
Brunton U.S.A., 620 E. Monroe Ave., Riverton, WY 82501 / 307-856-6559; FAX: 307-857-4702 info@brunton.com www.brunton.com
Bryan & Assoc., R D Sauls, PO Box 5772, Anderson, SC 29623-5772 / 864-261-6810 bryanandac@aol.com www.huntersweb.com/bryanandac
Brynin, Milton, P.O. Box 383, Yonkers, NY 10710 / 914-779-4333
BSA Guns Ltd., Armoury Rd. Small Heath, Birmingham B11 2PP, ENGLAND / 011-021-772-8543; FAX: 011-021-773-0845 sales@bsagun.com www.bsagun.com
BSA Optics, 3911 SW 47th Ave., Ste. 914, Ft. Lauderdale, FL 33314 / 954-581-2144; FAX: 954-581-3165 4info@basaoptics.com www.bsaoptics.com
B-Square Company, Inc., P.O. Box 11281, 2708 St. Louis Ave., Ft. Worth, TX 76110 / 817-923-0964 or 800-433-2909; FAX: 817-926-7012
Buchsenmachermeister, Peter Hofer Jagdwaffen, Buchsenmachermeister, Kirchgasse 24 A-9170, Ferlach, AUSTRIA / 43 4227 3683; FAX: 43 4227 368330 peterhofer@hoferwaffen.com www.hoferwaffen.com
Buck Knives, Inc., 1900 Weld Blvd., P.O. Box 1267, El Cajon, CA 92020 / 619-449-1100; or 800-326-2825; FAX: 619-562-5774
Buck Stix-SOS Products Co., Box 3, Neenah, WI 54956
Buck Stop Lure Co., Inc., 3600 Grow Rd. NW, P.O. Box 636, Stanton, MI 48888 / 989-762-5091; FAX: 989-762-5124 buckstop@nethawk.com www.buckstopscents.com
Buckeye Custom Bullets, 6490 Stewart Rd., Elida, OH 45807 / 419-641-4463
Buckhorn Gun Works, 8109 Woodland Dr., Black Hawk, SD 57718 / 605-787-6472
Buckskin Bullet Co., P.O. Box 1893, Cedar City, UT 84721 / 435-586-3286
Budin, Dave, 817 Main St., P.O. Box 685, Margaretville, NY 12455 / 914-568-4103; FAX: 914-586-4105
Budin, Dave. See: DEL-SPORTS, INC.
Buenger Enterprises/Goldenrod Dehumidifier, 3600 S. Harbor Blvd., Oxnard, CA 93035 / 800-451-6797; or 805-985-5828; FAX: 805-985-1534
Buffalo Arms Co., 660 Vermeer Ct., Ponderay, ID 83852 / 208-263-6953; FAX: 208-265-2096 www.buffaloarms.com
Buffalo Bullet Co., Inc., 12637 Los Nietos Rd., Unit A, Santa Fe Springs, CA 90670 / 800-423-8069; FAX: 562-944-5054
Buffalo Gun Center, 3385 Harlem Rd., Buffalo, NY 14225 / 716-833-2581; FAX: 716-833-2265 www.buffaloguncenter.com
Buffalo Rock Shooters Supply, R.R. 1, Ottawa, IL 61350 / 815-433-2471
Buffer Technologies, P.O. Box 104930, Jefferson City, MO 65110 / 573-634-8529; FAX: 573-634-8522
Bull Mountain Rifle Co., 6327 Golden West Terrace, Billings, MT 59106 / 406-656-0778
Bullberry Barrel Works, Ltd., 2430 W. Bullberry Ln., Hurricane, UT 84737 / 435-635-9866; FAX: 435-635-0348 fred@bullberry.com www.bullberry.com
Bullet Metals, Bill Ferguson, P.O. Box 1238, Sierra Vista, AZ 85636 / 520-458-5321; FAX: 520-458-1421 info@theantimonyman.com www.bullet-metals.com
Bullet N Press, 1210 Jones St., Gastonia, NC 28052 / 704-853-0265 bnpress@quik.com www.clt.quik.com/bnpress
Bullet Swaging Supply, Inc., P.O. Box 1056, 303 McMillan Rd., West Monroe, LA 71291 / 318-387-3266; FAX: 318-387-7779 leblackmon@colla.com
Bull-X, Inc., 411 E. Water St., Farmer City, IL 61842-1556 / 309-928-2574 or 800-248-3845; FAX: 309-928-2130
Burkhart Gunsmithing, Don, P.O. Box 852, Rawlins, WY 82301 / 307-324-6007
Burnham Bros., P.O. Box 1148, Menard, TX 78659 / 915-396-4572; FAX: 915-396-4574
Burris Co., Inc., PO Box 1747, 331 E. 8th St., Greeley, CO 80631 / 970-356-1670; FAX: 970-356-8702
Bushmaster Firearms, Inc., 999 Roosevelt Trail, Windham, ME 04062 / 800-998-7928; FAX: 207-892-8068 info@bushmaster.com www.bushmaster.com
Bushmaster Hunting & Fishing, 451 Alliance Ave., Toronto, ON M6N 2J1 CANADA / 416-763-4040; FAX: 416-763-0623
Bushnell Sports Optics Worldwide, 9200 Cody, Overland Park, KS 66214 / 913-752-3400 or 800-423-3537; FAX: 913-752-3550
Buster's Custom Knives, P.O. Box 214, Richfield, UT 84701 / 435-896-5319; FAX: 435-896-8333 www.warenskiknives.com
Butler Creek Corp., 2100 S. Silverstone Way, Meridian, ID 83642-8151 / 800-423-8327 or 406-388-1356; FAX: 406-388-7204
Butler Enterprises, 834 Oberting Rd., Lawrenceburg, IN 47025 / 812-537-3584
Buzz Fletcher Custom Stockmaker, 117 Silver Road, P.O. Box 189, Taos, NM 87571 / 505-758-3486

C

C&D Special Products (See Claybuster Wads & Harvester Bullets)
C&H Research, 115 Sunnyside Dr., Box 351, Lewis, KS 67552 / 316-324-5445; or 888-324-5445; FAX: 620-324-5984 info@mercuryrecoil.com www.mercuryrecoil.com
C. Palmer Manufacturing Co., Inc., P.O. Box 220, West Newton, PA 15089 / 412-872-8200; FAX: 412-872-8302
C. Sharps Arms Co. Inc./Montana Armory, 100 Centennial Dr., PO Box 885, Big Timber, MT 59011 / 406-932-4353; FAX: 406-932-4443
C.S. Van Gorden & Son, Inc., 1815 Main St., Bloomer, WI 54724 / 715-568-2612 vangorden@bloomer.net
C.W. Erickson's L.L.C., 530 Garrison Ave. NE, PO Box 522, Buffalo, MN 55313 / 763-682-3665; FAX: 763-682-4328 www.archerhunter.com
Cabanas (See U.S. Importer-Mandall Shooting Supply
Cabela's, One Cabela Drive, Sidney, NE 69160 / 308-254-5505; FAX: 308-254-8420
Cabinet Mtn. Outfitters Scents & Lures, P.O. Box 766, Plains, MT 59859 / 406-826-3970
Cache La Poudre Rifleworks, 140 N. College, Ft. Collins, CO 80524 / 920-482-6913
Calhoon Mfg., 4343 U.S. Highway 87, Havre, MT 59501 / 406-395-4079 www.jamescalhoon.com
Cali'co Hardwoods, Inc., 3580 Westwind Blvd., Santa Rosa, CA 95403 / 707-546-4045; FAX: 707-546-4027 calicohardwoods@msn.com
Calico Light Weapon Systems, 1489 Greg St., Sparks, NV 89431
California Sights (See Fautheree, Andy)
Cambos Outdoorsman, 532 E. Idaho Ave., Ontario, OR 97914 / 541-889-3135; FAX: 541-889-2633
Cambos Outdoorsman, Fritz Hallberg, 532 E. Idaho Ave, Ontario, OR 97914 / 541-889-3135; FAX: 541-889-2633
Camdex, Inc., 2330 Alger, Troy, MI 48083 / 810-528-2300; FAX: 810-528-0989
Cameron's, 16690 W. 11th Ave., Golden, CO 80401 / 303-279-7365; FAX: 303-628-5413 ncnoremac@aol.com
Camillus Cutlery Co., 54 Main St., Camillus, NY 13031 / 315-672-8111; FAX: 315-672-8832
Campbell, Dick, 20000 Silver Ranch Rd., Conifer, CO 80433 / 303-697-0150; FAX: 303-697-0150 dicksknives@aol.com
Camp-Cap Products, P.O. Box 3805, Chesterfield, MO 63006 / 314-532-4340; FAX: 314-532-4340
Cannon Safe, Inc., 216 S. 2nd Ave. #BLD-932, San Bernardino, CA 92400 / 310-692-0636; or 800-242-1055; FAX: 310-692-7252
Canons Delcour, Rue J.B. Cools, B-4040, Herstal, BELGIUM / 32.(0)42.40.61.40; FAX: 32(0)42.40.22.88
Canyon Cartridge Corp., P.O. Box 152, Albertson, NY 11507 FAX: 516-294-8946
Cape Outfitters, 599 County Rd. 206, Cape Girardeau, MO 63701 / 573-335-4103; FAX: 573-335-1555
Caraville Manufacturing, P.O. Box 4545, Thousand Oaks, CA 91359 / 805-499-1234
Carbide Checkering Tools (See J&R Engineering)
Carhartt, Inc., P.O. Box 600, 3 Parklane Blvd., Dearborn, MI 48121 / 800-358-3825; or 313-271-8460; FAX: 313-271-3455
Carl Walther GmbH, B.P. 4325, D-89033, Ulm, GERMANY
Carl Zeiss Inc., 13005 N. Kingston Ave., Chester, VA 23836 / 800-441-3005; FAX: 804-530-8481
Carlson, Douglas R, Antique American Firearms, P.O. Box 71035, Dept GD, Des Moines, IA 50325 / 515-224-6552
Carolina Precision Rifles, 1200 Old Jackson Hwy., Jackson, SC 29831 / 803-827-2069
Carrell, William. See: CARRELL'S PRECISION FIREARMS
Carrell's Precision Firearms, William Carrell, 1952 W.Silver Falls Ct., Meridian, ID 83642-3837
Carry-Lite, Inc., P.O. Box 1587, Fort Smith, AR 72902 / 479-782-8971; FAX: 479-783-0234
Carter's Gun Shop, 225 G St., Penrose, CO 81240 / 719-372-6240
Cascade Bullet Co., Inc., 2355 South 6th St., Klamath Falls, OR 97601 / 503-884-9316
Cascade Shooters, 2155 N.W. 12th St., Redwood, OR 97756
Case & Sons Cutlery Co., W R, Owens Way, Bradford, PA 16701 / 814-368-4123; or 800-523-6350; FAX: 814-768-5369
Case Sorting System, 12695 Cobblestone Creek Rd., Poway, CA 92064 / 619-486-9340
Cash Mfg. Co., Inc., P.O. Box 130, 201 S. Klein Dr., Waunakee, WI 53597-0130 / 608-849-5664; FAX: 608-849-5664
Caspian Arms, Ltd., 14 North Main St., Hardwick, VT 05843 / 802-472-6454; FAX: 802-472-6709
Cast Performance Bullet Company, P.O. Box 153, Riverton, WY 82501 / 307-857-2940; FAX: 307-857-3132 castperform@wyoming.com castperformance.com
Casull Arms Corp., P.O. Box 1629, Afton, WY 83110 / 307-886-0200
Caswell International, 720 Industrial Dr. No. 112, Cary, IL 60013 / 847-639-7666; FAX: 847-639-7694 www.caswellintl.com
Cathey Enterprises, Inc., P.O. Box 2202, Brownwood, TX 76804 / 915-643-2553; FAX: 915-643-3653
Cation, 2341 Alger St., Troy, MI 48083 / 810-689-0658; FAX: 810-689-7558
Caywood, Shane J., P.O. Box 321, Minocqua, WI 54548 / 715-277-3866
Caywood Gunmakers, 18 Kings Hill Estates, Berryville, AR 72616 / 870-423-4741 www.caywoodguns.com
CBC, Avenida Humberto de Campos 3220, 09400-000, Ribeirao Pires, SP, BRAZIL / 55 11 4822 8378; FAX: 55 11 4822 8323 export@cbc.com.bc www.cbc.com.bc
CBC-BRAZIL, 3 Cuckoo Lane, Honley, Yorkshire HD7 2BR, ENGLAND / 44-1484-661062; FAX: 44-1484-663709
CCG Enterprises, 5217 E. Belknap St., Halton City, TX 76117 / 800-819-7464
CCI/Speer Div of ATK, P.O. Box 856, 2299 Snake River Ave., Lewiston, ID 83501 / 800-627-3640 or 208-746-2351
CCL Security Products, 199 Whiting St, New Britain, CT 06051 / 800-733-8588
Cedar Hill Game Calls, Inc., 238 Vic Allen Rd, Downsville, LA 71234 / 318-982-5632; FAX: 318-368-2245
Centaur Systems, Inc., 1602 Foothill Rd., Kalispell, MT 59901 / 406-755-8609; FAX: 406-755-8609
Center Lock Scope Rings, 9901 France Ct., Lakeville, MN 55044 / 952-461-2114; FAX: 952-461-2194 marklee55044@usfamily.net
Central Specialties Ltd (See Trigger Lock Division
Century Gun Dist. Inc., 1467 Jason Rd., Greenfield, IN 46140 / 317-462-4524
Century International Arms, Inc., 1161 Holland Dr, Boca Raton, FL 33487 / 800-527-1252; FAX: 561-998-1993 support@centuryarms.com www.centuryarms.com
CFVentures, 509 Harvey Dr., Bloomington, IN 47403-1715 paladinwilltravel@yahoo.com www.caversam16.freeserve.co.uk
CH Tool & Die Co. (See 4-D Custom Die Co.), 711 N Sandusky St., P.O. Box 889, Mt. Vernon, OH 43050-0889 / 740-397-7214; FAX: 740-397-6600
Chace Leather Products, 507 Alden St., Fall River, MA 02722 / 508-678-7556; FAX: 508-675-9666 chacelea@aol.com www.chaceleather.com
Chadick's Ltd., P.O. Box 100, Terrell, TX 75160 / 214-563-7577

REFERENCE

MANUFACTURER'S DIRECTORY

Chambers Flintlocks Ltd., Jim, 116 Sams Branch Rd., Candler, NC 28715 / 828-667-8361; FAX: 828-665-0852 www.flintlocks.com
Champion Shooters' Supply, P.O. Box 303, New Albany, OH 43054 / 614-855-1603; FAX: 614-855-1209
Champion Target Co., 232 Industrial Parkway, Richmond, IN 47374 / 800-441-4971
Champion's Choice, Inc., 201 International Blvd., LaVergne, TN 37086 / 615-793-4066; FAX: 615-793-4070 champ.choice@earthlink.net www.champchoice.com
Champlin Firearms, Inc., P.O. Box 3191, Woodring Airport, Enid, OK 73701 / 580-237-7388; FAX: 580-242-6922 info@champlinarms.com www.champlinarms.com
Chapman Academy of Practical Shooting, 4350 Academy Rd., Hallsville, MO 65255 / 573-696-5544; FAX: 573-696-2266 ha@chapmanacademy.com
Chapman, J Ken. See: OLD WEST BULLET MOULDS
Chapman Manufacturing Co., 471 New Haven Rd., P.O. Box 250, Durham, CT 06422 / 860-349-9228; FAX: 860-349-0084 sales@chapmanmfg.com www.chapmanmfg.com
Chapuis Armes, 21 La Gravoux, BP15, 42380, St. Bonnet-le-Chatea, FRANCE / (33)77.50.06.96
Chapuis USA, 416 Business Park, Bedford, KY 40006
Charter 2000, 273 Canal St, Shelton, CT 06484 / 203-922-1652
Checkmate Refinishing, 370 Champion Dr., Brooksville, FL 34601 / 352-799-5774; FAX: 352-799-2986 checkmatecustom.com
Cheddite, France S.A., 99 Route de Lyon, F-26501, Bourg-les-Valence, FRANCE / 33-75-56-4545; FAX: 33-75-56-3587 export@cheddite.com
Chelsea Gun Club of New York City Inc., 237 Ovington Ave., Apt. D53, Brooklyn, NY 11209 / 718-836-9422; or 718-833-2704
Cherry Creek State Park Shooting Center, 12500 E. Belleview Ave., Englewood, CO 80111 / 303-693-1765
CheVron Bullets, RR1, Ottawa, IL 61350 / 815-433-2471
Cheyenne Pioneer Products, PO Box 28425, Kansas City, MO 64188 / 816-413-9196; FAX: 816-455-2859 cheyennepp@aol.com www.cartridgeboxes.com
Chicago Cutlery Co., 1536 Beech St., Terre Haute, IN 47804 / 800-457-2665
Chicasaw Gun Works, 4 Mi. Mkr., Pluto Rd., Box 868, Shady Spring, WV 25918-0868 / 304-763-2848; FAX: 304-763-3725
Chip McCormick Corp., P.O. Box 1560, Manchaca, TX 78652 / 800-328-2447; FAX: 512-280-4282 www.chipmccormick.com
Chipmunk (See Oregon Arms, Inc.)
Choate Machine & Tool Co., Inc., P.O. Box 218, 116 Lovers Ln., Bald Knob, AR 72010 / 501-724-6193; or 800-972-6390; FAX: 501-724-5873
Christensen Arms, 192 East 100 North, Fayette, UT 84630 / 435-528-7999; FAX: 435-528-7494 www.christensenarms.com
Christie's East, 20 Rockefeller Plz., New York, NY 10020-1902 / 212-606-0406 christics.com
Chu Tani Ind., Inc., P.O. Box 2064, Cody, WY 82414-2064
Chuck's Gun Shop, P.O. Box 597, Waldo, FL 32694 / 904-468-2264
Chuilli, Stephen, 8895 N. Military Trl. Ste., Ste. 201E, Palm Beach Gardens, FL 33410
Churchill (See U.S. Importer-Ellett Bros.)
Churchill, Winston G., 2838 20 Mile Stream Rd., Proctorville, VT 05153 / 802-226-7772
Churchill Glove Co., James, PO Box 298, Centralia, WA 98531 / 360-736-2816; FAX: 360-330-0151
CIDCO, 21480 Pacific Blvd., Sterling, VA 22170 / 703-444-5353
Cimarron F.A. Co., P.O. Box 906, Fredericksburg, TX 78624-0906 / 830-997-9090; FAX: 830-997-0802 cimgraph@koc.com www.cimarron-firearms.com
Cincinnati Swaging, 2605 Marlington Ave., Cincinnati, OH 45208
Clark Custom Guns, Inc., 336 Shootout Lane, Princeton, LA 71067 / 318-949-9884; FAX: 318-949-9829
Clark Firearms Engraving, P.O. Box 80746, San Marino, CA 91118 / 818-287-1652
Clarkfield Enterprises, Inc., 1032 10th Ave., Clarkfield, MN 56223 / 612-669-7140
Claro Walnut Gunstock Co., 1235 Stanley Ave., Chico, CA 95928 / 530-342-5188; FAX: 530-342-5199 wally@clarowalnutgunstocks.com www.clarowalnutgunstocks.com
Classic Arms Company, Rt 1 Box 120F, Burnet, TX 78611 / 512-756-4001
Classic Arms Corp., P.O. Box 106, Dunsmuir, CA 96025-0106 / 530-235-2000
Classic Old West Styles, 1060 Doniphan Park Circle C, El Paso, TX 79936 / 915-587-0684
Claybuster Wads & Harvester Bullets, 309 Sequoya Dr., Hopkinsville, KY 42240 / 800-922-6287; or 800-284-1746; FAX: 502-885-8088
Clean Shot Technologies, 21218 St. Andrews Blvd. Ste 504, Boca Raton, FL 33433 / 888-866-2532
Clearview Mfg. Co., Inc., 413 S. Oakley St., Fordyce, AR 71742 / 501-352-8557; FAX: 501-352-7120
Clearview Products, 3021 N. Portland, Oklahoma City, OK 73107
Cleland's Outdoor World, Inc, 10306 Airport Hwy., Swanton, OH 43558 / 419-865-4713; FAX: 419-865-5865
Clements' Custom Leathercraft, Chas, 1741 Dallas St., Aurora, CO 80010-2018 / 303-364-0403; FAX: 303-739-9824 gryphons@home.com kuntaoslcat.com
Clenzoil Worldwide Corp, Jack Fitzgerald, 25670 1st St., Westlake, OH 44145-1430 / 440-899-0482; FAX: 440-899-0483
Clift Mfg., L. R., 3821 Hammonton Rd., Marysville, CA 95901 / 916-755-3390; FAX: 916-755-3393
Clymer Mfg. Co., 1645 W. Hamlin Rd., Rochester Hills, MI 48309-3312 / 248-853-5555; FAX: 248-853-1530
C-More Systems, P.O. Box 1750, 7553 Gary Rd., Manassas, VA 20108 / 703-361-2663; FAX: 703-361-5881
Cobra Enterprises, Inc., 1960 S. Milestone Drive, Suite F, Salt Lake City, UT 84104 FAX: 801-908-8301 www.cobrapistols@networld.com
Cobra Sport S.R.I., Via Caduti Nei Lager No. 1, 56020 San Romano, Montopoli v/Arno (Pi, ITALY / 0039-571-450490; FAX: 0039-571-450492
Coffin, Charles H., 3719 Scarlet Ave., Odessa, TX 79762 / 915-366-4729; FAX: 915-366-4729
Coffin, Jim (See Working Guns)
Coffin, Jim. See: WORKING GUNS
Cogar's Gunsmithing, 206 Redwine Dr., Houghton Lake, MI 48629 / 517-422-4591
Coghlan's Ltd., 121 Irene St., Winnipeg, MB R3T 4C7 CANADA / 204-284-9550; FAX: 204-475-4127
Cold Steel Inc., 3036 Seaborg Ave. Ste. A, Ventura, CA 93003 / 800-255-4716; or 800-624-2363; FAX: 805-642-9727
Cole-Grip, 16135 Cohasset St., Van Nuys, CA 91406 / 818-782-4424
Coleman Co., Inc., 3600 N. Hydraulic, Wichita, KS 67219 / 1-800-835-3278; www.coleman.com
Cole's Gun Works, Old Bank Building, Rt. 4 Box 250, Moyock, NC 27958 / 919-435-2345
Collector's Armoury, Ltd., Tom Nelson, 9404 Gunston Cove Rd., Lorton, VA 22079 / 703-493-9120; FAX: 703-493-9424 www.collectorsarmoury.com
Collings, Ronald, 1006 Cielta Linda, Vista, CA 92083
Colonial Arms, Inc., P.O. Box 636, Selma, AL 36702-0636 / 334-872-9455; FAX: 334-872-9540 colonialarms@mindspring.com www.colonialarms.com
Colonial Repair, 47 Navarre St., Roslindale, MA 02131-4725 / 617-469-4951
Colorado Gunsmithing Academy, RR 3 Box 79B, El Campo, TX 77437 / 719-336-4099; or 800-754-2046; FAX: 719-336-9642
Colorado School of Trades, 1575 Hoyt St., Lakewood, CO 80215 / 800-234-4594; FAX: 303-233-4723
Colt Blackpowder Arms Co., 110 8th Street, Brooklyn, NY 11215 / 718-499-4678; FAX: 718-768-8056
Colt's Mfg. Co., Inc., PO Box 1868, Hartford, CT 06144-1868 / 800-962-COLT; or 860-236-6311; FAX: 860-244-1449
Compass Industries, Inc., 104 East 25th St., New York, NY 10010 / 212-473-2614 or 800-221-9904; FAX: 212-353-0826
Compasseco, Ltd., 151 Atkinson Hill Ave., Bardtown, KY 40004 / 502-349-0910
Competition Electronics, Inc., 3469 Precision Dr., Rockford, IL 61109 / 815-874-8001; FAX: 815-874-8181
Competitor Corp., Inc., 26 Knight St. Unit 3, Jaffrey, NH 03452 / 603-532-9483; FAX: 603-532-8209 competitorcorp@aol.com competitor-pistol.com
Component Concepts, Inc., 530 S. Springbrook Road, Newberg, OR 97132 / 503-554-8095; FAX: 503-554-9370 cci@cybcon.com www.phantomonline.com
Concept Development Corp., 16610 E. Laser Drive, Suite 5, Fountain Hills, AZ 85268-6644
Conetrol Scope Mounts, 10225 Hwy. 123 S., Seguin, TX 78155 / 830-379-3030; or 800-CONETROL; FAX: 830-379-3030 email@conetrol.com www.conetrol.com
Connecticut Shotgun Mfg. Co., P.O. Box 1692, 35 Woodland St., New Britain, CT 06051 / 860-225-6581; FAX: 860-832-8707
Connecticut Valley Classics (See CVC, BPI)
Conrad, C. A., 3964 Ebert St., Winston-Salem, NC 27127 / 919-788-5469
Cook Engineering Service, 891 Highbury Rd., Vict, 3133 AUSTRALIA
Cooper Arms, P.O. Box 114, Stevensville, MT 59870 / 406-777-0373; FAX: 406-777-5228
Cooper-Woodward Perfect Lube, 4120 Oesterle Rd., Helena, MT 59602 / 406-459-2287 cwperfectlube@mt.net cwperfectlube.com
Corbin Mfg. & Supply, Inc., 600 Industrial Circle, P.O. Box 2659, White City, OR 97503 / 541-826-5211; FAX: 541-826-8669 sales@corbins.com www.corbins.com
Cor-Bon Inc./Glaser LLC, P.O. Box 173, 1311 Industry Rd., Sturgis, SD 57785 / 605-347-4544; or 800-221-3489; FAX: 605-347-5055 email@corbon.com www.corbon.com
Corkys Gun Clinic, 4401 Hot Springs Dr., Greeley, CO 80634-9226 / 970-330-0516
Corry, John, 861 Princeton Ct., Neshanic Station, NJ 08853 / 908-369-8019
Cosmi Americo & Figlio S.N.C., Via Flaminia 307, Ancona, ITALY / 071-888208; FAX: 39-071-887008
Coulston Products, Inc., P.O. Box 30, 201 Ferry St. Suite 212, Easton, PA 18044-0030 / 215-253-0167; or 800-445-9927; FAX: 215-252-1511
Counter Assault, 120 Industrial Court, Kalispell, MT 59901 / 406-257-4740; FAX: 406-257-6674
Cousin Bob's Mountain Products, 7119 Ohio River Blvd., Ben Avon, PA 15202 / 412-766-5114; FAX: 412-766-5114
CP Bullets, 1310 Industrial Hwy #5-6, South Hampton, PA 18966 / 215-953-7264; FAX: 215-953-7275
CQB Training, P.O. Box 1739, Manchester, MO 63011
Craftguard, 3624 Logan Ave., Waterloo, IA 50703 / 319-232-2959; FAX: 319-234-0804
Crandall Tool & Machine Co., 19163 21 Mile Rd., Tustin, MI 49688 / 616-829-4430
Creedmoor Sports, Inc., P.O. Box 1040, Oceanside, CA 92051 / 767-757-5529; FAX: 760-757-5558 shoot@creedmoorsports.com www.creedmoorsports.com
Creek Side Metal & Woodcrafters, Fishers Hill, VA 22626 / 703-465-3903
Creighton Audette, 19 Highland Circle, Springfield, VT 05156 / 802-885-2331
Crimson Trace Lasers, 8090 SW Cirrus Dr., Beverton, OR 97008 / 800-442-2406; FAX: 503-627-0166 www.crimsontrace.com
Crit'R Call (See Rocky Mountain Wildlife Products)
Crosman Airguns, Rts. 5 and 20, E. Bloomfield, NY 14443 / 716-657-6161; FAX: 716-657-5405
Crosman Blades (See Coleman Co., Inc.)
Crouse's Country Cover, P.O. Box 160, Storrs, CT 06268 / 860-423-8736
CRR, Inc./Marble's Inc., 420 Industrial Park, P.O. Box 111, Gladstone, MI 49837 / 906-428-3710; FAX: 906-428-3711
Crucelegui, Hermanos (See U.S. Importer-Mandall)
Cubic Shot Shell Co., Inc., 98 Fatima Dr., Campbell, OH 44405 / 330-755-0349
Cullity Restoration, 209 Old Country Rd., East Sandwich, MA 02537 / 508-888-1147
Cumberland Arms, 514 Shafer Road, Manchester, TN 37355 / 800-797-8414

REFERENCE

MANUFACTURER'S DIRECTORY

Cumberland Mountain Arms, P.O. Box 710, Winchester, TN 37398 / 615-967-8414; FAX: 615-967-9199
Cummings Bullets, 1417 Esperanza Way, Escondido, CA 92027
Cupp, Alana, Custom Engraver, P.O. Box 207, Annabella, UT 84711 / 801-896-4834
Curly Maple Stock Blanks (See Tiger-Hunt)
Curtis Cast Bullets, 527 W. Babcock St., Bozeman, MT 59715 / 406-587-8117; FAX: 406-587-8117
Curtis Gun Shop (See Curtis Cast Bullets)
Custom Bullets by Hoffman, 2604 Peconic Ave., Seaford, NY 11783
Custom Calls, 607 N. 5th St., Burlington, IA 52601 / 319-752-4465
Custom Checkering Service, Kathy Forster, 2124 S.E. Yamhill St., Portland, OR 97214 / 503-236-5874
Custom Chronograph, Inc., 5305 Reese Hill Rd., Sumas, WA 98295 / 360-988-7801
Custom Firearms (See Ahrends, Kim)
Custom Products (See Jones Custom Products)
Custom Quality Products, Inc., 345 W. Girard Ave., P.O. Box 71129, Madison Heights, MI 48071 / 810-585-1616; FAX: 810-585-0644
Custom Riflestocks, Inc., Michael M. Kokolus, 7005 Herber Rd., New Tripoli, PA 18066 / 610-298-3013; FAX: 610-298-2431 mkokolus@prodigy.net
Custom Single Shot Rifles, 9651 Meadows Lane, Guthrie, OK 73044 / 405-282-3634
Custom Tackle and Ammo, P.O. Box 1886, Farmington, NM 87499 / 505-632-3539
Cutco Cutlery, P.O. Box 810, Olean, NY 14760 / 716-372-3111
CVA, 5988 Peachtree Corners East, Norcross, GA 30071 / 770-449-4687; FAX: 770-242-8546 info@cva.com www.cva.com
Cylinder & Slide, Inc., William R. Laughridge, 245 E. 4th St., Fremont, NE 68025 / 402-721-4277; FAX: 402-721-0263 bill@cylinder-slide.com www.clinder-slide.com
CZ USA, PO Box 171073, Kansas City, KS 66117 / 913-321-1811; FAX: 913-321-4901

D

D&D Gunsmiths, Ltd., 363 E. Elmwood, Troy, MI 48083 / 810-583-1512; FAX: 810-583-1524
D&G Precision Duplicators (See Greene Precision)
D&H Precision Tooling, 7522 Barnard Mill Rd., Ringwood, IL 60072 / 815-653-4011
D&L Industries (See D.J. Marketing)
D&L Sports, P.O. Box 651, Gillette, WY 82717 / 307-686-4008
D.C.C. Enterprises, 259 Wynburn Ave., Athens, GA 30601
D.J. Marketing, 10602 Horton Ave., Downey, CA 90241 / 310-806-0891; FAX: 310-806-6231
D.L. Unmussig Bullets, 7862 Brentford Dr., Richmond, VA 23225 / 804-320-1165; FAX: 804-320-4587
Dade Screw Machine Products, 2319 NW 7th Ave., Miami, FL 33127 / 305-573-5050
Daisy Outdoor Products, P.O. Box 220, Rogers, AR 72757 / 479-636-1200; FAX: 479-636-0573 www.daisy.com
Dakota (See U.S. Importer-EMF Co., Inc.)
Dakota Arms, Inc., 130 Industry Road, Sturgis, SD 57785 / 605-347-4686; FAX: 605-347-4459 info@dakotaarms.com www.dakotaarms.com
Dakota Corp., 77 Wales St., P.O. Box 543, Rutland, VT 05701 / 802-775-6062; or 800-451-4167; FAX: 802-773-3919
Daly, Charles/KBI, P.O. Box 6625, Harrisburg, PA 17112 / 866-DALY GUN
Da-Mar Gunsmith's, Inc., 102 1st St., Solvay, NY 13209
damascususa@inteliport.com, 149 Deans Farm Rd., Tyner, NC 27980 / 252-221-2010; FAX: 252-221-2010 damascususa@inteliport.com
Dan Wesson Firearms, 5169 Rt. 12 South, Norwich, NY 13815 / 607-336-1174; FAX: 607-336-2730 danwessonfirearms@citlink.net danwessonfirearms.com
Danforth, Mikael. See: VEKTOR USA
Dangler, Homer L., 2870 Lee Marie Dr., Adrian, MI 49221 / 517-266-1997
Danner Shoe Mfg. Co., 12722 NE Airport Way, Portland, OR 97230 / 503-251-1100; or 800-345-0430; FAX: 503-251-1119
Dan's Whetstone Co., Inc., 130 Timbs Place, Hot Springs, AR 71913 / 501-767-1616; FAX: 501-767-9598 questions@danswhetstone.com www.danswhetstone.com
Danuser Machine Co., 550 E. Third St., P.O. Box 368, Fulton, MO 65251 / 573-642-2246; FAX: 573-642-2240 sales@danuser.com www.danuser.com
Dara-Nes, Inc. (See Nesci Enterprises, Inc.)
D'Arcy Echols & Co., P.O. Box 421, Millville, UT 84326 / 435-755-6842
Darlington Gun Works, Inc., P.O. Box 698, 516 S. 52 Bypass, Darlington, SC 29532 / 803-393-3931
Dart Bell/Brass (See MAST Technology)
Darwin Hensley Gunmaker, P.O. Box 329, Brightwood, OR 97011 / 503-622-5411
Data Tech Software Systems, 19312 East Eldorado Drive, Aurora, CO 80013
Dave Norin Schrank's Smoke & Gun, 2010 Washington St., Waukegan, IL 60085 / 708-662-4034
Dave's Gun Shop, P.O. Box 2824, Casper, WY 82602-2824 / 307-754-9724
David Clark Co., Inc., P.O. Box 15054, Worcester, MA 01615 / 508-756-6216; FAX: 508-753-5827 sales@davidclark.com www.davidclark.com
David Condon, Inc., 109 E. Washington St., Middleburg, VA 22117 / 703-687-5642
David Miller Co., 3131 E. Greenlee Rd., Tucson, AZ 85716 / 520-326-3117
David R. Chicoine, 1210 Jones Street, Gastonia, NC 28052 / 704-853-0265 bnpress@quik.com www.icxquik.com/bnpress
David W. Schwartz Custom Guns, 2505 Waller St., Eau Claire, WI 54703 / 715-832-1735
Davide Pedersoli and Co., Via Artigiani 57, Gardone VT, Brescia 25063, ITALY / 030-8915000; FAX: 030-8911019 info@davidepedersoli.com www.davide_pedersoli.com
Davis, Don, 1619 Heights, Katy, TX 77493 / 713-391-3090
Davis Industries (See Cobra Enterprises, Inc.)
Davis Products, Mike, 643 Loop Dr., Moses Lake, WA 98837 / 509-765-6178; or 509-766-7281
Daystate Ltd., Birch House Lanee, Cotes Heath Staffs, ST15.022, ENGLAND / 01782-791755; FAX: 01782-791617
Dayton Traister, 4778 N. Monkey Hill Rd., P.O. Box 593, Oak Harbor, WA 98277 / 360-679-4657; FAX: 360-675-1114
DBI Books Division of Krause Publications, 700 E. State St., Iola, WI 54990-0001 / 715-445-2214
D-Boone Ent., Inc., 5900 Colwyn Dr., Harrisburg, PA 17109
Dead Eye's Sport Center, 76 Baer Rd., Shickshinny, PA 18655 / 570-256-7432 deadeyeprizz@aol.com
Deepeeka Exports Pvt. Ltd., D-78, Saket, Meerut-250-006, INDIA / 011-91-121-640363 or ; FAX: 011-91-121-640988 deepeeka@poboxes.com www.deepeeka.com
Defense Training International, Inc., 749 S. Lemay, Ste. A3-337, Ft. Collins, CO 80524 / 303-482-2520; FAX: 303-482-0548
Degen Inc. (See Aristocrat Knives)
deHaas Barrels, 20049 W. State Hwy. Z, Ridgeway, MO 64481 / 660-872-6308
Del Rey Products, P.O. Box 5134, Playa Del Rey, CA 90296-5134 / 213-823-0494
Delhi Gun House, 1374 Kashmere Gate, New Delhi 110 006, INDIA / 2940974; or 394-0974; FAX: 2917344 dgh@vsnl.com
Delorge, Ed, 6734 W. Main, Houma, LA 70360 / 985-223-0206 delorge@triparish.net www.eddelorge.com
Del-Sports, Inc., Dave Budin, Box 685, 817 Main St., Margaretville, NY 12455 / 845-586-4103; FAX: 845-586-4105
Delta Arms Ltd., P.O. Box 1000, Delta, VT 84624-1000
Delta Enterprises, 284 Hagemann Drive, Livermore, CA 94550
Delta Frangible Ammunition LLC, P.O. Box 2350, Stafford, VA 22555-2350 / 540-720-5778; or 800-339-1933; FAX: 540-720-5667 dfa@dfanet.com www.dfanet.com
Dem-Bart Checkering Tools, Inc., 1825 Bickford Ave., Snohomish, WA 98290 / 360-568-7356 walt@dembartco.com www.dembartco.com
Denver Instrument Co., 6542 Fig St., Arvada, CO 80004 / 800-321-1135; or 303-431-7255; FAX: 303-423-4831
DeSantis Holster & Leather Goods, Inc., P.O. Box 2039, 149 Denton Ave., New Hyde Park, NY 11040-0701 / 516-354-8000; FAX: 516-354-7501
Desert Mountain Mfg., P.O. Box 130184, Coram, MT 59913 / 800-477-0762; or 406-387-5361; FAX: 406-387-5361
Detonics USA, 53 Perimeter Center East #200, Atlanta, GA 30346 / 866-759-1169
DGR Custom Rifles, 4191 37th Ave. SE, Tappen, ND 58487 / 701-327-8135
DGS, Inc., Dale A. Storey, 1117 E. 12th, Casper, WY 82601 / 307-237-2414; FAX: 307-237-2414 dalest@trib.com www.dgsrifle.com
DHB Products, 336 River View Dr., Verona, VA 24482-2547 / 703-836-2648
Diamond Machining Technology, Inc. (See DMT)
Diamond Mfg. Co., P.O. Box 174, Wyoming, PA 18644 / 800-233-9601
Dibble, Derek A., 555 John Downey Dr., New Britain, CT 06051 / 203-224-2630
Dietz Gun Shop & Range, Inc., 421 Range Rd., New Braunfels, TX 78132 / 210-885-4662
Dilliott Gunsmithing, Inc., 657 Scarlett Rd., Dandridge, TN 37725 / 865-397-9204 gunsmithd@aol.com dilliottgunsmithing.com
Dillon Precision Products, Inc., 8009 East Dillon's Way, Scottsdale, AZ 85260 / 480-948-8009; or 800-762-3845; FAX: 480-998-2786 sales@dillonprecision.com www.dillonprecision.com
Dina Arms Corporation, P.O. Box 46, Royersford, PA 19468 / 610-287-0266; FAX: 610-287-0266
Dixie Gun Works, P.O. Box 130, Union City, TN 38281 / 731-885-0700; FAX: 731-885-0440 info@dixiegunworks.com www.dixiegunworks.com
Dixon Muzzleloading Shop, Inc., 9952 Kunkels Mill Rd., Kempton, PA 19529 / 610-756-6271 dixonmuzzleloading.com
DKT, Inc., 14623 Vera Drive, Union, MI 49130-9744 / 800-741-7083 orders; FAX: 616-641-2015
DLO Mfg., 10807 SE Foster Ave., Arcadia, FL 33821-7304
DMT--Diamond Machining Technology Inc., 85 Hayes Memorial Dr., Marlborough, MA 01752 FAX: 508-485-3924
Dohring Bullets, 100 W. 8 Mile Rd., Ferndale, MI 48220
Dolbare, Elizabeth, P.O. Box 502, Dubois, WY 82513-0502 / 307-450-7500 edolbare@hotmail.com www.scrimshaw-engraving.com
Domino, P.O. Box 108, 20019 Settimo Milanese, Milano, ITALY / 1-39-2-33512040; FAX: 1-39-2-33511587
Don Klein Custom Guns, 433 Murray Park Dr., Ripon, WI 54971 / 920-748-2931 daklein@charter.net www.donkleincustomguns.com
Donnelly, C. P., 405 Kubli Rd., Grants Pass, OR 97527 / 541-846-6604
Doskocil Mfg. Co., Inc., P.O. Box 1246, 4209 Barnett, Arlington, TX 76017 / 817-467-5116; FAX: 817-472-9810
Douglas Barrels, Inc., 5504 Big Tyler Rd., Charleston, WV 25313-1398 / 304-776-1341; FAX: 304-776-8560 www.benchrest.com/douglas
Downsizer Corp., P.O. Box 710316, Santee, CA 92072-0316 / 619-448-5510 www.downsizer.com
DPMS (Defense Procurement Manufacturing Services, Inc.), 13983 Industry Avenue, Becker, MN 55308 / 800-578-DPMS; or 763-261-5600; FAX: 763-261-5599
Dr. O's Products Ltd., P.O. Box 111, Niverville, NY 12130 / 518-784-3333; FAX: 518-784-2800
Drain, Mark, SE 3211 Kamilche Point Rd., Shelton, WA 98584 / 206-426-5452
Dremel Mfg. Co., 4915-21st St., Racine, WI 53406
Dri-Slide, Inc., 411 N. Darling, Fremont, MI 49412 / 616-924-3950
Dropkick, 1460 Washington Blvd., Williamsport, PA 17701 / 717-326-6561; FAX: 717-326-4950
DS Arms, Inc., P.O. Box 370, 27 West 990 Industrial Ave., Barrington, IL 60010 / 847-277-7258; FAX: 847-277-7259 www.dsarms.com
DTM International, Inc., 40 Joslyn Rd., P.O. Box 5, Lake Orion, MI 48362 / 313-693-6670

MANUFACTURER'S DIRECTORY

Duane A. Hobbie Gunsmithing, 2412 Pattie Ave., Wichita, KS 67216 / 316-264-8266

Duane's Gun Repair (See DGR Custom Rifles)

Dubber, Michael W., P.O. Box 312, Evansville, IN 47702 / 812-424-9000; FAX: 812-424-6551

Duck Call Specialists, P.O. Box 124, Jerseyville, IL 62052 / 618-498-9855

Duffy, Charles E. (See Guns Antique & Modern DBA), Williams Lane, P.O. Box 2, West Hurley, NY 12491 / 914-679-2997

Du-Lite Corp., 171 River Rd., Middletown, CT 06457 / 203-347-2505; FAX: 203-347-9404

Dumoulin, Ernest, Rue Florent Boclinville 8-10, 13-4041, Votten, BELGIUM / 41 27 78 92

Duncan's Gun Works, Inc., 1619 Grand Ave., San Marcos, CA 92069 / 760-727-0515

DunLyon R&D, Inc., 52151 E. US Hwy. 60, Miami, AZ 85539 / 928-473-9027

Duofold, Inc., RD 3 Rt. 309, Valley Square Mall, Tamaqua, PA 18252 / 717-386-2666; FAX: 717-386-3652

Dutchman's Firearms, Inc., 4143 Taylor Blvd., Louisville, KY 40215 / 502-366-0555

Dybala Gun Shop, P.O. Box 1024, FM 3156, Bay City, TX 77414 / 409-245-0866

Dykstra, Doug, 411 N. Darling, Fremont, MI 49412 / 616-924-3950

Dynalite Products, Inc., 215 S. Washington St., Greenfield, OH 45123 / 513-981-2124

Dynamit Nobel-RWS, Inc., 81 Ruckman Rd., Closter, NJ 07624 / 201-767-7971; FAX: 201-767-1589

E

E&L Mfg., Inc., 4177 Riddle Bypass Rd., Riddle, OR 97469 / 541-874-2137; FAX: 541-874-3107

E. Arthur Brown Co., 3404 Pawnee Dr., Alexandria, MN 56308 / 320-762-8847

E.A.A. Corp., P.O. Box 1299, Sharpes, FL 32959 / 407-639-4842; or 800-536-4442; FAX: 407-639-7006

Eagan, Donald V., P.O. Box 196, Benton, PA 17814 / 717-925-6134

Eagle Arms, Inc. (See ArmaLite, Inc.)

Eagle Grips, Eagle Business Center, 460 Randy Rd., Carol Stream, IL 60188 / 800-323-6144; or 708-260-0400; FAX: 708-260-0486

Eagle Imports, Inc., 1750 Brielle Ave., Unit B1, Wanamassa, NJ 07712 / 732-493-0333; FAX: 732-493-0301 gsodini@aol.com www.bersa-11ama.com

E-A-R, Inc., Div. of Cabot Safety Corp., 5457 W. 79th St., Indianapolis, IN 46268 / 800-327-3431; FAX: 800-488-8007

EAW (See U.S. Importer-New England Custom Gun Serv

Eckelman Gunsmithing, 3125 133rd St. SW, Fort Ripley, MN 56449 / 218-829-3176

Eclectic Technologies, Inc., 45 Grandview Dr., Suite A, Farmington, CT 06034

Ed Brown Products, Inc., P.O. Box 492, Perry, MO 63462 / 573-565-3261; FAX: 573-565-2791 edbrown@edbrown.com www.edbrown.com

Edenpine, Inc. c/o Six Enterprises, Inc., 320 D Turtle Creek Ct., San Jose, CA 95125 / 408-999-0201; FAX: 408-999-0216

EdgeCraft Corp., S. Weiner, 825 Southwood Road, Avondale, PA 19311 / 610-268-0500; or 800-342-3255; FAX: 610-268-3545 www.edgecraft.com

Edmisten Co., P.O. Box 1293, Boone, NC 28607

Edmund Scientific Co., 101 E. Gloucester Pike, Barrington, NJ 08033 / 609-543-6250

Ednar, Inc., 2-4-8 Kayabacho, Nihonbashi Chuo-ku, Tokyo, JAPAN / 81-3-3667-1651; FAX: 81-3-3661-8113

Ed's Gun House, Ed Kukowski, P.O. Box 62, Minnesota City, MN 55959 / 507-689-2925

Effebi SNC-Dr. Franco Beretta, via Rossa, 4, 25062, ITALY / 030-2751955; FAX: 030-2180414

Eggleston, Jere D., 400 Saluda Ave., Columbia, SC 29205 / 803-799-3402

Eichelberger Bullets, Wm., 158 Crossfield Rd., King Of Prussia, PA 19406

Ekol Leather Care, P.O. Box 2652, West Lafayette, IN 47906 / 317-463-2250; FAX: 317-463-7004

El Paso Saddlery Co., P.O. Box 27194, El Paso, TX 79926 / 915-544-2233; FAX: 915-544-2535 epsaddlery.com www.epsaddlery.com

Electro Prismatic Collimators, Inc., 1441 Manatt St., Lincoln, NE 68521

Electronic Shooters Protection, Inc., 15290 Gadsden Ct., Brighton, CO 80603 / 800-797-7791; FAX: 303-659-8668 esp@usa.net espamerican.com

Electronic Trigger Systems, Inc., P.O. Box 645, Park Rapids, MN 56470 / 218-732-5333

Eley Ltd., P.O. Box 705, Witton, Birmingham, B6 7UT ENGLAND / 021-356-8899; FAX: 021-331-4173

Elite Ammunition, P.O. Box 3251, Oakbrook, IL 60522 / 708-366-9006

Ellett Bros., 267 Columbia Ave., P.O. Box 128, Chapin, SC 29036 / 803-345-3751; or 800-845-3711; FAX: 803-345-1820

Ellicott Arms, Inc. / Woods Pistolsmithing, 8390 Sunset Dr., Ellicott City, MD 21043 / 410-465-7979

Elliott, Inc., G. W., 514 Burnside Ave, East Hartford, CT 06108 / 203-289-5741; FAX: 203-289-3137

EMAP USA, 6420 Wilshire Blvd., Los Angeles, CA 90048 / 213-782-2000; FAX: 213-782-2867

Emerging Technologies, Inc. (See Laseraim Technologies, Inc.)

EMF Co., Inc., 1900 E. Warner Ave., Suite 1-D, Santa Ana, CA 92705 / 949-261-6611; FAX: 949-756-0133

Empire Cutlery Corp., 12 Kruger Ct., Clifton, NJ 07013 / 201-472-5155; FAX: 201-779-0759

English, Inc., A.G., 708 S. 12th St., Broken Arrow, OK 74012 / 918-251-3399 agenglish@wedzone.net www.agenglish.com

Engraving Artistry, 36 Alto Rd., Burlington, CT 06013 / 860-673-6837 bobburt44@hotmail.com

Engraving Only, Box 55 Rabbit Gulch, Hill City, SD 57745 / 605-574-2239

Enguix Import-Export, Alpujarras 58, Alzira, Valencia, SPAIN / (96) 241 43 95; FAX: (96) 241 43 95

Enhanced Presentations, Inc., 5929 Market St., Wilmington, NC 28405 / 910-799-1622; FAX: 910-799-5004

Enlow, Charles, 895 Box, Beaver, OK 73932 / 405-625-4487

Entre`prise Arms, Inc., 15861 Business Center Dr., Irwindale, CA 91706

EPC, 1441 Manatt St., Lincoln, NE 68521 / 402-476-3946

Erhardt, Dennis, 4508 N. Montana Ave., Helena, MT 59602 / 406-442-4533

Essex Arms, P.O. Box 363, Island Pond, VT 05846 / 802-723-6203; FAX: 802-723-6203

Estate Cartridge, Inc., 900 Bob Ehlen Dr., Anoka, MN 55303-7502 / 409-856-7277; FAX: 409-856-5486

Euber Bullets, No. Orwell Rd., Orwell, VT 05760 / 802-948-2621

Euroarms of America, Inc., P.O. Box 3277, Winchester, VA 22604 / 540-662-1863; FAX: 540-662-4464 www.euroarms.net

Euro-Imports, 2221 Upland Ave. S., Pahrump, NV 89048 / 775-751-6671; FAX: 775-751-6671

European American Armory Corp. (See E.A.A. Corp.)

Eversull Co., Inc., 1 Tracemont, Boyce, LA 71409 / 318-793-8728; FAX: 318-793-5483 bestguns@aol.com

Evolution Gun Works, Inc., 4050 B-8 Skyron Dr., Doylestown, PA 18901 / 215-348-9892; FAX: 215-348-1056 egw@pil.net www.egw-guns.com

Excalibur Electro Optics, Inc., P.O. Box 400, Fogelsville, PA 18051-0400 / 610-391-9105; FAX: 610-391-9220

Excalibur Publications, P.O. Box 89667, Tucson, AZ 85752 / 520-575-9057 excaliburedítor@earthlink.net

Excel Industries, Inc., 4510 Carter Ct., Chino, CA 91710 / 909-627-2404; FAX: 909-627-7817

Executive Protection Institute, P.O. Box 802, Berryville, VA 22611 / 540-554-2540; FAX: 540-554-2558 ruk@crosslink.net www.personalprotecion.com

Eze-Lap Diamond Prods., P.O. Box 2229, 15164 West State St., Westminster, CA 92683 / 714-847-1555; FAX: 714-897-0280

E-Z-Way Systems, P.O. Box 4310, Newark, OH 43058-4310 / 614-345-6645; or 800-848-2072; FAX: 614-345-6600

F

F.A.I.R., Via Gitti, 41, 25060 Marcheno Bresc, ITALY / 030/861162-8610344; FAX: 030/8610179 info@fair.it www.fair.it

Fabarm S.p.A., Via Averolda 31, 25039 Travagliato, Brescia, ITALY / 030-6863629; FAX: 030-6863684 info@fabarm.com www.fabarm.com

Fagan Arms, 22952 15 Mile Rd, Clinton Township, MI 48035 / 810-465-4637; FAX: 810-792-6996

Faith Associates, P.O. Box 549, Flat Rock, NC 28731-0549 FAX: 828-697-6827

Falcon Industries, Inc., P.O. Box 1060, Tijeras, NM 87059 / 505-281-3783; FAX: 505-281-3991 shines@ergogrips.net www.ergogrips.net

Far North Outfitters, Box 1252, Bethel, AK 99559

Farm Form Decoys, Inc., 1602 Biovu, P.O. Box 748, Galveston, TX 77553 / 409-744-0762; or 409-765-6361; FAX: 409-765-8513

Farr Studio, Inc., 183 Hunters Rd., Washington, VA 22747-2001 / 615-638-8825

Farrar Tool Co., Inc., 11855 Cog Hill Dr., Whittier, CA 90601-1902 / 310-863-4367; FAX: 310-863-5123

Faulhaber Wildlocker, Dipl.-Ing. Norbert Wittasek, Seilergasse 2, A-1010 Wien, AUSTRIA / 43-1-5137001; FAX: 43-1-5137001 faulhaber1@utanet.at

Faulk's Game Call Co., Inc., 616 18th St., Lake Charles, LA 70601 / 337-436-9726; FAX: 337-494-7205

Faust Inc., T. G., 544 Minor St, Reading, PA 19602 / 610-375-8549; FAX: 610-375-4488

Fautheree, Andy, P.O. Box 4607, Pagosa Springs, CO 81157 / 970-731-5003; FAX: 970-731-5009

Feather, Flex Decoys, 4500 Doniphan Dr., Neosho, MO 64850 / 318-746-8596; FAX: 318-742-4815

Federal Arms Corp. of America, 7928 University Ave., Fridley, MN 55432 / 612-780-8780; FAX: 612-780-8780

Federal Cartridge Co., 900 Ehlen Dr., Anoka, MN 55303 / 612-323-2300; FAX: 612-323-2506

Federal Champion Target Co., 232 Industrial Parkway, Richmond, IN 47374 / 800-441-4971; FAX: 317-966-7747

Federated-Fry (See Fry Metals)

FEG, Budapest, Soroksariut 158, H-1095, HUNGARY

Feinwerkbau Westinger & Altenburger, Neckarstrasse 43, 78727, Oberndorf a. N., GERMANY / 07423-814-00; FAX: 07423-814-200 info@feinwerkbau.de www.feinwerkbau.de

Feken, Dennis, Rt. 2, Box 124, Perry, OK 73077 / 405-336-5611

Felk Pistols, Inc., 2121 Castlebridge Rd., Midlothian, VA 23113 / 804-794-3744; FAX: 208-988-4834

Ferguson, Bill, P.O. Box 1238, Sierra Vista, AZ 85636 / 520-458-5321; FAX: 520-458-9125

Ferguson, Bill. See: BULLET METALS

FERLIB, Via Parte 33 Marcheno/BS, Marcheno/BS, ITALY / 00390308610191; FAX: 00390308966882 info@ferlib.com www.ferlib.com

Ferris Firearms, 7110 F.M. 1863, Bulverde, TX 78163 / 210-980-4424

Fibron Products, Inc., P.O. Box 430, Buffalo, NY 14209-0430 / 716-886-2378; FAX: 716-886-2394

Fieldsport Ltd., Bryan Bilinski, 3313 W. South Airport Rd., Traverse City, MI 49684 / 616-933-0767

Fiocchi Munizioni S.P.A. (See U.S. Importer-Fiocch

Fiocchi of America, Inc., 5030 Fremont Rd., Ozark, MO 65721 / 417-725-4118; or 800-721-2666; FAX: 417-725-1039

Firearms Co. Ltd. / Alpine (See U.S. Importer-Mandall

Firearms Engraver's Guild of America, 332 Vine St., Oregon City, OR 97045 / 503-656-5693

Firearms International, 5709 Hartsdale, Houston, TX 77036 / 713-460-2447

Fisher, Jerry A., 631 Crane Mt. Rd., Big Fork, MT 59911 / 406-837-2722

Fisher Custom Firearms, 2199 S. Kittredge Way, Aurora, CO 80013 / 303-755-3710

Fitzgerald, Jack. See: CLENZOIL WORLDWIDE CORP

Flambeau, Inc., 15981 Valplast Rd., Middlefield, OH 44062 / 216-632-1631; FAX: 216-632-1581 www.flambeau.com

Flayderman & Co., Inc., P.O. Box 2446, Ft. Lauderdale, FL 33303 / 954-761-8855

REFERENCE

MANUFACTURER'S DIRECTORY

Fleming Firearms, 7720 E. 126th St. N., Collinsville, OK 74021-7016 / 918-665-3624
Fletcher-Bidwell, LLC., 305 E. Terhune St., Viroqua, WI 54665-1631 / 866-637-1860 fbguns@netscape.net
Flintlocks, Etc., 160 Rossiter Rd., P.O. Box 181, Richmond, MA 01254 / 413-698-3822; FAX: 413-698-3866 flintetc@berkshire.rr.com
Flitz International Ltd., 821 Mohr Ave., Waterford, WI 53185 / 414-534-5898; FAX: 414-534-2991
Fluoramics, Inc., 18 Industrial Ave., Mahwah, NJ 07430 / 800-922-0075; FAX: 201-825-7035
Flynn's Custom Guns, P.O. Box 7461, Alexandria, LA 71306 / 318-455-7130
FN Manufacturing, P.O. Box 24257, Columbia, SC 29224 / 803-736-0522
Folks, Donald E., 205 W. Lincoln St., Pontiac, IL 61764 / 815-844-7901
Foothills Video Productions, Inc., P.O. Box 651, Spartanburg, SC 29304 / 803-573-7023; or 800-782-5358
Foredom Electric Co., Rt. 6, 16 Stony Hill Rd., Bethel, CT 06801 / 203-792-8622
Forgett, Valmore. See: NAVY ARMS COMPANY
Forgreens Tool & Mfg., Inc., P.O. Box 955, Robert Lee, TX 76945 / 915-453-2800; FAX: 915-453-2460
Forkin Custom Classics, 205 10th Avenue S.W., White Sulphur Spring, MT 59645 / 406-547-2344
Forrest Tool Co., P.O. Box 768, 44380 Gordon Lane, Mendocino, CA 95460 / 707-937-2141; FAX: 717-937-1817
Forster, Kathy (See Custom Checkering)
Forster, Larry L., Box 212, 216 Highway 13 E., Gwinner, ND 58040-0212 / 701-678-2475
Forster Products, 310 E. Lanark Ave., Lanark, IL 61046 / 815-493-6360; FAX: 815-493-2371
Fort Hill Gunstocks, 12807 Fort Hill Rd., Hillsboro, OH 45133 / 513-466-2763
Fort Knox Security Products, 1051 N. Industrial Park Rd., Orem, UT 84057 / 801-224-7233; or 800-821-5216; FAX: 801-226-5493
Forthofer's Gunsmithing & Knifemaking, 5535 U.S. Hwy. 93S, Whitefish, MT 59937-8411 / 406-862-2674
Fortune Products, Inc., 205 Hickory Creek Rd., Marble Falls, TX 78654 / 210-693-6111; FAX: 210-693-6394 randy@accusharp.com
Forty-Five Ranch Enterprises, Box 1080, Miami, OK 74355-1080 / 918-542-5875
Foster, See: ACCURACY INTERNATIONAL
Fountain Products, 492 Prospect Ave., West Springfield, MA 01089 / 413-781-4651; FAX: 413-733-8217
4-D Custom Die Co., 711 N. Sandusky St., PO Box 889, Mt. Vernon, OH 43050-0889 / 740-397-7214; FAX: 740-397-6600 info@ch4d.com ch4d.com
Fowler Bullets, 806 Dogwood Dr., Gastonia, NC 28054 / 704-867-3259
Fowler, Bob (See Black Powder Products)
Fox River Mills, Inc., P.O. Box 298, 227 Poplar St., Osage, IA 50461 / 515-732-3798; FAX: 515-732-5128
Francotte & Cie S.A. Auguste, rue de Trois Juin 109, 4400 Herstal-Liege, BELGIUM / 32-4-248-13-18; FAX: 32-4-248-11-79
Frank Knives, 13868 NW Keleka Pl., Seal Rock, OR 97376 / 541-563-3041; FAX: 541-563-3041
Frank Mittermeier, Inc., P.O. Box 1, Bronx, NY 10465
Franzen International, Inc. (See U.S. Importer for)
Fred F. Wells/Wells Sport Store, 110 N Summit St., Prescott, AZ 86301 / 928-445-3655 www.wellssportstore@cableone-net
Freedom Arms, Inc., P.O. Box 150, Freedom, WY 83120 / 307-883-2468; FAX: 307-883-2005
Fremont Tool Works, 1214 Prairie, Ford, KS 67842 / 316-369-2327
Front Sight Firearms Training Institute, P.O. Box 2619, Aptos, CA 95001 / 800-987-7719; FAX: 408-684-2137
Frontier, 2910 San Bernardo, Laredo, TX 78040 / 956-723-5409; FAX: 956-723-1774
Frontier Arms Co., Inc., 401 W. Rio Santa Cruz, Green Valley, AZ 85614-3932
Frontier Products Co., 2401 Walker Rd., Roswell, NM 88201-8950 / 614-262-9357
Frontier Safe Co., 3201 S. Clinton St., Fort Wayne, IN 46806 / 219-744-7233; FAX: 219-744-6678
Frost Cutlery Co., P.O. Box 22636, Chattanooga, TN 37422 / 615-894-6079; FAX: 615-894-9576
Fry Metals, 4100 6th Ave., Altoona, PA 16602 / 814-946-1611
Fujinon, Inc., 10 High Point Dr., Wayne, NJ 07470 / 201-633-5600; FAX: 201-633-5216
Fullmer, Geo. M., 2499 Mavis St., Oakland, CA 94601 / 510-533-4193
Fulton Armory, 8725 Bollman Place No. 1, Savage, MD 20763 / 301-490-9485; FAX: 301-490-9547 www.fulton.armory.com
Furr Arms, 91 N. 970 W., Orem, UT 84057 / 801-226-3877; FAX: 801-226-3877

G

G&H Decoys, Inc., P.O. Box 1208, Hwy. 75 North, Henryetta, OK 74437 / 918-652-3314; FAX: 918-652-3400
G.C. Bullet Co., Inc., 40 Mokelumne River Dr., Lodi, CA 95240
G.G. & G., 3602 E. 42nd Stravenue, Tucson, AZ 85713 / 520-748-7167; FAX: 520-748-7583 ggg&3@aol.com www.ggg&3.com
G.H. Enterprises Ltd., Bag 10, Okotoks, AB T0L 1T0 CANADA / 403-938-6070
G.U., Inc. (See U.S. Importer for New SKB Arms Co.)
G.W. Elliott, Inc., 514 Burnside Ave., East Hartford, CT 06108 / 203-289-5741; FAX: 203-289-3137
G96 Products Co., Inc., 85 5th Ave., Bldg. #6, Paterson, NJ 07544 / 973-684-4050; FAX: 973-684-3848 g96prod@aol
Gage Manufacturing, 663 W. 7th St., A, San Pedro, CA 90731 / 310-832-3546
Gaillard Barrels, P.O. Box 21, Pathlow, SK S0K 3B0 CANADA / 306-752-3769; FAX: 306-752-5969
Gain Twist Barrel Co., Rifle Works and Armory, 707 12th St., Cody, WY 82414 / 307-587-4919; FAX: 307-527-6097
Galati International, P.O. Box 10, 616 Burley Ridge Rd., Wesco, MO 65586 / 636-584-0785; FAX: 573-775-4308 support@galatiinternational.com www.galatiinternational.com
Galaxy Imports Ltd., Inc., P.O. Box 3361, Victoria, TX 77903 / 361-573-4867; FAX: 361-576-9622 galaxy@cox-internet.com
GALCO International Ltd., 2019 W. Quail Ave., Phoenix, AZ 85027 / 623-474-7070; FAX: 623-582-6854 customerservice@usgalco.com www.usgalco.com
Galena Industries AMT, 5463 Diaz St., Irwindale, CA 91706 / 626-856-8883; FAX: 626-856-8878
Gamba S.p.A. Societa Armi Bresciane Srl, Renato, Via Artigiani 93, ITALY / 30-8911640; FAX: 30-8911648
Gamba, USA, P.O. Box 60452, Colorado Springs, CO 80960 / 719-578-1145; FAX: 719-444-0731
Game Haven Gunstocks, 13750 Shire Rd., Wolverine, MI 49799 / 616-525-8257
Gamebore Division, Polywad, Inc., P.O. Box 7916, Macon, GA 31209 / 478-477-0669; or 800-998-0669
Gamo (See U.S. Importers-Arms United Corp, Daisy M
Gamo USA, Inc., 3911 SW 47th Ave., Suite 914, Ft. Lauderdale, FL 33314 / 954-581-5822; FAX: 954-581-3165 gamousa@gate.net www.gamo.com
Gander Mountain, Inc., 12400 Fox River Rd., Wilmont, WI 53192 / 414-862-6848
GAR, 590 McBride Ave., West Paterson, NJ 07424 / 973-754-1114; FAX: 973-754-1114 garreloading@aol.com www.garreloading.com
Garcia National Gun Traders, Inc., 225 SW 22nd Ave., Miami, FL 33135 / 305-642-2355
Garrett Cartridges, Inc., P.O. Box 178, Chehalis, WA 98532 / 360-736-0702 www.garrettcartridges.com
Garthwaite Pistolsmith, Inc., Jim, 12130 State Route 405, Watsontown, PA 17777 / 570-538-1566; FAX: 570-538-2965 www.garthwaite.com
Gary Goudy Classic Stocks, 1512 S. 5th St., Dayton, WA 99328 / 509-382-2726 goudy@innw.net
Gary Reeder Custom Guns, 2601 7th Avenue East, Flagstaff, AZ 86004 / 928-526-3313; FAX: 928-527-0840 gary@reedercustomguns.com www.reedercustomguns.com
Gator Guns & Repair, 7952 Kenai Spur Hwy., Kenai, AK 99611-8311
Gaucher Armes, S.A., 46 rue Desjoyaux, 42000, Saint-Etienne, FRANCE / 04-77-33-38-92; FAX: 04-77-61-95-72
GDL Enterprises, 409 Le Gardeur, Slidell, LA 70460 / 504-649-0693
Gehmann, Walter (See Huntington Die Specialties)
Genco, P.O. Box 5704, Asheville, NC 28803
Genecco Gun Works, 10512 Lower Sacramento Rd., Stockton, CA 95210 / 209-951-0706; FAX: 209-931-3872
Gene's Custom Guns, P.O. Box 10534, White Bear Lake, MN 55110 / 651-429-5105; FAX: 651-429-7365
Gentex Corp., 5 Tinkham Ave., Derry, NH 03038 / 603-434-0311; FAX: 603-434-3002 sales@derry.gentexcorp.com www.derry.gentexcorp.com
Gentner Bullets, 109 Woodlawn Ave., Upper Darby, PA 19082 / 610-352-9396
Gentry Custom LLC, 314 N. Hoffman, Belgrade, MT 59714 / 406-388-GUNS davidgent@mcn.net www.gentrycustom.com
George & Roy's, P.O. Box 2125, Sisters, OR 97759-2125 / 503-228-5424; or 800-553-3022; FAX: 503-225-9409
George Hoenig, Inc., 6521 Morton Dr., Boise, ID 83704 / 208-375-1116; FAX: 208-375-1116
George Ibberson (Sheffield) Ltd., 25-31 Allen St., Sheffield, S3 7AW ENGLAND / 0114-2766123; FAX: 0114-2738465 sales@eggintongroupco.uk www.eggintongroup.co.uk
George Madis Winchester Consultants, George Madis, P.O. Box 545, Brownsboro, TX 75756 / 903-852-6480; FAX: 903-852-3045 gmadis@earthlink.com www.georgemadis.com
Gerber Legendary Blades, 14200 SW 72nd Ave., Portland, OR 97223 / 503-639-6161; or 800-950-6161; FAX: 503-684-7008
Gervais, Mike, 3804 S. Cruise Dr., Salt Lake City, UT 84109 / 801-277-7729
Getz Barrel Company, P.O. Box 88, 426 E. Market St., Beavertown, PA 17813 / 570-658-7263; FAX: 570-658-4110 www.getzbrl.com
Giacomo Sporting USA, 6234 Stokes Lee Center Rd., Lee Center, NY 13363
Gibbs Rifle Co., Inc., 219 Lawn St., Martinsburg, WV 25401 / 304-262-1651; FAX: 304-262-1658 support@gibbsrifle.com www.gibbsrifle.com
Gil Hebard Guns, Inc., 125 Public Square, Knoxville, IL 61448 / 309-289-2700; FAX: 309-289-2233
Gilbert Equipment Co., Inc., 960 Downtowner Rd., Mobile, AL 36609 / 205-344-3322
Gillmann, Edwin, 33 Valley View Dr., Hanover, PA 17331 / 717-632-1662 gillmaned@super-pa.net
Gilmore Sports Concepts, Inc., 5949 S. Garnett Rd., Tulsa, OK 74146 / 918-250-3810; FAX: 918-250-3845 info@gilmoresports.com www.gilmoresports.com
Giron, Robert E., 12671 Cousins Rd.., Peosta, IA 52068 / 412-731-6041
Glacier Glove, 4890 Aircenter Circle, Suite 210, Reno, NV 89502 / 702-825-8225; FAX: 702-825-6544
Glaser LLC, P.O. Box 173, Sturgis, SD 57785 / 605-347-4544; or 800-221-3489; FAX: 605-347-5055 email@corbon.com www.safetyslug.com
Glaser Safety Slug, Inc., P.O. Box 8223, Foster City, CA 94404 / 800-221-3489; FAX: 510-785-6685 safetyslug.com
Glass, Herb, P.O. Box 25, Bullville, NY 10915 / 914-361-3021
Glimm, Jerome. See: GLIMM'S CUSTOM GUN ENGRAVING
Glimm's Custom Gun Engraving, Jerome C. Glimm, 19 S. Maryland, Conrad, MT 59425 / 406-278-3574 jandlglimm@mcn.net
Glock GmbH, P.O. Box 50, A-2232, Deutsch Wagram, AUSTRIA
Glock, Inc., P.O. Box 369, Smyrna, GA 30081 / 770-432-1202; FAX: 770-433-8719
Glynn Scobey Duck & Goose Calls, Rt. 3, Box 37, Newbern, TN 38059 / 731-643-6128
GML Products, Inc., 394 Laredo Dr., Birmingham, AL 35226 / 205-979-4867
Gner's Hard Cast Bullets, 1107 11th St., LaGrande, OR 97850 / 503-963-8796

MANUFACTURER'S DIRECTORY

Goens, Dale W., P.O. Box 224, Cedar Crest, NM 87008 / 505-281-5419
Goergen's Gun Shop, Inc., 17985 538th Ave., Austin, MN 55912 / 507-433-9280
GOEX, Inc., P.O. Box 659, Doyline, LA 71023-0659 / 318-382-9300; FAX: 318-382-9303 mfahringer@goexpowder.com www.goexpowder.com
Golden Age Arms Co., 115 E. High St., Ashley, OH 43003 / 614-747-2488
Golden Bear Bullets, 3065 Fairfax Ave., San Jose, CA 95148 / 408-238-9515
Gonic Arms/North American Arms, Inc., 134 Flagg Rd., Gonic, NH 03839 / 603-332-8456; or 603-332-8457
Goodling's Gunsmithing, 1950 Stoverstown Rd., Spring Grove, PA 17362 / 717-225-3350
Goodwin, Fred. See: GOODWIN'S PAWN SHOP
Goodwin's Pawn Shop, Fred Goodwin, Silver Ridge, ME 04776 / 207-365-4451
Gotz Bullets, 11426 Edgemere Ter., Roscoe, IL 61073-8232
Gould & Goodrich, 709 E. McNeil, Lillington, NC 27546 / 910-893-2071; FAX: 910-893-4742
Gournet Artistic Engraving, Geoffroy Gournet, 820 Paxinosa Ave., Easton, PA 18042 / 610-559-0710 www.geoffroygournet.com
Gournet, Geoffroy. See: GOURNET ARTISTIC ENGRAVING
Grace, Charles E., 718 E. 2nd, Trinidad, CO 81082 / 719-846-9435 chuckgrace@sensonics.org
Grace Metal Products, P.O. Box 67, Elk Rapids, MI 49629 / 616-264-8133
Graf & Sons, 4050 S. Clark St., Mexico, MO 65265 / 573-581-2266; FAX: 573-581-2875 customerservice@grafs.com www.grafs.com
Grand Slam Hunting Products, Box 121, 25454 Military Rd., Cascade, MD 21719 / 301-241-4900; FAX: 301-241-4900 rlj6call@aol.com
Granite Mountain Arms, Inc., 3145 W. Hidden Acres Trail, Prescott, AZ 86305 / 520-541-9758; FAX: 520-445-6826
Grant, Howard V., Hiawatha 15, Woodruff, WI 54568 / 715-356-7146
Graphics Direct, P.O. Box 372421, Reseda, CA 91337-2421 / 818-344-9002
Graves Co., 1800 Andrews Ave., Pompano Beach, FL 33069 / 800-327-9103; FAX: 305-960-0301
Grayback Wildcats, Mike Beeks, 5306 Bryant Ave., Klamath Falls, OR 97603 / 541-884-1072; FAX: 541-884-1072 graybackwildcats@aol.com
Graybill's Gun Shop, 1035 Ironville Pike, Columbia, PA 17512 / 717-684-2739
Great American Gunstock Co., 3420 Industrial Drive, Yuba City, CA 95993 / 800-784-4867; FAX: 530-671-3906 gunstox@hotmail.com www.gunstocks.com
Great Lakes Airguns, 6175 S. Park Ave., Hamburg, NY 14075 / 716-648-6666; FAX: 716-648-6666 www.greatlakesairguns.com
Green, Arthur S., 485 S. Robertson Blvd., Beverly Hills, CA 90211 / 310-274-1283
Green, Roger M., P.O. Box 984, 435 E. Birch, Glenrock, WY 82637 / 307-436-9804
Green Head Game Call Co., RR 1, Box 33, Lacon, IL 61540 / 309-246-2155
Green Mountain Rifle Barrel Co., Inc., P.O. Box 2670, 153 West Main St., Conway, NH 03818 / 603-447-1095; FAX: 603-447-1099 www.gmriflebarrel.com
Greenwood Precision, P.O. Box 407, Rogersville, MO 65742 / 417-725-2330
Greg Gunsmithing Repair, 3732 26th Ave. North, Robbinsdale, MN 55422 / 612-529-8103
Greg's Superior Products, P.O. Box 46219, Seattle, WA 98146
Greider Precision, 431 Santa Marina Ct., Escondido, CA 92029 / 760-480-8892; FAX: 760-480-9800 greider@msn.com
Gre-Tan Rifles, 29742 W.C.R. 50, Kersey, CO 80644 / 970-353-6176; FAX: 970-356-5940 www.gtrtooling.com
Grier's Hard Cast Bullets, 1107 11th St., LaGrande, OR 97850 / 503-963-8796
Griffin & Howe, Inc., 36 W. 44th St., Suite 1011, New York, NY 10036 / 212-921-0980 info@griffinhowe.com www.griffinhowe.com
Griffin & Howe, Inc., 340 W. Putnam Ave., Greenwich, CT 06830 / 203-618-0270 info@griffinhowe.com www.griffinhowe.com
Griffin & Howe, Inc., 33 Claremont Rd., Bernardsville, NJ 07924 / 908-766-2287; FAX: 908-766-1068 info@griffinhowe.com www.griffinhowe.com
Grifon, Inc., 58 Guinam St., Waltham, MS 02154
Groenewold, John, P.O. Box 830, Mundelein, IL 60060 / 847-566-2365; FAX: 847-566-4065 jgairguns@direcway.com http://jgairguns.tripod.com/airgun
GRS / Glendo Corp., P.O. Box 1153, 900 Overlander St., Emporia, KS 66801 / 620-343-1084; or 800-836-3519; FAX: 620-343-9640 glendo@glendo.com www.glendo.com
Grulla Armes, Apartado 453, Avda Otaloa 12, Eiber, SPAIN
Gruning Precision, Inc., 7101 Jurupa Ave., No. 12, Riverside, CA 92504 / 909-289-4371; FAX: 909-689-7791 gruningprecision@earthlink.net www.gruningprecision.com
GSI, Inc., 7661 Commerce Ln., Trussville, AL 35173 / 205-655-8299
GTB-Custom Bullets, 482 Comerwood Court, S. San Francisco, CA 94080 / 650-583-1550
Guarasi, Robert. See: WILCOX INDUSTRIES CORP.
Guardsman Products, 411 N. Darling, Fremont, MI 49412 / 616-924-3950
Gun City, 212 W. Main Ave., Bismarck, ND 58501 / 701-223-2304
Gun Hunter Books (See Gun Hunter Trading Co.), 5075 Heisig St., Beaumont, TX 77705 / 409-835-3006; FAX: 409-838-2266 gunhuntertrading@hotmail.com
Gun Hunter Trading Co., 5075 Heisig St., Beaumont, TX 77705 / 409-835-3006; FAX: 409-838-2266 gunhuntertrading@hotmail.com
Gun Leather Limited, 116 Lipscomb, Ft. Worth, TX 76104 / 817-334-0225; FAX: 800-247-0609
Gun List (See Krause Publications), 700 E State St., Iola, WI 54990 / 715-445-2214; FAX: 715-445-4087
Gun South, Inc. (See GSI, Inc.)
Gun Vault, 7339 E. Acoma Dr., Ste. 7, Scottsdale, AZ 85260 / 602-951-6855
Gun-Alert, 1010 N. Maclay Ave., San Fernando, CA 91340 / 818-365-0864; FAX: 818-365-1308
Guncraft Books (See Guncraft Sports, Inc.), 10737 Dutchtown Rd., Knoxville, TN 37932 / 865-966-4545; FAX: 865-966-4500 findit@guncraft.com www.guncraft.com
Guncraft Sports, Inc., 10737 Dutchtown Rd., Knoxville, TN 37932 / 865-966-4545; FAX: 865-966-4500 findit@guncraft.com www.usit.net/guncraft
Guncraft Sports, Inc., Marie C. Wiest, 10737 Dutchtown Rd., Knoxville, TN 37932 / 865-966-4545; FAX: 865-966-4500 findit@guncraft.com www.guncraft.com
Guncrafter Industries, 171 Madison 1510, Huntsville, AR 72740 / 479-665-2466 www.guncrafterindustries.com
Gun-Ho Sports Cases, 110 E. 10th St., St. Paul, MN 55101 / 612-224-9491
Gunline Tools, 2950 Saturn St., "O", Brea, CA 92821 / 714-993-5100; FAX: 714-572-4128
Gunnerman Books, P.O. Box 81697, Rochester Hills, MI 48308 / 248-608-2856
Guns Antique & Modern DBA / Charles E. Duffy, Williams Lane, West Hurley, NY 12491 / 914-679-2997
Guns Div. of D.C. Engineering, Inc., 8633 Southfield Fwy., Detroit, MI 48228 / 313-271-7111; or 800-886-7623; FAX: 313-271-7112 guns@rifletech.com www.rifletech.com
GUNS Magazine, 591 Camino de la Reina, Suite 200, San Diego, CA 92108 / 619-297-5350; FAX: 619-297-5353
Gunsite Training Center, P.O. Box 700, Paulden, AZ 86334 / 520-636-4565; FAX: 520-636-1236
Gunsmithing Ltd., 57 Unquowa Rd., Fairfield, CT 06824 / 203-254-0436; FAX: 203-254-1535
Gunsmithing, Inc., 30 West Buchanan St., Colorado Springs, CO 80907 / 719-632-3795; FAX: 719-632-3493
Gurney, F. R., Box 13, Sooke, BC V0S 1N0 CANADA / 604-642-5282; FAX: 604-642-7859

H

H&B Forge Co., Rt. 2, Geisinger Rd., Shiloh, OH 44878 / 419-895-1856
H&P Publishing, 7174 Hoffman Rd., San Angelo, TX 76905 / 915-655-5953
H&R 1871.LLC, 60 Industrial Rowe, Gardner, MA 01440 / 508-632-9393; FAX: 508-632-2300 hr1871@hr1871.com www.hr1871.com
H. Krieghoff Gun Co., Boschstrasse 22, D-89079, Ulm, GERMANY / 731-401820; FAX: 731-4018270
H.K.S. Products, 7841 Founion Dr., Florence, KY 41042 / 606-342-7841; or 800-354-9814; FAX: 606-342-5865
H.P. White Laboratory, Inc., 3114 Scarboro Rd., Street, MD 21154 / 410-838-6550; FAX: 410-838-2802
Hafner World Wide, Inc., P.O. Box 1987, Lake City, FL 32055 / 904-755-6481; FAX: 904-755-6595 hafner@isgroupe.net
Hakko Co. Ltd., 1-13-12, Narimasu, Itabashiku Tokyo, JAPAN / 03-5997-7870/2; FAX: 81-3-5997-7840
Half Moon Rifle Shop, 490 Halfmoon Rd., Columbia Falls, MT 59912 / 406-892-4409 halfmoonrs@centurytel.net
Hall Manufacturing, 142 CR 406, Clanton, AL 35045 / 205-755-4094
Hall Plastics, Inc., John, P.O. Box 1526, Alvin, TX 77512 / 713-489-8709
Hallberg, Fritz. See: CAMBOS OUTDOORSMAN
Hallowell & Co., P.O. Box 1445, Livingston, MT 59047 / 406-222-4770; FAX: 406-222-4792 morris@hallowellco.com www.hallowellco.com
Hally Caller, 443 Wells Rd., Doylestown, PA 18901 / 215-345-6354; FAX: 215-345-8892 info@hallycaller.com www.hallycaller.com
Hamilton, Alex B. (See Ten-Ring Precision, Inc.)
Hammans, Charles E., P.O. Box 788, 2022 McCracken, Stuttgart, AR 72160-0788 / 870-673-1388
Hammerli Ltd., Seonerstrasse 37, CH-5600, SWITZERLAND / 064-50 11 44; FAX: 064-51 38 27
Hammerli Service-Precision Mac, Rudolf Marent, 9711 Tiltree St., Houston, TX 77075 / 713-946-7028 rmarent@webtv.net
Hammerli USA, 19296 Oak Grove Circle, Groveland, CA 95321 FAX: 209-962-5311
Hammond Custom Guns Ltd., 619 S. Pandora, Gilbert, AZ 85234 / 602-892-3437
HandCrafts Unltd. (See Clements' Custom Leather), 1741 Dallas St., Aurora, CO 80010-2018 / 303-364-0403; FAX: 303-739-9824 gryphons@home.com kuntaoslcat.com
Handgun Press, P.O. Box 406, Glenview, IL 60025 / 847-657-6500; FAX: 847-724-8831 handgunpress@earthlink.net
Hank's Gun Shop, Box 370, 50 West 100 South, Monroe, UT 84754 / 801-527-4456
Hanned Precision (See The Hanned Line)
Hansen & Co., 244-246 Old Post Rd., Southport, CT 06490 / 203-259-6222; FAX: 203-254-3832
Hanson's Gun Center, Dick, 233 Everett Dr., Colorado Springs, CO 80911
Harford (See U.S. Importer-EMF Co. Inc.)
Harper's Custom Stocks, 928 Lombrano St., San Antonio, TX 78207 / 210-732-7174
Harrell's Precision, 5756 Hickory Dr., Salem, VA 24153 / 540-380-2683
Harrington & Richardson (See H&R 1871, Inc.)
Harris Engineering Inc., Dept GD54, Barlow, KY 42024 / 502-334-3633; FAX: 502-334-3000
Harris Enterprises, P.O. Box 105, Bly, OR 97622 / 503-353-2625
Harris Hand Engraving, Paul A., 113 Rusty Ln., Boerne, TX 78006-5746 / 512-391-5121
Harris Publications, 1115 Broadway, New York, NY 10010 / 212-807-7100; FAX: 212-627-4678
Harrison Bullets, 6437 E. Hobart St., Mesa, AZ 85205
Harry Lawson Co., 3328 N. Richey Blvd., Tucson, AZ 85716 / 520-326-1117; FAX: 520-326-1117
Hart & Son, Inc., Robert W., 401 Montgomery St., Nescopeck, PA 18635 / 717-752-3655; FAX: 717-752-1088
Hart Rifle Barrels, Inc., P.O. Box 182, 1690 Apulia Rd., Lafayette, NY 13084 / 315-677-9841; FAX: 315-677-9610 hartrb@aol.com hartbarrels.com
Hartford (See U.S. Importer-EMF Co. Inc.)
Hartmann & Weiss GmbH, Rahlstedter Bahnhofstr. 47, 22143, Hamburg, GERMANY / (40) 677 55 85; FAX: (40) 677 55 92 hartmannundweisst-online.de
Harvey, Frank, 218 Nightfall, Terrace, NV 89015 / 702-558-6998

REFERENCE

MANUFACTURER'S DIRECTORY

Harwood, Jack O., 1191 S. Pendlebury Lane, Blackfoot, ID 83221 / 208-785-5368
Hastings, P.O. Box 224, Clay Center, KS 67432 / 785-632-3169; FAX: 785-632-6554
Hatfield Gun, 224 N. 4th St., St. Joseph, MO 64501
Hawk Laboratories, Inc. (See Hawk, Inc.), 849 Hawks Bridge Rd., Salem, NJ 08079 / 609-299-2700; FAX: 609-299-2800
Hawk, Inc., 849 Hawks Bridge Rd., Salem, NJ 08079 / 609-299-2700; FAX: 609-299-2800 info@hawkbullets.com www.hawkbullets.com
Hawken Shop, The (See Dayton Traister)
Haydel's Game Calls, Inc., 5018 Hazel Jones Rd., Bossier City, LA 71111 / 318-746-3586; FAX: 318-746-3711
Heatbath Corp., P.O. Box 2978, Springfield, MA 01101 / 413-543-3381
Hecht, Hubert J., Waffen-Hecht, P.O. Box 2635, Fair Oaks, CA 95628 / 916-966-1020
Heckler & Koch GmbH, PO Box 1329, 78722 Oberndorf, Neckar, GERMANY / 49-7423179-0; FAX: 49-7423179-2406
Heckler & Koch, Inc., 21480 Pacific Blvd., Sterling, VA 20166-8900 / 703-450-1900; FAX: 703-450-8160 www.hecklerkoch-usa.com
Hege Jagd-u. Sporthandels GmbH, P.O. Box 101461, W-7770, Ueberlingen a. Boden, GERMANY
Heidenstrom Bullets, Dalghte 86-3660 Rjukan, 35091818, NORWAY, olau.joh@online.tuo
Heilmann, Stephen, P.O. Box 657, Grass Valley, CA 95945 / 530-272-8758; FAX: 530-274-0285 sheilmann@jps.net www.metalwood.com
Heinie Specialty Products, 301 Oak St., Quincy, IL 62301-2500 / 217-228-9500; FAX: 217-228-9502 rheinie@heinie.com www.heinie.com
Helwan (See U.S. Importer-Interarms)
Henigson & Associates, Steve, PO Box 2726, Culver City, CA 90231 / 310-305-8288; FAX: 310-305-1905
Henriksen Tool Co., Inc., 8515 Wagner Creek Rd., Talent, OR 97540 / 541-535-2309; FAX: 541-535-2309
Henry Repeating Arms Co., 110 8th St., Brooklyn, NY 11215 / 718-499-5600; FAX: 718-768-8056 info@henryrepeating.com www.henryrepeating.com
Hensley, Gunmaker, Darwin, PO Box 329, Brightwood, OR 97011 / 503-622-5411
Heppler, Keith. See: KEITH'S CUSTOM GUNSTOCKS
Hercules, Inc. (See Alliant Techsystems, Smokeless)
Heritage Firearms (See Heritage Mfg., Inc.)
Heritage Manufacturing, Inc., 4600 NW 135th St., Opa Locka, FL 33054 / 305-685-5966; FAX: 305-687-6721 infohmi@heritagemfg.com www.heritagemfg.com
Heritage/VSP Gun Books, P.O. Box 887, McCall, ID 83638 / 208-634-4104; FAX: 208-634-3101 heritage@gunbooks.com www.gunbooks.com
Herrett's Stocks, Inc., P.O. Box 741, Twin Falls, ID 83303 / 208-733-1498
Herter's Manufacturing Inc., 111 E. Burnett St., P.O. Box 518, Beaver Dam, WI 53916-1811 / 414-887-1765; FAX: 414-887-8444
Hesco-Meprolight, 2139 Greenville Rd., LaGrange, GA 30241 / 706-884-7967; FAX: 706-882-4683
Hesse Arms, Robert Hesse, 1126 70th Street E., Inver Grove Heights, MN 55077-2416 / 651-455-5760; FAX: 612-455-5760
Hesse, Robert. See: HESSE ARMS
Heydenberk, Warren R., 1059 W. Sawmill Rd., Quakertown, PA 18951 / 215-538-2682
Hickman, Jaclyn, Box 1900, Glenrock, WY 82637
Hidalgo, Tony, 12701 SW 9th Pl., Davie, FL 33325 / 954-476-7645
High Bridge Arms, Inc., 3185 Mission St., San Francisco, CA 94110 / 415-282-8358
High North Products, Inc., P.O. Box 2, Antigo, WI 54409 / 715-627-2331; FAX: 715-623-5451
High Performance International, 5734 W. Florist Ave., Milwaukee, WI 53218 / 414-466-9040
High Precision, Bud Welsh, 80 New Road, E. Amherst, NY 14051 / 716-688-6344; FAX: 716-688-0425 welsh5168@aol.com www.high-precision.com
High Standard Mfg. Co./F.I., Inc., 5200 Mitchelldale St., Ste. E17, Houston, TX 77092-7222 / 713-462-4200; or 800-272-7816; FAX: 713-681-5665 info@highstandard.com www.highstandard.com
High Tech Specialties, Inc., P.O. Box 839, 293 E Main St., Rear, Adamstown, PA 19501 / 717-484-0405; FAX: 717-484-0523 bansner@aol.com www.bansmersrifle.com/hightech
Highline Machine Co., Randall Thompson, Randall Thompson, 654 Lela Place, Grand Junction, CO 81504 / 970-434-4971
Highwood Special Products, 1531 E. Highwood, Pontiac, MI 48340
Hi-Grade Imports, 8655 Monterey Rd., Gilroy, CA 95021 / 408-842-9301; FAX: 408-842-2374
Hill, Loring F., 304 Cedar Rd., Elkins Park, PA 19027
Hill Speed Leather, Ernie, 4507 N 195th Ave., Litchfield Park, AZ 85340 / 602-853-9222; FAX: 602-853-9235
Hinman Outfitters, Bob, 107 N Sanderson Ave., Bartonville, IL 61607-1839 / 309-691-8132
Hi-Performance Ammunition Company, 484 State Route 366, Apollo, PA 15613 / 412-327-8100
HIP-GRIP Barami Corp., P.O. Box 252224, West Bloomfield, MI 48325-2224 / 248-738-0462; FAX: 248-738-2542 hipgripja@aol.com www.hipgrip.com
Hi-Point Firearms/MKS Supply, 8611-A North Dixie Dr., Dayton, OH 45414 / 877-425-4867; FAX: 937-454-0503 www.hi-pointfirearms.com
Hiptmayer, Armurier, RR 112 750, P.O. Box 136, Eastman, PQ J0E 1P0 CANADA / 514-297-2492
Hiptmayer, Heidemarie, RR 112 750, P.O. Box 136, Eastman, PQ J0E 1P0 CANADA / 514-297-2492
Hiptmayer, Klaus, RR 112 750, P.O. Box 136, Eastman, PQ J0E 1P0 CANADA / 514-297-2492
Hirtenberger AG, Leobersdorferstrasse 31, A-2552, Hirtenberg, AUSTRIA / 43(0)2256 81184; FAX: 43(0)2256 81808 www.hirtenberger.ot
HJS Arms, Inc., P.O. Box 3711, Brownsville, TX 78523-3711 / 956-542-2767; FAX: 956-542-2767
Hoag, James W., 8523 Canoga Ave., Suite C, Canoga Park, CA 91304 / 818-998-1510
Hobson Precision Mfg. Co., 210 Big Oak Ln., Brent, AL 35034 / 205-926-4662; FAX: 205-926-3193 cahobbob@dbtech.net
Hodgdon Powder Co., 6231 Robinson, Shawnee Mission, KS 66202 / 913-362-9455; FAX: 913-362-1307
Hodgman, Inc., 1750 Orchard Rd., Montgomery, IL 60538 / 708-897-7555; FAX: 708-897-7558
Hodgson, Richard, 9081 Tahoe Lane, Boulder, CO 80301
Hoehn Sales, Inc., 2045 Kohn Road, Wright City, MO 63390 / 636-745-8144; FAX: 636-745-7868 hoehnsal@usmo.com
Hofer Jagdwaffen, P., Buchsenmachermeister, Kirchgasse 24, A-9170 Ferlach, AUSTRIA / 43 4227 3683; FAX: 43 4227 368330 peterhofer@hoferwaffen.com www.hoferwaffen.com
Hoffman New Ideas, 821 Northmoor Rd., Lake Forest, IL 60045 / 312-234-4075
Hogue Grips, P.O. Box 1138, Paso Robles, CA 93447 / 800-438-4747 or 805-239-1440; FAX: 805-239-2553
Holland & Holland Ltd., 33 Bruton St., London, ENGLAND / 44-171-499-4411; FAX: 44-171-408-7962
Holland's Gunsmithing, P.O. Box 69, Powers, OR 97466 / 541-439-5155; FAX: 541-439-5155
Hollinger, Jon. See: ASPEN OUTFITTING CO.
Hollywood Engineering, 10642 Arminta St., Sun Valley, CA 91352 / 818-842-8376; FAX: 818-504-4168 cadqueenel1@aol.com
Homak, 5151 W. 73rd St., Chicago, IL 60638-6613 / 312-523-3100; FAX: 312-523-9455
Home Shop Machinist, The Village Press Publications, P.O. Box 1810, Traverse City, MI 49685 / 800-447-7367; FAX: 616-946-3289
Hondo Ind., 510 S. 52nd St., I04, Tempe, AZ 85281
Hoppe's Div. Penguin Industries, Inc., P.O. Box 1690, Oregon City, OR 97045-0690 / 610-384-6000
Horizons Unlimited, P.O. Box 426, Warm Springs, GA 31830 / 706-655-3603; FAX: 706-655-3603
Hornady Mfg. Co., P.O. Box 1848, Grand Island, NE 68802 / 800-338-3220 or 308-382-1390; FAX: 308-382-5761
Horseshoe Leather Products, Andy Arratoonian, The Cottage Sharow, Ripon U.K., ENGLAND U.K. / 44-1765-605858 andy@horseshoe.co.uk www.holsters.org
House of Muskets, Inc., The, PO Box 4640, Pagosa Springs, CO 81157 / 970-731-2295
Houtz & Barwick, P.O. Box 435, W. Church St., Elizabeth City, NC 27909 / 800-775-0337; or 919-335-4191; FAX: 919-335-1152
Howa Machinery, Ltd., Sukaguchi, Shinkawa-cho Nishikasugai-gun, Aichi 452-8601, JAPAN / 81-52-408-1231; FAX: 81-52-401-4999 howa@howa.co.jp http://www.howa.cojpl
Howell Machine, 815 1/2 D St., Lewiston, ID 83501 / 208-743-7418
H-S Precision, Inc., 1301 Turbine Dr., Rapid City, SD 57701 / 605-341-3006; FAX: 605-342-8964
HT Bullets, 244 Belleville Rd., New Bedford, MA 02745 / 508-999-3338
Hubert J. Hecht Waffen-Hecht, P.O. Box 2635, Fair Oaks, CA 95628 / 916-966-1020
Huebner, Corey O., P.O. Box 564, Frenchtown, MT 59834 / 406-721-7168 bugsboys@hotmail.com
Huey Gun Cases, 820 Indiana St., Lawrence, KS 66044-2645 / 816-444-1637; FAX: 816-444-1637 hueycases@aol.com www.hueycases.com
Hume, Don, P.O. Box 351, Miami, OK 74355 / 800-331-2686; FAX: 918-542-4340 info@donhume.com www.donhume.com
Hunkeler, A. (See Buckskin Machine Works), 3235 S 358th St., Auburn, WA 98001 / 206-927-5412
Hunter Co., Inc., 3300 W. 71st Ave., Westminster, CO 80030 / 303-427-4626; FAX: 303-428-3980 debbiet@huntercompany.com www.huntercompany.com
Hunterjohn, PO Box 771457, St. Louis, MO 63177 / 314-531-7250 www.hunterjohn.com
Hunter's Specialties Inc., 6000 Huntington Ct. NE, Cedar Rapids, IA 52402-1268 / 319-395-0321; FAX: 319-395-0326
Hunters Supply, Inc., P.O. Box 313, Tioga, TX 76271 / 940-437-2458; FAX: 940-437-2228 hunterssupply@hotmail.com www.hunterssupply.net
Huntington Die Specialties, 601 Oro Dam Blvd., Oroville, CA 95965 / 530-534-1210; FAX: 530-534-1212 buy@huntingtons.com www.huntingtons.com
Hutton Rifle Ranch, P.O. Box 170317, Boise, ID 83717 / 208-345-8781 www.martinbrevik@aol.com
Hydrosorbent Products, PO Box 437, Ashley Falls, MA 01222 / 800-448-7903; FAX: 413-229-8743 orders@dehumidify.com www.dehumidify.com

I

I.A.B. (See U.S. Importer-Taylor's & Co. Inc.)
I.D.S.A. Books, 1324 Stratford Drive, Piqua, OH 45356 / 937-773-4203; FAX: 937-778-1922
I.N.C. Inc. (See Kickeez I.N.C., Inc.)
I.S.S., P.O. Box 185234, Ft. Worth, TX 76181 / 817-595-2090; FAX: 817-595-2090 iss@concentric.net
I.S.W., 106 E. Cairo Dr., Tempe, AZ 85282
IAR Inc., 33171 Camino Capistrano, San Juan Capistrano, CA 92675 / 949-443-3642; FAX: 949-443-3647 sales@iar-arms.com iar-arms.com
Ide, Ken. See: STURGEON VALLEY SPORTERS
IGA (See U.S. Importer-Stoeger Industries)
Image Ind. Inc., 382 Balm Court, Wood Dale, IL 60191 / 630-766-2402; FAX: 630-766-7373
Impact Case & Container, Inc., P.O. Box 1129, Rathdrum, ID 83858 / 877-687-2452; FAX: 208-687-0632 bradk@icc-case.com www.icc-case.com
Imperial (See E-Z-Way Systems), P.O. Box 4310, Newark, OH 43058-4310 / 614-345-6645; FAX: 614-345-6600 ezway@infinet.com www.jcunald.com
Imperial Magnum Corp., P.O. Box 249, Oroville, WA 98844 / 604-495-3131; FAX: 604-495-2816
Imperial Miniature Armory, 10547 S. Post Oak Road, Houston, TX 77035-3305 / 713-729-8428; FAX: 713-729-2274 miniguns@aol.com www.1800miniature.com
Imperial Schrade Corp., 7 Schrade Ct., Box 7000, Ellenville, NY 12428 / 914-647-7601; FAX: 914-647-8701 csc@schradeknives.com www.schradeknives.com
Import Sports Inc., 1750 Brielle Ave., Unit B1, Wanamassa, NJ 07712 / 732-493-0302; FAX: 732-493-0301 gsodini@aol.com www.bersa-11ama.com
IMR Powder Co., 1080 Military Turnpike, Suite 2, Plattsburgh, NY 12901 / 518-563-2253; FAX: 518-563-6916

Info-Arm, P.O. Box 1262, Champlain, NY 12919 / 514-955-0355; FAX: 514-955-0357 infoarm@qc.aira.com

Ingle, Ralph W., Engraver, 112 Manchester Ct., Centerville, GA 31028 / 478-953-5824 riengraver@aol.com www.fega.com

Innovative Weaponry Inc., 2513 E. Loop 820 N., Fort Worth, TX 76118 / 817-284-0099 or 800-334-3573

INTEC International, Inc., P.O. Box 5708, Scottsdale, AZ 85261 / 602-483-1708

Inter Ordnance of America LP, 3305 Westwood Industrial Dr., Monroe, NC 28110-5204 / 704-821-8337; FAX: 704-821-8523

Intercontinental Distributors, Ltd., PO Box 815, Beulah, ND 58523

Intrac Arms International, 5005 Chapman Hwy., Knoxville, TN 37920

Ion Industries, Inc., 3508 E Allerton Ave., Cudahy, WI 53110 / 414-486-2007; FAX: 414-486-2017

Iosso Products, 1485 Lively Blvd., Elk Grove Village, IL 60007 / 847-437-8400; FAX: 847-437-8478

Iron Bench, 12619 Bailey Rd., Redding, CA 96003 / 916-241-4623

Ironside International Publishers, Inc., P.O. Box 1050, Lorton, VA 22199

Ironsighter Co., P.O. Box 85070, Westland, MI 48185 / 734-326-8731; FAX: 734-326-3378 www.ironsighter.com

Irwin, Campbell H., 140 Hartland Blvd., East Hartland, CT 06027 / 203-653-3901

Island Pond Gun Shop, Cross St., Island Pond, VT 05846 / 802-723-4546

Israel Arms Inc., 5625 Star Ln. #B, Houston, TX 77057 / 713-789-0745; FAX: 713-914-9515 www.israelarms.com

Ithaca Classic Doubles, Stephen Lamboy, No. 5 Railroad St., Victor, NY 14564 / 716-924-2710; FAX: 716-924-2737 ithacadoubles.com

Ithaca Gun Company LLC, 901 Rt. 34 B, King Ferry, NY 13081 / 315-364-7171; FAX: 315-364-5134 info@ithacagun.com

Ivanoff, Thomas G. (See Tom's Gun Repair)

J

J J Roberts Firearm Engraver, 7808 Lake Dr, Manassas, VA 20111 / 703-330-0448; FAX: 703-264-8600 james..roberts@angelfire.com www.angelfire.com/va2/engraver

J&D Components, 75 East 350 North, Orem, UT 84057-4719 / 801-225-7007 www.jdcomponents.com

J&J Products, Inc., 9240 Whitmore, El Monte, CA 91731 / 818-571-5228; FAX: 800-927-8361

J&J Sales, 1501 21st Ave. S., Great Falls, MT 59405 / 406-727-9789 mtshootingbench@yahoo.com www.j&jsales.us

J&L Superior Bullets (See Huntington Die Special)

J&R Engineering, P.O. Box 77, 200 Lyons Hill Rd., Athol, MA 01331 / 508-249-9241

J&R Enterprises, 4550 Scotts Valley Rd., Lakeport, CA 95453

J&S Heat Treat, 803 S. 16th St., Blue Springs, MO 64015 / 816-229-2149; FAX: 816-228-1135

J. Dewey Mfg. Co., Inc., P.O. Box 2014, Southbury, CT 06488 / 203-264-3064; FAX: 203-262-6907 deweyrods@worldnet.att.net www.deweyrods.com

J. Korzinek Riflesmith, RD 2, Box 73D, Canton, PA 17724 / 717-673-8512

J.A. Blades, Inc. (See Christopher Firearms Co.)

J.A. Henckels Zwillingswerk Inc., 9 Skyline Dr., Hawthorne, NY 10532 / 914-592-7370

J.G. Anschutz GmbH & Co. KG, Daimlerstr. 12, D-89079 Ulm, Ulm, GERMANY / 49 731 40120; FAX: 49 731 4012700 JGA-info@anschuetz-sport.com www.anschuetz-sport.com

J.G. Dapkus Co., Inc., Commerce Circle, P.O. Box 293, Durham, CT 06422 www.explodingtargets.com

J.I.T. Ltd., P.O. Box 230, Freedom, WY 83120 / 708-494-0937

J.J. Roberts / Engraver, 7808 Lake Dr., Manassas, VA 20111 / 703-330-0448 jjrengraver@aol.com www.angelfire.com/va2/engraver

J.P. Enterprises Inc., P.O. Box 378, Hugo, MN 55110 / 612-486-9064; FAX: 612-482-0970

J.R. Williams Bullet Co., 2008 Tucker Rd., Perry, GA 31069 / 912-987-0274

J.W. Morrison Custom Rifles, 4015 W. Sharon, Phoenix, AZ 85029 / 602-978-3754

J/B Adventures & Safaris Inc., 2275 E. Arapahoe Rd., Ste. 109, Littleton, CO 80122-1521 / 303-771-0977

Jack A. Rosenberg & Sons, 12229 Cox Ln., Dallas, TX 75234 / 214-241-6302

Jack Dever Co., 8520 NW 90th St., Oklahoma City, OK 73132 / 405-721-6393 jbdever1@home.com

Jack First, Inc., 1201 Turbine Dr., Rapid City, SD 57703 / 605-343-8481; FAX: 605-343-9420

Jack Jonas Appraisals & Taki, 13952 E. Marina Dr., #604, Aurora, CO 80014

Jackalope Gun Shop, 1048 S. 5th St., Douglas, WY 82633 / 307-358-3441

Jaffin, Harry. See: BRIDGEMAN PRODUCTS

Jagdwaffen, Peter. See: BUCHSENMACHERMEISTER

James Churchill Glove Co., PO Box 298, Centralia, WA 98531 / 360-736-2816; FAX: 360-330-0151 churchillglove@localaccess.com

James Wayne Firearms for Collectors and Investors, 2608 N. Laurent, Victoria, TX 77901 / 361-578-1258; FAX: 361-578-3559

Jamison International, Marc Jamison, 3551 Mayer Ave., Sturgis, SD 57785 / 605-347-5090; FAX: 605-347-4704 jbell2@masttechnology.com

Jamison, Marc. See: JAMISON INTERNATIONAL

Jamison's Forge Works, 4527 Rd. 6.5 NE, Moses Lake, WA 98837 / 509-762-2659

Jantz Supply, 309 West Main Dept HD, Davis, OK 73030-0584 / 580-369-2316; FAX: 580-369-3082 jantz@brightok.net www.knifemaking.com

Jarrett Rifles, Inc., 383 Brown Rd., Jackson, SC 29831 / 803-471-3616 www.jarrettrifles.com

Jarvis, Inc., 1123 Cherry Orchard Lane, Hamilton, MT 59840 / 406-961-4392

Javelina Lube Products, P.O. Box 337, San Bernardino, CA 92402 / 909-350-9556; FAX: 909-429-1211

Jay McCament Custom Gunmaker, Jay McCament, 1730-134th St. Ct. S., Tacoma, WA 98444 / 253-531-8832

JB Custom, P.O. Box 6912, Leawood, KS 66206 / 913-381-2329

Jeff Flannery Engraving, 11034 Riddles Run Rd., Union, KY 41091 / 859-384-3127; FAX: 859-384-2222 engraving@fuse.net http://home.fuse.net/engraving/

Jeffredo Gunsight, P.O. Box 669, San Marcos, CA 92079 / 760-728-2695

Jena Eur, PO Box 319, Dunmore, PA 18512

Jenco Sales, Inc., P.O. Box 1000, Manchaca, TX 78652 / 800-531-5301; FAX: 800-266-2373 jencosales@sbcglobal.net

Jenkins Recoil Pads, 5438 E. Frontage Ln., Olney, IL 62450 / 618-395-3416

Jensen Bullets, RR 1 Box 187, Arco, ID 83213 / 208-785-5590

Jensen's Custom Ammunition, 5146 E. Pima, Tucson, AZ 85712 / 602-325-3346; FAX: 602-322-5704

Jensen's Firearms Academy, 1280 W. Prince, Tucson, AZ 85705 / 602-293-8516

Jericho Tool & Die Co., Inc., 2917 St. Hwy. 7, Bainbridge, NY 13733 / 607-563-8222; FAX: 607-563-8560 jerichotool.com www.jerichotool.com

Jerry Phillips Optics, P.O. Box L632, Langhorne, PA 19047 / 215-757-5037; FAX: 215-757-7097

Jesse W. Smith Saddlery, 0499 County Road J, Pritchett, CO 81064 / 509-325-0622

Jester Bullets, Rt. 1 Box 27, Orienta, OK 73737

Jewell Triggers, Inc., 3620 Hwy. 123, San Marcos, TX 78666 / 512-353-2999; FAX: 512-392-0543

JGS Precision Tool Mfg., LLC, 60819 Selander Rd., Coos Bay, OR 97420 / 541-267-4331; FAX: 541-267-5996 jgstools@harborside.com www.jgstools.com

Jim Blair Engraving, P.O. Box 64, Glenrock, WY 82637 / 307-436-8115 jblairengrav@msn.com

Jim Noble Co., 1305 Columbia St., Vancouver, WA 98660 / 360-695-1309; FAX: 360-695-6835 jnobleco@aol.com

Jim Norman Custom Gunstocks, 14281 Cane Rd., Valley Center, CA 92082 / 619-749-6252

Jim's Precision, Jim Ketchum, 1725 Moclips Dr., Petaluma, CA 94952 / 707-762-3014

JLK Bullets, 414 Turner Rd., Dover, AR 72837 / 501-331-4194

Johanssons Vapentillbehor, Bert, S-430 20, Veddige, SWEDEN

John Hall Plastics, Inc., P.O. Box 1526, Alvin, TX 77512 / 713-489-8709

John J. Adams & Son Engravers, 7040 VT Rt 113, Vershire, VT 05079 / 802-685-0019

John Masen Co. Inc., 1305 Jelmak, Grand Prairie, TX 75050 / 817-430-8732; FAX: 817-430-1715

John Partridge Sales Ltd., Trent Meadows Rugeley, Staffordshire, WS15 2HS ENGLAND

John Rigby & Co., 500 Linne Rd. Ste. D, Paso Robles, CA 93446 / 805-227-4236; FAX: 805-227-4723 jribgy@calinet www.johnrigbyandco.com

John's Custom Leather, 523 S. Liberty St., Blairsville, PA 15717 / 724-459-6802; FAX: 724-459-5996

Johnson Wood Products, 34897 Crystal Road, Strawberry Point, IA 52076 / 563-933-6504 johnsonwoodproducts@yahoo.com

Johnston Bros. (See C&T Corp. TA Johnson Brothers)

Jonad Corp., 2091 Lakeland Ave., Lakewood, OH 44107 / 216-226-3161

Jonathan Arthur Ciener, Inc., 8700 Commerce St., Cape Canaveral, FL 32920 / 321-868-2200; FAX: 321-868-2201 www.22lrconversions.com

Jones Co., Dale, 680 Hoffman Draw, Kila, MT 59920 / 406-755-4684

Jones Custom Products, Neil A., 17217 Brookhouser Rd., Saegertown, PA 16433 / 814-763-2769; FAX: 814-763-4228

Jones, J. See: SSK INDUSTRIES

Jones Moulds, Paul, 4901 Telegraph Rd., Los Angeles, CA 90022 / 213-262-1510

JP Sales, Box 307, Anderson, TX 77830

JRP Custom Bullets, RR2 2233 Carlton Rd., Whitehall, NY 12887 / 518-282-0084 or 802-438-5548

JSL Ltd. (See U.S. Importer-Specialty Shooters)

Juenke, Vern, 25 Bitterbush Rd., Reno, NV 89523 / 702-345-0225

Jungkind, Reeves C., 509 E. Granite St., Llano, TX 78643-3055 / 325-247-1151

Jurras, L. See: L. E. JURRAS & ASSOC.

Justin Phillippi Custom Bullets, P.O. Box 773, Ligonier, PA 15658 / 412-238-9671

K

K&M Industries, Inc., Box 66, 510 S. Main, Troy, ID 83871 / 208-835-2281; FAX: 208-835-5211

K&M Services, 5430 Salmon Run Rd., Dover, PA 17315 / 717-292-3175; FAX: 717-292-3175

K. Eversull Co., Inc., 1 Tracemont, Boyce, LA 71409 / 318-793-8728; FAX: 318-793-5483 bestguns@aol.com

K.B.I. Inc., P.O. Box 6625, Harrisburg, PA 17112 / 717-540-8518; FAX: 717-540-8567

K.L. Null Holsters Ltd., 161 School St. NW, Hill City Station, Resaca, GA 30735 / 706-625-5643; FAX: 706-625-9392 ken@klnullholsters.com www.klnullholsters.com

Ka Pu Kapili, P.O. Box 745, Honokaa, HI 96727 / 808-776-1644; FAX: 808-776-1731

KA-BAR Knives, 200 Homer St., Olean, NY 14760 / 800-282-0130; FAX: 716-790-7188 info@ka-bar.com www.ka-bar.com

Kahles A. Swarovski Company, 2 Slater Rd., Cranston, RI 02920 / 401-946-2220; FAX: 401-946-2587

Kahr Arms, PO Box 220, 630 Route 303, Blauvelt, NY 10913 / 845-353-7770; FAX: 845-353-7833 www.kahr.com

Kailua Custom Guns Inc., 51 N. Dean Street, Coquille, OR 97423 / 541-396-5413 kailuacustom@aol.com www.kailuacustom.com

Kalispel Case Line, P.O. Box 267, Cusick, WA 99119 / 509-445-1121

Kamik Outdoor Footwear, 554 Montee de Liesse, Montreal, PQ H4T 1P1 CANADA / 514-341-3950; FAX: 514-341-1861

Kane, Edward, P.O. Box 385, Ukiah, CA 95482 / 707-462-2937

Kapro Mfg. Co. Inc. (See R.E.I.)

MANUFACTURER'S DIRECTORY

Kasenit Co., Inc., 39 Park Ave., Highland Mills, NY 10930 / 845-928-9595; FAX: 845-986-8038
Kaswer Custom, Inc., 13 Surrey Drive, Brookfield, CT 06804 / 203-775-0564; FAX: 203-775-6872
KDF, Inc., 2485 Hwy. 46 N., Seguin, TX 78155 / 830-379-8141; FAX: 830-379-5420
KeeCo Impressions, Inc., 346 Wood Ave., North Brunswick, NJ 08902 / 800-468-0546
Kehr, Roger, 2131 Agate Ct. SE, Lacy, WA 98503 / 360-491-0691
Keith's Bullets, 942 Twisted Oak, Algonquin, IL 60102 / 708-658-3520
Keith's Custom Gunstocks, Keith M. Heppler, 540 Banyan Circle, Walnut Creek, CA 94598 / 925-934-3509; FAX: 925-934-3143 kmheppler@hotmail.com
Kelbly, Inc., 7222 Dalton Fox Lake Rd., North Lawrence, OH 44666 / 216-683-4674; FAX: 216-683-7349
Kelley's, P.O. Box 125, Woburn, MA 01801-0125 / 800-879-7273; FAX: 781-272-7077 kels@star.net www.kelsmilitary.com
Kellogg's Professional Products, 325 Pearl St., Sandusky, OH 44870 / 419-625-6551; FAX: 419-625-6167 skwigton@aol.com
Kelly, Lance, 1723 Willow Oak Dr., Edgewater, FL 32132 / 904-423-4933
Kel-Tec CNC Industries, Inc., PO Box 236009, Cocoa, FL 32923 / 407-631-0068; FAX: 407-631-1169
Kemen America, 2550 Hwy. 23, Wrenshall, MN 55797 / 218-384-3670 patrickl@midwestshootingschool.com midwestshootingschool.com
Ken Eyster Heritage Gunsmiths, Inc., 6441 Bisop Rd., Centerburg, OH 43011 / 740-625-6131; FAX: 740-625-7811
Ken Starnes Gunmaker, 15940 SW Holly Hill Rd., Hillsboro, OR 97123-9033 / 503-628-0705; FAX: 503-443-2096 kstarnes@kdsa.com
Keng's Firearms Specialty, Inc./US Tactical Systems, 875 Wharton Dr., P.O. Box 44405, Atlanta, GA 30336-1405 / 404-691-7611; FAX: 404-505-8445
Kennebec Journal, 274 Western Ave., Augusta, ME 04330 / 207-622-6288
Kennedy Firearms, 10 N. Market St., Muncy, PA 17756 / 717-546-6695
Kenneth W. Warren Engraver, P.O. Box 2842, Wenatchee, WA 98807 / 509-663-6123; FAX: 509-665-6123
Ken's Kustom Kartridges, 331 Jacobs Rd., Hubbard, OH 44425 / 216-534-4595
Kent Cartridge America, Inc., PO Box 849, 1000 Zigor Rd., Kearneysville, WV 25430
Keowee Game Calls, 608 Hwy. 25 North, Travelers Rest, SC 29690 / 864-834-7204; FAX: 864-834-7831
Kershaw Knives, 25300 SW Parkway Ave., Wilsonville, OR 97070 / 503-682-1966; or 800-325-2891; FAX: 503-682-7168
Kesselring Gun Shop, 4024 Old Hwy. 99N, Burlington, WA 98233 / 360-724-3113; FAX: 360-724-7003 info@kesselrings.com www.kesselrings.com
Ketchum, Jim (See Jim's Precision)
Keystone Sporting Arms, Inc. (Crickett Rifles), 8920 State Route 405, Milton, PA 17847 / 800-742-2777; FAX: 570-742-1455
Kickeez I.N.C., Inc., 301 Industrial Dr., Carl Junction, MO 64834-8806 / 419-649-2100; FAX: 417-649-2200 kickey@ipa.net
Kilham & Co., Main St., P.O. Box 37, Lyme, NH 03768 / 603-795-4112
Kim Ahrends Custom Firearms, Inc., Box 203, Clarion, IA 50525 / 515-532-3449; FAX: 515-532-3926
Kimar (See U.S. Importer-IAR,Inc)
Kimber of America, Inc., 1 Lawton St., Yonkers, NY 10705 / 800-880-2418; FAX: 914-964-9340
King & Co., P.O. Box 1242, Bloomington, IL 61702 / 309-473-3964; FAX: 309-473-2161
King's Gun Works, 1837 W. Glenoaks Blvd., Glendale, CA 91201 / 818-956-6010; FAX: 818-548-8606
Kirkpatrick Leather Co., PO Box 677, Laredo, TX 78040 / 956-723-6631; FAX: 956-725-0672 mike@kirkpatrickleather.com www.kirkpatrickleather.com
KK Air International (See Impact Case & Container Co.)
Kleen-Bore, Inc., 16 Industrial Pkwy., Easthampton, MA 01027 / 413-527-0300; FAX: 413-527-2522 info@kleen-bore.com www.kleen-bore.com
Kleinendorst, K. W., RR 1, Box 1500, Hop Bottom, PA 18824 / 717-289-4687
Klingler Woodcarving, P.O. Box 141, Thistle Hill, Cabot, VT 05647 / 802-426-3811
Knifeware, Inc., P.O. Box 3, Greenville, WV 24945 / 304-832-6878
Knight Rifles, 21852 Hwy. J46, P.O. Box 130, Centerville, IA 52544 / 515-856-2626; FAX: 515-856-2628 www.knightrifles.com
Knight Rifles (See Modern Muzzle Loading, Inc.)
Knight's Mfg. Co., 7750 Ninth St. SW, Vero Beach, FL 32968 / 561-562-5697; FAX: 561-569-2955 civiliansales@knightarmco.com
Knock on Wood Antiques, 355 Post Rd., Darien, CT 06820 / 203-655-9031
Knoell, Doug, 9737 McCardle Way, Santee, CA 92071 / 619-449-5189
Knopp, Gary. See: SUPER 6 LLC
KOGOT, 410 College, Trinidad, CO 81082 / 719-846-9406; FAX: 719-846-9406
Kolar, 1925 Roosevelt Ave., Racine, WI 53406 / 414-554-0800; FAX: 414-554-9093
Kolpin Outdoors, Inc., P.O. Box 107, 205 Depot St., Fox Lake, WI 53933 / 414-928-3118; FAX: 414-928-3687 cdutton@kolpin.com www.kolpin.com
Korth Germany GmbH, Robert Bosch Strasse, 11, D-23909, 23909 Ratzeburg, GERMANY / 4541-840363; FAX: 4541-84 05 35 info@korthwaffen.de www.korthwaffen.com
Korth USA, 437R Chandler St., Tewksbury, MA 01876 / 978-851-8656; FAX: 978-851-9462 info@kortusa.com www.korthusa.com
Korzinek Riflesmith, J., RD 2 Box 73D, Canton, PA 17724 / 717-673-8512
Koval Knives, 5819 Zarley St., Suite A, New Albany, OH 43054 / 614-855-0777; FAX: 614-855-0945 koval@kovalknives.com www.kovalknives.com
Kowa Optimed, Inc., 20001 S. Vermont Ave., Torrance, CA 90502 / 310-327-1913; FAX: 310-327-4177 scopekowa@kowa.com www.kowascope.com
Kramer Designs, P.O. Box 129, Clancy, MT 59634 / 406-933-8658; FAX: 406-933-8658
Kramer Handgun Leather, P.O. Box 112154, Tacoma, WA 98411 / 800-510-2666; FAX: 253-564-1214 www.kramerleather.com
Krause Publications, Inc., 700 E. State St., Iola, WI 54990 / 715-445-2214; FAX: 715-445-4087
Krico Deutschland GmbH, Nurnbergerstrasse 6, D-90602, Pyrbaum, GERMANY / 09180-2780; FAX: 09180-2661
Krieger Barrels, Inc., 2024 Mayfield Rd, Richfield, WI 53076 / 262-628-8558; FAX: 262-628-8748
Krieghoff Gun Co., H., Boschstrasse 22, D-89079 Elm, GERMANY / 731-4018270
Krieghoff International,Inc., 7528 Easton Rd., Ottsville, PA 18942 / 610-847-5173; FAX: 610-847-8691
Kukowski, Ed. See: ED'S GUN HOUSE
Kulis Freeze Dry Taxidermy, 725 Broadway Ave., Bedford, OH 44146 / 216-232-8352; FAX: 216-232-7305 jkulis@kastaway.com kastaway.com
KVH Industries, Inc., 110 Enterprise Center, Middletown, RI 02842 / 401-847-3327; FAX: 401-849-0045
Kwik-Site Co., 5555 Treadwell St., Wayne, MI 48184 / 734-326-1500; FAX: 734-326-4120 kwiksiteco@aol.com

L

L&R Lock Co., 1137 Pocalla Rd., Sumter, SC 29150 / 803-775-6127; FAX: 803-775-5171
L&S Technologies Inc. (See Aimtech Mount Systems)
L. Bengtson Arms Co., 6345-B E. Akron St., Mesa, AZ 85205 / 602-981-6375
L. E. Jurras & Assoc., L. E. Jurras, P.O. Box 680, Washington, IN 47501 / 812-254-6170; FAX: 812-254-6170 jurasgun@rtcc.net
L.A.R. Mfg., Inc., 4133 W. Farm Rd., West Jordan, UT 84088 / 801-280-3505; FAX: 801-280-1972
L.B.T., Judy Smith, HCR 62, Box 145, Moyie Springs, ID 83845 / 208-267-3588
L.E. Wilson, Inc., Box 324, 404 Pioneer Ave., Cashmere, WA 98815 / 509-782-1328; FAX: 509-782-7200
L.L. Bean, Inc., Freeport, ME 04032 / 207-865-4761; FAX: 207-552-2802
L.P.A. Inc., Via Alfieri 26, Gardone V.T., Brescia, ITALY / 30-891-14-81; FAX: 30-891-09-51
L.R. Clift Mfg., 3821 Hammonton Rd., Marysville, CA 95901 / 916-755-3390; FAX: 916-755-3393
L.W. Seecamp Co., Inc., PO Box 255, New Haven, CT 06502 / 203-877-3429; FAX: 203-877-3429 seecamp@optonline.net
La Clinique du .45, 1432 Rougemont, Chambly, PQ J3L 2L8 CANADA / 514-658-1144
Labanu, Inc., 2201-F Fifth Ave., Ronkonkoma, NY 11779 / 516-467-6197; FAX: 516-981-4112
LaBoone, Pat. See: THE MIDWEST SHOOTING SCHOOL
LaBounty Precision Reboring, Inc, 7968 Silver Lake Rd., PO Box 186, Maple Falls, WA 98266 / 360-599-2047; FAX: 360-599-3018
LaCrosse Footwear, Inc., 18550 NE Riverside Parkway, Portland, OR 97230 / 503-766-1010; or 800-323-2668; FAX: 503-766-1015
LaFrance Specialties, P.O. Box 87933, San Diego, CA 92138 / 619-293-3373; FAX: 619-293-0819 timlafrance@att.net lafrancespecialties.com
Lake Center Marina, PO Box 670, St. Charles, MO 63302 / 314-946-7500
Lakefield Arms Ltd. (See Savage Arms, Inc.)
Lakewood Products LLC, 275 June St., Berlin, WI 54923 / 800-872-8458; FAX: 920-361-7719 lakewood@centurytel.net www.lakewoodproducts.com
Lamboy, Stephen. See: ITHACA CLASSIC DOUBLES
Lampert, Ron, Rt. 1, 44857 Schoolcraft Trl., Guthrie, MN 56461 / 218-854-7345
Lamson & Goodnow Mfg. Co., 45 Conway St., Shelburne Falls, MA 03170 / 413-625-6564; or 800-872-6564; FAX: 413-625-9816 www.lamsonsharp.com
Lansky Levine, Arthur. See: LANSKY SHARPENERS
Lansky Sharpeners, Arthur Lansky Levine, PO Box 50830, Las Vegas, NV 89016 / 702-361-7511; FAX: 702-896-9511
LaPrade, PO Box 250, Ewing, VA 24248 / 423-733-2615
Lapua Ltd., P.O. Box 5, Lapua, FINLAND / 6-310111; FAX: 6-4388991
LaRocca Gun Works, 51 Union Place, Worcester, MA 01608 / 508-754-2887; FAX: 508-754-2887 www.laroccagunworks.com
Larry Lyons Gunworks, 110 Hamilton St., Dowagiac, MI 49047 / 616-782-9478
Laser Devices, Inc., 2 Harris Ct. A-4, Monterey, CA 93940 / 831-373-0701; FAX: 831-373-0903 sales@laserdevices.com www.laserdevices.com
Laseraim Technologies, Inc., P.O. Box 3548, Little Rock, AR 72203 / 501-375-2227
Laserlyte, 2201 Amapola Ct., Torrance, CA 90501
LaserMax, Inc., 3495 Winton Place, Bldg. B, Rochester, NY 14623-2807 / 800-527-3703; FAX: 716-272-5427 customerservice@lasermax-inc.com www.lasermax-inc.com
Lassen Community College, Gunsmithing Dept., P.O. Box 3000, Hwy. 139, Susanville, CA 96130 / 916-251-8800; FAX: 916-251-8838
Lathrop's, Inc., 5146 E. Pima, Tucson, AZ 85712 / 520-881-0266; or 800-875-4867; FAX: 520-322-5704
Laughridge, William R. (See Cylinder & Slide Inc.)
Laurel Mountain Forge, P.O. Box 52, Crown Point, IN 46308 / 219-548-2950; FAX: 219-548-2950
Laurona Armas Eibar, S.A.L., Avenida de Otaola 25, P.O. Box 260, Eibar 20600, SPAIN / 34-43-700600; FAX: 34-43-700616
Lawrence Brand Shot (See Precision Reloading)
Lawrence Leather Co., P.O. Box 1479, Lillington, NC 27546 / 910-893-2071; FAX: 910-893-4742
Lawson Co., Harry, 3328 N Richey Blvd., Tucson, AZ 85716 / 520-326-1117; FAX: 520-326-1117
Lawson, John. See: THE SIGHT SHOP
Lawson, John G. (See Sight Shop, The)
Lazzeroni Arms Co., PO Box 26696, Tucson, AZ 85726 / 888-492-7247; FAX: 520-624-4250
Le Clear Industries (See E-Z-Way Systems), P.O. Box 4310, Newark, OH 43058-4310 / 614-345-6645; FAX: 614-345-6600
Leapers, Inc., 7675 Five Mile Rd., Northville, MI 48167 / 248-486-1231; FAX: 248-486-1430
Leatherman Tool Group, Inc., 12106 NE Ainsworth Cir., P.O. Box 20595, Portland, OR 97294 / 503-253-7826; FAX: 503-253-7830

MANUFACTURER'S DIRECTORY

Lebeau-Courally, Rue St. Gilles, 386 4000, Liege, BELGIUM / 042-52-48-43; FAX: 32-4-252-2008 info@lebeau-courally.com www.lebeau-courally.com
Leckie Professional Gunsmithing, 546 Quarry Rd., Ottsville, PA 18942 / 215-847-8594
Ledbetter Airguns, Riley, 1804 E Sprague St, Winston Salem, NC 27107-3521 / 919-784-0676
Lee Precision, Inc., 4275 Hwy. U, Hartford, WI 53027 / 262-673-3075; FAX: 262-673-9273 info@leeprecision.com www.leeprecision.com
Lee Supplies, Mark, 9901 France Ct., Lakeville, MN 55044 / 612-461-2114
LeFever Arms Co., Inc., 6234 Stokes, Lee Center Rd., Lee Center, NY 13363 / 315-337-6722; FAX: 315-337-1543
Legacy Sports International, 206 S. Union St., Alexandria, VA 22314 / 703-548-4837 www.legacysports.com
Leibowitz, Leonard, 1205 Murrayhill Ave., Pittsburgh, PA 15217 / 412-361-5455
Leica USA, Inc., 156 Ludlow Ave., Northvale, NJ 07647 / 201-767-7500; FAX: 201-767-8666
LEM Gun Specialties, Inc. The Lewis Lead Remover, P.O. Box 2855, Peachtree City, GA 30269-2024 / 770-487-0556
Leonard Day, 6 Linseed Rd Box 1, West Hatfield, MA 01088-7505 / 413-337-8369
Les Baer Custom, Inc., 29601 34th Ave., Hillsdale, IL 61257 / 309-658-2716; FAX: 309-658-2610 www.lesbaer.com
LesMerises, Felix. See: ROCKY MOUNTAIN ARMOURY
Lethal Force Institute (See Police Bookshelf), PO Box 122, Concord, NH 03301 / 603-224-6814; FAX: 603-226-3554
Lett Custom Grips, 672 Currier Rd., Hopkinton, NH 03229-2652 / 800-421-5388; FAX: 603-226-4580 info@lettgrips.com www.lettgrips.com
Leupold & Stevens, Inc., 14400 NW Greenbrier Pky., Beaverton, OR 97006 / 503-646-9171; FAX: 503-526-1455
Lever Arms Service Ltd., 2131 Burrard St., Vancouver, BC V6J 3H7 CANADA / 604-736-2711; FAX: 604-738-3503 leverarms@leverarms.com www.leverarms.com
Lew Horton Dist. Co., Inc., 15 Walkup Dr., Westboro, MA 01581 / 508-366-7400; FAX: 508-366-5332
Liberty Metals, 2233 East 16th St., Los Angeles, CA 90021 / 213-581-9171; FAX: 213-581-9351 libertymfgsolder@hotmail.com
Liberty Safe, 999 W. Utah Ave., Payson, UT 84651-1744 / 800-247-5625; FAX: 801-489-6409
Liberty Shooting Supplies, P.O. Box 357, Hillsboro, OR 97123 / 503-640-5518; FAX: 503-640-5518 info@libertyshootingsupplies.com www.libertyshootingsupplies.com
Lightning Performance Innovations, Inc., RD1 Box 555, Mohawk, NY 13407 / 315-866-8819; FAX: 315-867-5701
Lilja Precision Rifle Barrels, P.O. Box 372, Plains, MT 59859 / 406-826-3084; FAX: 406-826-3083 lilja@riflebarrels.com www.riflebarrels.com
Lincoln, Dean, Box 1886, Farmington, NM 87401
Linder Solingen Knives, 4401 Sentry Dr. #B, Tucker, GA 30084 / 770-939-6915; FAX: 770-939-6738
Lindsay Engraving & Tools, Steve Lindsay, 3714 W. Cedar Hills, Kearney, NE 68845 / 308-236-7885 steve@lindsayengraving.com www.handgravers.com
Lindsay, Steve. See: LINDSAY ENGRAVING & TOOLS
Lindsley Arms Cartridge Co., P.O. Box 757, 20 College Hill Rd., Henniker, NH 03242 / 603-428-3127
Linebaugh Custom Sixguns, P.O. Box 455, Cody, WY 82414 / 307-645-3332 www.sixgunner.com
Lion Country Supply, P.O. Box 480, Port Matilda, PA 16870
List Precision Engineering, Unit 1 Ingley Works, 13 River Road, Barking, ENGLAND / 011-081-594-1686
Lithi Bee Bullet Lube, 1728 Carr Rd., Muskegon, MI 49442 / 616-788-4479 lithibee@att.net
"Little John's" Antique Arms, 1740 W. Laveta, Orange, CA 92668
Little Trees Ramble (See Scott Pilkington)
Littler Sales Co., 20815 W. Chicago, Detroit, MI 48228 / 313-273-6888; FAX: 313-273-1099 littlerptg@aol.com
Littleton, J. F., 275 Pinedale Ave., Oroville, CA 95966 / 916-533-6084
Ljutic Industries, Inc., 732 N. 16th Ave., Suite 22, Yakima, WA 98902 / 509-248-0476; FAX: 509-576-8233 ljuticgun@earthlink.net www.ljuticgun.com
Llama Gabilondo Y Cia, Apartado 290, E-01080, Victoria, SPAIN
Loch Leven Industries/Convert-A-Pell, P.O. Box 2751, Santa Rosa, CA 95405 / 707-573-8735; FAX: 707-573-0369
Lock's Philadelphia Gun Exchange, 6700 Rowland Ave., Philadelphia, PA 19149 / 215-332-6225; FAX: 215-332-4800 locks.gunshop@verizon.net
Lodewick, Walter H., 2816 NE Halsey St., Portland, OR 97232 / 503-284-2554 wlodewick@aol.com
Lodgewood Mfg., P.O. Box 611, Whitewater, WI 53190 / 262-473-5444; FAX: 262-473-6448 lodgewd@idcnet.com lodgewood.com
Log Cabin Sport Shop, 8010 Lafayette Rd., Lodi, OH 44254 / 330-948-1082; FAX: 330-948-4307 logcabin@logcabinshop.com www.logcabinshop.com
Logan, Harry M., Box 745, Honokaa, HI 96727 / 808-776-1644
Logdewood Mfg., P.O. Box 611, Whitewater, WI 53190 / 262-473-5444; FAX: 262-473-6448 lodgewd@idcnet.com www.lodgewood.com
Lohman Mfg. Co., Inc., 4500 Doniphan Dr., P.O. Box 220, Neosho, MO 64850 / 417-451-4438; FAX: 417-451-2576
Lomont Precision Bullets, 278 Sandy Creek Rd., Salmon, ID 83467 / 208-756-6819; FAX: 208-756-6824 www.klomont.com
London Guns Ltd., Box 3750, Santa Barbara, CA 93130 / 805-683-4141; FAX: 805-683-1712
Lone Star Gunleather, 1301 Brushy Bend Dr., Round Rock, TX 78681 / 512-255-1805
Lone Star Rifle Company, 11231 Rose Road, Conroe, TX 77303 / 936-856-3363; FAX: 936-856-3363 dave@lonestar.com
Long, George F., 1500 Rogue River Hwy., Ste. F, Grants Pass, OR 97527 / 541-476-7552
Lortone Inc., 2856 NW Market St., Seattle, WA 98107
Lothar Walther Precision Tool Inc., 3425 Hutchinson Rd., Cumming, GA 30040 / 770-889-9998; FAX: 770-889-4919 lotharwalther@mindspring.com www.lothar-walther.com
LPS Laboratories, Inc., 4647 Hugh Howell Rd., P.O. Box 3050, Tucker, GA 30084 / 404-934-7800
Lucas, Edward E, 32 Garfield Ave., East Brunswick, NJ 08816 / 201-251-5526
Lupton, Keith. See: PAWLING MOUNTAIN CLUB
Lyman Instant Targets, Inc. (See Lyman Products)
Lyman Products Corp., 475 Smith Street, Middletown, CT 06457-1541 / 800-423-9704; FAX: 860-632-1699 lymansales@cshore.com www.lymanproducts.com

M

M.H. Canjar Co., 6510 Raleigh St., Arvada, CO 80003 / 303-295-2638; FAX: 303-295-2638
MA Systems, Inc., P.O. Box 894, Pryor, OK 74362-0894 / 918-824-3705; FAX: 918-824-3710
Mac-1 Airgun Distributors, 13974 Van Ness Ave., Gardena, CA 90249-2900 / 310-327-3581; FAX: 310-327-0238 mac1@maclairgun.com www.mac1airgun.com
Madis Books, 2453 West Five Mile Pkwy., Dallas, TX 75233 / 214-330-7168
Madis, George. See: GEORGE MADIS WINCHESTER CONSULTANTS
MAG Instrument, Inc., 1635 S. Sacramento Ave., Ontario, CA 91761 / 909-947-1006; FAX: 909-947-3116
Magma Engineering Co., P.O. Box 161, 20955 E. Ocotillo Rd., Queen Creek, AZ 85242 / 602-987-9008; FAX: 602-987-0148
Mag-Na-Port International, Inc., 41302 Executive Dr., Harrison Twp., MI 48045-1306 / 586-469-6727; FAX: 586-469-0425 email@magnaport.com www.magnaport.com
Magnolia Sports, Inc., 211 W. Main, Magnolia, AR 71753 / 501-234-8410; or 800-530-7816; FAX: 501-234-8117
Magnum Power Products, Inc., P.O. Box 17768, Fountain Hills, AZ 85268
Magnum Research, Inc., 7110 University Ave. NE, Minneapolis, MN 55432 / 800-772-6168 or 763-574-1868; FAX: 763-574-0109 info@magnumresearch.com
Magnus Bullets, P.O. Box 239, Toney, AL 35773 / 256-420-8359; FAX: 256-420-8360
Mag-Pack Corp., P.O. Box 846, Chesterland, OH 44026 / 440-285-9480 magpack@hotmail.com
MagSafe Ammo Co., 4700 S US Highway 17/92, Casselberry, FL 32707-3814 / 407-834-9966; FAX: 407-834-8185 www.magsafeonline.com
Magtech Ammunition Co. Inc., 6845 20th Ave. S., Ste. 120, Centerville, MN 55038
Mahony, Philip Bruce, 67 White Hollow Rd., Lime Rock, CT 06039-2418 / 203-435-9341 filbalony-redbeard@snet.net
Mahovsky's Metalife, R.D. 1, Box 149a Eureka Road, Grand Valley, PA 16420 / 814-436-7747
Maine Custom Bullets, RFD 1, Box 1755, Brooks, ME 04921
Makinson, Nicholas, RR 3, Komoka, ON N0L 1R0 CANADA / 519-471-5462
Mallardtone Game Calls, 10406 96th St., Court West, Taylor Ridge, IL 61284 / 309-798-2481; FAX: 309-798-2501
Mandall Shooting Supplies Inc., 3616 N. Scottsdale Rd., Scottsdale, AZ 85251 / 480-945-2553; FAX: 480-949-0734
Marble Arms (See CRR, Inc./Marble's Inc.)
Marchmon Bullets, 6502 Riverdale Rd., Whitmore Lake, MI 48189
Marent, Rudolf. See: HAMMERLI SERVICE-PRECISION MAC
Mark Lee Supplies, 9901 France Ct., Lakeville, MN 55044 / 952-461-2114; FAX: 952-461-2194 marklee55044@usfamily.net
Markell, Inc., 422 Larkfield Center 235, Santa Rosa, CA 95403 / 707-573-0792; FAX: 707-573-9867
Markesbery Muzzle Loaders, Inc., 7785 Foundation Dr., Ste. 6, Florence, KY 41042 / 606-342-5553 or 606-342-2380
Marksman Products, 5482 Argosy Dr., Huntington Beach, CA 92649 / 714-898-7535; or 800-822-8005; FAX: 714-891-0782
Marlin Firearms Co., 100 Kenna Dr., North Haven, CT 06473 / 203-239-5621; FAX: 203-234-7991 www.marlinfirearms.com
MarMik, Inc., 2116 S. Woodland Ave., Michigan City, IN 46360 / 219-872-7231; FAX: 219-872-7231
Marocchi F.lli S.p.A, Via Galileo Galilei 8, I-25068 Zanano, ITALY
Marquart Precision Co., P.O. Box 1740, Prescott, AZ 86302 / 520-445-5646
Marsh, Mike, Croft Cottage, Main St., Derbyshire, DE4 2BY ENGLAND / 01629 650 669
Marshall Enterprises, 792 Canyon Rd., Redwood City, CA 94062
Marshall Fish Mfg. Gunsmith Sptg. Co., Rd. Box 2439, Westport, NY 12993 / 518-962-4897; FAX: 518-962-4897
Martin B. Retting Inc., 11029 Washington, Culver City, CA 90232 / 213-837-2412
Martini & Hagn, 1264 Jimsmith Lake Rd, Cranbrook, BC V1C 6V6 CANADA / 250-417-2926; FAX: 250-417-2928
Martin's Gun Shop, 937 S. Sheridan Blvd., Lakewood, CO 80226 / 303-922-2184
Martz, John V., 8060 Lakeview Lane, Lincoln, CA 95648 FAX: 916-645-3815
Marvel, Alan, 3922 Madonna Rd., Jarretsville, MD 21084 / 301-557-6545
Marx, Harry (See U.S. Importer for FERLIB)
Maryland Paintball Supply, 8507 Harford Rd., Parkville, MD 21234 / 410-882-5607
MAST Technology, Inc., 14555 US Hwy. 95 S., P.O. Box 60969, Boulder City, NV 89006 / 702-293-6969; FAX: 702-293-7255 info@masttechnology.com www.bellammo.com
Master Lock Co., 2600 N. 32nd St., Milwaukee, WI 53245 / 414-444-2800
Match Prep-Doyle Gracey, P.O. Box 155, Tehachapi, CA 93581 / 661-822-5383; FAX: 661-823-8680
Mathews Gun Shop & Gunsmithing, Inc., 10224 S. Paramount Blvd., Downey, CA 90241 / 562-928-2129; FAX: 562-928-8629
Matthews Cutlery, 4401 Sentry Dr. #B, Tucker, GA 30084 / 770-939-6915

MANUFACTURER'S DIRECTORY

Mauser Werke Oberndorf Waffensysteme GmbH, Postfach 1349, 78722, Oberndorf/N., GERMANY
Maverick Arms, Inc., 7 Grasso Ave., P.O. Box 497, North Haven, CT 06473 / 203-230-5300; FAX: 203-230-5420
Maxi-Mount Inc., P.O. Box 291, Willoughby Hills, OH 44096-0291 / 440-944-9456; FAX: 440-944-9456 maximount454@yahoo.com
Mayville Engineering Co. (See MEC, Inc.)
Mazur Restoration, Pete, 13083 Drummer Way, Grass Valley, CA 95949 / 530-268-2412
McBros Rifle Co., P.O. Box 86549, Phoenix, AZ 85080 / 602-582-3713; FAX: 602-581-3825
McCament, Jay. See: JAY MCCAMENT CUSTOM GUNMAKER
McCann, Tom, 14 Walton Dr., New Hope, PA 18938 / 215-862-2728
McCann Industries, P.O. Box 641, Spanaway, WA 98387 / 253-537-6919; FAX: 253-537-6919 mccann.machine@worldnet.att.net www.mccannindustries.com
McCluskey Precision Rifles, 10502 14th Ave. NW, Seattle, WA 98177 / 206-781-2776
McCombs, Leo, 1862 White Cemetery Rd., Patriot, OH 45658 / 740-256-1714
McDonald, Dennis, 8359 Brady St., Peosta, IA 52068 / 319-556-7940
McFarland, Stan, 2221 Idella Ct., Grand Junction, CO 81505 / 970-243-4704
McGhee, Larry. See: B.C. OUTDOORS
McGowen Rifle Barrels, 5961 Spruce Lane, St. Anne, IL 60964 / 815-937-9816; FAX: 815-937-4024
Mchalik, Gary. See: ROSSI FIREARMS
McKenzie, Lynton, 6940 N. Alvernon Way, Tucson, AZ 85718 / 520-299-5090
McMillan Fiberglass Stocks, Inc., 1638 W. Knudsen Dr. #102, Phoenix, AZ 85027 / 623-582-9635; FAX: 623-581-3825 mfsinc@mcmfamily.com www.mcmfamily.com
McMillan Optical Gunsight Co., 28638 N. 42nd St., Cave Creek, AZ 85331 / 602-585-7868; FAX: 602-585-7872
McMillan Rifle Barrels, P.O. Box 3427, Bryan, TX 77805 / 409-690-3456; FAX: 409-690-0156
McMurdo, Lynn (See Specialty Gunsmithing), PO Box 404, Afton, WY 83110 / 307-886-5535
MCS, Inc., 166 Pocono Rd., Brookfield, CT 06804-2023 / 203-775-1013; FAX: 203-775-9462
McWelco Products, 6730 Santa Fe Ave., Hesperia, CA 92345 / 619-244-8876; FAX: 619-244-9398 products@mcwelco.com www.mawelco.com
MDS, P.O. Box 1441, Brandon, FL 33509-1441 / 813-653-1180; FAX: 813-684-5953
Measurement Group Inc., Box 27777, Raleigh, NC 27611
Measures, Leon. See: SHOOT WHERE YOU LOOK
MEC, Inc., 715 South St., Mayville, WI 53050 / 414-387-4500; FAX: 414-387-5802 reloaders@mayul.com www.mayvl.com
MEC-Gar S.R.L., Via Madonnina 64, Gardone V.T. Brescia, ITALY / 39-30-8912687; FAX: 39-30-8910065
MEC-Gar U.S.A., Inc., Hurley Farms Industr. Park, 115, Hurley Road 6G, Oxford, CT 06478 / 203-262-1525; FAX: 203-262-1719 mecgar@aol.com www.mec-gar.com
Mech-Tech Systems, Inc., 1602 Foothill Rd., Kalispell, MT 59901 / 406-755-8055
Meister Bullets (See Gander Mountain)
Mele, Frank, 201 S. Wellow Ave., Cookeville, TN 38501 / 615-526-4860
Menck, Gunsmith Inc., T.W., 5703 S 77th St., Ralston, NE 68127
Mendez, John A., P.O. Box 620984, Orlando, FL 32862 / 407-344-2791
Men-Metallwerk Elisenhuette GmbH, P.O. Box 1263, Nassau/Lahn, D-56372 GERMANY / 2604-7819
Meprolight (See Hesco-Meprolight)
Mercer Custom Guns, 216 S. Whitewater Ave., Jefferson, WI 53549 / 920-674-3839
Merit Corp., PO Box 9044, Schenectady, NY 12309 / 518-346-1420 sales@meritcorporation.com www.meritcorporation.com
Merkel, Schutzenstrasse 26, D-98527 Suhl, Suhl, GERMANY FAX: 011-49-3681-854-203 www.merkel-waffen.de
Merkuria Ltd., Argentinska 38, 17005, Praha 7, CZECH REPUBLIC / 422-875117; FAX: 422-809152
Metal Merchants, PO Box 186, Walled Lake, MI 48390-0186
Metalife Industries (See Mahovsky's Metalife)
Michael's Antiques, Box 591, Waldoboro, ME 04572
Michaels Of Oregon, Co., P.O. Box 1690, Oregon City, OR 97045 www.michaels-oregon.com
Micro Sight Co., 242 Harbor Blvd., Belmont, CA 94002 / 415-591-0769; FAX: 415-591-7531
Microfusion Alfa S.A., Paseo San Andres N8, P.O. Box 271, Eibar, 20600 SPAIN / 34-43-11-89-16; FAX: 34-43-11-40-38
Mid-America Recreation, Inc., 1328 5th Ave., Moline, IL 61265 / 309-764-5089; FAX: 309-764-5089 fmilcusguns@aol.com www.midamericarecreation.com
Middlebrooks Custom Shop, 7366 Colonial Trail East, Surry, VA 23883 / 757-357-0881; FAX: 757-365-0442
Midway Arms, Inc., 5875 W. Van Horn Tavern Rd., Columbia, MO 65203 / 800-243-3220; or 573-445-6363; FAX: 573-446-1018
Midwest Gun Sport, 1108 Herbert Dr., Zebulon, NC 27597 / 919-269-5570
Midwest Sport Distributors, Box 129, Fayette, MO 65248
Mike Davis Products, 643 Loop Dr., Moses Lake, WA 98837 / 509-765-6178; or 509-766-7281
Mike Yee Custom Stocking, 29927 56 Pl. S., Auburn, WA 98001 / 253-839-3991
Military Armament Corp., P.O. Box 120, Mt. Zion Rd., Lingleville, TX 76461 / 817-965-3253
Millennium Designed Muzzleloaders, PO Box 536, Routes 11 & 25, Limington, ME 04049 / 207-637-2316
Miller Arms, Inc., P.O. Box 260 Purl St., St. Onge, SD 57779 / 605-642-5160; FAX: 605-642-5160
Miller Custom, 210 E. Julia, Clinton, IL 61727 / 217-935-9362
Miller Single Trigger Mfg. Co., 6680 Rt. 5-20, P.O. Box 471, Bloomfield, NY 14469 / 585-657-6338
Millett Sights, 7275 Murdy Circle, Adm. Office, Huntington Beach, CA 92647 / 714-842-5575 or 800-645-5388; FAX: 714-843-5707
Mills Jr., Hugh B., 3615 Canterbury Rd., New Bern, NC 28560 / 919-637-4631
Milstor Corp., 80-975 Indio Blvd. C-7, Indio, CA 92201 / 760-775-9998; FAX: 760-775-5229 milstor@webtv.net
Minute Man High Tech Industries, 10611 Canyon Rd. E., Suite 151, Puyallup, WA 98373 / 800-233-2734
Mirador Optical Corp., P.O. Box 11614, Marina Del Rey, CA 90295-7614 / 310-821-5587; FAX: 310-305-0386
Mitchell, Jack, c/o Geoff Gaebe, Addieville East Farm, 200 Pheasant Dr., Mapleville, RI 02839 / 401-568-3185
Mitchell Bullets, R.F., 430 Walnut St., Westernport, MD 21562
Mitchell Mfg. Corp., P.O. Box 9295, Fountain Valley, CA 92728 / 714-444-2220
Mitchell Optics, Inc., 2072 CR 1100 N, Sidney, IL 61877 / 217-688-2219; or 217-621-3018; FAX: 217-688-2505 mitche1@attglobal.net
Mitchell's Accuracy Shop, 68 Greenridge Dr., Stafford, VA 22554 / 703-659-0165
Mitchell's Mauser, P.O. Box 9295, Fountain Valley, CA 92728 / 714-979-7663; FAX: 714-899-3660
MI-TE Bullets, 1396 Ave. K, Ellsworth, KS 67439 / 785-472-4575; FAX: 785-472-5579
Mittleman, William, P.O. Box 65, Etna, CA 96027
Mixson Corp., 7635 W. 28th Ave., Hialeah, FL 33016 / 305-821-5190; or 800-327-0078; FAX: 305-558-9318
MJK Gunsmithing, Inc., 417 N. Huber Ct., E. Wenatchee, WA 98802 / 509-884-7683
MKS Supply, Inc. (See Hi-Point Firearms)
MMC, 5050 E. Belknap St., Haltom City, TX 76117 / 817-831-9557; FAX: 817-834-5508
MOA Corporation, 2451 Old Camden Pike, Eaton, OH 45320 / 937-456-3669 www.moaguns
Modern Gun Repair School, PO Box 846, Saint Albans, VT 05478 / 802-524-2223; FAX: 802-524-2053 jfwp@dlilearn.com www.mgsinfoadlifearn.com
Modern Muzzleloading, Inc., P.O. Box 130, Centerville, IA 52544 / 515-856-2626
Moeller, Steve, 1213 4th St., Fulton, IL 61252 / 815-589-2300
Mogul Co./Life Jacket, 500 N. Kimball Rd., Ste. 109, South Lake, TX 76092
Molin Industries, Tru-Nord Division, P.O. Box 365, 204 North 9th St., Brainerd, MN 56401 / 218-829-2870
Monell Custom Guns, 228 Red Mills Rd., Pine Bush, NY 12566 / 914-744-3021
Moneymaker Guncraft Corp., 1420 Military Ave., Omaha, NE 68131 / 402-556-0226
Montana Armory, Inc. (See C. Sharps Arms Co. Inc.), 100 Centennial Dr., P.O. Box 885, Big Timber, MT 59011 / 406-932-4353; FAX: 406-932-4443
Montana Outfitters, Lewis E. Yearout, 308 Riverview Dr. E., Great Falls, MT 59404 / 406-761-0859; or 406-727-4560
Montana Precision Swaging, P.O. Box 4746, Butte, MT 59702 / 406-494-0600; FAX: 406-494-0600
Montana Rifleman, Inc., 2593A Hwy. 2 East, Kalispell, MT 59901 / 406-755-4867
Montana Vintage Arms, 2354 Bear Canyon Rd., Bozeman, MT 59715
Morini (See U.S. Importers-Mandall Shooting Supply)
Morrison Custom Rifles, J. W., 4015 W Sharon, Phoenix, AZ 85029 / 602-978-3754
Morrison Precision, 6719 Calle Mango, Hereford, AZ 85615 / 520-378-6207 morprec@c2i2.com
Morrow, Bud, 11 Hillside Lane, Sheridan, WY 82801-9729 / 307-674-8360
Morton Booth Co., P.O. Box 123, Joplin, MO 64802 / 417-673-1962; FAX: 417-673-3642
Mo's Competitor Supplies (See MCS, Inc.)
Moss Double Tone, Inc., P.O. Box 1112, 2101 S. Kentucky, Sedalia, MO 65301 / 816-827-0827
Mountain Plains Industries, 3720 Otter Place, Lynchburg, VA 24503 / 800-687-3000; FAX: 434-845-6594 mpitargets@cstone.net
Mountain State Muzzleloading Supplies, Inc., Box 154-1, Rt. 2, Williamstown, WV 26187 / 304-375-7842; FAX: 304-375-3737
Mowrey Gun Works, P.O. Box 246, Waldron, IN 46182 / 317-525-6181; FAX: 317-525-9595
Mowrey's Guns & Gunsmithing, 119 Fredericks St., Canajoharie, NY 13317 / 518-673-3483
MPC, P.O. Box 450, McMinnville, TN 37110-0450 / 615-473-5513; FAX: 615-473-5516 thebox@blomand.net www.mpc-thebox.com
MPI Stocks, PO Box 83266, Portland, OR 97283 / 503-226-1215; FAX: 503-226-2661
MSR Targets, P.O. Box 1042, West Covina, CA 91793 / 818-331-7840
MTM Molded Products Co., Inc., 3370 Obco Ct., Dayton, OH 45414 / 937-890-7461; FAX: 937-890-1747
Mulberry House Publishing, P.O. Box 2180, Apache Junction, AZ 85217 / 888-738-1567; FAX: 480-671-1015
Mulhern, Rick, Rt. 5, Box 152, Rayville, LA 71269 / 318-728-2688
Mullins Ammunition, Rt. 2 Box 304N, Clintwood, VA 24228 / 276-926-6772; FAX: 276-926-6092 mammo@extremeshockusa.com www.extremeshockusa
Mullis Guncraft, 3523 Lawyers Road E., Monroe, NC 28110 / 704-283-6683
Multiplex International, 26 S. Main St., Concord, NH 03301 FAX: 603-796-2223
Multipropulseurs, La Bertrandiere, 42580, FRANCE / 77 74 01 30; FAX: 77 93 19 34
Mundy, Thomas A., 69 Robbins Road, Somerville, NJ 08876 / 201-722-2199
Murmur Corp., 2823 N. Westmoreland Ave., Dallas, TX 75222 / 214-630-5400
Murphy, R.R. Murphy Co., Inc. See: MURPHY, R.R. CO., INC.
Murphy, R.R. Co., Inc., R.R. Murphy Co., Inc. Murphy, P.O. Box 102, Ripley, TN 38063 / 901-635-4003; FAX: 901-635-2320
Murray State College, 1 Murray Campus St., Tishomingo, OK 73460 / 508-371-2371 darnold@mscok.edu
Muscle Products Corp., 112 Fennell Dr., Butler, PA 16002 / 800-227-7049; or 724-283-0567; FAX: 724-283-8310 mpc@mpc_home.com www.mpc_home.com
Muzzleloaders Etcetera, Inc., 9901 Lyndale Ave. S., Bloomington, MN 55420 / 952-884-1161 www.muzzleloaders-etcetera.com
MWG Co., P.O. Box 971202, Miami, FL 33197 / 800-428-9394; or 305-253-8393; FAX: 305-232-1247

MANUFACTURER'S DIRECTORY

N

N.B.B., Inc., 24 Elliot Rd., Sterling, MA 01564 / 508-422-7538; or 800-942-9444

N.C. Ordnance Co., P.O. Box 3254, Wilson, NC 27895 / 919-237-2440; FAX: 919-243-9845

Nagel's Custom Bullets, 100 Scott St., Baytown, TX 77520-2849

Nalpak, 1937-C Friendship Drive, El Cajon, CA 92020 / 619-258-1200

Nastoff, Steve. See: NASTOFFS 45 SHOP, INC.

Nastoffs 45 Shop, Inc., Steve Nastoff, 1057 Laverne Dr., Youngstown, OH 44511

National Bullet Co., 1585 E. 361 St., Eastlake, OH 44095 / 216-951-1854; FAX: 216-951-7761

National Target Co., 4690 Wyaconda Rd., Rockville, MD 20852 / 800-827-7060 or 301-770-7060; FAX: 301-770-7892

Nationwide Airgun Repair, 2310 Windsor Forest Dr., Louisville, KY 40272 / 502-937-2614; FAX: 812-637-1463 shortshoestring@insightbb.com

Naval Ordnance Works, Rt. 2, Box 919, Sheperdstown, WV 25443 / 304-876-0998

Navy Arms Co., 219 Lawn St., Martinsburg, WV 25401 / 304-262-9870; FAX: 304-262-1658

Navy Arms Company, Valmore J. Forgett Jr., 815 22nd Street, Union City, NJ 07087 / 201-863-7100; FAX: 201-863-8770 info@navyarms.com www.navyarms.com

NCP Products, Inc., 3500 12th St. N.W., Canton, OH 44708 / 330-456-5130; FAX: 330-456-5234

Necessary Concepts, Inc., P.O. Box 571, Deer Park, NY 11729 / 516-667-8509; FAX: 516-667-8588

NEI Handtools, Inc., 10960 Gary Player Dr., El Paso, TX 79935

Neil A. Jones Custom Products, 17217 Brookhouser Road, Saegertown, PA 16433 / 814-763-2769; FAX: 814-763-4228

Nelson, Gary K., 975 Terrace Dr., Oakdale, CA 95361 / 209-847-4590

Nelson, Stephen. See: NELSON'S CUSTOM GUNS, INC.

Nelson's Custom Guns, Inc., Stephen Nelson, 7430 Valley View Dr. N.W., Corvallis, OR 97330 / 541-745-5232 nelsons-custom@attbi.com

Nesci Enterprises Inc., P.O. Box 119, Summit St., East Hampton, CT 06424 / 203-267-2588

Nesika Bay Precision, 22239 Big Valley Rd., Poulsbo, WA 98370 / 206-697-3830

Nettestad Gun Works, 38962 160th Avenue, Pelican Rapids, MN 56572 / 218-863-4301

Neumann GmbH, Am Galgenberg 6, 90575, GERMANY / 09101/8258; FAX: 09101/6356

Nevada Pistol Academy, Inc., 4610 Blue Diamond Rd., Las Vegas, NV 89139 / 702-897-1100

New England Ammunition Co., 1771 Post Rd. East, Suite 223, Westport, CT 06880 / 203-254-8048

New England Arms Co., Box 278, Lawrence Lane, Kittery Point, ME 03905 / 207-439-0593; FAX: 207-439-0525 info@newenglandarms.com www.newenglandarms.com

New England Custom Gun Service, 438 Willow Brook Rd., Plainfield, NH 03781 / 603-469-3450; FAX: 603-469-3471 bestguns@cyborportal.net www.newenglandcustom.com

New Orleans Jewelers Supply Co., 206 Charters St., New Orleans, LA 70130 / 504-523-3839; FAX: 504-523-3836

New SKB Arms Co., C.P.O. Box 1401, Tokyo, JAPAN / 81-3-3943-9550; FAX: 81-3-3943-0695

New Ultra Light Arms, LLC, P.O. Box 340, Granville, WV 26534

Newark Electronics, 4801 N. Ravenswood Ave., Chicago, IL 60640

Newell, Robert H., 55 Coyote, Los Alamos, NM 87544 / 505-662-7135

Newman Gunshop, 2035 Chester Ave. #411, Ottumwa, IA 52501-3715 / 515-937-5775

Nicholson Custom, 17285 Thornlay Road, Hughesville, MO 65334 / 816-826-8746

Nickels, Paul R., 4328 Seville St., Las Vegas, NV 89121 / 702-435-5318

Nicklas, Ted, 5504 Hegel Rd., Goodrich, MI 48438 / 810-797-4493

Niemi Engineering, W. B., Box 126 Center Rd., Greensboro, VT 05841 / 802-533-7180; FAX: 802-533-7141

Nikon, Inc., 1300 Walt Whitman Rd., Melville, NY 11747 / 516-547-8623; FAX: 516-547-0309

Nitex Gun Shop, P.O. Box 1706, Uvalde, TX 78801 / 830-278-8843

Noreen, Peter H., 5075 Buena Vista Dr., Belgrade, MT 59714 / 406-586-7383

Norica, Avnda Otaola, 16 Apartado 68, Eibar, SPAIN

Norinco, 7A Yun Tan N, Beijing, CHINA

Norincoptics (See BEC, Inc.)

Norma Precision AB (See U.S. Importers-Dynamit)

Normark Corp., 10395 Yellow Circle Dr., Minnetonka, MN 55343-9101 / 612-933-7060; FAX: 612-933-0046

North American Arms, Inc., 2150 South 950 East, Provo, UT 84606-6285 / 800-821-5783; or 801-374-9990; FAX: 801-374-9998

North American Correspondence Schools The Gun Pro, Oak & Pawney St., Scranton, PA 18515 / 717-342-7701

North American Shooting Systems, P.O. Box 306, Osoyoos, BC V0H 1V0 CANADA / 250-495-3131; FAX: 250-495-3131 rifle@cablerocket.com

North Devon Firearms Services, 3 North St., Braunton, EX33 1AJ ENGLAND / 01271 813624; FAX: 01271 813624

North Mountain Pine Training Center (See Executive

North Star West, P.O. Box 488, Glencoe, CA 95232 / 209-293-7010 northstarwest.com

Northern Precision, 329 S. James St., Carthage, NY 13619 / 315-493-1711

Northlake Outdoor Footwear, P.O. Box 10, Franklin, TN 37065-0010 / 615-794-1556; FAX: 615-790-8005

Northside Gun Shop, 2725 NW 109th, Oklahoma City, OK 73120 / 405-840-2353

Northwest Arms, 26884 Pearl Rd., Parma, ID 83660 / 208-722-6771; FAX: 208-722-1062

No-Sho Mfg. Co., 10727 Glenfield Ct., Houston, TX 77096 / 713-723-5332

Nosler, Inc., P.O. Box 671, Bend, OR 97709 / 800-285-3701; or 541-382-3921; FAX: 541-388-4667 www.nosler.com

Novak's, Inc., 1206 1/2 30th St., P.O. Box 4045, Parkersburg, WV 26101 / 304-485-9295; FAX: 304-428-6722

Nowlin Mfg. Co., 20622 S 4092 Rd., Claremore, OK 74017 / 918-342-0689; FAX: 918-342-0624 nowlinguns@msn.com nowlinguns.com

NRI Gunsmith School, P.O. Box 182968, Columbus, OH 43218-2968

Nu-Line Guns,Inc., 1053 Caulks Hill Rd., Harvester, MO 63304 / 314-441-4500; or 314-447-4501; FAX: 314-447-5018

Null Holsters Ltd. K.L., 161 School St NW, Resaca, GA 30735 / 706-625-5643; FAX: 706-625-9392

Numrich Gun Parts Corporation, 226 Williams Lane, P.O. Box 299, West Hurley, NY 12491 / 866-686-7424; FAX: 877-GUNPART info@gunpartscorp.com www.@-gunparts.com

Nygord Precision Products, Inc., P.O. Box 12578, Prescott, AZ 86304 / 928-717-2315; FAX: 928-717-2198 nygords@northlink.com www.nygordprecision.com

O

O.F. Mossberg & Sons, Inc., 7 Grasso Ave., North Haven, CT 06473 / 203-230-5300; FAX: 203-230-5420

Oakman Turkey Calls, RD 1, Box 825, Harrisonville, PA 17228 / 717-485-4620

Obermeyer Rifled Barrels, 23122 60th St., Bristol, WI 53104 / 262-843-3537; FAX: 262-843-2129

October Country Muzzleloading, P.O. Box 969, Dept. GD, Hayden, ID 83835 / 208-772-2068; FAX: 208-772-9230 ocinfo@octobercountry.com www.octobercountry.com

Oehler Research, Inc., P.O. Box 9135, Austin, TX 78766 / 512-327-6900; or 800-531-5125; FAX: 512-327-6903 www.oehler-research.com

Oil Rod and Gun Shop, 69 Oak St., East Douglas, MA 01516 / 508-476-3687

OK Weber, Inc., P.O. Box 7485, Eugene, OR 97401 / 541-747-0458; FAX: 541-747-5927 okweber@pacinfo www.okweber.com

Oker's Engraving, P.O. Box 126, Shawnee, CO 80475 / 303-838-6042

Oklahoma Ammunition Co., 3701A S. Harvard Ave., No. 367, Tulsa, OK 74135-2265 / 918-396-3187; FAX: 918-396-4270

Oklahoma Leather Products, Inc., 500 26th NW, Miami, OK 74354 / 918-542-6651; FAX: 918-542-6653

Olathe Gun Shop, 716-A South Rogers Road, Olathe, KS 66062 / 913-782-6900; FAX: 913-782-6902 info@olathegunshop.com www.olathegunshop.com

Old Wagon Bullets, 32 Old Wagon Rd., Wilton, CT 06897

Old West Bullet Moulds, J Ken Chapman, P.O. Box 519, Flora Vista, NM 87415 / 505-334-6970

Old West Reproductions, Inc. R.M. Bachman, 446 Florence S. Loop, Florence, MT 59833 / 406-273-2615; FAX: 406-273-2615 rick@oldwestreproductions.com www.oldwestreproductions.com

Old Western Scrounger Ammunition Inc., 50 Industrial Parkway, Carson City, NV 89706 / 775-246-2091; FAX: 775-246-2095 www.ows-ammunition.com

Old World Gunsmithing, 2901 SE 122nd St., Portland, OR 97236 / 503-760-7681

Old World Oil Products, 3827 Queen Ave. N., Minneapolis, MN 55412 / 612-522-5037

Ole Frontier Gunsmith Shop, 2617 Hwy. 29 S., Cantonment, FL 32533 / 904-477-8074

Olson, Myron, 989 W. Kemp, Watertown, SD 57201 / 605-886-9787

Olson, Vic, 5002 Countryside Dr., Imperial, MO 63052 / 314-296-8086

Olympic Arms Inc., 620-626 Old Pacific Hwy. SE, Olympia, WA 98513 / 360-456-3471; FAX: 360-491-3447 info@olyarms.com www.olyarms.com

Olympic Optical Co., P.O. Box 752377, Memphis, TN 38175-2377 / 901-794-3890; or 800-238-7120; FAX: 901-794-0676 80

Omega Sales, P.O. Box 1066, Mt. Clemens, MI 48043 / 810-469-7323; FAX: 810-469-0425

100 Straight Products, Inc., P.O. Box 6148, Omaha, NE 68106 / 402-556-1055; FAX: 402-556-1055

One Of A Kind, 15610 Purple Sage, San Antonio, TX 78255 / 512-695-3364

One Ragged Hole, P.O. Box 13624, Tallahassee, FL 32317-3624

Op-Tec, P.O. Box L632, Langhorn, PA 19047 / 215-757-5037; FAX: 215-757-7097

Optical Services Co., P.O. Box 1174, Santa Teresa, NM 88008-1174 / 505-589-3833

Orchard Park Enterprise, P.O. Box 563, Orchard Park, NY 14127 / 616-656-0356

Oregon Arms, Inc. (See Rogue Rifle Co., Inc.)

Oregon Trail Bullet Company, PO Box 529, Dept. P, Baker City, OR 97814 / 800-811-0548; FAX: 514-523-1803

Original Box, Inc., 700 Linden Ave., York, PA 17404 / 717-854-2897; FAX: 717-845-4276

Original Deer Formula Co., The, P.O. Box 1705, Dickson, TN 37056 / 800-874-6965; FAX: 615-446-0646 deerformula1@aol.com www.deerformula

Orion Rifle Barrel Co., RR2, 137 Cobler Village, Kalispell, MT 59901 / 406-257-5649

Otis Technology, Inc., RR 1 Box 84, Boonville, NY 13309 / 315-942-3320

Ottmar, Maurice, Box 657, 113 E. Fir, Coulee City, WA 99115 / 509-632-5717

Outa-Site Gun Carriers, 219 Market St., Laredo, TX 78040 / 210-722-4678; or 800-880-9715; FAX: 210-726-4858

Outdoor Edge Cutlery Corp., 4699 Nautilus Ct. S. Ste. 503, Boulder, CO 80301-5310 / 303-652-8212; FAX: 303-652-8238

Outdoor Enthusiast, 3784 W. Woodland, Springfield, MO 65807 / 417-883-9841

Outdoor Sports Headquarters, Inc., 967 Watertower Ln., West Carrollton, OH 45449 / 513-865-5855; FAX: 513-865-5962

Outers Laboratories Div. of ATK, Route 2, P.O. Box 39, Onalaska, WI 54650 / 608-781-5800; FAX: 608-781-0368

Ox-Yoke Originals, Inc., 34 Main St., Milo, ME 04463 / 800-231-8313; or 207-943-7351; FAX: 207-943-2416

Ozark Gun Works, 11830 Cemetery Rd., Rogers, AR 72756 / 479-631-1024; FAX: 479-631-1024 ogw@hotmail.com www.eocities.com/ocarkgunworks

MANUFACTURER'S DIRECTORY

P

P&M Sales & Services, LLC, 4697 Tote Rd. Bldg. H-B, Comins, MI 48619 / 989-848-8364; FAX: 989-848-8364 info@pmsales-online.com
P.A.C.T., Inc., P.O. Box 531525, Grand Prairie, TX 75053 / 214-641-0049
P.S.M.G. Gun Co., 10 Park Ave., Arlington, MA 02174 / 781-646-1699; FAX: 781-643-7212 psmg2@aol.com
Pachmayr Div. Lyman Products, 475 Smith St., Middletown, CT 06457 / 860-632-2020; or 800-225-9626; FAX: 860-632-1699 lymansales@cshore.com www.pachmayr.com
Pacific Armament Corp, 4813 Enterprise Way, Unit K, Modesto, CA 95356 / 209-545-2800 gunsparts@att.net
Pacific Rifle Co., P.O. Box 841, Carlton, OR 97111 / 503-852-6276 pacificrifle@aol.com
PAC-NOR Barreling, 99299 Overlook Rd., P.O. Box 6188, Brookings, OR 97415 / 503-469-7330; FAX: 503-469-7331 info@pac-nor.com www.pac-nor.com
Paco's (See Small Custom Mould & Bullet Co.)
Page Custom Bullets, P.O. Box 25, Port Moresby, NEW GUINEA
Pagel Gun Works, Inc., 2 SE 1st St., Grand Rapids, MN 55744
Pager Pal, 200 W Pleasantview, Hurst, TX 76054 / 800-561-1603; FAX: 817-285-8769 www.pagerpal.com
Paintball Games International Magazine Aceville, Castle House 97 High St., Essex, ENGLAND / 011-44-206-564840
Palsa Outdoor Products, P.O. Box 81336, Lincoln, NE 68501 / 402-488-5288; FAX: 402-488-2321
Pansch, Robert F, 1004 Main St. #10, Neenah, WI 54956 / 920-725-8175
Paragon Sales & Services, Inc., 2501 Theodore St., Crest Hill, IL 60435-1613 / 815-725-9212; FAX: 815-725-8974
Para-Ordnance Mfg., Inc., 980 Tapscott Rd., Scarborough, ON M1X 1E7 CANADA / 416-297-7855; FAX: 416-297-1289
Para-Ordnance, Inc., 1919 NE 45th St., Ste 215, Ft. Lauderdale, FL 33308 info@paraord.com www.paraord.com
Pardini Armi Srl, Via Italica 154, 55043, Lido Di Camaiore Lu, ITALY / 584-90121; FAX: 584-90122
Paris, Frank J., 17417 Pershing St., Livonia, MI 48152-3822
Parker & Sons Shooting Supply, 9337 Smoky Row Road, Strawberry Plains, TN 37871 / 865-933-3286; FAX: 865-932-8586
Parker Gun Finishes, 9337 Smokey Row Rd., Strawberry Plains, TN 37871 / 865-933-3286; FAX: 865-932-8586
Parsons Optical Mfg. Co., PO Box 192, Ross, OH 45061 / 513-867-0820; FAX: 513-867-8380 psscopes@concentric.net
Partridge Sales Ltd., John, Trent Meadows, Rugeley, ENGLAND
Pasadena Gun Center, 206 E. Shaw, Pasadena, TX 77506 / 713-472-0417; FAX: 713-472-1322
Passive Bullet Traps, Inc. (See Savage Range Systems, Inc.)
Paterson Gunsmithing, 438 Main St., Paterson, NJ 07502 / 201-345-4100
Pathfinder Sports Leather, 2920 E. Chambers St., Phoenix, AZ 85040 / 602-276-0016
Patrick W. Price Bullets, 16520 Worthley Drive, San Lorenzo, CA 94580 / 510-278-1547
Pattern Control, 114 N. Third St., P.O. Box 462105, Garland, TX 75046 / 214-494-3551; FAX: 214-272-8447
Paul A. Harris Hand Engraving, 113 Rusty Lane, Boerne, TX 78006-5746 / 512-391-5121
Paul and Sharon Dressel, 209 N. 92nd Ave., Yakima, WA 98908 / 509-966-9233; FAX: 509-966-3365 dressels@nwinfo.net www.dressels.com
Paul D. Hillmer Custom Gunstocks, 7251 Hudson Heights, Hudson, IA 50643 / 319-988-3941
Paul Jones Moulds, 4901 Telegraph Rd., Los Angeles, CA 90022 / 213-262-1510
Paulsen Gunstocks, Rt. 71, Box 11, Chinook, MT 59523 / 406-357-3403
Pawling Mountain Club, Keith Lupton, PO Box 573, Pawling, NY 12564 / 914-855-3825
Paxton Quigley's Personal Protection Strategies, 9903 Santa Monica Blvd., 300, Beverly Hills, CA 90212 / 310-281-1762 www.defend-net.com/paxton
Payne Photography, Robert, Robert, P.O. Box 141471, Austin, TX 78714 / 512-272-4554
Peacemaker Specialists, P.O. Box 157, Whitmore, CA 96096 / 530-472-3438 www.peacemakerspecialists.com
Pearce Grip, Inc., P.O. Box 40367, Fort Worth, TX 76140 / 817-568-9704; FAX: 817-568-9707 info@pearcegrip.com www.pearcegrip.com
Pease Accuracy, Bob, P.O. Box 310787, New Braunfels, TX 78131 / 210-625-1342
PECAR Herbert Schwarz GmbH, Kreuzbergstrasse 6, 10965, Berlin, GERMANY / 004930-785-7383; FAX: 004930-785-1934 michael.schwart@pecar-berlin.de www.pecar-berlin.de
Pecatonica River Longrifle, 5205 Nottingham Dr., Rockford, IL 61111 / 815-968-1995; FAX: 815-968-1996
Pedersen, C. R., 2717 S. Pere Marquette Hwy., Ludington, MI 49431 / 231-843-2061; FAX: 231-845-7695 fega@fega.com
Pedersen, Rex C., 2717 S. Pere Marquette Hwy., Ludington, MI 49431 / 231-843-2061; FAX: 231-845-7695 fega@fega.com
Peifer Rifle Co., P.O. Box 220, Nokomis, IL 62075
Pejsa Ballistics, 1314 Marquette Ave., Apt 906, Minneapolis, MN 55403 / 612-332-5073; FAX: 612-332-5204 pejsa@sprintmail.com pejsa.com
Pelaire Products, 5346 Bonky Ct., W. Palm Beach, FL 33415 / 561-439-0691; FAX: 561-967-0052
Peltor, Inc. (See Aero Peltor)
PEM's Mfg. Co., 5063 Waterloo Rd., Atwater, OH 44201 / 216-947-3721
Pence Precision Barrels, 7567 E. 900 S., S. Whitley, IN 46787 / 219-839-4745
Pendleton Royal, c/o Swingler Buckland Ltd., 4/7 Highgate St., Birmingham, ENGLAND / 44 121 440 3060; or 44 121 446 5898; FAX: 44 121 446 4165
Pendleton Woolen Mills, P.O. Box 3030, 220 N.W. Broadway, Portland, OR 97208 / 503-226-4801
Penn Bullets, P.O. Box 756, Indianola, PA 15051
Pennsylvania Gun Parts Inc., RR 7 Box 150, Mount Pleasant, PA 15666
Pennsylvania Gunsmith School, 812 Ohio River Blvd., Avalon, Pittsburgh, PA 15202 / 412-766-1812; FAX: 412-766-0855 pgs@pagunsmith.com www.pagunsmith.com
Penrod Precision, 312 College Ave., P.O. Box 307, N. Manchester, IN 46962 / 260-982-8385; FAX: 260-982-1819
Pentax Corp., 35 Inverness Dr. E., Englewood, CO 80112 / 303-799-8000; FAX: 303-790-1131
Pentheny de Pentheny, c/o H.P. Okelly, 321 S. Main St., Sebastopol, CA 95472 / 707-824-1637; FAX: 707-824-1637
Perazone-Gunsmith, Brian, Cold Spring Rd., Roxbury, NY 12474 / 607-326-4088; FAX: 607-326-3140 bpgunsmith@catskill.net www.bpgunsmith@catskill.net
Perazzi U.S.A. Inc., 1010 West Tenth, Azusa, CA 91702 / 626-334-1234; FAX: 626-334-0344 perazziusa@aol.com
Performance Specialists, 308 Eanes School Rd., Austin, TX 78746 / 512-327-0119
Perugini Visini & Co. S.r.l., Via Camprelle, 126, 25080 Nuvolera, ITALY / 30-6897535; FAX: 30-6897821 peruvisi@virgilia.it
Pete de Coux Auction House, HC 30 Box 932 G, Prescott, AZ 86305-7447 / 928-776-8285; FAX: 928-776-8276 pdbullets@commspeed.net
Pete Mazur Restoration, 13083 Drummer Way, Grass Valley, CA 95949 / 530-268-2412; FAX: 530-268-2412
Pete Rickard, Inc., 115 Roy Walsh Rd, Cobleskill, NY 12043 / 518-234-2731: FAX: 518-234-2454 rickard@telenet.net www.peterickard.com
Peter Dyson & Son Ltd., 3 Cuckoo Lane, Honley, Holmfirth, Yorkshire, HD9 6AS ENGLAND / 44-1484-661062; FAX: 44-1484-663709 peter@peterdyson.co.uk www.peterdyson.co.uk
Peter Hale/Engraver, 800 E. Canyon Rd., Spanish Fork, UT 84660 / 801-798-8215
Peters Stahl GmbH, Stettiner Strasse 42, D-33106, Paderborn, GERMANY / 05251-750025; FAX: 05251-75611
Peterson Gun Shop, Inc., A.W., 4255 W. Old U.S. 441, Mt. Dora, FL 32757-3299 / 352-383-4258; FAX: 352-735-1001
Petro-Explo Inc., 7650 U.S. Hwy. 287, Suite 100, Arlington, TX 76017 / 817-478-8888
Pettinger Books, Gerald, 47827 300th Ave., Russell, IA 50238 / 641-535-2239 gpettinger@lisco.com
Pflumm Mfg. Co., 10662 Widmer Rd., Lenexa, KS 66215 / 800-888-4867; FAX: 913-451-7857
PFRB Co., P.O. Box 1242, Bloomington, IL 61702 / 309-473-3964; or 800-914-5464; FAX: 309-473-2161
Philip S. Olt Co., P.O. Box 550, 12662 Fifth St., Pekin, IL 61554 / 309-348-3633; FAX: 309-348-3300
Phillippi Custom Bullets, Justin, P.O. Box 773, Ligonier, PA 15658 / 724-238-2962; FAX: 724-238-9671 jrp@wpa.net http://www.wpa.net~jrphil
Phillips & Rogers, Inc., 100 Hilbig #C, Conroe, TX 77301 / 409-435-0011
Phoenix Arms, 4231 Brickell St., Ontario, CA 91761 / 909-937-6900; FAX: 909-937-0060
Photronic Systems Engineering Company, 6731 Via De La Reina, Bonsall, CA 92003 / 619-758-8000
Piedmont Community College, P.O. Box 1197, Roxboro, NC 27573 / 336-599-1181; FAX: 336-597-3817 www.piedmont.cc.nc.us
Pierce Pistols, 55 Sorrellwood Lane, Sharpsburg, GA 30277-9523 / 404-253-8192
Pietta (See U.S. Importers-Navy Arms Co, Taylor's
Pilgrim Pewter, Inc. (See Bell Originals Inc. Sid)
Pilkington, Scott (See Little Trees Ramble)
Pine Technical College, 1100 4th St., Pine City, MN 55063 / 800-521-7463; FAX: 612-629-6766
Pinetree Bullets, 133 Skeena St., Kitimat, BC V8C 1Z1 CANADA / 604-632-3768; FAX: 604-632-3768
Pioneer Arms Co., 355 Lawrence Rd., Broomall, PA 19008 / 215-356-5203
Piotti (See U.S. Importer-Moore & Co., Wm. Larkin)
Piquette, Paul. See: PIQUETTE'S CUSTOM ENGRAVING
Piquette's Custom Engraving, Paul R. Piquette, 80 Bradford Dr., Feeding Hills, MA 01030 / 413-789-4582; FAX: 413-786-8118 ppiquette@aol.com www.pistoldynamics.com
Plaza Cutlery, Inc., 3333 Bristol, 161 South Coast Plaza, Costa Mesa, CA 92626 / 714-549-3932
Plum City Ballistic Range, N2162 80th St., Plum City, WI 54761 / 715-647-2539
PlumFire Press, Inc., 30-A Grove Ave., Patchogue, NY 11772-4112 / 800-695-7246; FAX: 516-758-4071
PMC/Eldorado Cartridge Corp., P.O. Box 62508, 12801 U.S. Hwy. 95 S., Boulder City, NV 89005 / 702-294-0025; FAX: 702-294-0121 kbauer@pmcammo.com www.pmcammo.com
Poburka, Philip (See Bison Studios)
Pointing Dog Journal, Village Press Publications, P.O. Box 968, Dept. PGD, Traverse City, MI 49685 / 800-272-3246; FAX: 616-946-3289
Police Bookshelf, PO Box 122, Concord, NH 03301 / 603-224-6814; FAX: 603-226-3554
Polywad, Inc., P.O. Box 7916, Macon, GA 31209 / 478-477-0669; or 800-998-0669 FAX: 478-477-0666 polywadmpb@aol.com www.polywad.com
Ponsness/Warren, 768 Ohio St., Rathdrum, ID 83858 / 800-732-0706; FAX: 208-687-2233
Pony Express Reloaders, 608 E. Co. Rd. D, Suite 3, St. Paul, MN 55117 / 612-483-9406; FAX: 612-483-9884
Pony Express Sport Shop, 23404 Lyons Ave., PMB 448, Newhall, CA 91321-2511 / 818-895-1231
Potts, Wayne E., 912 Poplar St., Denver, CO 80220 / 303-355-5462
Powder Horn Ltd., PO Box 565, Glenview, IL 60025 / 305-565-6060
Powell & Son (Gunmakers) Ltd., William, 35-37 Carrs Lane, Birmingham, B4 7SX ENGLAND / 121-643-0689; FAX: 121-631-3504 sales@william-powell.co.uk www.william-powell.co.uk
Powell Agency, William, 22 Circle Dr., Bellmore, NY 11710 / 516-679-1158
Power Custom, Inc., 29739 Hwy. J, Gravois Mills, MO 65037 / 573-372-5684; FAX: 573-372-5799 rwpowers@laurie.net www.powercustom.com
Power Plus Enterprises, Inc., PO Box 38, Warm Springs, GA 31830 / 706-655-2132
Powley Computer (See Hutton Rifle Ranch)

MANUFACTURER'S DIRECTORY

Practical Tools, Inc., 7067 Easton Rd., P.O. Box 133, Pipersville, PA 18947 / 215-766-7301; FAX: 215-766-8681

Prairie Gun Works, 1-761 Marion St., Winnipeg, MB R2J 0K6 CANADA / 204-231-2976; FAX: 204-231-8566

Prairie River Arms, 1220 N. Sixth St., Princeton, IL 61356 / 815-875-1616; or 800-445-1541; FAX: 815-875-1402

Pranger, Ed G., 1414 7th St., Anacortes, WA 98221 / 206-293-3488

Precision Airgun Sales, Inc., 5247 Warrensville Ctr Rd., Maple Hts., OH 44137 / 216-587-5005; FAX: 216-587-5005

Precision Cast Bullets, 101 Mud Creek Lane, Ronan, MT 59864 / 406-676-5135

Precision Delta Corp., PO Box 128, Ruleville, MS 38771 / 662-756-2810; FAX: 662-756-2590

Precision Firearm Finishing, 25 N.W. 44th Avenue, Des Moines, IA 50313 / 515-288-8680; FAX: 515-244-3925

Precision Gun Works, 104 Sierra Rd., Dept. GD, Kerrville, TX 78028 / 830-367-4587

Precision Reloading, Inc., P.O. Box 122, Stafford Springs, CT 06076 / 860-684-7979; FAX: 860-684-6788 info@precisionreloading.com www.precisionreloading.com

Precision Sales International, Inc., PO Box 1776, Westfield, MA 01086 / 413-562-5055; FAX: 413-562-5056 precision-sales.com

Precision Shooting, Inc., 222 McKee St., Manchester, CT 06040 / 860-645-8776; FAX: 860-643-8215 www.theaccuraterifle.com

Precision Small Arms Inc., 9272 Jeronimo Rd, Ste 121, Irvine, CA 92618 / 800-554-5515; or 949-768-3530; FAX: 949-768-4808 www.tcbebe.com

Precision Specialties, 131 Hendom Dr., Feeding Hills, MA 01030 / 413-786-3365; FAX: 413-786-3365

Precision Sport Optics, 15571 Producer Lane, Unit G, Huntington Beach, CA 92649 / 714-891-1309; FAX: 714-892-6920

Premier Reticles, 920 Breckinridge Lane, Winchester, VA 22601-6707 / 540-722-0601; FAX: 540-722-3522

Prescott Projectile Co., 1808 Meadowbrook Road, Prescott, AZ 86303

Preslik's Gunstocks, 4245 Keith Ln., Chico, CA 95926 / 916-891-8236

Price Bullets, Patrick W., 16520 Worthley Dr., San Lorenzo, CA 94580 / 510-278-1547

Prime Reloading, 30 Chiswick End, Meldreth, ROYSTON UK / 0763-260636

Primedia Publishing Co., 6420 Wilshire Blvd., Los Angeles, CA 90048 / 213-782-2000; FAX: 213-782-2867

Primos Hunting Calls, 4436 North State St., Ste. A-7, Jackson, MS 39206 / 601-366-1288; FAX: 601-362-3274 www.primos.com

PRL Bullets, c/o Blackburn Enterprises, 114 Stuart Rd., Ste. 110, Cleveland, TN 37312 / 423-559-0340

Pro Load Ammunition, Inc., 5180 E. Seltice Way, Post Falls, ID 83854 / 208-773-9444; FAX: 208-773-9441

Professional Gunsmiths of America, Rt 1 Box 224, Lexington, MO 64067 / 660-259-2636

Professional Hunter Supplies (See Star Custom Bullets), P.O. Box 608, 468 Main St., Ferndale, CA 95536 / 707-786-9140; FAX: 707-786-9117 wmebride@humboldt.com

PrOlixr Lubricants, P.O. Box 1348, Victorville, CA 92393 / 760-243-3129; FAX: 760-241-0148 prolix@accex.net www.prolixlubricant.com

Pro-Mark Div. of Wells Lamont, 6640 W. Touhy, Chicago, IL 60648 / 312-647-8200

Proofmark Corp., P.O. Box 357, Burgess, VA 22432 / 804-453-4337; FAX: 804-453-4337 proofmark@rivnet.net www.proofmarkbullets.com

Pro-Port Ltd., 41302 Executive Dr., Harrison Twp., MI 48045-1306 / 586-469-6727; FAX: 586-469-0425 e-mail@magnaport.com www.magnaport.com

Pro-Shot Products, Inc., P.O. Box 763, Taylorville, IL 62568 / 217-824-9133; FAX: 217-824-8861 www.proshotproducts.com

Protektor Model, 1-11 Bridge St., Galeton, PA 16922 / 814-435-2442 mail@protektormodel.com www.protektormodel.com

Prototech Industries, Inc., 10532 E Road, Delia, KS 66418 / 785-771-3571 prototec@grapevine.net

ProWare, Inc., 15847 NE Hancock St., Portland, OR 97230 / 503-239-0159

PWL Gunleather, P.O. Box 450432, Atlanta, GA 31145 / 800-960-4072; FAX: 770-822-1704 covert@pwlusa.com www.pwlusa.com

PWM Sales Ltd., N.D.F.S., Gowdall Lane, Pollington DN14 0AU, ENGLAND / 01405862688; FAX: 01405862622 Paulwelburn9@aol.com

Pyramyd Stone Inter. Corp., 2447 Suffolk Lane, Pepper Pike, OH 44124-4540

Q

Quack Decoy & Sporting Clays, 4 Ann & Hope Way, P.O. Box 98, Cumberland, RI 02864 / 401-723-8202; FAX: 401-722-5910

Quaker Boy, Inc., 5455 Webster Rd., Orchard Parks, NY 14127 / 716-662-3979; FAX: 716-662-9426

Quality Arms, Inc., Box 19477, Dept. GD, Houston, TX 77224 / 281-870-8377 arrieta2@excite.com www.gunshop.com

Quality Cartridge, P.O. Box 445, Hollywood, MD 20636 / 301-373-3719 www.qual-cart.com

Quality Custom Firearms, Stepehn Billeb, 22 Vista View Drive, Cody, WY 82414 / 307-587-4278; FAX: 307-587-4297 stevebilleb@wyoming.com

Quarton Beamshot, 4538 Centerview Dr., Ste. 149, San Antonio, TX 78228 / 800-520-8435; FAX: 210-735-1326 www.beamshot.com

Que Industries, Inc., PO Box 2471, Everett, WA 98203 / 425-303-9088; FAX: 206-514-3266 queinfo@queindustries.com

Queen Cutlery Co., PO Box 500, Franklinville, NY 14737 / 800-222-5233; FAX: 800-299-2618

R

R&C Knives & Such, 2136 CANDY CANE WALK, Manteca, CA 95336-9501 / 209-239-3722; FAX: 209-825-6947

R&D Gun Repair, Kenny Howell, RR1 Box 283, Beloit, WI 53511

R&J Gun Shop, 337 S. Humbolt St., Canyon City, OR 97820 / 541-575-2130 rjgunshop@highdestertnet.com

R&S Industries Corp., 8255 Brentwood Industrial Dr., St. Louis, MO 63144 / 314-781-5169 ron@miraclepolishingcloth.com www.miraclepolishingcloth.com

R. Murphy Co., Inc., 13 Groton-Harvard Rd., P.O. Box 376, Ayer, MA 01432 / 617-772-3481 www.r.murphyknives.com

R.A. Wells Custom Gunsmith, 3452 1st Ave., Racine, WI 53402 / 414-639-5223

R.E. Seebeck Assoc., P.O. Box 59752, Dallas, TX 75229

R.E.I., P.O. Box 88, Tallevast, FL 34270 / 813-755-0085

R.E.T. Enterprises, 2608 S. Chestnut, Broken Arrow, OK 74012 / 918-251-GUNS; FAX: 918-251-0587

R.F. Mitchell Bullets, 430 Walnut St., Westernport, MD 21562

R.I.S. Co., Inc., 718 Timberlake Circle, Richardson, TX 75080 / 214-235-0933

R.T. Eastman Products, P.O. Box 1531, Jackson, WY 83001 / 307-733-3217; or 800-624-4311

Rabeno, Martin, 530 The Eagle Pass, Durango, CO 81301 / 970-382-0353 fancygun@aol.com

Radack Photography, Lauren, 21140 Jib Court L-12, Aventura, FL 33180 / 305-931-3110

Radiator Specialty Co., 1900 Wilkinson Blvd., P.O. Box 34689, Charlotte, NC 28234 / 800-438-6947; FAX: 800-421-9525

Radical Concepts, P.O. Box 1473, Lake Grove, OR 97035 / 503-538-7437

Rainier Ballistics, 4500 15th St. East, Tacoma, WA 98424 / 800-638-8722; FAX: 253-922-7854 sales@rainierballistics.com www.rainierballistics.com

Ralph Bone Engraving, 718 N. Atlanta St., Owasso, OK 74055 / 918-272-9745

Ram-Line ATK, P.O. Box 39, Onalaska, WI 54650

Ramon B. Gonzalez Guns, P.O. Box 370, Monticello, NY 12701 / 914-794-4515; FAX: 914-794-4515

Rampart International, 2781 W. MacArthur Blvd., B-283, Santa Ana, CA 92704 / 800-976-7240 or 714-557-6405

Ranch Products, P.O. Box 145, Malinta, OH 43535 / 313-277-3118; FAX: 313-565-8536

Randall-Made Knives, P.O. Box 1988, Orlando, FL 32802 / 407-855-8075

Randco UK, 286 Gipsy Rd., Welling, DA16 1JJ ENGLAND / 44 81 303 4118

Randolph Engineering, Inc., Ranger Shooting Glasses, 26 Thomas Patten Dr., Randolph, MA 02368 / 800-541-1405; FAX: 781-986-0337 sales@randolphusa.com www.randolphusa.com

Randy Duane Custom Stocks, 7822 Church St., Middletown, VA 22645-9521

Range Brass Products Company, P.O. Box 218, Rockport, TX 78381

Ransom International Corp., 1027 Spire Dr, Prescott, AZ 86302 / 520-778-7899; FAX: 520-778-7993 ransom@primenet.com www.ransom-intl.com

Rapine Bullet Mould Mfg. Co., 9503 Landis Lane, East Greenville, PA 18041 / 215-679-5413; FAX: 215-679-9795

Ravell Ltd., 289 Diputacion St., 08009, Barcelona, SPAIN / 34(3) 4874486; FAX: 34(3) 4881394

Ray Riling Arms Books Co., 6844 Gorsten St., Philadelphia, PA 19119 / 215-438-2456; FAX: 215-438-5395 sales@rayrilingarmsbooks.com www.rayrilingarmsbooks.com

Ray's Gunsmith Shop, 3199 Elm Ave., Grand Junction, CO 81504 / 970-434-6162; FAX: 970-434-6162

Raytech Div. of Lyman Products Corp., 475 Smith Street, Middletown, CT 06457-1541 / 860-632-2020 or 800-225-9626; FAX: 860-632-1699 raysales@cshore.com www.raytech-ind.com

RCBS Operations/ATK, 605 Oro Dam Blvd., Oroville, CA 95965 / 530-533-5191 or 800-533-5000; FAX: 530-533-1647 www.rcbs.com

Reardon Products, P.O. Box 126, Morrison, IL 61270 / 815-772-3155

Red Diamond Dist. Co., 1304 Snowdon Dr., Knoxville, TN 37912

Redding Reloading Equipment, 1089 Starr Rd., Cortland, NY 13045 / 607-753-3331; FAX: 607-756-8445 techline@redding-reloading.com www.redding-reloading.com

Redfield Media Resource Center, 4607 N.E. Cedar Creek Rd., Woodland, WA 98674 / 360-225-5000; FAX: 360-225-7616

Redman's Rifling & Reboring, 189 Nichols Rd., Omak, WA 98841 / 509-826-5512

Redwood Bullet Works, 3559 Bay Rd., Redwood City, CA 94063 / 415-367-6741

Reed, Dave, Rt. 1, Box 374, Minnesota City, MN 55959 / 507-689-2944

Reimer Johannsen, Inc., 438 Willow Brook Rd., Plainfield, NH 03781 / 603-469-3450; FAX: 603-469-3471

Reloaders Equipment Co., 4680 High St., Ecorse, MI 48229

Reloading Specialties, Inc., Box 1130, Pine Island, MN 55463 / 507-356-8500; FAX: 507-356-8800

Remington Arms Co., Inc., 870 Remington Drive, P.O. Box 700, Madison, NC 27025-0700 / 800-243-9700; FAX: 910-548-8700

Remington Double Shotguns, 7885 Cyd Dr., Denver, CO 80221 / 303-429-6947

Renato Gamba S.p.A.-Societa Armi Bresciane Srl., Via Artigiani 93, 25063 Gardone, Val Trompia (BS), ITALY / 30-8911640; FAX: 30-8911648

Renegade, P.O. Box 31546, Phoenix, AZ 85046 / 602-482-6777; FAX: 602-482-1952

Renfrew Guns & Supplies, R.R. 4, Renfrew, ON K7V 3Z7 CANADA / 613-432-7080

Reno, Wayne, 2808 Stagestop Road, Jefferson, CO 80456

Republic Arms, Inc. (See Cobra Enterprises, Inc.)

Retting, Inc., Martin B., 11029 Washington, Culver City, CA 90232 / 213-837-2412

RG-G, Inc., P.O. Box 935, Trinidad, CO 81082 / 719-845-1436

RH Machine & Consulting Inc., P.O. Box 394, Pacific, MO 63069 / 314-271-8465

Rhino, P.O. Box 787, Locust, NC 28097 / 704-753-2198

Rhodeside, Inc., 1704 Commerce Dr., Piqua, OH 45356 / 513-773-5781

Rice, Keith (See White Rock Tool & Die)

Richards Micro-Fit Stocks, 8331 N. San Fernando Ave., Sun Valley, CA 91352 / 818-767-6097; FAX: 818-767-7121

REFERENCE

MANUFACTURER'S DIRECTORY

Ridgeline, Inc., Bruce Sheldon, P.O. Box 930, Dewey, AZ 86327-0930 / 800-632-5900; FAX: 520-632-5900
Ridgetop Sporting Goods, P.O. Box 306, 42907 Hilligoss Ln. East, Eatonville, WA 98328 / 360-832-6422; FAX: 360-832-6422
Ries, Chuck, 415 Ridgecrest Dr., Grants Pass, OR 97527 / 503-476-5623
Rifles, Inc., 3580 Leal Rd., Pleasanton, TX 78064 / 830-569-2055; FAX: 830-569-2297
Riggs, Jim, 206 Azalea, Boerne, TX 78006 / 210-249-8567
Riley Ledbetter Airguns, 1804 E. Sprague St., Winston Salem, NC 27107-3521 / 919-784-0676
Rim Pac Sports, Inc., 1034 N. Soldano Ave., Azusa, CA 91702-2135
Ringler Custom Leather Co., 31 Shining Mtn. Rd., Powell, WY 82435 / 307-645-3255
Ripley Rifles, 42 Fletcher Street, Ripley, Derbyshire, DE5 3LP ENGLAND / 011-0773-748353
Rizzini F.lli (See U.S. Importers-Moore & C England)
Rizzini SNC, Via 2 Giugno, 7/7Bis-25060, Marcheno (Brescia), ITALY
RLCM Enterprises, 110 Hill Crest Drive, Burleson, TX 76028
RMS Custom Gunsmithing, 4120 N. Bitterwell, Prescott Valley, AZ 86314 / 520-772-7626
Robert Evans Engraving, 332 Vine St., Oregon City, OR 97045 / 503-656-5693
Robert Valade Engraving, 931 3rd Ave., Seaside, OR 97138 / 503-738-7672
Robinett, R. G., P.O. Box 72, Madrid, IA 50156 / 515-795-2906
Robinson, Don, Pennsylvania Hse, 36 Fairfax Crescent, W Yorkshire, ENGLAND / 0422-364458 donrobinsonuk@yahoo.co.uk www.guns4u2.co.uk
Robinson Armament Co., PO Box 16776, Salt Lake City, UT 84116 / 801-355-0401; FAX: 801-355-0402 zdf@robarm.com www.robarm.com
Robinson Firearms Mfg. Ltd., 1699 Blondeaux Crescent, Kelowna, BC V1Y 4J8 CANADA / 604-868-9596
Robinson H.V. Bullets, 3145 Church St., Zachary, LA 70791 / 504-654-4029
Rochester Lead Works, 76 Anderson Ave., Rochester, NY 14607 / 716-442-8500; FAX: 716-442-4712
Rock River Arms, 101 Noble St., Cleveland, IL 61241
Rockwood Corp., Speedwell Division, 136 Lincoln Blvd., Middlesex, NJ 08846 / 800-243-8274; FAX: 980-560-7475
Rocky Mountain Armoury, Mr. Felix LesMerises, 610 Main Street, P.O. Box 691, Frisco, CO 80443-0691 / 970-668-0136; FAX: 970-668-4484 felix@rockymountainarmoury.com
Rocky Mountain Arms, Inc., 1813 Sunset Pl, Unit D, Longmont, CO 80501 / 800-375-0846; FAX: 303-678-8766
Rocky Mountain Target Co., 3 Aloe Way, Leesburg, FL 34788 / 352-365-9598
Rocky Mountain Wildlife Products, P.O. Box 999, La Porte, CO 80535 / 970-484-2768; FAX: 970-484-0807 critrcall@earthlink.net www.critrcall.com
Rocky Shoes & Boots, 294 Harper St., Nelsonville, OH 45764 / 800-848-9452; or 614-753-1951; FAX: 614-753-4024
Rogue Rifle Co., Inc., 1140 36th St. N., Ste. B, Lewiston, ID 83501 / 208-743-4355; FAX: 208-743-4163
Rogue River Rifleworks, 500 Linne Road #D, Paso Robles, CA 93446 / 805-227-4706; FAX: 805-227-4723 rrrifles@calinet.com
Rohner, Hans, 1148 Twin Sisters Ranch Rd., Nederland, CO 80466-9600
Rohner, John, 186 Virginia Ave, Asheville, NC 28806 / 303-444-3841
Rohrbaugh, P.O. Box 785, Bayport, NY 11705 / 631-363-2843; FAX: 631-363-2681 API380@aol.com
Romain's Custom Guns, Inc., RD 1, Whetstone Rd., Brockport, PA 15823 / 814-265-1948 romwhetstone@penn.com
Ron Frank Custom Classic Arms, 7131 Richland Rd., Ft. Worth, TX 76118 / 817-284-9300; FAX: 817-284-9300 rfrank3974@aol.com
Rooster Laboratories, P.O. Box 414605, Kansas City, MO 64141 / 816-474-1622; FAX: 816-474-7622
Rorschach Precision Products, 417 Keats Cir., Irving, TX 75061 / 214-790-3487
Rosenberg & Son, Jack A., 12229 Cox Ln., Dallas, TX 75234 / 214-241-6302
Ross, Don, 12813 West 83 Terrace, Lenexa, KS 66215 / 913-492-6982
Rosser, Bob, 2809 Crescent Ave., Suite 20, Homewood, AL 35209 / 205-870-4422; FAX: 205-870-4421 www.hand-engravers.com
Rossi Firearms, Gary Mchalik, 16175 NW 49th Ave., Miami, FL 33014-6314 / 305-474-0401; FAX: 305-623-7506
Rottweil Compe, 1330 Glassell, Orange, CA 92667
Roy Baker's Leather Goods, PO Box 893, Magnolia, AR 71754 / 870-234-0344
Royal Arms Gunstocks, 919 8th Ave. NW, Great Falls, MT 59404 / 406-453-1149 royalarms@lmt.net www.lmt.net/~royalarms
Royal Arms International, R J Brill, P.O. Box 6083, Woodland Hills, CA 91365 / 818-704-5110; FAX: 818-887-2059 royalarms.com
Roy's Custom Grips, 793 Mt. Olivet Church Rd., Lynchburg, VA 24504 / 434-993-3470
RPM, 15481 N. Twin Lakes Dr., Tucson, AZ 85739 / 520-825-1233; FAX: 520-825-3333
Rubright Bullets, 1008 S. Quince Rd., Walnutport, PA 18088 / 215-767-1339
Rucker Dist. Inc., P.O. Box 479, Terrell, TX 75160 / 214-563-2094
Ruger (See Sturm, Ruger & Co., Inc.)
Ruger, Chris. See: RUGER'S CUSTOM GUNS
Ruger's Custom Guns, Chris Ruger, 1050 Morton Blvd., Kingston, NY 12401 / 845-336-7106; FAX: 845-336-7106 rugerscustom@outdrs.net rugergunsmith.com
Rundell's Gun Shop, 6198 Frances Rd., Clio, MI 48420 / 313-687-0559
Rupert's Gun Shop, 2202 Dick Rd., Suite B, Fenwick, MI 48834 / 517-248-3252 17rupert@pathwaynet.com
Russ Haydon's Shooters' Supply, 15018 Goodrich Dr. NW, Gig Harbor, WA 98329 / 877-663-6249; FAX: 253-857-7884 www.shooters-supply.com
Russ, William. See: BILL RUSS TRADING POST
Rusteprufe Laboratories, 1319 Jefferson Ave., Sparta, WI 54656 / 608-269-4144; FAX: 608-366-1972 rusteprufe@centurytel.net www.rusteprufe.com
Rusty Duck Premium Gun Care Products, 7785 Foundation Dr., Suite 6, Florence, KY 41042 / 606-342-5553; FAX: 606-342-5556
Rutgers Book Center, 127 Raritan Ave., Highland Park, NJ 08904 / 732-545-4344; FAX: 732-545-6686 gunbooks@rutgersgunbooks.com www.rutgersgunbooks.com
Rutten (See U.S. Importer-Labanu Inc)
RWS (See U.S. Importer-Dynamit Nobel-RWS, Inc.), 81 Ruckman Rd., Closter, NJ 07624 / 201-767-7971; FAX: 201-767-1589

S

S&K Scope Mounts, RD 2 Box 72E, Sugar Grove, PA 16350 / 814-489-3091; or 800-578-9862; FAX: 814-489-5466 comments@scopemounts.com www.scopemounts.com
S&S Firearms, 74-11 Myrtle Ave., Glendale, NY 11385 / 718-497-1100; FAX: 718-497-1105 info@ssfirearms.com ssfirearms.com
S.A.R.L. G. Granger, 66 cours Fauriel, 42100, Saint Etienne, FRANCE / 04 77 25 14 73; FAX: 04 77 38 66 99
S.C.R.C., P.O. Box 660, Katy, TX 77492-0660 FAX: 281-492-6332
S.D. Meacham, 1070 Angel Ridge, Peck, ID 83545
S.I.A.C.E. (See U.S. Importer-IAR Inc)
Sabatti SPA, Via A Volta 90, 25063 Gandome V.T.(BS), Brescia, ITALY / 030-8912207-831312; FAX: 030-8912059 info@sabatti.it www.sabatti.com
SAECO (See Redding Reloading Equipment)
Safari Arms/Schuetzen Pistol Works, 620-626 Old Pacific Hwy. SE, Olympia, WA 98513 / 360-459-3471; FAX: 360-491-3447 info@yarms.com www.olyarms.com
Safari Press, Inc., 15621 Chemical Lane B, Huntington Beach, CA 92649 / 714-894-9080; FAX: 714-894-4949 info@safaripress.com www.safaripress.com
Safariland Ltd., Inc., 3120 E. Mission Blvd., P.O. Box 51478, Ontario, CA 91761 / 909-923-7300; FAX: 909-923-7400
SAFE, PO Box 864, Post Falls, ID 83877 / 208-773-3624; FAX: 208-773-6819 staysafe@safe-llc.com www.safe-llc.com
Safety Speed Holster, Inc., 910 S. Vail Ave., Montebello, CA 90640 / 323-723-4140; FAX: 323-726-6973 e-mail@safetyspeedholster.com www.safetyspeedholster.com
Sako Ltd (See U.S. Importer-Stoeger Industries)
Sam Welch Gun Engraving, Sam Welch, HC 64 Box 2110, Moab, UT 84532 / 435-259-8131
Samco Global Arms, Inc., 6995 NW 43rd St., Miami, FL 33166 / 305-593-9782; FAX: 305-593-1014 samco@samcoglobal.com www.samcoglobal.com
Sampson, Roger, 2316 Mahogany St., Mora, MN 55051 / 612-679-4868
San Marco (See U.S. Importers-Cape Outfitters-EMF
Sandia Die & Cartridge Co., 37 Atancacio Rd. NE, Albuquerque, NM 87123 / 505-298-5729
Sarco, Inc., 323 Union St., Stirling, NJ 07980 / 908-647-3800; FAX: 908-647-9413
Sarsilmaz Shotguns - Turkey (see B.C. Outdoors)
Sauer (See U.S. Importers-Paul Co., The, Sigarms I
Sauls, R. See: BRYAN & ASSOC.
Saunders Gun & Machine Shop, 145 Delhi Rd, Manchester, IA 52057 / 563-927-4026
Savage Arms (Canada), Inc., 248 Water St., P.O. Box 1240, Lakefield, ON K0L 2H0 CANADA / 705-652-8000; FAX: 705-652-8431 www.savagearms.com
Savage Arms, Inc., 100 Springdale Rd., Westfield, MA 01085 / 413-568-7001; FAX: 413-562-7764
Savage Range Systems, Inc., 100 Springdale Rd., Westfield, MA 01085 / 413-568-7001; FAX: 413-562-1152 snailtraps@savagearms.com www.snailtraps.com
Saville Iron Co. (See Greenwood Precision)
Savino, Barbara J., P.O. Box 51, West Burke, VT 05871-0051
Scansport, Inc., P.O. Box 700, Enfield, NH 03748 / 603-632-7654
Sceery Game Calls, P.O. Box 6520, Sante Fe, NM 87502 / 505-471-9110; FAX: 505-471-3476
Schaefer Shooting Sports, P.O. Box 1515, Melville, NY 11747-0515 / 516-643-5466; FAX: 516-643-2426 robert@robertschaefer.com www.schaefershooting.com
Scharch Mfg., Inc.-Top Brass, 10325 Co. Rd. 120, Salida, CO 81201 / 719-539-7242; or 800-836-4683; FAX: 719-539-3021 scharch@chaffee.net www.topbraass.tv
Scherer, Liz. See: SCHERER SUPPLIES
Scherer Supplies, Liz Scherer, Box 250, Ewing, VA 24248 FAX: 423-733-2073
Schiffman, Curt, 2938 S. Greenwood, Mesa, AZ 85212
Schiffman, Mike, 8233 S. Crystal Springs, McCammon, ID 83250 / 208-254-9114
Schmidt & Bender, Inc., P.O. Box 134, Meriden, NH 03770 / 603-469-3565; FAX: 603-469-3471 scopes@cyberportal.net www.schmidtbender.com
Schmidtke Group, 17050 W. Salentine Dr., New Berlin, WI 53151-7349
Schneider Bullets, 3655 West 214th St., Fairview Park, OH 44126
Schneider Rifle Barrels, Inc., 1403 W Red Baron Rd., Payson, AZ 85541 / 602-948-2525
Schroeder Bullets, 1421 Thermal Ave., San Diego, CA 92154 / 619-423-3523; FAX: 619-423-8124
Schulz Industries, 16247 Minnesota Ave., Paramount, CA 90723 / 213-439-5903
Schumakers Gun Shop, 512 Prouty Corner Lp. A, Colville, WA 99114 / 509-684-4848
Scope Control, Inc., 5775 Co. Rd. 23 SE, Alexandria, MN 56308 / 612-762-7295
Score High Gunsmithing, 9812-A, Cochiti SE, Albuquerque, NM 087123 / 800-326-5632 or 505-292-5532; FAX: 505-292-2592
Scot Powder, Rt.1 Box 167, McEwen, TN 37101 / 800-416-3006; FAX: 615-729-4211
Scott Fine Guns Inc., Thad, P.O. Box 412, Indianola, MS 38751 / 601-887-5929
Searcy Enterprises, P.O. Box 584, Boron, CA 93596 / 760-762-6771; FAX: 760-762-0191
Second Chance Body Armor, P.O. Box 578, Central Lake, MI 49622 / 616-544-5721; FAX: 616-544-9824
Seebeck Assoc., R.E., P. O. Box 59752, Dallas, TX 75229

MANUFACTURER'S DIRECTORY

Seecamp Co. Inc., L. W., PO Box 255, New Haven, CT 06502 / 203-877-3429; FAX: 203-877-3429
Segway Industries, P.O. Box 783, Suffern, NY 10901-0783 / 914-357-5510
Seligman Shooting Products, Box 133, Seligman, AZ 86337 / 602-422-3607 shootssp@yahoo.com
Sellier & Bellot, USA, Inc., P.O. Box 27006, Shawnee Mission, KS 66225 / 913-685-0916; FAX: 913-685-0917
Selsi Co., Inc., P.O. Box 10, Midland Park, NJ 07432-0010 / 201-935-0388; FAX: 201-935-5851
Semmer, Charles (See Remington Double Shotguns), 7885 Cyd Dr, Denver, CO 80221 / 303-429-6947
Sentinel Arms, P.O. Box 57, Detroit, MI 48231 / 313-331-1951; FAX: 313-331-1456
Servus Footwear Co., 1136 2nd St., Rock Island, IL 61204 / 309-786-7741; FAX: 309-786-9808
Shappy Bullets, 76 Milldale Ave., Plantsville, CT 06479 / 203-621-3704
Sharp Shooter Supply, 4970 Lehman Road, Delphos, OH 45833 / 419-695-3179
Sharps Arms Co., Inc., C., 100 Centennial, Box 885, Big Timber, MT 59011 / 406-932-4353
Shaw, Inc., E. R. (See Small Arms Mfg. Co.)
Shay's Gunsmithing, 931 Marvin Ave., Lebanon, PA 17042
Sheffield Knifemakers Supply, Inc., P.O. Box 741107, Orange City, FL 32774-1107 / 386-775-6453; FAX: 386-774-5754
Sheldon, Bruce. See: RIDGELINE, INC.
Shepherd Enterprises, Inc., Box 189, Waterloo, NE 68069 / 402-779-2424; FAX: 402-779-4010 sshepherd@shepherdscopes.com www.shepherdscopes.com
Sherwood, George, 46 N. River Dr., Roseburg, OR 97470 / 541-672-3159
Shilen, Inc., 205 Metro Park Blvd., Ennis, TX 75119 / 972-875-5318; FAX: 972-875-5402
Shiloh Rifle Mfg., P.O. Box 279, Big Timber, MT 59011
Shockley, Harold H., 204 E. Farmington Rd., Hanna City, IL 61536 / 309-565-4524
Shoot Where You Look, Leon Measures, Dept GD, 408 Fair, Livingston, TX 77351
Shooters Arms Manufacturing, Inc., Rivergate Mall, Gen. Maxilom Ave., Cebu City 6000, PHILIPPINES / 6332-254-8478 www.shootersarms.com.ph
Shooter's Choice Gun Care, 15050 Berkshire Ind. Pky., Middlefield, OH 44062 / 440-834-8888; FAX: 440-834-3388 www.shooterschoice.com
Shooter's Edge Inc., 3313 Creekstone Dr., Fort Collins, CO 80525
Shooters Supply, 1120 Tieton Dr., Yakima, WA 98902 / 509-452-1181
Shooter's World, 3828 N. 28th Ave., Phoenix, AZ 85017 / 602-266-0170
Shooters, Inc., 5139 Stanart St., Norfolk, VA 23502 / 757-461-9152; FAX: 757-461-9155 gflocker@aol.com
Shootin' Shack, 357 Cypress Drive, No. 10, Tequesta, FL 33469 / 561-842-0990; FAX: 561-545-4861
Shooting Specialties (See Titus, Daniel)
Shooting Star, 1715 FM 1626 Ste 105, Manchaca, TX 78652 / 512-462-0009
Shoot-N-C Targets (See Birchwood Casey)
Shotgun Sports, P.O. Box 6810, Auburn, CA 95604 / 530-889-2220; FAX: 530-889-9106 custsrv@shotgunsportsmagazine.com shotgunsportsmagazine.com
Shotgun Sports Magazine, dba Shootin' Accessories Ltd., P.O. Box 6810, Auburn, CA 95604 / 916-889-2220 custsrv@shotgunsportsmagazine.com shotgunspotsmagazine.com
Shotguns Unlimited, 2307 Fon Du Lac Rd., Richmond, VA 23229 / 804-752-7115
Siegrist Gun Shop, 8752 Turtle Road, Whittemore, MI 48770 / 989-873-3929
Sierra Bullets, 1400 W. Henry St., Sedalia, MO 65301 / 816-827-6300; FAX: 816-827-6300
Sierra Specialty Prod. Co., 1344 Oakhurst Ave., Los Altos, CA 94024 FAX: 415-965-1536
SIG, CH-8212 Neuhausen, SWITZERLAND
Sigarms, Inc., 18 Industrial Dr., Exeter, NH 03833 / 603-772-2302; FAX: 603-772-9082 www.sigarms.com
Sightron, Inc., 1672B Hwy. 96, Franklinton, NC 27525 / 919-528-8783; FAX: 919-528-0995 info@sightron.com www.sightron.com

SIG-Sauer (See U.S. Importer-Sigarms Inc.)
Silencio/Safety Direct, 56 Coney Island Dr., Sparks, NV 89431 / 800-648-1812 or 702-354-4451; FAX: 702-359-1074
Silent Hunter, 1100 Newton Ave., W. Collingswood, NJ 08107 / 609-854-3276
Silhouette Leathers, P.O. Box 1161, Gunnison, CO 81230 / 970-641-6630 oldshooter@yahoo.com
Silver Eagle Machining, 18007 N. 69th Ave., Glendale, AZ 85308
Silver Ridge Gun Shop (See Goodwin, Fred)
Simmons, Jerry, 715 Middlebury St., Goshen, IN 46528-2717 / 574-533-8546
Simmons Gun Repair, Inc., 700 S. Rogers Rd., Olathe, KS 66062 / 913-782-3131; FAX: 913-782-4189
Simmons Outdoor Corp., 6001 Oak Canyon, Irvine, CA 92618 / 949-451-1450; FAX: 949-451-1460 www.meade.com
Sinclair International, Inc., 2330 Wayne Haven St., Fort Wayne, IN 46803 / 260-493-1858; FAX: 260-493-2530 sales@sinclairintl.com www.sinclairintl.com
Singletary, Kent, 4538 W Carol Ave., Glendale, AZ 85302 / 602-526-6836 kent@kscustom www.kscustom.com
Siskiyou Gun Works (See Donnelly, C. P.)
Six Enterprises, 320-D Turtle Creek Ct., San Jose, CA 95125 / 408-999-0201; FAX: 408-999-0216
SKB Shotguns, 4325 S. 120th St., Omaha, NE 68137 / 800-752-2767; FAX: 402-330-8040 skb@skbshotguns.com www.skbshotguns.com
Skeoch, Brian R., P.O. Box 279, Glenrock, WY 82637 / 307-436-9655 brianskeoch@aol.com
Skip's Machine, 364 29 Road, Grand Junction, CO 81501 / 303-245-5417
Sklany's Machine Shop, 566 Birch Grove Dr., Kalispell, MT 59901 / 406-755-4257
Slezak, Jerome F., 1290 Marlowe, Lakewood (Cleveland), OH 44107 / 216-221-1668
Slug Site, Ozark Wilds, 21300 Hwy. 5, Versailles, MO 65084 / 573-378-6430 john@ebeling.com john.ebeling.com
Small Arms Mfg. Co., 5312 Thoms Run Rd., Bridgeville, PA 15017 / 412-221-4343; FAX: 412-221-4303
Small Arms Specialists, 443 Firchburg Rd., Mason, NH 03048 / 603-878-0427; FAX: 603-878-3905 miniguns@empire.net miniguns.com
Small Custom Mould & Bullet Co., Box 17211, Tucson, AZ 85731
Smart Parts, 1203 Spring St., Latrobe, PA 15650 / 412-539-2660; FAX: 412-539-2298
Smires, C. L., 5222 Windmill Lane, Columbia, MD 21044-1328
Smith & Wesson, 2100 Roosevelt Ave., Springfield, MA 01104 / 413-781-8300; FAX: 413-731-8980
Smith, Art, P.O. Box 645, Park Rapids, MN 56470 / 218-732-5333;
Smith, Mark A., P.O. Box 182, Sinclair, WY 82334 / 307-324-7929
Smith, Michael, 2612 Ashmore Ave., Red Bank, TN 37415 / 615-267-8341
Smith, Ron, 5869 Straley, Ft. Worth, TX 76114 / 817-732-6768
Smith, Sharmon, 4545 Speas Rd., Fruitland, ID 83619 / 208-452-6329 sharmon@fmtc.com
Smith Abrasives, Inc., 1700 Sleepy Valley Rd., P.O. Box 5095, Hot Springs, AR 71902-5095 / 501-321-2244; FAX: 501-321-9232
Smith, Judy. See: L.B.T.
Smith Saddlery, Jesse W., 0499 County Road J, Pritchett, CO 81064 / 509-325-0622
Smokey Valley Rifles, E1976 Smokey Valley Rd., Scandinavia, WI 54977 / 715-467-2674
Snapp's Gunshop, 6911 E. Washington Rd., Clare, MI 48617 / 989-386-9226 snapp@glccomputers.com
Sno-Seal, Inc. (See Atsko/Sno-Seal, Inc.)
Societa Armi Bresciane Srl (See U.S. Importer-Cape
SOS Products Co. (See Buck Stix-SOS Products Co.), Box 3, Neenah, WI 54956
Sotheby's, 1334 York Ave. at 72nd St., New York, NY 10021 / 212-606-7260
Sound Tech Silencers, Box 391, Pelham, AL 35124 / 205-664-5860 silenceio@wmconnect.com www.soundtechsilencers.com

South Bend Replicas, Inc., 61650 Oak Rd.., South Bend, IN 46614 / 219-289-4500
Southeastern Community College, 1015 S. Gear Ave., West Burlington, IA 52655 / 319-752-2731
Southern Ammunition Co., Inc., 4232 Meadow St., Loris, SC 29569-3124 / 803-756-3262; FAX: 803-756-3583
Southern Bloomer Mfg. Co., P.O. Box 1621, Bristol, TN 37620 / 615-878-6660; FAX: 615-878-8761
Southern Security, 1700 Oak Hills Dr., Kingston, TN 37763 / 423-376-6297; FAX: 800-251-9992
Sparks, Milt, 605 E. 44th St. No. 2, Boise, ID 83714-4800
Spartan-Realtree Products, Inc., 1390 Box Circle, Columbus, GA 31907 / 706-569-9101; FAX: 706-569-0042
Specialty Gunsmithing, Lynn McMurdo, P.O. Box 404, Afton, WY 83110 / 307-886-5535
Specialty Shooters Supply, Inc., 3325 Griffin Rd., Suite 9mm, Fort Lauderdale, FL 33317
Speer Bullets, P.O. Box 856, Lewiston, ID 83501 / 208-746-2351; www.speer-bullets.com
Spegel, Craig, P.O. Box 387, Nehalem, OR 97131 / 503-368-5653
Speiser, Fred D., 2229 Dearborn, Missoula, MT 59801 / 406-549-8133
Spencer Reblue Service, 1820 Tupelo Trail, Holt, MI 48842 / 517-694-7474
Spencer's Rifle Barrels, Inc., 4107 Jacobs Creek Dr., Scottsville, VA 24590 / 804-293-6836; FAX: 804-293-6836 www.spencerriflebarrels.com
SPG LLC, P.O. Box 1625, Cody, WY 82414 / 307-587-7621; FAX: 307-587-7695 spg@cody.wtp.net www.blackpowderspg.com
Sphinx Systems Ltd., Gesteigtstrasse 12, CH-3800, Matten, BRNE, SWITZERLAND
Splitfire Sporting Goods, L.L.C., P.O. Box 1044, Orem, UT 84059-1044 / 801-932-7950; FAX: 801-932-7959 www.splitfireguns.com
Spolar Power Load, Inc., 17376 Filbert, Fontana, CA 92335 / 800-227-9667
Sport Flite Manufacturing Co., P.O. Box 1082, Bloomfield Hills, MI 48303 / 248-647-3747
Sporting Clays Of America, 9257 Bluckeye Rd, Sugar Grove, OH 43155-9632 / 740-746-8334; FAX: 740-746-8605
Sports Afield Magazine, 15621 Chemical Lane B, Huntington Beach, CA 92649 / 714-894-9080; FAX: 714-894-4949 info@sportsafield.com www.sportsafield.com
Sports Innovations, Inc., P.O. Box 5181, 8505 Jacksboro Hwy., Wichita Falls, TX 76307 / 817-723-6015
Sportsman Safe Mfg. Co., 6309-6311 Paramount Blvd., Long Beach, CA 90805 / 800-266-7150; or 310-984-5445
Sportsman's Communicators, 588 Radcliffe Ave., Pacific Palisades, CA 90272 / 800-538-3752
Sportsmatch U.K. Ltd., 16 Summer St. Leighton,, Buzzard Beds, Bedfordshire, LU7 8HT ENGLAND / 4401525-381638; FAX: 4401525-851236 info@sportsmatch-uk.com www.sportsmatch-uk.com
Sportsmen's Exchange & Western Gun Traders, Inc., 560 S. C St., Oxnard, CA 93030 / 805-483-1917
Spradlin's, 457 Shannon Rd., Texas CreekCotopaxi, CO 81223 / 719-275-7105; FAX: 719-275-3852 spradlins@prodigy.net www.spradlins.net
Springfield Armory, 420 W. Main St, Geneseo, IL 61254 / 309-944-5631; FAX: 309-944-3676 sales@springfield-armory.com www.springfieldarmory.com
Springfield Sporters, Inc., RD 1, Penn Run, PA 15765 / 412-254-2626; FAX: 412-254-9173
Springfield, Inc., 420 W. Main St., Geneseo, IL 61254 / 309-944-5631; FAX: 309-944-3676
Spyderco, Inc., 820 Spyderco Way, Golden, CO 80403 / 800-525-7770; or 800-525-7770; FAX: 303-278-2229 sales@spyderco.com www.spyderco.com
SSK Industries, J. D. Jones, 590 Woodvue Lane, Wintersville, OH 43953 / 740-264-0176; FAX: 740-264-2257 www.sskindustries.com
Stackpole Books, 5067 Ritter Rd., Mechanicsburg, PA 17055-6921 / 717-796-0411; or 800-732-3669; FAX: 717-796-0412 tmanney@stackpolebooks.com www.stackpolebooks.com

MANUFACTURER'S DIRECTORY

Stalker, Inc., P.O. Box 21, Fishermans Wharf Rd., Malakoff, TX 75148 / 903-489-1010

Stalwart Corporation, P.O. Box 46, Evanston, WY 82931 / 307-789-7687; FAX: 307-789-7688

Stan Baker Sports, Stan Baker, 10000 Lake City Way, Seattle, WA 98125 / 206-522-4575

Stan De Treville & Co., 4129 Normal St., San Diego, CA 92103 / 619-298-3393

Stanley Bullets, 2085 Heatheridge Ln., Reno, NV 89509

Star Ammunition, Inc., 5520 Rock Hampton Ct., Indianapolis, IN 46268 / 800-221-5927; FAX: 317-872-5847

Star Custom Bullets, P.O. Box 608, 468 Main St., Ferndale, CA 95536 / 707-786-9140; FAX: 707-786-9117 wmebridge@humboldt.com

Star Machine Works, P.O. Box 1872, Pioneer, CA 95666 / 209-295-5000

Starke Bullet Company, P.O. Box 400, 605 6th St. NW, Cooperstown, ND 58425 / 888-797-3431

Starkey Labs, 6700 Washington Ave. S., Eden Prairie, MN 55344

Starkey's Gun Shop, 9430 McCombs, El Paso, TX 79924 / 915-751-3030

Starlight Training Center, Inc., Rt. 1, P.O. Box 88, Bronaugh, MO 64728 / 417-843-3555

Starline, Inc., 1300 W. Henry St., Sedalia, MO 65301 / 660-827-6640; FAX: 660-827-6650 info@starlinebrass.com http://www.starlinebrass.com

Starr Trading Co., Jedediah, P.O. Box 2007, Farmington Hills, MI 48333 / 810-683-4343; FAX: 810-683-3282

Starrett Co., L. S., 121 Crescent St., Athol, MA 01331 / 978-249-3551; FAX: 978-249-8495

Steelman's Gun Shop, 10465 Beers Rd., Swartz Creek, MI 48473 / 810-735-4884

Steffens, Ron, 18396 Mariposa Creek Rd., Willits, CA 95490 / 707-485-0873

Stegall, James B., 26 Forest Rd., Wallkill, NY 12589

Steve Henigson & Associates, P.O. Box 2726, Culver City, CA 90231 / 310-305-8288; FAX: 310-305-1905

Steve Kamyk Engraver, 9 Grandview Dr., Westfield, MA 01085-1810 / 413-568-0457 stevek201@attbi

Steven Dodd Hughes, P.O. Box 545, Livingston, MT 59047 / 406-222-9377; FAX: 406-222-9377

Steves House of Guns, Rt. 1, Minnesota City, MN 55959 / 507-689-2573

Stewart Game Calls, Inc., Johnny, P.O. Box 7954, 5100 Fort Ave., Waco, TX 76714 / 817-772-3261; FAX: 817-772-3670

Stewart's Gunsmithing, P.O. Box 5854, Pietersburg North 0750, Transvaal, SOUTH AFRICA / 01521-89401

Steyr Mannlicher GmbH & Co KG, Mannlicherstrasse 1, 4400 Steyr, Steyr, AUSTRIA / 0043-7252-896-0; FAX: 0043-7252-78620 office@steyr-mannlicher.com www.steyr-mannlicher.com

STI International, 114 Halmar Cove, Georgetown, TX 78628 / 800-959-8201; FAX: 512-819-0465 www.stiguns.com

Stiles Custom Guns, 76 Cherry Run Rd., Box 1605, Homer City, PA 15748 / 712-479-9945

Stillwell, Robert, 421 Judith Ann Dr., Schertz, TX 78154

Stoeger Industries, 17603 Indian Head Hwy., Suite 200, Accokeek, MD 20607-2501 / 301-283-6300; FAX: 301-283-6986 www.stoegerindustries.com

Stoeger Publishing Co. (See Stoeger Industries)

Stone Enterprises Ltd., 426 Harveys Neck Rd., P.O. Box 335, Wicomico Church, VA 22579 / 804-580-5114; FAX: 804-580-8421

Stone Mountain Arms, 5988 Peachtree Corners E., Norcross, GA 30071 / 800-251-9412

Stoney Point Products, Inc., P.O. Box 234, 1822 N Minnesota St., New Ulm, MN 56073-0234 / 507-354-3360; FAX: 507-354-7236 stoney@newulmtel.net www.stoneypoint.com

Storm, Gary, P.O. Box 5211, Richardson, TX 75083 / 214-385-0862

Stott's Creek Armory, Inc., 2526 S. 475W, Morgantown, IN 46160 / 317-878-5489; FAX: 317-878-9489 sccalendar@aol.com www.Sccalendar.aol.com

Stratco, Inc., P.O. Box 2270, Kalispell, MT 59901 / 406-755-1221; FAX: 406-755-1226

Strayer, Sandy. See: STRAYER-VOIGT, INC.

Strayer-Voigt, Inc., Sandy Strayer, 3435 Ray Orr Blvd, Grand Prairie, TX 75050 / 972-513-0575

Strong Holster Co., 39 Grove St., Gloucester, MA 01930 / 508-281-3300; FAX: 508-281-6321

Strutz Rifle Barrels, Inc., W. C., P.O. Box 611, Eagle River, WI 54521 / 715-479-4766

Stuart, V. Pat, Rt.1, Box 447-S, Greenville, VA 24440 / 804-556-3845

Sturgeon Valley Sporters, Ken Ide, P.O. Box 283, Vanderbilt, MI 49795 / 517-983-4338 k.ide@mail.com

Sturm Ruger & Co. Inc., 200 Ruger Rd., Prescott, AZ 86301 / 928-541-8820; FAX: 520-541-8850 www.ruger.com

"Su-Press-On", Inc., P.O. Box 09161, Detroit, MI 48209 / 313-842-4222

Sullivan, David S. (See Westwind Rifles, Inc.)

Sun Welding Safe Co., 290 Easy St. No.3, Simi Valley, CA 93065 / 805-584-6678; or 800-729-SAFE; FAX: 805-584-6169 sunwelding.com

Sunny Hill Enterprises, Inc., W1790 Cty. HHH, Malone, WI 53049 / 920-795-4722; FAX: 920-795-4822

Super 6 LLC, Gary Knopp, 3806 W. Lisbon Ave., Milwaukee, WI 53208 / 414-344-3343; FAX: 414-344-0304

Sure-Shot Game Calls, Inc., P.O. Box 816, 6835 Capitol, Groves, TX 77619 / 409-962-1636; FAX: 409-962-5465

Svon Corp., 2107 W. Blue Heron Blvd., Riviera Beach, FL 33404 / 508-881-8852

Swann, D. J., 5 Orsova Close, Eltham North Vic., 3095 AUSTRALIA / 03-431-0323

Swanndri New Zealand, 152 Elm Ave., Burlingame, CA 94010 / 415-347-6158

Swanson, Mark, 975 Heap Avenue, Prescott, AZ 86301 / 928-778-4423

Swarovski Optik North America Ltd., 2 Slater Rd., Cranston, RI 02920 / 401-946-2220; or 800-426-3089; FAX: 401-946-2587

Sweet Home, Inc., P.O. Box 900, Orrville, OH 44667-0900

Swenson's 45 Shop, A. D., 3839 Ladera Vista Rd, Fallbrook, CA 92028-9431

Swift Bullet Co., P.O. Box 27, 201 Main St., Quinter, KS 67752 / 913-754-3959; FAX: 913-754-2359

Swift Instruments, Inc., 952 Dorchester Ave., Boston, MA 02125 / 617-436-2960; FAX: 617-436-3232

Swift River Gunworks, 450 State St., Belchertown, MA 01007 / 413-323-4052

Szweda, Robert (See RMS Custom Gunsmithing)

T

T&S Industries, Inc., 1027 Skyview Dr., W. Carrollton, OH 45449 / 513-859-8414

T.F.C. S.p.A., Via G. Marconi 118, B, Villa Carcina 25069, ITALY / 030-881271; FAX: 030-881826

T.G. Faust, Inc., 544 Minor St., Reading, PA 19602 / 610-375-8549; FAX: 610-375-4488

T.K. Lee Co., 1282 Branchwater Ln., Birmingham, AL 35216 / 205-913-5222 odonmich@aol.com www.scopedot.com

T.W. Menck Gunsmith, Inc., 5703 S. 77th St., Ralston, NE 68127 guntools@cox.net http://llwww.members.cox.net/guntools

Tabler Marketing, 2554 Lincoln Blvd., Suite 555, Marina Del Rey, CA 90291 / 818-755-4565; FAX: 818-755-0972

Taconic Firearms Ltd., Perry Lane, P.O. Box 553, Cambridge, NY 12816 / 518-677-2704; FAX: 518-677-5974

Tactical Defense Institute, 2174 Bethany Ridges, West Union, OH 45693 / 937-544-7228; FAX: 937-544-2887 tdiohio@dragonbbs.com www.tdiohio.com

Talley, Dave, P.O. Box 821, Glenrock, WY 82637 / 307-436-8724; or 307-436-9315

Talon Industries Inc. (See Cobra Enterprises, Inc.)

Tamarack Products, Inc., P.O. Box 625, Wauconda, IL 60084 / 708-526-9333; FAX: 708-526-9353

Tanfoglio Fratelli S.r.l., via Valtrompia 39, 41, Brescia, ITALY / 30-8910361; FAX: 30-8910183

Tanglefree Industries, 1261 Heavenly Dr., Martinez, CA 94553 / 800-982-4868; FAX: 510-825-3874

Tank's Rifle Shop, P.O. Box 474, Fremont, NE 68026-0474 / 402-727-1317 jtank@tanksrifleshop.com www.tanksrifleshop.com

Tanner (See U.S. Importer-Mandall Shooting Supply)

Taracorp Industries, Inc., 1200 Sixteenth St., Granite City, IL 62040 / 618-451-4400

Target Shooting, Inc., P.O. Box 773, Watertown, SD 57201 / 605-882-6955; FAX: 605-882-8840

Tar-Hunt Custom Rifles, Inc., 101 Dogtown Rd., Bloomsburg, PA 17815 / 570-784-6368; FAX: 570-389-9150 www.tar-hunt.com

Tarnhelm Supply Co., Inc., 431 High St., Boscawen, NH 03303 / 603-796-2551; FAX: 603-796-2918 info@tarnhelm.com www.tarnhelm.com

Tasco Sales, Inc., 2889 Commerce Pky., Miramar, FL 33025

Taurus Firearms, Inc., 16175 NW 49th Ave., Miami, FL 33014 / 305-624-1115; FAX: 305-623-7506

Taurus International Firearms (See U.S. Importer)

Taurus S.A. Forjas, Avenida Do Forte 511, Porto Alegre, RS BRAZIL 91360 / 55-51-347-4050; FAX: 55-51-347-3065

Taylor & Robbins, P.O. Box 164, Rixford, PA 16745 / 814-966-3233

Taylor's & Co., Inc., 304 Lenoir Dr., Winchester, VA 22603 / 540-722-2017; FAX: 540-722-2018

TCCI, P.O. Box 302, Phoenix, AZ 85001 / 602-237-3823; FAX: 602-237-3858

TCSR, 3998 Hoffman Rd., White Bear Lake, MN 55110-4626 / 800-328-5323; FAX: 612-429-0526

TDP Industries, Inc., P.O. Box 249, Ottsville, PA 18942-0249 / 215-345-8687; FAX: 215-345-6057

Techno Arms (See U.S. Importer- Auto-Ordnance Corp

Tecnolegno S.p.A., Via A. Locatelli, 6 10, 24019 Zogno, I ITALY / 0345-55111; FAX: 0345-55155

Ted Blocker Holsters, Inc., 9396 S.W. Tigard St., Tigard, OR 97223 / 800-650-9742; FAX: 503-670-9692 www.tedblocker.com

Tele-Optics, 630 E. Rockland Rd., P.O. Box 6313, Libertyville, IL 60048 / 847-362-7757; FAX: 847-362-7757

Tennessee Valley Mfg., 14 County Road 521, Corinth, MS 38834 / 601-286-5014 tvm@avsia.com www.avsia.com/tvm

Ten-Ring Precision, Inc., Alex B. Hamilton, 1449 Blue Crest Lane, San Antonio, TX 78232 / 210-494-3063; FAX: 210-494-3066

TEN-X Products Group, 1905 N Main St, Suite 133, Cleburne, TX 76031-1305 / 972-243-4016; or 800-433-2225; FAX: 972-243-4112

Tepeco, P.O. Box 342, Friendswood, TX 77546 / 713-482-2702

Terry K. Kopp Professional Gunsmithing, Rt 1 Box 224, Lexington, MO 64067 / 816-259-2636

Testing Systems, Inc., 220 Pegasus Ave., Northvale, NJ 07647

Tetra Gun Care, 8 Vreeland Rd., Florham Park, NJ 07932 / 973-443-0004; FAX: 973-443-0263

Tex Shoemaker & Sons, Inc., 714 W. Cienega Ave., San Dimas, CA 91773 / 909-592-2071; FAX: 909-592-2378 texshoemaker@texshoemaker.com www.texshoemaker.com

Texas Armory (See Bond Arms, Inc.)

Texas Platers Supply Co., 2453 W. Five Mile Parkway, Dallas, TX 75233 / 214-330-7168

Thad Rybka Custom Leather Equipment, 2050 Canoe Creek Rd., Springvale, AL 35146-6709

Thad Scott Fine Guns, Inc., P.O. Box 412, Indianola, MS 38751 / 601-887-5929

The A.W. Peterson Gun Shop, Inc., 4255 West Old U.S. 441, Mount Dora, FL 32757-3299 / 352-383-4258

The Accuracy Den, 25 Bitterbrush Rd., Reno, NV 89523 / 702-345-0225

The Ballistic Program Co., Inc., 2417 N. Patterson St., Thomasville, GA 31792 / 912-228-5739 or 800-368-0835

The BulletMakers Workshop, RFD 1 Box 1755, Brooks, ME 04921

The Competitive Pistol Shop, 5233 Palmer Dr., Ft. Worth, TX 76117-2433 / 817-834-8479

The Concealment Shop, Inc., 3550 E. Hwy. 80, Mesquite, TX 75149 / 972-289-8997; or 800-444-7090; FAX: 972-289-4410 info@theconcealmentshop.com www.theconcealmentshop.com

The Country Armourer, P.O. Box 308, Ashby, MA 01431-0308 / 508-827-6797; FAX: 508-827-4845

The Creative Craftsman, Inc., 95 Highway 29 North, P.O. Box 331, Lawrenceville, GA 30246 / 404-963-2112; FAX: 404-513-9488

Manufacturer's Directory

The Custom Shop, 890 Cochrane Crescent, Peterborough, ON K9H 5N3 CANADA / 705-742-6693

The Ensign-Bickford Co., 660 Hopmeadow St., Simsbury, CT 06070

The Firearm Training Center, 9555 Blandville Rd., West Paducah, KY 42086 / 502-554-5886

The Fouling Shot, 6465 Parfet St., Arvada, CO 80004

The Gun Doctor, 435 East Maple, Roselle, IL 60172 / 708-894-0668

The Gun Room, 1121 Burlington, Muncie, IN 47302 / 765-282-9073; FAX: 765-282-5270 bshstleguns@aol.com

The Gun Room Press, 127 Raritan Ave., Highland Park, NJ 08904 / 732-545-4344; FAX: 732-545-6686 gunbooks@rutgersgunbooks.com www.rutgersgunbooks.com

The Gun Shop, 62778 Spring Creek Rd., Montrose, CO 81401

The Gun Shop, 5550 S. 900 East, Salt Lake City, UT 84117 / 801-263-3633

The Gun Works, 247 S. 2nd St., Springfield, OR 97477 / 541-741-4118; FAX: 541-988-1097 gunworks@worldnet.att.net www.thegunworks.com

The Gunsight, 1712 North Placentia Ave., Fullerton, CA 92631

The Hanned Line, 4463 Madoc Way, San Jose, CA 95130 smith@hanned.com www.hanned.com

The Hawken Shop, P.O. Box 593, Oak Harbor, WA 98277 / 206-679-4657; FAX: 206-675-1114

The Keller Co., P.O. Box 4057, Port Angeles, WA 98363-0997 / 214-770-8585

The Lewis Lead Remover (See LEM Gun Specialties)

The Midwest Shooting School, Pat LaBoone, 2550 Hwy. 23, Wrenshall, MN 55797 / 218-384-3670 shootingschool@starband.net

The NgraveR Co., 67 Wawecus Hill Rd., Bozrah, CT 06334 / 860-823-1533; FAX: 860-887-6252 ngraver98@aol.com www.ngraver.com

The Ordnance Works, 2969 Pidgeon Point Road, Eureka, CA 95501 / 707-443-3252

The Orvis Co., Rt. 7, Manchester, VT 05254 / 802-362-3622; FAX: 802-362-3525

The Outdoor Connection, Inc., 7901 Panther Way, Waco, TX 76712-6556 / 800-533-6076 or 254-772-5575; FAX: 254-776-3553 floyd@outdoorconnection.com www.outdoorconnection.com

The Park Rifle Co., Ltd., Unit 6a Dartford Trade Park, Power Mill Lane, Dartford DA7 7NX, ENGLAND / 011-0322-222512

The Paul Co., 27385 Pressonville Rd., Wellsville, KS 66092 / 785-883-4444; FAX: 785-883-2525

The Protector Mfg. Co., Inc., 443 Ashwood Place, Boca Raton, FL 33431 / 407-394-6011

The Robar Co., Inc., 21438 N. 7th Ave., Suite B, Phoenix, AZ 85027 / 623-581-2648; FAX: 623-582-0059 info@robarguns.com www.robarguns.com

The School of Gunsmithing, 6065 Roswell Rd., Atlanta, GA 30328 / 800-223-4542

The Shooting Gallery, 8070 Southern Blvd., Boardman, OH 44512 / 216-726-7788

The Sight Shop, John G. Lawson, 1802 E. Columbia Ave., Tacoma, WA 98404 / 253-474-5465 parahellum9@aol.com www.thesightshop.org

The Southern Armory, 25 Millstone Road, Woodlawn, VA 24381 / 703-238-1343; FAX: 703-238-1453

The Surecase Co., 233 Wilshire Blvd., Ste. 900, Santa Monica, CA 90401 / 800-92ARMLOC

The Swampfire Shop (See Peterson Gun Shop, Inc.)

The Wilson Arms Co., 63 Leetes Island Rd., Branford, CT 06405 / 203-488-7297; FAX: 203-488-0135

Theis, Terry, 21452 FM 2093, Harper, TX 78631 / 830-864-4438

Thiewes, George W., 14329 W. Parada Dr., Sun City West, AZ 85375

Things Unlimited, 235 N. Kimbau, Casper, WY 82601 / 307-234-5277

Thirion Gun Engraving, Denise, PO Box 408, Graton, CA 95444 / 707-829-1876

Thomas, Charles C., 2600 S. First St., Springfield, IL 62704 / 217-789-8980; FAX: 217-789-9130 books@ccthomas.com ccthomas.com

Thompson Bullet Lube Co., P.O. Box 409, Wills Point, TX 75169 / 866-476-1500; FAX: 866-476-1500 thompsonbulletlube.com www.thompsonbulletlube.com

Thompson Precision, 110 Mary St., P.O. Box 251, Warren, IL 61087 / 815-745-3625

Thompson, Randall. See: HIGHLINE MACHINE CO.

Thompson Target Technology, 4804 Sherman Church Ave. S.W., Canton, OH 44710 / 330-484-6480; FAX: 330-491-1087 www.thompsontarget.com

Thompson Tool Mount, 1550 Solomon Rd., Santa Maria, CA 93455 / 805-934-1281 ttm@pronet.net www.thompsontoolmount.com

Thompson/Center Arms, P.O. Box 5002, Rochester, NH 03866 / 603-332-2394; FAX: 603-332-5133 tech@tcarms.com www.tcarms.com

3-Ten Corp., P.O. Box 269, Feeding Hills, MA 01030 / 413-789-2086; FAX: 413-789-1549

Thunden Ranch, HCR 1, Box 53, Mt. Home, TX 78058 / 830-640-3138

Thurston Sports, Inc., RD 3 Donovan Rd., Auburn, NY 13021 / 315-253-0966

Tiger-Hunt Gunstocks, Box 379, Beaverdale, PA 15921 / 814-472-5161 tigerhunt4@aol.com www.gunstockwood.com

Tikka (See U.S. Importer-Stoeger Industries)

Time Precision, 4 Nicholas Sq., New Milford, CT 06776-3506 / 203-775-8343

Tinks & Ben Lee Hunting Products (See Wellington)

Tink's Safariland Hunting Corp., P.O. Box 244, 1140 Monticello Rd., Madison, GA 30650 / 706-342-4915; FAX: 706-342-7568

Tioga Engineering Co., Inc., P.O. Box 913, 13 Cone St., Wellsboro, PA 16901 / 570-724-3533; FAX: 570-724-3895 tiogaeng@epix.net

Tippman Pneumatics, Inc., 2955 Adams Center Rd., Fort Wayne, IN 46803

Tirelli, Snc Di Tirelli Primo E.C., Via Matteotti No. 359, Gardone V.T. Brescia, I ITALY / 030-8912819; FAX: 030-832240

TM Stockworks, 6355 Maplecrest Rd., Fort Wayne, IN 46835 / 219-485-5389

TMI Products (See Haselbauer Products, Jerry)

Tom Forrest, Inc., P.O. Box 326, Lakeside, CA 92040 / 619-561-5800; FAX: 888-GUN-CLIP info@gunmag.com www.gunmags.com

Tombstone Smoke`n' Deals, PO Box 31298, Phoenix, AZ 85046 / 602-905-7013; FAX: 602-443-1998

Tom's Gun Repair, Thomas G. Ivanoff, 76-6 Rt. Southfork Rd., Cody, WY 82414 / 307-587-6949

Tom's Gunshop, 3601 Central Ave., Hot Springs, AR 71913 / 501-624-3856

Tonoloway Tack Drives, HCR 81, Box 100, Needmore, PA 17238

Torel, Inc., 1708 N. South St., P.O. Box 592, Yoakum, TX 77995 / 512-293-2341; FAX: 512-293-3413

TOZ (See U.S. Importer-Nygord Precision Products)

Track of the Wolf, Inc., 18308 Joplin St. NW, Elk River, MN 55330-1773 / 763-633-2500; FAX: 763-633-2550

Traditions Performance Firearms, P.O. Box 776, 1375 Boston Post Rd., Old Saybrook, CT 06475 / 860-388-4656; FAX: 860-388-4657 info@traditionsfirearms.com www.traditionsfirearms.com

Trafalgar Square, P.O. Box 257, N. Pomfret, VT 05053 / 802-457-1911

Trail Visions, 5800 N. Ames Terrace, Glendale, WI 53209 / 414-228-1328

Trax America, Inc., PO Box 898, 1150 Eldridge, Forrest City, AR 72335 / 870-633-0410; or 800-232-2327; FAX: 870-633-4788 trax@ipa.net www.traxamerica.com

Treadlok Gun Safe, Inc., 1764 Granby St. NE, Roanoke, VA 24012 / 800-729-8732; or 703-982-6881; FAX: 703-982-1059

Treemaster, P.O. Box 247, Guntersville, AL 35976 / 205-878-3597

Trevallion Gunstocks, 9 Old Mountain Rd., Cape Neddick, ME 03902 / 207-361-1130

Trico Plastics, 28061 Diaz Rd., Temecula, CA 92590 / 909-676-7714; FAX: 909-676-0267 ustinfo@ustplastics.com www.tricoplastics.com

Trigger Lock Division / Central Specialties Ltd., 220-D Exchange Dr., Crystal Lake, IL 60014 / 847-639-3900; FAX: 847-639-3972

Trijicon, Inc., 49385 Shafer Ave., P.O. Box 930059, Wixom, MI 48393-0059 / 248-960-7700 or 800-338-0563

Trilby Sport Shop, 1623 Hagley Rd., Toledo, OH 43612-2024 / 419-472-6222

Trilux, Inc., P.O. Box 24608, Winston-Salem, NC 27114 / 910-659-9438; FAX: 910-768-7720

Trinidad St. Jr. Col. Gunsmith Dept., 600 Prospect St., Trinidad, CO 81082 / 719-846-5631; FAX: 719-846-5667

Triple-K Mfg. Co., Inc., 2222 Commercial St., San Diego, CA 92113 / 619-232-2066; FAX: 619-232-7675 sales@triplek.com www.triplek.com

Tristar Sporting Arms, Ltd., 1814 Linn St. #16, N. Kansas City, MO 64116-3627 / 816-421-1400; FAX: 816-421-4182 tristar@blitz-it.net www.tristarsportingarms

Trius Traps, Inc., P.O. Box 25, 221 S. Miami Ave., Cleves, OH 45002 / 513-941-5682; FAX: 513-941-7970 triustraps@fuse.net www.triustraps.com

Trooper Walsh, 2393 N. Edgewood St., Arlington, VA 22207

Trotman, Ken, 135 Ditton Walk, Unit 11, Cambridge, CB5 8PY ENGLAND / 01223-211030; FAX: 01223-212317 www.kentrolman.com

Tru-Balance Knife Co., P.O. Box 140555, Grand Rapids, MI 49514 / 616-647-1215

True Flight Bullet Co., 5581 Roosevelt St., Whitehall, PA 18052 / 610-262-7630; FAX: 610-262-7806

Truglo, Inc., P.O. Box 1612, McKinna, TX 75070 / 972-774-0300; FAX: 972-774-0323 www.truglosights.com

Trulock Tool, P.O. Box 530, Whigham, GA 31797 / 229-762-4678; FAX: 229-762-4050 trulockchokes@hotmail.com trulockchokes.com

Tru-Square Metal Products, Inc., 640 First St. SW, P.O. Box 585, Auburn, WA 98071 / 253-833-2310; or 800-225-1017; FAX: 253-833-2349 t-tumbler@qwest.net

Tucker, James C., P.O. Box 366, Medford, OR 97501 / 541-245-3887 jctstocker@yahoo.com

Tucson Mold, Inc., 930 S. Plumer Ave., Tucson, AZ 85719 / 520-792-1075; FAX: 520-792-1075

Turk's Head Productions, Mustafa Bilal, 908 NW 50th St., Seattle, WA 98107-3634 / 206-782-4164; FAX: 206-783-5677 info@turkshead.com www.turkshead.com

Turnbull Restoration, Doug, 6680 Rt. 5 & 20, P.O. Box 471, Bloomfield, NY 14469 / 585-657-6338; FAX: 585-657-6338 turnbullrest@mindspring.com www.turnbullrestoration.com

Tuttle, Dale, 4046 Russell Rd., Muskegon, MI 49445 / 616-766-2250

Tyler Manufacturing & Distributing, 3804 S. Eastern, Oklahoma City, OK 73129 / 405-677-1487; or 800-654-8415

U

U.S. Fire Arms Mfg. Co., Inc., 55 Van Dyke Ave., Hartford, CT 06106 / 877-227-6901; FAX: 800-644-7265 usfirearms.com

U.S. Importer-Wm. Larkin Moore, 8430 E. Raintree Ste. B-7, Scottsdale, AZ 85260

U.S. Optics, A Division of Zeitz Optics U.S.A., 5900 Dale St., Buena Park, CA 90621 / 714-994-4901; FAX: 714-994-4904 www.usoptics.com

U.S. Repeating Arms Co., Inc., 275 Winchester Ave., Morgan, UT 84050-9333 / 801-876-3440; FAX: 801-876-3737 www.winchester-guns.com

U.S. Tactical Systems (See Keng's Firearms Specialty)

Ugartechea S. A., Ignacio, Chonta 26, Eibar, SPAIN / 43-121257; FAX: 43-121669

Ultra Dot Distribution, P.O. Box 362, 6304 Riverside Dr., Yankeetown, FL 34498 / 352-447-2255; FAX: 352-447-2266

Ultralux (See U.S. Importer-Keng's Firearms)

UltraSport Arms, Inc., 1955 Norwood Ct., Racine, WI 53403 / 414-554-3237; FAX: 414-554-9731

Uncle Bud's, HCR 81, Box 100, Needmore, PA 17238 / 717-294-6000; FAX: 717-294-6005

Uncle Mike's (See Michaels of Oregon Co.)

MANUFACTURER'S DIRECTORY

Unertl Optical Co., Inc., 103 Grand Avenue, P.O. Box 895, Mars, PA 16046-0895 / 724-625-3810; FAX: 724-625-3819 unertl@nauticom.net www.unertloptics.net
Unique/M.A.P.F., 10 Les Allees, 64700, Hendaye, FRANCE / 33-59 20 71 93
UniTec, 1250 Bedford SW, Canton, OH 44710 / 216-452-4017
United Binocular Co., 9043 S. Western Ave., Chicago, IL 60620
United Cutlery Corp., 1425 United Blvd., Sevierville, TN 37876 / 865-428-2532; or 800-548-0835; FAX: 865-428-2267
United States Products Co., 518 Melwood Ave., Pittsburgh, PA 15213-1136 / 412-621-2130; FAX: 412-621-8740 sales@us-products.com www.us-products.com
Universal Sports, P.O. Box 532, Vincennes, IN 47591 / 812-882-8680; FAX: 812-882-8680
Upper Missouri Trading Co., P.O. Box 100, 304 Harold St., Crofton, NE 68730-0100 / 402-388-4844
USAC, 4500-15th St. East, Tacoma, WA 98424 / 206-922-7589
Uselton/Arms, Inc., 842 Conference Dr., Goodlettsville, TN 37072 / 615-851-4919
Utica Cutlery Co., 820 Noyes St., Utica, NY 13503 / 315-733-4663; FAX: 315-733-6602

V

V.H. Blackinton & Co., Inc., 221 John L. Dietsch, Attleboro Falls, MA 02763-0300 / 508-699-4436; FAX: 508-695-5349
Valdada Enterprises, P.O. Box 773122, 31733 County Road 35, Steamboat Springs, CO 80477 / 970-879-2983; FAX: 970-879-0851 www.valdada.com
Valtro USA, Inc., 1281 Andersen Dr., San Rafael, CA 94901 / 415-256-2575; FAX: 415-256-2576
VAM Distribution Co. LLC, 1141-B Mechanicsburg Rd., Wooster, OH 44691 www.rex10.com
Van Gorden & Son Inc., C. S., 1815 Main St., Bloomer, WI 54724 / 715-568-2612
Van Horn, Gil, P.O. Box 207, Llano, CA 93544
Van Patten, J. W., P.O. Box 145, Foster Hill, Milford, PA 18337 / 717-296-7069
Vann Custom Bullets, 2766 N. Willowside Way, Meridian, ID 83642
Van's Gunsmith Service, 224 Route 69-A, Parish, NY 13131 / 315-625-7251
Varmint Masters, LLC, Rick Vecqueray, P.O. Box 6724, Bend, OR 97708 / 541-318-7306; FAX: 541-318-7306 varmintmasters@bendcable.com www.varmintmasters.net
Vecqueray, Rick. See: VARMINT MASTERS, LLC
Vega Tool Co., c/o T.R. Ross, 4865 Tanglewood Ct., Boulder, CO 80301 / 303-530-0174 clanlaird@aol.com www.vegatool.com
Vektor USA, Mikael Danforth, 5139 Stanart St, Norfolk, VA 23502 / 888-740-0837; or 757-455-8895; FAX: 757-461-9155
Venco Industries, Inc. (See Shooter's Choice Gun Care)
Venus Industries, P.O. Box 246, Sialkot-1, PAKISTAN FAX: 92 432 85579
Verney-Carron, BP 72-54 Boulevard Thiers, 42002 St Etienne Cedex 1, St Etienne Cedex 1, FRANCE / 33-477791500; FAX: 33-477790702 email@verney-carron.com www.verney-carron.com
Vest, John, 1923 NE 7th St., Redmond, OR 97756 / 541-923-8898
VibraShine, Inc., P.O. Box 577, Taylorsville, MS 39168 / 601-785-9854; FAX: 601-785-9874 rdbekevibrashine.com www.vibrashine.com
Vibra-Tek Co., 1844 Arroya Rd., Colorado Springs, CO 80906 / 719-634-8611; FAX: 719-634-6886
Vic's Gun Refinishing, 6 Pineview Dr., Dover, NH 03820-6422 / 603-742-0013
Victory Ammunition, P.O. Box 1022, Milford, PA 18337 / 717-296-5768; FAX: 717-296-9298
Victory USA, P.O. Box 1021, Pine Bush, NY 12566 / 914-744-2060; FAX: 914-744-5181
Vihtavuori Oy, FIN-41330 Vihtavuori, FINLAND, / 358-41-3779211; FAX: 358-41-3771643
Vihtavuori Oy/Kaltron-Pettibone, 1241 Ellis St., Bensenville, IL 60106 / 708-350-1116; FAX: 708-350-1606
Viking Video Productions, P.O. Box 251, Roseburg, OR 97470
Village Restorations & Consulting, Inc., P.O. Box 569, Claysburg, PA 16625 / 814-239-8200; FAX: 814-239-2165 www.villagerestoration@yahoo.com
Vincent's Shop, 210 Antoinette, Fairbanks, AK 99701
Vintage Industries, Inc., 2772 Depot St., Sanford, FL 32773
Viper Bullet and Brass Works, 11 Brock St., Box 582, Norwich, ON N0J 1P0 CANADA
Viramontez Engraving, Ray Viramontez, 601 Springfield Dr., Albany, GA 31721 / 229-432-9683 sgtvira@aol.com
Viramontez, Ray. See: VIRAMONTEZ ENGRAVING
Virgin Valley Custom Guns, 450 E 800 N #20, Hurricane, UT 84737 / 435-635-8941; FAX: 435-635-8943 vvcguns@infowest.com www.virginvalleyguns.com
Visible Impact Targets, Rts. 5 & 20, E. Bloomfield, NY 14443 / 716-657-6161; FAX: 716-657-5405
Vitt/Boos, 1195 Buck Hill Rd., Townshend, VT 05353 / 802-365-9232
Voere-KGH GmbH, Untere Sparchen 56, A-6330 Kufstein, Tirol, AUSTRIA / 0043-5372-62547; FAX: 0043-5372-65752 voere@aon.com www.voere.com
Volquartsen Custom Ltd., 24276 240th Street, PO Box 397, Carroll, IA 51401 / 712-792-4238; FAX: 712-792-2542 vcl@netins.net www.volquartsen.com
Vorhes, David, 3042 Beecham St., Napa, CA 94558 / 707-226-9116; FAX: 707-253-7334
VSP Publishers (See Heritage/VSP Gun Books), P.O. Box 887, McCall, ID 83638 / 208-634-4104; FAX: 208-634-3101 heritage@gunbooks.com www.gunbooks.com
VTI Gun Parts, P.O. Box 509, Lakeville, CT 06039 / 860-435-8068; FAX: 860-435-8146 mail@vtigunparts.com www.vtigunparts.com
Vulpes Ventures, Inc., Fox Cartridge Division, P.O. Box 1363, Bolingbrook, IL 60440-7363 / 630-759-1229

W

W. Square Enterprises, 9826 Sagedale Dr., Houston, TX 77089 / 281-484-0935; FAX: 281-464-9940 lfdw@pdq.net www.loadammo.com
W. Waller & Son, Inc., 2221 Stoney Brook Rd., Grantham, NH 03753-7706 / 603-863-4177 www.wallerandson.com
W.B. Niemi Engineering, Box 126 Center Road, Greensboro, VT 05841 / 802-533-7180 or 802-533-7141
W.C. Wolff Co., P.O. Box 458, Newtown Square, PA 19073 / 610-359-9600; or 800-545-0077; mail@gunsprings.com www.gunsprings.com
W.E. Birdsong & Assoc., 1435 Monterey Rd., Florence, MS 39073-9748 / 601-366-8270
W.E. Brownell Checkering Tools, 9390 Twin Mountain Cir., San Diego, CA 92126 / 858-695-2479; FAX: 858-695-2479
W.J. Riebe Co., 3434 Tucker Rd., Boise, ID 83703
W.R. Case & Sons Cutlery Co., Owens Way, Bradford, PA 16701 / 814-368-4123; or 800-523-6350; FAX: 814-368-1736 jsullivan@wrcase.com www.wrcase.com
Wagoner, Vernon G., 2325 E. Encanto St., Mesa, AZ 85213-5917 / 480-835-1307
Wakina by Pic, 24813 Alderbrook Dr., Santa Clarita, CA 91321 / 800-295-8194
Waldron, Herman, Box 475, 80 N. 17th St., Pomeroy, WA 99347 / 509-843-1404
Walker Arms Co., Inc., 499 County Rd. 820, Selma, AL 36701 / 334-872-6231; FAX: 334-872-6262
Wallace, Terry, 385 San Marino, Vallejo, CA 94589 / 707-642-7041
Walls Industries, Inc., P.O. Box 98, 1905 N. Main, Cleburne, TX 76033 / 817-645-4366; FAX: 817-645-7946 www.wallsoutdoors.com
Walters Industries, 6226 Park Lane, Dallas, TX 75225 / 214-691-6973
Walters, John. See: WALTERS WADS
Walters Wads, John Walters, 500 N. Avery Dr., Moore, OK 73160 / 405-799-0376; FAX: 405-799-7727 www.tinwadman@cs.com
Walther America, P.O. Box 22, Springfield, MA 01102 / 413-747-3443 www.walther-usa.com
Walther GmbH, Carl, B.P. 4325, D-89033 Ulm, GERMANY
Walt's Custom Leather, Walt Whinnery, 1947 Meadow Creek Dr., Louisville, KY 40218 / 502-458-4361
WAMCO-New Mexico, P.O. Box 205, Peralta, NM 87042-0205 / 505-869-0826
Ward & Van Valkenburg, 114 32nd Ave. N., Fargo, ND 58102 / 701-232-2351
Ward Machine, 5620 Lexington Rd., Corpus Christi, TX 78412 / 512-992-1221
Wardell Precision Handguns Ltd., 48851 N. Fig Springs Rd., New River, AZ 85027-8513 / 602-465-7995
Warenski Engraving, Julie Warenski, 590 E. 500 N., Richfield, UT 84701 / 435-896-5319; FAX: 435-896-8333 julie@warenskiknives.com
Warenski, Julie. See: WARENSKI ENGRAVING
Warne Manufacturing Co., 9057 SE Jannsen Rd., Clackamas, OR 97015 / 503-657-5590 or 800-683-5590; FAX: 503-657-5695 info@warnescopemounts.com www.warnescopemounts.com
Warren Muzzleloading Co., Inc., Hwy. 21 North, P.O. Box 100, Ozone, AR 72854 / 501-292-3268
Washita Mountain Whetstone Co., P.O. Box 378, Lake Hamilton, AR 71951 / 501-525-3914
Wasmundt, Jim, P.O. Box 511, Fossil, OR 97830
Watson Bros., 39 Redcross Way, SE1 1H6, London, ENGLAND FAX: 44-171-403-336
Watson Bullets, 231 Allies Pass, Frostproof, FL 33843 / 863-635-7948 cbestbullet@aol.com
Wayne E. Schwartz Custom Guns, 970 E. Britton Rd., Morrice, MI 48857 / 517-625-4079
Wayne Firearms For Collectors & Investors
Wayne Specialty Services, 260 Waterford Drive, Florissant, MO 63033 / 413-831-7083
WD-40 Co., 1061 Cudahy Pl., San Diego, CA 92110 / 619-275-1400; FAX: 619-275-5823
Weatherby, Inc., 3100 El Camino Real, Atascadero, CA 93422 / 805-466-1767; FAX: 805-466-2527 www.weatherby.com
Weaver Products ATK, P.O. Box 39, Onalaska, WI 54650 / 800-648-9624 or 608-781-5800; FAX: 608-781-0368
Weaver Scope Repair Service, 1121 Larry Mahan Dr., Suite B, El Paso, TX 79925 / 915-593-1005
Webb, Bill, 6504 North Bellefontaine, Kansas City, MO 64119 / 816-453-7431
Weber & Markin Custom Gunsmiths, 4-1691 Powick Rd., Kelowna, BC V1X 4L1 CANADA / 250-762-7575; FAX: 250-861-3655 www.weberandmarkinguns.com
Webley and Scott Ltd., Frankley Industrial Park, Tay Rd., Birmingham, B45 0PA ENGLAND / 011-021-453-1864; FAX: 0121-457-7846 guns@webley.co.uk www.webley.co.uk
Webster Scale Mfg. Co., P.O. Box 188, Sebring, FL 33870 / 813-385-6362
Weems, Cecil, 510 W Hubbard St., Mineral Wells, TX 76067-4847 / 817-325-1462
Weigand Combat Handguns, Inc., 1057 South Main Rd., Mountain Top, PA 18707 / 570-868-8358; FAX: 570-868-5218 sales@jackweigand.com www.jackweigand.com
Weihrauch KG, Hermann, Industriestrasse 11, 8744 Mellrichstadt, Mellrichstadt, GERMANY
Welch, Sam. See: SAM WELCH GUN ENGRAVING
Wellington Outdoors, P.O. Box 244, 1140 Monticello Rd., Madison, GA 30650 / 706-342-4915; FAX: 706-342-7568
Wells, Rachel, 110 N. Summit St., Prescott, AZ 86301 / 928-445-3655 wellssportstore@cableone.net wellssportstore@cableone-net
Wells Creek Knife & Gun Works, 32956 State Hwy. 38, Scottsburg, OR 97473 / 541-587-4202; FAX: 541-587-4223
Welsh, Bud. See: HIGH PRECISION
Wenger North America/Precise Int'l., 15 Corporate Dr., Orangeburg, NY 10962 / 800-431-2996; FAX: 914-425-4700
Wenig Custom Gunstocks, 103 N. Market St., P.O. Box 249, Lincoln, MO 65338 / 660-547-3334; FAX: 660-547-2881 gustock@wenig.com www.wenig.com
Werth, T. W., 1203 Woodlawn Rd., Lincoln, IL 62656 / 217-732-1300

REFERENCE

MANUFACTURER'S DIRECTORY

Wescombe, Bill (See North Star West)
Wessinger Custom Guns & Engraving, 268 Limestone Rd., Chapin, SC 29036 / 803-345-5677
West, Jack L., 1220 W. Fifth, P.O. Box 427, Arlington, OR 97812
Western Cutlery (See Camillus Cutlery Co.)
Western Design (See Alpha Gunsmith Division)
Western Mfg. Co., 550 Valencia School Rd., Aptos, CA 95003 / 831-688-5884 lotsabears@eathlink.net
Western Missouri Shooters Alliance, P.O. Box 11144, Kansas City, MO 64119 / 816-597-3950; FAX: 816-229-7350
Western Nevada West Coast Bullets, P.O. BOX 2270, DAYTON, NV 89403-2270 / 702-246-3941; FAX: 702-246-0836
Westley Richards & Co. Ltd., 40 Grange Rd., Birmingham, ENGLAND / 010-214722953; FAX: 010-214141138 sales@westleyrichards.com www.westleyrichards.com
Westley Richards Agency USA (See U.S. Importer for
Westwind Rifles, Inc., David S. Sullivan, P.O. Box 261, 640 Briggs St., Erie, CO 80516 / 303-828-3823
Weyer International, 2740 Nebraska Ave., Toledo, OH 43607 / 419-534-2020; FAX: 419-534-2697
Whildin & Sons Ltd, E.H., RR 2 Box 119, Tamaqua, PA 18252 / 717-668-6743; FAX: 717-668-6745
Whinnery, Walt (See Walt's Custom Leather)
Whiscombe (See U.S. Importer-Pelaire Products)
White Barn Wor, 431 County Road, Broadlands, IL 61816
White Pine Photographic Services, Hwy. 60, General Delivery, Wilno, ON K0J 2N0 CANADA / 613-756-3452
White Rifles, Inc., 234 S.1250 W., Linden, UT 84042 / 801-932-7950 www.whiterifles.com
White Rock Tool & Die, 6400 N. Brighton Ave., Kansas City, MO 64119 / 816-454-0478
Whitestone Lumber Corp., 148-02 14th Ave., Whitestone, NY 11357 / 718-746-4400; FAX: 718-767-1748 whstco@aol.com
Wichita Arms, Inc., 923 E. Gilbert, P.O. Box 11371, Wichita, KS 67211 / 316-265-0661; FAX: 316-265-0760 sales@wichitaarms.com www.wichitaarms.com
Wick, David E., 1504 Michigan Ave., Columbus, IN 47201 / 812-376-6960
Widener's Reloading & Shooting Supply, Inc., P.O. Box 3009 CRS, Johnson City, TN 37602 / 615-282-6786; FAX: 615-282-6651
Wideview Scope Mount Corp., 13535 S. Hwy. 16, Rapid City, SD 57702 / 605-341-3220; FAX: 605-341-9142 wvdon@rapidnet.com www.jii.to
Wiebe, Duane, 5300 Merchant Cir. #2, Placerville, CA 95667 / 530-344-1357; FAX: 530-344-1357 wiebe@d-wdb.com
Wiest, Marie. See: GUNCRAFT SPORTS, INC.
Wilcox All-Pro Tools & Supply, 4880 147th St., Montezuma, IA 50171 / 515-623-3138; FAX: 515-623-3104
Wilcox Industries Corp., Robert F Guarasi, 53 Durham St., Portsmouth, NH 03801 / 603-431-1331; FAX: 603-431-1221
Wild Bill's Originals, P.O. Box 13037, Burton, WA 98013 / 206-463-5738; FAX: 206-465-5925 wildbill@halcyon.com
Wild West Guns, 7521 Old Seward Hwy., Unit A, Anchorage, AK 99518 / 800-992-4570 or 907-344-4500; FAX: 907-344-4005 wwguns@ak.net www.wildwestguns.com
Wilderness Sound Products Ltd., 4015 Main St. A, Springfield, OR 97478 / 800-47-0006; FAX: 541-741-0263
Wildey, Inc., 45 Angevine Rd, Warren, CT 06754-1818 / 203-355-9000; FAX: 203-354-7759
Wildlife Research Center, Inc., 1050 McKinley St., Anoka, MN 55303 / 763-427-3350; or 800-USE-LURE; FAX: 763-427-8354
Will-Burt Co., 169 S. Main, Orrville, OH 44667
William E. Phillips Firearms, 38 Avondale Rd., Wigston, Leicester, ENGLAND / 0116 2886334; FAX: 0116 2810644 wephillips@aol.com
William Powell Agency, 22 Circle Dr., Bellmore, NY 11710 / 516-679-1158
Williams Gun Sight Co., 7389 Lapeer Rd., Box 329, Davison, MI 48423 / 810-653-2131 or 800-530-9028; FAX: 810-658-2140 williamsgunsight.com
Williams Mfg. of Oregon, 110 East B St., Drain, OR 97435 / 503-836-7461; FAX: 503-836-7245
Williams Shootin' Iron Service, The Lynx-Line, Rt. 2 Box 223A, Mountain Grove, MO 65711 / 417-948-0902; FAX: 417-948-0902
Williamson Precision Gunsmithing, 117 W. Pipeline, Hurst, TX 76053 / 817-285-0064; FAX: 817-280-0044
Willow Bend, P.O. Box 203, Chelmsford, MA 01824 / 978-256-8508; FAX: 978-256-8508
Wilsom Combat, 2234 CR 719, Berryville, AR 72616-4573 / 800-955-4856; FAX: 870-545-3310
Wilson Case, Inc., P.O. Box 1106, Hastings, NE 68902-1106 / 800-322-5493; FAX: 402-463-5276 sales@wilsoncase.com www.wilsoncase.com
Wilson Combat, 2234 CR 719, Berryville, AR 72616-4573 / 800-955-4856
Winchester Div. Olin Corp., 427 N. Shamrock, E. Alton, IL 62024 / 618-258-3566; FAX: 618-258-3599
Winchester Sutler, Inc., The, 270 Shadow Brook Lane, Winchester, VA 22603 / 540-888-3595; FAX: 540-888-4632
Windish, Jim, 2510 Dawn Dr., Alexandria, VA 22306 / 703-765-1994
Wingshooting Adventures, 0-1845 W. Leonard, Grand Rapids, MI 49544 / 616-677-1980; FAX: 616-677-1986
Winkle Bullets, R.R. 1, Box 316, Heyworth, IL 61745
Winter, Robert M., P.O. Box 484, 42975-287th St., Menno, SD 57045 / 605-387-5322
Wise Custom Guns, 1402 Blanco Rd., San Antonio, TX 78212-2716 / 210-828-3388
Wise Guns, Dale, 1402 Blanco Rd., San Antonio, TX 78212 / 210-734-9999
Wiseman and Co., Bill, P.O. Box 3427, Bryan, TX 77805 / 409-690-3456; FAX: 409-690-0156
Wisners, Inc., P.O. Box 58, Adna, WA 98522 / 360-748-4590; FAX: 360-748-6028 parts@gunpartsspecialist.com www.wisnersinc.com
Wolf (See J.R. Distributing)
Wolf Performance Ammunition, 2201 E. Winston Rd., Ste. K, Anaheim, CA 92806-5537 / 702-837-8506; FAX: 702-837-9250
Wolfe Publishing Co., 2625 Stearman Rd., Ste. A, Prescott, AZ 86301 / 928-445-7810; or 800-899-7810; FAX: 928-778-5124
Wolf's Western Traders, 1250 Santa Cora Ave. #613, Chula Vista, CA 91913 / 619-482-1701 patwolf4570book@aol.com
Wolverine Footwear Group, 9341 Courtland Dr. NE, Rockford, MI 49351 / 616-866-5500; FAX: 616-866-5658
Wood, Frank (See Classic Guns, Inc.), 5305 Peachtree Ind. Blvd., Norcross, GA 30092 / 404-242-7944
Woodleigh (See Huntington Die Specialties)
Woods Wise Products, P.O. Box 681552, Franklin, TN 37068 / 800-735-8182; FAX: 615-726-2637
Woodstream, P.O. Box 327, Lititz, PA 17543 / 717-626-2125; FAX: 717-626-1912
Woodworker's Supply, 1108 North Glenn Rd., Casper, WY 82601 / 307-237-5354
Woolrich, Inc., Mill St., Woolrich, PA 17701 / 800-995-1299; FAX: 717-769-6234/6259
Working Guns, Jim Coffin, 1224 NW Fernwood Cir., Corvallis, OR 97330-2909 / 541-928-4391
World of Targets (See Birchwood Casey)
World Trek, Inc., 7170 Turkey Creek Rd., Pueblo, CO 81007-1046 / 719-546-2121; FAX: 719-543-6886
Worthy Products, Inc., RR 1, P.O. Box 213, Martville, NY 13111 / 315-324-5298
Wostenholm (See Ibberson [Sheffield] Ltd., George)
Wright's Gunstock Blanks, 8540 SE Kane Rd., Gresham, OR 97080 / 503-666-1705 doyal@wrightsguns.com www.wrightsguns.com
WTA Manufacturing, P.O. Box 164, Kit Carson, CO 80825 / 800-700-3054; FAX: 719-962-3570 wta@rebeltec.net http://www.members.aol.com/ductman249/wta.html
Wyant Bullets, Gen. Del., Swan Lake, MT 59911
Wyant's Outdoor Products, Inc., P.O. Box 9, Broadway, VA 22815
Wyoming Custom Bullets, 1626 21st St., Cody, WY 82414
Wyoming Knife Corp., 101 Commerce Dr., Ft. Collins, CO 80524 / 303-224-3454

X

X-Spand Target Systems, 26-10th St. SE, Medicine Hat, AB T1A 1P7 CANADA / 403-526-7997; FAX: 403-528-2362

Y

Yankee Gunsmith "Just Glocks", 2901 Deer Flat Dr., Copperas Cove, TX 76522 / 817-547-8433; FAX: 254-547-8887 ed@justglocks.com www.justglocks.com
Yavapai College, 1100 E. Sheldon St., Prescott, AZ 86301 / 520-776-2353; FAX: 520-776-2355
Yavapai Firearms Academy Ltd., P.O. Box 27290, Prescott Valley, AZ 86312 / 928-772-8262; FAX: 928-772-0062 info@yfainc.corn www.yfainc.com
Yearout, Lewis E. (See Montana Outfitters), 308 Riverview Dr. E., Great Falls, MT 59404 / 406-761-0859; or 406-727-4569
Yellowstone Wilderness Supply, P.O. Box 129, W. Yellowstone, MT 59758 / 406-646-7613
Yesteryear Armory & Supply, P.O. Box 408, Carthage, TN 37030
York M-1 Conversion, 12145 Mill Creek Run, Plantersville, TX 77363 / 936-894-2397; FAX: 936-894-2397 bmf25years@aol.com
Young Country Arms, William, 1409 Kuehner Dr. #13, Simi Valley, CA 93063-4478

Z

Zabala Hermanos S.A., P.O. Box 97, 20600 Elbar, Elgueta, Guipuzcoa, 20600 SPAIN / 943-768076; FAX: 943-768201 imanol@zabalahermanos.com www.zabalabermanos.com
Zander's Sporting Goods, 7525 Hwy 154 West, Baldwin, IL 62217-9706 / 800-851-4373; FAX: 618-785-2320
Zanotti Armor, Inc., 123 W. Lone Tree Rd., Cedar Falls, IA 50613 / 319-232-9650 www.zanottiarmor.com
Zeeryp, Russ, 1601 Foard Dr., Lynn Ross Manor, Morristown, TN 37814 / 615-586-2357
Zero Ammunition Co., Inc., 1601 22nd St. SE, P.O. Box 1188, Cullman, AL 35056-1188 / 800-545-9376; FAX: 205-739-4683
Ziegel Engineering, 1390 E. Bunnett St. "F", Signal Hill, CA 90755 / 562-596-9481; FAX: 562-598-4734 ziegel@aol.com www.ziegeleng.com
Zim's, Inc., 4370 S. 3rd West, Salt Lake City, UT 84107 / 801-268-2505
Z-M Weapons, 203 South St., Bernardston, MA 01337 / 413-648-9501; FAX: 413-648-0219
Zufall, Joseph F., P.O. Box 304, Golden, CO 80402-0304

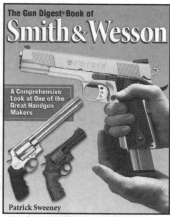

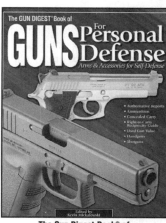

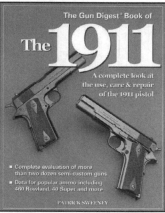

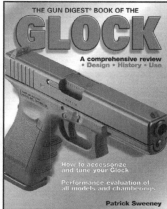

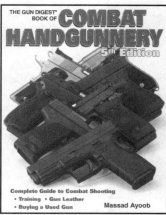

Gun Digest® Book of Firearms Assembly/Disassembly

by J.B. Wood

This five-part series provides step-by-step photos and simple language to guide you through field stripping basics and thoroughly explains all take-down components and finishes with reassembly instructions for hundreds of popular firearms, including automatic pistols, revolvers, rimfire rifles, centerfire rifles and shotguns. Clear photos and easy-to-understand instructions guide you every step of the way. Author J.B. Wood has revised and expanded these volumes, so each contains hundreds of variants. More than 2,500 pages of hands-on information will help you increase your accuracy and speed. You'll save yourself time and money and money with these must-have guides!

Part I:
Automatic Pistols
2nd Edition
Softcover
8¼ x 10¹¹⁄₁₆
592 pages
1,700 b&w photos
Item# AS1R2 • $24.95

Part IV:
Centerfire Rifles
2nd Edition
Softcover
8½ x 11
576 pages
1,750 b&w photos
Item# AS4R2 • $24.99

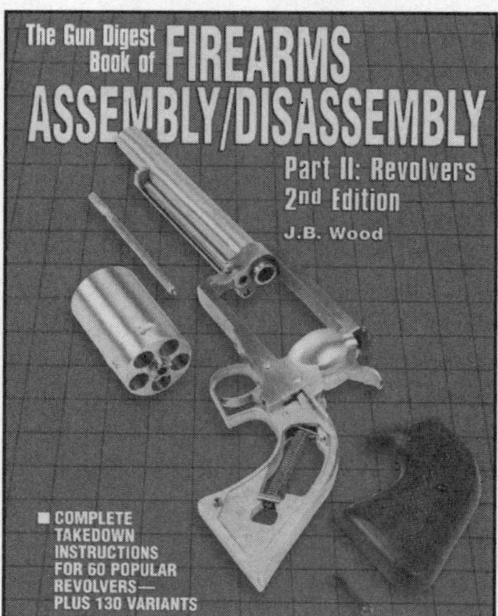

Part II:
Revolvers
2nd Edition
Softcover
8½ x 11
576 pages
1,605 b&w photos
Item# AS2R2 • $27.95

Part V:
Shotguns
Second Edition
Softcover
8½ x 11
592 pages
1,600+ b&w photos
Item# AS5R2 • $24.95

Part III:
Rimfire Rifles
Revised Edition
Softcover
8¼ x 10¹¹⁄₁₆
480 pages
1,590 b&w photos
Item# AS3R • $19.95

To order call 800-258-0929
Offer GNB4

Krause Publications
a division of F+W Publications, Inc.
Offer GNB4
P.O. Box 5009
Iola WI 54945-5009
www.krausebooks.com

Please add $4.00 for the first book and $2.25 each additional for shipping & handling to U.S. addresses. Non-U.S. addresses please add $20.95 for the first book and $5.95 each additional.

Residents of CA, IA, IL, KS, NJ, PA, SD, TN, VA, WI please add appropriate sales tax.